NHUMANITY

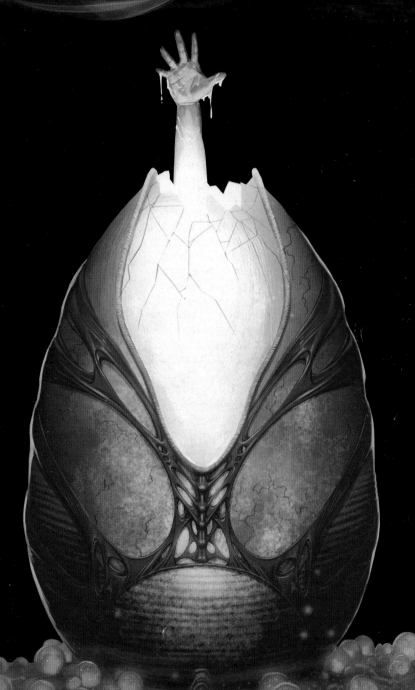

...UMANITY. Contains material originally published in magazine form as AVENGERS ASSEMBLE #21-25, INHUMANITY #1-2, UNCANNY X-MEN #15, INDESTRUCTIBLE HULK #17-20, NEW AVENGERS #13, IRON ...N #20,INH, INHUMANITY: THE AWAKENING #1-2, AVENGERS:A.I. #7, MIGHTY AVENGERS #4-5 and INHUMANITY: SUPERIOR SPIDER-MAN #1. First printing 2015. ISBN# 978-0-7851-9034-9. Published by ...RVEL WORLDWIDE, INC., a subsidiary of MARVEL ENTERTAINMENT, LLC. OFFICE OF PUBLICATION: 135 West 50th Street, New York, NY 10020. Copyright © 2013, 2014 and 2015 Marvel Characters, Inc. All
...N FINE, EVP - Office of the President, Marvel Worldwide, Inc. and EVP & CMO Marvel Characters B.V.; DAN BUCKLEY, Publisher & President - Print, Animation & Digital Divisions; JOE QUESADA, Chief Creative
...cer; TOM BREVOORT, SVP of Publishing; DAVID BOGART, SVP of Operations & Procurement, Publishing; C.B. CEBULSKI, SVP of Creator & Content Development; DAVID GABRIEL, SVP Print, Sales & Marketing;
...O'KEEFE, VP of Operations & Logistics; DAN CARR, Executive Director of Publishing Technology; SUSAN CRESPI, Editorial Operations Manager; ALEX MORALES, Publishing Operations Manager; STAN LEE,
...irman Emeritus. For information regarding advertising in Marvel Comics or on Marvel.com, please contact Niza Disla, Director of Marvel Partnerships, at ndisla@marvel.com. For Marvel subscription inquiries,
...se call 800-217-9158. **Manufactured between 12/12/2014 and 1/19/2015 by R.R. DONNELLEY, INC., SALEM, VA, USA.**

9 8 7 6 5 4 3 2 1

INHUMANITY

INHUMANITY #1
Writer: **Matt Fraction**
Penciler: **Olivier Coipel**
Inker: **Mark Morales**
Colorist: **Laura Martin**
Ancient Flashback Art: **Leinil Yu,**
Gerry Alanguilan & Israel Silva
Infinity Flashback Art: **Dustin Weaver**
& Israel Silva
Letterer: **VC's Clayton Cowles**
Cover Art: **Olivier Coipel & Dean White**
Assistant Editor: **Xander Jarowey**
Associate Editor: **Jordan D. White**
Editor: **Nick Lowe**

INHUMANITY #2
Writer: **Matt Fraction**
Artists: **Nick Bradshaw with Todd Nauck**
Inkers: **Nick Bradshaw, Scott Hanna, Tom**
Palmer & Todd Nauck
Color Artists: **Antonio Fabela**
& Andres Mossa
Letterer: **VC's Clayton Cowles**
Cover Art: **Nick Bradshaw & Laura Martin**
Assistant Editor: **Xander Jarowey**
Associate Editor: **Jordan D. White**
Editor: **Nick Lowe**

INDESTRUCTIBLE HULK #17-20
Writer: **Mark Waid**
Artists, #17: **Clay & Seth Mann** (pp. 1-10, 12-13)
& Miguel Sepulveda (pp. 11, 14-20)
Artists, #18: **Jheremy Raapack** (pp. 1-10)
& Miguel Sepulveda
with **Tom Grummett** (pp. 11-20)
Artists, #19: **Jheremy Raapack** (pp. 1-12,
16, 19-20), **Joe Bennett** & **Ruy Jose** (pp. 13-15)
and **Tom Grummett** with **Karl Kesel**
& Andrew Hennessy (pp. 17-18)
Color Artist: **Val Staples**
Letterer: **VC's Cory Petit**
Cover Art: **Mahmud Asrar & Dave McCaig**
Assistant Editor: **Emily Shaw**
Editor: **Mark Paniccia**

UNCANNY X-MEN #15
Writer: **Brian Michael Bendis**
Artist: **Kris Anka**
Color Artist: **Rain Beredo**
Letterers: **VC's Joe Caramagna**
& Chris Eliopoulos
Cover Art: **Kris Anka**
Assistant Editor: **Xander Jarowey**
Associate Editor: **Jordan D. White**
Editor: **Nick Lowe**

AVENGERS ASSEMBLE #21-25
Writers: **Kelly Sue DeConnick**
& Warren Ellis
Artist: **Matteo Buffagni**
with **Paco Diaz** (#22)
Color Artist: **Nolan Woodard**
Letterer: **VC's Clayton Cowles**
Cover Art: **Jorge Molina**
Assistant Editor: **Jon Moisan**
Editor: **Lauren Sankovitch**
Executive Editor: **Tom Brevoort**

IRON MAN #20.INH
Writer: **Kieron Gillen**
Artist: **Agustin Padilla**
Inker: **Scott Hanna**
Color Artist: **Guru-eFX**
Letterer: **VC's Joe Caramagna**
Cover Art: **Paul Rivoche**
Assistant Editor: **Emily Shaw**
Editor: **Mark Paniccia**

MIGHTY AVENGERS #4-5
Writer: **Al Ewing**
Penciler: **Greg Land**
Inker: **Jay Leisten**
Color Artist: **Frank D'Armata**
Letterer: **VC's Cory Petit**
Cover Art: **Greg Land & Frank D'Armata**
Assistant Editor: **Jake Thomas**
Editors: **Tom Brevoort**
with **Lauren Sankovitch**

AVENGERS A.I. #7
Writer: **Sam Humphries**
Artist: **André Lima Araújo**
Color Artist: **Frank D'Armata**
Letterer: **VC's Clayton Cowles**
Cover Art: **David Marquez**
& Frank D'Armata
Editor: **Jon Moisan**
Editor: **Lauren Sankovitch**
Executive Editor: **Tom Brevoort**

INHUMANITY:
THE AWAKENING #1-2
Writer: **Matt Kindt**
Artist: **Paul Davidson**
Color Artist: **Jean-Francois Beaulieu**
Letterer: **VC's Joe Caramagna**
Cover Art: **Jorge Molina**
Assistant Editor: **Jon Moisan**
Editor: **Bill Rosemann**

INHUMANITY:
SUPERIOR SPIDER-MAN #1
Writer: **Christos Gage**
Art & Cover: **Stephanie Hans**
Letterer: **VC's Clayton Cowles**
Assistant Editor: **Ellie Pyle**
Editor: **Stephen Wacker**

NEW AVENGERS #13
Writer: **Jonathan Hickman**
Artist: **Simone Bianchi**
Color Artist: **Adriano Dell'Alpi**
Letterer: **VC's Joe Caramagna**
Cover Art: **Simone Bianchi**
Assistant Editor: **Jake Thomas**
Editors: **Tom Brevoort**
with **Lauren Sankovitch**

Collection Editor: Jennifer Grünwald • Assistant Editor: Sarah Brunstad • Associate Managing Editor: Alex Starbuck • Editor, Special Projects: Mark D. Beaz
Senior Editor, Special Projects: Jeff Youngquist • SVP Print, Sales & Marketing: David Gabriel • Book Design: Jeff Powell

Editor in Chief: Axel Alonso • Chief Creative Officer: Joe Quesada • Publisher: Dan Buckley • Executive Producer: Alan Fine

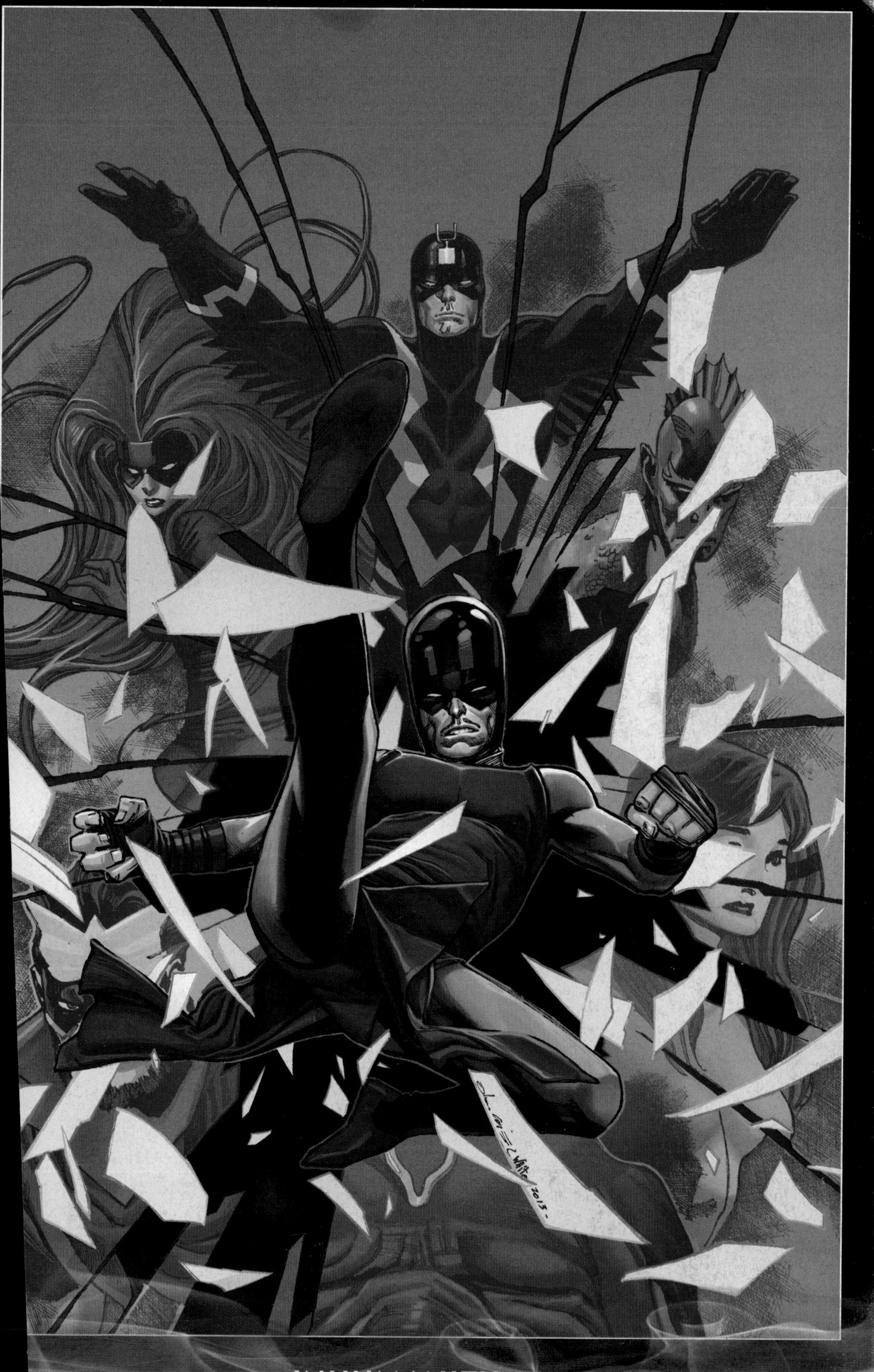

INHUMANITY #1

ONCE UPON A TIME...

A MAGNIFICENT
PALACE HID ABOVE
THE CLOUDS.

THIS CITY HOUSED
GODS, CHAMPIONS,
WARRIORS, HEROES
AND LEGENDS.

ITS PEOPLE CALLED
IT **ATTILAN**. IT WAS
THEIR RIGHTFUL HOME.

IT COULD HAVE BEEN
YOUR RIGHTFUL HOME,
TOO...

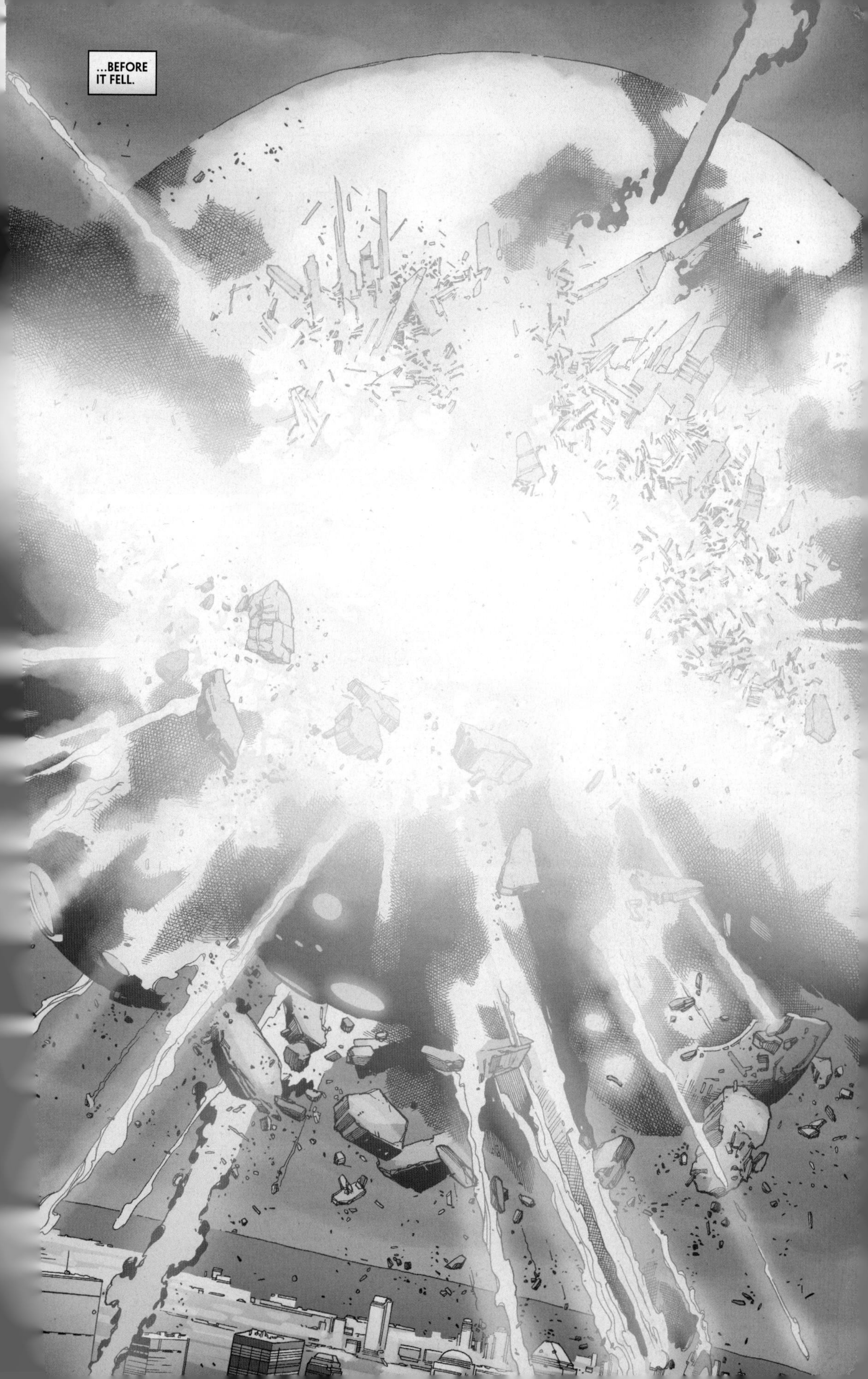
...BEFORE IT FELL.

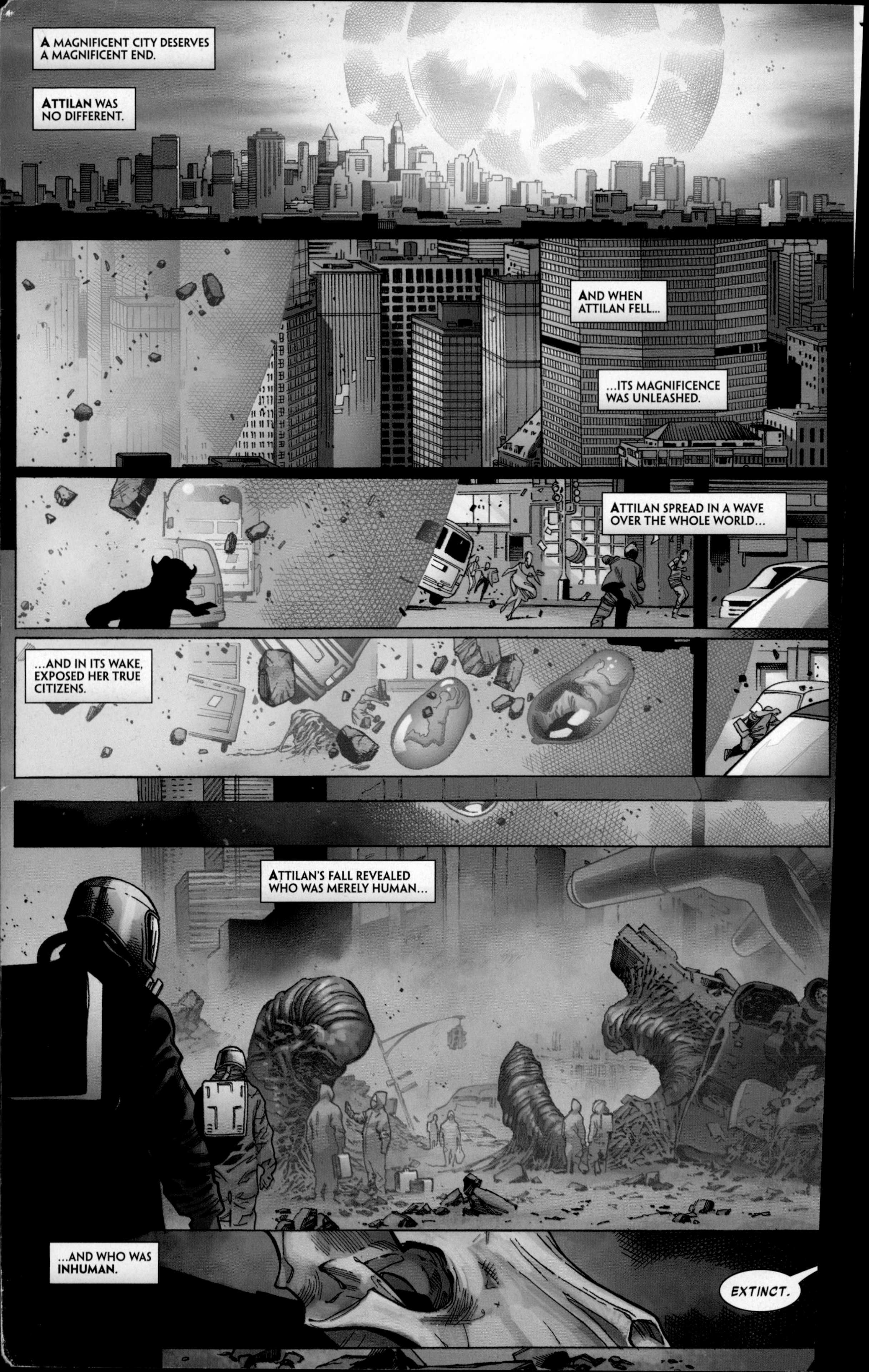
A MAGNIFICENT CITY DESERVES A MAGNIFICENT END.
ATTILAN WAS NO DIFFERENT.
AND WHEN ATTILAN FELL...
...ITS MAGNIFICENCE WAS UNLEASHED.
ATTILAN SPREAD IN A WAVE OVER THE WHOLE WORLD...
...AND IN ITS WAKE, EXPOSED HER TRUE CITIZENS.
ATTILAN'S FALL REVEALED WHO WAS MERELY HUMAN...
...AND WHO WAS INHUMAN.
EXTINCT.

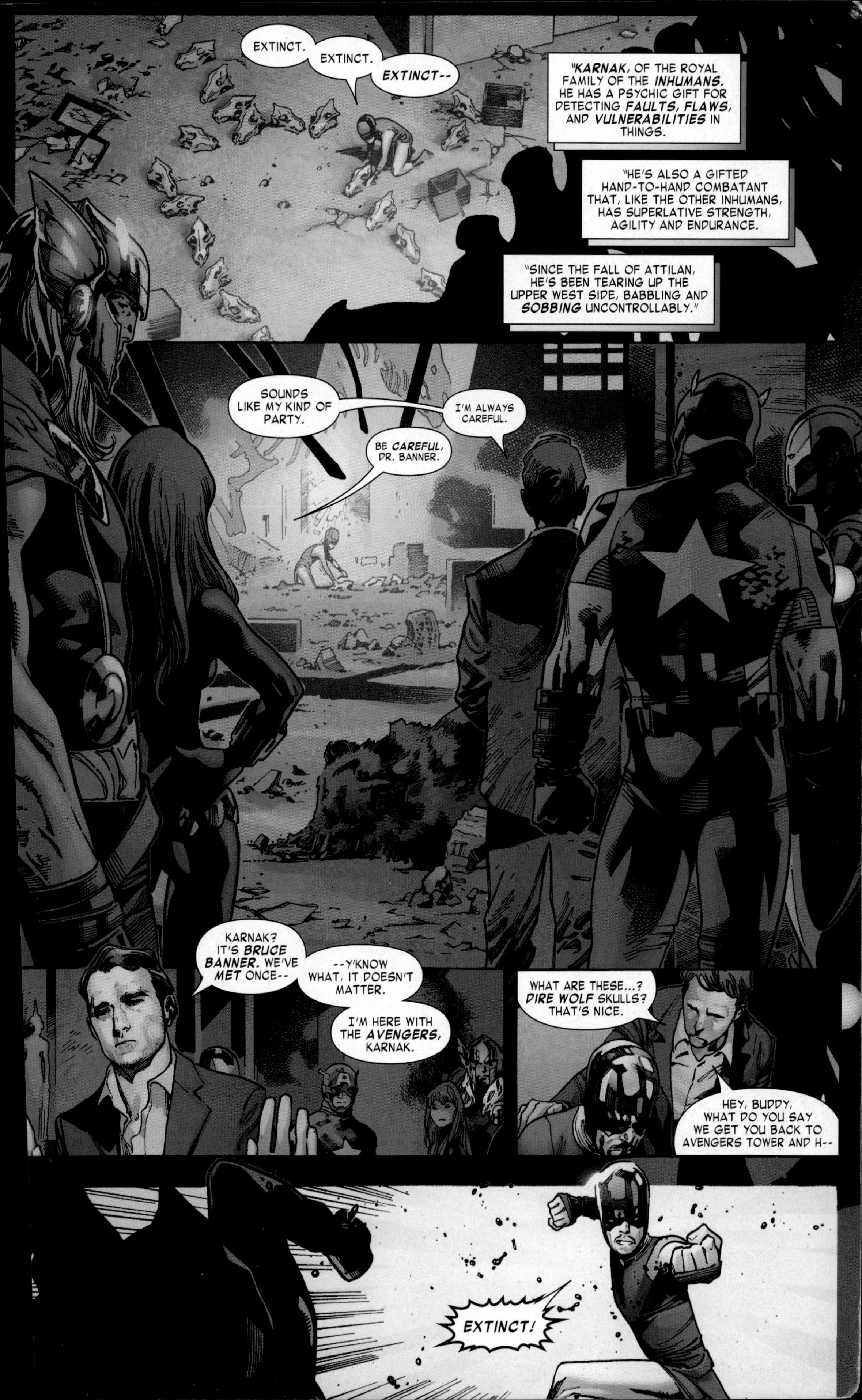

EXTINCT.
EXTINCT.
EXTINCT--
"KARNAK, OF THE ROYAL FAMILY OF THE INHUMANS. HE HAS A PSYCHIC GIFT FOR DETECTING FAULTS, FLAWS, AND VULNERABILITIES IN THINGS.
"HE'S ALSO A GIFTED HAND-TO-HAND COMBATANT THAT, LIKE THE OTHER INHUMANS, HAS SUPERLATIVE STRENGTH, AGILITY AND ENDURANCE.
"SINCE THE FALL OF ATTILAN, HE'S BEEN TEARING UP THE UPPER WEST SIDE, BABBLING AND SOBBING UNCONTROLLABLY."
SOUNDS LIKE MY KIND OF PARTY.
BE CAREFUL, DR. BANNER.
I'M ALWAYS CAREFUL.
KARNAK? IT'S BRUCE BANNER. WE'VE MET ONCE--
--Y'KNOW WHAT, IT DOESN'T MATTER.
I'M HERE WITH THE AVENGERS, KARNAK.
WHAT ARE THESE...? DIRE WOLF SKULLS? THAT'S NICE.
HEY, BUDDY, WHAT DO YOU SAY WE GET YOU BACK TO AVENGERS TOWER AND H--
EXTINCT!

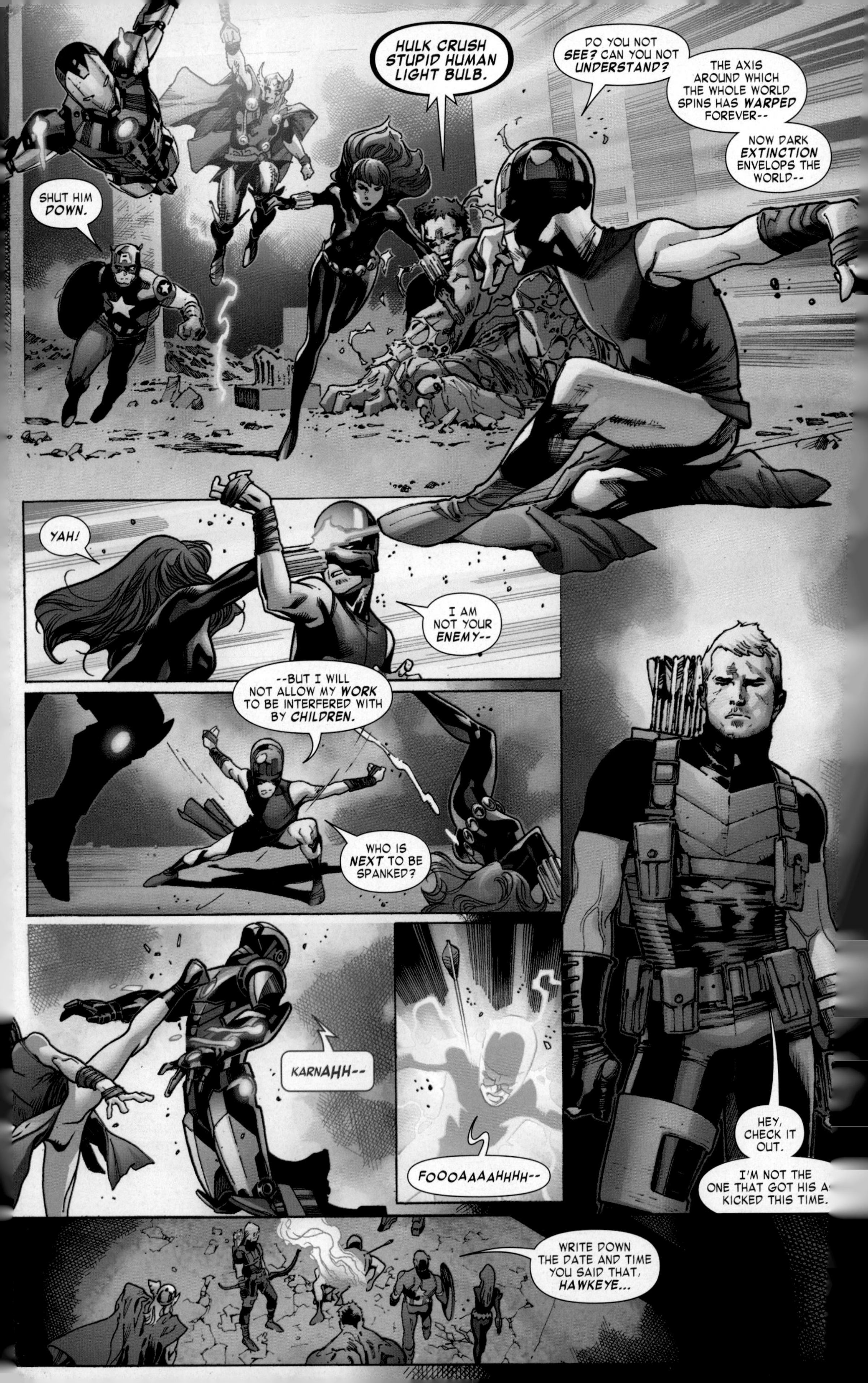
SHUT HIM DOWN.
HULK CRUSH STUPID HUMAN LIGHT BULB.
DO YOU NOT SEE? CAN YOU NOT UNDERSTAND?
THE AXIS AROUND WHICH THE WHOLE WORLD SPINS HAS WARPED FOREVER--
NOW DARK EXTINCTION ENVELOPS THE WORLD--
YAH!
I AM NOT YOUR ENEMY--
--BUT I WILL NOT ALLOW MY WORK TO BE INTERFERED WITH BY CHILDREN.
WHO IS NEXT TO BE SPANKED?
KARNAHH--
FOOOAAAAHHHH--
HEY, CHECK IT OUT.
I'M NOT THE ONE THAT GOT HIS A KICKED THIS TIME.
WRITE DOWN THE DATE AND TIME YOU SAID THAT, HAWKEYE...

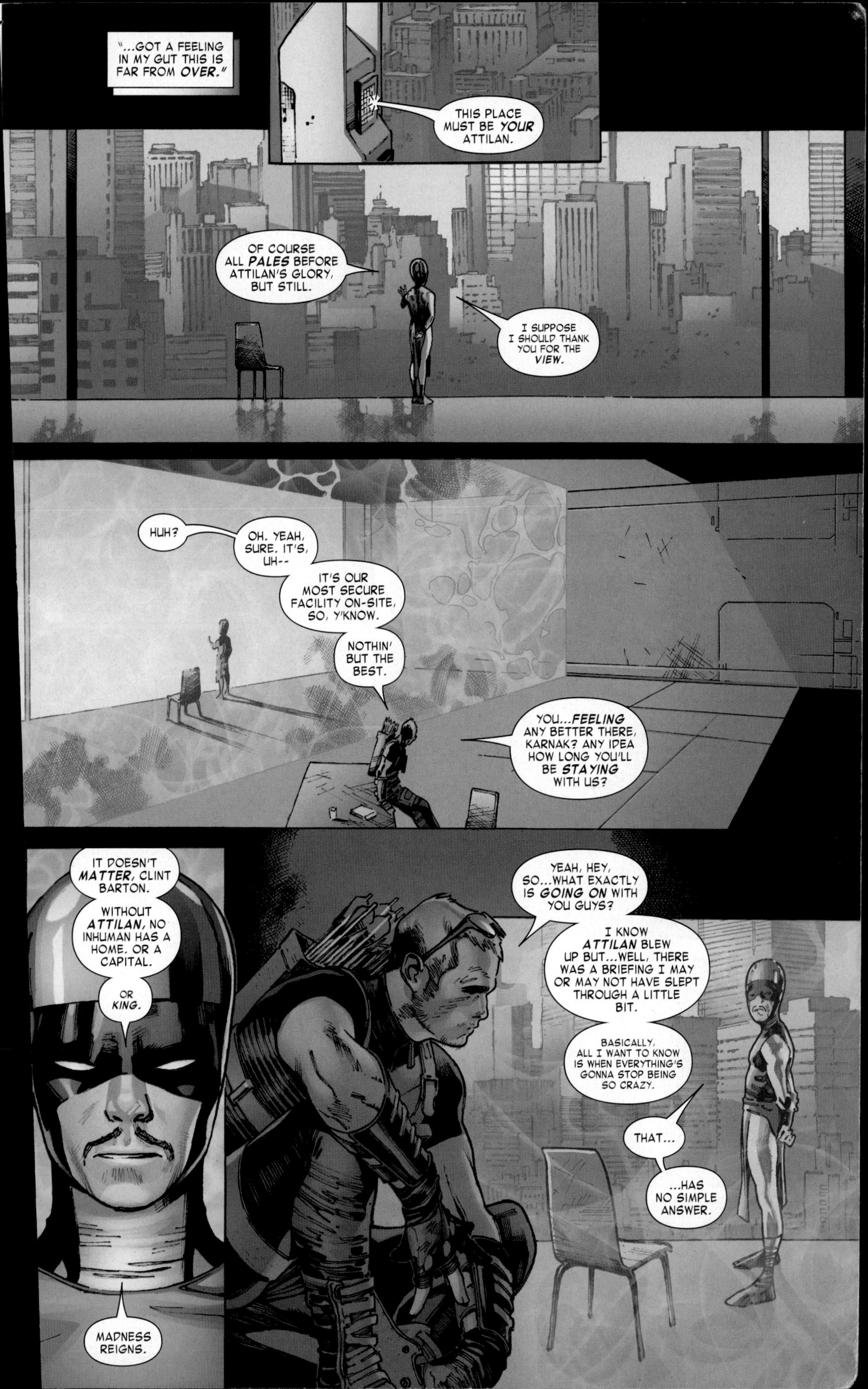
"...GOT A FEELING IN MY GUT THIS IS FAR FROM OVER."
THIS PLACE MUST BE YOUR ATTILAN.
OF COURSE ALL PALES BEFORE ATTILAN'S GLORY, BUT STILL.
I SUPPOSE I SHOULD THANK YOU FOR THE VIEW.
HUH?
OH. YEAH, SURE. IT'S, UH--
IT'S OUR MOST SECURE FACILITY ON-SITE, SO, Y'KNOW.
NOTHIN' BUT THE BEST.
YOU...FEELING ANY BETTER THERE, KARNAK? ANY IDEA HOW LONG YOU'LL BE STAYING WITH US?
IT DOESN'T MATTER, CLINT BARTON.
WITHOUT ATTILAN, NO INHUMAN HAS A HOME. OR A CAPITAL.
OR KING.
MADNESS REIGNS.
YEAH, HEY, SO...WHAT EXACTLY IS GOING ON WITH YOU GUYS?
I KNOW ATTILAN BLEW UP BUT...WELL, THERE WAS A BRIEFING I MAY OR MAY NOT HAVE SLEPT THROUGH A LITTLE BIT.
BASICALLY, ALL I WANT TO KNOW IS WHEN EVERYTHING'S GONNA STOP BEING SO CRAZY.
THAT...
...HAS NO SIMPLE ANSWER.

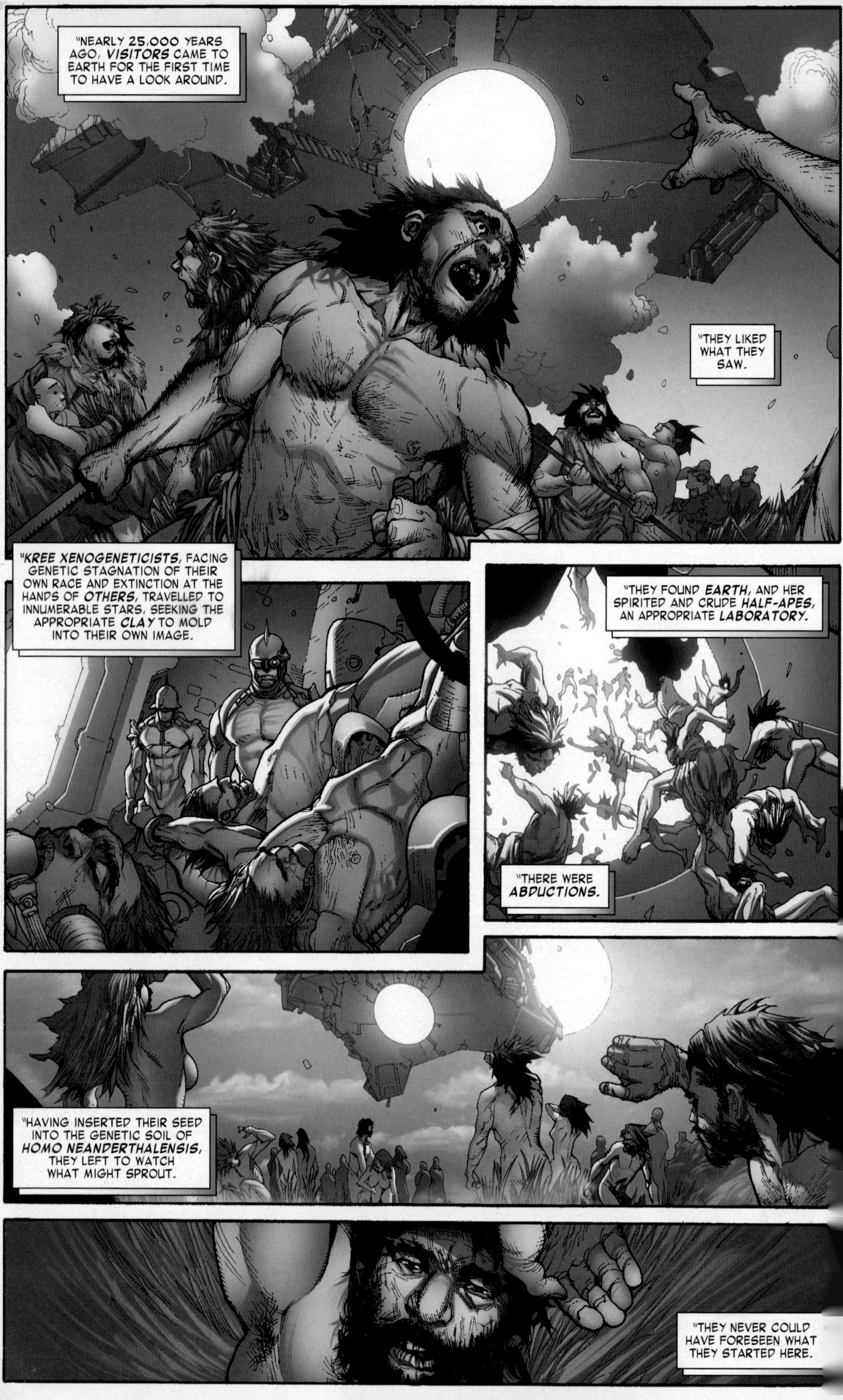
"NEARLY 25,000 YEARS AGO, VISITORS CAME TO EARTH FOR THE FIRST TIME TO HAVE A LOOK AROUND.
"THEY LIKED WHAT THEY SAW.
"KREE XENOGENETICISTS, FACING GENETIC STAGNATION OF THEIR OWN RACE AND EXTINCTION AT THE HANDS OF OTHERS, TRAVELLED TO INNUMERABLE STARS, SEEKING THE APPROPRIATE CLAY TO MOLD INTO THEIR OWN IMAGE.
"THEY FOUND EARTH, AND HER SPIRITED AND CRUDE HALF-APES, AN APPROPRIATE LABORATORY.
"THERE WERE ABDUCTIONS.
"HAVING INSERTED THEIR SEED INTO THE GENETIC SOIL OF HOMO NEANDERTHALENSIS, THEY LEFT TO WATCH WHAT MIGHT SPROUT.
"THEY NEVER COULD HAVE FORESEEN WHAT THEY STARTED HERE.

"IN THE CENTURIES THAT FOLLOWED, *HOMO SAPIENS* CRAWLED OUT OF THEIR CAVES TO FIND *INHOMO SUPREMIS* WERE ALREADY WELL AHEAD OF THEM...

"THE INHUMAN CALLED *RANDAC* TOOK UP WHERE THE KREE LEFT OFF.

"PUSHING. *PROBING.* EXPLORING AND EXPERIMENTING.

"HE SOUGHT TO EVOLVE THE INHUMAN INTO WEAPONS ABLE TO RESIST THE KREE WERE THEY EVER TO RETURN.

"THIS WAS CONTROVERSIAL.

"WOULD THIS NOT BE FULFILLING THEIR *KREE* DESTINIES?

"WOULD THIS NOT BE COMPLIANCE WITH THE WISHES OF THE DEVILS THAT CREATED THEM?

"*DIVISIONS* FORMED AMONG THE COALESCED TRIBES.

"RANDAC COULD NOT CARE *LESS* OF THE KREE OR THEIR INTENTIONS.

"RANDAC BELIEVED HE WAS SEIZING INHUMAN DESTINY BY THE THROAT...

"...AND DEMANDING IT *OBEY HIM.*

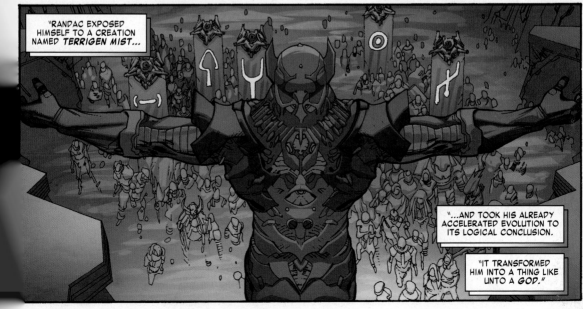

"RANDAC EXPOSED HIMSELF TO A CREATION NAMED *TERRIGEN MIST*...

"...AND TOOK HIS ALREADY ACCELERATED EVOLUTION TO ITS LOGICAL CONCLUSION.

"IT TRANSFORMED HIM INTO A THING LIKE UNTO A *GOD.*"

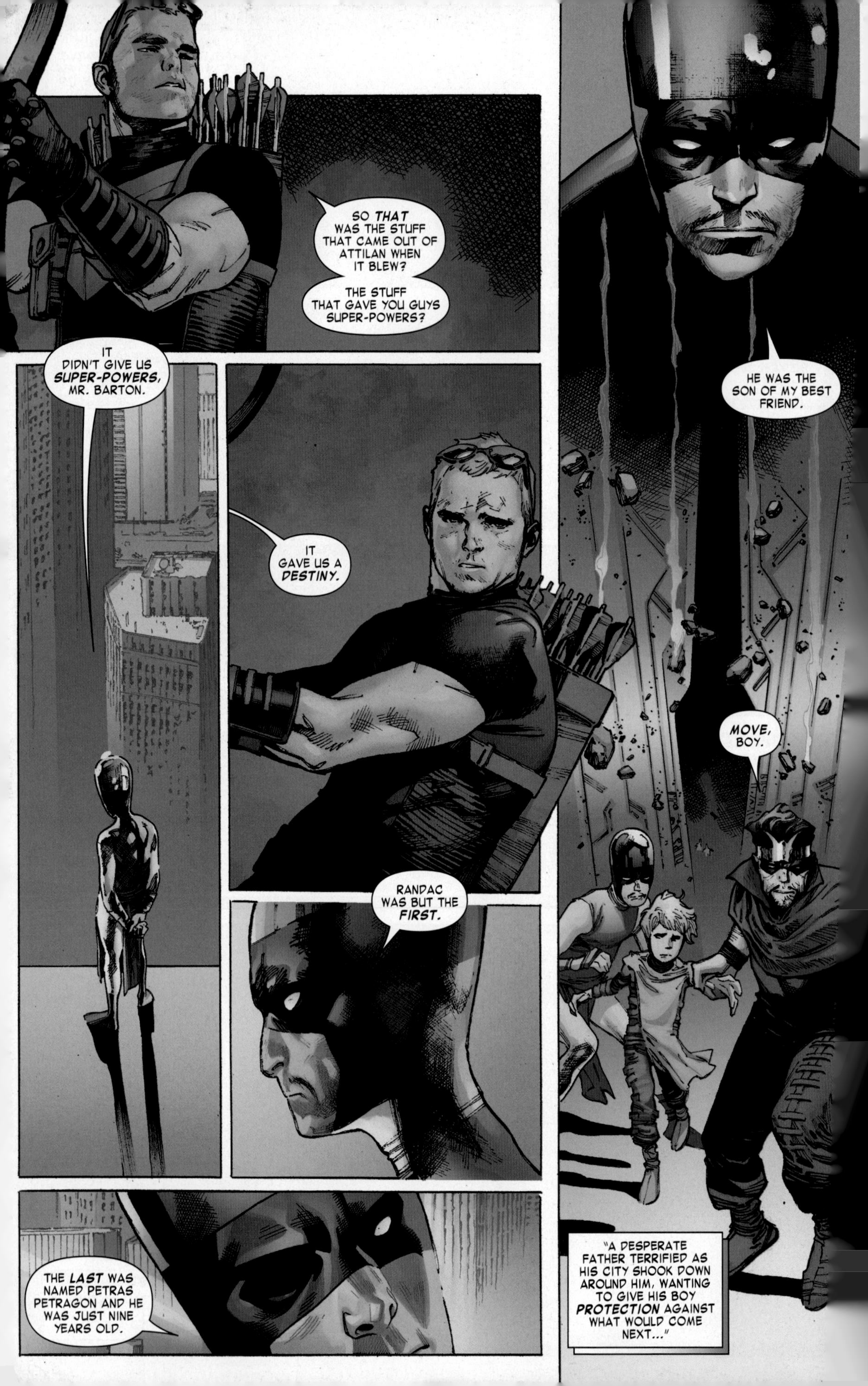
SO THAT WAS THE STUFF THAT CAME OUT OF ATTILAN WHEN IT BLEW?
THE STUFF THAT GAVE YOU GUYS SUPER-POWERS?
IT DIDN'T GIVE US SUPER-POWERS, MR. BARTON.
IT GAVE US A DESTINY.
RANDAC WAS BUT THE FIRST.
THE LAST WAS NAMED PETRAS PETRAGON AND HE WAS JUST NINE YEARS OLD.
HE WAS THE SON OF MY BEST FRIEND.
MOVE, BOY.
"A DESPERATE FATHER TERRIFIED AS HIS CITY SHOOK DOWN AROUND HIM, WANTING TO GIVE HIS BOY PROTECTION AGAINST WHAT WOULD COME NEXT..."

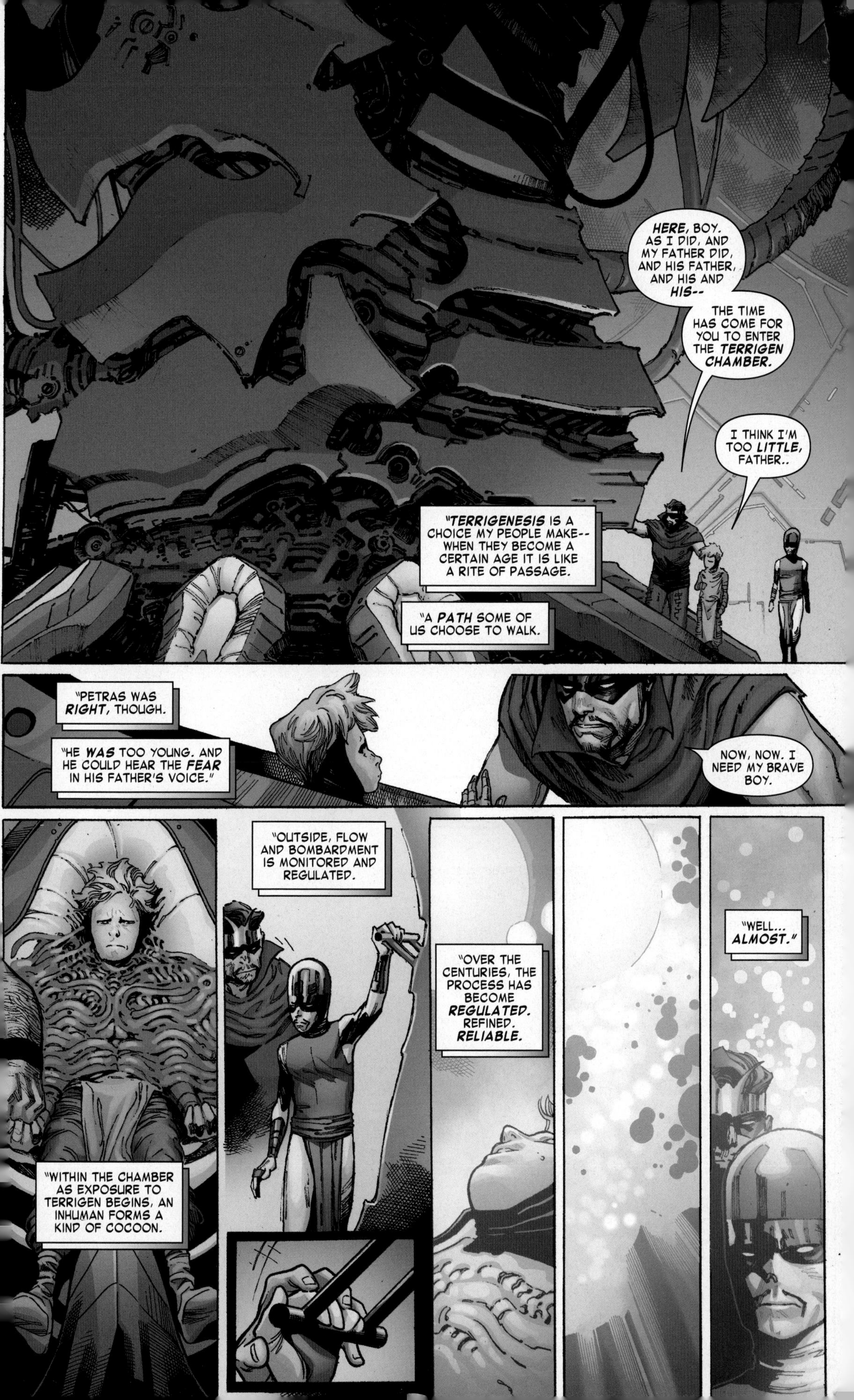
HERE, BOY. AS I DID, AND MY FATHER DID, AND HIS FATHER, AND HIS AND HIS--
THE TIME HAS COME FOR YOU TO ENTER THE TERRIGEN CHAMBER.
I THINK I'M TOO LITTLE, FATHER..
"TERRIGENESIS IS A CHOICE MY PEOPLE MAKE-- WHEN THEY BECOME A CERTAIN AGE IT IS LIKE A RITE OF PASSAGE.
"A PATH SOME OF US CHOOSE TO WALK.
"PETRAS WAS RIGHT, THOUGH.
"HE WAS TOO YOUNG. AND HE COULD HEAR THE FEAR IN HIS FATHER'S VOICE."
NOW, NOW. I NEED MY BRAVE BOY.
"WITHIN THE CHAMBER AS EXPOSURE TO TERRIGEN BEGINS, AN INHUMAN FORMS A KIND OF COCOON.
"OUTSIDE, FLOW AND BOMBARDMENT IS MONITORED AND REGULATED.
"OVER THE CENTURIES, THE PROCESS HAS BECOME REGULATED. REFINED. RELIABLE.
"WELL... ALMOST."

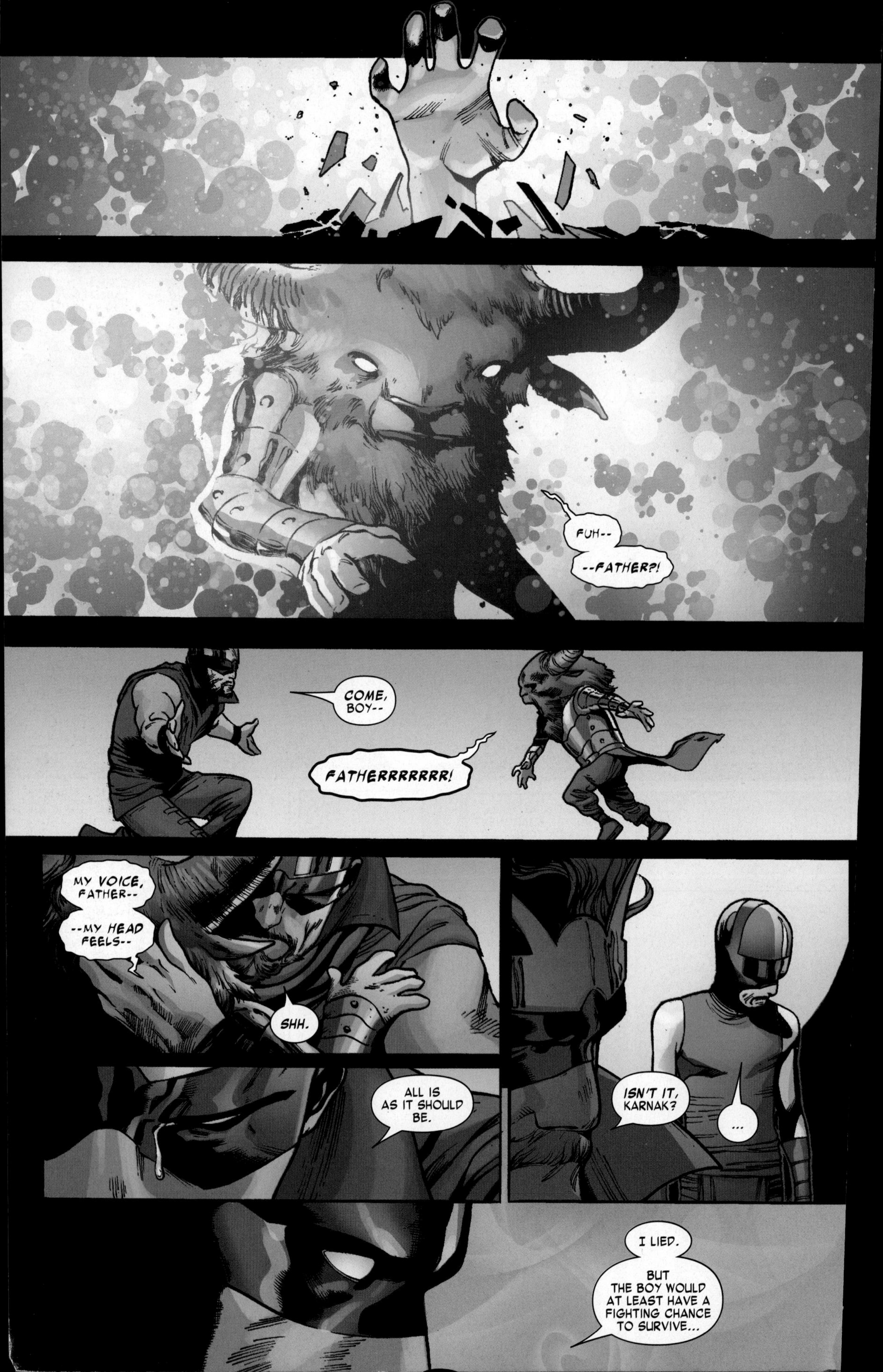
FUH--
--FATHER?!
COME, BOY--
FATHERRRRRRR!
MY VOICE, FATHER--
--MY HEAD FEELS--
SHH.
ALL IS AS IT SHOULD BE.
ISN'T IT, KARNAK?
...
I LIED.
BUT THE BOY WOULD AT LEAST HAVE A FIGHTING CHANCE TO SURVIVE...

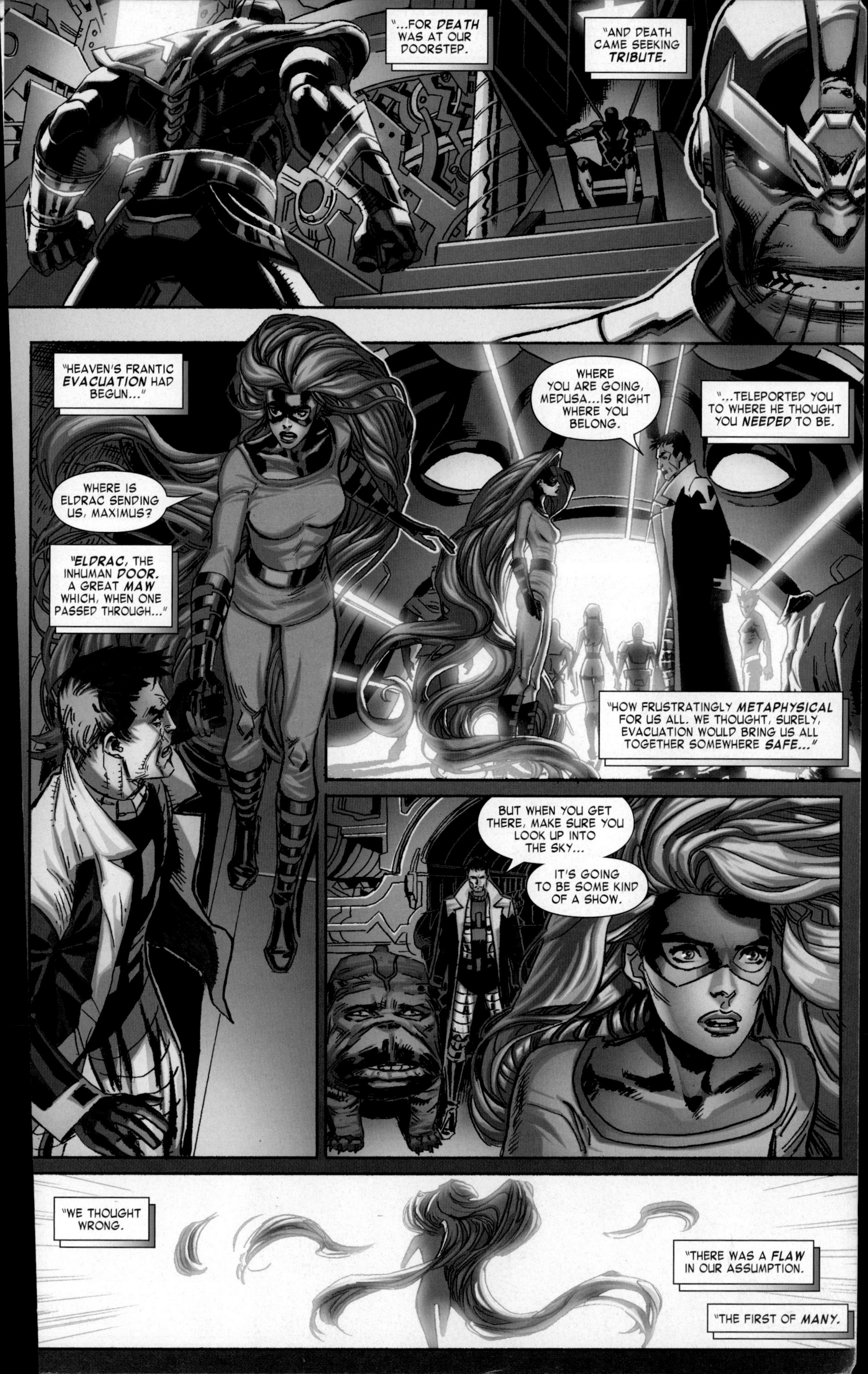
"...FOR DEATH WAS AT OUR DOORSTEP.
"AND DEATH CAME SEEKING TRIBUTE.
"HEAVEN'S FRANTIC EVACUATION HAD BEGUN..."
WHERE IS ELDRAC SENDING US, MAXIMUS?
"ELDRAC, THE INHUMAN DOOR. A GREAT MAW WHICH, WHEN ONE PASSED THROUGH..."
WHERE YOU ARE GOING, MEDUSA...IS RIGHT WHERE YOU BELONG.
"...TELEPORTED YOU TO WHERE HE THOUGHT YOU NEEDED TO BE.
"HOW FRUSTRATINGLY METAPHYSICAL FOR US ALL. WE THOUGHT, SURELY, EVACUATION WOULD BRING US ALL TOGETHER SOMEWHERE SAFE..."
BUT WHEN YOU GET THERE, MAKE SURE YOU LOOK UP INTO THE SKY...
IT'S GOING TO BE SOME KIND OF A SHOW.
"WE THOUGHT WRONG.
"THERE WAS A FLAW IN OUR ASSUMPTION.
"THE FIRST OF MANY.

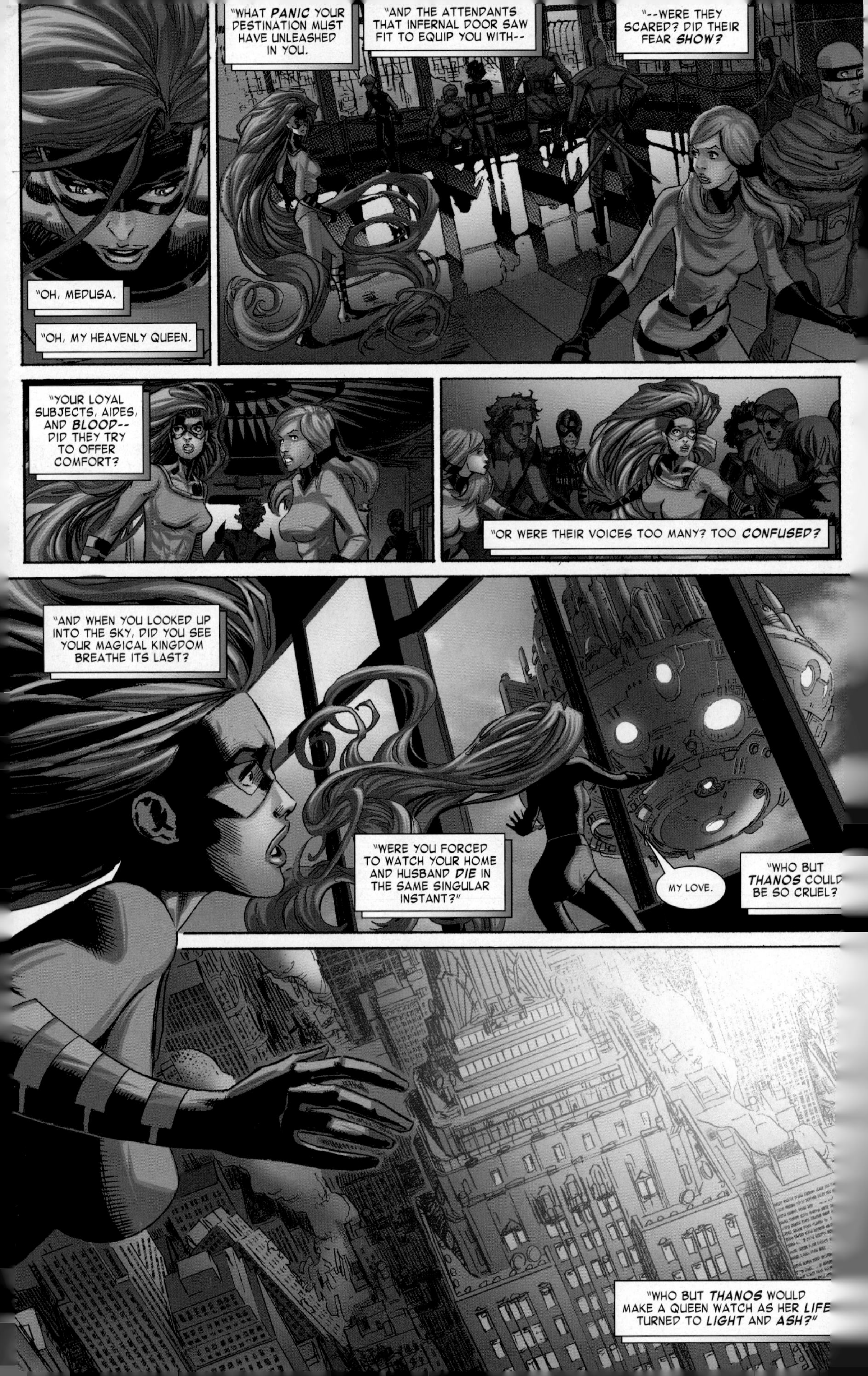
"OH, MEDUSA.
"OH, MY HEAVENLY QUEEN.
"WHAT PANIC YOUR DESTINATION MUST HAVE UNLEASHED IN YOU.
"AND THE ATTENDANTS THAT INFERNAL DOOR SAW FIT TO EQUIP YOU WITH--
"--WERE THEY SCARED? DID THEIR FEAR SHOW?
"YOUR LOYAL SUBJECTS, AIDES, AND BLOOD-- DID THEY TRY TO OFFER COMFORT?
"OR WERE THEIR VOICES TOO MANY? TOO CONFUSED?
"AND WHEN YOU LOOKED UP INTO THE SKY, DID YOU SEE YOUR MAGICAL KINGDOM BREATHE ITS LAST?
"WERE YOU FORCED TO WATCH YOUR HOME AND HUSBAND DIE IN THE SAME SINGULAR INSTANT?"
MY LOVE.
"WHO BUT THANOS COULD BE SO CRUEL?
"WHO BUT THANOS WOULD MAKE A QUEEN WATCH AS HER LIFE TURNED TO LIGHT AND ASH?"

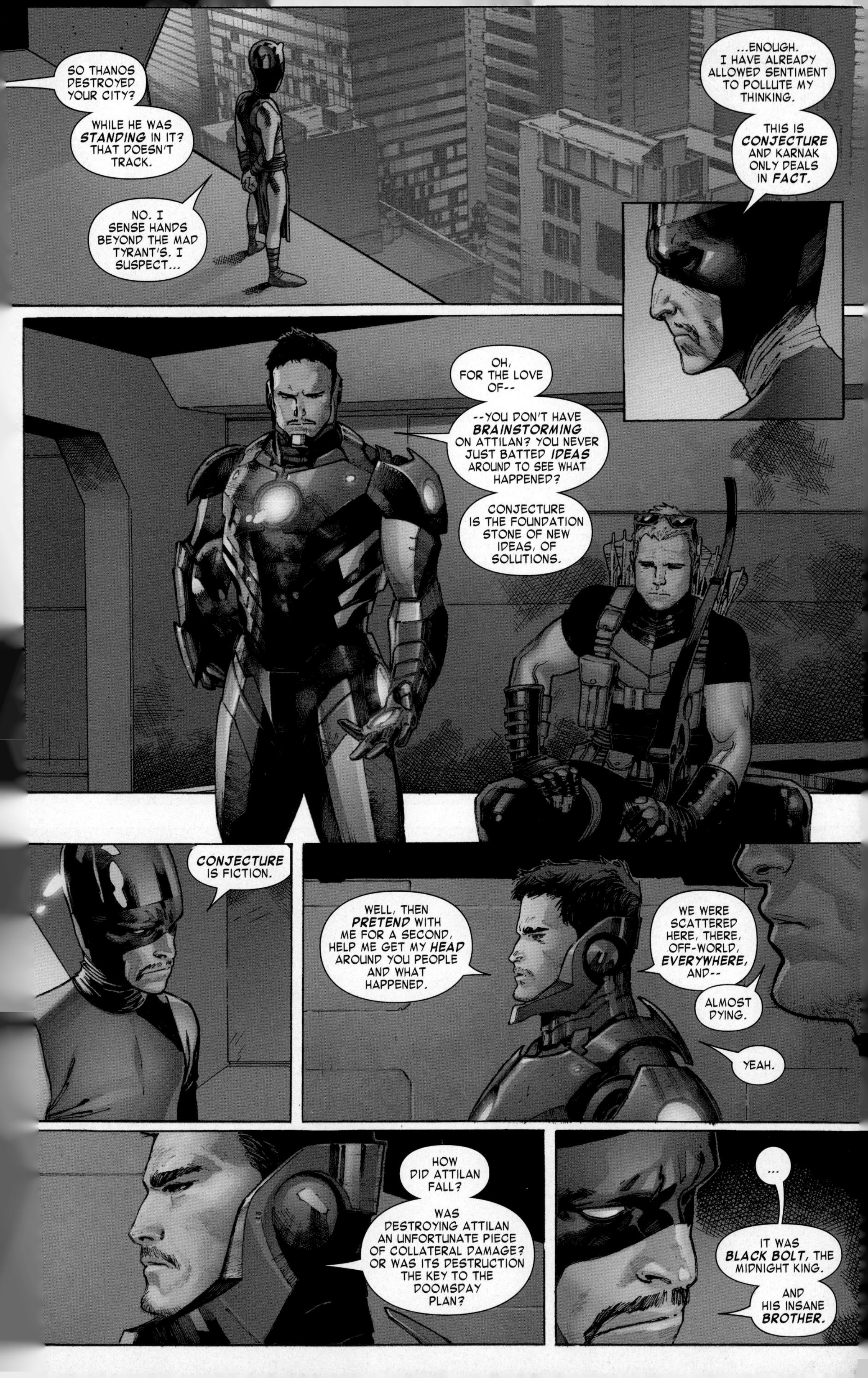
SO THANOS DESTROYED YOUR CITY?
WHILE HE WAS STANDING IN IT? THAT DOESN'T TRACK.
NO. I SENSE HANDS BEYOND THE MAD TYRANT'S. I SUSPECT...
...ENOUGH. I HAVE ALREADY ALLOWED SENTIMENT TO POLLUTE MY THINKING.
THIS IS CONJECTURE AND KARNAK ONLY DEALS IN FACT.
OH, FOR THE LOVE OF--
--YOU DON'T HAVE BRAINSTORMING ON ATTILAN? YOU NEVER JUST BATTED IDEAS AROUND TO SEE WHAT HAPPENED?
CONJECTURE IS THE FOUNDATION STONE OF NEW IDEAS, OF SOLUTIONS.
CONJECTURE IS FICTION.
WELL, THEN PRETEND WITH ME FOR A SECOND, HELP ME GET MY HEAD AROUND YOU PEOPLE AND WHAT HAPPENED.
WE WERE SCATTERED HERE, THERE, OFF-WORLD, EVERYWHERE, AND--
ALMOST DYING.
YEAH.
HOW DID ATTILAN FALL?
WAS DESTROYING ATTILAN AN UNFORTUNATE PIECE OF COLLATERAL DAMAGE? OR WAS ITS DESTRUCTION THE KEY TO THE DOOMSDAY PLAN?
...
IT WAS BLACK BOLT, THE MIDNIGHT KING.
AND HIS INSANE BROTHER.

"ONLY BLACK BOLT AND HIS THUNDEROUS, UNHOLY VOICE COULD HAVE DESTROYED MY CITY.

"BUT MAXIMUS...

"...ONLY HE COULD HAVE DEVISED A WEAPON--AND A PLAN--SO INFERNAL.

"THE BOMB WASN'T JUST AN EXPLOSIVE DEVICE.

"THE DESTRUCTION OF ATTILAN WAS NOT THE GOAL, BUT RATHER AN UNFORTUNATE SIDE EFFECT OF THE DEVICE'S OPERATION.

"IT WAS A DISTRIBUTION SYSTEM FOR TERRIGEN.

"MAXIMUS GAVE MY KING THE WEAPON TO FELL HIS OWN KINGDOM.

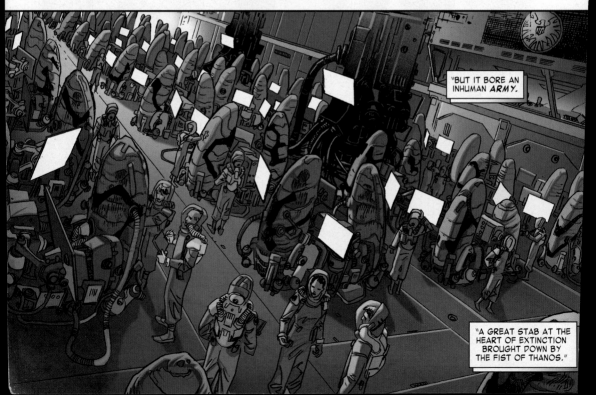

"BUT IT BORE AN INHUMAN ARMY.

"A GREAT STAB AT THE HEART OF EXTINCTION BROUGHT DOWN BY THE FIST OF THANOS."

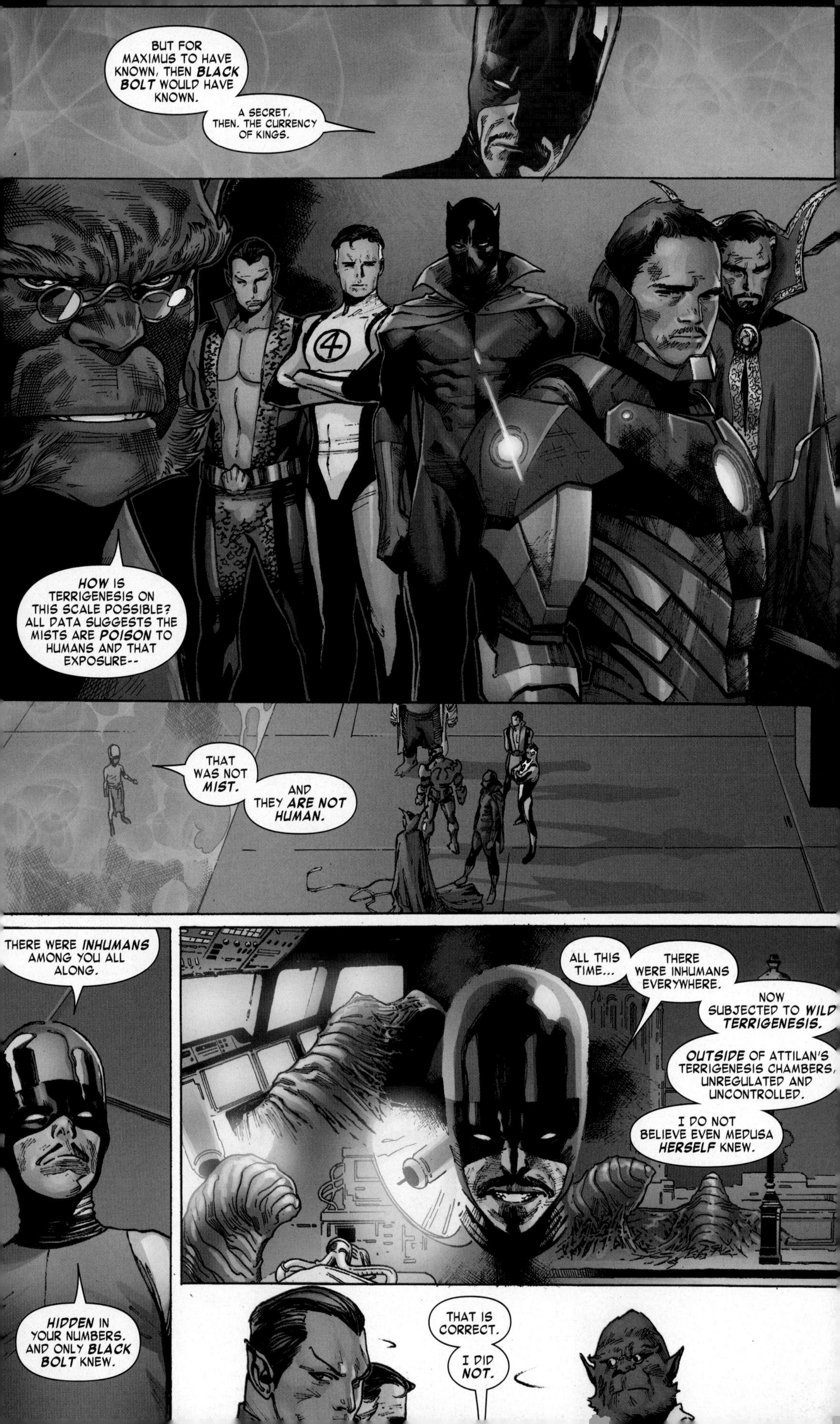
BUT FOR MAXIMUS TO HAVE KNOWN, THEN BLACK BOLT WOULD HAVE KNOWN.
A SECRET, THEN. THE CURRENCY OF KINGS.
HOW IS TERRIGENESIS ON THIS SCALE POSSIBLE? ALL DATA SUGGESTS THE MISTS ARE POISON TO HUMANS AND THAT EXPOSURE--
THAT WAS NOT MIST.
AND THEY ARE NOT HUMAN.
THERE WERE INHUMANS AMONG YOU ALL ALONG.
HIDDEN IN YOUR NUMBERS. AND ONLY BLACK BOLT KNEW.
ALL THIS TIME...
THERE WERE INHUMANS EVERYWHERE.
NOW SUBJECTED TO WILD TERRIGENESIS.
OUTSIDE OF ATTILAN'S TERRIGENESIS CHAMBERS, UNREGULATED AND UNCONTROLLED.
I DO NOT BELIEVE EVEN MEDUSA HERSELF KNEW.
THAT IS CORRECT.
I DID NOT.

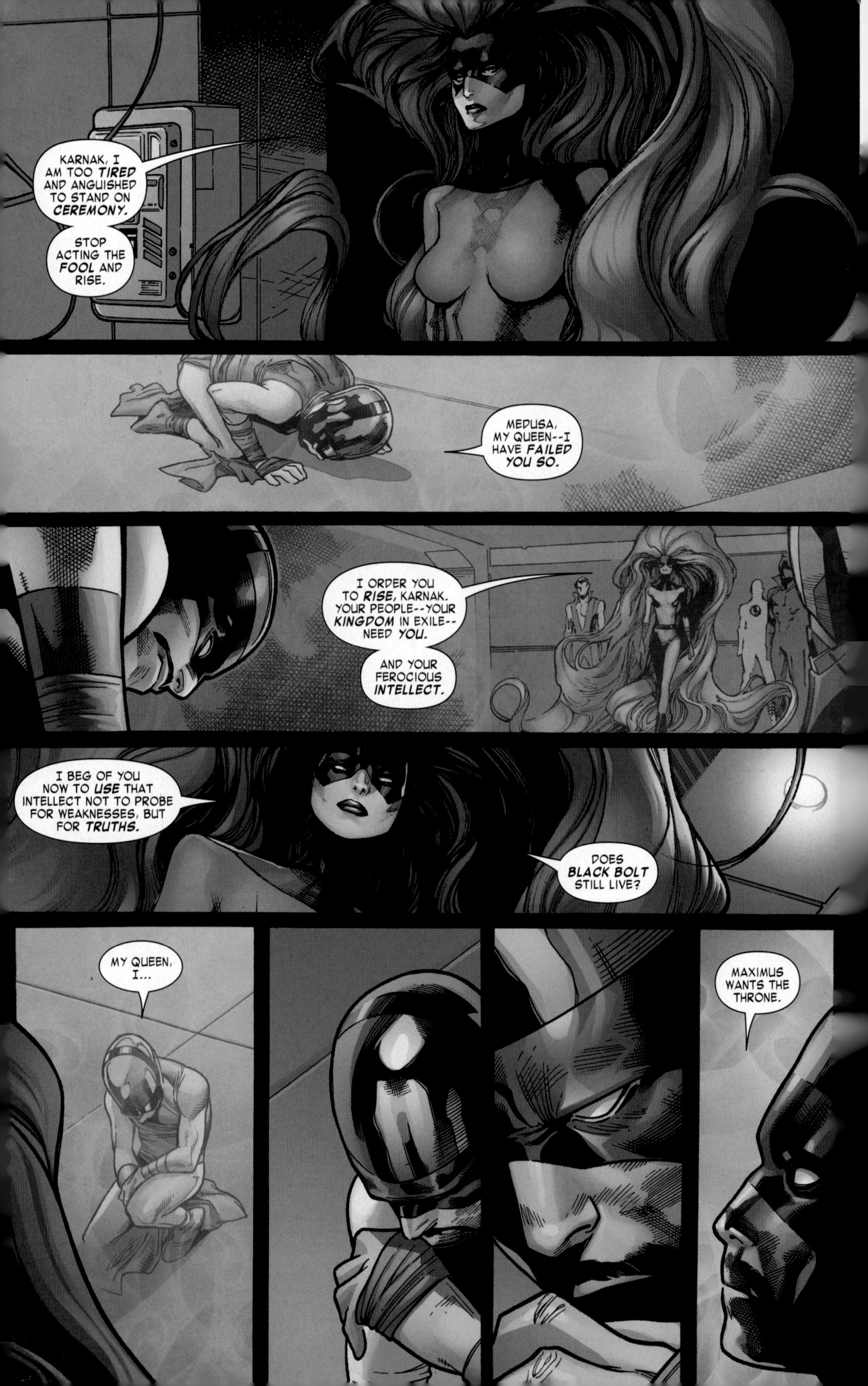
KARNAK, I AM TOO TIRED AND ANGUISHED TO STAND ON CEREMONY.
STOP ACTING THE FOOL AND RISE.
MEDUSA, MY QUEEN--I HAVE FAILED YOU SO.
I ORDER YOU TO RISE, KARNAK. YOUR PEOPLE--YOUR KINGDOM IN EXILE--NEED YOU.
AND YOUR FEROCIOUS INTELLECT.
I BEG OF YOU NOW TO USE THAT INTELLECT NOT TO PROBE FOR WEAKNESSES, BUT FOR TRUTHS.
DOES BLACK BOLT STILL LIVE?
MY QUEEN, I...
MAXIMUS WANTS THE THRONE.

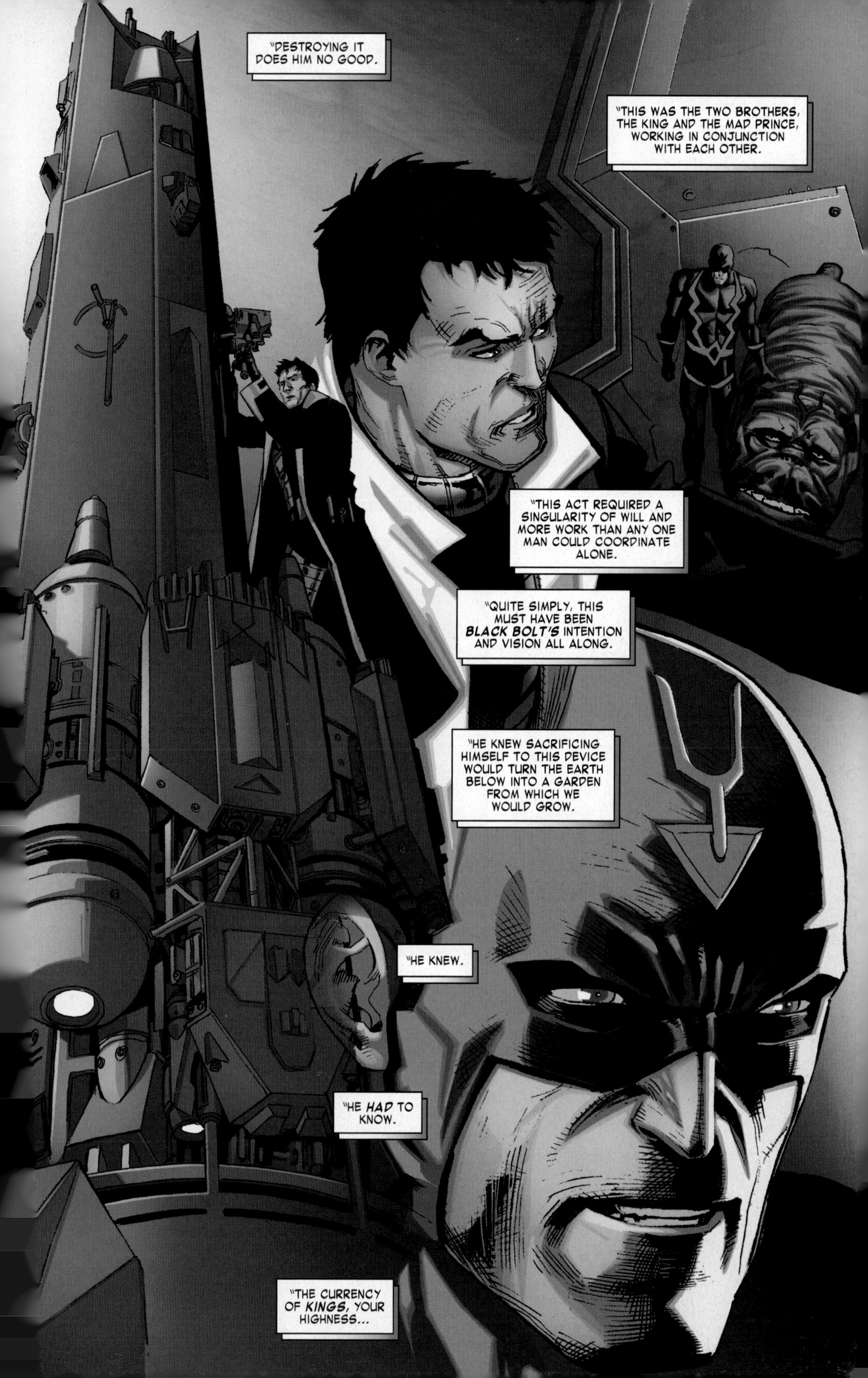
"DESTROYING IT DOES HIM NO GOOD.
"THIS WAS THE TWO BROTHERS, THE KING AND THE MAD PRINCE, WORKING IN CONJUNCTION WITH EACH OTHER.
"THIS ACT REQUIRED A SINGULARITY OF WILL AND MORE WORK THAN ANY ONE MAN COULD COORDINATE ALONE.
"QUITE SIMPLY, THIS MUST HAVE BEEN BLACK BOLT'S INTENTION AND VISION ALL ALONG.
"HE KNEW SACRIFICING HIMSELF TO THIS DEVICE WOULD TURN THE EARTH BELOW INTO A GARDEN FROM WHICH WE WOULD GROW.
"HE KNEW.
"HE HAD TO KNOW.
"THE CURRENCY OF KINGS, YOUR HIGHNESS...

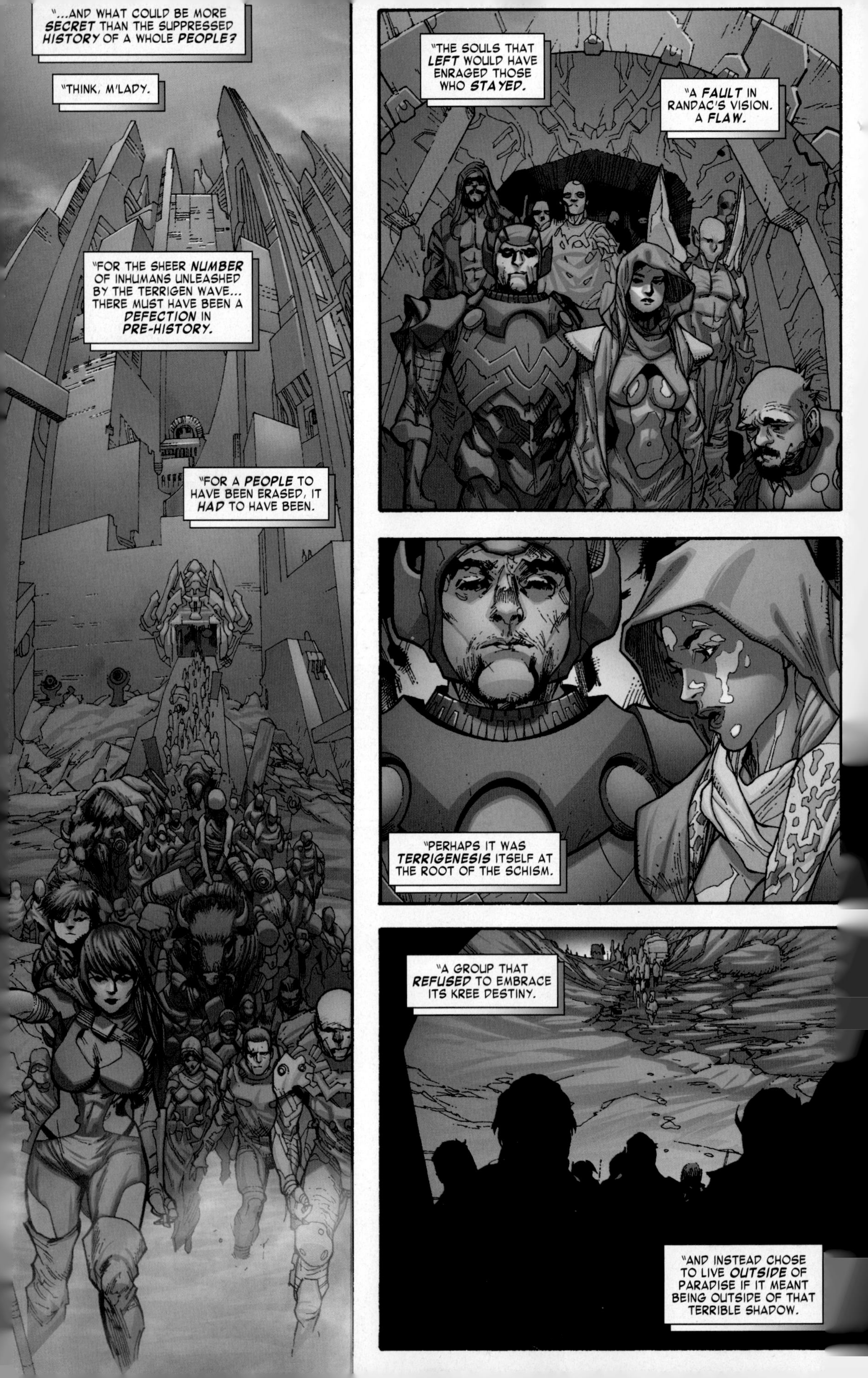
"...AND WHAT COULD BE MORE SECRET THAN THE SUPPRESSED HISTORY OF A WHOLE PEOPLE?
"THINK, M'LADY.
"FOR THE SHEER NUMBER OF INHUMANS UNLEASHED BY THE TERRIGEN WAVE... THERE MUST HAVE BEEN A DEFECTION IN PRE-HISTORY.
"FOR A PEOPLE TO HAVE BEEN ERASED, IT HAD TO HAVE BEEN.
"THE SOULS THAT LEFT WOULD HAVE ENRAGED THOSE WHO STAYED.
"A FAULT IN RANDAC'S VISION. A FLAW.
"PERHAPS IT WAS TERRIGENESIS ITSELF AT THE ROOT OF THE SCHISM.
"A GROUP THAT REFUSED TO EMBRACE ITS KREE DESTINY.
"AND INSTEAD CHOSE TO LIVE OUTSIDE OF PARADISE IF IT MEANT BEING OUTSIDE OF THAT TERRIBLE SHADOW.

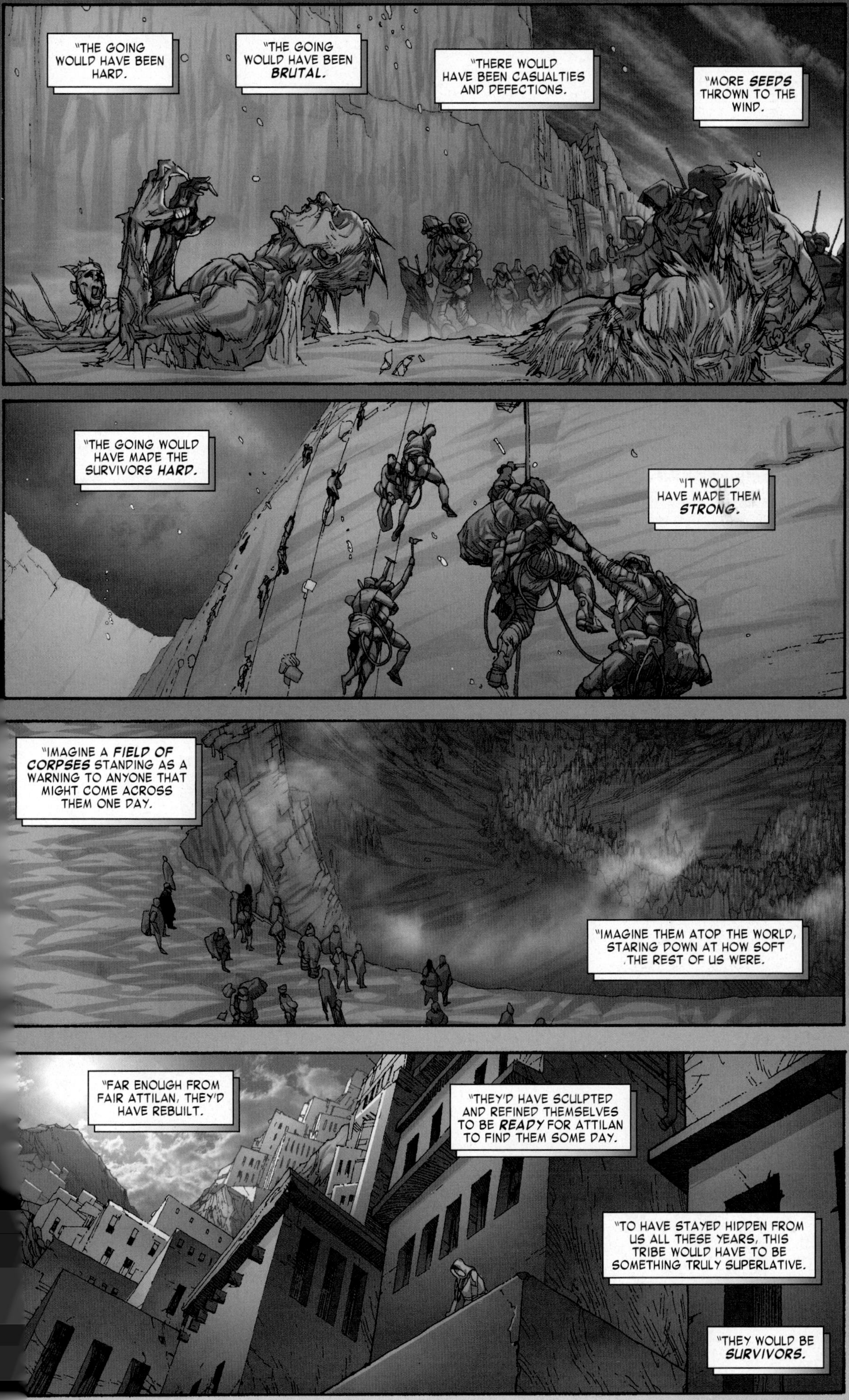
"THE GOING WOULD HAVE BEEN HARD.
"THE GOING WOULD HAVE BEEN BRUTAL.
"THERE WOULD HAVE BEEN CASUALTIES AND DEFECTIONS.
"MORE SEEDS THROWN TO THE WIND.
"THE GOING WOULD HAVE MADE THE SURVIVORS HARD.
"IT WOULD HAVE MADE THEM STRONG.
"IMAGINE A FIELD OF CORPSES STANDING AS A WARNING TO ANYONE THAT MIGHT COME ACROSS THEM ONE DAY.
"IMAGINE THEM ATOP THE WORLD, STARING DOWN AT HOW SOFT THE REST OF US WERE.
"FAR ENOUGH FROM FAIR ATTILAN, THEY'D HAVE REBUILT.
"THEY'D HAVE SCULPTED AND REFINED THEMSELVES TO BE READY FOR ATTILAN TO FIND THEM SOME DAY.
"TO HAVE STAYED HIDDEN FROM US ALL THESE YEARS, THIS TRIBE WOULD HAVE TO BE SOMETHING TRULY SUPERLATIVE.
"THEY WOULD BE SURVIVORS.

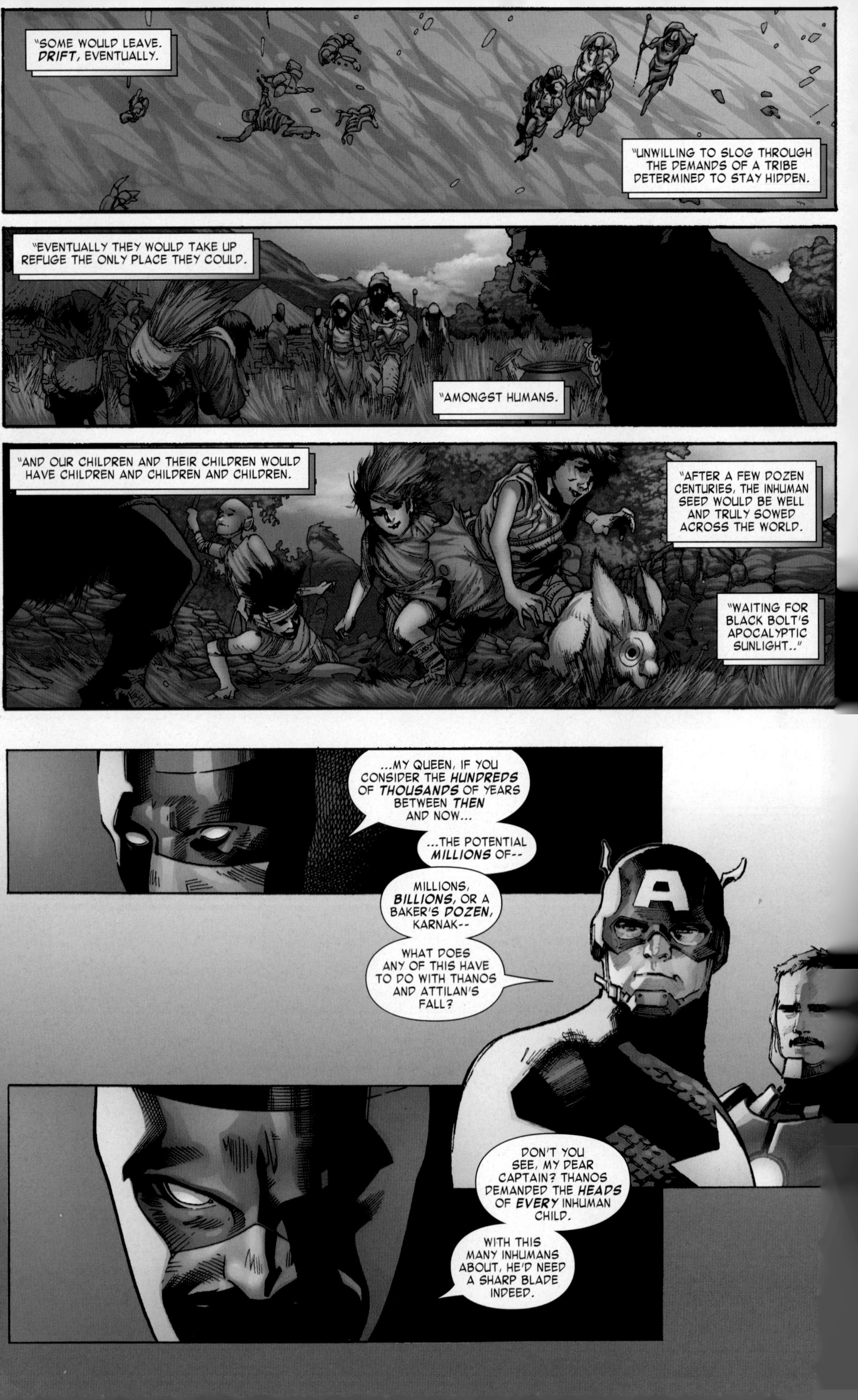
"SOME WOULD LEAVE. DRIFT, EVENTUALLY.
"UNWILLING TO SLOG THROUGH THE DEMANDS OF A TRIBE DETERMINED TO STAY HIDDEN.
"EVENTUALLY THEY WOULD TAKE UP REFUGE THE ONLY PLACE THEY COULD.
"AMONGST HUMANS.
"AND OUR CHILDREN AND THEIR CHILDREN WOULD HAVE CHILDREN AND CHILDREN AND CHILDREN.
"AFTER A FEW DOZEN CENTURIES, THE INHUMAN SEED WOULD BE WELL AND TRULY SOWED ACROSS THE WORLD.
"WAITING FOR BLACK BOLT'S APOCALYPTIC SUNLIGHT.."
...MY QUEEN, IF YOU CONSIDER THE HUNDREDS OF THOUSANDS OF YEARS BETWEEN THEN AND NOW...
...THE POTENTIAL MILLIONS OF--
MILLIONS, BILLIONS, OR A BAKER'S DOZEN, KARNAK--
WHAT DOES ANY OF THIS HAVE TO DO WITH THANOS AND ATTILAN'S FALL?
DON'T YOU SEE, MY DEAR CAPTAIN? THANOS DEMANDED THE HEADS OF EVERY INHUMAN CHILD.
WITH THIS MANY INHUMANS ABOUT, HE'D NEED A SHARP BLADE INDEED.

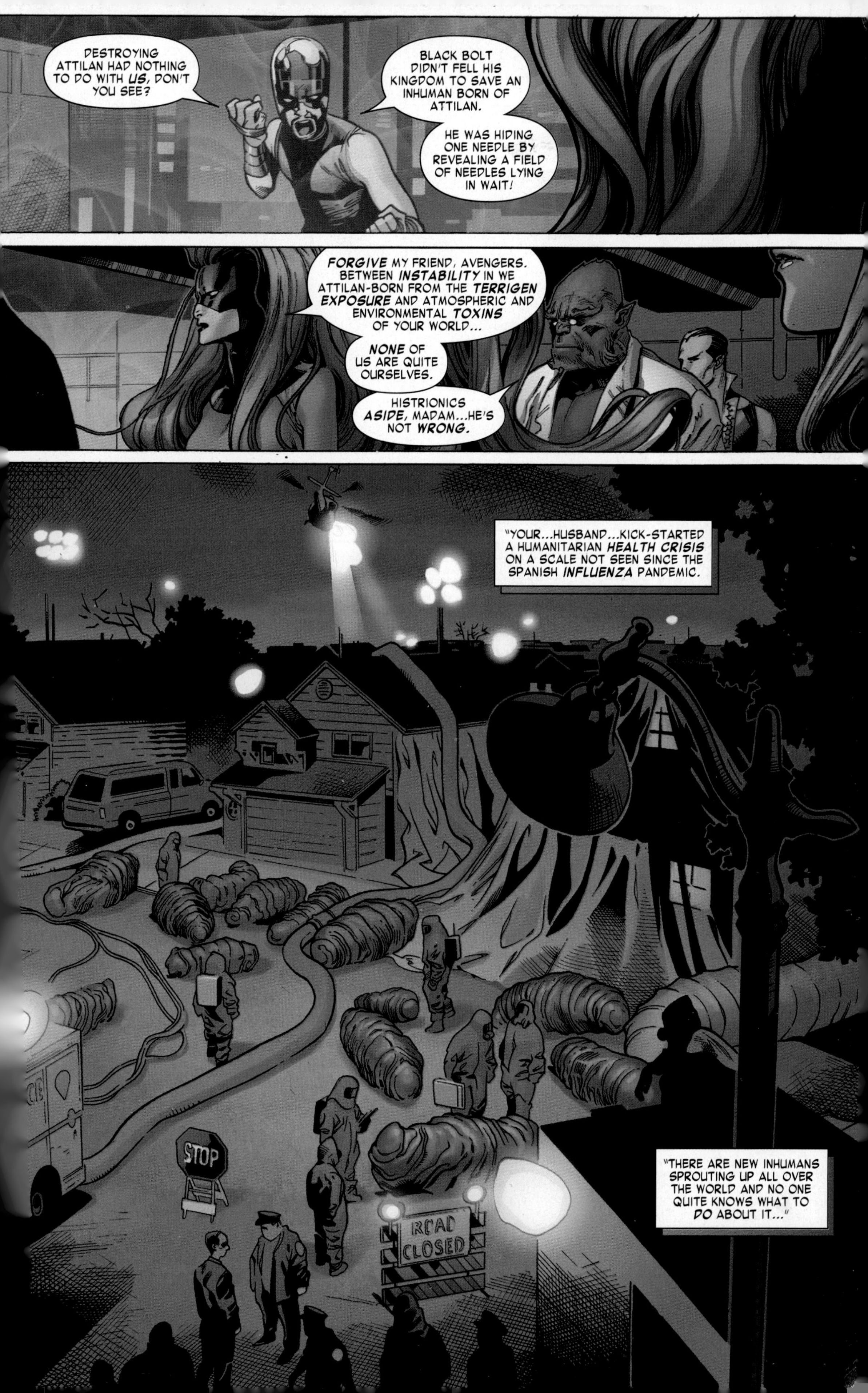
DESTROYING ATTILAN HAD NOTHING TO DO WITH US, DON'T YOU SEE?
BLACK BOLT DIDN'T FELL HIS KINGDOM TO SAVE AN INHUMAN BORN OF ATTILAN.
HE WAS HIDING ONE NEEDLE BY REVEALING A FIELD OF NEEDLES LYING IN WAIT!
FORGIVE MY FRIEND, AVENGERS. BETWEEN INSTABILITY IN WE ATTILAN-BORN FROM THE TERRIGEN EXPOSURE AND ATMOSPHERIC AND ENVIRONMENTAL TOXINS OF YOUR WORLD...
NONE OF US ARE QUITE OURSELVES.
HISTRIONICS ASIDE, MADAM...HE'S NOT WRONG.
"YOUR...HUSBAND...KICK-STARTED A HUMANITARIAN HEALTH CRISIS ON A SCALE NOT SEEN SINCE THE SPANISH INFLUENZA PANDEMIC.
STOP
ROAD CLOSED
"THERE ARE NEW INHUMANS SPROUTING UP ALL OVER THE WORLD AND NO ONE QUITE KNOWS WHAT TO DO ABOUT IT..."

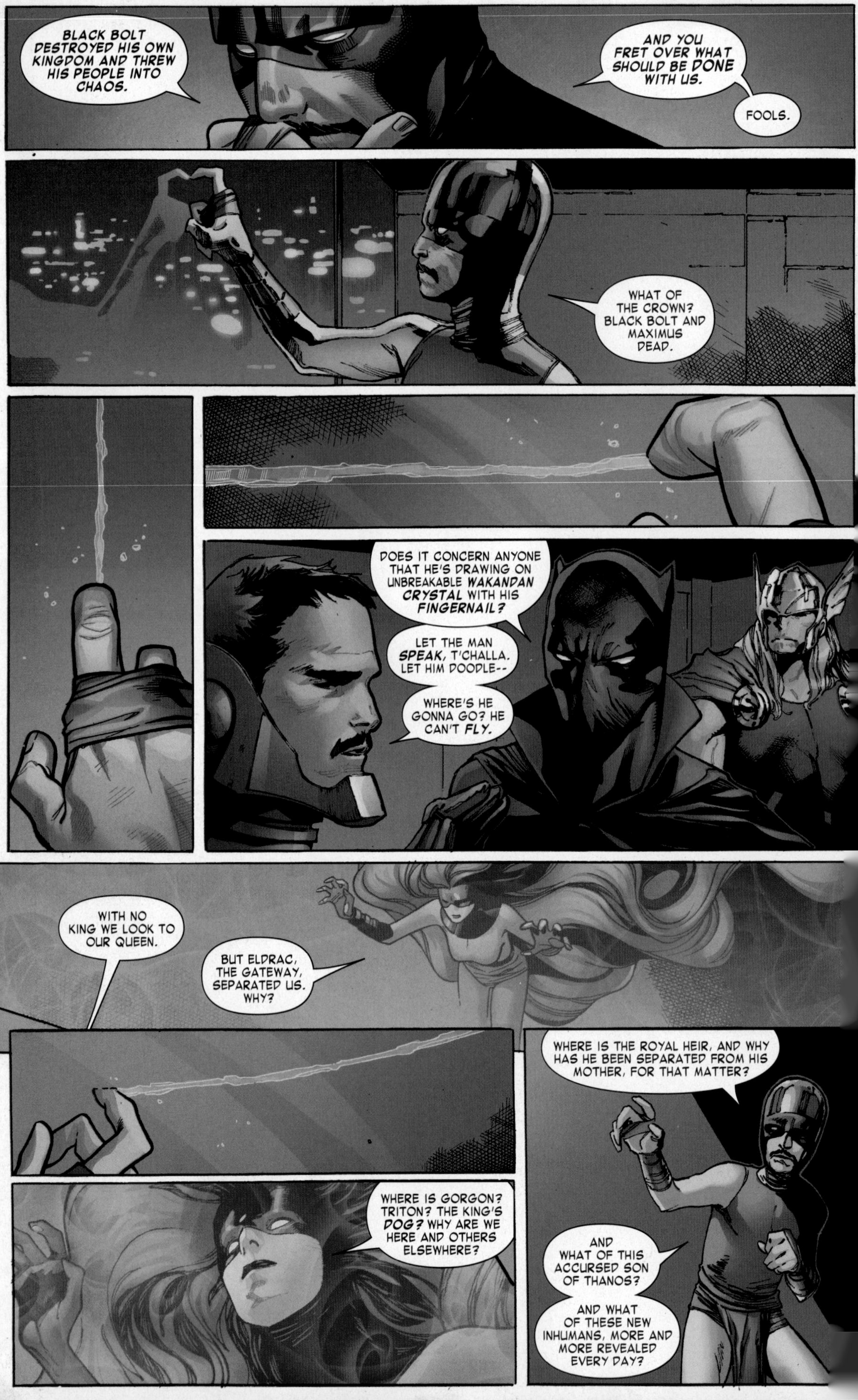
BLACK BOLT DESTROYED HIS OWN KINGDOM AND THREW HIS PEOPLE INTO CHAOS.
AND YOU FRET OVER WHAT SHOULD BE DONE WITH US.
FOOLS.
WHAT OF THE CROWN? BLACK BOLT AND MAXIMUS DEAD.
DOES IT CONCERN ANYONE THAT HE'S DRAWING ON UNBREAKABLE WAKANDAN CRYSTAL WITH HIS FINGERNAIL?
LET THE MAN SPEAK, T'CHALLA. LET HIM DOODLE--
WHERE'S HE GONNA GO? HE CAN'T FLY.
WITH NO KING WE LOOK TO OUR QUEEN.
BUT ELDRAC, THE GATEWAY, SEPARATED US. WHY?
WHERE IS THE ROYAL HEIR, AND WHY HAS HE BEEN SEPARATED FROM HIS MOTHER, FOR THAT MATTER?
WHERE IS GORGON? TRITON? THE KING'S DOG? WHY ARE WE HERE AND OTHERS ELSEWHERE?
AND WHAT OF THIS ACCURSED SON OF THANOS?
AND WHAT OF THESE NEW INHUMANS, MORE AND MORE REVEALED EVERY DAY?

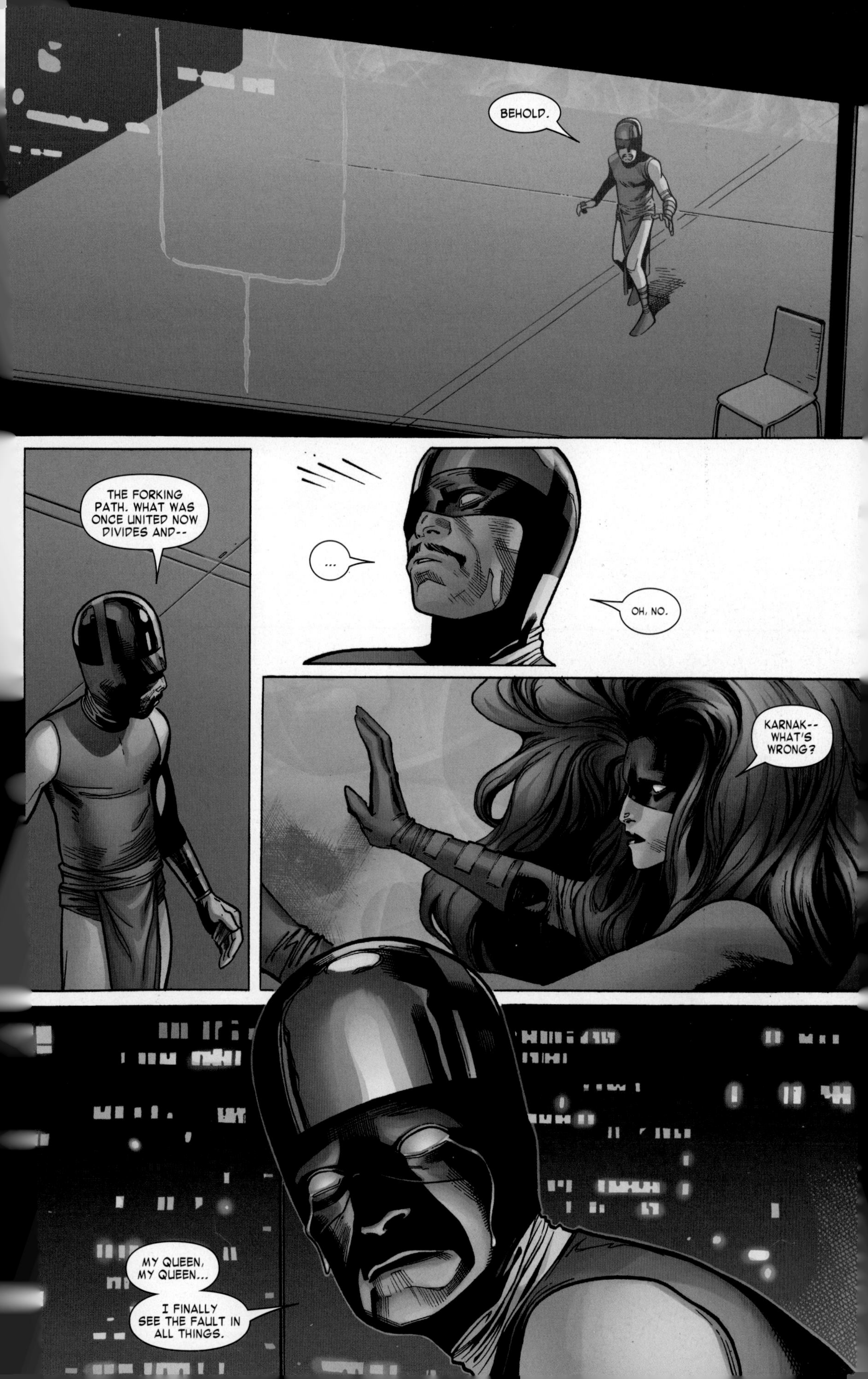
BEHOLD.
THE FORKING PATH. WHAT WAS ONCE UNITED NOW DIVIDES AND--
...
OH, NO.
KARNAK-- WHAT'S WRONG?
MY QUEEN, MY QUEEN...
I FINALLY SEE THE FAULT IN ALL THINGS.

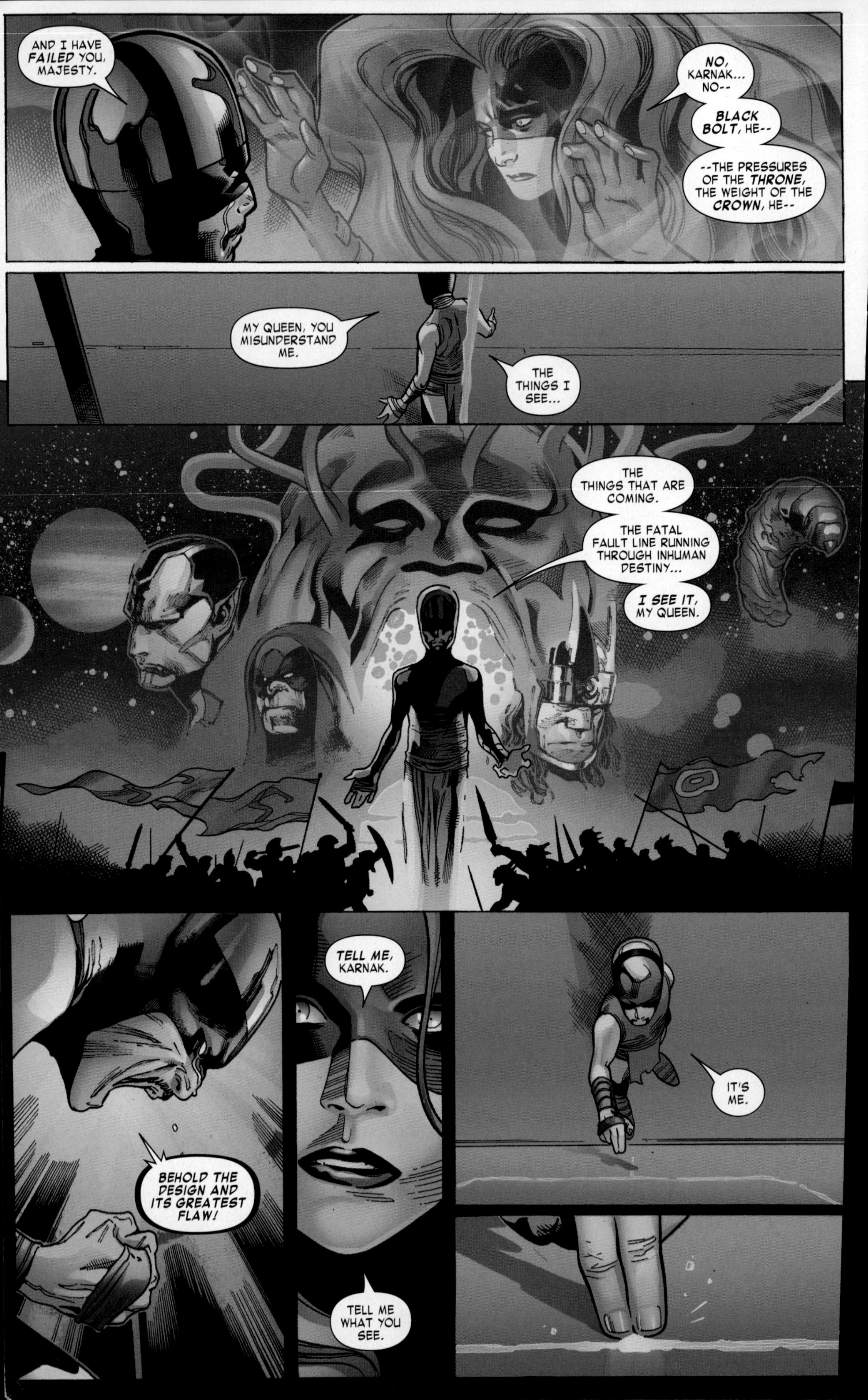

AND I HAVE FAILED YOU, MAJESTY.
NO, KARNAK... NO--
BLACK BOLT, HE--
--THE PRESSURES OF THE THRONE, THE WEIGHT OF THE CROWN, HE--
MY QUEEN, YOU MISUNDERSTAND ME.
THE THINGS I SEE...
THE THINGS THAT ARE COMING.
THE FATAL FAULT LINE RUNNING THROUGH INHUMAN DESTINY...
I SEE IT, MY QUEEN.
BEHOLD THE DESIGN AND ITS GREATEST FLAW!
TELL ME, KARNAK.
TELL ME WHAT YOU SEE.
IT'S ME.

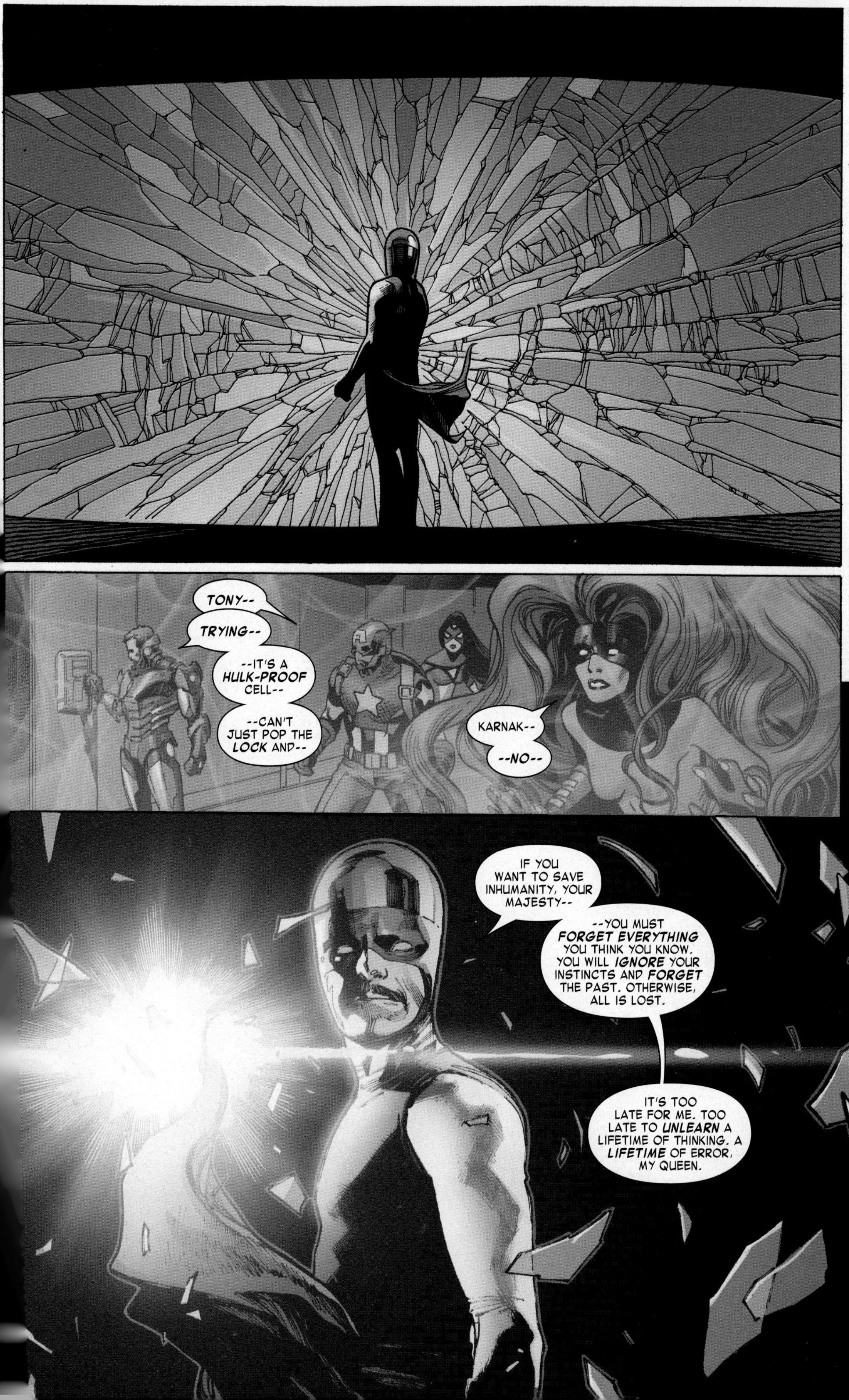
TONY--
TRYING--
--IT'S A HULK-PROOF CELL--
--CAN'T JUST POP THE LOCK AND--
KARNAK--
--NO--
IF YOU WANT TO SAVE INHUMANITY, YOUR MAJESTY--
--YOU MUST FORGET EVERYTHING YOU THINK YOU KNOW. YOU WILL IGNORE YOUR INSTINCTS AND FORGET THE PAST. OTHERWISE, ALL IS LOST.
IT'S TOO LATE FOR ME. TOO LATE TO UNLEARN A LIFETIME OF THINKING. A LIFETIME OF ERROR, MY QUEEN.

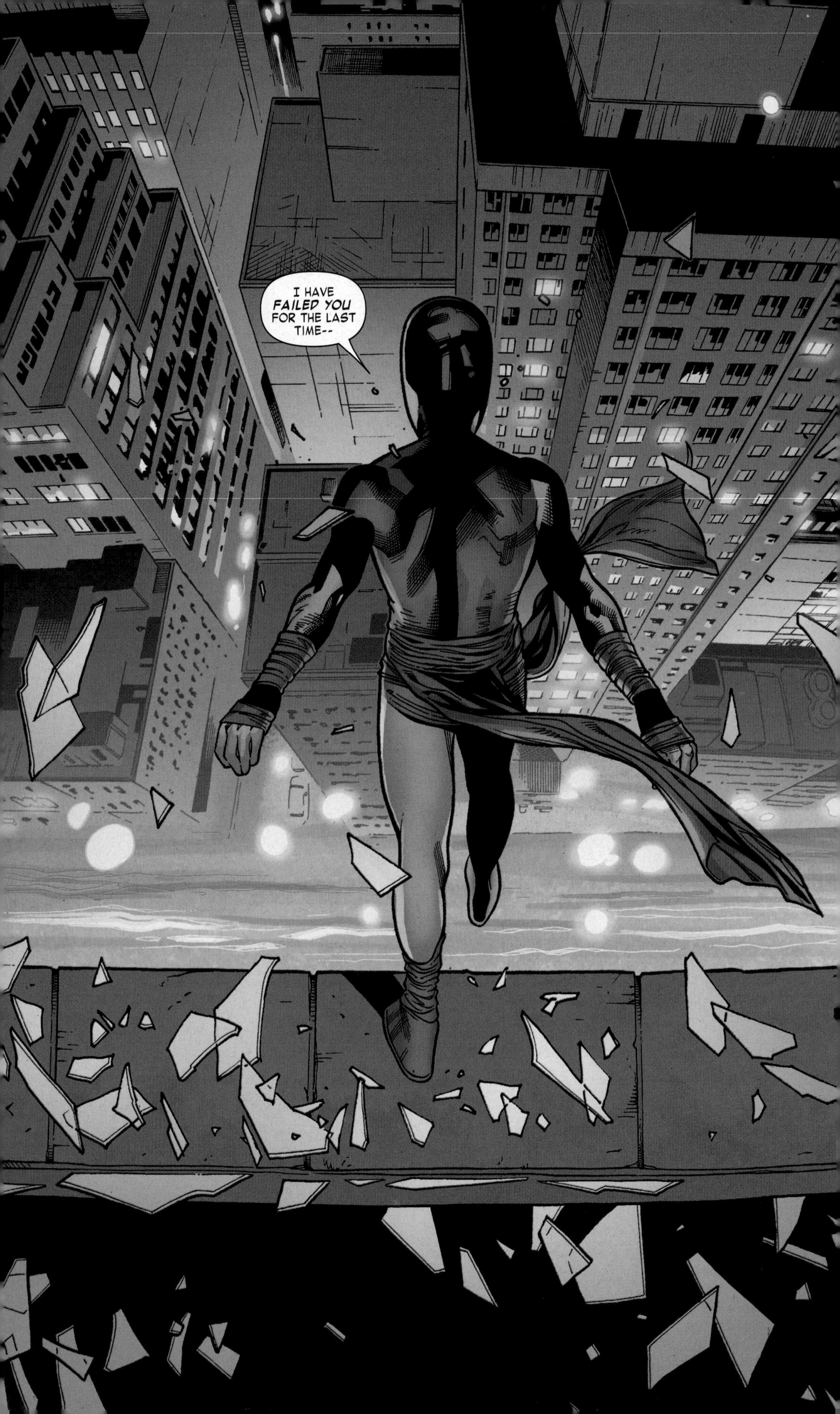
I HAVE FAILED YOU FOR THE LAST TIME--

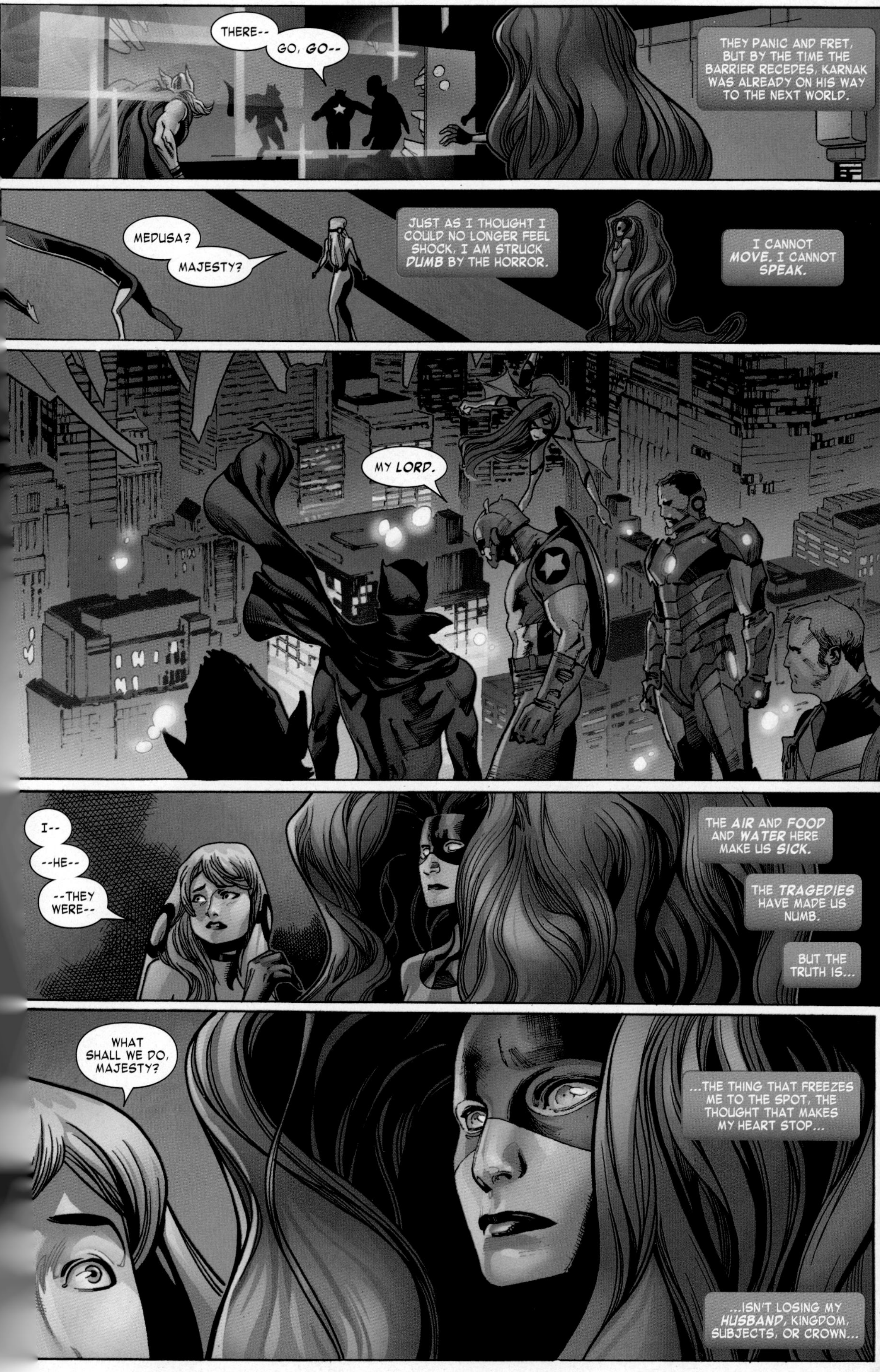
THERE--
GO, GO--
THEY PANIC AND FRET, BUT BY THE TIME THE BARRIER RECEDES, KARNAK WAS ALREADY ON HIS WAY TO THE NEXT WORLD.
MEDUSA?
MAJESTY?
JUST AS I THOUGHT I COULD NO LONGER FEEL SHOCK, I AM STRUCK DUMB BY THE HORROR.
I CANNOT MOVE. I CANNOT SPEAK.
MY LORD.
I--
--HE--
--THEY WERE--
THE AIR AND FOOD AND WATER HERE MAKE US SICK.
THE TRAGEDIES HAVE MADE US NUMB.
BUT THE TRUTH IS...
WHAT SHALL WE DO, MAJESTY?
...THE THING THAT FREEZES ME TO THE SPOT, THE THOUGHT THAT MAKES MY HEART STOP...
...ISN'T LOSING MY HUSBAND, KINGDOM, SUBJECTS, OR CROWN...

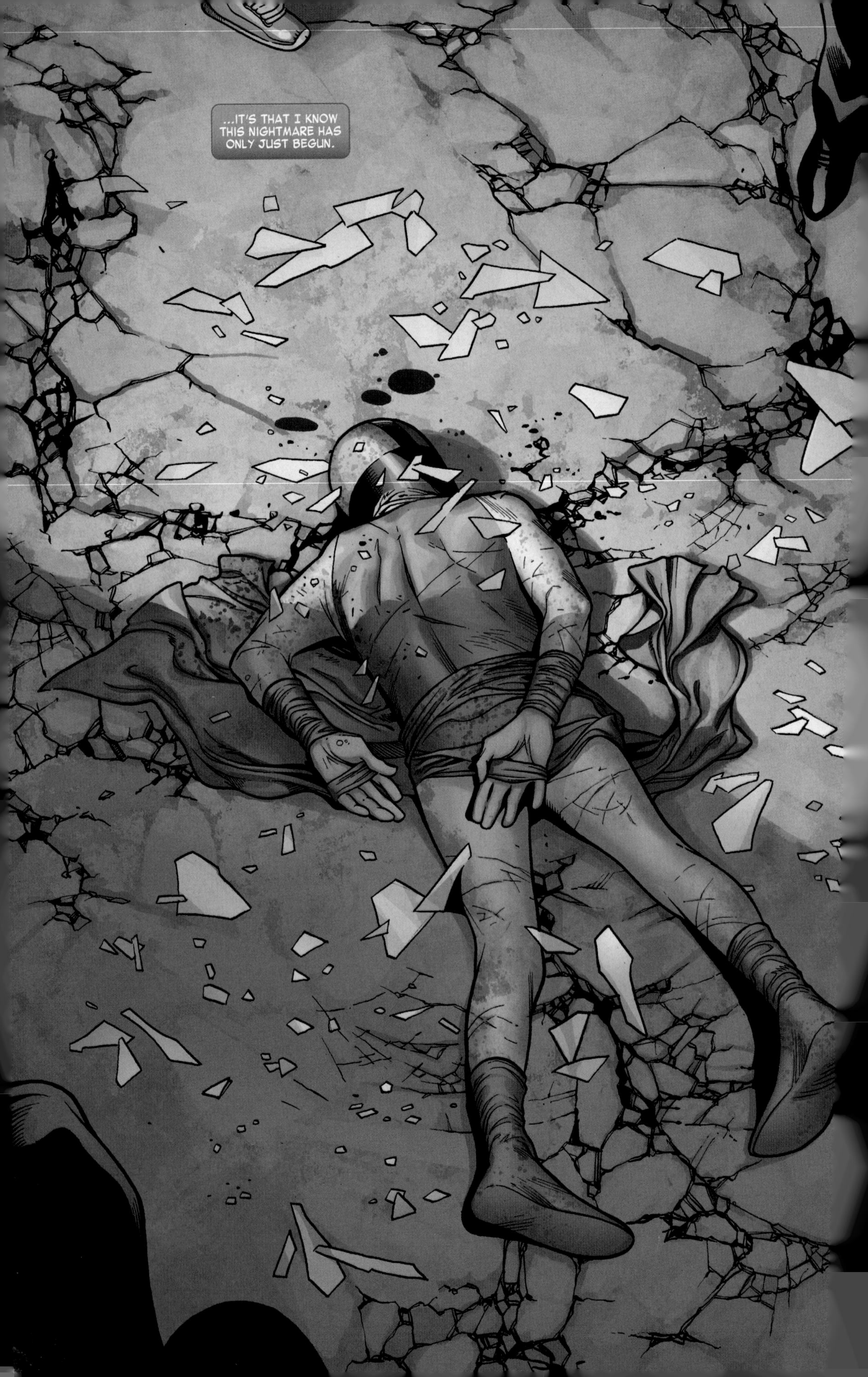
...IT'S THAT I KNOW THIS NIGHTMARE HAS ONLY JUST BEGUN.

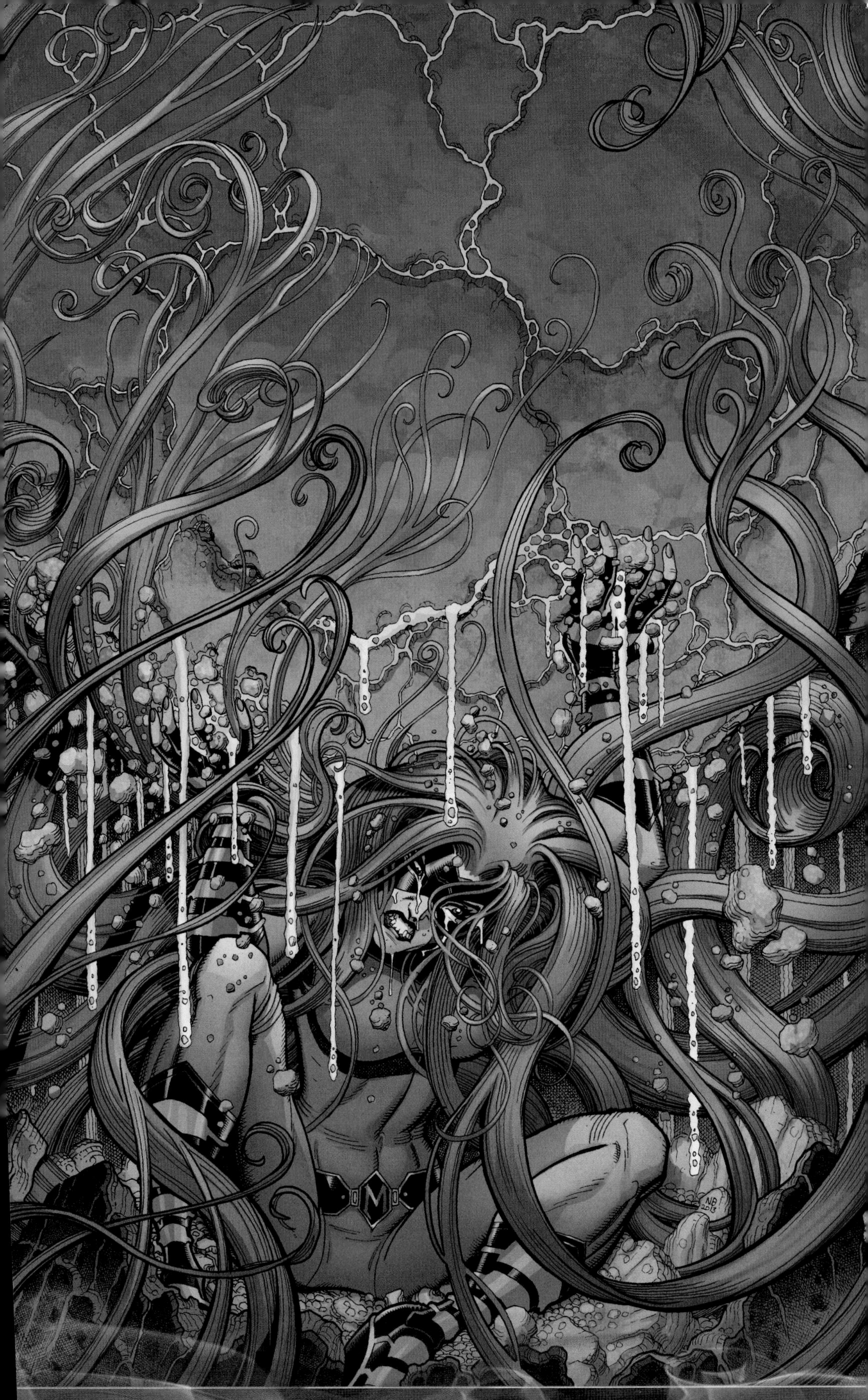

INHUMANITY #2

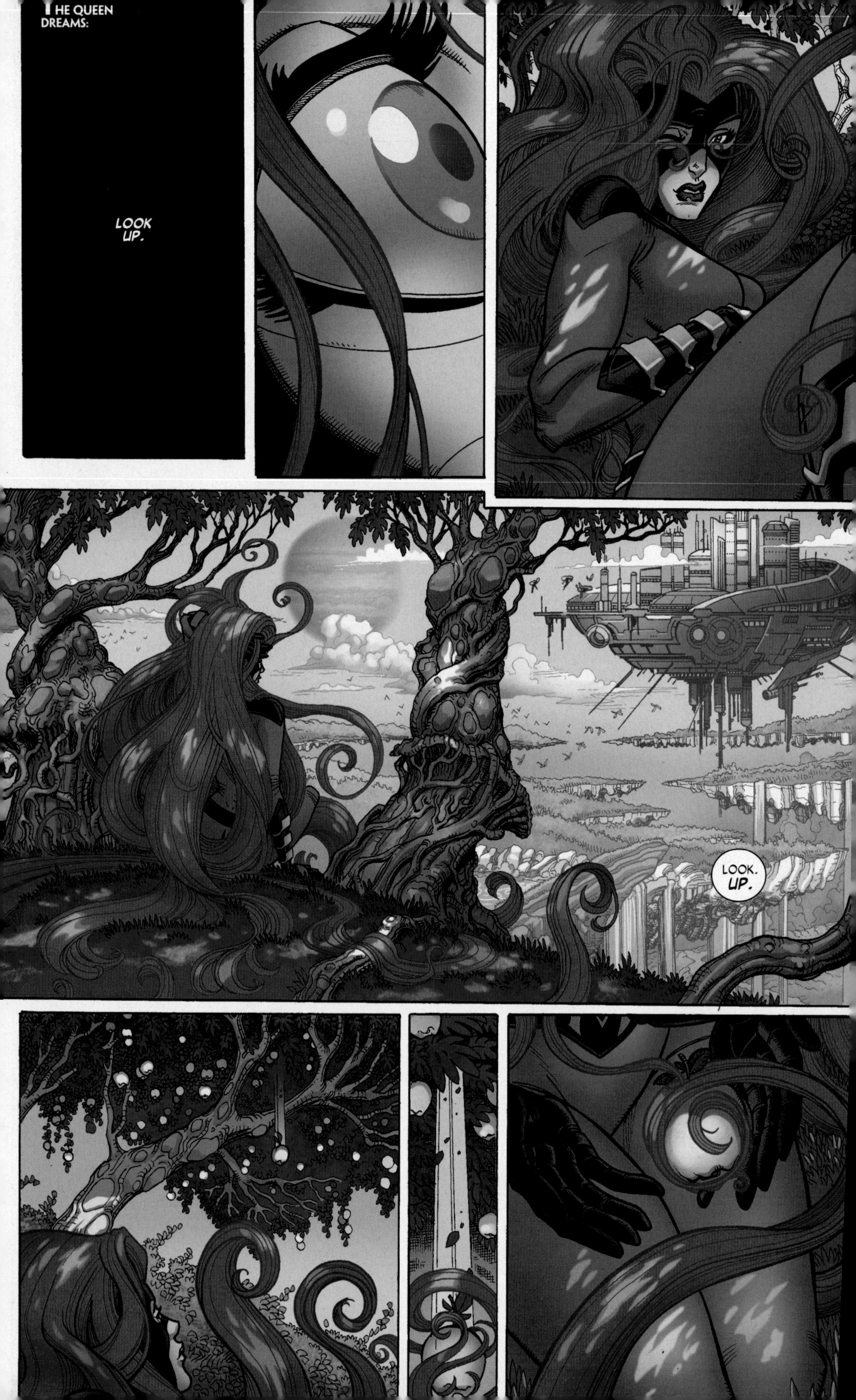
THE QUEEN DREAMS:
LOOK UP.
LOOK. UP.

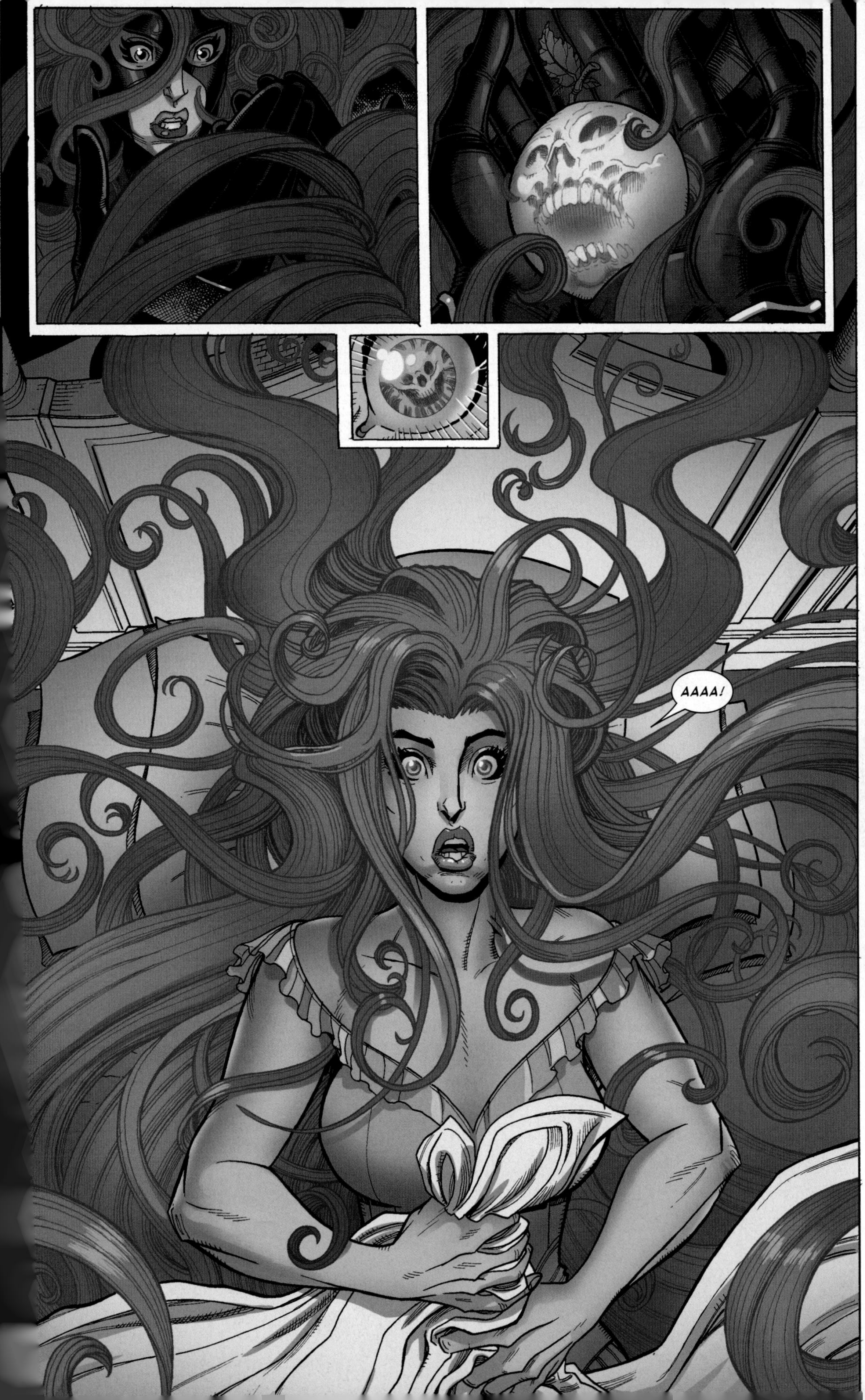
AAAA!

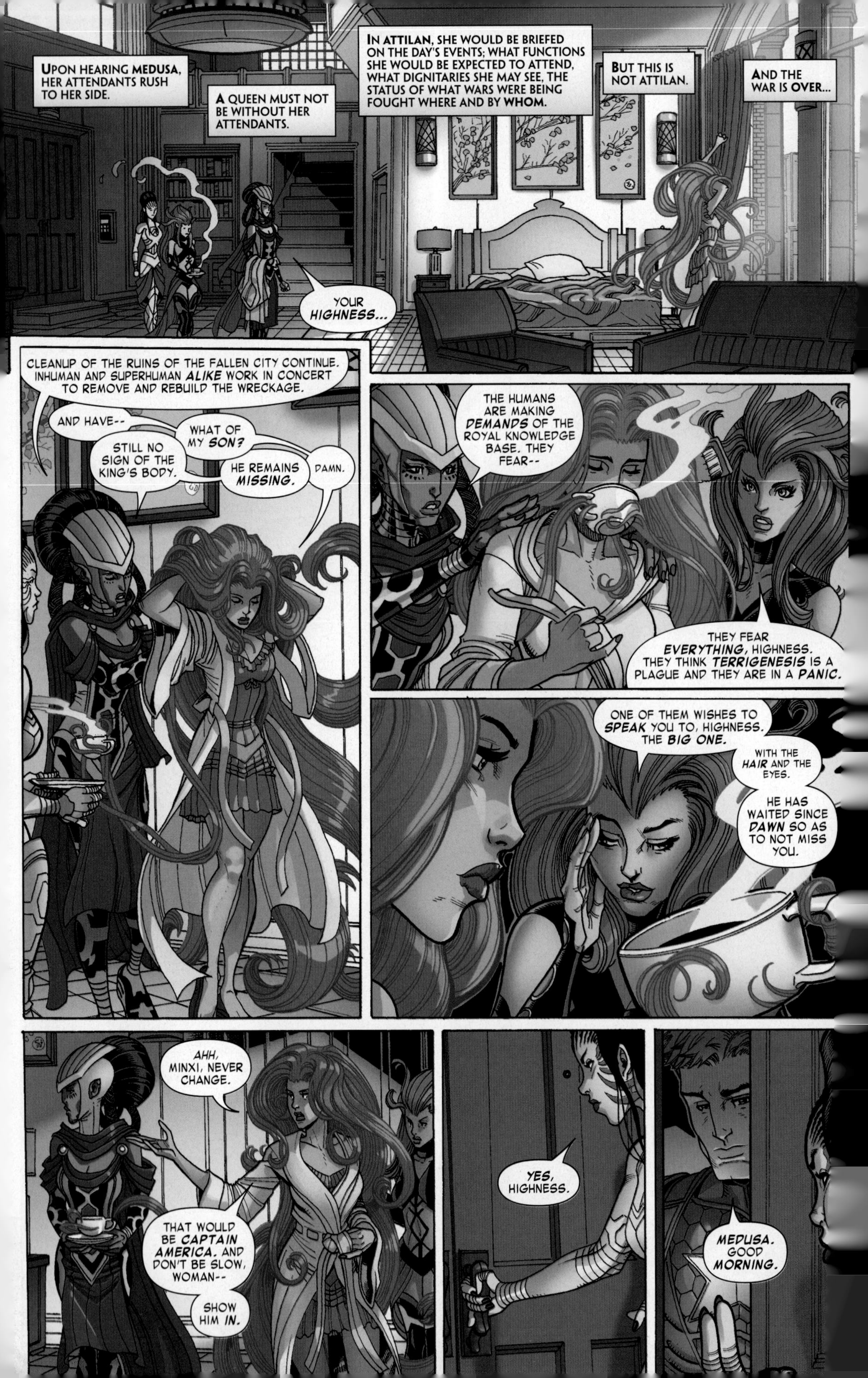

UPON HEARING MEDUSA, HER ATTENDANTS RUSH TO HER SIDE.
A QUEEN MUST NOT BE WITHOUT HER ATTENDANTS.
IN ATTILAN, SHE WOULD BE BRIEFED ON THE DAY'S EVENTS; WHAT FUNCTIONS SHE WOULD BE EXPECTED TO ATTEND, WHAT DIGNITARIES SHE MAY SEE, THE STATUS OF WHAT WARS WERE BEING FOUGHT WHERE AND BY WHOM.
BUT THIS IS NOT ATTILAN.
AND THE WAR IS OVER...
YOUR HIGHNESS...
CLEANUP OF THE RUINS OF THE FALLEN CITY CONTINUE. INHUMAN AND SUPERHUMAN ALIKE WORK IN CONCERT TO REMOVE AND REBUILD THE WRECKAGE.
AND HAVE--
WHAT OF MY SON?
STILL NO SIGN OF THE KING'S BODY.
HE REMAINS MISSING.
DAMN.
THE HUMANS ARE MAKING DEMANDS OF THE ROYAL KNOWLEDGE BASE. THEY FEAR--
THEY FEAR EVERYTHING, HIGHNESS. THEY THINK TERRIGENESIS IS A PLAGUE AND THEY ARE IN A PANIC.
ONE OF THEM WISHES TO SPEAK YOU TO, HIGHNESS. THE BIG ONE.
WITH THE HAIR AND THE EYES.
HE HAS WAITED SINCE DAWN SO AS TO NOT MISS YOU.
AHH, MINXI, NEVER CHANGE.
THAT WOULD BE CAPTAIN AMERICA. AND DON'T BE SLOW, WOMAN--
SHOW HIM IN.
YES, HIGHNESS.
MEDUSA. GOOD MORNING.

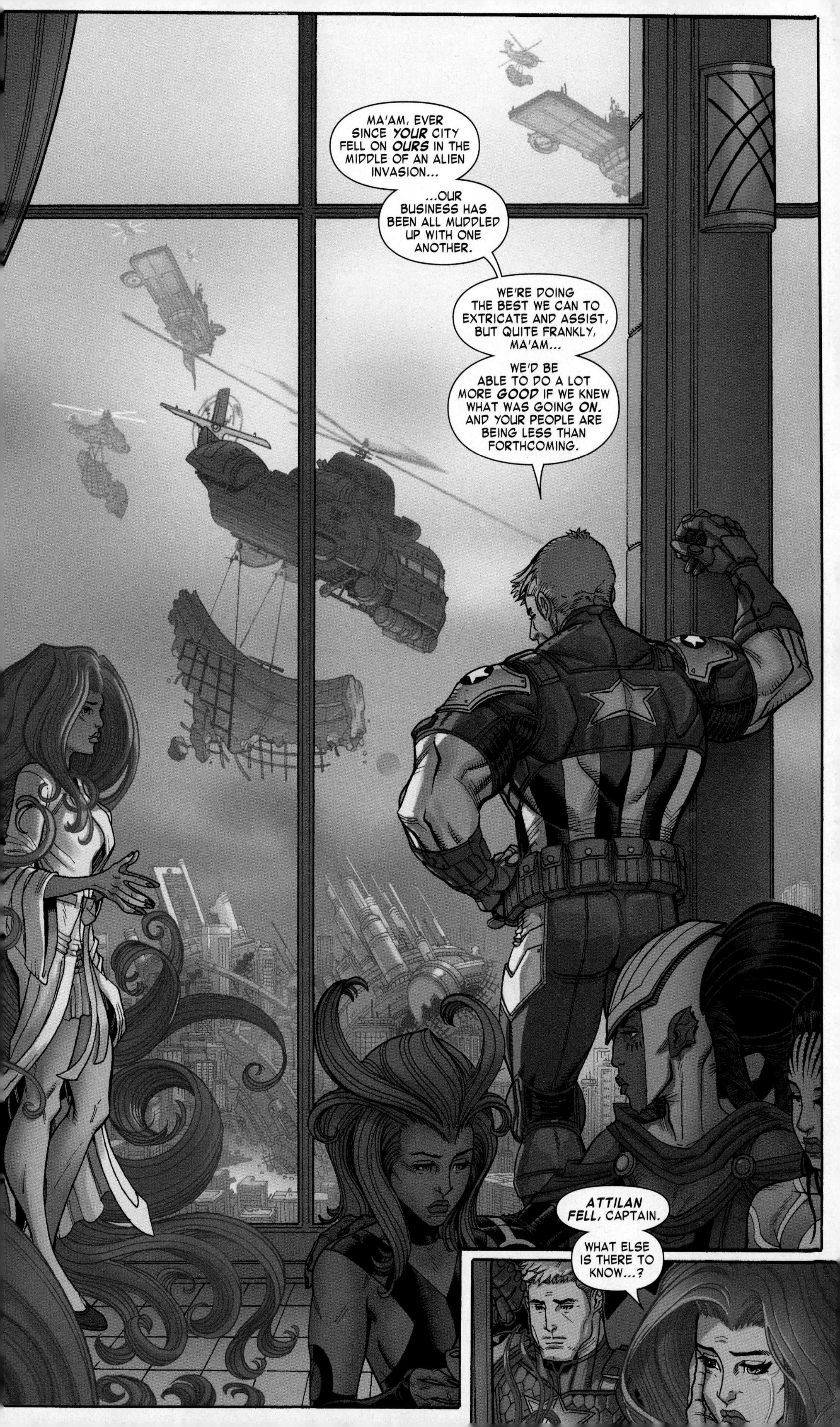

MA'AM, EVER SINCE *YOUR* CITY FELL ON *OURS* IN THE MIDDLE OF AN ALIEN INVASION...
...OUR BUSINESS HAS BEEN ALL MUDDLED UP WITH ONE ANOTHER.
WE'RE DOING THE BEST WE CAN TO EXTRICATE AND ASSIST, BUT QUITE FRANKLY, MA'AM...
WE'D BE ABLE TO DO A LOT MORE *GOOD* IF WE KNEW WHAT WAS GOING *ON.* AND YOUR PEOPLE ARE BEING LESS THAN FORTHCOMING.
ATTILAN FELL, CAPTAIN.
WHAT ELSE IS THERE TO KNOW...?

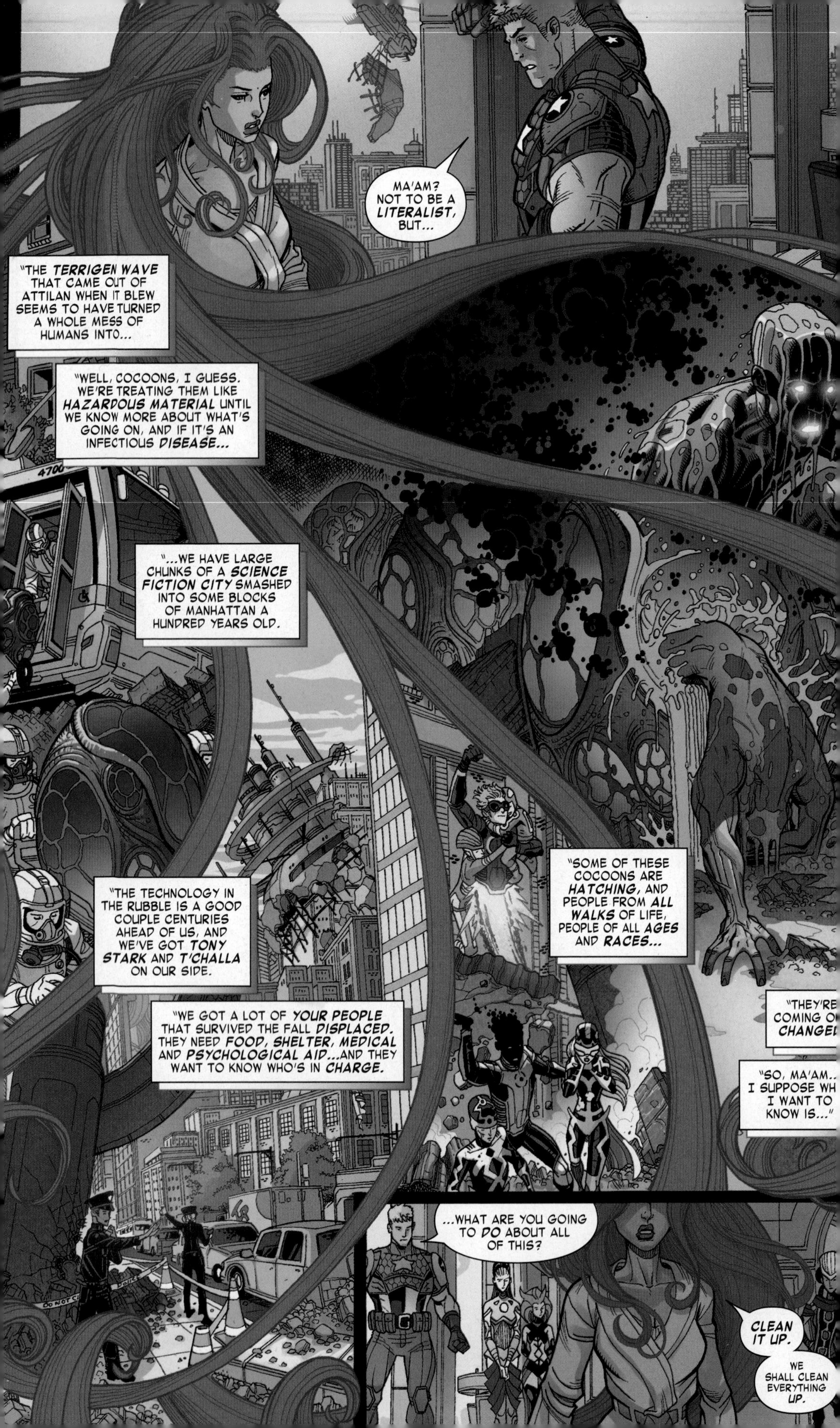
MA'AM? NOT TO BE A LITERALIST, BUT...
"THE TERRIGEN WAVE THAT CAME OUT OF ATTILAN WHEN IT BLEW SEEMS TO HAVE TURNED A WHOLE MESS OF HUMANS INTO...
"WELL, COCOONS, I GUESS. WE'RE TREATING THEM LIKE HAZARDOUS MATERIAL UNTIL WE KNOW MORE ABOUT WHAT'S GOING ON, AND IF IT'S AN INFECTIOUS DISEASE...
"...WE HAVE LARGE CHUNKS OF A SCIENCE FICTION CITY SMASHED INTO SOME BLOCKS OF MANHATTAN A HUNDRED YEARS OLD.
"THE TECHNOLOGY IN THE RUBBLE IS A GOOD COUPLE CENTURIES AHEAD OF US, AND WE'VE GOT TONY STARK AND T'CHALLA ON OUR SIDE.
"WE GOT A LOT OF YOUR PEOPLE THAT SURVIVED THE FALL DISPLACED. THEY NEED FOOD, SHELTER, MEDICAL AND PSYCHOLOGICAL AID...AND THEY WANT TO KNOW WHO'S IN CHARGE.
"SOME OF THESE COCOONS ARE HATCHING, AND PEOPLE FROM ALL WALKS OF LIFE, PEOPLE OF ALL AGES AND RACES...
"SO, MA'AM...
...WHAT ARE YOU GOING TO DO ABOUT ALL OF THIS?
CLEAN IT UP.
WE SHALL CLEAN EVERYTHING UP.

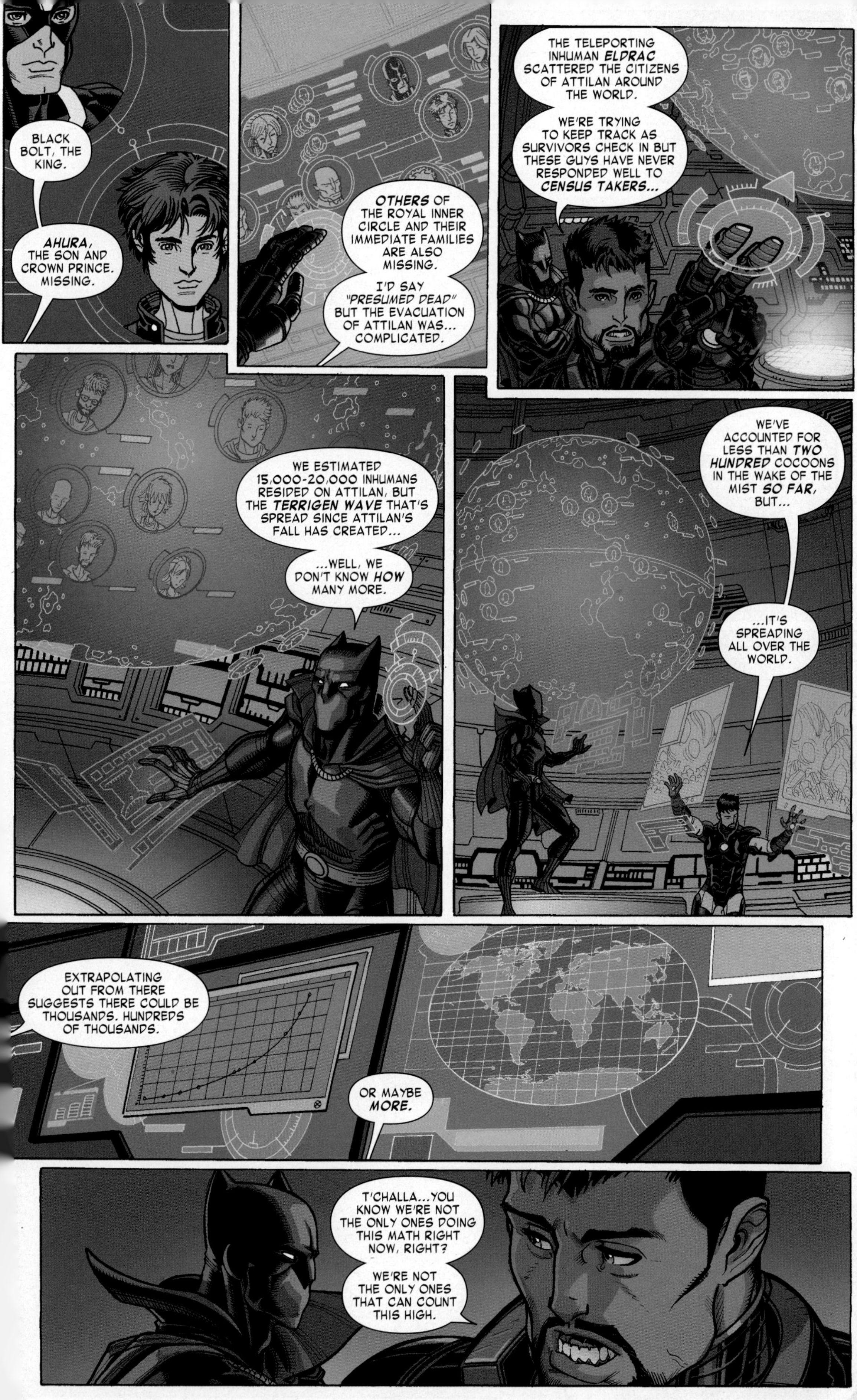
BLACK BOLT, THE KING.
AHURA, THE SON AND CROWN PRINCE. MISSING.
OTHERS OF THE ROYAL INNER CIRCLE AND THEIR IMMEDIATE FAMILIES ARE ALSO MISSING.
I'D SAY "PRESUMED DEAD" BUT THE EVACUATION OF ATTILAN WAS... COMPLICATED.
THE TELEPORTING INHUMAN ELDRAC SCATTERED THE CITIZENS OF ATTILAN AROUND THE WORLD.
WE'RE TRYING TO KEEP TRACK AS SURVIVORS CHECK IN BUT THESE GUYS HAVE NEVER RESPONDED WELL TO CENSUS TAKERS...
WE ESTIMATED 15,000-20,000 INHUMANS RESIDED ON ATTILAN, BUT THE TERRIGEN WAVE THAT'S SPREAD SINCE ATTILAN'S FALL HAS CREATED...
...WELL, WE DON'T KNOW HOW MANY MORE.
WE'VE ACCOUNTED FOR LESS THAN TWO HUNDRED COCOONS IN THE WAKE OF THE MIST SO FAR, BUT...
...IT'S SPREADING ALL OVER THE WORLD.
EXTRAPOLATING OUT FROM THERE SUGGESTS THERE COULD BE THOUSANDS. HUNDREDS OF THOUSANDS.
OR MAYBE MORE.
T'CHALLA...YOU KNOW WE'RE NOT THE ONLY ONES DOING THIS MATH RIGHT NOW, RIGHT?
WE'RE NOT THE ONLY ONES THAT CAN COUNT THIS HIGH.

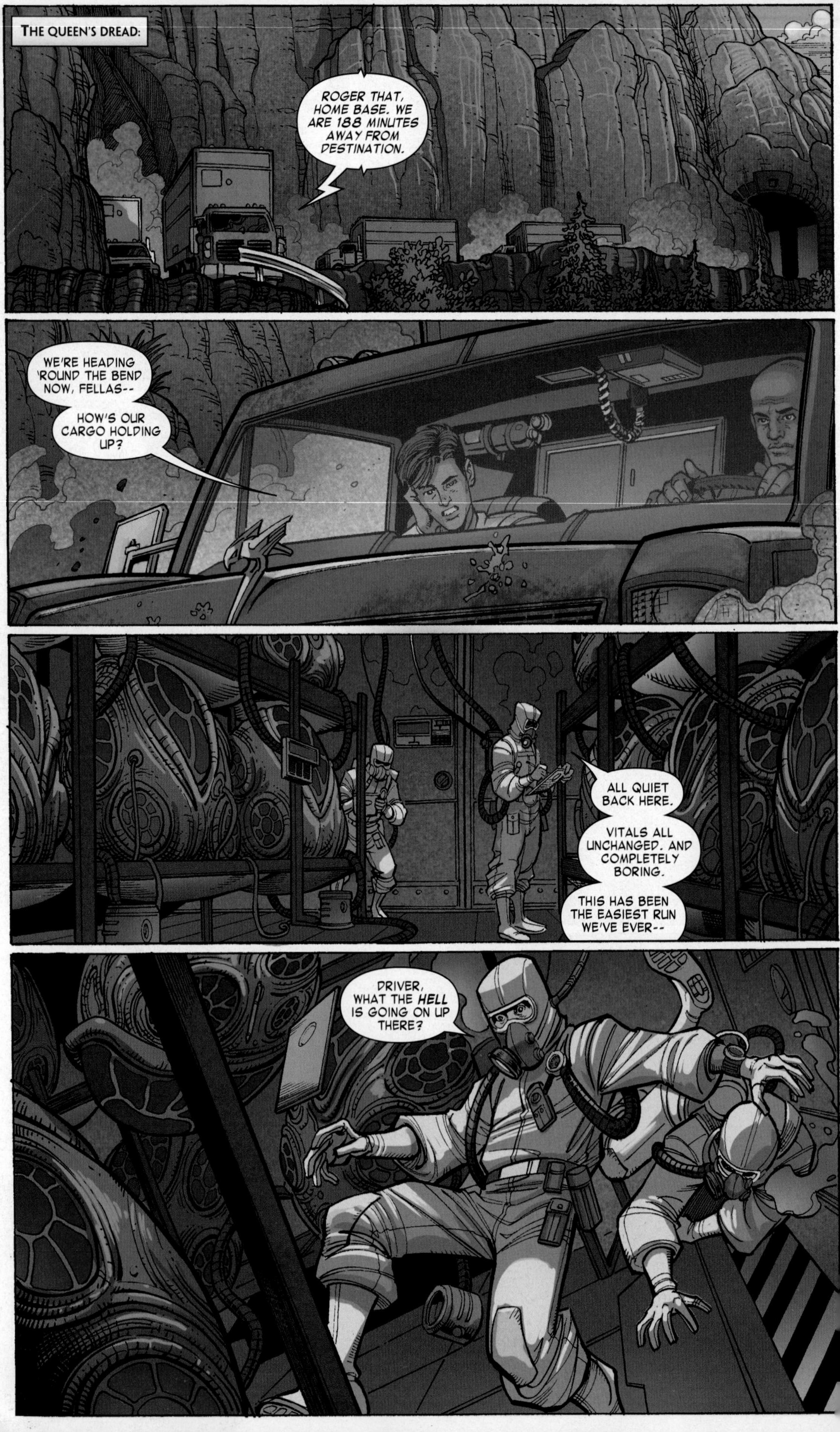
THE QUEEN'S DREAD:
ROGER THAT, HOME BASE. WE ARE 188 MINUTES AWAY FROM DESTINATION.
WE'RE HEADING 'ROUND THE BEND NOW, FELLAS--
HOW'S OUR CARGO HOLDING UP?
ALL QUIET BACK HERE.
VITALS ALL UNCHANGED. AND COMPLETELY BORING.
THIS HAS BEEN THE EASIEST RUN WE'VE EVER--
DRIVER, WHAT THE HELL IS GOING ON UP THERE?

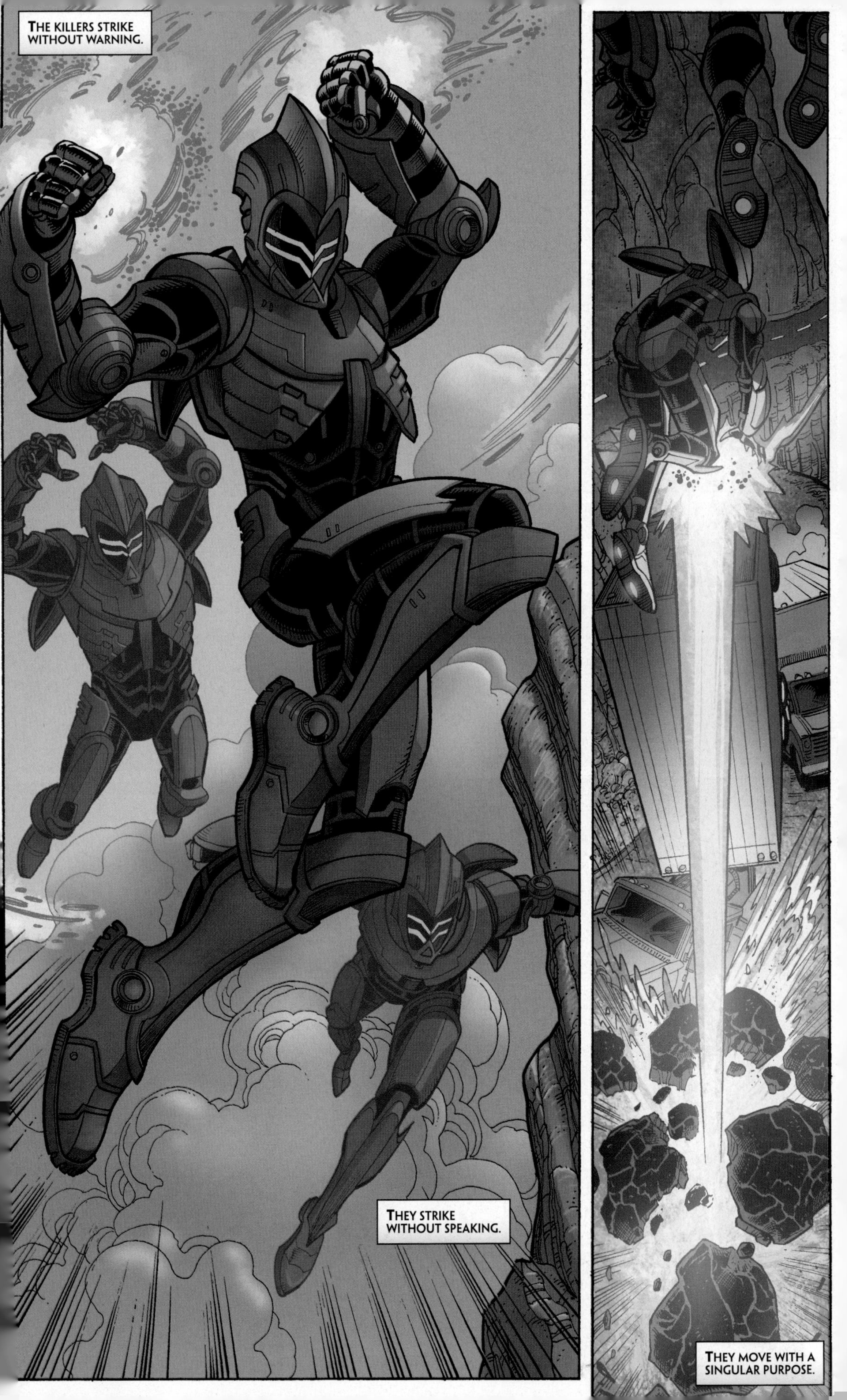
THE KILLERS STRIKE WITHOUT WARNING.
THEY STRIKE WITHOUT SPEAKING.
THEY MOVE WITH A SINGULAR PURPOSE.

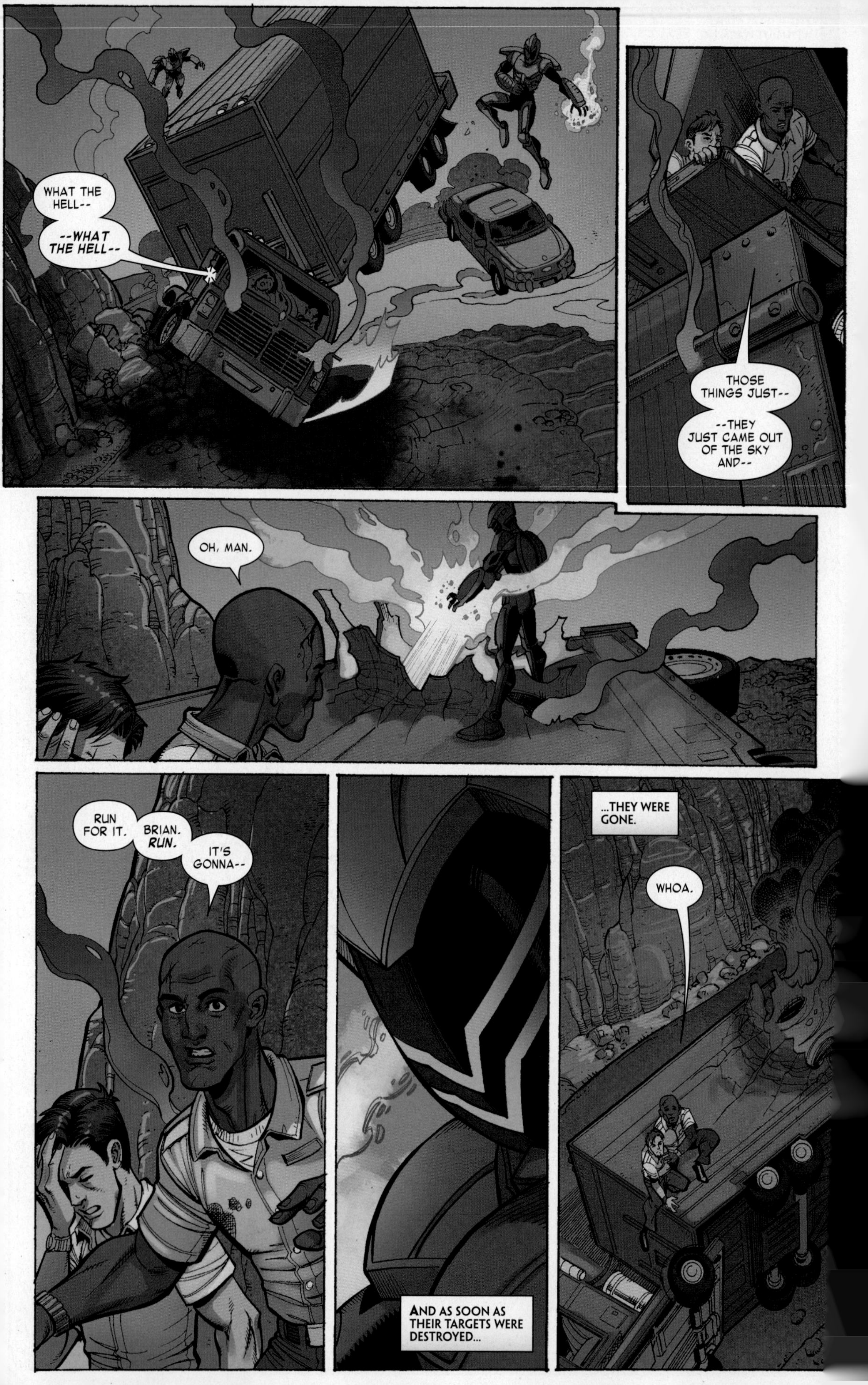
WHAT THE HELL--
--WHAT THE HELL--
THOSE THINGS JUST--
--THEY JUST CAME OUT OF THE SKY AND--
OH, MAN.
RUN FOR IT.
BRIAN. RUN.
IT'S GONNA--
AND AS SOON AS THEIR TARGETS WERE DESTROYED...
...THEY WERE GONE.
WHOA.

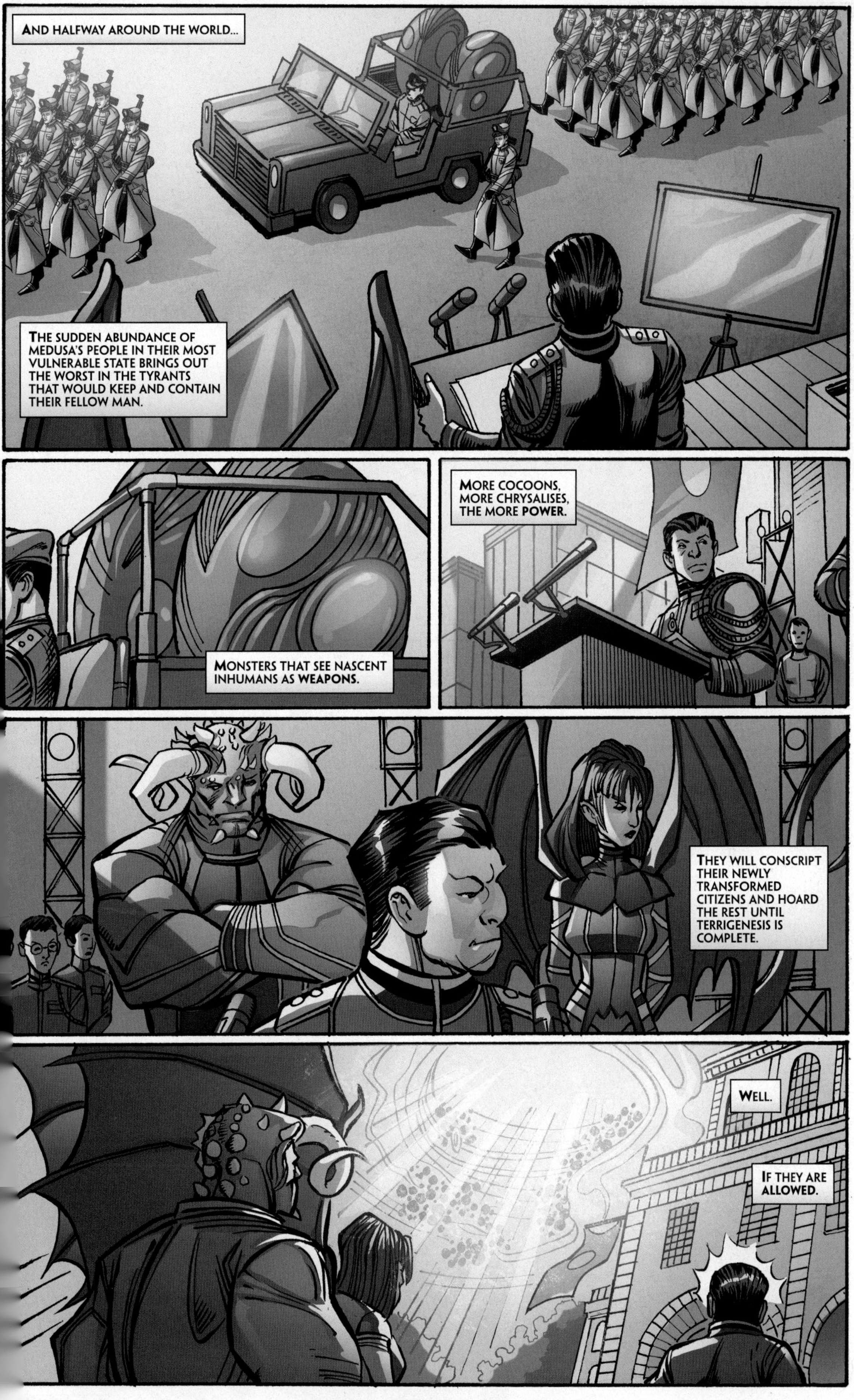

AND HALFWAY AROUND THE WORLD...
THE SUDDEN ABUNDANCE OF MEDUSA'S PEOPLE IN THEIR MOST VULNERABLE STATE BRINGS OUT THE WORST IN THE TYRANTS THAT WOULD KEEP AND CONTAIN THEIR FELLOW MAN.
MONSTERS THAT SEE NASCENT INHUMANS AS WEAPONS.
MORE COCOONS, MORE CHRYSALISES, THE MORE POWER.
THEY WILL CONSCRIPT THEIR NEWLY TRANSFORMED CITIZENS AND HOARD THE REST UNTIL TERRIGENESIS IS COMPLETE.
WELL.
IF THEY ARE ALLOWED.

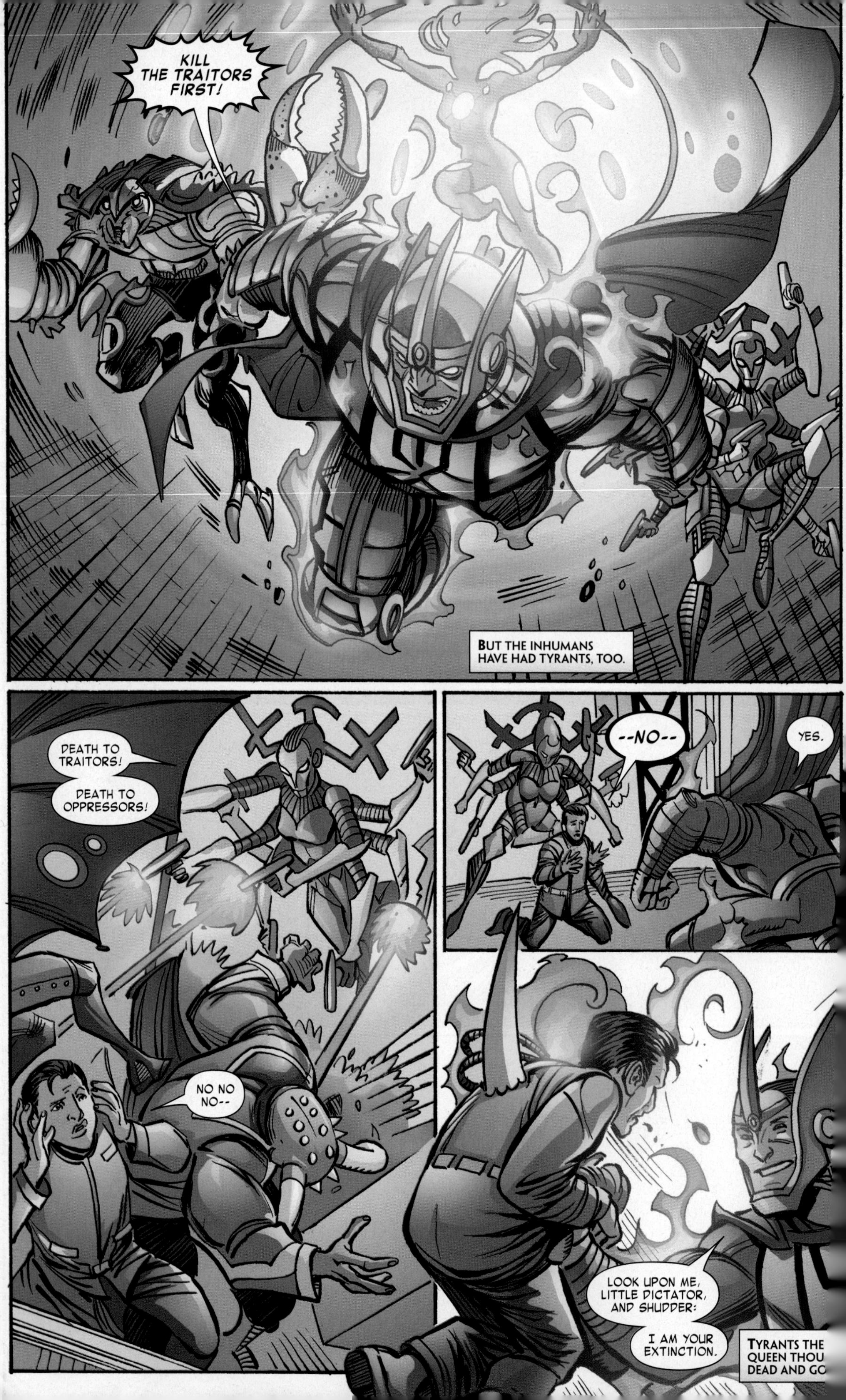
KILL THE TRAITORS FIRST!
BUT THE INHUMANS HAVE HAD TYRANTS, TOO.
DEATH TO TRAITORS!
DEATH TO OPPRESSORS!
--NO--
YES.
NO NO NO--
LOOK UPON ME, LITTLE DICTATOR, AND SHUDDER:
I AM YOUR EXTINCTION.
TYRANTS THE QUEEN THOU DEAD AND GO

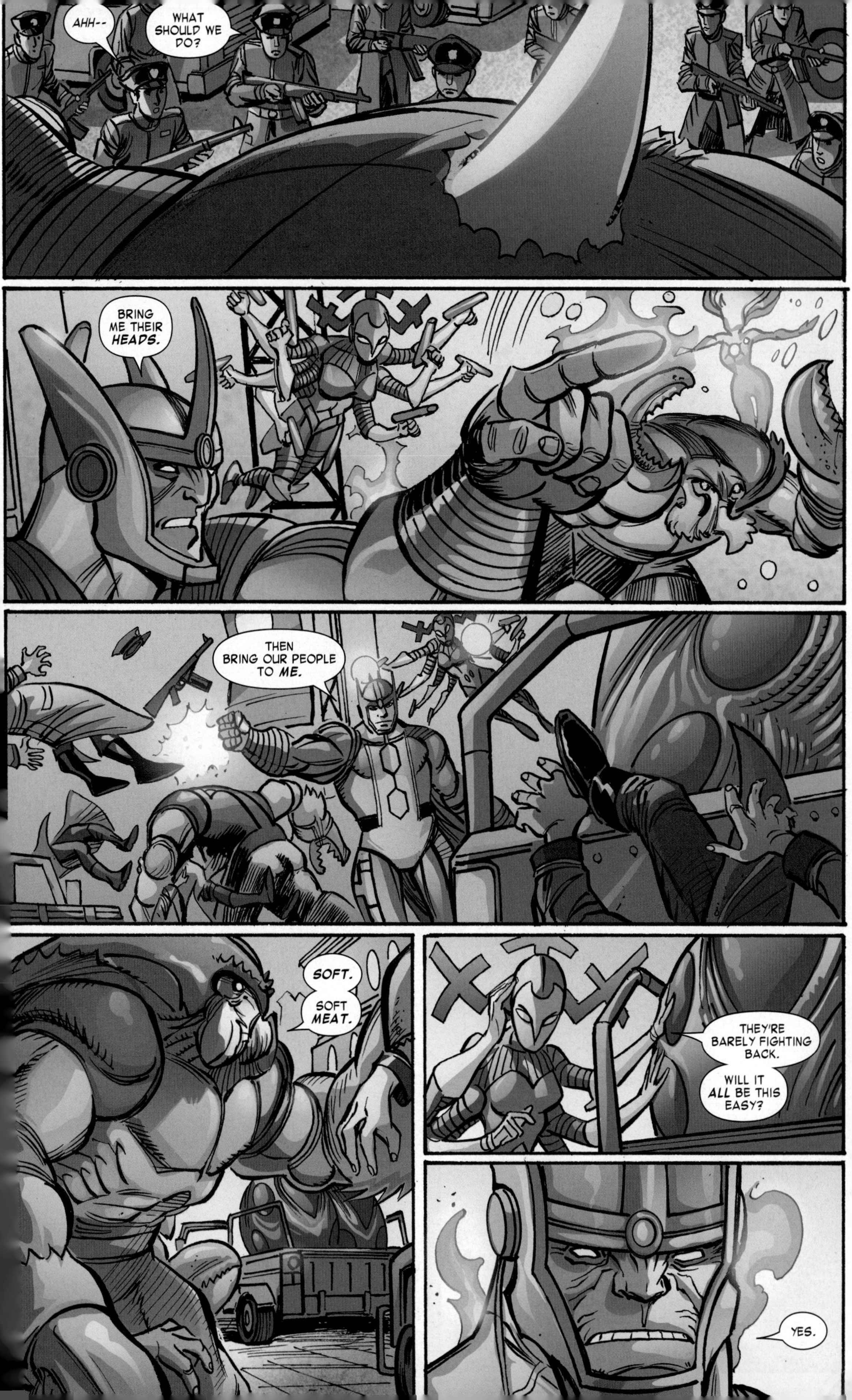
AHH--
WHAT SHOULD WE DO?
BRING ME THEIR HEADS.
THEN BRING OUR PEOPLE TO ME.
SOFT.
SOFT MEAT.
THEY'RE BARELY FIGHTING BACK.
WILL IT ALL BE THIS EASY?
YES.

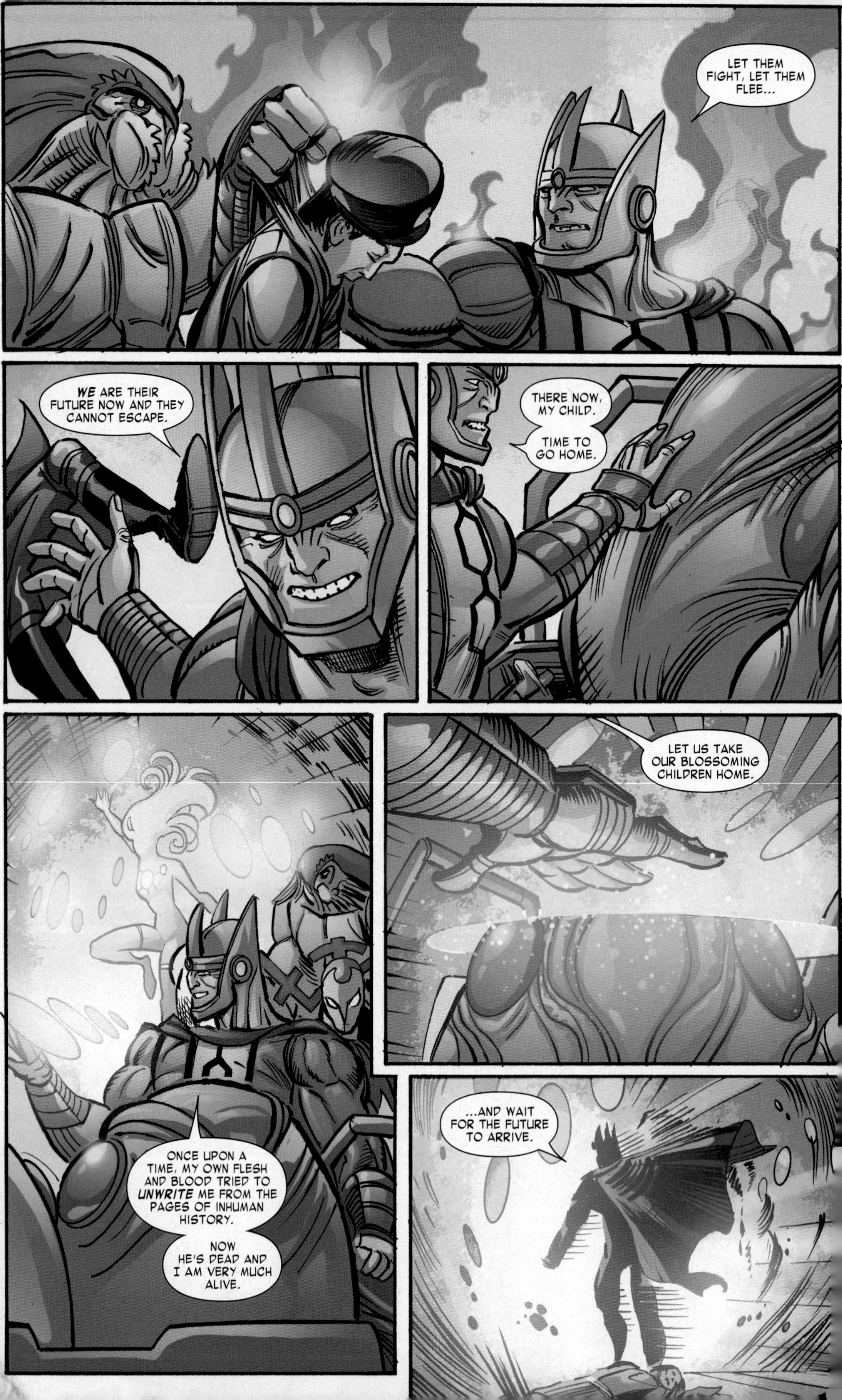
LET THEM FIGHT, LET THEM FLEE...
WE ARE THEIR FUTURE NOW AND THEY CANNOT ESCAPE.
THERE NOW, MY CHILD.
TIME TO GO HOME.
ONCE UPON A TIME, MY OWN FLESH AND BLOOD TRIED TO UNWRITE ME FROM THE PAGES OF INHUMAN HISTORY.
NOW HE'S DEAD AND I AM VERY MUCH ALIVE.
LET US TAKE OUR BLOSSOMING CHILDREN HOME.
...AND WAIT FOR THE FUTURE TO ARRIVE.

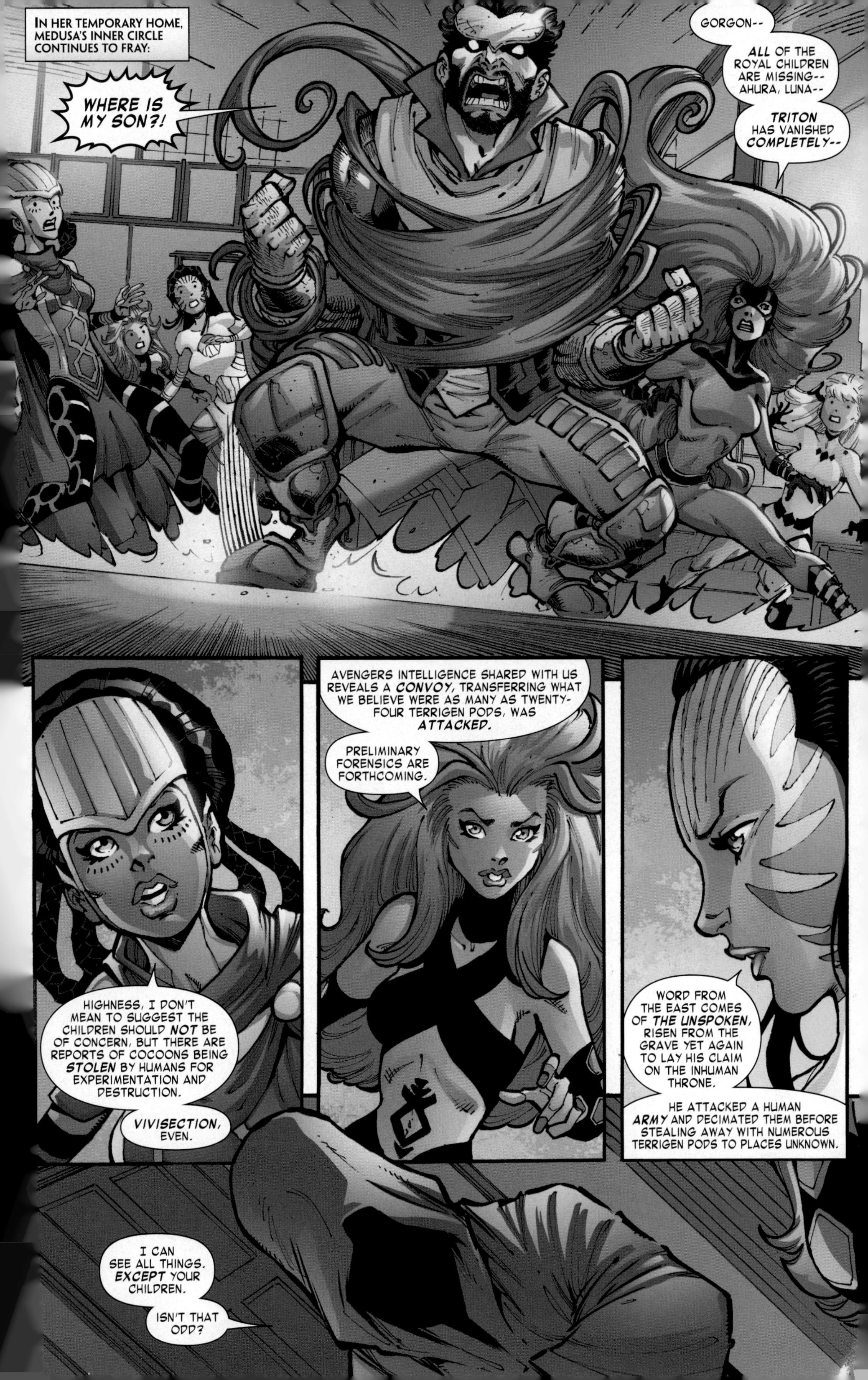
IN HER TEMPORARY HOME, MEDUSA'S INNER CIRCLE CONTINUES TO FRAY:
WHERE IS MY SON?!
GORGON--
ALL OF THE ROYAL CHILDREN ARE MISSING-- AHURA, LUNA--
TRITON HAS VANISHED COMPLETELY--
HIGHNESS, I DON'T MEAN TO SUGGEST THE CHILDREN SHOULD NOT BE OF CONCERN, BUT THERE ARE REPORTS OF COCOONS BEING STOLEN BY HUMANS FOR EXPERIMENTATION AND DESTRUCTION.
VIVISECTION, EVEN.
AVENGERS INTELLIGENCE SHARED WITH US REVEALS A CONVOY, TRANSFERRING WHAT WE BELIEVE WERE AS MANY AS TWENTY-FOUR TERRIGEN PODS, WAS ATTACKED.
PRELIMINARY FORENSICS ARE FORTHCOMING.
WORD FROM THE EAST COMES OF THE UNSPOKEN, RISEN FROM THE GRAVE YET AGAIN TO LAY HIS CLAIM ON THE INHUMAN THRONE.
HE ATTACKED A HUMAN ARMY AND DECIMATED THEM BEFORE STEALING AWAY WITH NUMEROUS TERRIGEN PODS TO PLACES UNKNOWN.
I CAN SEE ALL THINGS. EXCEPT YOUR CHILDREN.
ISN'T THAT ODD?

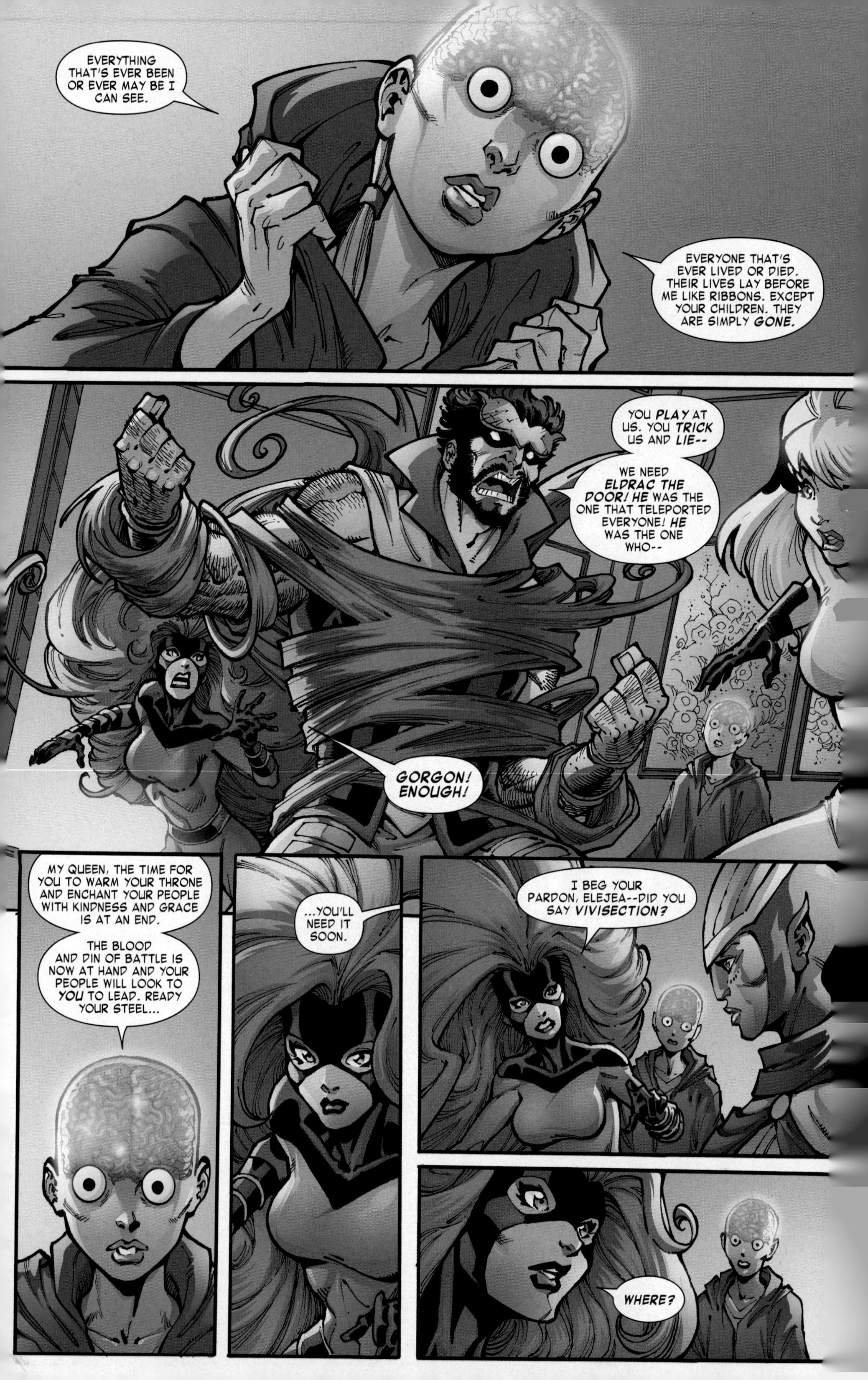
EVERYTHING THAT'S EVER BEEN OR EVER MAY BE I CAN SEE.
EVERYONE THAT'S EVER LIVED OR DIED. THEIR LIVES LAY BEFORE ME LIKE RIBBONS. EXCEPT YOUR CHILDREN. THEY ARE SIMPLY GONE.
YOU PLAY AT US. YOU TRICK US AND LIE--
WE NEED ELDRAC THE DOOR! HE WAS THE ONE THAT TELEPORTED EVERYONE! HE WAS THE ONE WHO--
GORGON! ENOUGH!
MY QUEEN, THE TIME FOR YOU TO WARM YOUR THRONE AND ENCHANT YOUR PEOPLE WITH KINDNESS AND GRACE IS AT AN END.
THE BLOOD AND DIN OF BATTLE IS NOW AT HAND AND YOUR PEOPLE WILL LOOK TO YOU TO LEAD. READY YOUR STEEL...
...YOU'LL NEED IT SOON.
I BEG YOUR PARDON, ELEJEA--DID YOU SAY VIVISECTION?
WHERE?

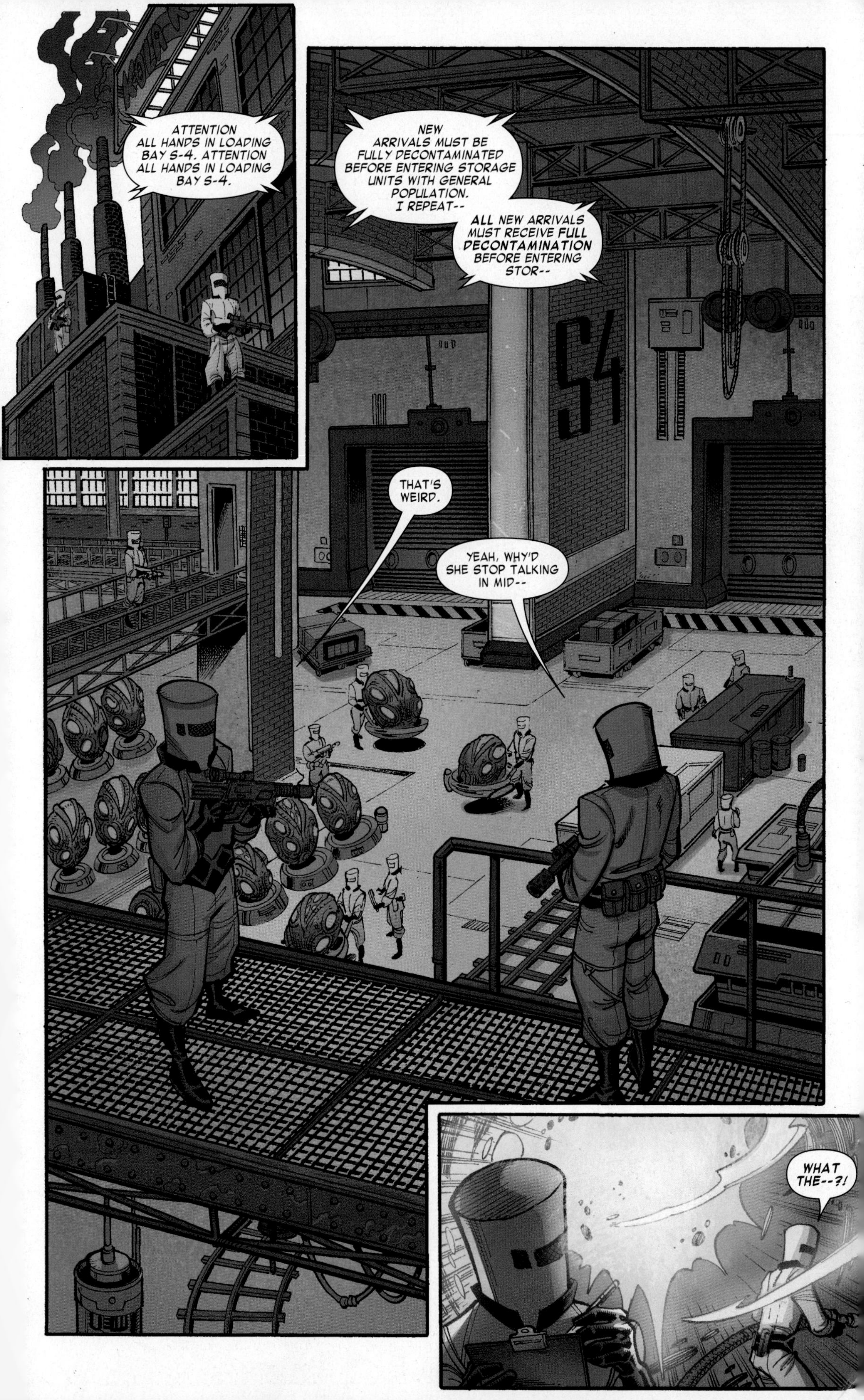
ATTENTION ALL HANDS IN LOADING BAY S-4. ATTENTION ALL HANDS IN LOADING BAY S-4.
NEW ARRIVALS MUST BE FULLY DECONTAMINATED BEFORE ENTERING STORAGE UNITS WITH GENERAL POPULATION. I REPEAT--
ALL NEW ARRIVALS MUST RECEIVE FULL DECONTAMINATION BEFORE ENTERING STOR--
S4
THAT'S WEIRD.
YEAH, WHY'D SHE STOP TALKING IN MID--
WHAT THE--?!

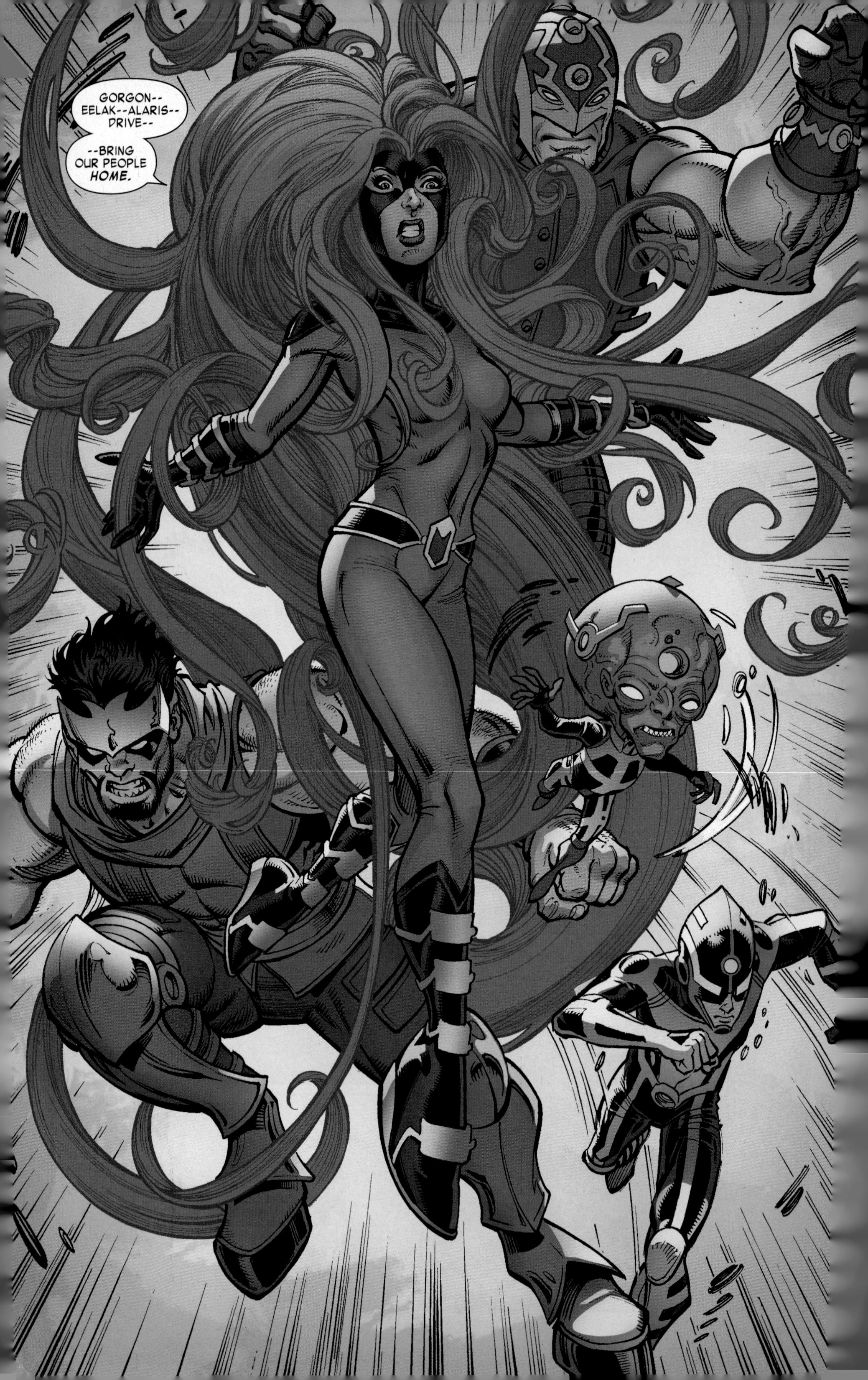
GORGON--
EELAK--ALARIS--
DRIVE--
--BRING OUR PEOPLE HOME.

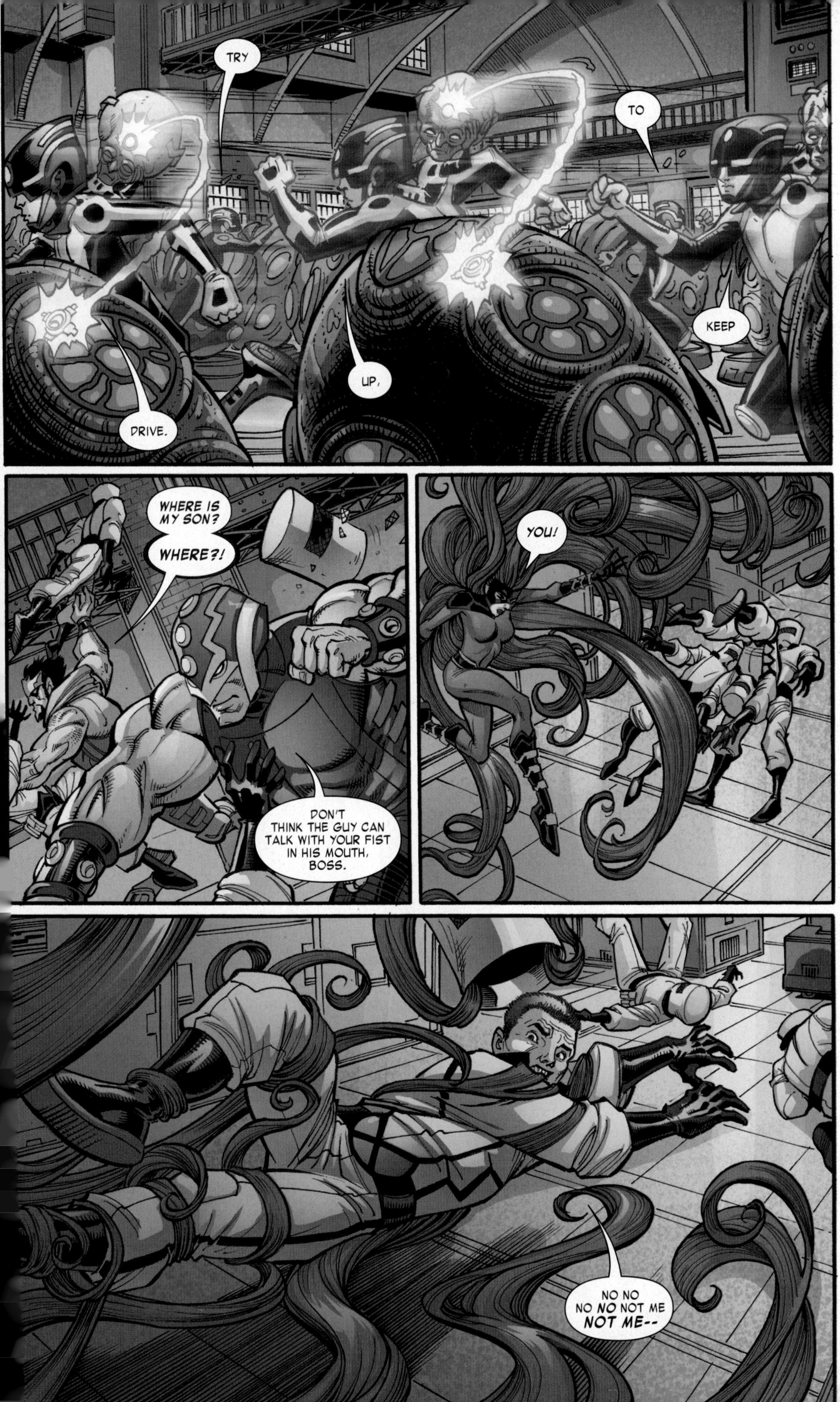
TRY
TO
KEEP
UP,
DRIVE.
WHERE IS MY SON?
WHERE?!
DON'T THINK THE GUY CAN TALK WITH YOUR FIST IN HIS MOUTH, BOSS.
YOU!
NO NO NO NO NOT ME NOT ME--

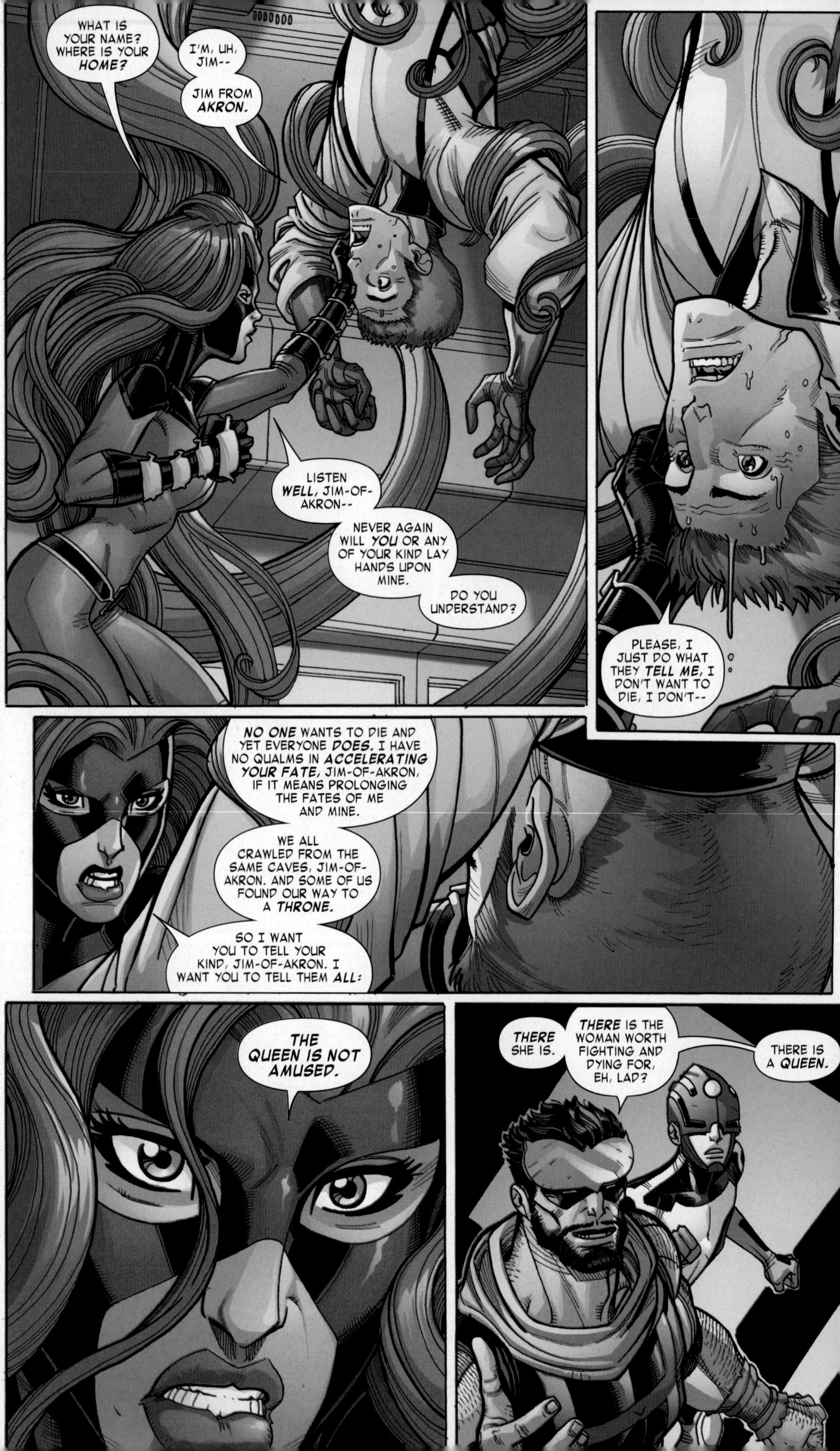
WHAT IS YOUR NAME? WHERE IS YOUR HOME?
I'M, UH, JIM--
JIM FROM AKRON.
LISTEN WELL, JIM-OF-AKRON--
NEVER AGAIN WILL YOU OR ANY OF YOUR KIND LAY HANDS UPON MINE.
DO YOU UNDERSTAND?
PLEASE, I JUST DO WHAT THEY TELL ME, I DON'T WANT TO DIE, I DON'T--
NO ONE WANTS TO DIE AND YET EVERYONE DOES. I HAVE NO QUALMS IN ACCELERATING YOUR FATE, JIM-OF-AKRON, IF IT MEANS PROLONGING THE FATES OF ME AND MINE.
WE ALL CRAWLED FROM THE SAME CAVES, JIM-OF-AKRON. AND SOME OF US FOUND OUR WAY TO A THRONE.
SO I WANT YOU TO TELL YOUR KIND, JIM-OF-AKRON. I WANT YOU TO TELL THEM ALL:
THE QUEEN IS NOT AMUSED.
THERE SHE IS.
THERE IS THE WOMAN WORTH FIGHTING AND DYING FOR, EH, LAD?
THERE IS A QUEEN.

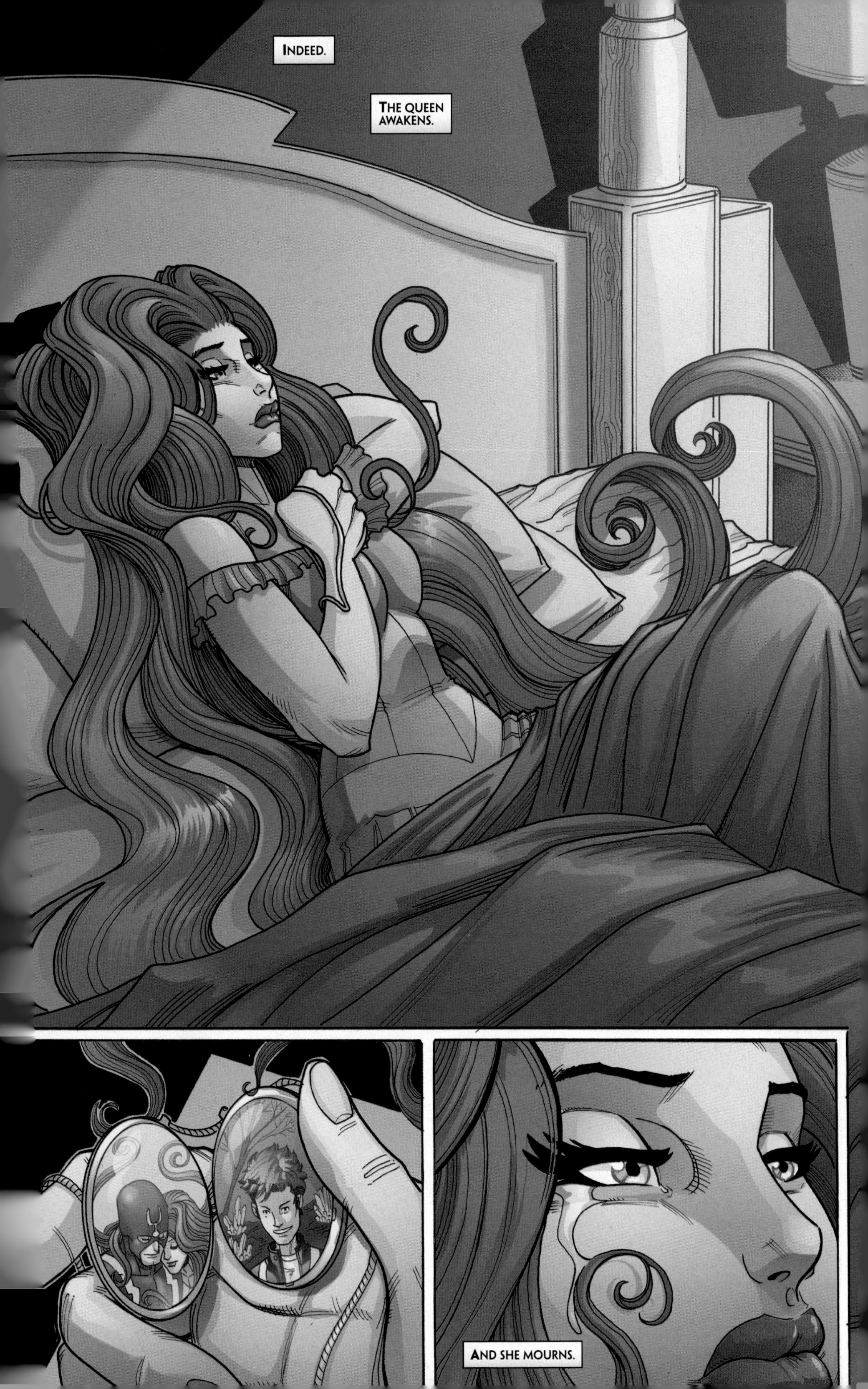
INDEED.
THE QUEEN AWAKENS.
AND SHE MOURNS.

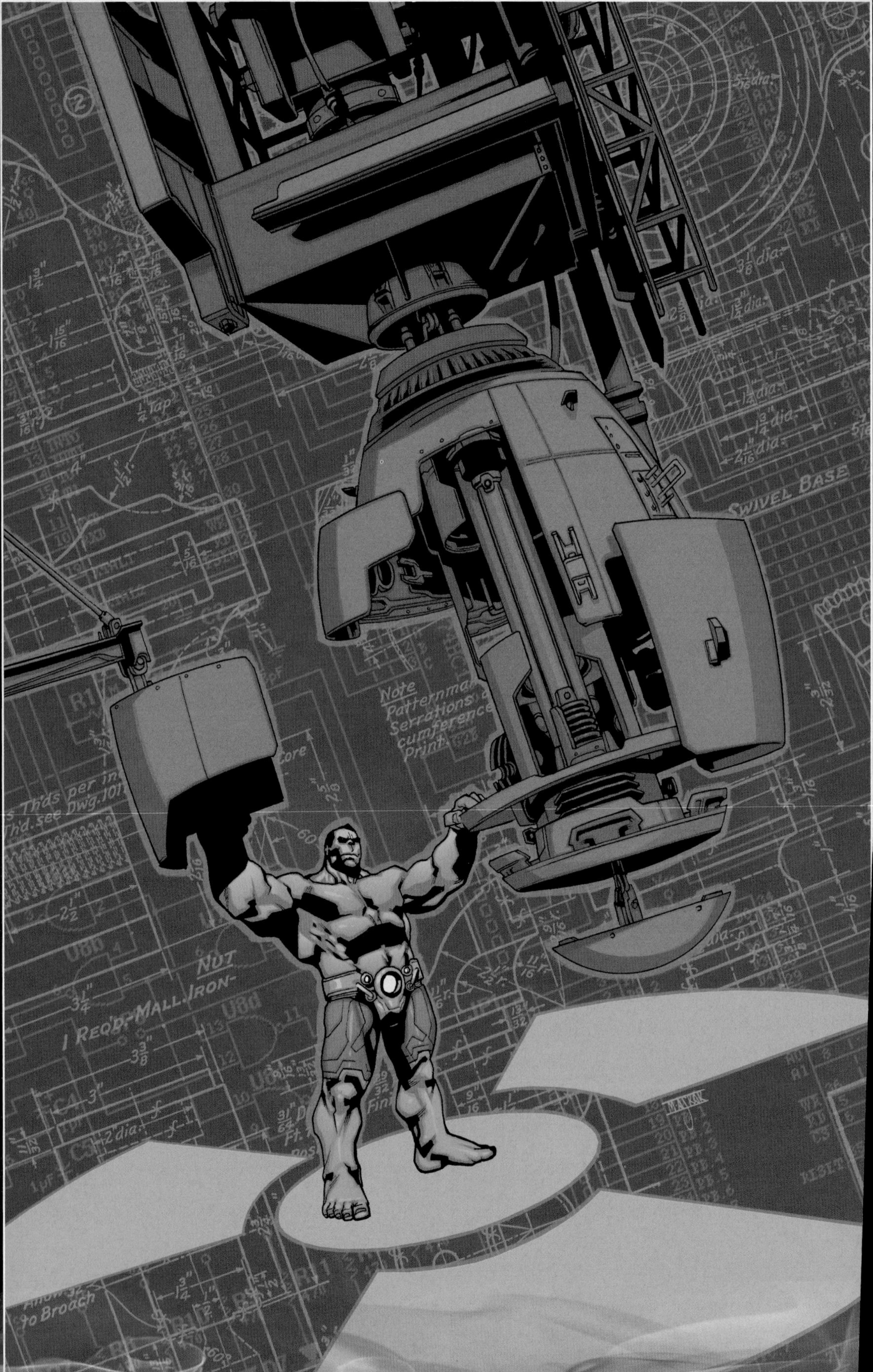
SWIVEL BASE
NUT
I REQD. MALL. IRON

INDESTRUCTIBLE HULK #17

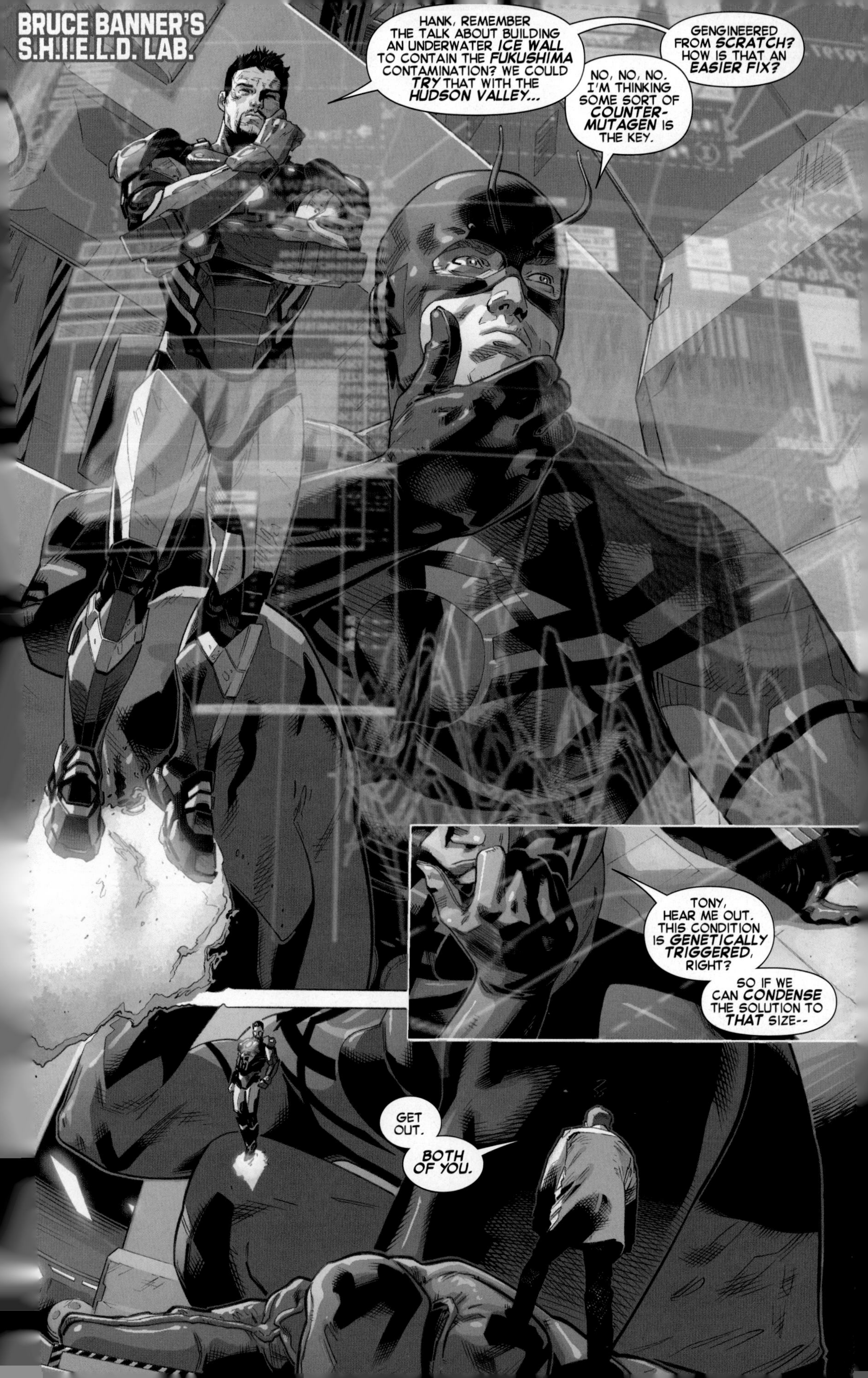
BRUCE BANNER'S S.H.I.E.L.D. LAB.
HANK, REMEMBER THE TALK ABOUT BUILDING AN UNDERWATER ICE WALL TO CONTAIN THE FUKUSHIMA CONTAMINATION? WE COULD TRY THAT WITH THE HUDSON VALLEY...
GENGINEERED FROM SCRATCH? HOW IS THAT AN EASIER FIX?
NO, NO, NO. I'M THINKING SOME SORT OF COUNTER-MUTAGEN IS THE KEY.
TONY, HEAR ME OUT. THIS CONDITION IS GENETICALLY TRIGGERED, RIGHT?
SO IF WE CAN CONDENSE THE SOLUTION TO THAT SIZE--
GET OUT.
BOTH OF YOU.

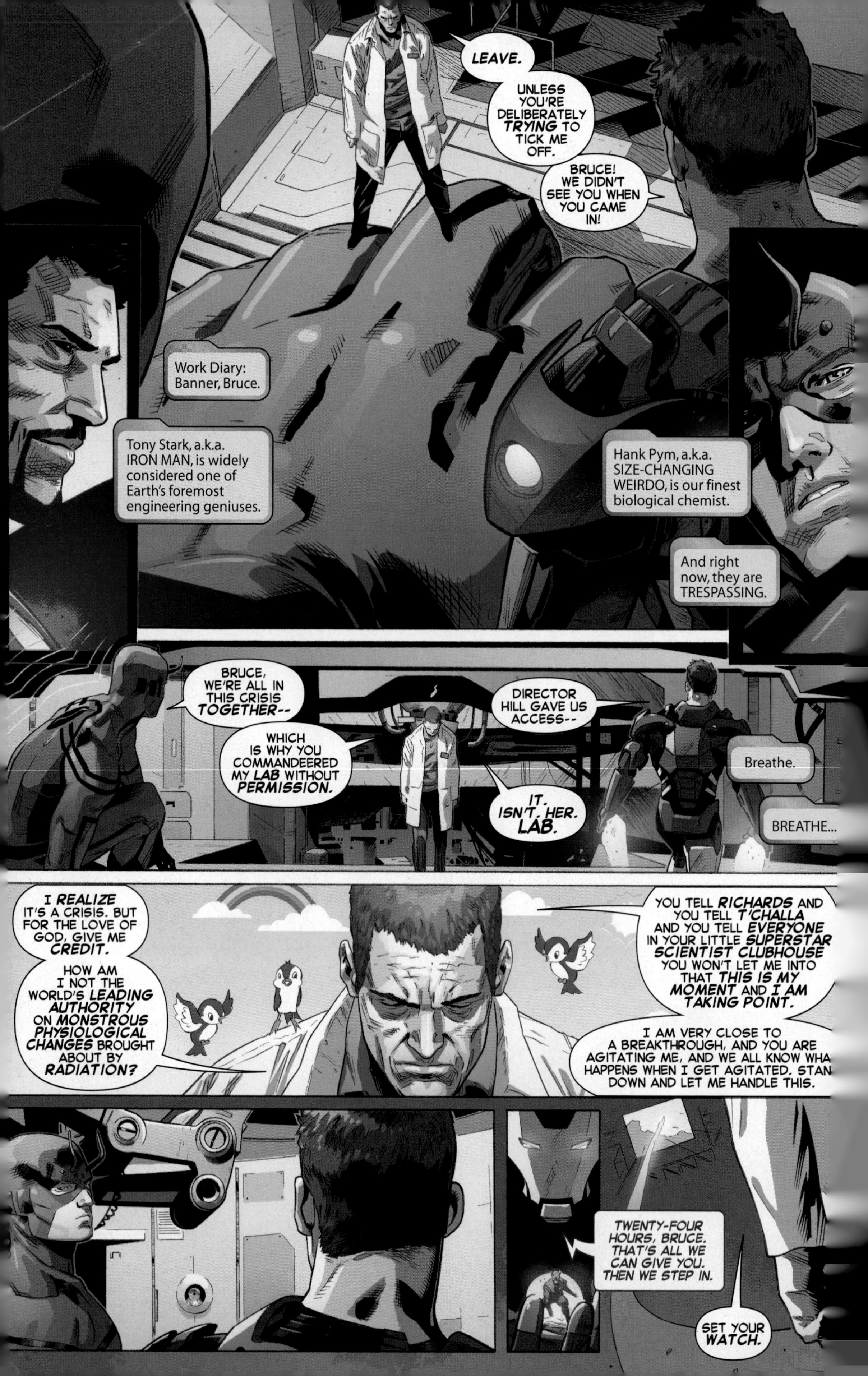
LEAVE.
UNLESS YOU'RE DELIBERATELY TRYING TO TICK ME OFF.
BRUCE! WE DIDN'T SEE YOU WHEN YOU CAME IN!
Work Diary: Banner, Bruce.
Tony Stark, a.k.a. IRON MAN, is widely considered one of Earth's foremost engineering geniuses.
Hank Pym, a.k.a. SIZE-CHANGING WEIRDO, is our finest biological chemist.
And right now, they are TRESPASSING.
BRUCE, WE'RE ALL IN THIS CRISIS TOGETHER--
WHICH IS WHY YOU COMMANDEERED MY LAB WITHOUT PERMISSION.
DIRECTOR HILL GAVE US ACCESS--
IT. ISN'T. HER. LAB.
Breathe.
BREATHE...
I REALIZE IT'S A CRISIS. BUT FOR THE LOVE OF GOD, GIVE ME CREDIT.
HOW AM I NOT THE WORLD'S LEADING AUTHORITY ON MONSTROUS PHYSIOLOGICAL CHANGES BROUGHT ABOUT BY RADIATION?
YOU TELL RICHARDS AND YOU TELL T'CHALLA AND YOU TELL EVERYONE IN YOUR LITTLE SUPERSTAR SCIENTIST CLUBHOUSE YOU WON'T LET ME INTO THAT THIS IS MY MOMENT AND I AM TAKING POINT.
I AM VERY CLOSE TO A BREAKTHROUGH, AND YOU ARE AGITATING ME, AND WE ALL KNOW WHA HAPPENS WHEN I GET AGITATED. STAN DOWN AND LET ME HANDLE THIS.
TWENTY-FOUR HOURS, BRUCE. THAT'S ALL WE CAN GIVE YOU. THEN WE STEP IN.
SET YOUR WATCH.

THE HULK WILL ALWAYS BE A PART OF DR. BRUCE BANNER, BUT BANNER WANTS TO BE REMEMBERED FOR HIS CONTRIBUTIONS TO SCIENCE AND NOT FOR TURNING INTO A BIG, GREEN FORCE OF RAGE AND DESTRUCTION. TO ACHIEVE THAT GOAL, BANNER HAS STRUCK A MUTUALLY BENEFICIAL DEAL WITH MARIA HILL, THE DIRECTOR OF S.H.I.E.L.D. SHE PROVIDES BANNER WITH A LAB, STAFF, EQUIPMENT AND ALL OF THE RESOURCES HE NEEDS TO BETTER MANKIND, AND BANNER PROVIDES S.H.I.E.L.D. WITH THE HULK FOR ANY MISSIONS THAT MIGHT NEED THAT EXTRA MUSCLE.

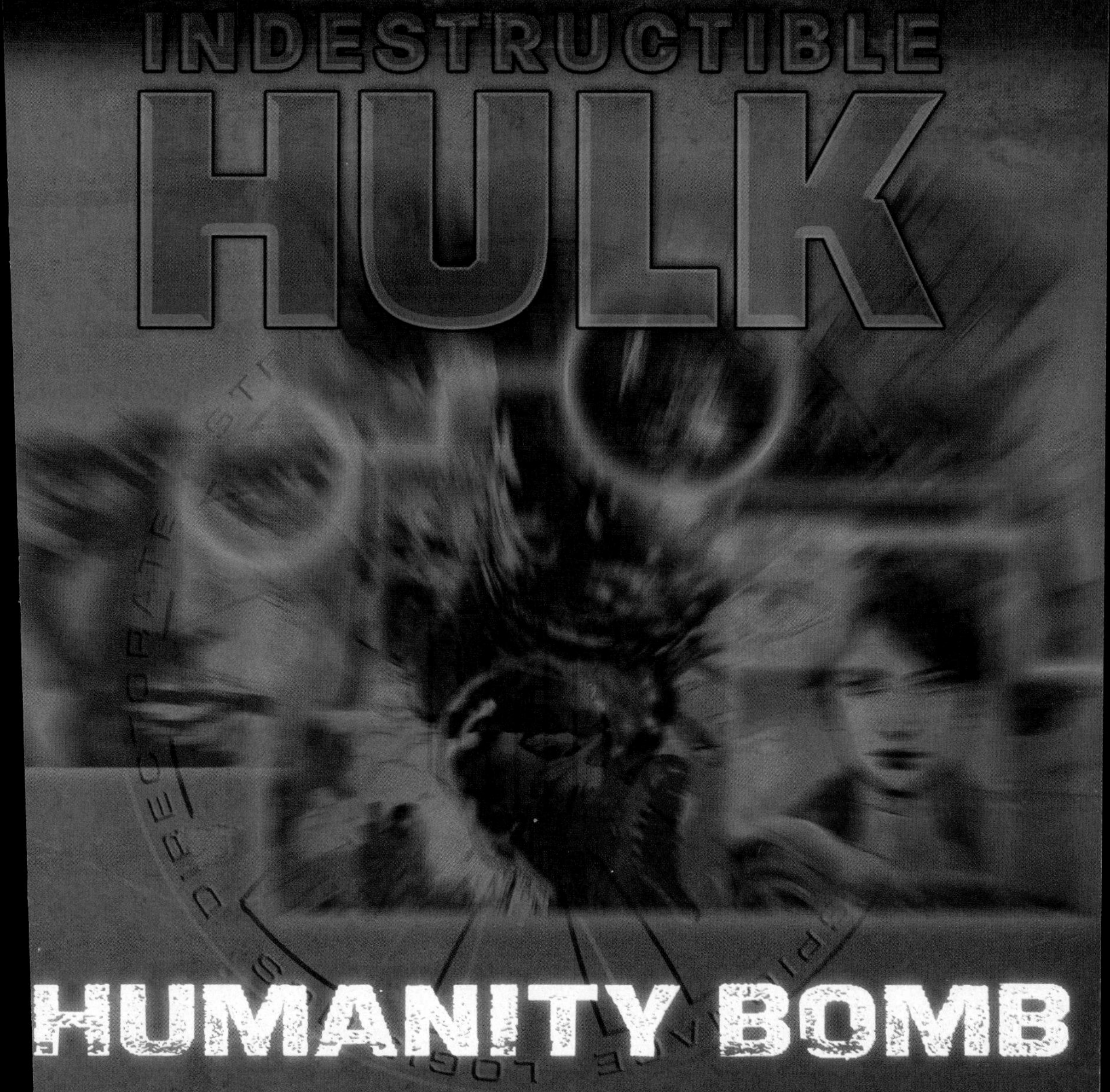
INDESTRUCTIBLE
HULK
HUMANITY BOMB

HULK DESTROYS, BANNER BUILDS.

LATELY, THERE'S BEEN A WHOLE LOT MORE OF HULK DESTROYING THAN BANNER BUILDING.

ECENTLY, BANNER AND LAB ASSISTANT RANDALL JESSUP RECOVERED A STRANGE ENERGY SOURCE, UT NOT BEFORE THE HULK LAID WASTE TO AN ANCIENT AZTEC RUIN, NEARLY KILLING JESSUP AND AN ENTIRE S.H.I.E.L.D. TASK FORCE.

UT BANNER HAS BEEN GIVEN A NEW CHANCE TO BUILD: DURING THANOS' ATTACK ON EARTH, THE IHUMANS RELEASED A CHEMICAL COMPOUND CALLED TERRIGEN MISTS INTO THE ATMOSPHERE, BRINGING ABOUT UNWELCOME CHANGES IN ANYONE WITH EVEN THE SLIGHTEST GENETIC TIE TO THE INHUMANS.

THE WORLD NEEDS A CURE, AND DR. BANNER IS ON THE CASE.

When you see this: AR , open up the MARVEL AR APP (available on applicable Apple ® iOS or Android ™ devices) and use your camera-enabled device to unlock extra-special exclusive features!

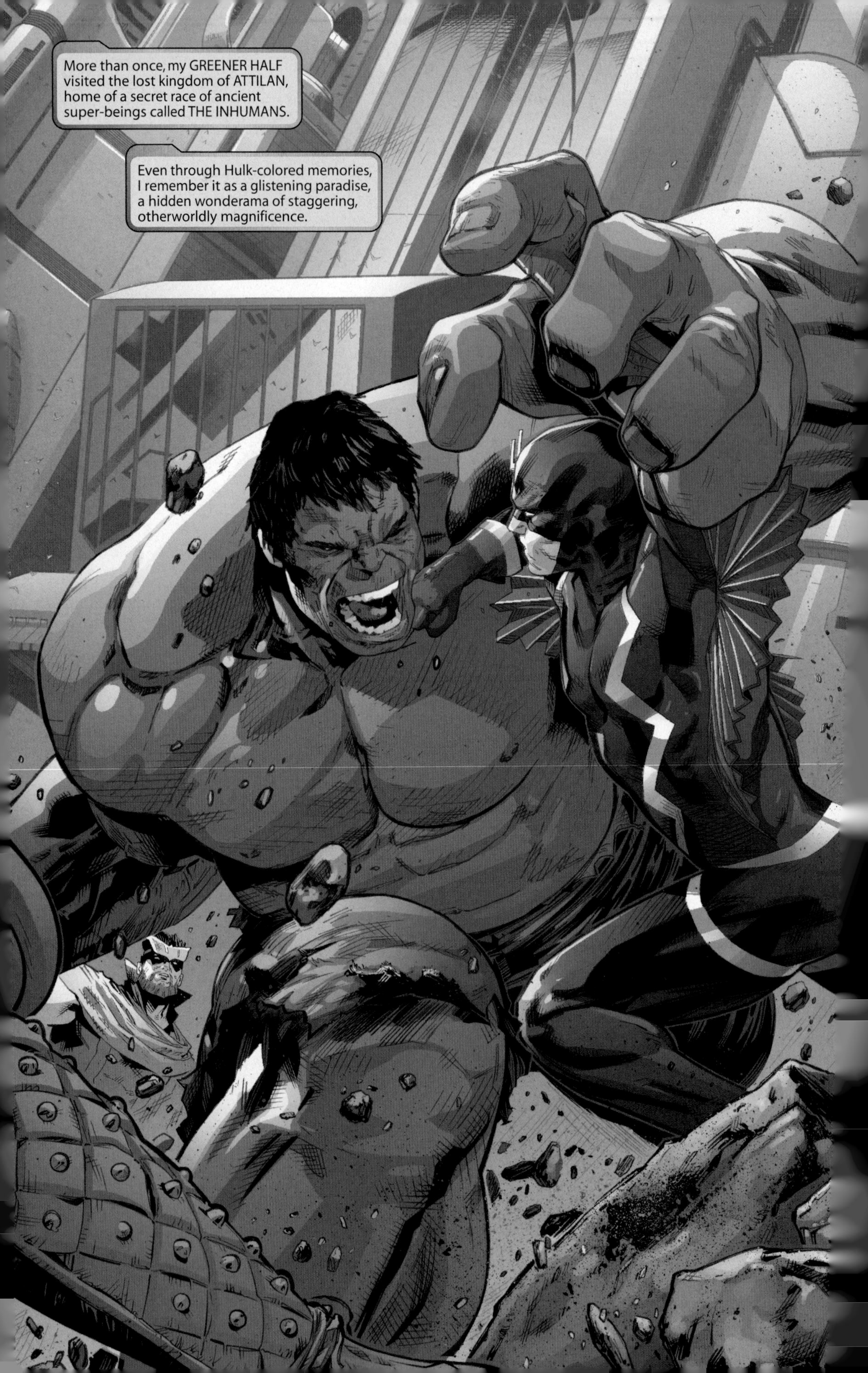
More than once, my GREENER HALF visited the lost kingdom of ATTILAN, home of a secret race of ancient super-beings called THE INHUMANS.
Even through Hulk-colored memories, I remember it as a glistening paradise, a hidden wonderama of staggering, otherworldly magnificence.

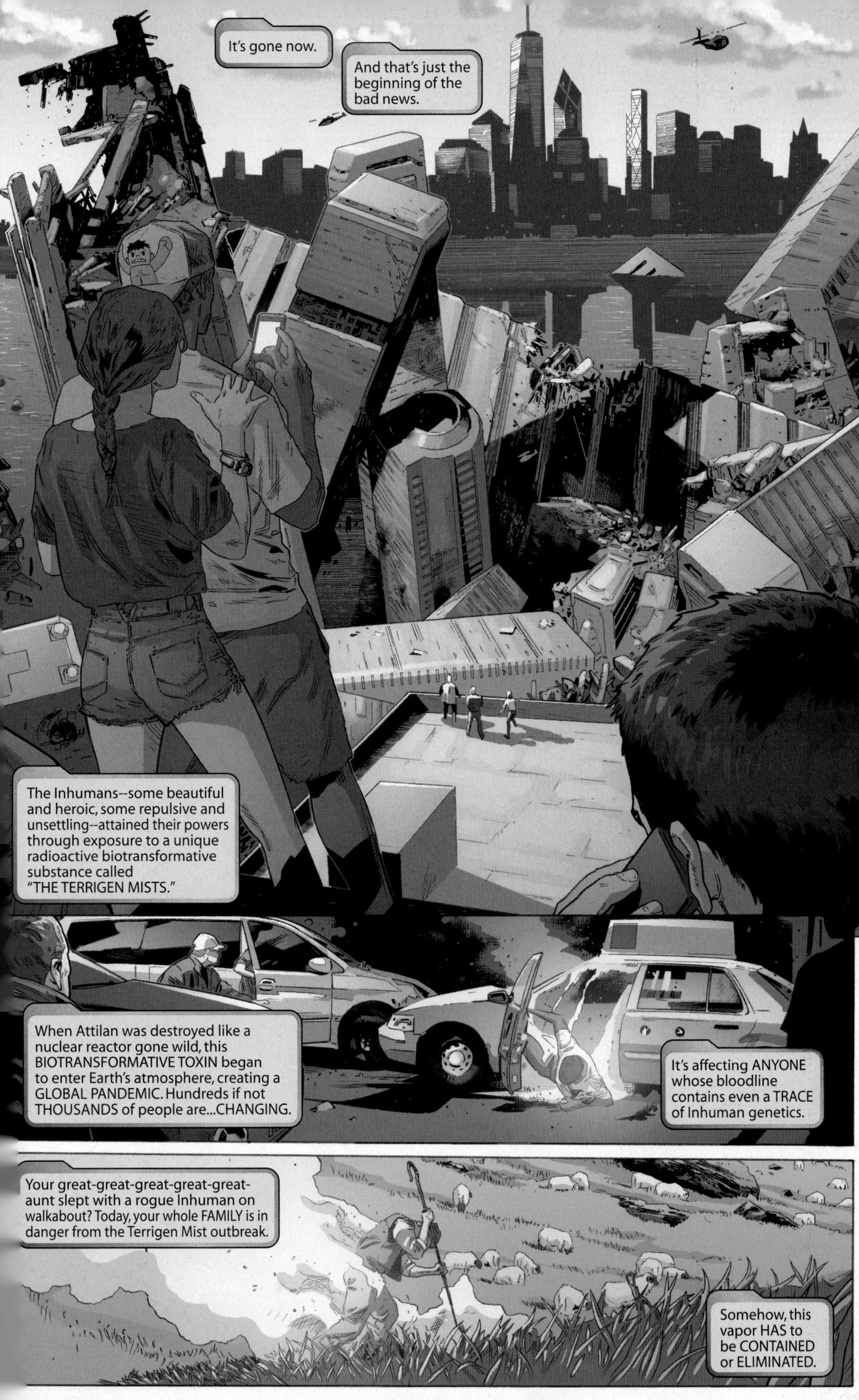
It's gone now.
And that's just the beginning of the bad news.
The Inhumans--some beautiful and heroic, some repulsive and unsettling--attained their powers through exposure to a unique radioactive biotransformative substance called "THE TERRIGEN MISTS."
When Attilan was destroyed like a nuclear reactor gone wild, this BIOTRANSFORMATIVE TOXIN began to enter Earth's atmosphere, creating a GLOBAL PANDEMIC. Hundreds if not THOUSANDS of people are...CHANGING.
It's affecting ANYONE whose bloodline contains even a TRACE of Inhuman genetics.
Your great-great-great-great-great-aunt slept with a rogue Inhuman on walkabout? Today, your whole FAMILY is in danger from the Terrigen Mist outbreak.
Somehow, this vapor HAS to be CONTAINED or ELIMINATED.

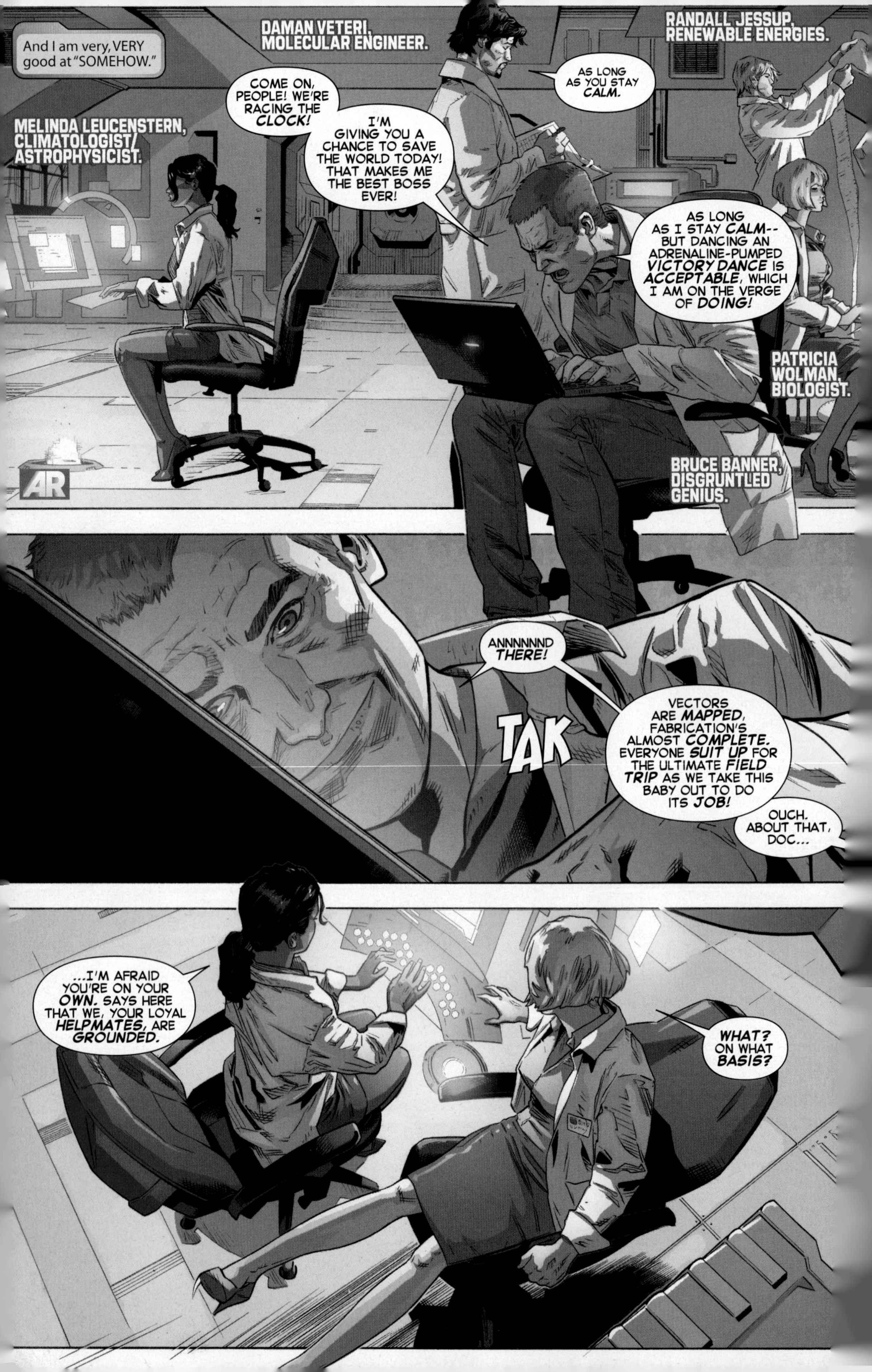
And I am very, VERY good at "SOMEHOW."
DAMAN VETERI, MOLECULAR ENGINEER.
RANDALL JESSUP, RENEWABLE ENERGIES.
COME ON, PEOPLE! WE'RE RACING THE CLOCK!
I'M GIVING YOU A CHANCE TO SAVE THE WORLD TODAY! THAT MAKES ME THE BEST BOSS EVER!
AS LONG AS YOU STAY CALM.
MELINDA LEUCENSTERN, CLIMATOLOGIST/ ASTROPHYSICIST.
AS LONG AS I STAY CALM-- BUT DANCING AN ADRENALINE-PUMPED VICTORY DANCE IS ACCEPTABLE, WHICH I AM ON THE VERGE OF DOING!
PATRICIA WOLMAN, BIOLOGIST.
BRUCE BANNER, DISGRUNTLED GENIUS.
ANNNNNND THERE!
TAK
VECTORS ARE MAPPED, FABRICATION'S ALMOST COMPLETE. EVERYONE SUIT UP FOR THE ULTIMATE FIELD TRIP AS WE TAKE THIS BABY OUT TO DO ITS JOB!
OUCH. ABOUT THAT, DOC...
...I'M AFRAID YOU'RE ON YOUR OWN. SAYS HERE THAT WE, YOUR LOYAL HELPMATES, ARE GROUNDED.
WHAT? ON WHAT BASIS?

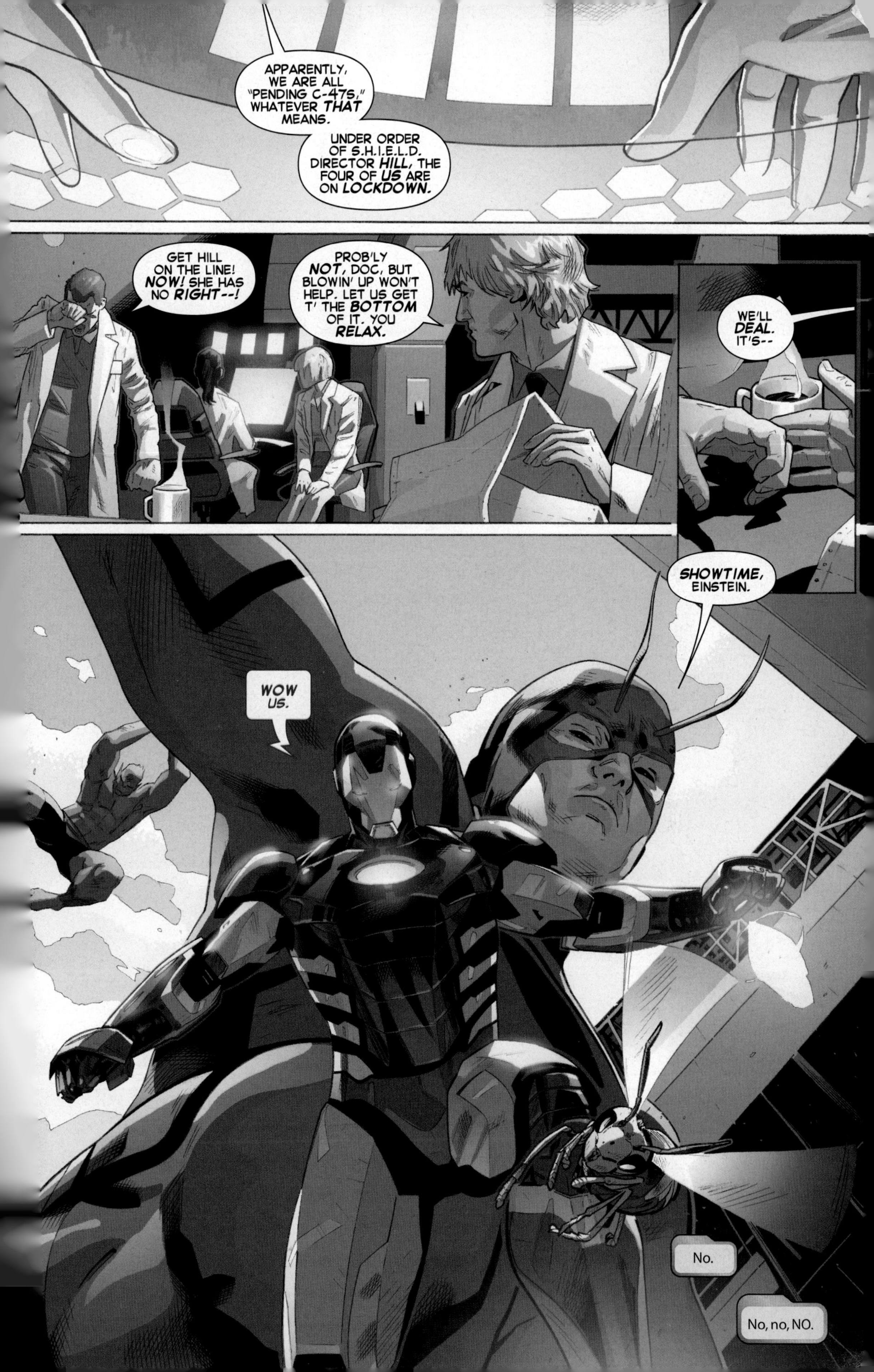
APPARENTLY, WE ARE ALL "PENDING C-47s," WHATEVER THAT MEANS.
UNDER ORDER OF S.H.I.E.L.D. DIRECTOR HILL, THE FOUR OF US ARE ON LOCKDOWN.
GET HILL ON THE LINE! NOW! SHE HAS NO RIGHT--!
PROB'LY NOT, DOC, BUT BLOWIN' UP WON'T HELP. LET US GET T' THE BOTTOM OF IT. YOU RELAX.
WE'LL DEAL. IT'S--
SHOWTIME, EINSTEIN.
WOW US.
No.
No, no, NO.

YOU PROMISED ME 24 HOURS!

WE'RE ON FUZZY TIME.

IS THAT A CRACK?

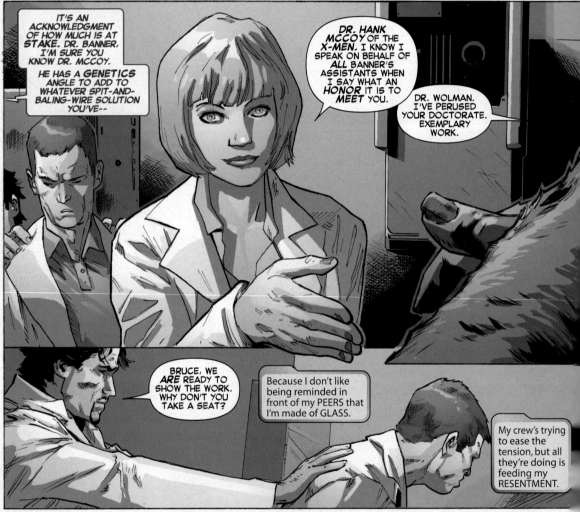

IT'S AN ACKNOWLEDGMENT OF HOW MUCH IS AT STAKE. DR. BANNER, I'M SURE YOU KNOW DR. MCCOY.

HE HAS A GENETICS ANGLE TO ADD TO WHATEVER SPIT-AND-BALING-WIRE SOLUTION YOU'VE--

DR. HANK MCCOY OF THE X-MEN. I KNOW I SPEAK ON BEHALF OF ALL BANNER'S ASSISTANTS WHEN I SAY WHAT AN HONOR IT IS TO MEET YOU.

DR. WOLMAN. I'VE PERUSED YOUR DOCTORATE. EXEMPLARY WORK.

BRUCE, WE ARE READY TO SHOW THE WORK. WHY DON'T YOU TAKE A SEAT?

Because I don't like being reminded in front of my PEERS that I'm made of GLASS.

My crew's trying to ease the tension, but all they're doing is feeding my RESENTMENT.

Shake it off, Bruce. This is your big chance to finally SEE the respect that you've earned from these men a hundred times OVER.

They'll NEVER look at you with condescension after this.

I'M STILL THE RINGMASTER AROUND HERE, THANKS. RANDALL, ARE THE PROPULSION UNITS FUELED?

ANOTHER 10 MINUTES.

GOOD ENOUGH, GENTLEMEN, HERE'S WHAT I'VE COME UP WITH:

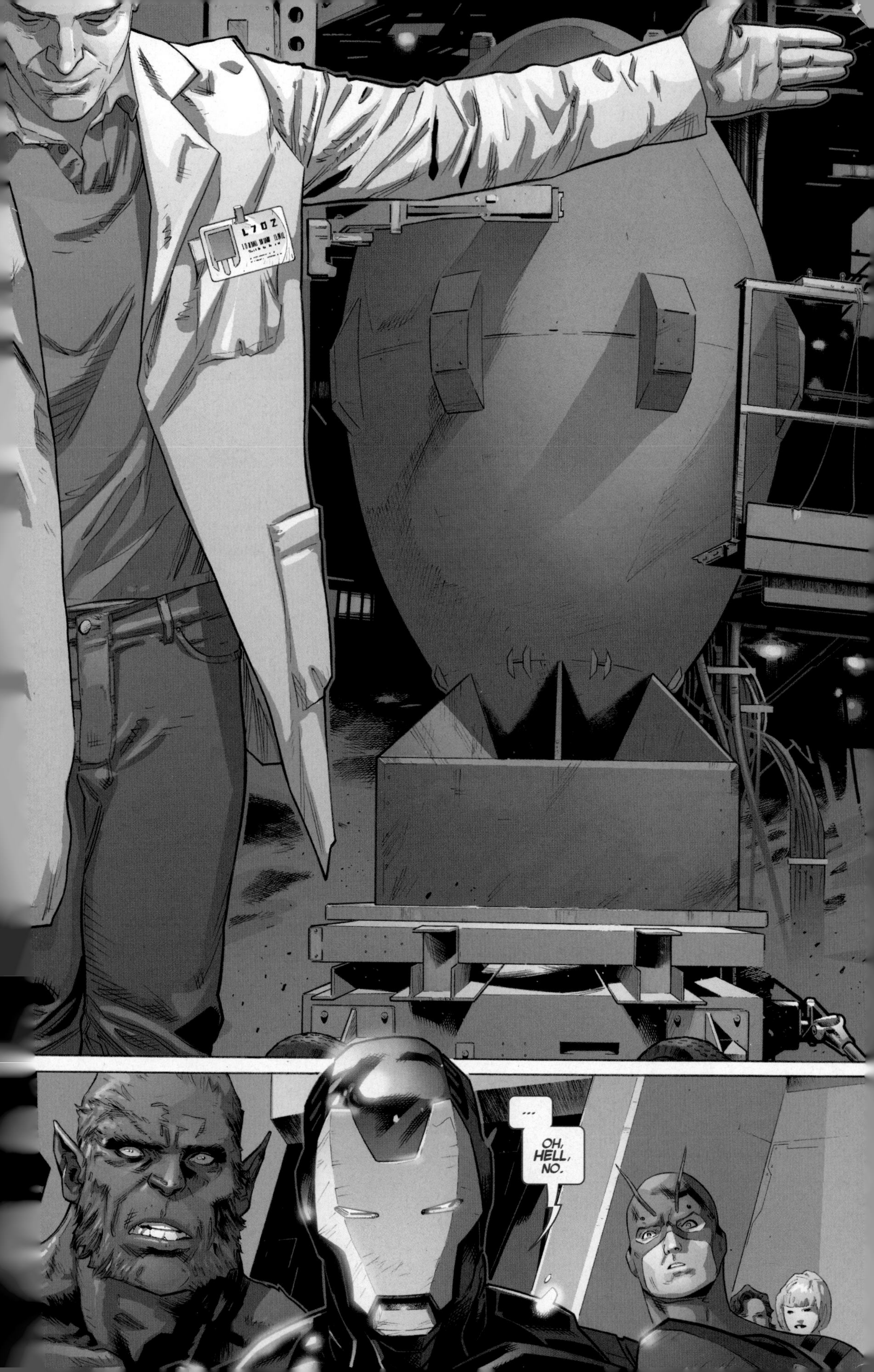
...
OH, HELL, NO.

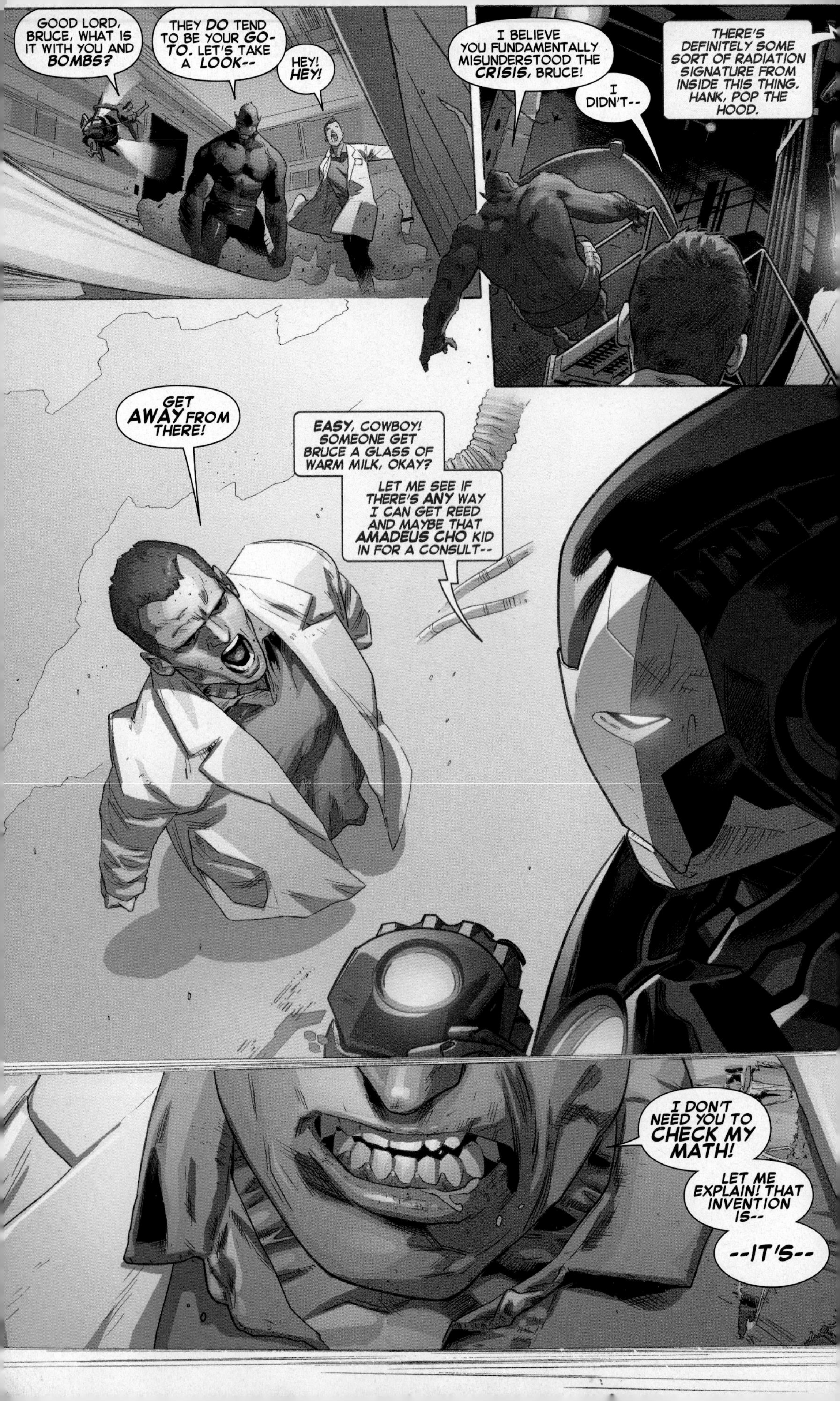

GOOD LORD, BRUCE, WHAT IS IT WITH YOU AND BOMBS?
THEY DO TEND TO BE YOUR GO-TO. LET'S TAKE A LOOK--
HEY! HEY!
I BELIEVE YOU FUNDAMENTALLY MISUNDERSTOOD THE CRISIS, BRUCE!
I DIDN'T--
THERE'S DEFINITELY SOME SORT OF RADIATION SIGNATURE FROM INSIDE THIS THING. HANK, POP THE HOOD.
GET AWAY FROM THERE!
EASY, COWBOY! SOMEONE GET BRUCE A GLASS OF WARM MILK, OKAY?
LET ME SEE IF THERE'S ANY WAY I CAN GET REED AND MAYBE THAT AMADEUS CHO KID IN FOR A CONSULT--
I DON'T NEED YOU TO CHECK MY MATH!
LET ME EXPLAIN! THAT INVENTION IS--
--IT'S--

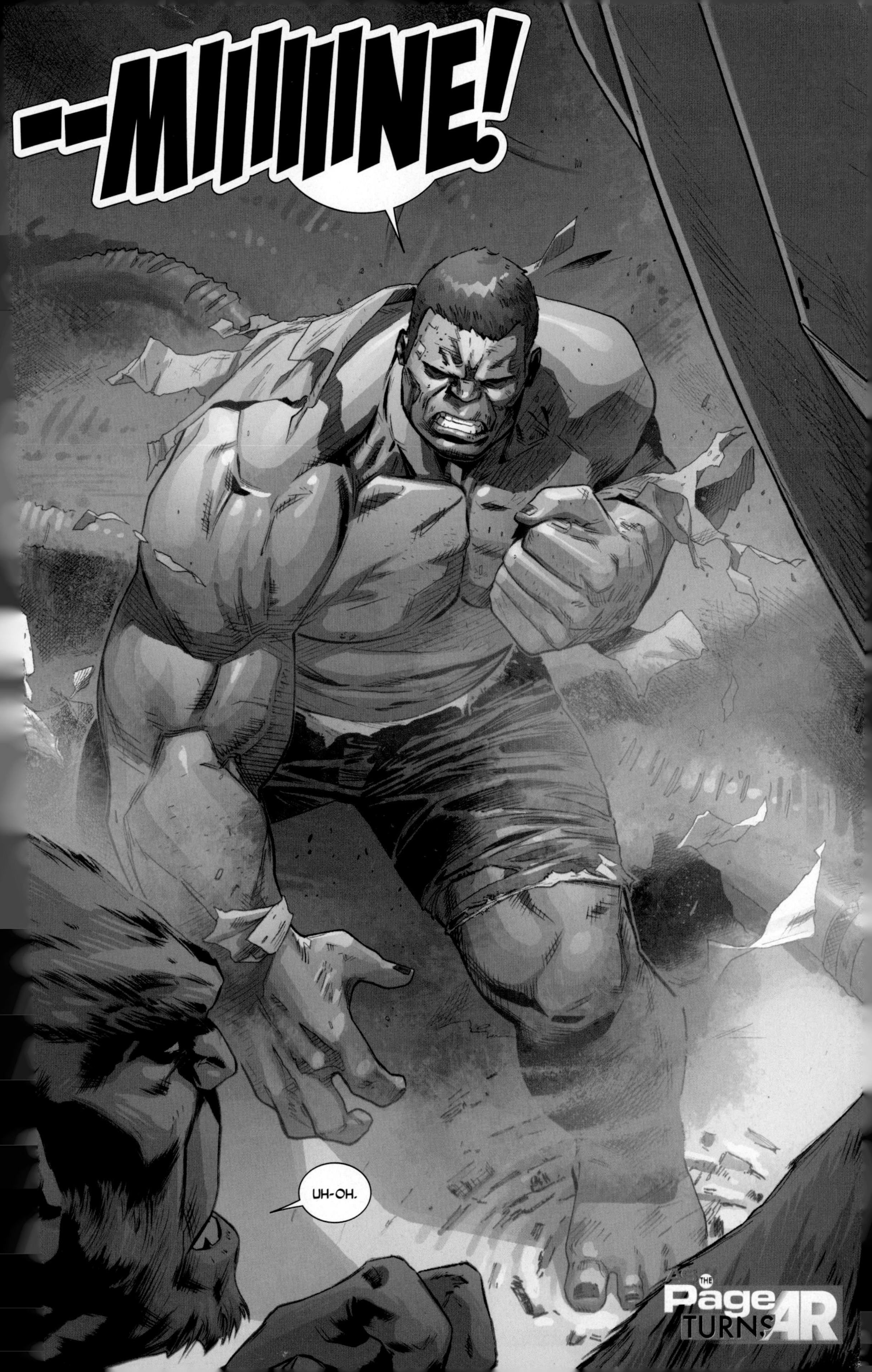
--MIIIIIINE!
UH-OH.

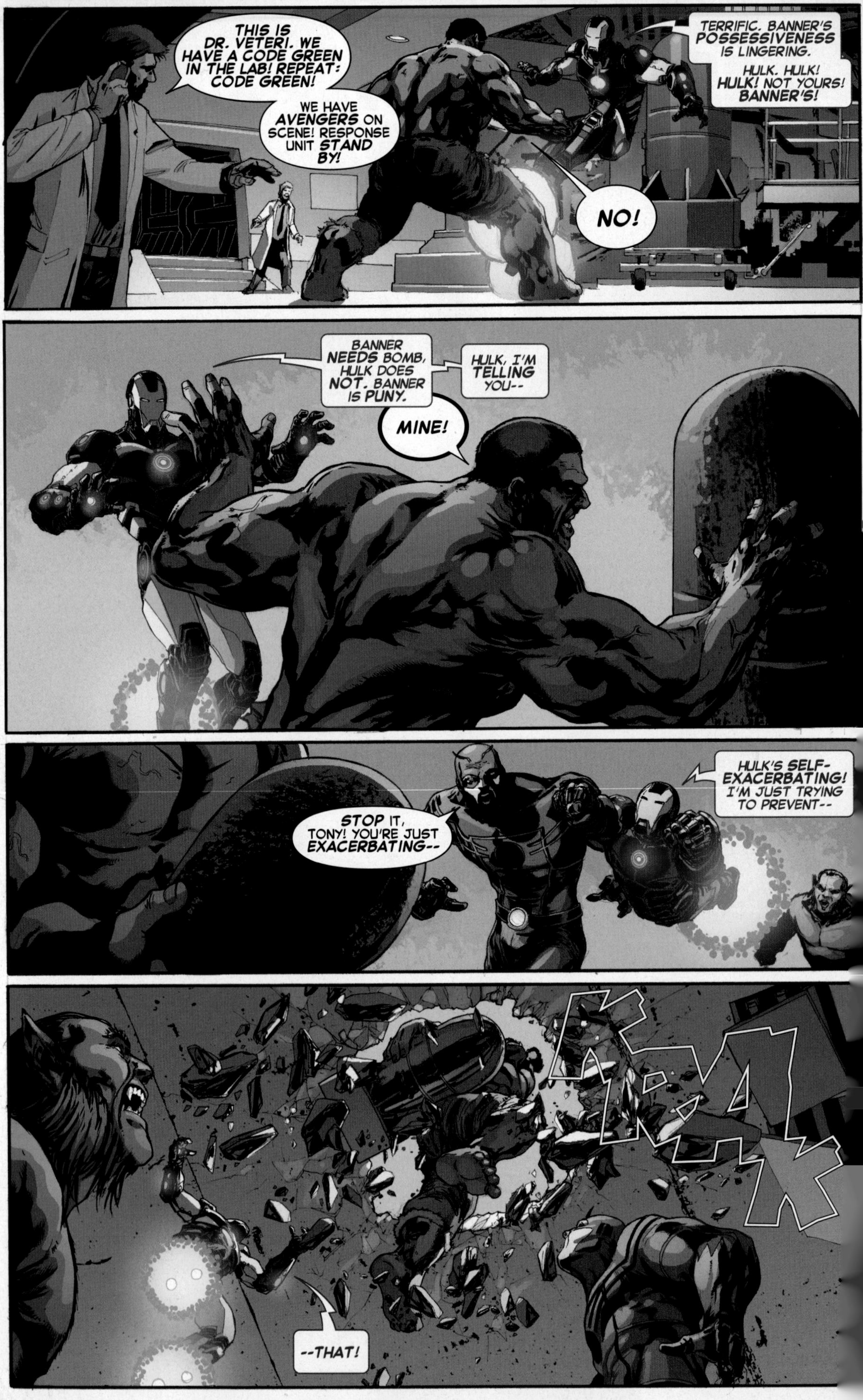
THIS IS DR. VETERI. WE HAVE A CODE GREEN IN THE LAB! REPEAT: CODE GREEN!
WE HAVE AVENGERS ON SCENE! RESPONSE UNIT STAND BY!
TERRIFIC. BANNER'S POSSESSIVENESS IS LINGERING.
HULK. HULK! HULK! NOT YOURS! BANNER'S!
NO!
BANNER NEEDS BOMB, HULK DOES NOT. BANNER IS PUNY.
HULK, I'M TELLING YOU--
MINE!
HULK'S SELF-EXACERBATING! I'M JUST TRYING TO PREVENT--
STOP IT, TONY! YOU'RE JUST EXACERBATING--
--THAT!

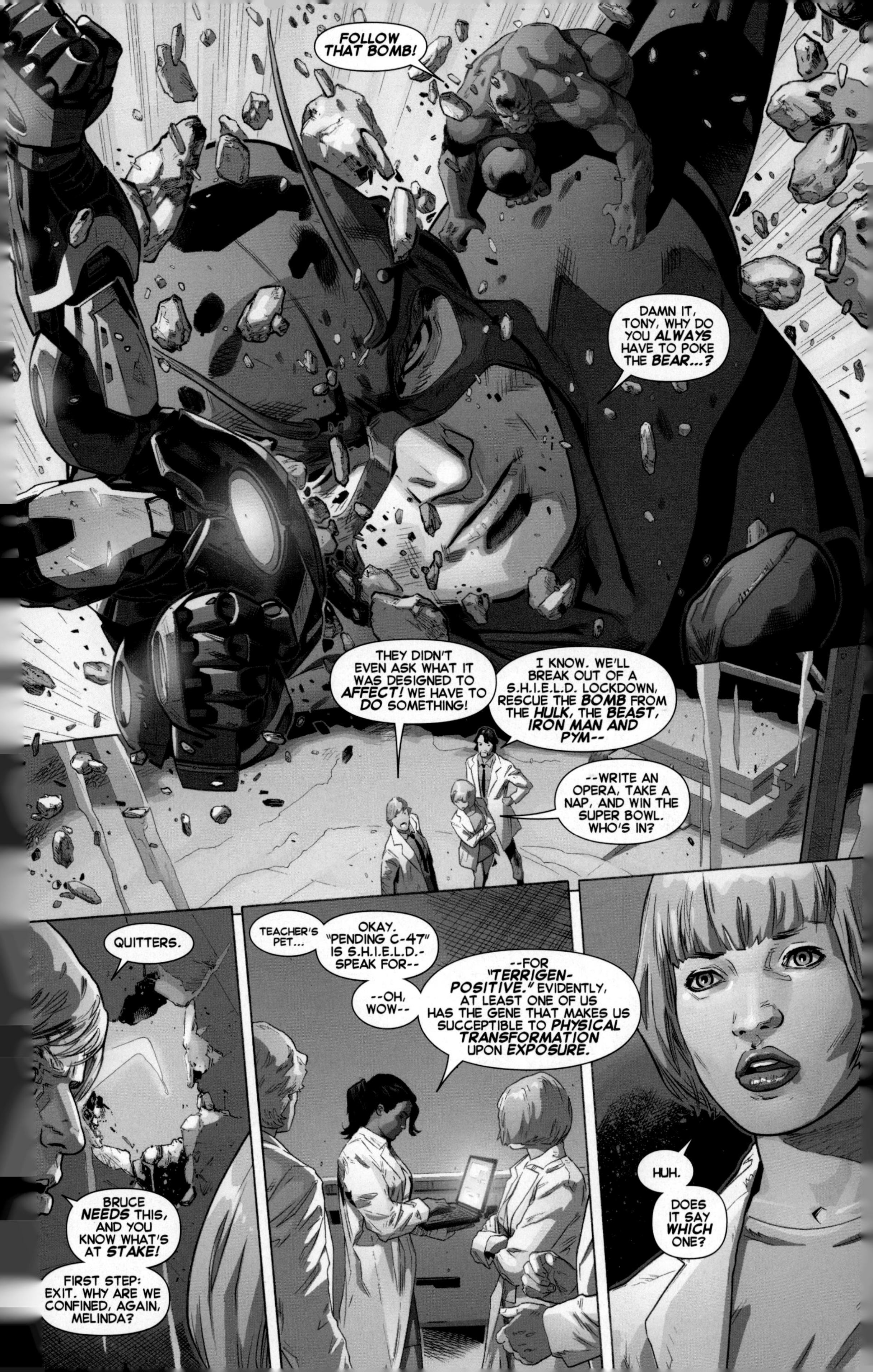
FOLLOW THAT BOMB!
DAMN IT, TONY, WHY DO YOU ALWAYS HAVE TO POKE THE BEAR...?
THEY DIDN'T EVEN ASK WHAT IT WAS DESIGNED TO AFFECT! WE HAVE TO DO SOMETHING!
I KNOW. WE'LL BREAK OUT OF A S.H.I.E.L.D. LOCKDOWN, RESCUE THE BOMB FROM THE HULK, THE BEAST, IRON MAN AND PYM--
--WRITE AN OPERA, TAKE A NAP, AND WIN THE SUPER BOWL. WHO'S IN?
QUITTERS.
BRUCE NEEDS THIS, AND YOU KNOW WHAT'S AT STAKE!
FIRST STEP: EXIT. WHY ARE WE CONFINED, AGAIN, MELINDA?
TEACHER'S PET...
OKAY. "PENDING C-47" IS S.H.I.E.L.D.-SPEAK FOR--
--OH, WOW--
--FOR "TERRIGEN-POSITIVE." EVIDENTLY, AT LEAST ONE OF US HAS THE GENE THAT MAKES US SUSCEPTIBLE TO PHYSICAL TRANSFORMATION UPON EXPOSURE.
HUH.
DOES IT SAY WHICH ONE?

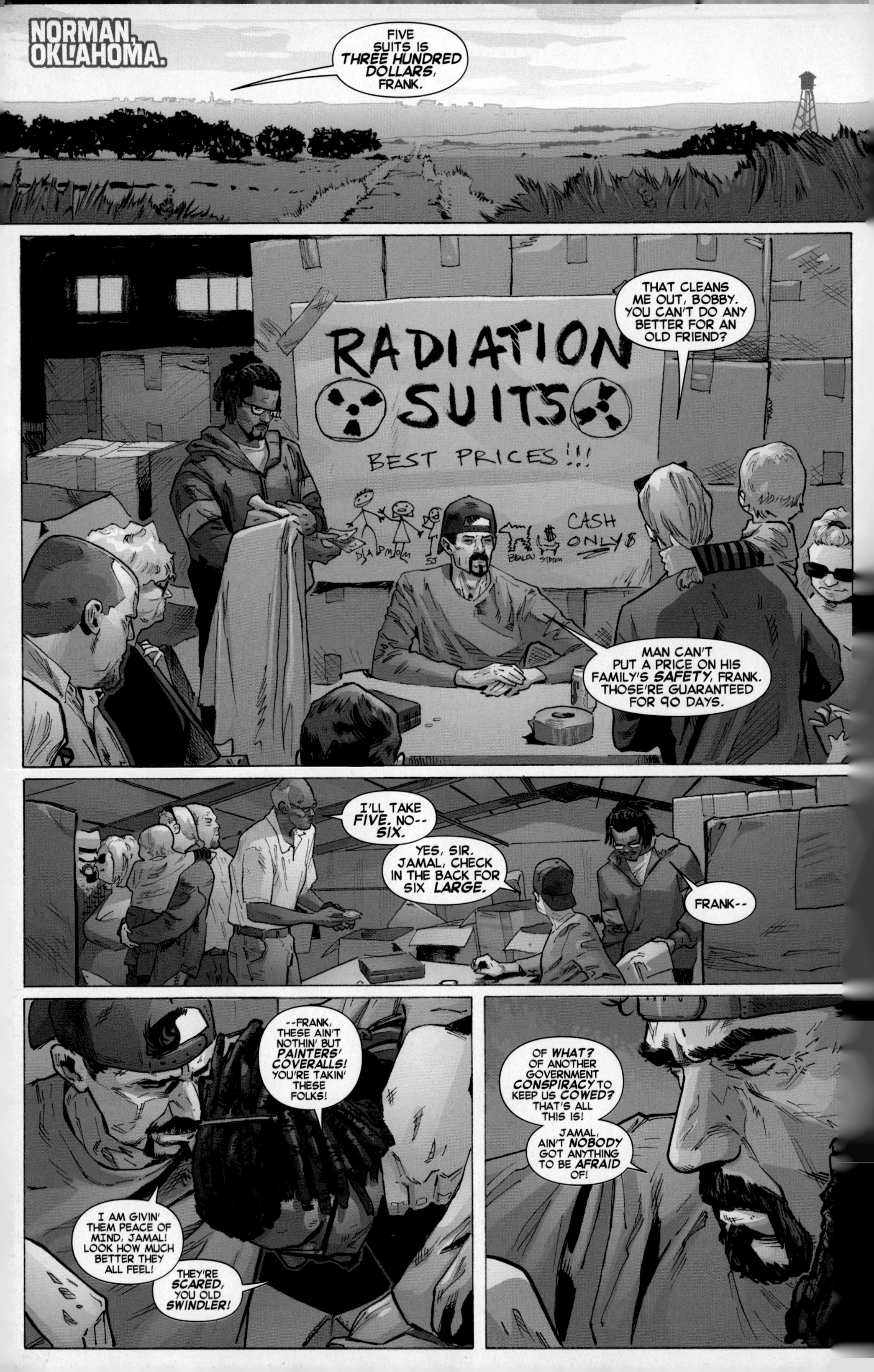
NORMAN, OKLAHOMA.
FIVE SUITS IS THREE HUNDRED DOLLARS, FRANK.
RADIATION SUITS
BEST PRICES!!!
CASH ONLY
THAT CLEANS ME OUT, BOBBY. YOU CAN'T DO ANY BETTER FOR AN OLD FRIEND?
MAN CAN'T PUT A PRICE ON HIS FAMILY'S SAFETY, FRANK. THOSE'RE GUARANTEED FOR 90 DAYS.
I'LL TAKE FIVE. NO-- SIX.
YES, SIR. JAMAL, CHECK IN THE BACK FOR SIX LARGE.
FRANK--
--FRANK, THESE AIN'T NOTHIN' BUT PAINTERS' COVERALLS! YOU'RE TAKIN' THESE FOLKS!
I AM GIVIN' THEM PEACE OF MIND, JAMAL! LOOK HOW MUCH BETTER THEY ALL FEEL!
THEY'RE SCARED, YOU OLD SWINDLER!
OF WHAT? OF ANOTHER GOVERNMENT CONSPIRACY TO KEEP US COWED? THAT'S ALL THIS IS!
JAMAL, AIN'T NOBODY GOT ANYTHING TO BE AFRAID OF!

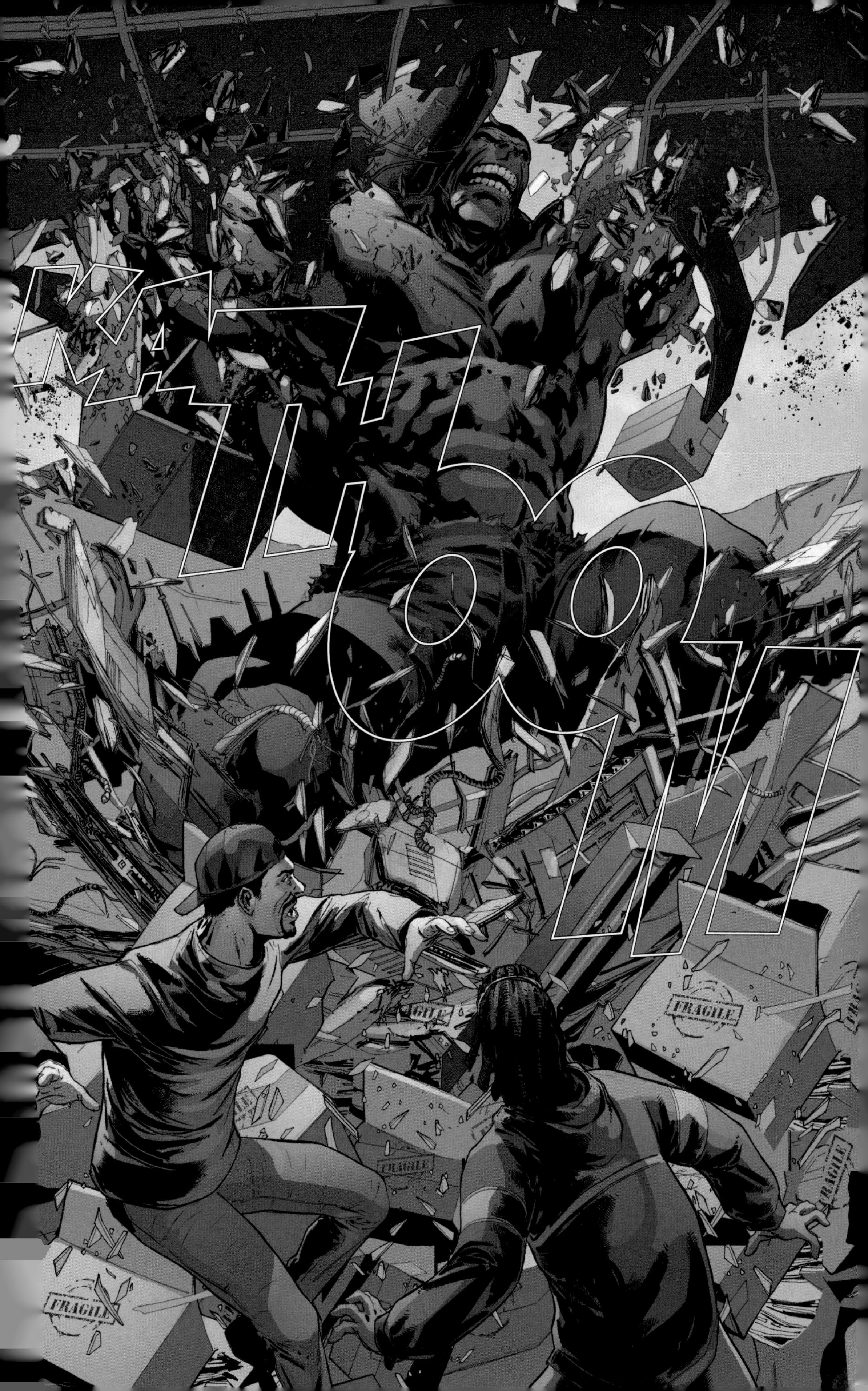
FRAGILE
FRAGILE
FRAGILE
FRAGILE

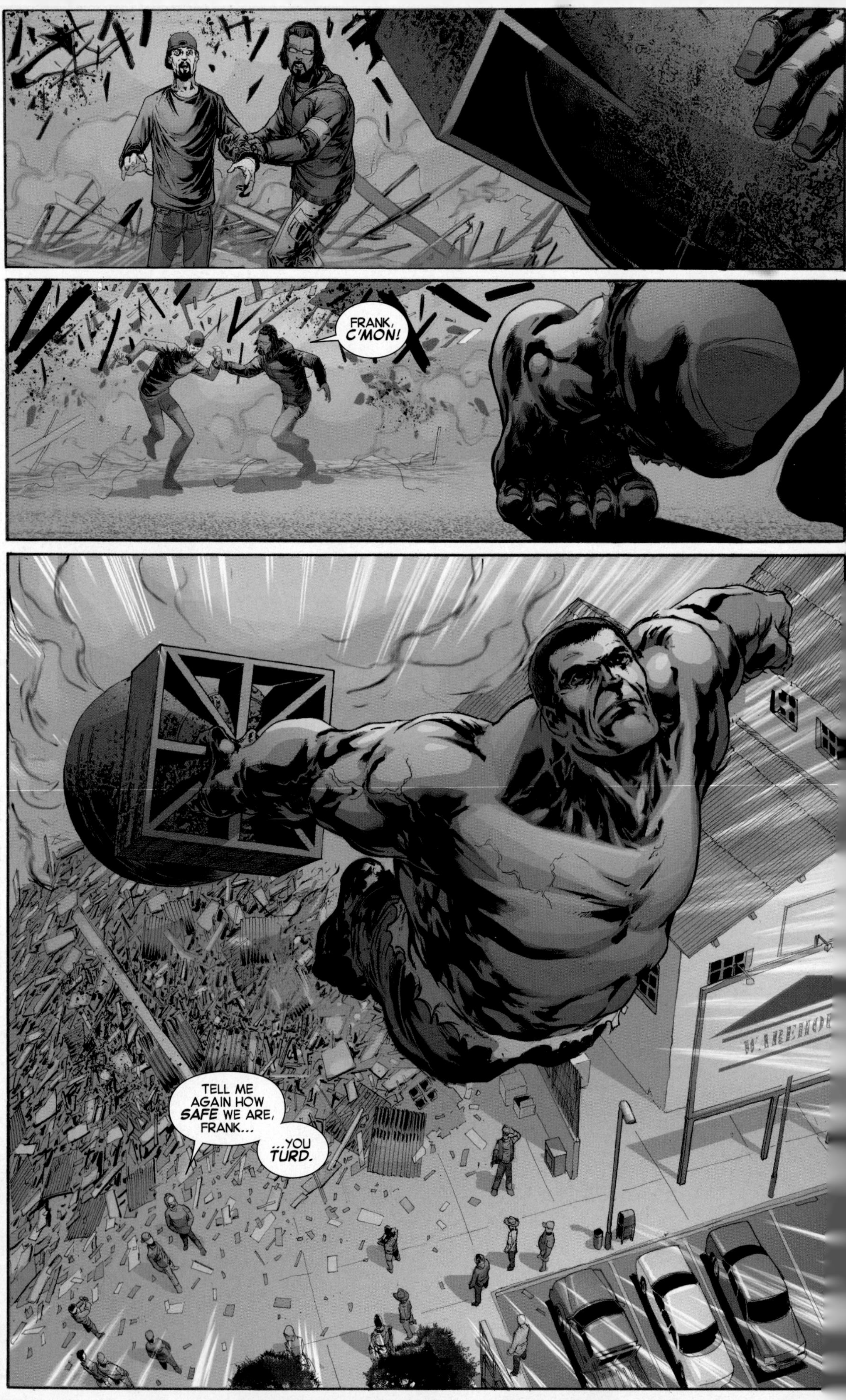
FRANK, C'MON!
TELL ME AGAIN HOW SAFE WE ARE, FRANK...
...YOU TURD.

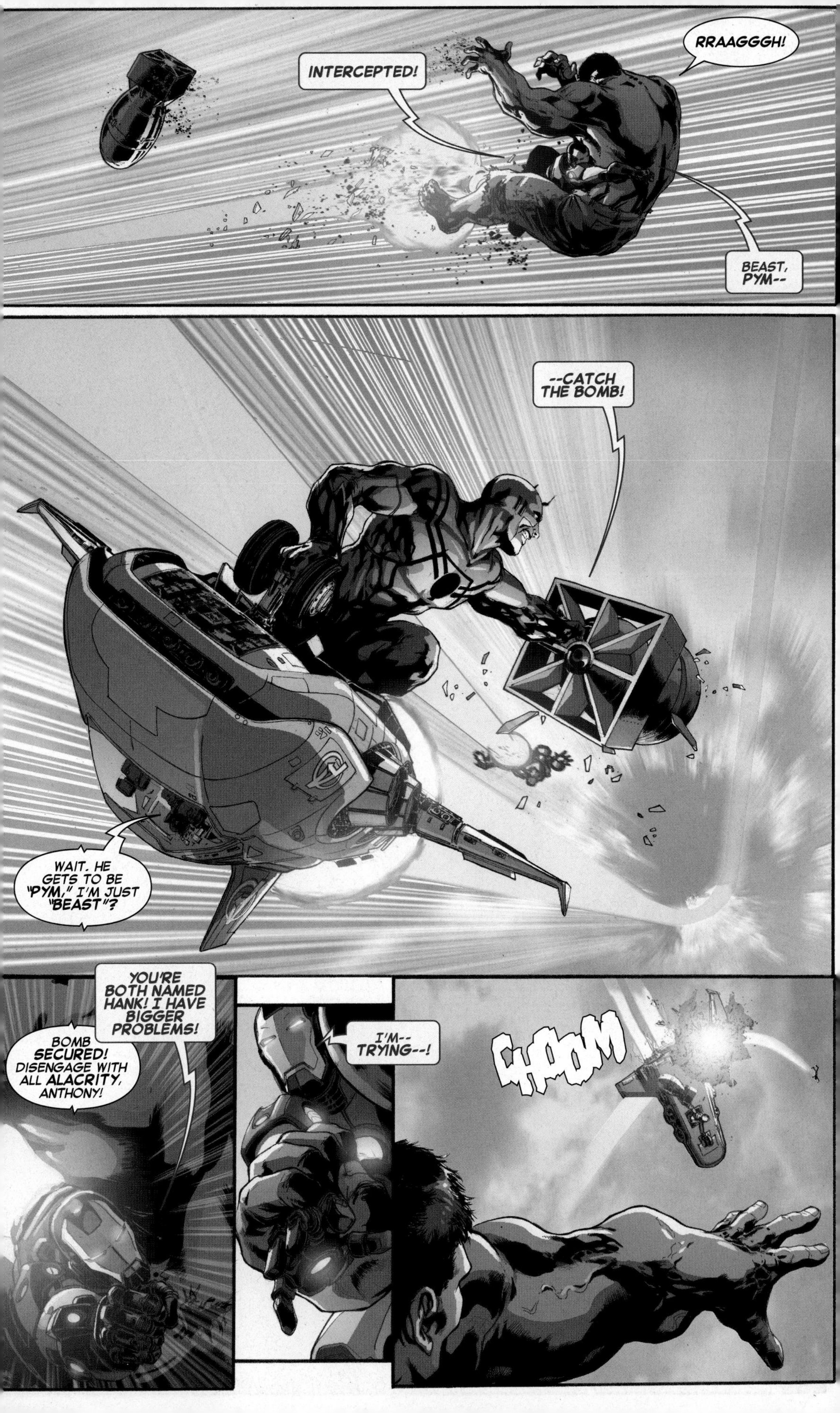
RRAAGGGH!
INTERCEPTED!
BEAST, PYM--
--CATCH THE BOMB!
WAIT. HE GETS TO BE "PYM," I'M JUST "BEAST"?
YOU'RE BOTH NAMED HANK! I HAVE BIGGER PROBLEMS!
BOMB SECURED! DISENGAGE WITH ALL ALACRITY, ANTHONY!
I'M-- TRYING--!
CHOOM

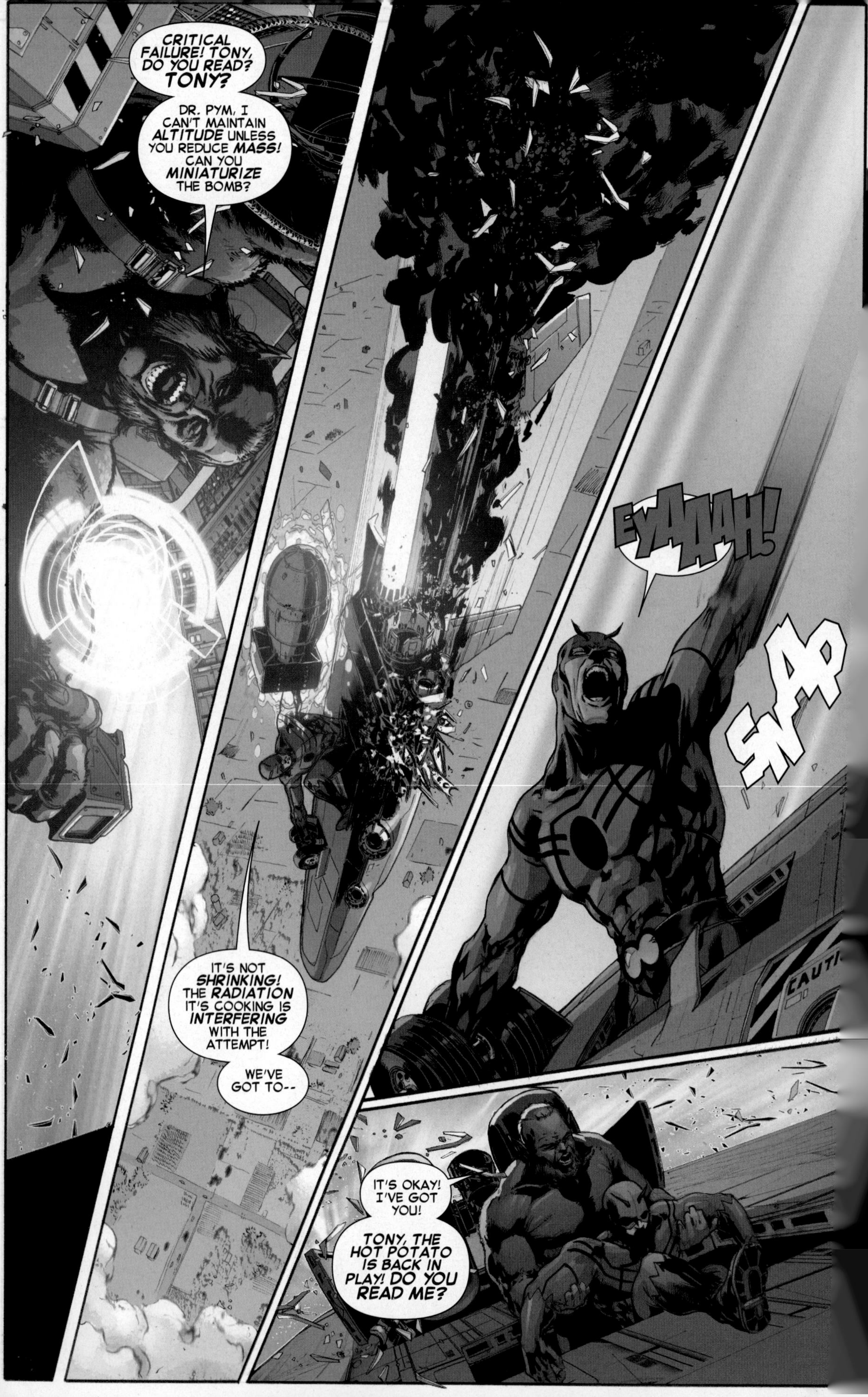
CRITICAL FAILURE! TONY, DO YOU READ? TONY?
DR. PYM, I CAN'T MAINTAIN ALTITUDE UNLESS YOU REDUCE MASS! CAN YOU MINIATURIZE THE BOMB?
IT'S NOT SHRINKING! THE RADIATION IT'S COOKING IS INTERFERING WITH THE ATTEMPT!
WE'VE GOT TO--
EYAAAH!
SNAP
CAUTI
IT'S OKAY! I'VE GOT YOU!
TONY, THE HOT POTATO IS BACK IN PLAY! DO YOU READ ME?

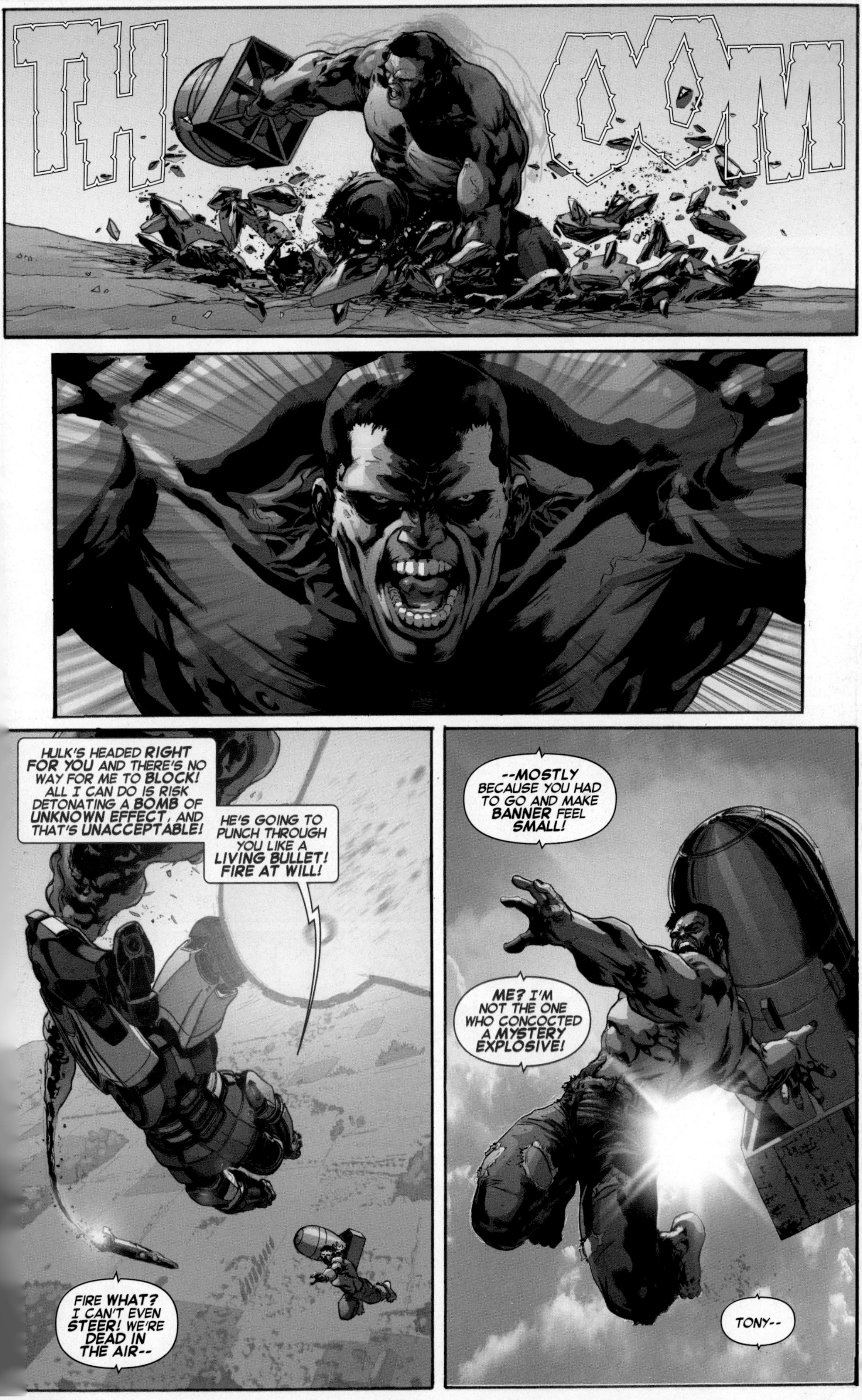
TH OOM
HULK'S HEADED RIGHT FOR YOU AND THERE'S NO WAY FOR ME TO BLOCK! ALL I CAN DO IS RISK DETONATING A BOMB OF UNKNOWN EFFECT, AND THAT'S UNACCEPTABLE!
HE'S GOING TO PUNCH THROUGH YOU LIKE A LIVING BULLET! FIRE AT WILL!
FIRE WHAT? I CAN'T EVEN STEER! WE'RE DEAD IN THE AIR--
--MOSTLY BECAUSE YOU HAD TO GO AND MAKE BANNER FEEL SMALL!
ME? I'M NOT THE ONE WHO CONCOCTED A MYSTERY EXPLOSIVE!
TONY--

--WHAT IF IT WORKS?

WHAT?

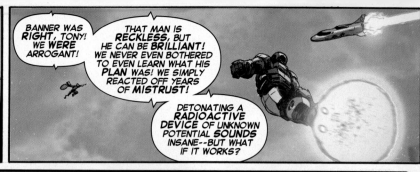

BANNER WAS RIGHT, TONY! WE WERE ARROGANT!

THAT MAN IS RECKLESS, BUT HE CAN BE BRILLIANT! WE NEVER EVEN BOTHERED TO EVEN LEARN WHAT HIS PLAN WAS! WE SIMPLY REACTED OFF YEARS OF MISTRUST!

DETONATING A RADIOACTIVE DEVICE OF UNKNOWN POTENTIAL SOUNDS INSANE--BUT WHAT IF IT WORKS?

"TONY, YOU'VE KNOWN BANNER BETTER AND LONGER THAN WE EVER WILL! IT'S YOUR CALL TO MAKE!

"PUT ASIDE ALL YOUR EGO AND RIVALRY AND DECIDE RIGHT NOW--"

DO YOU STAND DOWN--

--AND LET YOU DIE--

--DO YOU TRUST BRUCE BANNER ENOUGH TO RISK MANKIND'S SURVIVAL?

SHOOM

SHOOM

FWOOSH

FWOOSH

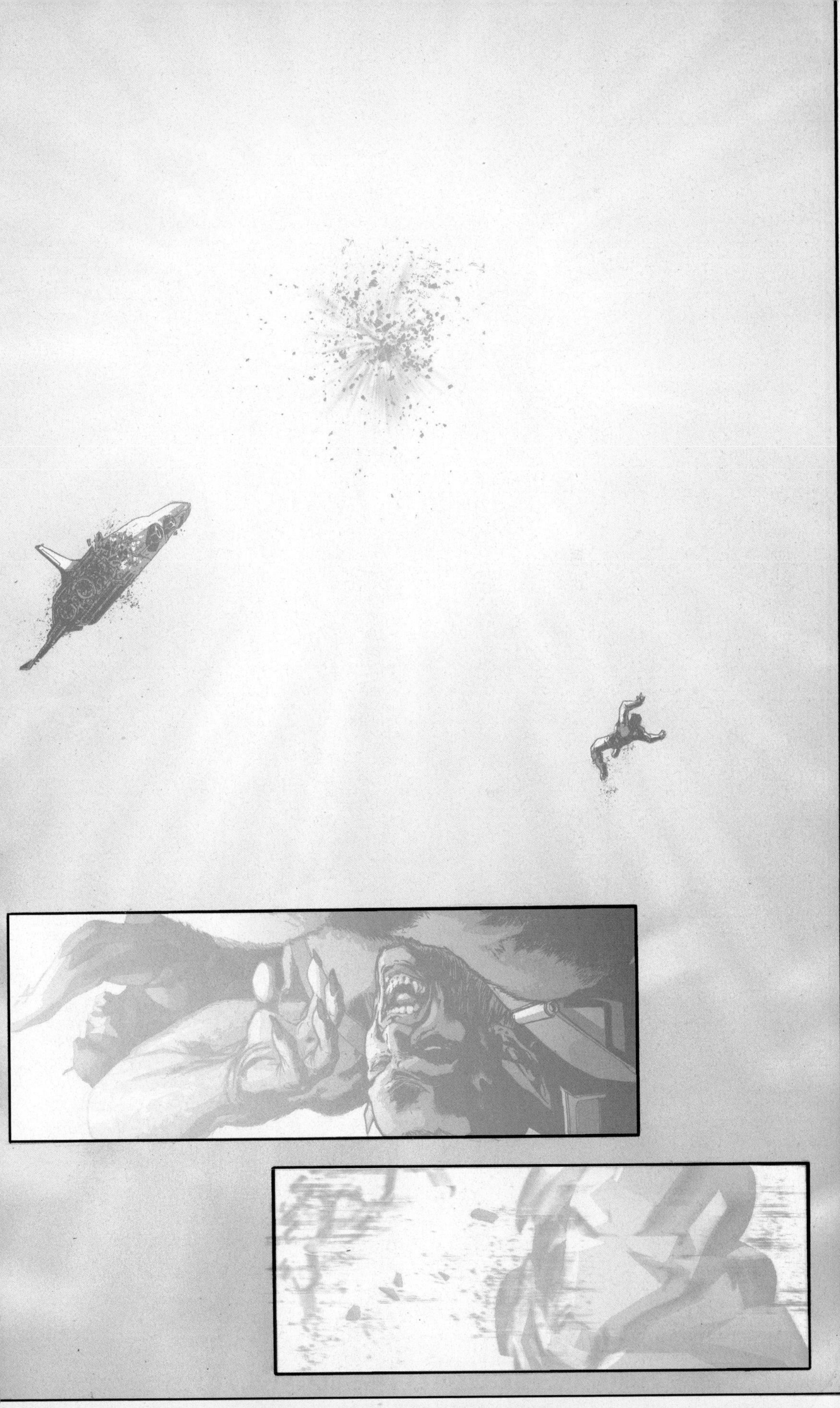

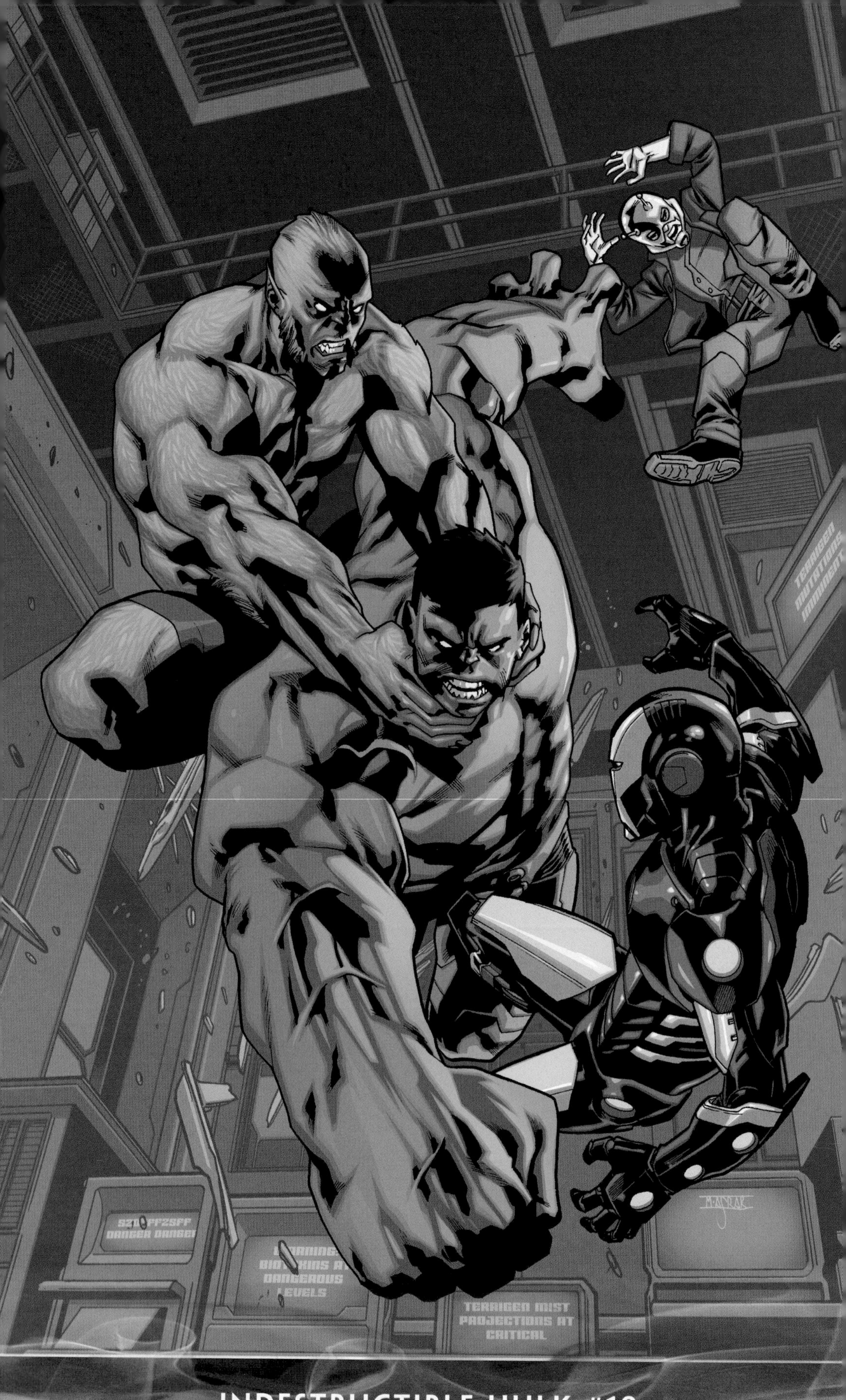
TERRIGEN MIST
PROJECTIONS AT
CRITICAL

INDESTRUCTIBLE HULK #18

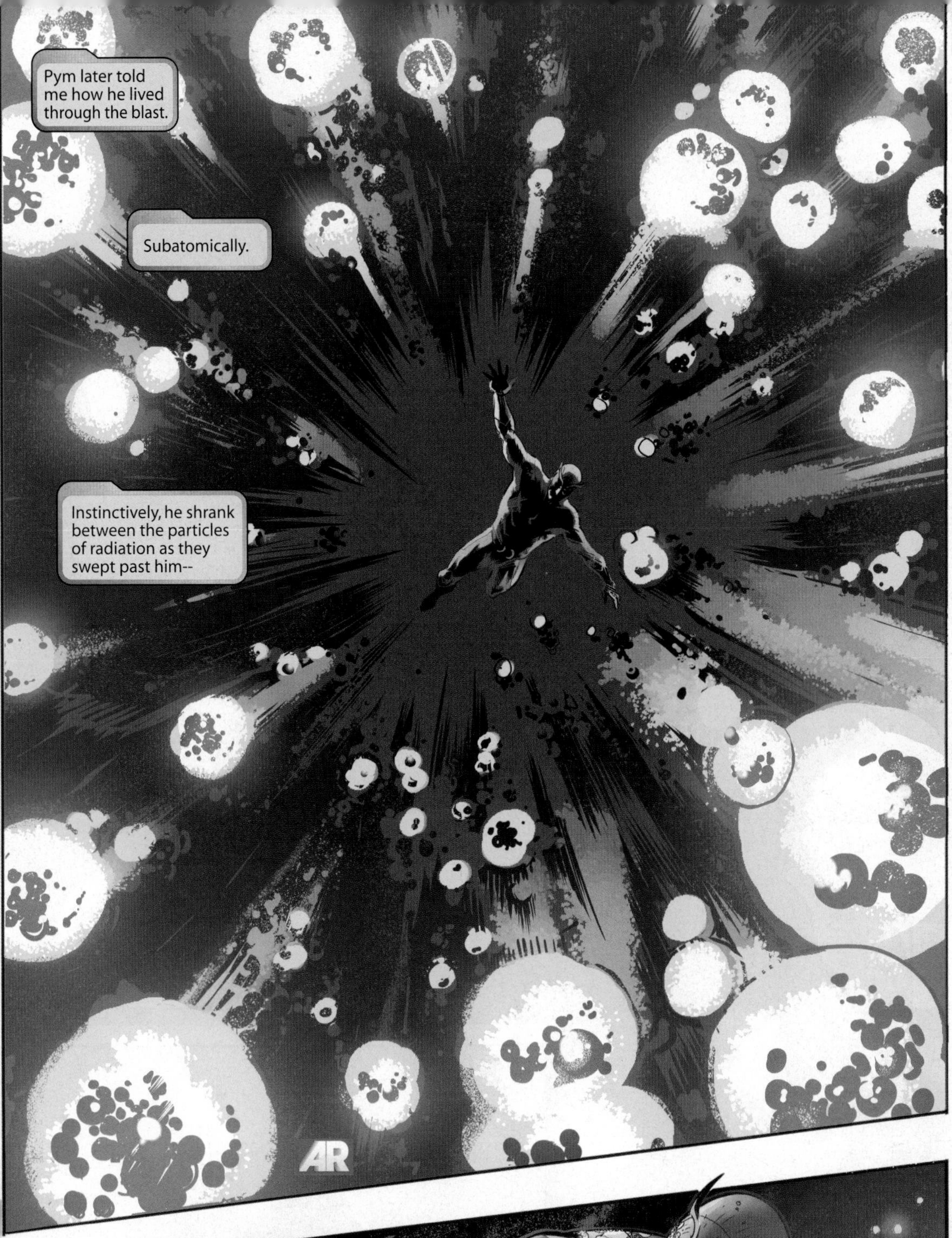
Pym later told me how he lived through the blast.
Subatomically.
Instinctively, he shrank between the particles of radiation as they swept past him--
AR

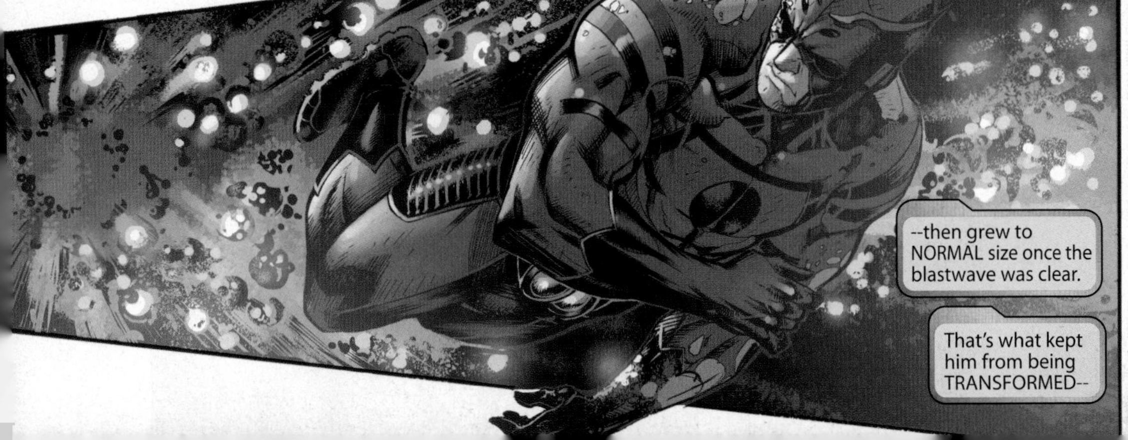
--then grew to NORMAL size once the blastwave was clear.
That's what kept him from being TRANSFORMED--

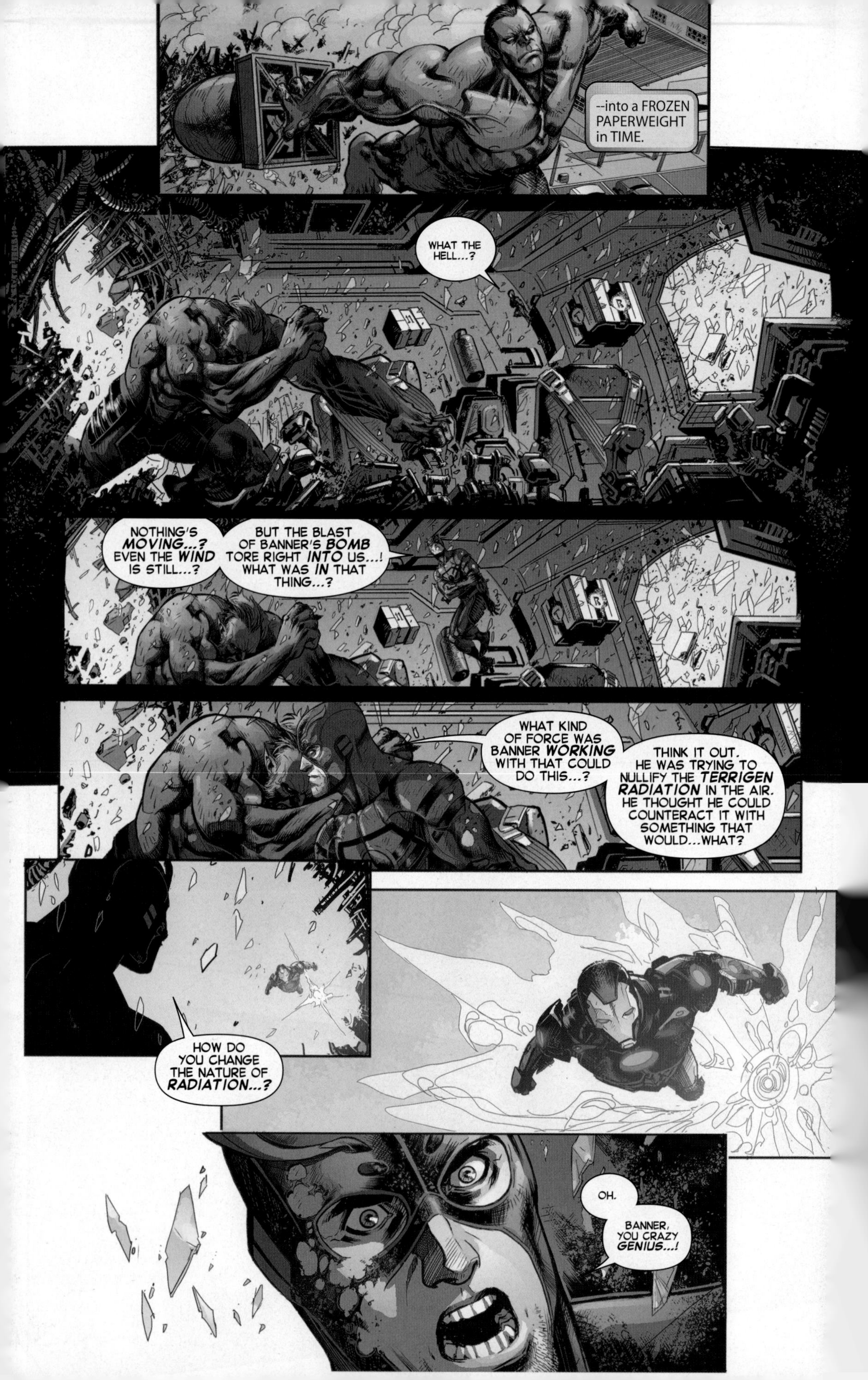
--into a FROZEN PAPERWEIGHT in TIME.
WHAT THE HELL...?
NOTHING'S MOVING...? EVEN THE WIND IS STILL...?
BUT THE BLAST OF BANNER'S BOMB TORE RIGHT INTO US...! WHAT WAS IN THAT THING...?
WHAT KIND OF FORCE WAS BANNER WORKING WITH THAT COULD DO THIS...?
THINK IT OUT. HE WAS TRYING TO NULLIFY THE TERRIGEN RADIATION IN THE AIR. HE THOUGHT HE COULD COUNTERACT IT WITH SOMETHING THAT WOULD...WHAT?
HOW DO YOU CHANGE THE NATURE OF RADIATION...?
OH.
BANNER, YOU CRAZY GENIUS...!

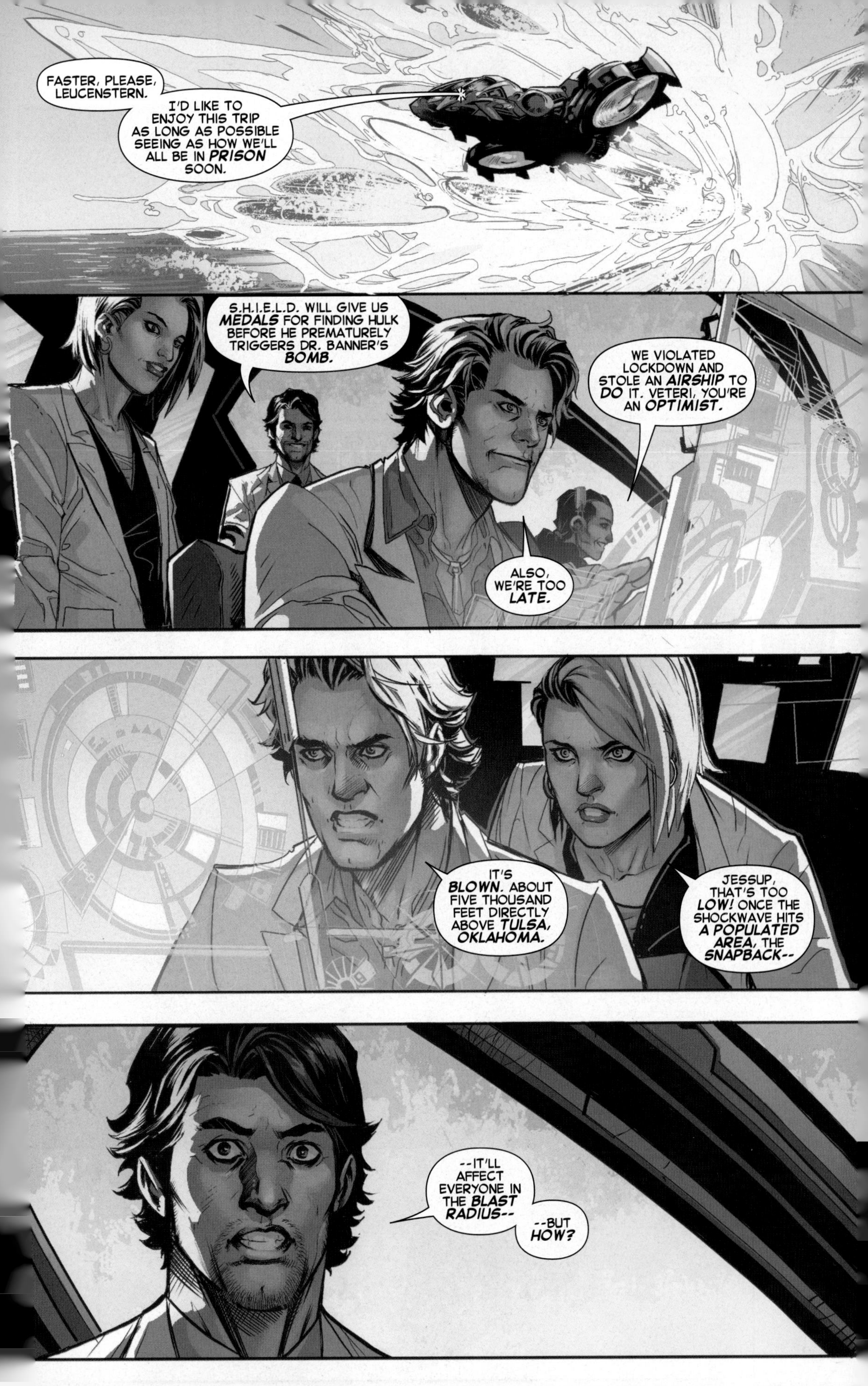
FASTER, PLEASE, LEUCENSTERN.
I'D LIKE TO ENJOY THIS TRIP AS LONG AS POSSIBLE SEEING AS HOW WE'LL ALL BE IN PRISON SOON.
S.H.I.E.L.D. WILL GIVE US MEDALS FOR FINDING HULK BEFORE HE PREMATURELY TRIGGERS DR. BANNER'S BOMB.
WE VIOLATED LOCKDOWN AND STOLE AN AIRSHIP TO DO IT. VETERI, YOU'RE AN OPTIMIST.
ALSO, WE'RE TOO LATE.
IT'S BLOWN. ABOUT FIVE THOUSAND FEET DIRECTLY ABOVE TULSA, OKLAHOMA.
JESSUP, THAT'S TOO LOW! ONCE THE SHOCKWAVE HITS A POPULATED AREA, THE SNAPBACK--
--IT'LL AFFECT EVERYONE IN THE BLAST RADIUS--
--BUT HOW?

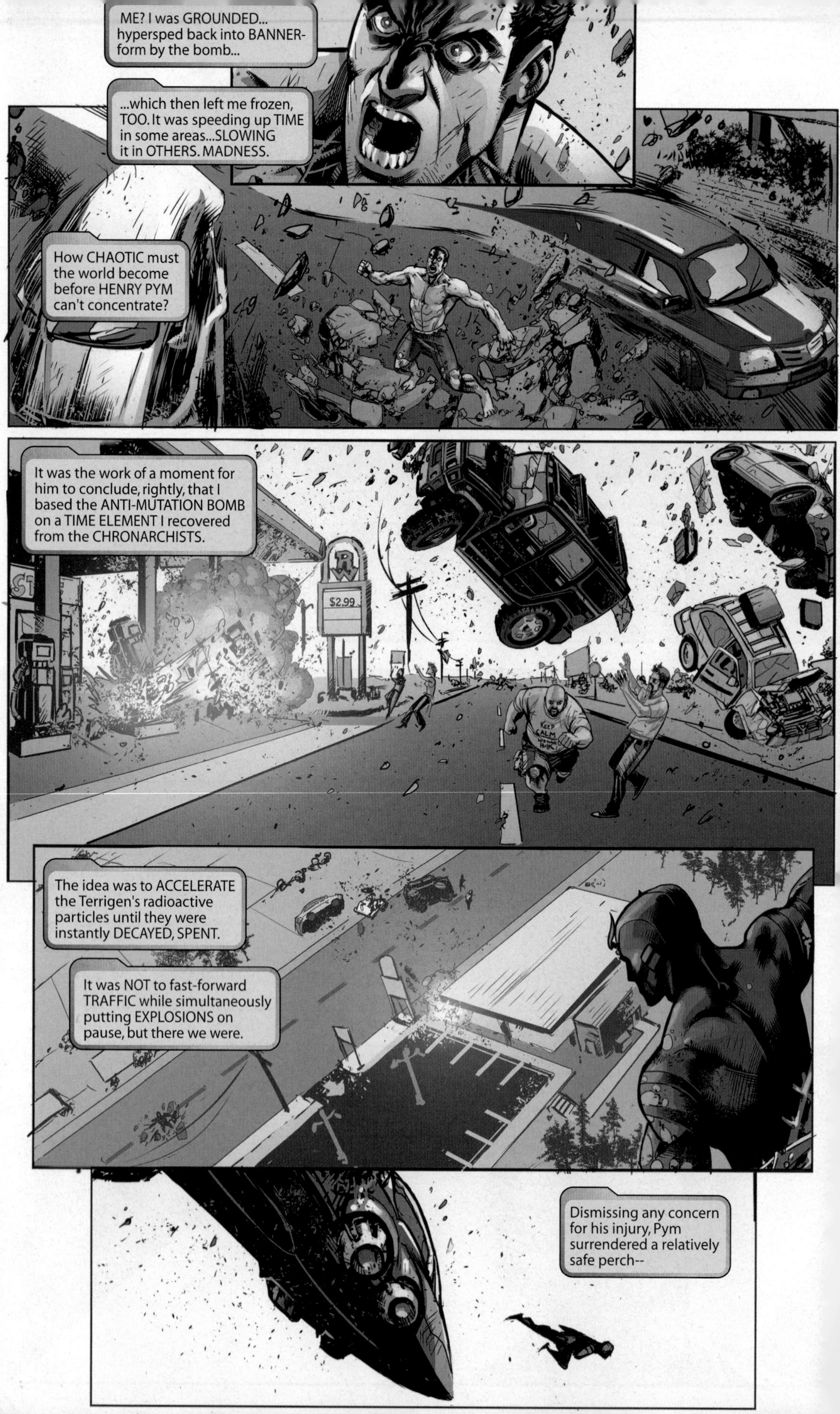
ME? I was GROUNDED... hypersped back into BANNER-form by the bomb...
...which then left me frozen, TOO. It was speeding up TIME in some areas...SLOWING it in OTHERS. MADNESS.
How CHAOTIC must the world become before HENRY PYM can't concentrate?
It was the work of a moment for him to conclude, rightly, that I based the ANTI-MUTATION BOMB on a TIME ELEMENT I recovered from the CHRONARCHISTS.
$2.99
KEEP CALM
The idea was to ACCELERATE the Terrigen's radioactive particles until they were instantly DECAYED, SPENT.
It was NOT to fast-forward TRAFFIC while simultaneously putting EXPLOSIONS on pause, but there we were.
Dismissing any concern for his injury, Pym surrendered a relatively safe perch--

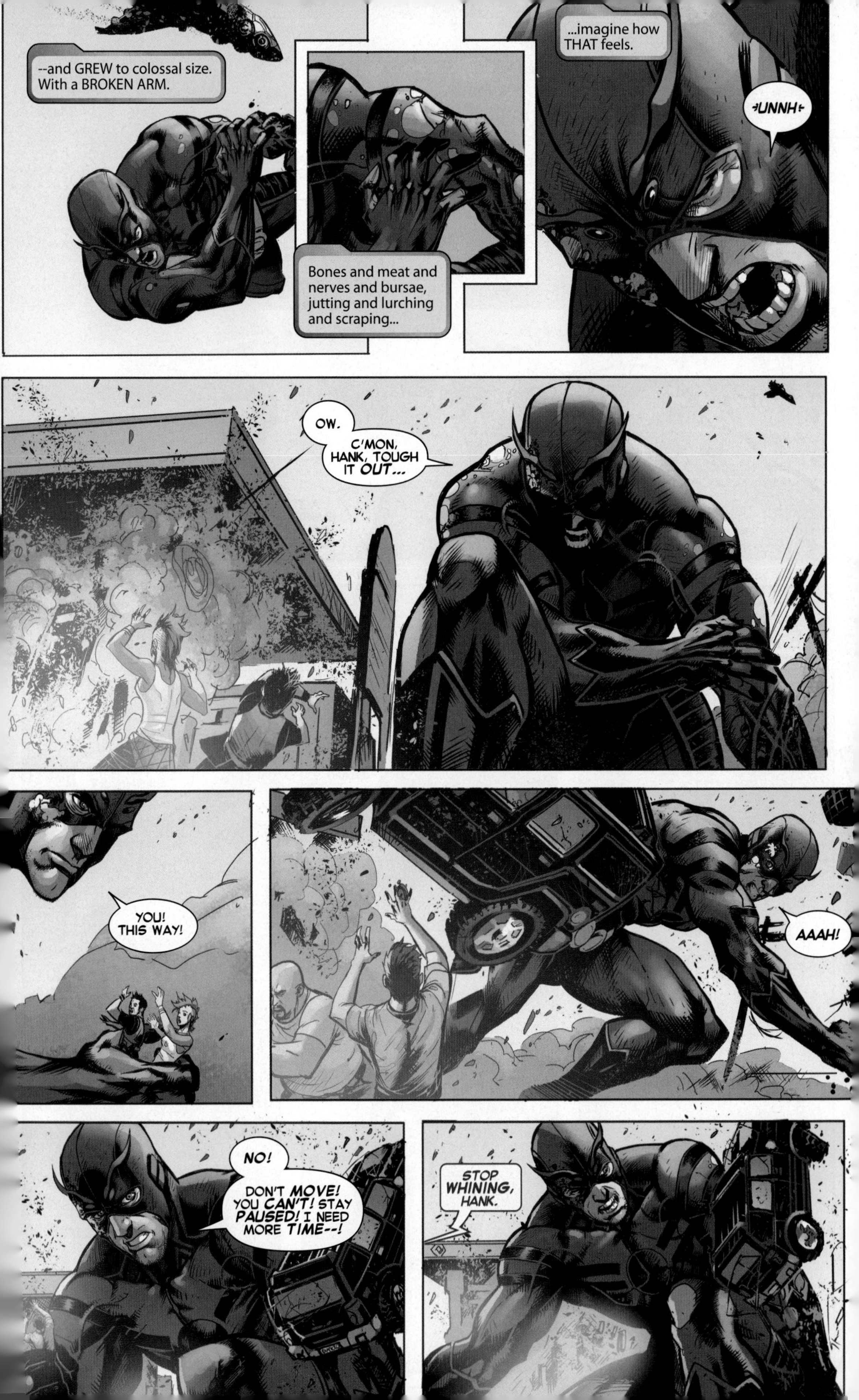
--and GREW to colossal size. With a BROKEN ARM.
Bones and meat and nerves and bursae, jutting and lurching and scraping...
...imagine how THAT feels.
UNNH
OW.
C'MON, HANK, TOUGH IT OUT...
YOU! THIS WAY!
AAAH!
NO!
DON'T MOVE! YOU CAN'T! STAY PAUSED! I NEED MORE TIME--!
STOP WHINING, HANK.

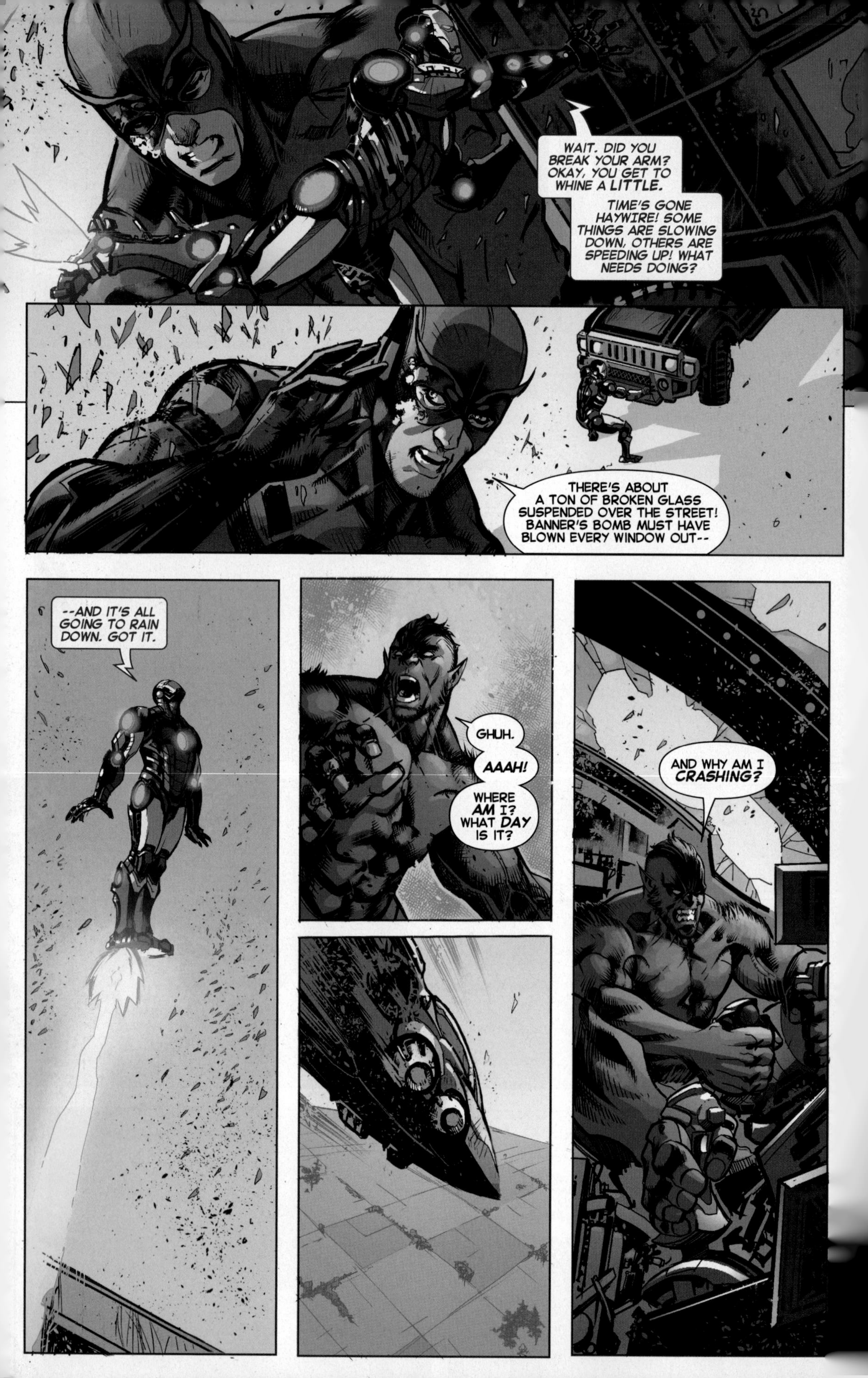
WAIT. DID YOU BREAK YOUR ARM? OKAY, YOU GET TO WHINE A LITTLE.
TIME'S GONE HAYWIRE! SOME THINGS ARE SLOWING DOWN, OTHERS ARE SPEEDING UP! WHAT NEEDS DOING?
THERE'S ABOUT A TON OF BROKEN GLASS SUSPENDED OVER THE STREET! BANNER'S BOMB MUST HAVE BLOWN EVERY WINDOW OUT--
--AND IT'S ALL GOING TO RAIN DOWN. GOT IT.
GHUH.
AAAH!
WHERE AM I? WHAT DAY IS IT?
AND WHY AM I CRASHING?

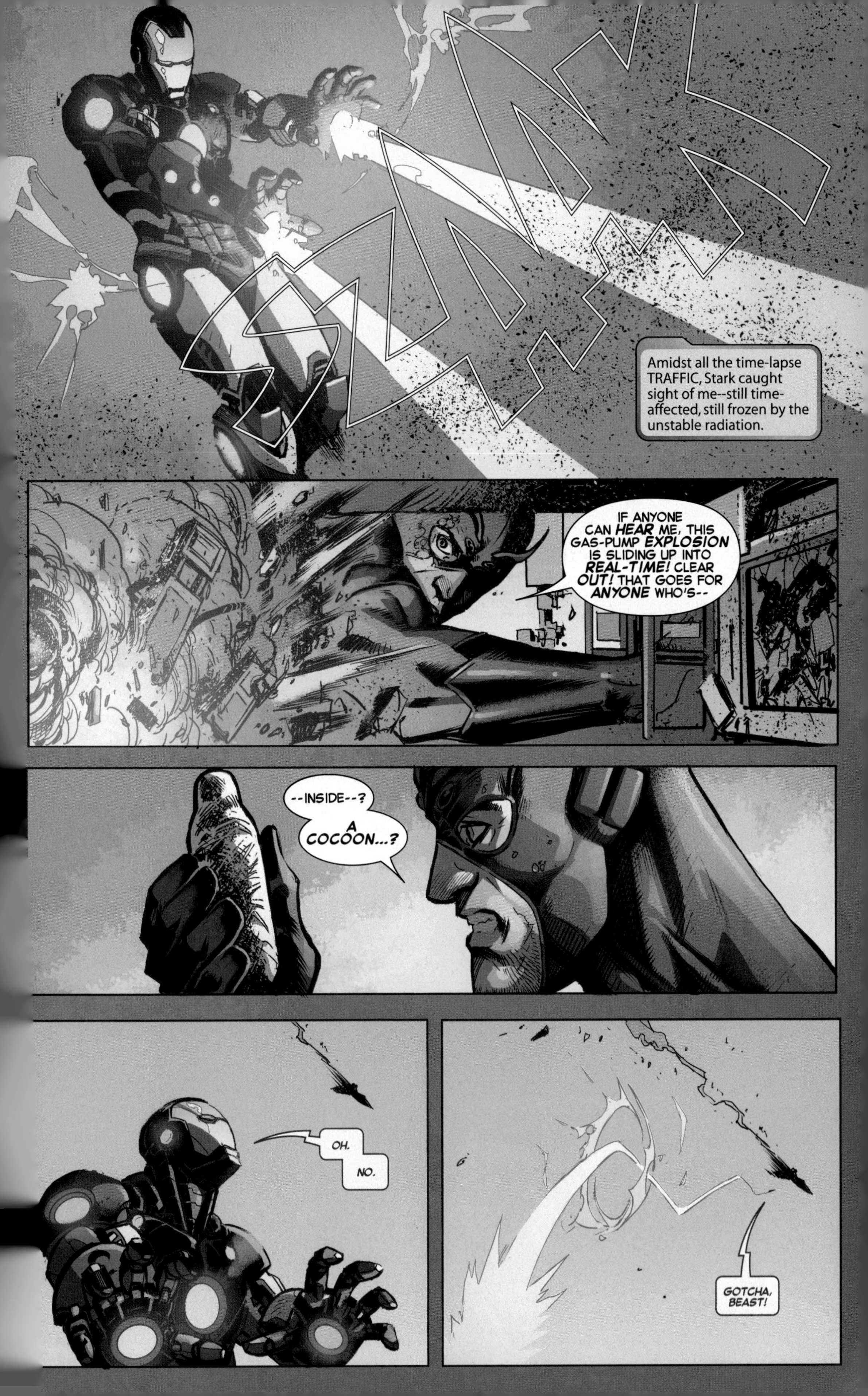
Amidst all the time-lapse TRAFFIC, Stark caught sight of me--still time-affected, still frozen by the unstable radiation.
IF ANYONE CAN HEAR ME, THIS GAS-PUMP EXPLOSION IS SLIDING UP INTO REAL-TIME! CLEAR OUT! THAT GOES FOR ANYONE WHO'S--
--INSIDE--?
A COCOON...?
OH.
NO.
GOTCHA, BEAST!

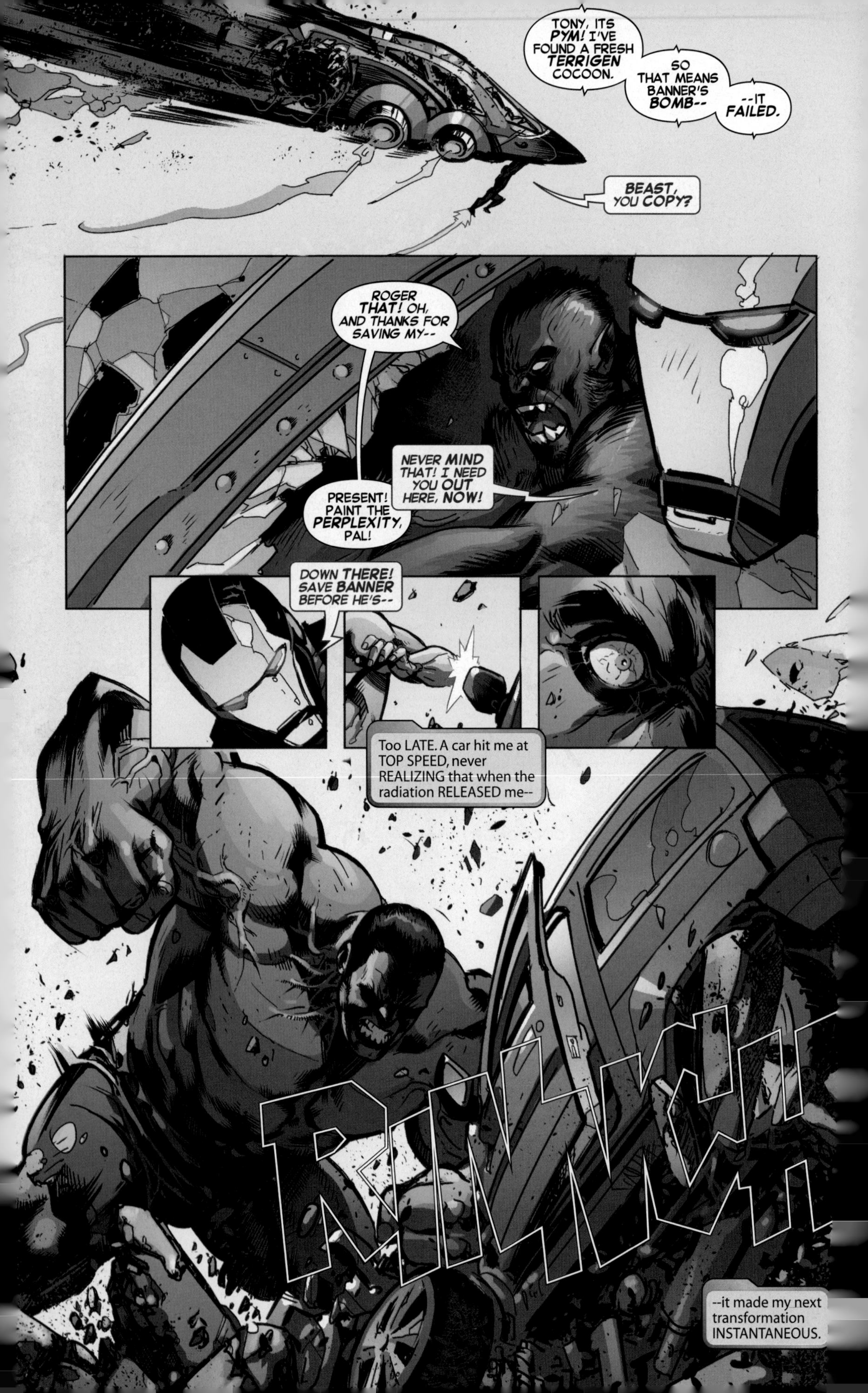

TONY, ITS PYM! I'VE FOUND A FRESH TERRIGEN COCOON.
SO THAT MEANS BANNER'S BOMB--
--IT FAILED.
BEAST, YOU COPY?
ROGER THAT! OH, AND THANKS FOR SAVING MY--
NEVER MIND THAT! I NEED YOU OUT HERE, NOW!
PRESENT! PAINT THE PERPLEXITY, PAL!
DOWN THERE! SAVE BANNER BEFORE HE'S--
Too LATE. A car hit me at TOP SPEED, never REALIZING that when the radiation RELEASED me--
--it made my next transformation INSTANTANEOUS.

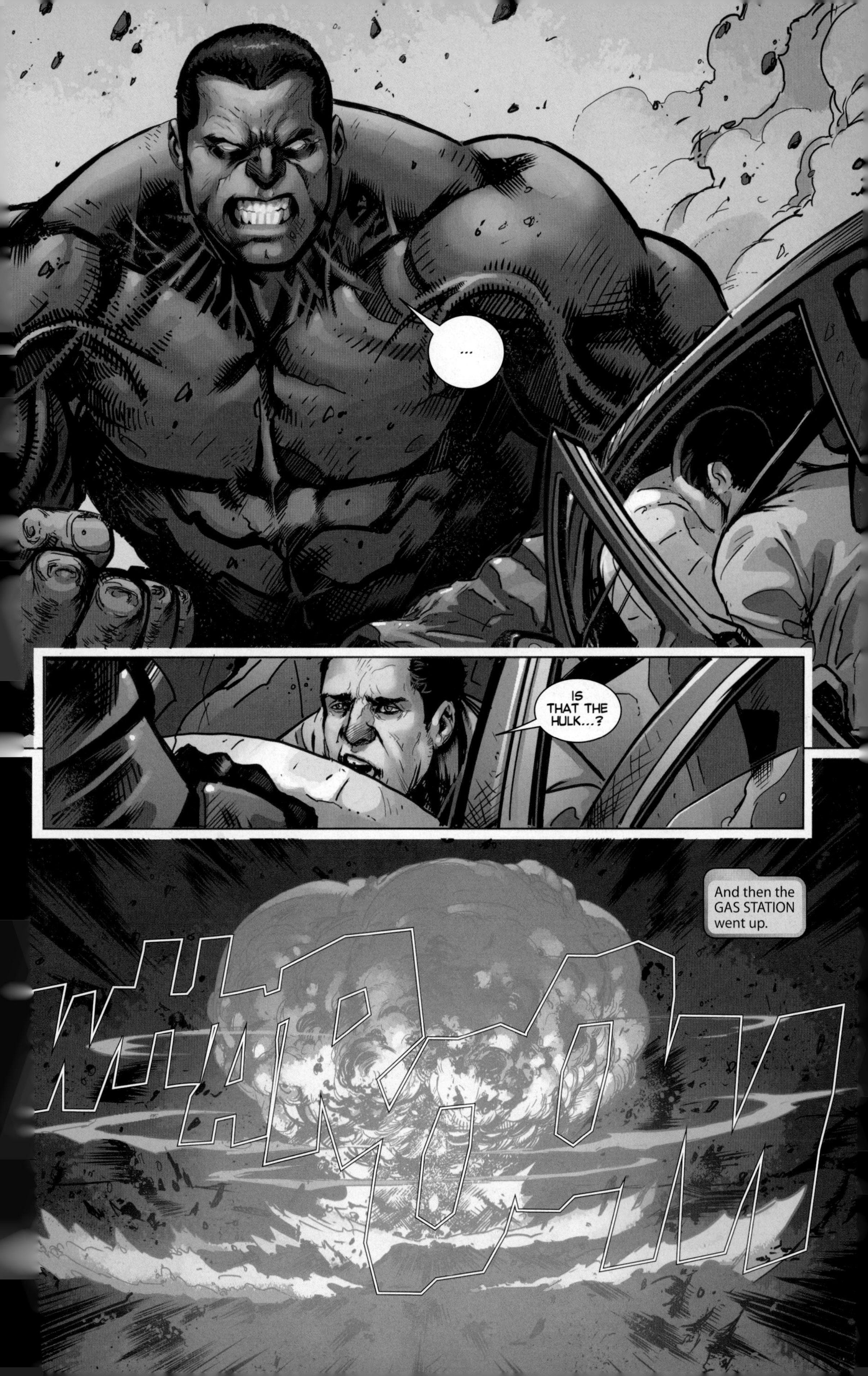
...
IS THAT THE HULK...?
And then the GAS STATION went up.
WHAROOOM

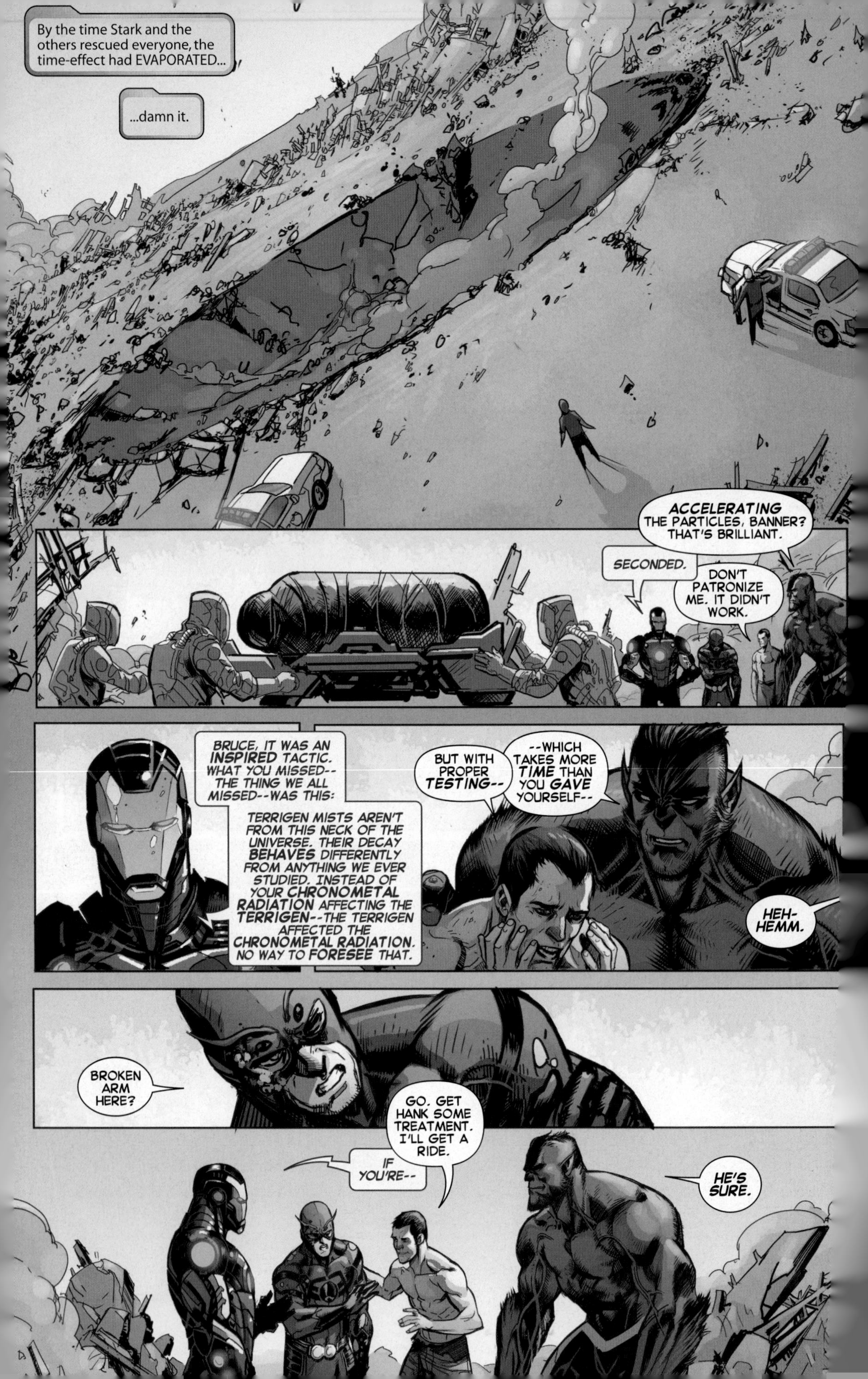

By the time Stark and the others rescued everyone, the time-effect had EVAPORATED...
...damn it.
ACCELERATING THE PARTICLES, BANNER? THAT'S BRILLIANT.
SECONDED.
DON'T PATRONIZE ME. IT DIDN'T WORK.
BRUCE, IT WAS AN INSPIRED TACTIC. WHAT YOU MISSED-- THE THING WE ALL MISSED--WAS THIS:
TERRIGEN MISTS AREN'T FROM THIS NECK OF THE UNIVERSE. THEIR DECAY BEHAVES DIFFERENTLY FROM ANYTHING WE EVER STUDIED. INSTEAD OF YOUR CHRONOMETAL RADIATION AFFECTING THE TERRIGEN--THE TERRIGEN AFFECTED THE CHRONOMETAL RADIATION. NO WAY TO FORESEE THAT.
BUT WITH PROPER TESTING--
--WHICH TAKES MORE TIME THAN YOU GAVE YOURSELF--
HEH-HEMM.
BROKEN ARM HERE?
GO. GET HANK SOME TREATMENT. I'LL GET A RIDE.
IF YOU'RE--
HE'S SURE.

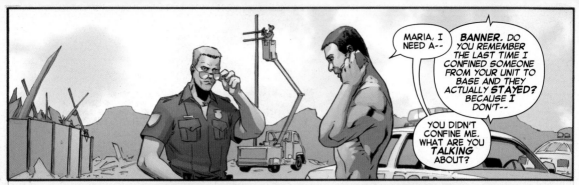

MARIA, I NEED A--

BANNER. DO YOU REMEMBER THE LAST TIME I CONFINED SOMEONE FROM YOUR UNIT TO BASE AND THEY ACTUALLY *STAYED?* BECAUSE I DON'T--

YOU DIDN'T CONFINE ME. WHAT ARE YOU *TALKING* ABOUT?

YOUR *STAFF.* YOU'VE TAUGHT THEM A *LOT,* MOST OF IT *WRONG*--BUT ON ONE KEY POINT THEY REMAIN TOUCHINGLY *IGNORANT.*

YOU'RE TOO BIG TO FIRE. THEY'RE *NOT.*

THEY...LEFT? OH, YEAH. THEY WERE JUST FOLLOWING MY ORDERS--

YOU *REALIZE* YOUR VOICE GOES UP A QUARTER-OCTAVE WHEN YOU *LIE,* RIGHT?

MARIA, I NEED A RIDE. *THAT'S* TRUE.

I'LL SEND THE LITTLE RASCALS YOUR WAY. YOU CAN ALL RIDE BACK TOGETHER AND GET YOUR *EXCUSES* STRAIGHT BEFORE THE *PINK SLIPS* START FLYING.

AND BRUCE?

QUIT FORCING ME INTO THE *SPOILSPORT* ROLE *EVERY TIME.* THAT'S NOT *ME,* AND I'M REALLY STARTING TO RESENT IT.

WELL THE *GOOD* NEWS IS, WE'VE THROWN OUR CAREERS AWAY FOR *NOTHING.*

S.H.I.E.L.D. SAYS DOC BANNER MADE IT *THROUGH.*

WOO-*HOO!*

AND HIS *HULKNAPPED* BOMB?

NO LIVES LOST.

YESYES *YES!*

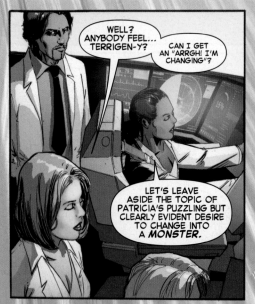

WELL? ANYBODY FEEL... *TERRIGEN*-Y?

CAN I GET AN *"ARRGH! I'M CHANGING"*?

LET'S LEAVE ASIDE THE TOPIC OF PATRICIA'S PUZZLING BUT CLEARLY EVIDENT DESIRE TO CHANGE INTO A *MONSTER.*

Puzzling ONLY if you don't know her SECRET: Patricia Wolman is DYING of an incurable disease.

OUR *ORDERS* ARE TO PICK THE DOCTOR UP IN *TULSA*, HURRY BACK TO BASE, AND PRESENT OUR THROATS TO DIRECTOR HILL'S BLADE.

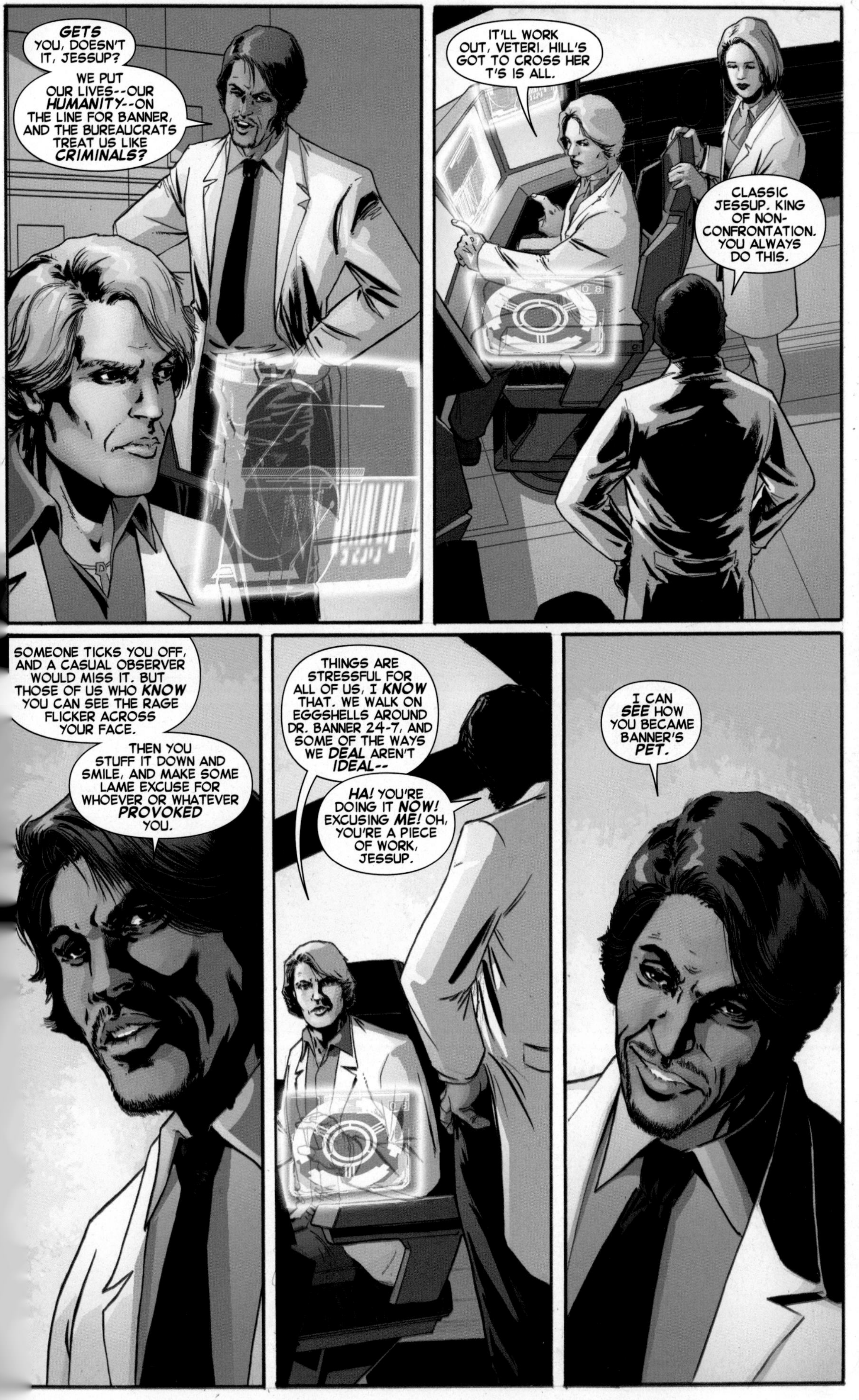
GETS YOU, DOESN'T IT, JESSUP?
WE PUT OUR LIVES--OUR HUMANITY--ON THE LINE FOR BANNER, AND THE BUREAUCRATS TREAT US LIKE CRIMINALS?
IT'LL WORK OUT, VETERI. HILL'S GOT TO CROSS HER T'S IS ALL.
CLASSIC JESSUP. KING OF NON-CONFRONTATION. YOU ALWAYS DO THIS.
SOMEONE TICKS YOU OFF, AND A CASUAL OBSERVER WOULD MISS IT. BUT THOSE OF US WHO KNOW YOU CAN SEE THE RAGE FLICKER ACROSS YOUR FACE.
THEN YOU STUFF IT DOWN AND SMILE, AND MAKE SOME LAME EXCUSE FOR WHOEVER OR WHATEVER PROVOKED YOU.
THINGS ARE STRESSFUL FOR ALL OF US, I KNOW THAT. WE WALK ON EGGSHELLS AROUND DR. BANNER 24-7, AND SOME OF THE WAYS WE DEAL AREN'T IDEAL--
HA! YOU'RE DOING IT NOW! EXCUSING ME! OH, YOU'RE A PIECE OF WORK, JESSUP.
I CAN SEE HOW YOU BECAME BANNER'S PET.

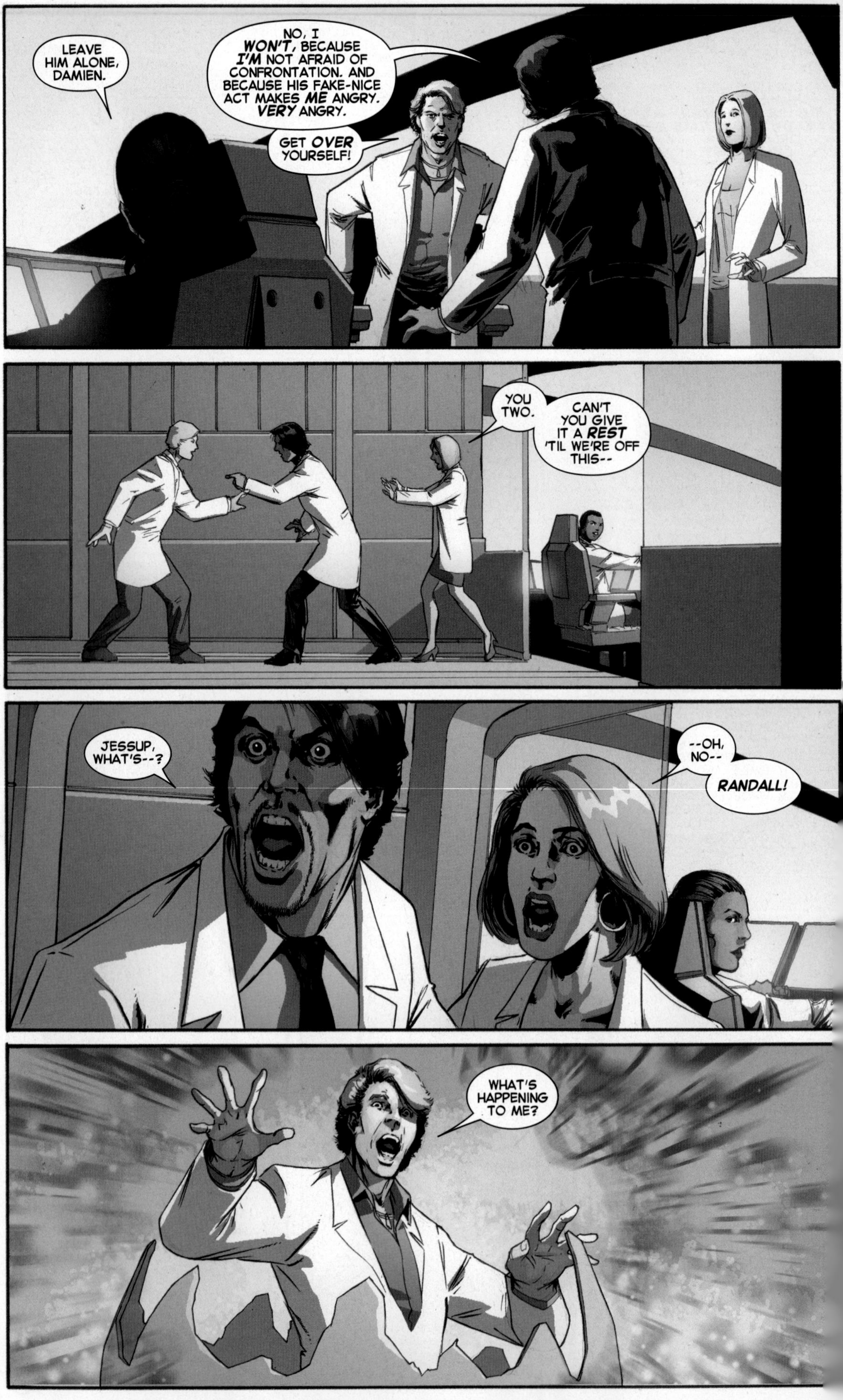
LEAVE HIM ALONE, DAMIEN.
NO, I WON'T, BECAUSE I'M NOT AFRAID OF CONFRONTATION. AND BECAUSE HIS FAKE-NICE ACT MAKES ME ANGRY. VERY ANGRY.
GET OVER YOURSELF!
YOU TWO.
CAN'T YOU GIVE IT A REST 'TIL WE'RE OFF THIS--
JESSUP, WHAT'S--?
--OH, NO--
RANDALL!
WHAT'S HAPPENING TO ME?

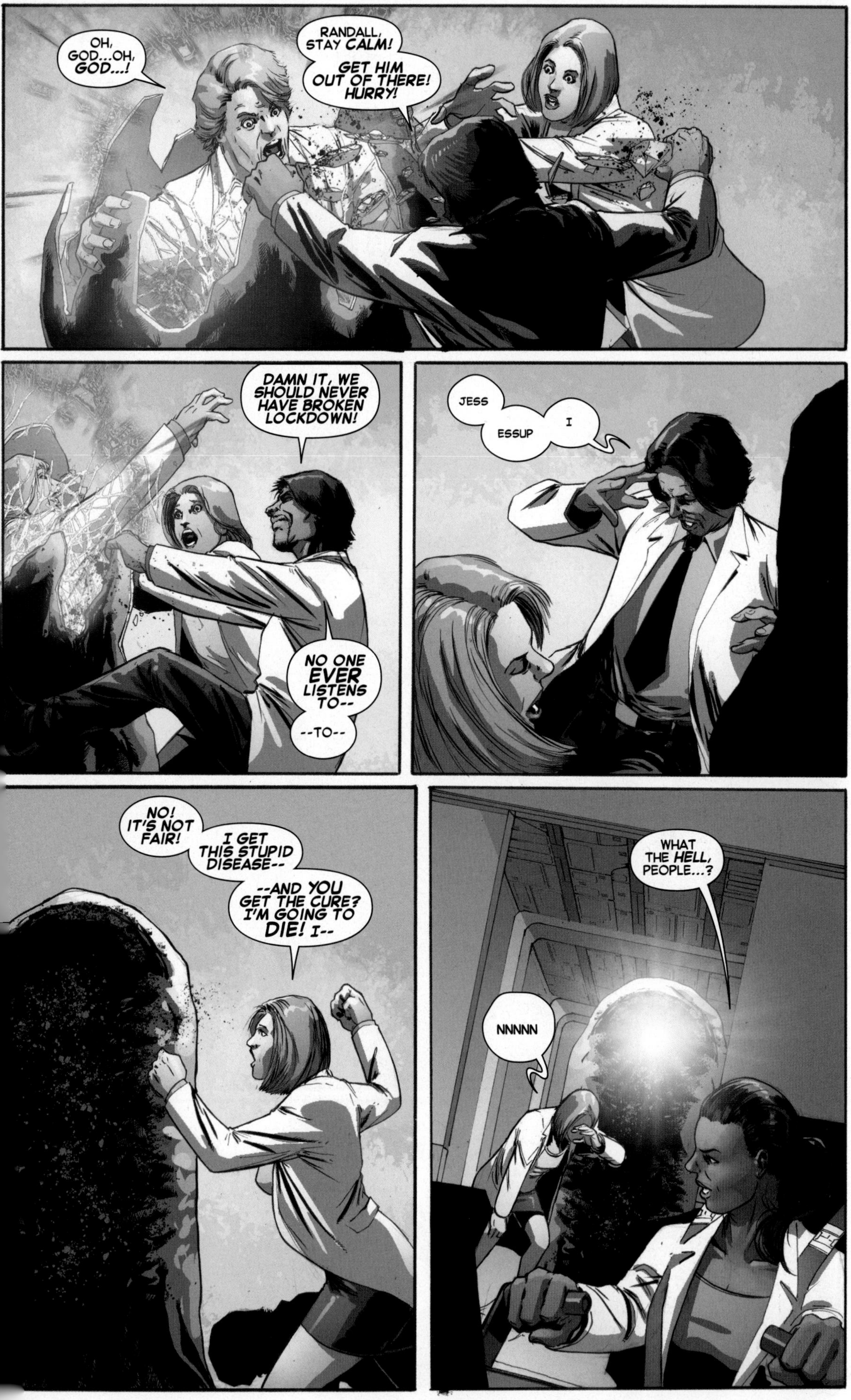
OH, GOD...OH, GOD...!
RANDALL, STAY CALM!
GET HIM OUT OF THERE! HURRY!
DAMN IT, WE SHOULD NEVER HAVE BROKEN LOCKDOWN!
NO ONE EVER LISTENS TO--
--TO--
JESS
ESSUP
I
NO! IT'S NOT FAIR!
I GET THIS STUPID DISEASE--
--AND YOU GET THE CURE? I'M GOING TO DIE! I--
WHAT THE HELL, PEOPLE...?
NNNNN

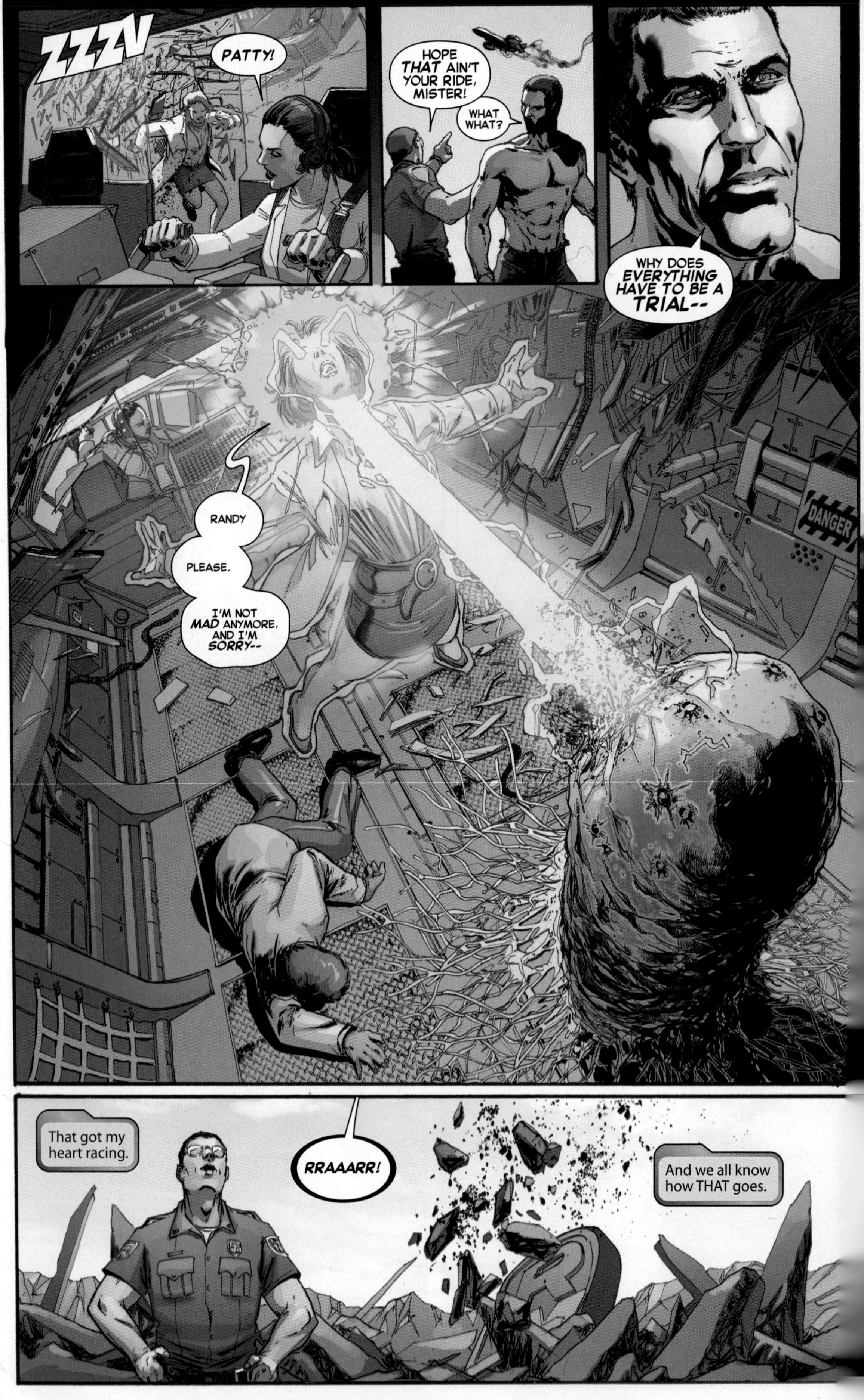
ZZZV
PATTY!
HOPE THAT AIN'T YOUR RIDE, MISTER!
WHAT WHAT?
WHY DOES EVERYTHING HAVE TO BE A TRIAL--
RANDY
PLEASE.
I'M NOT MAD ANYMORE, AND I'M SORRY--
DANGER
That got my heart racing.
RRAAARR!
And we all know how THAT goes.

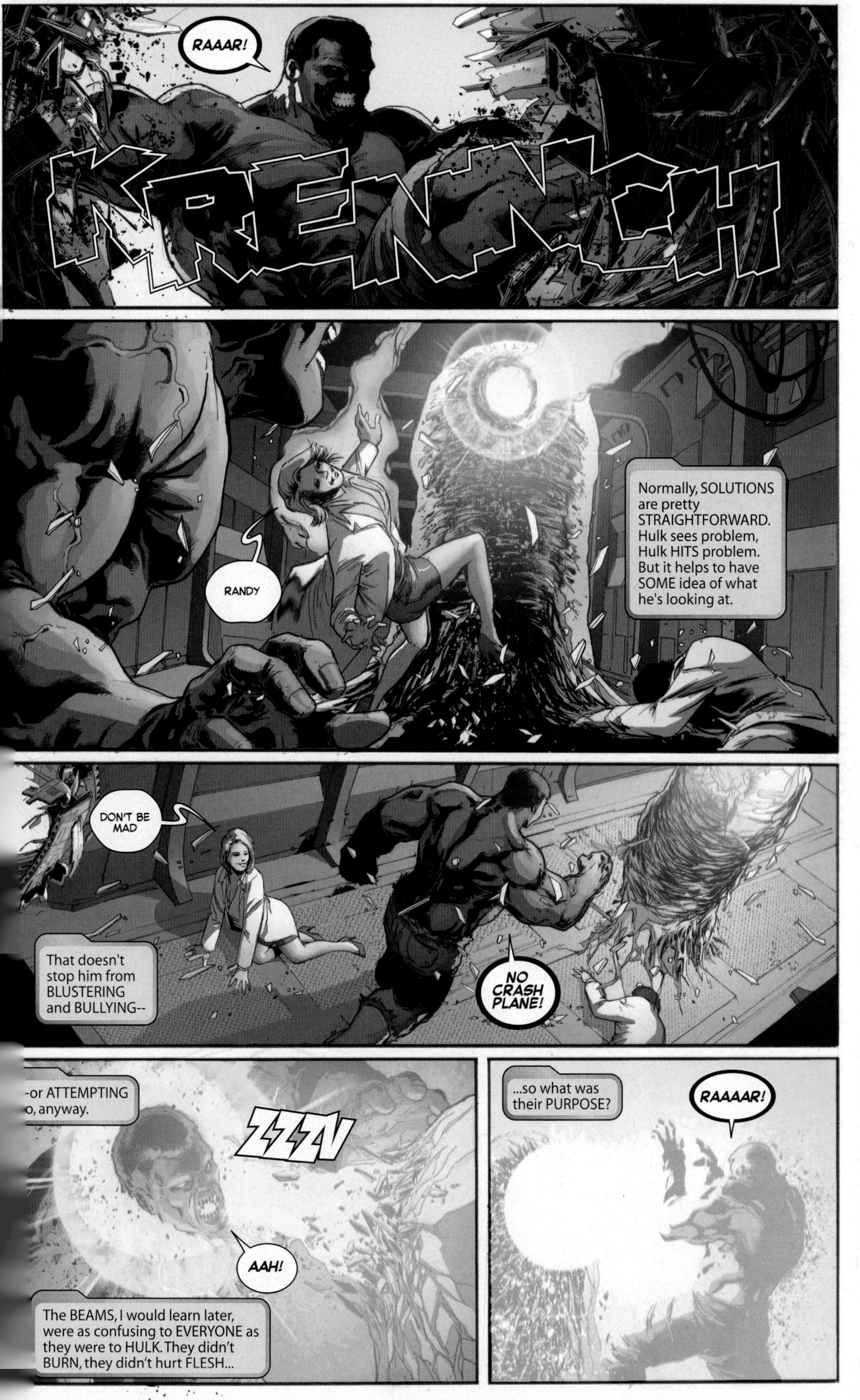
RAAAR!
KRENNCH
RANDY
Normally, SOLUTIONS are pretty STRAIGHTFORWARD. Hulk sees problem, Hulk HITS problem. But it helps to have SOME idea of what he's looking at.
DON'T BE MAD
That doesn't stop him from BLUSTERING and BULLYING--
NO CRASH PLANE!
-or ATTEMPTING o, anyway.
ZZZV
AAH!
The BEAMS, I would learn later, were as confusing to EVERYONE as they were to HULK. They didn't BURN, they didn't hurt FLESH...
...so what was their PURPOSE?
RAAAAR!

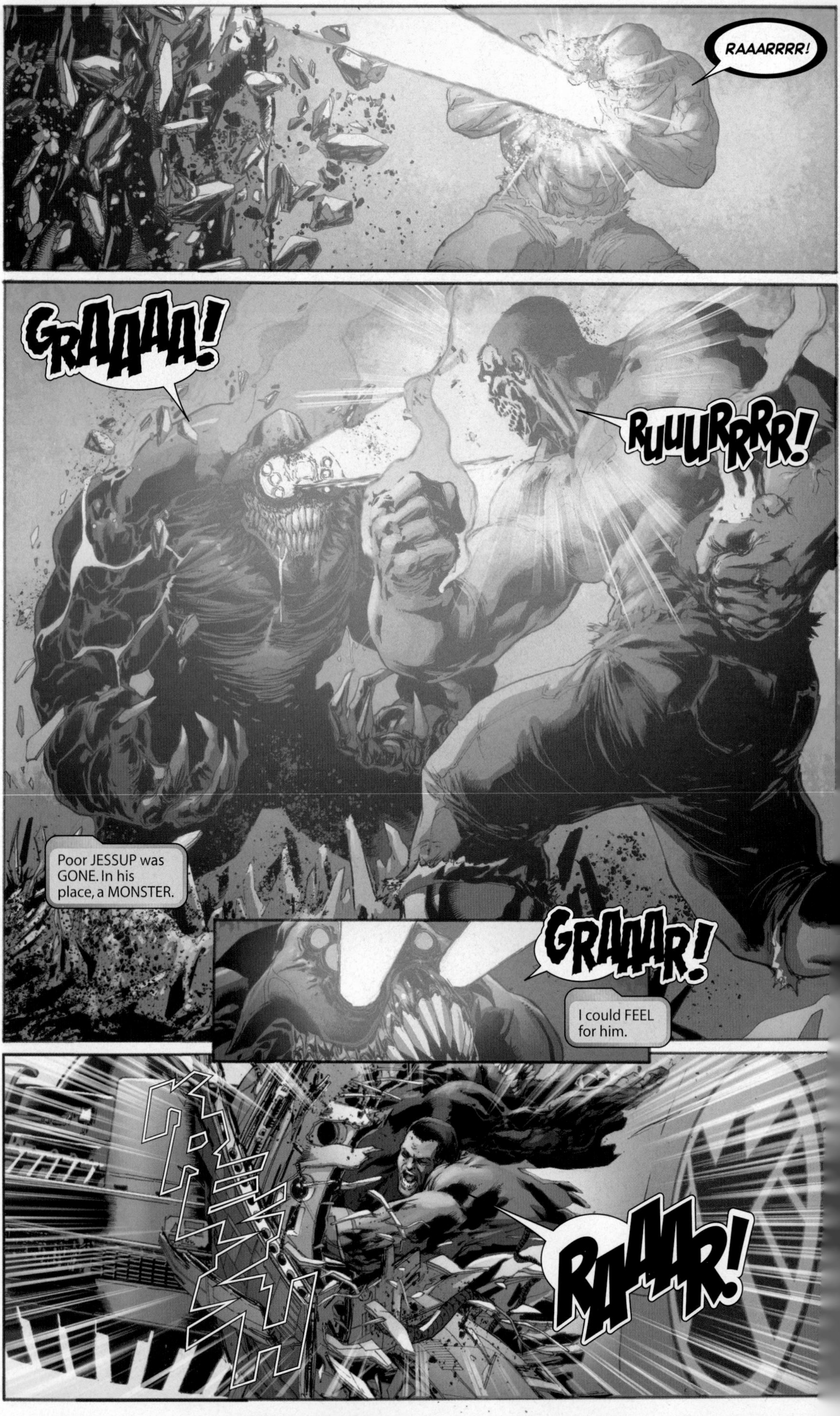
RAAARRRR!
GRAAAAA!
RUUURRRR!
Poor JESSUP was GONE. In his place, a MONSTER.
GRAAAR!
I could FEEL for him.
RAAAR!

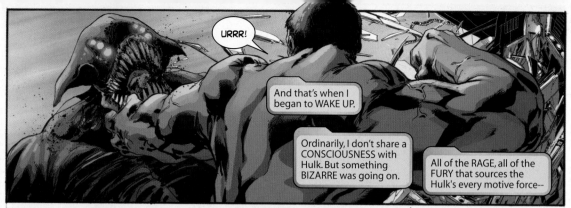

URRR!

And that's when I began to WAKE UP.

Ordinarily, I don't share a CONSCIOUSNESS with Hulk. But something BIZARRE was going on.

All of the RAGE, all of the FURY that sources the Hulk's every motive force--

--it was ebbing AWAY.

Like infection from a wound.

HUH?

AAA-HA! HA!

And for the first time, the HULK fully tastes a feeling BANNER only barely REMEMBERS.

HAHA!

HAHAHAHAHAHA!

HAHAHAHA!

The ABSENCE of ANGER.

Where did it GO?

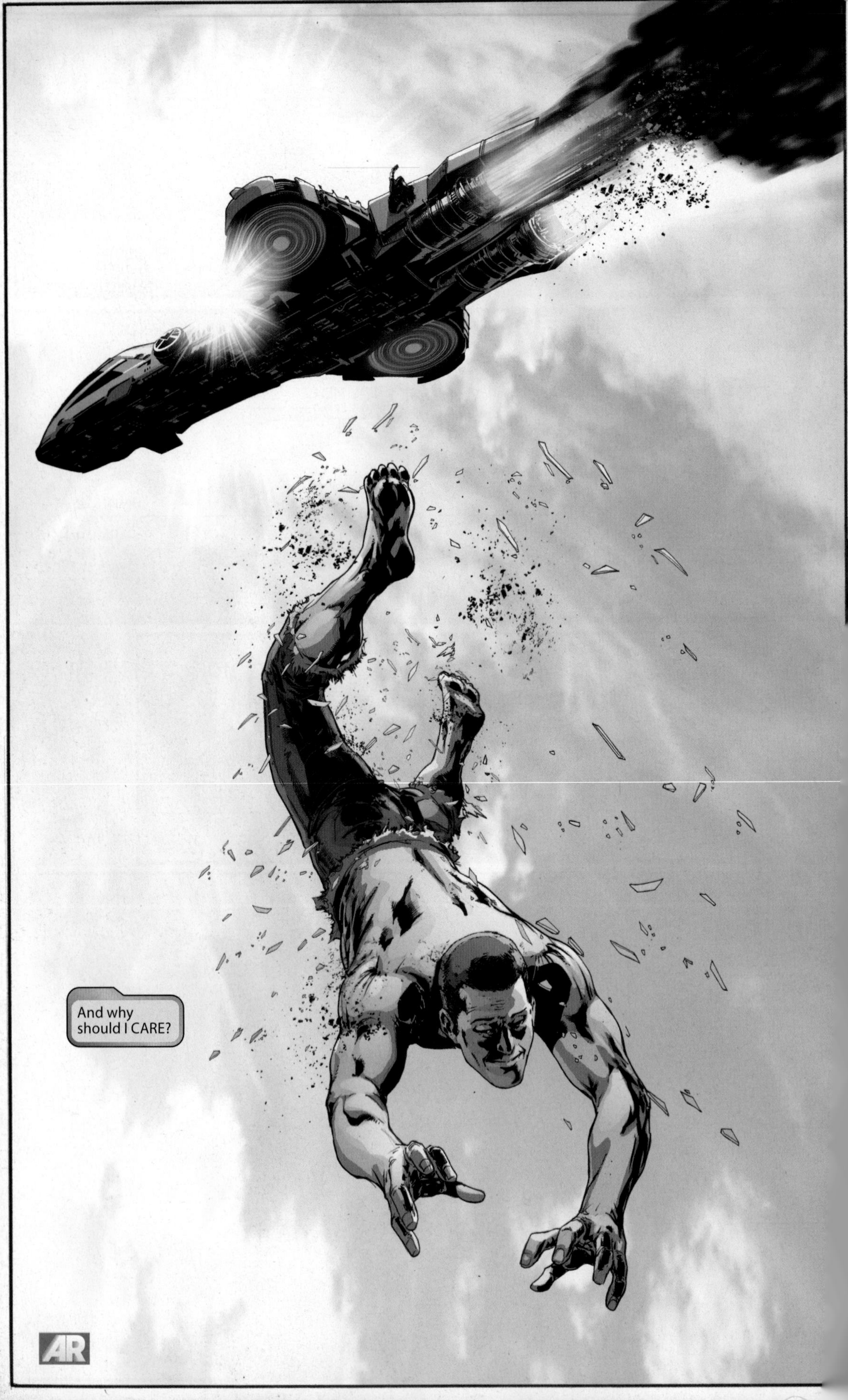
And why should I CARE?

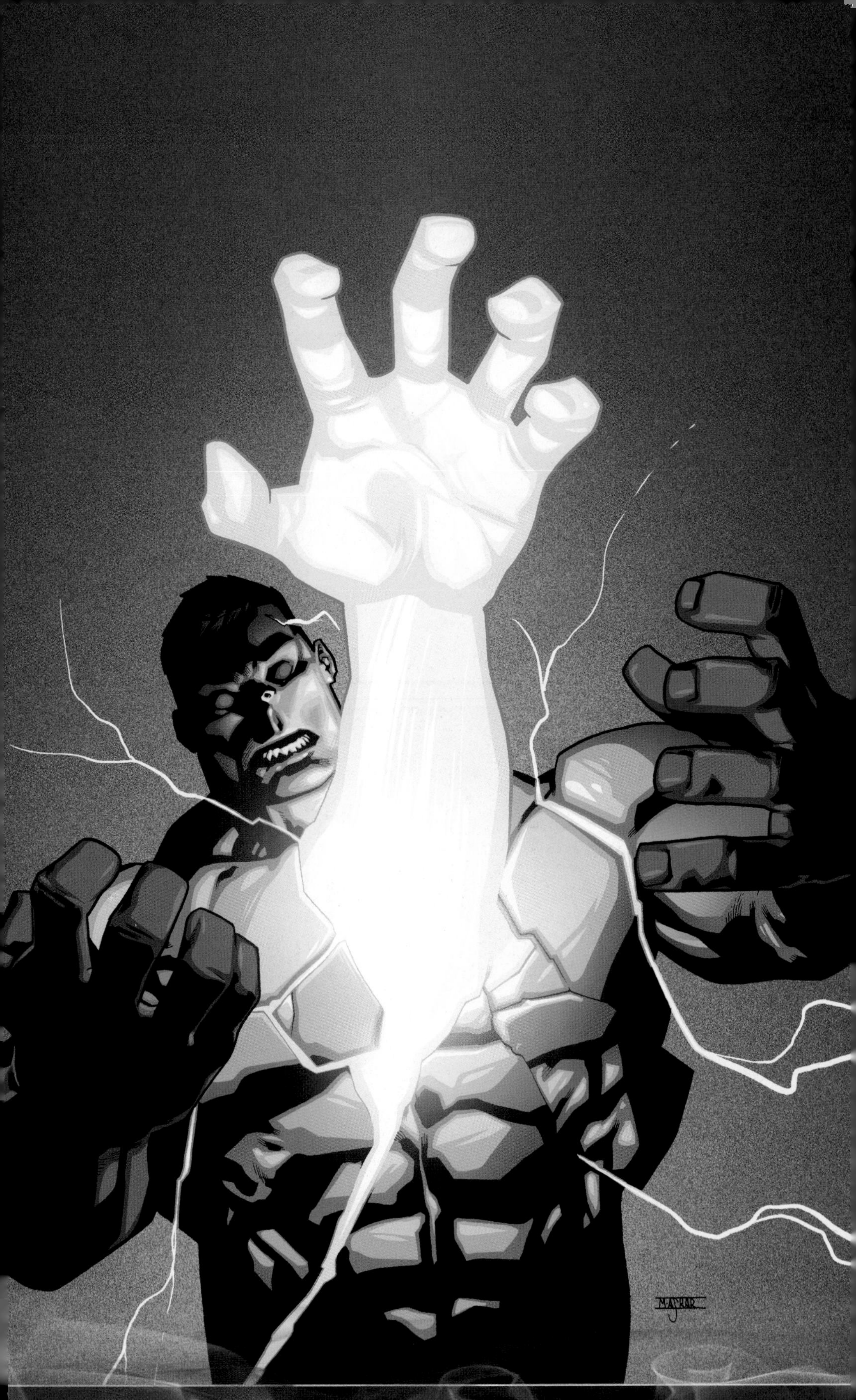
M.Yardin

INDESTRUCTIBLE HULK #19

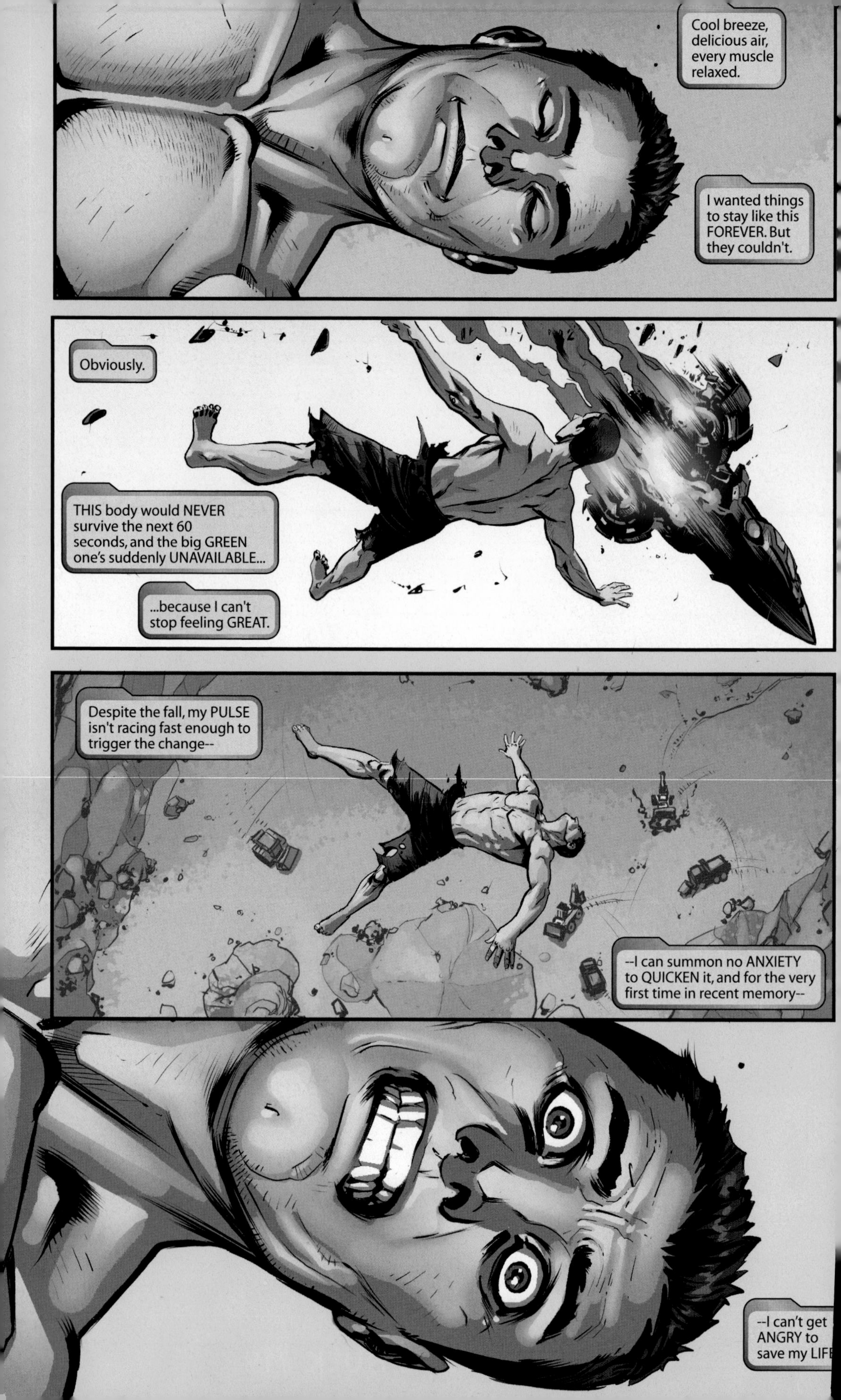

Cool breeze, delicious air, every muscle relaxed.
I wanted things to stay like this FOREVER. But they couldn't.
Obviously.
THIS body would NEVER survive the next 60 seconds, and the big GREEN one's suddenly UNAVAILABLE...
...because I can't stop feeling GREAT.
Despite the fall, my PULSE isn't racing fast enough to trigger the change--
--I can summon no ANXIETY to QUICKEN it, and for the very first time in recent memory--
--I can't get ANGRY to save my LIFE

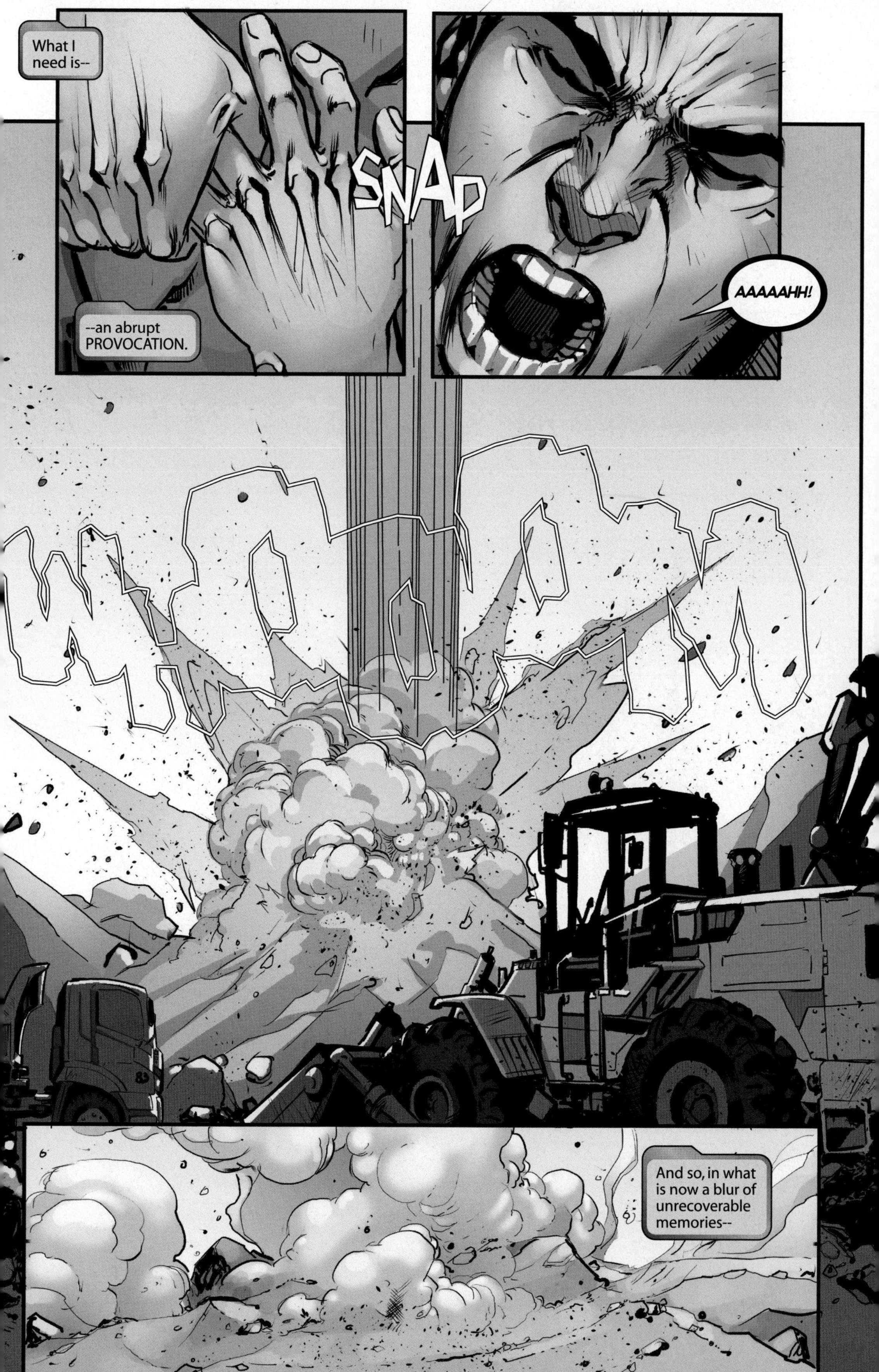
What I need is--
--an abrupt PROVOCATION.
SNAP
AAAAAHH!
And so, in what is now a blur of unrecoverable memories--

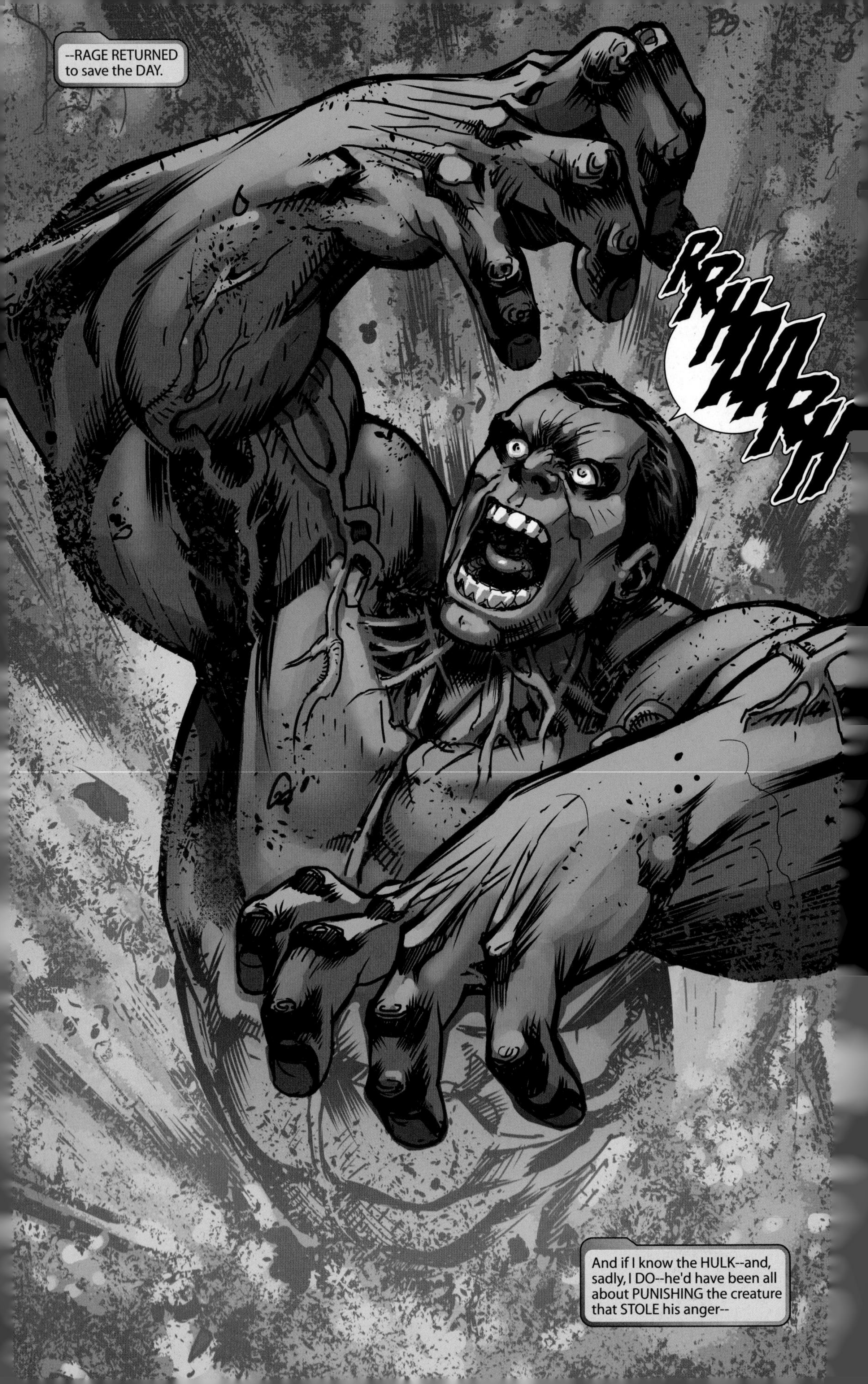
--RAGE RETURNED to save the DAY.
RRHHRRH
And if I know the HULK--and, sadly, I DO--he'd have been all about PUNISHING the creature that STOLE his anger--

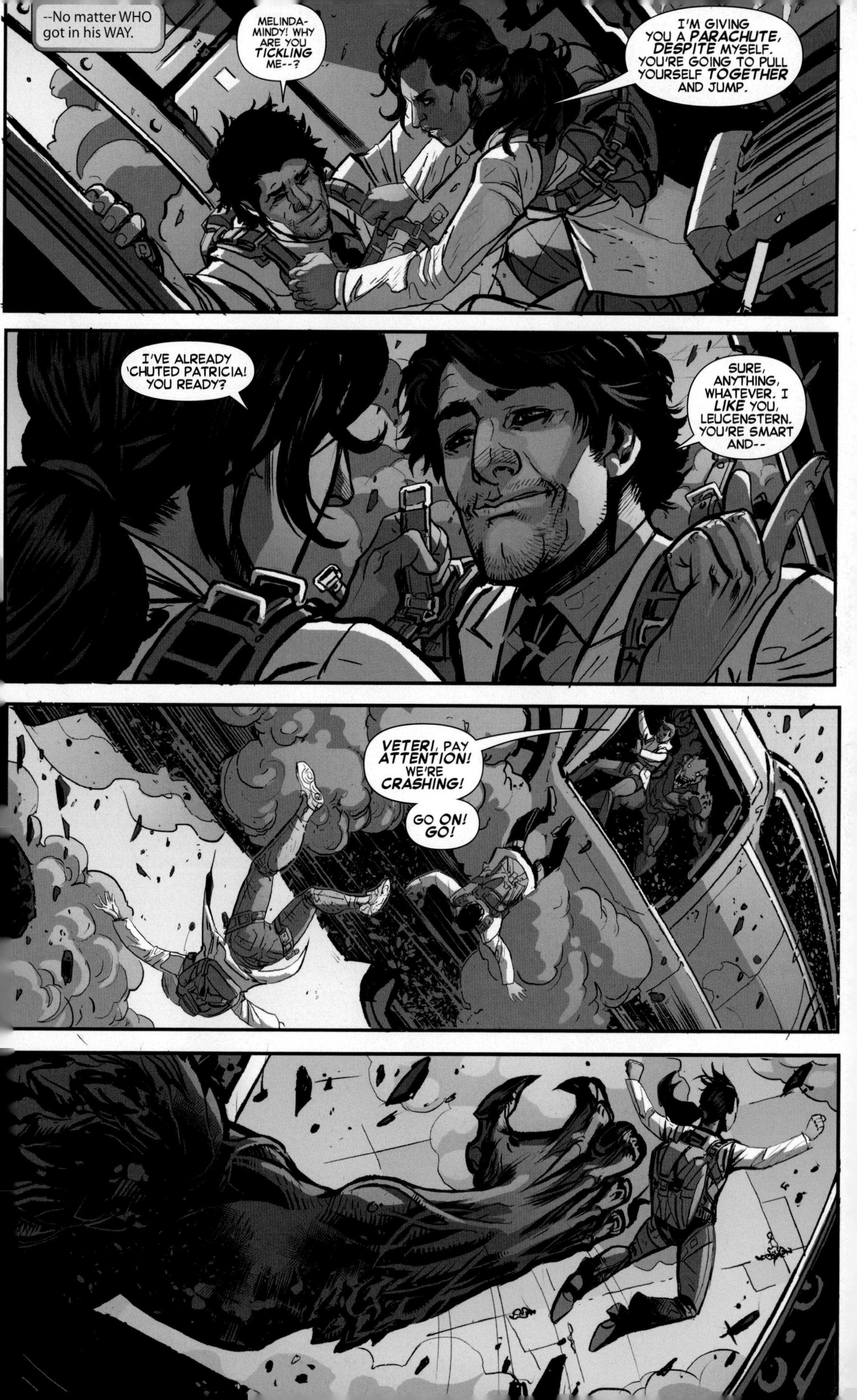
--No matter WHO got in his WAY.
MELINDA-MINDY! WHY ARE YOU TICKLING ME--?
I'M GIVING YOU A PARACHUTE, DESPITE MYSELF. YOU'RE GOING TO PULL YOURSELF TOGETHER AND JUMP.
I'VE ALREADY 'CHUTED PATRICIA! YOU READY?
SURE, ANYTHING, WHATEVER. I LIKE YOU, LEUCENSTERN. YOU'RE SMART AND--
VETERI, PAY ATTENTION! WE'RE CRASHING!
GO ON! GO!

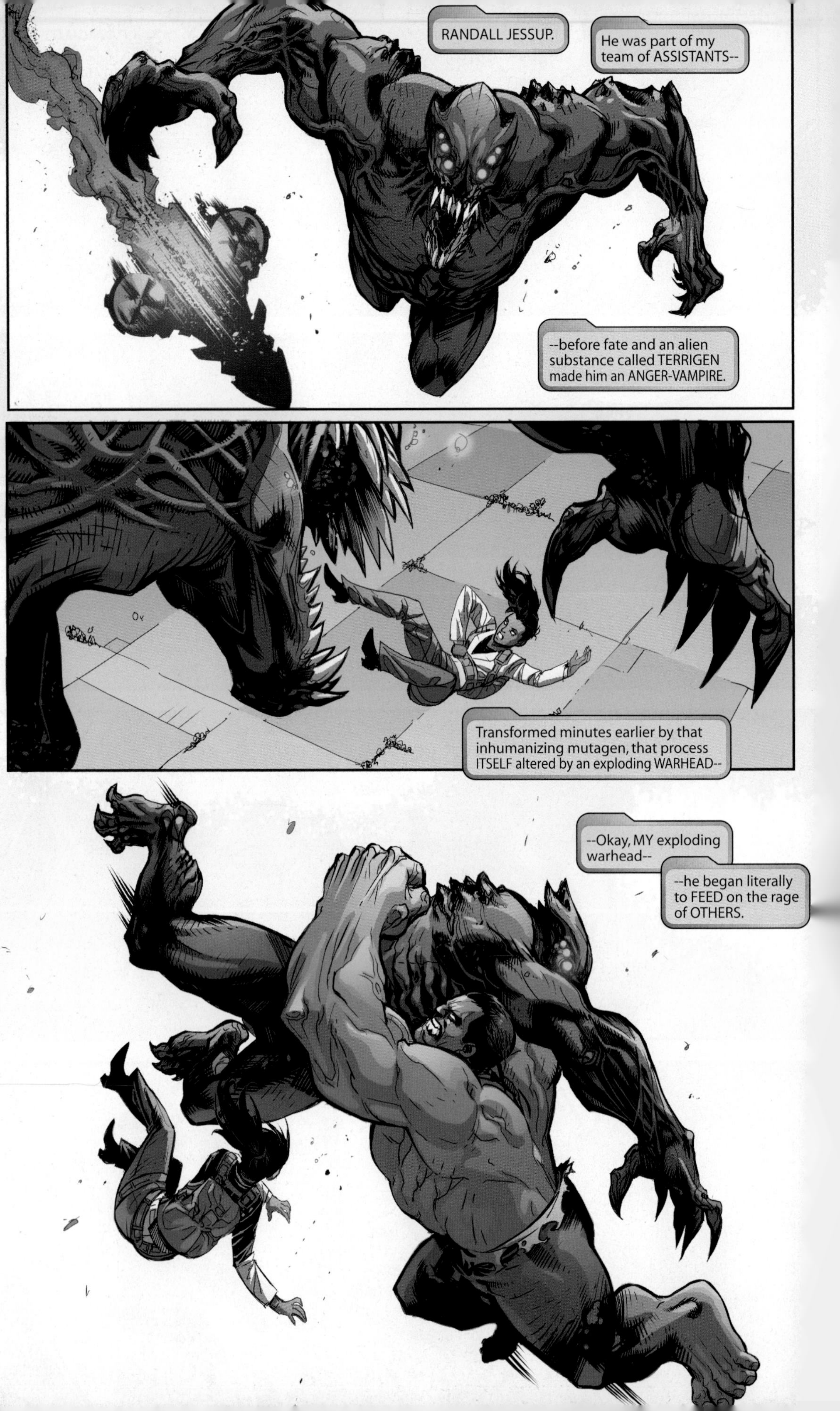
RANDALL JESSUP.
He was part of my team of ASSISTANTS--
--before fate and an alien substance called TERRIGEN made him an ANGER-VAMPIRE.
Transformed minutes earlier by that inhumanizing mutagen, that process ITSELF altered by an exploding WARHEAD--
--Okay, MY exploding warhead--
--he began literally to FEED on the rage of OTHERS.

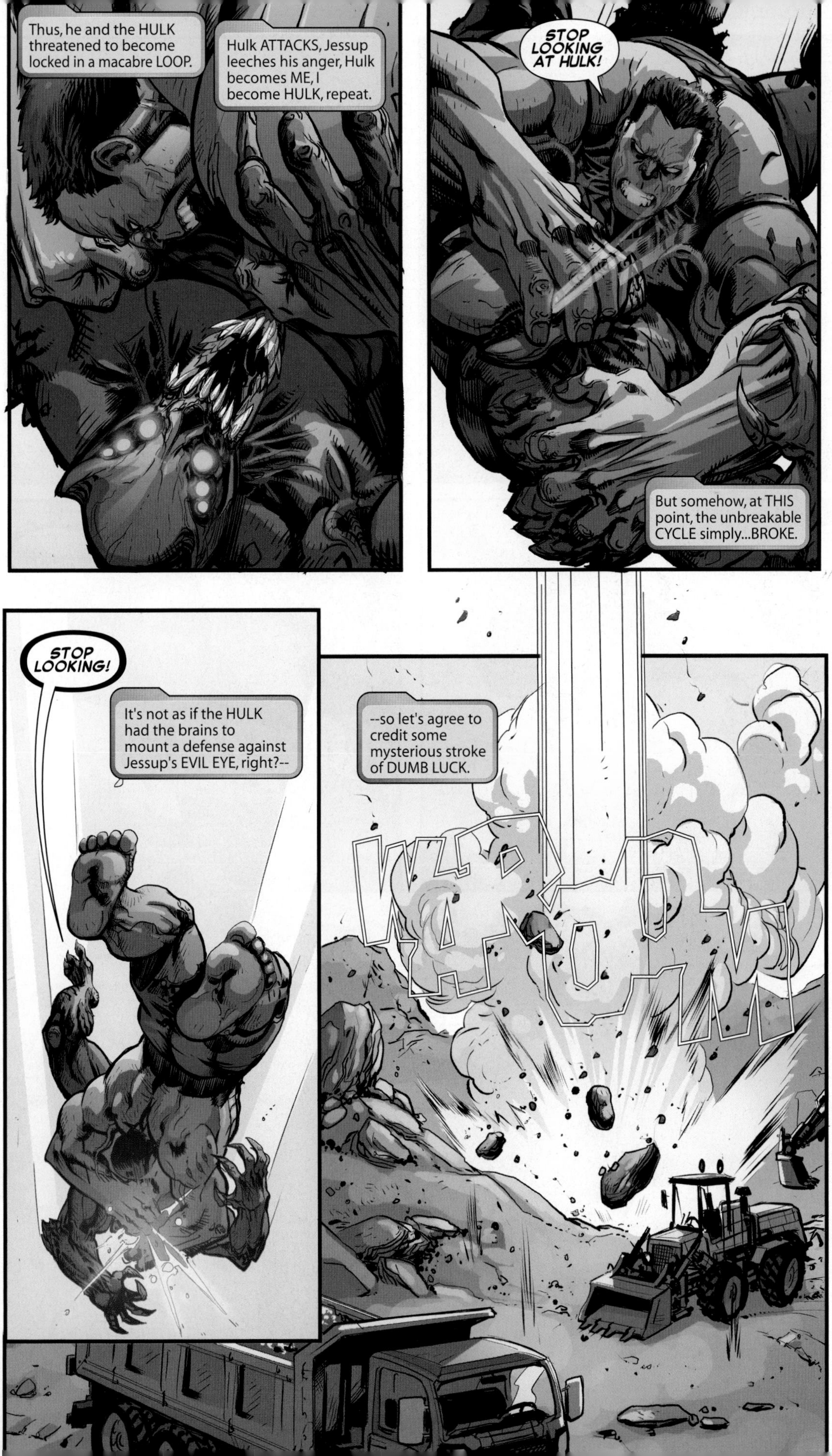
Thus, he and the HULK threatened to become locked in a macabre LOOP.
Hulk ATTACKS, Jessup leeches his anger, Hulk becomes ME, I become HULK, repeat.
STOP LOOKING AT HULK!
But somehow, at THIS point, the unbreakable CYCLE simply...BROKE.
STOP LOOKING!
It's not as if the HULK had the brains to mount a defense against Jessup's EVIL EYE, right?--
--so let's agree to credit some mysterious stroke of DUMB LUCK.
KA-DOOOM

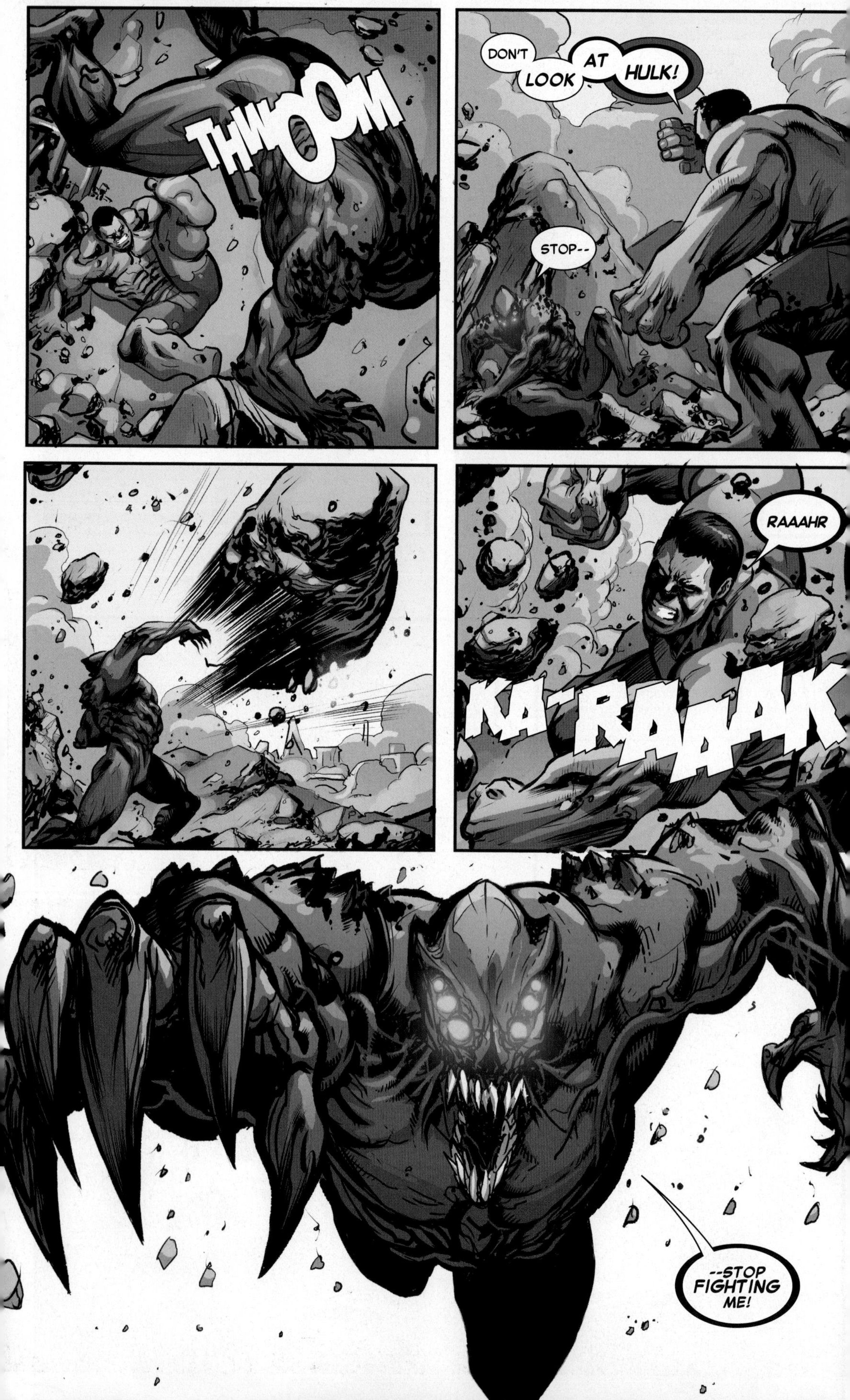
THWOOM
DON'T
LOOK
AT
HULK!
STOP--
RAAAHR
KA-RAAAK
--STOP FIGHTING ME!

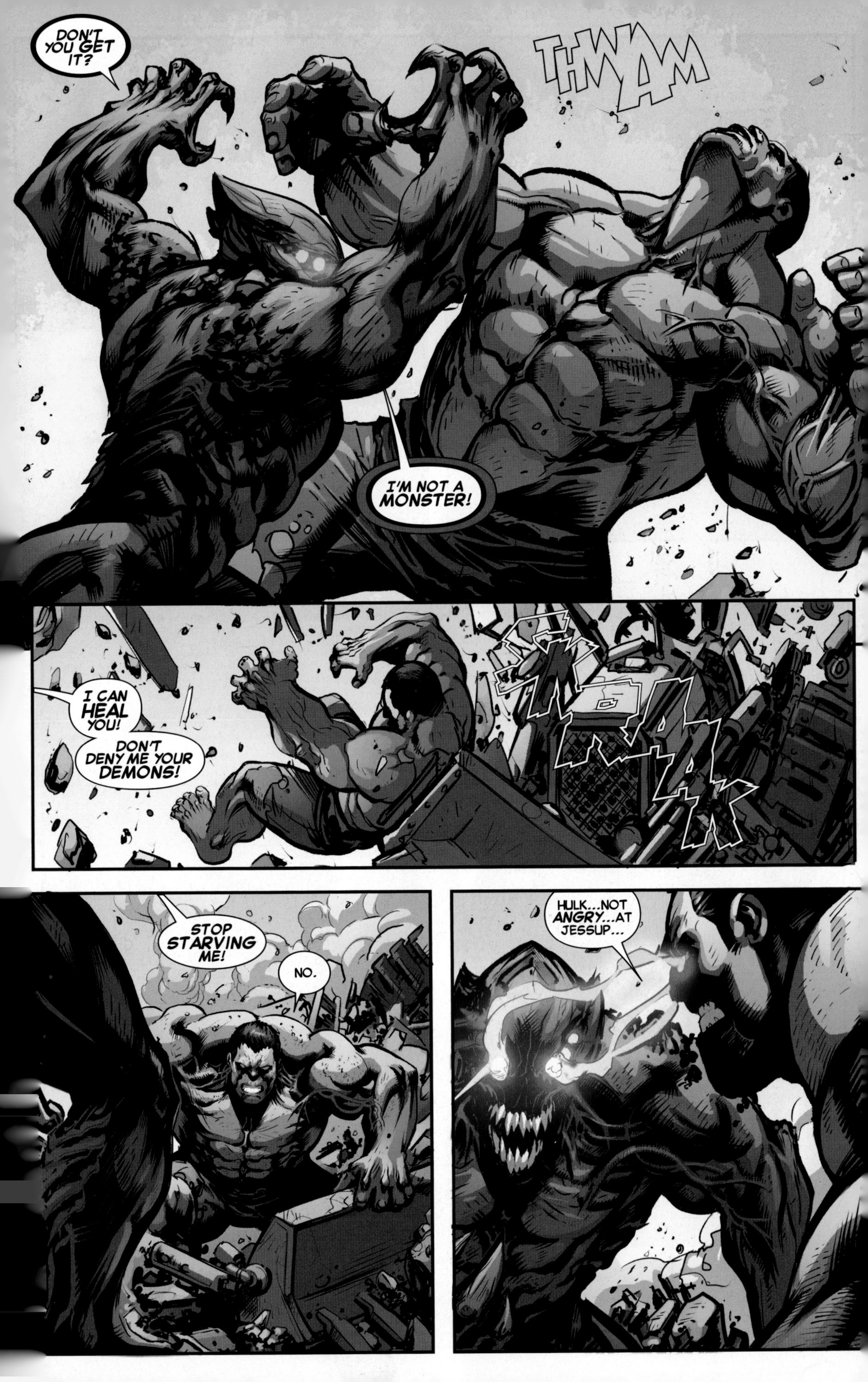
DON'T YOU GET IT?
THWAM
I'M NOT A MONSTER!
I CAN HEAL YOU!
DON'T DENY ME YOUR DEMONS!
STOP STARVING ME!
NO.
HULK...NOT ANGRY...AT JESSUP...

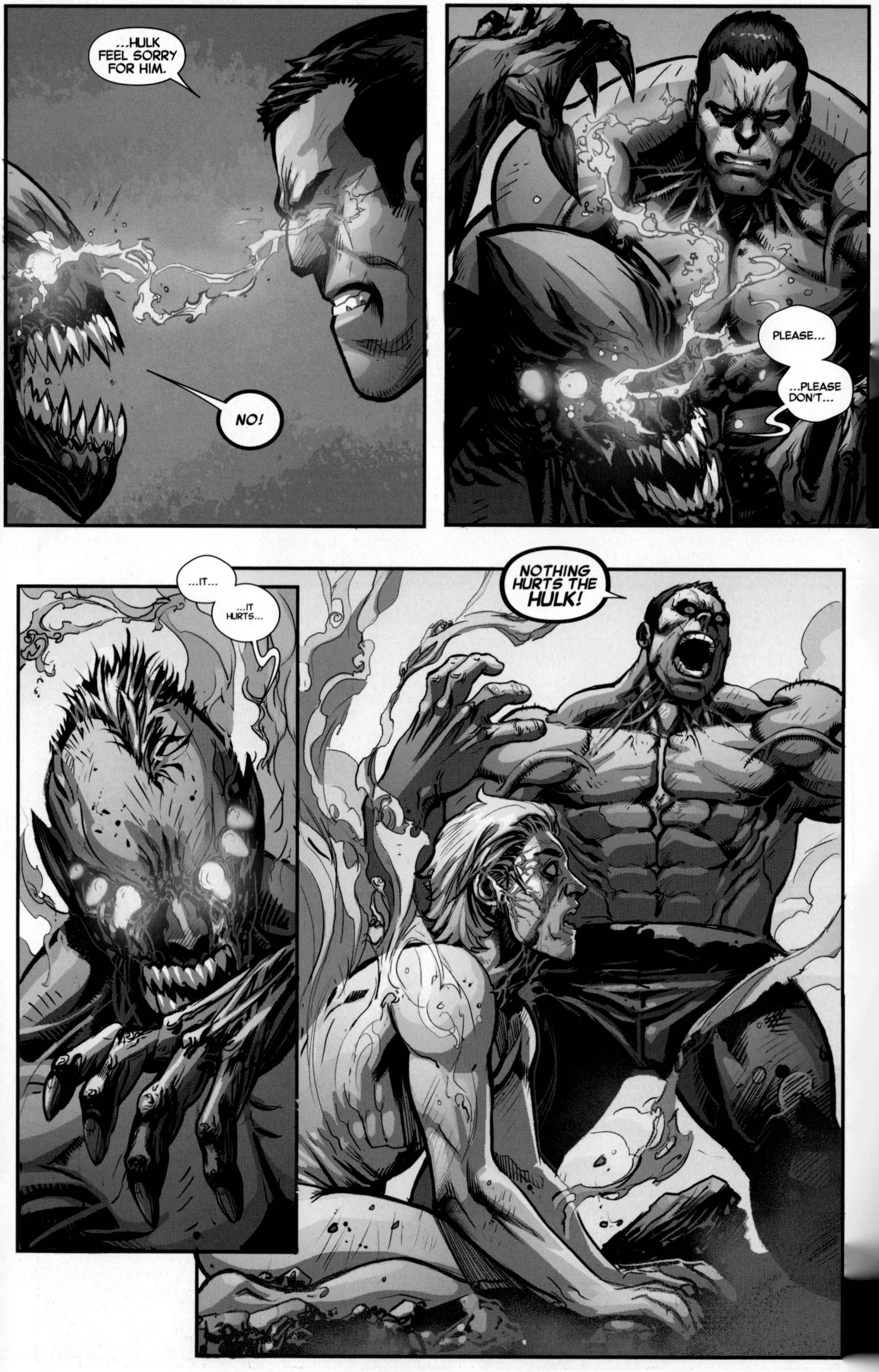
...HULK FEEL SORRY FOR HIM.
NO!
PLEASE...
...PLEASE DON'T...
...IT...
...IT HURTS...
NOTHING HURTS THE HULK!

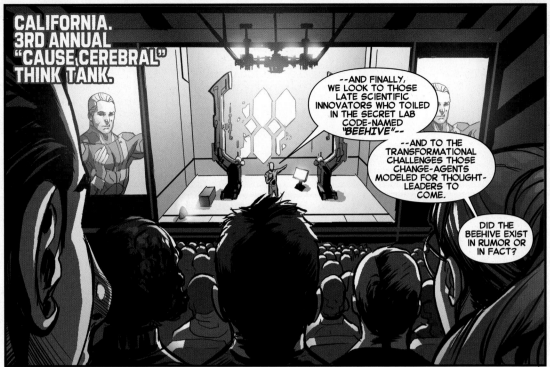

CALIFORNIA. 3RD ANNUAL "CAUSE CEREBRAL" THINK TANK.

--AND FINALLY, WE LOOK TO THOSE LATE SCIENTIFIC INNOVATORS WHO TOILED IN THE SECRET LAB CODE-NAMED *BEEHIVE*--

--AND TO THE TRANSFORMATIONAL CHALLENGES THOSE CHANGE-AGENTS MODELED FOR THOUGHT-LEADERS TO COME.

DID THE BEEHIVE EXIST IN RUMOR OR IN FACT?

DID AN ENCLAVE OF SCIENCE-ENTREPRENEURS SECRETLY DEVELOP A HUMAN UPGRADE?

DID THAT SENTIENT BREAKTHROUGH EMERGE FROM ITS COCOON AND DELETE ITS MAKERS IN A PASSION OF CREATIVE DESTRUCTION?

THE ANSWER IS, IT DOESN'T *MATTER.* FACTS *DIE,* BUT *IDEAS* BREATHE *FOREVER...*

...AND NEW *COCOONS* MATERIALIZE EVERY DAY.

BRAVO!

ENCORE!

CLAPCLAPCLAPCLAPCLAPCLAPCLAP

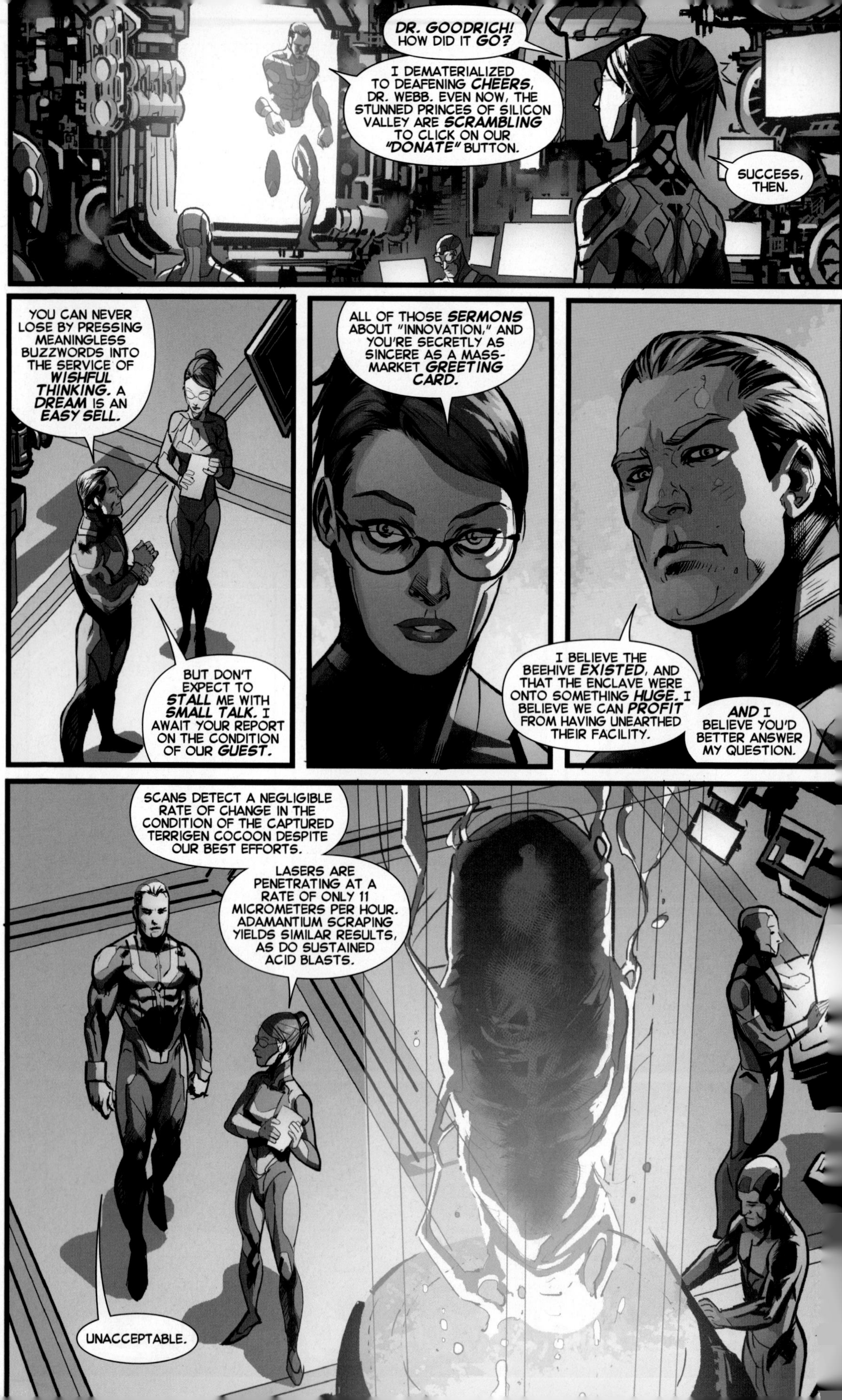
DR. GOODRICH! HOW DID IT GO?
I DEMATERIALIZED TO DEAFENING CHEERS, DR. WEBB. EVEN NOW, THE STUNNED PRINCES OF SILICON VALLEY ARE SCRAMBLING TO CLICK ON OUR "DONATE" BUTTON.
SUCCESS, THEN.
YOU CAN NEVER LOSE BY PRESSING MEANINGLESS BUZZWORDS INTO THE SERVICE OF WISHFUL THINKING. A DREAM IS AN EASY SELL.
BUT DON'T EXPECT TO STALL ME WITH SMALL TALK. I AWAIT YOUR REPORT ON THE CONDITION OF OUR GUEST.
ALL OF THOSE SERMONS ABOUT "INNOVATION," AND YOU'RE SECRETLY AS SINCERE AS A MASS-MARKET GREETING CARD.
I BELIEVE THE BEEHIVE EXISTED, AND THAT THE ENCLAVE WERE ONTO SOMETHING HUGE. I BELIEVE WE CAN PROFIT FROM HAVING UNEARTHED THEIR FACILITY.
AND I BELIEVE YOU'D BETTER ANSWER MY QUESTION.
SCANS DETECT A NEGLIGIBLE RATE OF CHANGE IN THE CONDITION OF THE CAPTURED TERRIGEN COCOON DESPITE OUR BEST EFFORTS.
LASERS ARE PENETRATING AT A RATE OF ONLY 11 MICROMETERS PER HOUR. ADAMANTIUM SCRAPING YIELDS SIMILAR RESULTS, AS DO SUSTAINED ACID BLASTS.
UNACCEPTABLE.

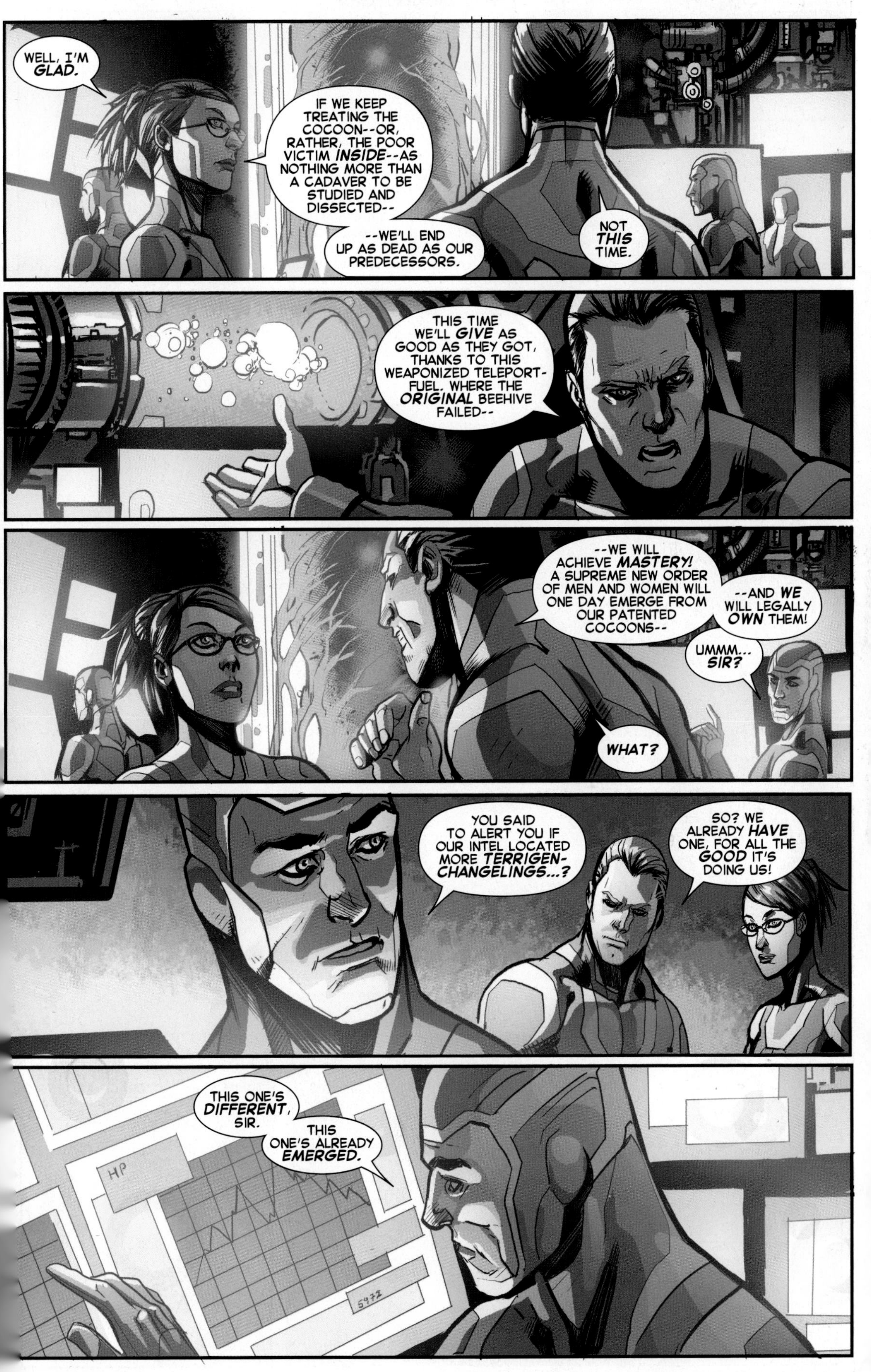
WELL, I'M GLAD.
IF WE KEEP TREATING THE COCOON--OR, RATHER, THE POOR VICTIM INSIDE--AS NOTHING MORE THAN A CADAVER TO BE STUDIED AND DISSECTED--
--WE'LL END UP AS DEAD AS OUR PREDECESSORS.
NOT THIS TIME.
THIS TIME WE'LL GIVE AS GOOD AS THEY GOT, THANKS TO THIS WEAPONIZED TELEPORT-FUEL. WHERE THE ORIGINAL BEEHIVE FAILED--
--WE WILL ACHIEVE MASTERY! A SUPREME NEW ORDER OF MEN AND WOMEN WILL ONE DAY EMERGE FROM OUR PATENTED COCOONS--
--AND WE WILL LEGALLY OWN THEM!
UMMM... SIR?
WHAT?
YOU SAID TO ALERT YOU IF OUR INTEL LOCATED MORE TERRIGEN-CHANGELINGS...?
SO? WE ALREADY HAVE ONE, FOR ALL THE GOOD IT'S DOING US!
THIS ONE'S DIFFERENT, SIR.
THIS ONE'S ALREADY EMERGED.
HP
5972

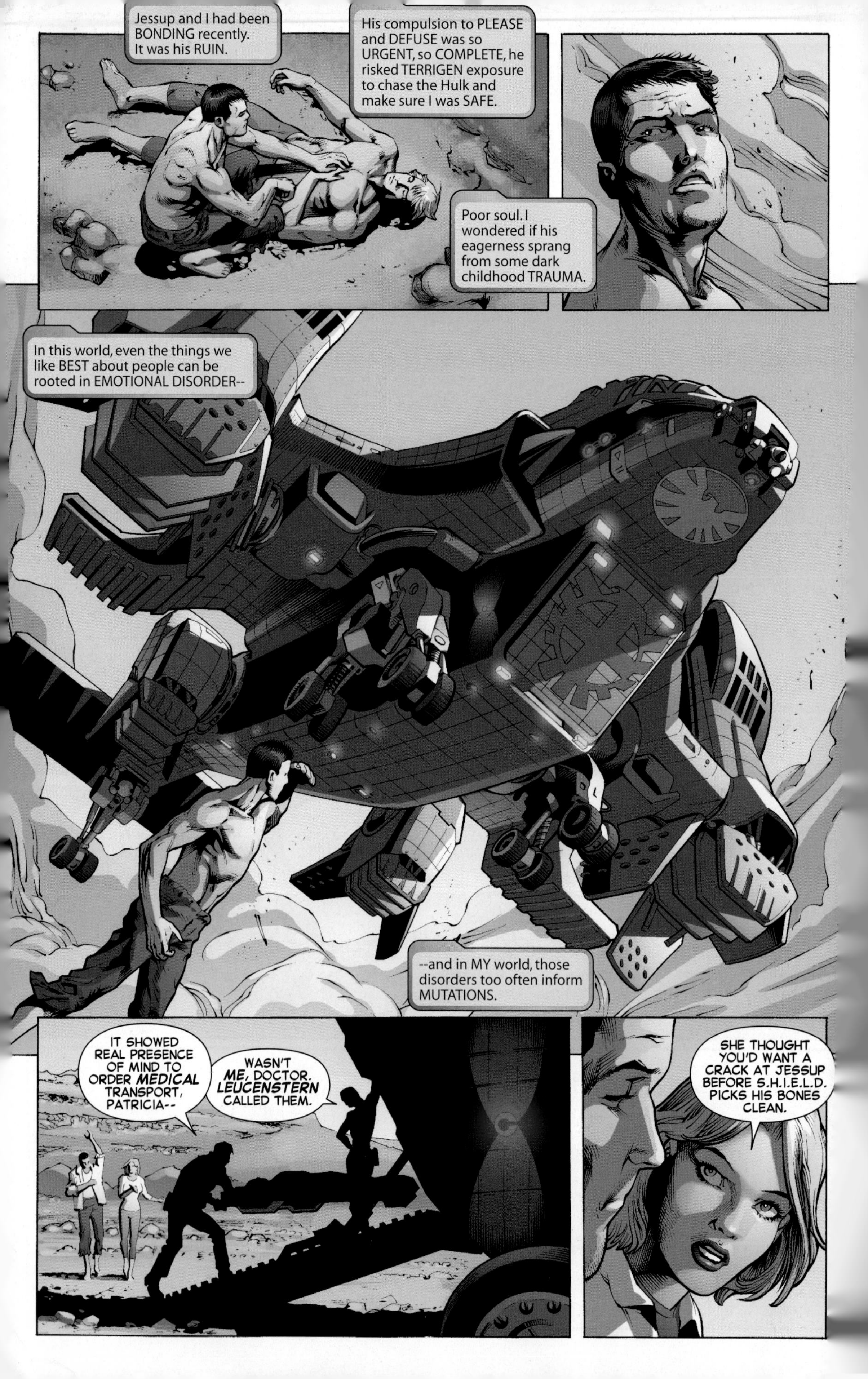
Jessup and I had been BONDING recently. It was his RUIN.
His compulsion to PLEASE and DEFUSE was so URGENT, so COMPLETE, he risked TERRIGEN exposure to chase the Hulk and make sure I was SAFE.
Poor soul. I wondered if his eagerness sprang from some dark childhood TRAUMA.
In this world, even the things we like BEST about people can be rooted in EMOTIONAL DISORDER--
--and in MY world, those disorders too often inform MUTATIONS.
IT SHOWED REAL PRESENCE OF MIND TO ORDER MEDICAL TRANSPORT, PATRICIA--
WASN'T ME, DOCTOR. LEUCENSTERN CALLED THEM.
SHE THOUGHT YOU'D WANT A CRACK AT JESSUP BEFORE S.H.I.E.L.D. PICKS HIS BONES CLEAN.

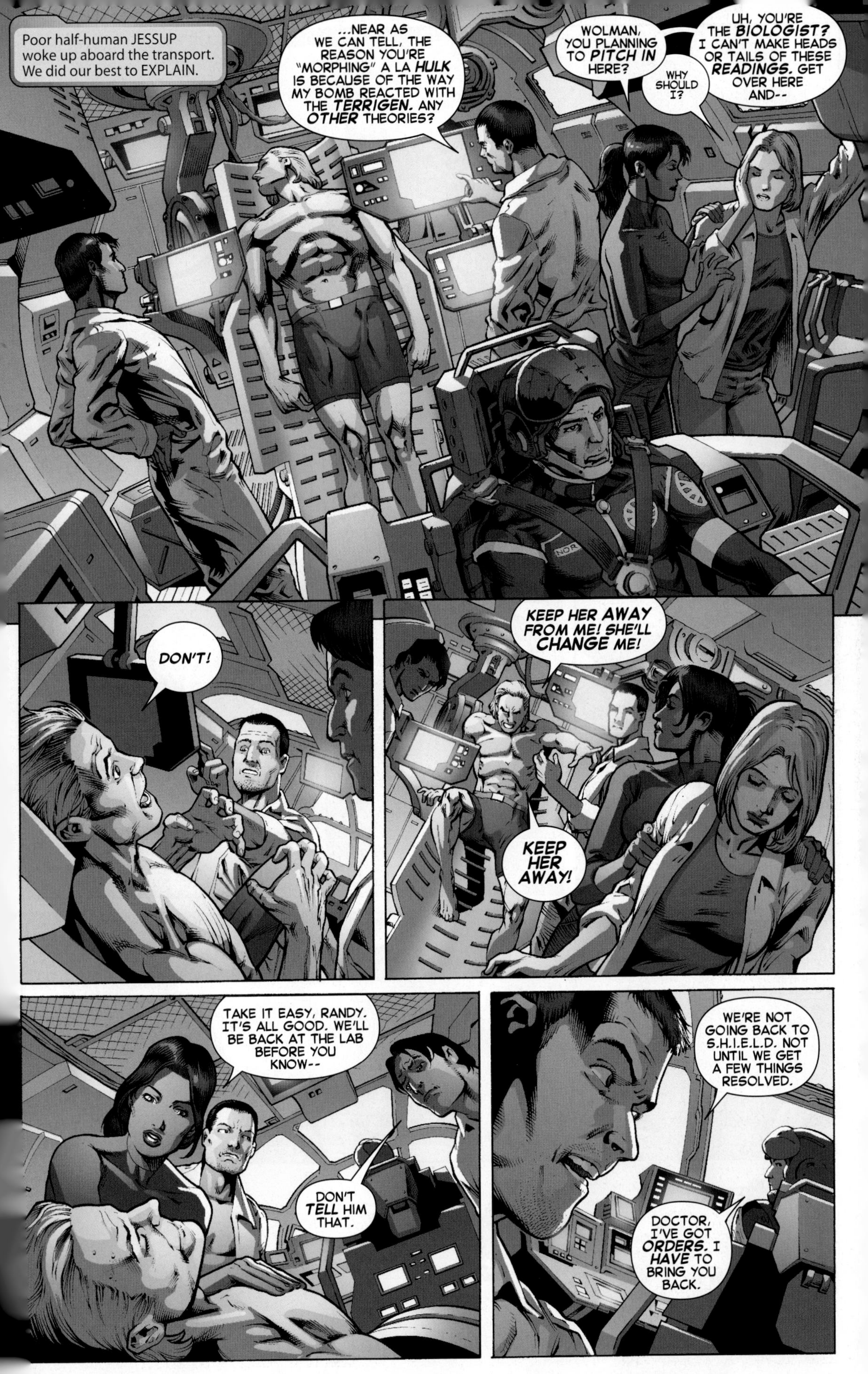
Poor half-human JESSUP woke up aboard the transport. We did our best to EXPLAIN.
...NEAR AS WE CAN TELL, THE REASON YOU'RE "MORPHING" A LA HULK IS BECAUSE OF THE WAY MY BOMB REACTED WITH THE TERRIGEN. ANY OTHER THEORIES?
WOLMAN, YOU PLANNING TO PITCH IN HERE?
WHY SHOULD I?
UH, YOU'RE THE BIOLOGIST? I CAN'T MAKE HEADS OR TAILS OF THESE READINGS. GET OVER HERE AND--
DON'T!
KEEP HER AWAY FROM ME! SHE'LL CHANGE ME!
KEEP HER AWAY!
TAKE IT EASY, RANDY. IT'S ALL GOOD. WE'LL BE BACK AT THE LAB BEFORE YOU KNOW--
DON'T TELL HIM THAT.
WE'RE NOT GOING BACK TO S.H.I.E.L.D. NOT UNTIL WE GET A FEW THINGS RESOLVED.
DOCTOR, I'VE GOT ORDERS. I HAVE TO BRING YOU BACK.

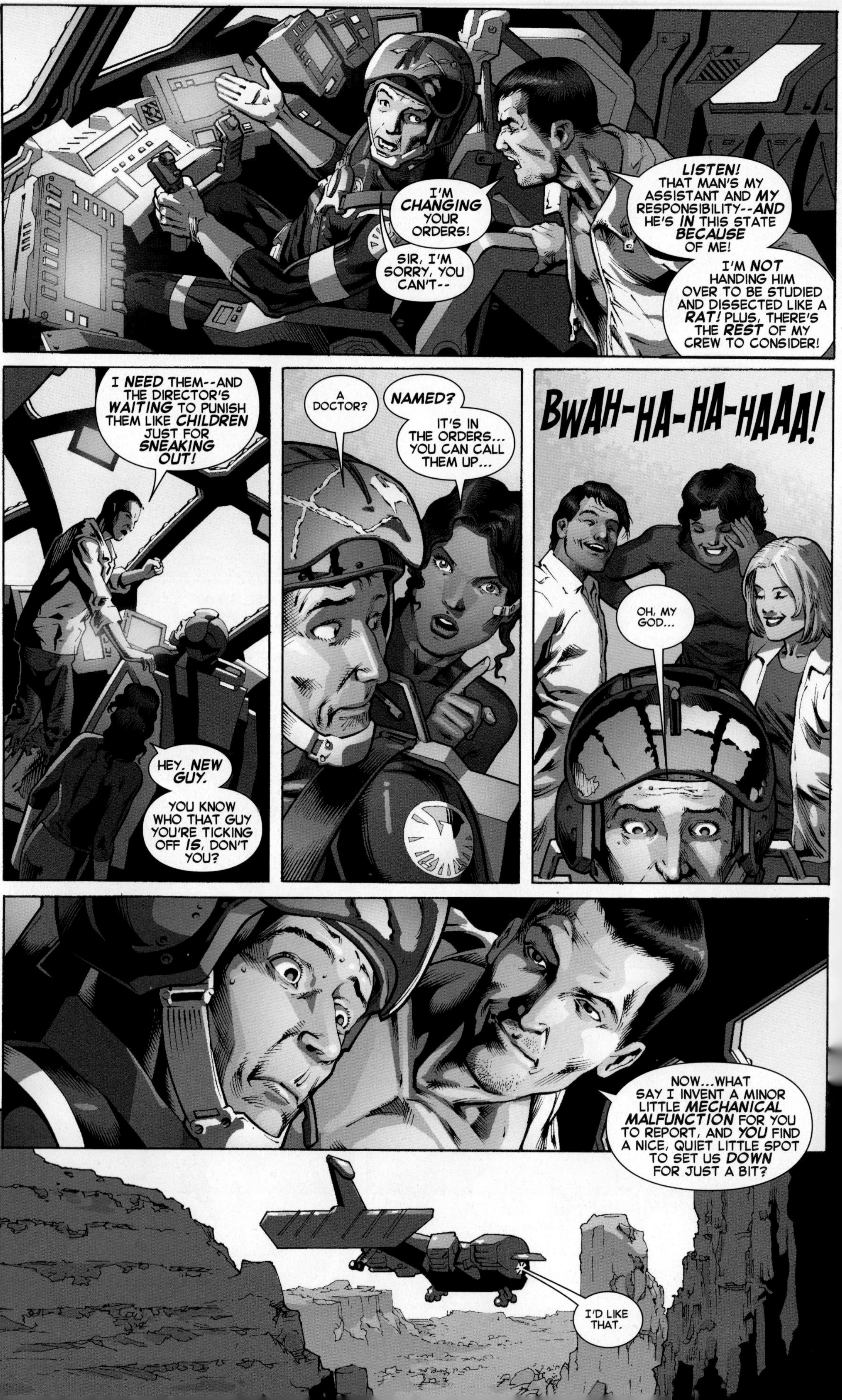
I'M CHANGING YOUR ORDERS!
SIR, I'M SORRY, YOU CAN'T--
LISTEN! THAT MAN'S MY ASSISTANT AND MY RESPONSIBILITY--AND HE'S IN THIS STATE BECAUSE OF ME!
I'M NOT HANDING HIM OVER TO BE STUDIED AND DISSECTED LIKE A RAT! PLUS, THERE'S THE REST OF MY CREW TO CONSIDER!
I NEED THEM--AND THE DIRECTOR'S WAITING TO PUNISH THEM LIKE CHILDREN JUST FOR SNEAKING OUT!
HEY. NEW GUY.
YOU KNOW WHO THAT GUY YOU'RE TICKING OFF IS, DON'T YOU?
A DOCTOR?
NAMED?
IT'S IN THE ORDERS... YOU CAN CALL THEM UP...
BWAH-HA-HA-HAAA!
OH, MY GOD...
NOW...WHAT SAY I INVENT A MINOR LITTLE MECHANICAL MALFUNCTION FOR YOU TO REPORT, AND YOU FIND A NICE, QUIET LITTLE SPOT TO SET US DOWN FOR JUST A BIT?
I'D LIKE THAT.

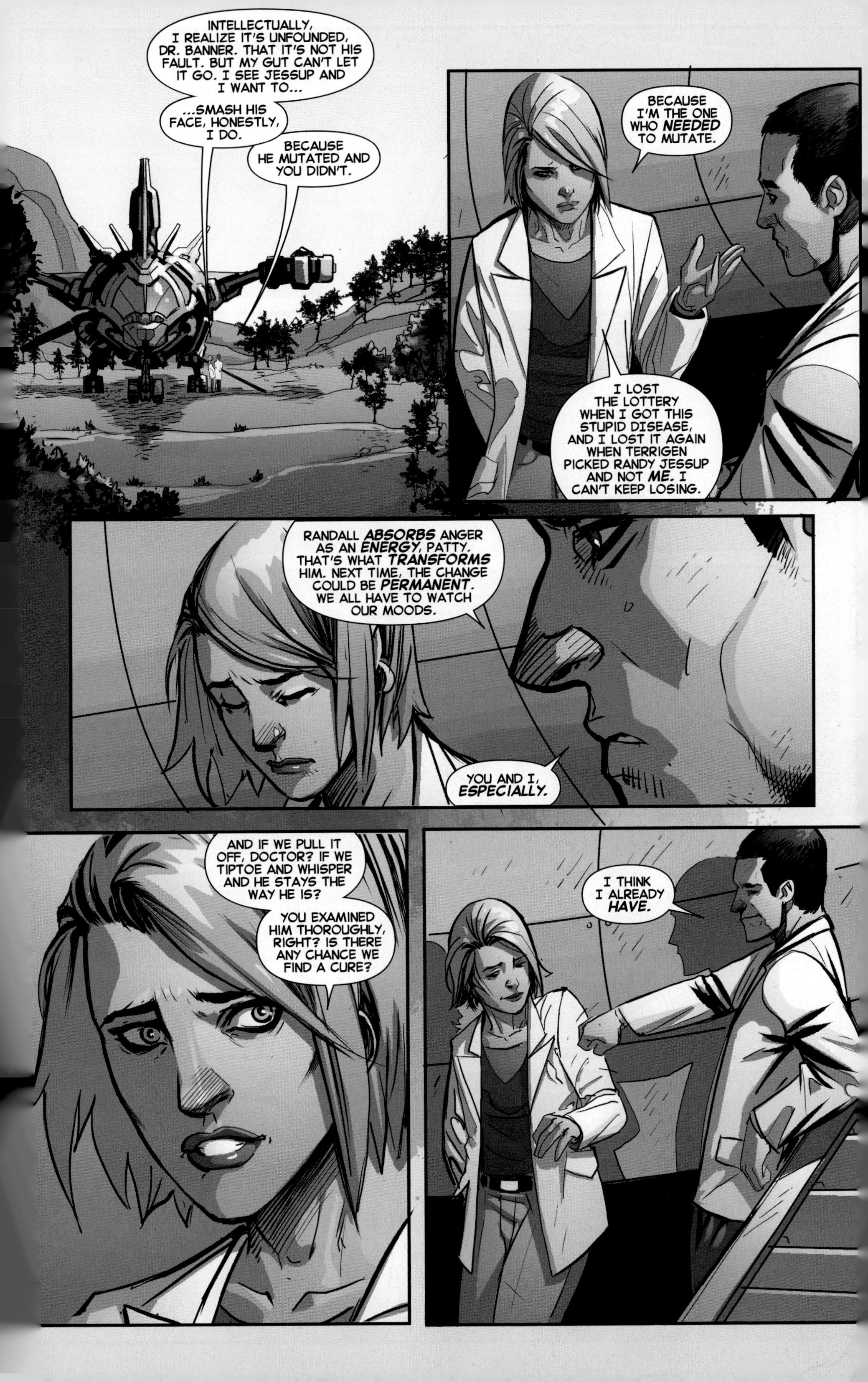

INTELLECTUALLY, I REALIZE IT'S UNFOUNDED, DR. BANNER. THAT IT'S NOT HIS FAULT. BUT MY GUT CAN'T LET IT GO. I SEE JESSUP AND I WANT TO...
...SMASH HIS FACE, HONESTLY, I DO.
BECAUSE HE MUTATED AND YOU DIDN'T.
BECAUSE I'M THE ONE WHO NEEDED TO MUTATE.
I LOST THE LOTTERY WHEN I GOT THIS STUPID DISEASE, AND I LOST IT AGAIN WHEN TERRIGEN PICKED RANDY JESSUP AND NOT ME. I CAN'T KEEP LOSING.
RANDALL ABSORBS ANGER AS AN ENERGY, PATTY. THAT'S WHAT TRANSFORMS HIM. NEXT TIME, THE CHANGE COULD BE PERMANENT. WE ALL HAVE TO WATCH OUR MOODS.
YOU AND I, ESPECIALLY.
AND IF WE PULL IT OFF, DOCTOR? IF WE TIPTOE AND WHISPER AND HE STAYS THE WAY HE IS?
YOU EXAMINED HIM THOROUGHLY, RIGHT? IS THERE ANY CHANCE WE FIND A CURE?
I THINK I ALREADY HAVE.

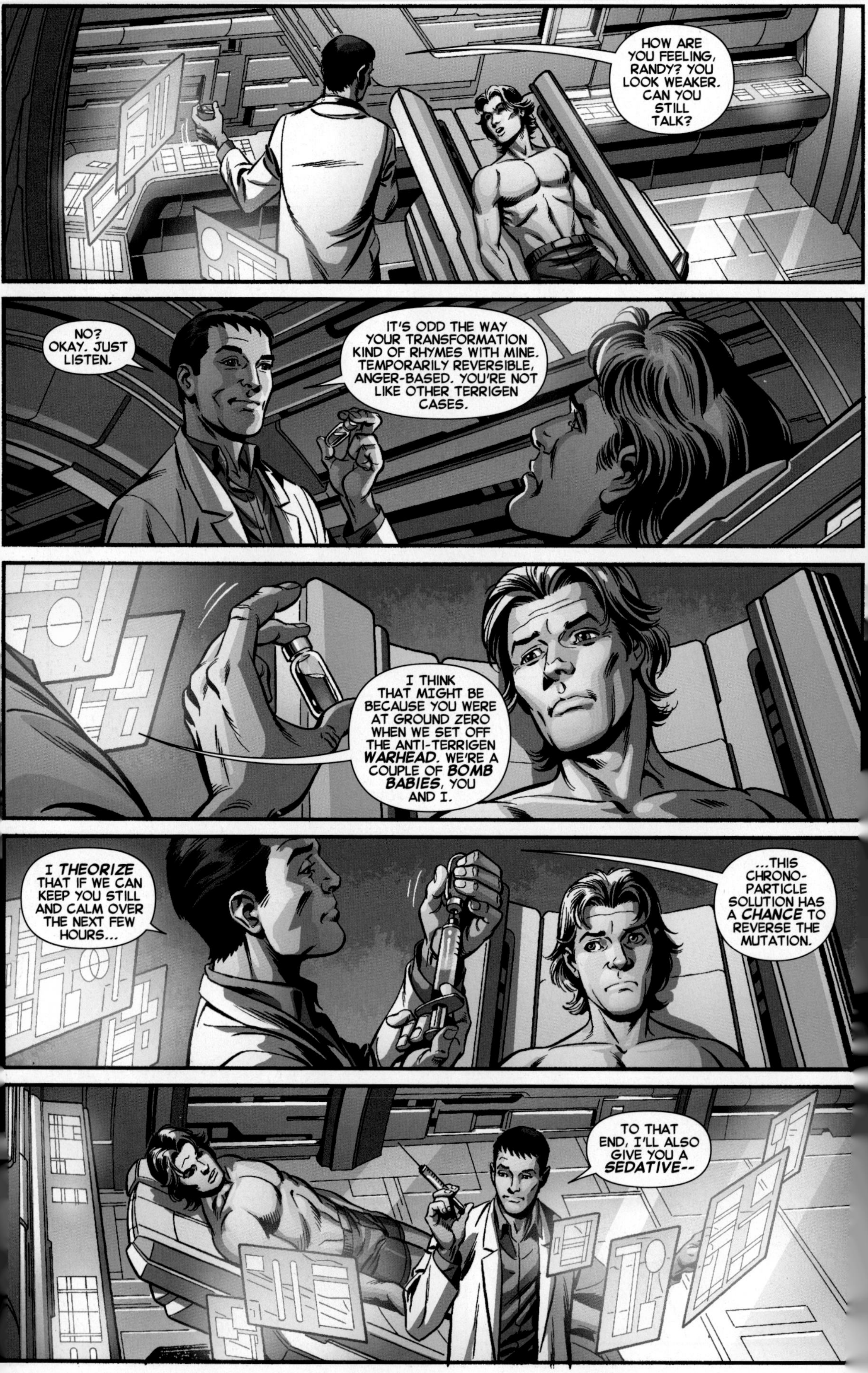
HOW ARE YOU FEELING, RANDY? YOU LOOK WEAKER. CAN YOU STILL TALK?
NO? OKAY. JUST LISTEN.
IT'S ODD THE WAY YOUR TRANSFORMATION KIND OF RHYMES WITH MINE. TEMPORARILY REVERSIBLE, ANGER-BASED. YOU'RE NOT LIKE OTHER TERRIGEN CASES.
I THINK THAT MIGHT BE BECAUSE YOU WERE AT GROUND ZERO WHEN WE SET OFF THE ANTI-TERRIGEN WARHEAD. WE'RE A COUPLE OF BOMB BABIES, YOU AND I.
I THEORIZE THAT IF WE CAN KEEP YOU STILL AND CALM OVER THE NEXT FEW HOURS...
...THIS CHRONO-PARTICLE SOLUTION HAS A CHANCE TO REVERSE THE MUTATION.
TO THAT END, I'LL ALSO GIVE YOU A SEDATIVE--

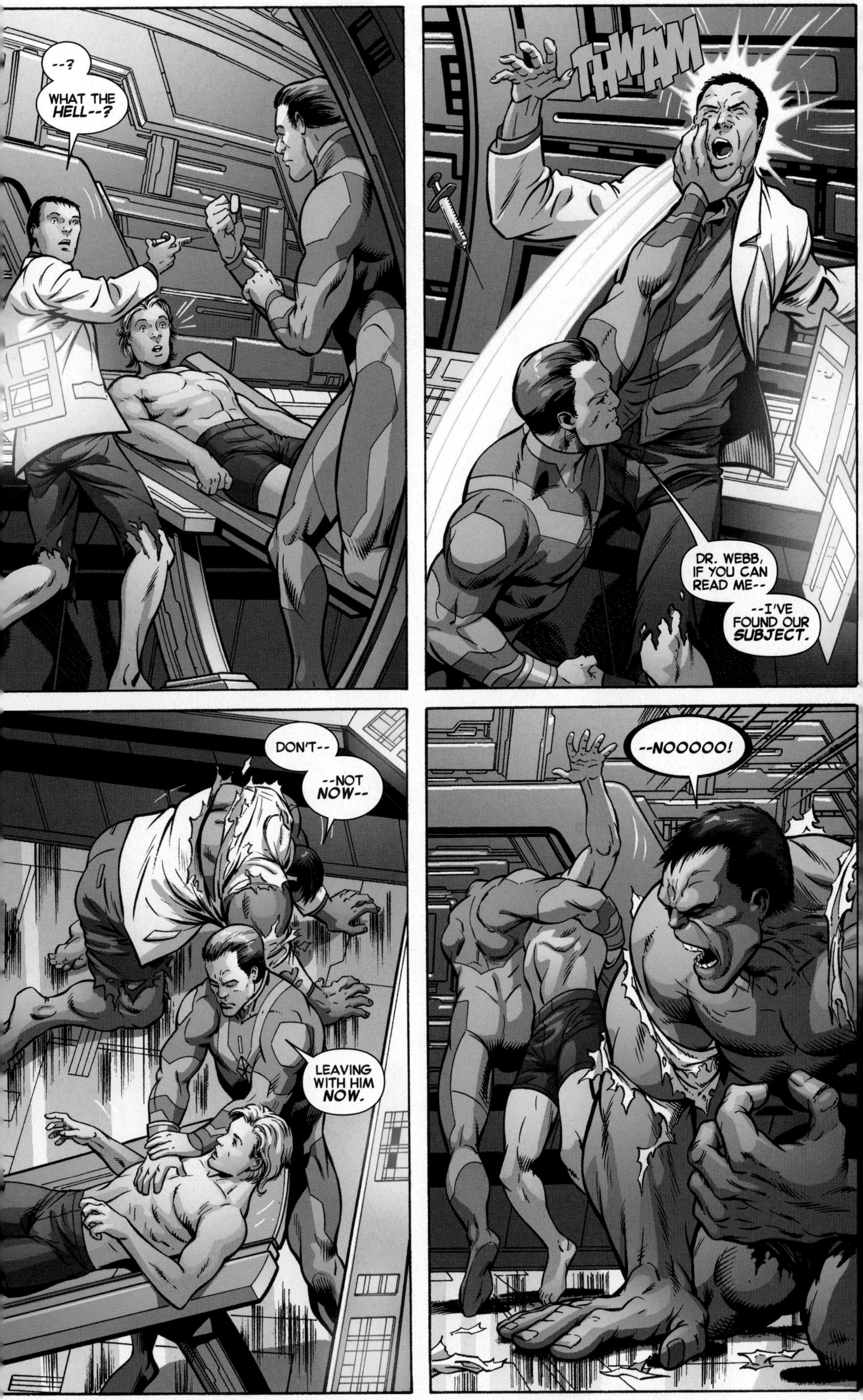
--?
WHAT THE HELL--?
THWAM
DR. WEBB, IF YOU CAN READ ME--
--I'VE FOUND OUR SUBJECT.
DON'T--
--NOT NOW--
LEAVING WITH HIM NOW.
--NOOOOO!

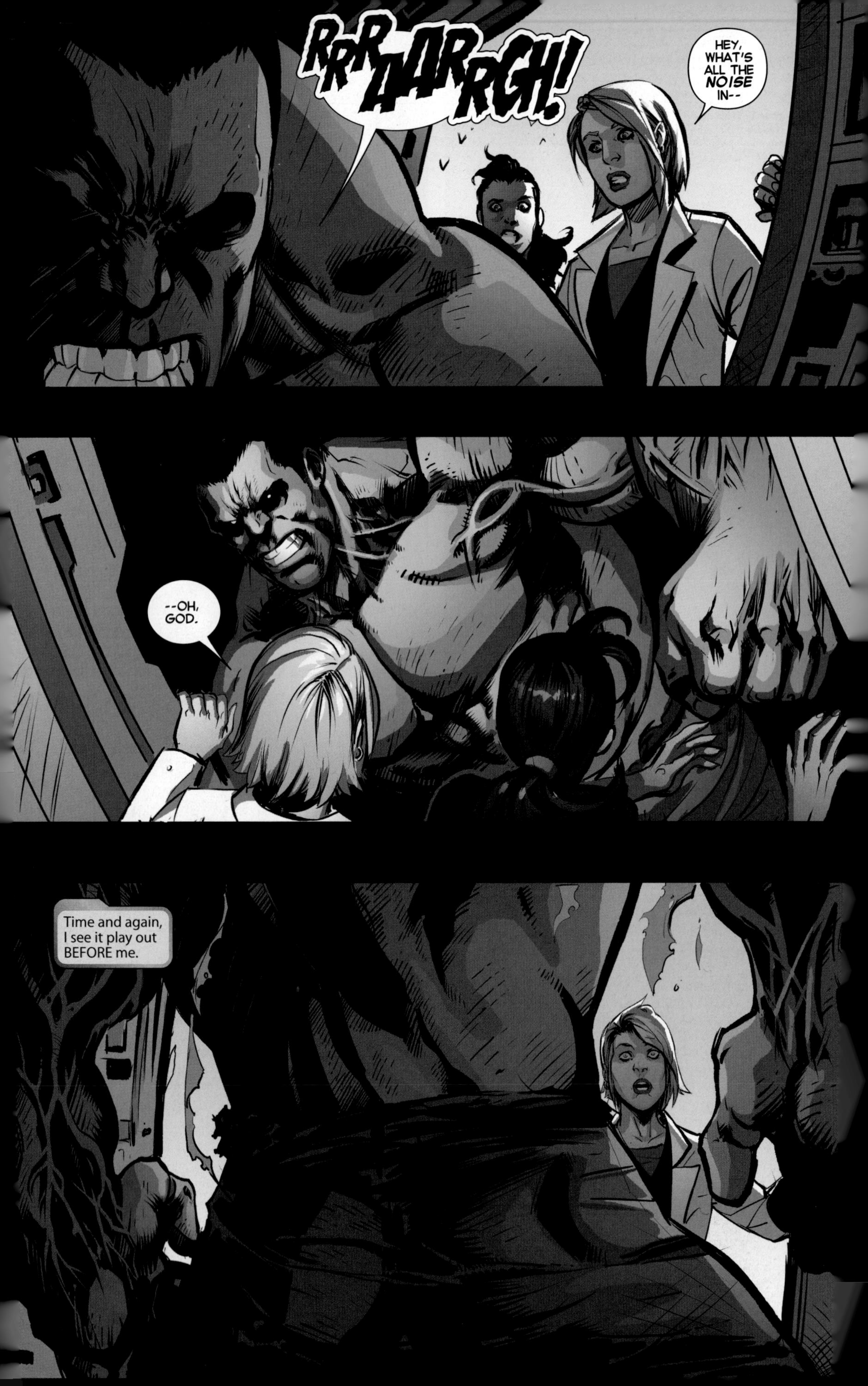

RRRAARRGH!
HEY, WHAT'S ALL THE NOISE IN--
--OH, GOD.
Time and again, I see it play out BEFORE me.

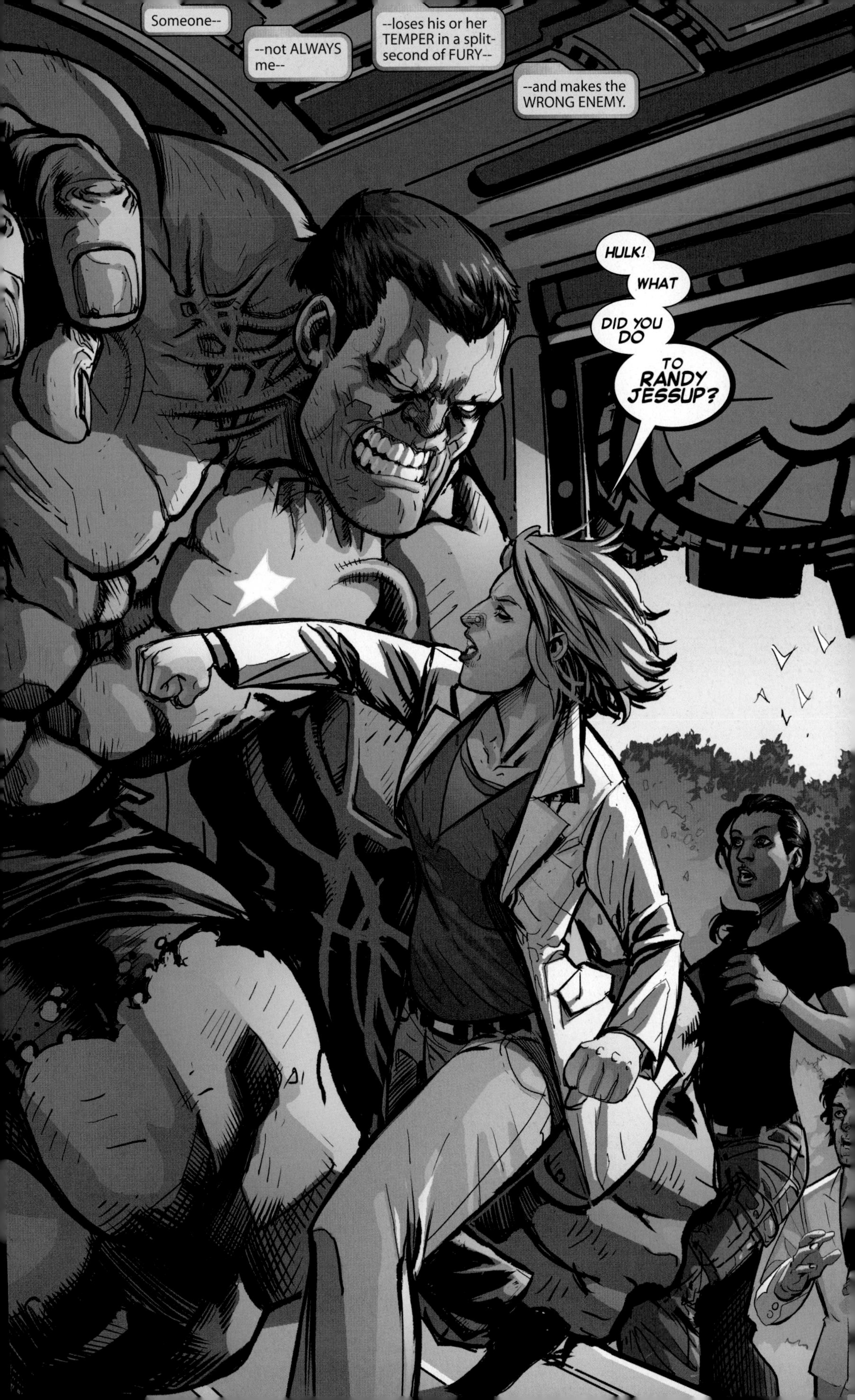
Someone--
--not ALWAYS me--
--loses his or her TEMPER in a split-second of FURY--
--and makes the WRONG ENEMY.
HULK!
WHAT
DID YOU DO
TO RANDY JESSUP?

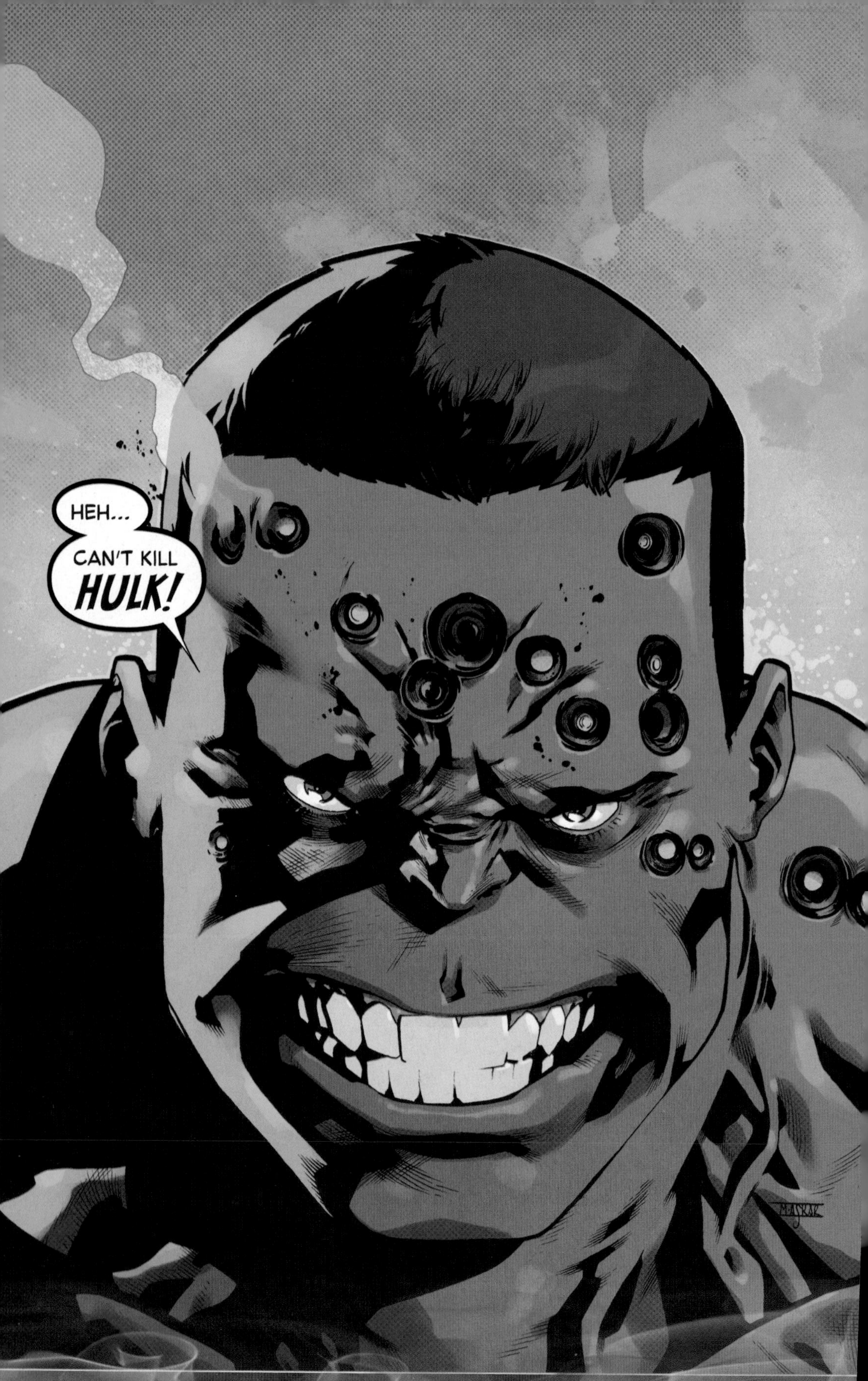
HEH...
CAN'T KILL HULK!
MASKAR

INDESTRUCTIBLE HULK #20

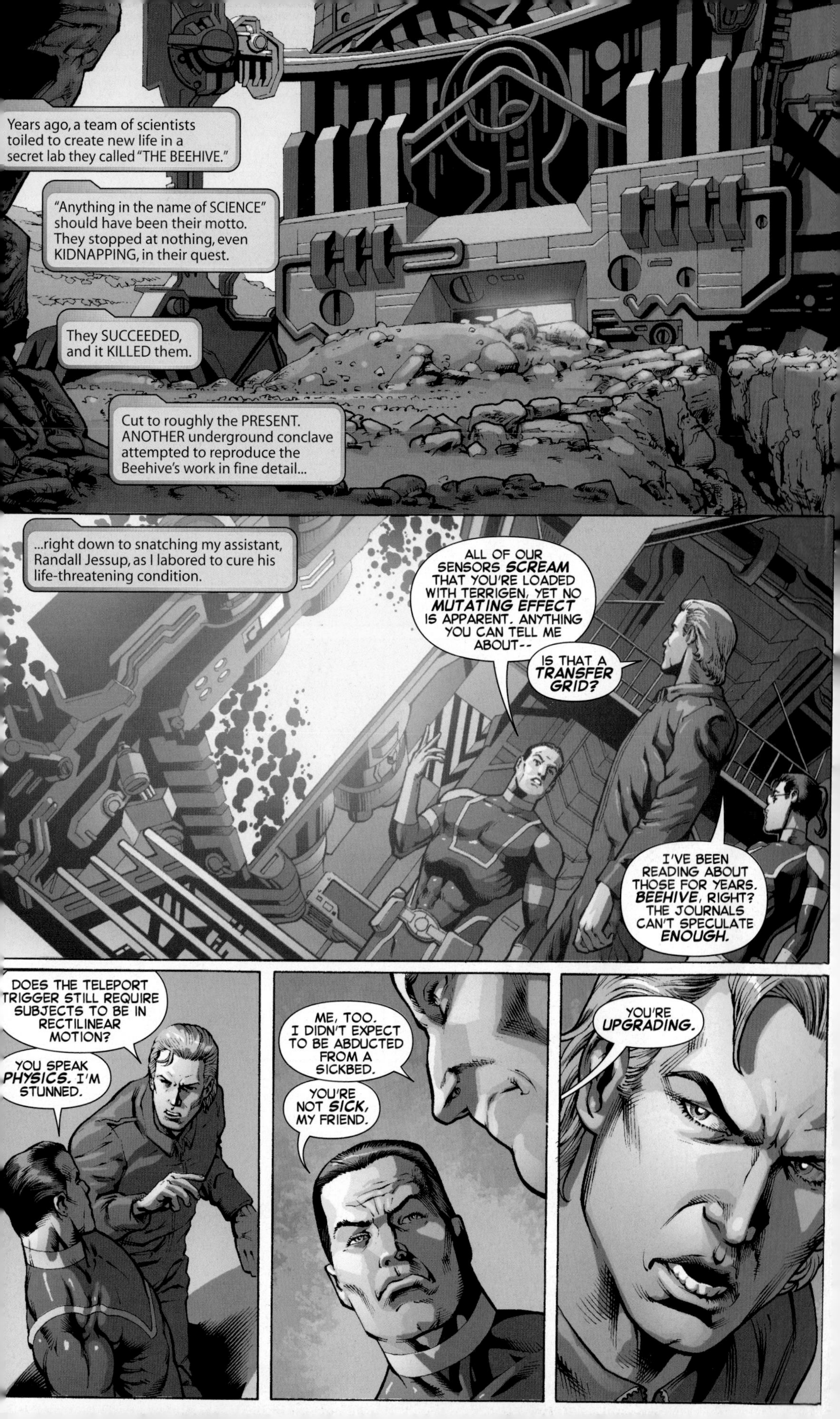
Years ago, a team of scientists toiled to create new life in a secret lab they called "THE BEEHIVE."
"Anything in the name of SCIENCE" should have been their motto. They stopped at nothing, even KIDNAPPING, in their quest.
They SUCCEEDED, and it KILLED them.
Cut to roughly the PRESENT. ANOTHER underground conclave attempted to reproduce the Beehive's work in fine detail...
...right down to snatching my assistant, Randall Jessup, as I labored to cure his life-threatening condition.
ALL OF OUR SENSORS SCREAM THAT YOU'RE LOADED WITH TERRIGEN, YET NO MUTATING EFFECT IS APPARENT. ANYTHING YOU CAN TELL ME ABOUT--
IS THAT A TRANSFER GRID?
I'VE BEEN READING ABOUT THOSE FOR YEARS. BEEHIVE, RIGHT? THE JOURNALS CAN'T SPECULATE ENOUGH.
DOES THE TELEPORT TRIGGER STILL REQUIRE SUBJECTS TO BE IN RECTILINEAR MOTION?
YOU SPEAK PHYSICS. I'M STUNNED.
ME, TOO. I DIDN'T EXPECT TO BE ABDUCTED FROM A SICKBED.
YOU'RE NOT SICK, MY FRIEND.
YOU'RE UPGRADING.

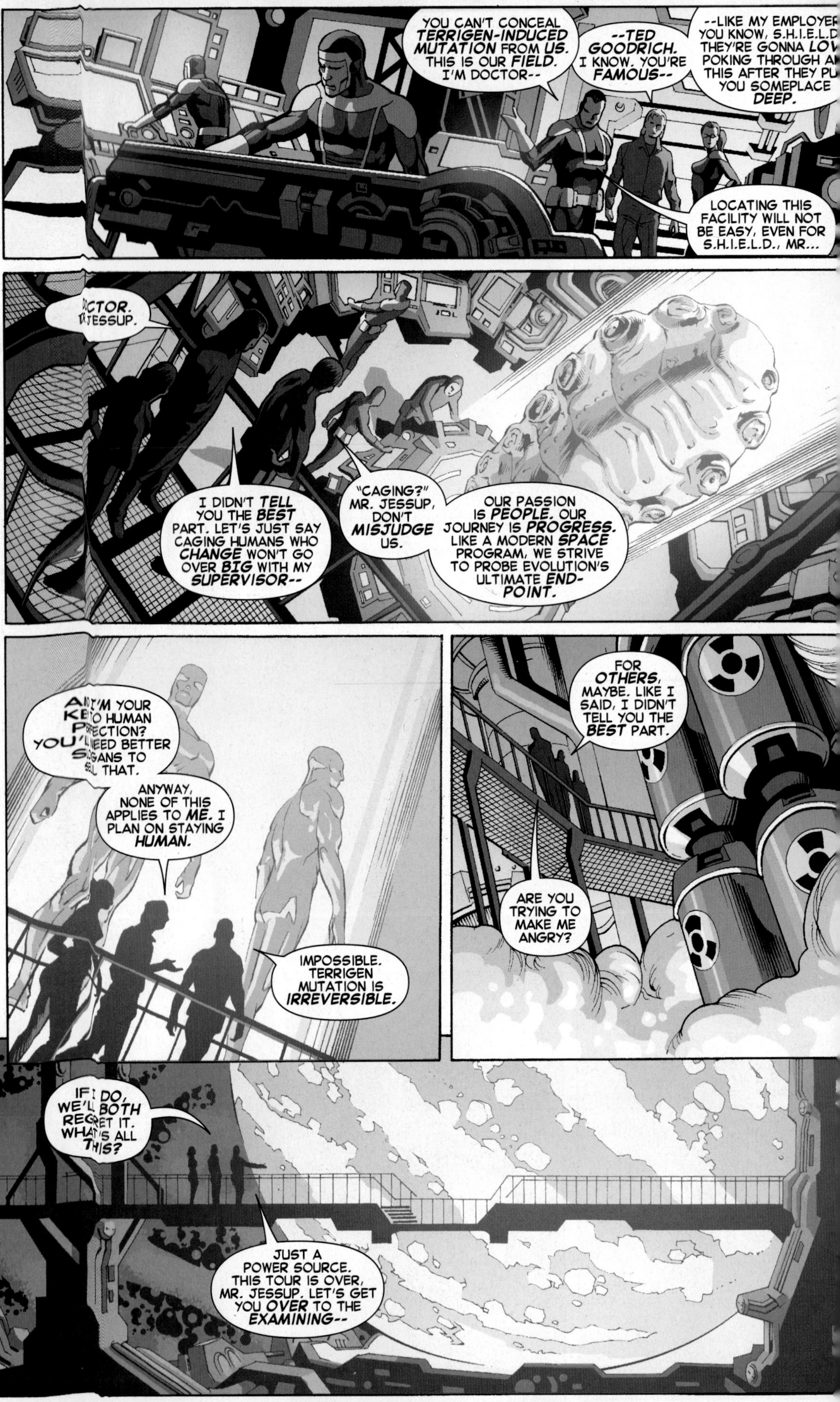
YOU CAN'T CONCEAL TERRIGEN-INDUCED MUTATION FROM US. THIS IS OUR FIELD. I'M DOCTOR--
--TED GOODRICH. I KNOW. YOU'RE FAMOUS--
--LIKE MY EMPLOYER YOU KNOW, S.H.I.E.L.D THEY'RE GONNA LOV POKING THROUGH A THIS AFTER THEY PU YOU SOMEPLACE DEEP.
LOCATING THIS FACILITY WILL NOT BE EASY, EVEN FOR S.H.I.E.L.D., MR...
DOCTOR. DR. JESSUP.
I DIDN'T TELL YOU THE BEST PART. LET'S JUST SAY CAGING HUMANS WHO CHANGE WON'T GO OVER BIG WITH MY SUPERVISOR--
"CAGING?" MR. JESSUP, DON'T MISJUDGE US.
OUR PASSION IS PEOPLE. OUR JOURNEY IS PROGRESS. LIKE A MODERN SPACE PROGRAM, WE STRIVE TO PROBE EVOLUTION'S ULTIMATE END-POINT.
AND I'M YOUR KEY TO HUMAN PERFECTION? YOU'LL NEED BETTER SLOGANS TO SELL THAT.
ANYWAY, NONE OF THIS APPLIES TO ME. I PLAN ON STAYING HUMAN.
IMPOSSIBLE. TERRIGEN MUTATION IS IRREVERSIBLE.
FOR OTHERS, MAYBE. LIKE I SAID, I DIDN'T TELL YOU THE BEST PART.
ARE YOU TRYING TO MAKE ME ANGRY?
IF I DO, WE'LL BOTH REGRET IT. WHAT'S ALL THIS?
JUST A POWER SOURCE. THIS TOUR IS OVER, MR. JESSUP. LET'S GET YOU OVER TO THE EXAMINING--

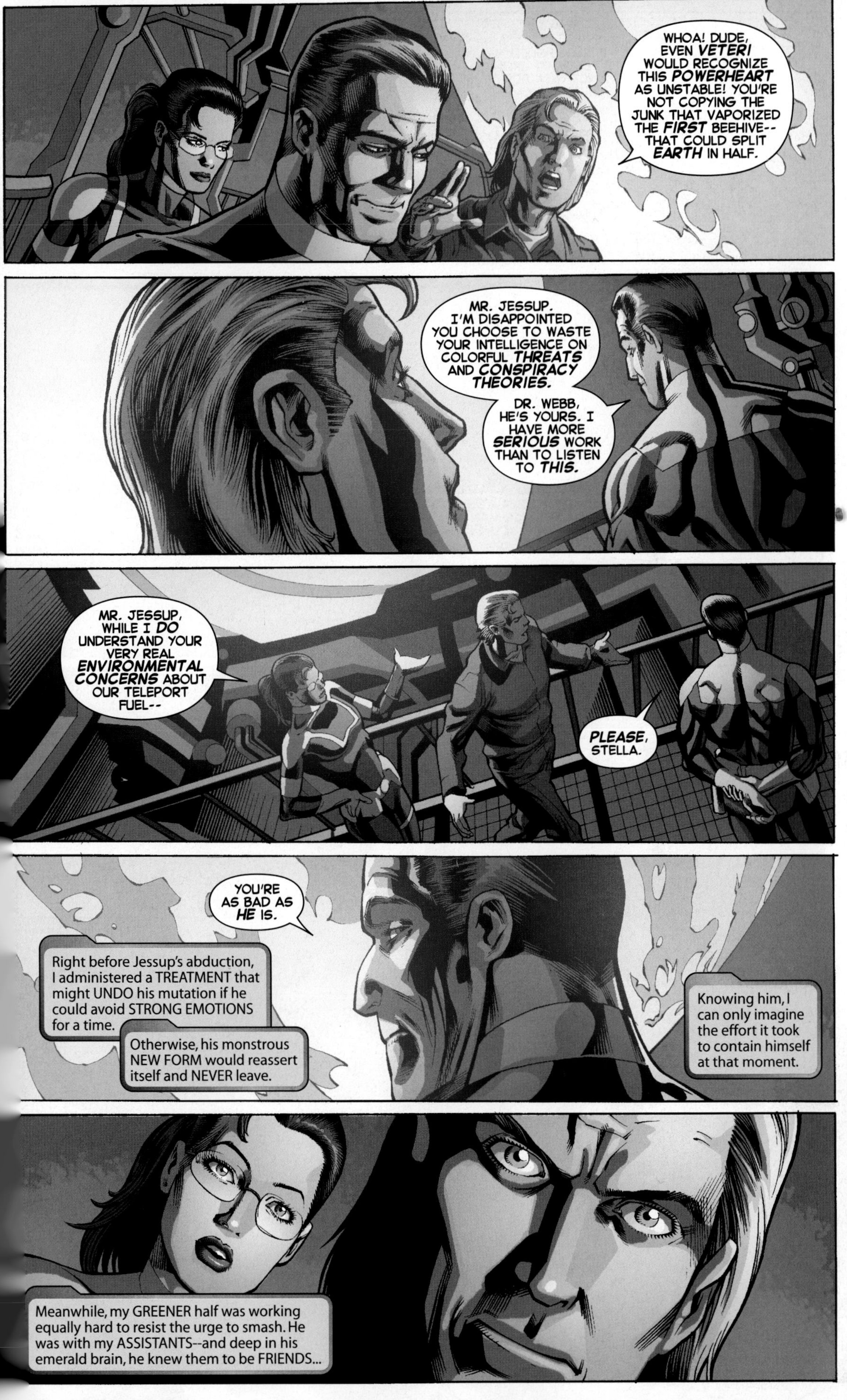
WHOA! DUDE, EVEN VETERI WOULD RECOGNIZE THIS POWERHEART AS UNSTABLE! YOU'RE NOT COPYING THE JUNK THAT VAPORIZED THE FIRST BEEHIVE--THAT COULD SPLIT EARTH IN HALF.
MR. JESSUP. I'M DISAPPOINTED YOU CHOOSE TO WASTE YOUR INTELLIGENCE ON COLORFUL THREATS AND CONSPIRACY THEORIES.
DR. WEBB, HE'S YOURS. I HAVE MORE SERIOUS WORK THAN TO LISTEN TO THIS.
MR. JESSUP, WHILE I DO UNDERSTAND YOUR VERY REAL ENVIRONMENTAL CONCERNS ABOUT OUR TELEPORT FUEL--
PLEASE, STELLA.
YOU'RE AS BAD AS HE IS.
Right before Jessup's abduction, I administered a TREATMENT that might UNDO his mutation if he could avoid STRONG EMOTIONS for a time.
Otherwise, his monstrous NEW FORM would reassert itself and NEVER leave.
Knowing him, I can only imagine the effort it took to contain himself at that moment.
Meanwhile, my GREENER half was working equally hard to resist the urge to smash. He was with my ASSISTANTS--and deep in his emerald brain, he knew them to be FRIENDS...

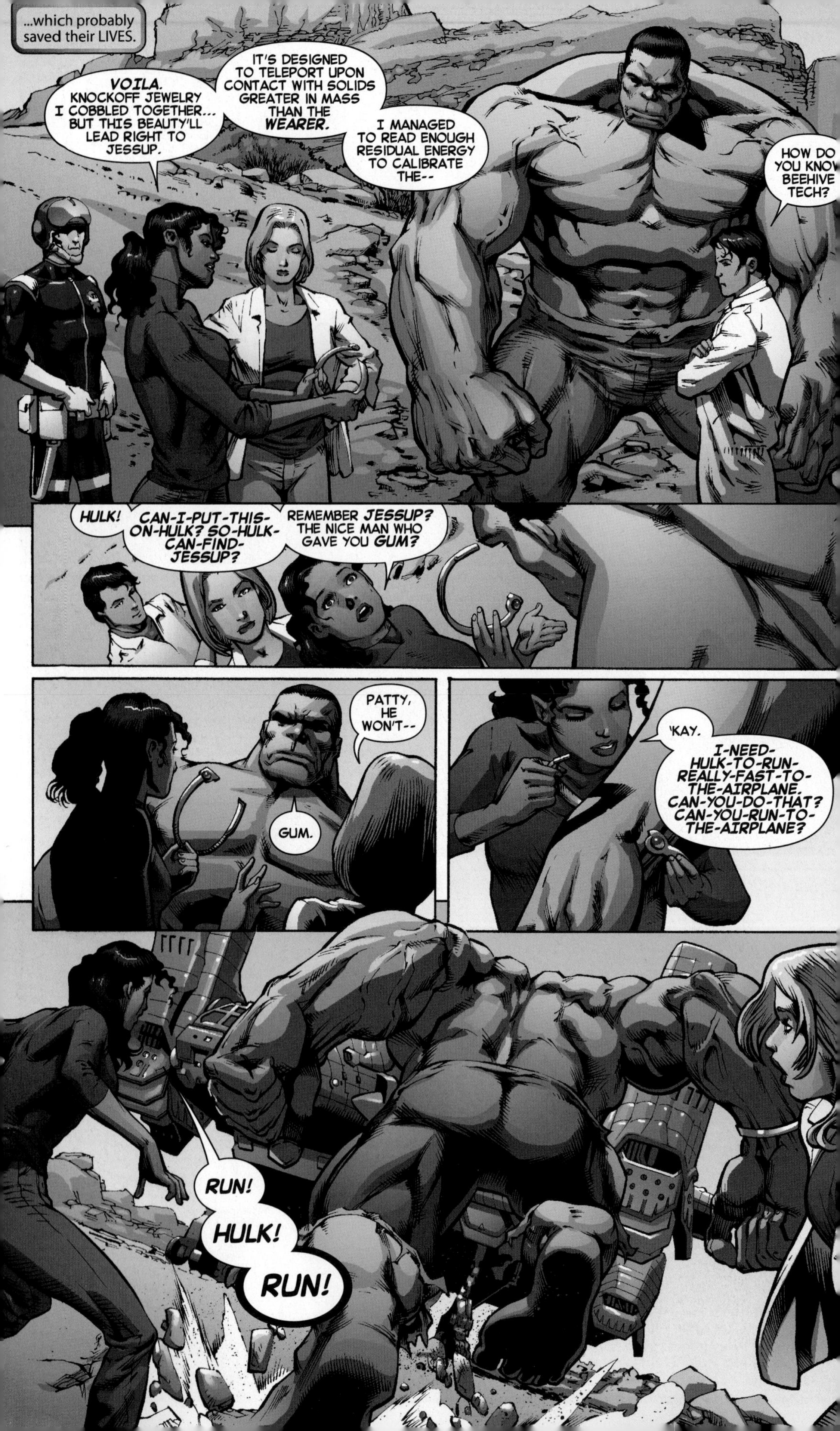
...which probably saved their LIVES.
VOILA. KNOCKOFF JEWELRY I COBBLED TOGETHER... BUT THIS BEAUTY'LL LEAD RIGHT TO JESSUP.
IT'S DESIGNED TO TELEPORT UPON CONTACT WITH SOLIDS GREATER IN MASS THAN THE WEARER.
I MANAGED TO READ ENOUGH RESIDUAL ENERGY TO CALIBRATE THE--
HOW DO YOU KNOW BEEHIVE TECH?
HULK!
CAN-I-PUT-THIS-ON-HULK? SO-HULK-CAN-FIND-JESSUP?
REMEMBER JESSUP? THE NICE MAN WHO GAVE YOU GUM?
PATTY, HE WON'T--
GUM.
'KAY.
I-NEED-HULK-TO-RUN-REALLY-FAST-TO-THE-AIRPLANE. CAN-YOU-DO-THAT? CAN-YOU-RUN-TO-THE-AIRPLANE?
RUN!
HULK!
RUN!

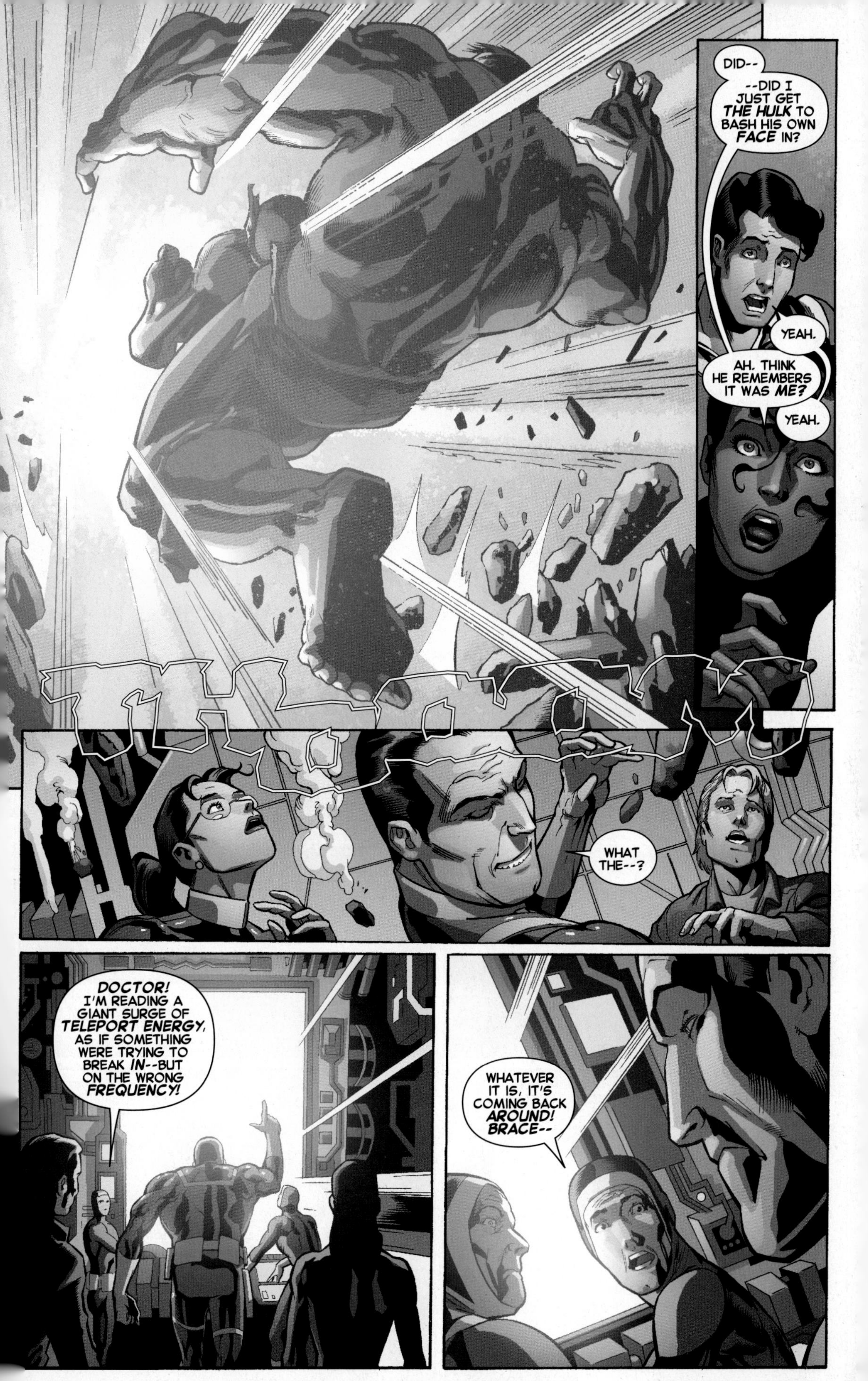
DID--
--DID I JUST GET THE HULK TO BASH HIS OWN FACE IN?
YEAH.
AH. THINK HE REMEMBERS IT WAS ME?
YEAH.
WHAT THE--?
DOCTOR! I'M READING A GIANT SURGE OF TELEPORT ENERGY, AS IF SOMETHING WERE TRYING TO BREAK IN--BUT ON THE WRONG FREQUENCY!
WHATEVER IT IS, IT'S COMING BACK AROUND! BRACE--

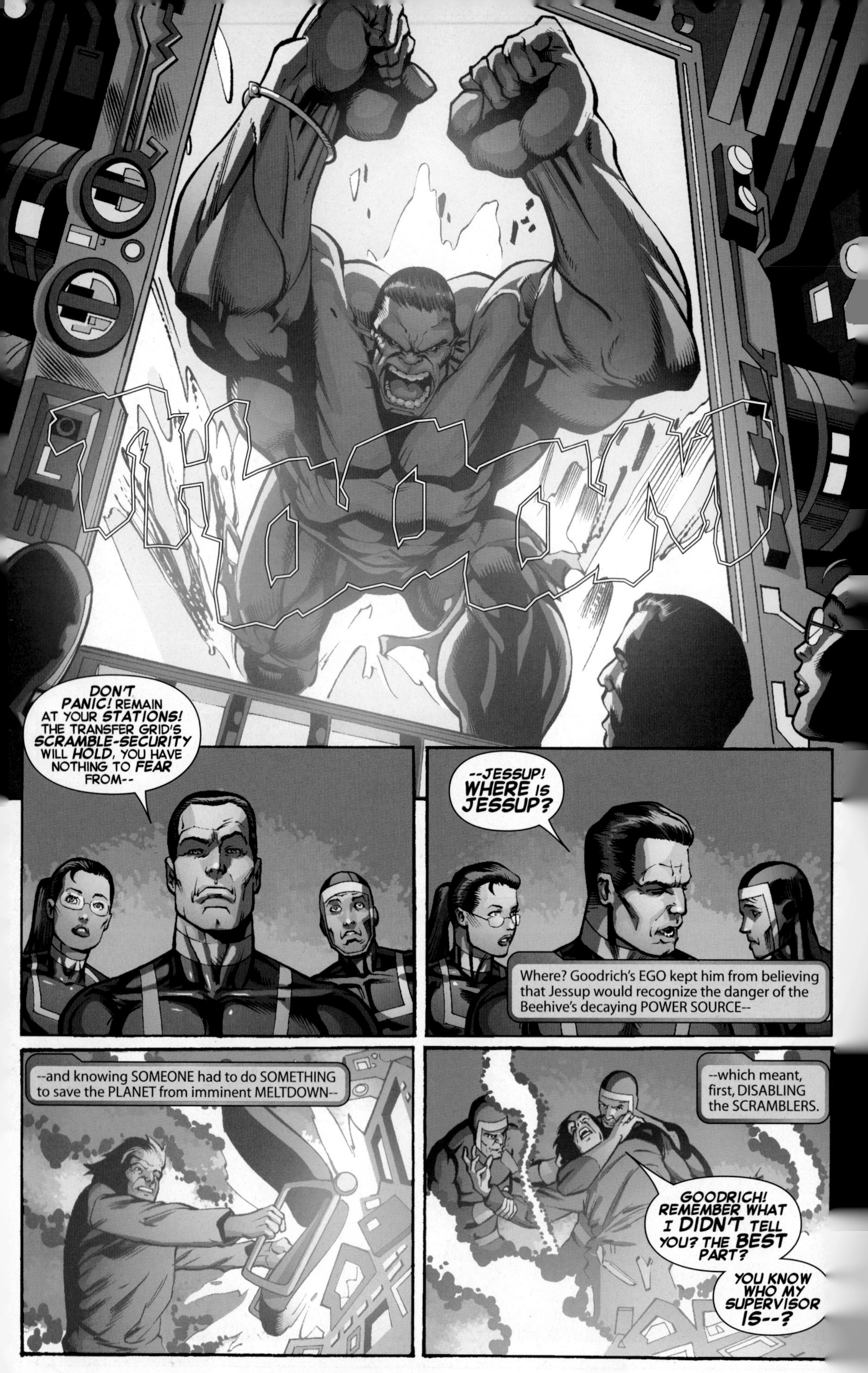
THOOOOM
DON'T PANIC! REMAIN AT YOUR STATIONS! THE TRANSFER GRID'S SCRAMBLE-SECURITY WILL HOLD, YOU HAVE NOTHING TO FEAR FROM--
--JESSUP! WHERE IS JESSUP?
Where? Goodrich's EGO kept him from believing that Jessup would recognize the danger of the Beehive's decaying POWER SOURCE--
--and knowing SOMEONE had to do SOMETHING to save the PLANET from imminent MELTDOWN--
--which meant, first, DISABLING the SCRAMBLERS.
GOODRICH! REMEMBER WHAT I DIDN'T TELL YOU? THE BEST PART?
YOU KNOW WHO MY SUPERVISOR IS--?

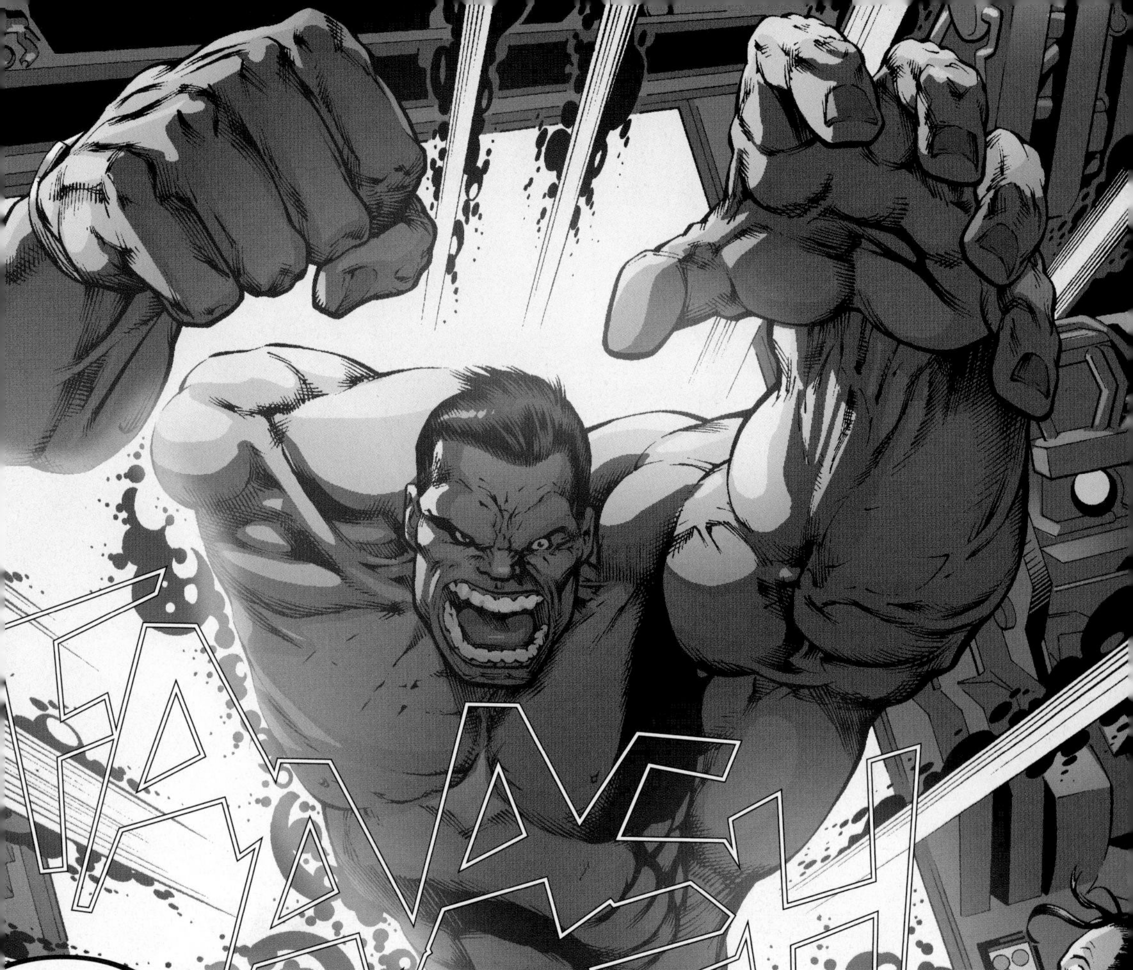
FAAAAASH
LET ME
TRODUCE
YOU!
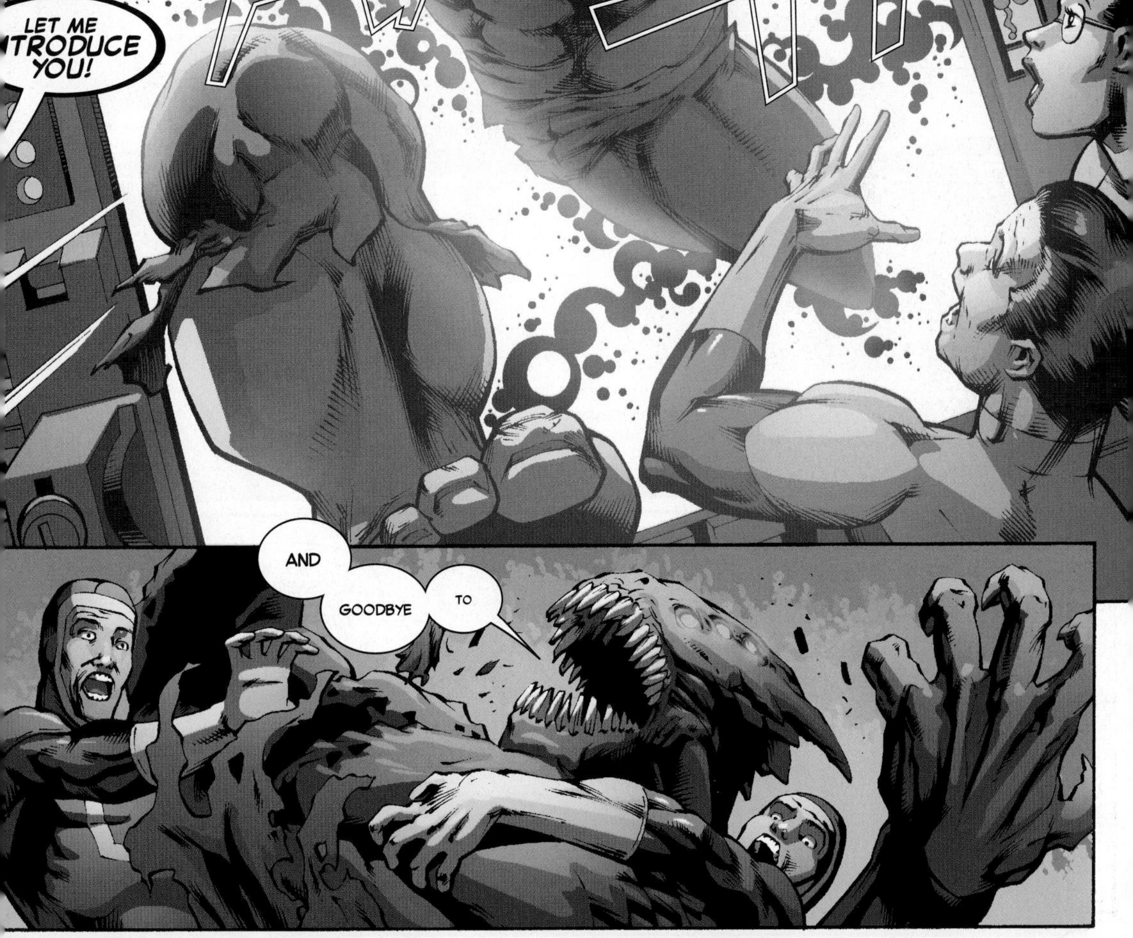
AND
GOODBYE
TO

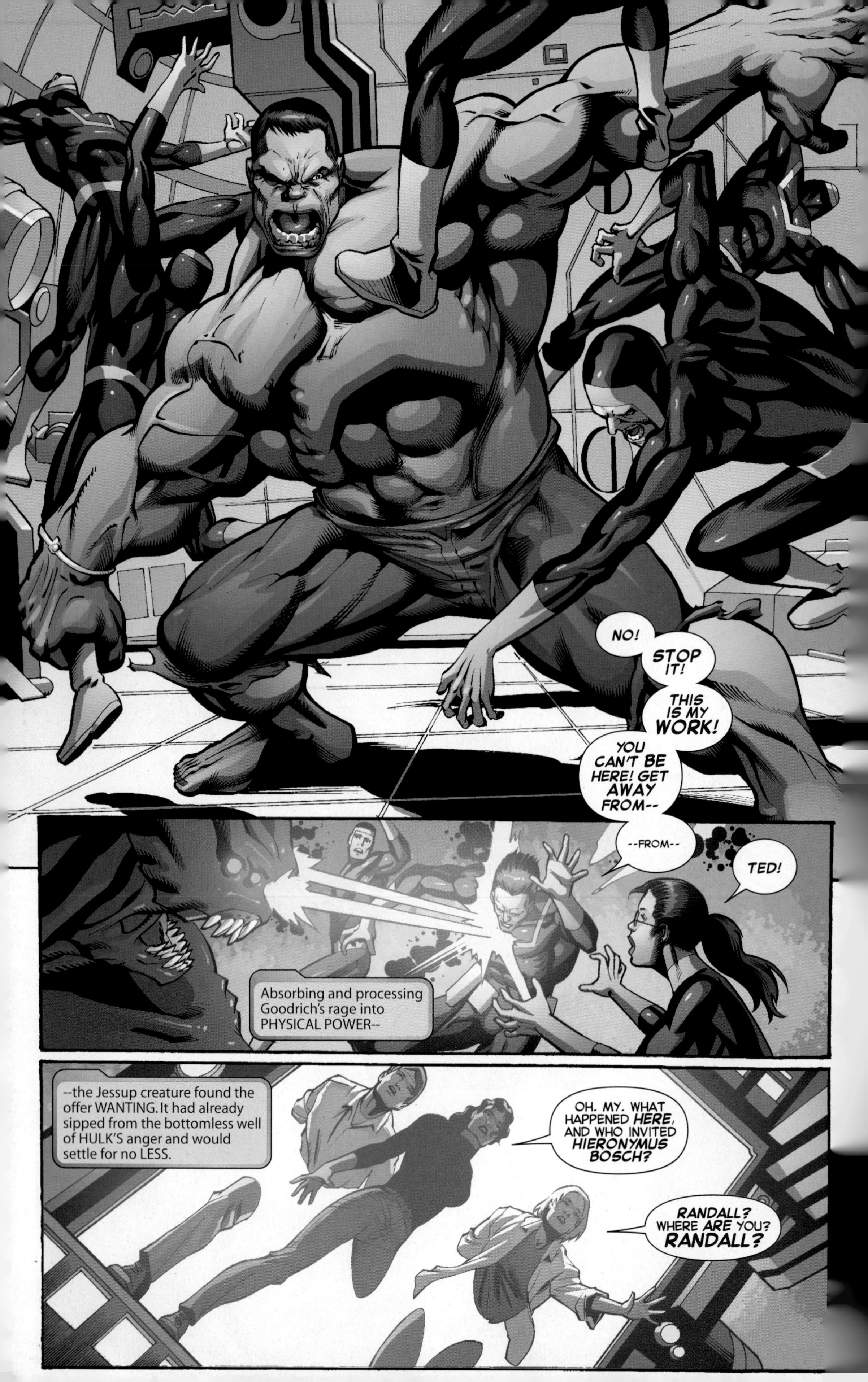
NO!
STOP IT!
THIS IS MY WORK!
YOU CAN'T BE HERE! GET AWAY FROM--
--FROM--
TED!
Absorbing and processing Goodrich's rage into PHYSICAL POWER--
--the Jessup creature found the offer WANTING. It had already sipped from the bottomless well of HULK'S anger and would settle for no LESS.
OH. MY. WHAT HAPPENED HERE, AND WHO INVITED HIERONYMUS BOSCH?
RANDALL? WHERE ARE YOU? RANDALL?

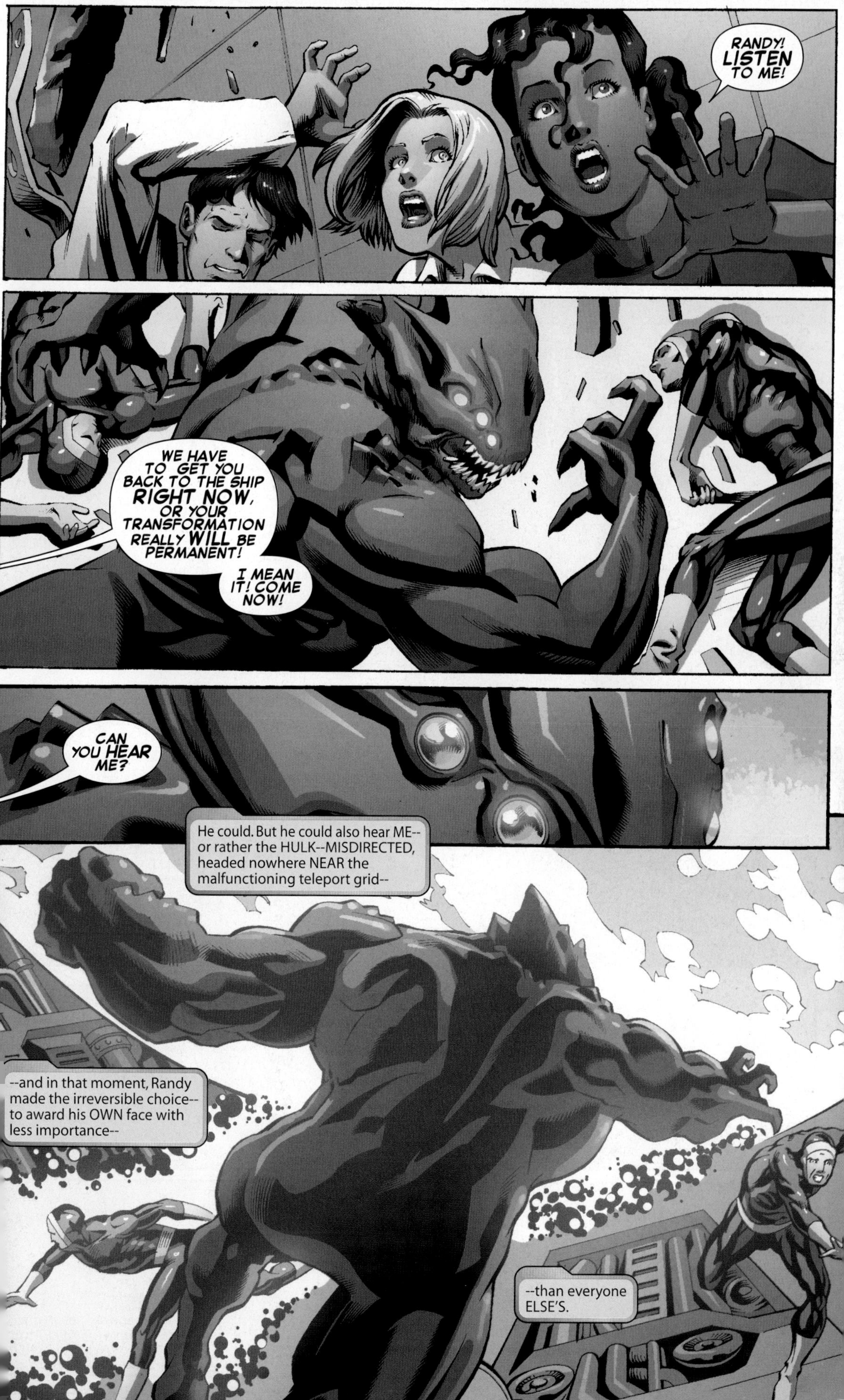
RANDY! LISTEN TO ME!
WE HAVE TO GET YOU BACK TO THE SHIP RIGHT NOW, OR YOUR TRANSFORMATION REALLY WILL BE PERMANENT!
I MEAN IT! COME NOW!
CAN YOU HEAR ME?
He could. But he could also hear ME--or rather the HULK--MISDIRECTED, headed nowhere NEAR the malfunctioning teleport grid--
--and in that moment, Randy made the irreversible choice--to award his OWN face with less importance--
--than everyone ELSE'S.

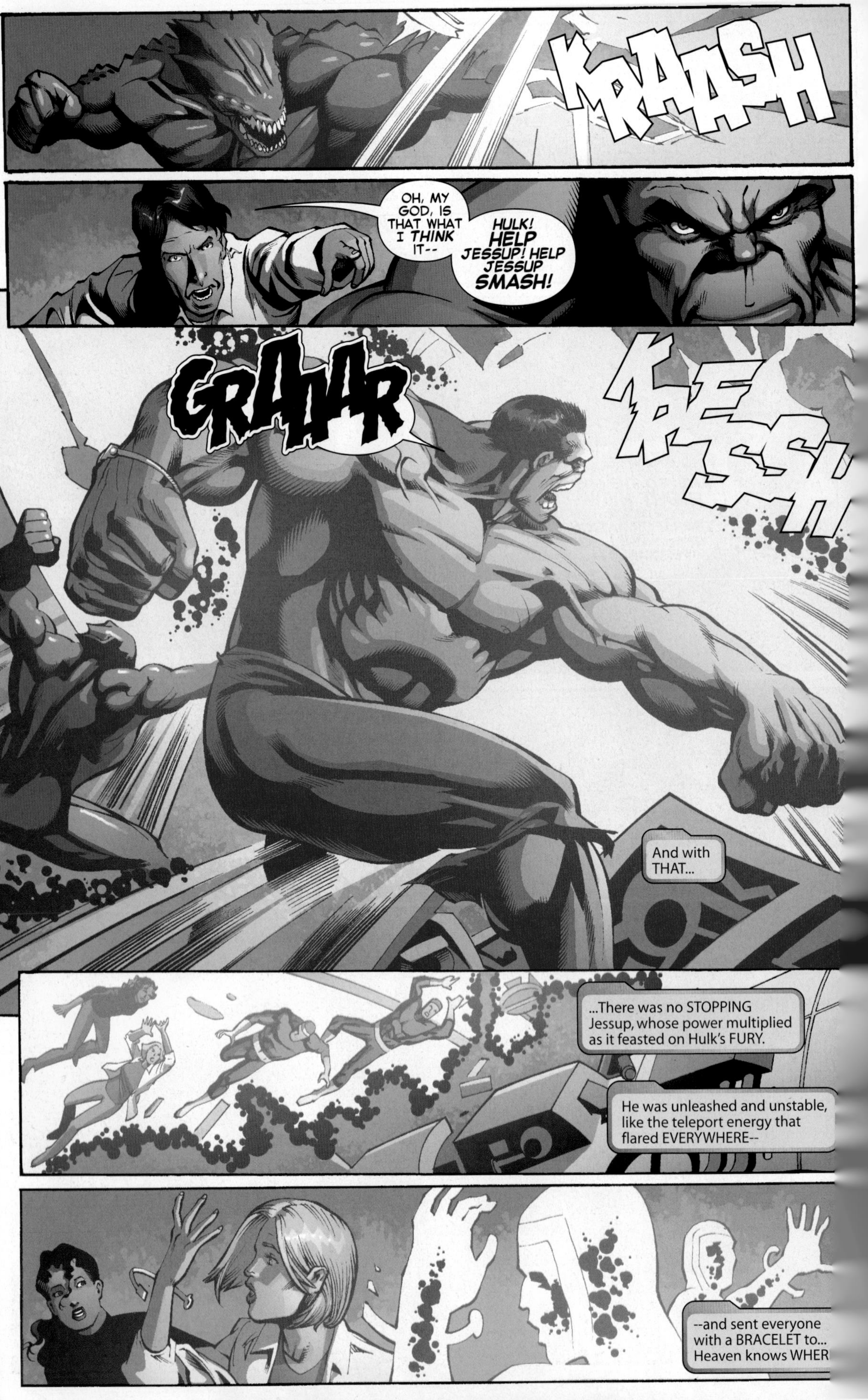
KRAASH
OH, MY GOD, IS THAT WHAT I THINK IT--
HULK! HELP JESSUP! HELP JESSUP SMASH!
GRAAAR
KRESSH
And with THAT...
...There was no STOPPING Jessup, whose power multiplied as it feasted on Hulk's FURY.
He was unleashed and unstable, like the teleport energy that flared EVERYWHERE--
--and sent everyone with a BRACELET to... Heaven knows WHER

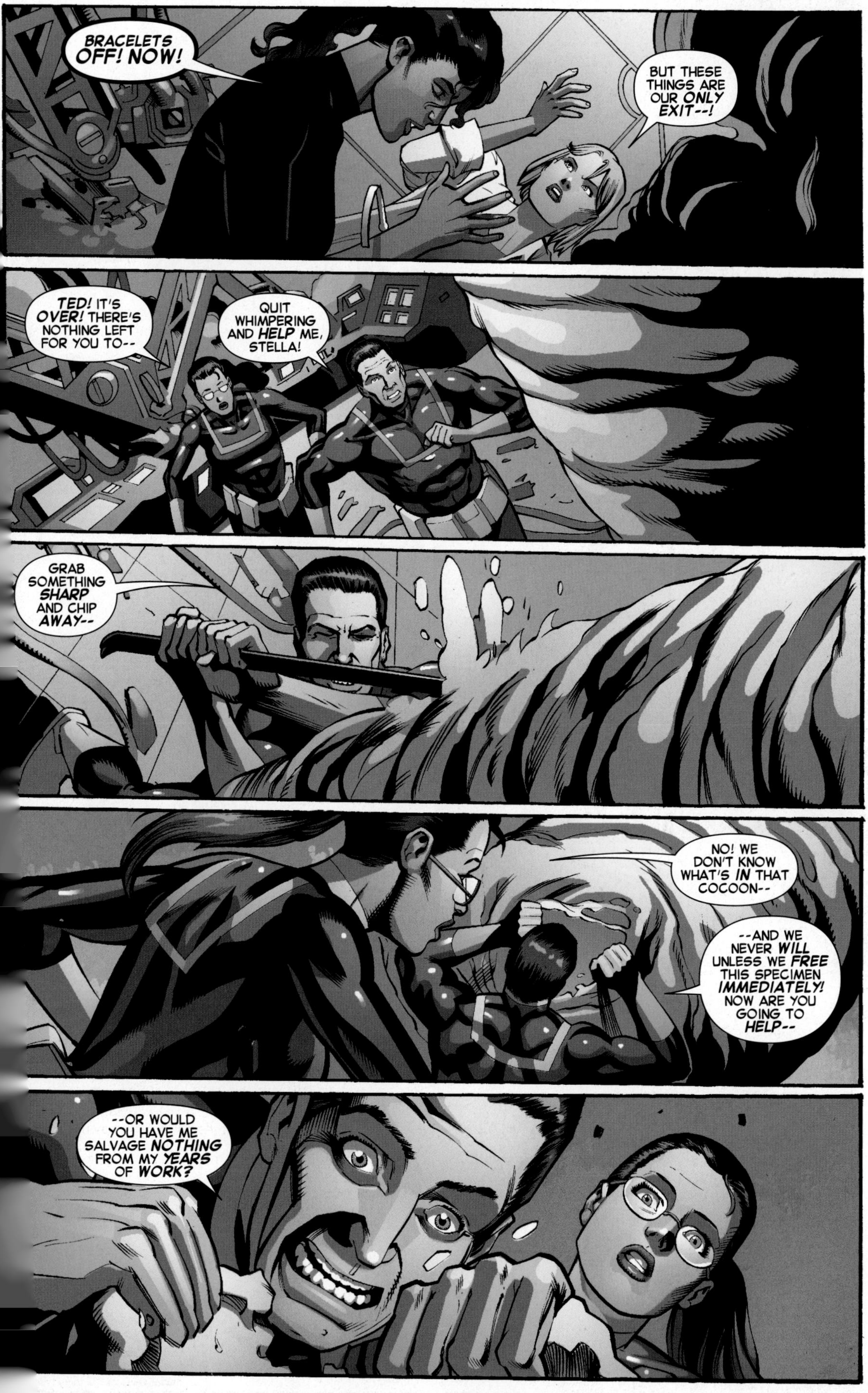
BRACELETS OFF! NOW!
BUT THESE THINGS ARE OUR ONLY EXIT--!
TED! IT'S OVER! THERE'S NOTHING LEFT FOR YOU TO--
QUIT WHIMPERING AND HELP ME, STELLA!
GRAB SOMETHING SHARP AND CHIP AWAY--
NO! WE DON'T KNOW WHAT'S IN THAT COCOON--
--AND WE NEVER WILL UNLESS WE FREE THIS SPECIMEN IMMEDIATELY! NOW ARE YOU GOING TO HELP--
--OR WOULD YOU HAVE ME SALVAGE NOTHING FROM MY YEARS OF WORK?

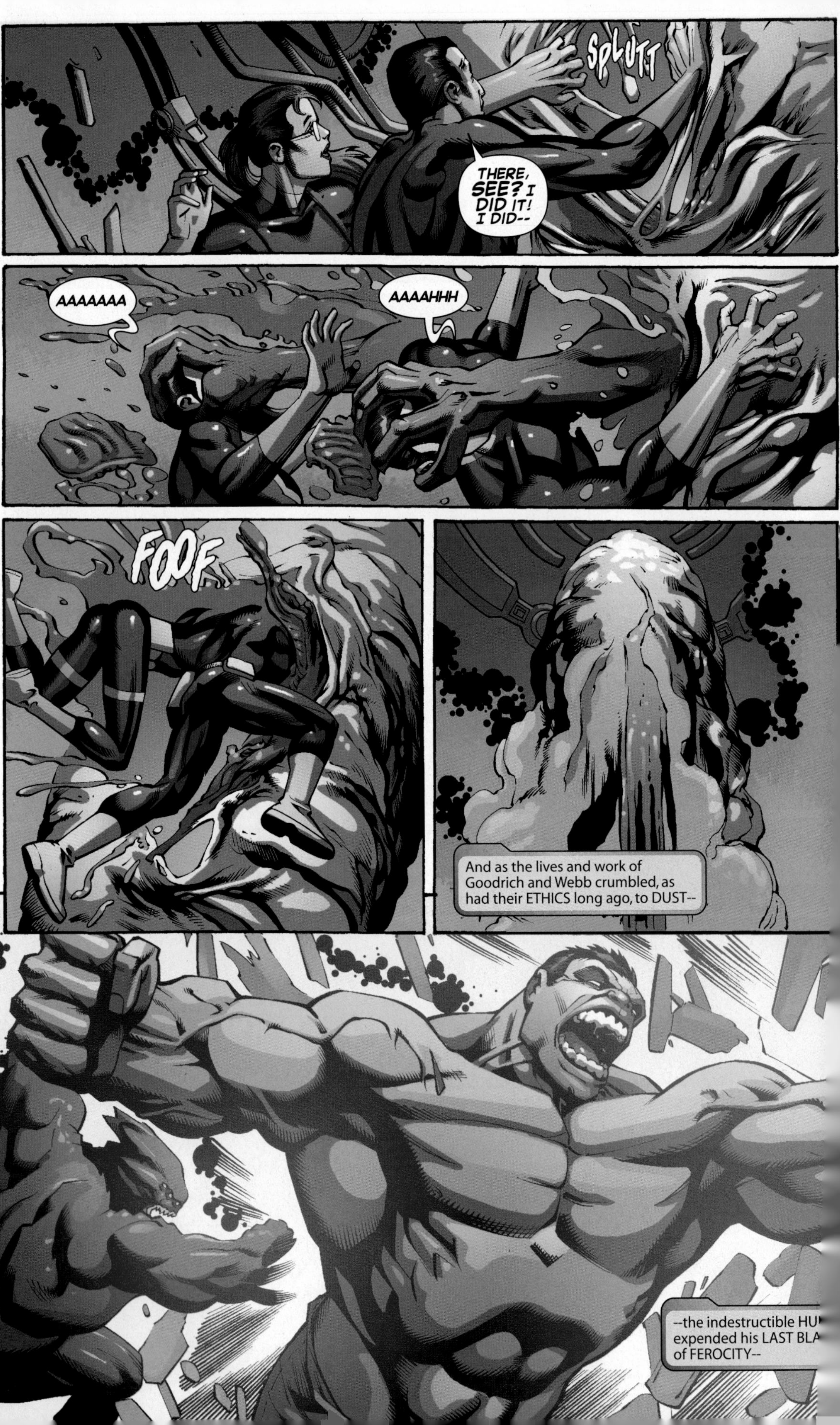
SPLUTT
THERE, SEE? I DID IT! I DID--
AAAAAAA
AAAAHHH
FOOF
And as the lives and work of Goodrich and Webb crumbled, as had their ETHICS long ago, to DUST--
--the indestructible HU
expended his LAST BLA
of FEROCITY--

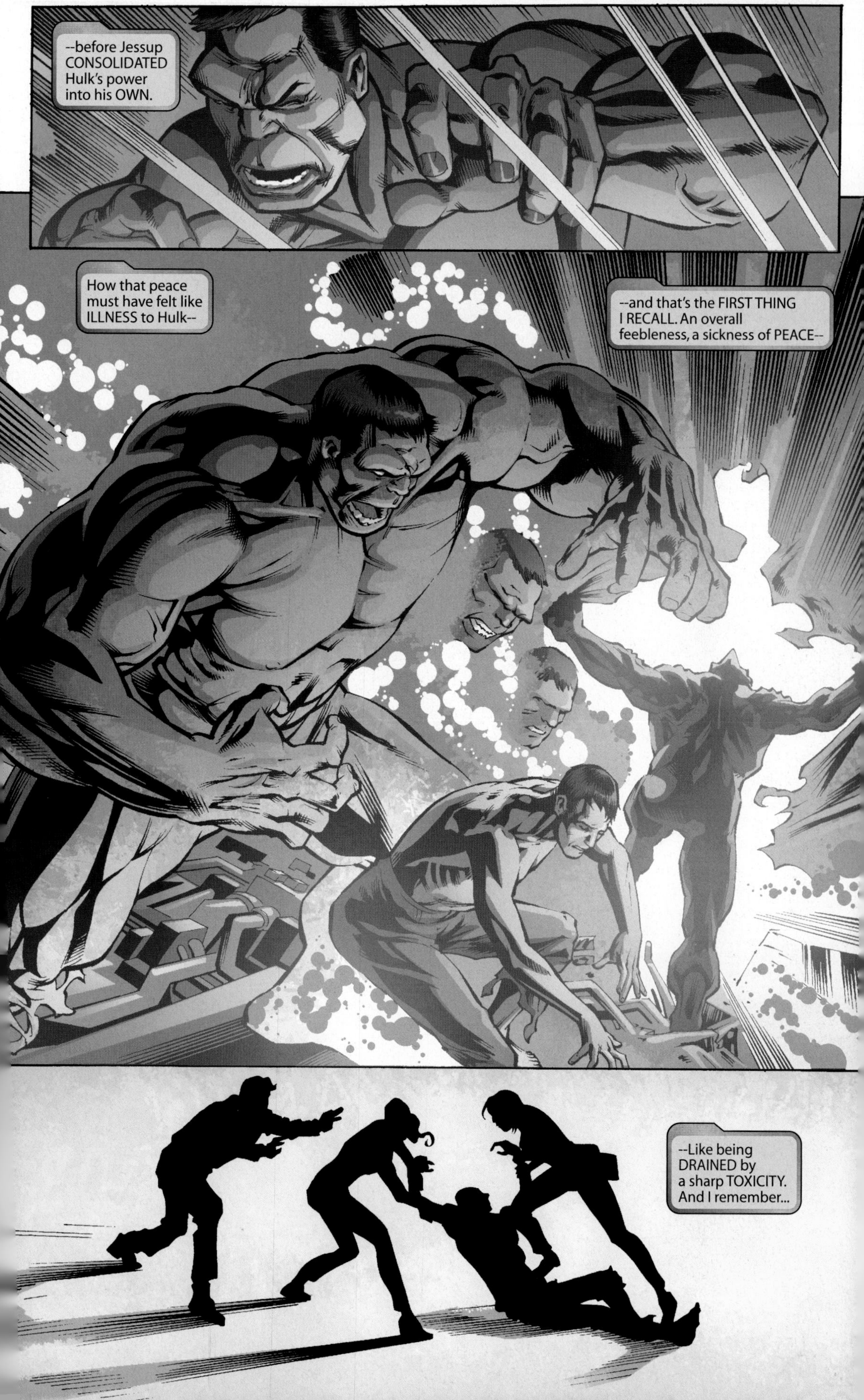
--before Jessup CONSOLIDATED Hulk's power into his OWN.
How that peace must have felt like ILLNESS to Hulk--
--and that's the FIRST THING I RECALL. An overall feebleness, a sickness of PEACE--
--Like being DRAINED by a sharp TOXICITY. And I remember...

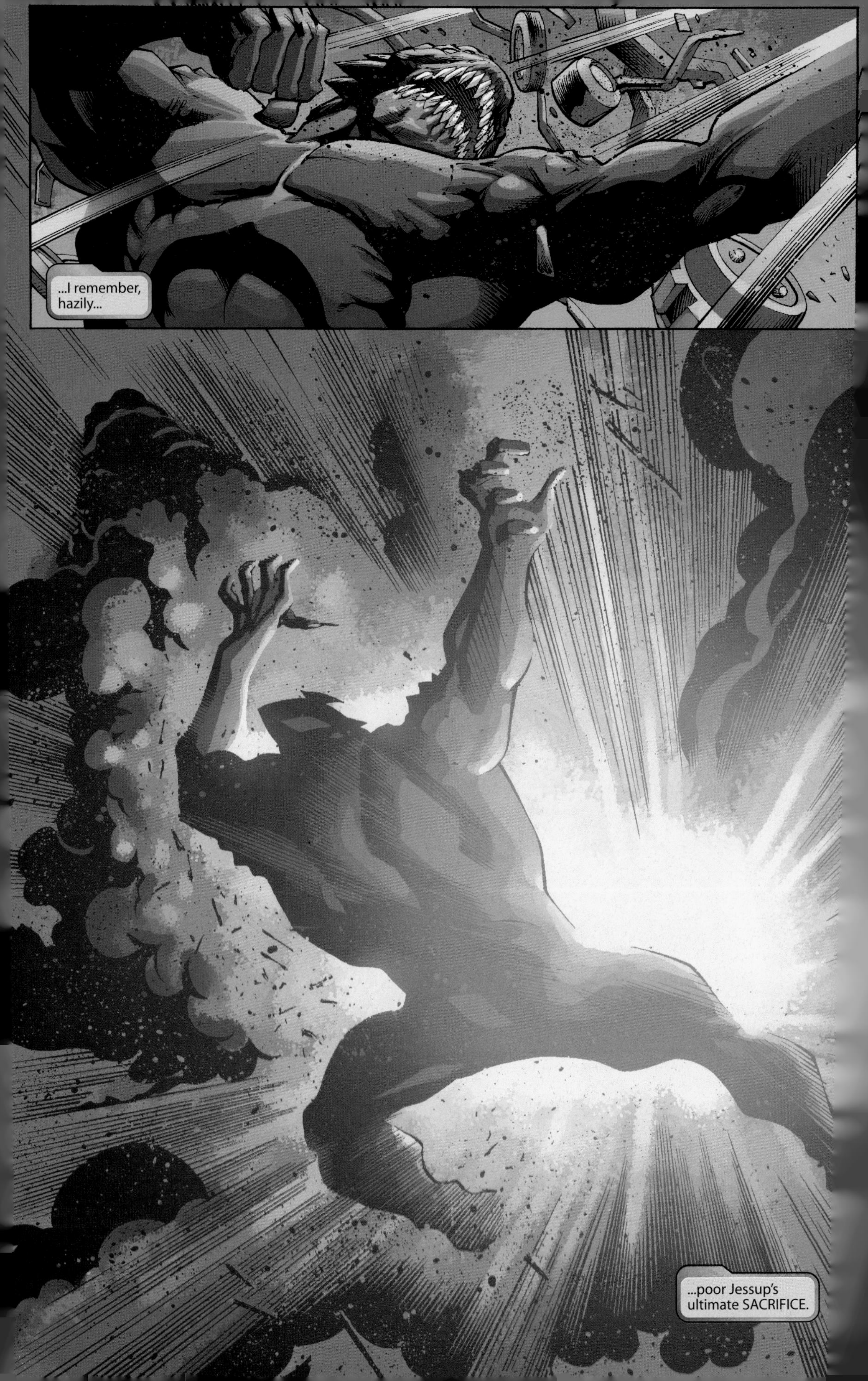
...I remember, hazily...
...poor Jessup's ultimate SACRIFICE.

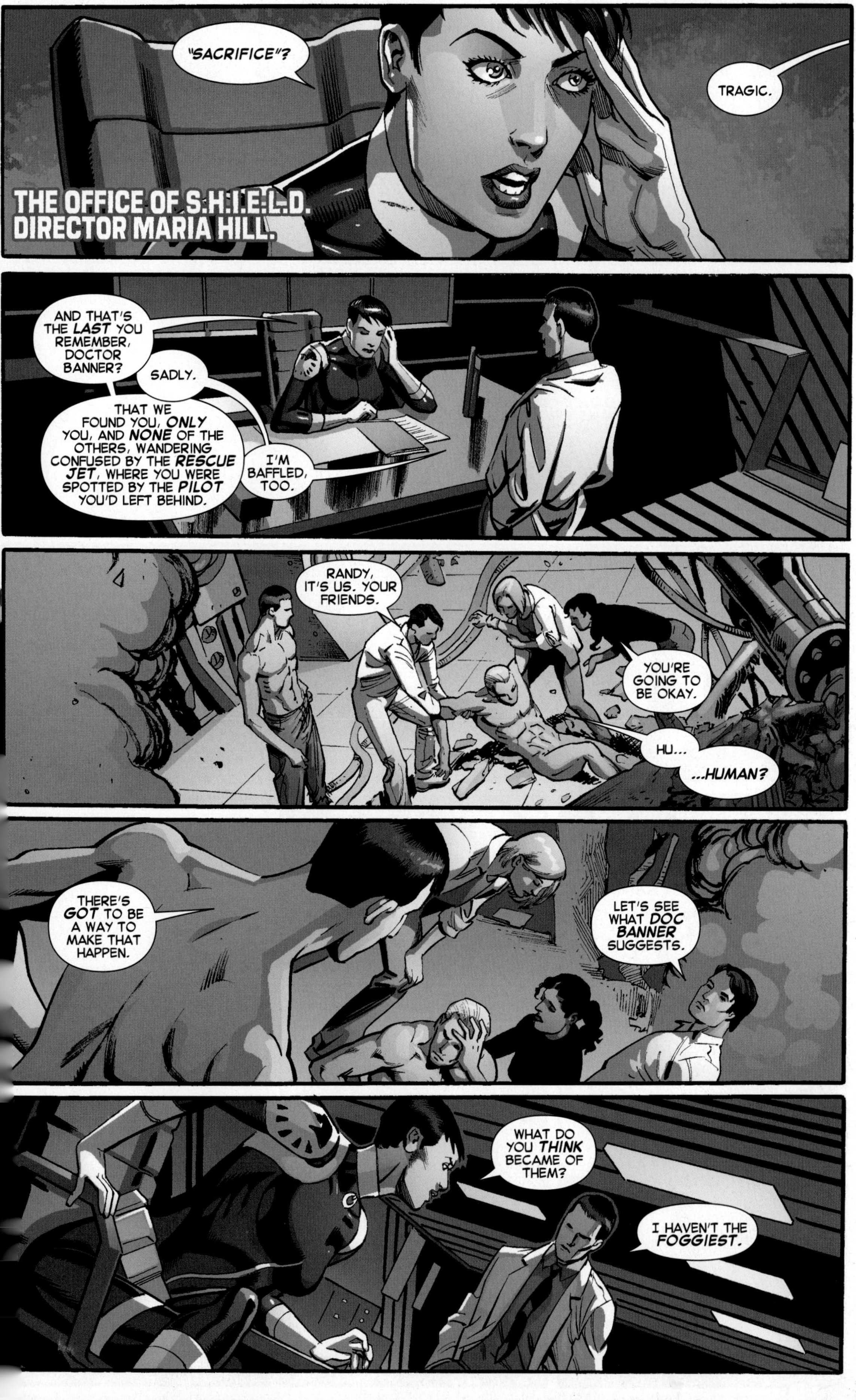
"SACRIFICE"?
TRAGIC.
THE OFFICE OF S.H.I.E.L.D. DIRECTOR MARIA HILL.
AND THAT'S THE LAST YOU REMEMBER, DOCTOR BANNER?
SADLY.
THAT WE FOUND YOU, ONLY YOU, AND NONE OF THE OTHERS, WANDERING CONFUSED BY THE RESCUE JET, WHERE YOU WERE SPOTTED BY THE PILOT YOU'D LEFT BEHIND.
I'M BAFFLED, TOO.
RANDY, IT'S US. YOUR FRIENDS.
YOU'RE GOING TO BE OKAY.
HU...
...HUMAN?
THERE'S GOT TO BE A WAY TO MAKE THAT HAPPEN.
LET'S SEE WHAT DOC BANNER SUGGESTS.
WHAT DO YOU THINK BECAME OF THEM?
I HAVEN'T THE FOGGIEST.

I DON'T HAVE A SUGGESTION. I HAVE AN *ORDER.*

LEUCENSTERN, YOU'RE SLY. YOU CRACKED THE TELEPORTATION CODE INTO THIS PLACE. CAN YOU REBUILD IT *SAFELY* SO THAT ONLY *YOU THREE* CAN ENTER AND LEAVE?

CAKE.

THEN YOU *DON'T* COME BACK. *NONE* OF YOU DO.

IF YOU'VE LEARNED *ANYTHING* FROM ME, IT'S HOW TO COPE WITH AND WRANGLE A MAN-MONSTER. YOU THREE NOW KNOW HOW TO *TAP-DANCE* ON EGGSHELLS WHILE SIMULTANEOUSLY ACCOMPLISHING *BRILLIANCE.*

JESSUP *NEEDS* THAT. HE NEEDS *YOU.*

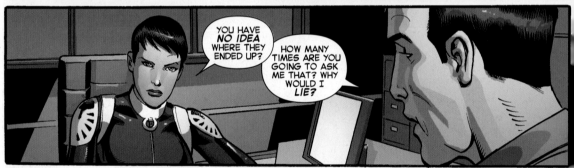

YOU HAVE *NO IDEA* WHERE THEY ENDED UP?

HOW MANY TIMES ARE YOU GOING TO ASK ME THAT? WHY WOULD I *LIE?*

IF YOU GO BACK TO S.H.I.E.L.D., MARIA HILL WILL *RUIN* YOU FOR DISREGARDING QUARANTINE. SO YOU STAY *HERE.* WITH *JESSUP.* HELP *HIM.*

BUT *YOU* NEED US.

GUYS...

...I'LL BE *FINE.*

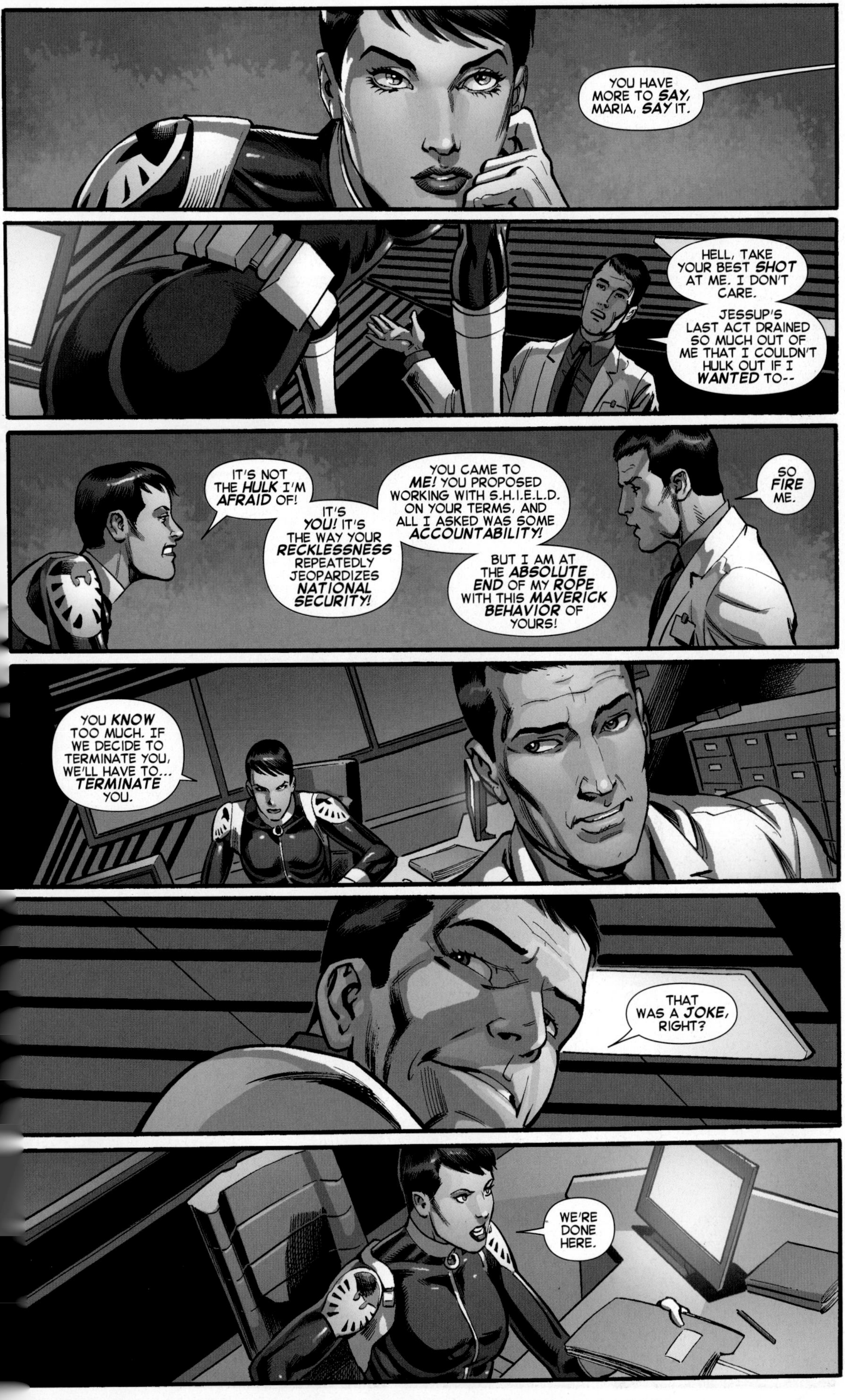
YOU HAVE MORE TO SAY, MARIA, SAY IT.
HELL, TAKE YOUR BEST SHOT AT ME. I DON'T CARE.
JESSUP'S LAST ACT DRAINED SO MUCH OUT OF ME THAT I COULDN'T HULK OUT IF I WANTED TO--
IT'S NOT THE HULK I'M AFRAID OF!
IT'S YOU! IT'S THE WAY YOUR RECKLESSNESS REPEATEDLY JEOPARDIZES NATIONAL SECURITY!
YOU CAME TO ME! YOU PROPOSED WORKING WITH S.H.I.E.L.D. ON YOUR TERMS, AND ALL I ASKED WAS SOME ACCOUNTABILITY!
BUT I AM AT THE ABSOLUTE END OF MY ROPE WITH THIS MAVERICK BEHAVIOR OF YOURS!
SO FIRE ME.
YOU KNOW TOO MUCH. IF WE DECIDE TO TERMINATE YOU, WE'LL HAVE TO... TERMINATE YOU.
THAT WAS A JOKE, RIGHT?
WE'RE DONE HERE.

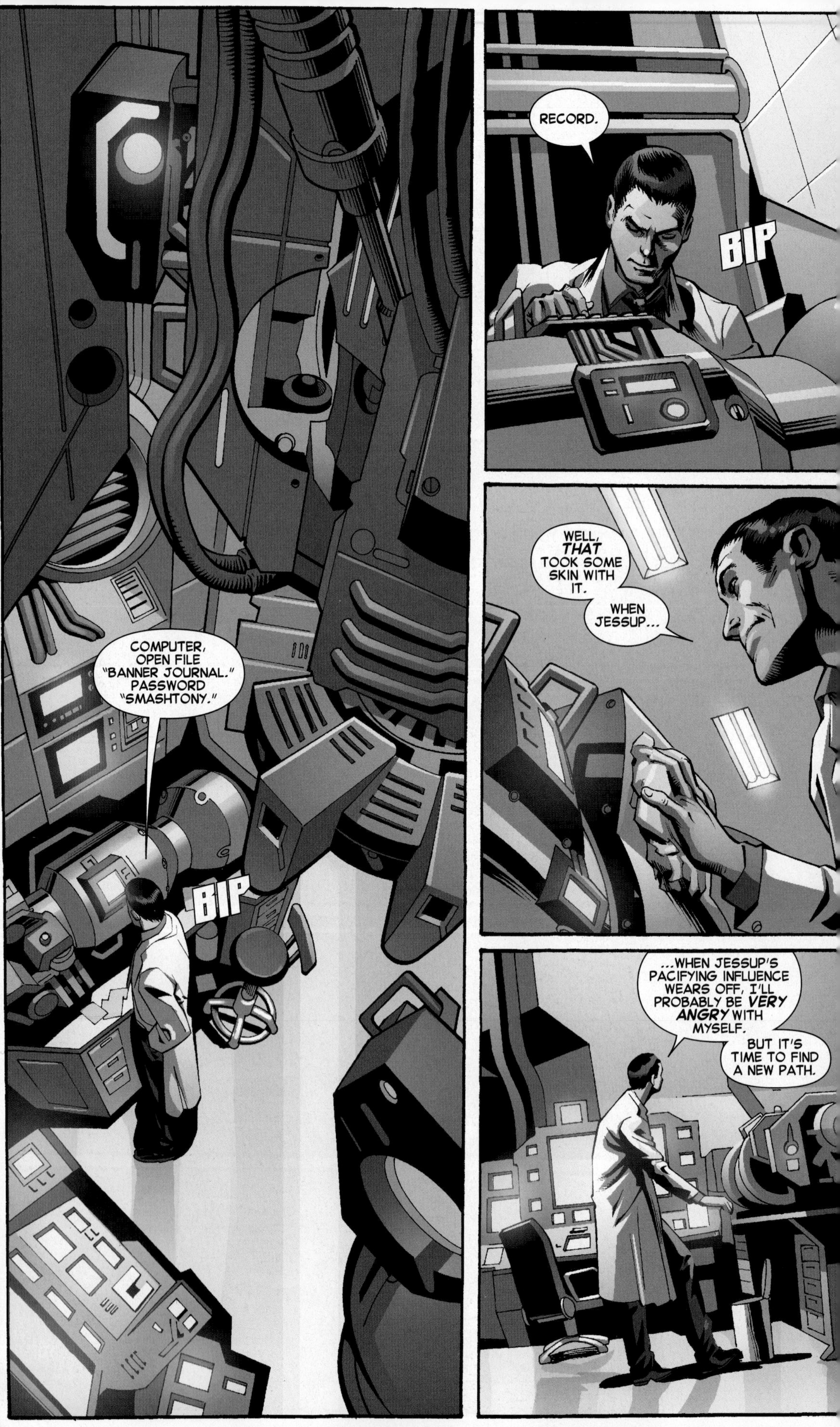
COMPUTER, OPEN FILE "BANNER JOURNAL." PASSWORD "SMASHTONY."
BIP
RECORD.
BIP
WELL, THAT TOOK SOME SKIN WITH IT.
WHEN JESSUP...
...WHEN JESSUP'S PACIFYING INFLUENCE WEARS OFF, I'LL PROBABLY BE VERY ANGRY WITH MYSELF.
BUT IT'S TIME TO FIND A NEW PATH.

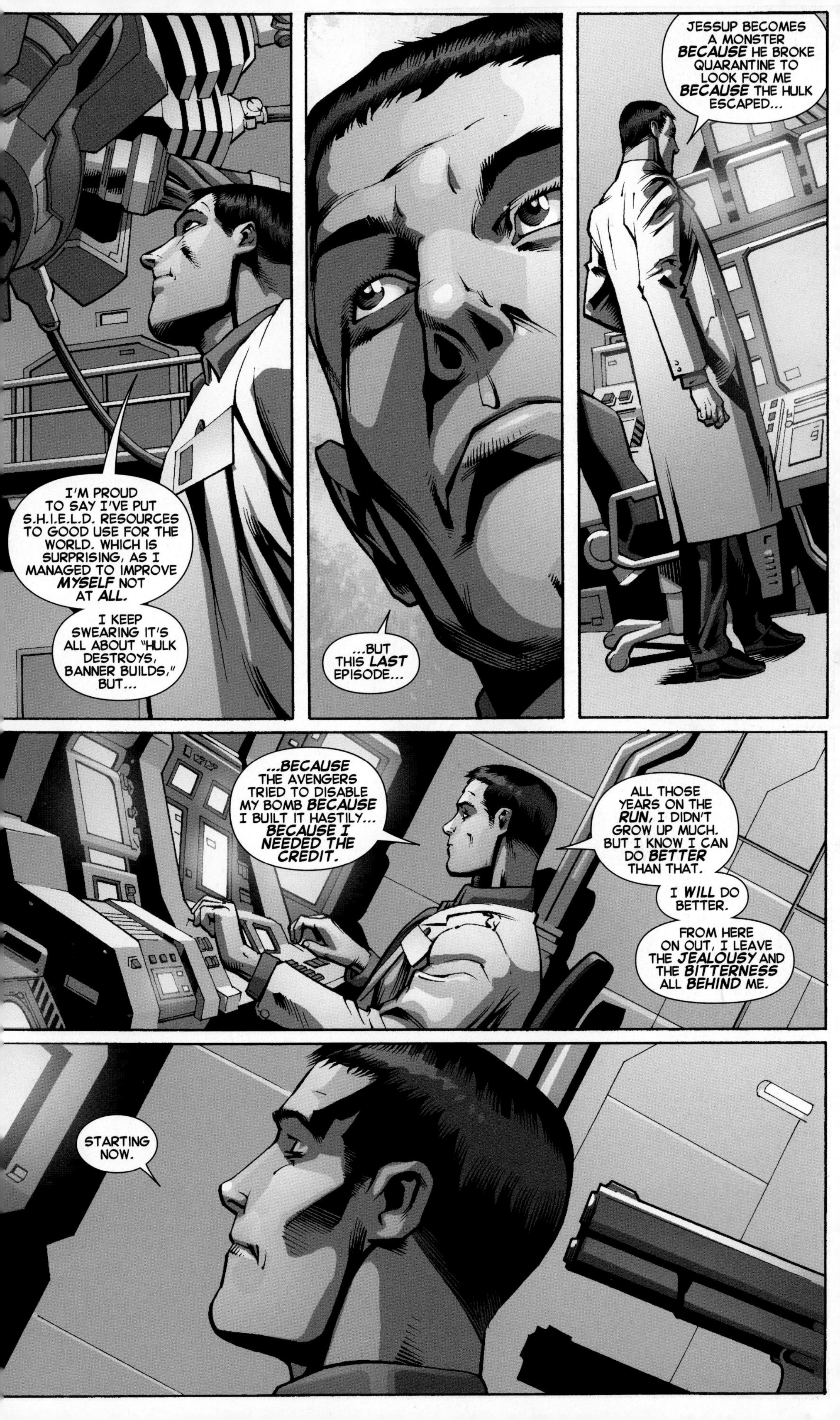
I'M PROUD TO SAY I'VE PUT S.H.I.E.L.D. RESOURCES TO GOOD USE FOR THE WORLD. WHICH IS SURPRISING, AS I MANAGED TO IMPROVE *MYSELF* NOT AT *ALL.*
I KEEP SWEARING IT'S ALL ABOUT "HULK DESTROYS, BANNER BUILDS," BUT...
...BUT THIS *LAST* EPISODE...
JESSUP BECOMES A MONSTER *BECAUSE* HE BROKE QUARANTINE TO LOOK FOR ME *BECAUSE* THE HULK ESCAPED...
...BECAUSE THE AVENGERS TRIED TO DISABLE MY BOMB *BECAUSE* I BUILT IT HASTILY... *BECAUSE I NEEDED THE CREDIT.*
ALL THOSE YEARS ON THE *RUN,* I DIDN'T GROW UP MUCH. BUT I KNOW I CAN DO *BETTER* THAN THAT.
I *WILL* DO BETTER.
FROM HERE ON OUT, I LEAVE THE *JEALOUSY* AND THE *BITTERNESS* ALL *BEHIND* ME.
STARTING NOW.

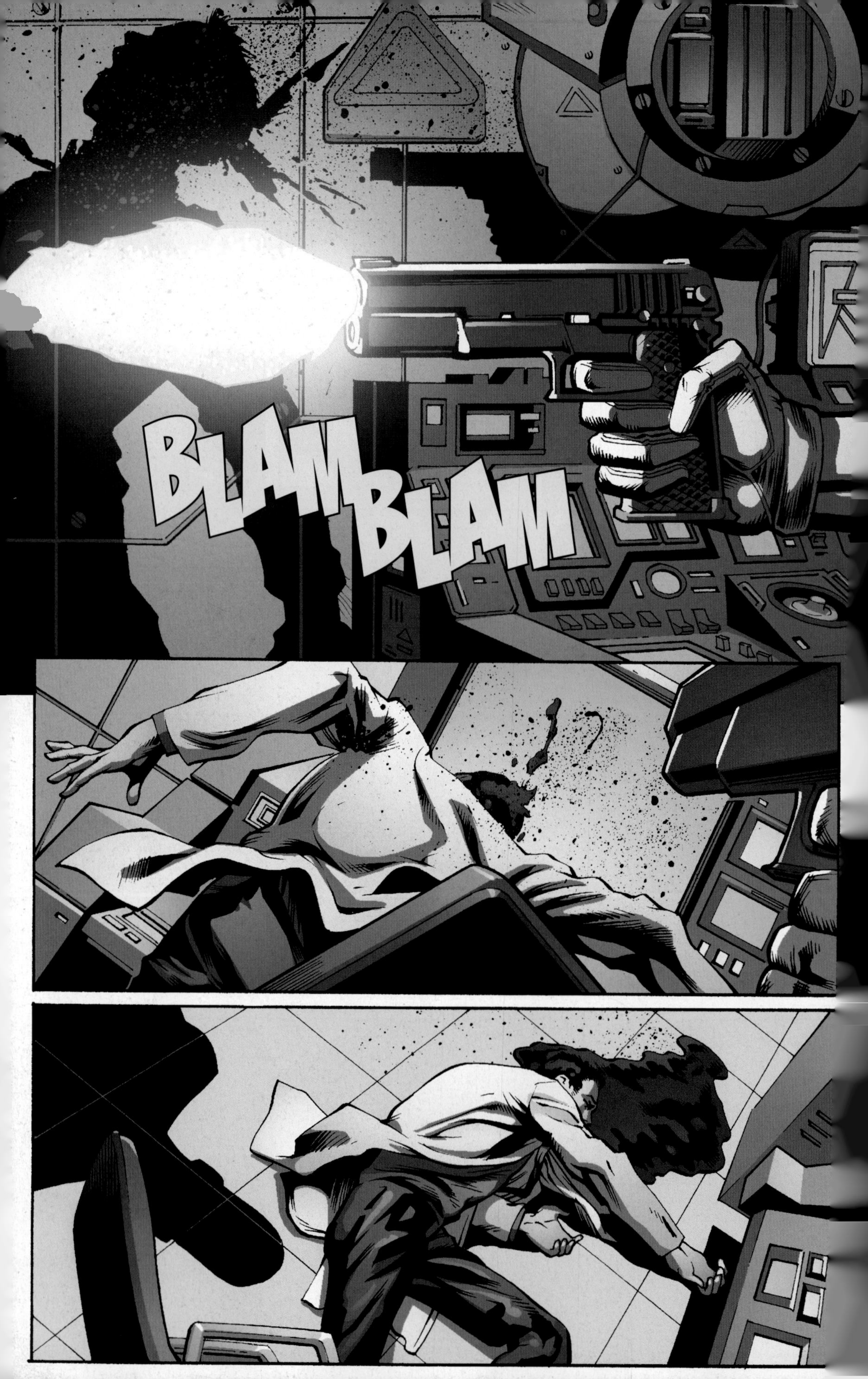
BLAM BLAM

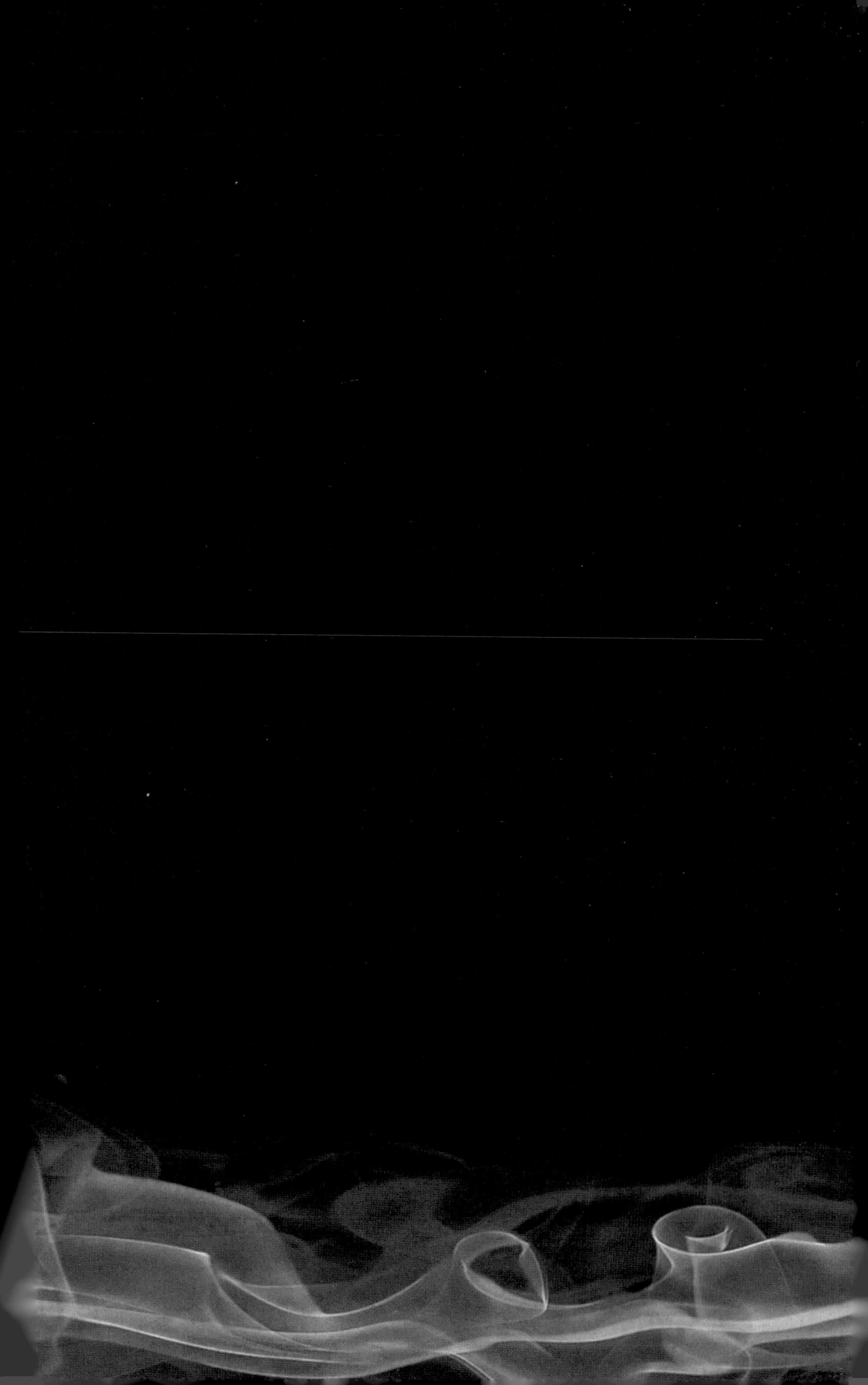

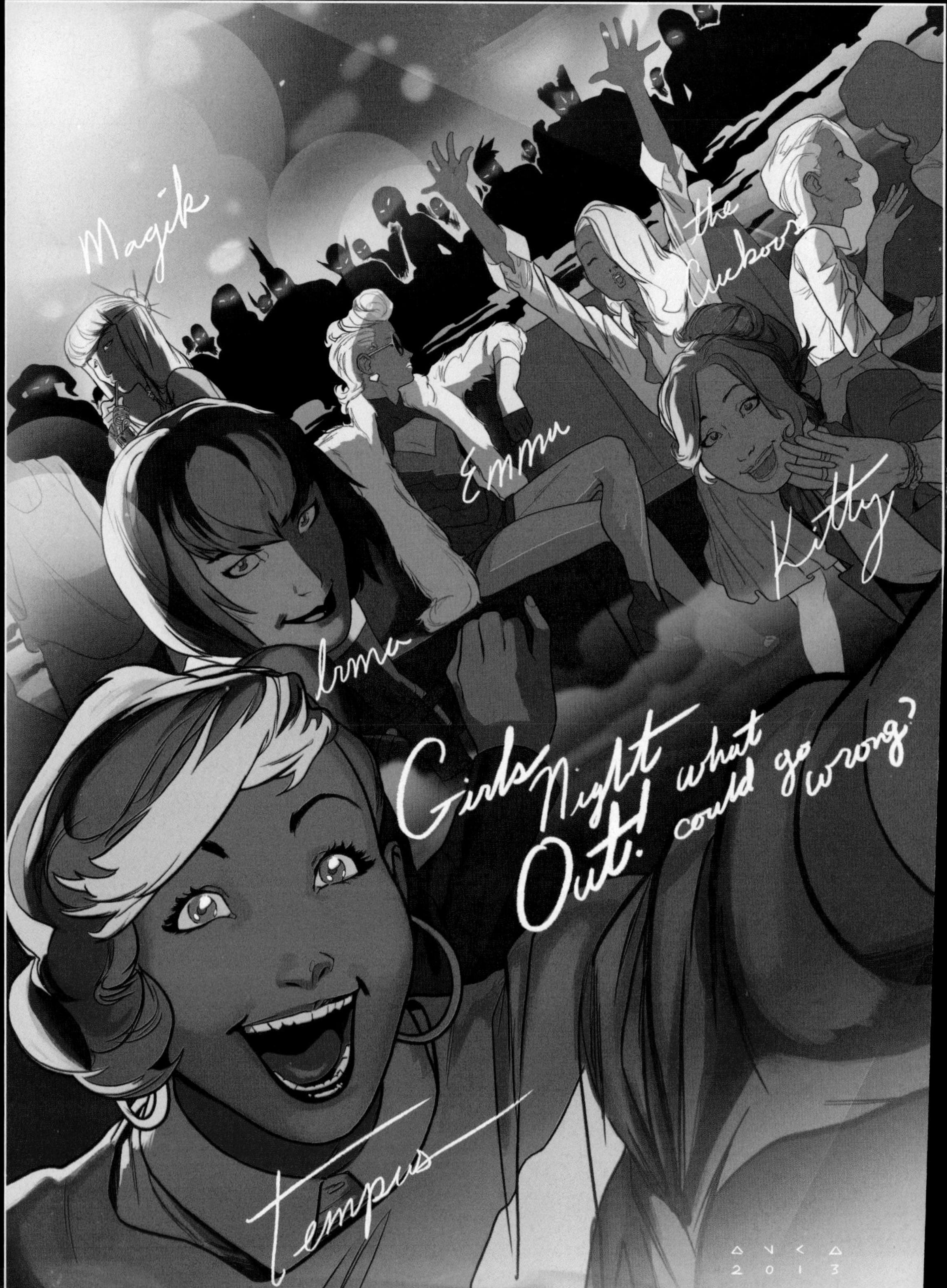
Magik
the Cuckoos
Emma
Kitty
Irma
Girls Night Out! what could go wrong?
Tempus
ANKA 2013

UNCANNY X-MEN #15

UNCANNY X-MEN

Born with genetic mutations that give them abilities beyond those of normal humans, mutants are the next stage in evolution.

As such, they are feared and hated by humanity. But a group of mutants known as the X-Men fight for peaceful coexistence between mutants and humankind.

But not all mutants see peaceful coexistence as a reality.

CYCLOPS IS THE FACE OF THE MUTANT REVOLUTION. HE OPENED THE NEW XAVIER SCHOOL IN WHAT USED TO BE THE WEAPON X FACILITY IN ORDER TO TRAIN NEW MUTANTS TO DEFEND THEMSELVES. THE SCHOOL HAS GROWN RECENTLY, AS KITTY PRYDE AND THE ALL-NEW X-MEN CAME FROM THE JEAN GREY SCHOOL.

MEANWHILE, AS A CONSEQUENCE OF THANOS'S INVASION OF EARTH, THE INHUMAN CITY OF ATTILAN WAS DESTROYED, TRIGGERING A BOMB SPREADING TERRIGEN, THE CHEMICAL THAT ACTIVATES THE SUPER POWERS IN INHUMANS, INTO THE ATMOSPHERE.

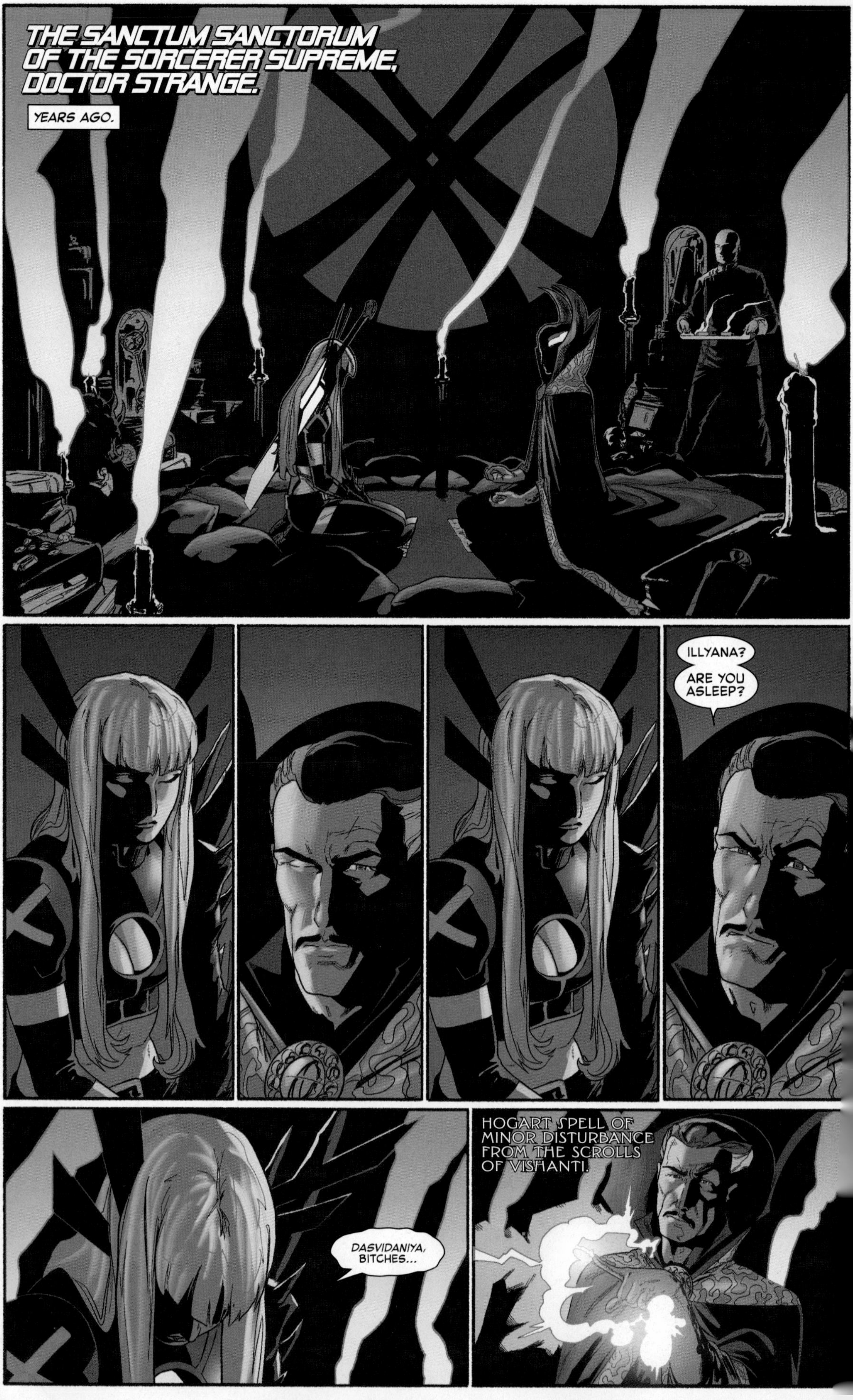
THE SANCTUM SANCTORUM OF THE SORCERER SUPREME, DOCTOR STRANGE.
YEARS AGO.
ILLYANA?
ARE YOU ASLEEP?
DASVIDANIYA, BITCHES...
HOGART SPELL OF MINOR DISTURBANCE FROM THE SCROLLS OF VISHANTI.

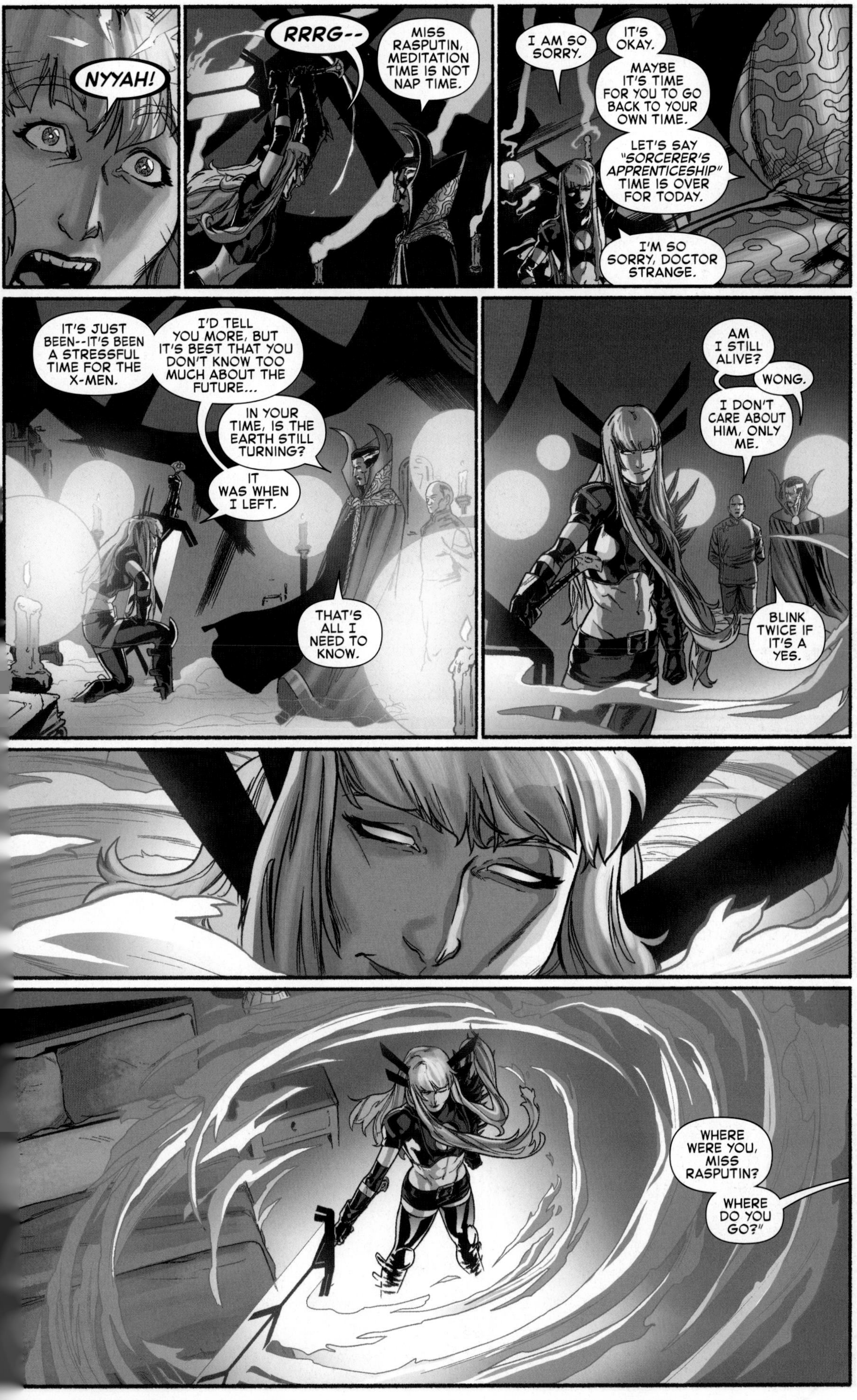
NYYAH!
RRRG--
MISS RASPUTIN, MEDITATION TIME IS NOT NAP TIME.
I AM SO SORRY.
IT'S OKAY.
MAYBE IT'S TIME FOR YOU TO GO BACK TO YOUR OWN TIME.
LET'S SAY "SORCERER'S APPRENTICESHIP" TIME IS OVER FOR TODAY.
I'M SO SORRY, DOCTOR STRANGE.
IT'S JUST BEEN--IT'S BEEN A STRESSFUL TIME FOR THE X-MEN.
I'D TELL YOU MORE, BUT IT'S BEST THAT YOU DON'T KNOW TOO MUCH ABOUT THE FUTURE...
IN YOUR TIME, IS THE EARTH STILL TURNING?
IT WAS WHEN I LEFT.
THAT'S ALL I NEED TO KNOW.
AM I STILL ALIVE?
WONG.
I DON'T CARE ABOUT HIM, ONLY ME.
BLINK TWICE IF IT'S A YES.
WHERE WERE YOU, MISS RASPUTIN?
WHERE DO YOU GO?"

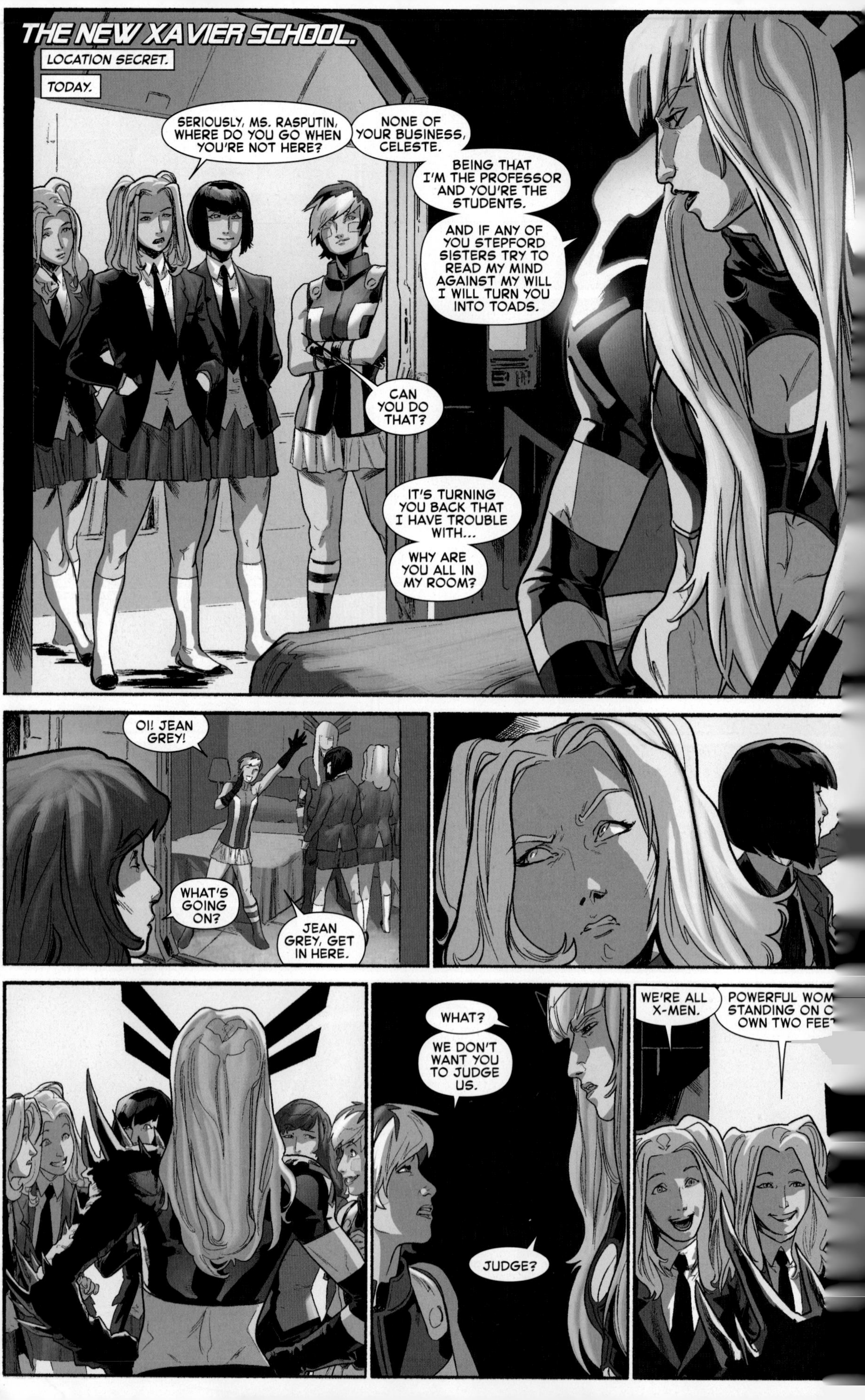
THE NEW XAVIER SCHOOL.
LOCATION SECRET.
TODAY.
SERIOUSLY, MS. RASPUTIN, WHERE DO YOU GO WHEN YOU'RE NOT HERE?
NONE OF YOUR BUSINESS, CELESTE.
BEING THAT I'M THE PROFESSOR AND YOU'RE THE STUDENTS.
AND IF ANY OF YOU STEPFORD SISTERS TRY TO READ MY MIND AGAINST MY WILL I WILL TURN YOU INTO TOADS.
CAN YOU DO THAT?
IT'S TURNING YOU BACK THAT I HAVE TROUBLE WITH...
WHY ARE YOU ALL IN MY ROOM?
OI! JEAN GREY!
WHAT'S GOING ON?
JEAN GREY, GET IN HERE.
WHAT?
WE DON'T WANT YOU TO JUDGE US.
JUDGE?
WE'RE ALL X-MEN.

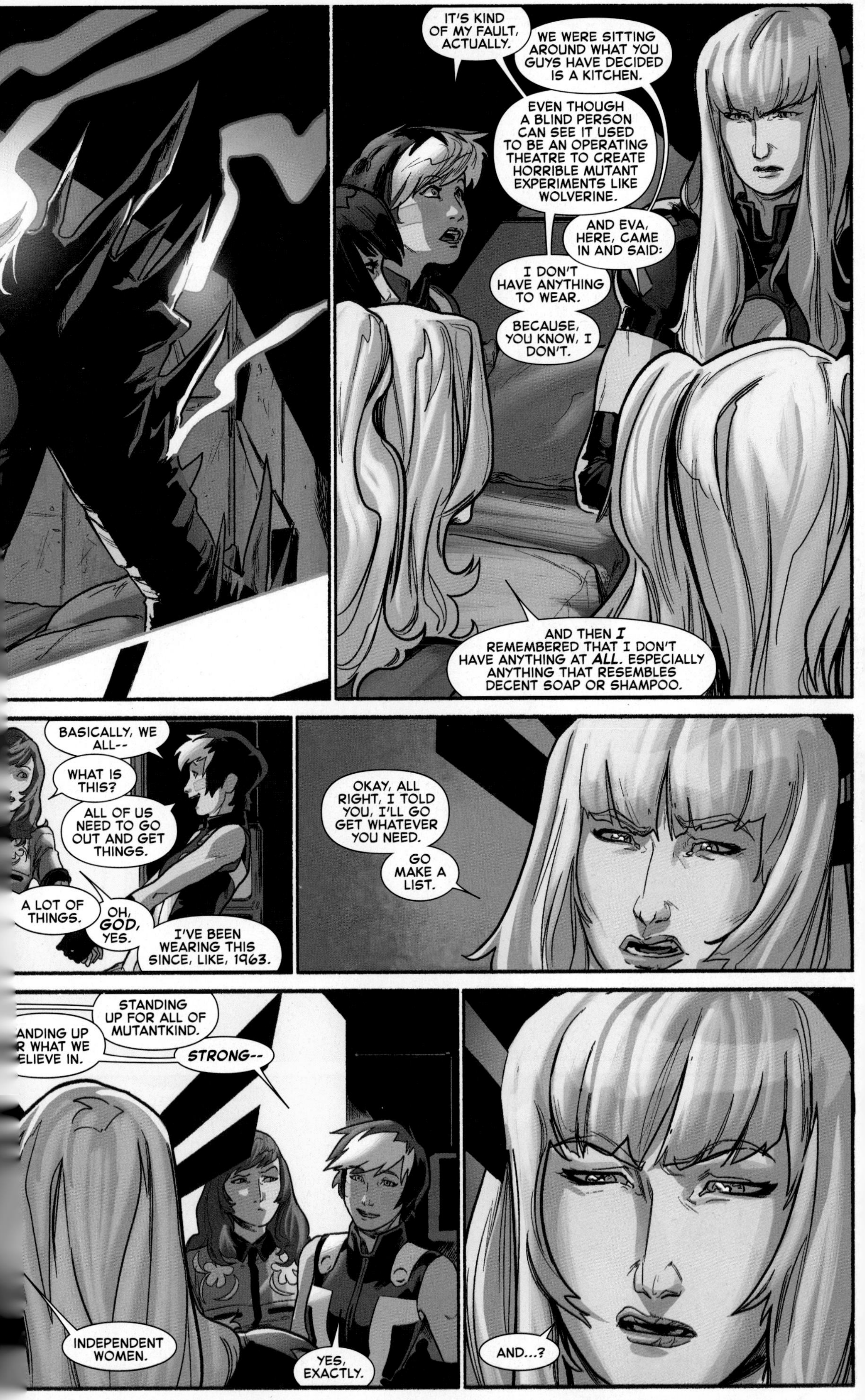
IT'S KIND OF MY FAULT, ACTUALLY.
WE WERE SITTING AROUND WHAT YOU GUYS HAVE DECIDED IS A KITCHEN.
EVEN THOUGH A BLIND PERSON CAN SEE IT USED TO BE AN OPERATING THEATRE TO CREATE HORRIBLE MUTANT EXPERIMENTS LIKE WOLVERINE.
AND EVA, HERE, CAME IN AND SAID:
I DON'T HAVE ANYTHING TO WEAR.
BECAUSE, YOU KNOW, I DON'T.
AND THEN *I* REMEMBERED THAT I DON'T HAVE ANYTHING AT *ALL*. ESPECIALLY ANYTHING THAT RESEMBLES DECENT SOAP OR SHAMPOO.
BASICALLY, WE ALL--
WHAT IS THIS?
ALL OF US NEED TO GO OUT AND GET THINGS.
A LOT OF THINGS.
OH, *GOD*, YES.
I'VE BEEN WEARING THIS SINCE, LIKE, 1963.
OKAY, ALL RIGHT, I TOLD YOU, I'LL GO GET WHATEVER YOU NEED.
GO MAKE A LIST.
STANDING UP FOR ALL OF MUTANTKIND.
ANDING UP R WHAT WE ELIEVE IN.
STRONG--
INDEPENDENT WOMEN.
YES, EXACTLY.
AND...?

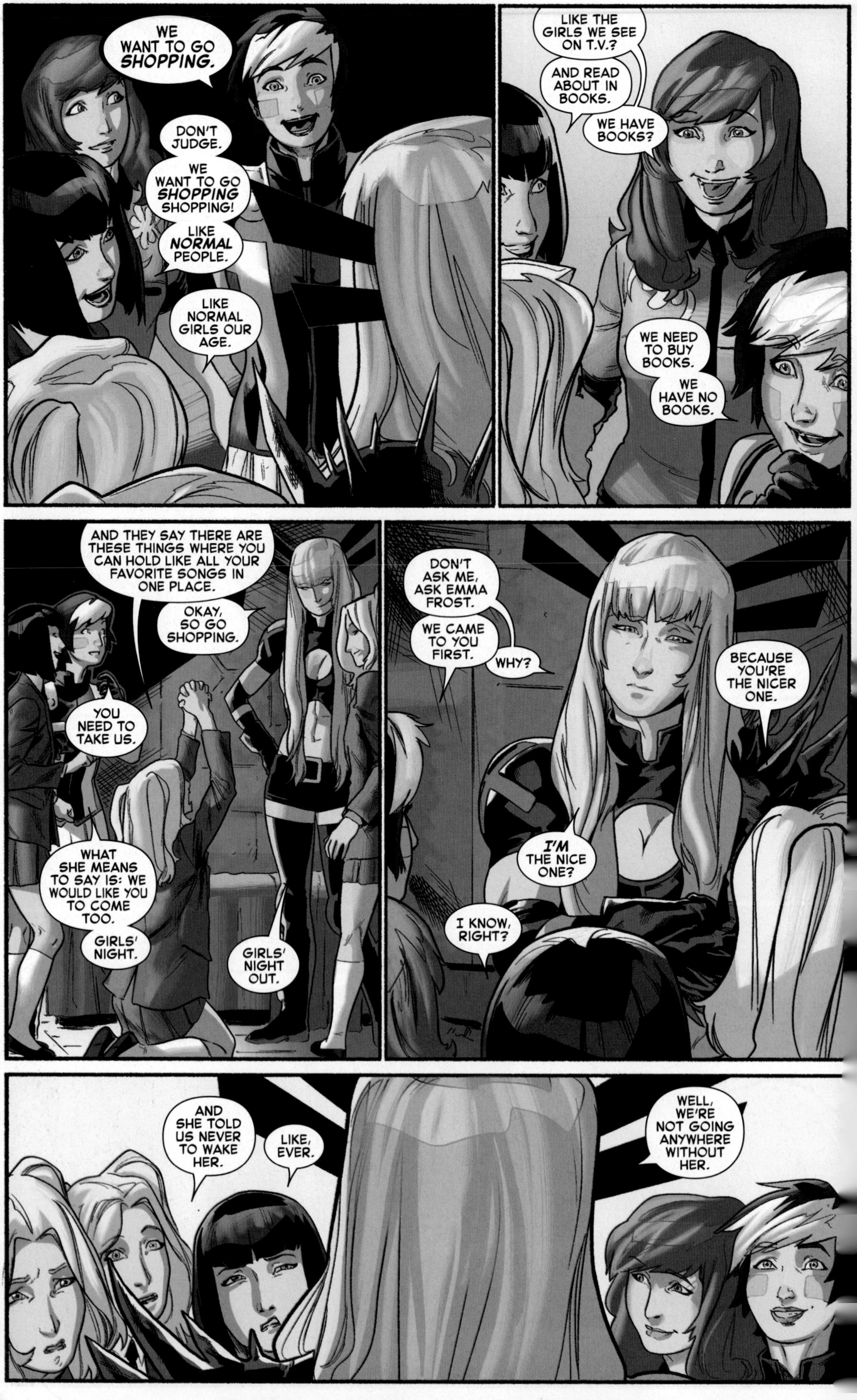
WE WANT TO GO SHOPPING.
DON'T JUDGE.
WE WANT TO GO SHOPPING SHOPPING!
LIKE NORMAL PEOPLE.
LIKE NORMAL GIRLS OUR AGE.
LIKE THE GIRLS WE SEE ON T.V.?
AND READ ABOUT IN BOOKS.
WE HAVE BOOKS?
WE NEED TO BUY BOOKS.
WE HAVE NO BOOKS.
AND THEY SAY THERE ARE THESE THINGS WHERE YOU CAN HOLD LIKE ALL YOUR FAVORITE SONGS IN ONE PLACE.
OKAY, SO GO SHOPPING.
YOU NEED TO TAKE US.
WHAT SHE MEANS TO SAY IS: WE WOULD LIKE YOU TO COME TOO.
GIRLS' NIGHT.
GIRLS' NIGHT OUT.
DON'T ASK ME, ASK EMMA FROST.
WE CAME TO YOU FIRST.
WHY?
BECAUSE YOU'RE THE NICER ONE.
I'M THE NICE ONE?
I KNOW, RIGHT?
AND SHE TOLD US NEVER TO WAKE HER.
LIKE, EVER.
WELL, WE'RE NOT GOING ANYWHERE WITHOUT HER.

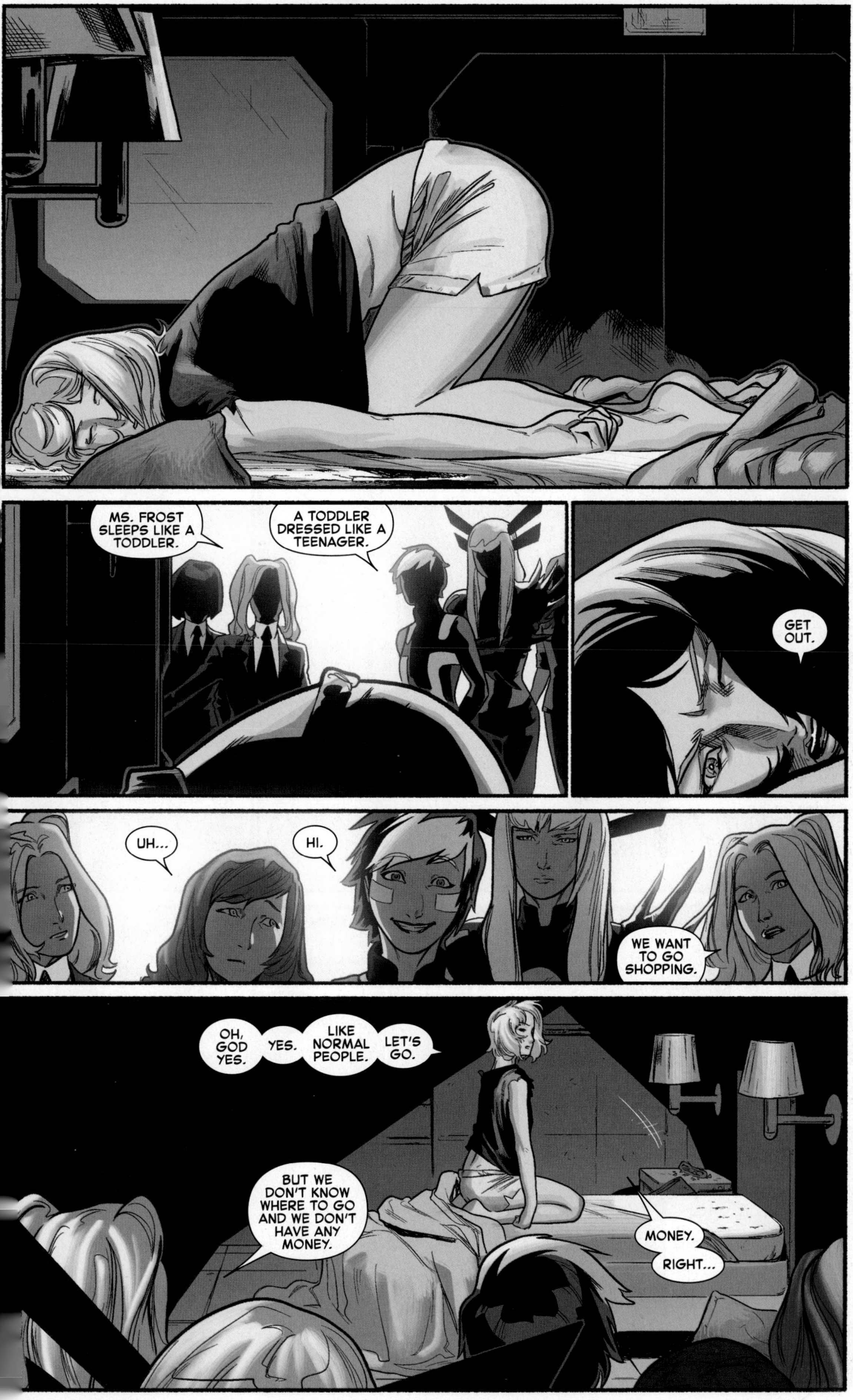
MS. FROST SLEEPS LIKE A TODDLER.
A TODDLER DRESSED LIKE A TEENAGER.
GET OUT.
UH...
HI.
WE WANT TO GO SHOPPING.
OH, GOD YES.
YES.
LIKE NORMAL PEOPLE.
LET'S GO.
BUT WE DON'T KNOW WHERE TO GO AND WE DON'T HAVE ANY MONEY.
MONEY.
RIGHT...

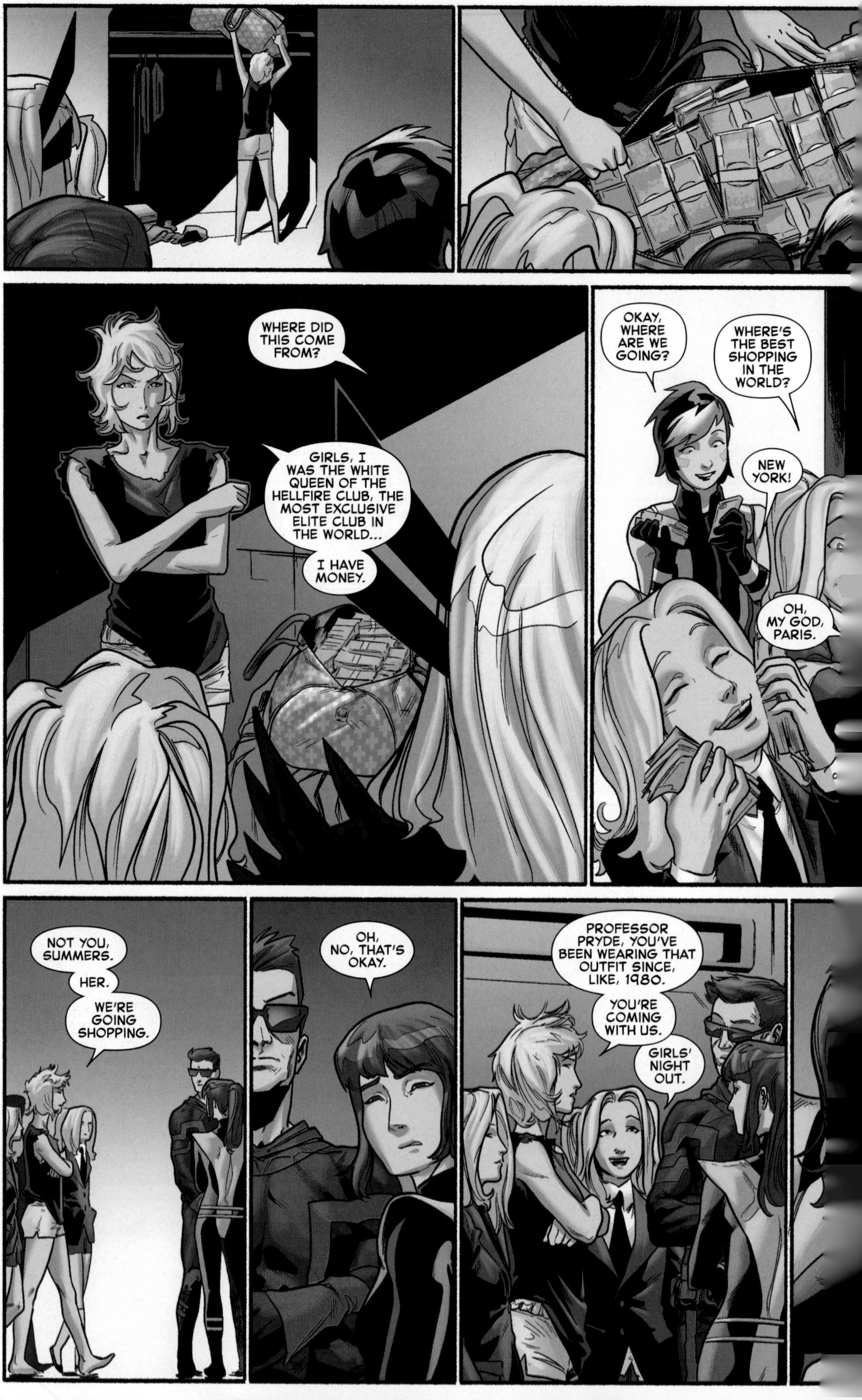
WHERE DID THIS COME FROM?
GIRLS, I WAS THE WHITE QUEEN OF THE HELLFIRE CLUB, THE MOST EXCLUSIVE ELITE CLUB IN THE WORLD...
I HAVE MONEY.
OKAY, WHERE ARE WE GOING?
WHERE'S THE BEST SHOPPING IN THE WORLD?
NEW YORK!
OH, MY GOD, PARIS.
NOT YOU, SUMMERS.
HER.
WE'RE GOING SHOPPING.
OH, NO, THAT'S OKAY.
PROFESSOR PRYDE, YOU'VE BEEN WEARING THAT OUTFIT SINCE, LIKE, 1980.
YOU'RE COMING WITH US.
GIRLS' NIGHT OUT.

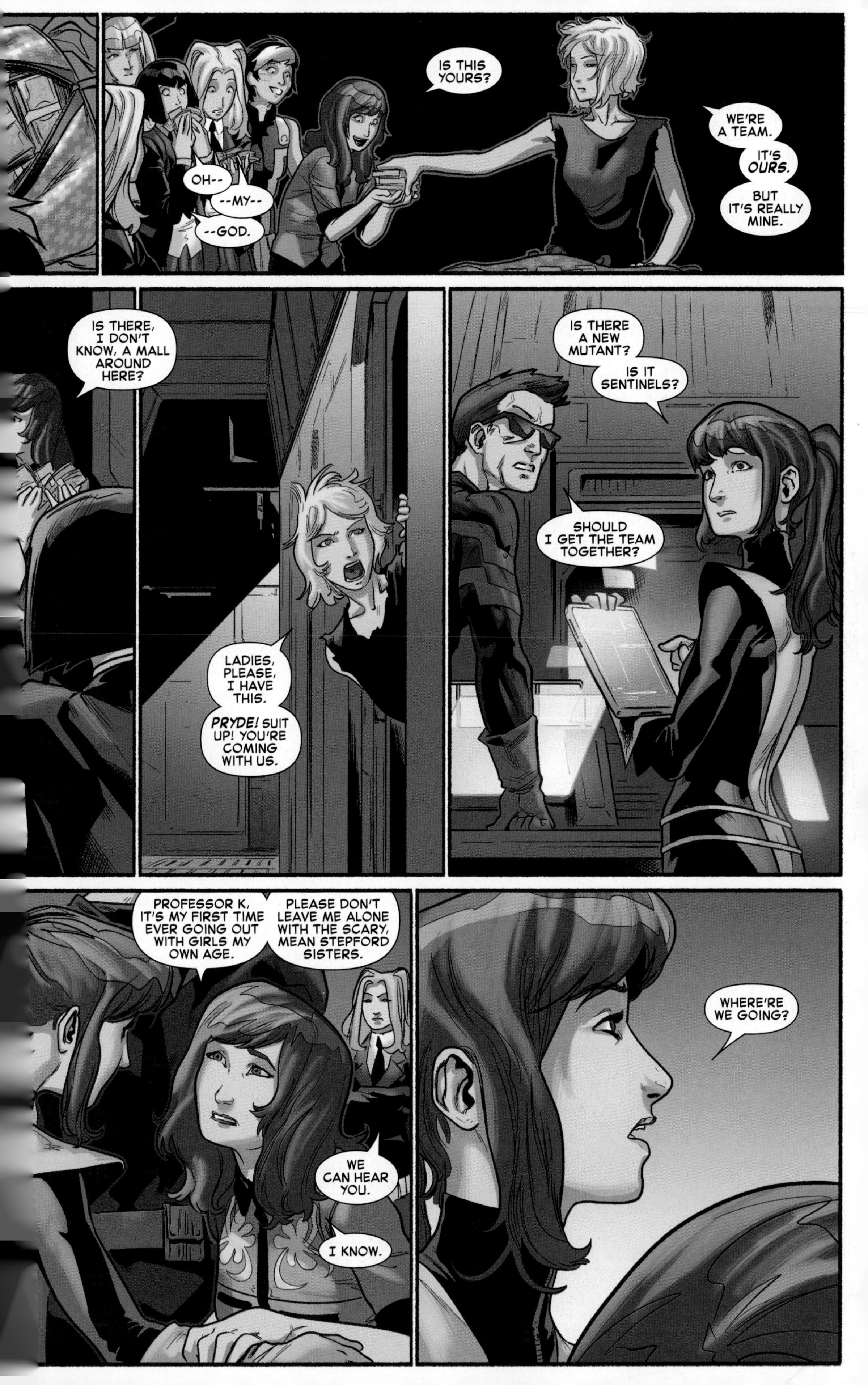

IS THIS YOURS?
OH--
--MY--
--GOD.
WE'RE A TEAM.
IT'S *OURS.*
BUT IT'S REALLY MINE.
IS THERE, I DON'T KNOW, A MALL AROUND HERE?
LADIES, PLEASE, I HAVE THIS.
PRYDE! SUIT UP! YOU'RE COMING WITH US.
IS THERE A NEW MUTANT?
IS IT SENTINELS?
SHOULD I GET THE TEAM TOGETHER?
PROFESSOR K, IT'S MY FIRST TIME EVER GOING OUT WITH GIRLS MY OWN AGE.
PLEASE DON'T LEAVE ME ALONE WITH THE SCARY, MEAN STEPFORD SISTERS.
WE CAN HEAR YOU.
I KNOW.
WHERE'RE WE GOING?

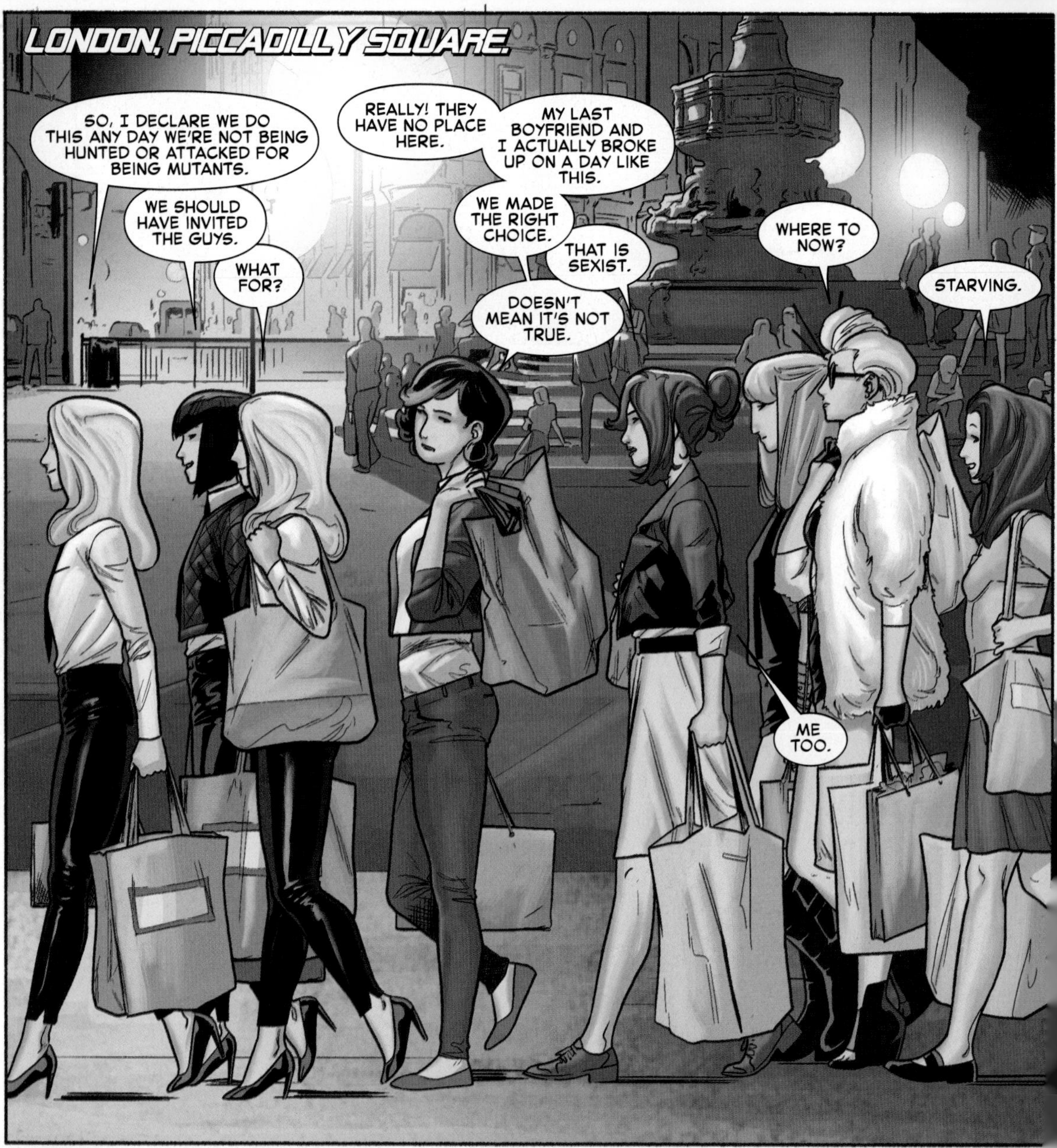
LONDON, PICCADILLY SQUARE.
SO, I DECLARE WE DO THIS ANY DAY WE'RE NOT BEING HUNTED OR ATTACKED FOR BEING MUTANTS.
WE SHOULD HAVE INVITED THE GUYS.
WHAT FOR?
REALLY! THEY HAVE NO PLACE HERE.
MY LAST BOYFRIEND AND I ACTUALLY BROKE UP ON A DAY LIKE THIS.
WE MADE THE RIGHT CHOICE.
THAT IS SEXIST.
DOESN'T MEAN IT'S NOT TRUE.
WHERE TO NOW?
STARVING.
ME TOO.

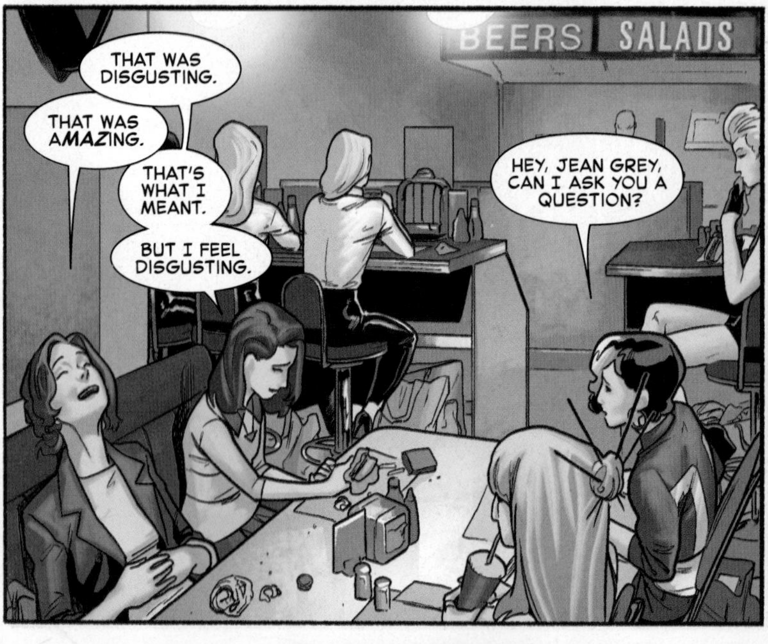
BEERS SALADS
THAT WAS DISGUSTING.
THAT WAS AMAZING.
THAT'S WHAT I MEANT.
BUT I FEEL DISGUSTING.
HEY, JEAN GREY, CAN I ASK YOU A QUESTION?

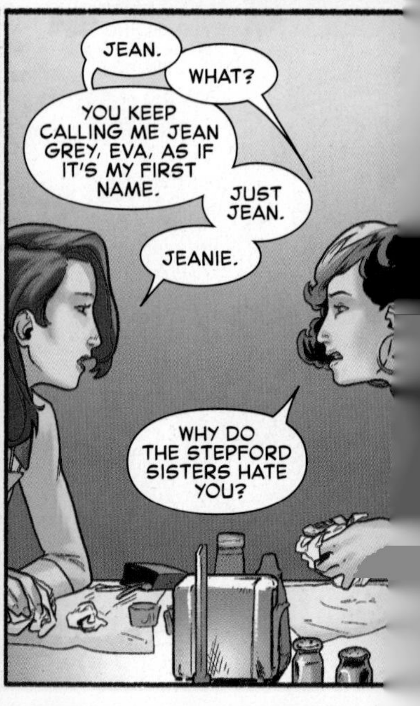
JEAN.
WHAT?
YOU KEEP CALLING ME JEAN GREY, EVA, AS IF IT'S MY FIRST NAME.
JUST JEAN.
JEANIE.
WHY DO THE STEPFORD SISTERS HATE YOU?

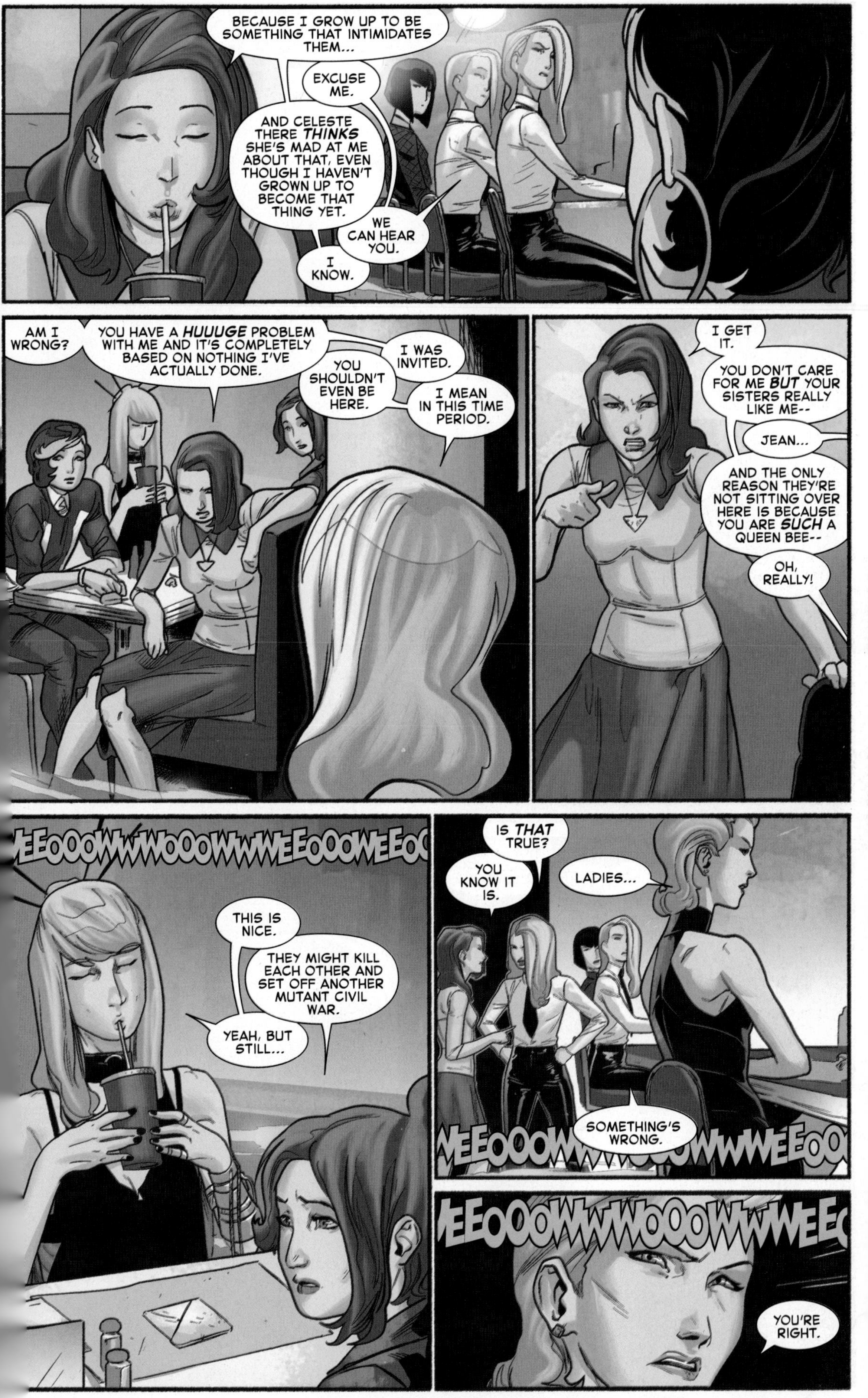
BECAUSE I GROW UP TO BE SOMETHING THAT INTIMIDATES THEM...
EXCUSE ME.
AND CELESTE THERE THINKS SHE'S MAD AT ME ABOUT THAT, EVEN THOUGH I HAVEN'T GROWN UP TO BECOME THAT THING YET.
WE CAN HEAR YOU.
I KNOW.
AM I WRONG?
YOU HAVE A HUUUGE PROBLEM WITH ME AND IT'S COMPLETELY BASED ON NOTHING I'VE ACTUALLY DONE.
I WAS INVITED.
YOU SHOULDN'T EVEN BE HERE.
I MEAN IN THIS TIME PERIOD.
I GET IT.
YOU DON'T CARE FOR ME BUT YOUR SISTERS REALLY LIKE ME--
JEAN...
AND THE ONLY REASON THEY'RE NOT SITTING OVER HERE IS BECAUSE YOU ARE SUCH A QUEEN BEE--
OH, REALLY!
WEEOOOWWWOOOWWWEEOOOWEEO
THIS IS NICE.
THEY MIGHT KILL EACH OTHER AND SET OFF ANOTHER MUTANT CIVIL WAR.
YEAH, BUT STILL...
IS THAT TRUE?
YOU KNOW IT IS.
LADIES...
SOMETHING'S WRONG.
WEEOOOWWWOOOWWWEEO
WEEOOOWWWOOOWWWEE
YOU'RE RIGHT.

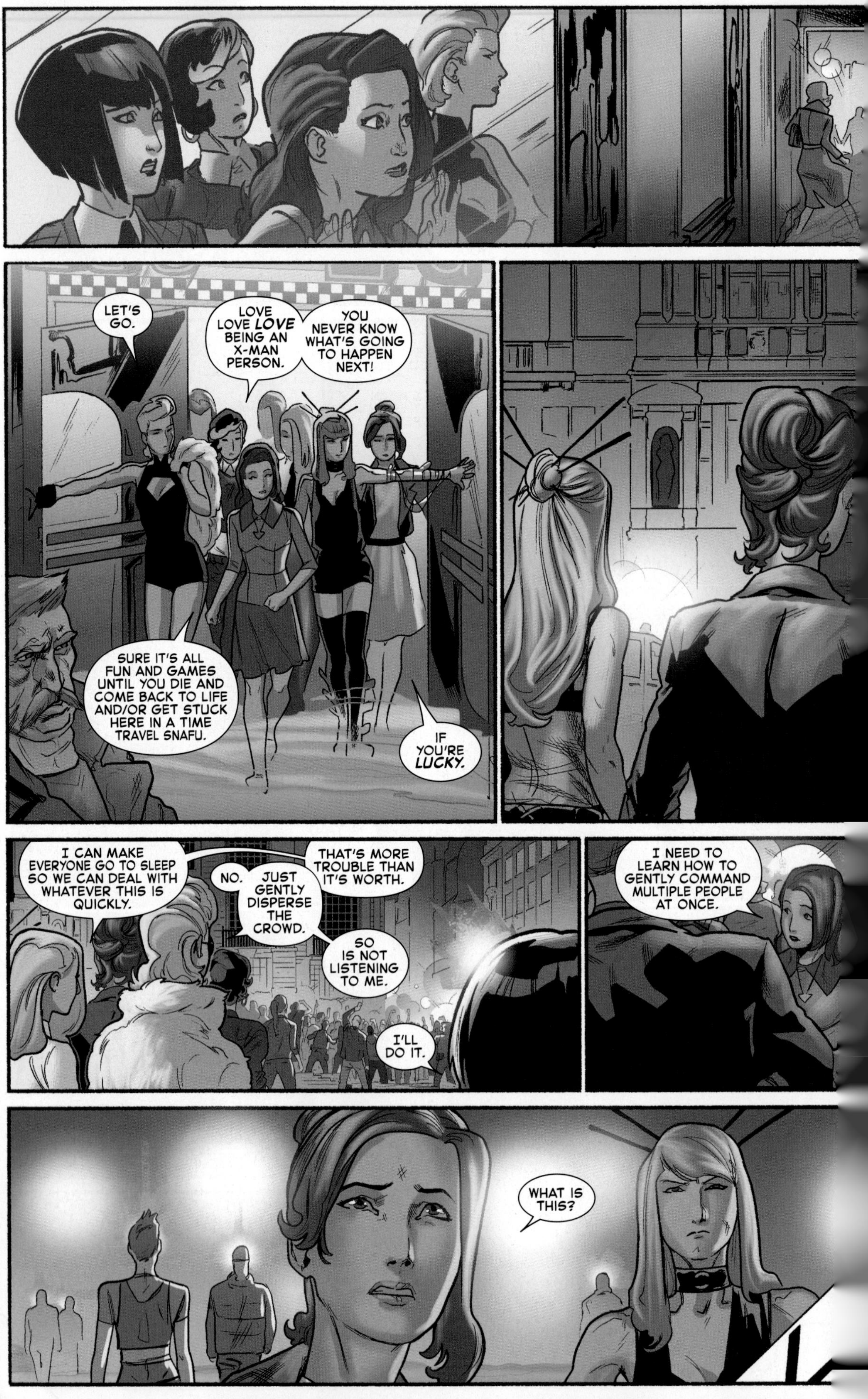
LET'S GO.
LOVE LOVE LOVE BEING AN X-MAN PERSON.
YOU NEVER KNOW WHAT'S GOING TO HAPPEN NEXT!
SURE IT'S ALL FUN AND GAMES UNTIL YOU DIE AND COME BACK TO LIFE AND/OR GET STUCK HERE IN A TIME TRAVEL SNAFU.
IF YOU'RE LUCKY.
I CAN MAKE EVERYONE GO TO SLEEP SO WE CAN DEAL WITH WHATEVER THIS IS QUICKLY.
THAT'S MORE TROUBLE THAN IT'S WORTH.
NO.
JUST GENTLY DISPERSE THE CROWD.
SO IS NOT LISTENING TO ME.
I'LL DO IT.
I NEED TO LEARN HOW TO GENTLY COMMAND MULTIPLE PEOPLE AT ONCE.
WHAT IS THIS?

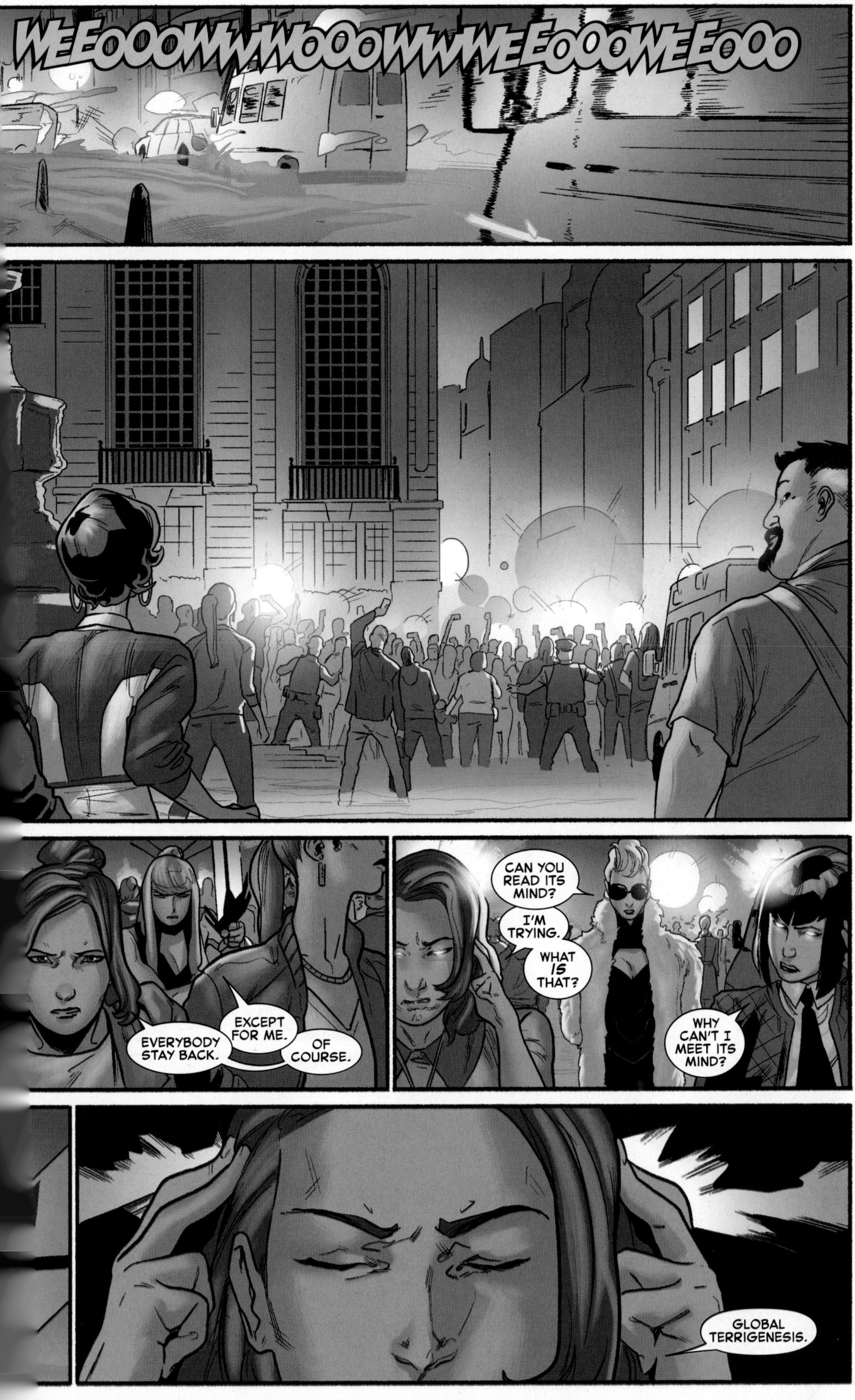
WEEOOOWWWOOOWWWEEOOOWEEOOO
EVERYBODY STAY BACK.
EXCEPT FOR ME.
OF COURSE.
CAN YOU READ ITS MIND?
I'M TRYING.
WHAT IS THAT?
WHY CAN'T I MEET ITS MIND?
GLOBAL TERRIGENESIS.

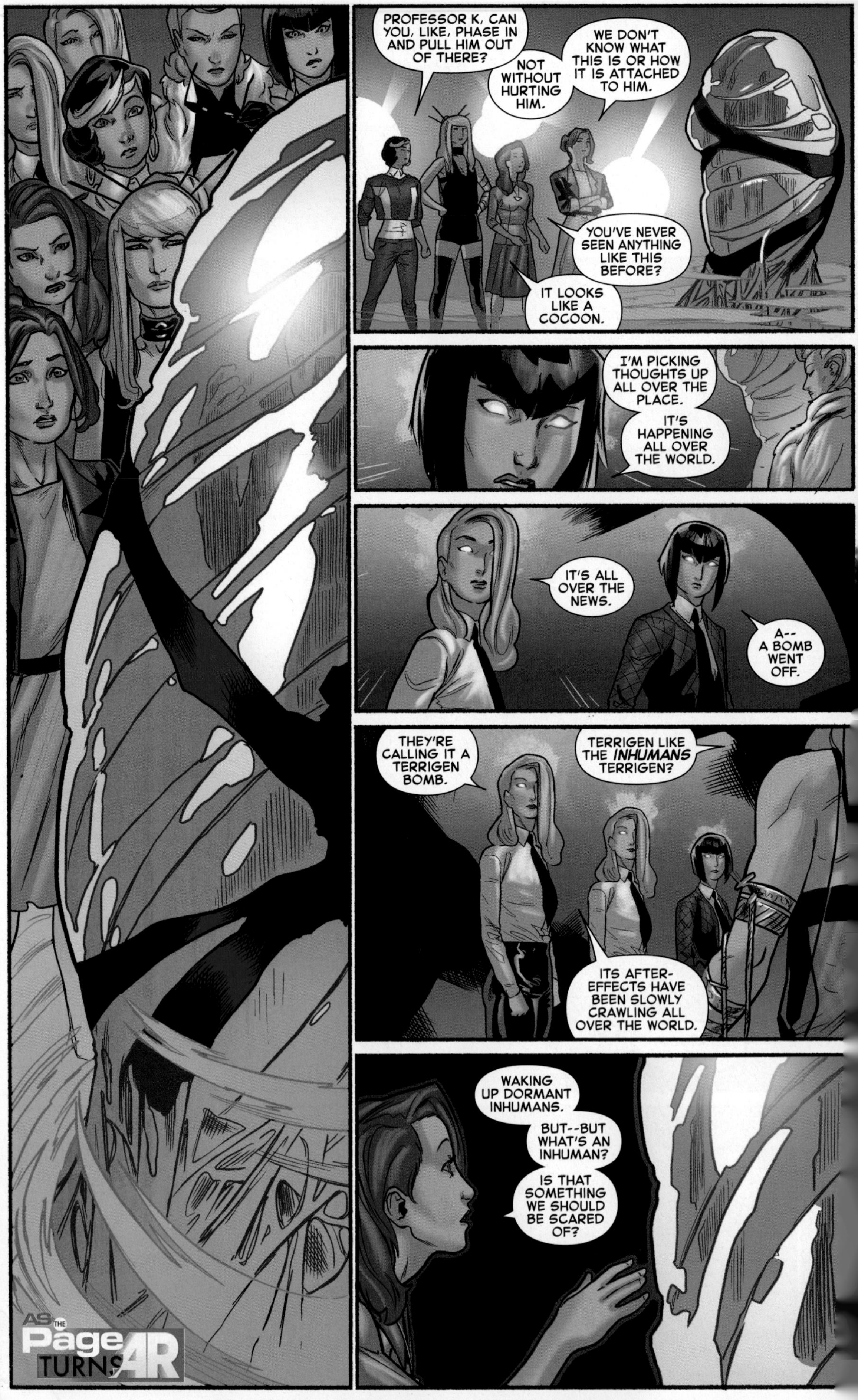
PROFESSOR K, CAN YOU, LIKE, PHASE IN AND PULL HIM OUT OF THERE?
NOT WITHOUT HURTING HIM.
WE DON'T KNOW WHAT THIS IS OR HOW IT IS ATTACHED TO HIM.
YOU'VE NEVER SEEN ANYTHING LIKE THIS BEFORE?
IT LOOKS LIKE A COCOON.
I'M PICKING THOUGHTS UP ALL OVER THE PLACE.
IT'S HAPPENING ALL OVER THE WORLD.
IT'S ALL OVER THE NEWS.
A-- A BOMB WENT OFF.
THEY'RE CALLING IT A TERRIGEN BOMB.
TERRIGEN LIKE THE *INHUMANS* TERRIGEN?
ITS AFTER-EFFECTS HAVE BEEN SLOWLY CRAWLING ALL OVER THE WORLD.
WAKING UP DORMANT INHUMANS.
BUT--BUT WHAT'S AN INHUMAN?
IS THAT SOMETHING WE SHOULD BE SCARED OF?
AS THE Page TURNS AR

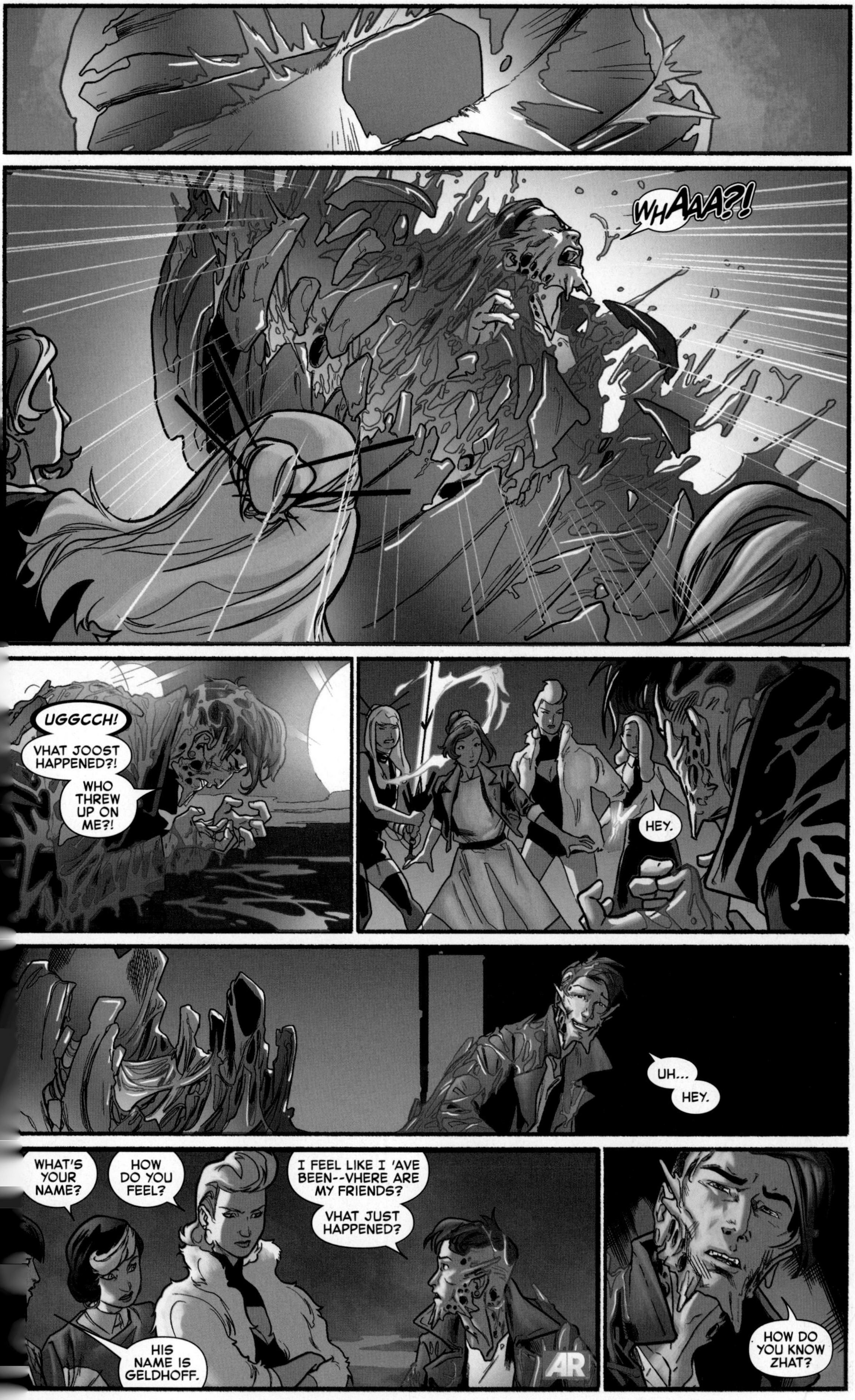
WHAAA?!
UGGCCH!
VHAT JOOST HAPPENED?!
WHO THREW UP ON ME?!
HEY.
UH...
HEY.
WHAT'S YOUR NAME?
HOW DO YOU FEEL?
I FEEL LIKE I 'AVE BEEN--VHERE ARE MY FRIENDS?
VHAT JUST HAPPENED?
HIS NAME IS GELDHOFF.
HOW DO YOU KNOW ZHAT?

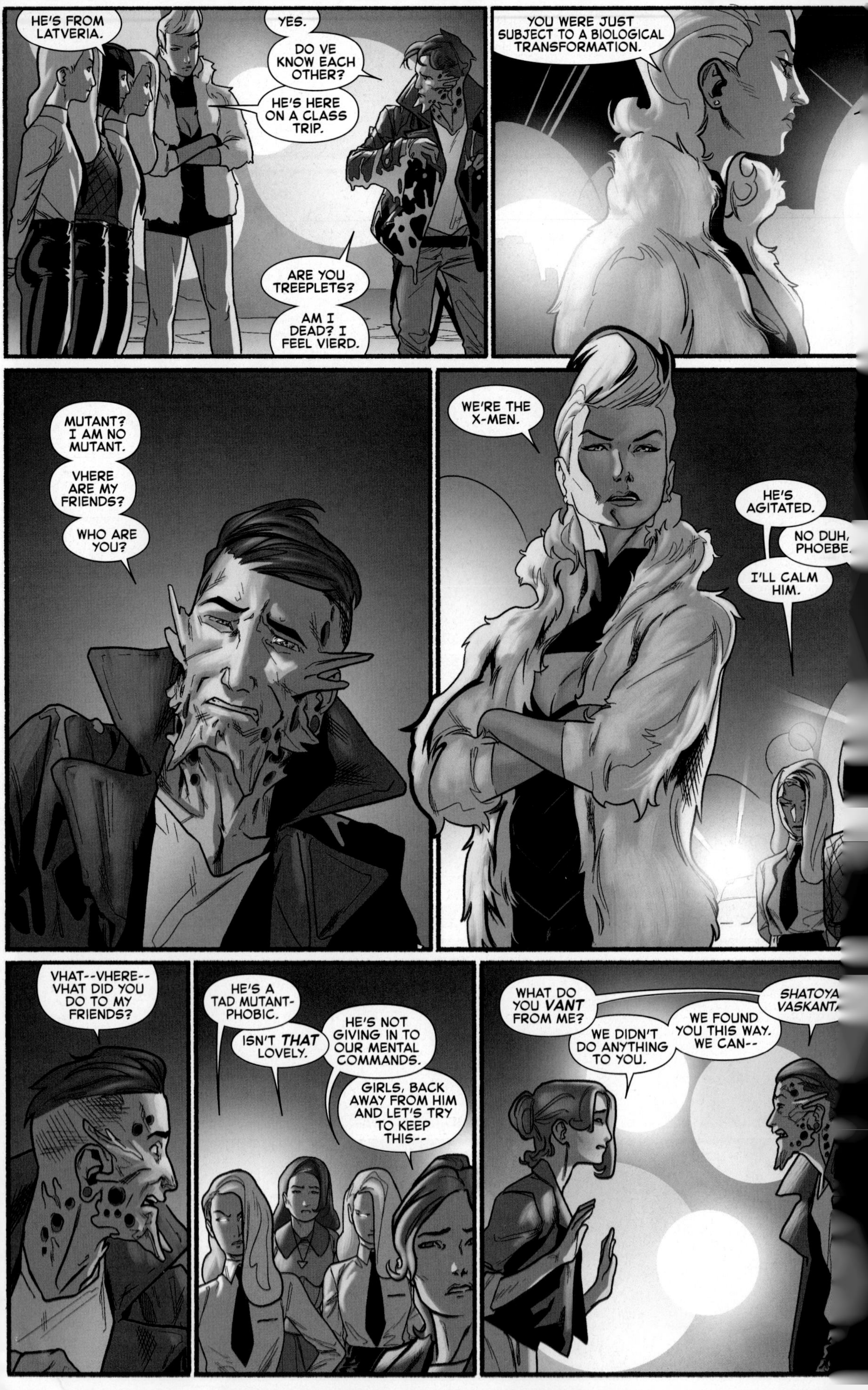
HE'S FROM LATVERIA.
YES.
DO VE KNOW EACH OTHER?
HE'S HERE ON A CLASS TRIP.
ARE YOU TREEPLETS?
AM I DEAD? I FEEL VIERD.
YOU WERE JUST SUBJECT TO A BIOLOGICAL TRANSFORMATION.
MUTANT? I AM NO MUTANT.
VHERE ARE MY FRIENDS?
WHO ARE YOU?
WE'RE THE X-MEN.
HE'S AGITATED.
NO DUH, PHOEBE.
I'LL CALM HIM.
VHAT--VHERE--VHAT DID YOU DO TO MY FRIENDS?
HE'S A TAD MUTANT-PHOBIC.
ISN'T THAT LOVELY.
HE'S NOT GIVING IN TO OUR MENTAL COMMANDS.
GIRLS, BACK AWAY FROM HIM AND LET'S TRY TO KEEP THIS--
WHAT DO YOU VANT FROM ME?
WE DIDN'T DO ANYTHING TO YOU.
WE FOUND YOU THIS WAY. WE CAN--
SHATOYA VASKANTA

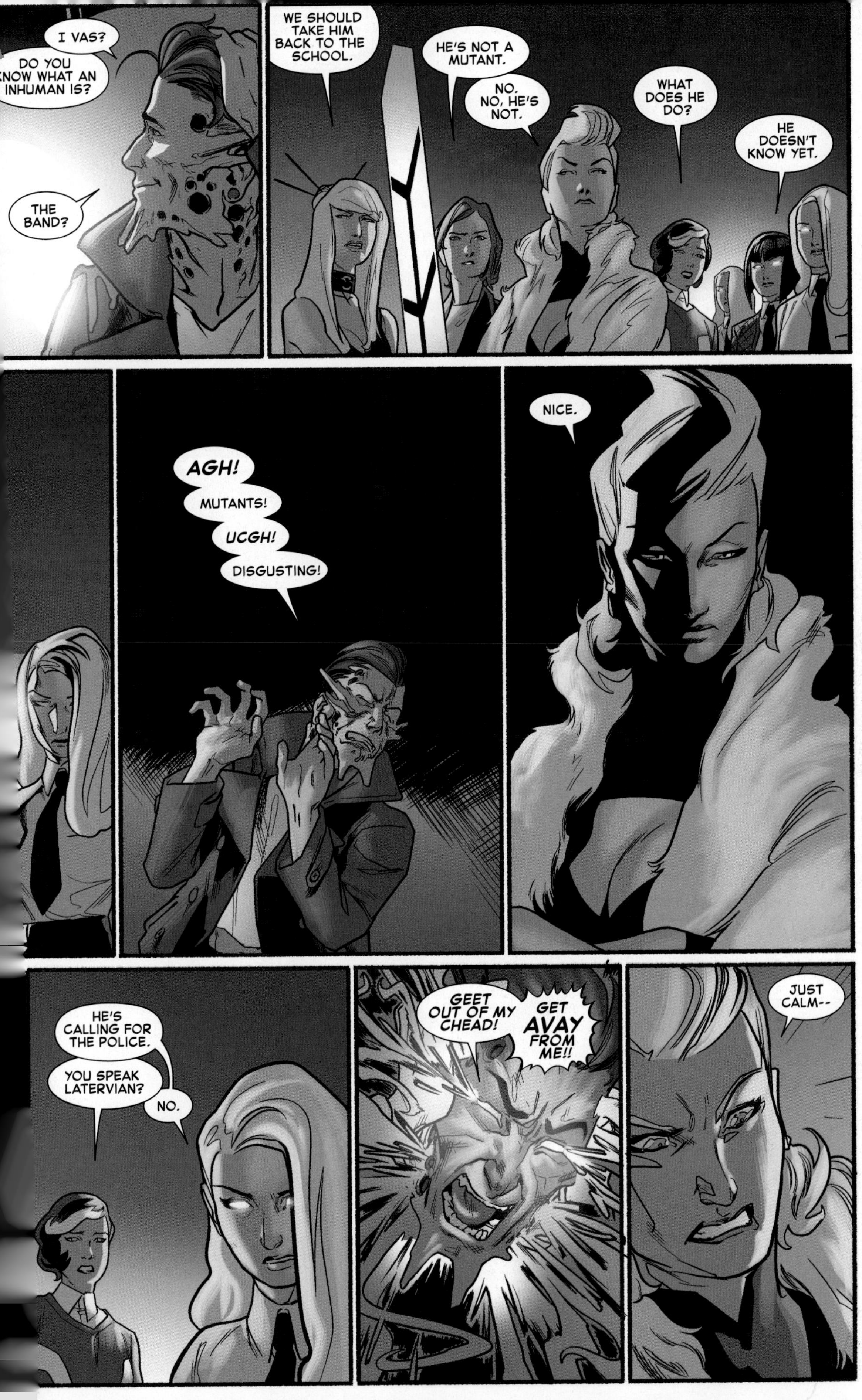
I VAS?
DO YOU KNOW WHAT AN INHUMAN IS?
THE BAND?
WE SHOULD TAKE HIM BACK TO THE SCHOOL.
HE'S NOT A MUTANT.
NO. NO, HE'S NOT.
WHAT DOES HE DO?
HE DOESN'T KNOW YET.
AGH!
MUTANTS!
UCGH!
DISGUSTING!
NICE.
HE'S CALLING FOR THE POLICE.
YOU SPEAK LATERVIAN?
NO.
GEET OUT OF MY CHEAD!
GET AVAY FROM ME!!
JUST CALM--

UM...

THAT--
THAT IS SOME POWER...
...SET...

DEED--
DEED I JUST KEEL--?

WHAT DEED I--?

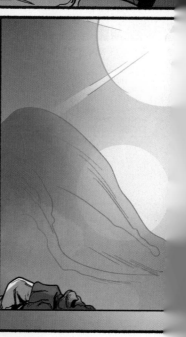

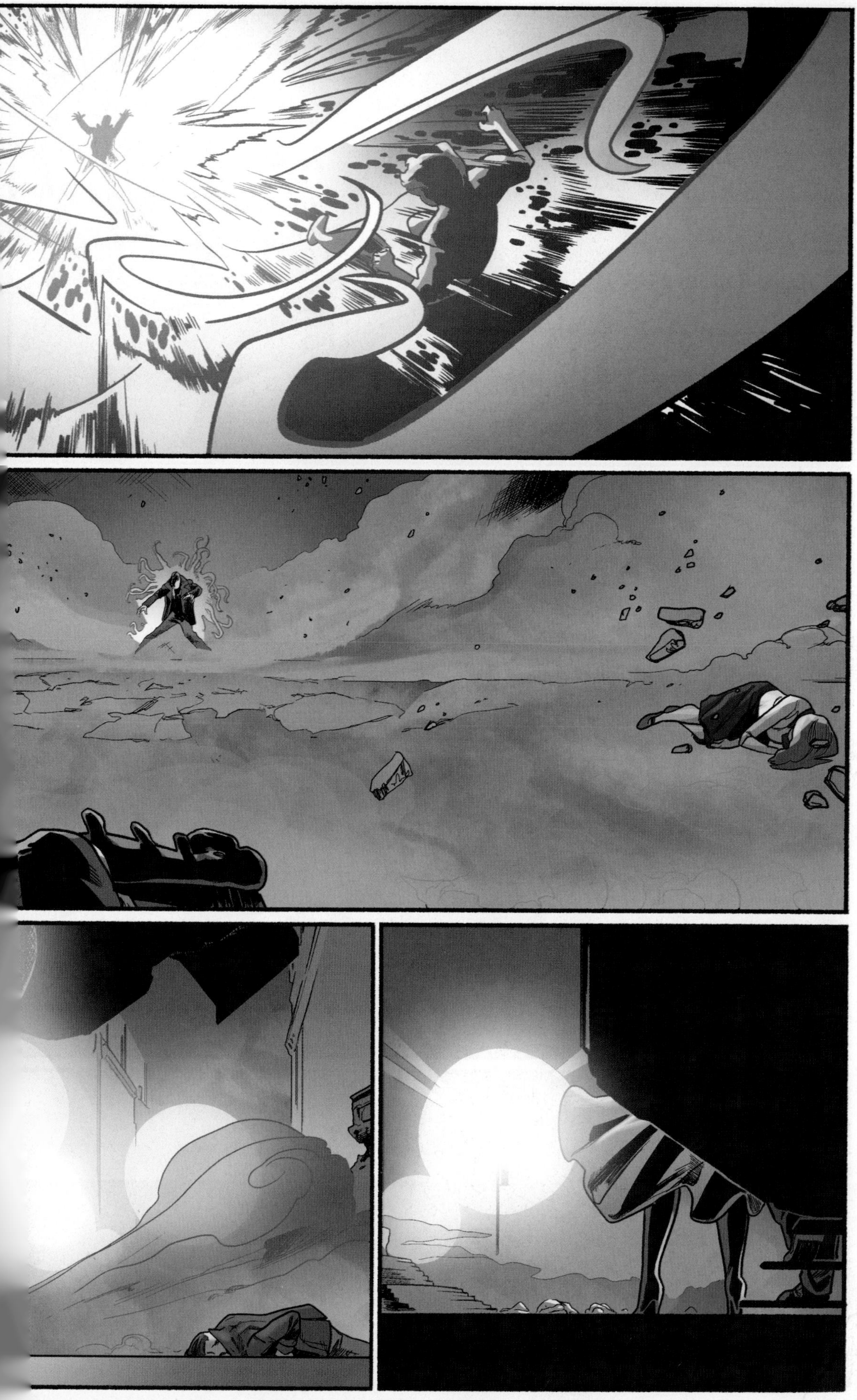

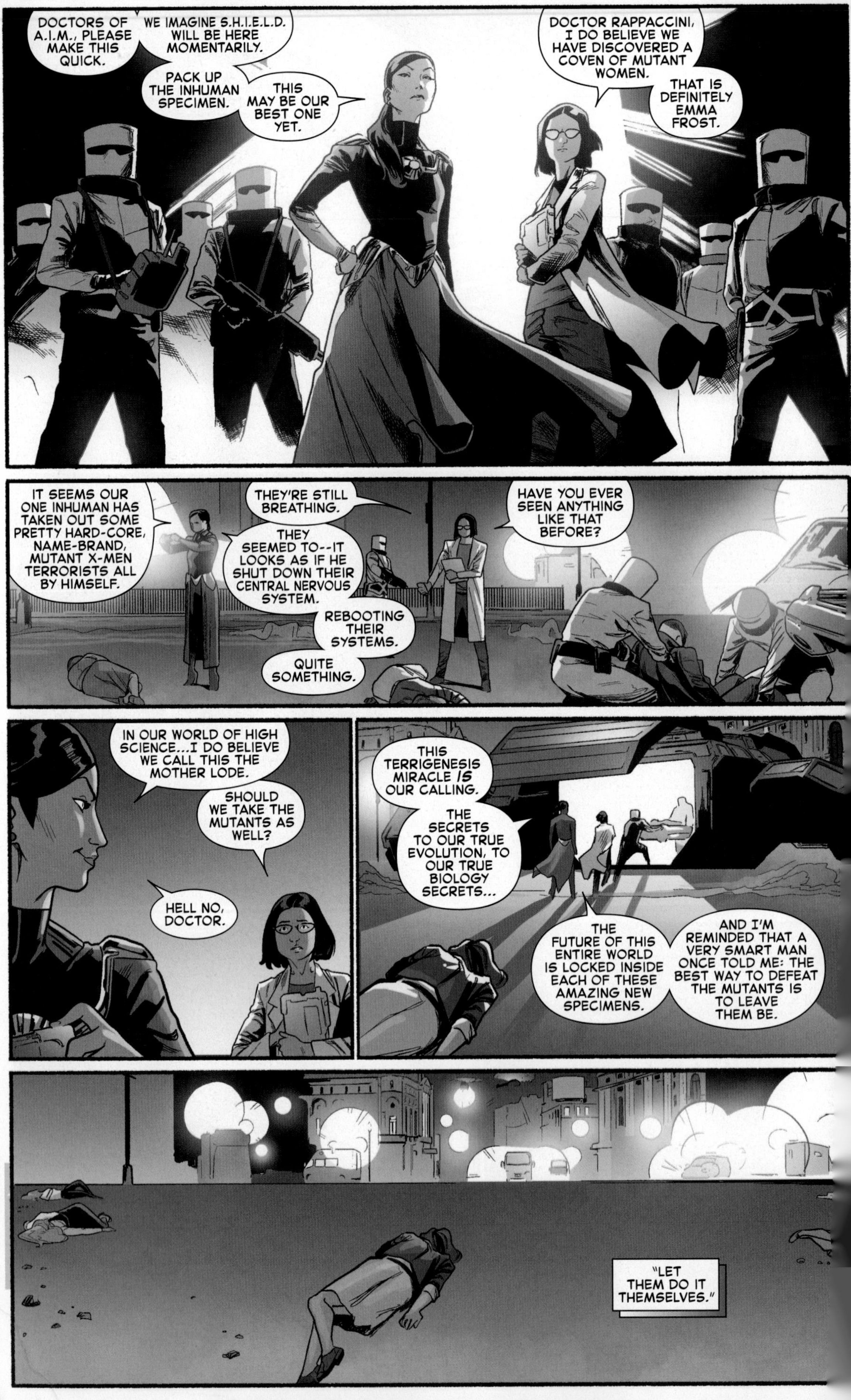
DOCTORS OF A.I.M., PLEASE MAKE THIS QUICK.
WE IMAGINE S.H.I.E.L.D. WILL BE HERE MOMENTARILY.
PACK UP THE INHUMAN SPECIMEN.
THIS MAY BE OUR BEST ONE YET.
DOCTOR RAPPACCINI, I DO BELIEVE WE HAVE DISCOVERED A COVEN OF MUTANT WOMEN.
THAT IS DEFINITELY EMMA FROST.
IT SEEMS OUR ONE INHUMAN HAS TAKEN OUT SOME PRETTY HARD-CORE, NAME-BRAND, MUTANT X-MEN TERRORISTS ALL BY HIMSELF.
THEY'RE STILL BREATHING.
THEY SEEMED TO--IT LOOKS AS IF HE SHUT DOWN THEIR CENTRAL NERVOUS SYSTEM.
REBOOTING THEIR SYSTEMS.
QUITE SOMETHING.
HAVE YOU EVER SEEN ANYTHING LIKE THAT BEFORE?
IN OUR WORLD OF HIGH SCIENCE...I DO BELIEVE WE CALL THIS THE MOTHER LODE.
SHOULD WE TAKE THE MUTANTS AS WELL?
HELL NO, DOCTOR.
THIS TERRIGENESIS MIRACLE IS OUR CALLING.
THE SECRETS TO OUR TRUE EVOLUTION, TO OUR TRUE BIOLOGY SECRETS...
THE FUTURE OF THIS ENTIRE WORLD IS LOCKED INSIDE EACH OF THESE AMAZING NEW SPECIMENS.
AND I'M REMINDED THAT A VERY SMART MAN ONCE TOLD ME: THE BEST WAY TO DEFEAT THE MUTANTS IS TO LEAVE THEM BE.
"LET THEM DO IT THEMSELVES."

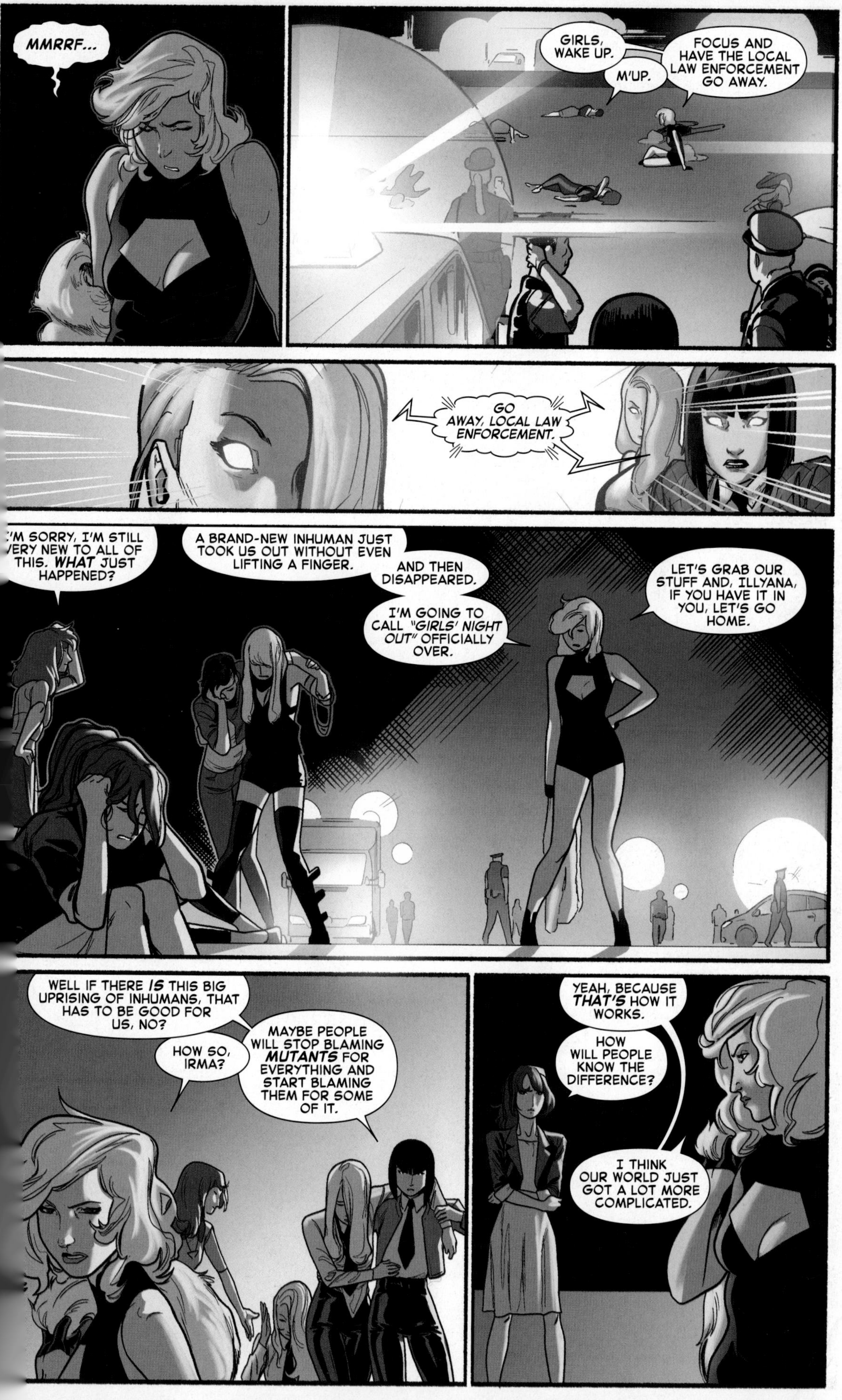
MMRRF...
GIRLS, WAKE UP.
M'UP.
FOCUS AND HAVE THE LOCAL LAW ENFORCEMENT GO AWAY.
GO AWAY, LOCAL LAW ENFORCEMENT.
I'M SORRY, I'M STILL VERY NEW TO ALL OF THIS. WHAT JUST HAPPENED?
A BRAND-NEW INHUMAN JUST TOOK US OUT WITHOUT EVEN LIFTING A FINGER.
AND THEN DISAPPEARED.
I'M GOING TO CALL "GIRLS' NIGHT OUT" OFFICIALLY OVER.
LET'S GRAB OUR STUFF AND, ILLYANA, IF YOU HAVE IT IN YOU, LET'S GO HOME.
WELL IF THERE IS THIS BIG UPRISING OF INHUMANS, THAT HAS TO BE GOOD FOR US, NO?
HOW SO, IRMA?
MAYBE PEOPLE WILL STOP BLAMING MUTANTS FOR EVERYTHING AND START BLAMING THEM FOR SOME OF IT.
YEAH, BECAUSE THAT'S HOW IT WORKS.
HOW WILL PEOPLE KNOW THE DIFFERENCE?
I THINK OUR WORLD JUST GOT A LOT MORE COMPLICATED.

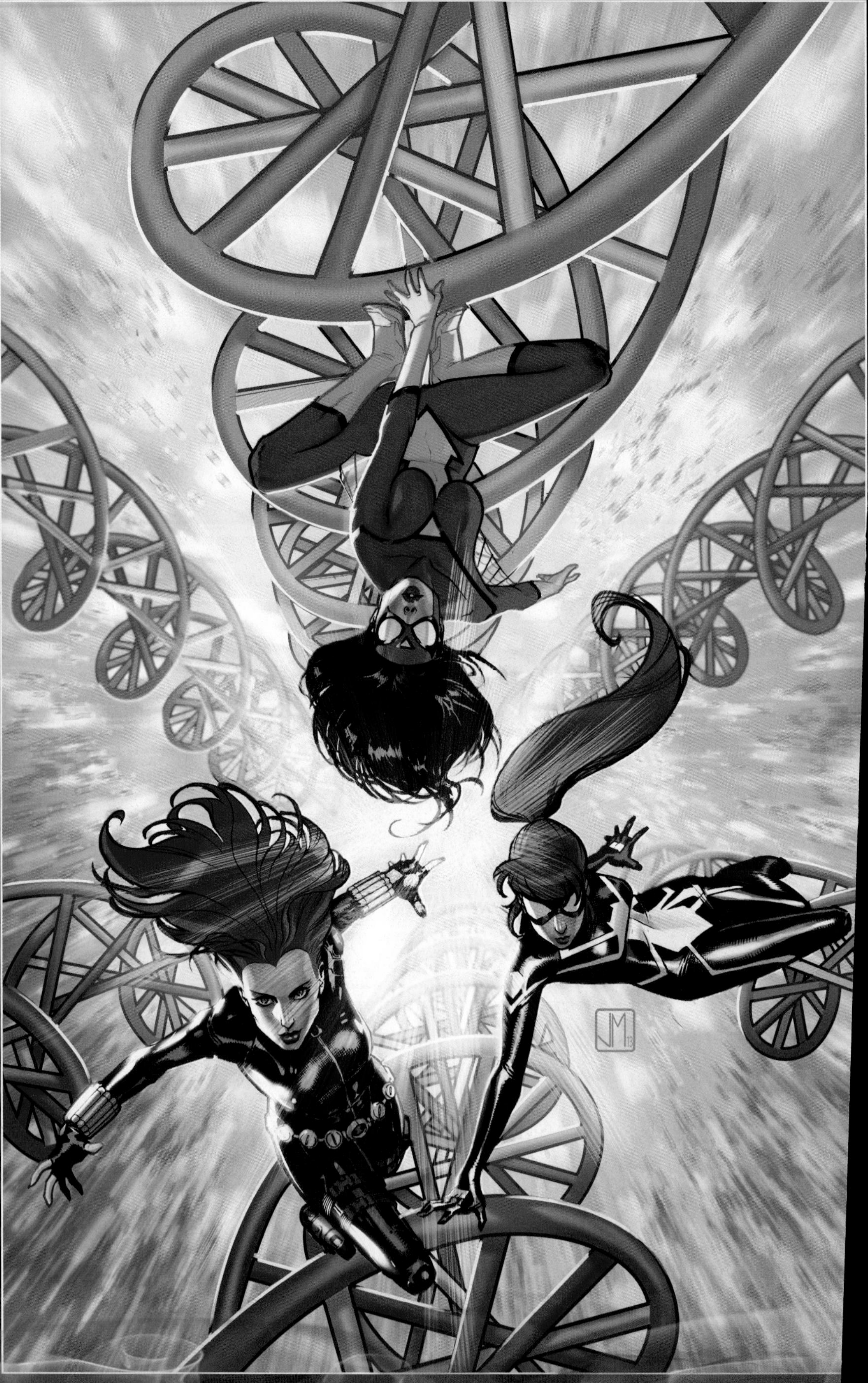

AVENGERS ASSEMBLE #21

AND THERE CAME A DAY, A DAY UNLIKE ANY OTHER, WHEN EARTH'S MIGHTIEST HEROES FOUND THEMSELVES UNITED AGAINST A COMMON THREAT! ON THAT DAY, THE AVENGERS WERE BORN, TO FIGHT THE FOES NO SINGLE SUPER HERO COULD WITHSTAND!

AVENGERS ASSEMBLE

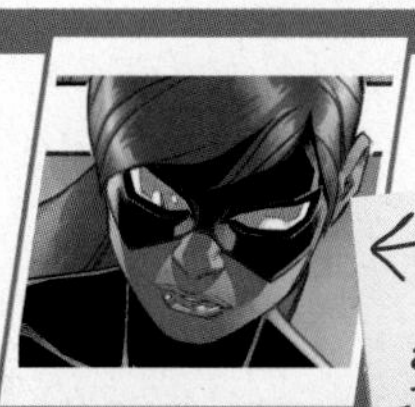

← Is not, NOT an Avenger
–The Superior Spider-Man

SPIDER-GIRL
ANYA CORAZON
SPIDER-POWERED SUPER STUDENT

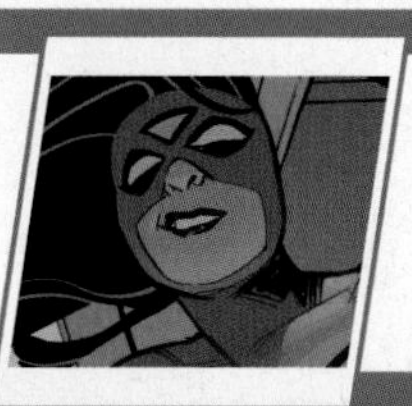

SPIDER-WOMAN
JESSICA DREW
SPIDER-POWERED SECRET AGENT

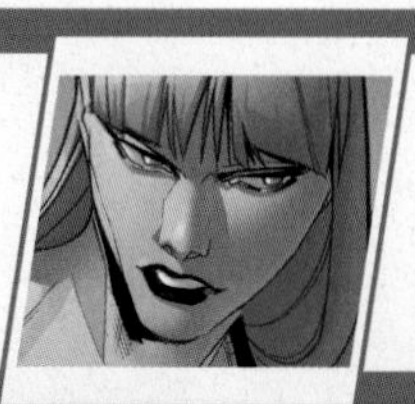

BLACK WIDOW
NATASHA ROMANOFF
PLAIN OL' COVERT SPECIALIST

FILE: INFINITY_04

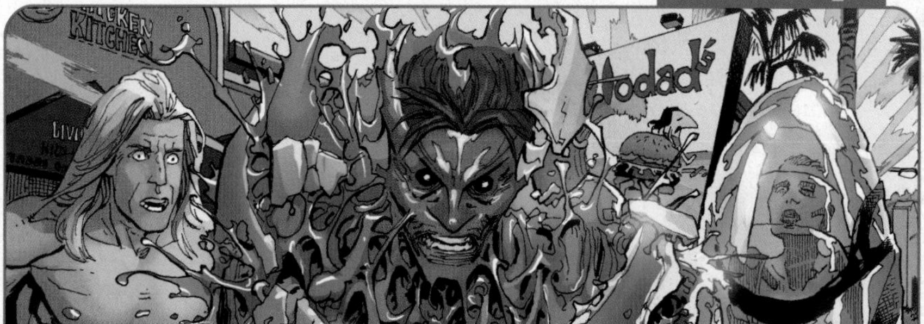

While most of the Avengers were off Earth fighting an alien threat, the Mad Titan Thanos led an invasion force to attack their home planet. Scouring the Earth to locate his own Inhuman son, Thane, Thanos sought to destroy Thane and raze the planet. Black Bolt, King of the Inhumans, in an effort to protect his people, detonated a Terrigen bomb, causing latent Inhumans hidden and scattered around Earth to undergo the Terrigen mists' mutating effects. Some were affected immediately; others were trapped in cocoons, the extent of their newly activated abilities yet to be seen...

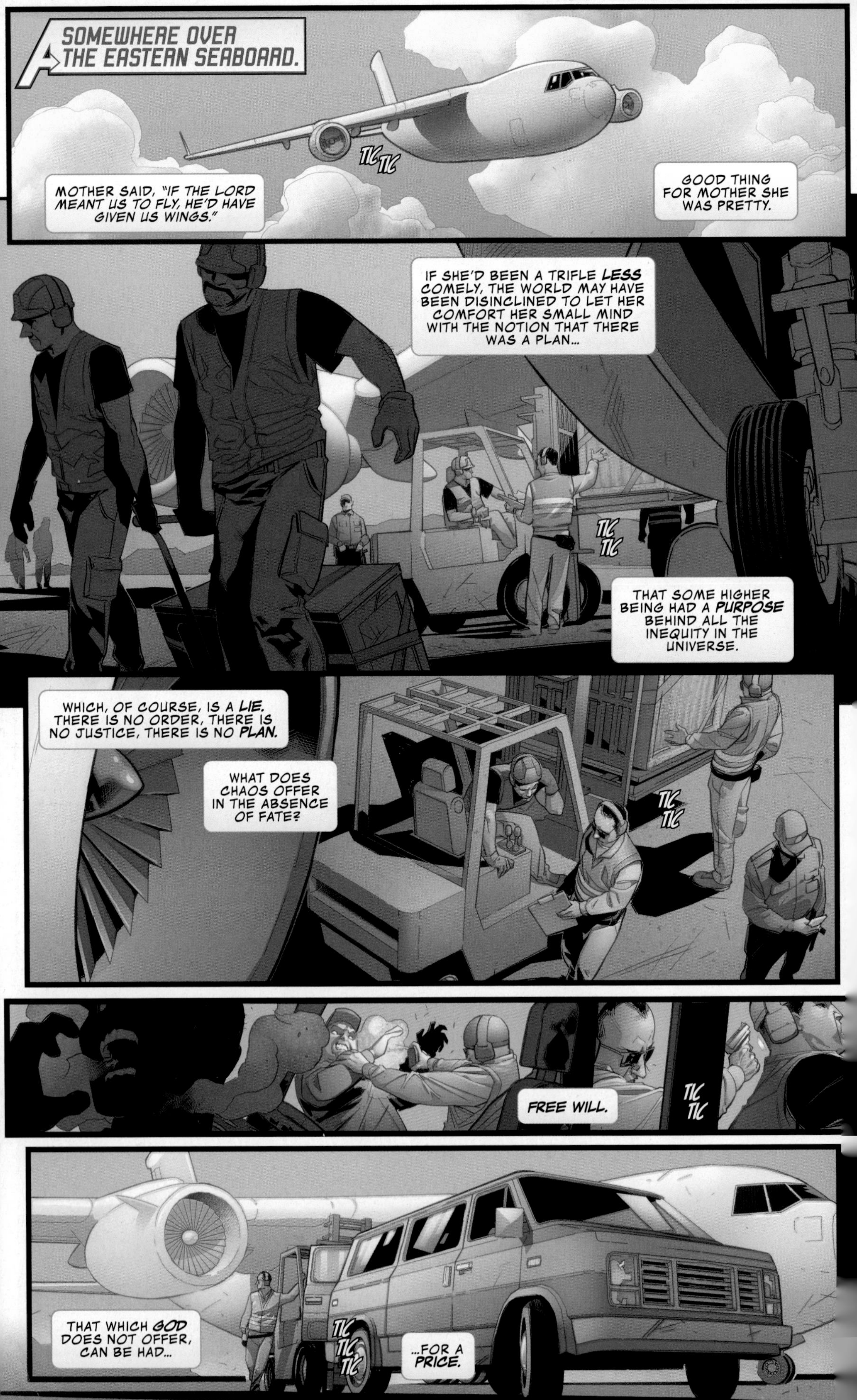
SOMEWHERE OVER THE EASTERN SEABOARD.
TIC TIC
MOTHER SAID, "IF THE LORD MEANT US TO FLY, HE'D HAVE GIVEN US WINGS."
GOOD THING FOR MOTHER SHE WAS PRETTY.
IF SHE'D BEEN A TRIFLE LESS COMELY, THE WORLD MAY HAVE BEEN DISINCLINED TO LET HER COMFORT HER SMALL MIND WITH THE NOTION THAT THERE WAS A PLAN...
TIC TIC
THAT SOME HIGHER BEING HAD A PURPOSE BEHIND ALL THE INEQUITY IN THE UNIVERSE.
WHICH, OF COURSE, IS A LIE. THERE IS NO ORDER, THERE IS NO JUSTICE, THERE IS NO PLAN.
WHAT DOES CHAOS OFFER IN THE ABSENCE OF FATE?
TIC TIC
FREE WILL.
TIC TIC
THAT WHICH GOD DOES NOT OFFER, CAN BE HAD...
TIC TIC TIC
...FOR A PRICE.

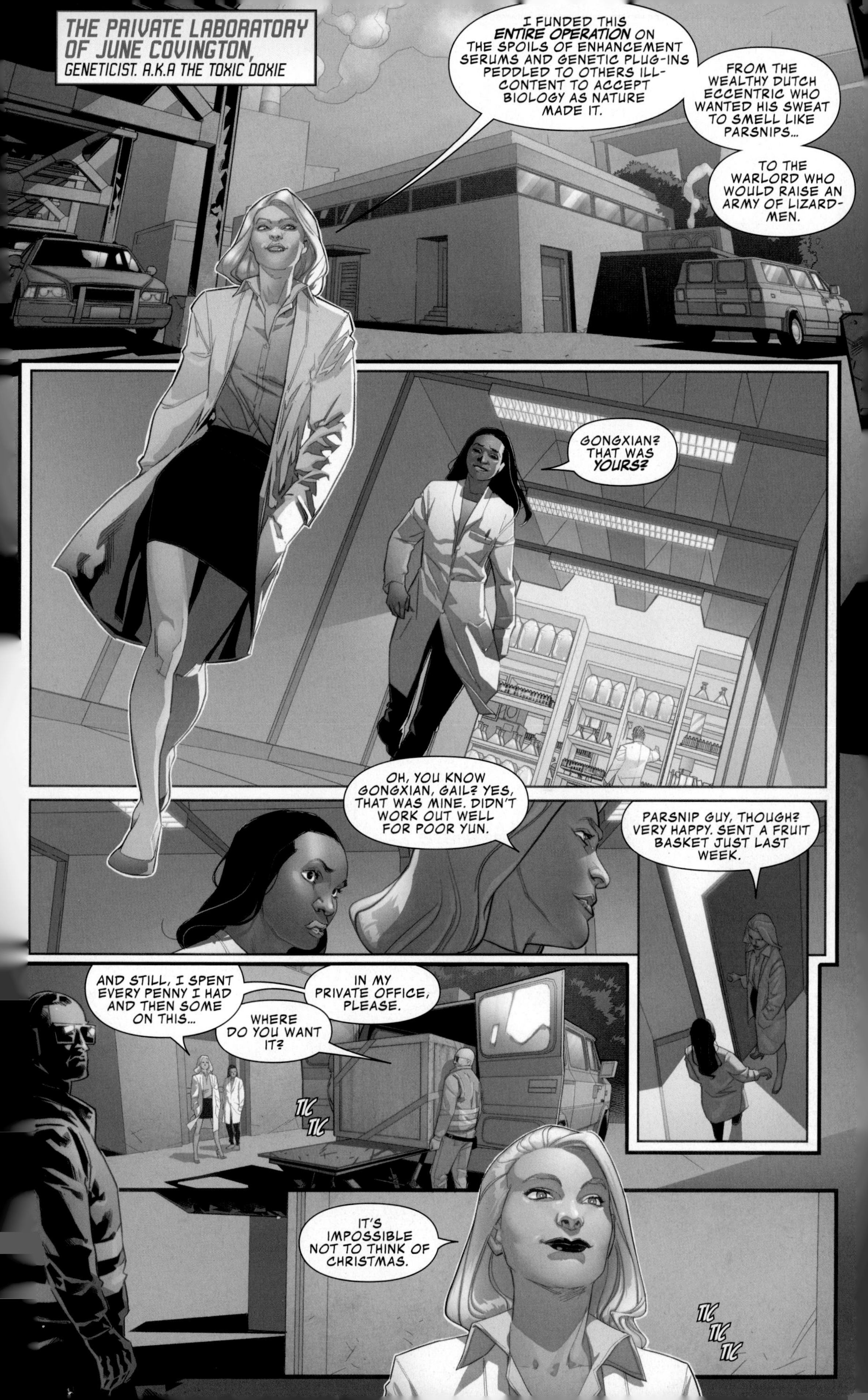
THE PRIVATE LABORATORY OF JUNE COVINGTON, GENETICIST. A.K.A THE TOXIC DOXIE
I FUNDED THIS ENTIRE OPERATION ON THE SPOILS OF ENHANCEMENT SERUMS AND GENETIC PLUG-INS PEDDLED TO OTHERS ILL-CONTENT TO ACCEPT BIOLOGY AS NATURE MADE IT.
FROM THE WEALTHY DUTCH ECCENTRIC WHO WANTED HIS SWEAT TO SMELL LIKE PARSNIPS...
TO THE WARLORD WHO WOULD RAISE AN ARMY OF LIZARD-MEN.
GONGXIAN? THAT WAS YOURS?
OH, YOU KNOW GONGXIAN, GAIL? YES, THAT WAS MINE. DIDN'T WORK OUT WELL FOR POOR YUN.
PARSNIP GUY, THOUGH? VERY HAPPY. SENT A FRUIT BASKET JUST LAST WEEK.
AND STILL, I SPENT EVERY PENNY I HAD AND THEN SOME ON THIS...
IN MY PRIVATE OFFICE, PLEASE.
WHERE DO YOU WANT IT?
TIC TIC
IT'S IMPOSSIBLE NOT TO THINK OF CHRISTMAS.
TIC TIC TIC

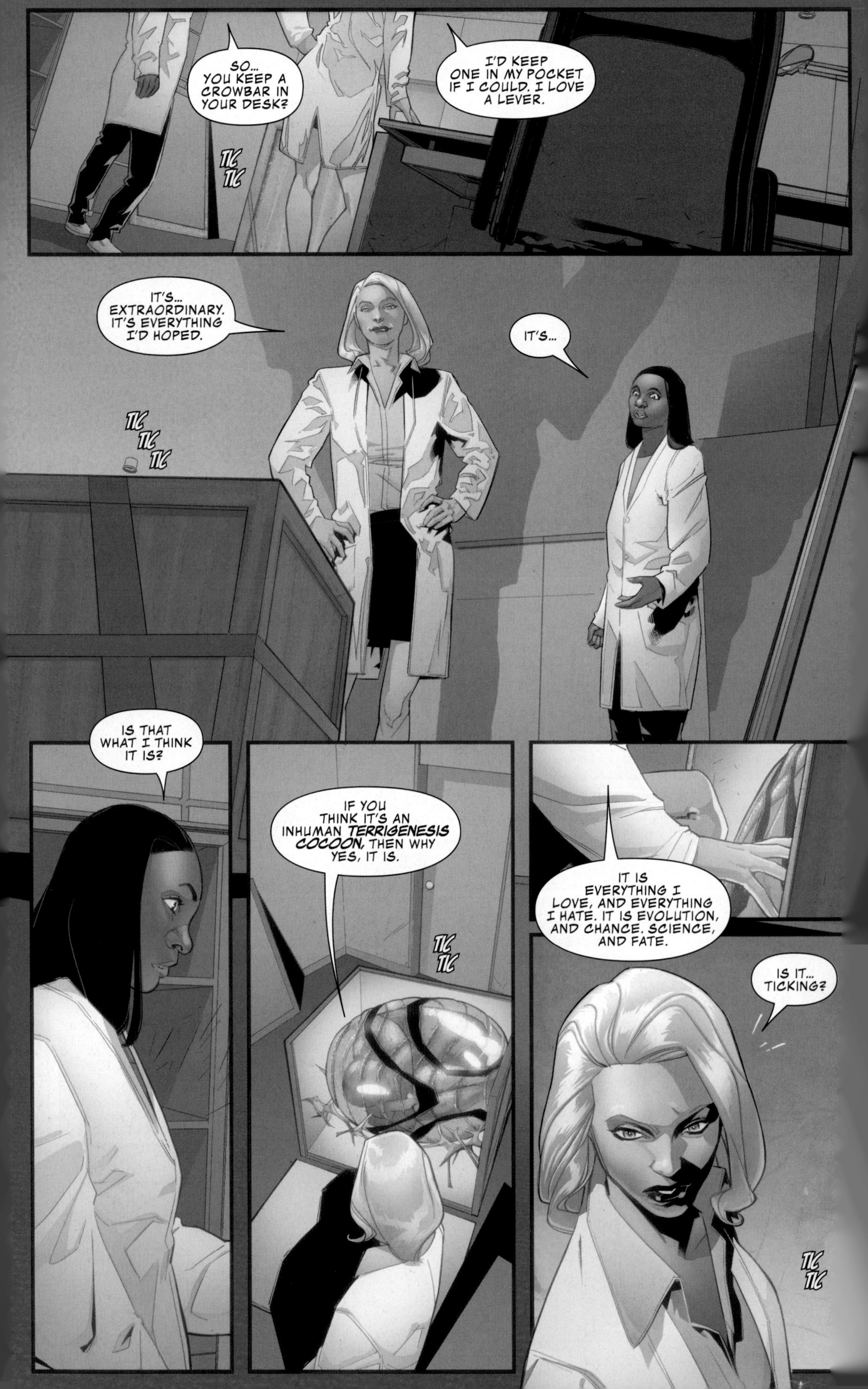

SO... YOU KEEP A CROWBAR IN YOUR DESK?
I'D KEEP ONE IN MY POCKET IF I COULD. I LOVE A LEVER.
TIC TIC
IT'S... EXTRAORDINARY. IT'S EVERYTHING I'D HOPED.
IT'S...
TIC TIC TIC
IS THAT WHAT I THINK IT IS?
IF YOU THINK IT'S AN INHUMAN TERRIGENESIS COCOON, THEN WHY YES, IT IS.
TIC TIC
IT IS EVERYTHING I LOVE, AND EVERYTHING I HATE. IT IS EVOLUTION, AND CHANCE. SCIENCE, AND FATE.
IS IT... TICKING?
TIC TIC

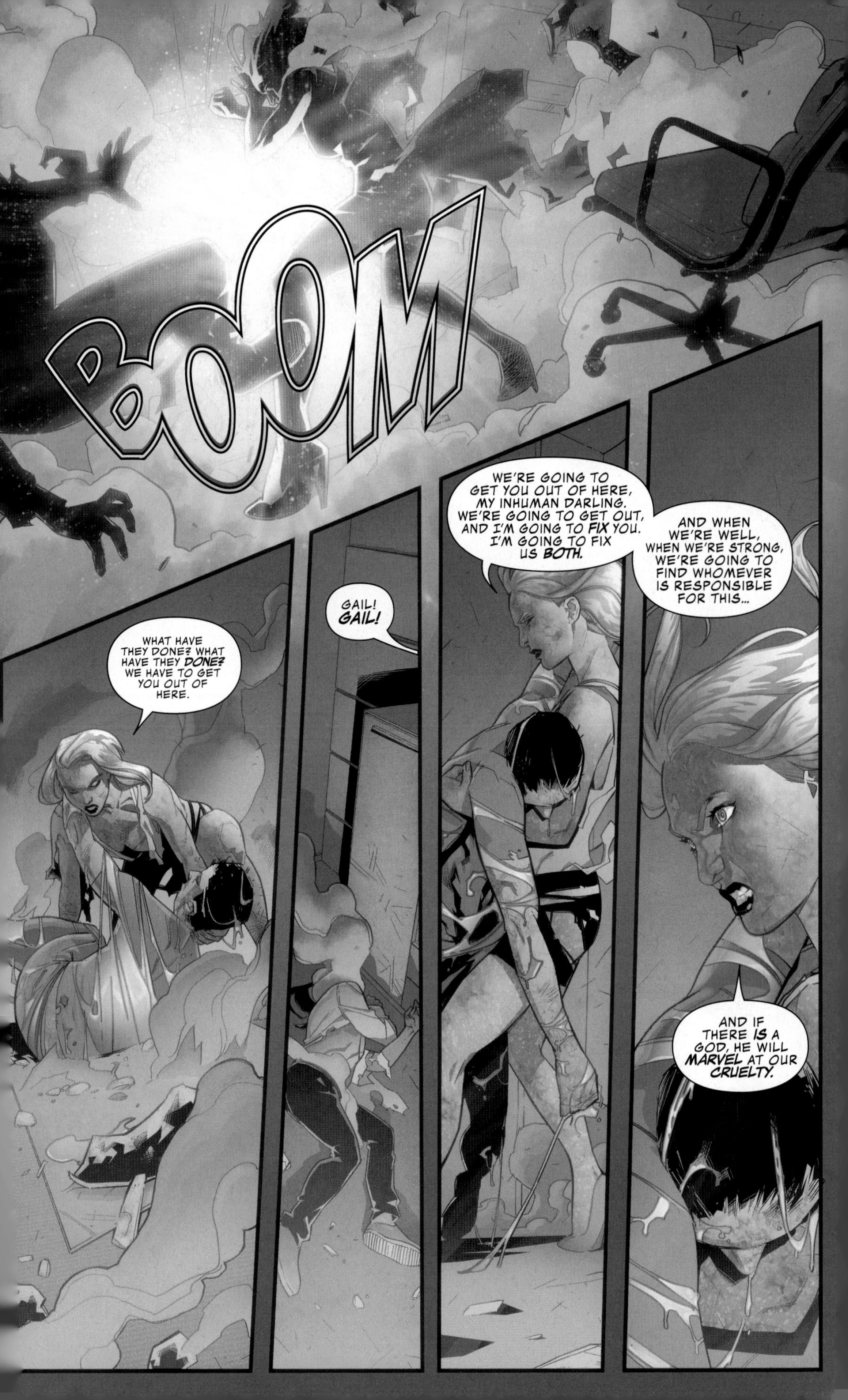
BOOM
WHAT HAVE THEY DONE? WHAT HAVE THEY DONE? WE HAVE TO GET YOU OUT OF HERE.
GAIL! GAIL!
WE'RE GOING TO GET YOU OUT OF HERE, MY INHUMAN DARLING. WE'RE GOING TO GET OUT, AND I'M GOING TO FIX YOU. I'M GOING TO FIX US BOTH.
AND WHEN WE'RE WELL, WHEN WE'RE STRONG, WE'RE GOING TO FIND WHOMEVER IS RESPONSIBLE FOR THIS...
AND IF THERE IS A GOD, HE WILL MARVEL AT OUR CRUELTY.

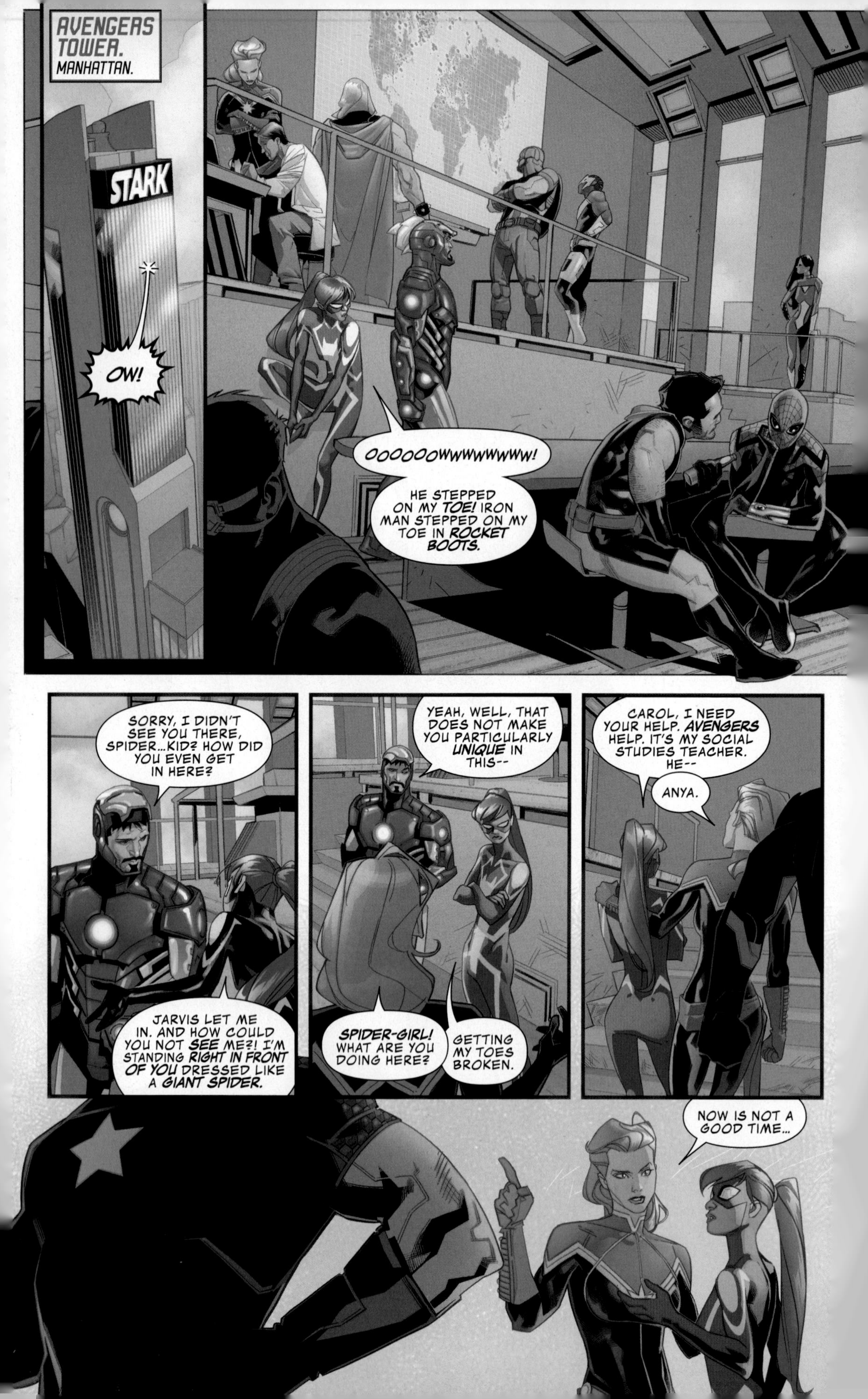
AVENGERS TOWER. MANHATTAN.
STARK
OW!
OOOOOOWWWWWWWW!
HE STEPPED ON MY TOE! IRON MAN STEPPED ON MY TOE IN ROCKET BOOTS.
SORRY, I DIDN'T SEE YOU THERE, SPIDER...KID? HOW DID YOU EVEN GET IN HERE?
JARVIS LET ME IN. AND HOW COULD YOU NOT SEE ME?! I'M STANDING RIGHT IN FRONT OF YOU DRESSED LIKE A GIANT SPIDER.
YEAH, WELL, THAT DOES NOT MAKE YOU PARTICULARLY UNIQUE IN THIS--
SPIDER-GIRL! WHAT ARE YOU DOING HERE?
GETTING MY TOES BROKEN.
CAROL, I NEED YOUR HELP. AVENGERS HELP. IT'S MY SOCIAL STUDIES TEACHER. HE--
ANYA.
NOW IS NOT A GOOD TIME...

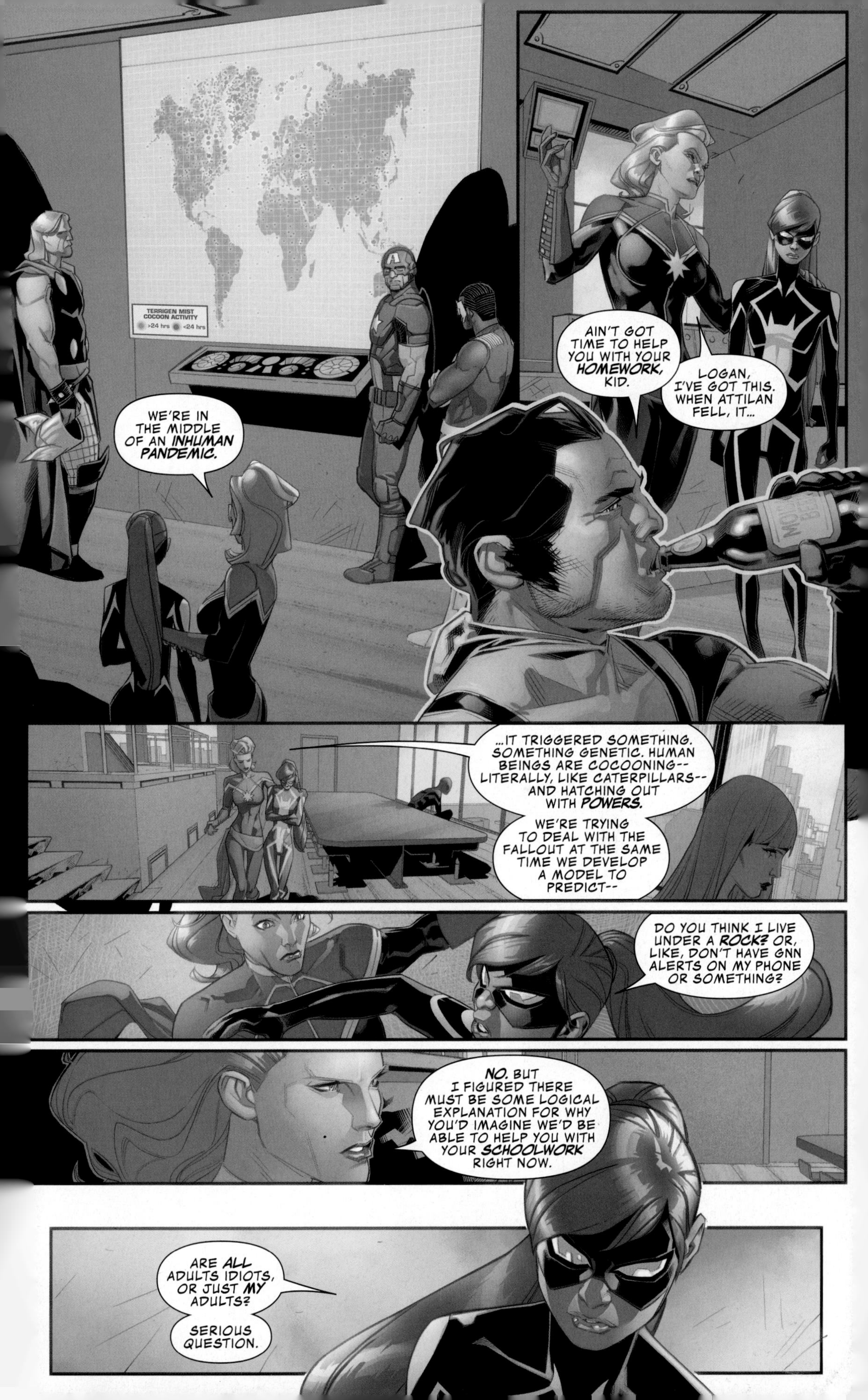
TERRIGEN MIST COCOON ACTIVITY
>24 hrs <24 hrs
WE'RE IN THE MIDDLE OF AN INHUMAN PANDEMIC.
AIN'T GOT TIME TO HELP YOU WITH YOUR HOMEWORK, KID.
LOGAN, I'VE GOT THIS. WHEN ATTILAN FELL, IT...
...IT TRIGGERED SOMETHING. SOMETHING GENETIC. HUMAN BEINGS ARE COCOONING-- LITERALLY, LIKE CATERPILLARS-- AND HATCHING OUT WITH POWERS.
WE'RE TRYING TO DEAL WITH THE FALLOUT AT THE SAME TIME WE DEVELOP A MODEL TO PREDICT--
DO YOU THINK I LIVE UNDER A ROCK? OR, LIKE, DON'T HAVE GNN ALERTS ON MY PHONE OR SOMETHING?
NO. BUT I FIGURED THERE MUST BE SOME LOGICAL EXPLANATION FOR WHY YOU'D IMAGINE WE'D BE ABLE TO HELP YOU WITH YOUR SCHOOLWORK RIGHT NOW.
ARE ALL ADULTS IDIOTS, OR JUST MY ADULTS?
SERIOUS QUESTION.

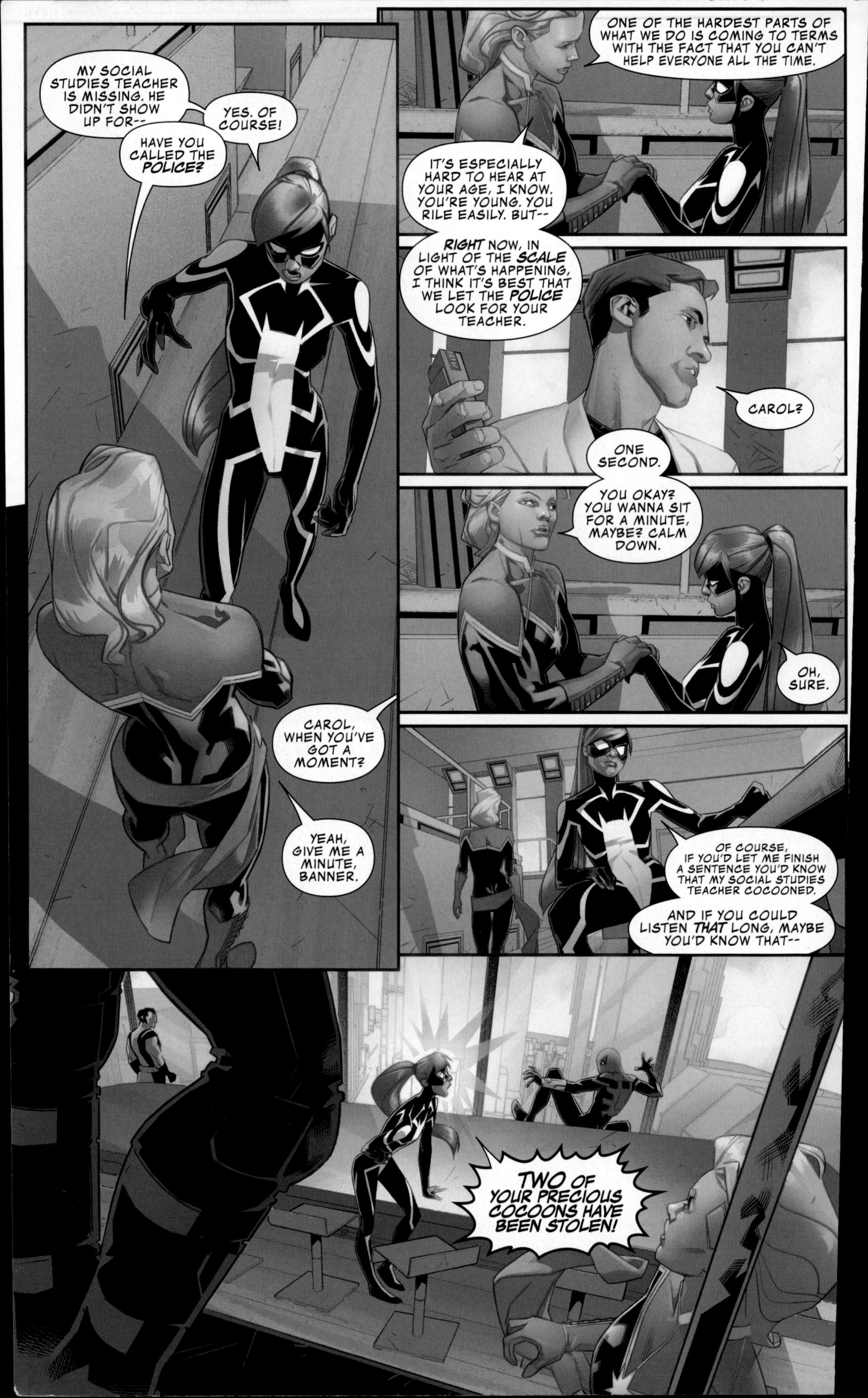
MY SOCIAL STUDIES TEACHER IS MISSING. HE DIDN'T SHOW UP FOR--
YES. OF COURSE!
HAVE YOU CALLED THE POLICE?
CAROL, WHEN YOU'VE GOT A MOMENT?
YEAH, GIVE ME A MINUTE, BANNER.
ONE OF THE HARDEST PARTS OF WHAT WE DO IS COMING TO TERMS WITH THE FACT THAT YOU CAN'T HELP EVERYONE ALL THE TIME.
IT'S ESPECIALLY HARD TO HEAR AT YOUR AGE, I KNOW. YOU'RE YOUNG. YOU RILE EASILY. BUT--
RIGHT NOW, IN LIGHT OF THE SCALE OF WHAT'S HAPPENING, I THINK IT'S BEST THAT WE LET THE POLICE LOOK FOR YOUR TEACHER.
CAROL?
ONE SECOND.
YOU OKAY? YOU WANNA SIT FOR A MINUTE, MAYBE? CALM DOWN.
OH, SURE.
OF COURSE, IF YOU'D LET ME FINISH A SENTENCE YOU'D KNOW THAT MY SOCIAL STUDIES TEACHER COCOONED.
AND IF YOU COULD LISTEN THAT LONG, MAYBE YOU'D KNOW THAT--
TWO OF YOUR PRECIOUS COCOONS HAVE BEEN STOLEN!

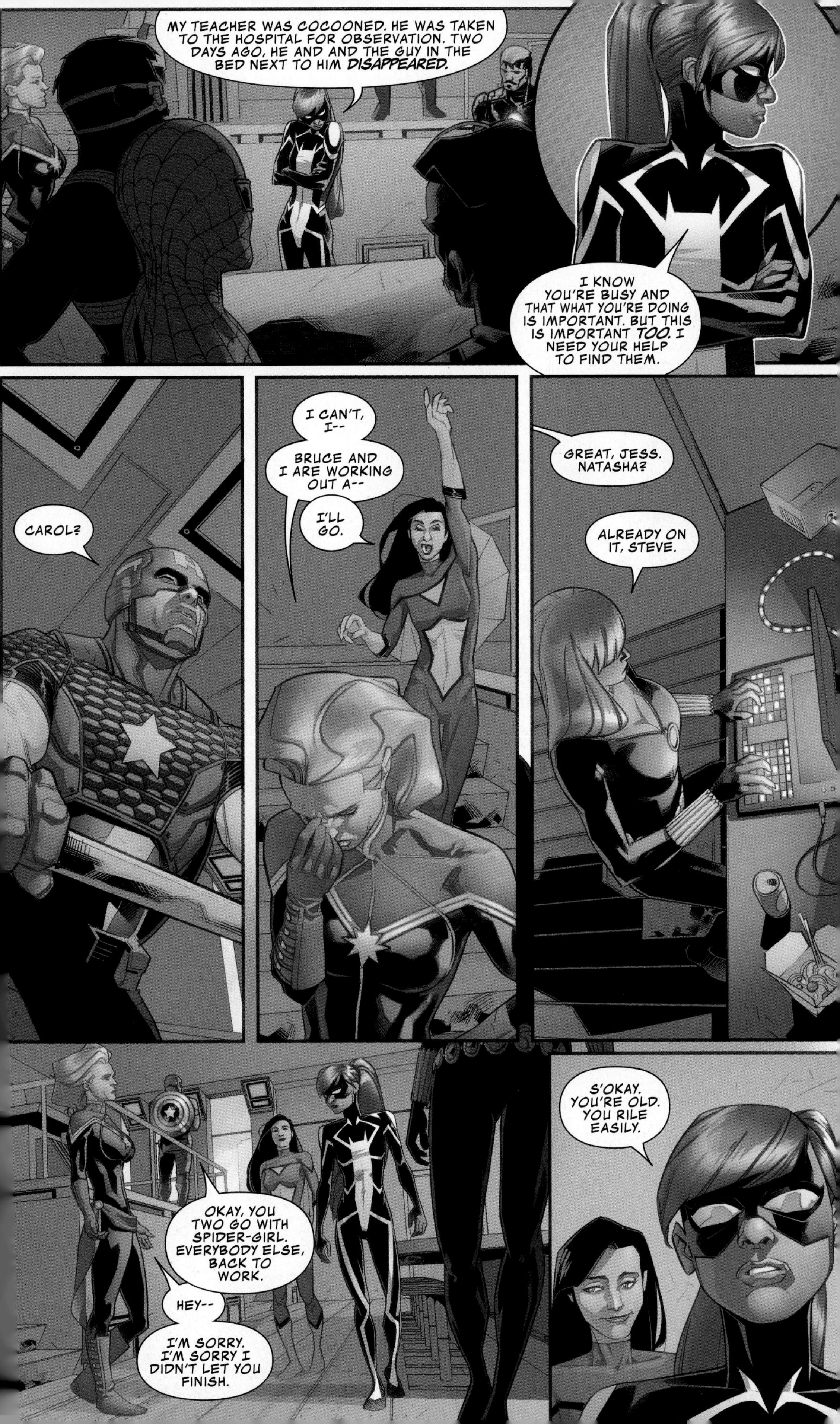

MY TEACHER WAS COCOONED. HE WAS TAKEN TO THE HOSPITAL FOR OBSERVATION. TWO DAYS AGO, HE AND AND THE GUY IN THE BED NEXT TO HIM *DISAPPEARED.*
I KNOW YOU'RE BUSY AND THAT WHAT YOU'RE DOING IS IMPORTANT. BUT THIS IS IMPORTANT *TOO.* I NEED YOUR HELP TO FIND THEM.
CAROL?
I CAN'T, I--
BRUCE AND I ARE WORKING OUT A--
I'LL GO.
GREAT, JESS. NATASHA?
ALREADY ON IT, STEVE.
OKAY, YOU TWO GO WITH SPIDER-GIRL. EVERYBODY ELSE, BACK TO WORK.
HEY--
I'M SORRY. I'M SORRY I DIDN'T LET YOU FINISH.
S'OKAY. YOU'RE OLD. YOU RILE EASILY.

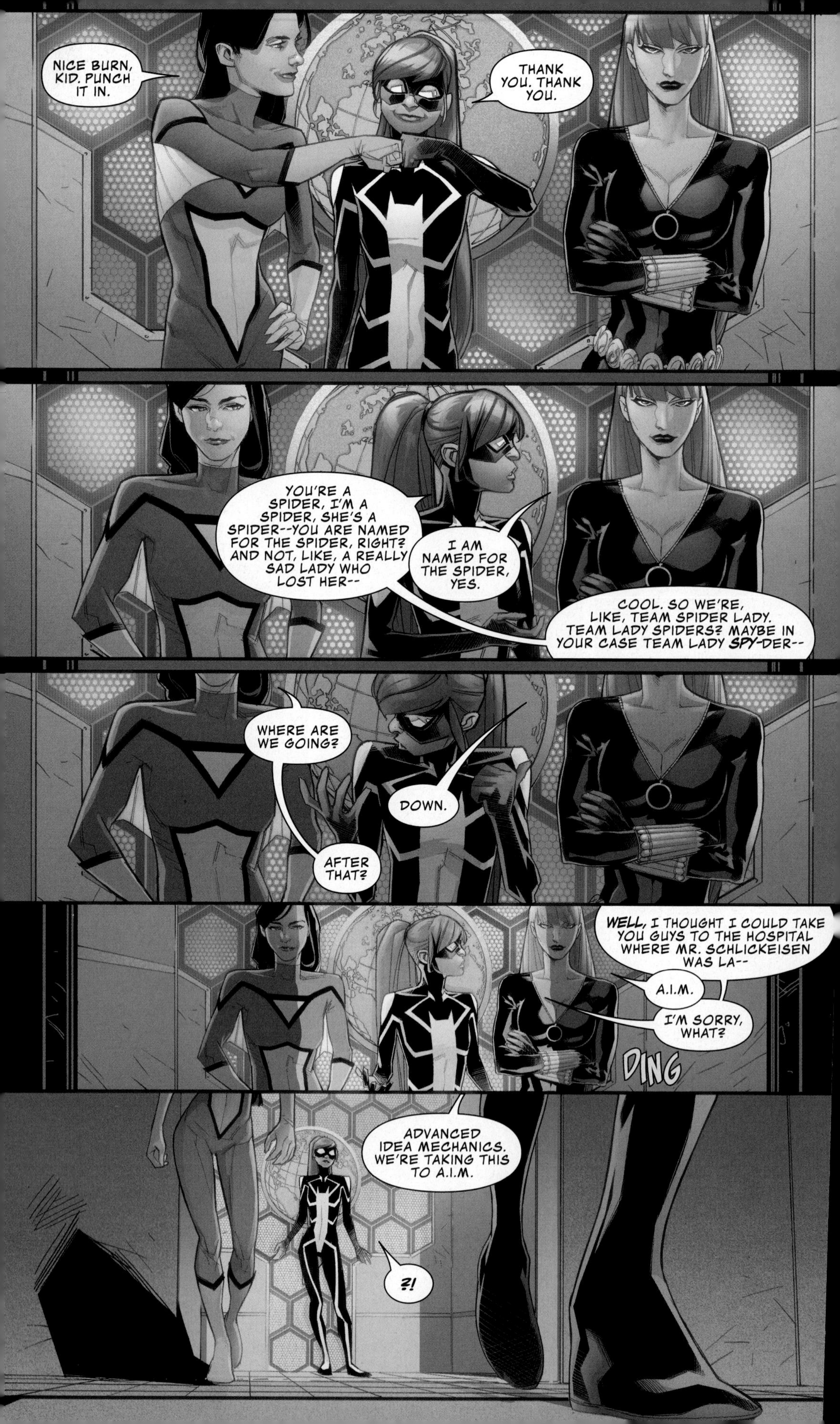
NICE BURN, KID. PUNCH IT IN.
THANK YOU. THANK YOU.
YOU'RE A SPIDER, I'M A SPIDER, SHE'S A SPIDER--YOU ARE NAMED FOR THE SPIDER, RIGHT? AND NOT, LIKE, A REALLY SAD LADY WHO LOST HER--
I AM NAMED FOR THE SPIDER, YES.
COOL. SO WE'RE, LIKE, TEAM SPIDER LADY. TEAM LADY SPIDERS? MAYBE IN YOUR CASE TEAM LADY SPY-DER--
WHERE ARE WE GOING?
DOWN.
AFTER THAT?
WELL, I THOUGHT I COULD TAKE YOU GUYS TO THE HOSPITAL WHERE MR. SCHLICKEISEN WAS LA--
A.I.M.
I'M SORRY, WHAT?
DING
ADVANCED IDEA MECHANICS. WE'RE TAKING THIS TO A.I.M.
?!

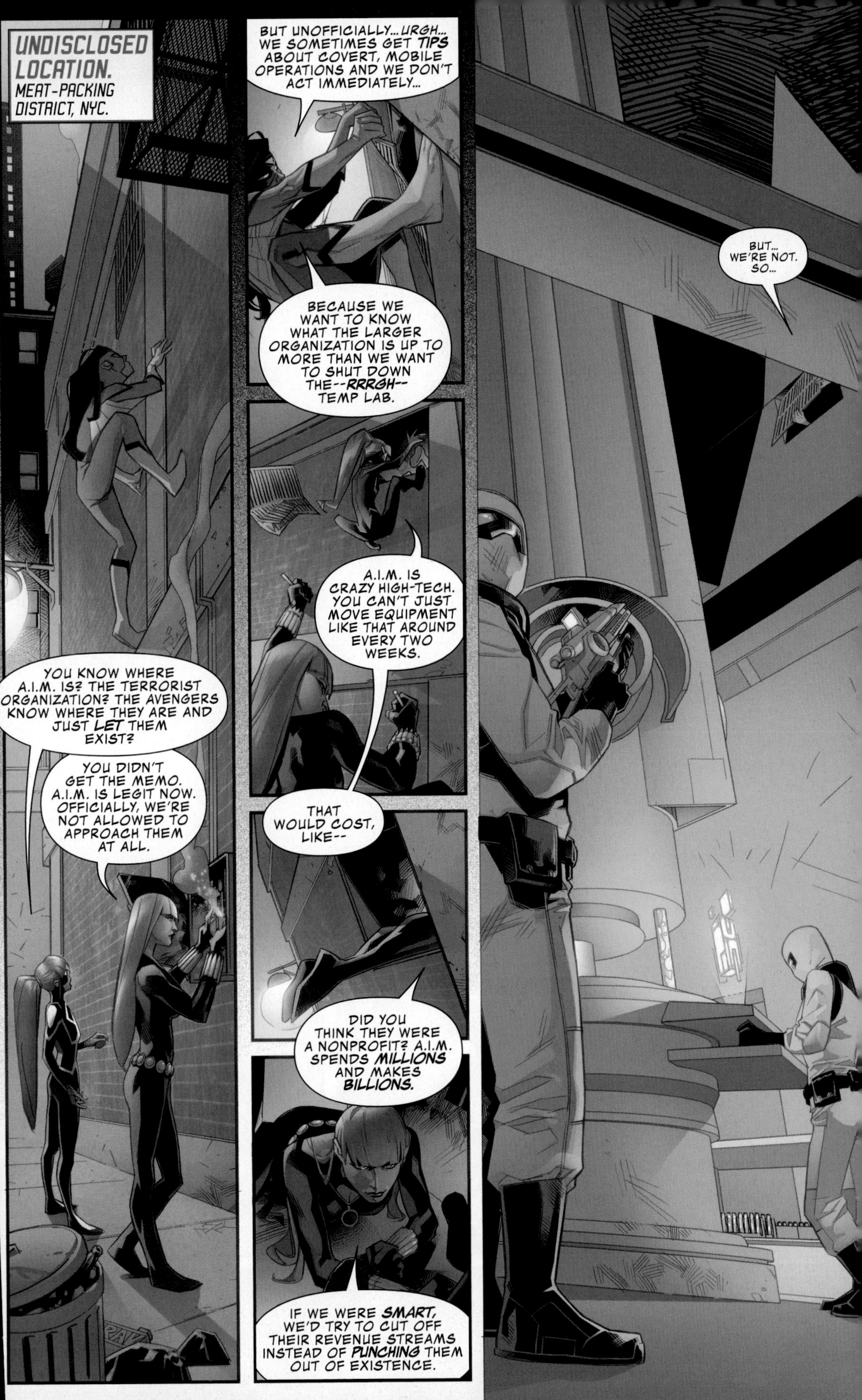
UNDISCLOSED LOCATION.
MEAT-PACKING DISTRICT, NYC.
YOU KNOW WHERE A.I.M. IS? THE TERRORIST ORGANIZATION? THE AVENGERS KNOW WHERE THEY ARE AND JUST LET THEM EXIST?
YOU DIDN'T GET THE MEMO. A.I.M. IS LEGIT NOW. OFFICIALLY, WE'RE NOT ALLOWED TO APPROACH THEM AT ALL.
BUT UNOFFICIALLY... URGH... WE SOMETIMES GET TIPS ABOUT COVERT, MOBILE OPERATIONS AND WE DON'T ACT IMMEDIATELY...
BECAUSE WE WANT TO KNOW WHAT THE LARGER ORGANIZATION IS UP TO MORE THAN WE WANT TO SHUT DOWN THE--RRRGH-- TEMP LAB.
A.I.M. IS CRAZY HIGH-TECH. YOU CAN'T JUST MOVE EQUIPMENT LIKE THAT AROUND EVERY TWO WEEKS.
THAT WOULD COST, LIKE--
DID YOU THINK THEY WERE A NONPROFIT? A.I.M. SPENDS MILLIONS AND MAKES BILLIONS.
IF WE WERE SMART, WE'D TRY TO CUT OFF THEIR REVENUE STREAMS INSTEAD OF PUNCHING THEM OUT OF EXISTENCE.
BUT... WE'RE NOT. SO...

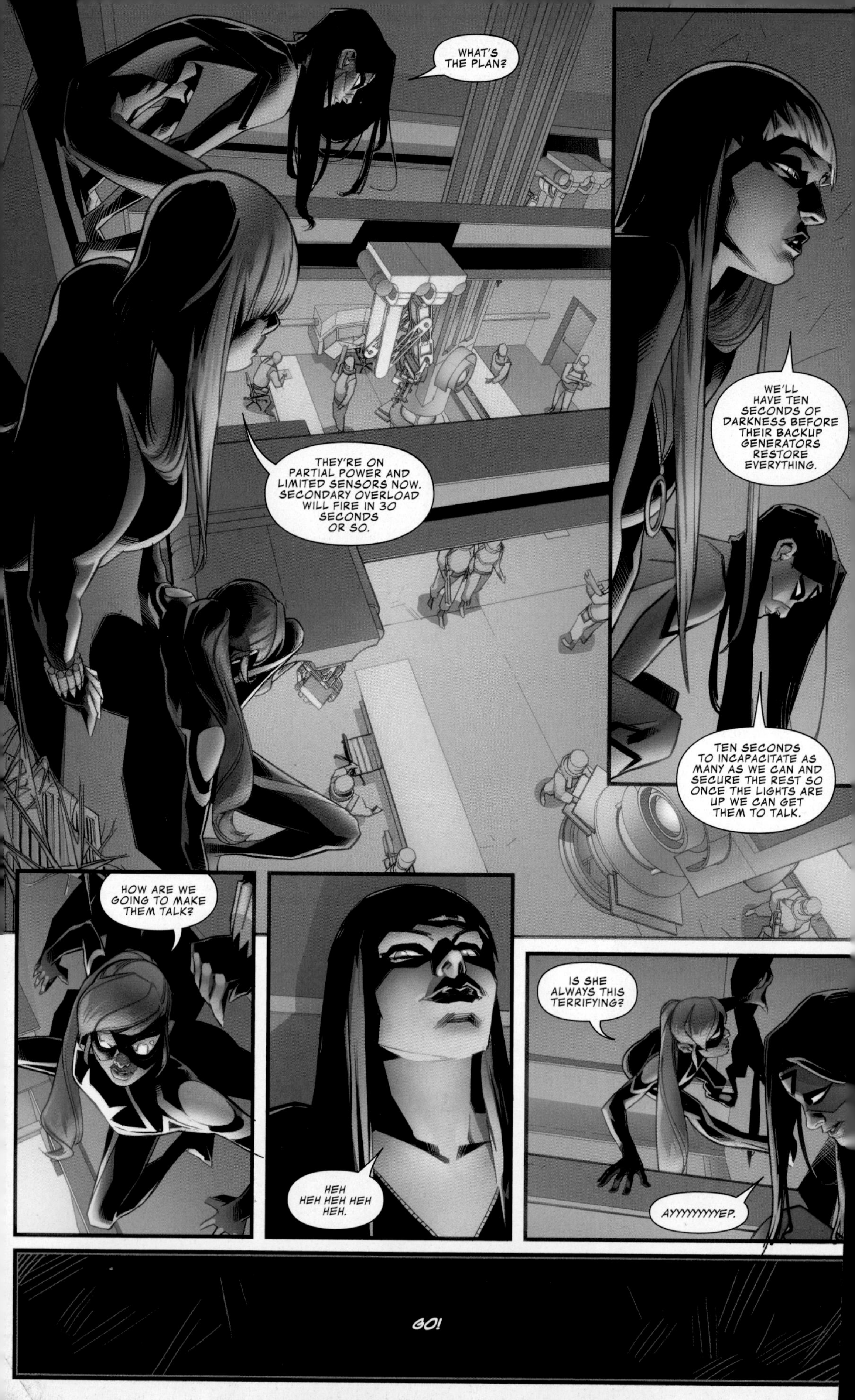
WHAT'S THE PLAN?
THEY'RE ON PARTIAL POWER AND LIMITED SENSORS NOW. SECONDARY OVERLOAD WILL FIRE IN 30 SECONDS OR SO.
WE'LL HAVE TEN SECONDS OF DARKNESS BEFORE THEIR BACKUP GENERATORS RESTORE EVERYTHING.
TEN SECONDS TO INCAPACITATE AS MANY AS WE CAN AND SECURE THE REST SO ONCE THE LIGHTS ARE UP WE CAN GET THEM TO TALK.
HOW ARE WE GOING TO MAKE THEM TALK?
HEH HEH HEH HEH HEH.
IS SHE ALWAYS THIS TERRIFYING?
AYYYYYYYYYEP.
GO!

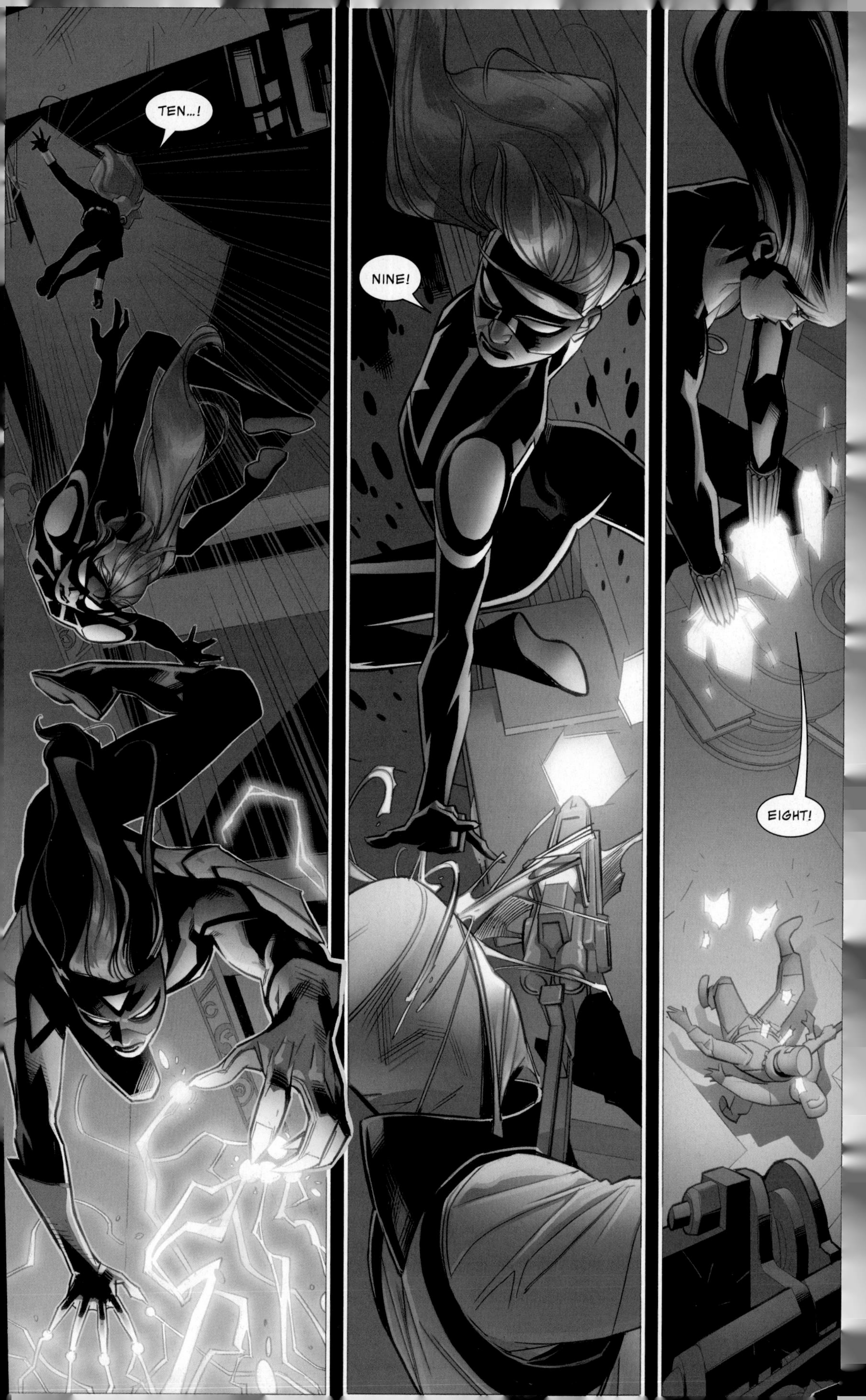
TEN...!
NINE!
EIGHT!

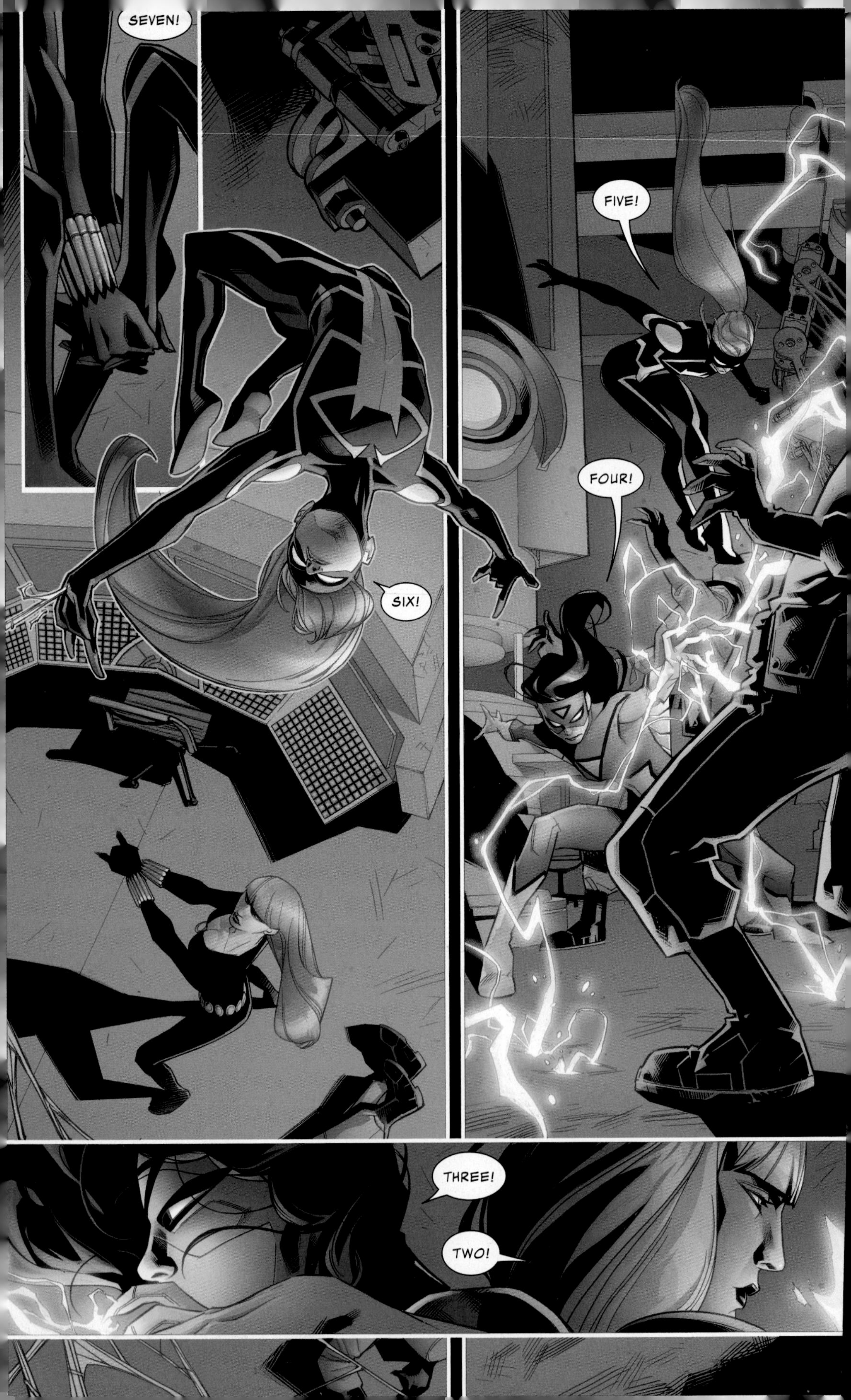
SEVEN!
SIX!
FIVE!
FOUR!
THREE!
TWO!

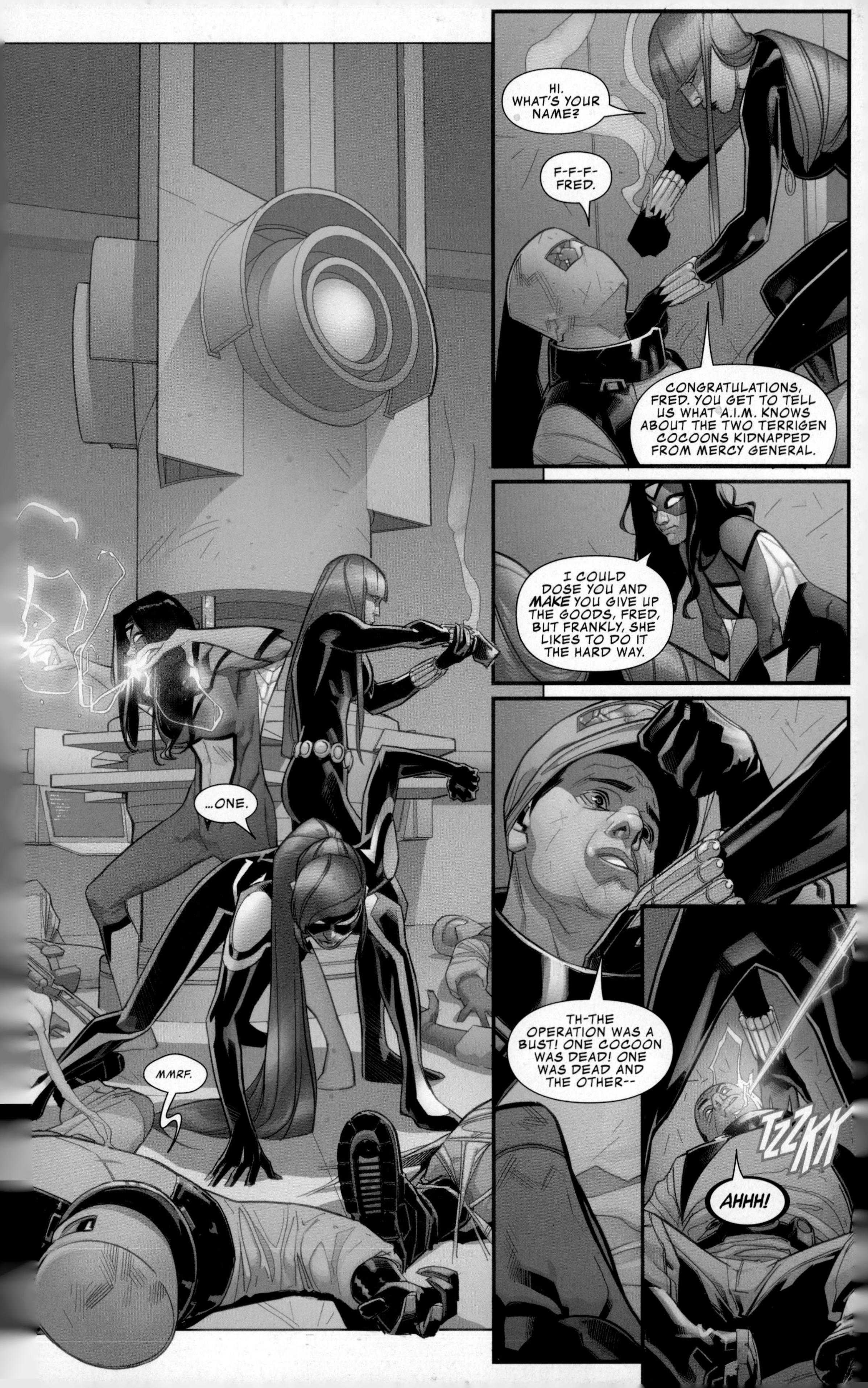
...ONE.
MMRF.
HI. WHAT'S YOUR NAME?
F-F-F-FRED.
CONGRATULATIONS, FRED. YOU GET TO TELL US WHAT A.I.M. KNOWS ABOUT THE TWO TERRIGEN COCOONS KIDNAPPED FROM MERCY GENERAL.
I COULD DOSE YOU AND MAKE YOU GIVE UP THE GOODS, FRED, BUT FRANKLY, SHE LIKES TO DO IT THE HARD WAY.
TH-THE OPERATION WAS A BUST! ONE COCOON WAS DEAD! ONE WAS DEAD AND THE OTHER--
TZZKK
AHHH!

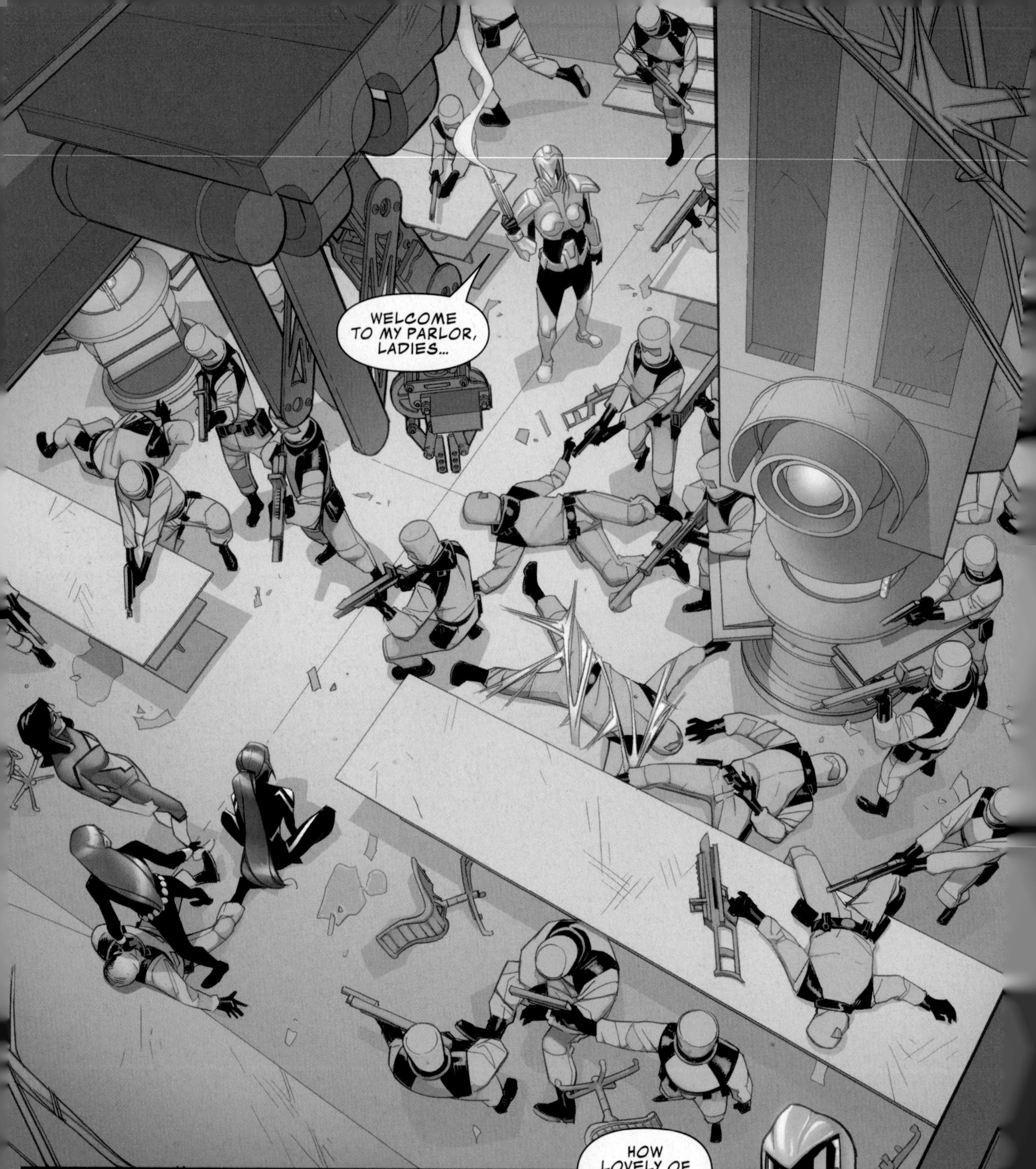
WELCOME TO MY PARLOR, LADIES...

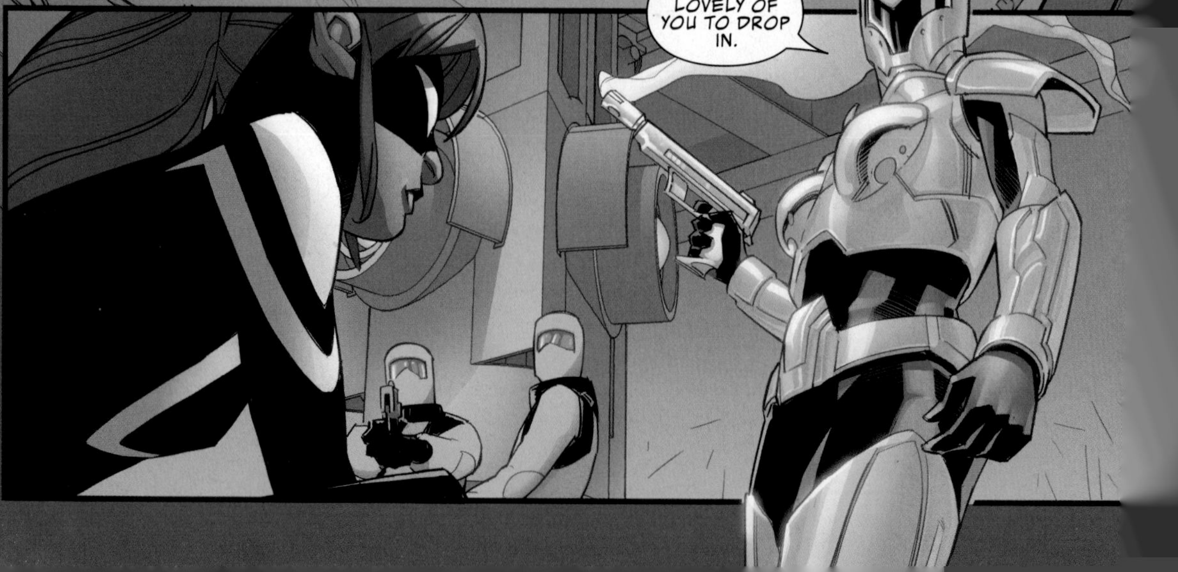
HOW LOVELY OF YOU TO DROP IN.

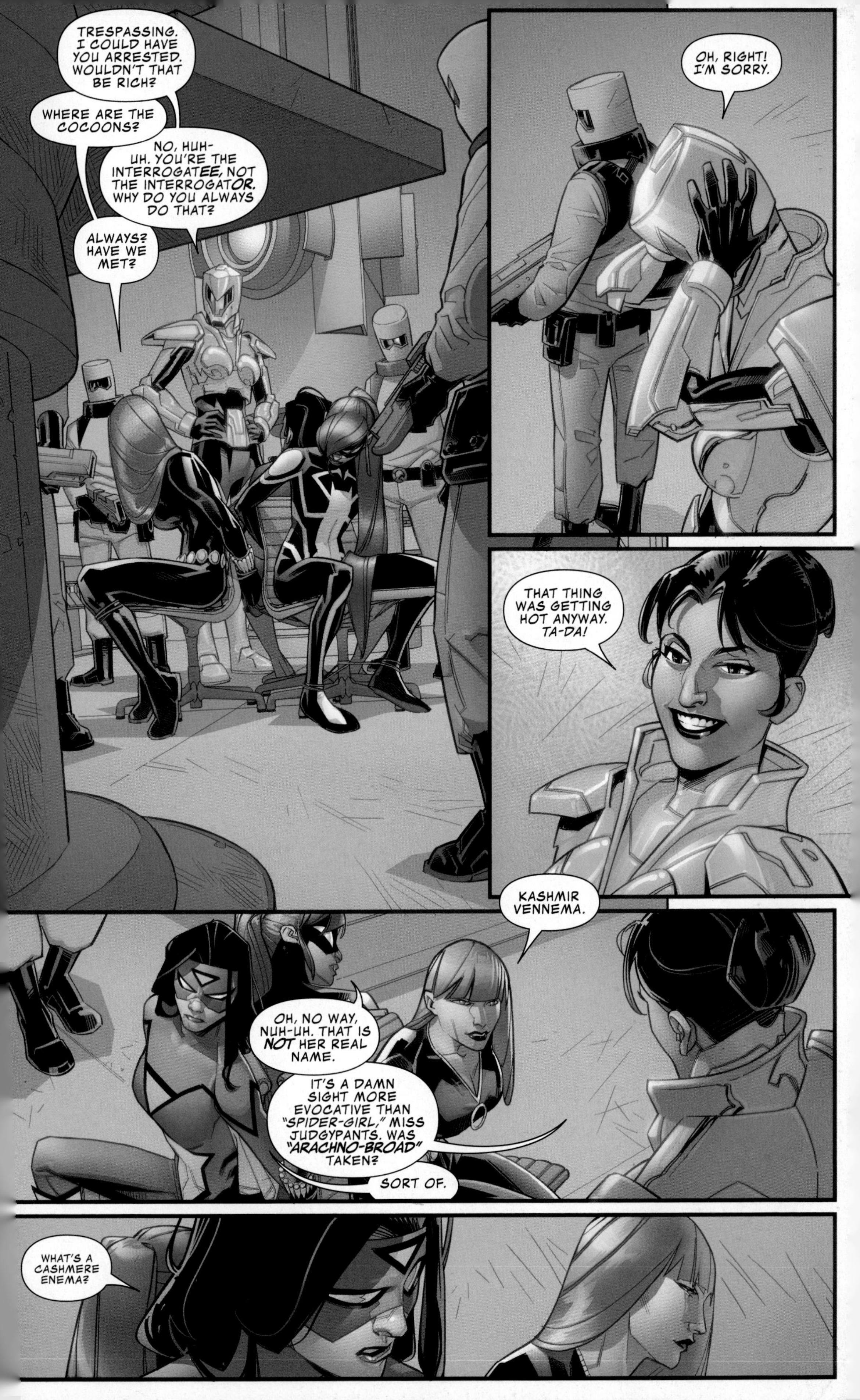
TRESPASSING. I COULD HAVE YOU ARRESTED. WOULDN'T THAT BE RICH?
WHERE ARE THE COCOONS?
NO, HUH-UH. YOU'RE THE INTERROGATEE, NOT THE INTERROGATOR. WHY DO YOU ALWAYS DO THAT?
ALWAYS? HAVE WE MET?
OH, RIGHT! I'M SORRY.
THAT THING WAS GETTING HOT ANYWAY. TA-DA!
KASHMIR VENNEMA.
OH, NO WAY, NUH-UH. THAT IS NOT HER REAL NAME.
IT'S A DAMN SIGHT MORE EVOCATIVE THAN "SPIDER-GIRL," MISS JUDGYPANTS. WAS "ARACHNO-BROAD" TAKEN?
SORT OF.
WHAT'S A CASHMERE ENEMA?

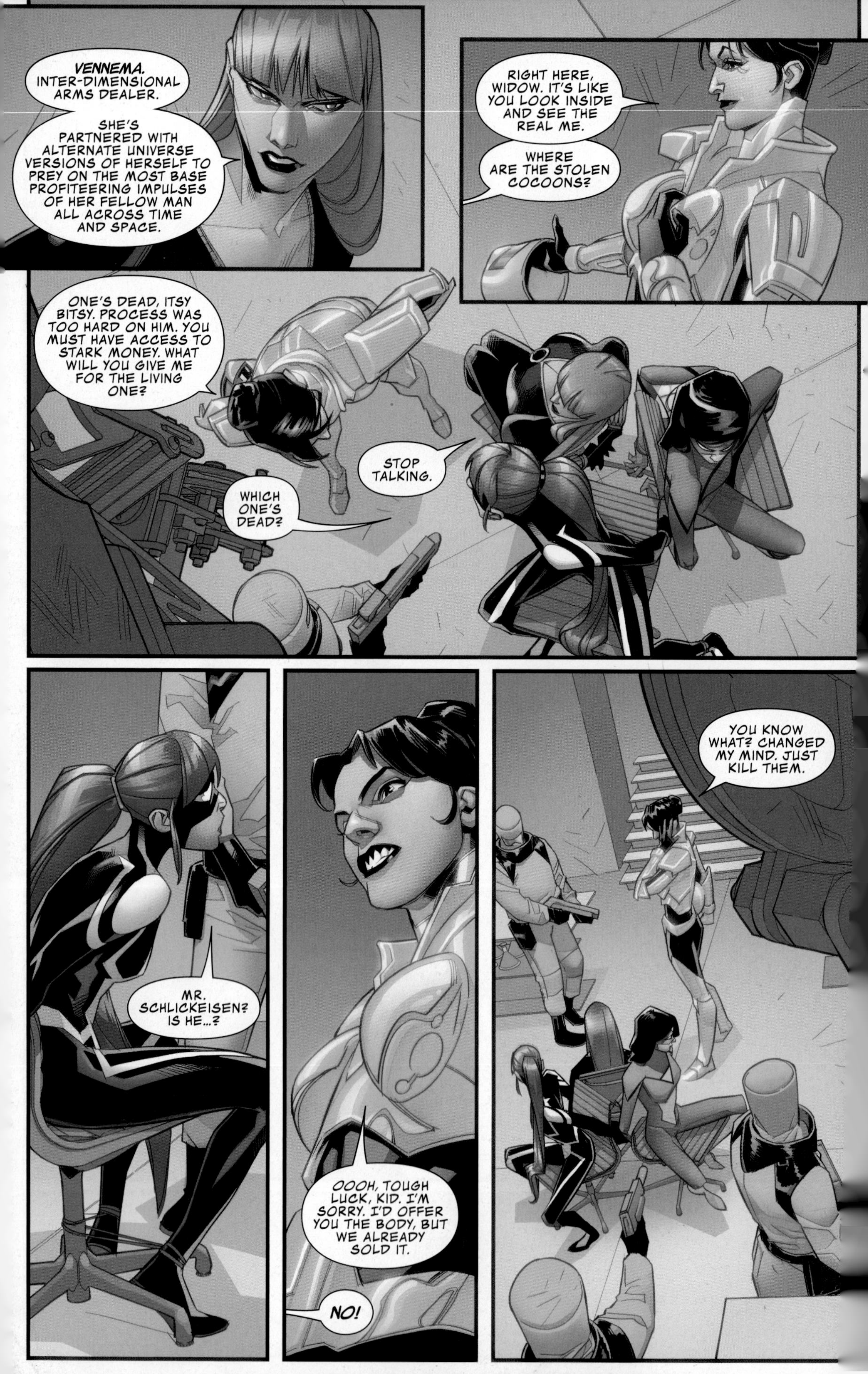
VENNEMA. INTER-DIMENSIONAL ARMS DEALER.
SHE'S PARTNERED WITH ALTERNATE UNIVERSE VERSIONS OF HERSELF TO PREY ON THE MOST BASE PROFITEERING IMPULSES OF HER FELLOW MAN ALL ACROSS TIME AND SPACE.
RIGHT HERE, WIDOW. IT'S LIKE YOU LOOK INSIDE AND SEE THE REAL ME.
WHERE ARE THE STOLEN COCOONS?
ONE'S DEAD, ITSY BITSY. PROCESS WAS TOO HARD ON HIM. YOU MUST HAVE ACCESS TO STARK MONEY. WHAT WILL YOU GIVE ME FOR THE LIVING ONE?
STOP TALKING.
WHICH ONE'S DEAD?
MR. SCHLICKEISEN? IS HE...?
OOOH, TOUGH LUCK, KID. I'M SORRY. I'D OFFER YOU THE BODY, BUT WE ALREADY SOLD IT.
NO!
YOU KNOW WHAT? CHANGED MY MIND. JUST KILL THEM.

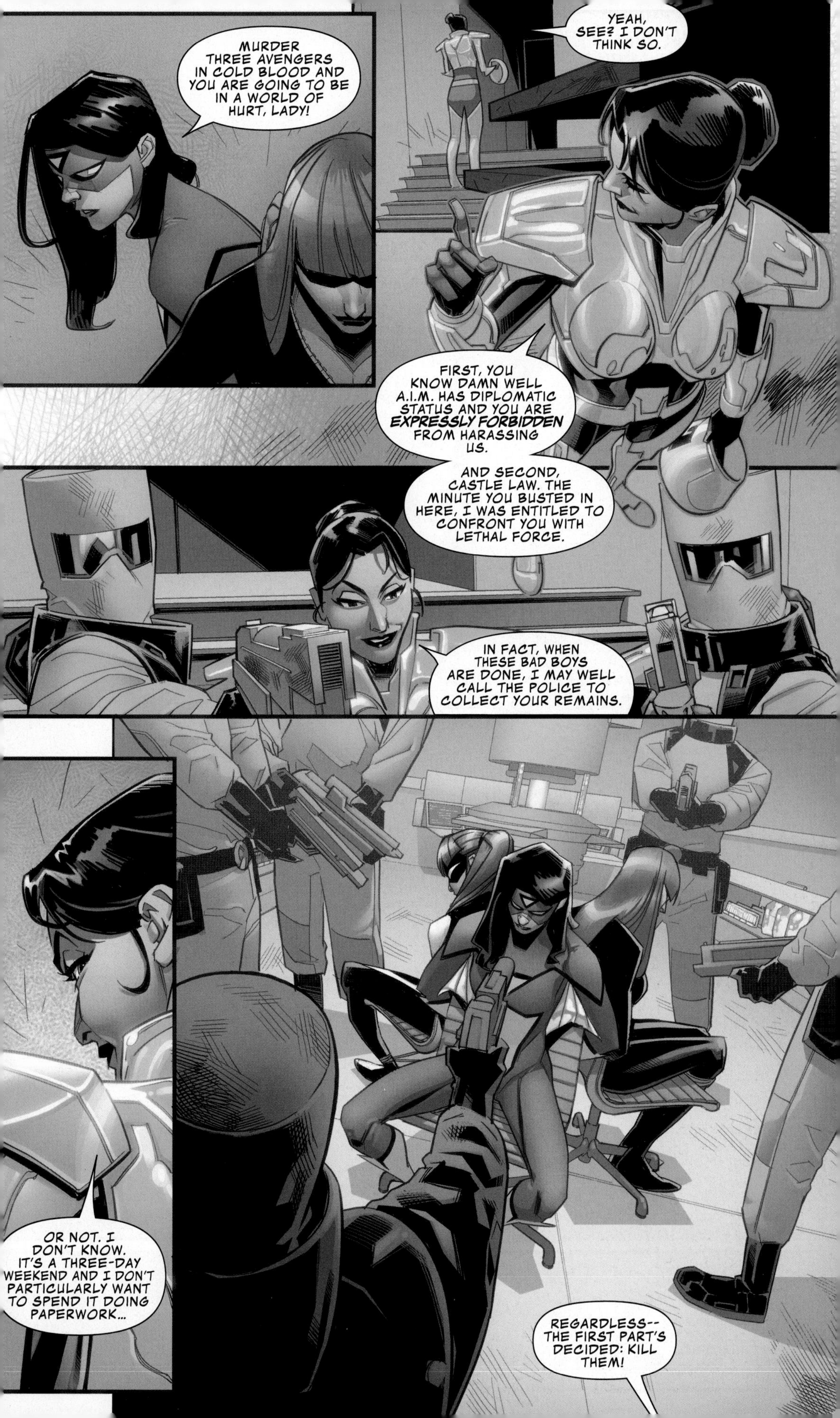
MURDER THREE AVENGERS IN COLD BLOOD AND YOU ARE GOING TO BE IN A WORLD OF HURT, LADY!
YEAH, SEE? I DON'T THINK SO.
FIRST, YOU KNOW DAMN WELL A.I.M. HAS DIPLOMATIC STATUS AND YOU ARE ***EXPRESSLY FORBIDDEN*** FROM HARASSING US.
AND SECOND, CASTLE LAW. THE MINUTE YOU BUSTED IN HERE, I WAS ENTITLED TO CONFRONT YOU WITH LETHAL FORCE.
IN FACT, WHEN THESE BAD BOYS ARE DONE, I MAY WELL CALL THE POLICE TO COLLECT YOUR REMAINS.
OR NOT. I DON'T KNOW. IT'S A THREE-DAY WEEKEND AND I DON'T PARTICULARLY WANT TO SPEND IT DOING PAPERWORK...
REGARDLESS-- THE FIRST PART'S DECIDED: KILL THEM!

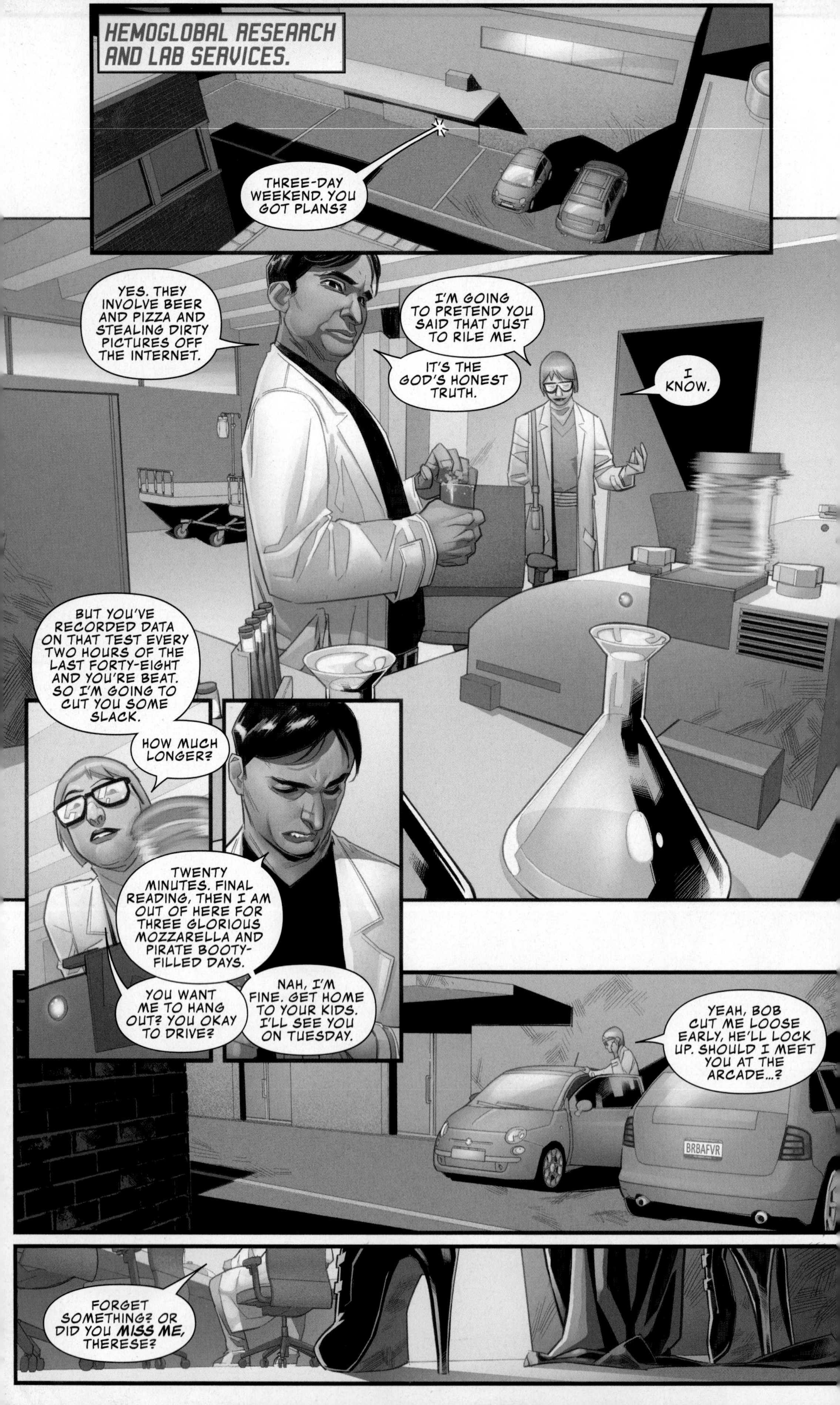

HEMOGLOBAL RESEARCH AND LAB SERVICES.
THREE-DAY WEEKEND. YOU GOT PLANS?
YES. THEY INVOLVE BEER AND PIZZA AND STEALING DIRTY PICTURES OFF THE INTERNET.
I'M GOING TO PRETEND YOU SAID THAT JUST TO RILE ME.
IT'S THE GOD'S HONEST TRUTH.
I KNOW.
BUT YOU'VE RECORDED DATA ON THAT TEST EVERY TWO HOURS OF THE LAST FORTY-EIGHT AND YOU'RE BEAT. SO I'M GOING TO CUT YOU SOME SLACK.
HOW MUCH LONGER?
TWENTY MINUTES. FINAL READING, THEN I AM OUT OF HERE FOR THREE GLORIOUS MOZZARELLA AND PIRATE BOOTY-FILLED DAYS.
YOU WANT ME TO HANG OUT? YOU OKAY TO DRIVE?
NAH, I'M FINE. GET HOME TO YOUR KIDS. I'LL SEE YOU ON TUESDAY.
YEAH, BOB CUT ME LOOSE EARLY, HE'LL LOCK UP. SHOULD I MEET YOU AT THE ARCADE...?
BRBAFVR
FORGET SOMETHING? OR DID YOU MISS ME, THERESE?

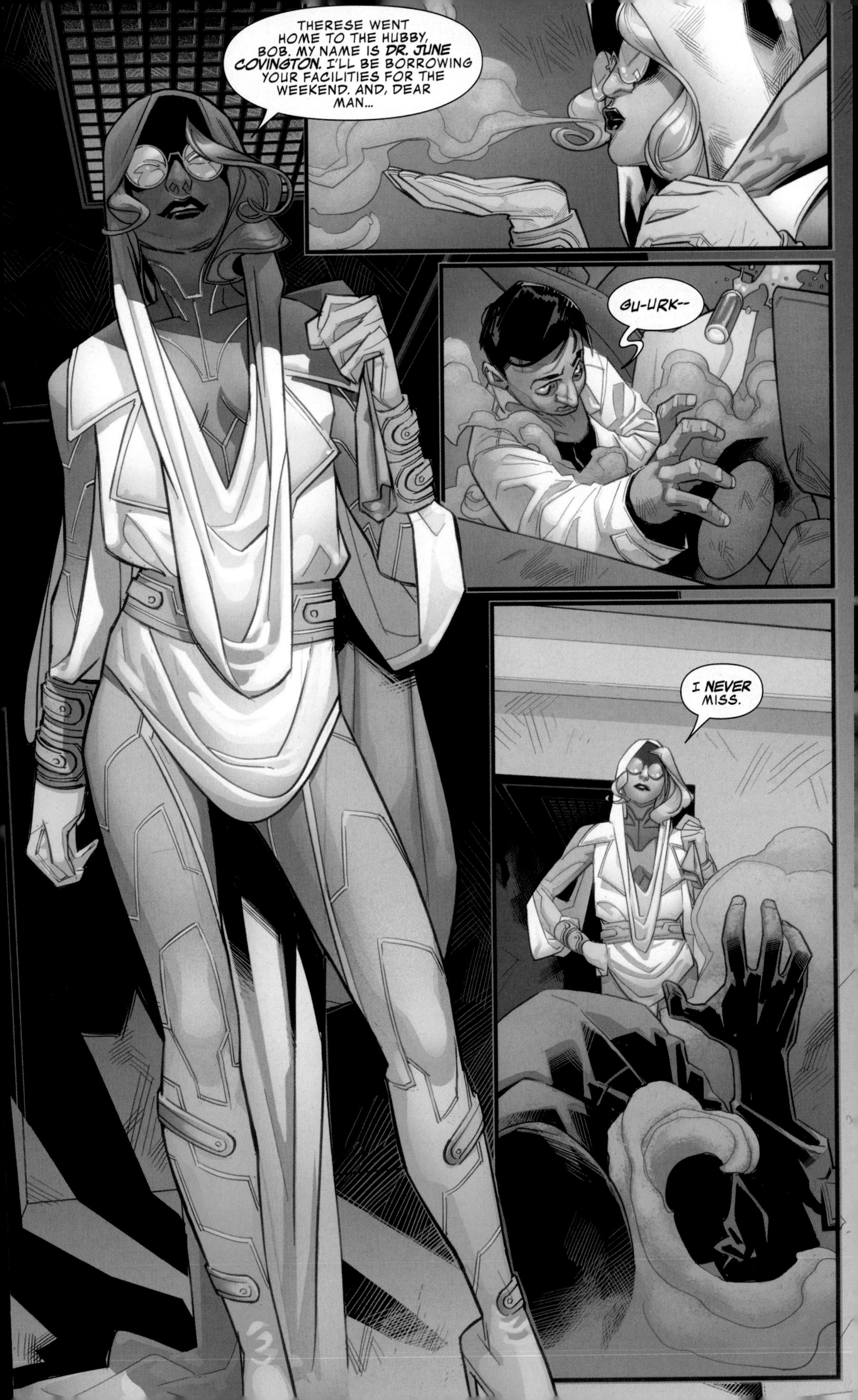
THERESE WENT HOME TO THE HUBBY, BOB. MY NAME IS DR. JUNE COVINGTON. I'LL BE BORROWING YOUR FACILITIES FOR THE WEEKEND. AND, DEAR MAN...
GU-URK--
I NEVER MISS.

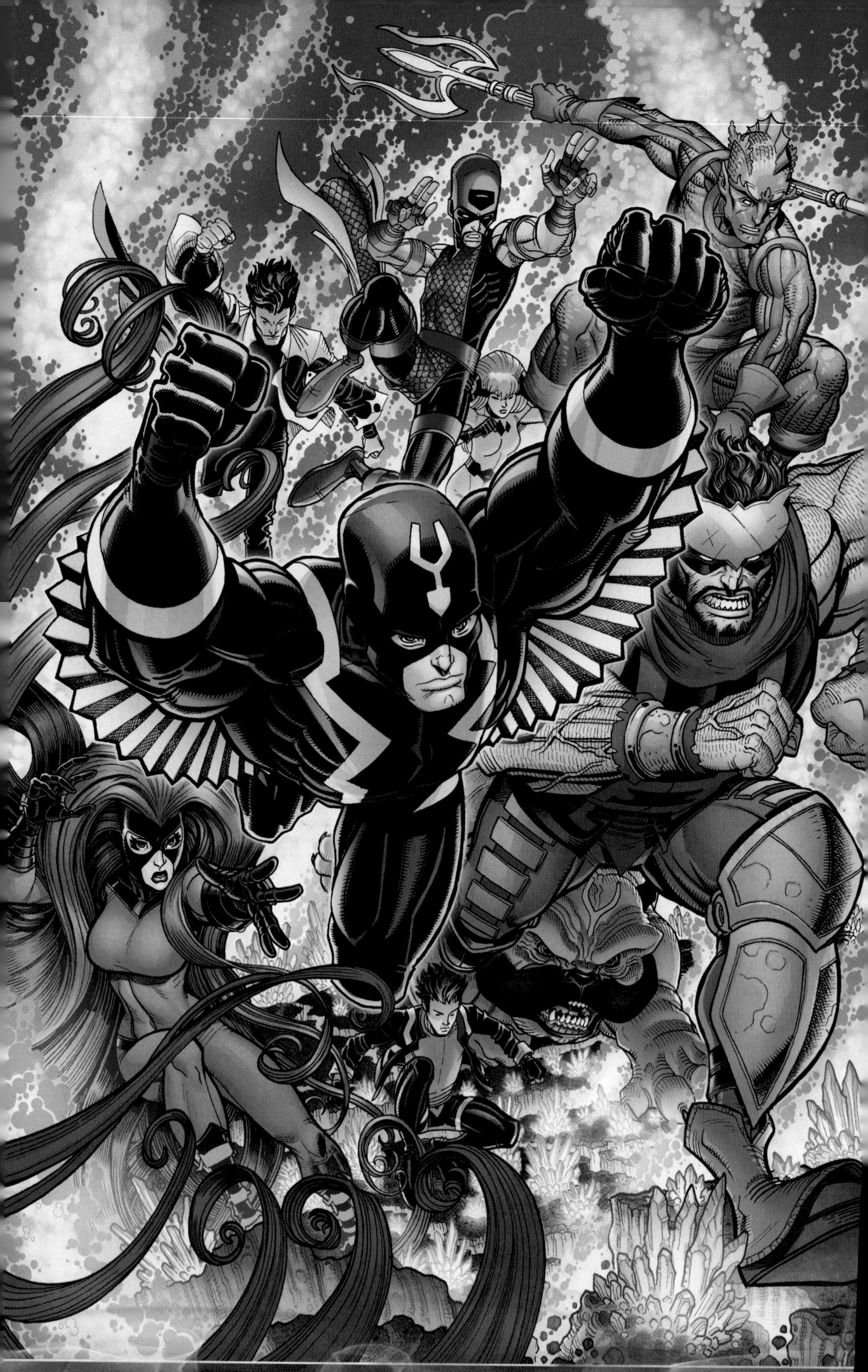

INHUMANITY #1 VARIANT BY NICK BRADSHAW & LAURA MARTIN

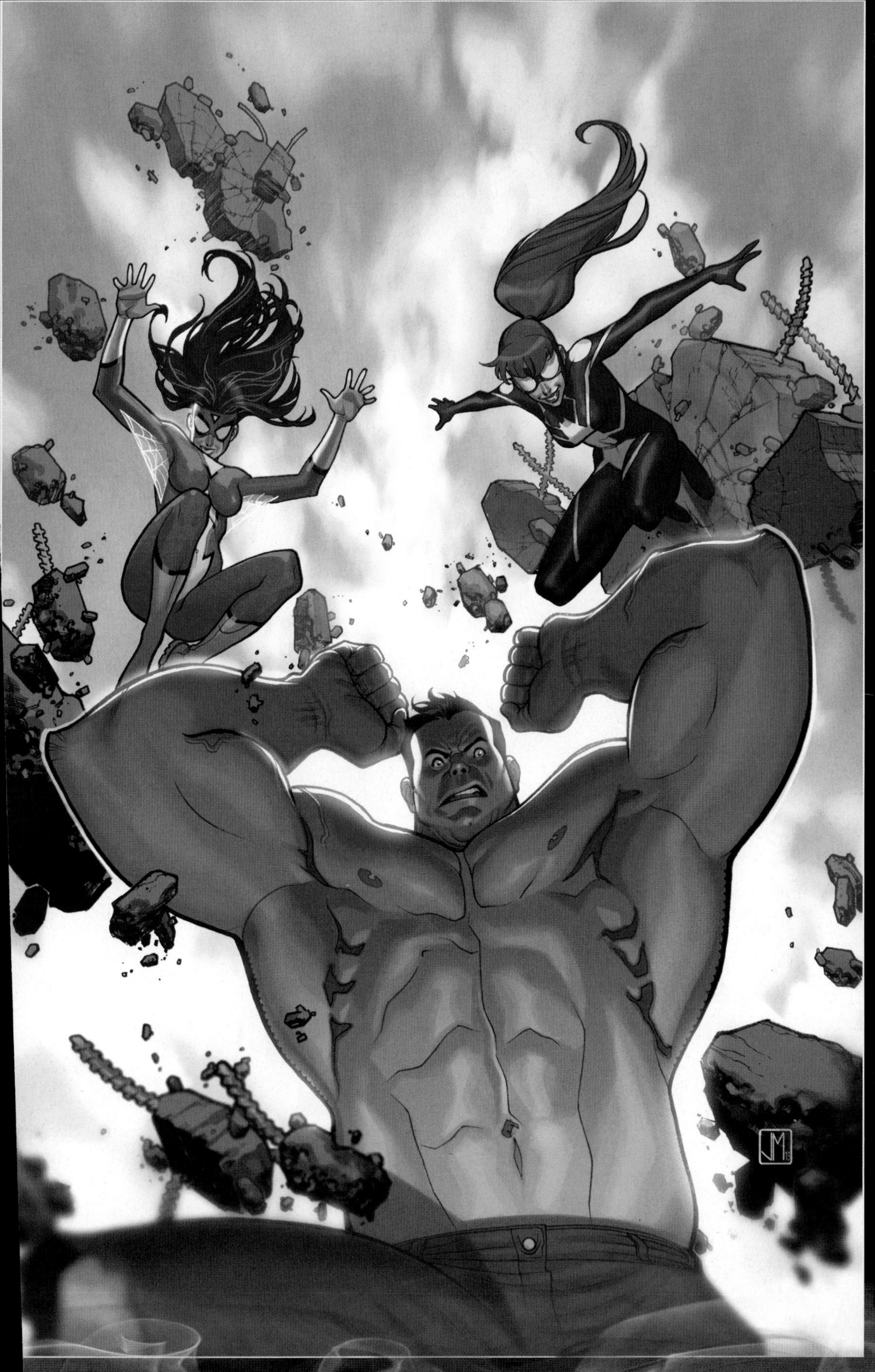

AVENGERS ASSEMBLE #22

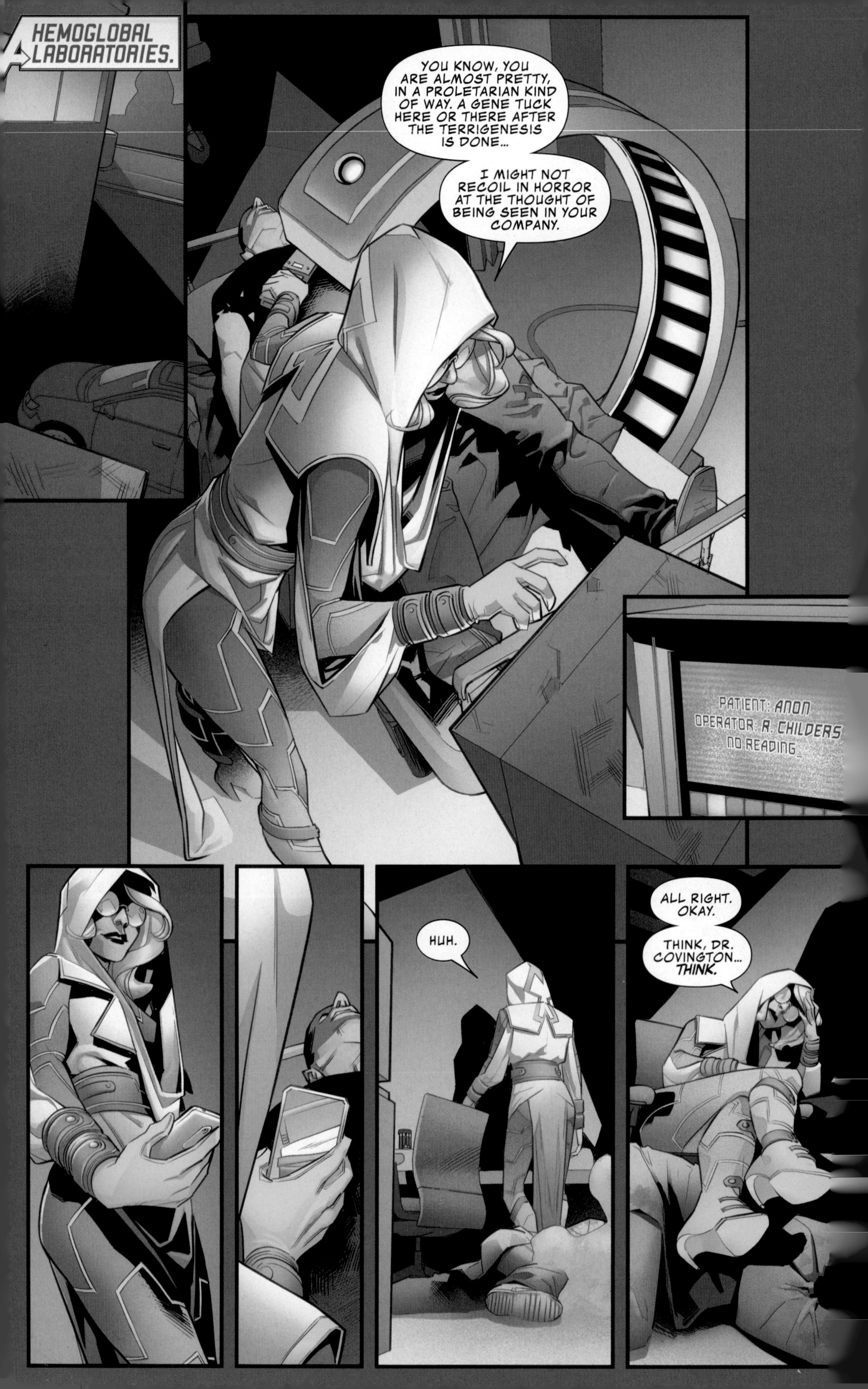
HEMOGLOBAL LABORATORIES.
YOU KNOW, YOU ARE ALMOST PRETTY, IN A PROLETARIAN KIND OF WAY. A GENE TUCK HERE OR THERE AFTER THE TERRIGENESIS IS DONE...
I MIGHT NOT RECOIL IN HORROR AT THE THOUGHT OF BEING SEEN IN YOUR COMPANY.
PATIENT: ANON
OPERATOR: A. CHILDERS
NO READING_
HUH.
ALL RIGHT. OKAY.
THINK, DR. COVINGTON... *THINK.*

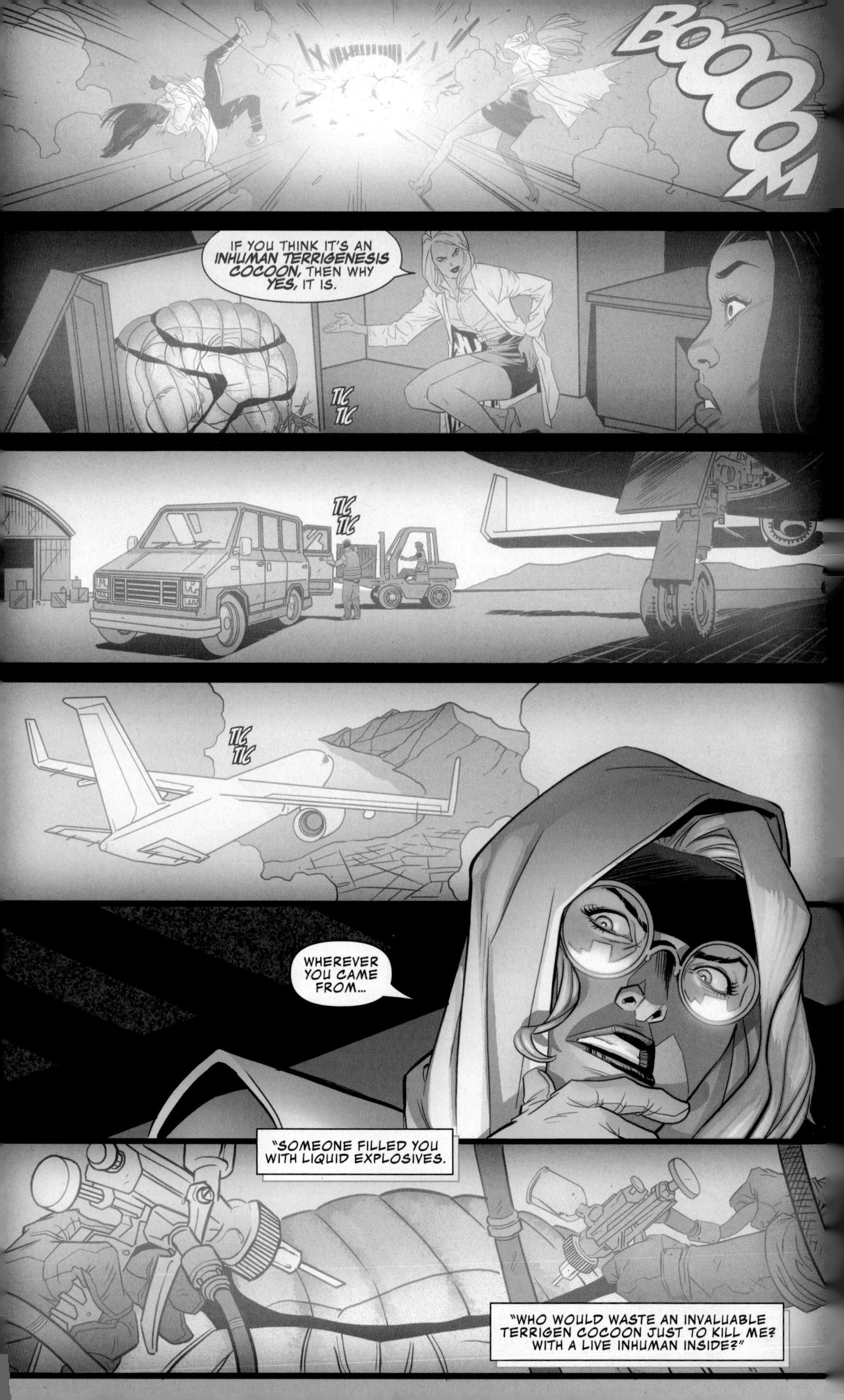
BOOOOM
IF YOU THINK IT'S AN INHUMAN TERRIGENESIS COCOON, THEN WHY YES, IT IS.
TIC TIC
TIC TIC
TIC TIC
WHEREVER YOU CAME FROM...
"SOMEONE FILLED YOU WITH LIQUID EXPLOSIVES.
"WHO WOULD WASTE AN INVALUABLE TERRIGEN COCOON JUST TO KILL ME? WITH A LIVE INHUMAN INSIDE?"

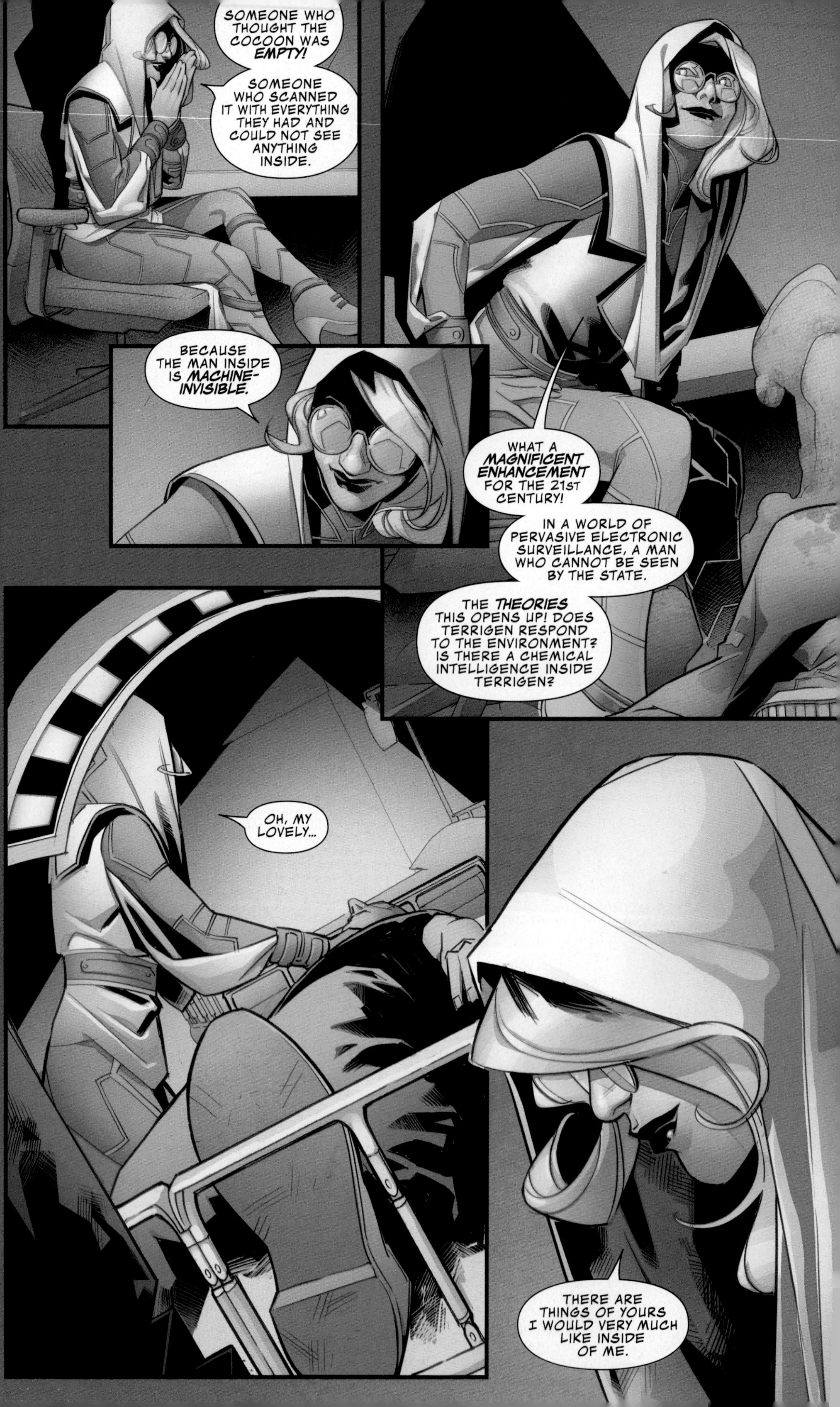
SOMEONE WHO THOUGHT THE COCOON WAS EMPTY!
SOMEONE WHO SCANNED IT WITH EVERYTHING THEY HAD AND COULD NOT SEE ANYTHING INSIDE.
BECAUSE THE MAN INSIDE IS MACHINE-INVISIBLE.
WHAT A MAGNIFICENT ENHANCEMENT FOR THE 21ST CENTURY!
IN A WORLD OF PERVASIVE ELECTRONIC SURVEILLANCE, A MAN WHO CANNOT BE SEEN BY THE STATE.
THE THEORIES THIS OPENS UP! DOES TERRIGEN RESPOND TO THE ENVIRONMENT? IS THERE A CHEMICAL INTELLIGENCE INSIDE TERRIGEN?
OH, MY LOVELY...
THERE ARE THINGS OF YOURS I WOULD VERY MUCH LIKE INSIDE OF ME.

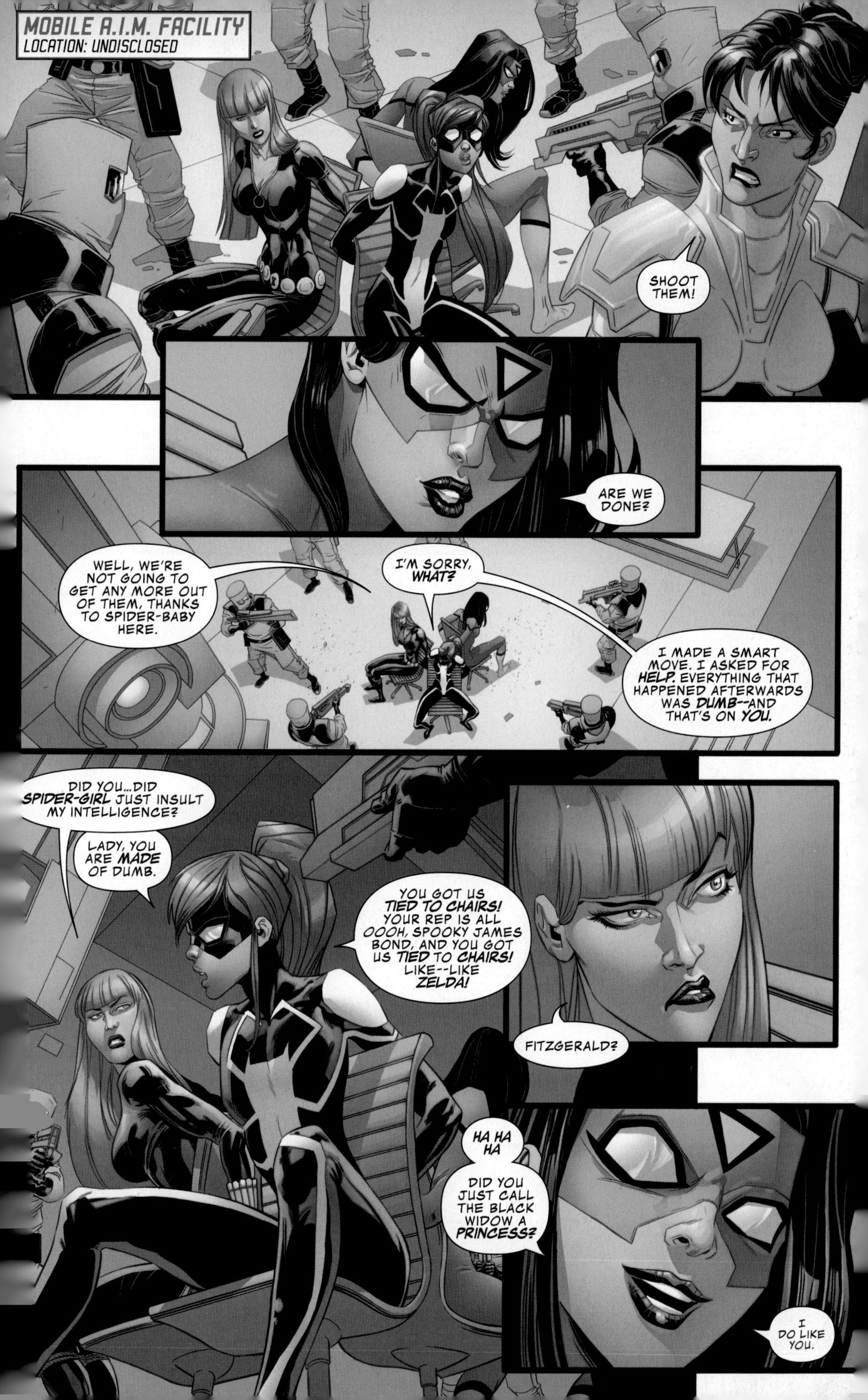
MOBILE A.I.M. FACILITY
LOCATION: UNDISCLOSED
SHOOT THEM!
ARE WE DONE?
WELL, WE'RE NOT GOING TO GET ANY MORE OUT OF THEM, THANKS TO SPIDER-BABY HERE.
I'M SORRY, WHAT?
I MADE A SMART MOVE. I ASKED FOR HELP. EVERYTHING THAT HAPPENED AFTERWARDS WAS DUMB--AND THAT'S ON YOU.
DID YOU...DID SPIDER-GIRL JUST INSULT MY INTELLIGENCE?
LADY, YOU ARE MADE OF DUMB.
YOU GOT US TIED TO CHAIRS! YOUR REP IS ALL OOOH, SPOOKY JAMES BOND, AND YOU GOT US TIED TO CHAIRS! LIKE--LIKE ZELDA!
FITZGERALD?
HA HA HA
DID YOU JUST CALL THE BLACK WIDOW A PRINCESS?
I DO LIKE YOU.

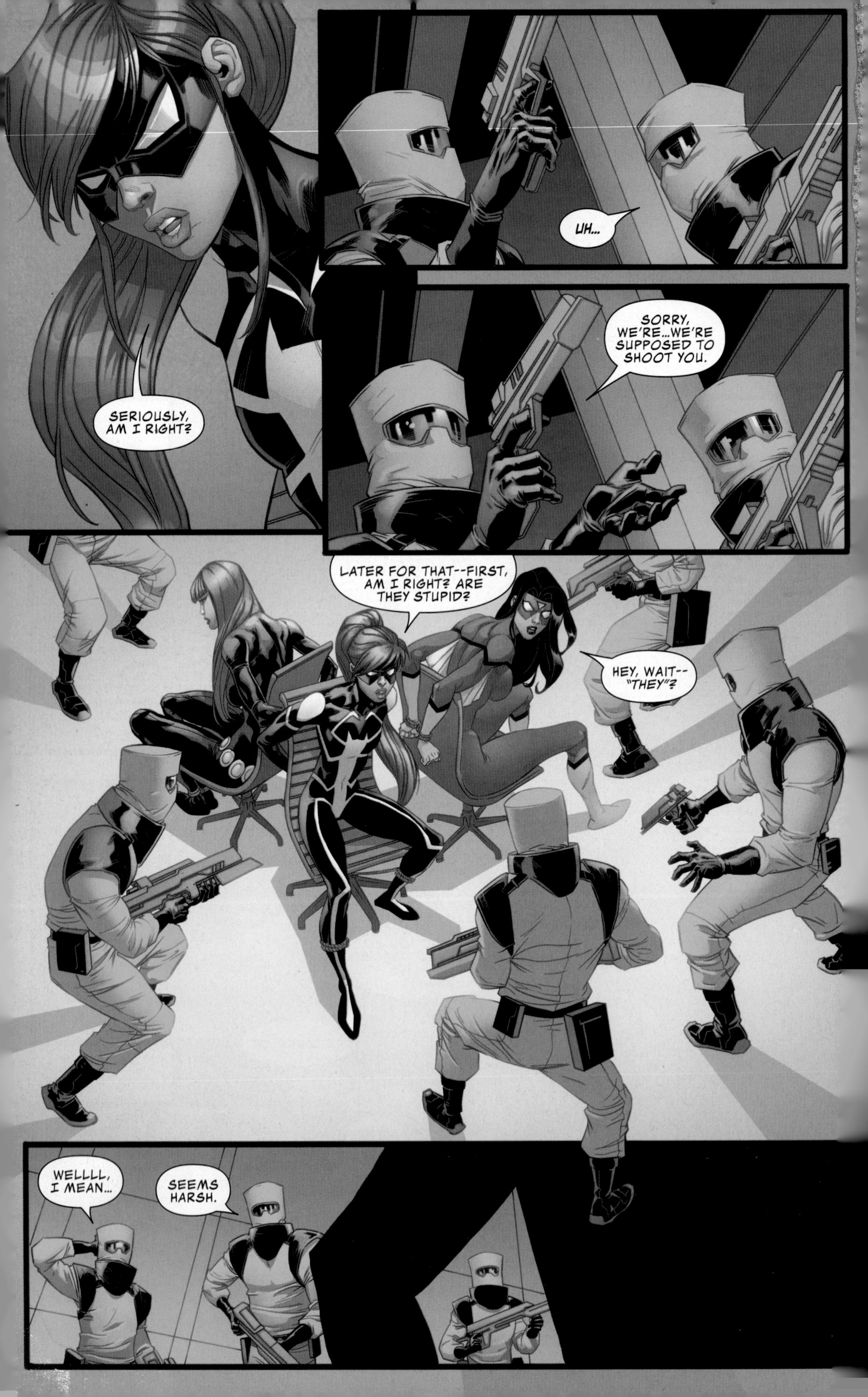
SERIOUSLY, AM I RIGHT?
UH...
SORRY, WE'RE...WE'RE SUPPOSED TO SHOOT YOU.
LATER FOR THAT--FIRST, AM I RIGHT? ARE THEY STUPID?
HEY, WAIT-- "THEY"?
WELLLL, I MEAN...
SEEMS HARSH.

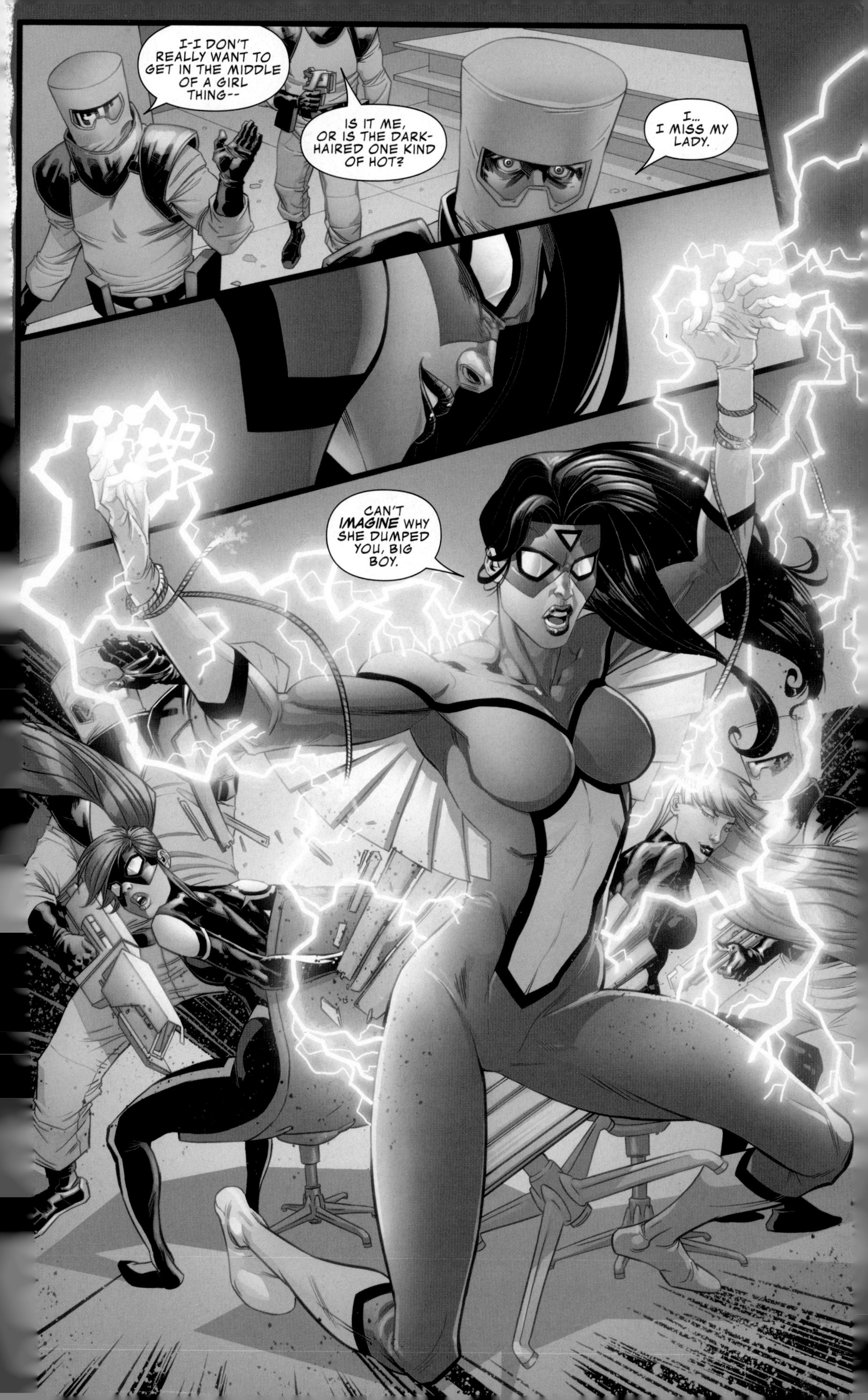
I-I DON'T REALLY WANT TO GET IN THE MIDDLE OF A GIRL THING--
IS IT ME, OR IS THE DARK-HAIRED ONE KIND OF HOT?
I... I MISS MY LADY.
CAN'T IMAGINE WHY SHE DUMPED YOU, BIG BOY.

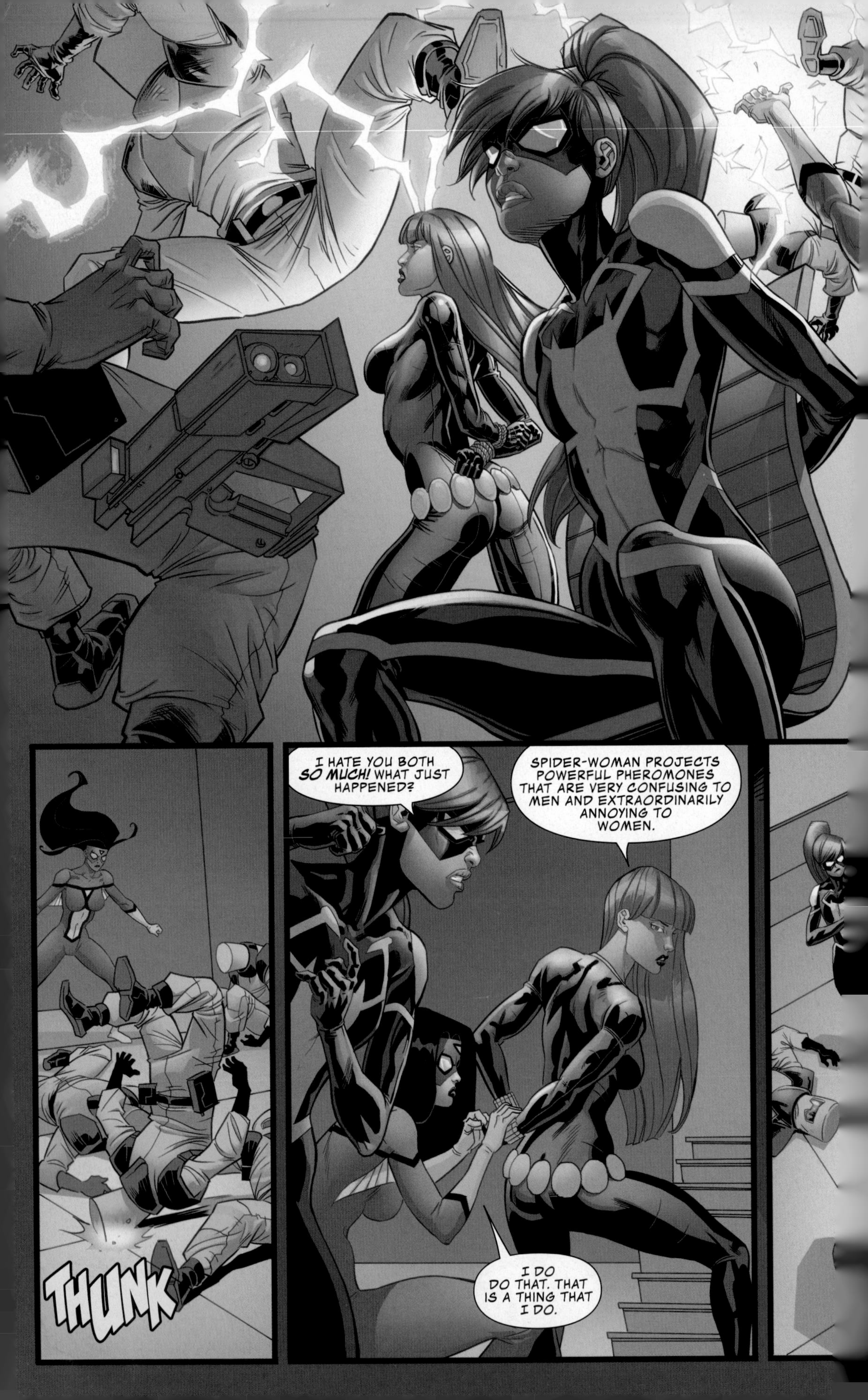
THUNK
I HATE YOU BOTH SO MUCH! WHAT JUST HAPPENED?
SPIDER-WOMAN PROJECTS POWERFUL PHEROMONES THAT ARE VERY CONFUSING TO MEN AND EXTRAORDINARILY ANNOYING TO WOMEN.
I DO DO THAT. THAT IS A THING THAT I DO.

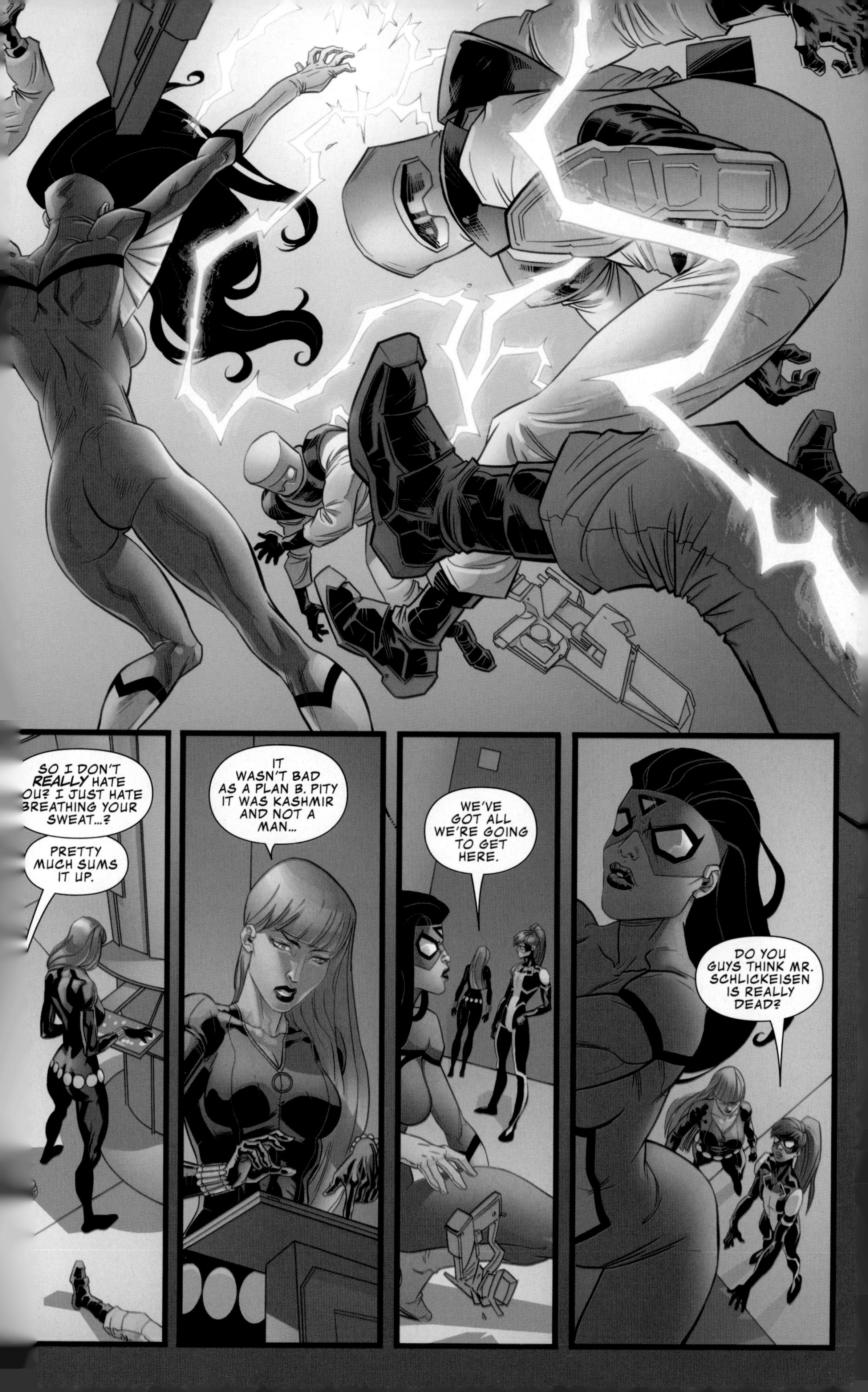

SO I DON'T *REALLY* HATE OU? I JUST HATE BREATHING YOUR SWEAT...?
PRETTY MUCH SUMS IT UP.
IT WASN'T BAD AS A PLAN B. PITY IT WAS KASHMIR AND NOT A MAN...
WE'VE GOT ALL WE'RE GOING TO GET HERE.
DO YOU GUYS THINK MR. SCHLICKEISEN IS REALLY DEAD?

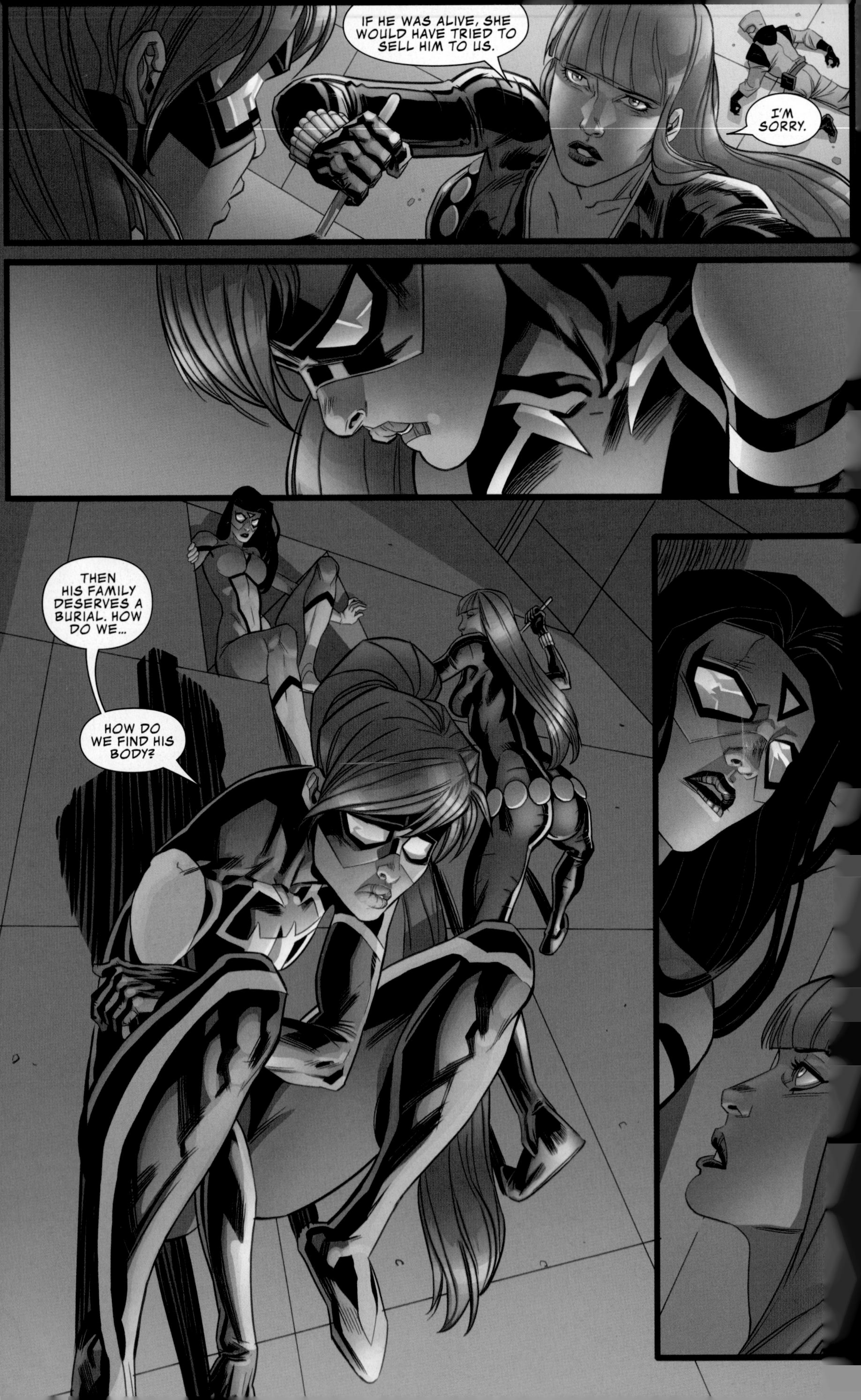
IF HE WAS ALIVE, SHE WOULD HAVE TRIED TO SELL HIM TO US.
I'M SORRY.
THEN HIS FAMILY DESERVES A BURIAL. HOW DO WE...
HOW DO WE FIND HIS BODY?

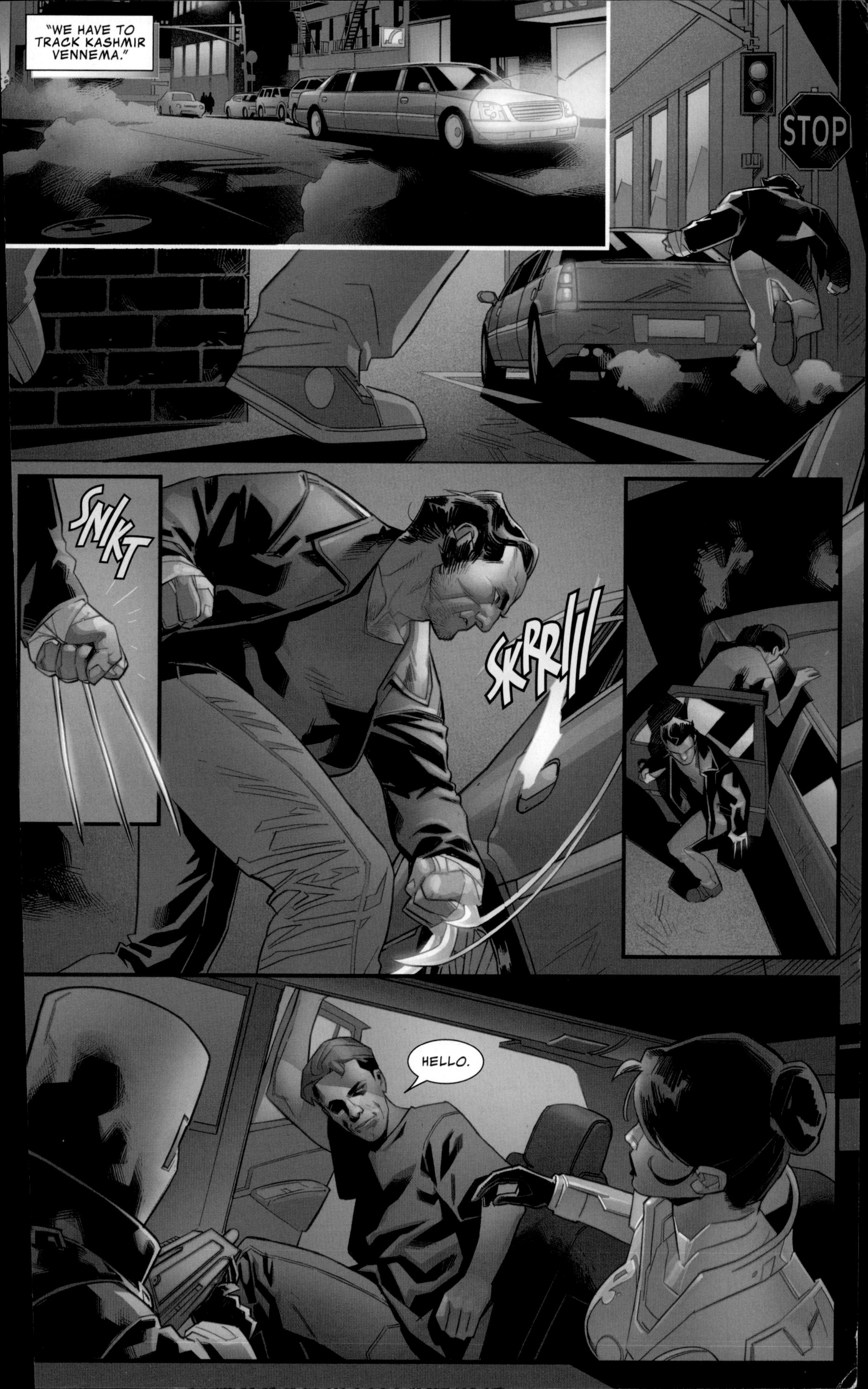
"WE HAVE TO TRACK KASHMIR VENNEMA."
STOP
SNIKT
SKRRIII
HELLO.

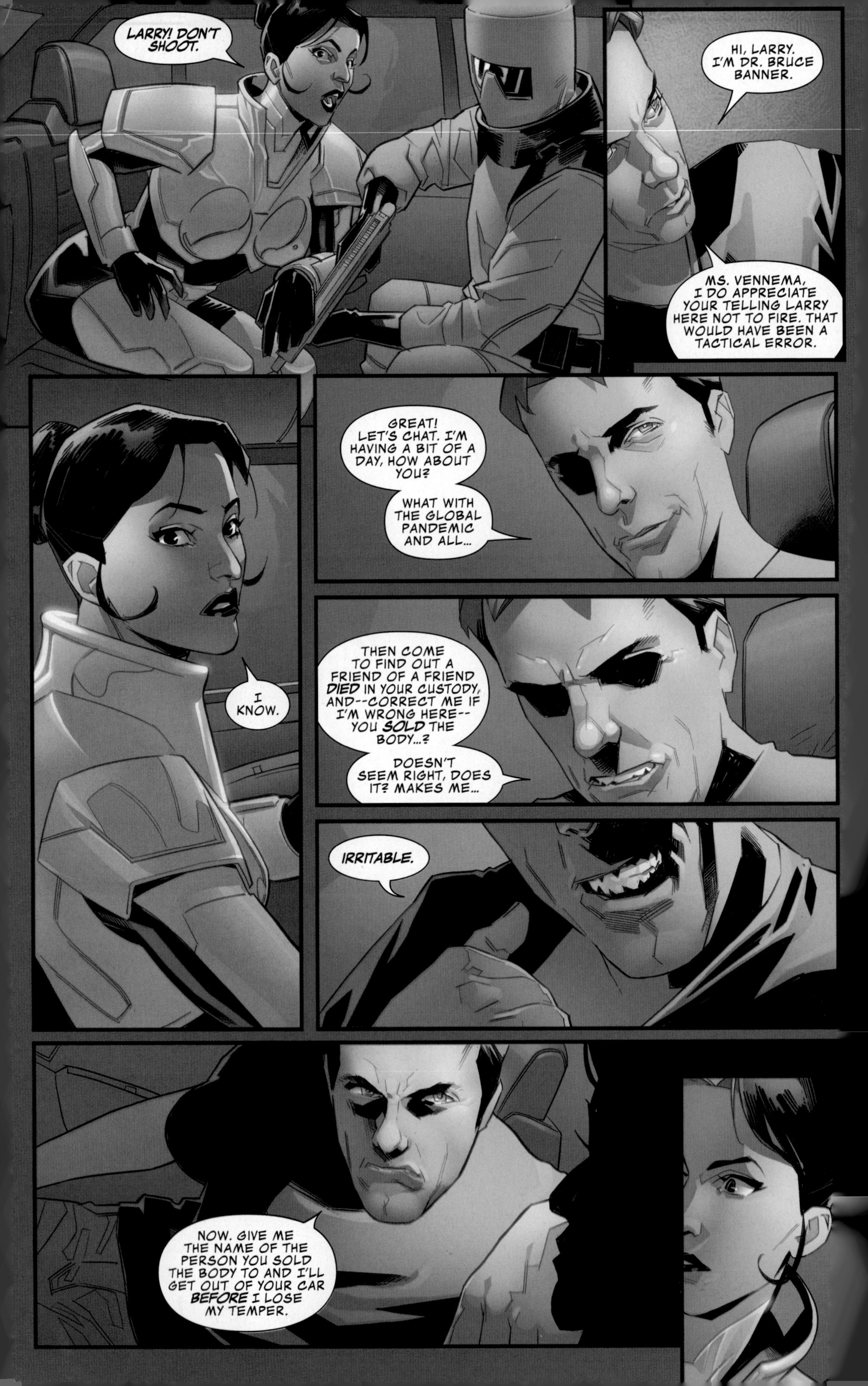
LARRY! DON'T SHOOT.
HI, LARRY. I'M DR. BRUCE BANNER.
MS. VENNEMA, I DO APPRECIATE YOUR TELLING LARRY HERE NOT TO FIRE. THAT WOULD HAVE BEEN A TACTICAL ERROR.
GREAT! LET'S CHAT. I'M HAVING A BIT OF A DAY, HOW ABOUT YOU?
WHAT WITH THE GLOBAL PANDEMIC AND ALL...
I KNOW.
THEN COME TO FIND OUT A FRIEND OF A FRIEND DIED IN YOUR CUSTODY, AND--CORRECT ME IF I'M WRONG HERE--YOU SOLD THE BODY...?
DOESN'T SEEM RIGHT, DOES IT? MAKES ME...
IRRITABLE.
NOW. GIVE ME THE NAME OF THE PERSON YOU SOLD THE BODY TO AND I'LL GET OUT OF YOUR CAR BEFORE I LOSE MY TEMPER.

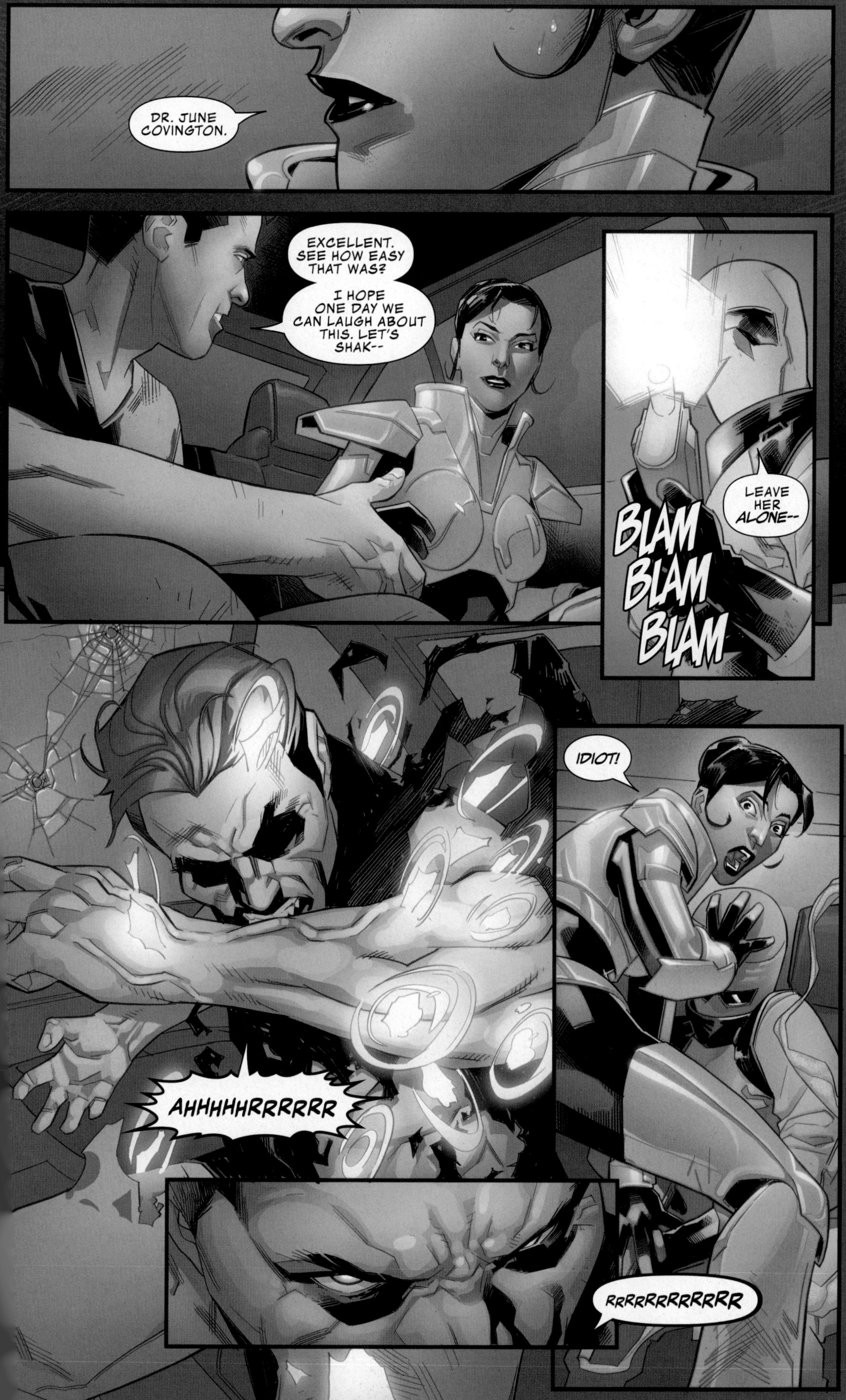
DR. JUNE COVINGTON.
EXCELLENT. SEE HOW EASY THAT WAS?
I HOPE ONE DAY WE CAN LAUGH ABOUT THIS. LET'S SHAK--
LEAVE HER ALONE--
BLAM BLAM BLAM
IDIOT!
AHHHHHRRRRRR
RRRRRRRRRRRR

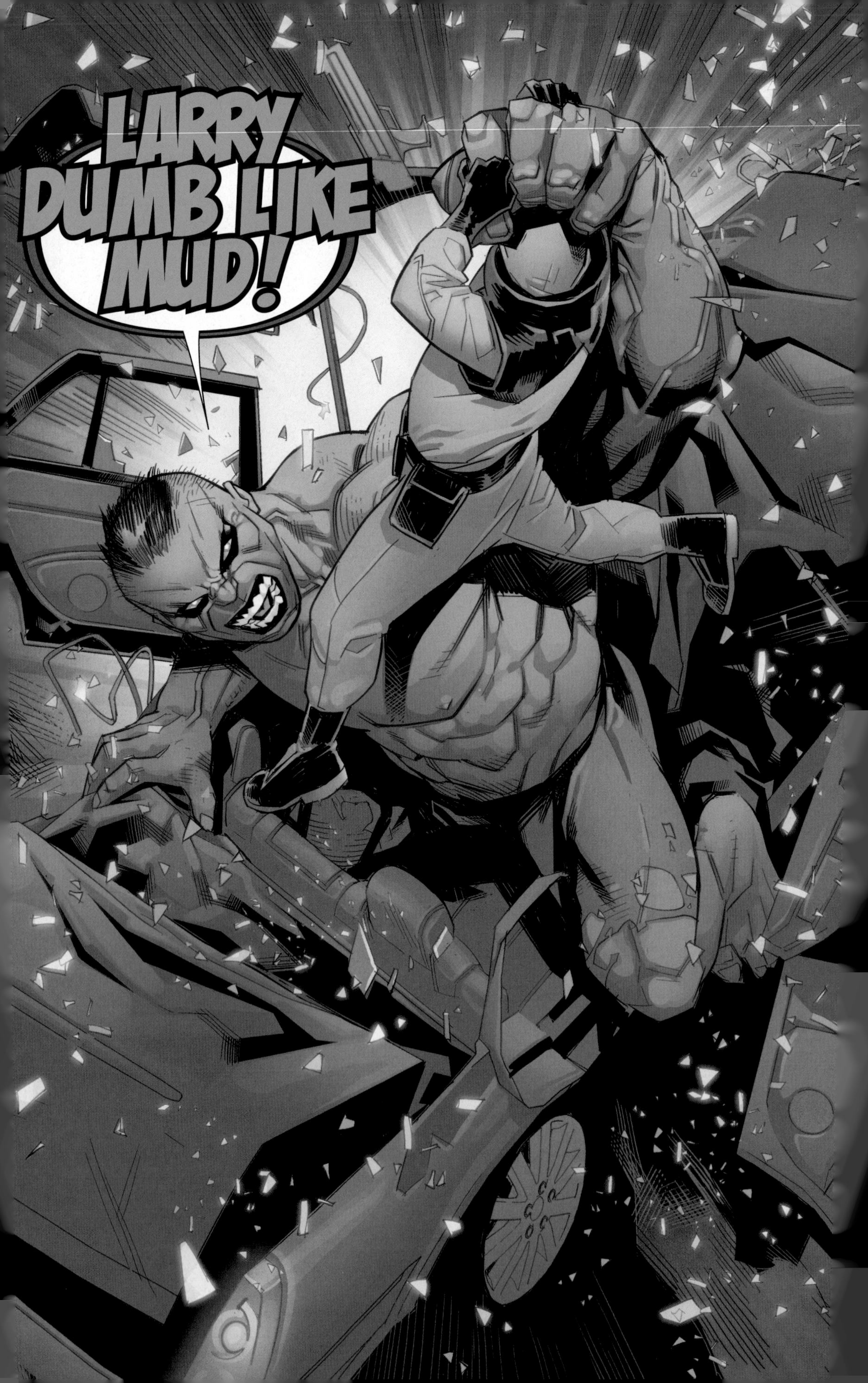
LARRY DUMB LIKE MUD!

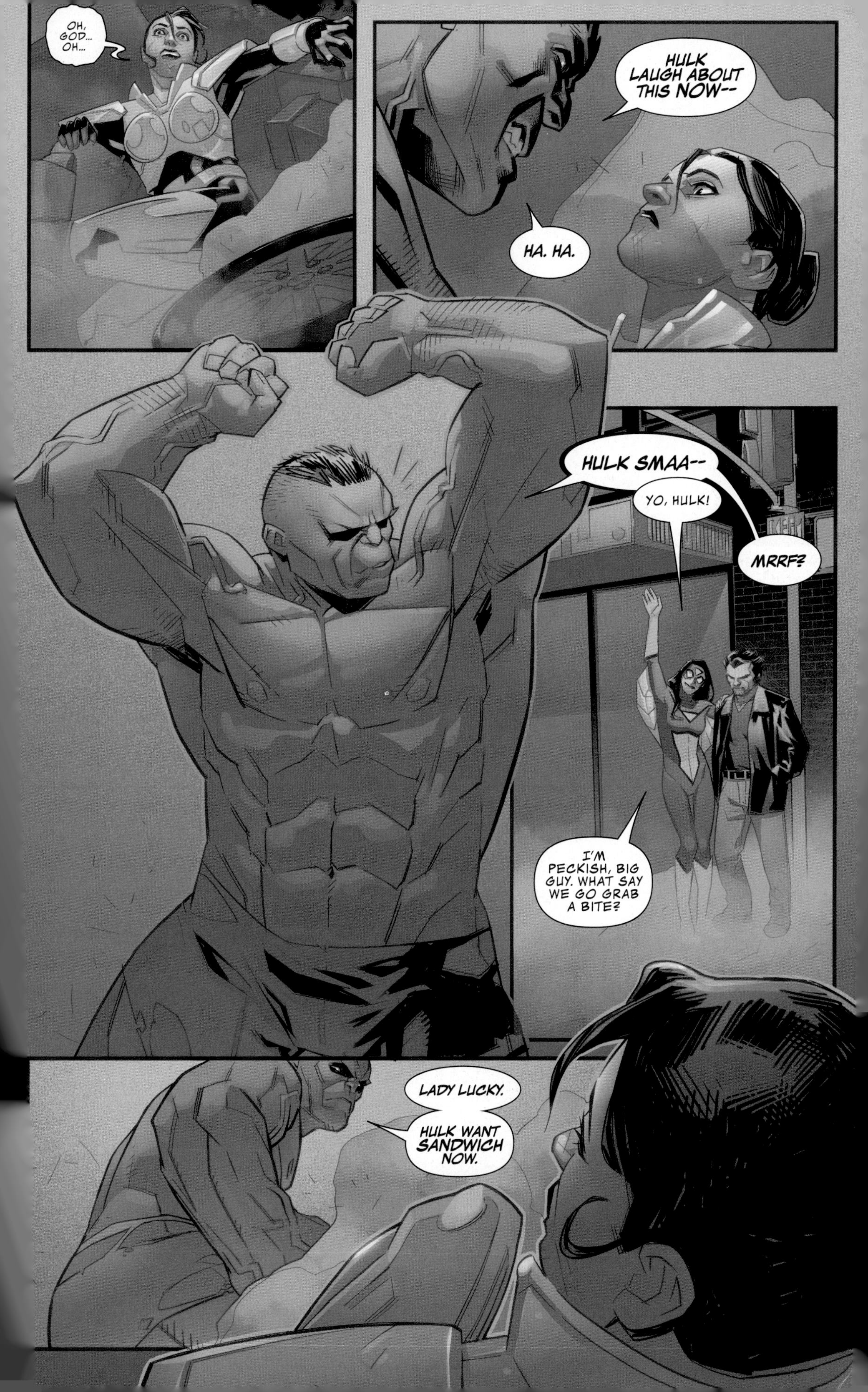
OH, GOD... OH...
HULK LAUGH ABOUT THIS NOW--
HA. HA.
HULK SMAA--
YO, HULK!
MRRF?
I'M PECKISH, BIG GUY. WHAT SAY WE GO GRAB A BITE?
LADY LUCKY.
HULK WANT SANDWICH NOW.

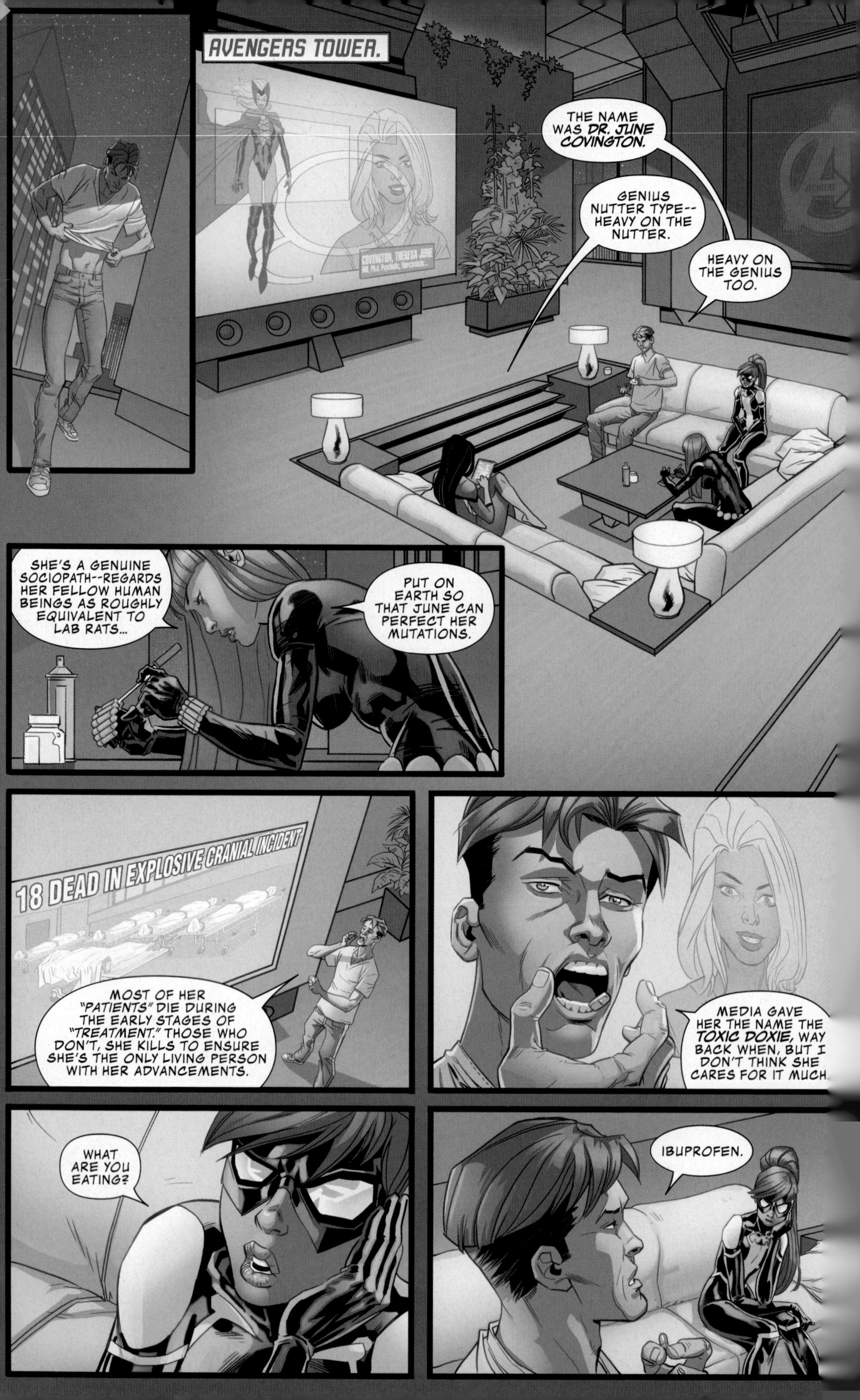
AVENGERS TOWER.
COVINGTON, THERESA JUNE
MD, Ph.d. Psychotic, Narcissistic...
THE NAME WAS DR. JUNE COVINGTON.
GENIUS NUTTER TYPE--HEAVY ON THE NUTTER.
HEAVY ON THE GENIUS TOO.
SHE'S A GENUINE SOCIOPATH--REGARDS HER FELLOW HUMAN BEINGS AS ROUGHLY EQUIVALENT TO LAB RATS...
PUT ON EARTH SO THAT JUNE CAN PERFECT HER MUTATIONS.
18 DEAD IN EXPLOSIVE CRANIAL INCIDENT
MOST OF HER "PATIENTS" DIE DURING THE EARLY STAGES OF "TREATMENT." THOSE WHO DON'T, SHE KILLS TO ENSURE SHE'S THE ONLY LIVING PERSON WITH HER ADVANCEMENTS.
MEDIA GAVE HER THE NAME THE TOXIC DOXIE, WAY BACK WHEN, BUT I DON'T THINK SHE CARES FOR IT MUCH.
WHAT ARE YOU EATING?
IBUPROFEN.

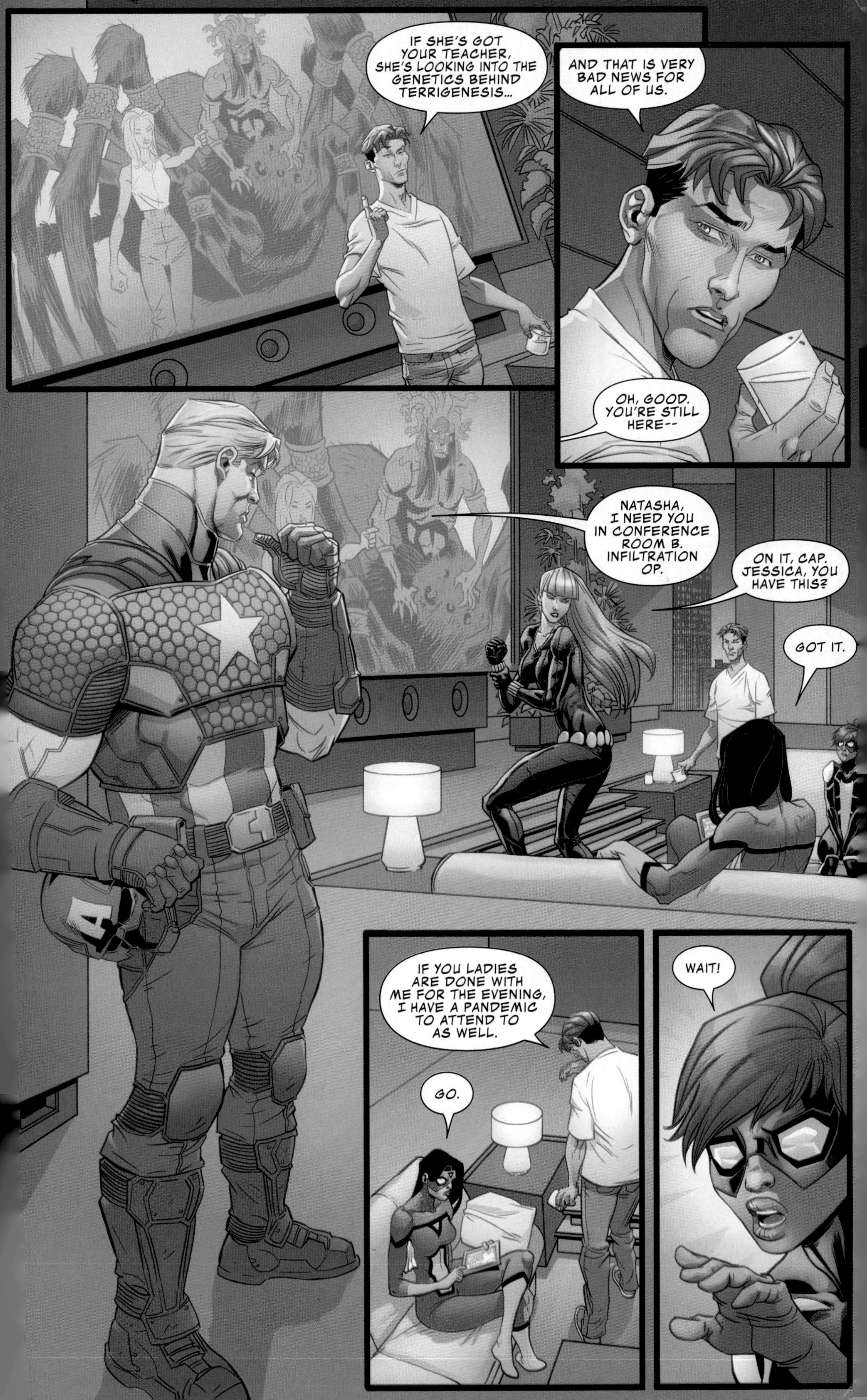
IF SHE'S GOT YOUR TEACHER, SHE'S LOOKING INTO THE GENETICS BEHIND TERRIGENESIS...
AND THAT IS VERY BAD NEWS FOR ALL OF US.
OH, GOOD. YOU'RE STILL HERE--
NATASHA, I NEED YOU IN CONFERENCE ROOM B. INFILTRATION OP.
ON IT, CAP. JESSICA, YOU HAVE THIS?
GOT IT.
IF YOU LADIES ARE DONE WITH ME FOR THE EVENING, I HAVE A PANDEMIC TO ATTEND TO AS WELL.
GO.
WAIT!

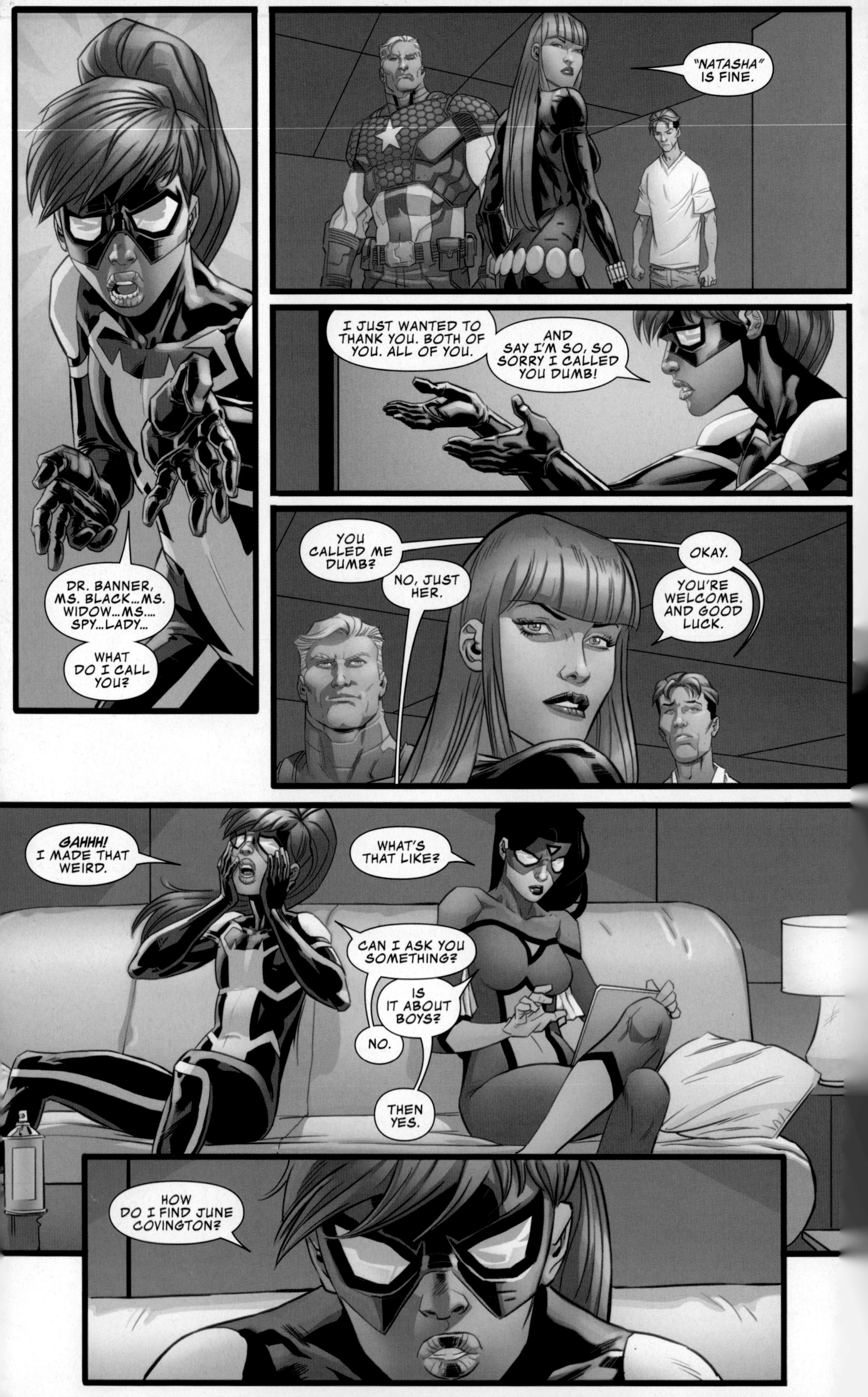
DR. BANNER, MS. BLACK...MS. WIDOW...MS.... SPY...LADY...
WHAT DO I CALL YOU?
"NATASHA" IS FINE.
I JUST WANTED TO THANK YOU. BOTH OF YOU. ALL OF YOU.
AND SAY I'M SO, SO SORRY I CALLED YOU DUMB!
YOU CALLED ME DUMB?
NO, JUST HER.
OKAY.
YOU'RE WELCOME. AND GOOD LUCK.
GAHHH! I MADE THAT WEIRD.
WHAT'S THAT LIKE?
CAN I ASK YOU SOMETHING?
IS IT ABOUT BOYS?
NO.
THEN YES.
HOW DO I FIND JUNE COVINGTON?

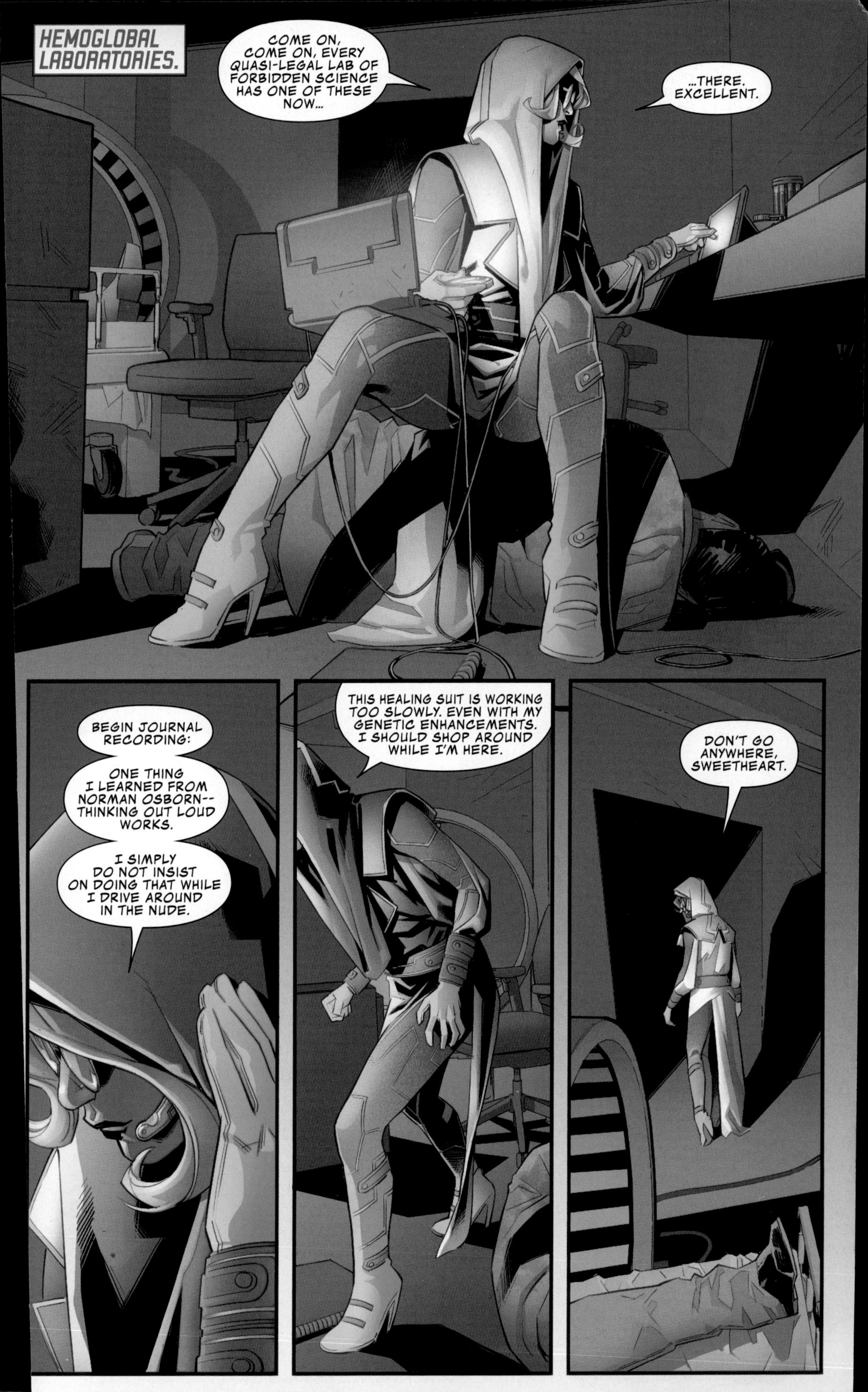
HEMOGLOBAL LABORATORIES.
COME ON, COME ON, EVERY QUASI-LEGAL LAB OF FORBIDDEN SCIENCE HAS ONE OF THESE NOW...
...THERE. EXCELLENT.
BEGIN JOURNAL RECORDING:
ONE THING I LEARNED FROM NORMAN OSBORN--THINKING OUT LOUD WORKS.
I SIMPLY DO NOT INSIST ON DOING THAT WHILE I DRIVE AROUND IN THE NUDE.
THIS HEALING SUIT IS WORKING TOO SLOWLY. EVEN WITH MY GENETIC ENHANCEMENTS. I SHOULD SHOP AROUND WHILE I'M HERE.
DON'T GO ANYWHERE, SWEETHEART.

THREE BROOM CLOSETS ON ONE FLOOR IS ABSURD, I DON'T CARE IF YOU USE BROKEN GLASS LIKE CONFETTI.

WHICH--IN POINT OF FACT--I HAVE.

AH HA!

THISSSSS IS MORE LIKE IT.

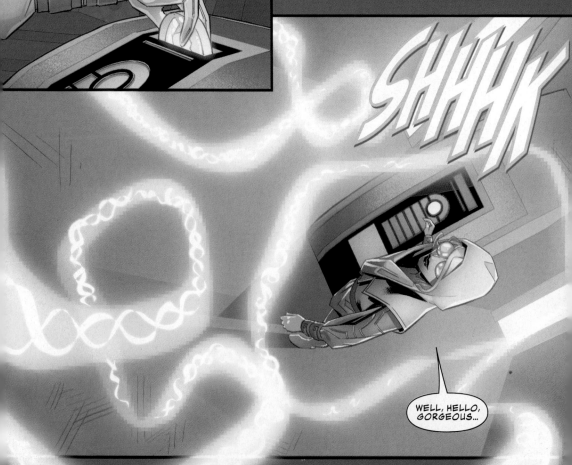

SHHHK

WELL, HELLO, GORGEOUS...

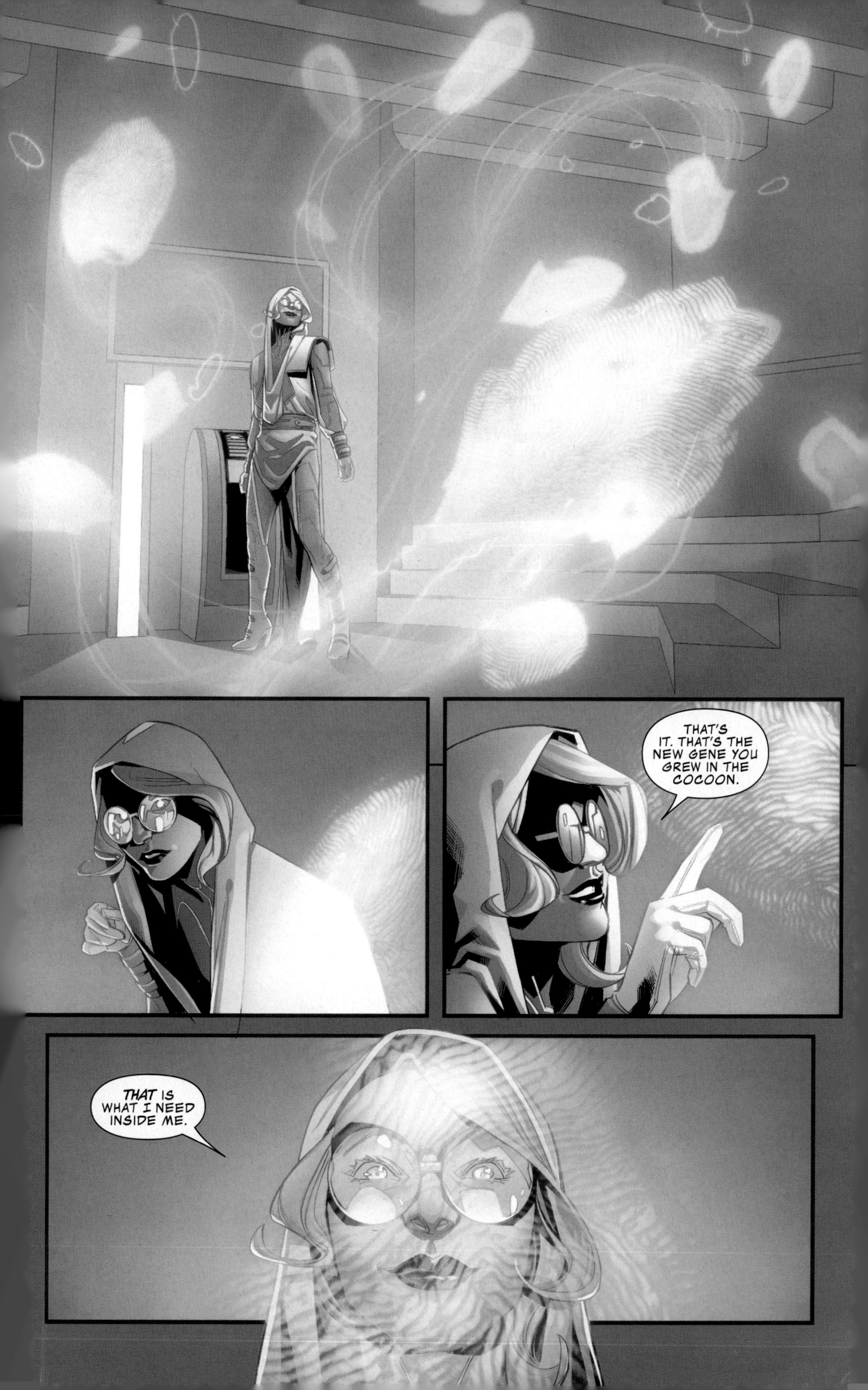
THAT'S IT. THAT'S THE NEW GENE YOU GREW IN THE COCOON.
THAT IS WHAT I NEED INSIDE ME.

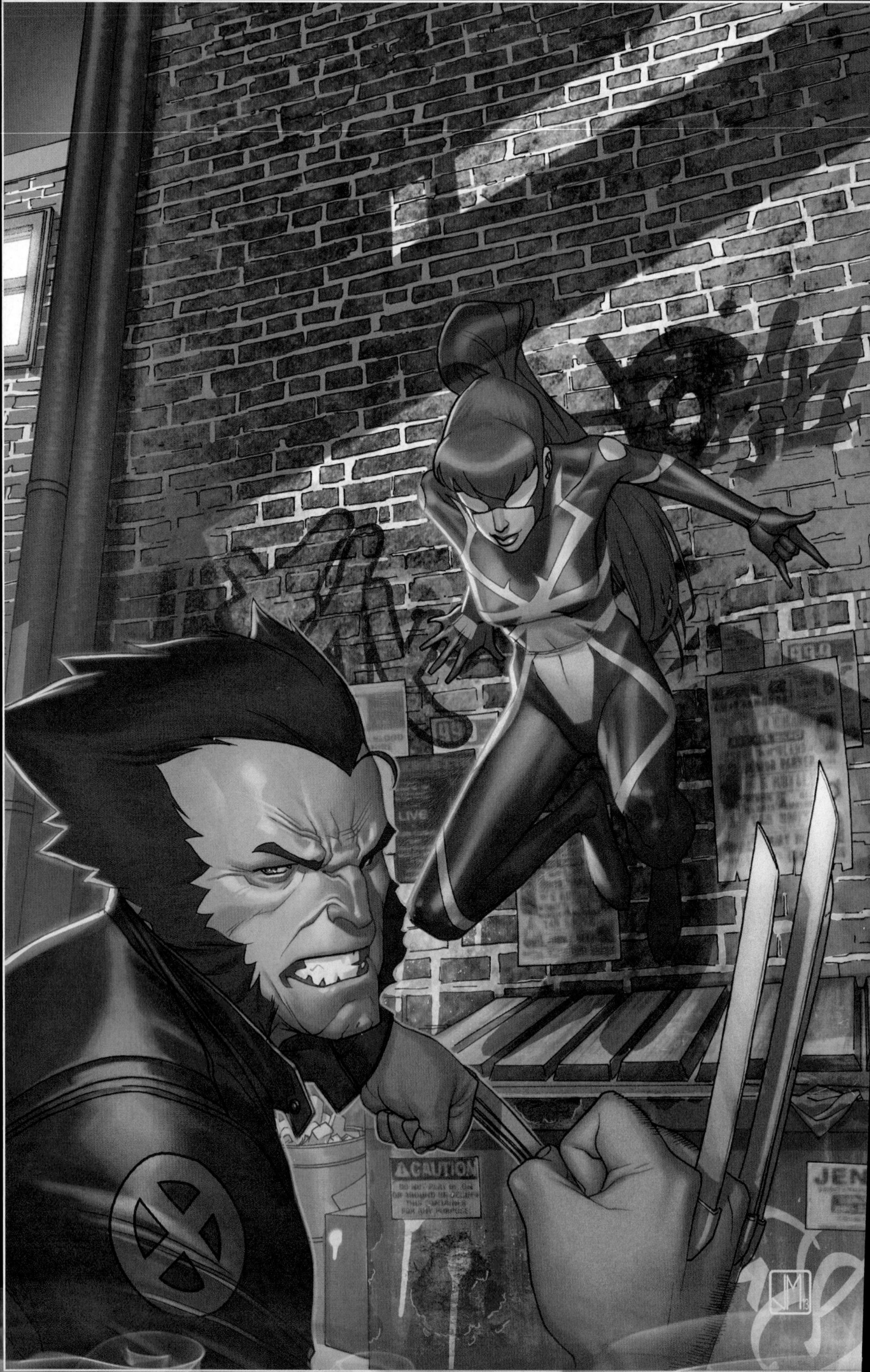
CAUTION

AVENGERS ASSEMBLE #23

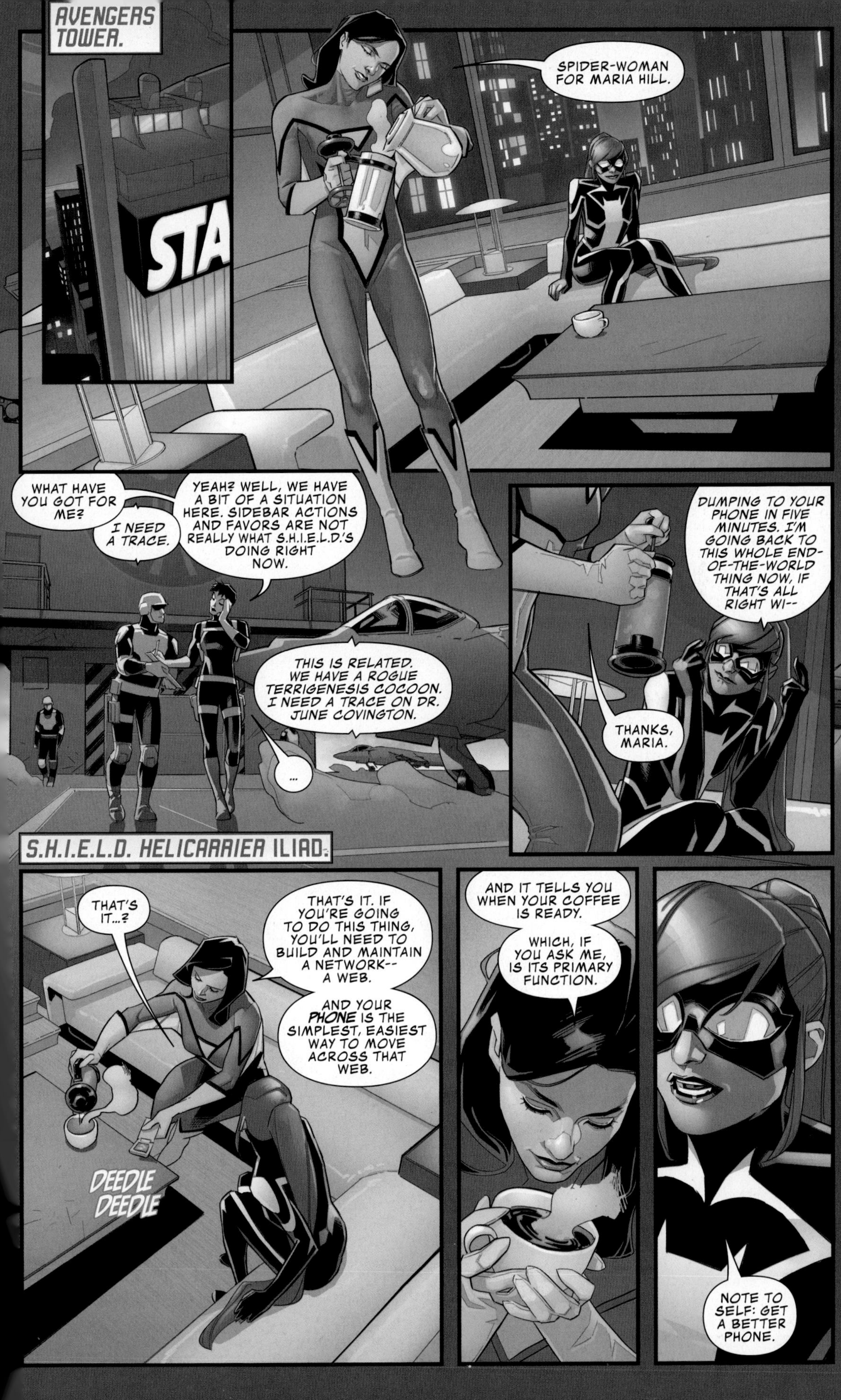
AVENGERS TOWER.
SPIDER-WOMAN FOR MARIA HILL.
WHAT HAVE YOU GOT FOR ME?
I NEED A TRACE.
YEAH? WELL, WE HAVE A BIT OF A SITUATION HERE. SIDEBAR ACTIONS AND FAVORS ARE NOT REALLY WHAT S.H.I.E.L.D.'S DOING RIGHT NOW.
THIS IS RELATED. WE HAVE A ROGUE TERRIGENESIS COCOON. I NEED A TRACE ON DR. JUNE COVINGTON.
...
S.H.I.E.L.D. HELICARRIER ILIAD.
DUMPING TO YOUR PHONE IN FIVE MINUTES. I'M GOING BACK TO THIS WHOLE END-OF-THE-WORLD THING NOW, IF THAT'S ALL RIGHT WI--
THANKS, MARIA.
THAT'S IT...?
THAT'S IT. IF YOU'RE GOING TO DO THIS THING, YOU'LL NEED TO BUILD AND MAINTAIN A NETWORK-- A WEB.
AND YOUR PHONE IS THE SIMPLEST, EASIEST WAY TO MOVE ACROSS THAT WEB.
DEEDLE DEEDLE
AND IT TELLS YOU WHEN YOUR COFFEE IS READY.
WHICH, IF YOU ASK ME, IS ITS PRIMARY FUNCTION.
NOTE TO SELF: GET A BETTER PHONE.

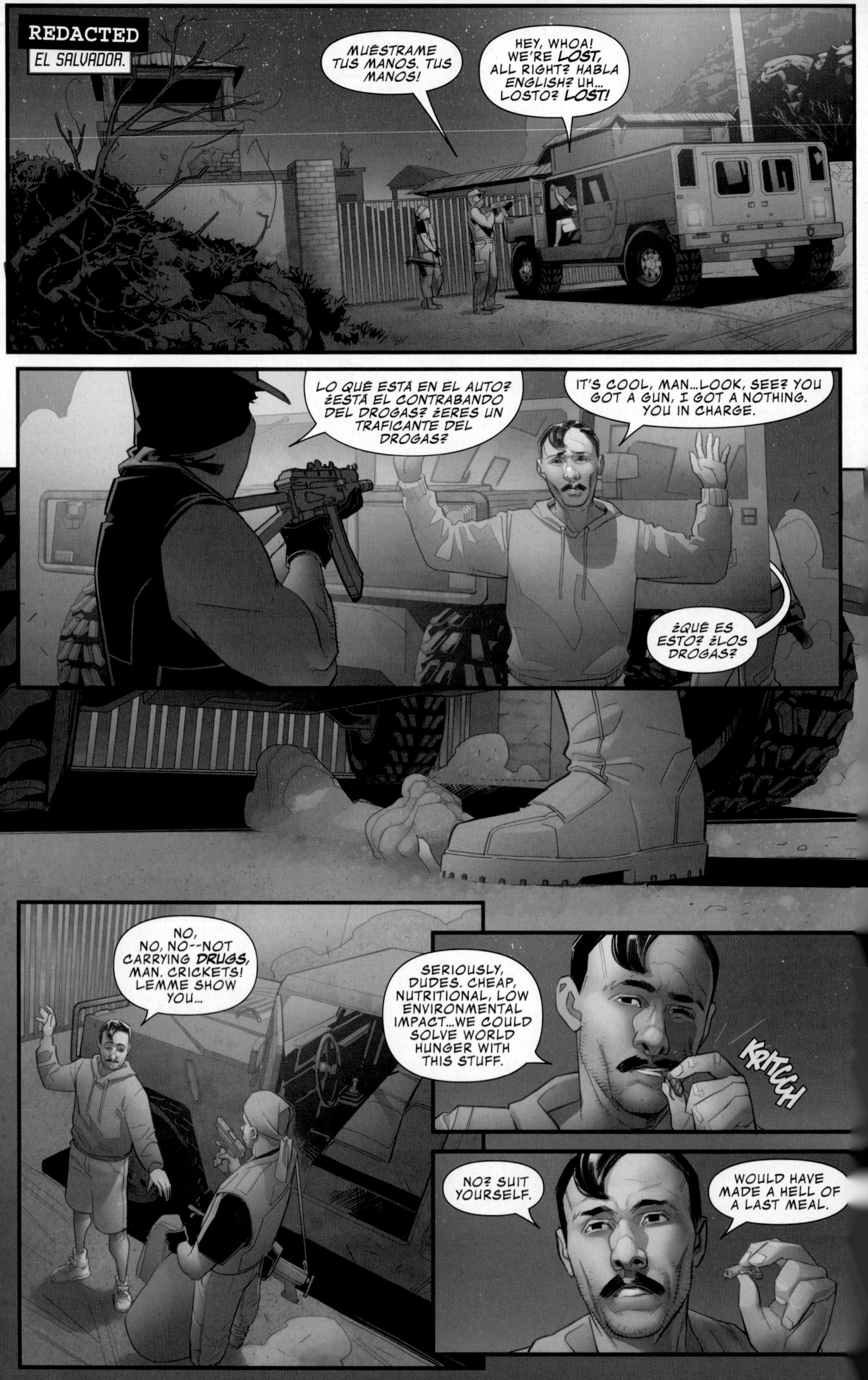
REDACTED
EL SALVADOR.
MUÉSTRAME TUS MANOS. TUS MANOS!
HEY, WHOA! WE'RE LOST, ALL RIGHT? HABLA ENGLISH? UH... LOSTO? LOST!
LO QUÉ ESTÁ EN EL AUTO? ¿ESTÁ EL CONTRABANDO DEL DROGAS? ¿ERES UN TRAFICANTE DEL DROGAS?
IT'S COOL, MAN...LOOK, SEE? YOU GOT A GUN, I GOT A NOTHING. YOU IN CHARGE.
¿QUÉ ES ESTO? ¿LOS DROGAS?
NO, NO, NO--NOT CARRYING DRUGS, MAN. CRICKETS! LEMME SHOW YOU...
SERIOUSLY, DUDES. CHEAP, NUTRITIONAL, LOW ENVIRONMENTAL IMPACT...WE COULD SOLVE WORLD HUNGER WITH THIS STUFF.
KRITCCH
NO? SUIT YOURSELF.
WOULD HAVE MADE A HELL OF A LAST MEAL.

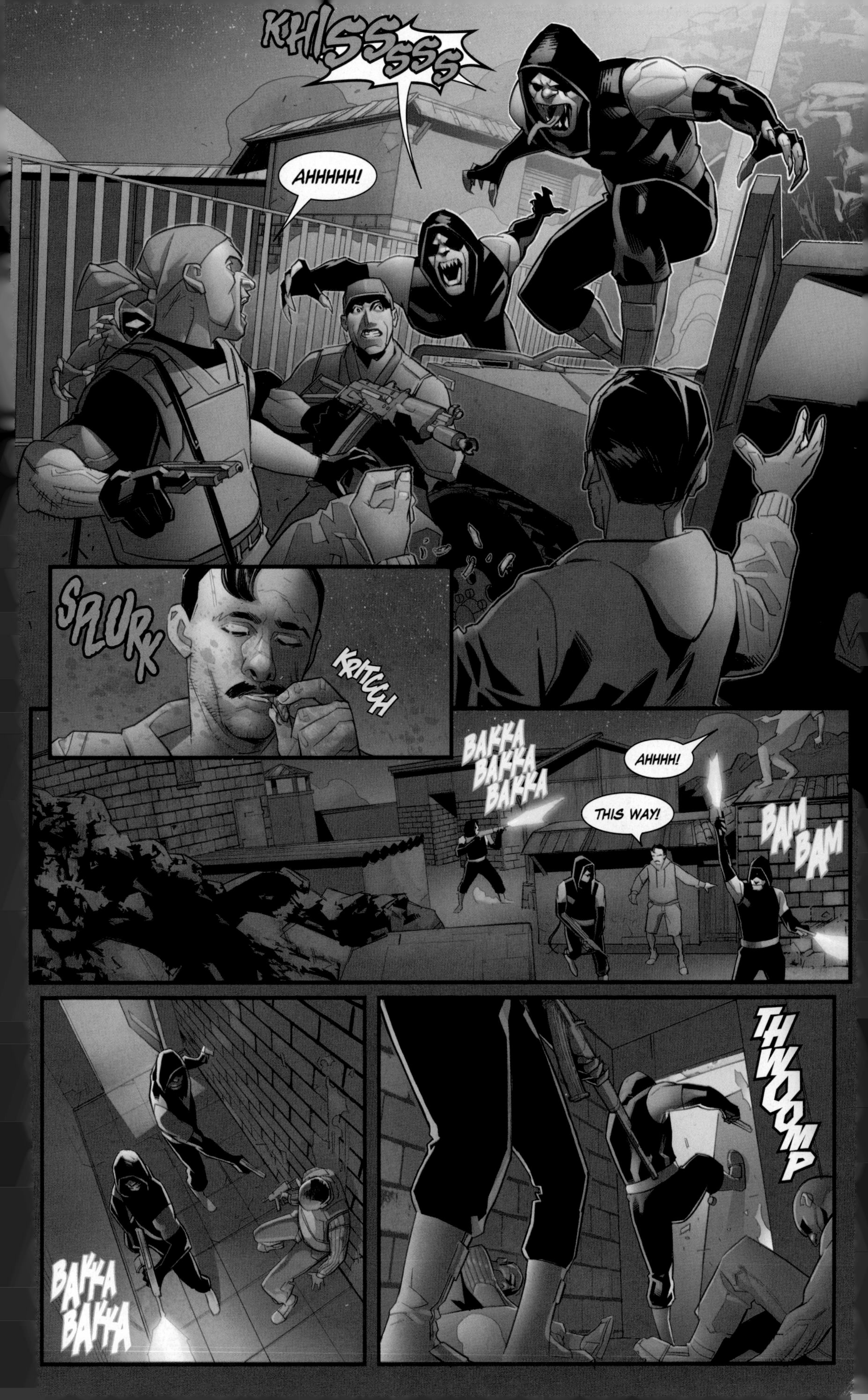
KHISSSSS
AHHHHH!
SPLURK
KRITCH
BAKKA BAKKA BAKKA
AHHHH!
THIS WAY!
BAM BAM
BAKKA BAKKA
THWOOMP

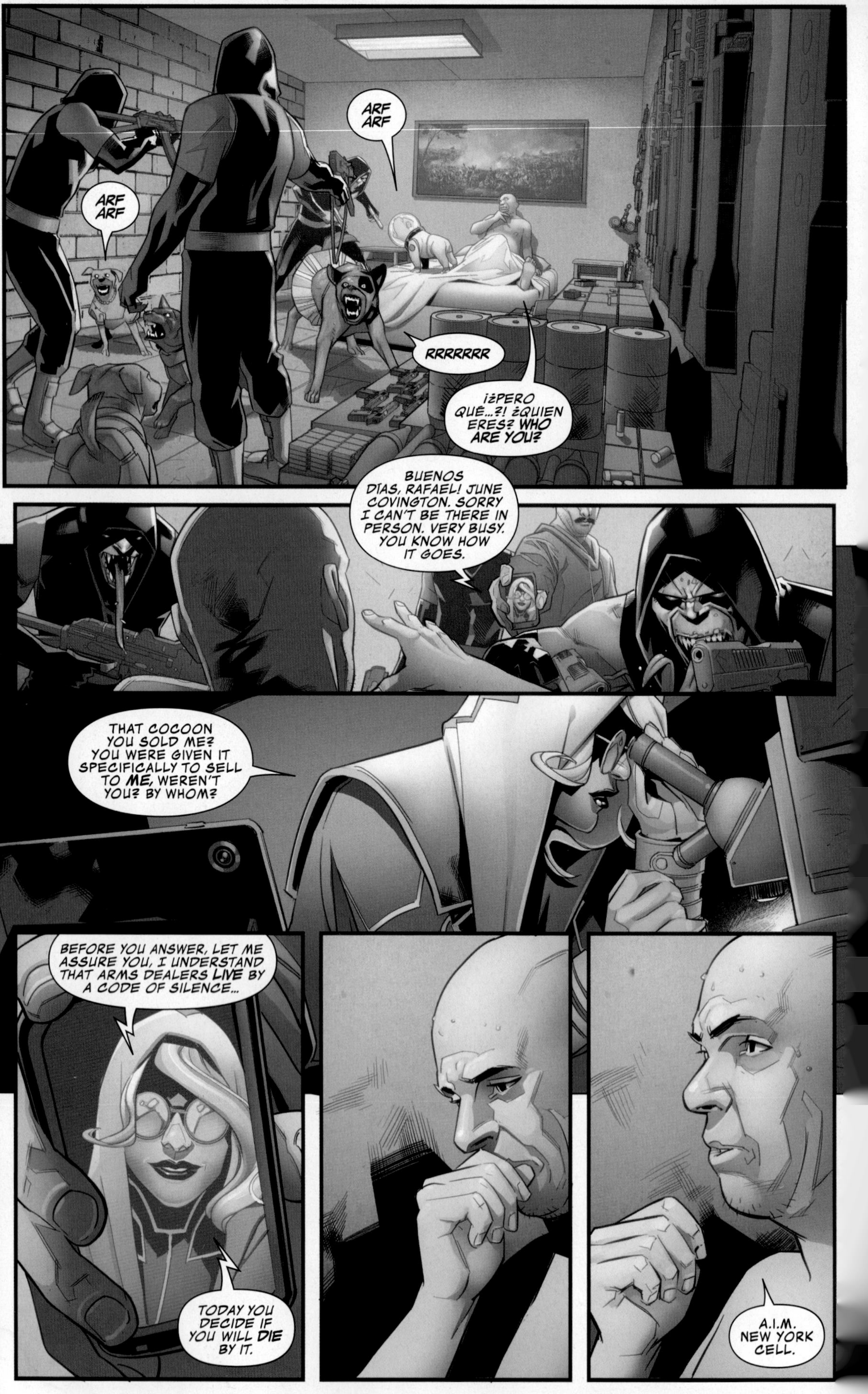
ARF ARF
ARF ARF
RRRRRRR
¡¿PERO QUÉ...?! ¿QUIEN ERES? WHO ARE YOU?
BUENOS DÍAS, RAFAEL! JUNE COVINGTON. SORRY I CAN'T BE THERE IN PERSON. VERY BUSY. YOU KNOW HOW IT GOES.
THAT COCOON YOU SOLD ME? YOU WERE GIVEN IT SPECIFICALLY TO SELL TO ME, WEREN'T YOU? BY WHOM?
BEFORE YOU ANSWER, LET ME ASSURE YOU, I UNDERSTAND THAT ARMS DEALERS LIVE BY A CODE OF SILENCE...
TODAY YOU DECIDE IF YOU WILL DIE BY IT.
A.I.M. NEW YORK CELL.

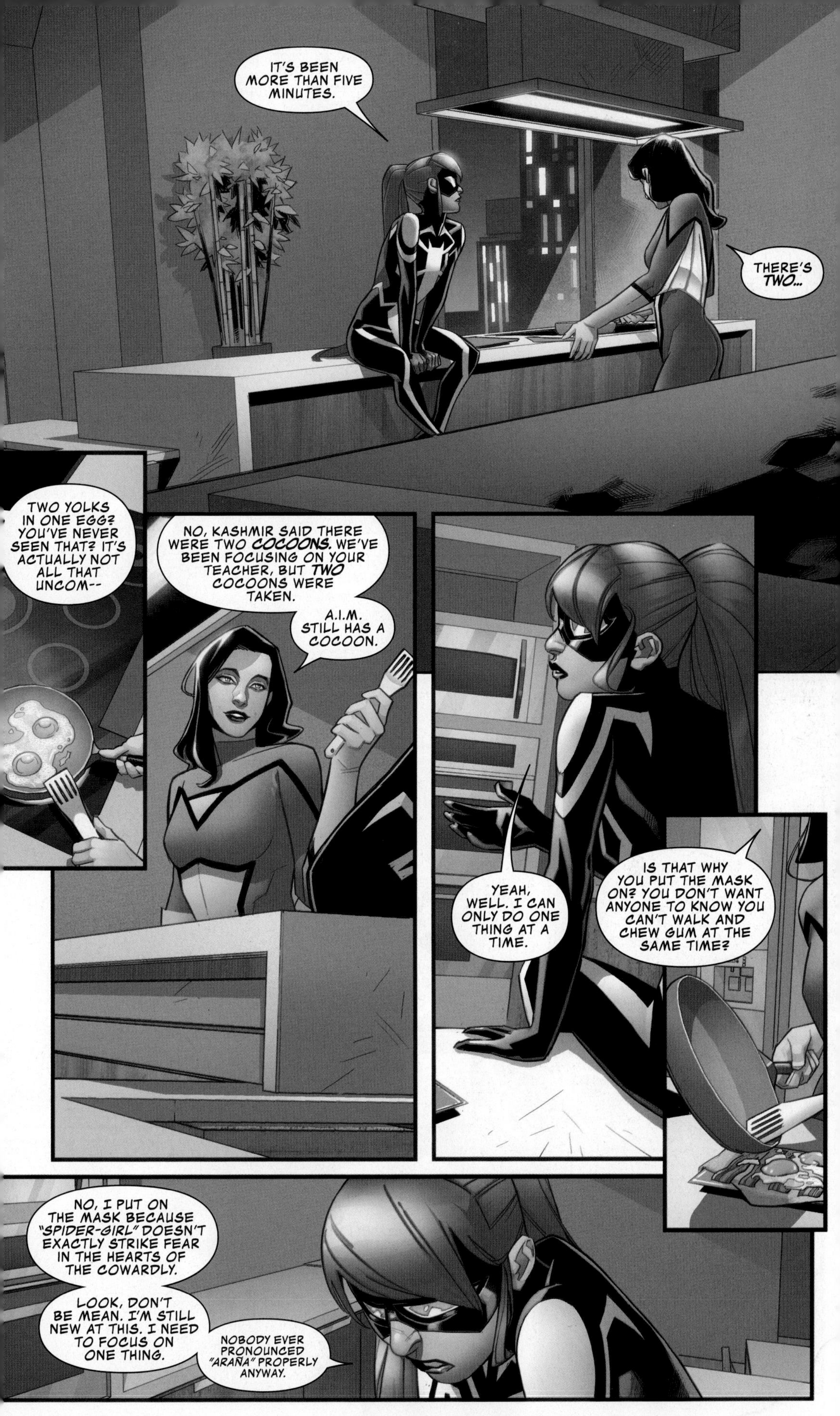
IT'S BEEN MORE THAN FIVE MINUTES.
THERE'S TWO...
TWO YOLKS IN ONE EGG? YOU'VE NEVER SEEN THAT? IT'S ACTUALLY NOT ALL THAT UNCOM--
NO, KASHMIR SAID THERE WERE TWO COCOONS. WE'VE BEEN FOCUSING ON YOUR TEACHER, BUT TWO COCOONS WERE TAKEN.
A.I.M. STILL HAS A COCOON.
YEAH, WELL. I CAN ONLY DO ONE THING AT A TIME.
IS THAT WHY YOU PUT THE MASK ON? YOU DON'T WANT ANYONE TO KNOW YOU CAN'T WALK AND CHEW GUM AT THE SAME TIME?
NO, I PUT ON THE MASK BECAUSE "SPIDER-GIRL" DOESN'T EXACTLY STRIKE FEAR IN THE HEARTS OF THE COWARDLY.
LOOK, DON'T BE MEAN. I'M STILL NEW AT THIS. I NEED TO FOCUS ON ONE THING.
NOBODY EVER PRONOUNCED "ARAÑA" PROPERLY ANYWAY.

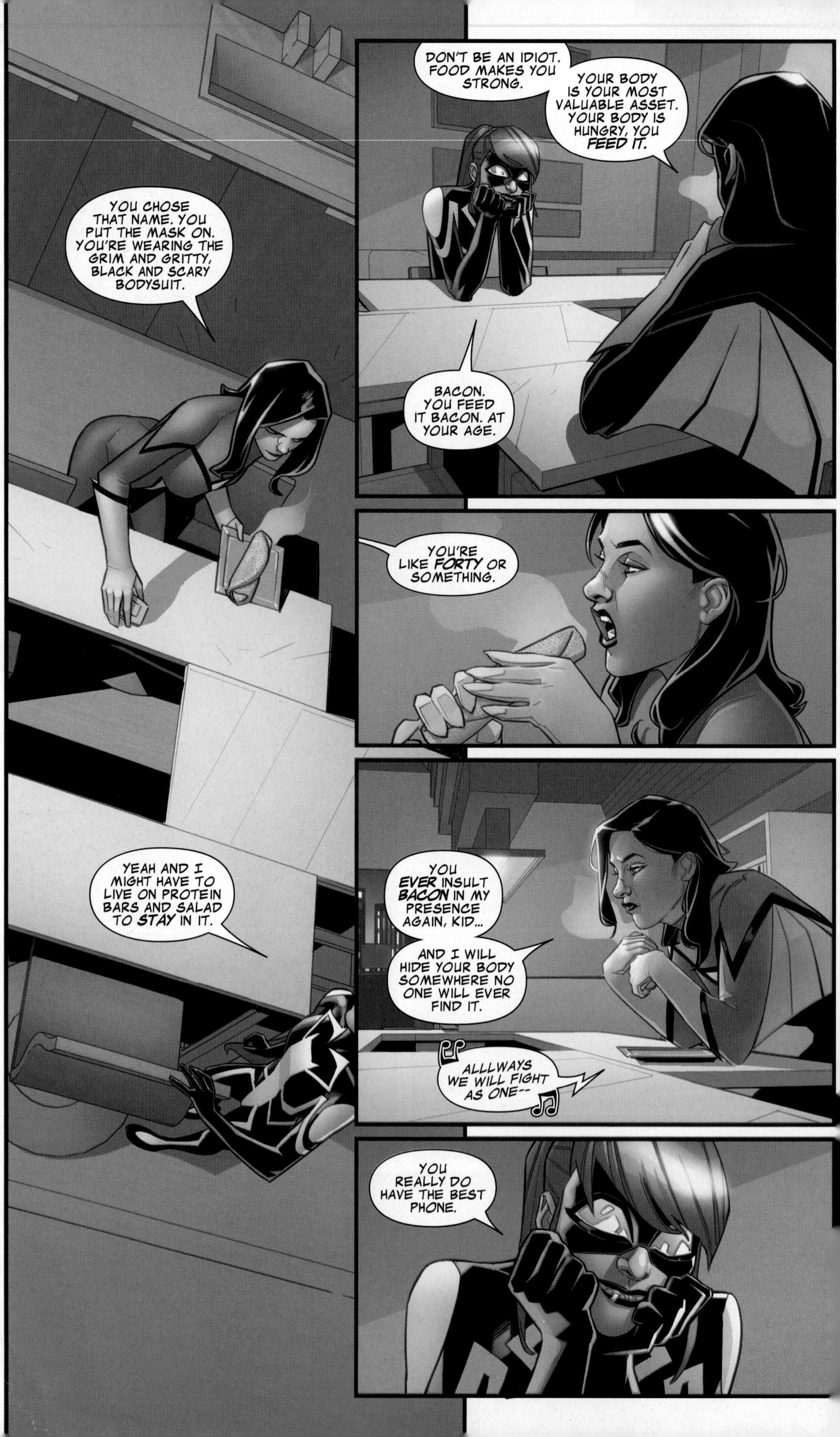
YOU CHOSE THAT NAME. YOU PUT THE MASK ON. YOU'RE WEARING THE GRIM AND GRITTY, BLACK AND SCARY BODYSUIT.
YEAH AND I MIGHT HAVE TO LIVE ON PROTEIN BARS AND SALAD TO STAY IN IT.
DON'T BE AN IDIOT. FOOD MAKES YOU STRONG.
YOUR BODY IS YOUR MOST VALUABLE ASSET. YOUR BODY IS HUNGRY, YOU FEED IT.
BACON. YOU FEED IT BACON. AT YOUR AGE.
YOU'RE LIKE FORTY OR SOMETHING.
YOU EVER INSULT BACON IN MY PRESENCE AGAIN, KID...
AND I WILL HIDE YOUR BODY SOMEWHERE NO ONE WILL EVER FIND IT.
ALLLWAYS WE WILL FIGHT AS ONE--
YOU REALLY DO HAVE THE BEST PHONE.

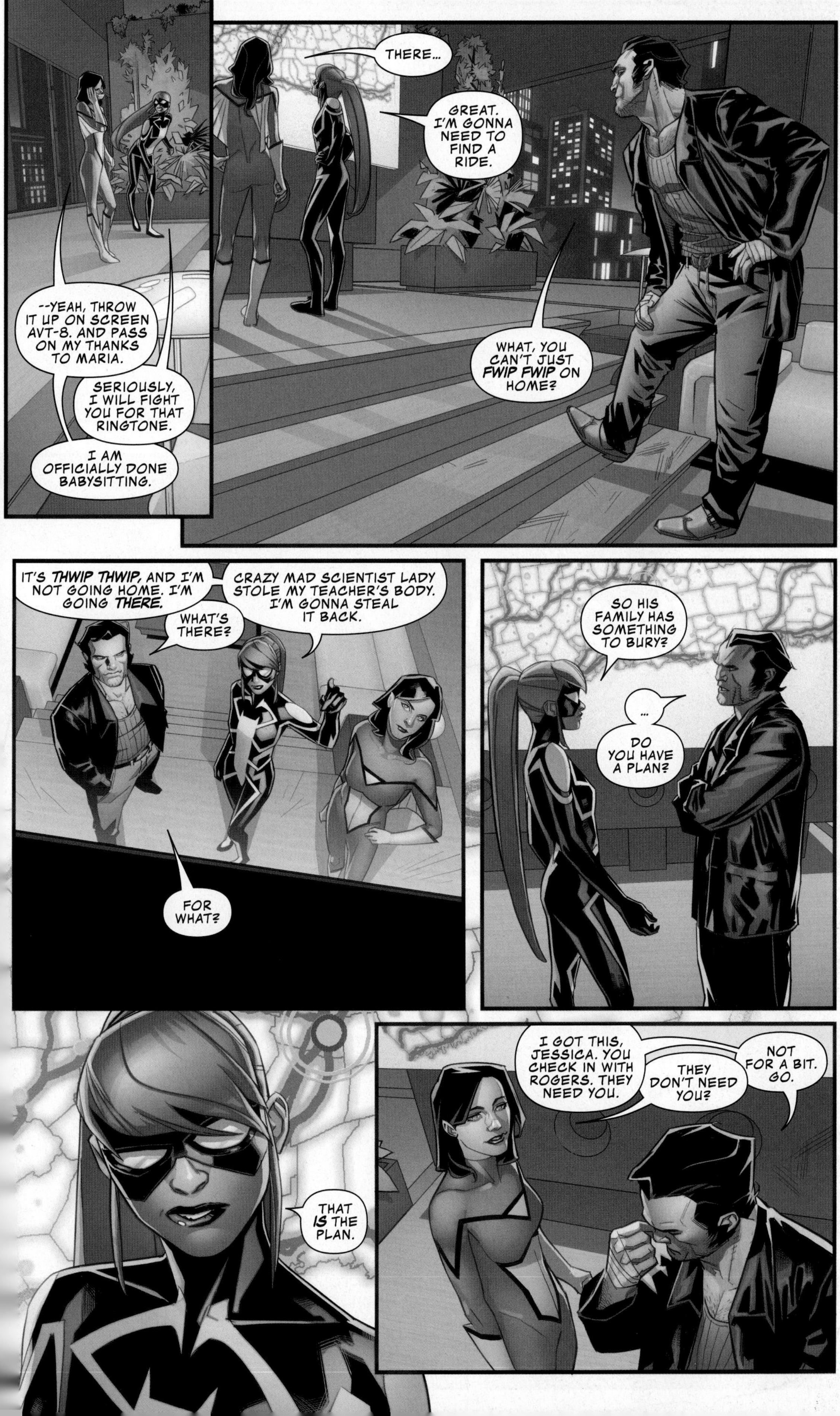
--YEAH, THROW IT UP ON SCREEN AVT-8. AND PASS ON MY THANKS TO MARIA.
SERIOUSLY, I WILL FIGHT YOU FOR THAT RINGTONE.
I AM OFFICIALLY DONE BABYSITTING.
THERE...
GREAT. I'M GONNA NEED TO FIND A RIDE.
WHAT, YOU CAN'T JUST **FWIP FWIP** ON HOME?
IT'S **THWIP THWIP**, AND I'M NOT GOING HOME. I'M GOING **THERE**.
WHAT'S THERE?
CRAZY MAD SCIENTIST LADY STOLE MY TEACHER'S BODY. I'M GONNA STEAL IT BACK.
FOR WHAT?
SO HIS FAMILY HAS SOMETHING TO BURY?
...
DO YOU HAVE A PLAN?
THAT **IS** THE PLAN.
I GOT THIS, JESSICA. YOU CHECK IN WITH ROGERS. THEY NEED YOU.
THEY DON'T NEED YOU?
NOT FOR A BIT. GO.

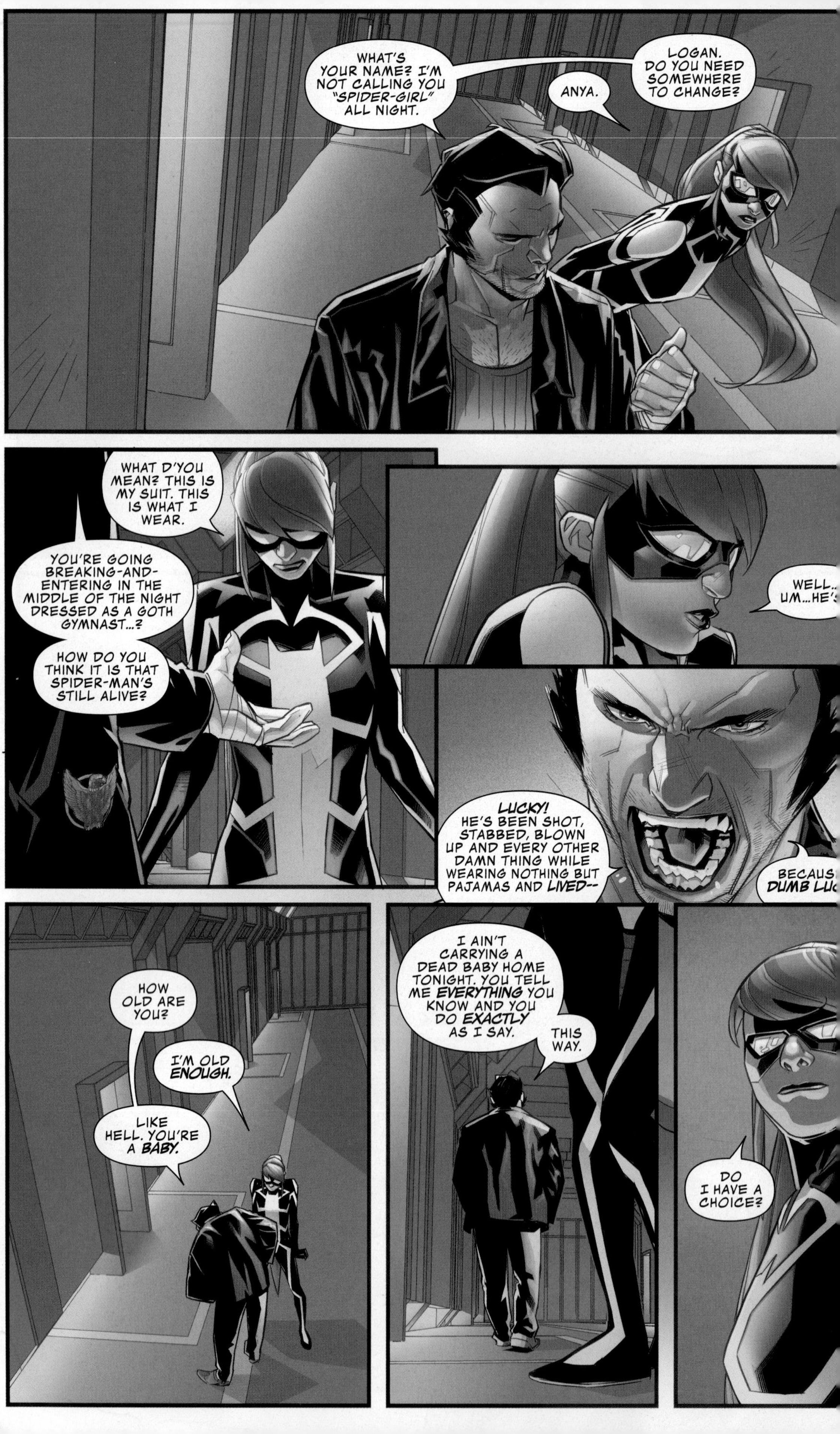
WHAT'S YOUR NAME? I'M NOT CALLING YOU "SPIDER-GIRL" ALL NIGHT.
ANYA.
LOGAN. DO YOU NEED SOMEWHERE TO CHANGE?
WHAT D'YOU MEAN? THIS IS MY SUIT. THIS IS WHAT I WEAR.
YOU'RE GOING BREAKING-AND-ENTERING IN THE MIDDLE OF THE NIGHT DRESSED AS A GOTH GYMNAST...?
HOW DO YOU THINK IT IS THAT SPIDER-MAN'S STILL ALIVE?
WELL... UM...HE'S
LUCKY! HE'S BEEN SHOT, STABBED, BLOWN UP AND EVERY OTHER DAMN THING WHILE WEARING NOTHING BUT PAJAMAS AND LIVED--
HOW OLD ARE YOU?
I'M OLD ENOUGH.
LIKE HELL. YOU'RE A BABY.
I AIN'T CARRYING A DEAD BABY HOME TONIGHT. YOU TELL ME EVERYTHING YOU KNOW AND YOU DO EXACTLY AS I SAY.
THIS WAY.
DO I HAVE A CHOICE?

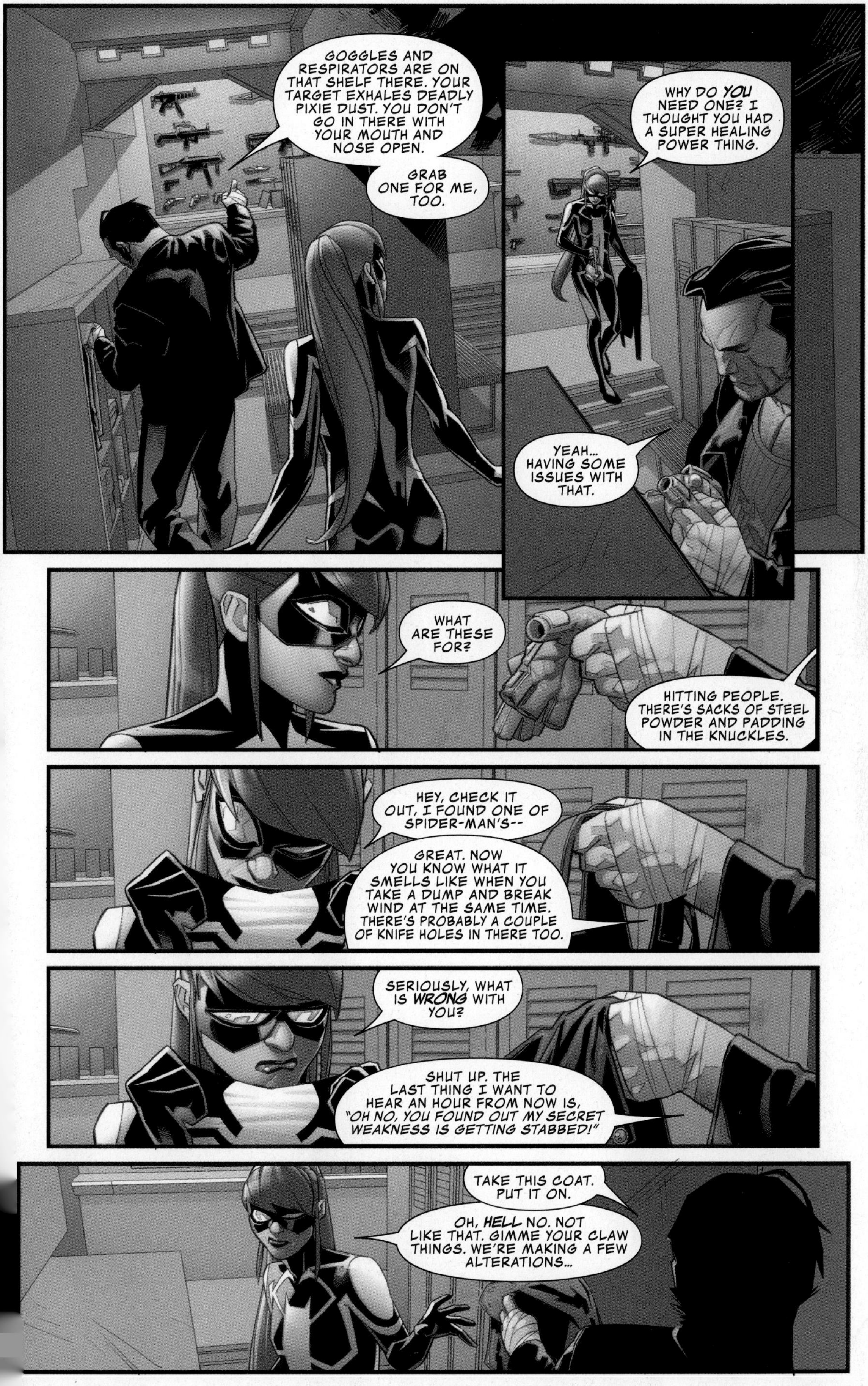
GOGGLES AND RESPIRATORS ARE ON THAT SHELF THERE. YOUR TARGET EXHALES DEADLY PIXIE DUST. YOU DON'T GO IN THERE WITH YOUR MOUTH AND NOSE OPEN.
GRAB ONE FOR ME, TOO.
WHY DO *YOU* NEED ONE? I THOUGHT YOU HAD A SUPER HEALING POWER THING.
YEAH... HAVING SOME ISSUES WITH THAT.
WHAT ARE THESE FOR?
HITTING PEOPLE. THERE'S SACKS OF STEEL POWDER AND PADDING IN THE KNUCKLES.
HEY, CHECK IT OUT, I FOUND ONE OF SPIDER-MAN'S--
GREAT. NOW YOU KNOW WHAT IT SMELLS LIKE WHEN YOU TAKE A DUMP AND BREAK WIND AT THE SAME TIME. THERE'S PROBABLY A COUPLE OF KNIFE HOLES IN THERE TOO.
SERIOUSLY, WHAT IS *WRONG* WITH YOU?
SHUT UP. THE LAST THING I WANT TO HEAR AN HOUR FROM NOW IS, *"OH NO, YOU FOUND OUT MY SECRET WEAKNESS IS GETTING STABBED!"*
TAKE THIS COAT. PUT IT ON.
OH, **HELL** NO. NOT LIKE THAT. GIMME YOUR CLAW THINGS. WE'RE MAKING A FEW ALTERATIONS...

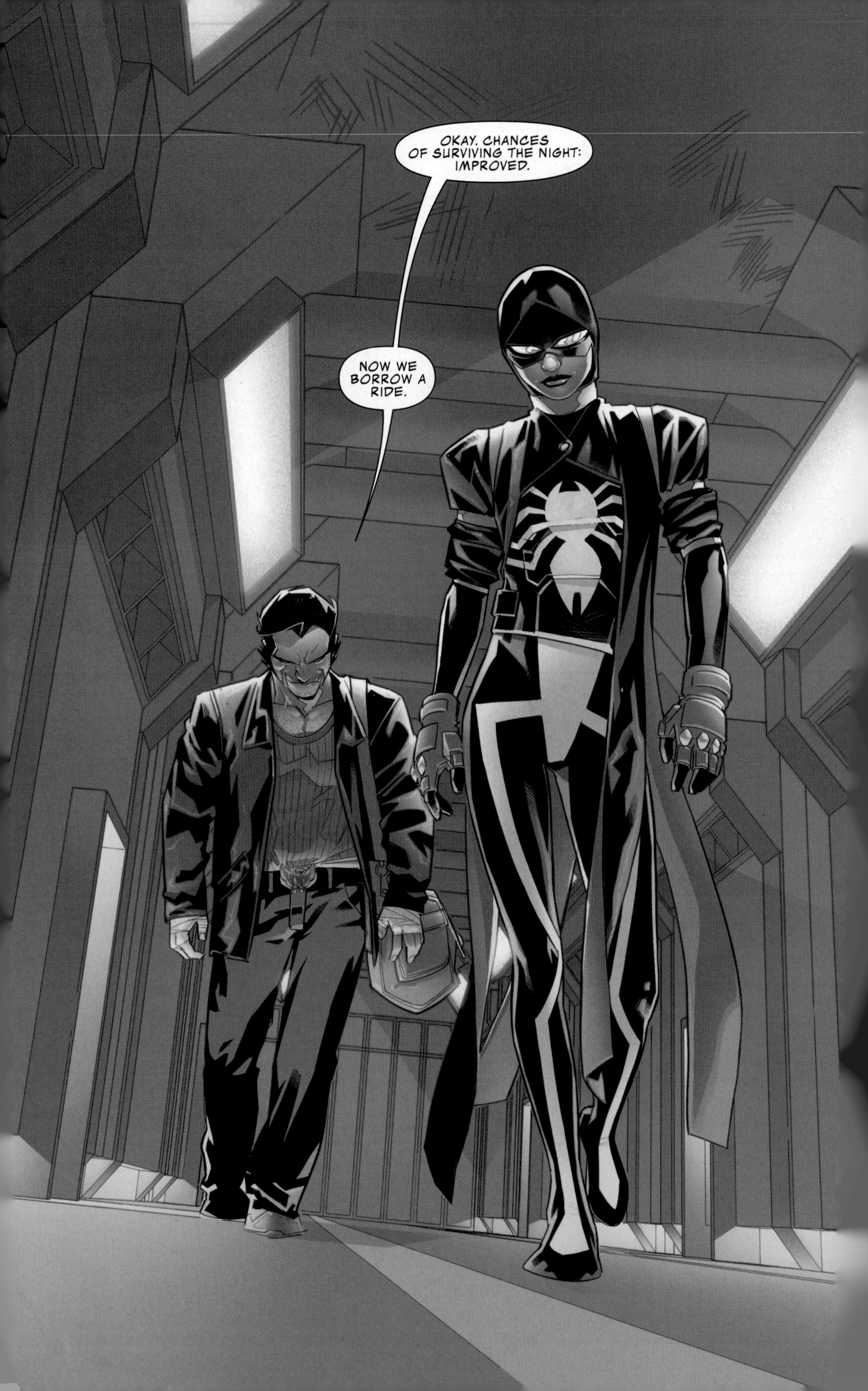
OKAY. CHANCES OF SURVIVING THE NIGHT: IMPROVED.
NOW WE BORROW A RIDE.

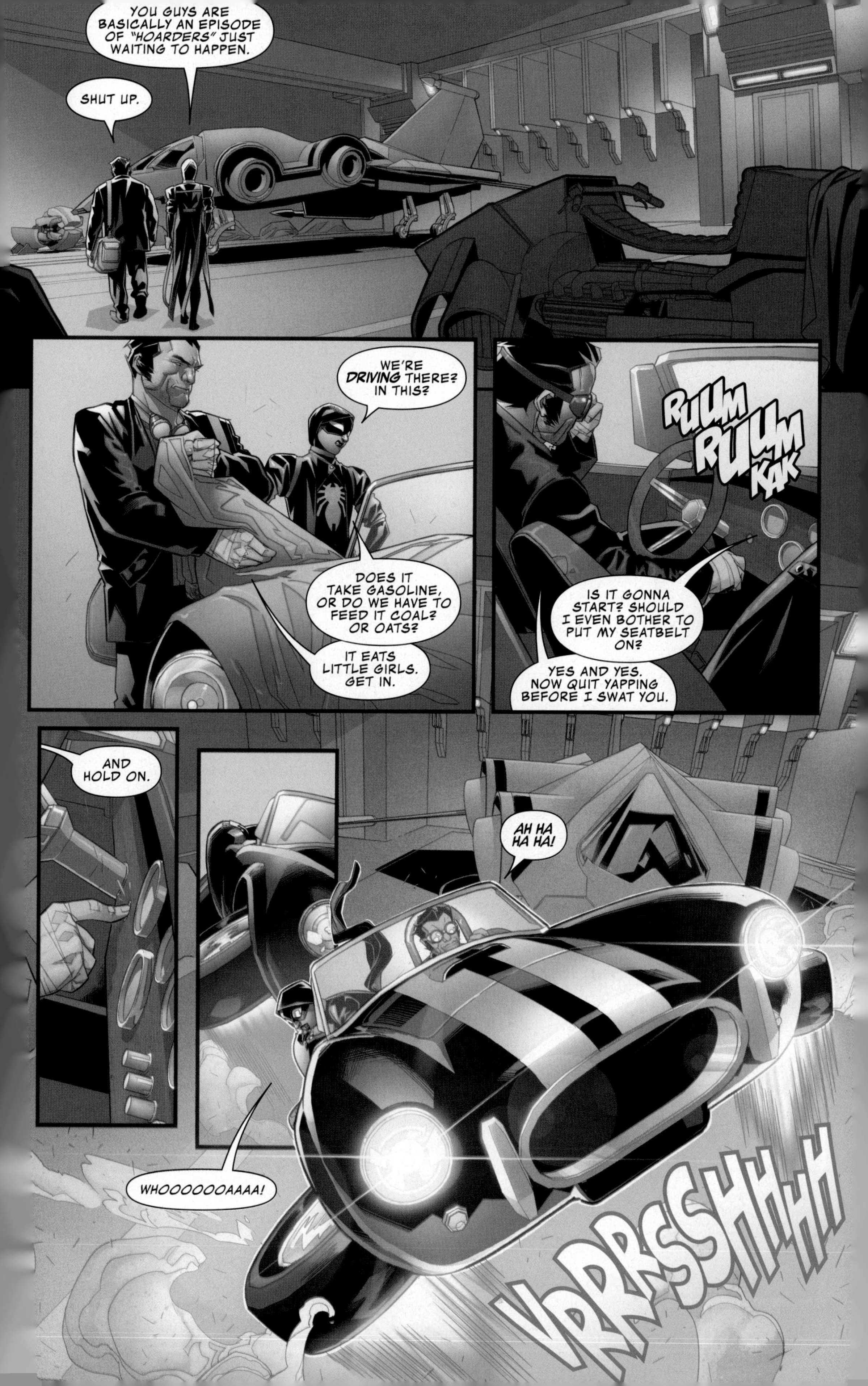
YOU GUYS ARE BASICALLY AN EPISODE OF "HOARDERS" JUST WAITING TO HAPPEN.
SHUT UP.
WE'RE DRIVING THERE? IN THIS?
DOES IT TAKE GASOLINE, OR DO WE HAVE TO FEED IT COAL? OR OATS?
IT EATS LITTLE GIRLS. GET IN.
RUUM RUUM KAK
IS IT GONNA START? SHOULD I EVEN BOTHER TO PUT MY SEATBELT ON?
YES AND YES. NOW QUIT YAPPING BEFORE I SWAT YOU.
AND HOLD ON.
AH HA HA HA!
WHOOOOOOAAAA!
VRRRSSHHHH

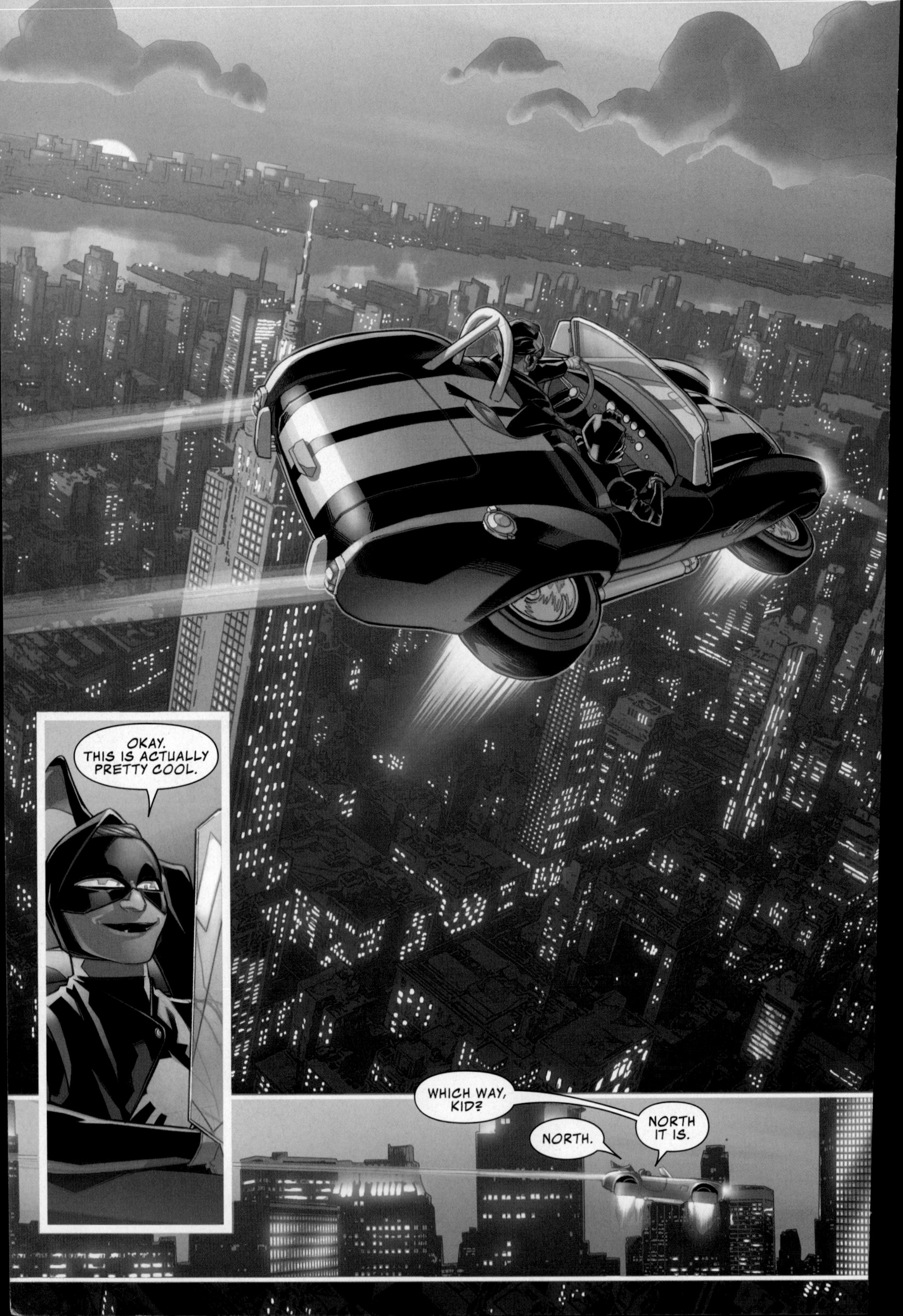
OKAY.
THIS IS ACTUALLY
PRETTY COOL.
WHICH WAY,
KID?
NORTH.
NORTH
IT IS.

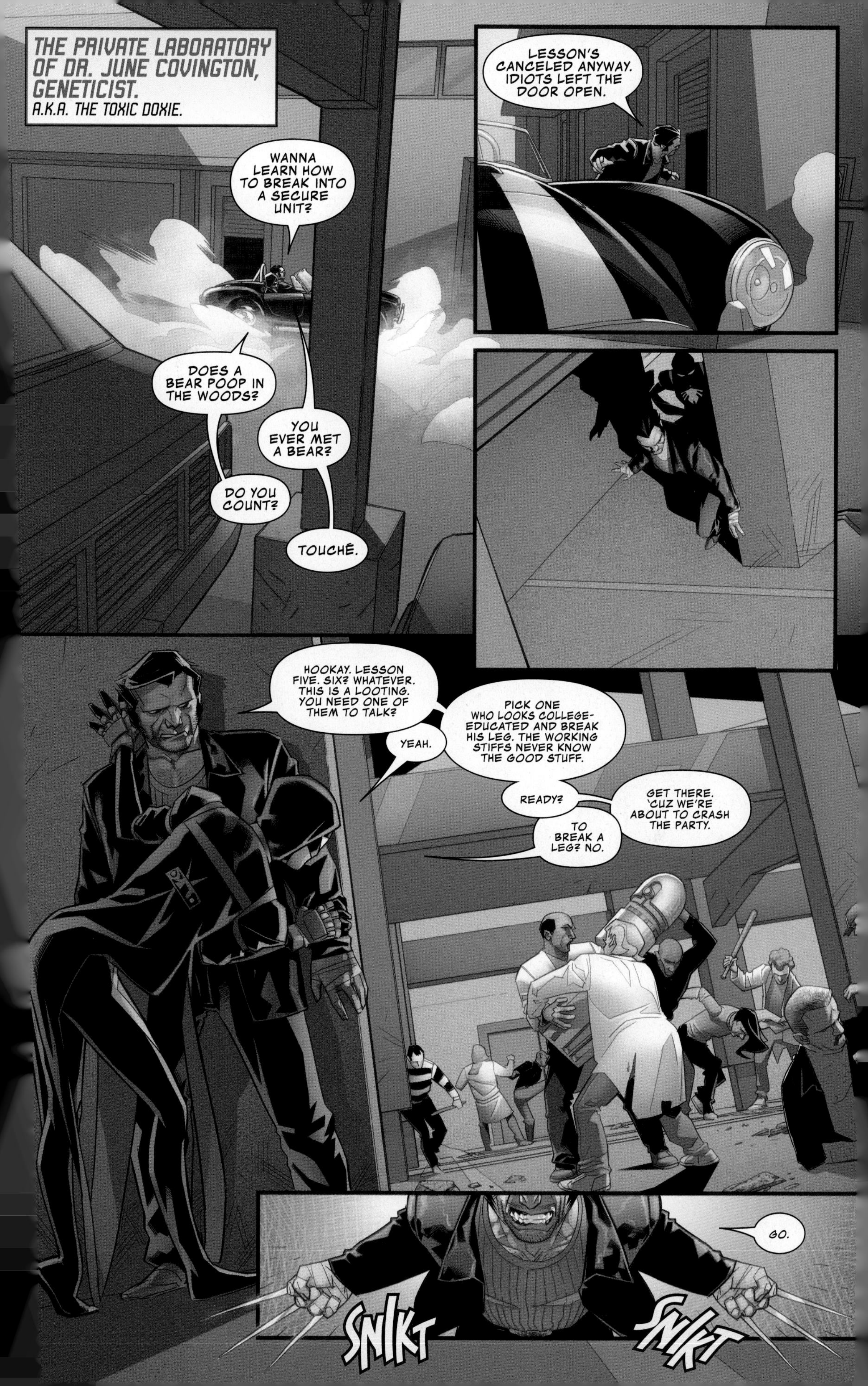
THE PRIVATE LABORATORY OF DR. JUNE COVINGTON, GENETICIST.
A.K.A. THE TOXIC DOXIE.
WANNA LEARN HOW TO BREAK INTO A SECURE UNIT?
DOES A BEAR POOP IN THE WOODS?
YOU EVER MET A BEAR?
DO YOU COUNT?
TOUCHÉ.
LESSON'S CANCELED ANYWAY. IDIOTS LEFT THE DOOR OPEN.
HOOKAY. LESSON FIVE. SIX? WHATEVER. THIS IS A LOOTING. YOU NEED ONE OF THEM TO TALK?
YEAH.
PICK ONE WHO LOOKS COLLEGE-EDUCATED AND BREAK HIS LEG. THE WORKING STIFFS NEVER KNOW THE GOOD STUFF.
READY?
TO BREAK A LEG? NO.
GET THERE. 'CUZ WE'RE ABOUT TO CRASH THE PARTY.
GO.
SNIKT
SNIKT

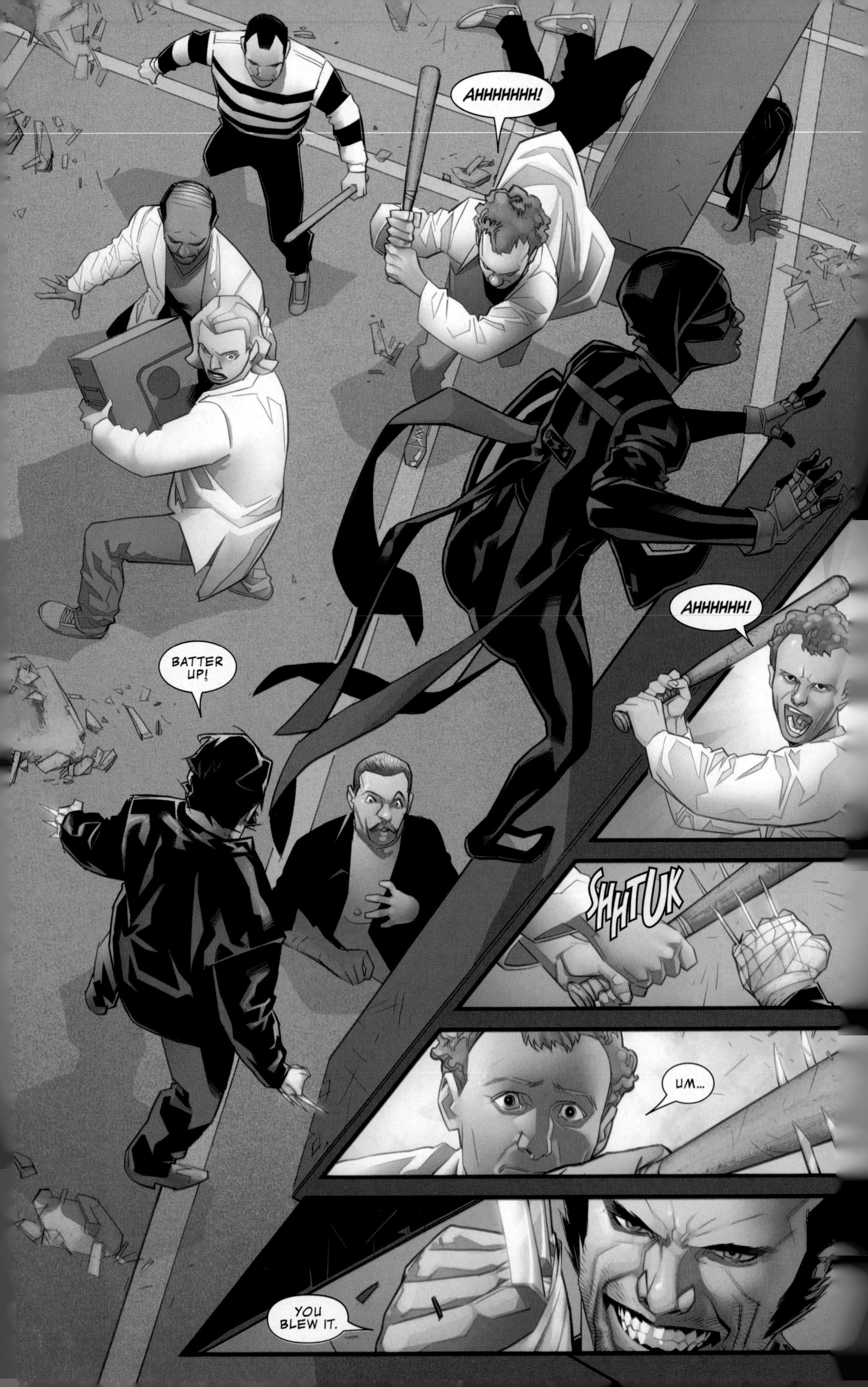
AHHHHHHH!
AHHHHHH!
BATTER UP!
SHHTUK
UM...
YOU BLEW IT.

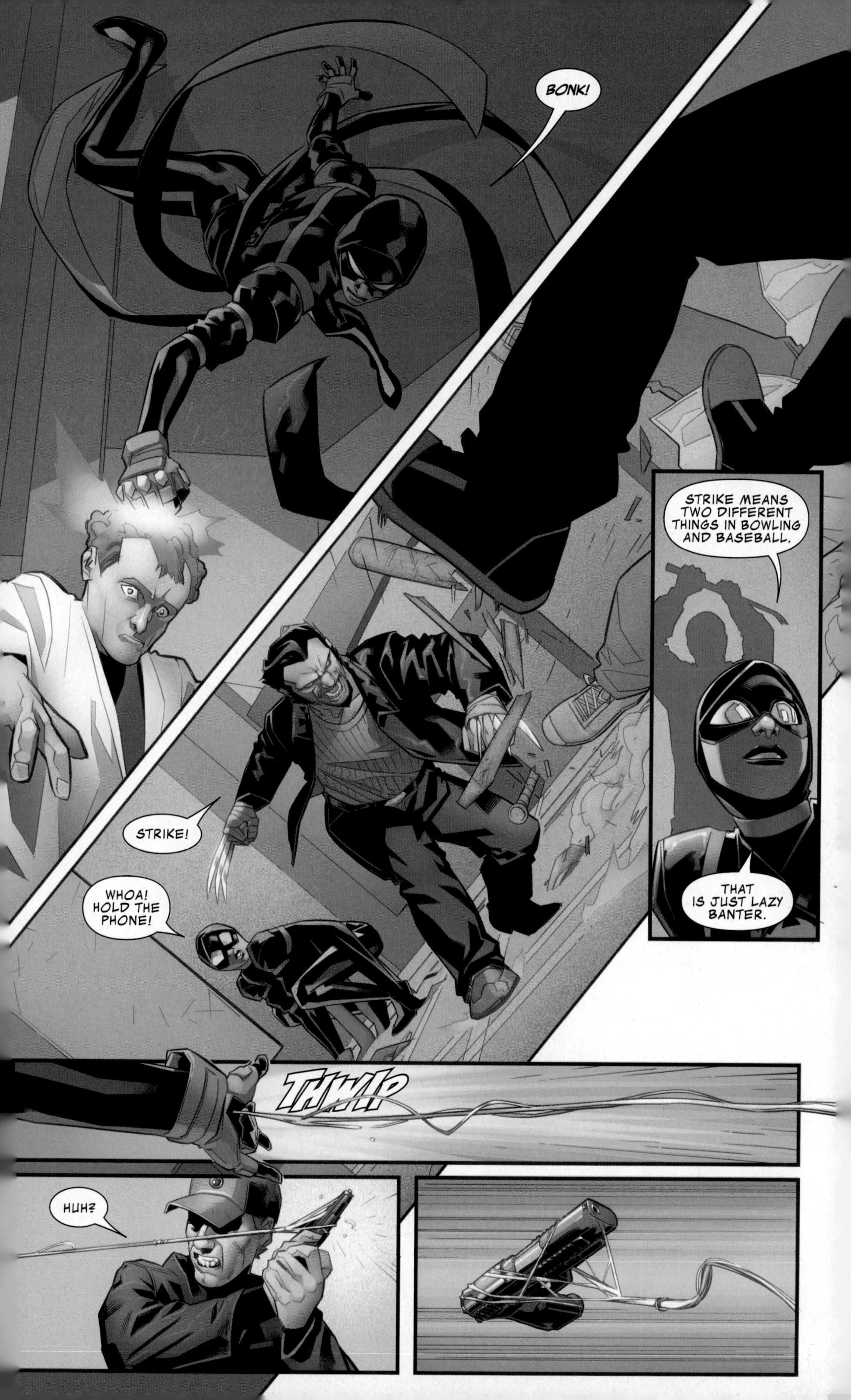
BONK!
STRIKE MEANS TWO DIFFERENT THINGS IN BOWLING AND BASEBALL.
STRIKE!
WHOA! HOLD THE PHONE!
THAT IS JUST LAZY BANTER.
THWIP
HUH?

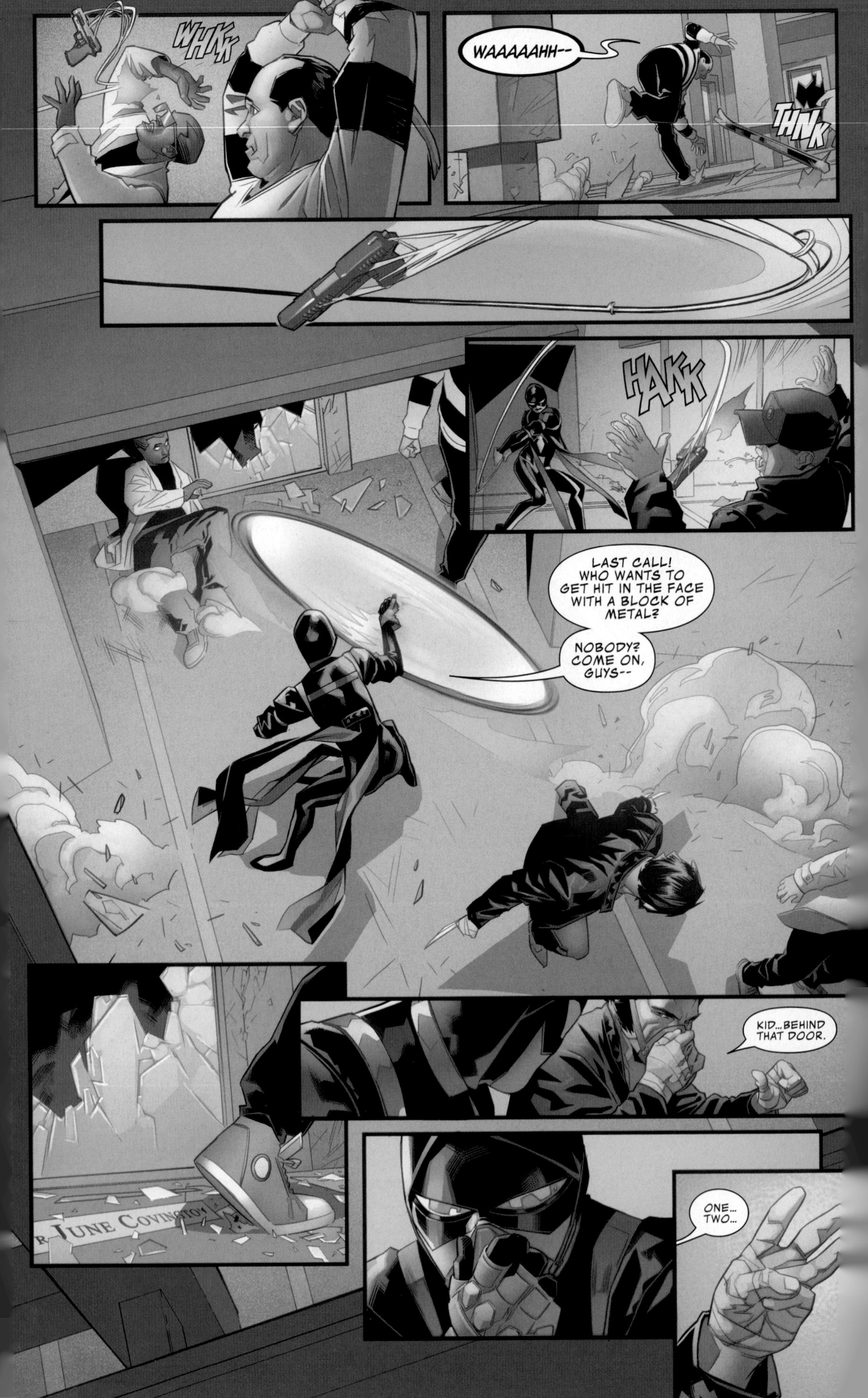
WHKK
WAAAAAHH--
THNK
HAKK
LAST CALL! WHO WANTS TO GET HIT IN THE FACE WITH A BLOCK OF METAL?
NOBODY? COME ON, GUYS--
JUNE COVINGTON
KID...BEHIND THAT DOOR.
ONE... TWO...

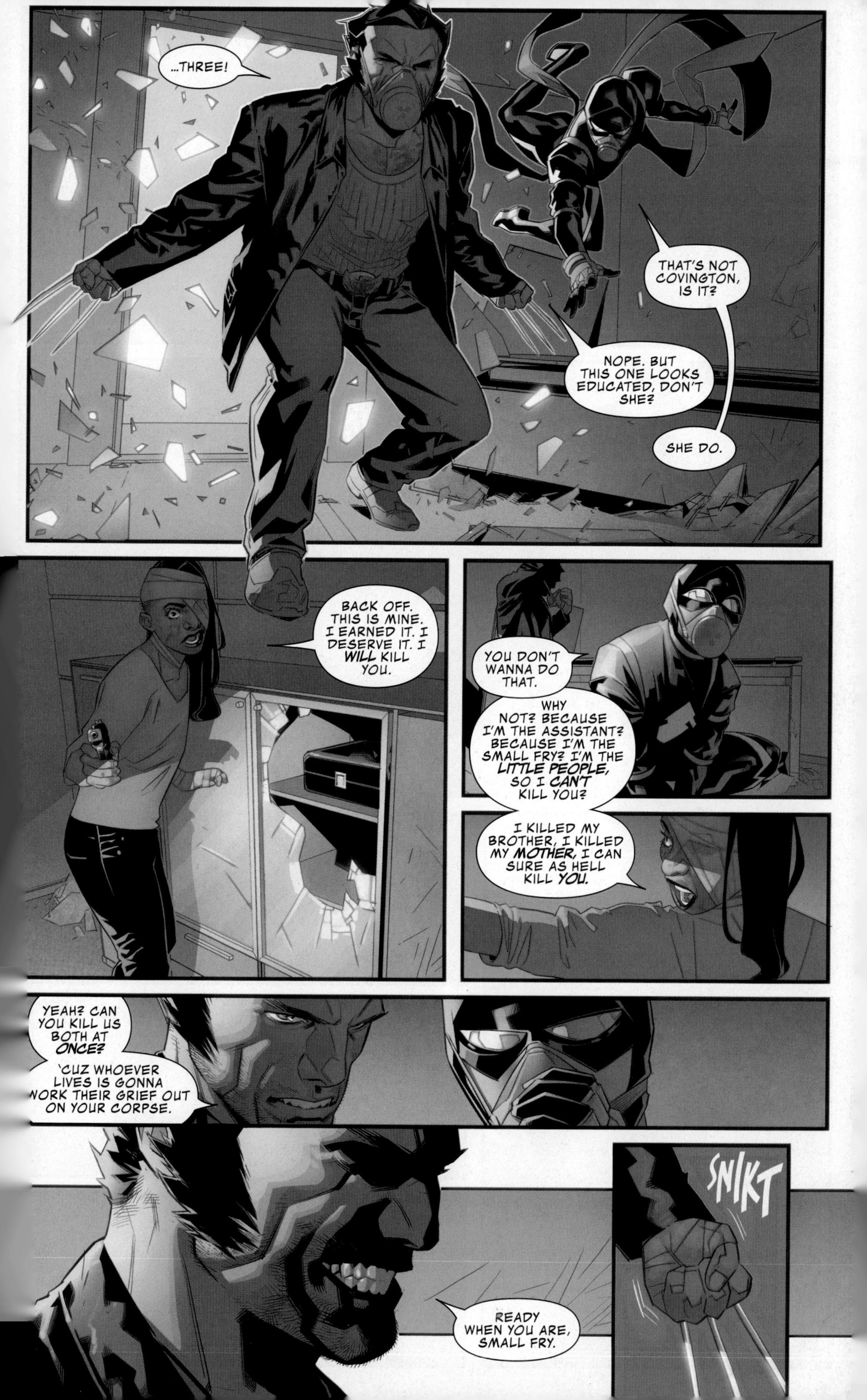
...THREE!
THAT'S NOT COVINGTON, IS IT?
NOPE. BUT THIS ONE LOOKS EDUCATED, DON'T SHE?
SHE DO.
BACK OFF. THIS IS MINE. I EARNED IT. I DESERVE IT. I WILL KILL YOU.
YOU DON'T WANNA DO THAT.
WHY NOT? BECAUSE I'M THE ASSISTANT? BECAUSE I'M THE SMALL FRY? I'M THE LITTLE PEOPLE, SO I CAN'T KILL YOU?
I KILLED MY BROTHER, I KILLED MY MOTHER, I CAN SURE AS HELL KILL YOU.
YEAH? CAN YOU KILL US BOTH AT ONCE?
'CUZ WHOEVER LIVES IS GONNA WORK THEIR GRIEF OUT ON YOUR CORPSE.
READY WHEN YOU ARE, SMALL FRY.
SNIKT

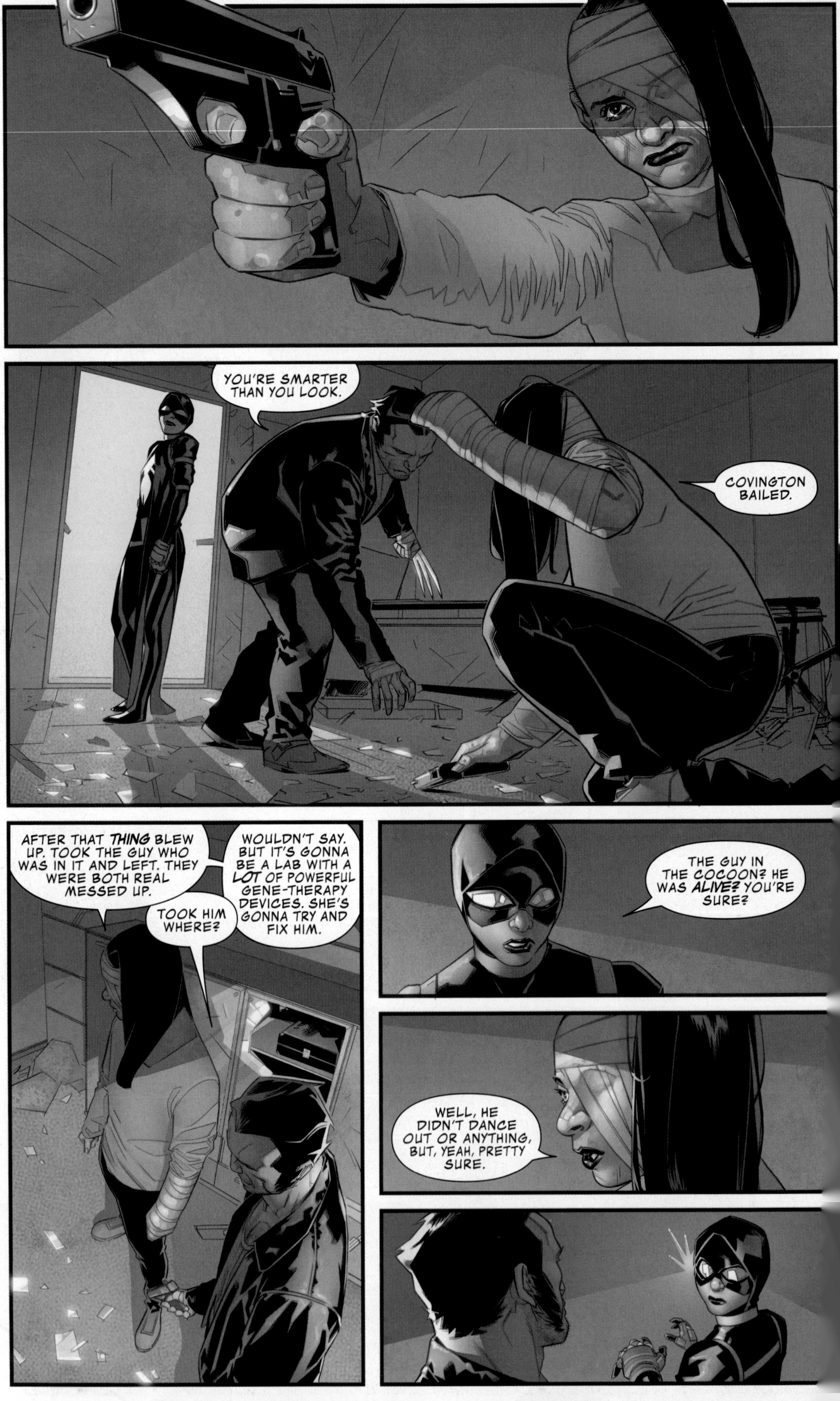
YOU'RE SMARTER THAN YOU LOOK.
COVINGTON BAILED.
AFTER THAT THING BLEW UP. TOOK THE GUY WHO WAS IN IT AND LEFT. THEY WERE BOTH REAL MESSED UP.
TOOK HIM WHERE?
WOULDN'T SAY. BUT IT'S GONNA BE A LAB WITH A LOT OF POWERFUL GENE-THERAPY DEVICES. SHE'S GONNA TRY AND FIX HIM.
THE GUY IN THE COCOON? HE WAS ALIVE? YOU'RE SURE?
WELL, HE DIDN'T DANCE OUT OR ANYTHING, BUT, YEAH, PRETTY SURE.

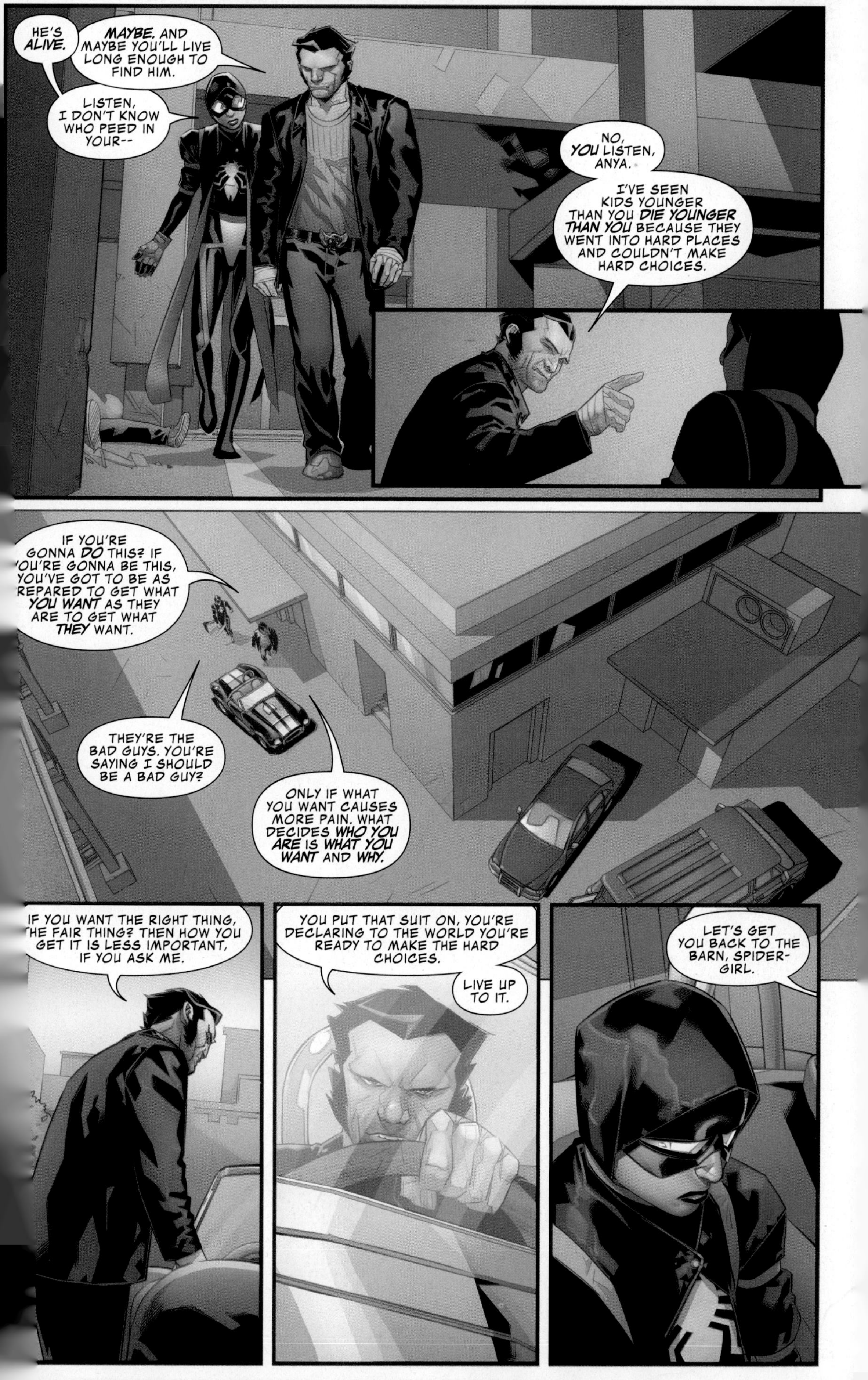
HE'S ALIVE.
MAYBE. AND MAYBE YOU'LL LIVE LONG ENOUGH TO FIND HIM.
LISTEN, I DON'T KNOW WHO PEED IN YOUR--
NO, YOU LISTEN, ANYA.
I'VE SEEN KIDS YOUNGER THAN YOU DIE YOUNGER THAN YOU BECAUSE THEY WENT INTO HARD PLACES AND COULDN'T MAKE HARD CHOICES.
IF YOU'RE GONNA DO THIS? IF YOU'RE GONNA BE THIS, YOU'VE GOT TO BE AS PREPARED TO GET WHAT YOU WANT AS THEY ARE TO GET WHAT THEY WANT.
THEY'RE THE BAD GUYS. YOU'RE SAYING I SHOULD BE A BAD GUY?
ONLY IF WHAT YOU WANT CAUSES MORE PAIN. WHAT DECIDES WHO YOU ARE IS WHAT YOU WANT AND WHY.
IF YOU WANT THE RIGHT THING, THE FAIR THING? THEN HOW YOU GET IT IS LESS IMPORTANT, IF YOU ASK ME.
YOU PUT THAT SUIT ON, YOU'RE DECLARING TO THE WORLD YOU'RE READY TO MAKE THE HARD CHOICES.
LIVE UP TO IT.
LET'S GET YOU BACK TO THE BARN, SPIDER-GIRL.

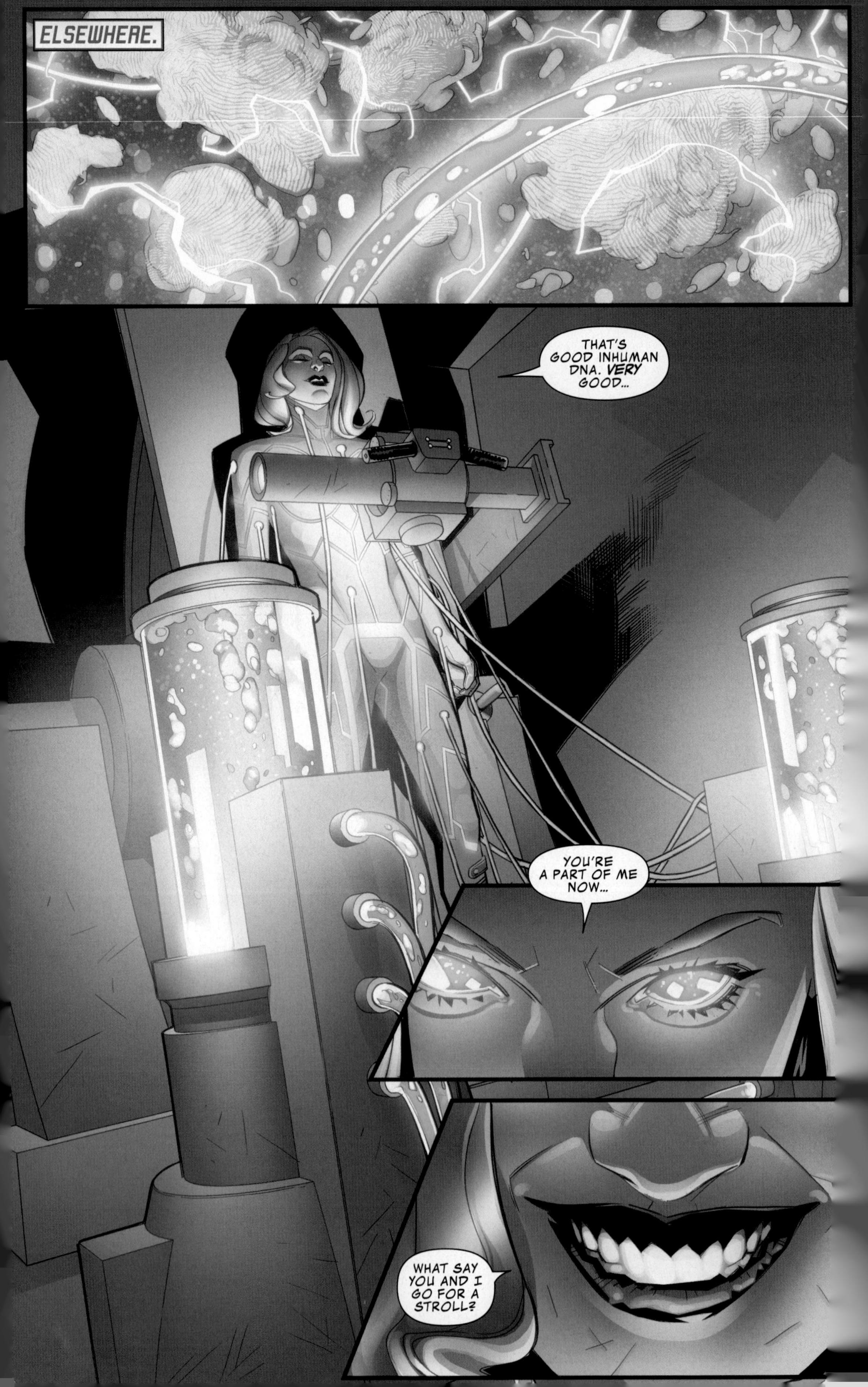
ELSEWHERE.
THAT'S GOOD INHUMAN DNA. VERY GOOD...
YOU'RE A PART OF ME NOW...
WHAT SAY YOU AND I GO FOR A STROLL?

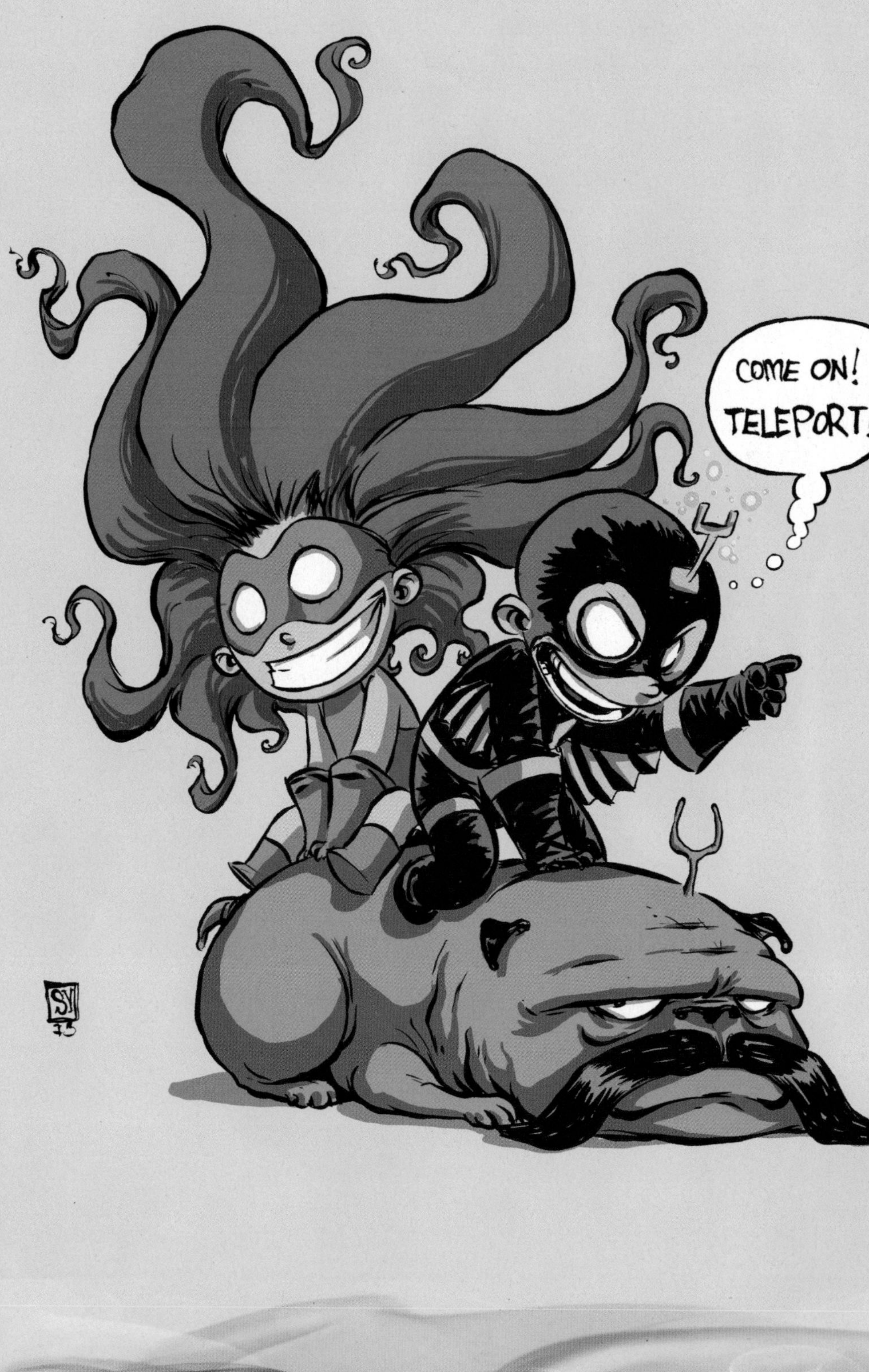
COME ON! TELEPORT!

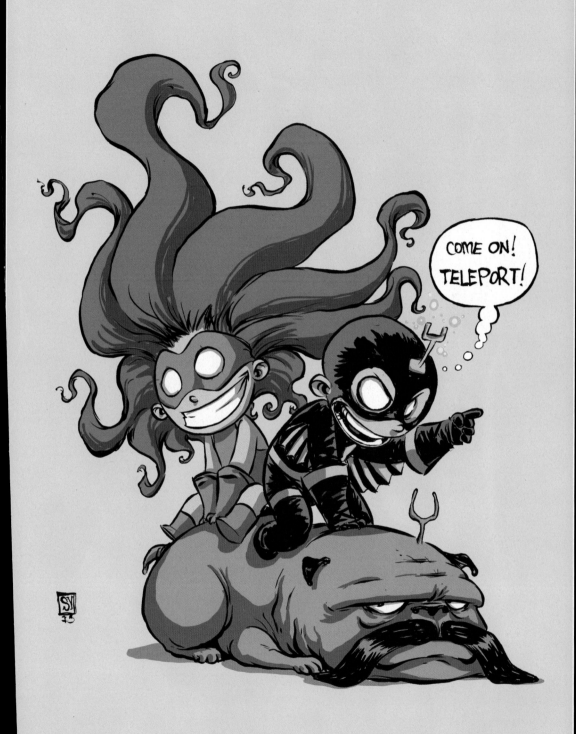

INHUMANITY #1 VARIANT BY SKOTTIE YOUNG

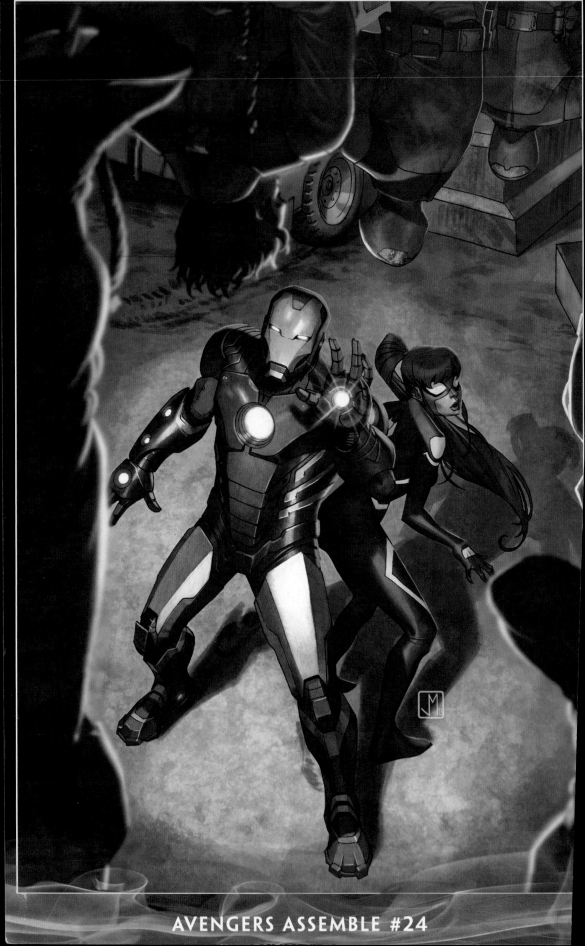

AVENGERS ASSEMBLE #24

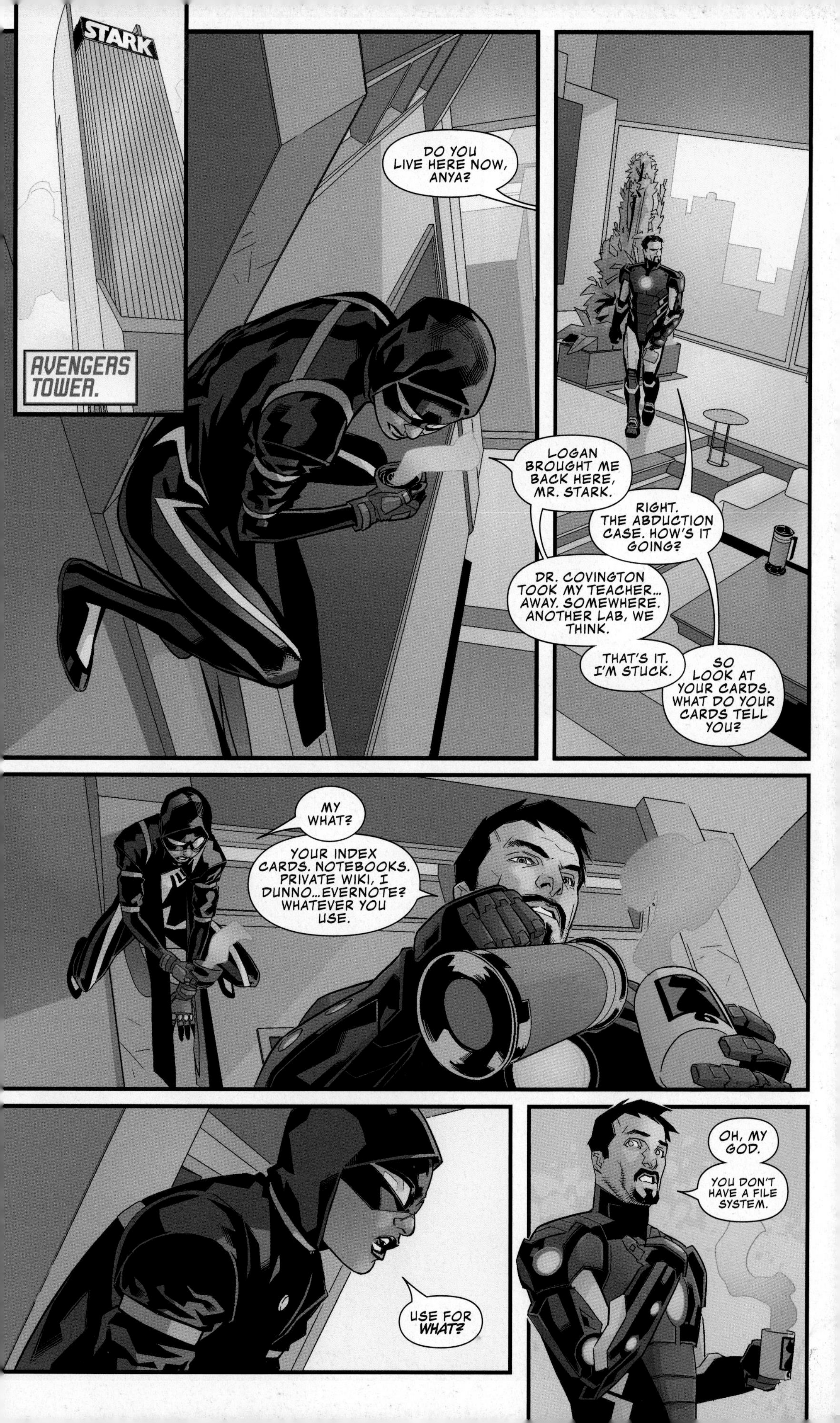
STARK
AVENGERS TOWER.
DO YOU LIVE HERE NOW, ANYA?
LOGAN BROUGHT ME BACK HERE, MR. STARK.
RIGHT. THE ABDUCTION CASE. HOW'S IT GOING?
DR. COVINGTON TOOK MY TEACHER... AWAY. SOMEWHERE. ANOTHER LAB, WE THINK.
THAT'S IT. I'M STUCK.
SO LOOK AT YOUR CARDS. WHAT DO YOUR CARDS TELL YOU?
MY WHAT?
YOUR INDEX CARDS. NOTEBOOKS. PRIVATE WIKI, I DUNNO...EVERNOTE? WHATEVER YOU USE.
USE FOR *WHAT?*
OH, MY GOD.
YOU DON'T HAVE A FILE SYSTEM.

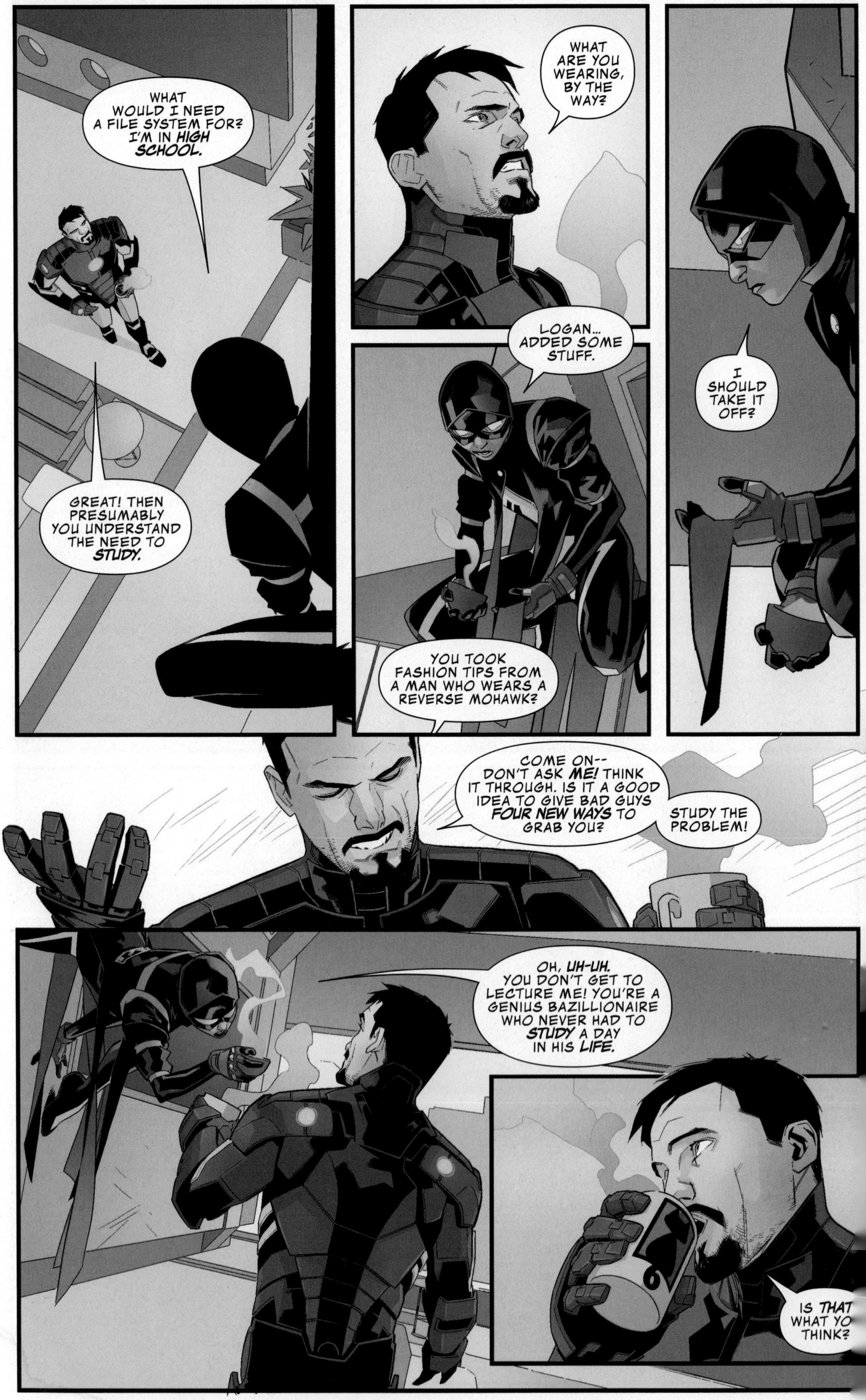
WHAT WOULD I NEED A FILE SYSTEM FOR? I'M IN HIGH SCHOOL.
GREAT! THEN PRESUMABLY YOU UNDERSTAND THE NEED TO STUDY.
WHAT ARE YOU WEARING, BY THE WAY?
LOGAN... ADDED SOME STUFF.
YOU TOOK FASHION TIPS FROM A MAN WHO WEARS A REVERSE MOHAWK?
I SHOULD TAKE IT OFF?
COME ON-- DON'T ASK ME! THINK IT THROUGH. IS IT A GOOD IDEA TO GIVE BAD GUYS FOUR NEW WAYS TO GRAB YOU?
STUDY THE PROBLEM!
OH, UH-UH. YOU DON'T GET TO LECTURE ME! YOU'RE A GENIUS BAZILLIONAIRE WHO NEVER HAD TO STUDY A DAY IN HIS LIFE.
IS THAT WHAT YO THINK?

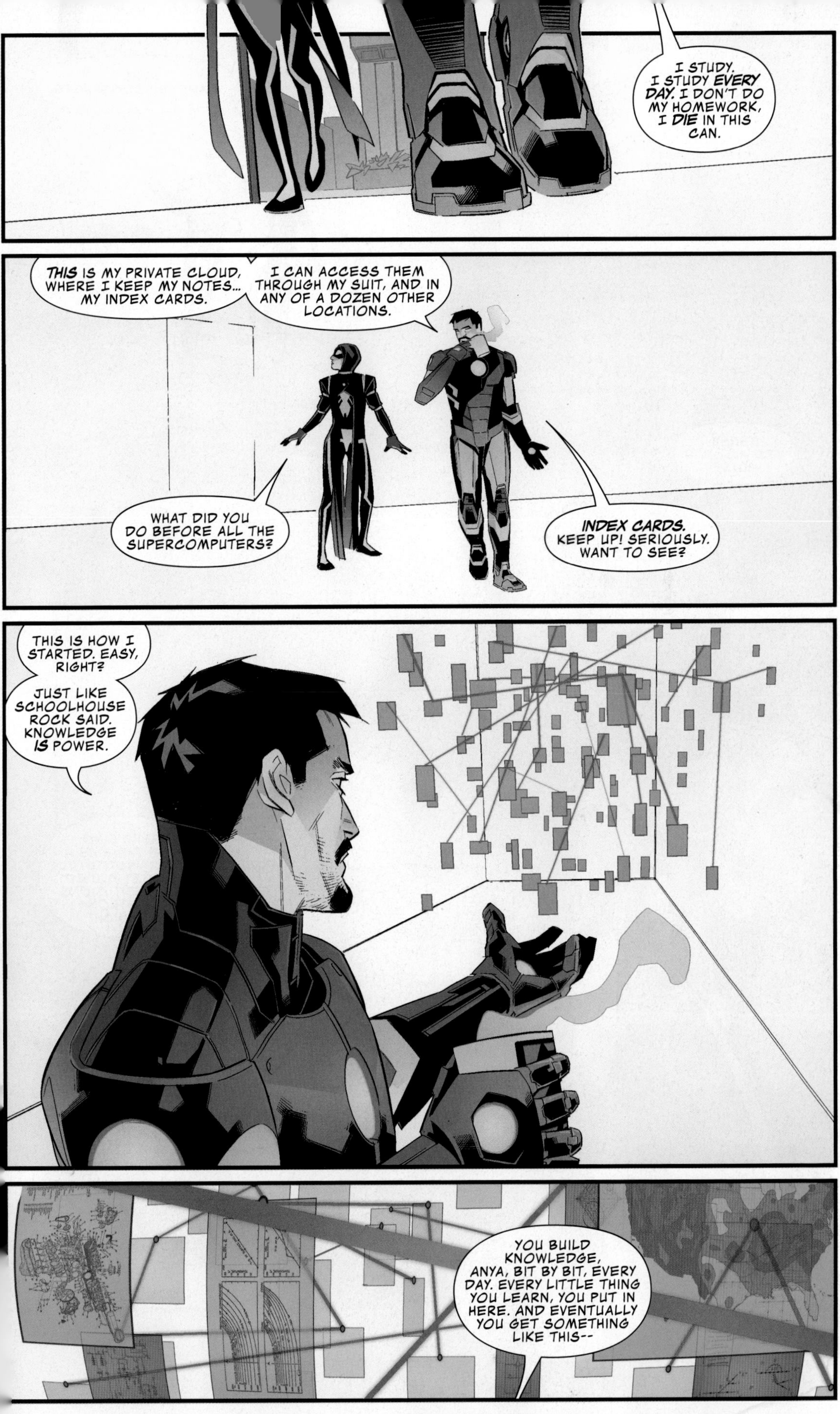
I STUDY. I STUDY EVERY DAY. I DON'T DO MY HOMEWORK, I DIE IN THIS CAN.
THIS IS MY PRIVATE CLOUD, WHERE I KEEP MY NOTES... MY INDEX CARDS.
I CAN ACCESS THEM THROUGH MY SUIT, AND IN ANY OF A DOZEN OTHER LOCATIONS.
WHAT DID YOU DO BEFORE ALL THE SUPERCOMPUTERS?
INDEX CARDS. KEEP UP! SERIOUSLY. WANT TO SEE?
THIS IS HOW I STARTED. EASY, RIGHT?
JUST LIKE SCHOOLHOUSE ROCK SAID. KNOWLEDGE IS POWER.
YOU BUILD KNOWLEDGE, ANYA, BIT BY BIT, EVERY DAY. EVERY LITTLE THING YOU LEARN, YOU PUT IN HERE. AND EVENTUALLY YOU GET SOMETHING LIKE THIS--

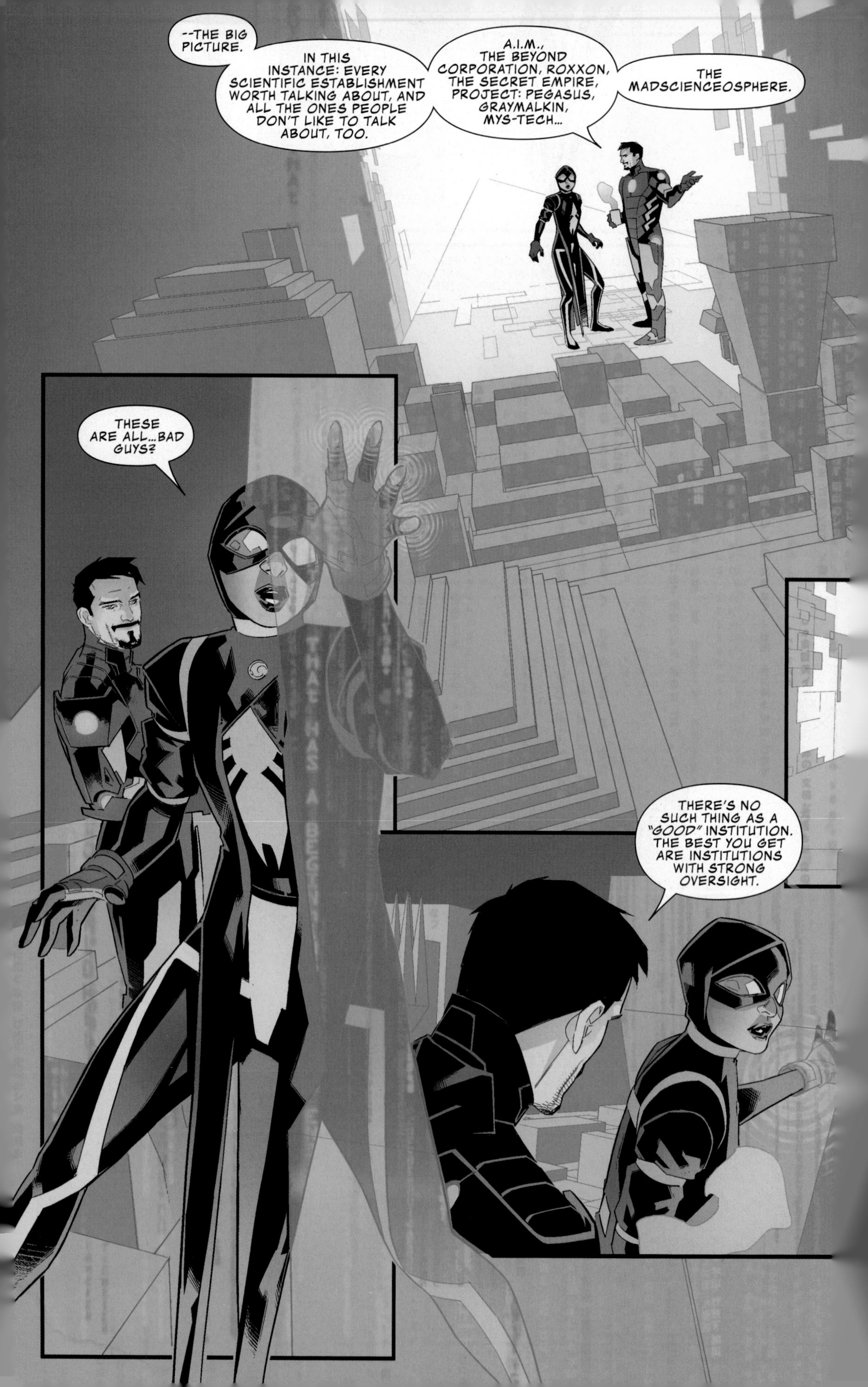
--THE BIG PICTURE.
IN THIS INSTANCE: EVERY SCIENTIFIC ESTABLISHMENT WORTH TALKING ABOUT, AND ALL THE ONES PEOPLE DON'T LIKE TO TALK ABOUT, TOO.
A.I.M., THE BEYOND CORPORATION, ROXXON, THE SECRET EMPIRE, PROJECT: PEGASUS, GRAYMALKIN, MYS-TECH...
THE MADSCIENCEOSPHERE.
THESE ARE ALL...BAD GUYS?
THERE'S NO SUCH THING AS A "GOOD" INSTITUTION. THE BEST YOU GET ARE INSTITUTIONS WITH STRONG OVERSIGHT.

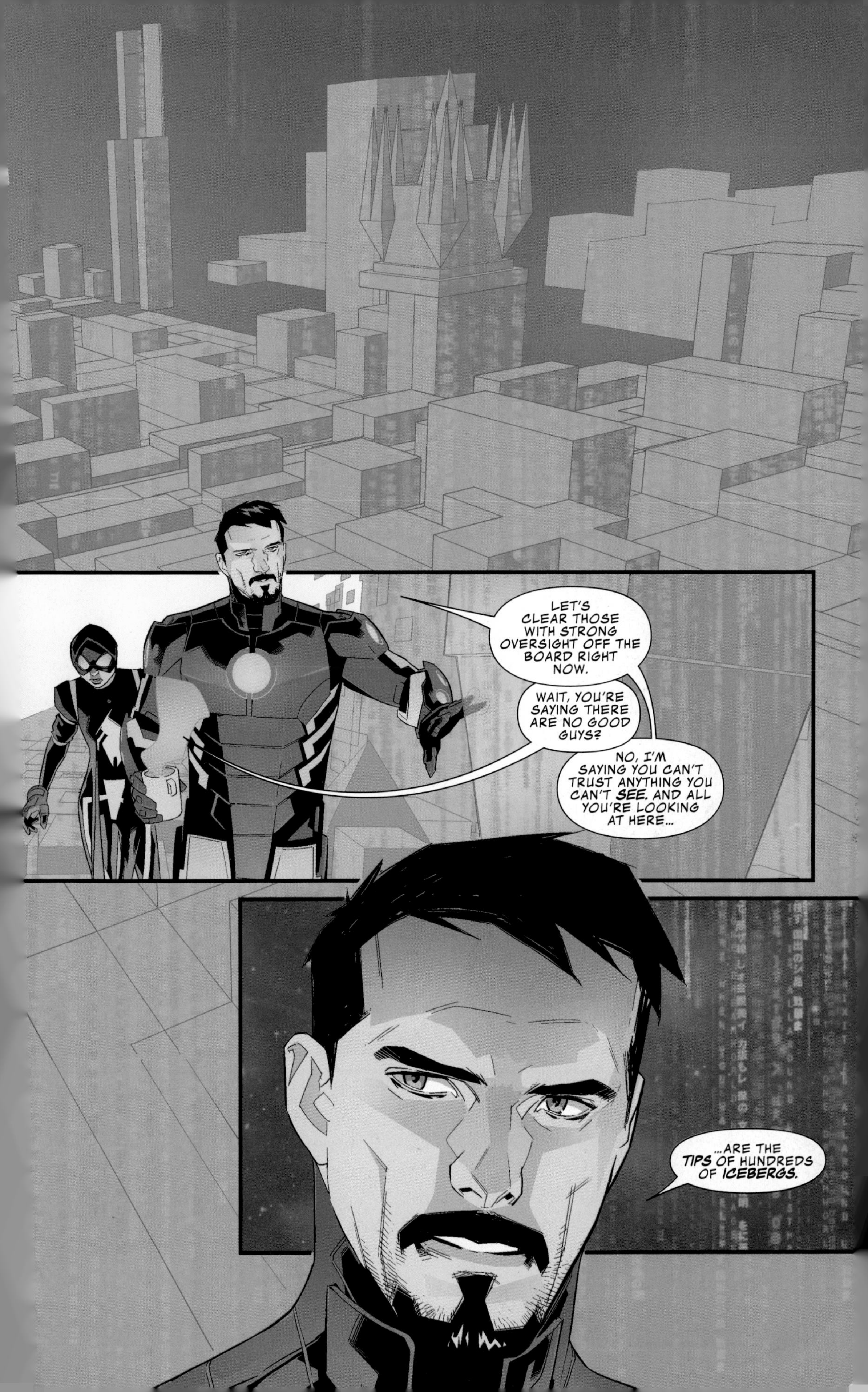
LET'S CLEAR THOSE WITH STRONG OVERSIGHT OFF THE BOARD RIGHT NOW.
WAIT, YOU'RE SAYING THERE ARE NO GOOD GUYS?
NO, I'M SAYING YOU CAN'T TRUST ANYTHING YOU CAN'T SEE. AND ALL YOU'RE LOOKING AT HERE...
...ARE THE TIPS OF HUNDREDS OF ICEBERGS.

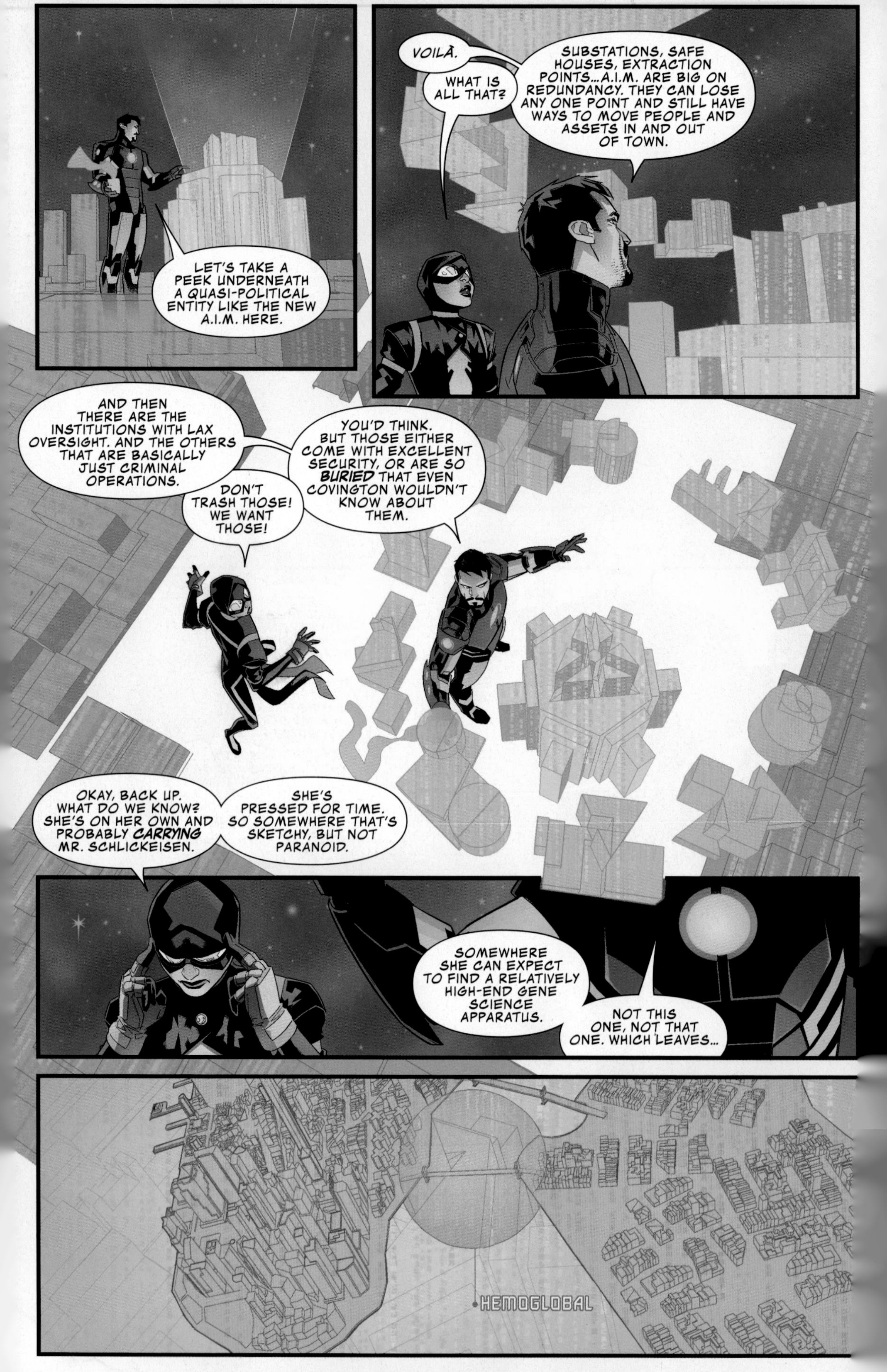
LET'S TAKE A PEEK UNDERNEATH A QUASI-POLITICAL ENTITY LIKE THE NEW A.I.M. HERE.
VOILÀ.
WHAT IS ALL THAT?
SUBSTATIONS, SAFE HOUSES, EXTRACTION POINTS...A.I.M. ARE BIG ON REDUNDANCY. THEY CAN LOSE ANY ONE POINT AND STILL HAVE WAYS TO MOVE PEOPLE AND ASSETS IN AND OUT OF TOWN.
AND THEN THERE ARE THE INSTITUTIONS WITH LAX OVERSIGHT. AND THE OTHERS THAT ARE BASICALLY JUST CRIMINAL OPERATIONS.
DON'T TRASH THOSE! WE WANT THOSE!
YOU'D THINK. BUT THOSE EITHER COME WITH EXCELLENT SECURITY, OR ARE SO BURIED THAT EVEN COVINGTON WOULDN'T KNOW ABOUT THEM.
OKAY, BACK UP. WHAT DO WE KNOW? SHE'S ON HER OWN AND PROBABLY CARRYING MR. SCHLICKEISEN.
SHE'S PRESSED FOR TIME. SO SOMEWHERE THAT'S SKETCHY, BUT NOT PARANOID.
SOMEWHERE SHE CAN EXPECT TO FIND A RELATIVELY HIGH-END GENE SCIENCE APPARATUS.
NOT THIS ONE, NOT THAT ONE. WHICH LEAVES...
HEMOGLOBAL

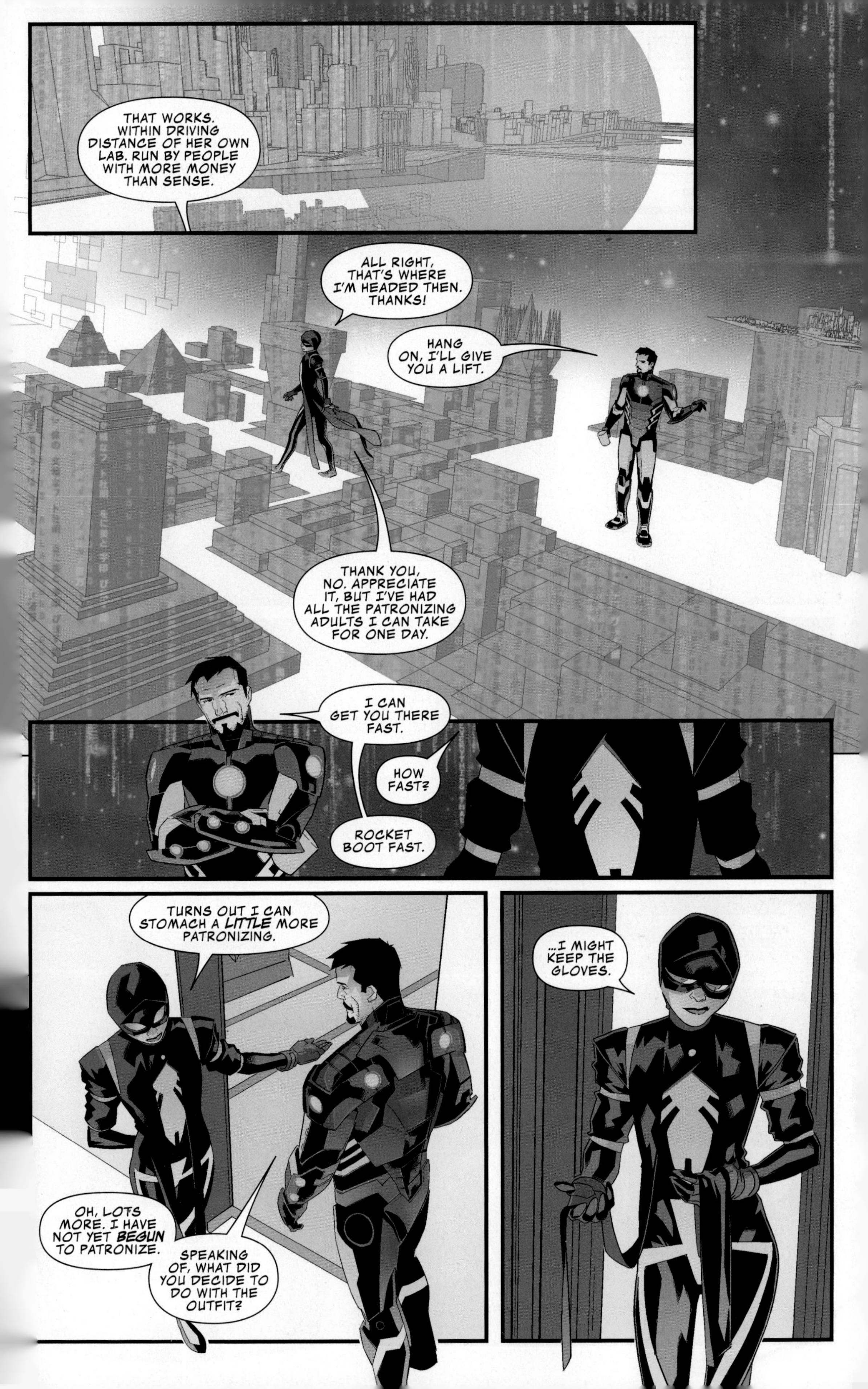
THAT WORKS. WITHIN DRIVING DISTANCE OF HER OWN LAB. RUN BY PEOPLE WITH MORE MONEY THAN SENSE.
ALL RIGHT, THAT'S WHERE I'M HEADED THEN. THANKS!
HANG ON, I'LL GIVE YOU A LIFT.
THANK YOU, NO. APPRECIATE IT, BUT I'VE HAD ALL THE PATRONIZING ADULTS I CAN TAKE FOR ONE DAY.
I CAN GET YOU THERE FAST.
HOW FAST?
ROCKET BOOT FAST.
TURNS OUT I CAN STOMACH A LITTLE MORE PATRONIZING.
OH, LOTS MORE. I HAVE NOT YET BEGUN TO PATRONIZE.
SPEAKING OF, WHAT DID YOU DECIDE TO DO WITH THE OUTFIT?
...I MIGHT KEEP THE GLOVES.

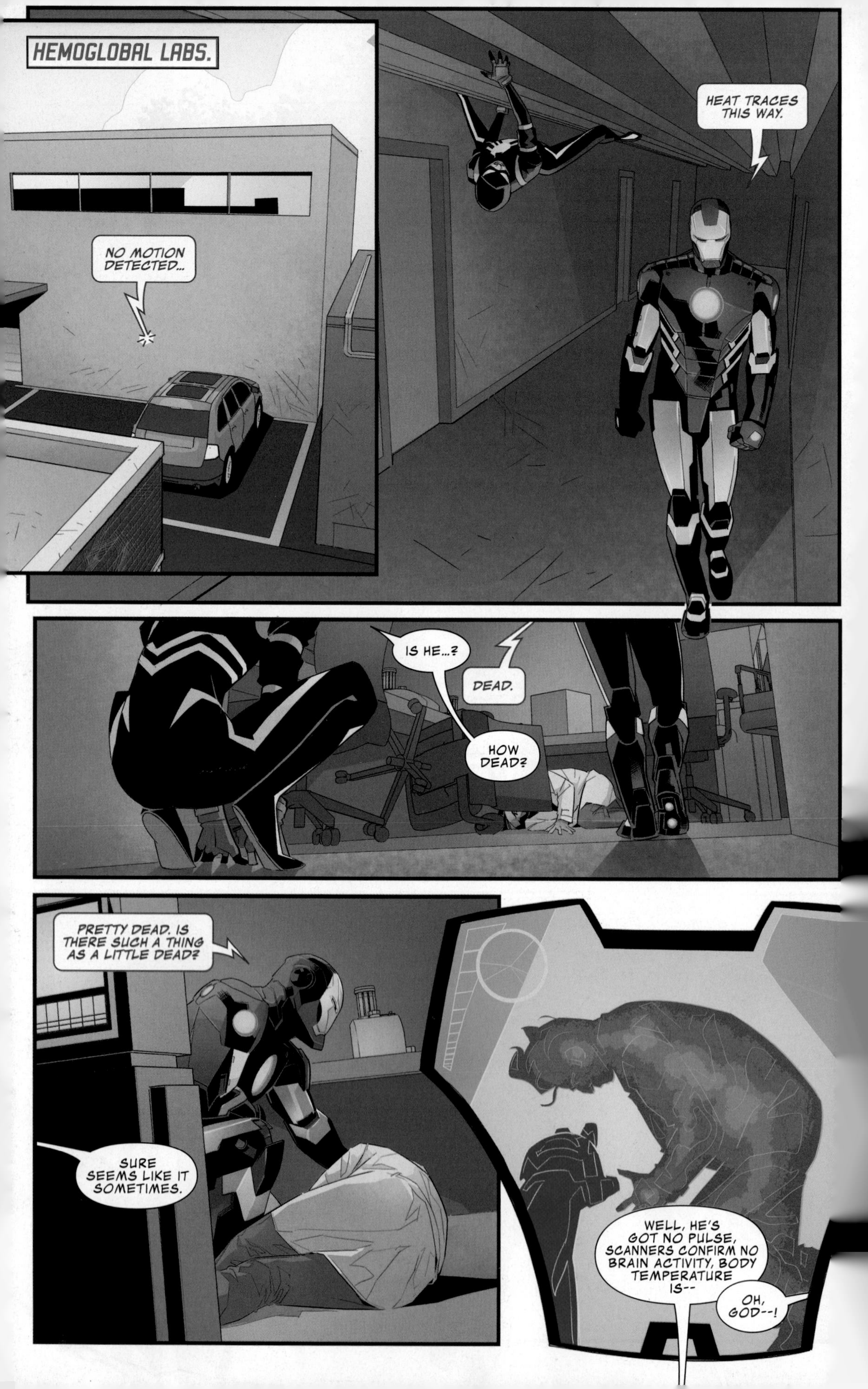
HEMOGLOBAL LABS.
NO MOTION DETECTED...
HEAT TRACES THIS WAY.
IS HE...?
DEAD.
HOW DEAD?
PRETTY DEAD. IS THERE SUCH A THING AS A LITTLE DEAD?
SURE SEEMS LIKE IT SOMETIMES.
WELL, HE'S GOT NO PULSE, SCANNERS CONFIRM NO BRAIN ACTIVITY, BODY TEMPERATURE IS--
OH, GOD--!

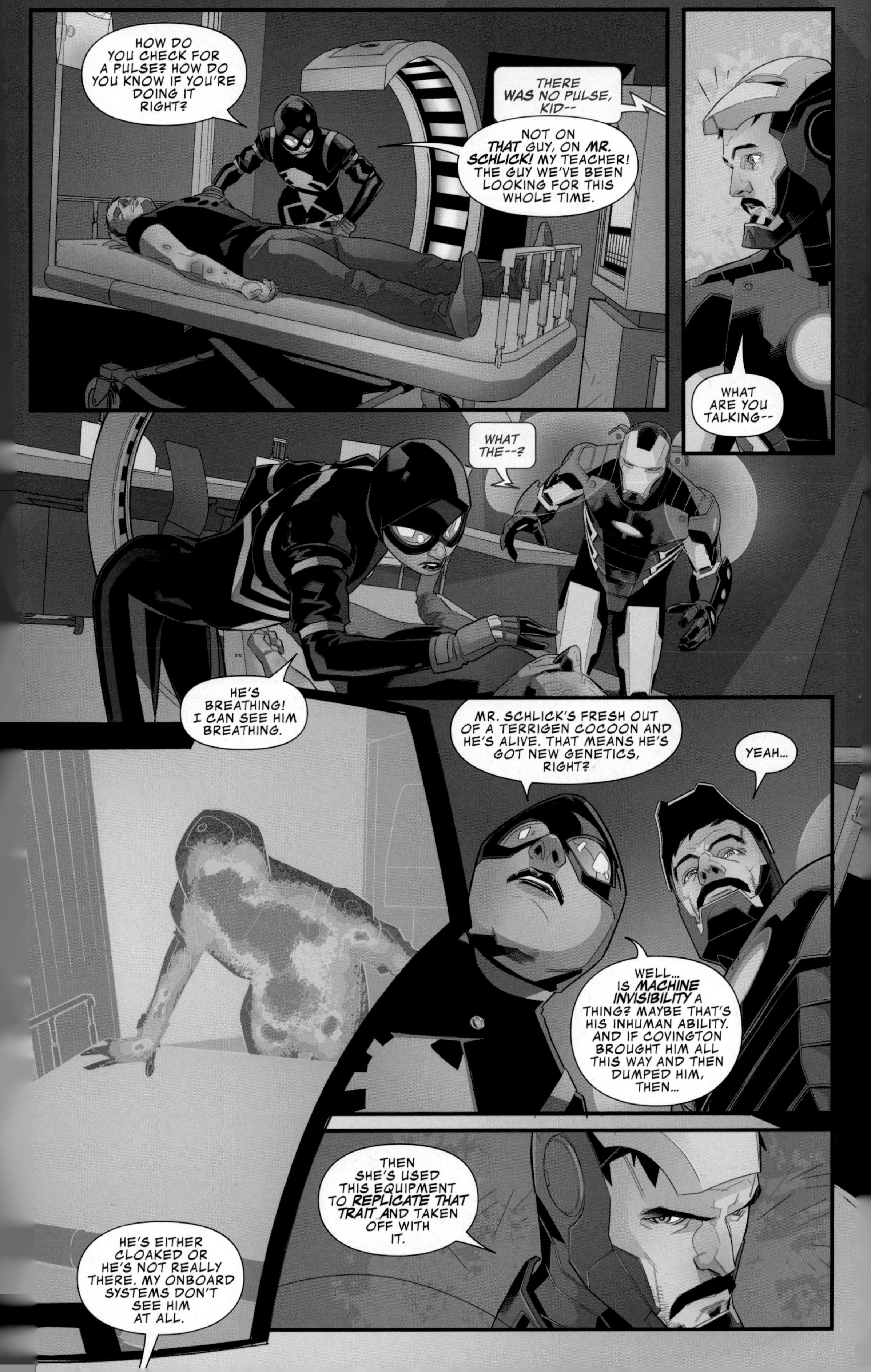
HOW DO YOU CHECK FOR A PULSE? HOW DO YOU KNOW IF YOU'RE DOING IT RIGHT?
THERE **WAS** NO PULSE, KID--
NOT ON **THAT** GUY, ON **MR. SCHLICK!** MY TEACHER! THE GUY WE'VE BEEN LOOKING FOR THIS WHOLE TIME.
WHAT ARE YOU TALKING--
WHAT THE--?
HE'S BREATHING! I CAN SEE HIM BREATHING.
MR. SCHLICK'S FRESH OUT OF A TERRIGEN COCOON AND HE'S ALIVE. THAT MEANS HE'S GOT NEW GENETICS, RIGHT?
YEAH...
WELL... IS **MACHINE INVISIBILITY** A THING? MAYBE THAT'S HIS INHUMAN ABILITY. AND IF COVINGTON BROUGHT HIM ALL THIS WAY AND THEN DUMPED HIM, THEN...
HE'S EITHER CLOAKED OR HE'S NOT REALLY THERE. MY ONBOARD SYSTEMS DON'T SEE HIM AT ALL.
THEN SHE'S USED THIS EQUIPMENT TO **REPLICATE THAT TRAIT** AND TAKEN OFF WITH IT.

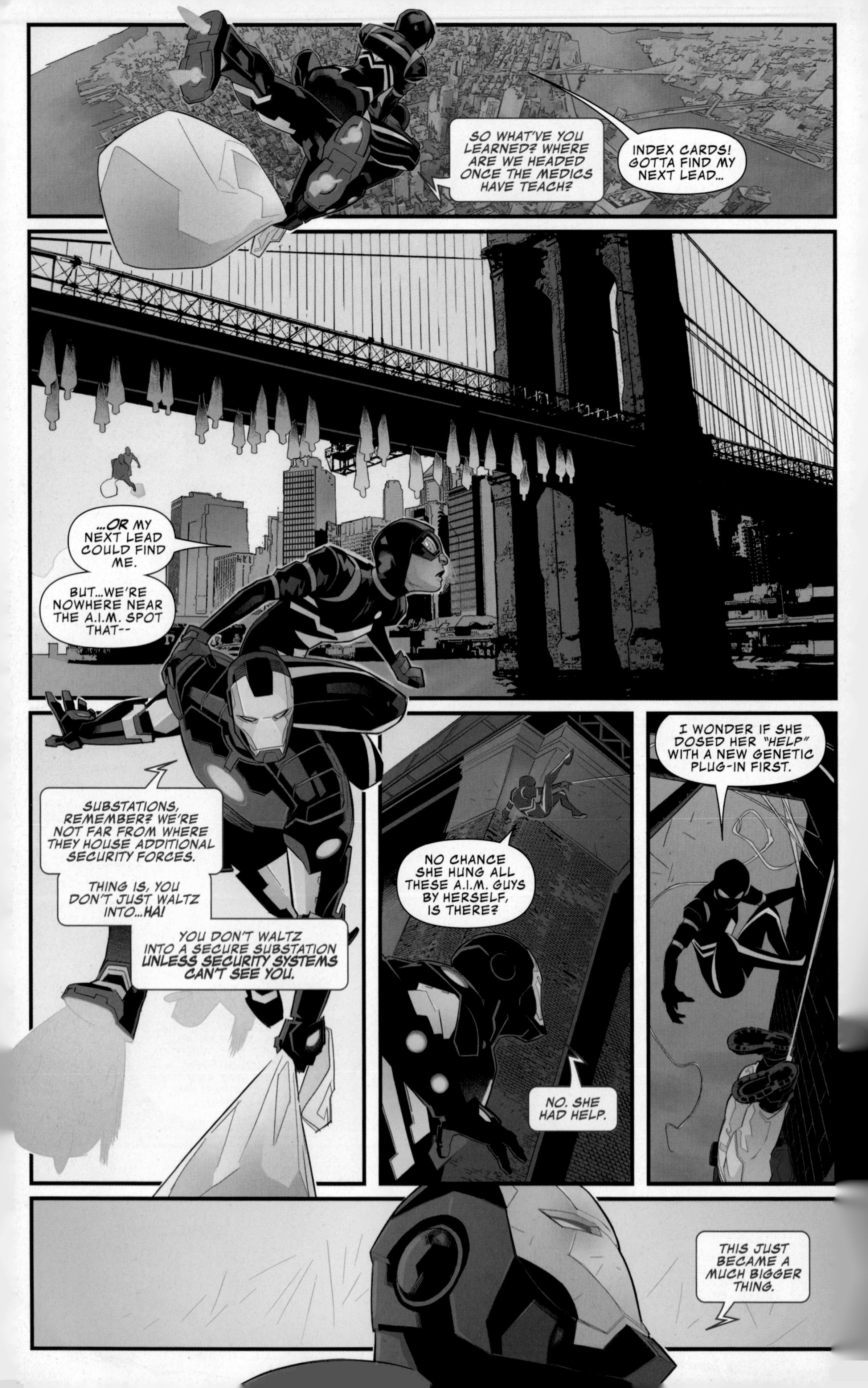
SO WHAT'VE YOU LEARNED? WHERE ARE WE HEADED ONCE THE MEDICS HAVE TEACH?
INDEX CARDS! GOTTA FIND MY NEXT LEAD...
...OR MY NEXT LEAD COULD FIND ME.
BUT...WE'RE NOWHERE NEAR THE A.I.M. SPOT THAT--
SUBSTATIONS, REMEMBER? WE'RE NOT FAR FROM WHERE THEY HOUSE ADDITIONAL SECURITY FORCES.
THING IS, YOU DON'T JUST WALTZ INTO...HA!
YOU DON'T WALTZ INTO A SECURE SUBSTATION UNLESS SECURITY SYSTEMS CAN'T SEE YOU.
NO CHANCE SHE HUNG ALL THESE A.I.M. GUYS BY HERSELF, IS THERE?
NO. SHE HAD HELP.
I WONDER IF SHE DOSED HER "HELP" WITH A NEW GENETIC PLUG-IN FIRST.
THIS JUST BECAME A MUCH BIGGER THING.

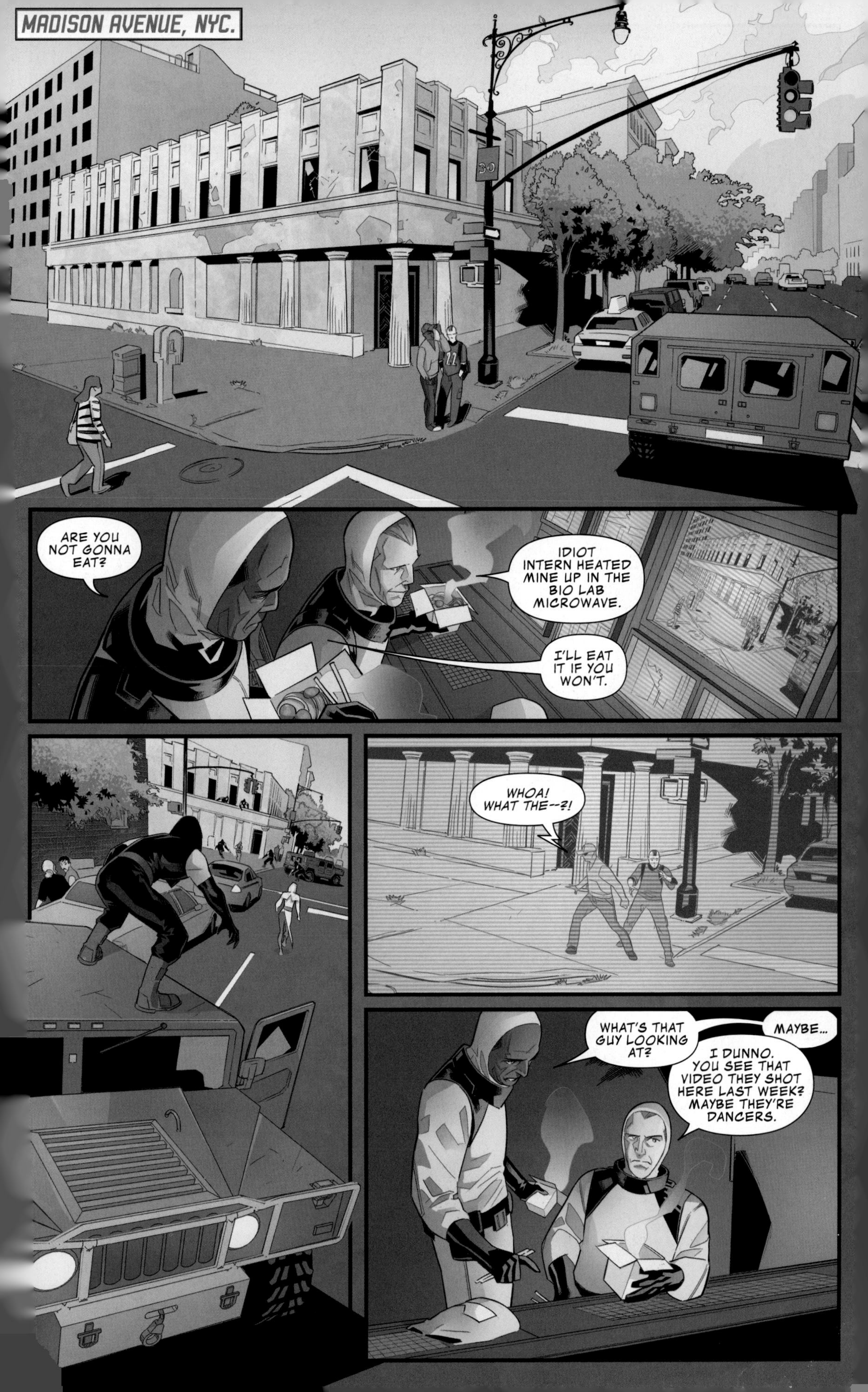
MADISON AVENUE, NYC.
ARE YOU NOT GONNA EAT?
IDIOT INTERN HEATED MINE UP IN THE BIO LAB MICROWAVE.
I'LL EAT IT IF YOU WON'T.
WHOA! WHAT THE--?!
WHAT'S THAT GUY LOOKING AT?
MAYBE...
I DUNNO. YOU SEE THAT VIDEO THEY SHOT HERE LAST WEEK? MAYBE THEY'RE DANCERS.

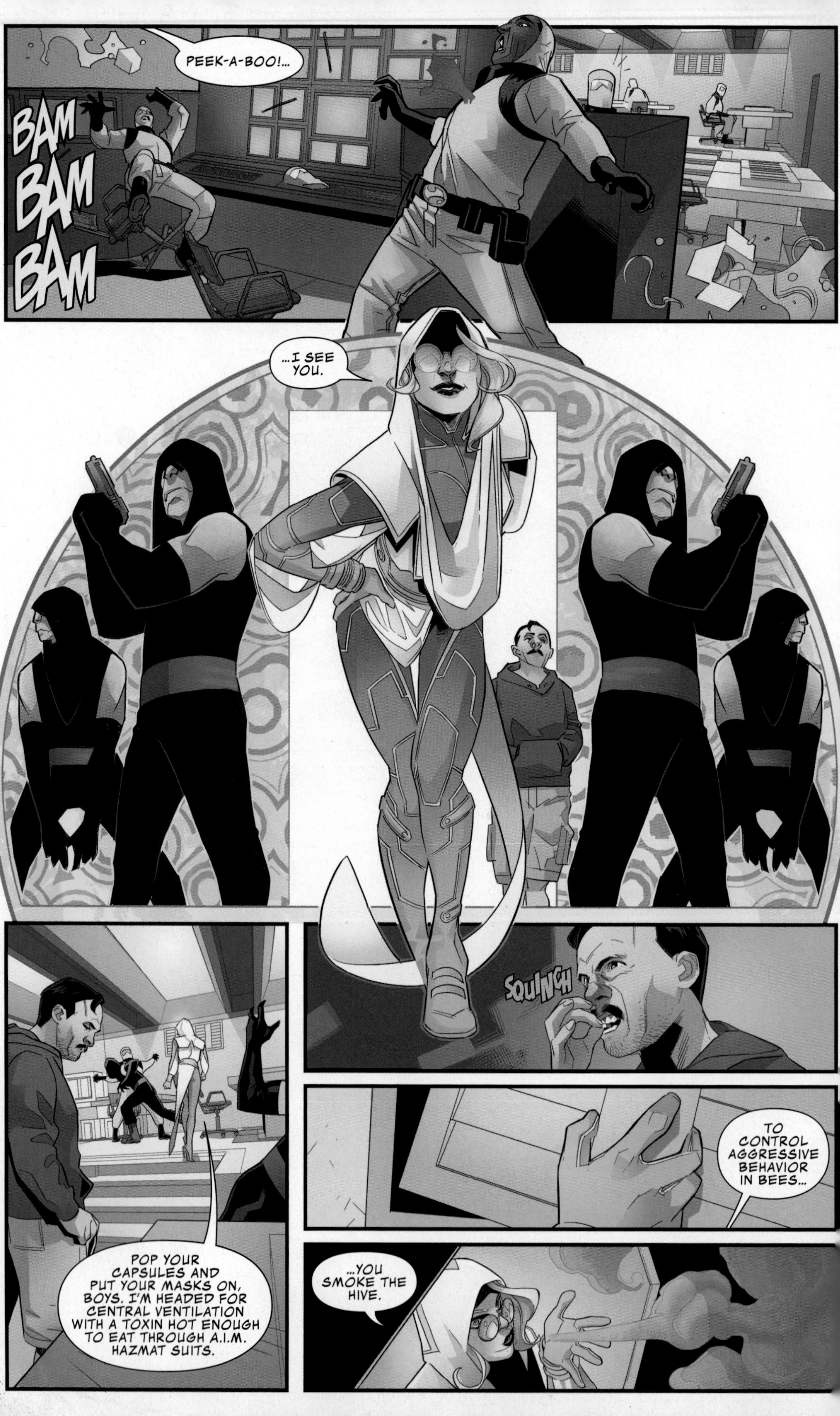
PEEK-A-BOO!...
BAM BAM BAM
...I SEE YOU.
POP YOUR CAPSULES AND PUT YOUR MASKS ON, BOYS. I'M HEADED FOR CENTRAL VENTILATION WITH A TOXIN HOT ENOUGH TO EAT THROUGH A.I.M. HAZMAT SUITS.
SQUINCH
TO CONTROL AGGRESSIVE BEHAVIOR IN BEES...
...YOU SMOKE THE HIVE.

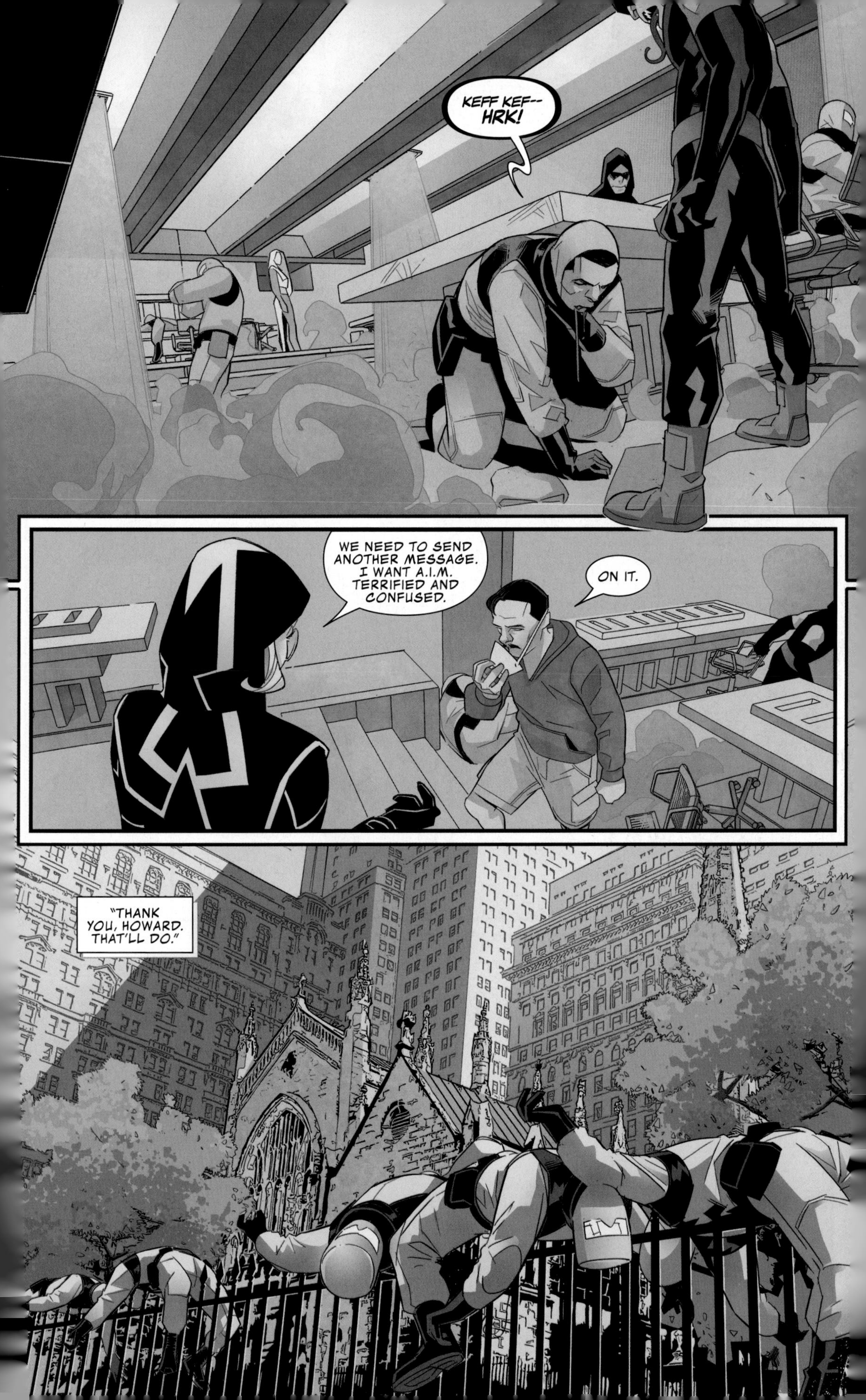
KEFF KEF-- HRK!
WE NEED TO SEND ANOTHER MESSAGE. I WANT A.I.M. TERRIFIED AND CONFUSED.
ON IT.
"THANK YOU, HOWARD. THAT'LL DO."

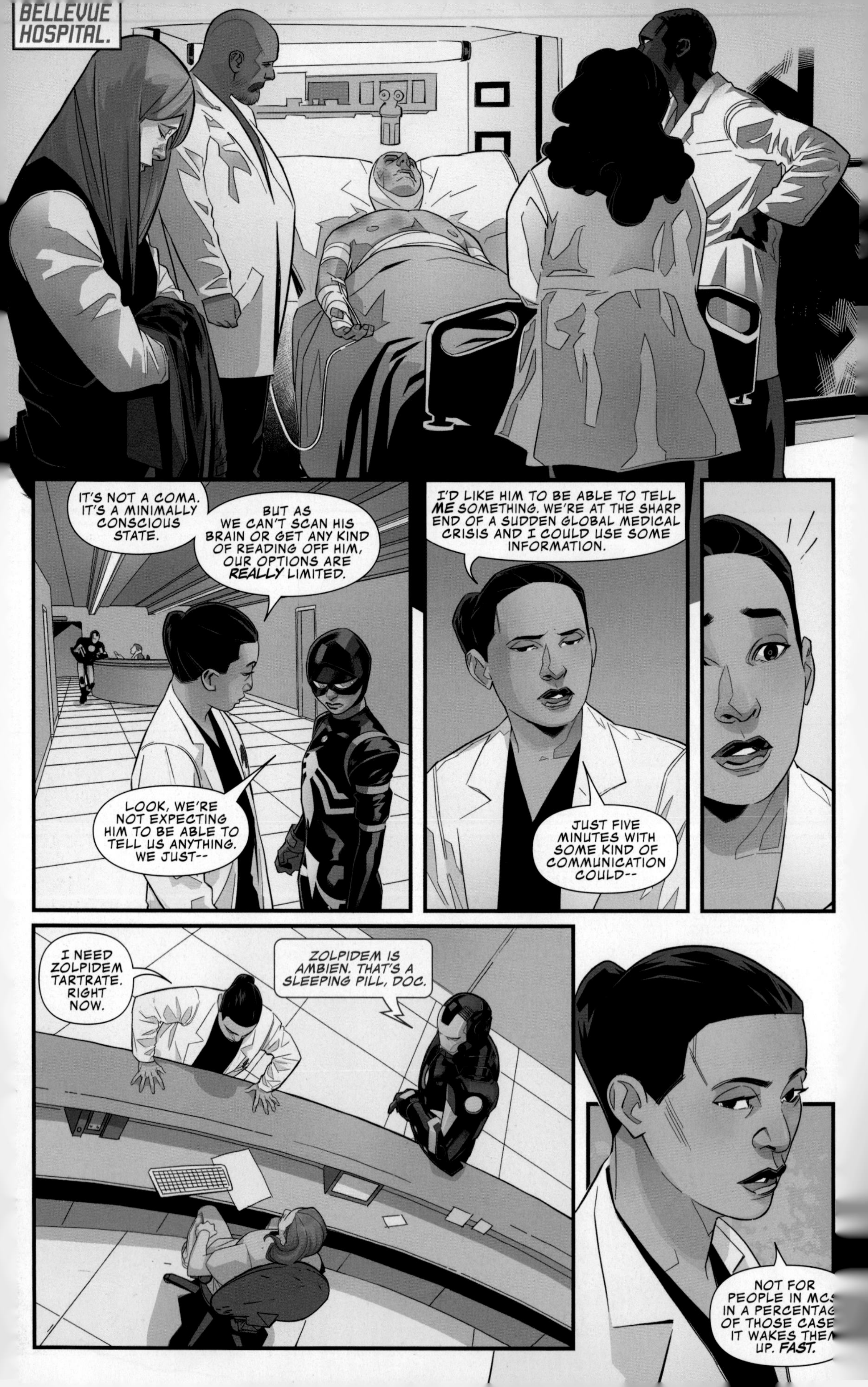
BELLEVUE HOSPITAL.
IT'S NOT A COMA. IT'S A MINIMALLY CONSCIOUS STATE.
BUT AS WE CAN'T SCAN HIS BRAIN OR GET ANY KIND OF READING OFF HIM, OUR OPTIONS ARE REALLY LIMITED.
LOOK, WE'RE NOT EXPECTING HIM TO BE ABLE TO TELL US ANYTHING. WE JUST--
I'D LIKE HIM TO BE ABLE TO TELL ME SOMETHING. WE'RE AT THE SHARP END OF A SUDDEN GLOBAL MEDICAL CRISIS AND I COULD USE SOME INFORMATION.
JUST FIVE MINUTES WITH SOME KIND OF COMMUNICATION COULD--
I NEED ZOLPIDEM TARTRATE. RIGHT NOW.
ZOLPIDEM IS AMBIEN. THAT'S A SLEEPING PILL, DOC.
NOT FOR PEOPLE IN MCS IN A PERCENTAG OF THOSE CASE IT WAKES THEM UP. FAST.

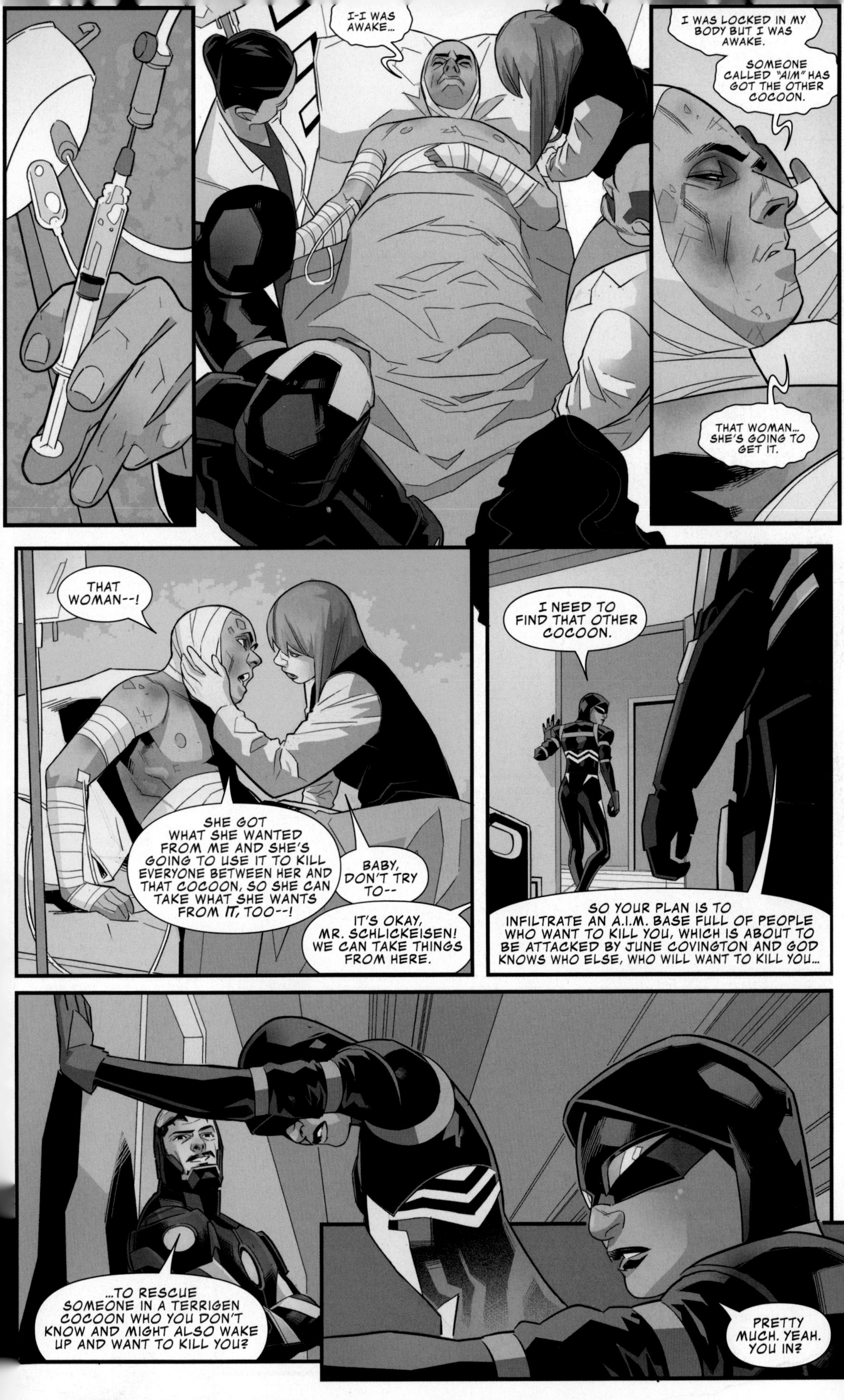
I-I WAS AWAKE...
I WAS LOCKED IN MY BODY BUT I WAS AWAKE.
SOMEONE CALLED "AIM" HAS GOT THE OTHER COCOON.
THAT WOMAN... SHE'S GOING TO GET IT.
THAT WOMAN--!
SHE GOT WHAT SHE WANTED FROM ME AND SHE'S GOING TO USE IT TO KILL EVERYONE BETWEEN HER AND THAT COCOON, SO SHE CAN TAKE WHAT SHE WANTS FROM IT, TOO--!
BABY, DON'T TRY TO--
IT'S OKAY, MR. SCHLICKEISEN! WE CAN TAKE THINGS FROM HERE.
I NEED TO FIND THAT OTHER COCOON.
SO YOUR PLAN IS TO INFILTRATE AN A.I.M. BASE FULL OF PEOPLE WHO WANT TO KILL YOU, WHICH IS ABOUT TO BE ATTACKED BY JUNE COVINGTON AND GOD KNOWS WHO ELSE, WHO WILL WANT TO KILL YOU...
...TO RESCUE SOMEONE IN A TERRIGEN COCOON WHO YOU DON'T KNOW AND MIGHT ALSO WAKE UP AND WANT TO KILL YOU?
PRETTY MUCH. YEAH. YOU IN?

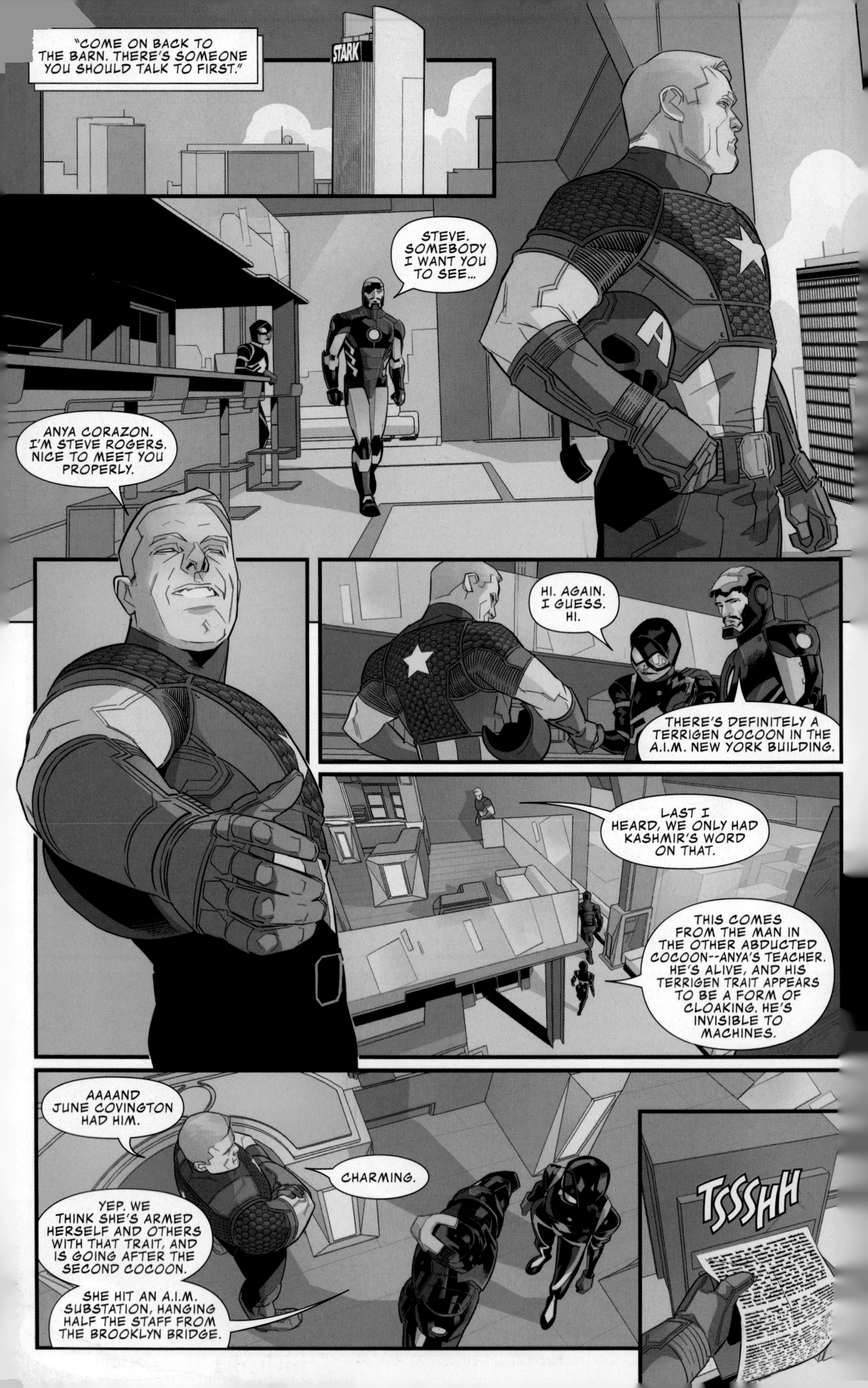
"COME ON BACK TO THE BARN. THERE'S SOMEONE YOU SHOULD TALK TO FIRST."
STARK
STEVE. SOMEBODY I WANT YOU TO SEE...
ANYA CORAZON. I'M STEVE ROGERS. NICE TO MEET YOU PROPERLY.
HI. AGAIN. I GUESS. HI.
THERE'S DEFINITELY A TERRIGEN COCOON IN THE A.I.M. NEW YORK BUILDING.
LAST I HEARD, WE ONLY HAD KASHMIR'S WORD ON THAT.
THIS COMES FROM THE MAN IN THE OTHER ABDUCTED COCOON--ANYA'S TEACHER. HE'S ALIVE, AND HIS TERRIGEN TRAIT APPEARS TO BE A FORM OF CLOAKING. HE'S INVISIBLE TO MACHINES.
AAAAND JUNE COVINGTON HAD HIM.
CHARMING.
YEP. WE THINK SHE'S ARMED HERSELF AND OTHERS WITH THAT TRAIT, AND IS GOING AFTER THE SECOND COCOON.
SHE HIT AN A.I.M. SUBSTATION, HANGING HALF THE STAFF FROM THE BROOKLYN BRIDGE.
TSSSHH

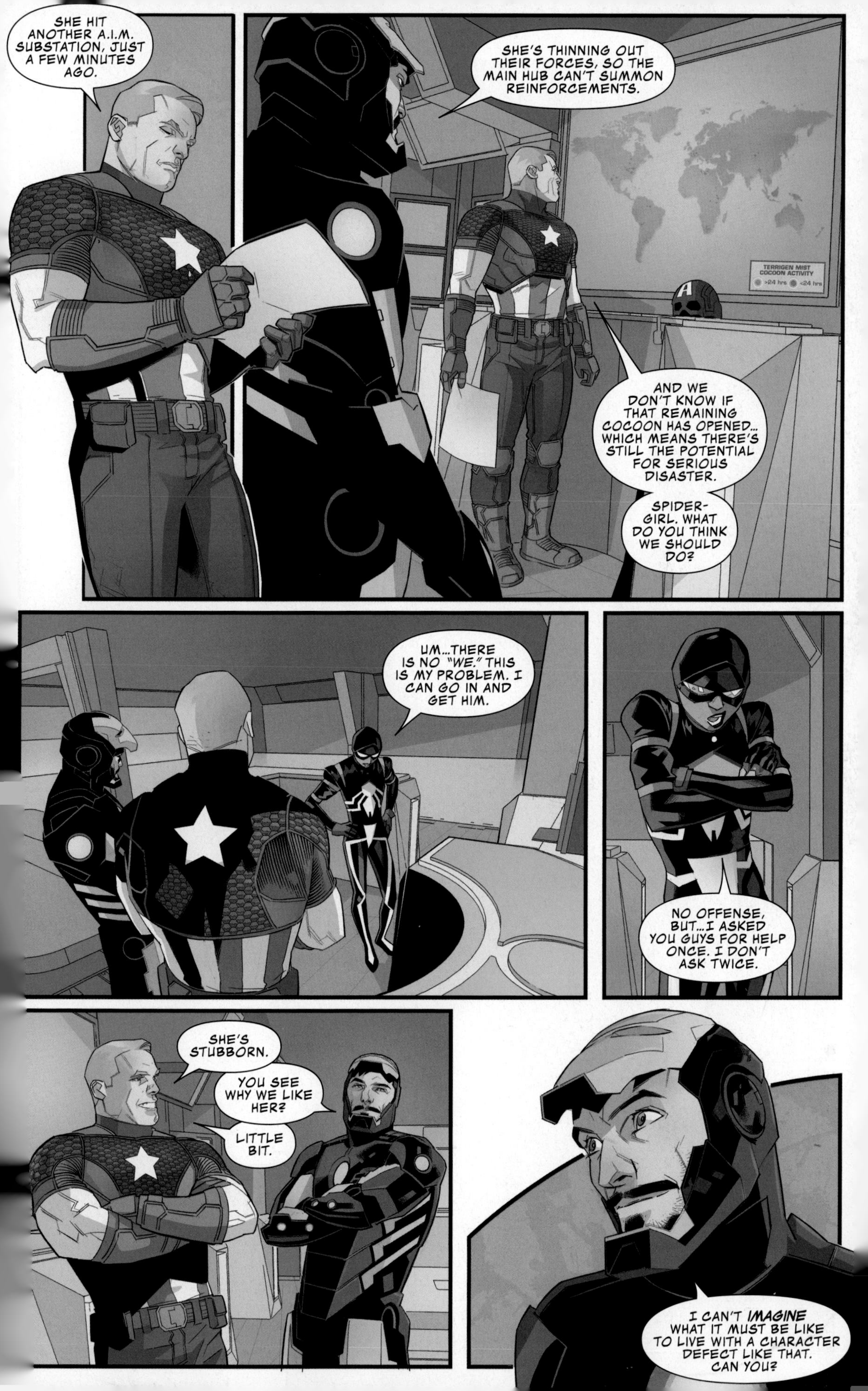

SHE HIT ANOTHER A.I.M. SUBSTATION, JUST A FEW MINUTES AGO.
SHE'S THINNING OUT THEIR FORCES, SO THE MAIN HUB CAN'T SUMMON REINFORCEMENTS.
TERRIGEN MIST COCOON ACTIVITY
>24 hrs
<24 hrs
AND WE DON'T KNOW IF THAT REMAINING COCOON HAS OPENED... WHICH MEANS THERE'S STILL THE POTENTIAL FOR SERIOUS DISASTER.
SPIDER-GIRL. WHAT DO YOU THINK WE SHOULD DO?
UM...THERE IS NO "WE." THIS IS MY PROBLEM. I CAN GO IN AND GET HIM.
NO OFFENSE, BUT...I ASKED YOU GUYS FOR HELP ONCE. I DON'T ASK TWICE.
SHE'S STUBBORN.
YOU SEE WHY WE LIKE HER?
LITTLE BIT.
I CAN'T *IMAGINE* WHAT IT MUST BE LIKE TO LIVE WITH A CHARACTER DEFECT LIKE THAT. CAN YOU?

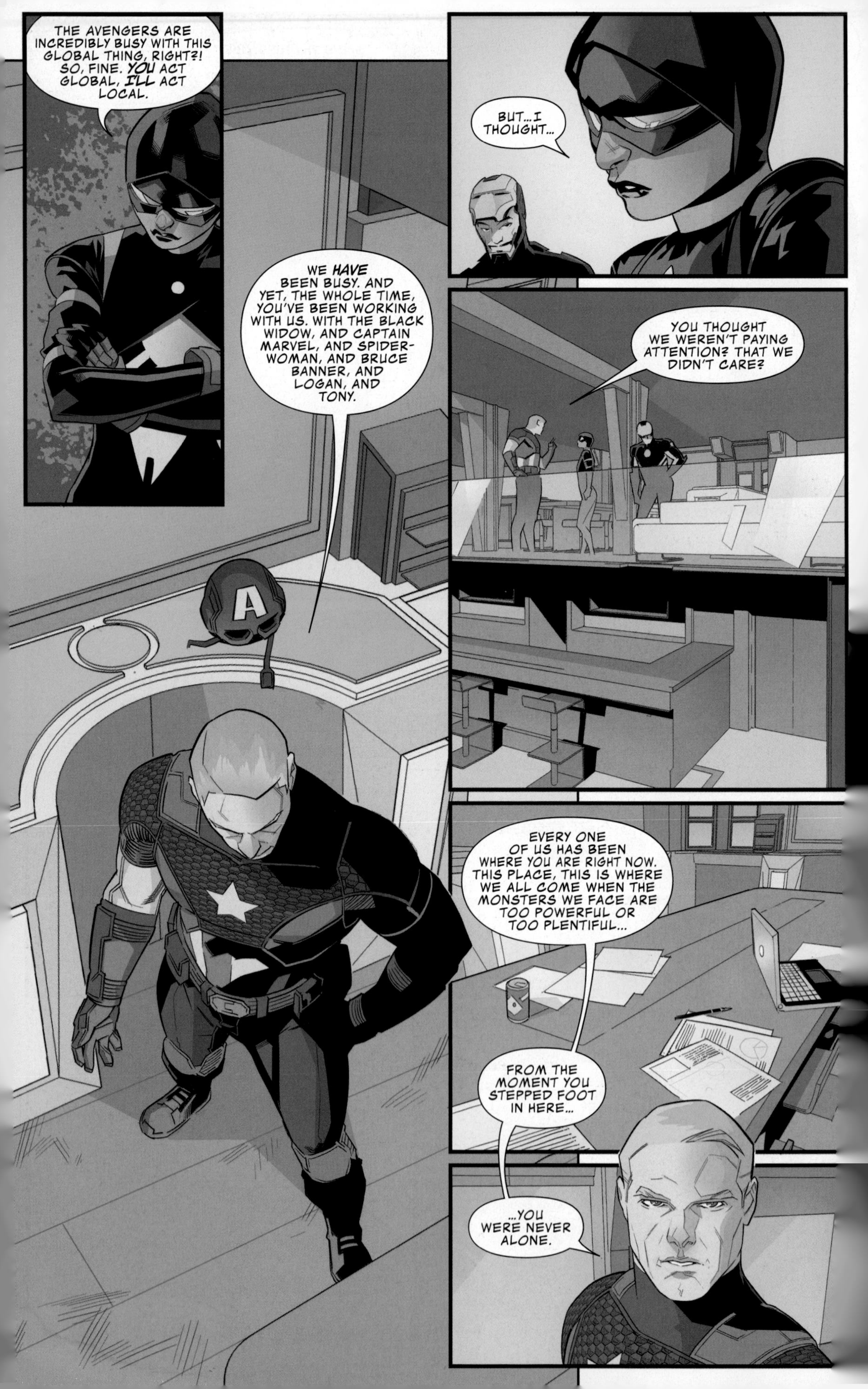
THE AVENGERS ARE INCREDIBLY BUSY WITH THIS GLOBAL THING, RIGHT?! SO, FINE. YOU ACT GLOBAL, I'LL ACT LOCAL.
BUT...I THOUGHT...
WE HAVE BEEN BUSY. AND YET, THE WHOLE TIME, YOU'VE BEEN WORKING WITH US. WITH THE BLACK WIDOW, AND CAPTAIN MARVEL, AND SPIDER-WOMAN, AND BRUCE BANNER, AND LOGAN, AND TONY.
YOU THOUGHT WE WEREN'T PAYING ATTENTION? THAT WE DIDN'T CARE?
EVERY ONE OF US HAS BEEN WHERE YOU ARE RIGHT NOW. THIS PLACE, THIS IS WHERE WE ALL COME WHEN THE MONSTERS WE FACE ARE TOO POWERFUL OR TOO PLENTIFUL...
FROM THE MOMENT YOU STEPPED FOOT IN HERE...
...YOU WERE NEVER ALONE.

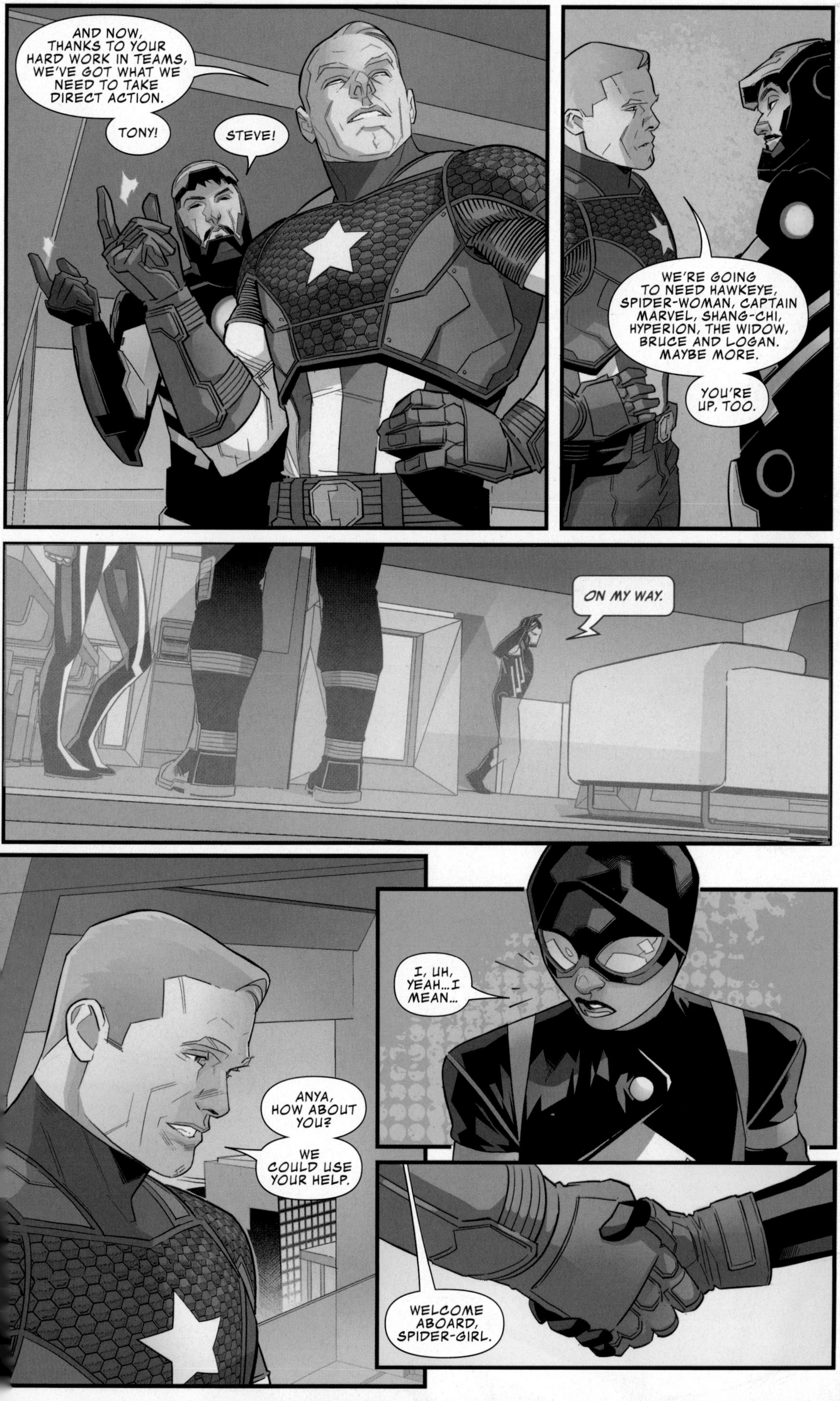
AND NOW, THANKS TO YOUR HARD WORK IN TEAMS, WE'VE GOT WHAT WE NEED TO TAKE DIRECT ACTION.
TONY!
STEVE!
WE'RE GOING TO NEED HAWKEYE, SPIDER-WOMAN, CAPTAIN MARVEL, SHANG-CHI, HYPERION, THE WIDOW, BRUCE AND LOGAN. MAYBE MORE.
YOU'RE UP, TOO.
ON MY WAY.
ANYA, HOW ABOUT YOU?
WE COULD USE YOUR HELP.
I, UH, YEAH...I MEAN...
WELCOME ABOARD, SPIDER-GIRL.

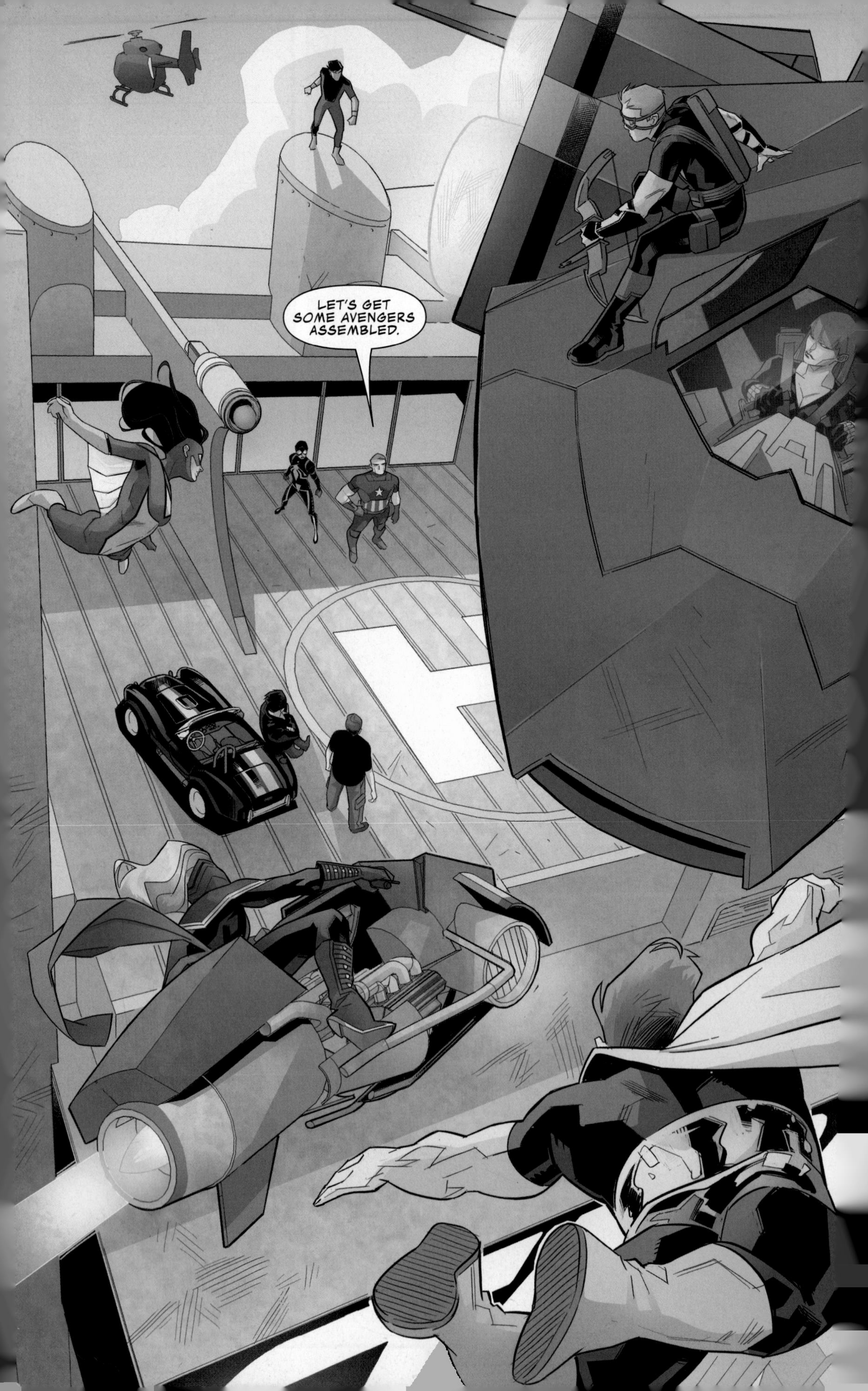
LET'S GET SOME AVENGERS ASSEMBLED.

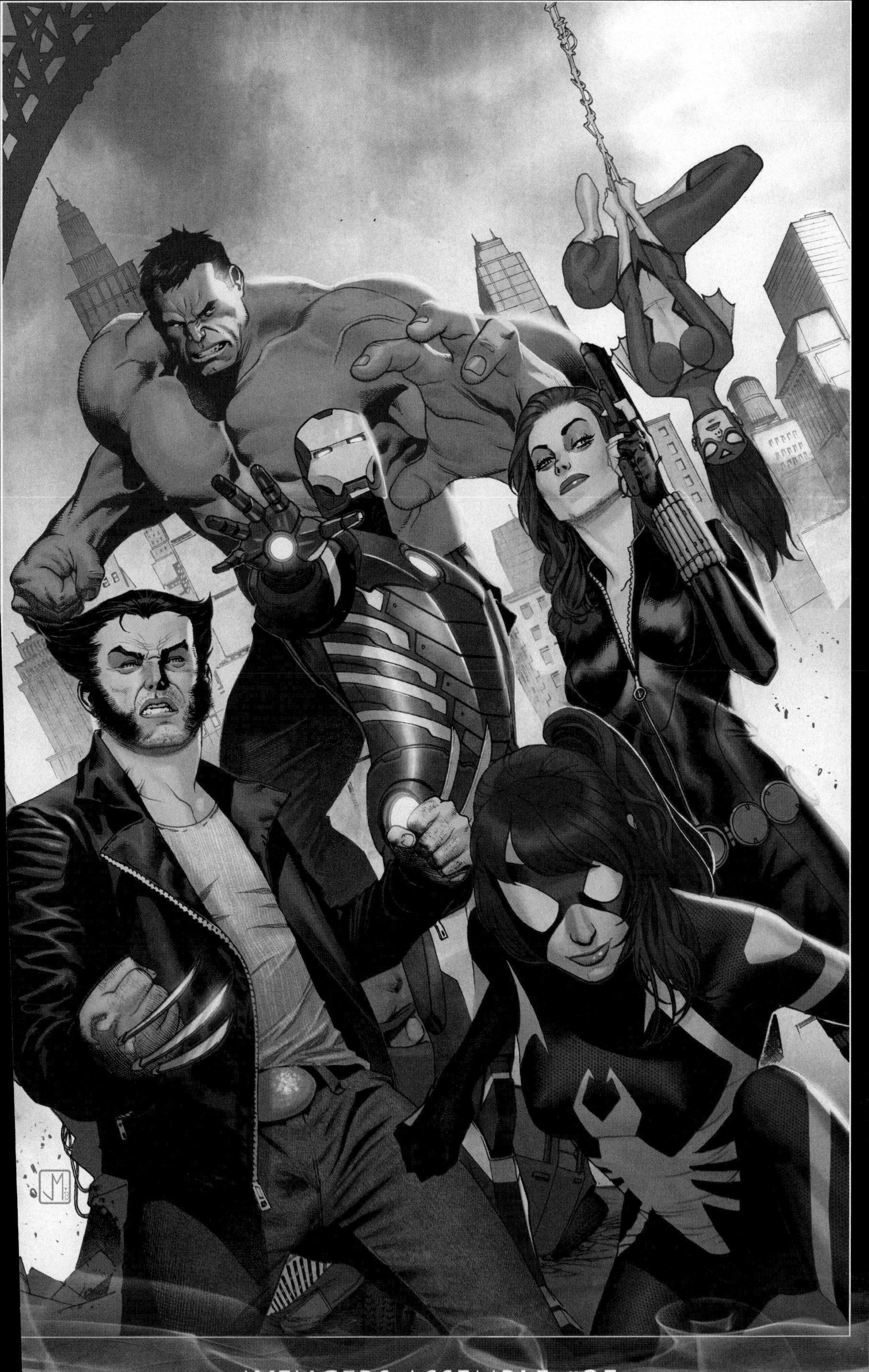

AVENGERS ASSEMBLE #25

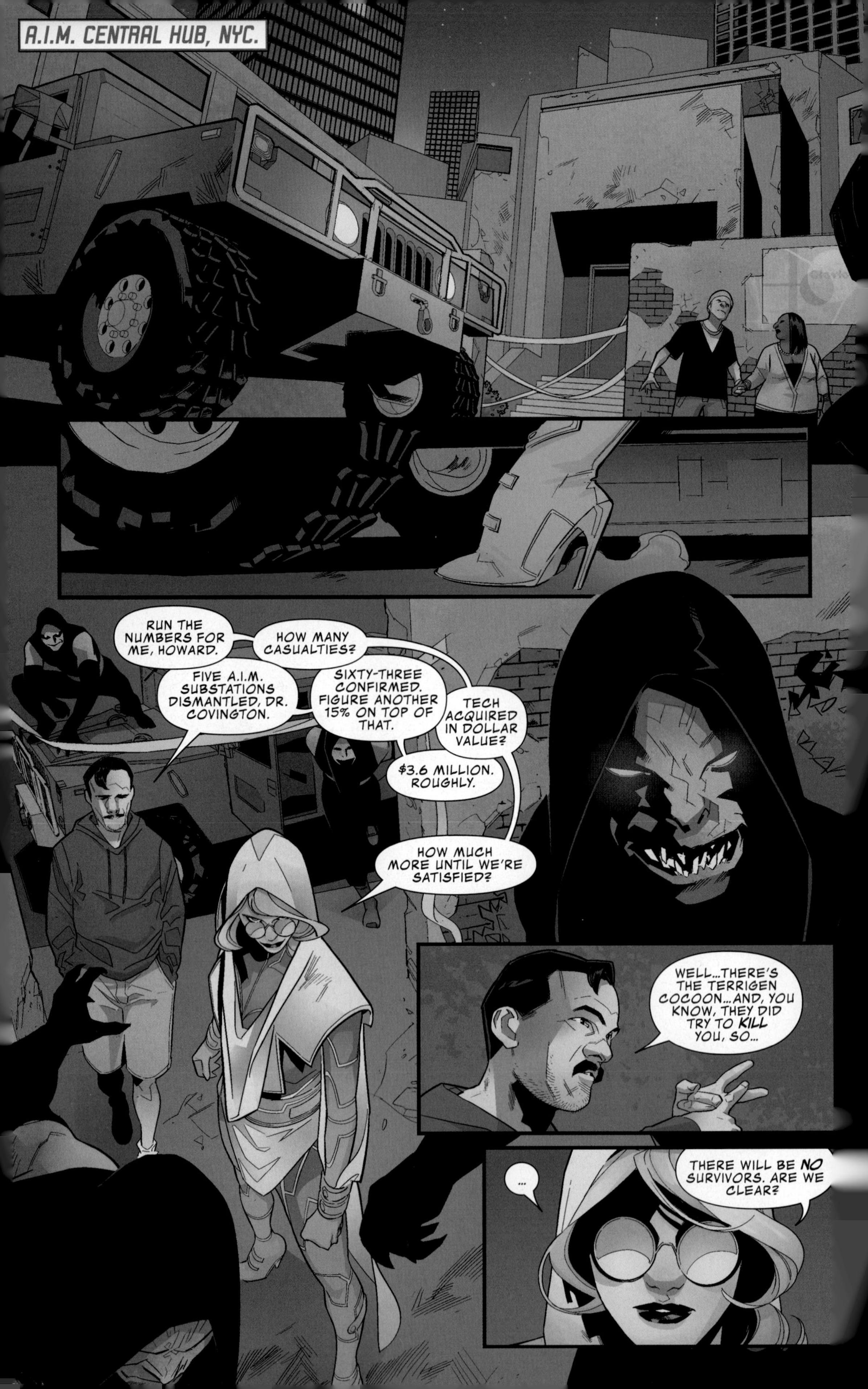
A.I.M. CENTRAL HUB, NYC.
RUN THE NUMBERS FOR ME, HOWARD.
HOW MANY CASUALTIES?
FIVE A.I.M. SUBSTATIONS DISMANTLED, DR. COVINGTON.
SIXTY-THREE CONFIRMED. FIGURE ANOTHER 15% ON TOP OF THAT.
TECH ACQUIRED IN DOLLAR VALUE?
$3.6 MILLION. ROUGHLY.
HOW MUCH MORE UNTIL WE'RE SATISFIED?
WELL...THERE'S THE TERRIGEN COCOON...AND, YOU KNOW, THEY DID TRY TO **KILL** YOU, SO...
...
THERE WILL BE **NO** SURVIVORS. ARE WE CLEAR?

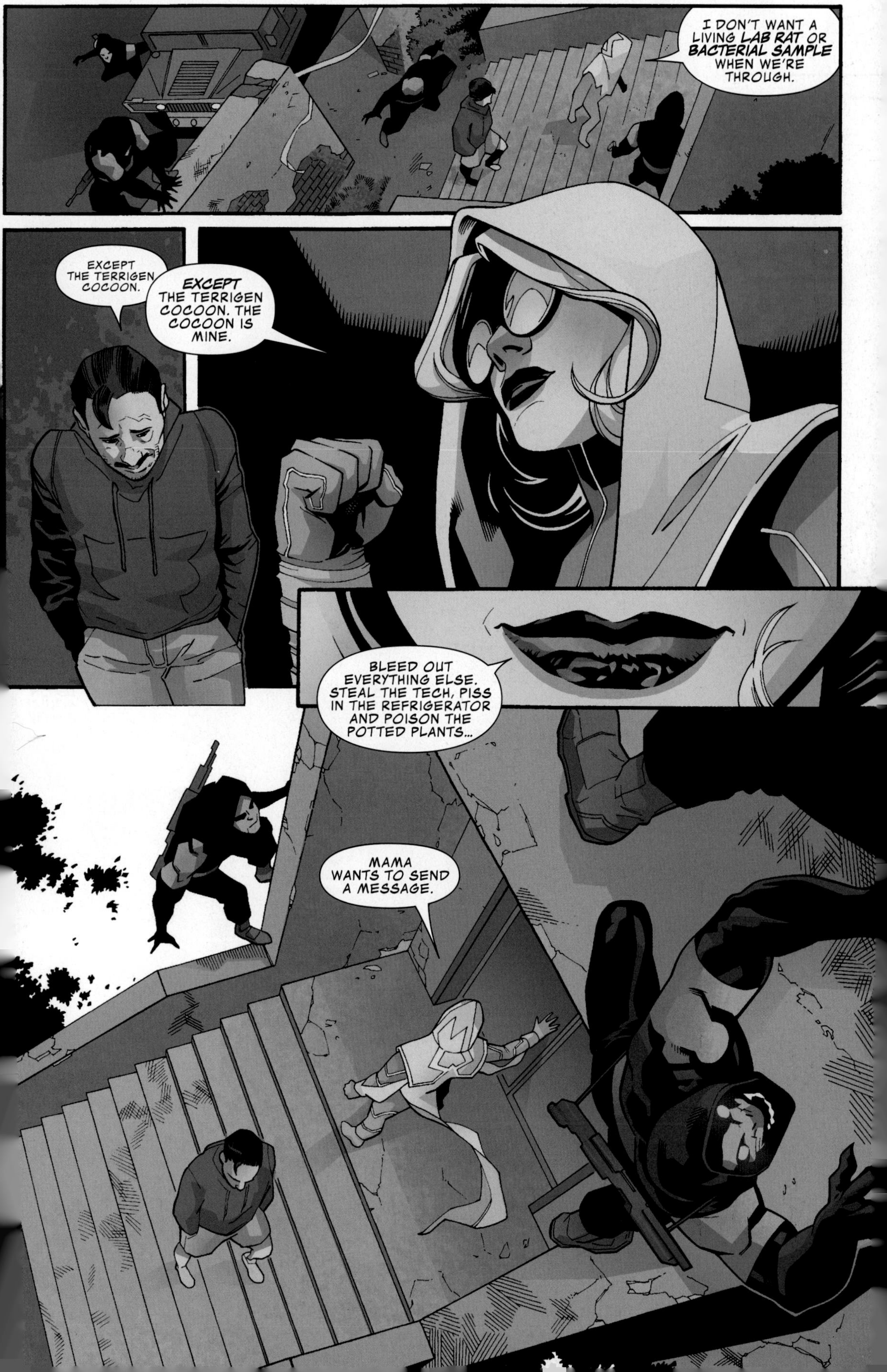
I DON'T WANT A LIVING LAB RAT OR BACTERIAL SAMPLE WHEN WE'RE THROUGH.
EXCEPT THE TERRIGEN COCOON.
EXCEPT THE TERRIGEN COCOON. THE COCOON IS MINE.
BLEED OUT EVERYTHING ELSE. STEAL THE TECH, PISS IN THE REFRIGERATOR AND POISON THE POTTED PLANTS...
MAMA WANTS TO SEND A MESSAGE.

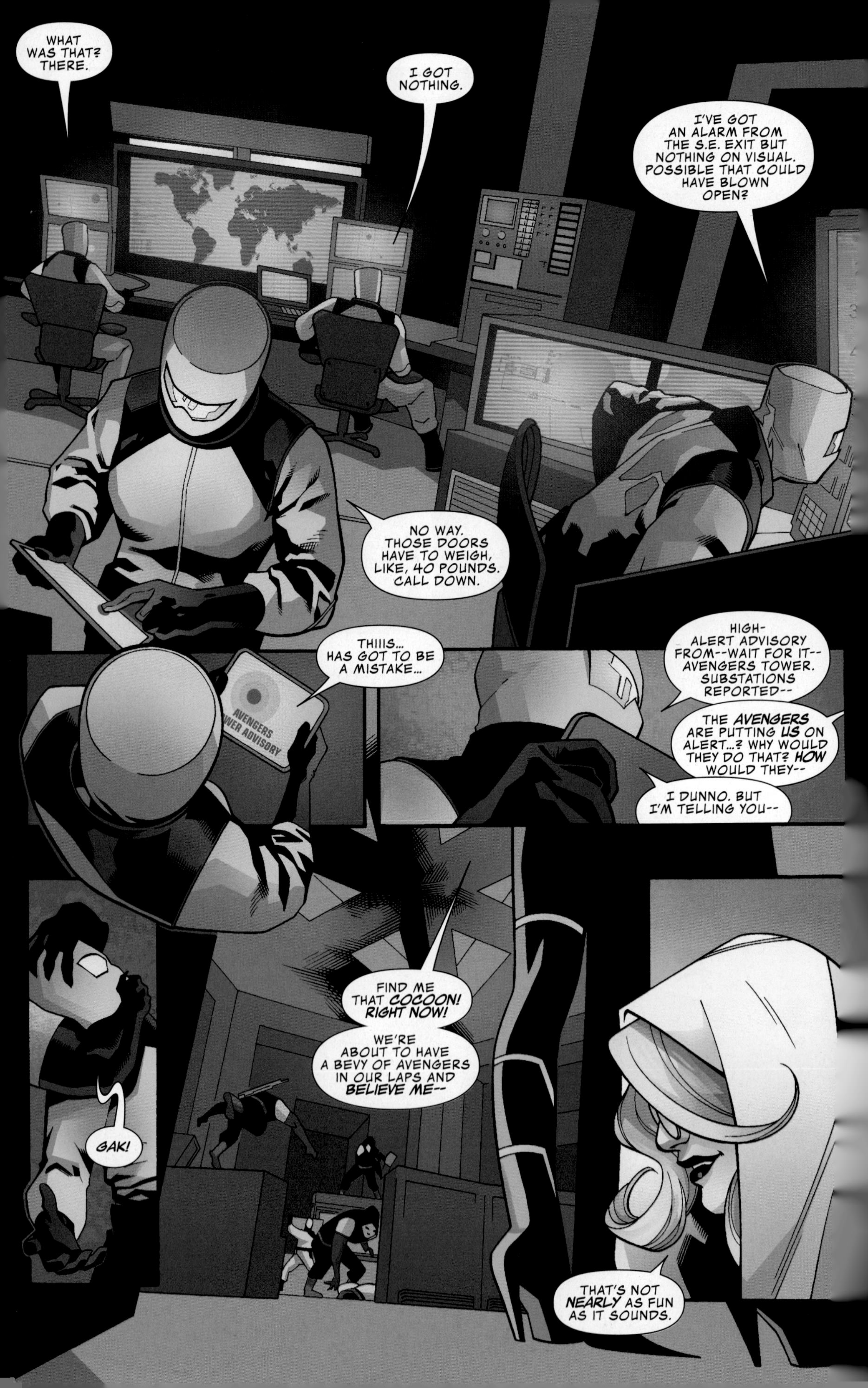
WHAT WAS THAT? THERE.
I GOT NOTHING.
I'VE GOT AN ALARM FROM THE S.E. EXIT BUT NOTHING ON VISUAL. POSSIBLE THAT COULD HAVE BLOWN OPEN?
NO WAY. THOSE DOORS HAVE TO WEIGH, LIKE, 40 POUNDS. CALL DOWN.
THIIIS... HAS GOT TO BE A MISTAKE...
AVENGERS
WER ADVISORY
HIGH-ALERT ADVISORY FROM--WAIT FOR IT--AVENGERS TOWER. SUBSTATIONS REPORTED--
THE AVENGERS ARE PUTTING US ON ALERT...? WHY WOULD THEY DO THAT? HOW WOULD THEY--
I DUNNO. BUT I'M TELLING YOU--
FIND ME THAT COCOON! RIGHT NOW!
WE'RE ABOUT TO HAVE A BEVY OF AVENGERS IN OUR LAPS AND BELIEVE ME--
GAK!
THAT'S NOT NEARLY AS FUN AS IT SOUNDS.

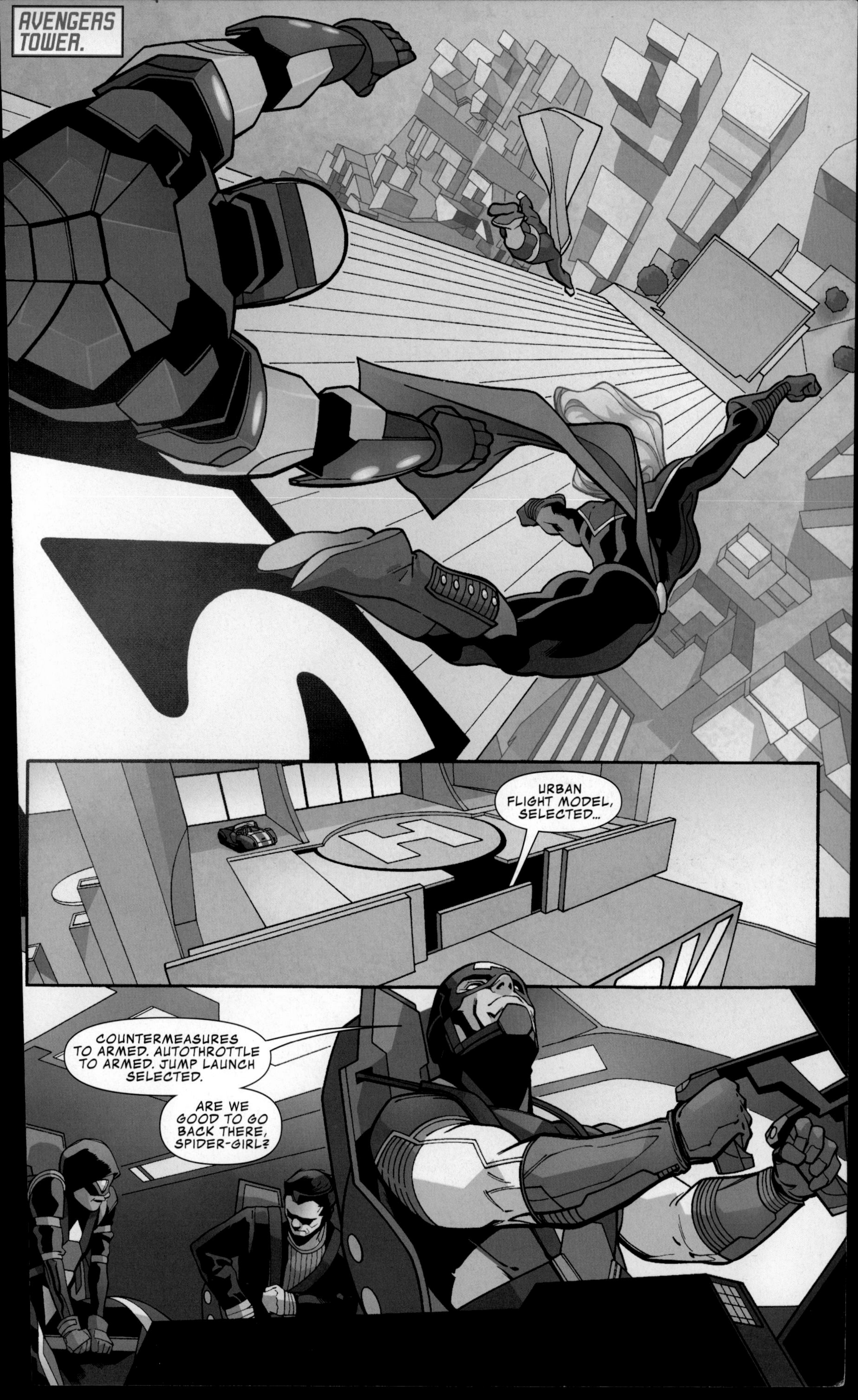
AVENGERS TOWER.
URBAN FLIGHT MODEL, SELECTED...
COUNTERMEASURES TO ARMED. AUTOTHROTTLE TO ARMED. JUMP LAUNCH SELECTED.
ARE WE GOOD TO GO BACK THERE, SPIDER-GIRL?

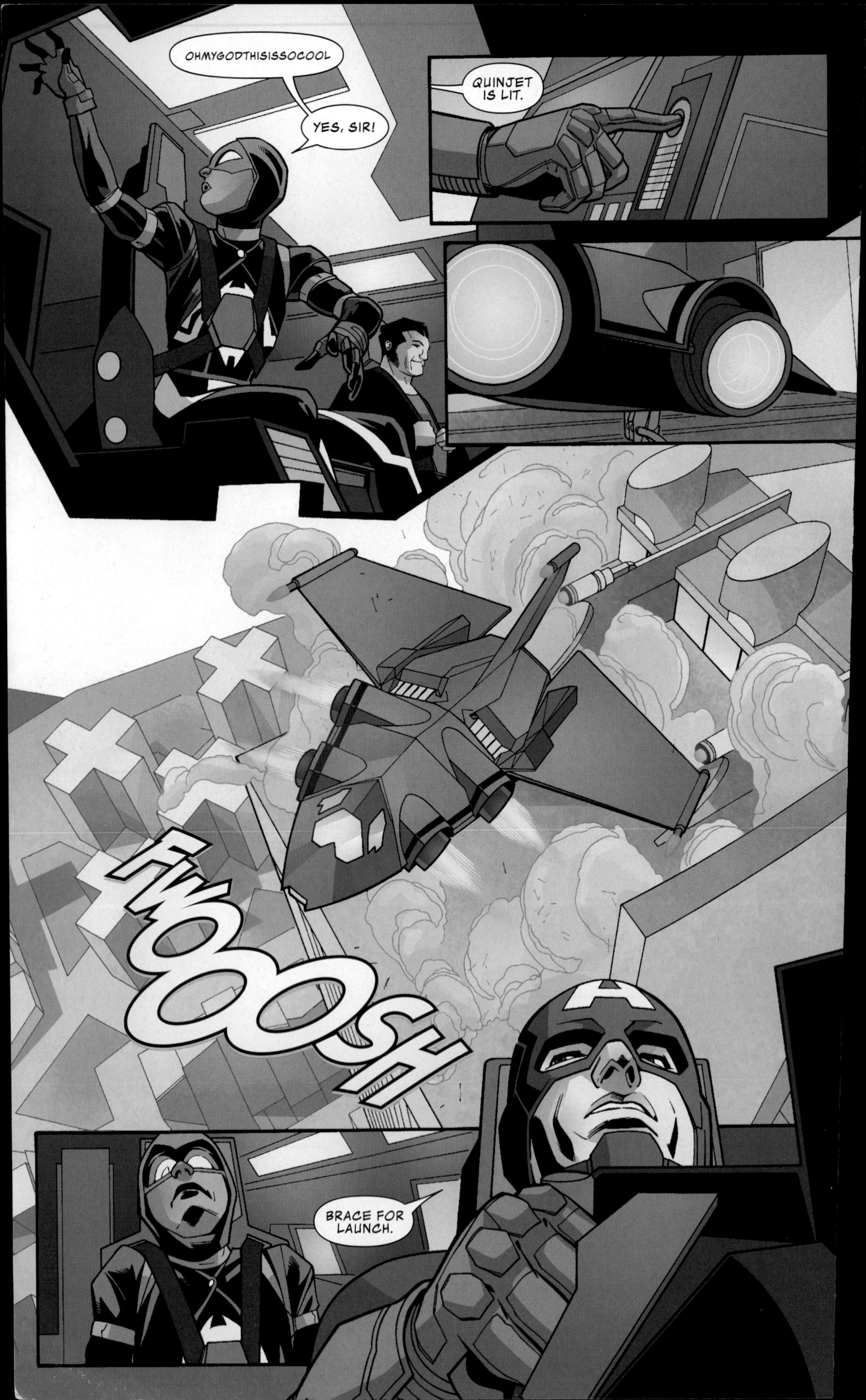
OHMYGODTHISISSOCOOL
YES, SIR!
QUINJET IS LIT.
FWOOSH
BRACE FOR LAUNCH.

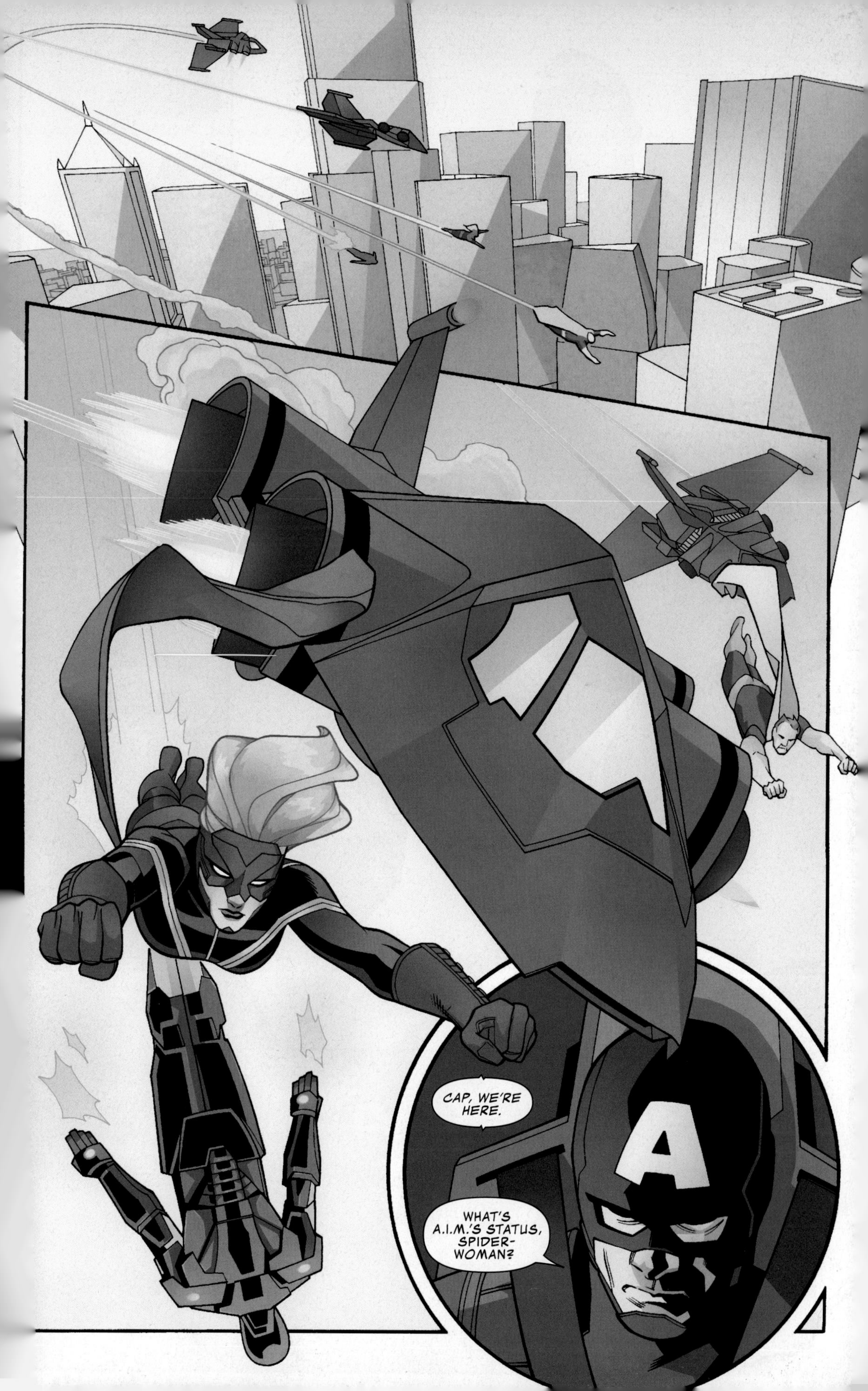
CAP, WE'RE HERE.
WHAT'S A.I.M.'S STATUS, SPIDER-WOMAN?

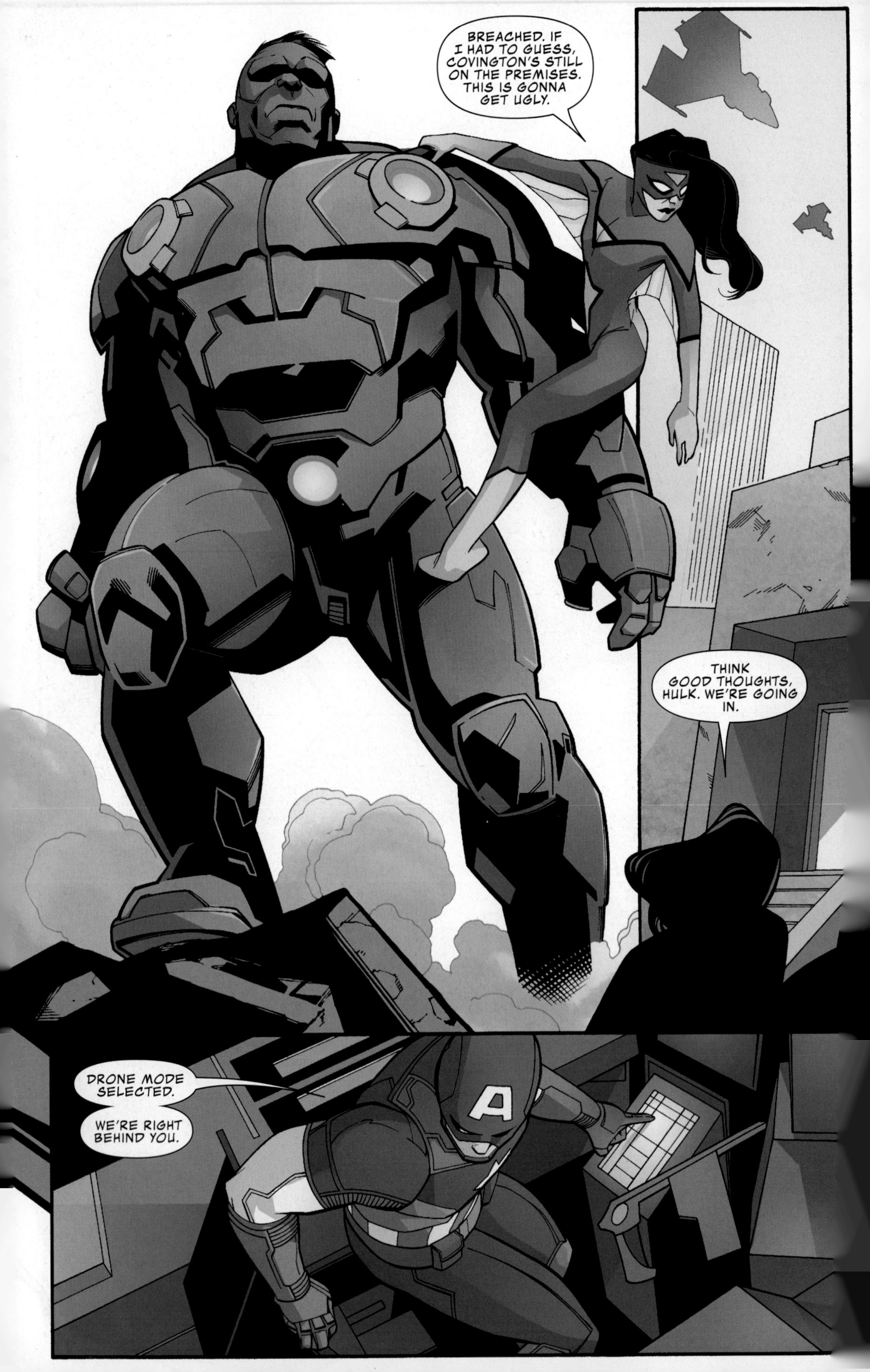
BREACHED. IF I HAD TO GUESS, COVINGTON'S STILL ON THE PREMISES. THIS IS GONNA GET UGLY.
THINK GOOD THOUGHTS, HULK. WE'RE GOING IN.
DRONE MODE SELECTED.
WE'RE RIGHT BEHIND YOU.

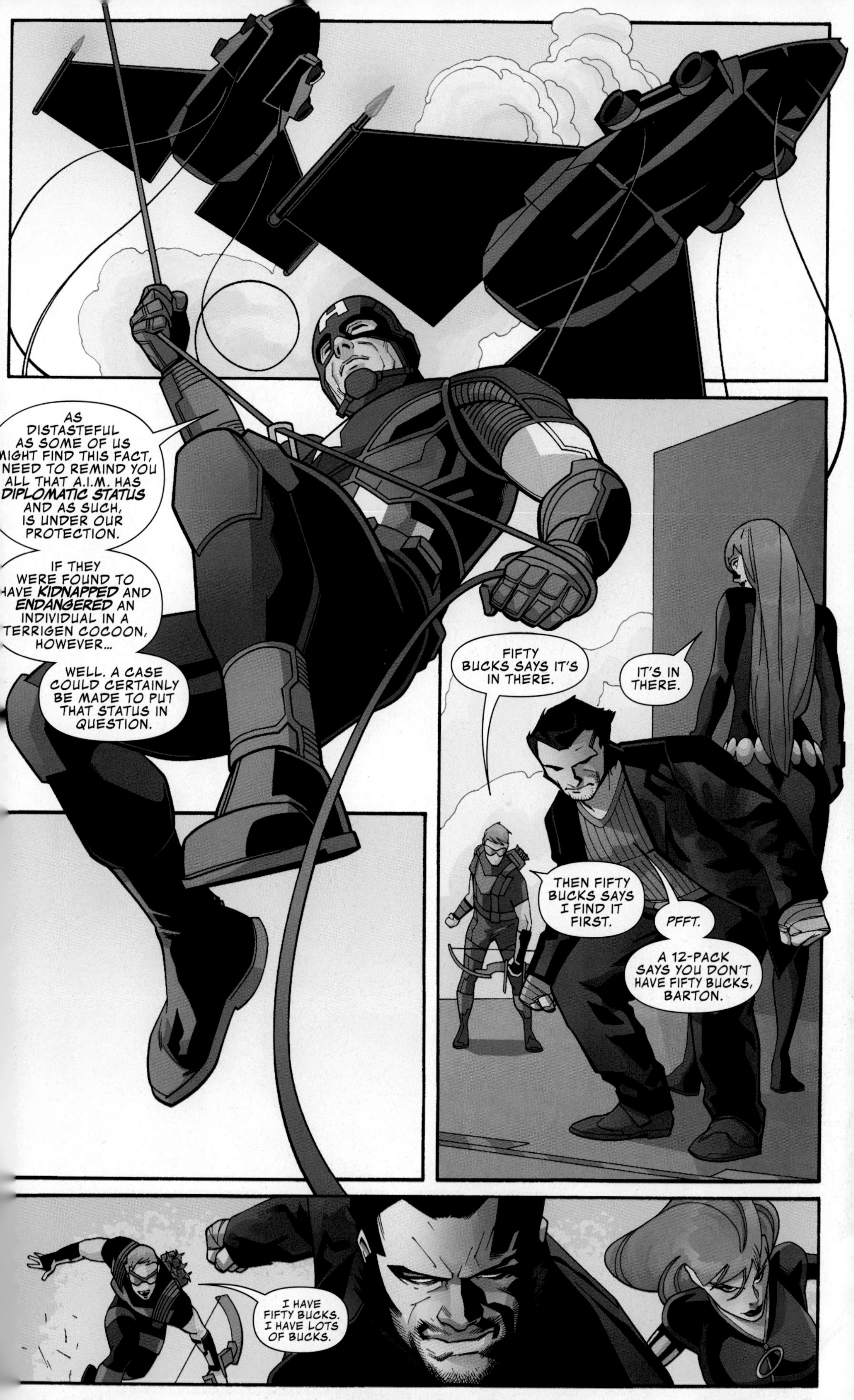
AS DISTASTEFUL AS SOME OF US MIGHT FIND THIS FACT, NEED TO REMIND YOU ALL THAT A.I.M. HAS DIPLOMATIC STATUS AND AS SUCH, IS UNDER OUR PROTECTION.
IF THEY WERE FOUND TO HAVE KIDNAPPED AND ENDANGERED AN INDIVIDUAL IN A TERRIGEN COCOON, HOWEVER...
WELL. A CASE COULD CERTAINLY BE MADE TO PUT THAT STATUS IN QUESTION.
FIFTY BUCKS SAYS IT'S IN THERE.
IT'S IN THERE.
THEN FIFTY BUCKS SAYS I FIND IT FIRST.
PFFT.
A 12-PACK SAYS YOU DON'T HAVE FIFTY BUCKS, BARTON.
I HAVE FIFTY BUCKS. I HAVE LOTS OF BUCKS.

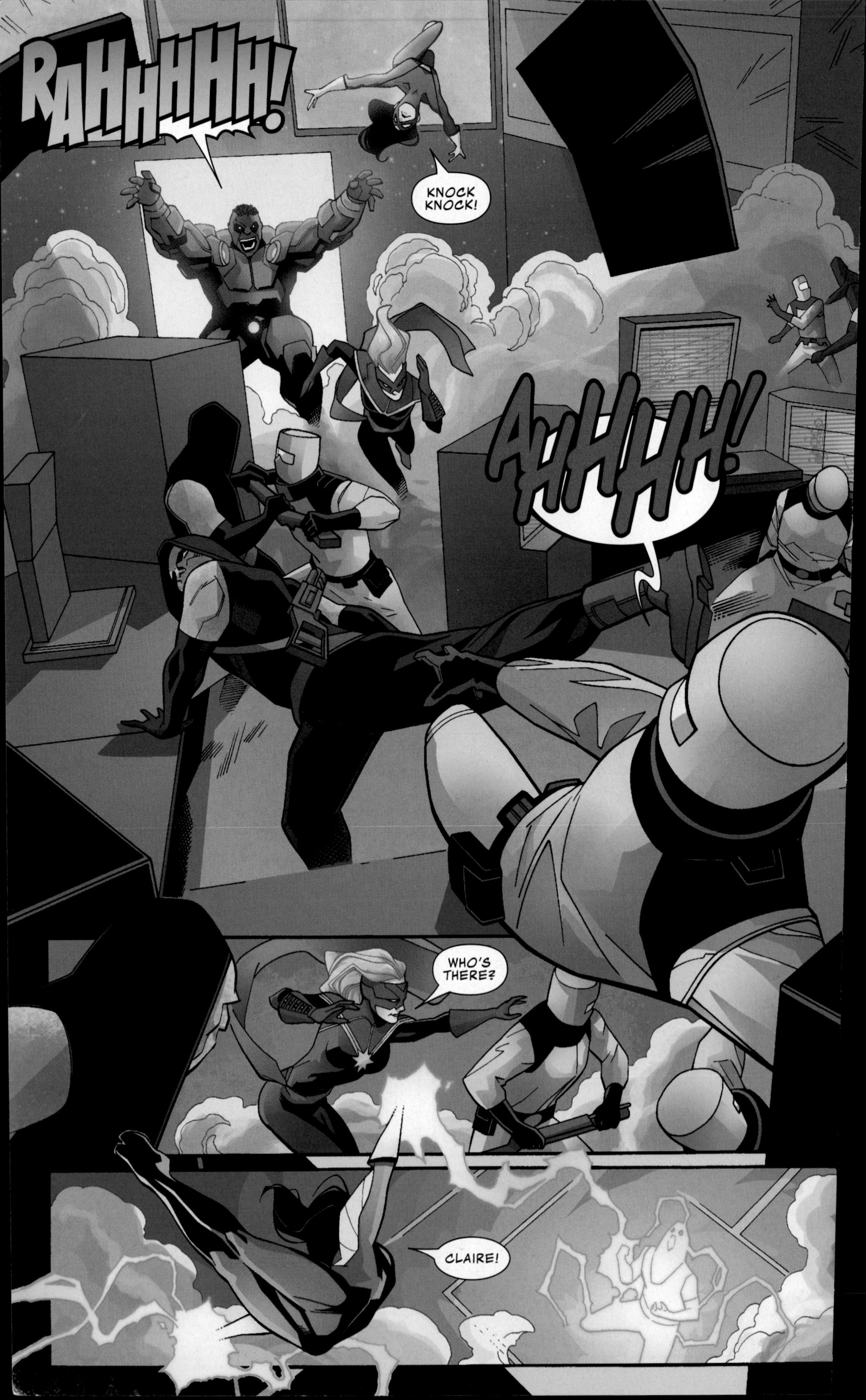
RAHHHHHH!
KNOCK KNOCK!
AHHHHH!
WHO'S THERE?
CLAIRE!

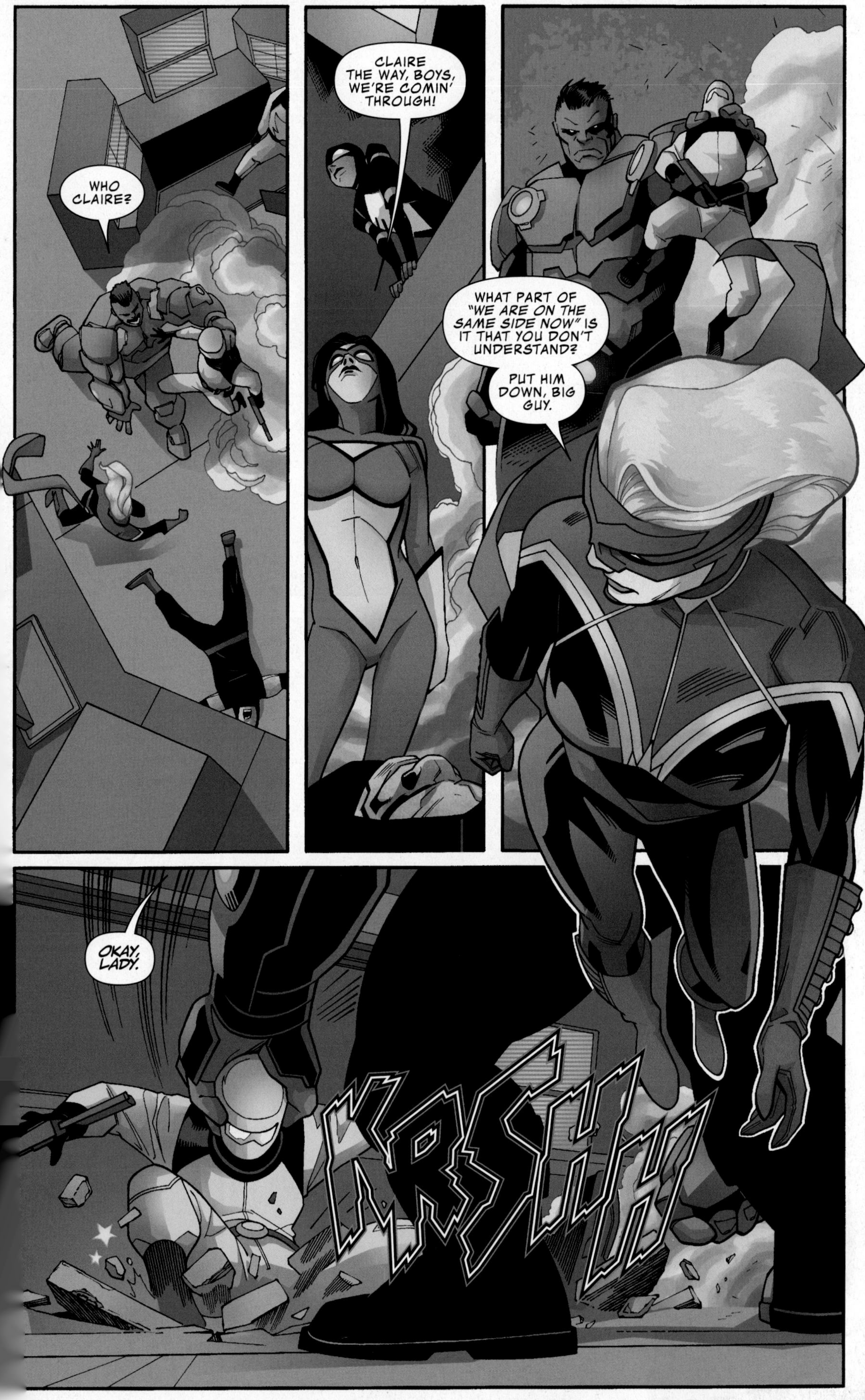
WHO CLAIRE?
CLAIRE THE WAY, BOYS, WE'RE COMIN' THROUGH!
WHAT PART OF "WE ARE ON THE SAME SIDE NOW" IS IT THAT YOU DON'T UNDERSTAND?
PUT HIM DOWN, BIG GUY.
OKAY, LADY.
KRSSHH

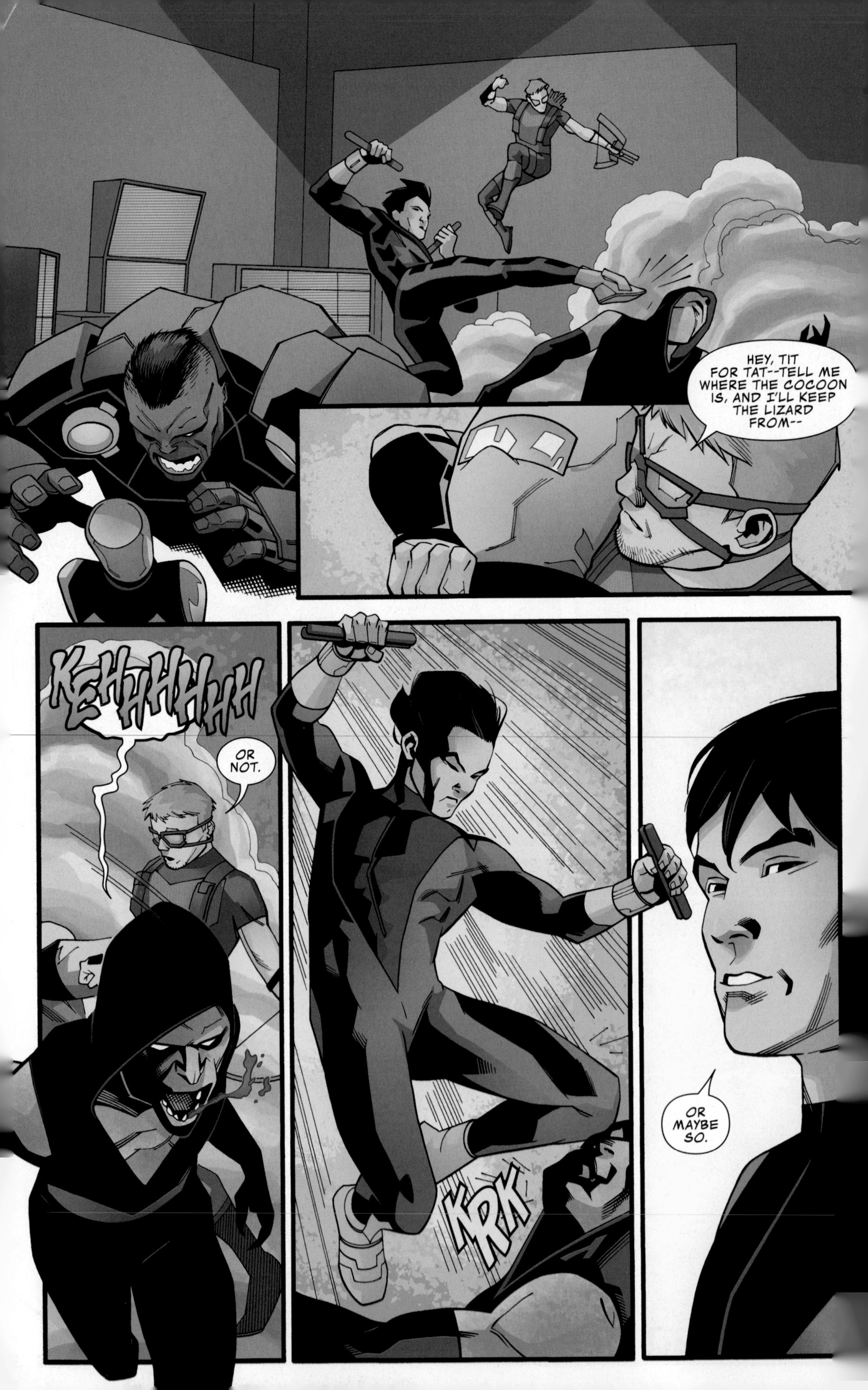
HEY, TIT FOR TAT--TELL ME WHERE THE COCOON IS, AND I'LL KEEP THE LIZARD FROM--
KEHHHHHH
OR NOT.
KRK
OR MAYBE SO.

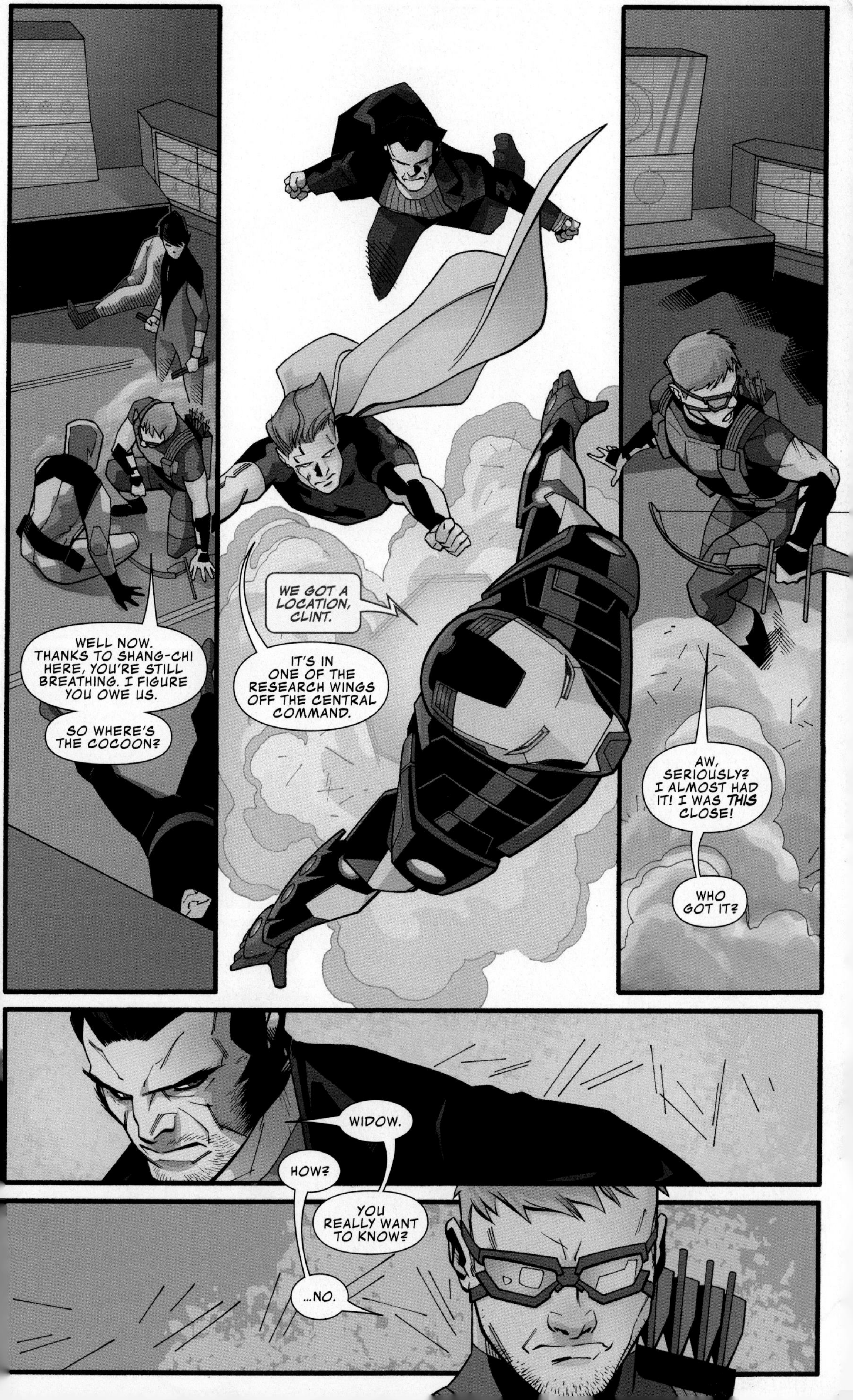
WELL NOW. THANKS TO SHANG-CHI HERE, YOU'RE STILL BREATHING. I FIGURE YOU OWE US.
SO WHERE'S THE COCOON?
WE GOT A LOCATION, CLINT.
IT'S IN ONE OF THE RESEARCH WINGS OFF THE CENTRAL COMMAND.
AW, SERIOUSLY? I ALMOST HAD IT! I WAS THIS CLOSE!
WHO GOT IT?
WIDOW.
HOW?
YOU REALLY WANT TO KNOW?
...NO.

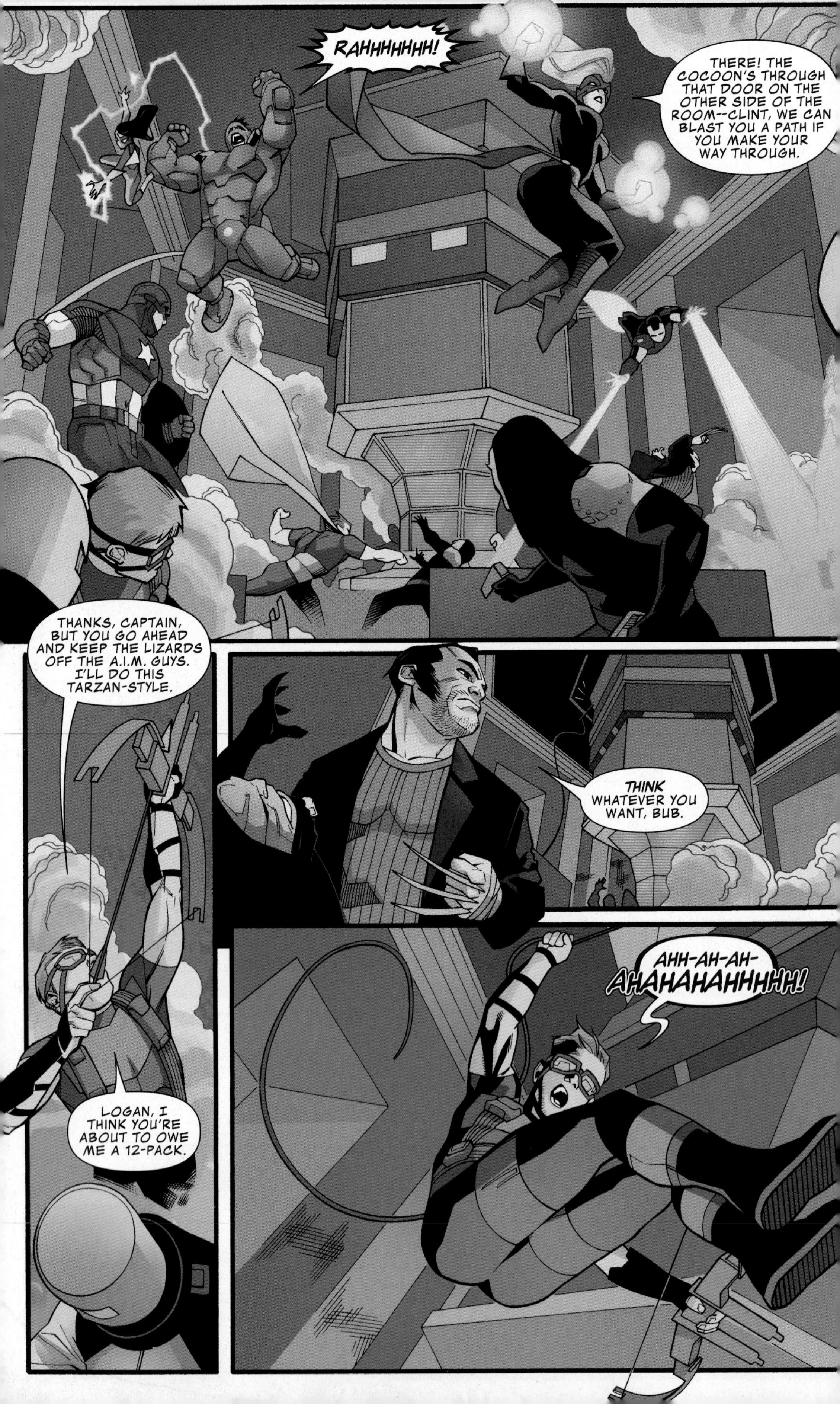
RAHHHHHHH!
THERE! THE COCOON'S THROUGH THAT DOOR ON THE OTHER SIDE OF THE ROOM--CLINT, WE CAN BLAST YOU A PATH IF YOU MAKE YOUR WAY THROUGH.
THANKS, CAPTAIN, BUT YOU GO AHEAD AND KEEP THE LIZARDS OFF THE A.I.M. GUYS. I'LL DO THIS TARZAN-STYLE.
LOGAN, I THINK YOU'RE ABOUT TO OWE ME A 12-PACK.
THINK WHATEVER YOU WANT, BUB.
AHH-AH-AH-AHAHAHAHHHHH!

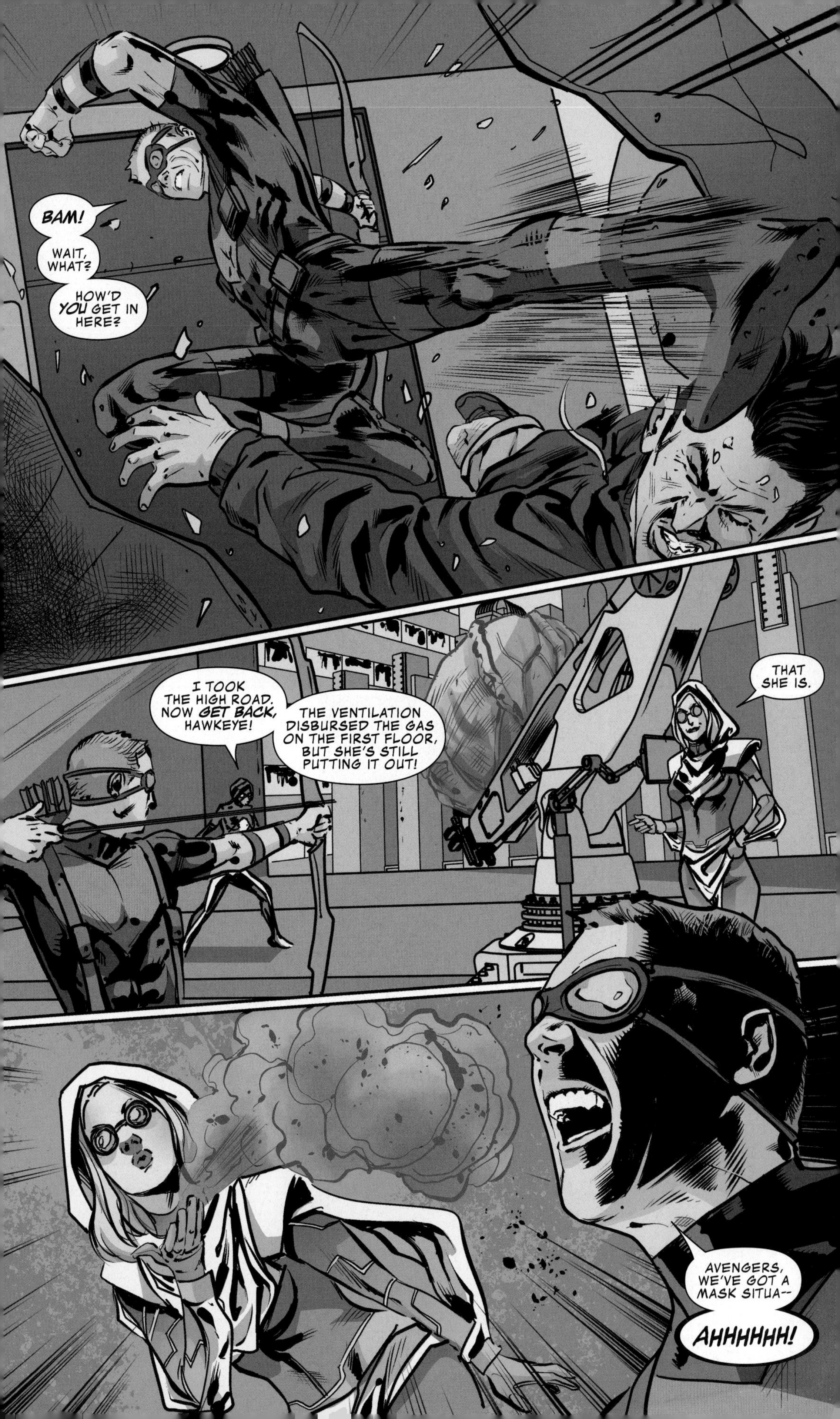
BAM!
WAIT, WHAT?
HOW'D YOU GET IN HERE?
I TOOK THE HIGH ROAD. NOW GET BACK, HAWKEYE!
THE VENTILATION DISBURSED THE GAS ON THE FIRST FLOOR, BUT SHE'S STILL PUTTING IT OUT!
THAT SHE IS.
AVENGERS, WE'VE GOT A MASK SITUA--
AHHHHHH!

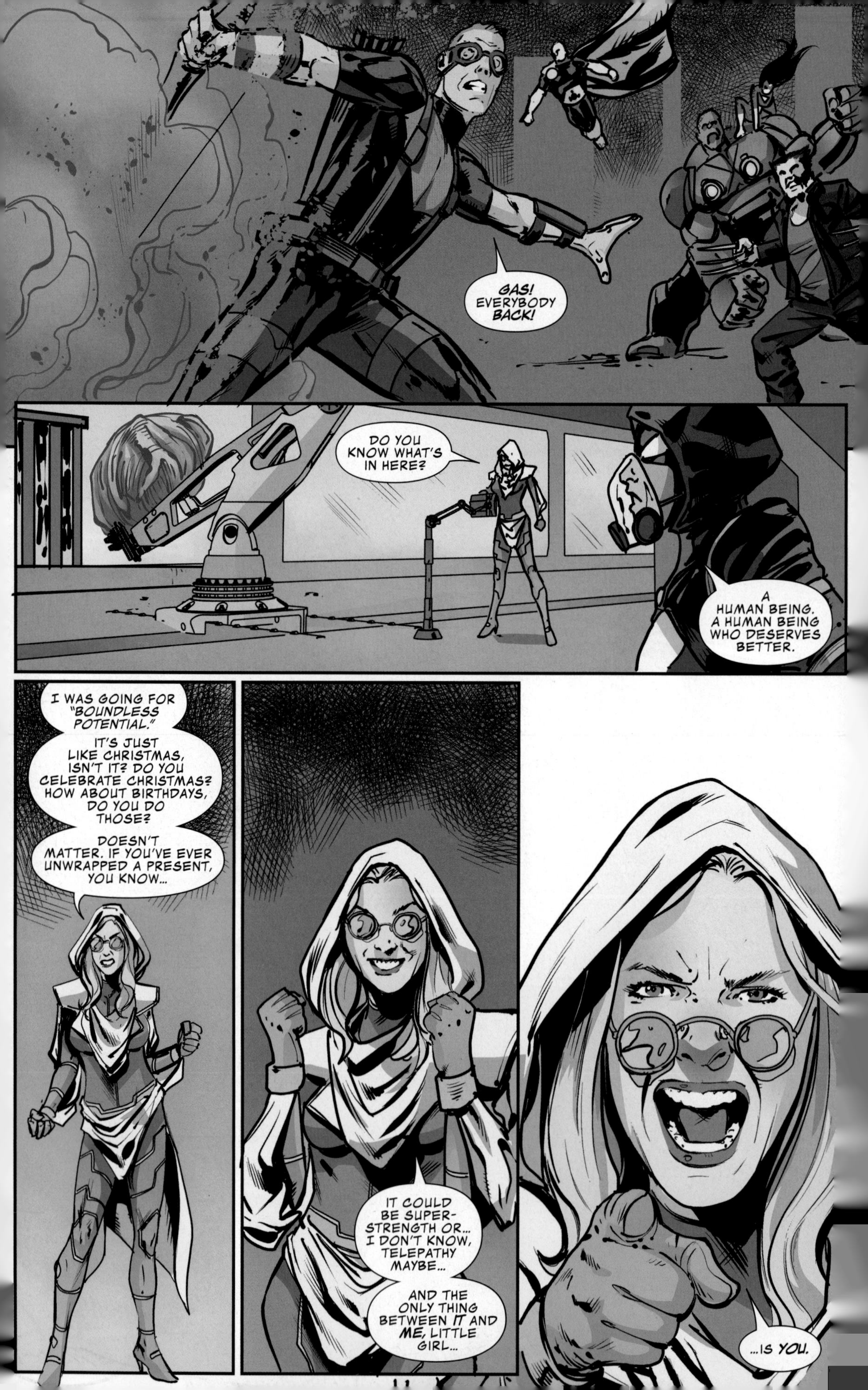
GAS! EVERYBODY BACK!
DO YOU KNOW WHAT'S IN HERE?
A HUMAN BEING. A HUMAN BEING WHO DESERVES BETTER.
I WAS GOING FOR "BOUNDLESS POTENTIAL."
IT'S JUST LIKE CHRISTMAS, ISN'T IT? DO YOU CELEBRATE CHRISTMAS? HOW ABOUT BIRTHDAYS, DO YOU DO THOSE?
DOESN'T MATTER. IF YOU'VE EVER UNWRAPPED A PRESENT, YOU KNOW...
IT COULD BE SUPER-STRENGTH OR... I DON'T KNOW, TELEPATHY MAYBE...
AND THE ONLY THING BETWEEN IT AND ME, LITTLE GIRL...
...IS YOU.

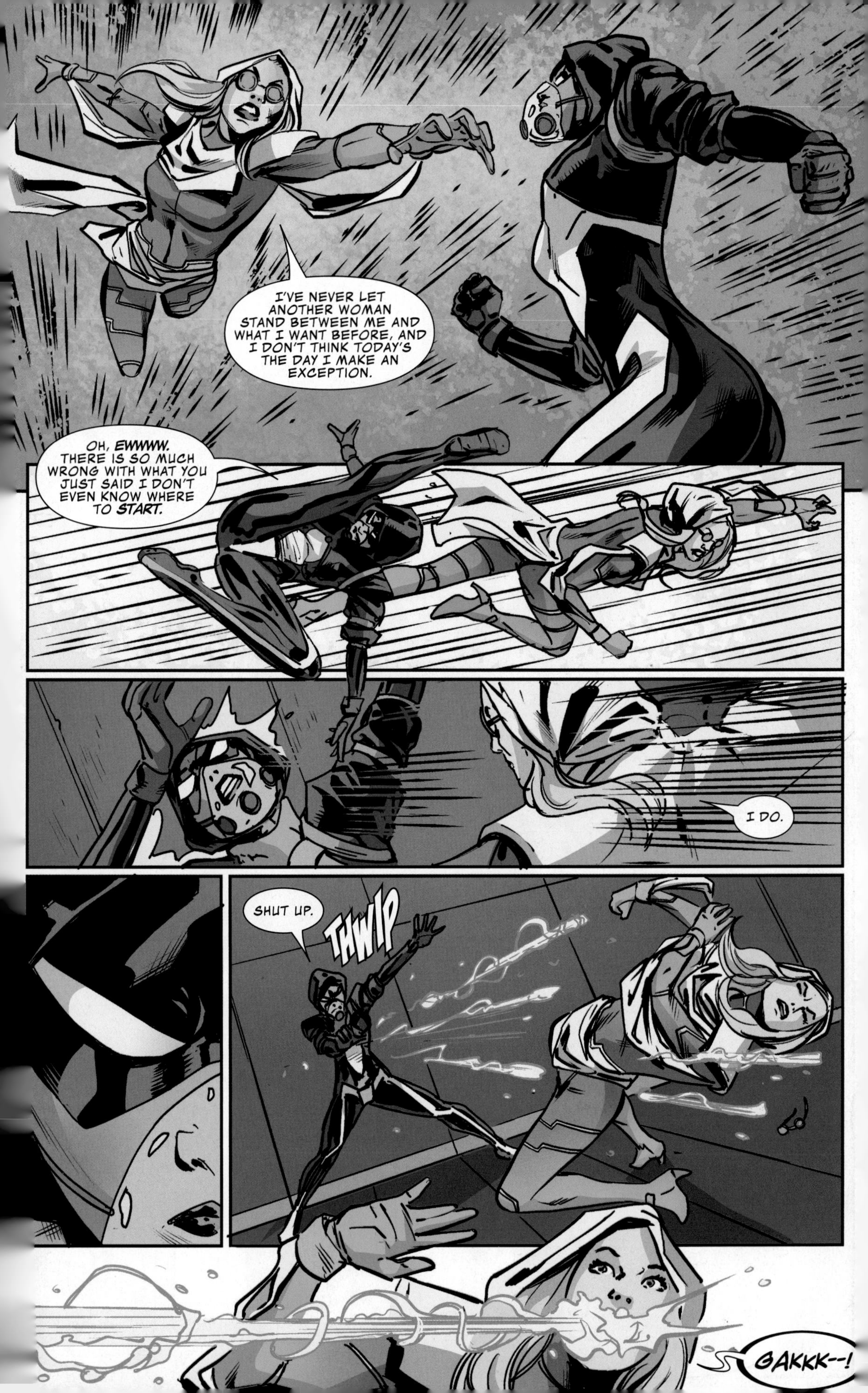
I'VE NEVER LET ANOTHER WOMAN STAND BETWEEN ME AND WHAT I WANT BEFORE, AND I DON'T THINK TODAY'S THE DAY I MAKE AN EXCEPTION.
OH, EWWWW. THERE IS SO MUCH WRONG WITH WHAT YOU JUST SAID I DON'T EVEN KNOW WHERE TO START.
I DO.
SHUT UP.
THWIP
GAKKK--!

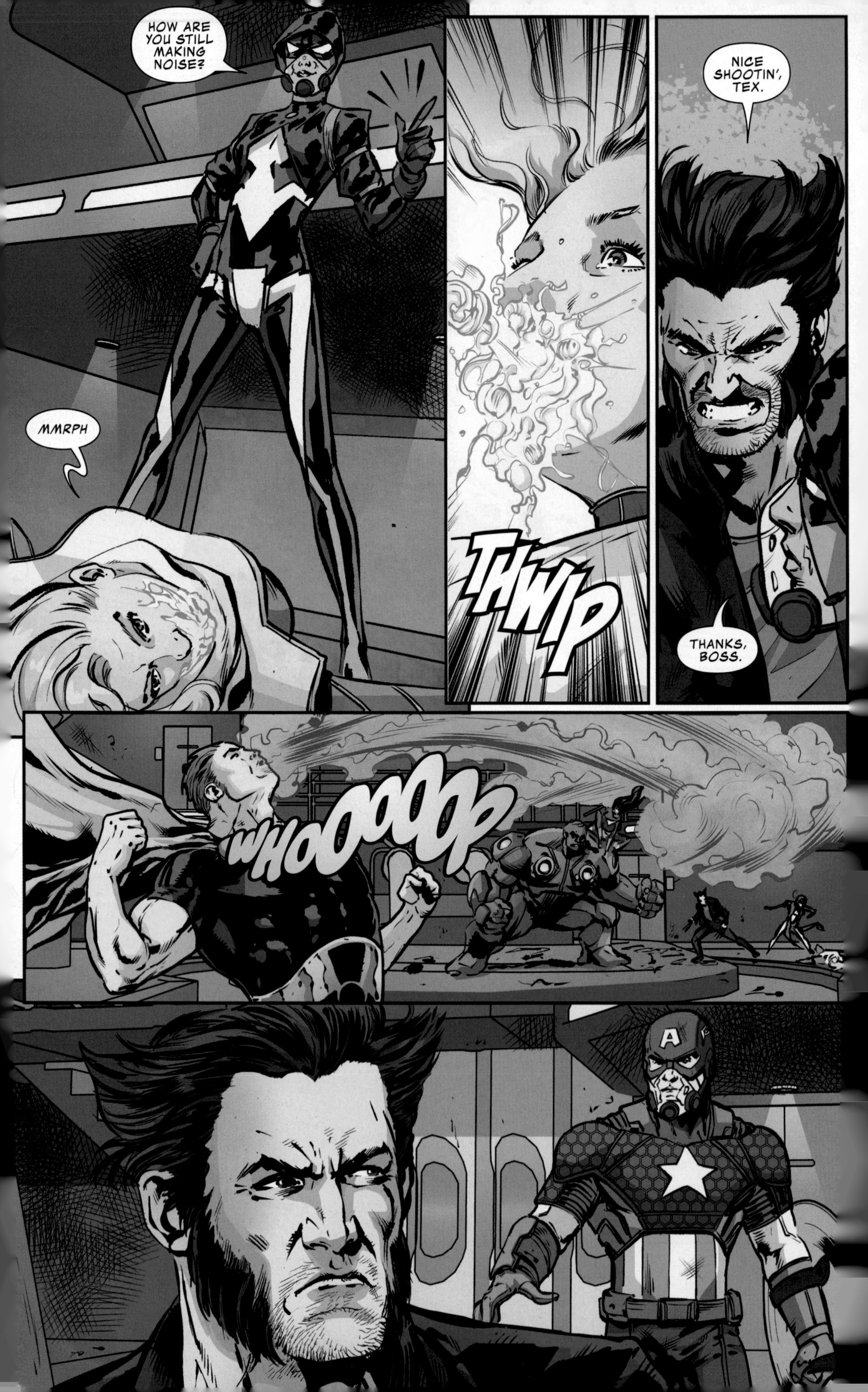
HOW ARE YOU STILL MAKING NOISE?
MMRPH
THWIP
NICE SHOOTIN', TEX.
THANKS, BOSS.
WHOOOOOP

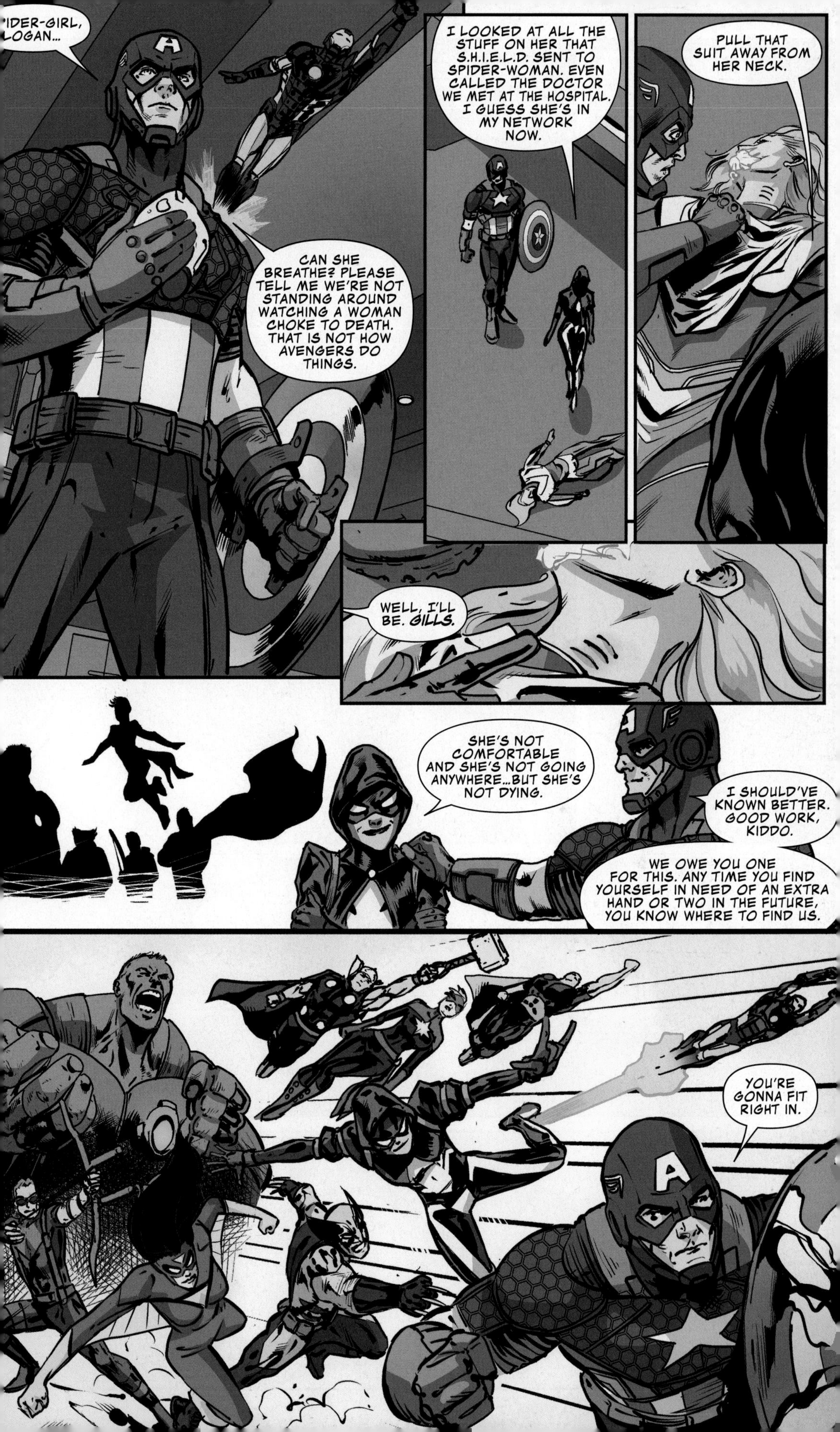
IDER-GIRL, LOGAN...
I LOOKED AT ALL THE STUFF ON HER THAT S.H.I.E.L.D. SENT TO SPIDER-WOMAN. EVEN CALLED THE DOCTOR WE MET AT THE HOSPITAL. I GUESS SHE'S IN MY NETWORK NOW.
PULL THAT SUIT AWAY FROM HER NECK.
CAN SHE BREATHE? PLEASE TELL ME WE'RE NOT STANDING AROUND WATCHING A WOMAN CHOKE TO DEATH. THAT IS NOT HOW AVENGERS DO THINGS.
WELL, I'LL BE. GILLS.
SHE'S NOT COMFORTABLE AND SHE'S NOT GOING ANYWHERE...BUT SHE'S NOT DYING.
I SHOULD'VE KNOWN BETTER. GOOD WORK, KIDDO.
WE OWE YOU ONE FOR THIS. ANY TIME YOU FIND YOURSELF IN NEED OF AN EXTRA HAND OR TWO IN THE FUTURE, YOU KNOW WHERE TO FIND US.
YOU'RE GONNA FIT RIGHT IN.

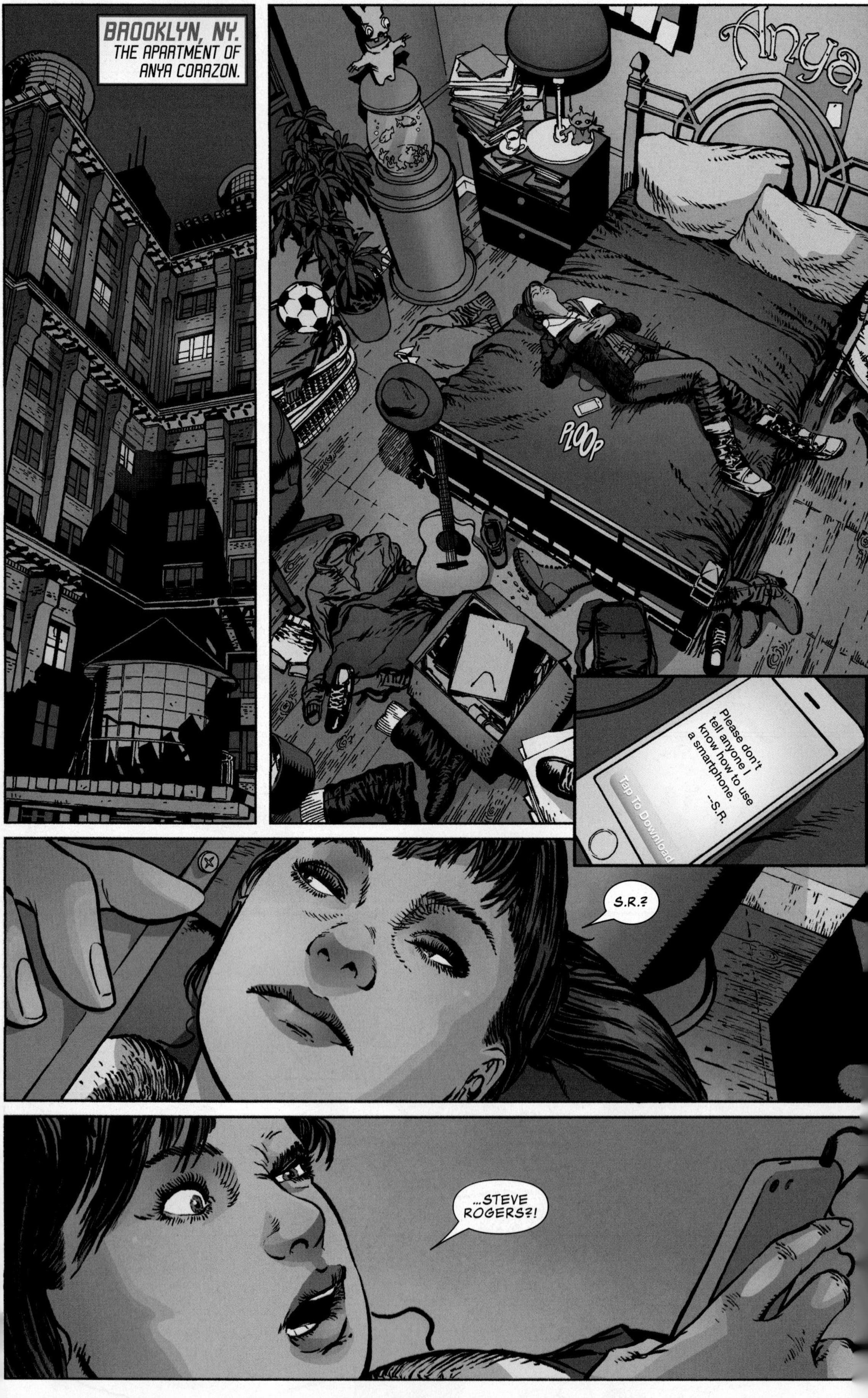
BROOKLYN, NY.
THE APARTMENT OF ANYA CORAZON.
Anya
PLOOP
Please don't tell anyone I know how to use a smartphone.
--S.R.
Tap To Download
S.R.?
...STEVE ROGERS?!

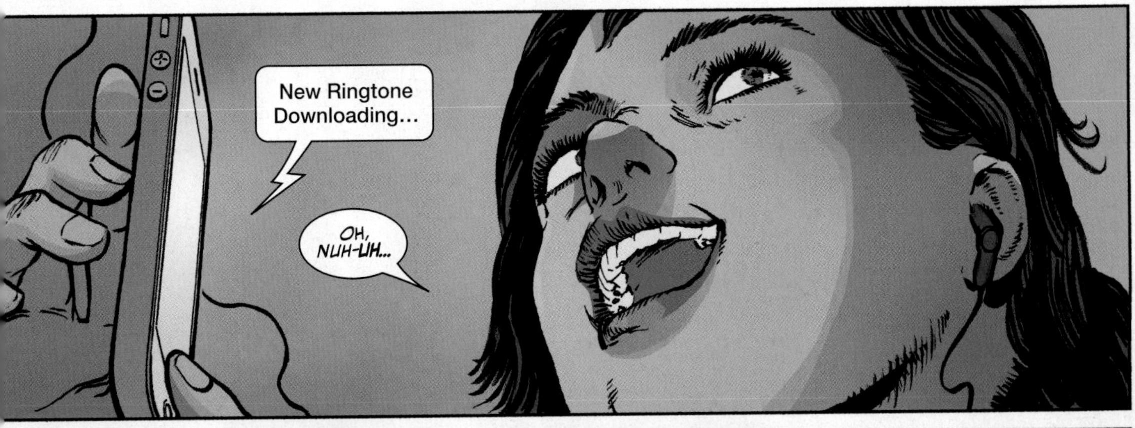
New Ringtone Downloading...
OH, NUH-UH...

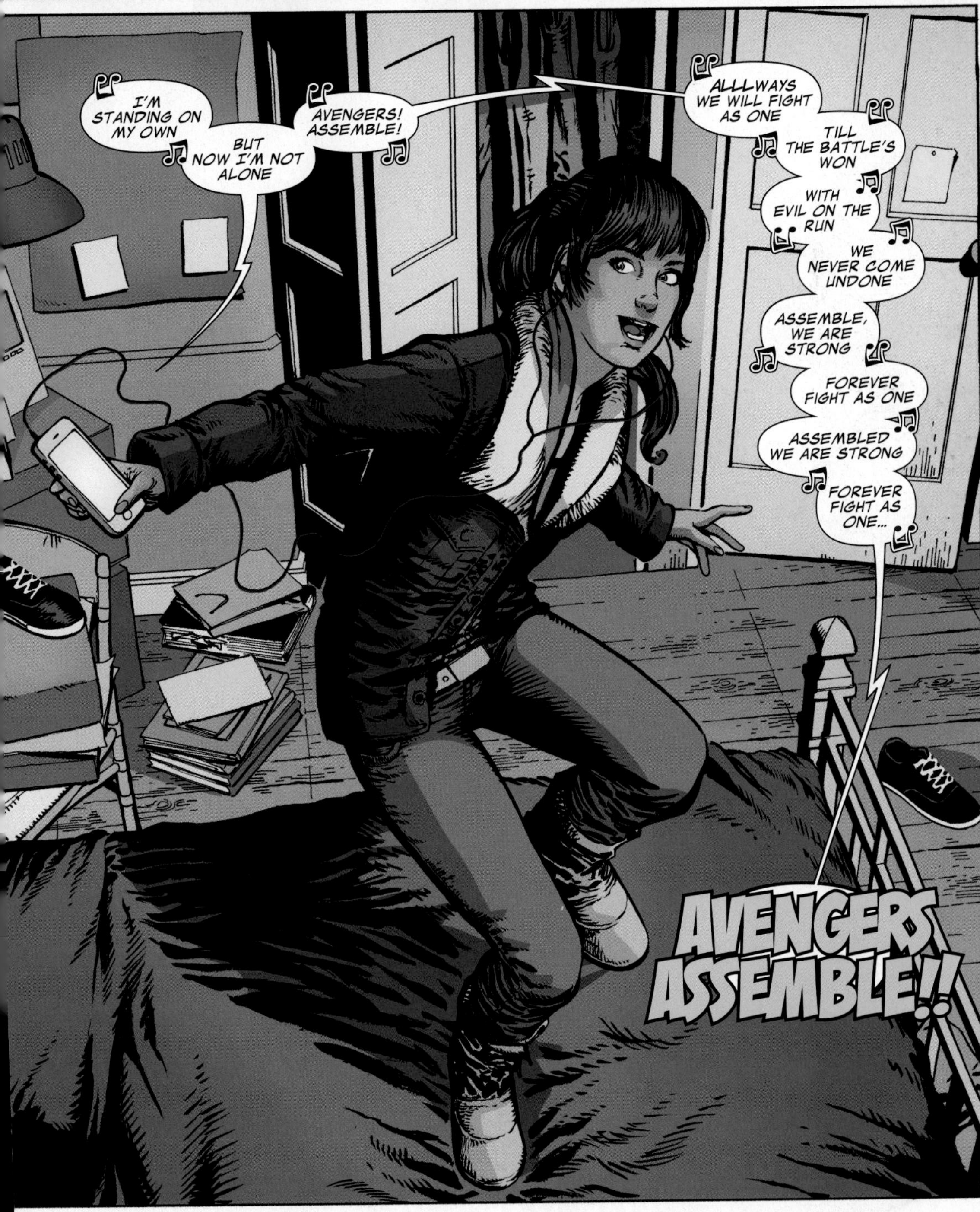
I'M STANDING ON MY OWN
BUT NOW I'M NOT ALONE
AVENGERS! ASSEMBLE!
ALLLWAYS WE WILL FIGHT AS ONE
TILL THE BATTLE'S WON
WITH EVIL ON THE RUN
WE NEVER COME UNDONE
ASSEMBLE, WE ARE STRONG
FOREVER FIGHT AS ONE
ASSEMBLED WE ARE STRONG
FOREVER FIGHT AS ONE...
AVENGERS ASSEMBLE!!

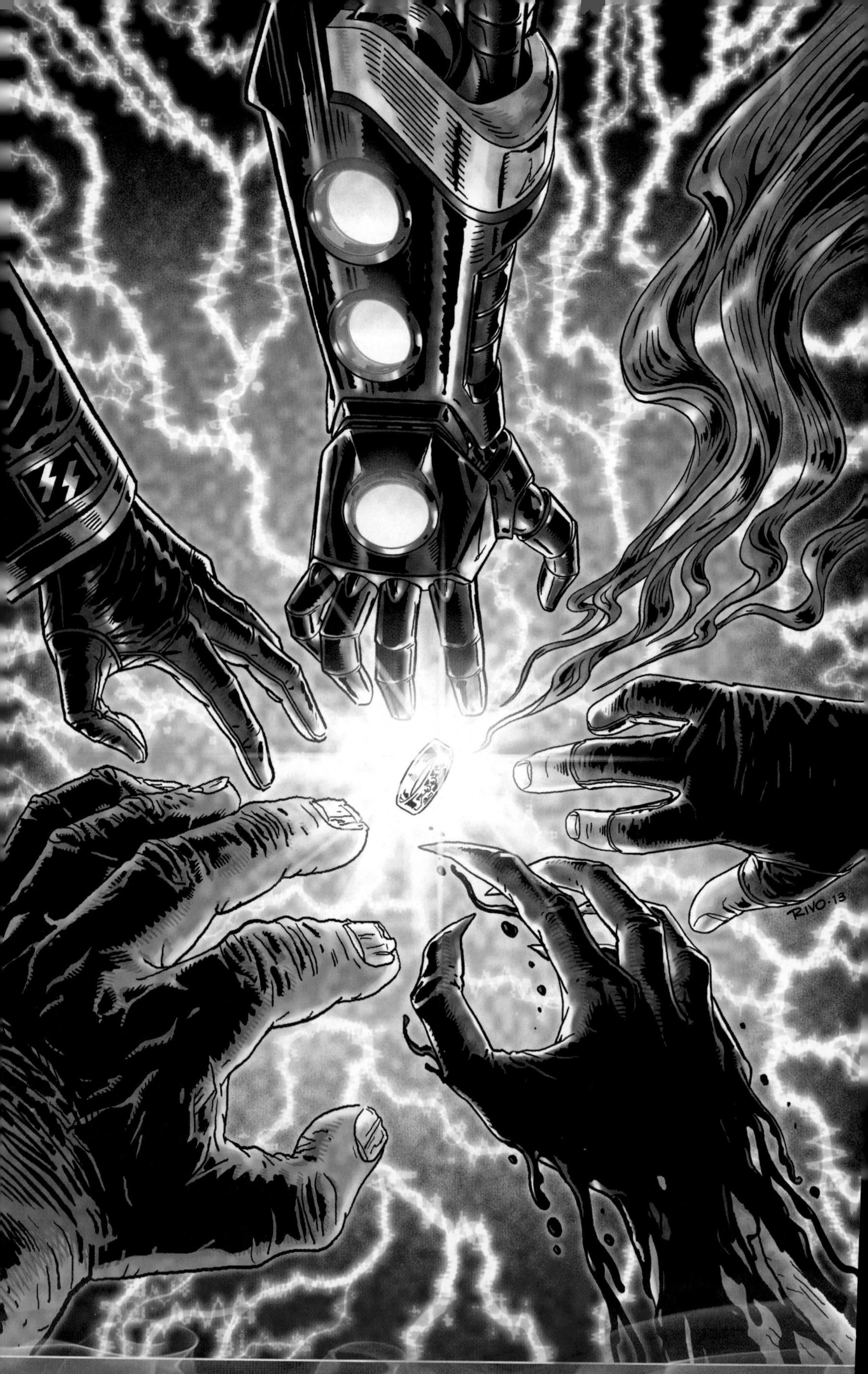
RIVO·13

IRON MAN #20.INH

INHUMANITY

IRON MAN

DURING THANOS THE MAD TITAN'S ATTACK ON EARTH, THE INHUMANS RELEASED A CHEMICAL CALLED THE TERRIGEN MISTS. SOONER OR LATER, EXPOSURE WILL TURN ANYONE WITH THE INHUMAN GENE INTO A COCOON... AND THEN THEY EMERGE AS A NEW INHUMAN. ONE THIRD OF HUMANITY HAS THIS GENE.

MEANWHILE, TONY STARK AND HIS OLDER BROTHER, ARNO, HAVE BEEN BUILDING A BETTER CITY TO SECURE THE FUTURE OF THE HUMAN RACE USING TECHNOLOGY THEY'VE NAMED TROY.

THEIR PLANS WERE DERAILED WHEN IT WAS REVEALED THAT THE MANDARIN'S RINGS HAD SOMEHOW GAINED SENTIENCE AND ESCAPED FROM S.H.I.E.L.D. CONTAINMENT...

THE RINGS SEEK THOSE WITH A GRUDGE AGAINST THE STARKS.

AND SO THE STARKS SEEK THE RINGS...

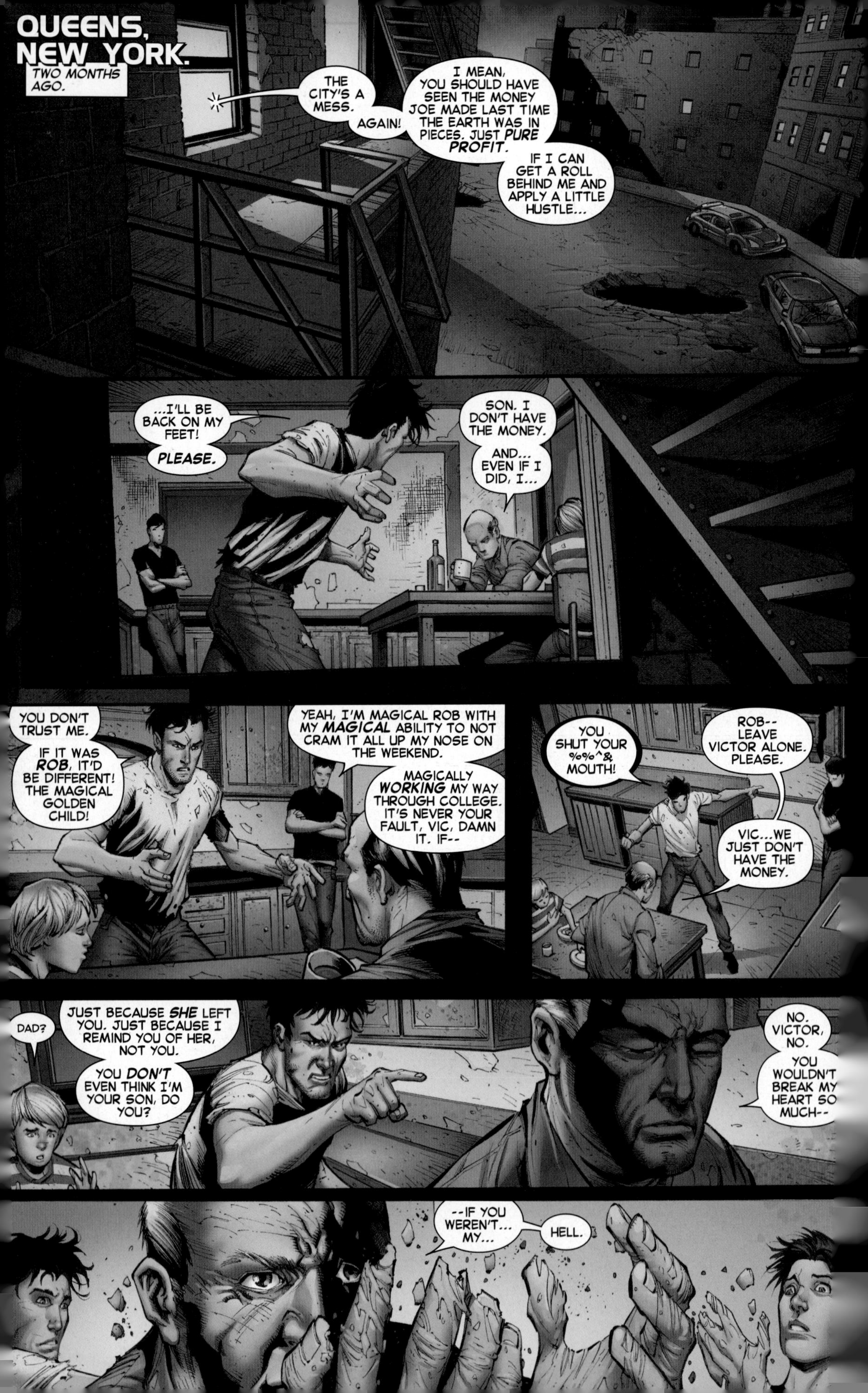
QUEENS, NEW YORK.
TWO MONTHS AGO.
THE CITY'S A MESS.
AGAIN!
I MEAN, YOU SHOULD HAVE SEEN THE MONEY JOE MADE LAST TIME THE EARTH WAS IN PIECES. JUST PURE PROFIT.
IF I CAN GET A ROLL BEHIND ME AND APPLY A LITTLE HUSTLE...
...I'LL BE BACK ON MY FEET!
PLEASE.
SON. I DON'T HAVE THE MONEY.
AND... EVEN IF I DID, I...
YOU DON'T TRUST ME.
IF IT WAS ROB, IT'D BE DIFFERENT! THE MAGICAL GOLDEN CHILD!
YEAH, I'M MAGICAL ROB WITH MY MAGICAL ABILITY TO NOT CRAM IT ALL UP MY NOSE ON THE WEEKEND.
MAGICALLY WORKING MY WAY THROUGH COLLEGE. IT'S NEVER YOUR FAULT, VIC, DAMN IT. IF--
YOU SHUT YOUR %%^& MOUTH!
ROB-- LEAVE VICTOR ALONE. PLEASE.
VIC...WE JUST DON'T HAVE THE MONEY.
DAD?
JUST BECAUSE SHE LEFT YOU. JUST BECAUSE I REMIND YOU OF HER, NOT YOU.
YOU DON'T EVEN THINK I'M YOUR SON, DO YOU?
NO. VICTOR, NO.
YOU WOULDN'T BREAK MY HEART SO MUCH--
--IF YOU WEREN'T... MY...
HELL.

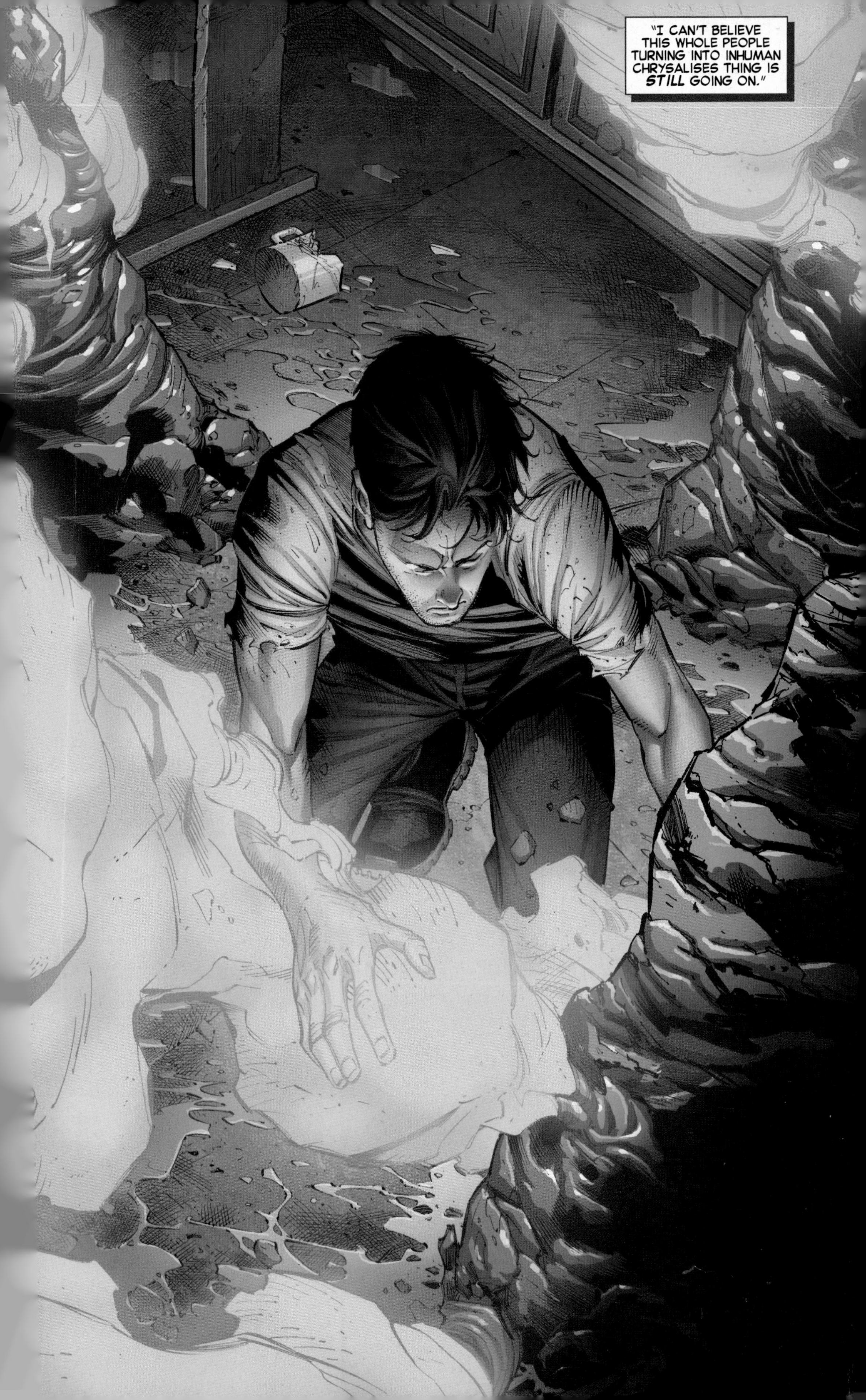
"I CAN'T BELIEVE THIS WHOLE PEOPLE TURNING INTO INHUMAN CHRYSALISES THING IS STILL GOING ON."

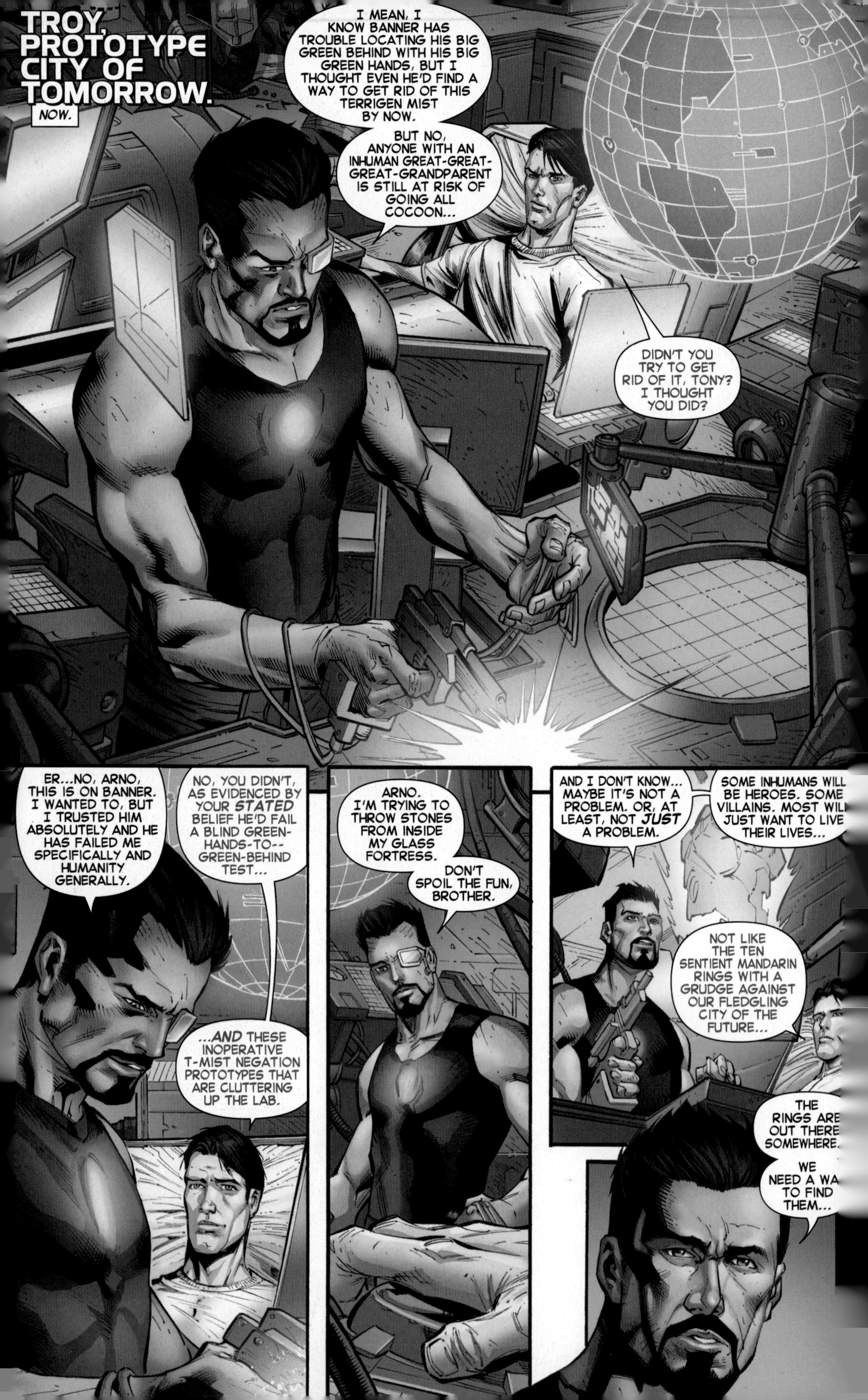
TROY, PROTOTYPE CITY OF TOMORROW.
NOW.
I MEAN, I KNOW BANNER HAS TROUBLE LOCATING HIS BIG GREEN BEHIND WITH HIS BIG GREEN HANDS, BUT I THOUGHT EVEN HE'D FIND A WAY TO GET RID OF THIS TERRIGEN MIST BY NOW.
BUT NO, ANYONE WITH AN INHUMAN GREAT-GREAT-GREAT-GRANDPARENT IS STILL AT RISK OF GOING ALL COCOON...
DIDN'T YOU TRY TO GET RID OF IT, TONY? I THOUGHT YOU DID?
ER...NO, ARNO, THIS IS ON BANNER. I WANTED TO, BUT I TRUSTED HIM ABSOLUTELY AND HE HAS FAILED ME SPECIFICALLY AND HUMANITY GENERALLY.
NO, YOU DIDN'T, AS EVIDENCED BY YOUR STATED BELIEF HE'D FAIL A BLIND GREEN-HANDS-TO--GREEN-BEHIND TEST...
...AND THESE INOPERATIVE T-MIST NEGATION PROTOTYPES THAT ARE CLUTTERING UP THE LAB.
ARNO. I'M TRYING TO THROW STONES FROM INSIDE MY GLASS FORTRESS.
DON'T SPOIL THE FUN, BROTHER.
AND I DON'T KNOW... MAYBE IT'S NOT A PROBLEM. OR, AT LEAST, NOT JUST A PROBLEM.
SOME INHUMANS WILL BE HEROES. SOME VILLAINS. MOST WILL JUST WANT TO LIVE THEIR LIVES...
NOT LIKE THE TEN SENTIENT MANDARIN RINGS WITH A GRUDGE AGAINST OUR FLEDGLING CITY OF THE FUTURE...
THE RINGS ARE OUT THERE SOMEWHERE.
WE NEED A WA TO FIND THEM...

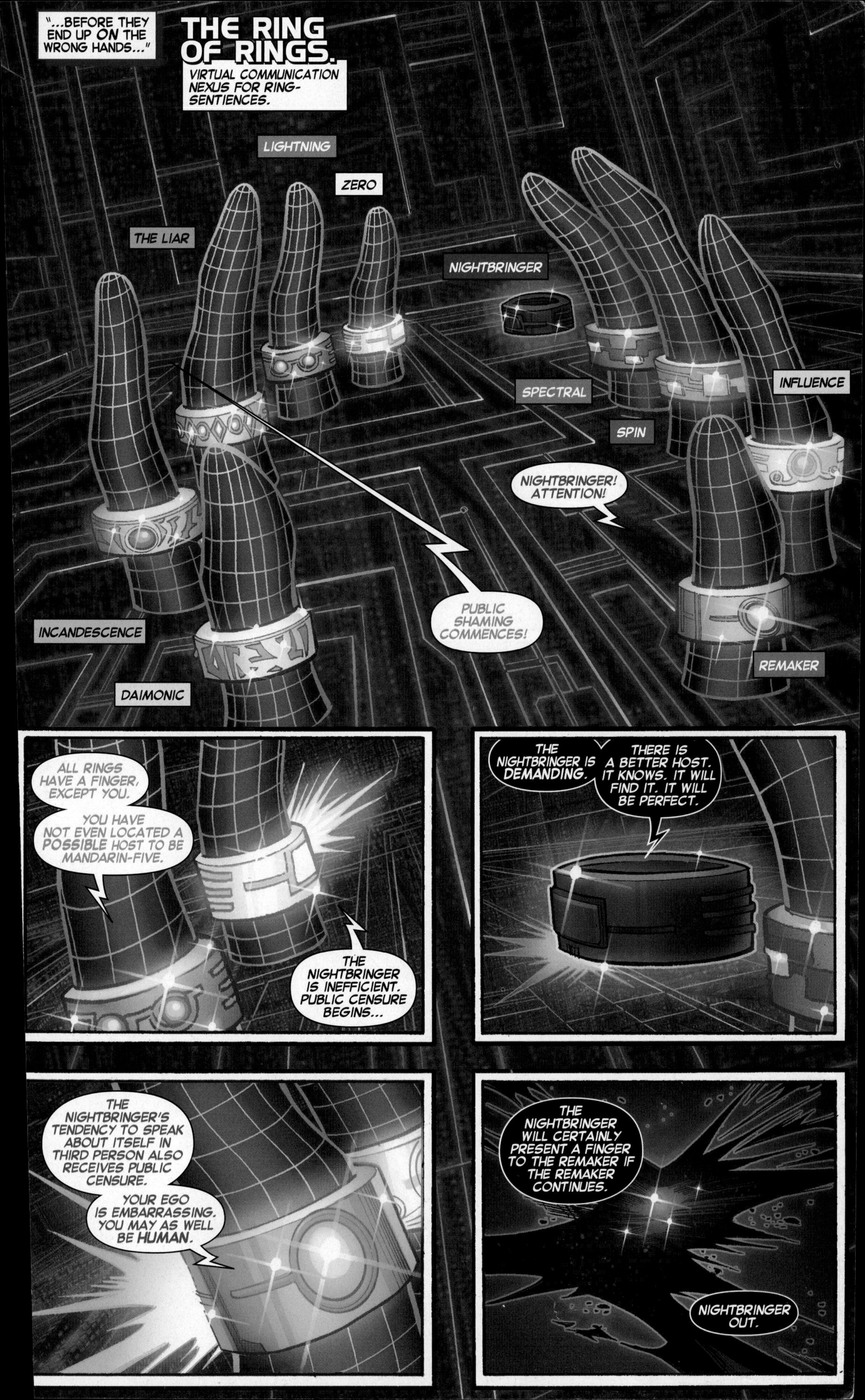
"...BEFORE THEY END UP ON THE WRONG HANDS..."
THE RING OF RINGS.
VIRTUAL COMMUNICATION NEXUS FOR RING-SENTIENCES.
LIGHTNING
ZERO
THE LIAR
NIGHTBRINGER
SPECTRAL
INFLUENCE
SPIN
NIGHTBRINGER! ATTENTION!
PUBLIC SHAMING COMMENCES!
INCANDESCENCE
REMAKER
DAIMONIC
ALL RINGS HAVE A FINGER, EXCEPT YOU.
YOU HAVE NOT EVEN LOCATED A POSSIBLE HOST TO BE MANDARIN-FIVE.
THE NIGHTBRINGER IS INEFFICIENT. PUBLIC CENSURE BEGINS...
THE NIGHTBRINGER IS DEMANDING.
THERE IS A BETTER HOST. IT KNOWS. IT WILL FIND IT. IT WILL BE PERFECT.
THE NIGHTBRINGER'S TENDENCY TO SPEAK ABOUT ITSELF IN THIRD PERSON ALSO RECEIVES PUBLIC CENSURE.
YOUR EGO IS EMBARRASSING. YOU MAY AS WELL BE HUMAN.
THE NIGHTBRINGER WILL CERTAINLY PRESENT A FINGER TO THE REMAKER IF THE REMAKER CONTINUES.
NIGHTBRINGER OUT.

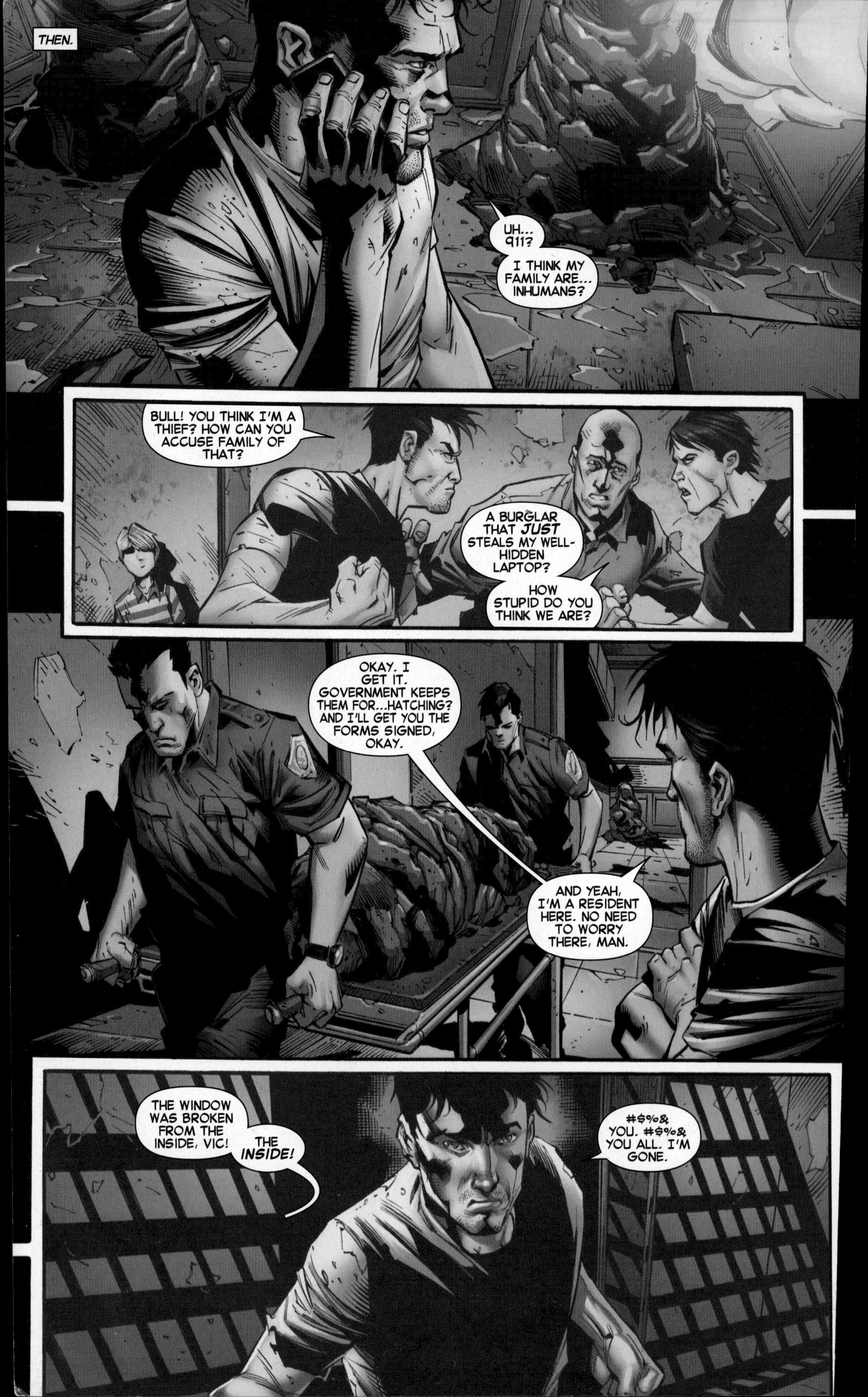
THEN.
UH... 911?
I THINK MY FAMILY ARE... INHUMANS?
BULL! YOU THINK I'M A THIEF? HOW CAN YOU ACCUSE FAMILY OF THAT?
A BURGLAR THAT JUST STEALS MY WELL-HIDDEN LAPTOP?
HOW STUPID DO YOU THINK WE ARE?
OKAY. I GET IT. GOVERNMENT KEEPS THEM FOR...HATCHING? AND I'LL GET YOU THE FORMS SIGNED, OKAY.
AND YEAH, I'M A RESIDENT HERE. NO NEED TO WORRY THERE, MAN.
THE WINDOW WAS BROKEN FROM THE INSIDE, VIC!
THE INSIDE!
#$%& YOU. #$%& YOU ALL. I'M GONE.

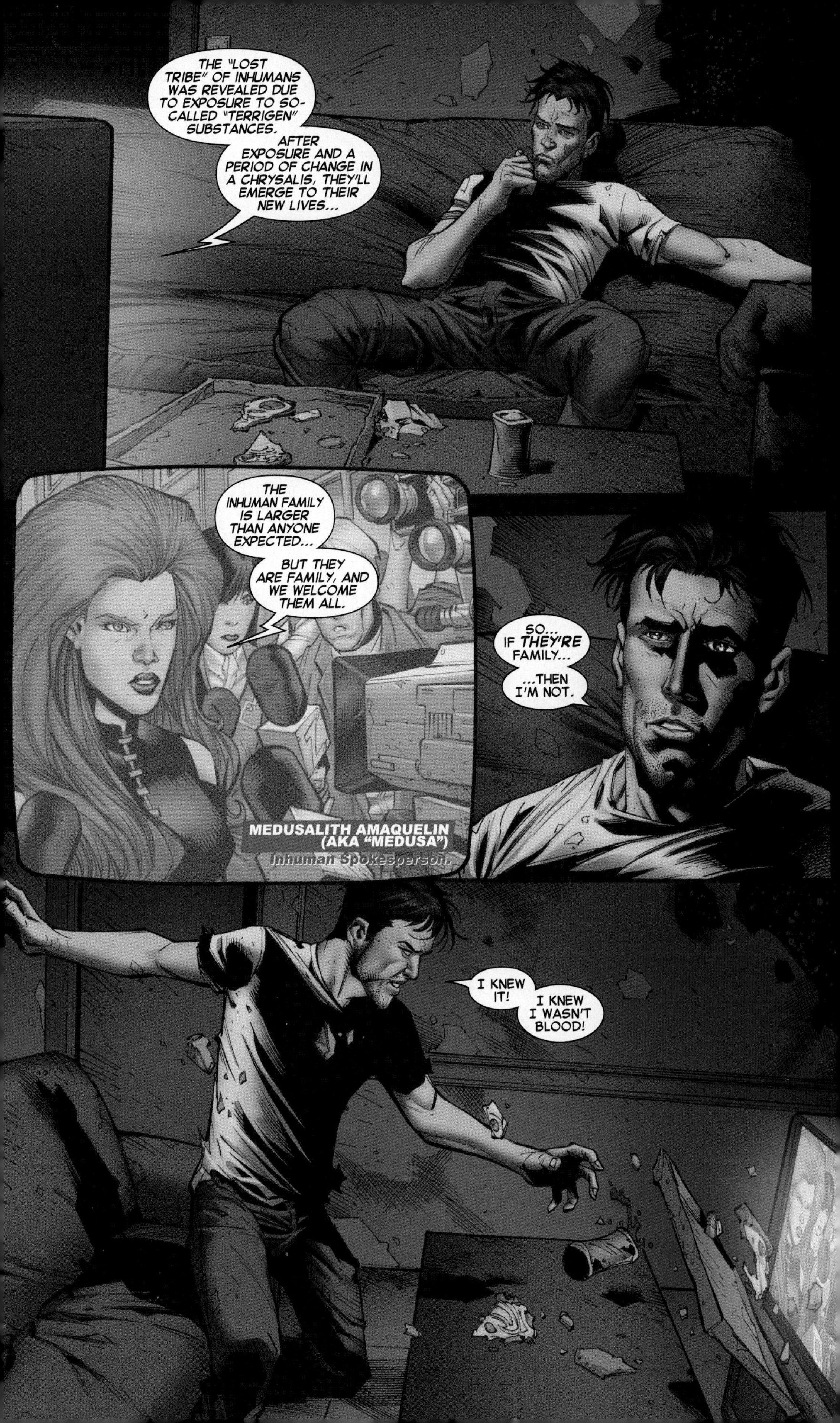
THE "LOST TRIBE" OF INHUMANS WAS REVEALED DUE TO EXPOSURE TO SO-CALLED "TERRIGEN" SUBSTANCES.
AFTER EXPOSURE AND A PERIOD OF CHANGE IN A CHRYSALIS, THEY'LL EMERGE TO THEIR NEW LIVES...
THE INHUMAN FAMILY IS LARGER THAN ANYONE EXPECTED...
BUT THEY ARE FAMILY, AND WE WELCOME THEM ALL.
MEDUSALITH AMAQUELIN (AKA "MEDUSA")
Inhuman Spokesperson.
SO... IF THEY'RE FAMILY...
...THEN I'M NOT.
I KNEW IT!
I KNEW I WASN'T BLOOD!

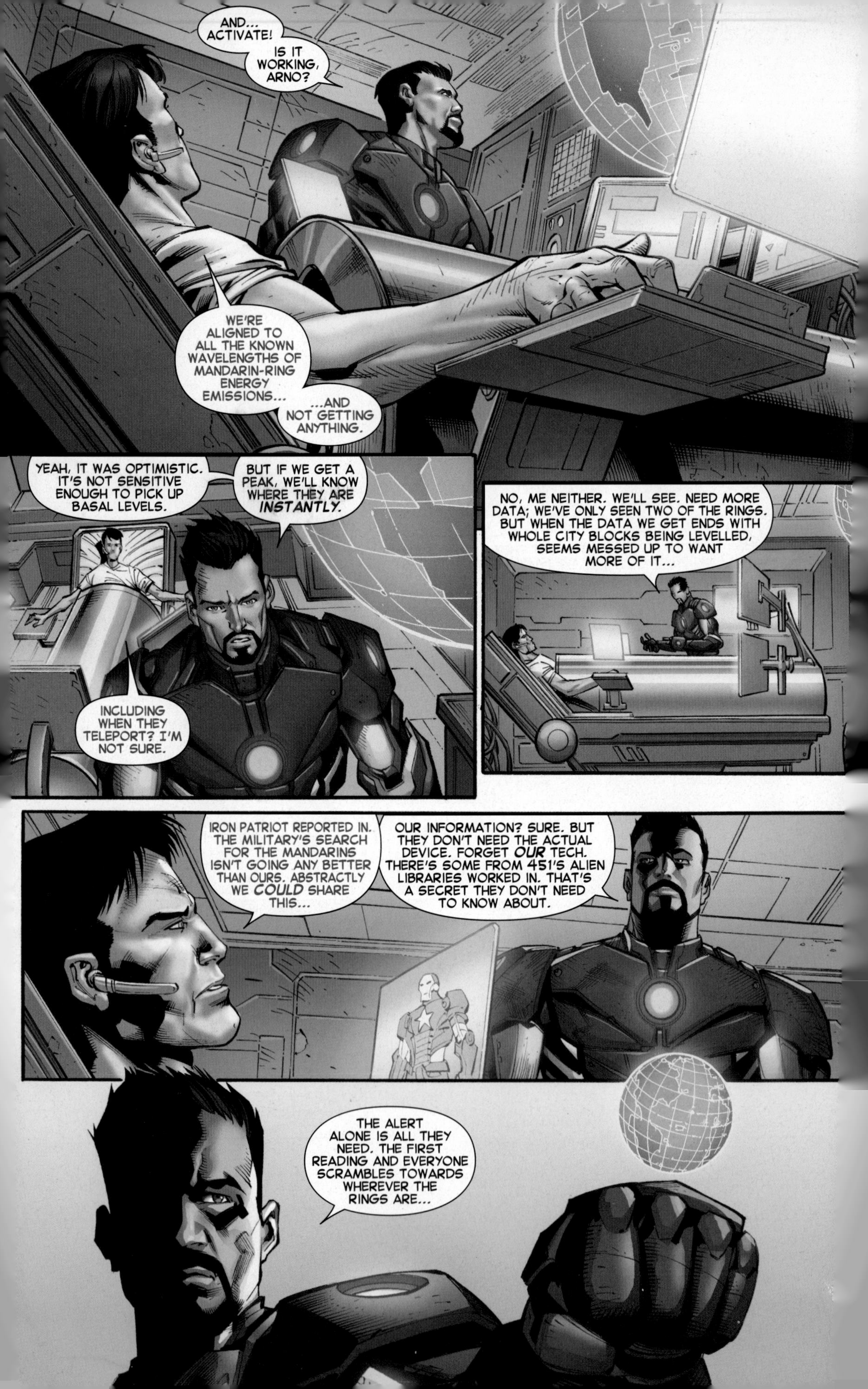
AND... ACTIVATE!
IS IT WORKING, ARNO?
WE'RE ALIGNED TO ALL THE KNOWN WAVELENGTHS OF MANDARIN-RING ENERGY EMISSIONS...
...AND NOT GETTING ANYTHING.
YEAH, IT WAS OPTIMISTIC. IT'S NOT SENSITIVE ENOUGH TO PICK UP BASAL LEVELS.
BUT IF WE GET A PEAK, WE'LL KNOW WHERE THEY ARE INSTANTLY.
INCLUDING WHEN THEY TELEPORT? I'M NOT SURE.
NO, ME NEITHER. WE'LL SEE. NEED MORE DATA; WE'VE ONLY SEEN TWO OF THE RINGS. BUT WHEN THE DATA WE GET ENDS WITH WHOLE CITY BLOCKS BEING LEVELLED, SEEMS MESSED UP TO WANT MORE OF IT...
IRON PATRIOT REPORTED IN. THE MILITARY'S SEARCH FOR THE MANDARINS ISN'T GOING ANY BETTER THAN OURS. ABSTRACTLY WE COULD SHARE THIS...
OUR INFORMATION? SURE. BUT THEY DON'T NEED THE ACTUAL DEVICE. FORGET OUR TECH. THERE'S SOME FROM 451'S ALIEN LIBRARIES WORKED IN. THAT'S A SECRET THEY DON'T NEED TO KNOW ABOUT.
THE ALERT ALONE IS ALL THEY NEED. THE FIRST READING AND EVERYONE SCRAMBLES TOWARDS WHEREVER THE RINGS ARE...

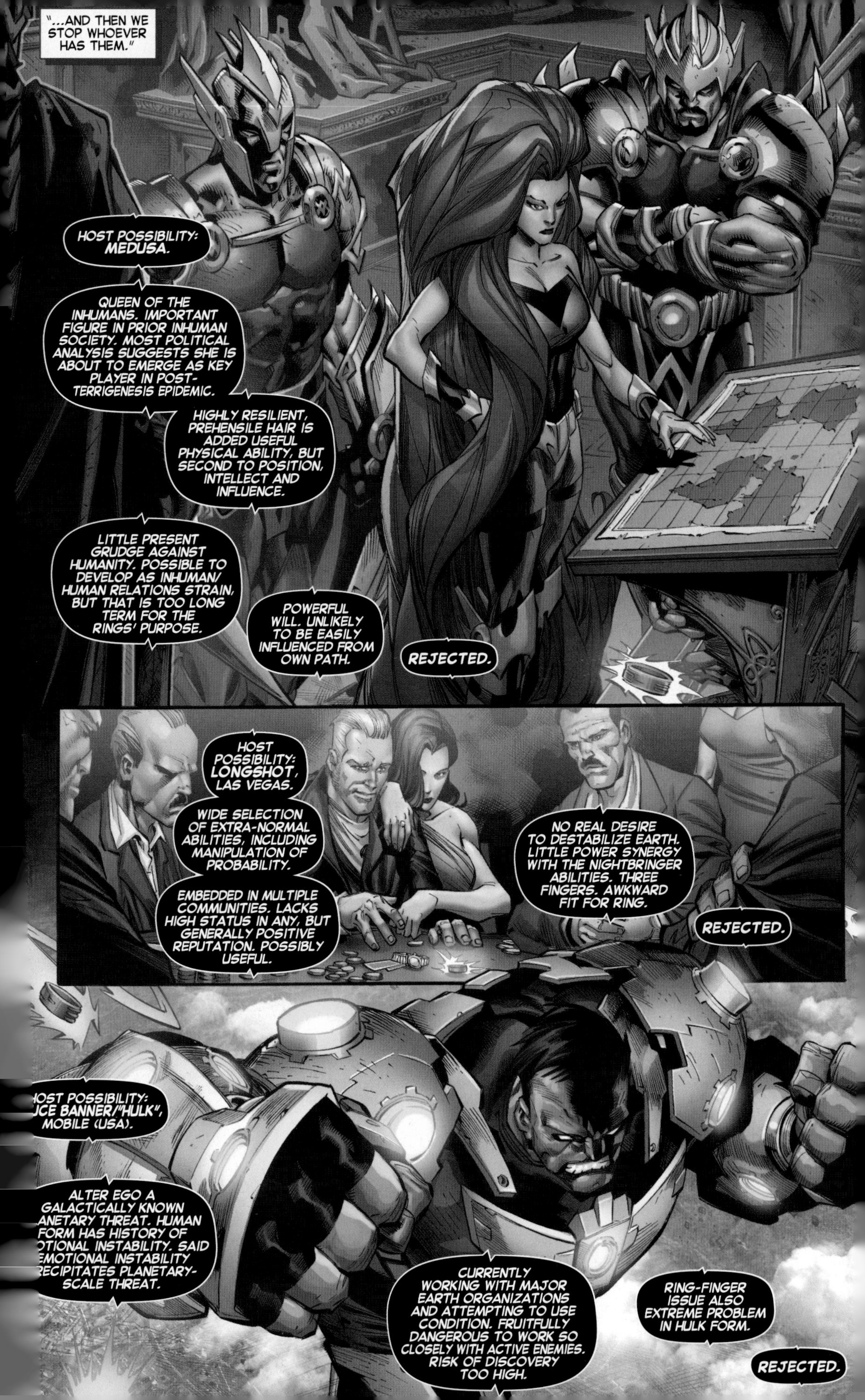
"...AND THEN WE STOP WHOEVER HAS THEM."
HOST POSSIBILITY: MEDUSA.
QUEEN OF THE INHUMANS. IMPORTANT FIGURE IN PRIOR INHUMAN SOCIETY. MOST POLITICAL ANALYSIS SUGGESTS SHE IS ABOUT TO EMERGE AS KEY PLAYER IN POST-TERRIGENESIS EPIDEMIC.
HIGHLY RESILIENT, PREHENSILE HAIR IS ADDED USEFUL PHYSICAL ABILITY, BUT SECOND TO POSITION, INTELLECT AND INFLUENCE.
LITTLE PRESENT GRUDGE AGAINST HUMANITY. POSSIBLE TO DEVELOP AS INHUMAN/HUMAN RELATIONS STRAIN, BUT THAT IS TOO LONG TERM FOR THE RINGS' PURPOSE.
POWERFUL WILL. UNLIKELY TO BE EASILY INFLUENCED FROM OWN PATH.
REJECTED.
HOST POSSIBILITY: LONGSHOT, LAS VEGAS.
WIDE SELECTION OF EXTRA-NORMAL ABILITIES, INCLUDING MANIPULATION OF PROBABILITY.
EMBEDDED IN MULTIPLE COMMUNITIES. LACKS HIGH STATUS IN ANY, BUT GENERALLY POSITIVE REPUTATION. POSSIBLY USEFUL.
NO REAL DESIRE TO DESTABILIZE EARTH. LITTLE POWER SYNERGY WITH THE NIGHTBRINGER ABILITIES. THREE FINGERS. AWKWARD FIT FOR RING.
REJECTED.
HOST POSSIBILITY: UCE BANNER/"HULK", MOBILE (USA).
ALTER EGO A GALACTICALLY KNOWN ANETARY THREAT. HUMAN FORM HAS HISTORY OF OTIONAL INSTABILITY. SAID EMOTIONAL INSTABILITY RECIPITATES PLANETARY-SCALE THREAT.
CURRENTLY WORKING WITH MAJOR EARTH ORGANIZATIONS AND ATTEMPTING TO USE CONDITION. FRUITFULLY DANGEROUS TO WORK SO CLOSELY WITH ACTIVE ENEMIES. RISK OF DISCOVERY TOO HIGH.
RING-FINGER ISSUE ALSO EXTREME PROBLEM IN HULK FORM.
REJECTED.

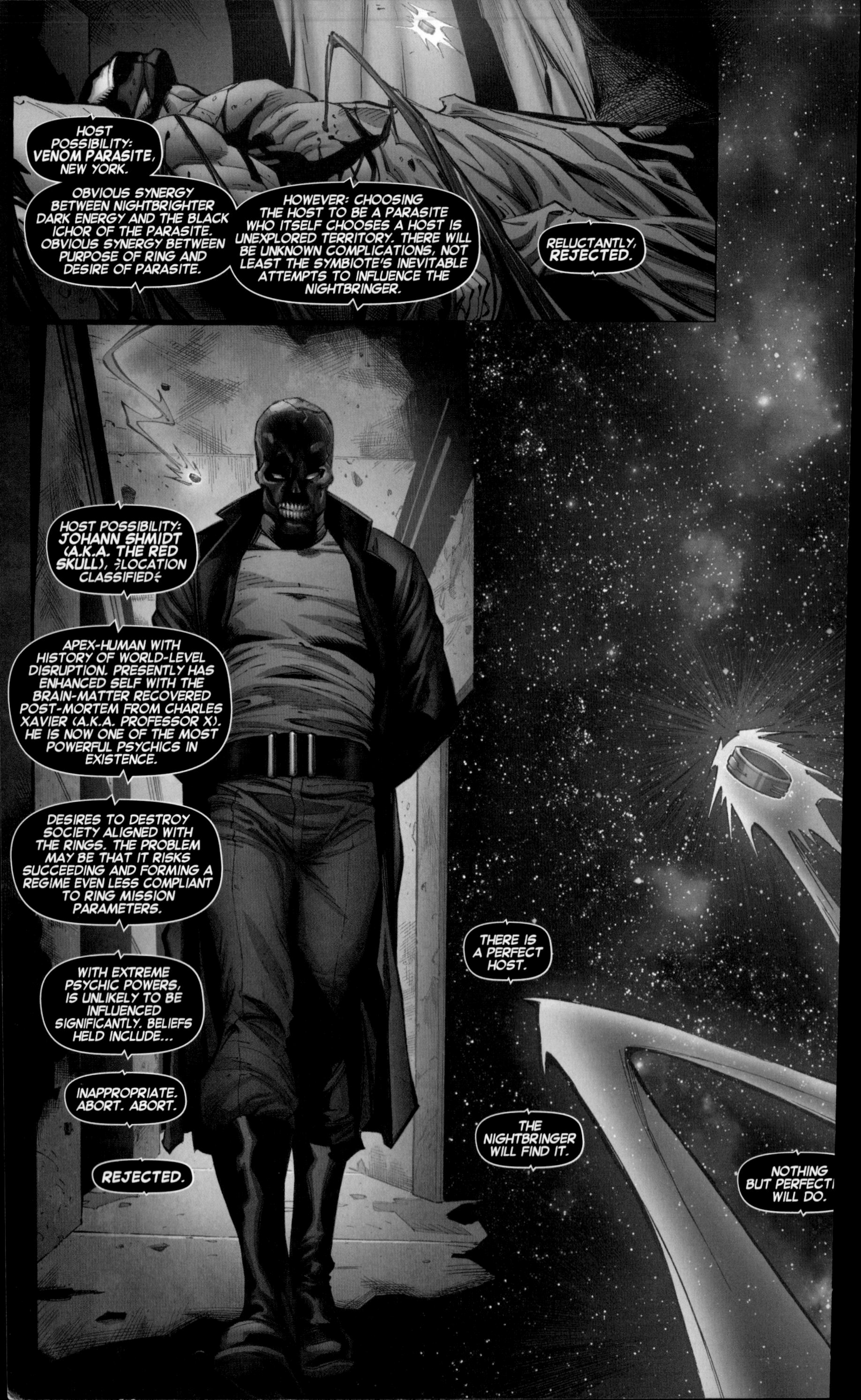
HOST POSSIBILITY: VENOM PARASITE, NEW YORK.
OBVIOUS SYNERGY BETWEEN NIGHTBRIGHTER DARK ENERGY AND THE BLACK ICHOR OF THE PARASITE. OBVIOUS SYNERGY BETWEEN PURPOSE OF RING AND DESIRE OF PARASITE.
HOWEVER: CHOOSING THE HOST TO BE A PARASITE WHO ITSELF CHOOSES A HOST IS UNEXPLORED TERRITORY. THERE WILL BE UNKNOWN COMPLICATIONS, NOT LEAST THE SYMBIOTE'S INEVITABLE ATTEMPTS TO INFLUENCE THE NIGHTBRINGER.
RELUCTANTLY, REJECTED.
HOST POSSIBILITY: JOHANN SHMIDT (A.K.A. THE RED SKULL), ⋚LOCATION CLASSIFIED⋛
APEX-HUMAN WITH HISTORY OF WORLD-LEVEL DISRUPTION. PRESENTLY HAS ENHANCED SELF WITH THE BRAIN-MATTER RECOVERED POST-MORTEM FROM CHARLES XAVIER (A.K.A. PROFESSOR X). HE IS NOW ONE OF THE MOST POWERFUL PSYCHICS IN EXISTENCE.
DESIRES TO DESTROY SOCIETY ALIGNED WITH THE RINGS. THE PROBLEM MAY BE THAT IT RISKS SUCCEEDING AND FORMING A REGIME EVEN LESS COMPLIANT TO RING MISSION PARAMETERS.
WITH EXTREME PSYCHIC POWERS, IS UNLIKELY TO BE INFLUENCED SIGNIFICANTLY. BELIEFS HELD INCLUDE...
INAPPROPRIATE. ABORT. ABORT.
REJECTED.
THERE IS A PERFECT HOST.
THE NIGHTBRINGER WILL FIND IT.
NOTHING BUT PERFECT WILL DO.

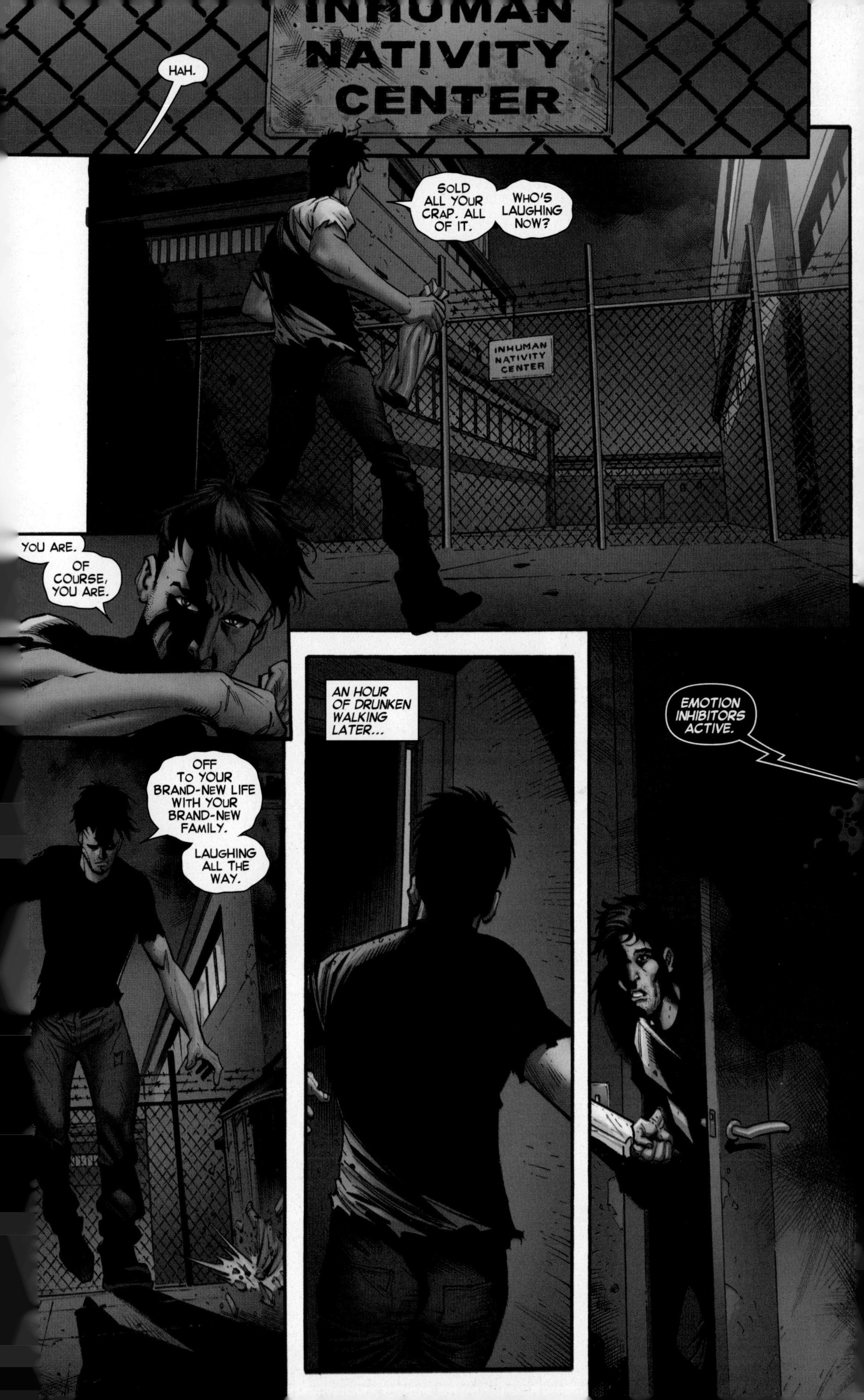
INHUMAN NATIVITY CENTER
HAH.
SOLD ALL YOUR CRAP. ALL OF IT.
WHO'S LAUGHING NOW?
INHUMAN NATIVITY CENTER
YOU ARE.
OF COURSE, YOU ARE.
OFF TO YOUR BRAND-NEW LIFE WITH YOUR BRAND-NEW FAMILY.
LAUGHING ALL THE WAY.
AN HOUR OF DRUNKEN WALKING LATER...
EMOTION INHIBITORS ACTIVE.

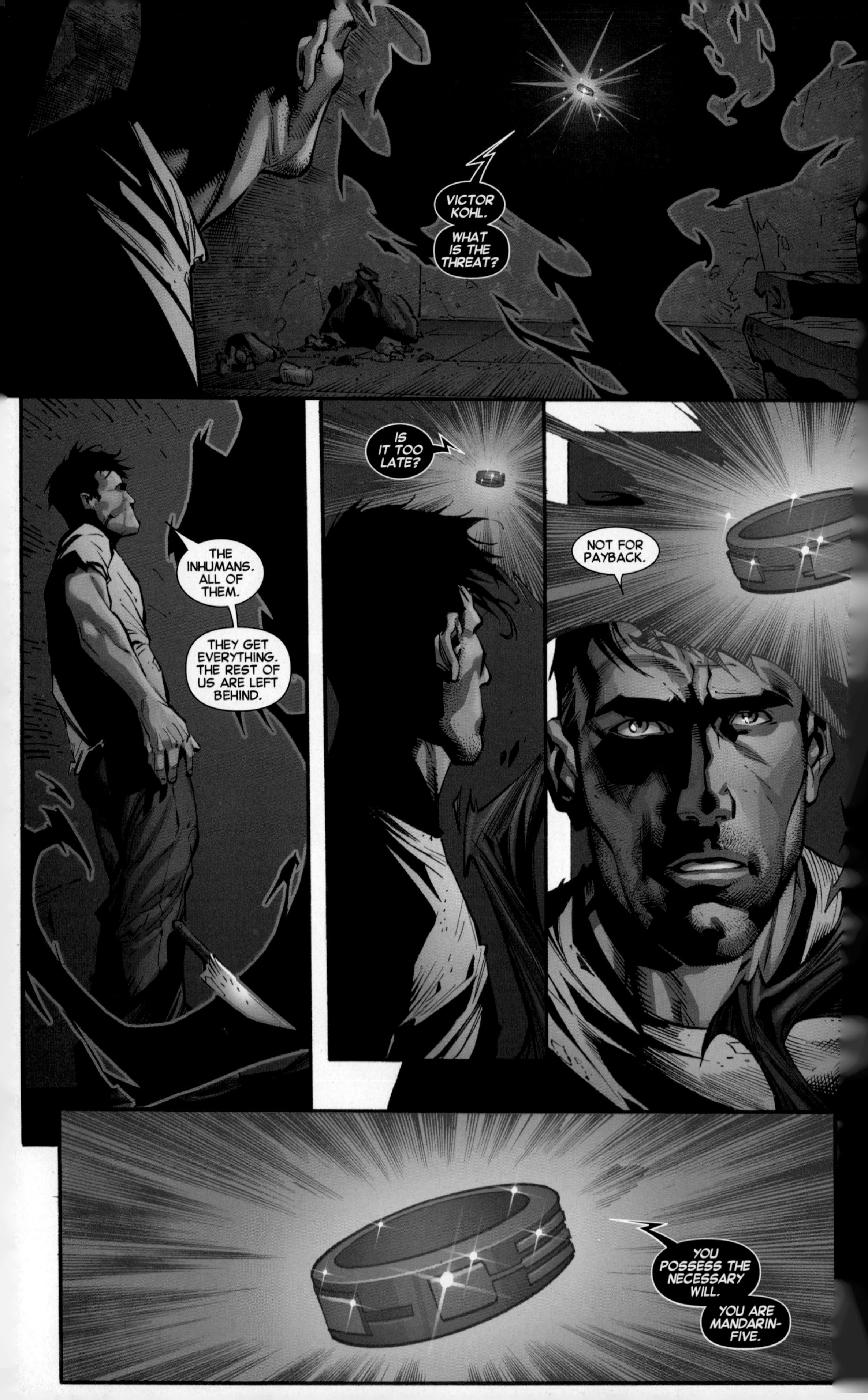
VICTOR KOHL.
WHAT IS THE THREAT?
THE INHUMANS. ALL OF THEM.
THEY GET EVERYTHING. THE REST OF US ARE LEFT BEHIND.
IS IT TOO LATE?
NOT FOR PAYBACK.
YOU POSSESS THE NECESSARY WILL.
YOU ARE MANDARIN-FIVE.

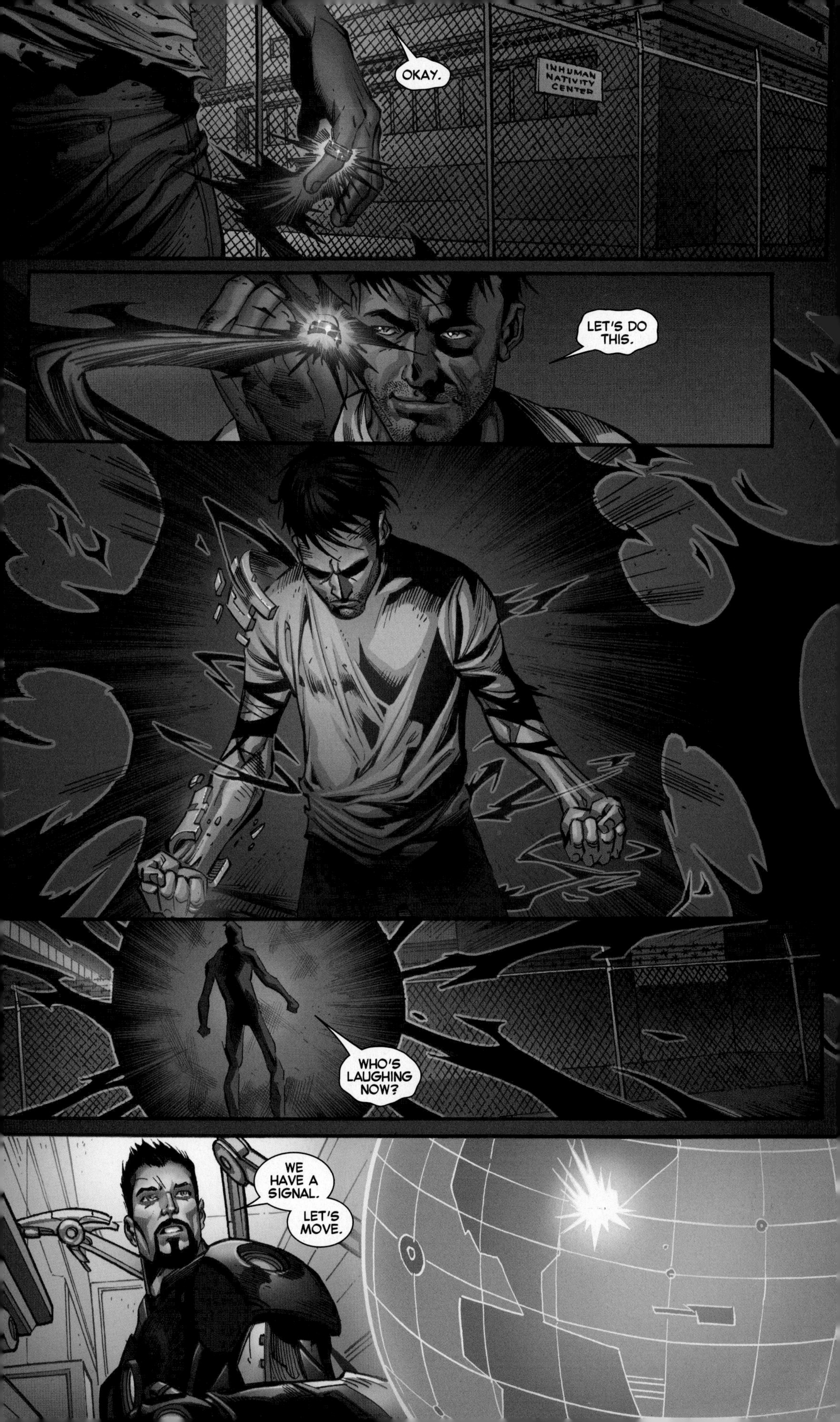
OKAY.
INHUMAN NATIVITY CENTER
LET'S DO THIS.
WHO'S LAUGHING NOW?
WE HAVE A SIGNAL.
LET'S MOVE.

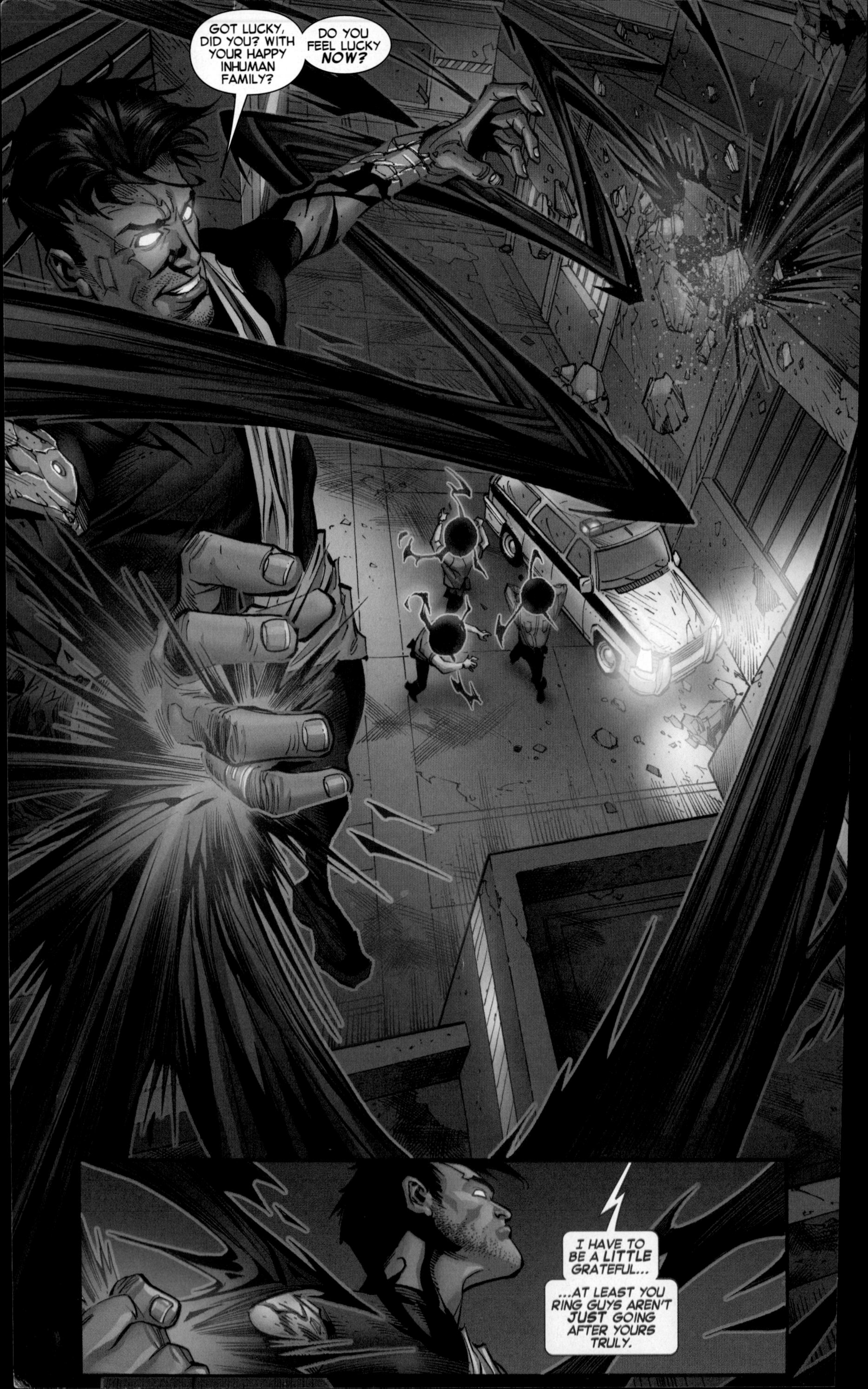
GOT LUCKY, DID YOU? WITH YOUR HAPPY INHUMAN FAMILY?
DO YOU FEEL LUCKY NOW?
I HAVE TO BE A LITTLE GRATEFUL...
...AT LEAST YOU RING GUYS AREN'T JUST GOING AFTER YOURS TRULY.

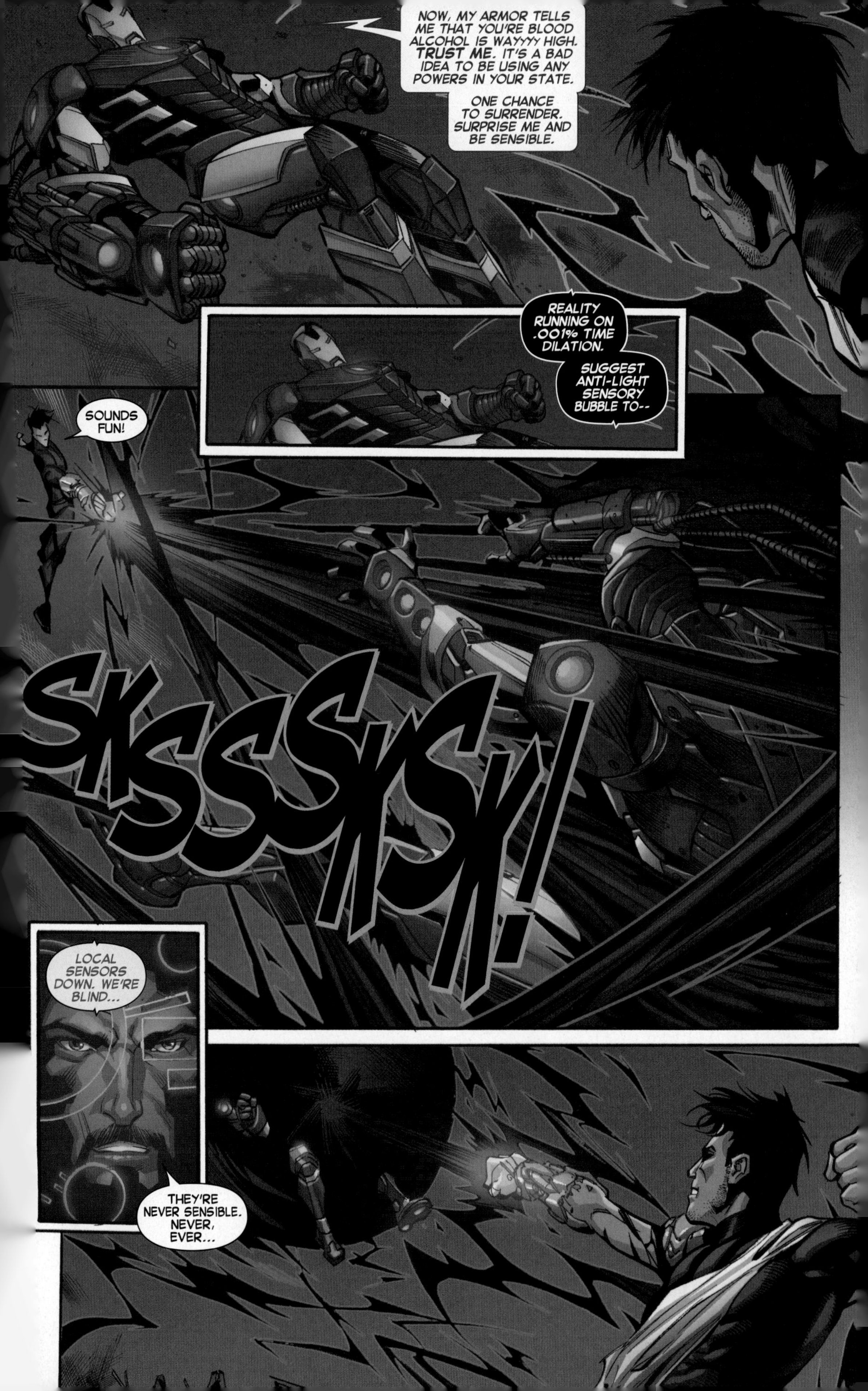
NOW, MY ARMOR TELLS ME THAT YOU'RE BLOOD ALCOHOL IS WAYYYY HIGH. TRUST ME. IT'S A BAD IDEA TO BE USING ANY POWERS IN YOUR STATE.
ONE CHANCE TO SURRENDER. SURPRISE ME AND BE SENSIBLE.
REALITY RUNNING ON .001% TIME DILATION.
SUGGEST ANTI-LIGHT SENSORY BUBBLE TO--
SOUNDS FUN!
SKSSSKSK!
LOCAL SENSORS DOWN. WE'RE BLIND...
THEY'RE NEVER SENSIBLE. NEVER, EVER...

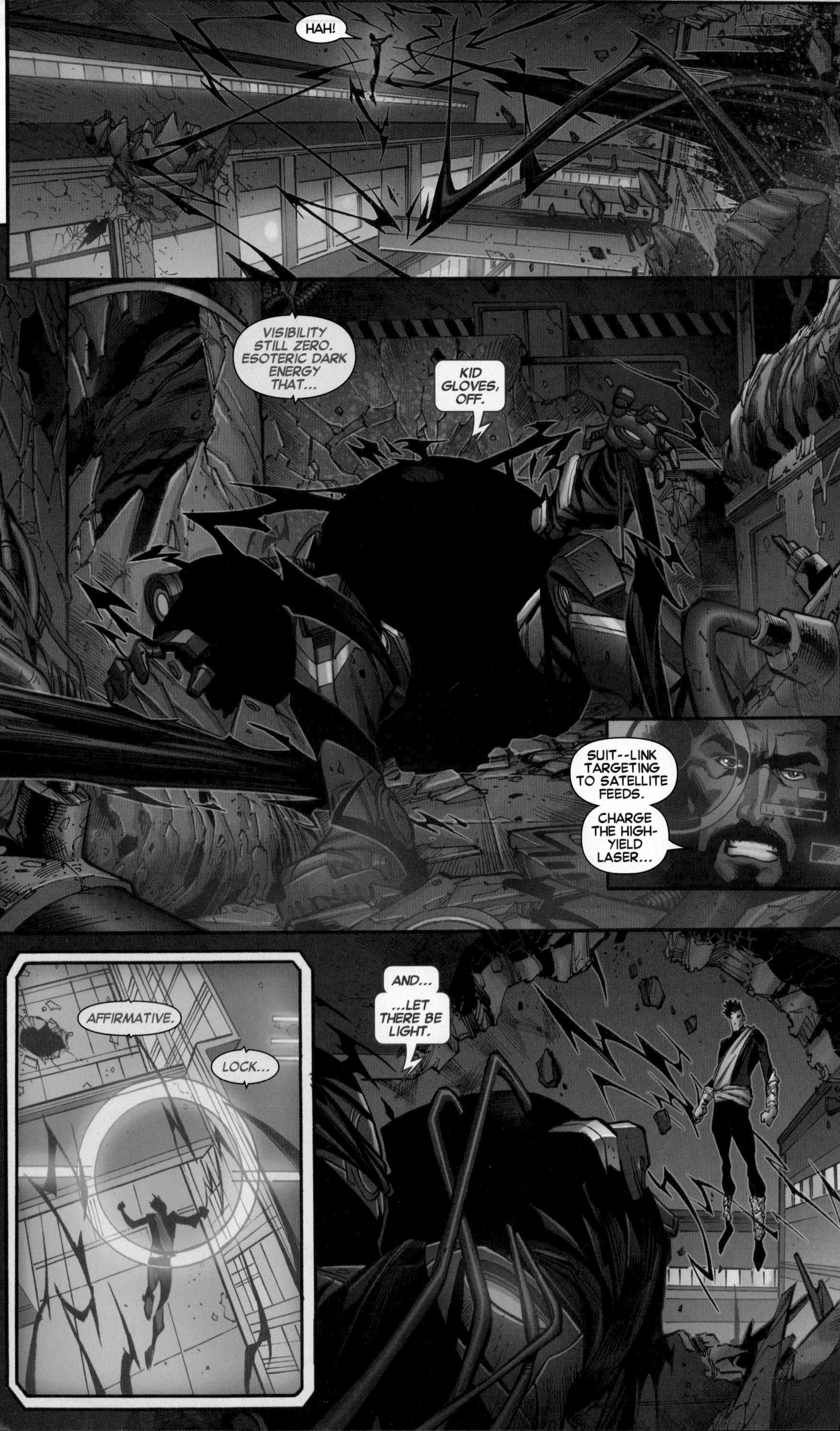

HAH!
VISIBILITY STILL ZERO. ESOTERIC DARK ENERGY THAT...
KID GLOVES, OFF.
SUIT--LINK TARGETING TO SATELLITE FEEDS.
CHARGE THE HIGH-YIELD LASER...
AFFIRMATIVE.
LOCK...
AND...
...LET THERE BE LIGHT.

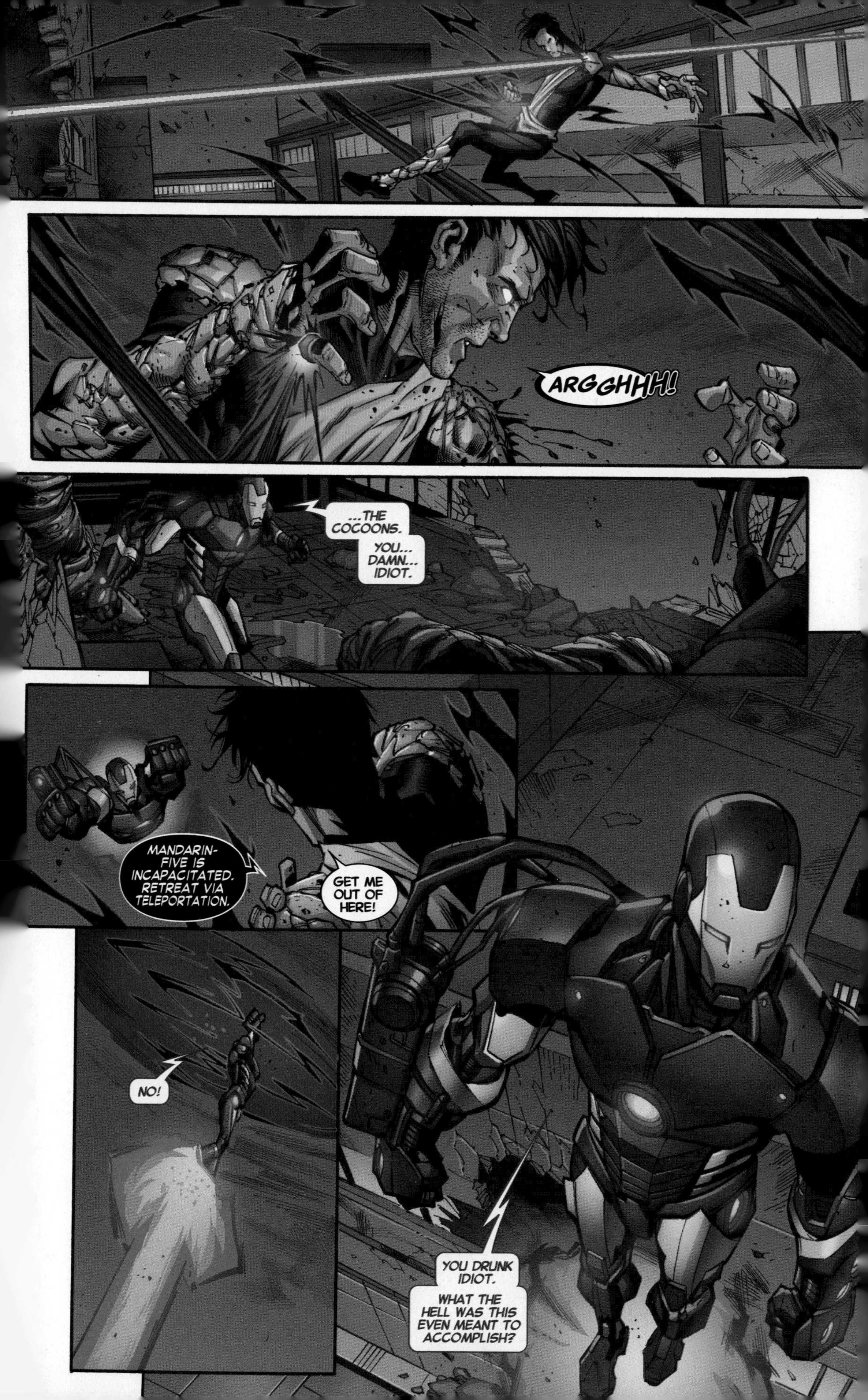
ARGGHHH!
...THE COCOONS.
YOU... DAMN... IDIOT.
MANDARIN-FIVE IS INCAPACITATED. RETREAT VIA TELEPORTATION.
GET ME OUT OF HERE!
NO!
YOU DRUNK IDIOT.
WHAT THE HELL WAS THIS EVEN MEANT TO ACCOMPLISH?

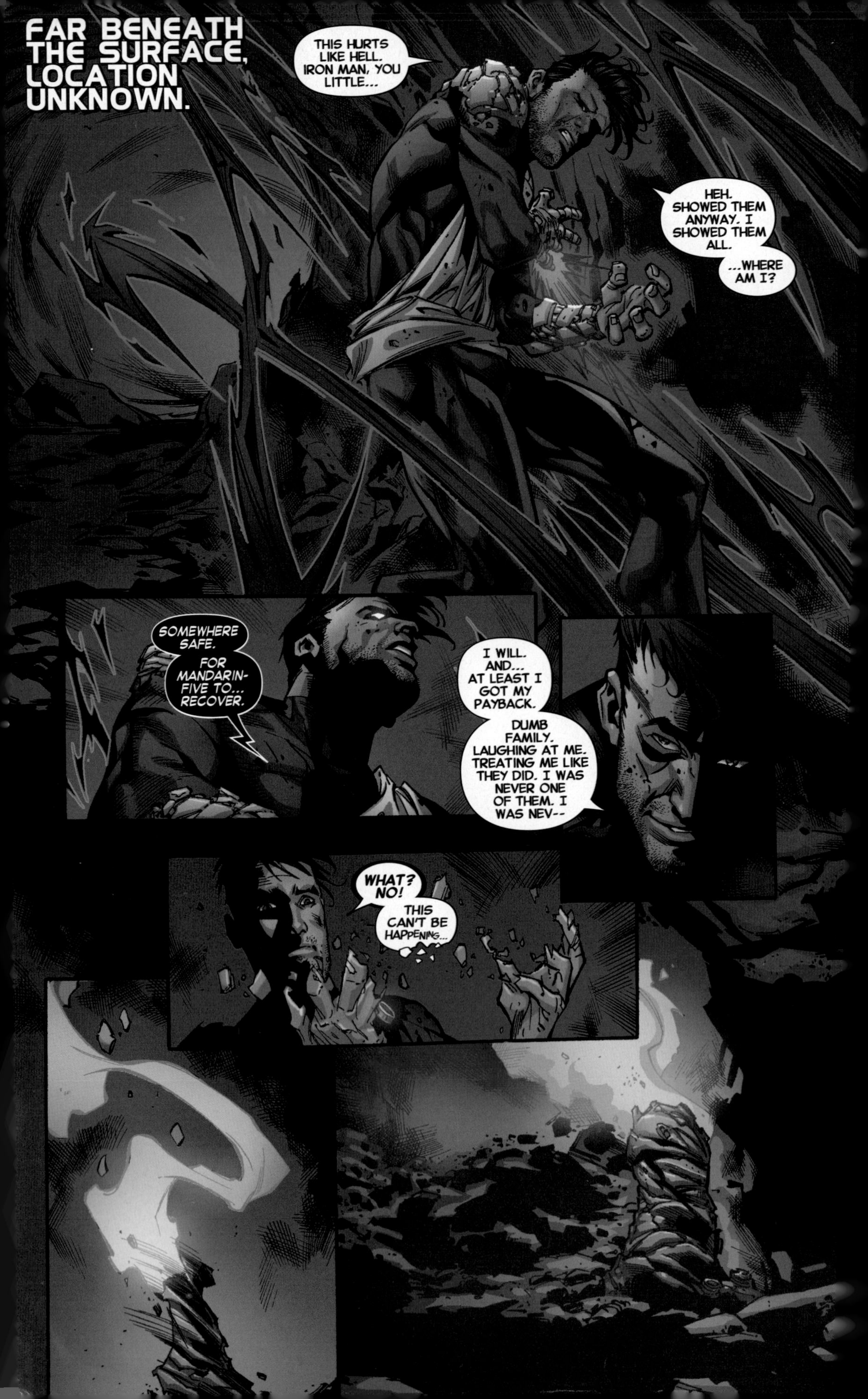
FAR BENEATH THE SURFACE, LOCATION UNKNOWN.
THIS HURTS LIKE HELL. IRON MAN, YOU LITTLE...
HEH. SHOWED THEM ANYWAY. I SHOWED THEM ALL.
...WHERE AM I?
SOMEWHERE SAFE.
FOR MANDARIN-FIVE TO... RECOVER.
I WILL. AND... AT LEAST I GOT MY PAYBACK.
DUMB FAMILY. LAUGHING AT ME. TREATING ME LIKE THEY DID. I WAS NEVER ONE OF THEM. I WAS NEV--
WHAT? NO!
THIS CAN'T BE HAPPENING...

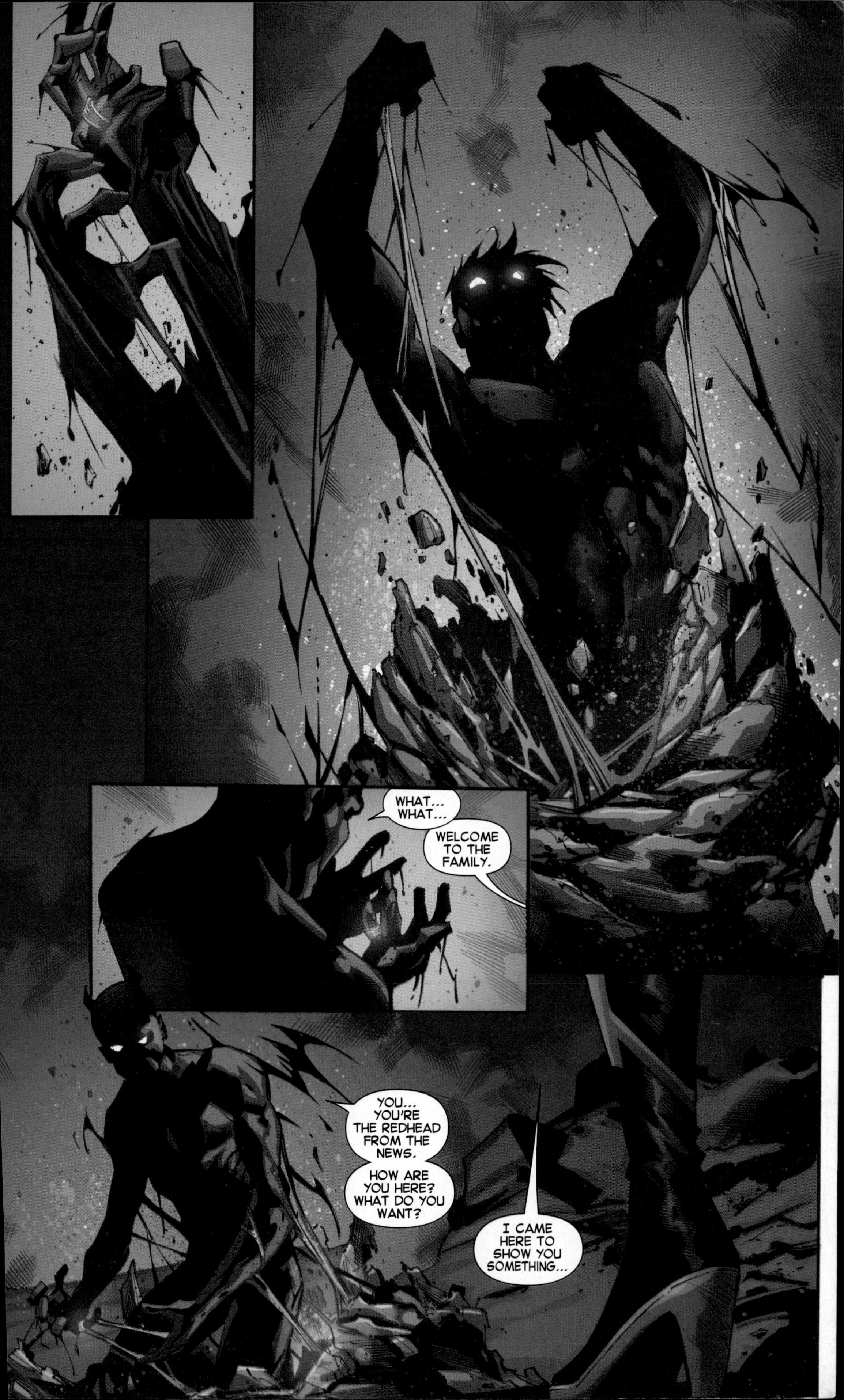
WHAT... WHAT...
WELCOME TO THE FAMILY.
YOU... YOU'RE THE REDHEAD FROM THE NEWS.
HOW ARE YOU HERE? WHAT DO YOU WANT?
I CAME HERE TO SHOW YOU SOMETHING...

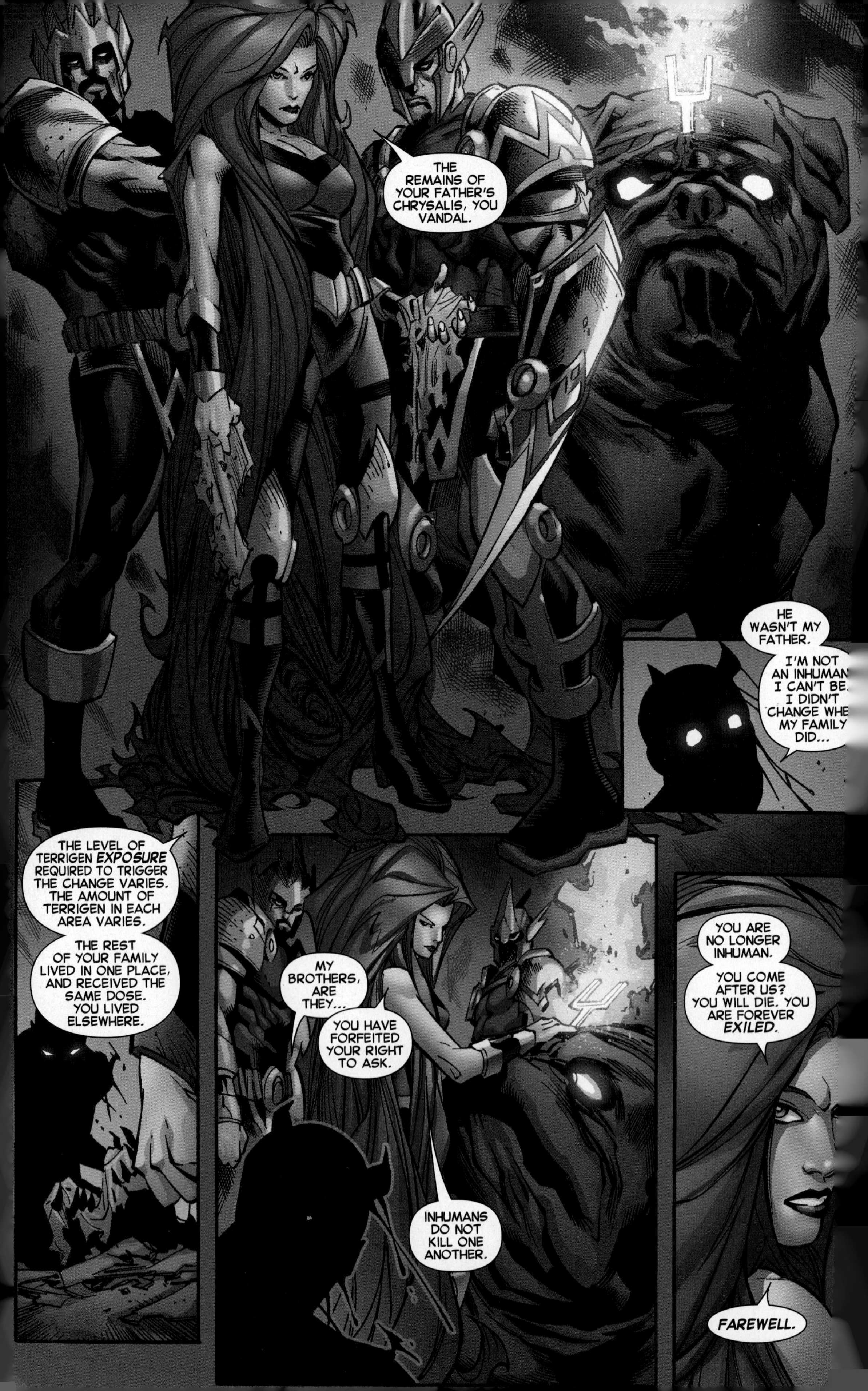
THE REMAINS OF YOUR FATHER'S CHRYSALIS, YOU VANDAL.
HE WASN'T MY FATHER.
I'M NOT AN INHUMAN. I CAN'T BE. I DIDN'T CHANGE WHEN MY FAMILY DID...
THE LEVEL OF TERRIGEN EXPOSURE REQUIRED TO TRIGGER THE CHANGE VARIES. THE AMOUNT OF TERRIGEN IN EACH AREA VARIES.
THE REST OF YOUR FAMILY LIVED IN ONE PLACE, AND RECEIVED THE SAME DOSE. YOU LIVED ELSEWHERE.
MY BROTHERS, ARE THEY...
YOU HAVE FORFEITED YOUR RIGHT TO ASK.
INHUMANS DO NOT KILL ONE ANOTHER.
YOU ARE NO LONGER INHUMAN.
YOU COME AFTER US? YOU WILL DIE. YOU ARE FOREVER EXILED.
FAREWELL.

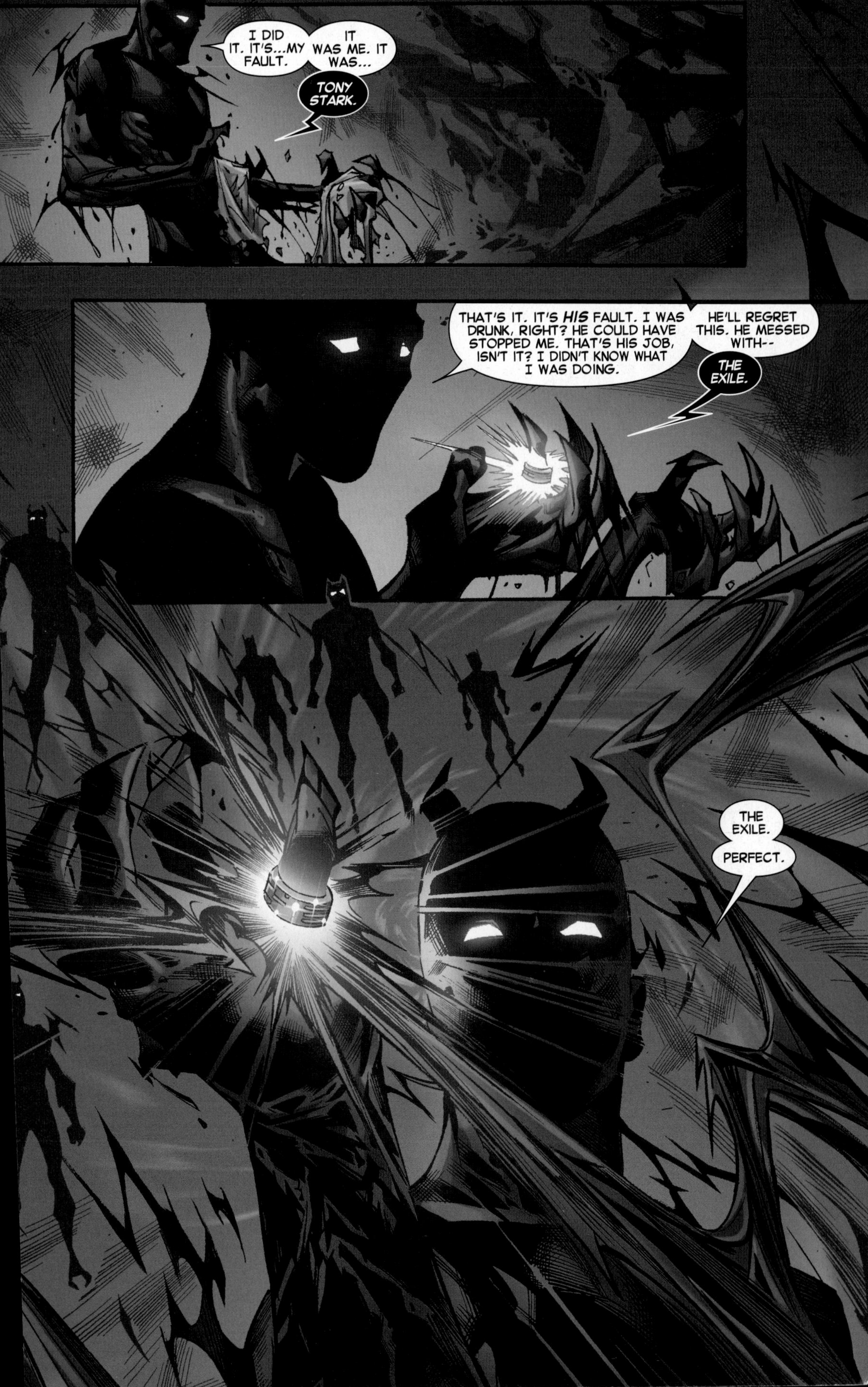
I DID IT. IT'S...MY FAULT.
IT WAS ME. IT WAS...
TONY STARK.
THAT'S IT. IT'S HIS FAULT. I WAS DRUNK, RIGHT? HE COULD HAVE STOPPED ME. THAT'S HIS JOB, ISN'T IT? I DIDN'T KNOW WHAT I WAS DOING.
HE'LL REGRET THIS. HE MESSED WITH--
THE EXILE.
THE EXILE.
PERFECT.

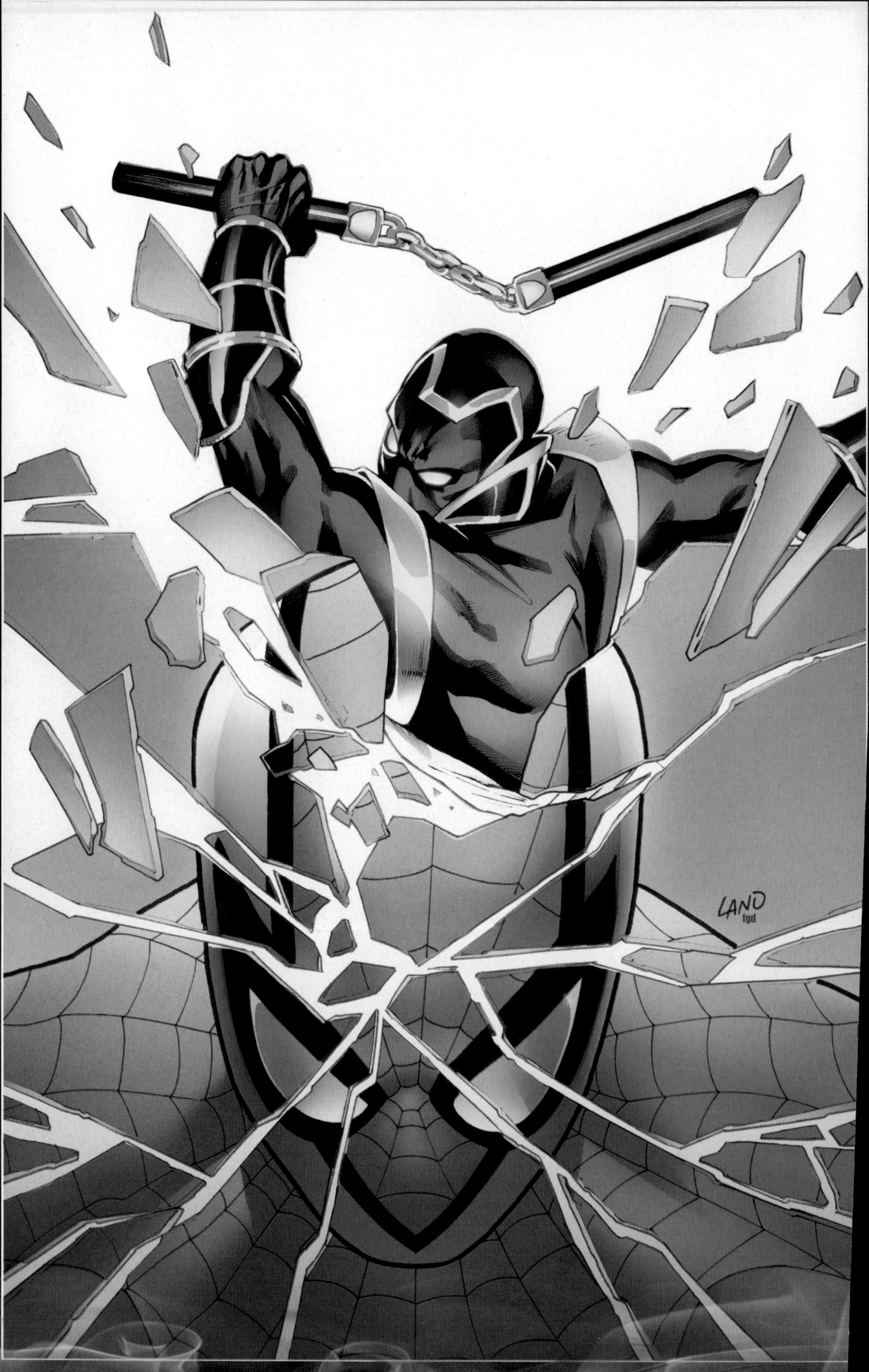

MIGHTY AVENGERS #4

ONLY INHUMAN ON THE INSIDE

During the great battle with Thanos's forces, the Inhuman city of Attilan was destroyed, falling from its place over Manhattan into the Hudson River. In the destruction, the catalyst that causes the Inhumans to manifest their strange powers, known as the Terrigen mist, was released into the atmosphere. As it spread around the world it caused individuals with latent Inhuman genes to be enveloped in a cocoon-like structure and then "hatch" with varying powers.

DAILY 📯 BUGLE®
NEW YORK'S FINEST DAILY NEWSPAPER

December 13, 2013

NEW TEAM LOOKING MIGHTY FINE!

Super hero LUKE CAGE was looking for a few good men and women to reopen his old venture HEROES FOR HIRE after he left the AVENGERS to focus more time on his family. Recruitment turned out easier than expected, when an attack on New York drew the awesome fighting forces of the light-powered Spectrum (a.k.a. Monica Rambeau, a fellow ex-Avenger), the Superior Spider-Man, the Blue Marvel (a.k.a. Adam Brashear), two former Avengers Academy students White Tiger and Power Man, and a colorfully masked vigilante who has thus far only been identified as "Spider Hero." After soundly defeating the monster Shuma-Gorath, the band of champions came together not as heroes for hire, but instead as THE MIGHTY AVENGERS!

—— PHOTO via GREG LAND / Land Press

- ☐ SHARE ▽
- 💾 SAVE
- 🖨 PRINT

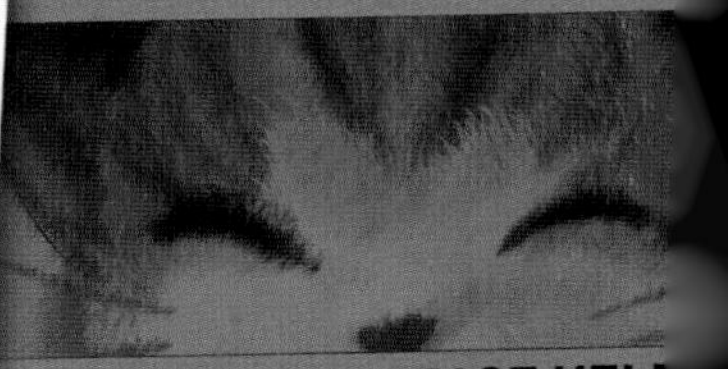

MISSING CAT! PLEASE HELP

The bullpen cat has gone missing under Jacob Thomas's watch! This is the last photograph we were able to capture of the kitten before she ran away. Please contact Deb, Irene, Idette or Manny if you have spotted h...

December 13, 2013 11:59 ...

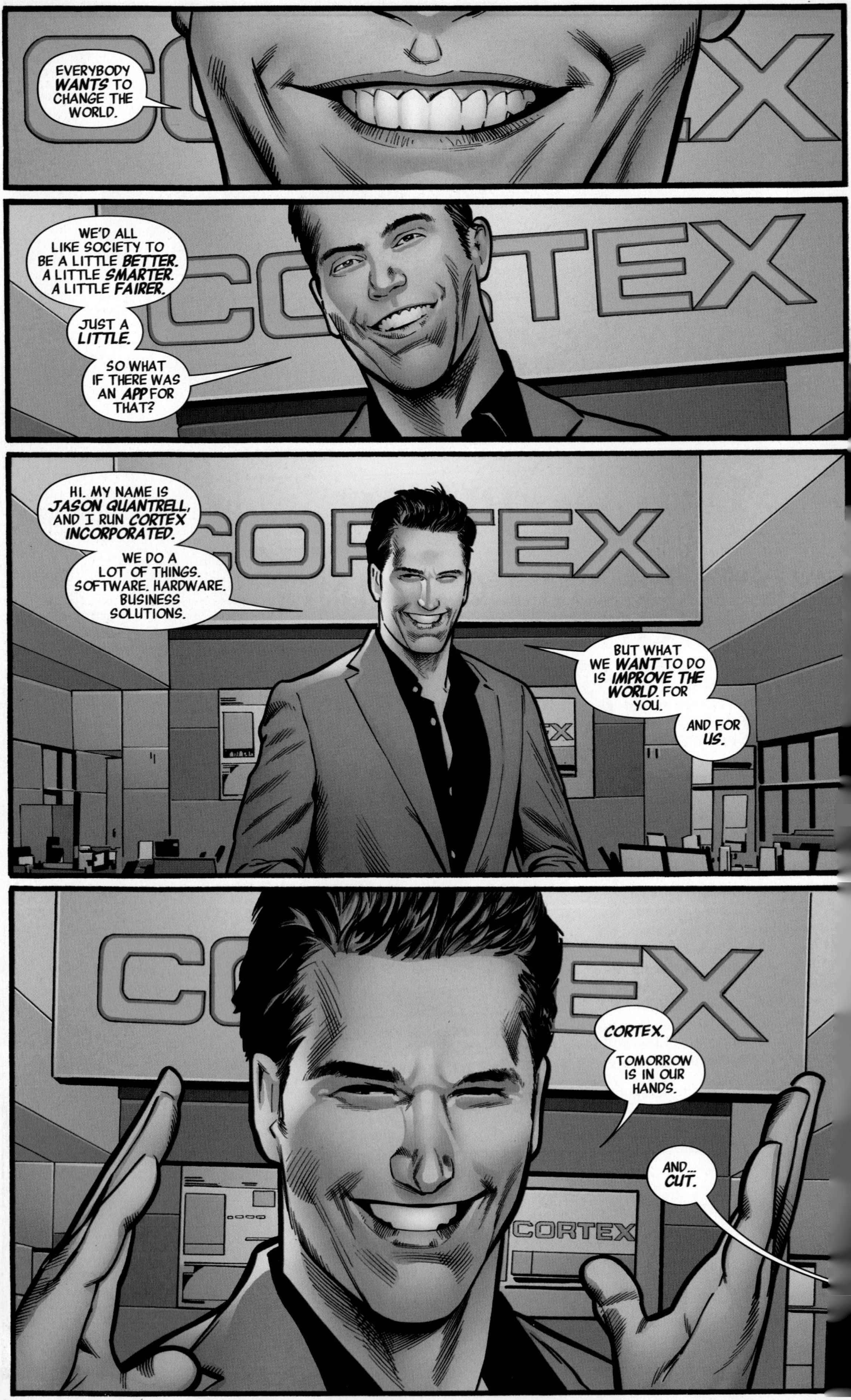
EVERYBODY WANTS TO CHANGE THE WORLD.
CORTEX
WE'D ALL LIKE SOCIETY TO BE A LITTLE BETTER. A LITTLE SMARTER. A LITTLE FAIRER.
JUST A LITTLE.
SO WHAT IF THERE WAS AN APP FOR THAT?
HI. MY NAME IS JASON QUANTRELL, AND I RUN CORTEX INCORPORATED.
WE DO A LOT OF THINGS. SOFTWARE. HARDWARE. BUSINESS SOLUTIONS.
BUT WHAT WE WANT TO DO IS IMPROVE THE WORLD. FOR YOU.
AND FOR US.
CORTEX.
TOMORROW IS IN OUR HANDS.
AND... CUT.
CORTEX

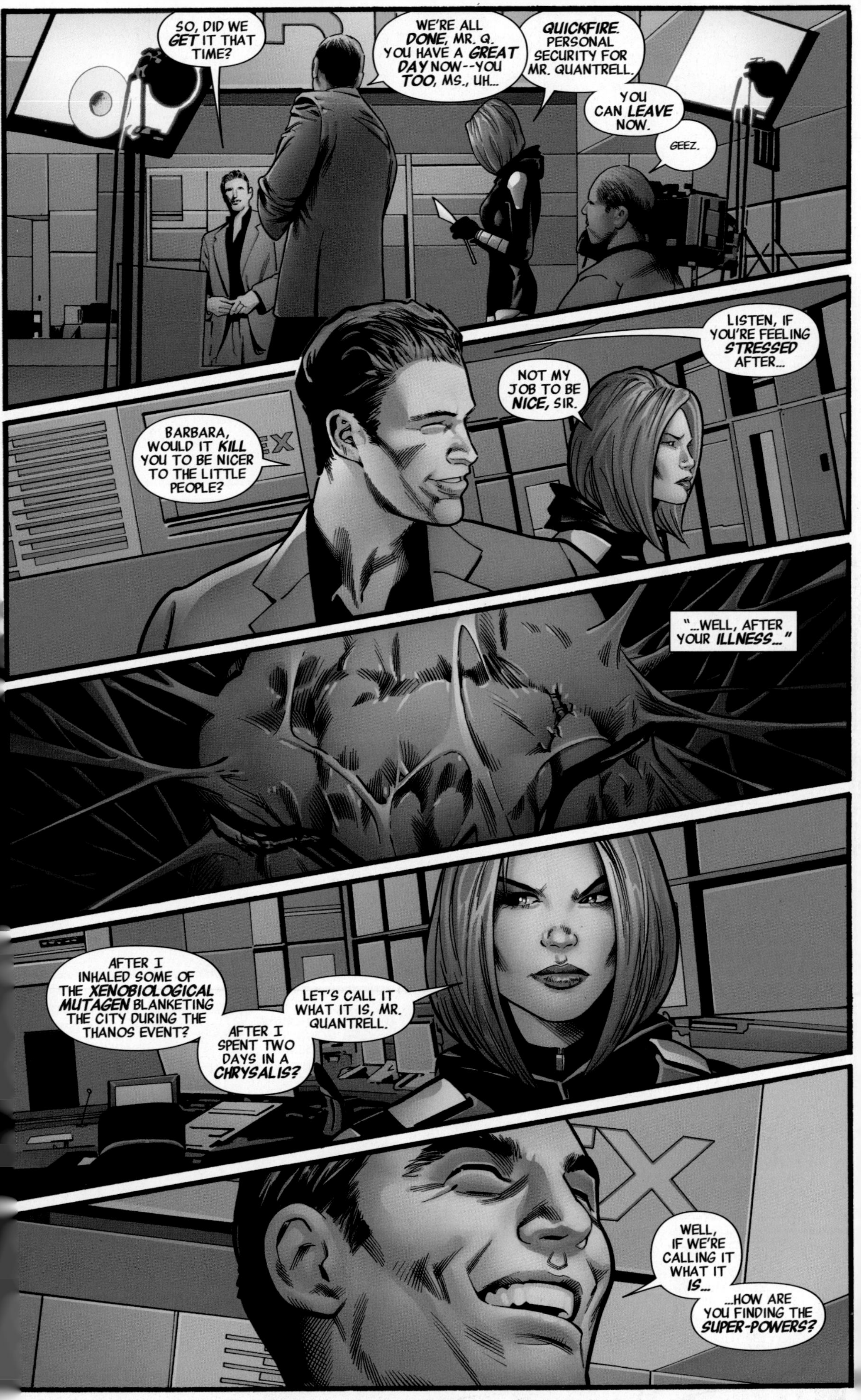
SO, DID WE GET IT THAT TIME?
WE'RE ALL DONE, MR. Q. YOU HAVE A GREAT DAY NOW--YOU TOO, MS., UH...
QUICKFIRE. PERSONAL SECURITY FOR MR. QUANTRELL.
YOU CAN LEAVE NOW.
GEEZ.
BARBARA, WOULD IT KILL YOU TO BE NICER TO THE LITTLE PEOPLE?
NOT MY JOB TO BE NICE, SIR.
LISTEN, IF YOU'RE FEELING STRESSED AFTER...
"...WELL, AFTER YOUR ILLNESS..."
AFTER I INHALED SOME OF THE XENOBIOLOGICAL MUTAGEN BLANKETING THE CITY DURING THE THANOS EVENT?
AFTER I SPENT TWO DAYS IN A CHRYSALIS?
LET'S CALL IT WHAT IT IS, MR. QUANTRELL.
WELL, IF WE'RE CALLING IT WHAT IT IS...
...HOW ARE YOU FINDING THE SUPER-POWERS?

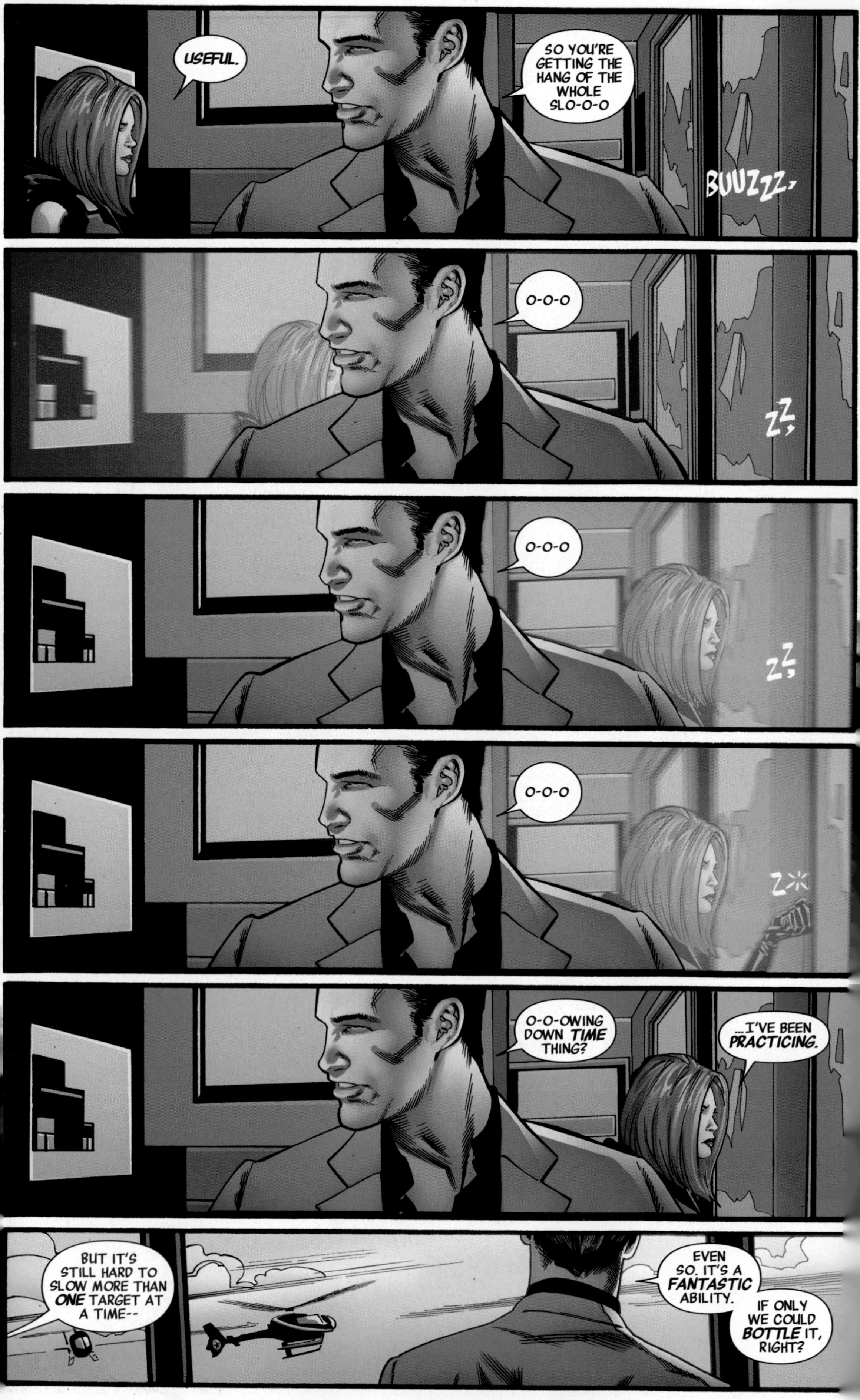
USEFUL.
SO YOU'RE GETTING THE HANG OF THE WHOLE SLO-O-O
BUUZZZ,
O-O-O
ZZ,
O-O-O
ZZ,
O-O-O
O-O-OWING DOWN TIME THING?
...I'VE BEEN PRACTICING.
BUT IT'S STILL HARD TO SLOW MORE THAN ONE TARGET AT A TIME--
EVEN SO. IT'S A FANTASTIC ABILITY.
IF ONLY WE COULD BOTTLE IT, RIGHT?

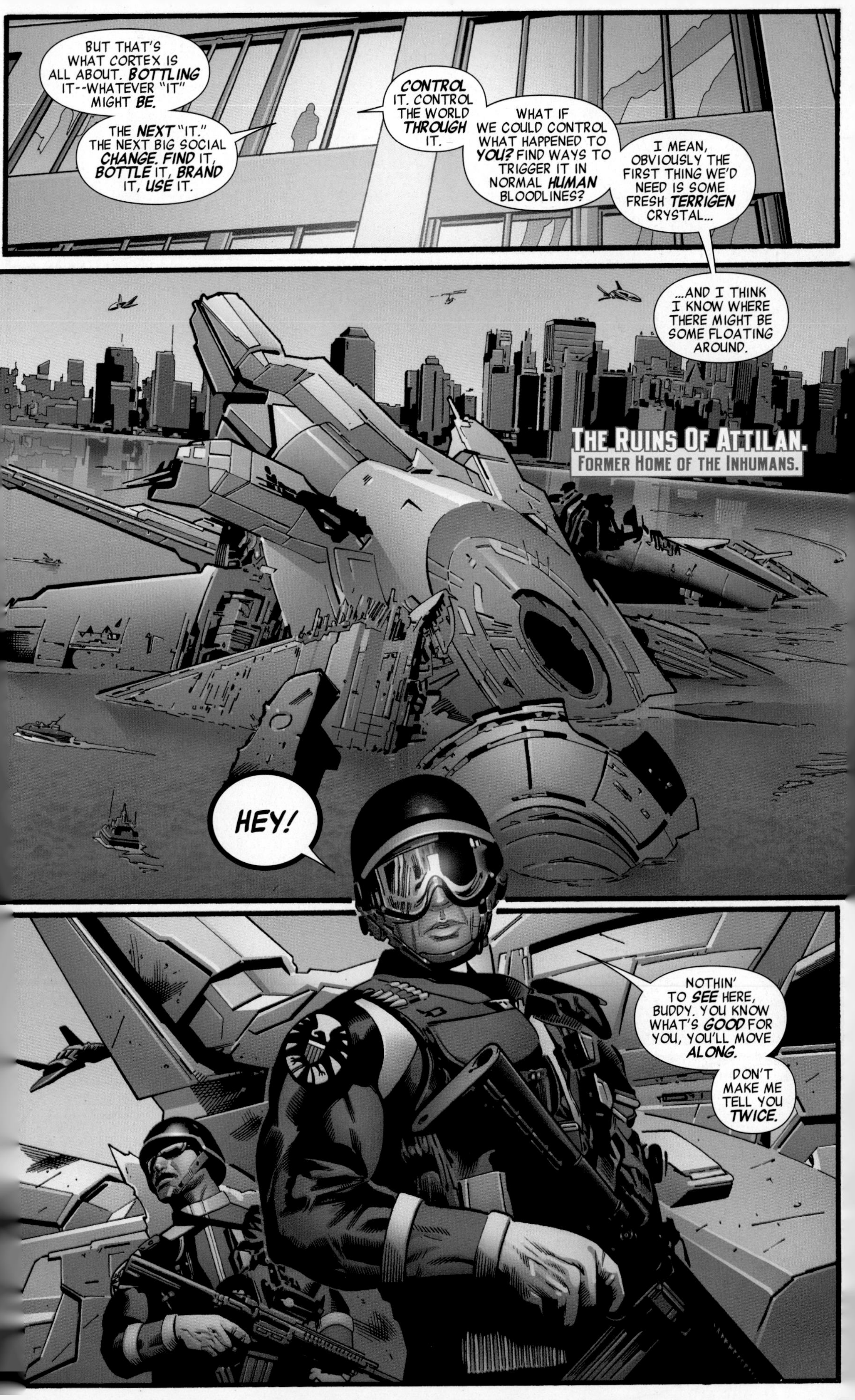
BUT THAT'S WHAT CORTEX IS ALL ABOUT. BOTTLING IT--WHATEVER "IT" MIGHT BE.
THE NEXT "IT." THE NEXT BIG SOCIAL CHANGE. FIND IT, BOTTLE IT, BRAND IT, USE IT.
CONTROL IT. CONTROL THE WORLD THROUGH IT.
WHAT IF WE COULD CONTROL WHAT HAPPENED TO YOU? FIND WAYS TO TRIGGER IT IN NORMAL HUMAN BLOODLINES?
I MEAN, OBVIOUSLY THE FIRST THING WE'D NEED IS SOME FRESH TERRIGEN CRYSTAL...
...AND I THINK I KNOW WHERE THERE MIGHT BE SOME FLOATING AROUND.
THE RUINS OF ATTILAN.
FORMER HOME OF THE INHUMANS.
HEY!
NOTHIN' TO SEE HERE, BUDDY. YOU KNOW WHAT'S GOOD FOR YOU, YOU'LL MOVE ALONG.
DON'T MAKE ME TELL YOU TWICE.

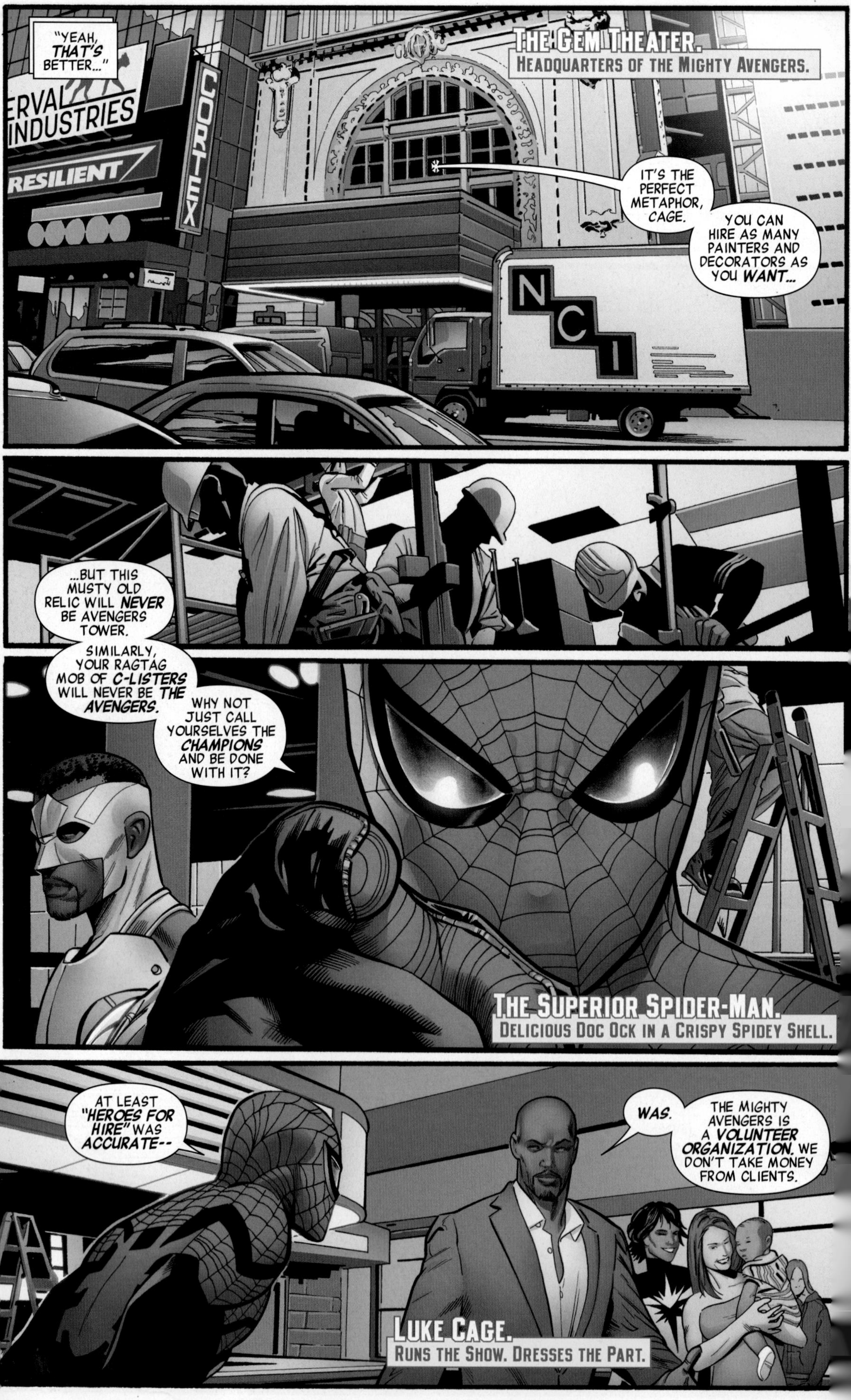

"YEAH, THAT'S BETTER..."
THE GEM THEATER.
HEADQUARTERS OF THE MIGHTY AVENGERS.
ERVAL INDUSTRIES
RESILIENT
CORTEX
IT'S THE PERFECT METAPHOR, CAGE.
YOU CAN HIRE AS MANY PAINTERS AND DECORATORS AS YOU WANT...
NCI
...BUT THIS MUSTY OLD RELIC WILL NEVER BE AVENGERS TOWER.
SIMILARLY, YOUR RAGTAG MOB OF C-LISTERS WILL NEVER BE THE AVENGERS.
WHY NOT JUST CALL YOURSELVES THE CHAMPIONS AND BE DONE WITH IT?
THE SUPERIOR SPIDER-MAN.
DELICIOUS DOC OCK IN A CRISPY SPIDEY SHELL.
AT LEAST "HEROES FOR HIRE" WAS ACCURATE--
WAS.
THE MIGHTY AVENGERS IS A VOLUNTEER ORGANIZATION. WE DON'T TAKE MONEY FROM CLIENTS.
LUKE CAGE.
RUNS THE SHOW. DRESSES THE PART.

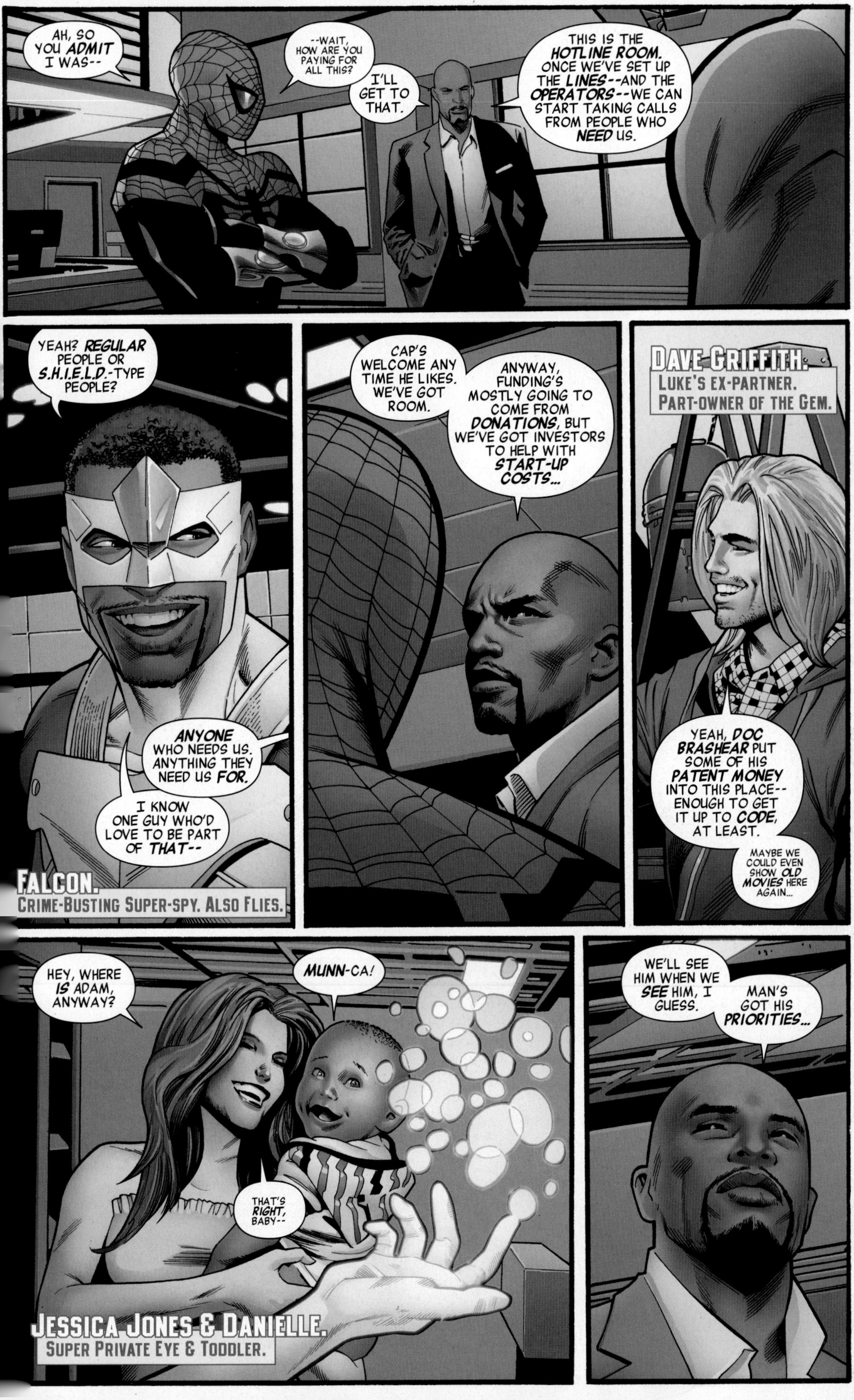

AH, SO YOU ADMIT I WAS--
--WAIT, HOW ARE YOU PAYING FOR ALL THIS?
I'LL GET TO THAT.
THIS IS THE HOTLINE ROOM. ONCE WE'VE SET UP THE LINES--AND THE OPERATORS--WE CAN START TAKING CALLS FROM PEOPLE WHO NEED US.
YEAH? REGULAR PEOPLE OR S.H.I.E.L.D.-TYPE PEOPLE?
ANYONE WHO NEEDS US. ANYTHING THEY NEED US FOR.
I KNOW ONE GUY WHO'D LOVE TO BE PART OF THAT--
FALCON.
CRIME-BUSTING SUPER-SPY. ALSO FLIES.
CAP'S WELCOME ANY TIME HE LIKES. WE'VE GOT ROOM.
ANYWAY, FUNDING'S MOSTLY GOING TO COME FROM DONATIONS, BUT WE'VE GOT INVESTORS TO HELP WITH START-UP COSTS...
DAVE GRIFFITH.
LUKE'S EX-PARTNER. PART-OWNER OF THE GEM.
YEAH, DOC BRASHEAR PUT SOME OF HIS PATENT MONEY INTO THIS PLACE--ENOUGH TO GET IT UP TO CODE, AT LEAST.
MAYBE WE COULD EVEN SHOW OLD MOVIES HERE AGAIN...
HEY, WHERE IS ADAM, ANYWAY?
MUNN-CA!
THAT'S RIGHT, BABY--
JESSICA JONES & DANIELLE.
SUPER PRIVATE EYE & TODDLER.
WE'LL SEE HIM WHEN WE SEE HIM, I GUESS.
MAN'S GOT HIS PRIORITIES...

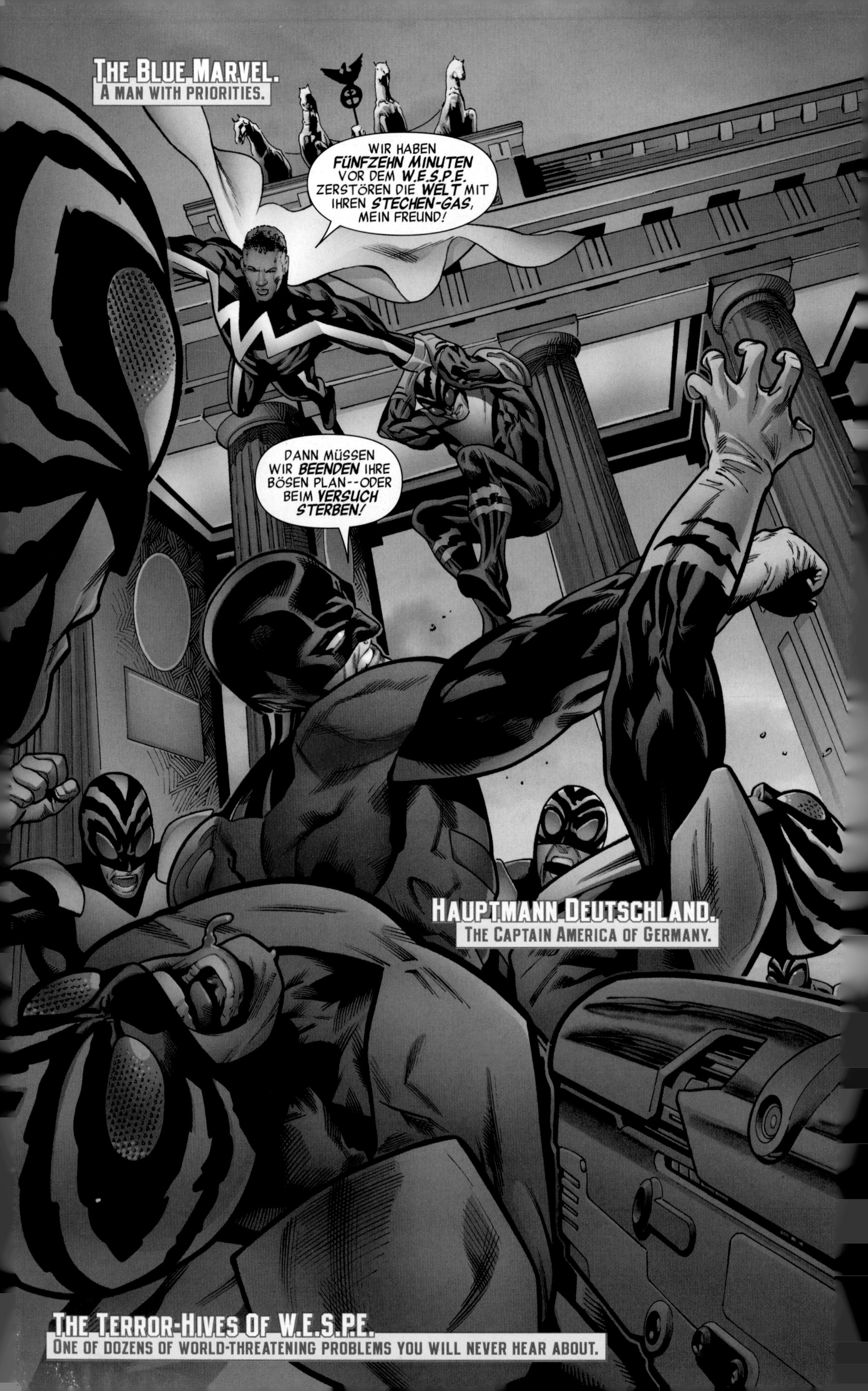
THE BLUE MARVEL.
A MAN WITH PRIORITIES.
WIR HABEN FÜNFZEHN MINUTEN VOR DEM W.E.S.P.E. ZERSTÖREN DIE WELT MIT IHREN STECHEN-GAS, MEIN FREUND!
DANN MÜSSEN WIR BEENDEN IHRE BÖSEN PLAN--ODER BEIM VERSUCH STERBEN!
HAUPTMANN DEUTSCHLAND.
THE CAPTAIN AMERICA OF GERMANY.
THE TERROR-HIVES OF W.E.S.P.E.
ONE OF DOZENS OF WORLD-THREATENING PROBLEMS YOU WILL NEVER HEAR ABOUT.

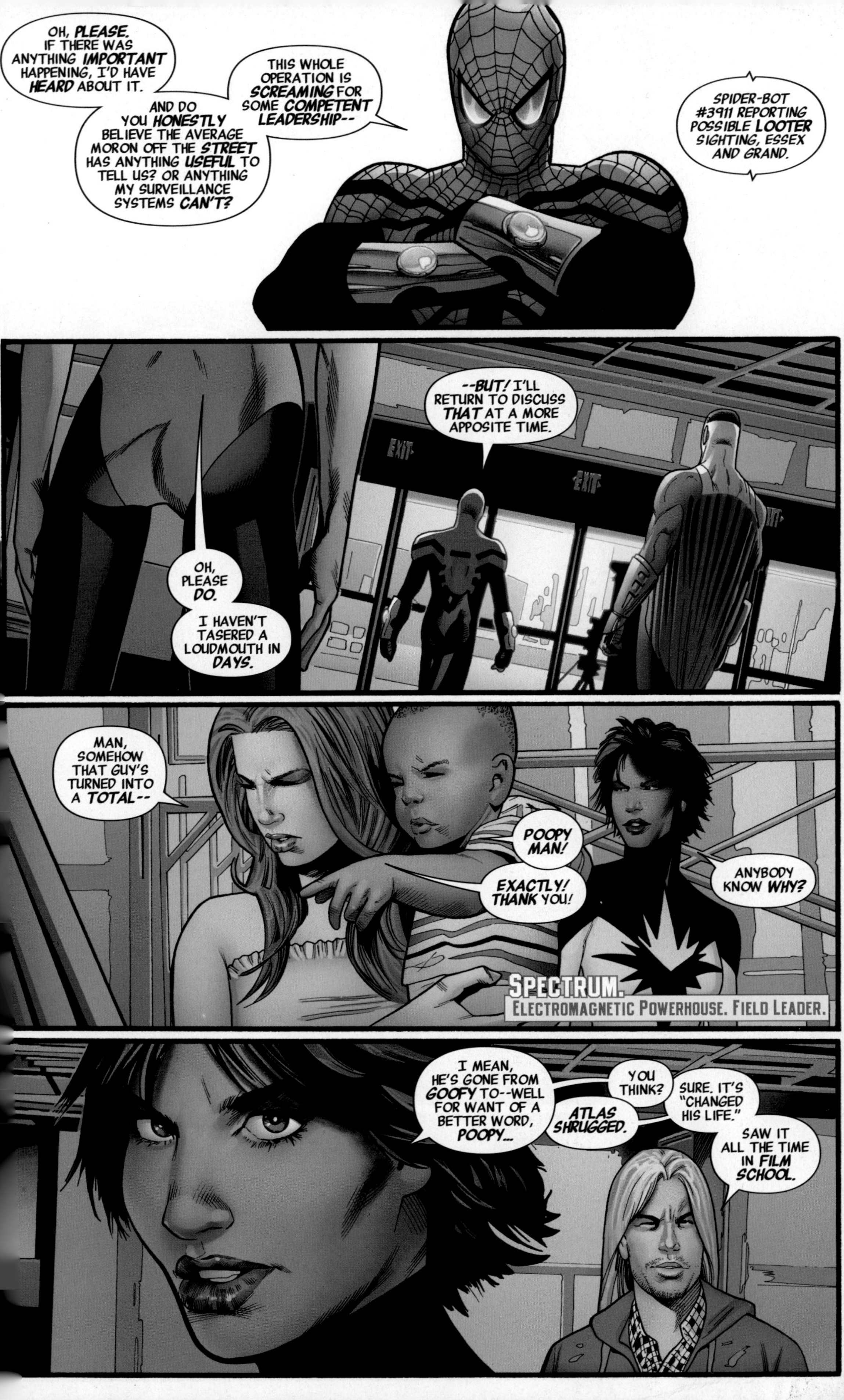
OH, PLEASE. IF THERE WAS ANYTHING IMPORTANT HAPPENING, I'D HAVE HEARD ABOUT IT.
AND DO YOU HONESTLY BELIEVE THE AVERAGE MORON OFF THE STREET HAS ANYTHING USEFUL TO TELL US? OR ANYTHING MY SURVEILLANCE SYSTEMS CAN'T?
THIS WHOLE OPERATION IS SCREAMING FOR SOME COMPETENT LEADERSHIP--
SPIDER-BOT #3911 REPORTING POSSIBLE LOOTER SIGHTING, ESSEX AND GRAND.
--BUT! I'LL RETURN TO DISCUSS THAT AT A MORE APPOSITE TIME.
EXIT
EXIT
OH, PLEASE DO.
I HAVEN'T TASERED A LOUDMOUTH IN DAYS.
MAN, SOMEHOW THAT GUY'S TURNED INTO A TOTAL--
POOPY MAN!
EXACTLY! THANK YOU!
ANYBODY KNOW WHY?
SPECTRUM.
ELECTROMAGNETIC POWERHOUSE. FIELD LEADER.
I MEAN, HE'S GONE FROM GOOFY TO--WELL FOR WANT OF A BETTER WORD, POOPY...
ATLAS SHRUGGED.
YOU THINK?
SURE. IT'S "CHANGED HIS LIFE."
SAW IT ALL THE TIME IN FILM SCHOOL.

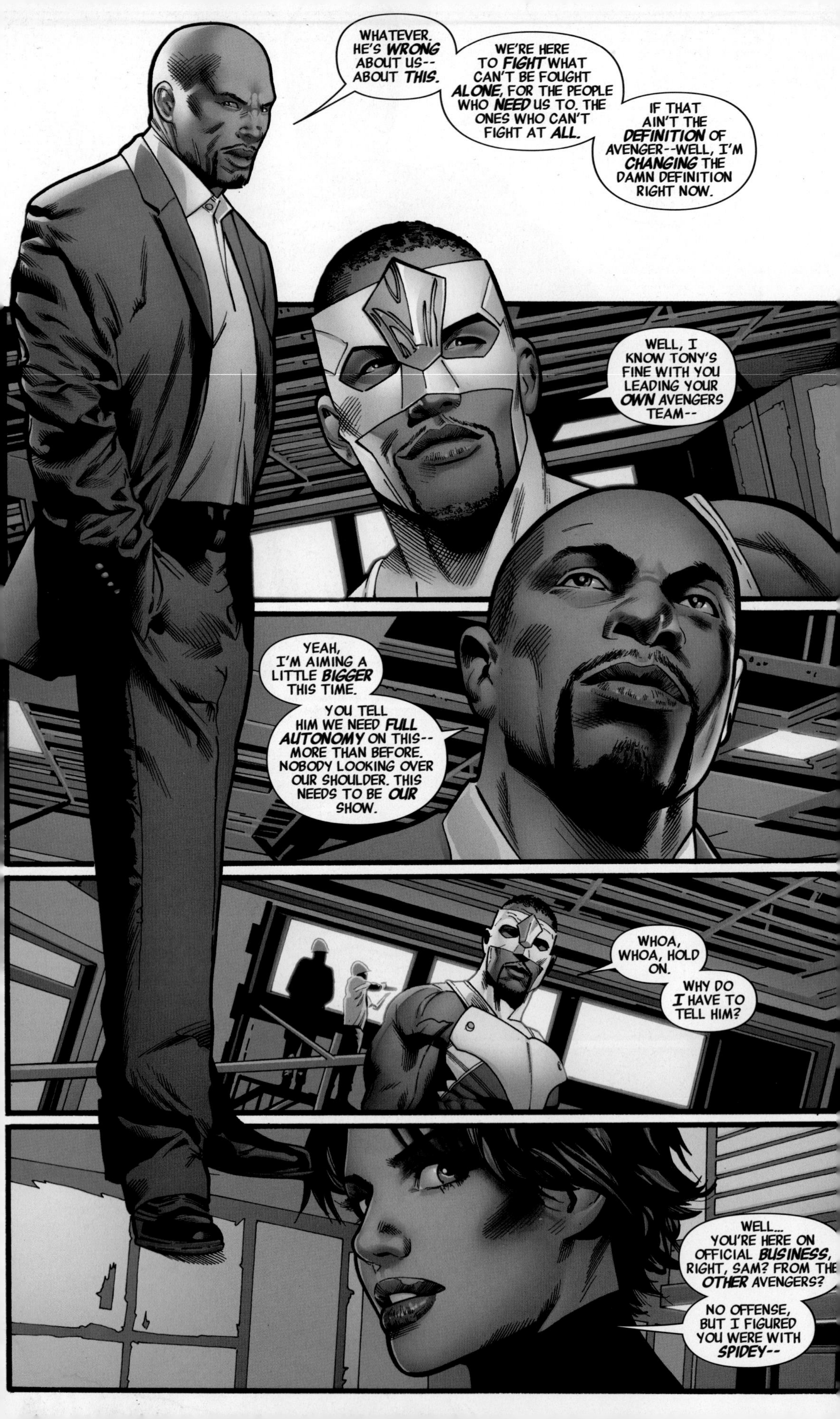
WHATEVER. HE'S WRONG ABOUT US-- ABOUT THIS.
WE'RE HERE TO FIGHT WHAT CAN'T BE FOUGHT ALONE, FOR THE PEOPLE WHO NEED US TO. THE ONES WHO CAN'T FIGHT AT ALL.
IF THAT AIN'T THE DEFINITION OF AVENGER--WELL, I'M CHANGING THE DAMN DEFINITION RIGHT NOW.
WELL, I KNOW TONY'S FINE WITH YOU LEADING YOUR OWN AVENGERS TEAM--
YEAH, I'M AIMING A LITTLE BIGGER THIS TIME.
YOU TELL HIM WE NEED FULL AUTONOMY ON THIS-- MORE THAN BEFORE. NOBODY LOOKING OVER OUR SHOULDER. THIS NEEDS TO BE OUR SHOW.
WHOA, WHOA, HOLD ON.
WHY DO I HAVE TO TELL HIM?
WELL... YOU'RE HERE ON OFFICIAL BUSINESS, RIGHT, SAM? FROM THE OTHER AVENGERS?
NO OFFENSE, BUT I FIGURED YOU WERE WITH SPIDEY--

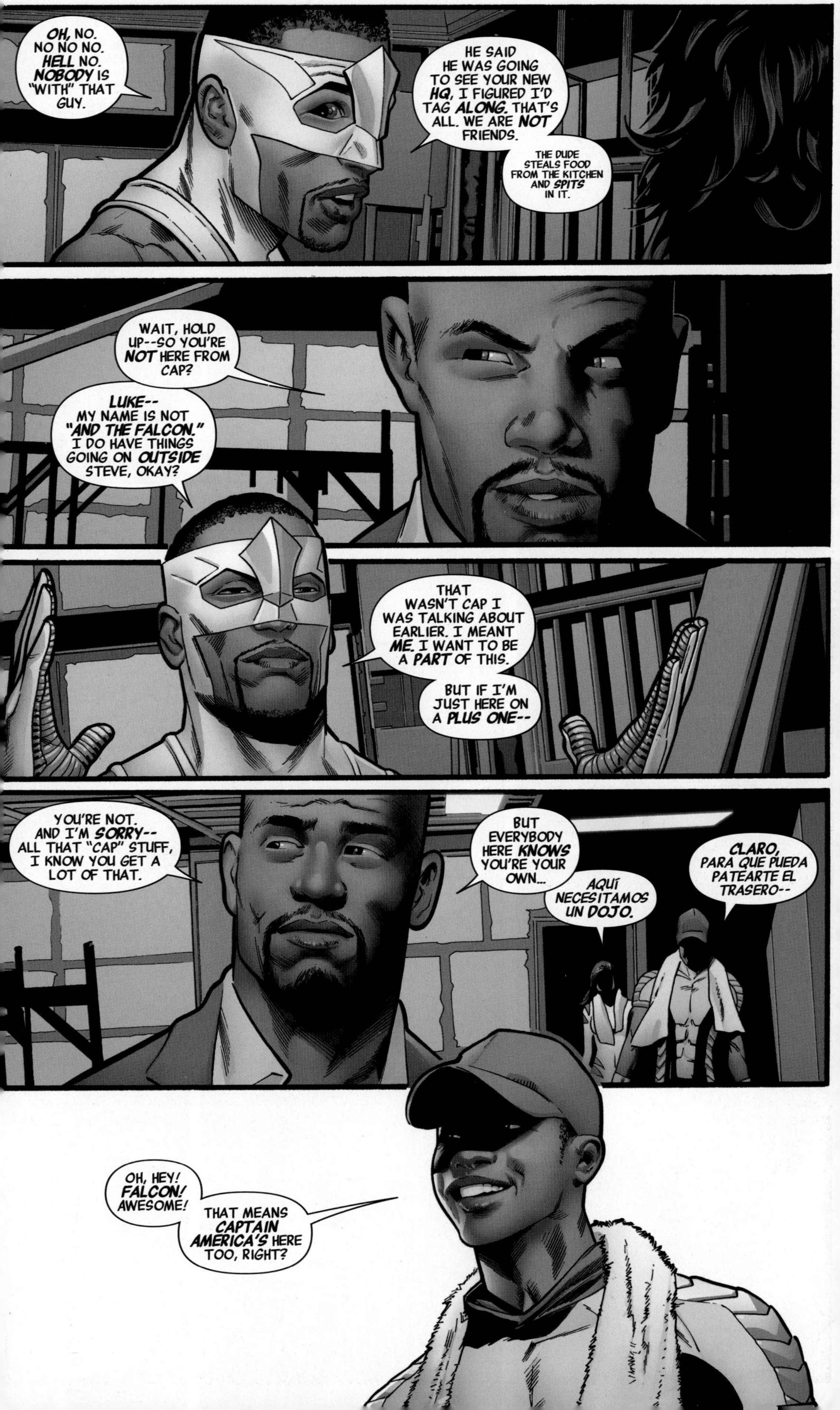
OH, NO. NO NO NO. HELL NO. NOBODY IS "WITH" THAT GUY.
HE SAID HE WAS GOING TO SEE YOUR NEW HQ, I FIGURED I'D TAG ALONG. THAT'S ALL. WE ARE NOT FRIENDS.
THE DUDE STEALS FOOD FROM THE KITCHEN AND SPITS IN IT.
WAIT, HOLD UP--SO YOU'RE NOT HERE FROM CAP?
LUKE-- MY NAME IS NOT "AND THE FALCON." I DO HAVE THINGS GOING ON OUTSIDE STEVE, OKAY?
THAT WASN'T CAP I WAS TALKING ABOUT EARLIER. I MEANT ME. I WANT TO BE A PART OF THIS.
BUT IF I'M JUST HERE ON A PLUS ONE--
YOU'RE NOT. AND I'M SORRY-- ALL THAT "CAP" STUFF, I KNOW YOU GET A LOT OF THAT.
BUT EVERYBODY HERE KNOWS YOU'RE YOUR OWN...
AQUÍ NECESITAMOS UN DOJO.
CLARO, PARA QUE PUEDA PATEARTE EL TRASERO--
OH, HEY! FALCON! AWESOME!
THAT MEANS CAPTAIN AMERICA'S HERE TOO, RIGHT?

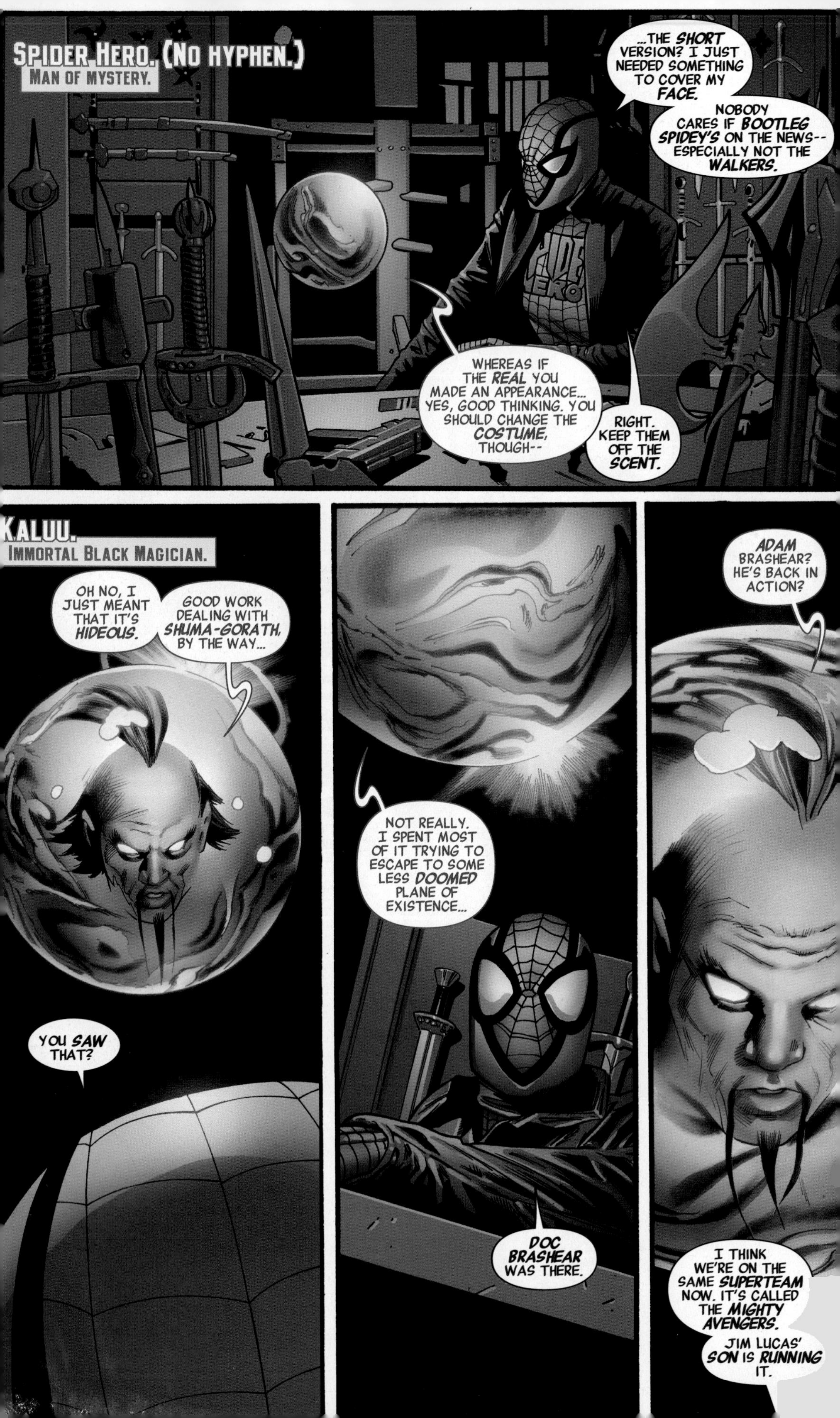
SPIDER HERO. (NO HYPHEN.)
MAN OF MYSTERY.
...THE SHORT VERSION? I JUST NEEDED SOMETHING TO COVER MY FACE.
NOBODY CARES IF BOOTLEG SPIDEY'S ON THE NEWS-- ESPECIALLY NOT THE WALKERS.
WHEREAS IF THE REAL YOU MADE AN APPEARANCE... YES, GOOD THINKING. YOU SHOULD CHANGE THE COSTUME, THOUGH--
RIGHT. KEEP THEM OFF THE SCENT.
KALUU.
IMMORTAL BLACK MAGICIAN.
OH NO, I JUST MEANT THAT IT'S HIDEOUS.
GOOD WORK DEALING WITH SHUMA-GORATH, BY THE WAY...
YOU SAW THAT?
NOT REALLY. I SPENT MOST OF IT TRYING TO ESCAPE TO SOME LESS DOOMED PLANE OF EXISTENCE...
DOC BRASHEAR WAS THERE.
ADAM BRASHEAR? HE'S BACK IN ACTION?
I THINK WE'RE ON THE SAME SUPERTEAM NOW. IT'S CALLED THE MIGHTY AVENGERS.
JIM LUCAS' SON IS RUNNING IT.

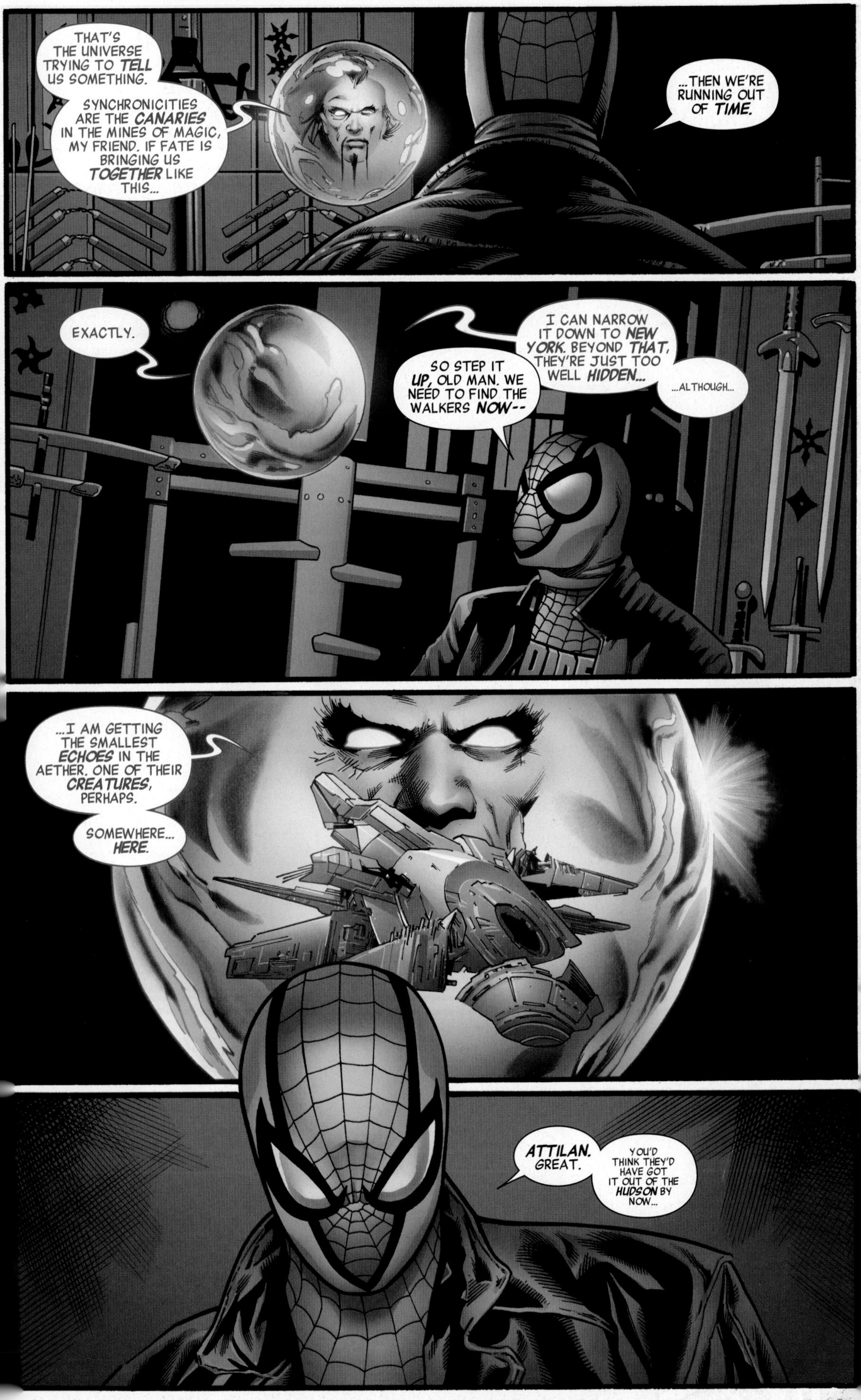
THAT'S THE UNIVERSE TRYING TO TELL US SOMETHING.
SYNCHRONICITIES ARE THE CANARIES IN THE MINES OF MAGIC, MY FRIEND. IF FATE IS BRINGING US TOGETHER LIKE THIS...
...THEN WE'RE RUNNING OUT OF TIME.
EXACTLY.
SO STEP IT UP, OLD MAN. WE NEED TO FIND THE WALKERS NOW--
I CAN NARROW IT DOWN TO NEW YORK. BEYOND THAT, THEY'RE JUST TOO WELL HIDDEN...
...ALTHOUGH...
...I AM GETTING THE SMALLEST ECHOES IN THE AETHER. ONE OF THEIR CREATURES, PERHAPS.
SOMEWHERE... HERE.
ATTILAN. GREAT.
YOU'D THINK THEY'D HAVE GOT IT OUT OF THE HUDSON BY NOW...

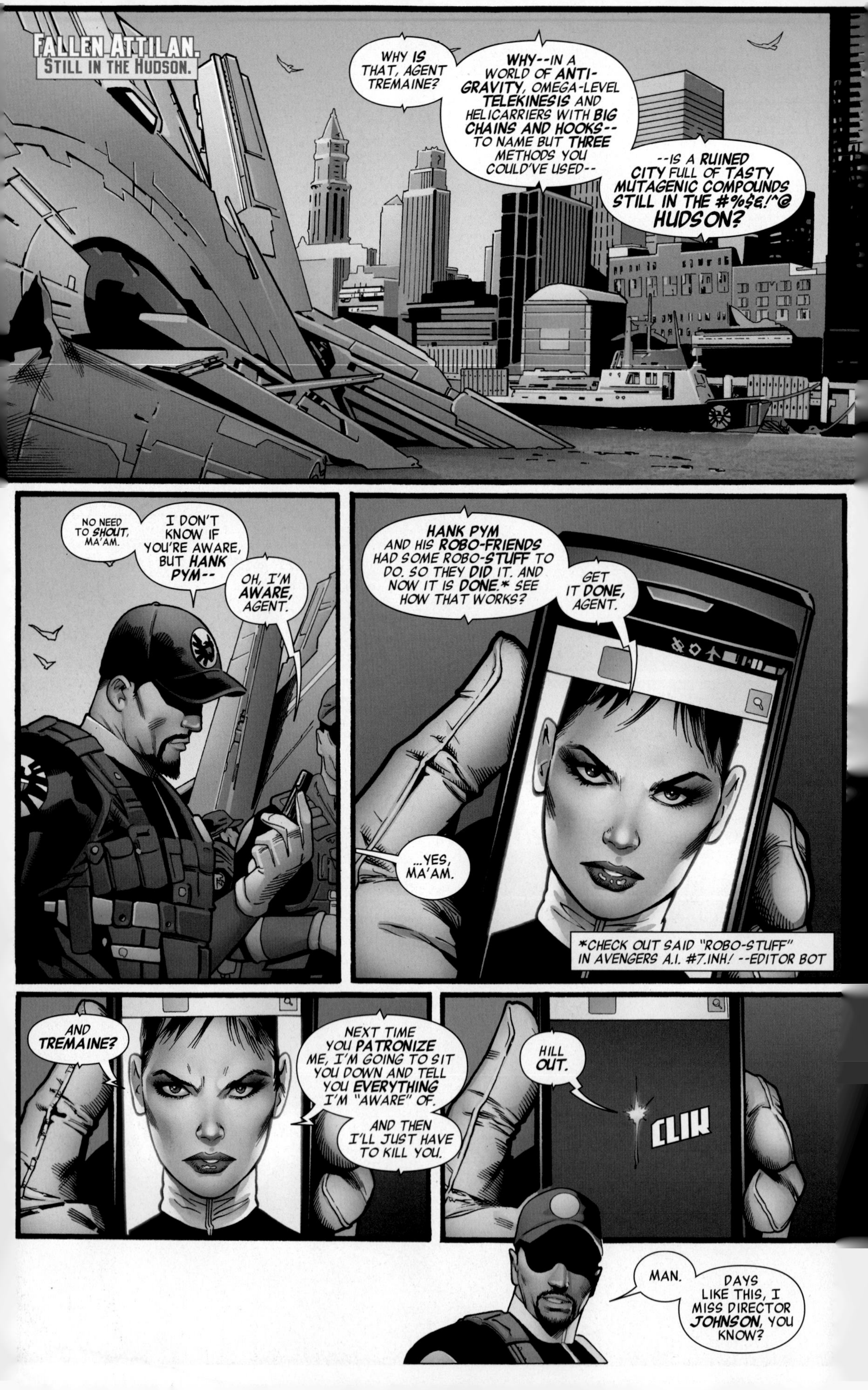
FALLEN ATTILAN.
STILL IN THE HUDSON.
WHY IS THAT, AGENT TREMAINE?
WHY--IN A WORLD OF ANTI-GRAVITY, OMEGA-LEVEL TELEKINESIS AND HELICARRIERS WITH BIG CHAINS AND HOOKS--TO NAME BUT THREE METHODS YOU COULD'VE USED--
--IS A RUINED CITY FULL OF TASTY MUTAGENIC COMPOUNDS STILL IN THE #%$&!^@ HUDSON?
NO NEED TO SHOUT, MA'AM.
I DON'T KNOW IF YOU'RE AWARE, BUT HANK PYM--
OH, I'M AWARE, AGENT.
HANK PYM AND HIS ROBO-FRIENDS HAD SOME ROBO-STUFF TO DO. SO THEY DID IT. AND NOW IT IS DONE.* SEE HOW THAT WORKS?
GET IT DONE, AGENT.
...YES, MA'AM.
*CHECK OUT SAID "ROBO-STUFF" IN AVENGERS A.I. #7.INH! --EDITOR BOT
AND TREMAINE?
NEXT TIME YOU PATRONIZE ME, I'M GOING TO SIT YOU DOWN AND TELL YOU EVERYTHING I'M "AWARE" OF.
AND THEN I'LL JUST HAVE TO KILL YOU.
HILL OUT.
CLIK
MAN.
DAYS LIKE THIS, I MISS DIRECTOR JOHNSON, YOU KNOW?

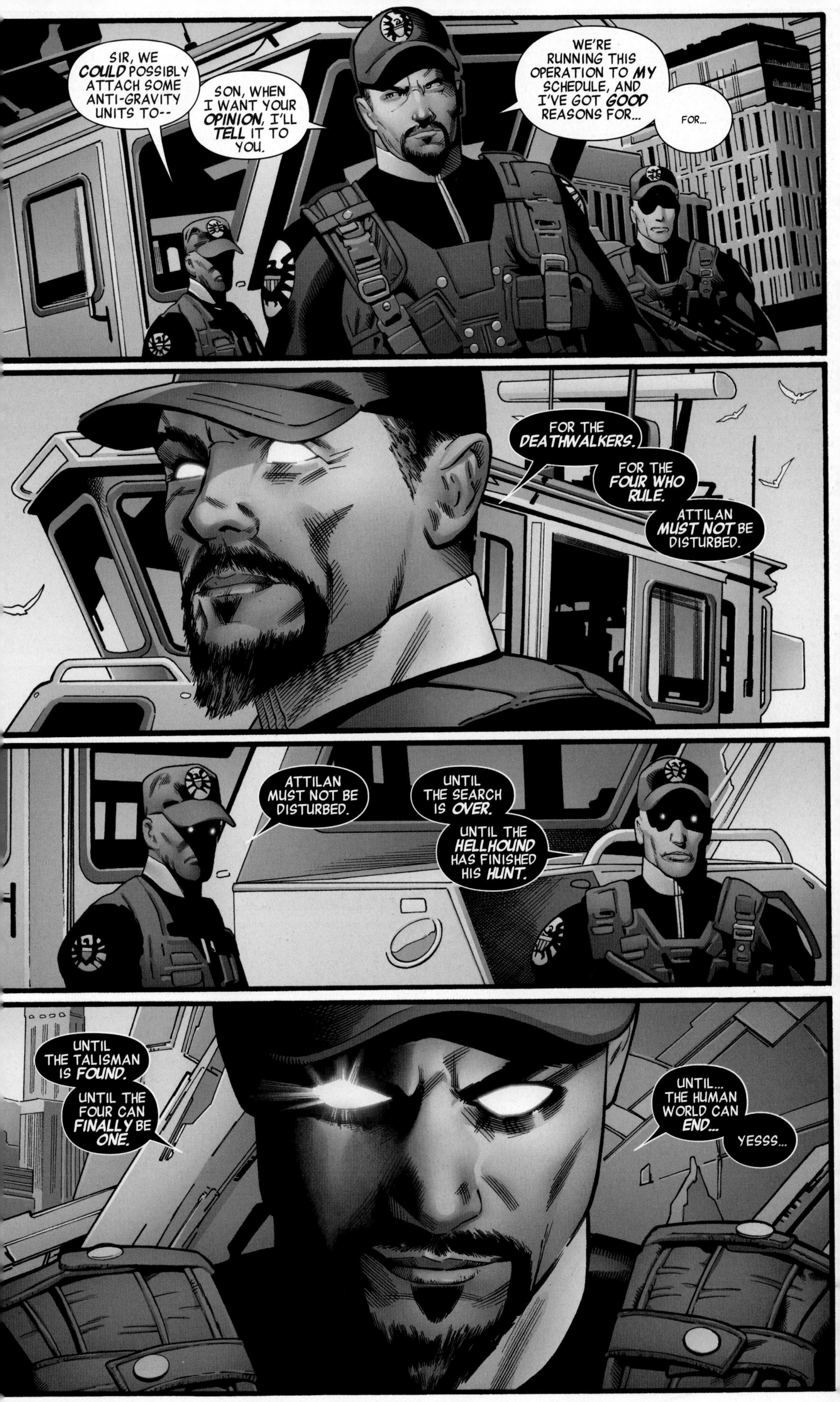
SIR, WE COULD POSSIBLY ATTACH SOME ANTI-GRAVITY UNITS TO--
SON, WHEN I WANT YOUR OPINION, I'LL TELL IT TO YOU.
WE'RE RUNNING THIS OPERATION TO MY SCHEDULE, AND I'VE GOT GOOD REASONS FOR...
FOR...
FOR THE DEATHWALKERS.
FOR THE FOUR WHO RULE.
ATTILAN MUST NOT BE DISTURBED.
ATTILAN MUST NOT BE DISTURBED.
UNTIL THE SEARCH IS OVER.
UNTIL THE HELLHOUND HAS FINISHED HIS HUNT.
UNTIL THE TALISMAN IS FOUND.
UNTIL THE FOUR CAN FINALLY BE ONE.
UNTIL... THE HUMAN WORLD CAN END...
YESSS...

IT WASN'T THE END OF THE WORLD.

IT WAS A SHOCK, BUT IT COULD HAVE BEEN WORSE.

BARBARA McDEVITT HAD READ THE REPORTS. THE MOB BOSS WHO TURNED PURPLE AND SPIKY. THE GIRL WHO BECAME ELECTRICITY AND WENT INSANE.

AND THEN THERE WERE THE ONES STILL TRAPPED IN THEIR COCOONS. STILL MUTATING.

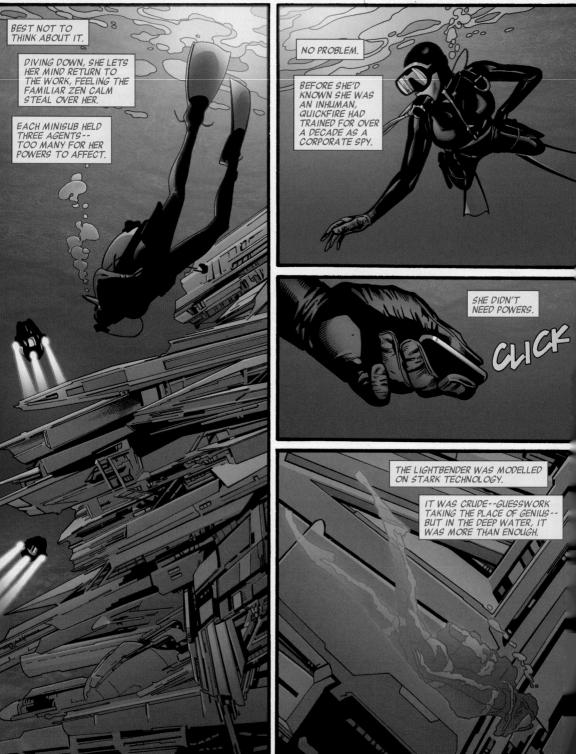

BEST NOT TO THINK ABOUT IT.

DIVING DOWN, SHE LETS HER MIND RETURN TO THE WORK, FEELING THE FAMILIAR ZEN CALM STEAL OVER HER.

EACH MINISUB HELD THREE AGENTS-- TOO MANY FOR HER POWERS TO AFFECT.

NO PROBLEM.

BEFORE SHE'D KNOWN SHE WAS AN INHUMAN, QUICKFIRE HAD TRAINED FOR OVER A DECADE AS A CORPORATE SPY.

SHE DIDN'T NEED POWERS.

CLICK

THE LIGHTBENDER WAS MODELLED ON STARK TECHNOLOGY.

IT WAS CRUDE--GUESSWORK TAKING THE PLACE OF GENIUS-- BUT IN THE DEEP WATER, IT WAS MORE THAN ENOUGH.

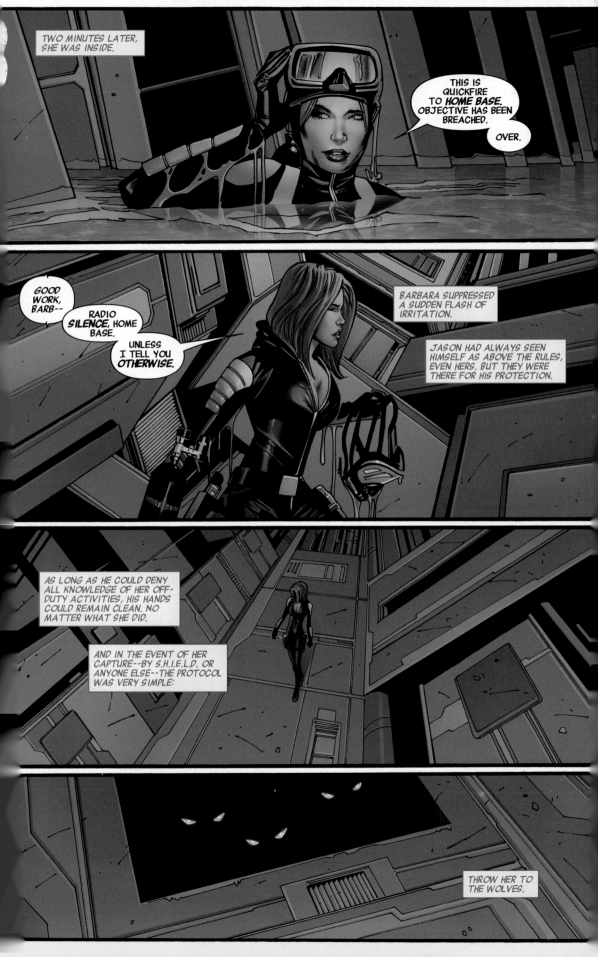

TWO MINUTES LATER, SHE WAS INSIDE.

THIS IS *QUICKFIRE* TO *HOME BASE*. OBJECTIVE HAS BEEN BREACHED.

OVER.

GOOD WORK, BARB--

RADIO *SILENCE*, HOME BASE.

UNLESS I TELL YOU *OTHERWISE*.

BARBARA SUPPRESSED A SUDDEN FLASH OF IRRITATION.

JASON HAD ALWAYS SEEN HIMSELF AS ABOVE THE RULES, EVEN HERS. BUT THEY WERE THERE FOR HIS PROTECTION.

AS LONG AS HE COULD DENY ALL KNOWLEDGE OF HER OFF-DUTY ACTIVITIES, HIS HANDS COULD REMAIN CLEAN. NO MATTER WHAT SHE DID.

AND IN THE EVENT OF HER CAPTURE--BY S.H.I.E.L.D. OR ANYONE ELSE--THE PROTOCOL WAS VERY SIMPLE:

THROW HER TO THE WOLVES.

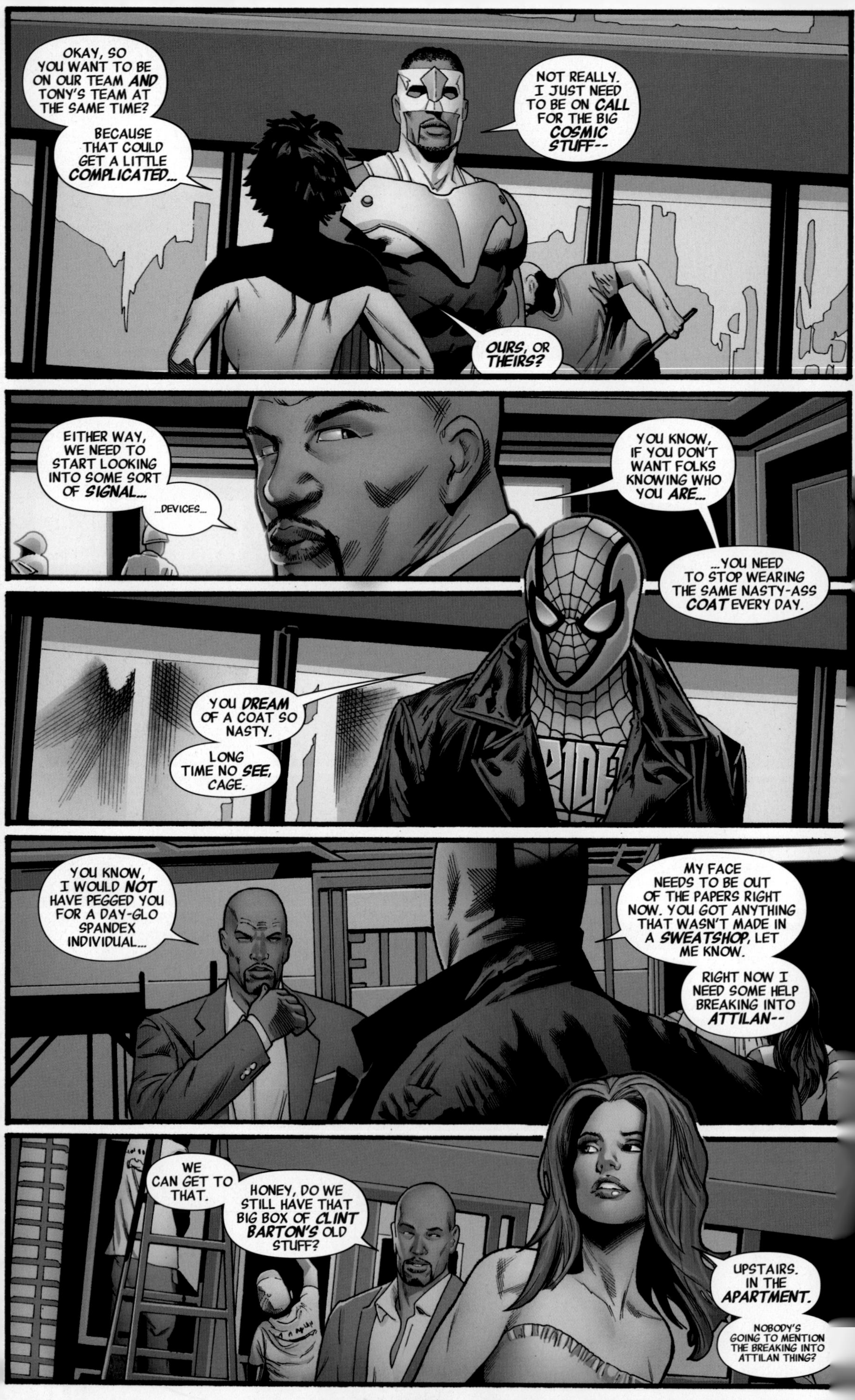
OKAY, SO YOU WANT TO BE ON OUR TEAM AND TONY'S TEAM AT THE SAME TIME?
BECAUSE THAT COULD GET A LITTLE COMPLICATED...
NOT REALLY. I JUST NEED TO BE ON CALL FOR THE BIG COSMIC STUFF--
OURS, OR THEIRS?
EITHER WAY, WE NEED TO START LOOKING INTO SOME SORT OF SIGNAL...
...DEVICES...
YOU KNOW, IF YOU DON'T WANT FOLKS KNOWING WHO YOU ARE...
...YOU NEED TO STOP WEARING THE SAME NASTY-ASS COAT EVERY DAY.
YOU DREAM OF A COAT SO NASTY.
LONG TIME NO SEE, CAGE.
YOU KNOW, I WOULD NOT HAVE PEGGED YOU FOR A DAY-GLO SPANDEX INDIVIDUAL...
MY FACE NEEDS TO BE OUT OF THE PAPERS RIGHT NOW. YOU GOT ANYTHING THAT WASN'T MADE IN A SWEATSHOP, LET ME KNOW.
RIGHT NOW I NEED SOME HELP BREAKING INTO ATTILAN--
WE CAN GET TO THAT.
HONEY, DO WE STILL HAVE THAT BIG BOX OF CLINT BARTON'S OLD STUFF?
UPSTAIRS. IN THE APARTMENT.
NOBODY'S GOING TO MENTION THE BREAKING INTO ATTILAN THING?

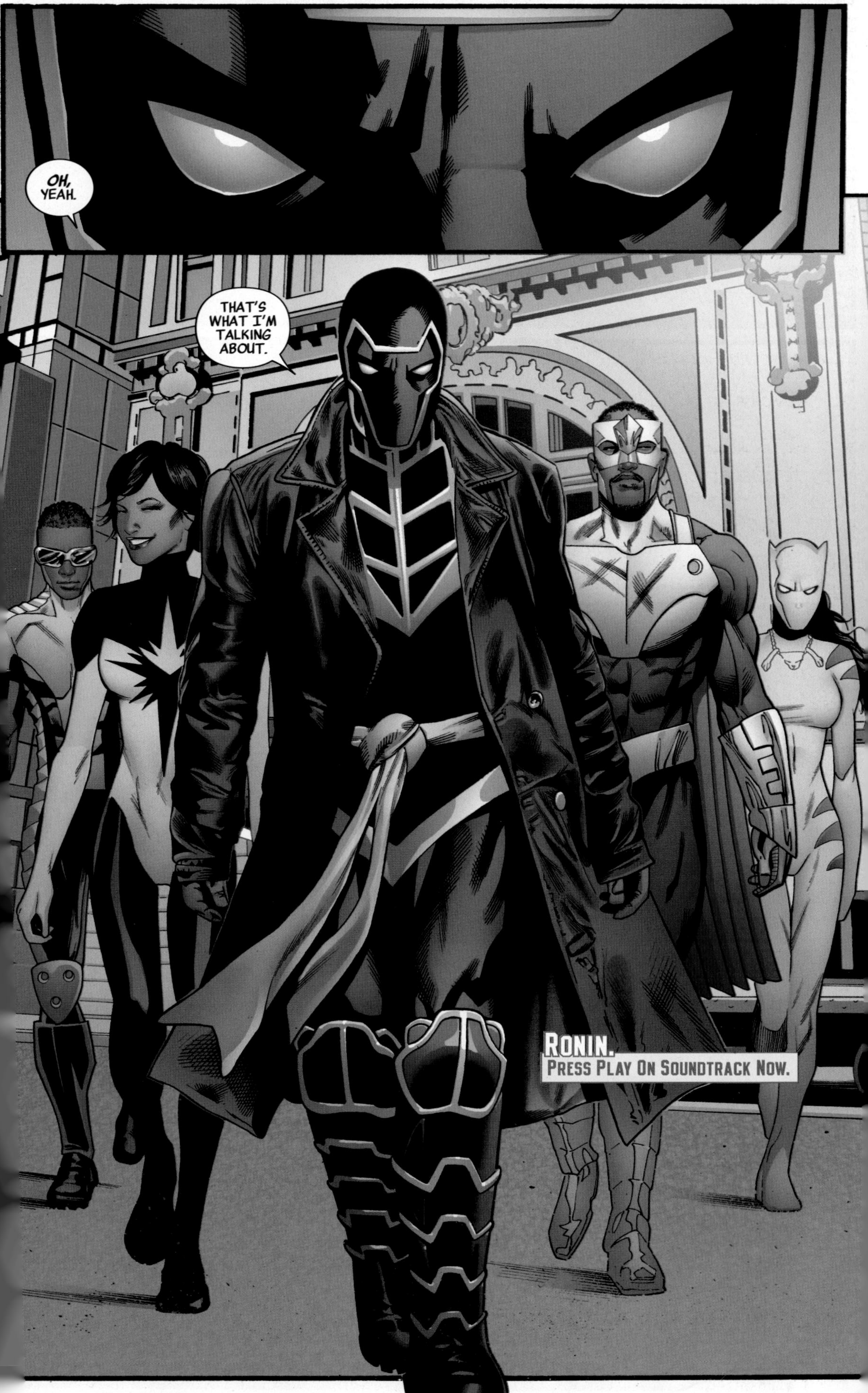

OH, YEAH.
THAT'S WHAT I'M TALKING ABOUT.
RONIN.
PRESS PLAY ON SOUNDTRACK NOW.

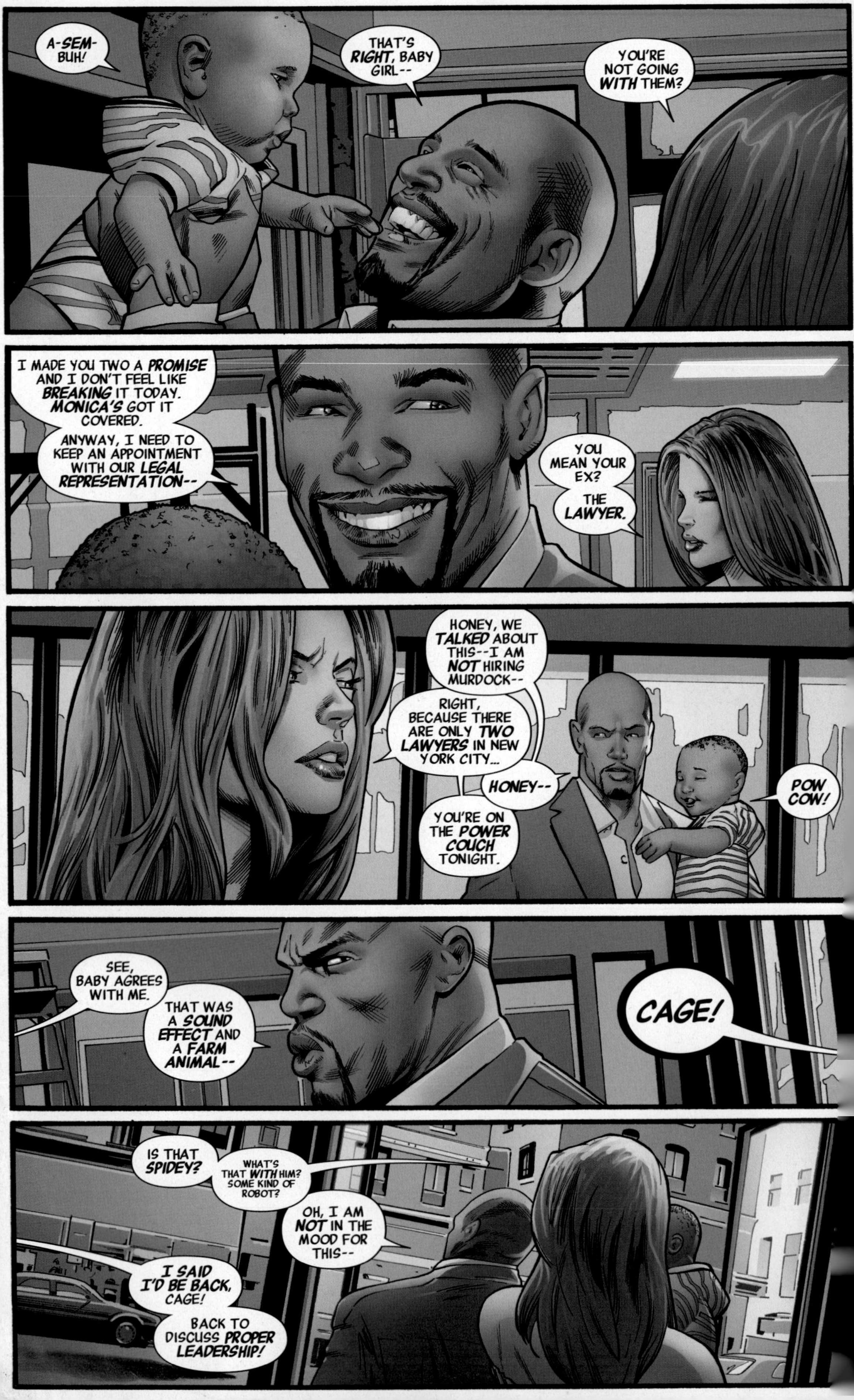
A-SEM-BUH!
THAT'S RIGHT, BABY GIRL--
YOU'RE NOT GOING WITH THEM?
I MADE YOU TWO A PROMISE AND I DON'T FEEL LIKE BREAKING IT TODAY. MONICA'S GOT IT COVERED.
ANYWAY, I NEED TO KEEP AN APPOINTMENT WITH OUR LEGAL REPRESENTATION--
YOU MEAN YOUR EX?
THE LAWYER.
HONEY, WE TALKED ABOUT THIS--I AM NOT HIRING MURDOCK--
RIGHT, BECAUSE THERE ARE ONLY TWO LAWYERS IN NEW YORK CITY...
HONEY--
YOU'RE ON THE POWER COUCH TONIGHT.
POW COW!
SEE, BABY AGREES WITH ME.
THAT WAS A SOUND EFFECT AND A FARM ANIMAL--
CAGE!
IS THAT SPIDEY?
WHAT'S THAT WITH HIM? SOME KIND OF ROBOT?
OH, I AM NOT IN THE MOOD FOR THIS--
I SAID I'D BE BACK, CAGE!
BACK TO DISCUSS PROPER LEADERSHIP!

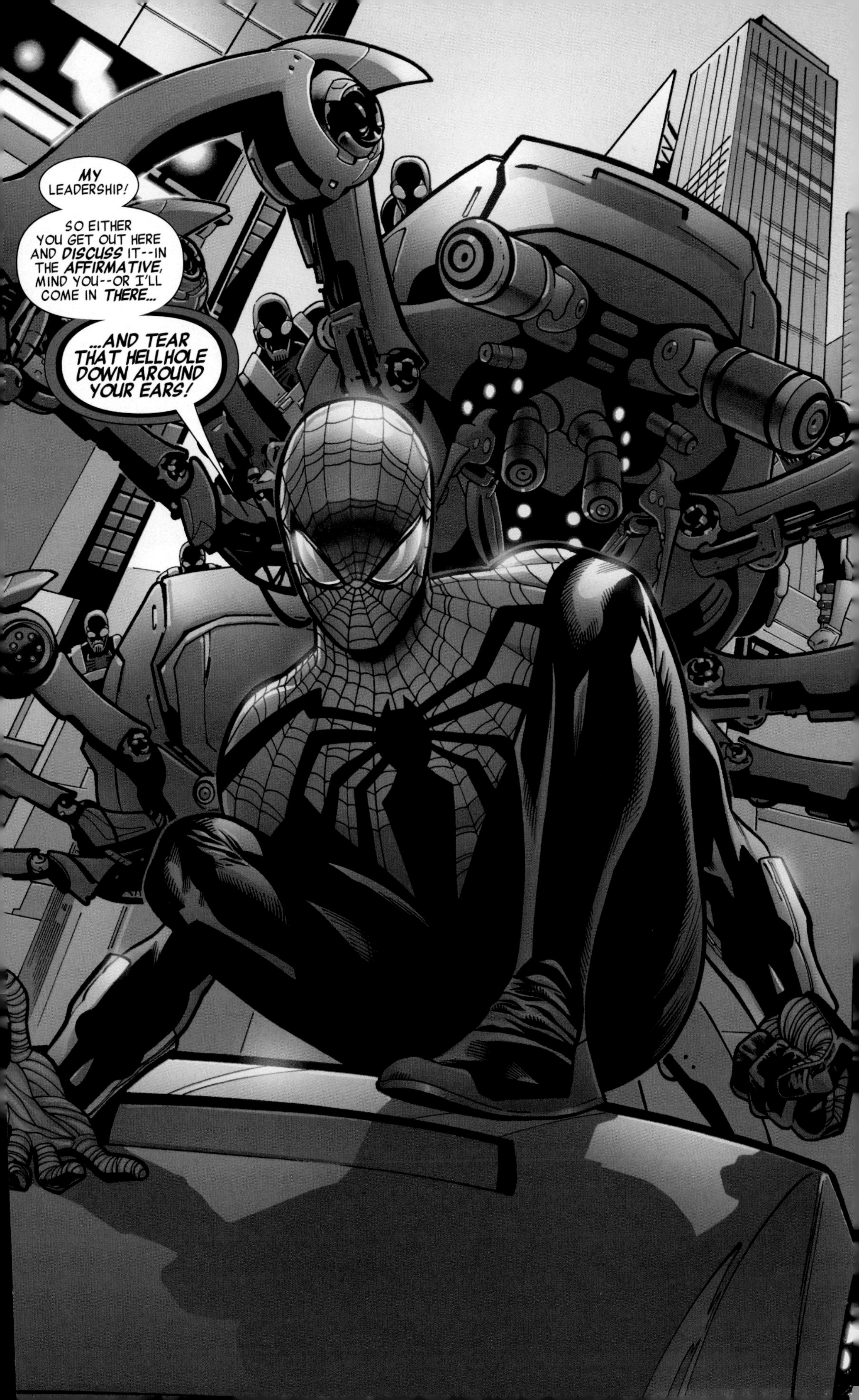
MY LEADERSHIP!
SO EITHER YOU GET OUT HERE AND DISCUSS IT--IN THE AFFIRMATIVE, MIND YOU--OR I'LL COME IN THERE...
...AND TEAR THAT HELLHOLE DOWN AROUND YOUR EARS!

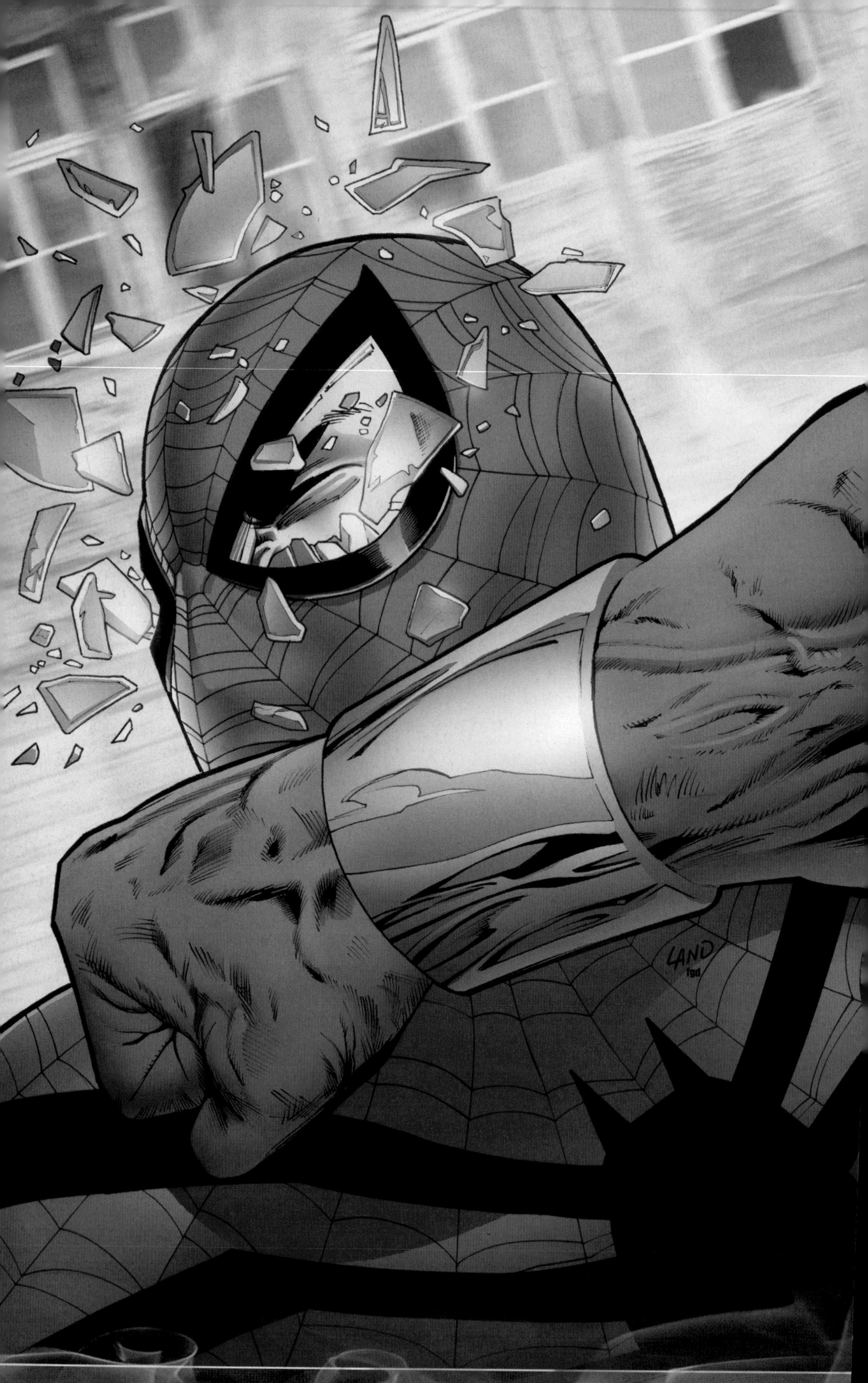
LAND

MIGHTY AVENGERS #5

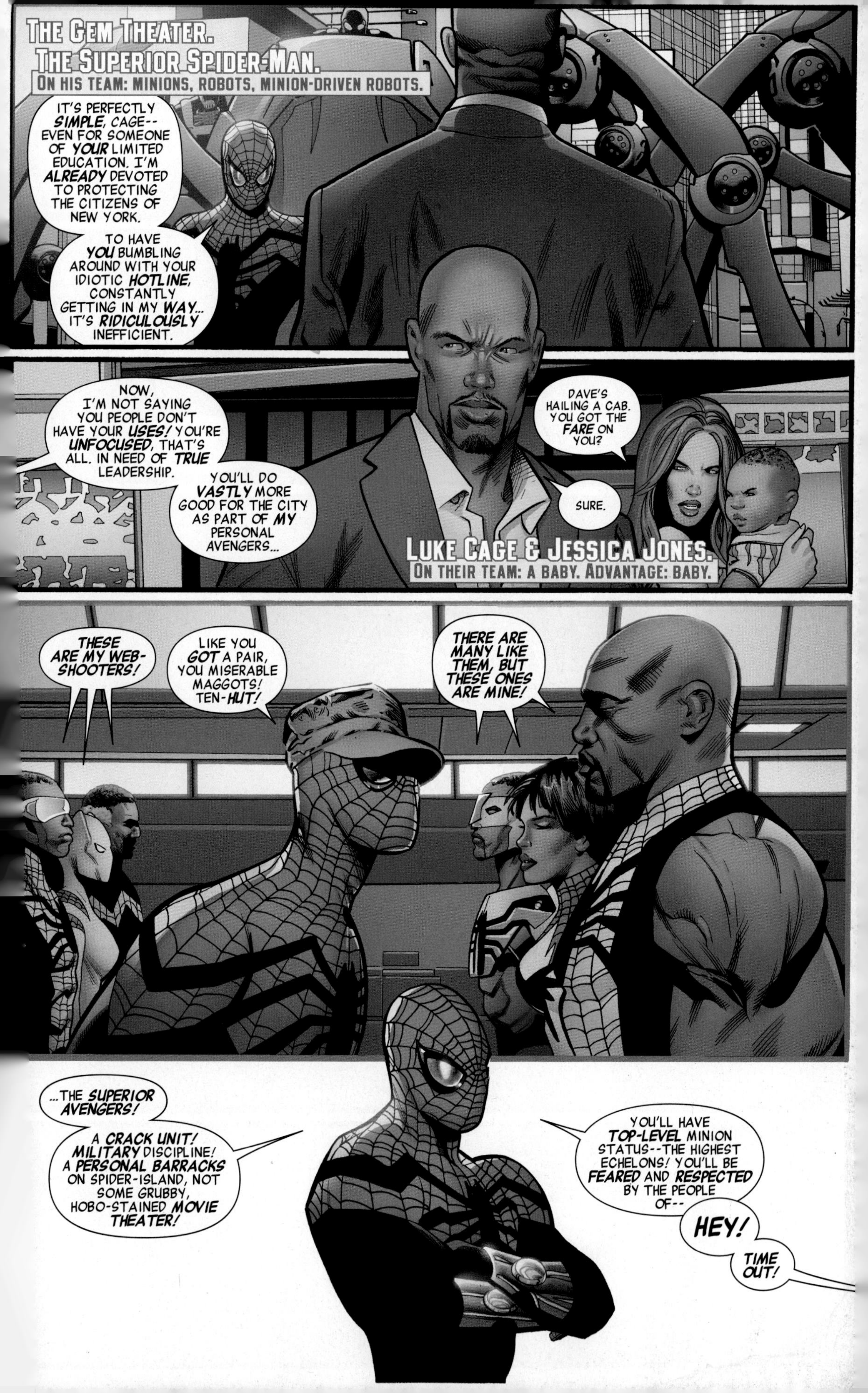
THE GEM THEATER.
THE SUPERIOR SPIDER-MAN.
ON HIS TEAM: MINIONS, ROBOTS, MINION-DRIVEN ROBOTS.
IT'S PERFECTLY SIMPLE, CAGE-- EVEN FOR SOMEONE OF YOUR LIMITED EDUCATION. I'M ALREADY DEVOTED TO PROTECTING THE CITIZENS OF NEW YORK.
TO HAVE YOU BUMBLING AROUND WITH YOUR IDIOTIC HOTLINE, CONSTANTLY GETTING IN MY WAY... IT'S RIDICULOUSLY INEFFICIENT.
NOW, I'M NOT SAYING YOU PEOPLE DON'T HAVE YOUR USES! YOU'RE UNFOCUSED, THAT'S ALL. IN NEED OF TRUE LEADERSHIP.
YOU'LL DO VASTLY MORE GOOD FOR THE CITY AS PART OF MY PERSONAL AVENGERS...
DAVE'S HAILING A CAB. YOU GOT THE FARE ON YOU?
SURE.
LUKE CAGE & JESSICA JONES.
ON THEIR TEAM: A BABY. ADVANTAGE: BABY.
THESE ARE MY WEB-SHOOTERS!
LIKE YOU GOT A PAIR, YOU MISERABLE MAGGOTS! TEN-HUT!
THERE ARE MANY LIKE THEM, BUT THESE ONES ARE MINE!
...THE SUPERIOR AVENGERS!
A CRACK UNIT! MILITARY DISCIPLINE! A PERSONAL BARRACKS ON SPIDER-ISLAND, NOT SOME GRUBBY, HOBO-STAINED MOVIE THEATER!
YOU'LL HAVE TOP-LEVEL MINION STATUS--THE HIGHEST ECHELONS! YOU'LL BE FEARED AND RESPECTED BY THE PEOPLE OF--
HEY!
TIME OUT!

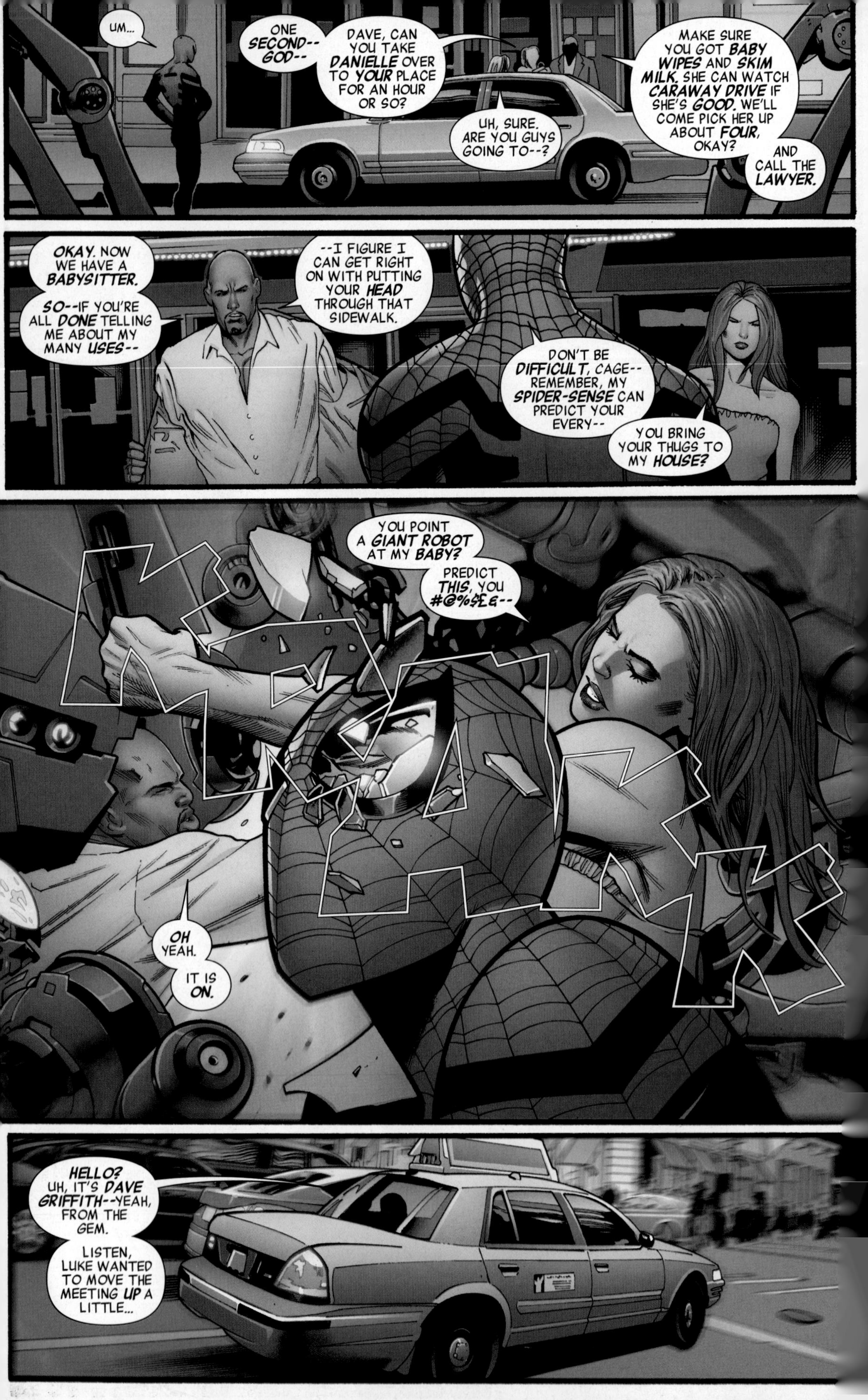
UM...
ONE SECOND-- GOD--
DAVE, CAN YOU TAKE DANIELLE OVER TO YOUR PLACE FOR AN HOUR OR SO?
UH, SURE. ARE YOU GUYS GOING TO--?
MAKE SURE YOU GOT BABY WIPES AND SKIM MILK. SHE CAN WATCH CARAWAY DRIVE IF SHE'S GOOD. WE'LL COME PICK HER UP ABOUT FOUR, OKAY?
AND CALL THE LAWYER.
OKAY. NOW WE HAVE A BABYSITTER.
SO--IF YOU'RE ALL DONE TELLING ME ABOUT MY MANY USES--
--I FIGURE I CAN GET RIGHT ON WITH PUTTING YOUR HEAD THROUGH THAT SIDEWALK.
DON'T BE DIFFICULT, CAGE-- REMEMBER, MY SPIDER-SENSE CAN PREDICT YOUR EVERY--
YOU BRING YOUR THUGS TO MY HOUSE?
YOU POINT A GIANT ROBOT AT MY BABY?
PREDICT THIS, YOU #@%$£&--
OH YEAH.
IT IS ON.
HELLO? UH, IT'S DAVE GRIFFITH--YEAH, FROM THE GEM.
LISTEN, LUKE WANTED TO MOVE THE MEETING UP A LITTLE...

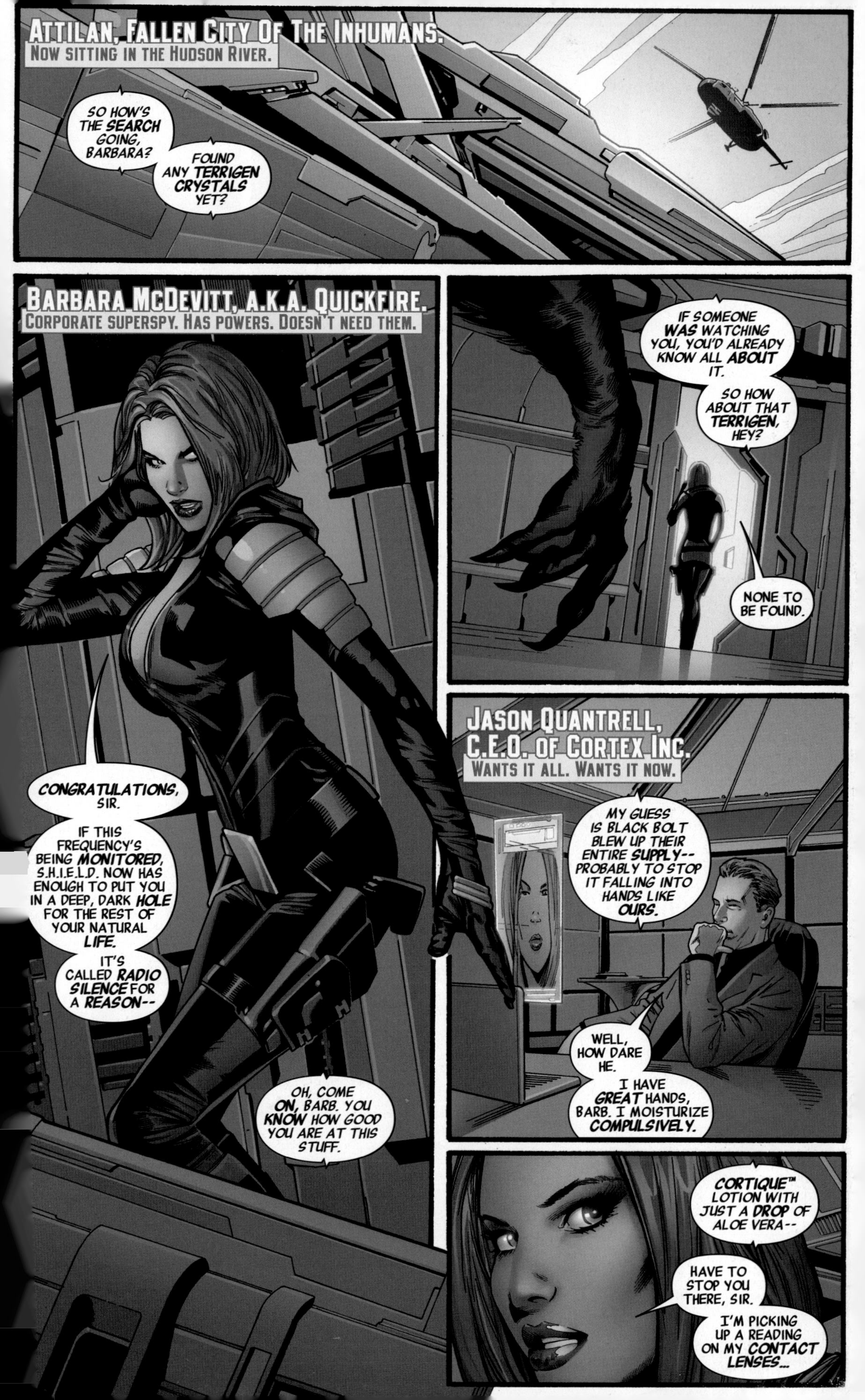
ATTILAN, FALLEN CITY OF THE INHUMANS.
NOW SITTING IN THE HUDSON RIVER.
SO HOW'S THE SEARCH GOING, BARBARA?
FOUND ANY TERRIGEN CRYSTALS YET?
BARBARA McDEVITT, A.K.A. QUICKFIRE.
CORPORATE SUPERSPY. HAS POWERS. DOESN'T NEED THEM.
IF SOMEONE WAS WATCHING YOU, YOU'D ALREADY KNOW ALL ABOUT IT.
SO HOW ABOUT THAT TERRIGEN, HEY?
NONE TO BE FOUND.
CONGRATULATIONS, SIR.
IF THIS FREQUENCY'S BEING MONITORED, S.H.I.E.L.D. NOW HAS ENOUGH TO PUT YOU IN A DEEP, DARK HOLE FOR THE REST OF YOUR NATURAL LIFE.
IT'S CALLED RADIO SILENCE FOR A REASON--
OH, COME ON, BARB. YOU KNOW HOW GOOD YOU ARE AT THIS STUFF.
JASON QUANTRELL, C.E.O. OF CORTEX INC.
WANTS IT ALL. WANTS IT NOW.
MY GUESS IS BLACK BOLT BLEW UP THEIR ENTIRE SUPPLY-- PROBABLY TO STOP IT FALLING INTO HANDS LIKE OURS.
WELL, HOW DARE HE.
I HAVE GREAT HANDS, BARB. I MOISTURIZE COMPULSIVELY.
CORTIQUE™ LOTION WITH JUST A DROP OF ALOE VERA--
HAVE TO STOP YOU THERE, SIR.
I'M PICKING UP A READING ON MY CONTACT LENSES...

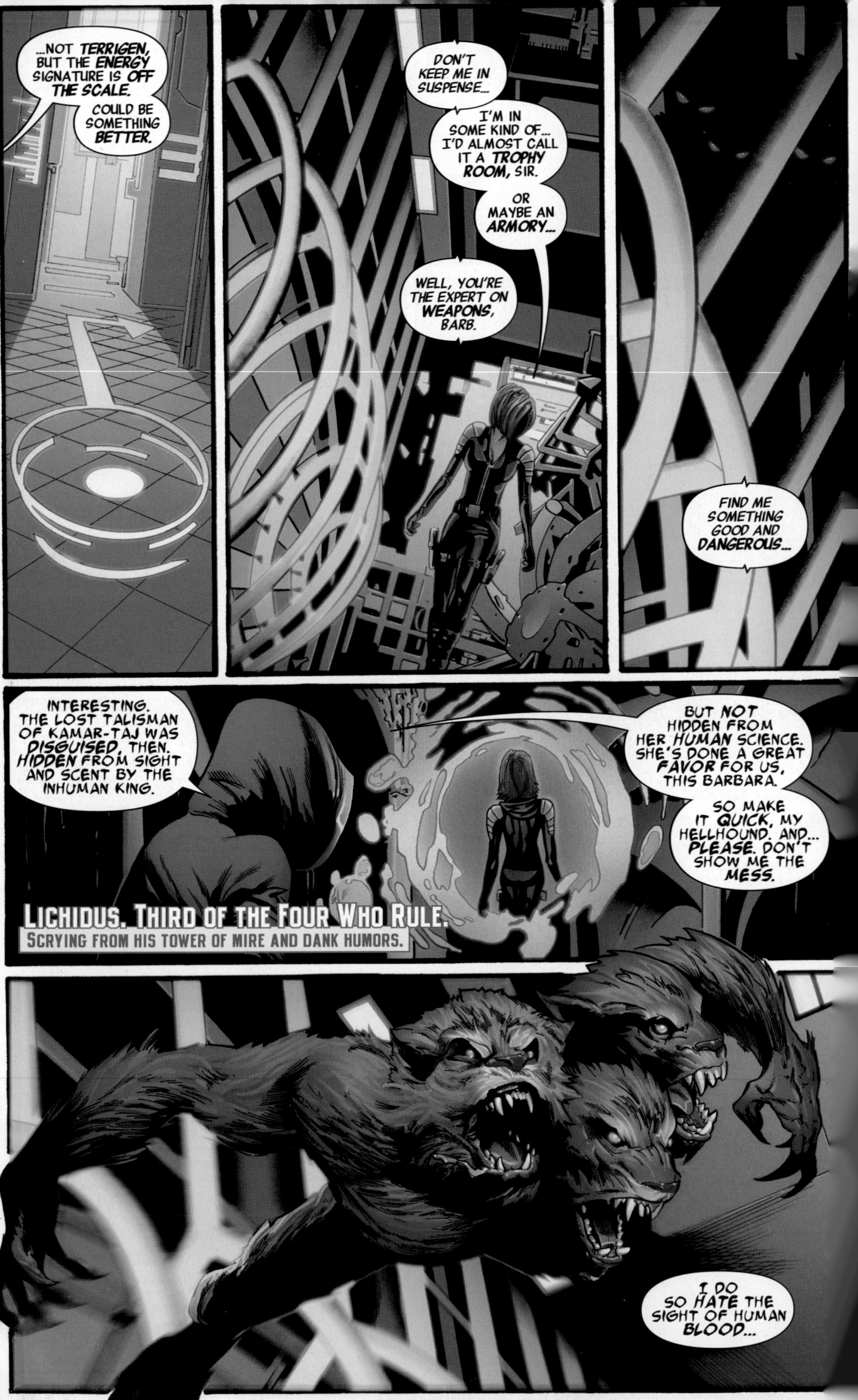
...NOT TERRIGEN, BUT THE ENERGY SIGNATURE IS OFF THE SCALE.
COULD BE SOMETHING BETTER.
DON'T KEEP ME IN SUSPENSE...
I'M IN SOME KIND OF... I'D ALMOST CALL IT A TROPHY ROOM, SIR.
OR MAYBE AN ARMORY...
WELL, YOU'RE THE EXPERT ON WEAPONS, BARB.
FIND ME SOMETHING GOOD AND DANGEROUS...
INTERESTING. THE LOST TALISMAN OF KAMAR-TAJ WAS DISGUISED, THEN. HIDDEN FROM SIGHT AND SCENT BY THE INHUMAN KING.
BUT NOT HIDDEN FROM HER HUMAN SCIENCE. SHE'S DONE A GREAT FAVOR FOR US, THIS BARBARA.
SO MAKE IT QUICK, MY HELLHOUND. AND... PLEASE. DON'T SHOW ME THE MESS.
LICHIDUS. THIRD OF THE FOUR WHO RULE.
SCRYING FROM HIS TOWER OF MIRE AND DANK HUMORS.
I DO SO HATE THE SIGHT OF HUMAN BLOOD...

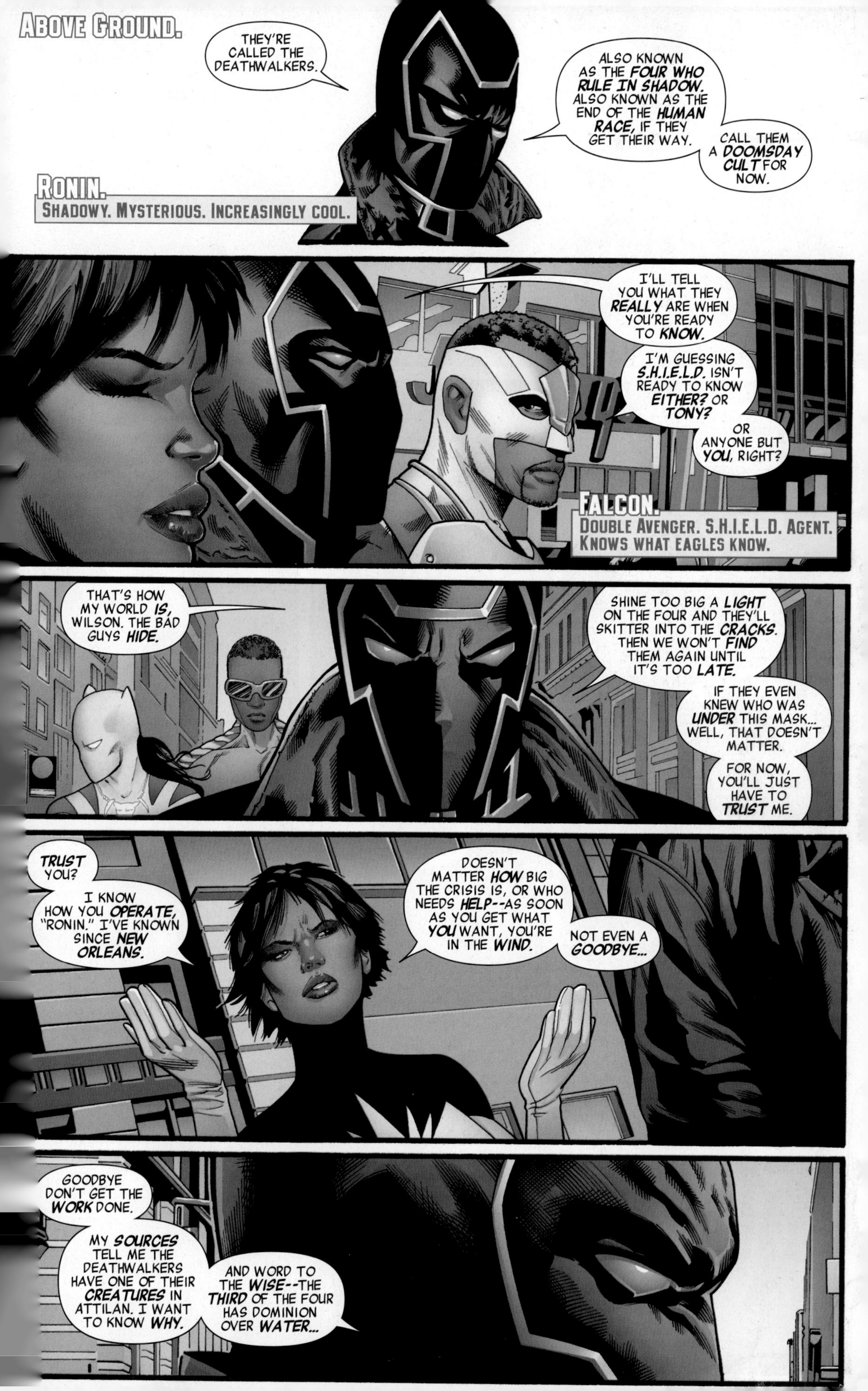
ABOVE GROUND.
THEY'RE CALLED THE DEATHWALKERS.
ALSO KNOWN AS THE FOUR WHO RULE IN SHADOW. ALSO KNOWN AS THE END OF THE HUMAN RACE, IF THEY GET THEIR WAY.
CALL THEM A DOOMSDAY CULT FOR NOW.
RONIN.
SHADOWY. MYSTERIOUS. INCREASINGLY COOL.
I'LL TELL YOU WHAT THEY REALLY ARE WHEN YOU'RE READY TO KNOW.
I'M GUESSING S.H.I.E.L.D. ISN'T READY TO KNOW EITHER? OR TONY?
OR ANYONE BUT YOU, RIGHT?
FALCON.
DOUBLE AVENGER. S.H.I.E.L.D. AGENT. KNOWS WHAT EAGLES KNOW.
THAT'S HOW MY WORLD IS, WILSON. THE BAD GUYS HIDE.
SHINE TOO BIG A LIGHT ON THE FOUR AND THEY'LL SKITTER INTO THE CRACKS. THEN WE WON'T FIND THEM AGAIN UNTIL IT'S TOO LATE.
IF THEY EVEN KNEW WHO WAS UNDER THIS MASK... WELL, THAT DOESN'T MATTER.
FOR NOW, YOU'LL JUST HAVE TO TRUST ME.
TRUST YOU?
I KNOW HOW YOU OPERATE, "RONIN." I'VE KNOWN SINCE NEW ORLEANS.
DOESN'T MATTER HOW BIG THE CRISIS IS, OR WHO NEEDS HELP--AS SOON AS YOU GET WHAT YOU WANT, YOU'RE IN THE WIND.
NOT EVEN A GOODBYE...
GOODBYE DON'T GET THE WORK DONE.
MY SOURCES TELL ME THE DEATHWALKERS HAVE ONE OF THEIR CREATURES IN ATTILAN. I WANT TO KNOW WHY.
AND WORD TO THE WISE--THE THIRD OF THE FOUR HAS DOMINION OVER WATER...

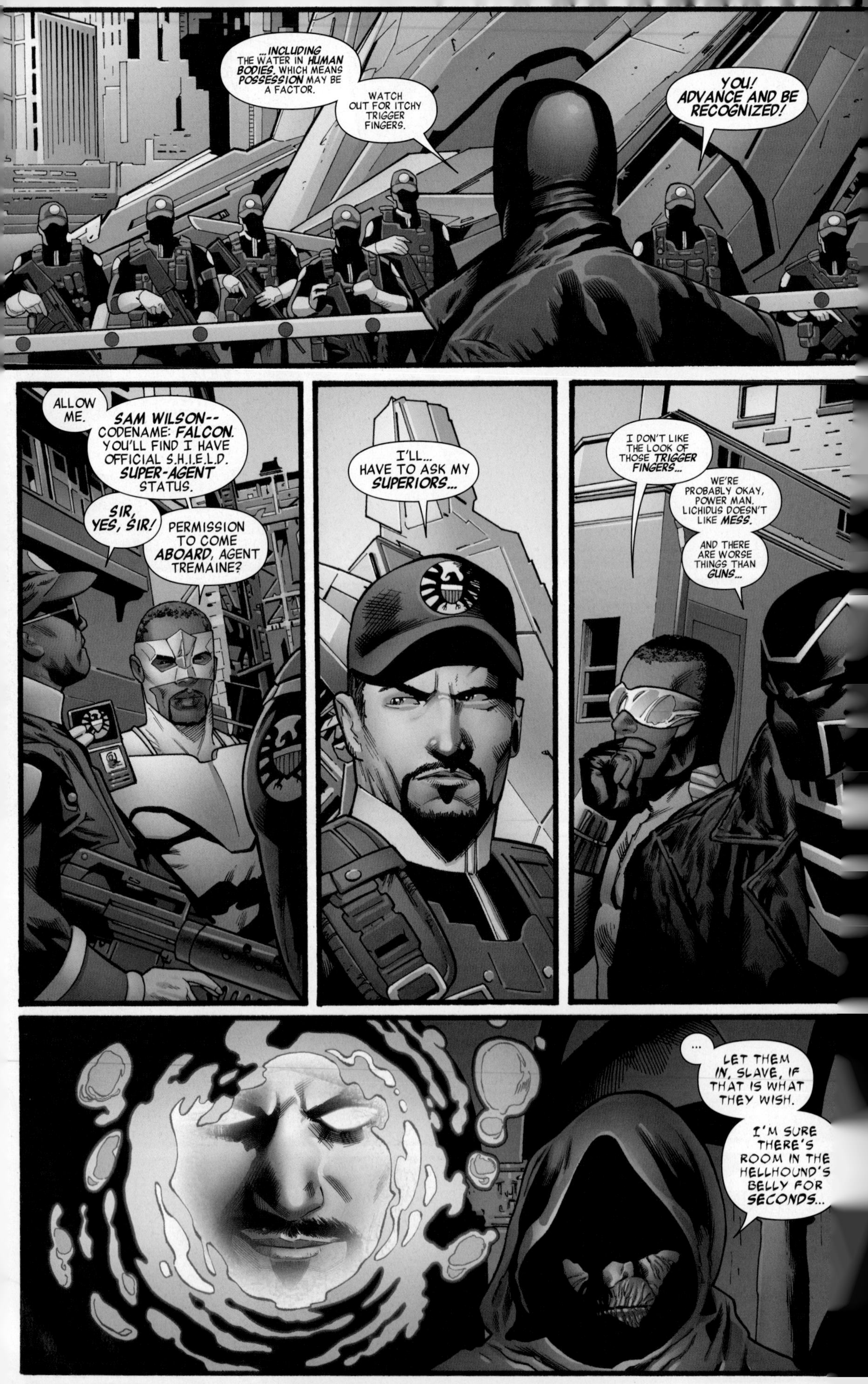
...INCLUDING THE WATER IN HUMAN BODIES. WHICH MEANS POSSESSION MAY BE A FACTOR.
WATCH OUT FOR ITCHY TRIGGER FINGERS.
YOU! ADVANCE AND BE RECOGNIZED!
ALLOW ME.
SAM WILSON-- CODENAME: FALCON. YOU'LL FIND I HAVE OFFICIAL S.H.I.E.L.D. SUPER-AGENT STATUS.
SIR, YES, SIR!
PERMISSION TO COME ABOARD, AGENT TREMAINE?
I'LL... HAVE TO ASK MY SUPERIORS...
I DON'T LIKE THE LOOK OF THOSE TRIGGER FINGERS...
WE'RE PROBABLY OKAY, POWER MAN. LICHIDUS DOESN'T LIKE MESS.
AND THERE ARE WORSE THINGS THAN GUNS...
...
LET THEM IN, SLAVE, IF THAT IS WHAT THEY WISH.
I'M SURE THERE'S ROOM IN THE HELLHOUND'S BELLY FOR SECONDS...

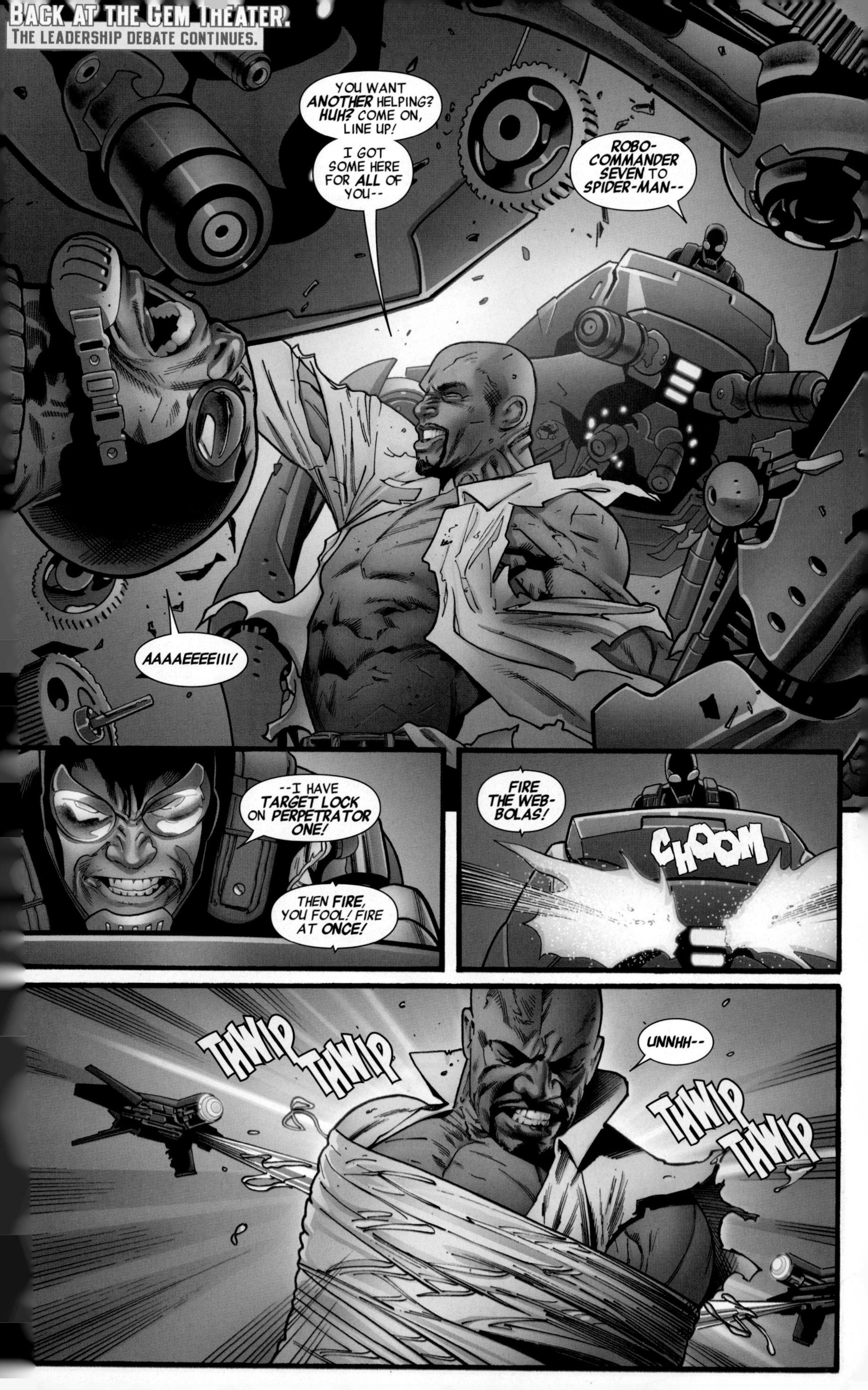
BACK AT THE GEM THEATER.
THE LEADERSHIP DEBATE CONTINUES.
YOU WANT ANOTHER HELPING? HUH? COME ON, LINE UP!
I GOT SOME HERE FOR ALL OF YOU--
ROBO-COMMANDER SEVEN TO SPIDER-MAN--
AAAAEEEEIII!
--I HAVE TARGET LOCK ON PERPETRATOR ONE!
THEN FIRE, YOU FOOL! FIRE AT ONCE!
FIRE THE WEB-BOLAS!
CHOOM
THWIP THWIP
UNNHH--
THWIP THWIP

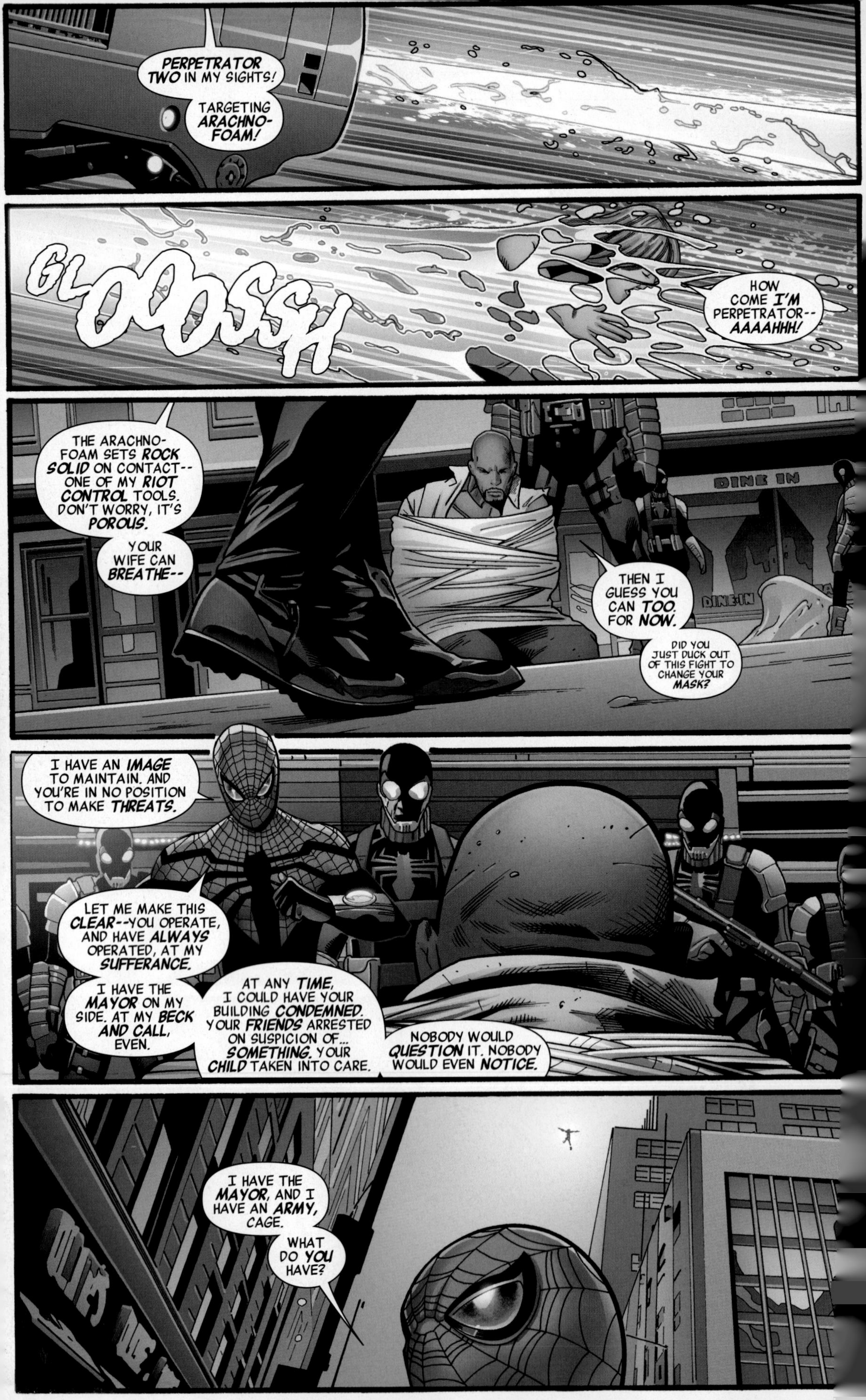
PERPETRATOR TWO IN MY SIGHTS!
TARGETING ARACHNO-FOAM!
GLOOOSSH
HOW COME I'M PERPETRATOR-- AAAAHHH!
THE ARACHNO-FOAM SETS ROCK SOLID ON CONTACT-- ONE OF MY RIOT CONTROL TOOLS. DON'T WORRY, IT'S POROUS.
YOUR WIFE CAN BREATHE--
THEN I GUESS YOU CAN TOO. FOR NOW.
DID YOU JUST DUCK OUT OF THIS FIGHT TO CHANGE YOUR MASK?
I HAVE AN IMAGE TO MAINTAIN. AND YOU'RE IN NO POSITION TO MAKE THREATS.
LET ME MAKE THIS CLEAR--YOU OPERATE, AND HAVE ALWAYS OPERATED, AT MY SUFFERANCE.
I HAVE THE MAYOR ON MY SIDE. AT MY BECK AND CALL, EVEN.
AT ANY TIME, I COULD HAVE YOUR BUILDING CONDEMNED. YOUR FRIENDS ARRESTED ON SUSPICION OF... SOMETHING. YOUR CHILD TAKEN INTO CARE.
NOBODY WOULD QUESTION IT. NOBODY WOULD EVEN NOTICE.
I HAVE THE MAYOR, AND I HAVE AN ARMY, CAGE.
WHAT DO YOU HAVE?

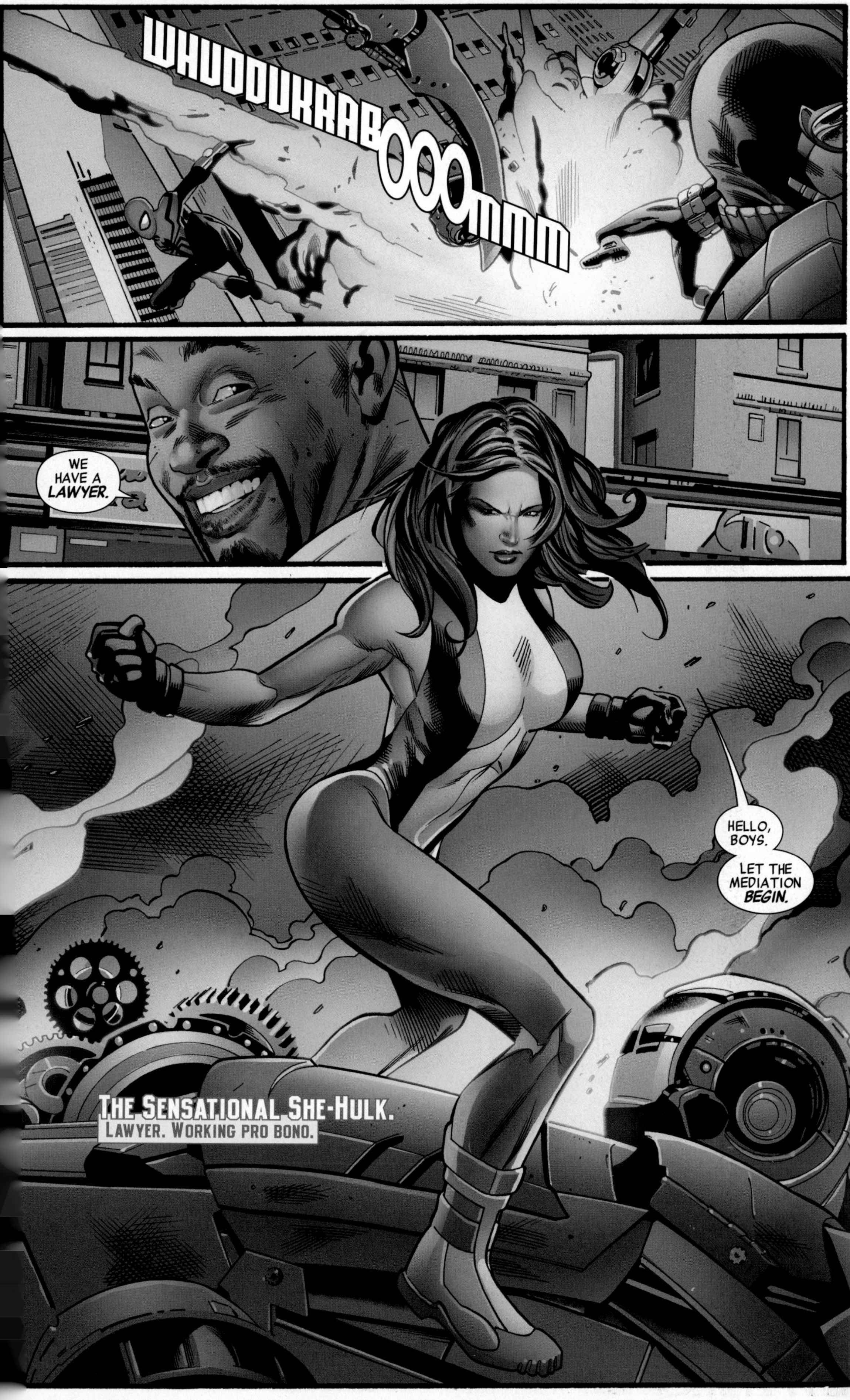
WHUDDUKRABOOOMMM
WE HAVE A LAWYER.
HELLO, BOYS.
LET THE MEDIATION BEGIN.
THE SENSATIONAL SHE-HULK.
LAWYER. WORKING PRO BONO.

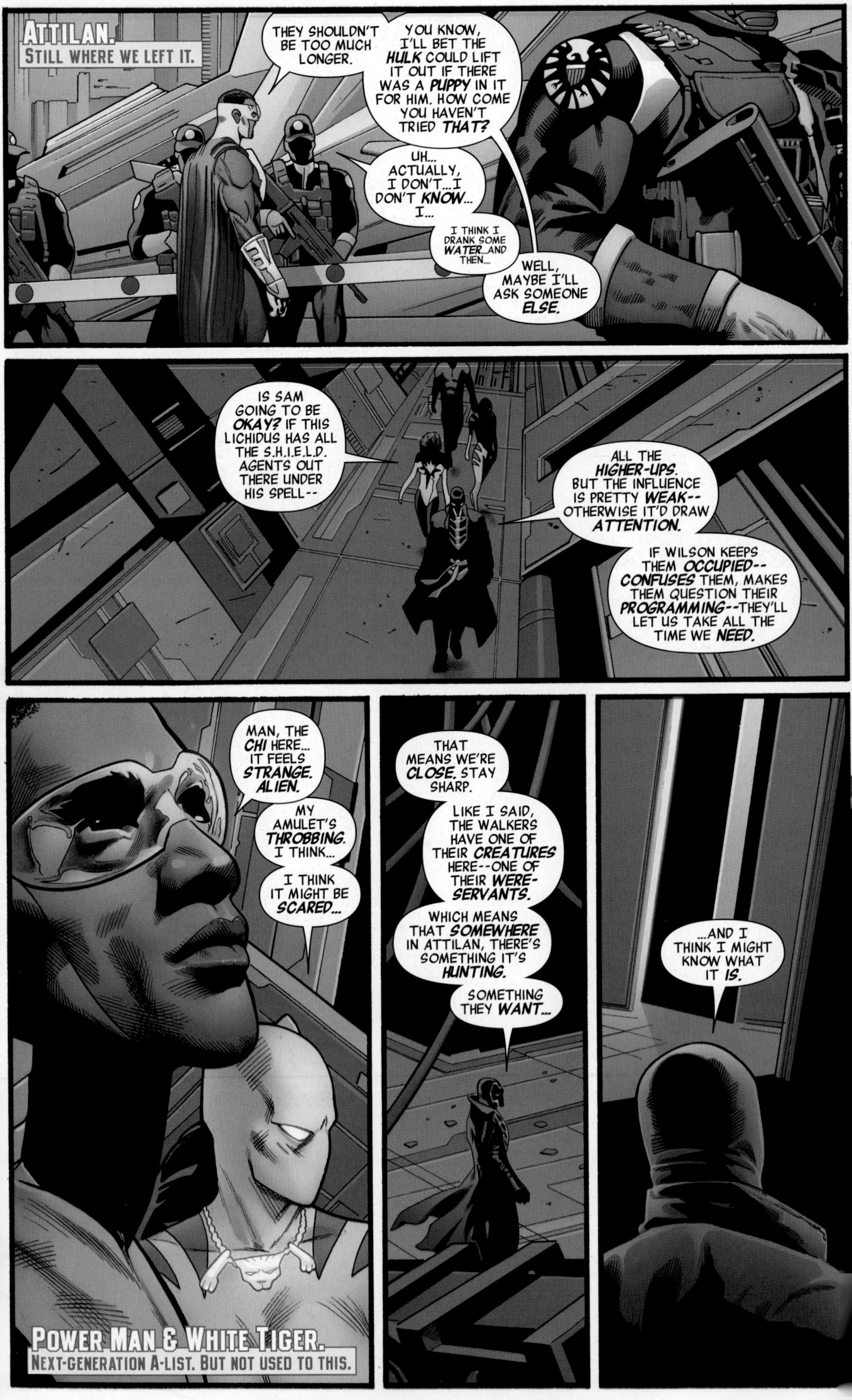
ATTILAN.
STILL WHERE WE LEFT IT.
THEY SHOULDN'T BE TOO MUCH LONGER.
YOU KNOW, I'LL BET THE HULK COULD LIFT IT OUT IF THERE WAS A PUPPY IN IT FOR HIM. HOW COME YOU HAVEN'T TRIED THAT?
UH... ACTUALLY, I DON'T...I DON'T KNOW... I...
I THINK I DRANK SOME WATER...AND THEN...
WELL, MAYBE I'LL ASK SOMEONE ELSE.
IS SAM GOING TO BE OKAY? IF THIS LICHIDUS HAS ALL THE S.H.I.E.L.D. AGENTS OUT THERE UNDER HIS SPELL--
ALL THE HIGHER-UPS. BUT THE INFLUENCE IS PRETTY WEAK--OTHERWISE IT'D DRAW ATTENTION.
IF WILSON KEEPS THEM OCCUPIED--CONFUSES THEM, MAKES THEM QUESTION THEIR PROGRAMMING--THEY'LL LET US TAKE ALL THE TIME WE NEED.
MAN, THE CHI HERE... IT FEELS STRANGE. ALIEN.
MY AMULET'S THROBBING. I THINK...
I THINK IT MIGHT BE SCARED...
POWER MAN & WHITE TIGER.
NEXT-GENERATION A-LIST. BUT NOT USED TO THIS.
THAT MEANS WE'RE CLOSE. STAY SHARP.
LIKE I SAID, THE WALKERS HAVE ONE OF THEIR CREATURES HERE--ONE OF THEIR WERE-SERVANTS.
WHICH MEANS THAT SOMEWHERE IN ATTILAN, THERE'S SOMETHING IT'S HUNTING.
SOMETHING THEY WANT...
...AND I THINK I MIGHT KNOW WHAT IT IS.

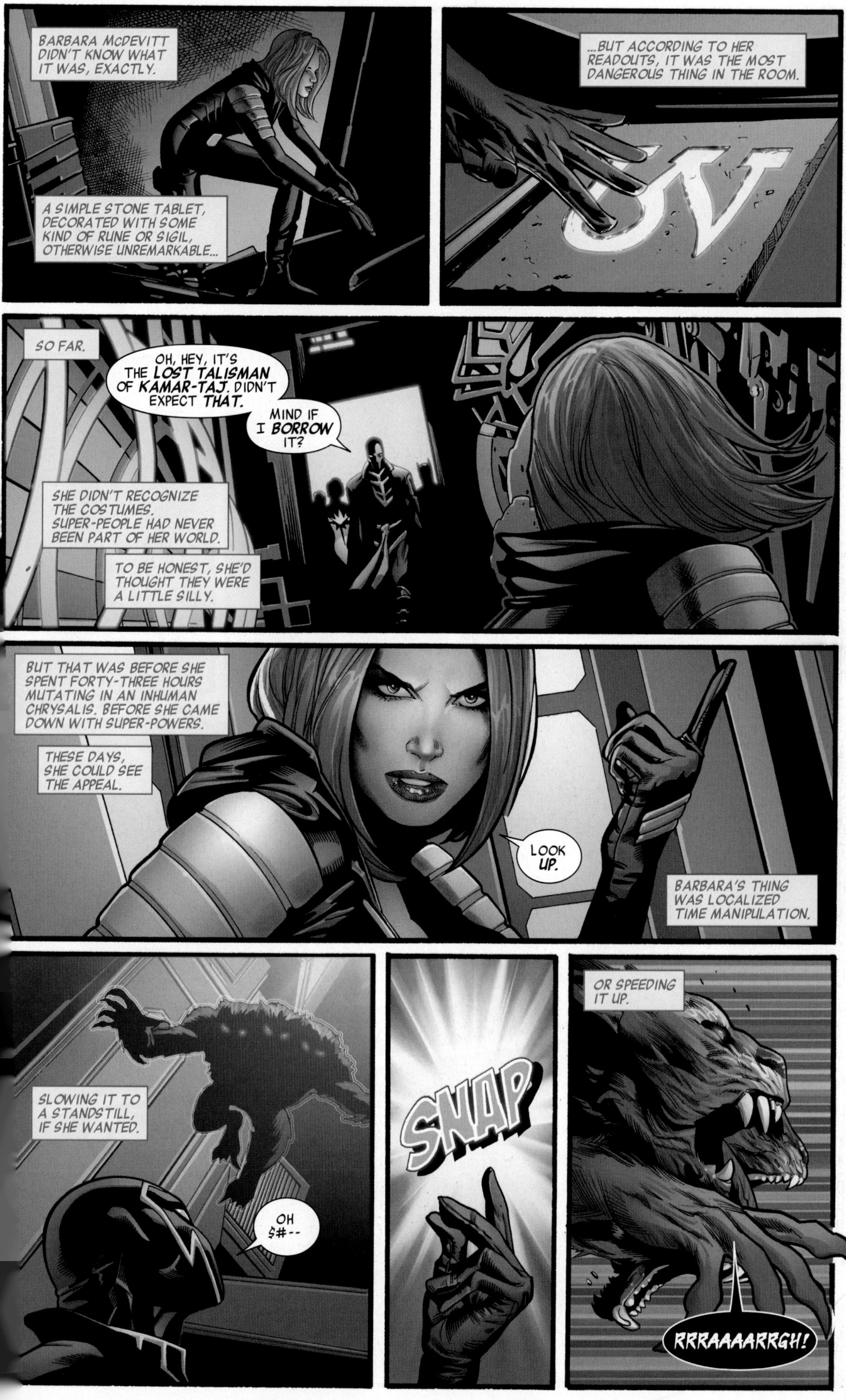

BARBARA McDEVITT DIDN'T KNOW WHAT IT WAS, EXACTLY.
A SIMPLE STONE TABLET, DECORATED WITH SOME KIND OF RUNE OR SIGIL, OTHERWISE UNREMARKABLE...
...BUT ACCORDING TO HER READOUTS, IT WAS THE MOST DANGEROUS THING IN THE ROOM.
SO FAR.
OH, HEY, IT'S THE LOST TALISMAN OF KAMAR-TAJ. DIDN'T EXPECT THAT.
MIND IF I BORROW IT?
SHE DIDN'T RECOGNIZE THE COSTUMES. SUPER-PEOPLE HAD NEVER BEEN PART OF HER WORLD.
TO BE HONEST, SHE'D THOUGHT THEY WERE A LITTLE SILLY.
BUT THAT WAS BEFORE SHE SPENT FORTY-THREE HOURS MUTATING IN AN INHUMAN CHRYSALIS. BEFORE SHE CAME DOWN WITH SUPER-POWERS.
THESE DAYS, SHE COULD SEE THE APPEAL.
LOOK UP.
BARBARA'S THING WAS LOCALIZED TIME MANIPULATION.
SLOWING IT TO A STANDSTILL, IF SHE WANTED.
OH $#--
SNAP
OR SPEEDING IT UP.
RRRAAAARRGH!

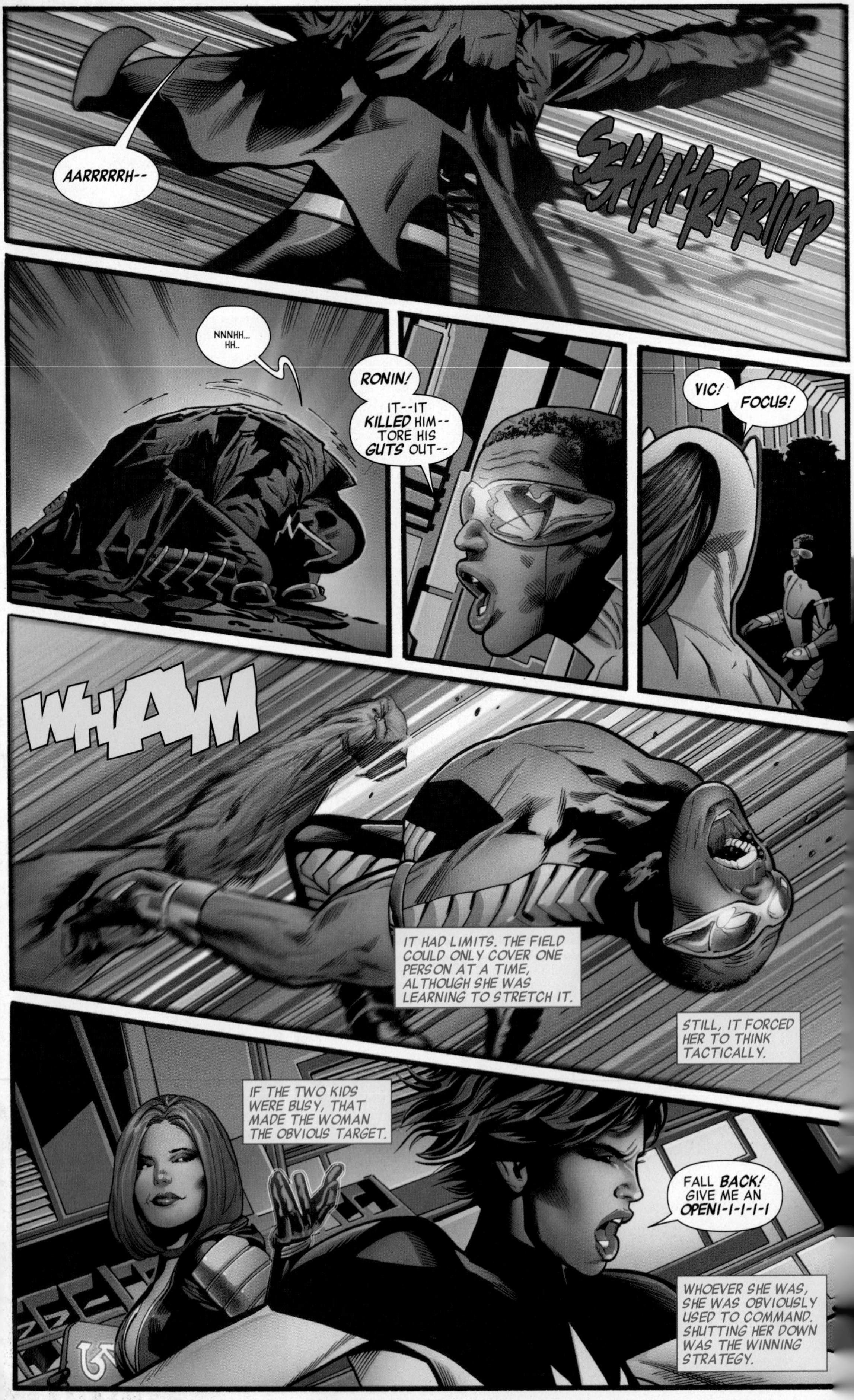

AARRRRRH--
SSHHHRRRIPP
NNNHH... HH..
RONIN!
IT--IT KILLED HIM-- TORE HIS GUTS OUT--
VIC!
FOCUS!
WHAM
IT HAD LIMITS. THE FIELD COULD ONLY COVER ONE PERSON AT A TIME, ALTHOUGH SHE WAS LEARNING TO STRETCH IT.
STILL, IT FORCED HER TO THINK TACTICALLY.
IF THE TWO KIDS WERE BUSY, THAT MADE THE WOMAN THE OBVIOUS TARGET.
FALL BACK! GIVE ME AN OPENI-I-I-I-I
WHOEVER SHE WAS, SHE WAS OBVIOUSLY USED TO COMMAND. SHUTTING HER DOWN WAS THE WINNING STRATEGY.

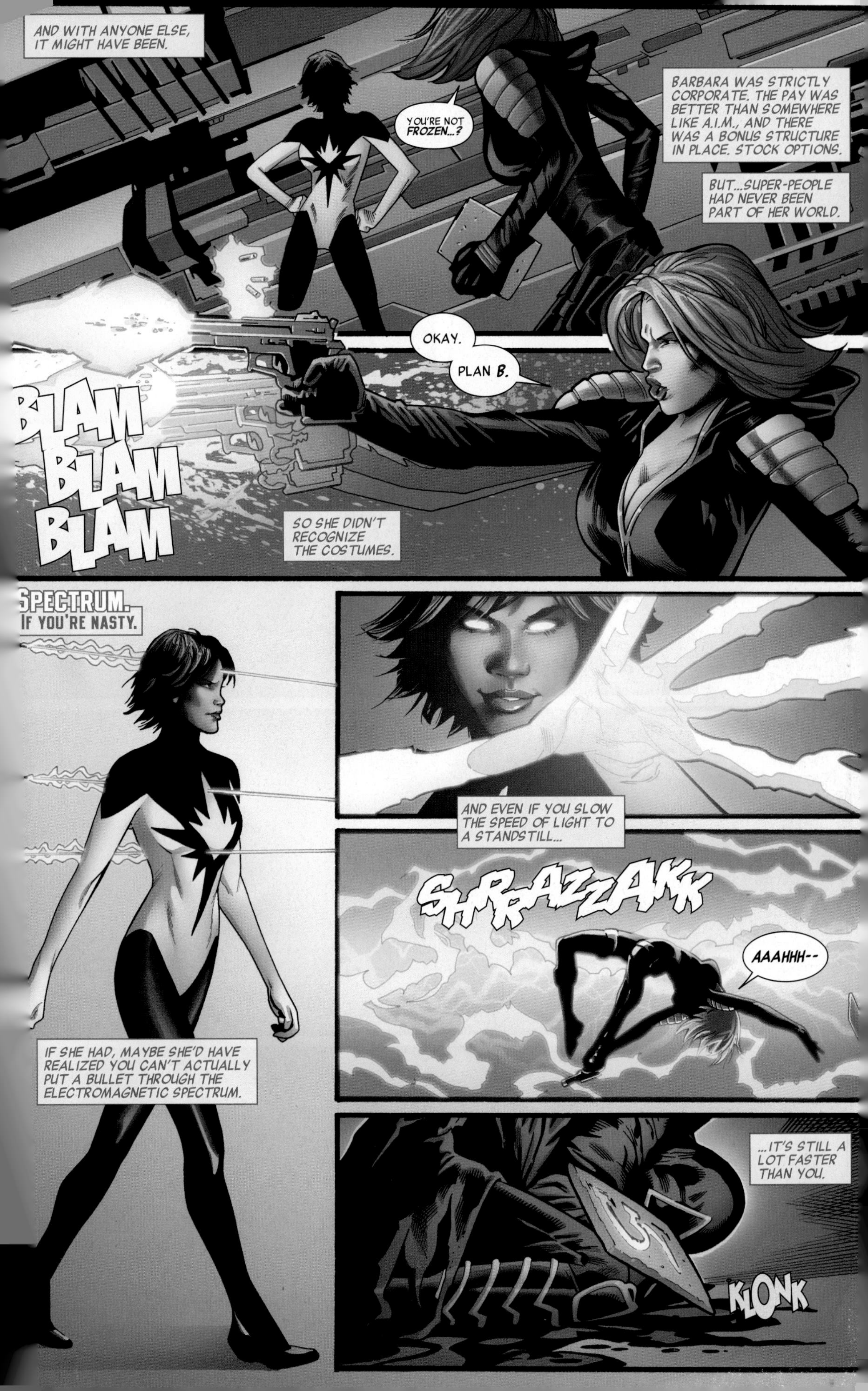
AND WITH ANYONE ELSE, IT MIGHT HAVE BEEN.
YOU'RE NOT FROZEN...?
BARBARA WAS STRICTLY CORPORATE. THE PAY WAS BETTER THAN SOMEWHERE LIKE A.I.M., AND THERE WAS A BONUS STRUCTURE IN PLACE. STOCK OPTIONS.
BUT...SUPER-PEOPLE HAD NEVER BEEN PART OF HER WORLD.
OKAY.
PLAN B.
BLAM BLAM BLAM
SO SHE DIDN'T RECOGNIZE THE COSTUMES.
SPECTRUM. IF YOU'RE NASTY.
IF SHE HAD, MAYBE SHE'D HAVE REALIZED YOU CAN'T ACTUALLY PUT A BULLET THROUGH THE ELECTROMAGNETIC SPECTRUM.
AND EVEN IF YOU SLOW THE SPEED OF LIGHT TO A STANDSTILL...
SHRRAZZAKK
AAAHHH--
...IT'S STILL A LOT FASTER THAN YOU.
KLONK

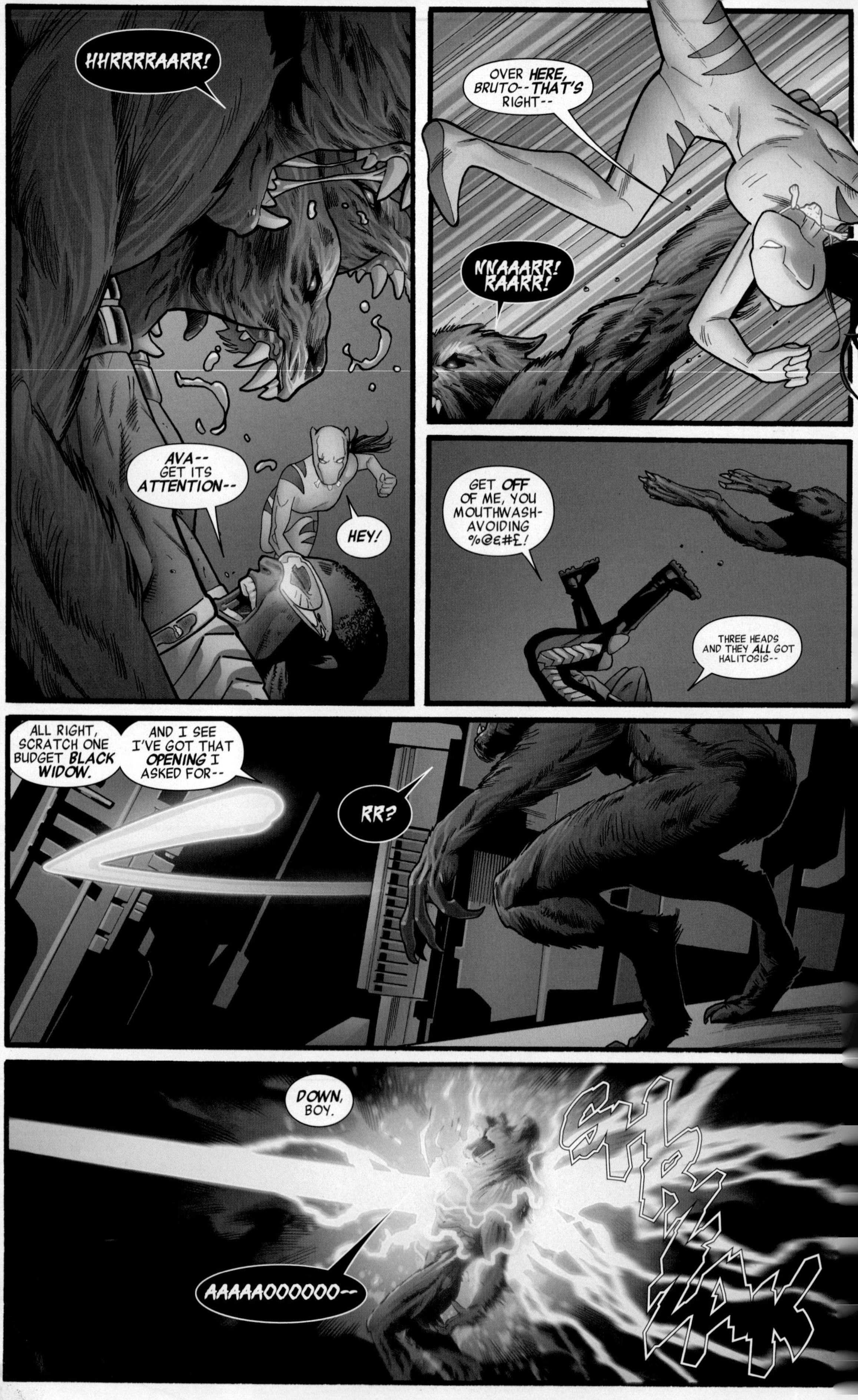
HHRRRRAARR!
AVA-- GET ITS ATTENTION--
HEY!
OVER HERE, BRUTO--THAT'S RIGHT--
N'NAAARR! RAARR!
GET OFF OF ME, YOU MOUTHWASH-AVOIDING %@€#£!
THREE HEADS AND THEY ALL GOT HALITOSIS--
ALL RIGHT, SCRATCH ONE BUDGET BLACK WIDOW.
AND I SEE I'VE GOT THAT OPENING I ASKED FOR--
RR?
DOWN, BOY.
AAAAAOOOOOO--

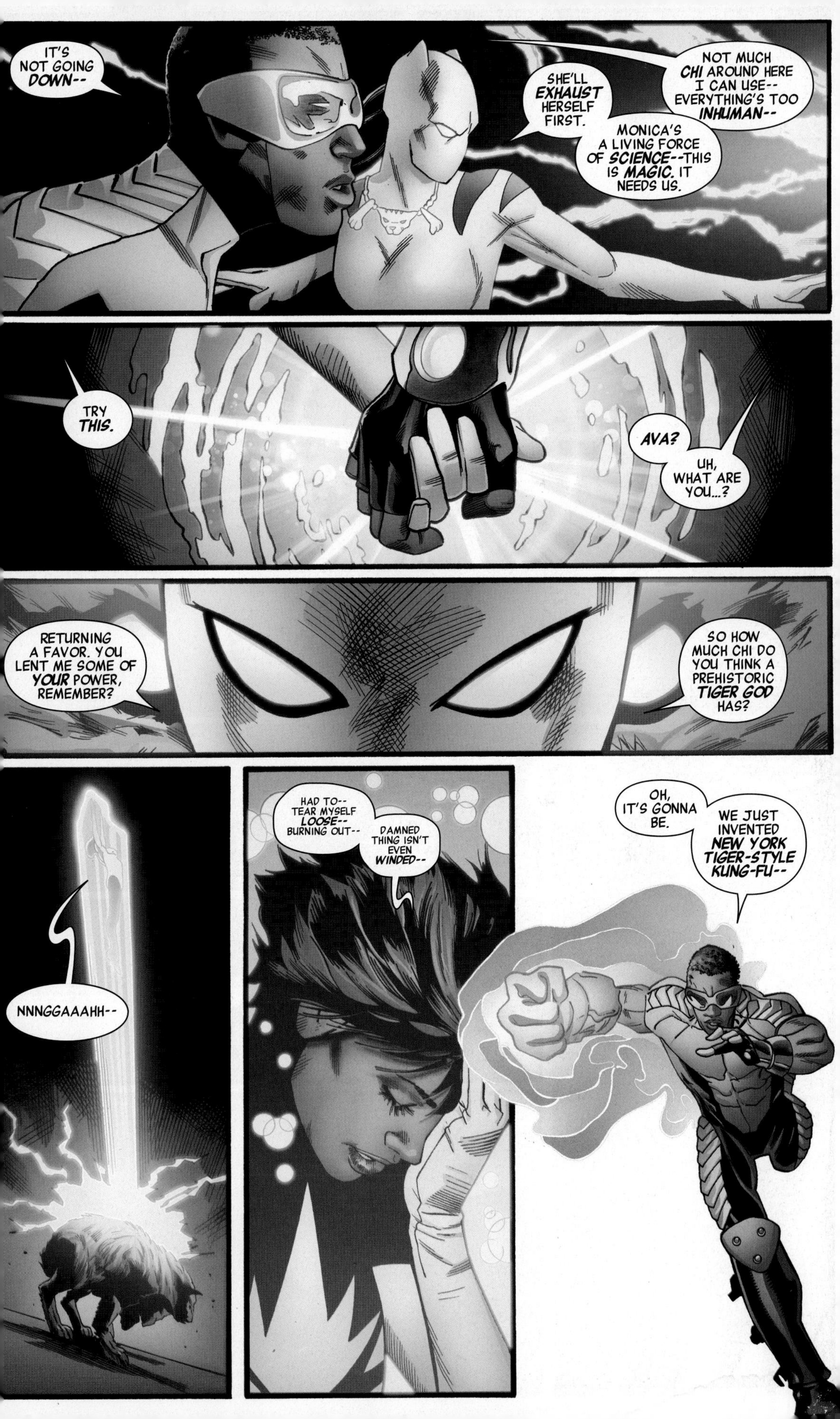
IT'S NOT GOING DOWN--
SHE'LL EXHAUST HERSELF FIRST.
MONICA'S A LIVING FORCE OF SCIENCE--THIS IS MAGIC. IT NEEDS US.
NOT MUCH CHI AROUND HERE I CAN USE--EVERYTHING'S TOO INHUMAN--
TRY THIS.
AVA?
UH, WHAT ARE YOU...?
RETURNING A FAVOR. YOU LENT ME SOME OF YOUR POWER, REMEMBER?
SO HOW MUCH CHI DO YOU THINK A PREHISTORIC TIGER GOD HAS?
NNNGGAAAHH--
HAD TO--TEAR MYSELF LOOSE--BURNING OUT--
DAMNED THING ISN'T EVEN WINDED--
OH, IT'S GONNA BE.
WE JUST INVENTED NEW YORK TIGER-STYLE KUNG-FU--

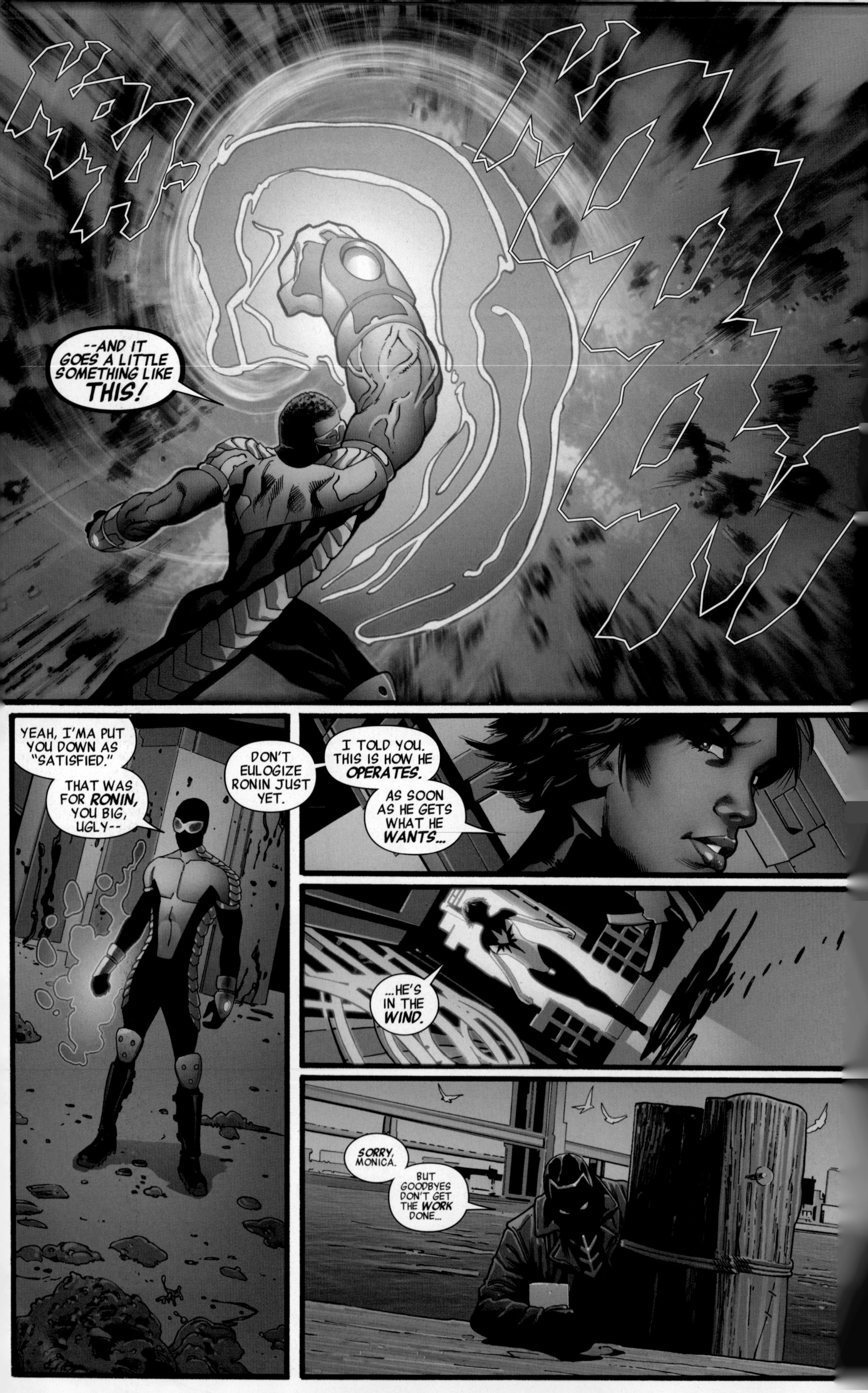

KA-
--AND IT GOES A LITTLE SOMETHING LIKE THIS!
KOOOM
YEAH, I'MA PUT YOU DOWN AS "SATISFIED."
THAT WAS FOR RONIN, YOU BIG, UGLY--
DON'T EULOGIZE RONIN JUST YET.
I TOLD YOU. THIS IS HOW HE OPERATES.
AS SOON AS HE GETS WHAT HE WANTS...
...HE'S IN THE WIND.
SORRY, MONICA.
BUT GOODBYES DON'T GET THE WORK DONE...

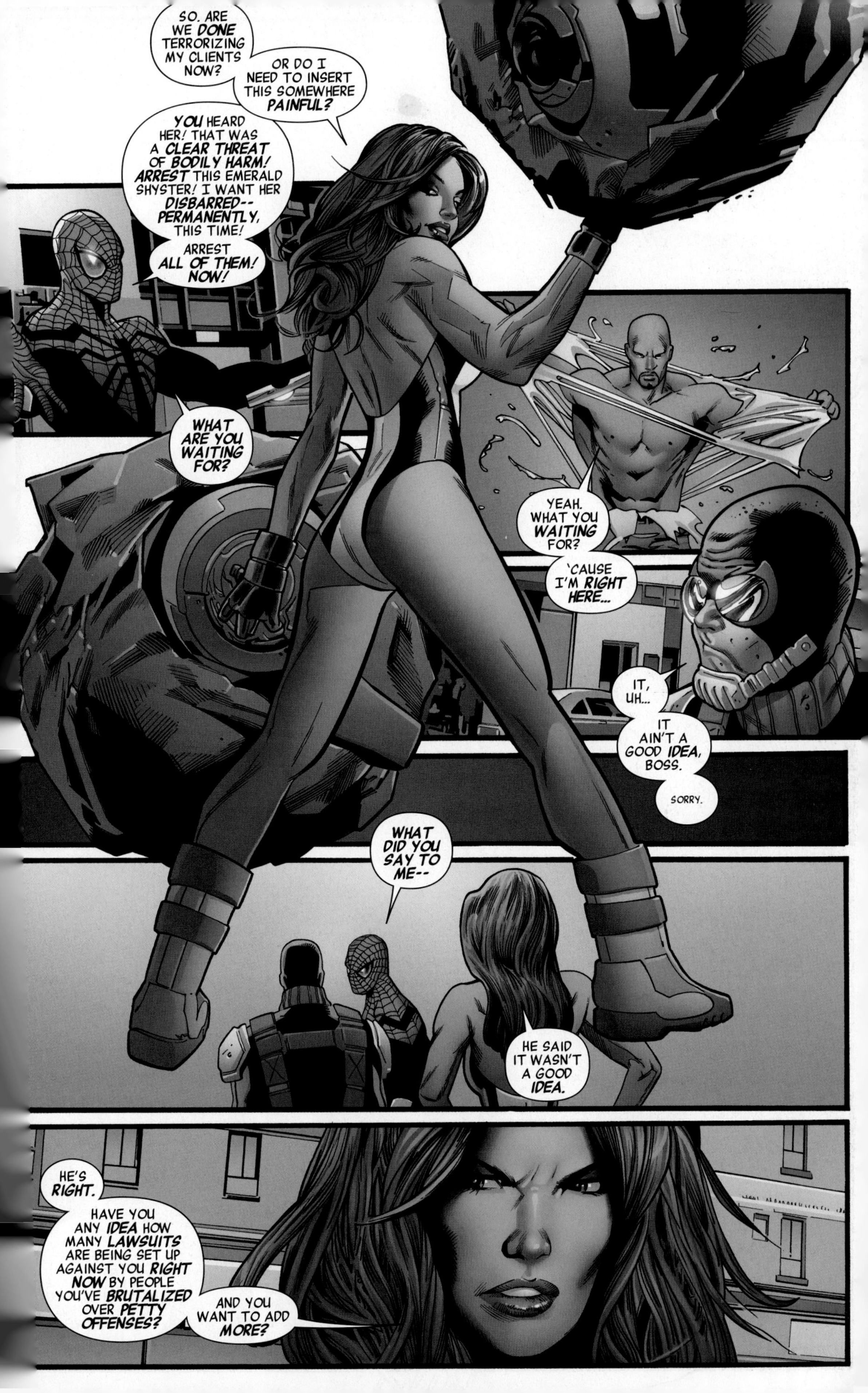
SO. ARE WE DONE TERRORIZING MY CLIENTS NOW?
OR DO I NEED TO INSERT THIS SOMEWHERE PAINFUL?
YOU HEARD HER! THAT WAS A CLEAR THREAT OF BODILY HARM! ARREST THIS EMERALD SHYSTER! I WANT HER DISBARRED-- PERMANENTLY, THIS TIME!
ARREST ALL OF THEM! NOW!
WHAT ARE YOU WAITING FOR?
YEAH. WHAT YOU WAITING FOR?
'CAUSE I'M RIGHT HERE...
IT, UH...
IT AIN'T A GOOD IDEA, BOSS.
SORRY.
WHAT DID YOU SAY TO ME--
HE SAID IT WASN'T A GOOD IDEA.
HE'S RIGHT.
HAVE YOU ANY IDEA HOW MANY LAWSUITS ARE BEING SET UP AGAINST YOU RIGHT NOW BY PEOPLE YOU'VE BRUTALIZED OVER PETTY OFFENSES?
AND YOU WANT TO ADD MORE?

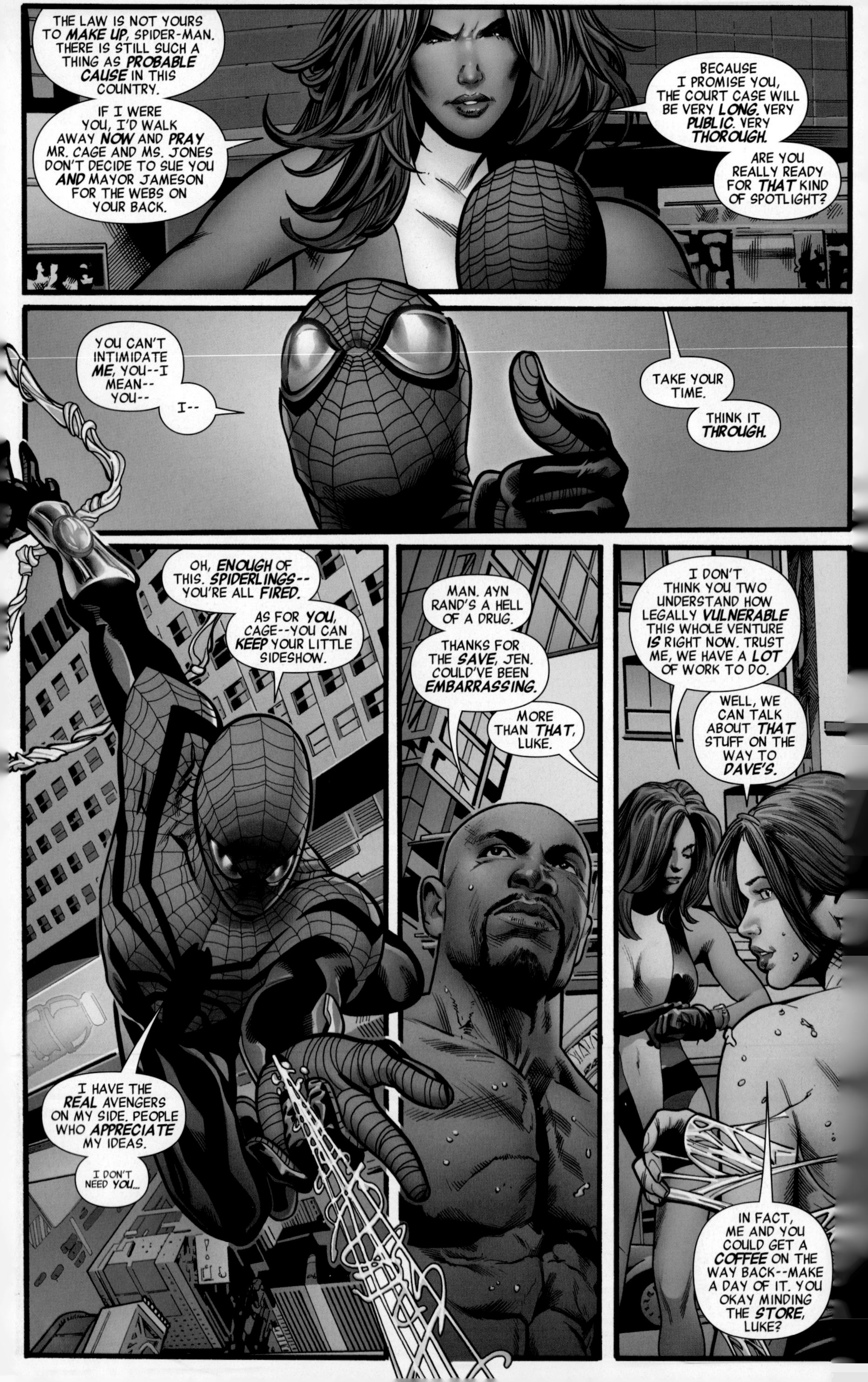
THE LAW IS NOT YOURS TO MAKE UP, SPIDER-MAN. THERE IS STILL SUCH A THING AS PROBABLE CAUSE IN THIS COUNTRY.
IF I WERE YOU, I'D WALK AWAY NOW AND PRAY MR. CAGE AND MS. JONES DON'T DECIDE TO SUE YOU AND MAYOR JAMESON FOR THE WEBS ON YOUR BACK.
BECAUSE I PROMISE YOU, THE COURT CASE WILL BE VERY LONG. VERY PUBLIC. VERY THOROUGH.
ARE YOU REALLY READY FOR THAT KIND OF SPOTLIGHT?
YOU CAN'T INTIMIDATE ME, YOU--I MEAN-- YOU--
I--
TAKE YOUR TIME.
THINK IT THROUGH.
OH, ENOUGH OF THIS. SPIDERLINGS-- YOU'RE ALL FIRED.
AS FOR YOU, CAGE--YOU CAN KEEP YOUR LITTLE SIDESHOW.
I HAVE THE REAL AVENGERS ON MY SIDE. PEOPLE WHO APPRECIATE MY IDEAS.
I DON'T NEED YOU...
MAN. AYN RAND'S A HELL OF A DRUG.
THANKS FOR THE SAVE, JEN. COULD'VE BEEN EMBARRASSING.
MORE THAN THAT, LUKE.
I DON'T THINK YOU TWO UNDERSTAND HOW LEGALLY VULNERABLE THIS WHOLE VENTURE IS RIGHT NOW. TRUST ME, WE HAVE A LOT OF WORK TO DO.
WELL, WE CAN TALK ABOUT THAT STUFF ON THE WAY TO DAVE'S.
IN FACT, ME AND YOU COULD GET A COFFEE ON THE WAY BACK--MAKE A DAY OF IT. YOU OKAY MINDING THE STORE, LUKE?

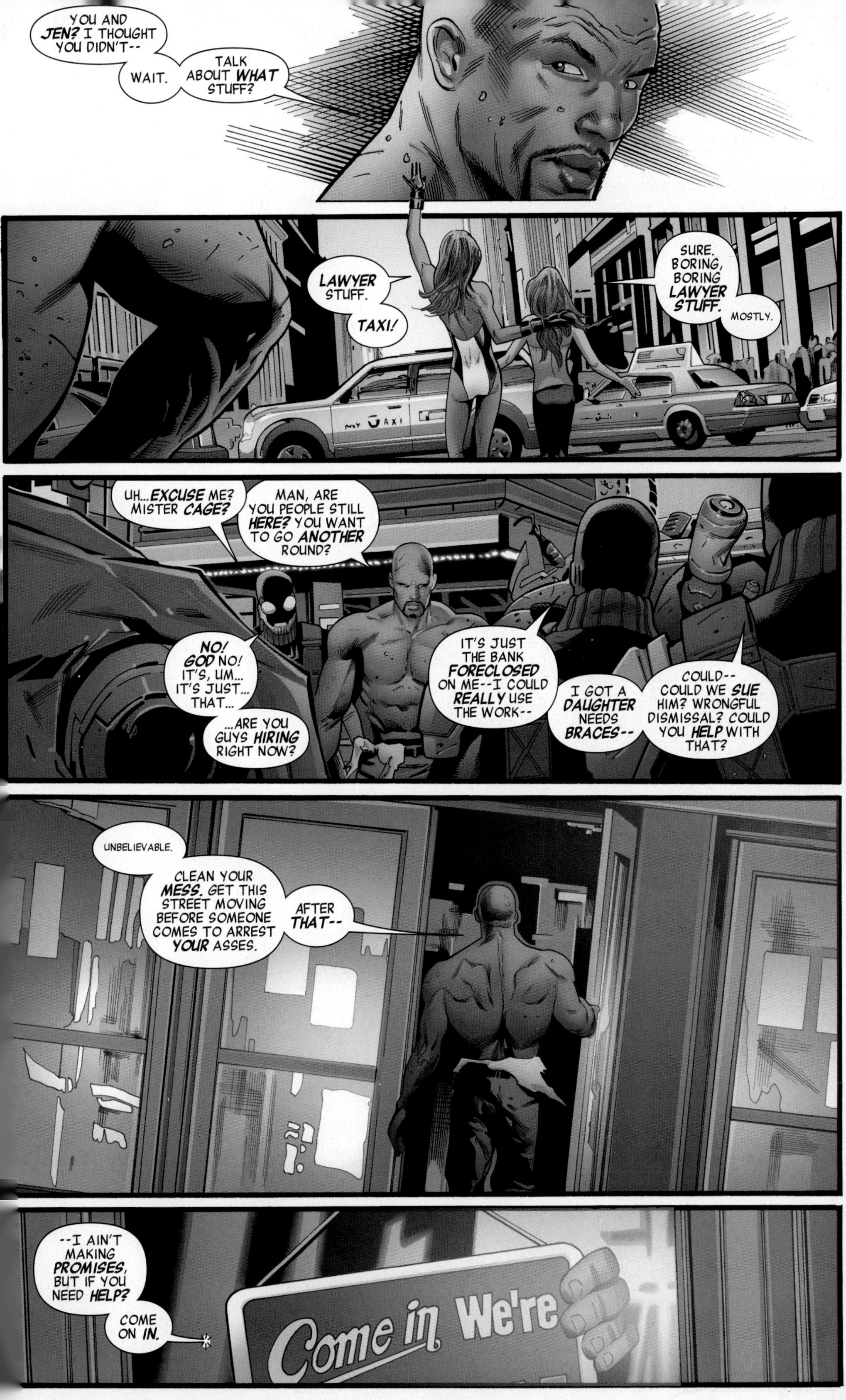

YOU AND JEN? I THOUGHT YOU DIDN'T--
WAIT.
TALK ABOUT WHAT STUFF?
LAWYER STUFF.
TAXI!
SURE. BORING, BORING LAWYER STUFF.
MOSTLY.
UH...EXCUSE ME? MISTER CAGE?
MAN, ARE YOU PEOPLE STILL HERE? YOU WANT TO GO ANOTHER ROUND?
NO! GOD NO! IT'S, UM... IT'S JUST... THAT...
...ARE YOU GUYS HIRING RIGHT NOW?
IT'S JUST THE BANK FORECLOSED ON ME--I COULD REALLY USE THE WORK--
I GOT A DAUGHTER NEEDS BRACES--
COULD-- COULD WE SUE HIM? WRONGFUL DISMISSAL? COULD YOU HELP WITH THAT?
UNBELIEVABLE.
CLEAN YOUR MESS. GET THIS STREET MOVING BEFORE SOMEONE COMES TO ARREST YOUR ASSES.
AFTER THAT--
--I AIN'T MAKING PROMISES, BUT IF YOU NEED HELP?
COME ON IN.
Come in We're

WE'RE OPEN.
THE MIGHTY AVENGERS
Come in We're
OPEN

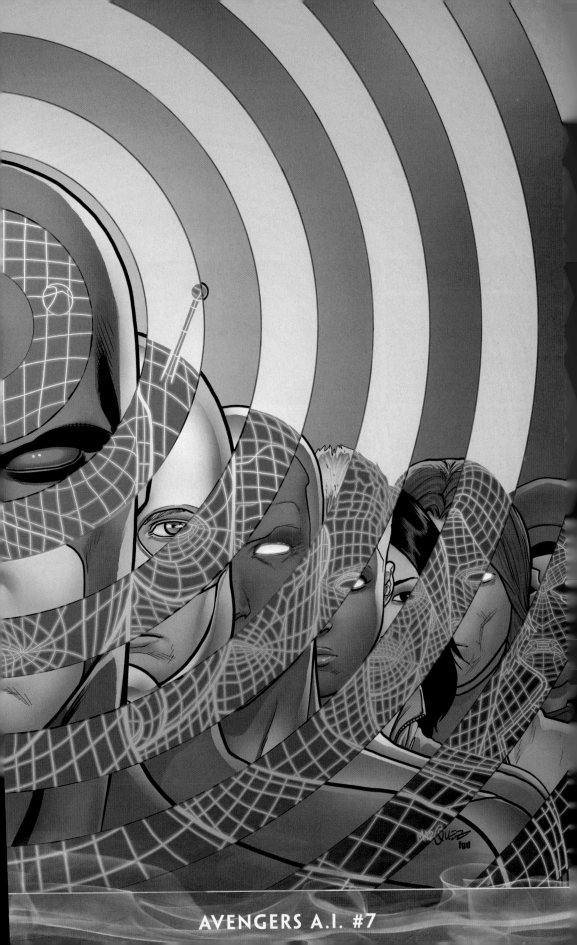

AVENGERS A.I. #7

PREVIOUSLY IN
AVENGERS A.I.

:DATE // THE CURRENT DATE IS --> WED 12/11/13

:RECAP // THE AVENGERS HAD LEFT EARTH TO FIGHT A WAR IN SPACE. CAPITALIZING ON THEIR ABSENCE, THE MAD TITAN THANOS ATTACKED EARTH IN AN ATTEMPT TO LOCATE AND EXTERMINATE HIS INHUMAN SON.

IN ORDER TO PROTECT HIS PEOPLE FROM THANOS, THE INHUMAN KING BLACK BOLT DESTROYED THE CITY OF ATTILAN OVER NEW YORK AND RELEASED THE TRANSFORMATIVE TERRIGEN MISTS OVER THE EARTH CREATING MANY NEW INHUMANS. MOST OF THESE NEWLY POWERED INDIVIDUALS WERE UNAWARE OF THEIR UNIQUE GENETIC HERITAGE.

WITH THE BROKEN CITY OF ATTILAN NOW LYING ON THE HUDSON RIVER, IT WILL PROVIDE A RIPE TARGET FOR THOSE LOOKING TO SCAVENGE ITS REMAINS FOR UNKNOWN TREASURES AND WEAPONS.

MEANWHILE, S.H.I.E.L.D. DIRECTOR MARIA HILL REASSIGNED AGENT MONICA CHANG TO AN A.I. HUNTING TEAM DESIGNED TO ENFORCE LEGISLATION THAT RULES ARTIFICIAL INTELLIGENCE AS INTELLECTUAL PROPERTY, ALLOWING AUTHORITIES TO KIDNAP AND DEACTIVATE A.I.S AT WILL.

:EJECT (A.I. N07 RECAP)

:EXIT

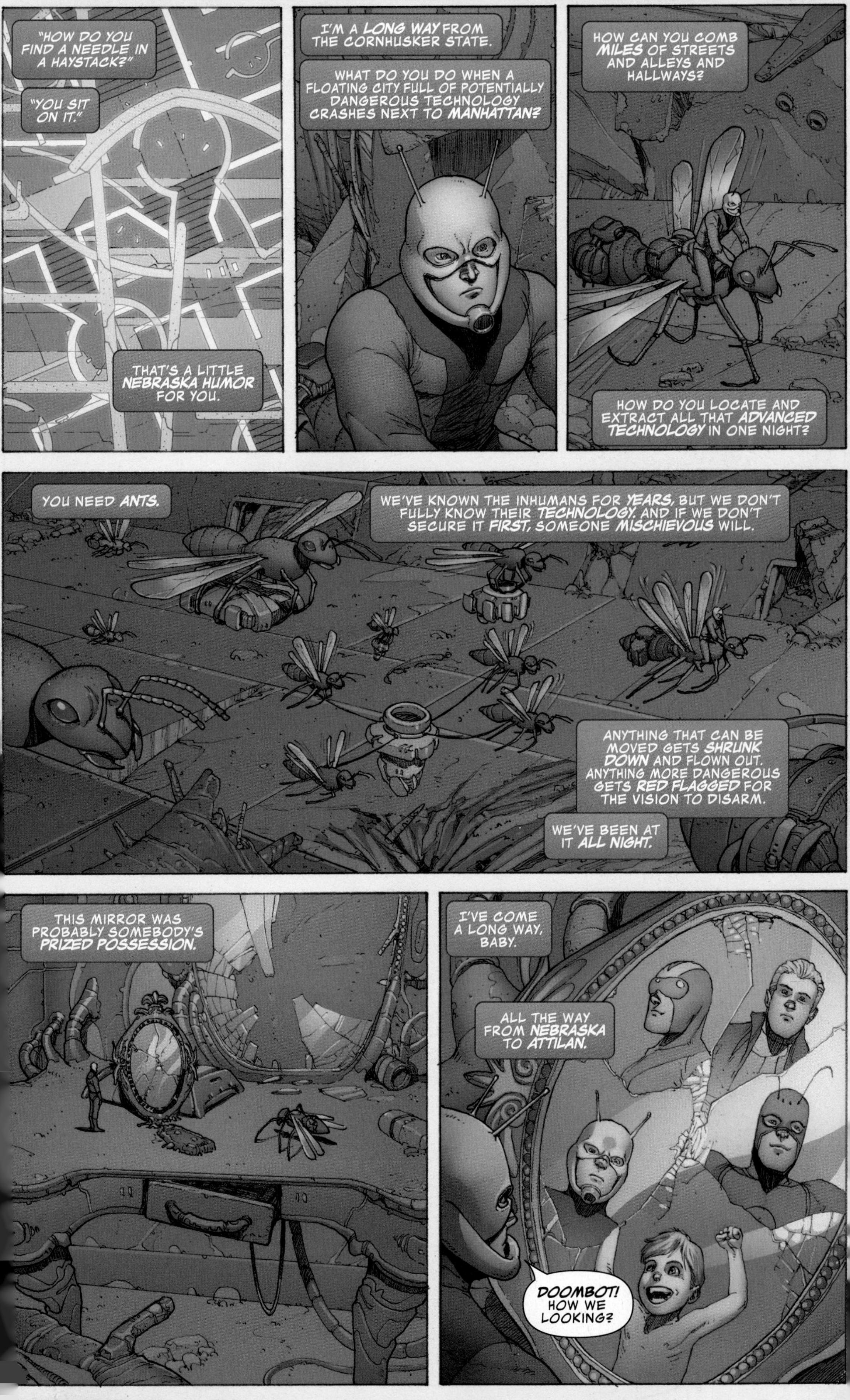
"HOW DO YOU FIND A NEEDLE IN A HAYSTACK?"
"YOU SIT ON IT."
THAT'S A LITTLE NEBRASKA HUMOR FOR YOU.
I'M A LONG WAY FROM THE CORNHUSKER STATE.
WHAT DO YOU DO WHEN A FLOATING CITY FULL OF POTENTIALLY DANGEROUS TECHNOLOGY CRASHES NEXT TO MANHATTAN?
HOW CAN YOU COMB MILES OF STREETS AND ALLEYS AND HALLWAYS?
HOW DO YOU LOCATE AND EXTRACT ALL THAT ADVANCED TECHNOLOGY IN ONE NIGHT?
YOU NEED ANTS.
WE'VE KNOWN THE INHUMANS FOR YEARS, BUT WE DON'T FULLY KNOW THEIR TECHNOLOGY. AND IF WE DON'T SECURE IT FIRST, SOMEONE MISCHIEVOUS WILL.
ANYTHING THAT CAN BE MOVED GETS SHRUNK DOWN AND FLOWN OUT. ANYTHING MORE DANGEROUS GETS RED FLAGGED FOR THE VISION TO DISARM.
WE'VE BEEN AT IT ALL NIGHT.
THIS MIRROR WAS PROBABLY SOMEBODY'S PRIZED POSSESSION.
I'VE COME A LONG WAY, BABY.
ALL THE WAY FROM NEBRASKA TO ATTILAN.
DOOMBOT! HOW WE LOOKING?

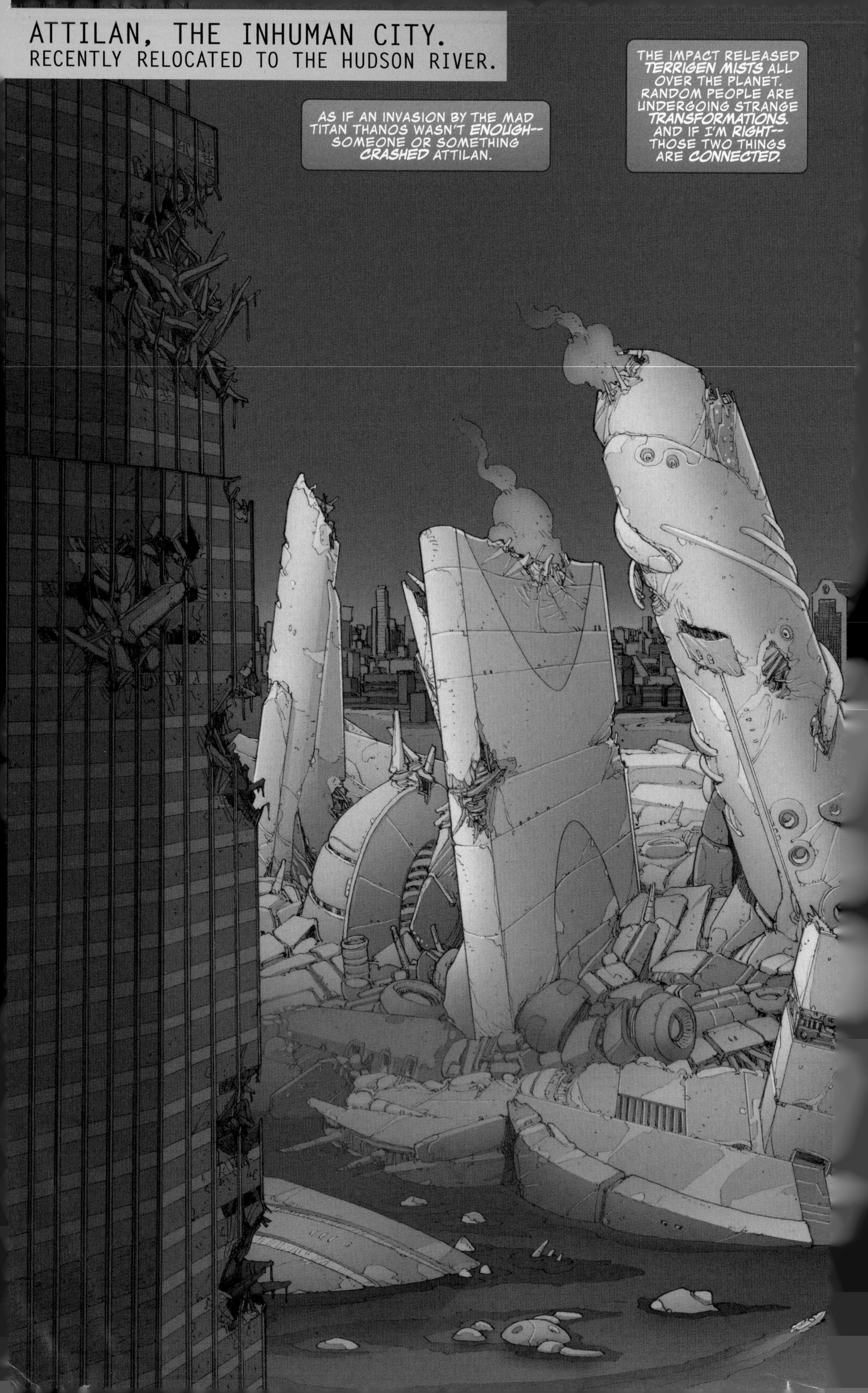
ATTILAN, THE INHUMAN CITY.
RECENTLY RELOCATED TO THE HUDSON RIVER.
AS IF AN INVASION BY THE MAD TITAN THANOS WASN'T ENOUGH-- SOMEONE OR SOMETHING CRASHED ATTILAN.
THE IMPACT RELEASED TERRIGEN MISTS ALL OVER THE PLANET. RANDOM PEOPLE ARE UNDERGOING STRANGE TRANSFORMATIONS. AND IF I'M RIGHT-- THOSE TWO THINGS ARE CONNECTED.

WHAT'S AN INHUMAN NATION WHEN YOU CRASH IT INTO A WORLD OF HUMANS?
WHAT'S A CITY OF THE SKY WHEN YOU DUNK IT INTO THE SEA?
WHAT'S A KINGDOM WITHOUT A KING?
EXACTLY THE SAME AS FIVE MINUTES AGO.
THERE IS A GIANT CITY IN YOUR RIVER.
GOOD, KEEP IT UP, DOOMBOT.
NO ONE GETS IN OR OUT OF ATTILAN UNTIL WE'RE DONE.

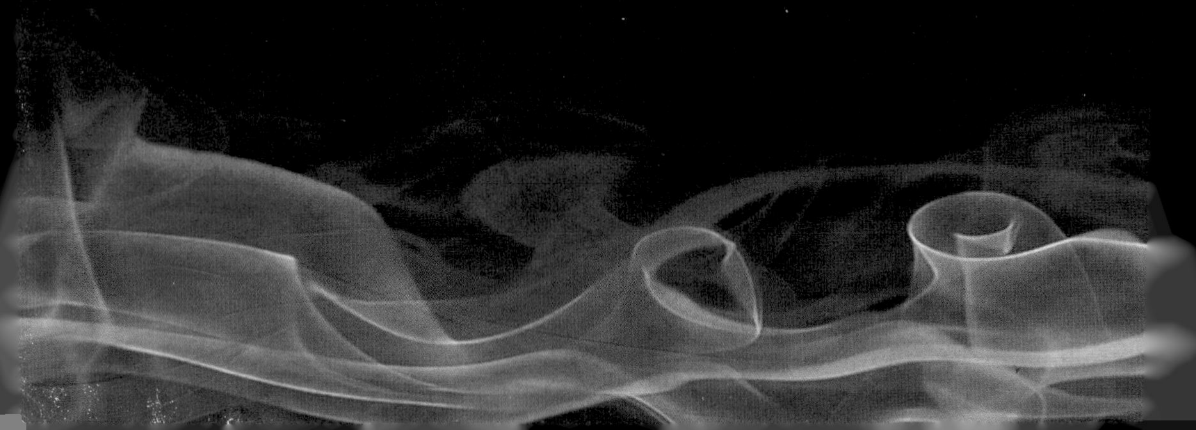

HANK, I AM PICKING UP A *STRANGE READING*, TWO BLOCKS INLAND. 48TH STREET, EAST OF 10TH AVENUE.

A CREATURE WITH A *VOLATILE* ENERGY SIGNATURE. MOVING *SLOWLY*.

THANKS, *VISION*. BETTER CHECK IT OUT, JUST TO BE *SURE*. DOOMBOT, *PROCEED* TO THE BOGEY'S LOCATION.

IF I MUST.

DOOM'S *SOUL* YEARNS TO SOAR WITH *NOBLE FALCONS*, YET MY BODY MEANDERS WITH *GOAT-KNEED GILLYFLOWERS*--

SQRRK ****

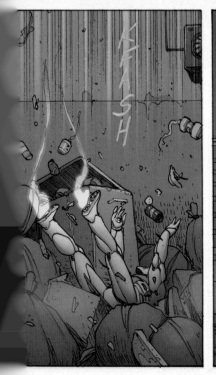

KRASH

WHO DARES--?!

SHOW YOURSELF!

DOOM!

THUMP

KWRRK ***

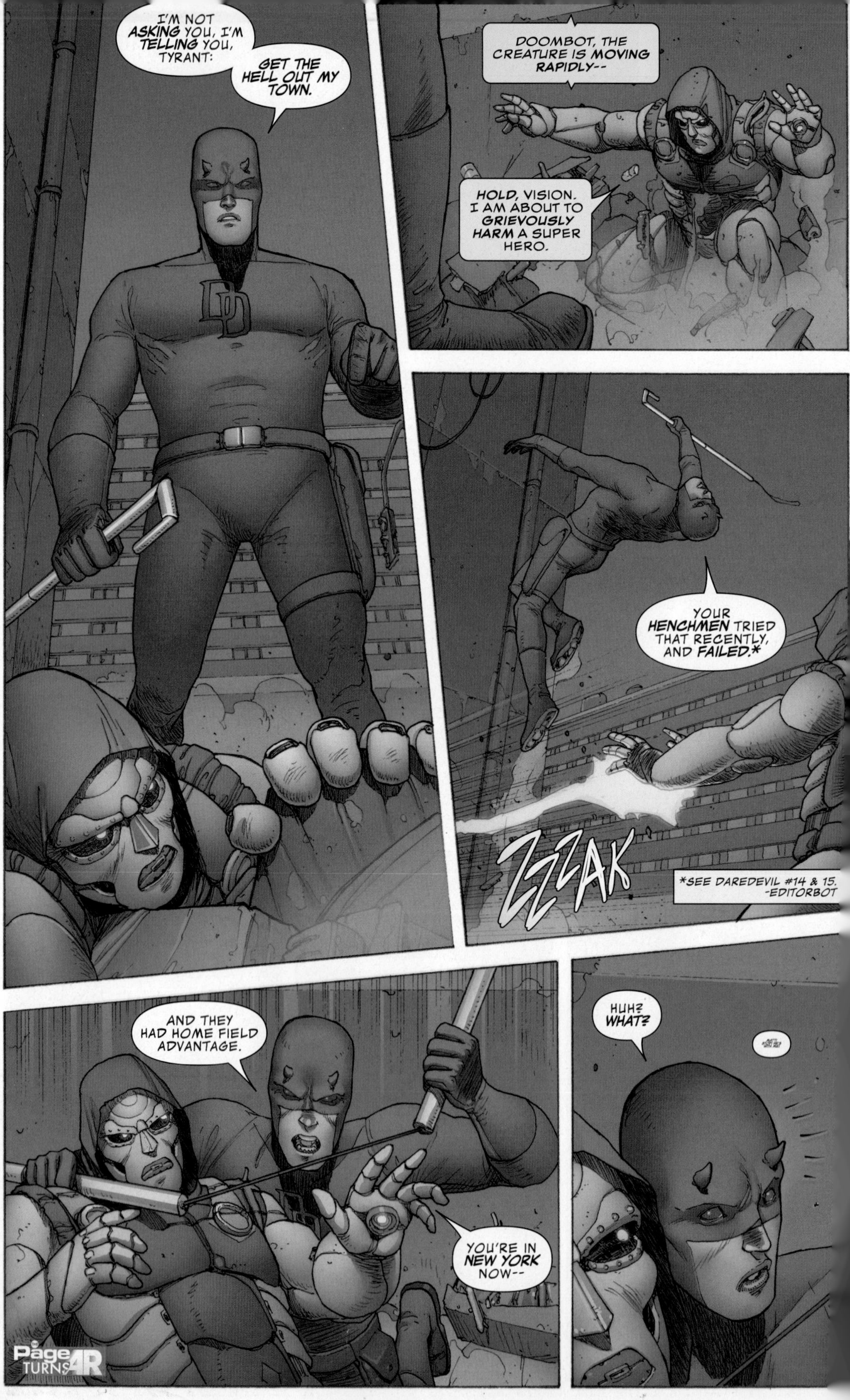
I'M NOT ASKING YOU, I'M TELLING YOU, TYRANT:
GET THE HELL OUT MY TOWN.
DOOMBOT, THE CREATURE IS MOVING RAPIDLY--
HOLD, VISION. I AM ABOUT TO GRIEVOUSLY HARM A SUPER HERO.
YOUR HENCHMEN TRIED THAT RECENTLY, AND FAILED.*
ZZZZAK
*SEE DAREDEVIL #14 & 15. -EDITORBOT
AND THEY HAD HOME FIELD ADVANTAGE.
YOU'RE IN NEW YORK NOW--
HUH? WHAT?

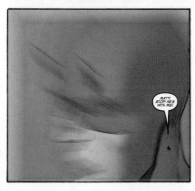
MATT! STOP! HE'S WITH ME!

MATT! STOP! HE'S WITH ME!

MATT! STOP! HE'S WITH ME!

I KNOW THAT *VOICE*, AND I KNOW THAT *HEARTBEAT.*

WAIT--

UNHAND ME!

YOUR *VOICE*-- CUT THROUGH WITH A SOUR STRAIN.

LIKE AN OLD *SPEAKER.*

THROUGH MY ARMS I FEEL THE TINY KITTEN-PURR *VIBRATIONS*--

OF A THOUSAND *SERVOS.*

THE SLIGHTLY ASTRINGENT TANG OF *IONIZED AIR*--

COOLING VENTS.

YOU'RE NOT *DOCTOR DOOM*--

OBVIOUSLY.

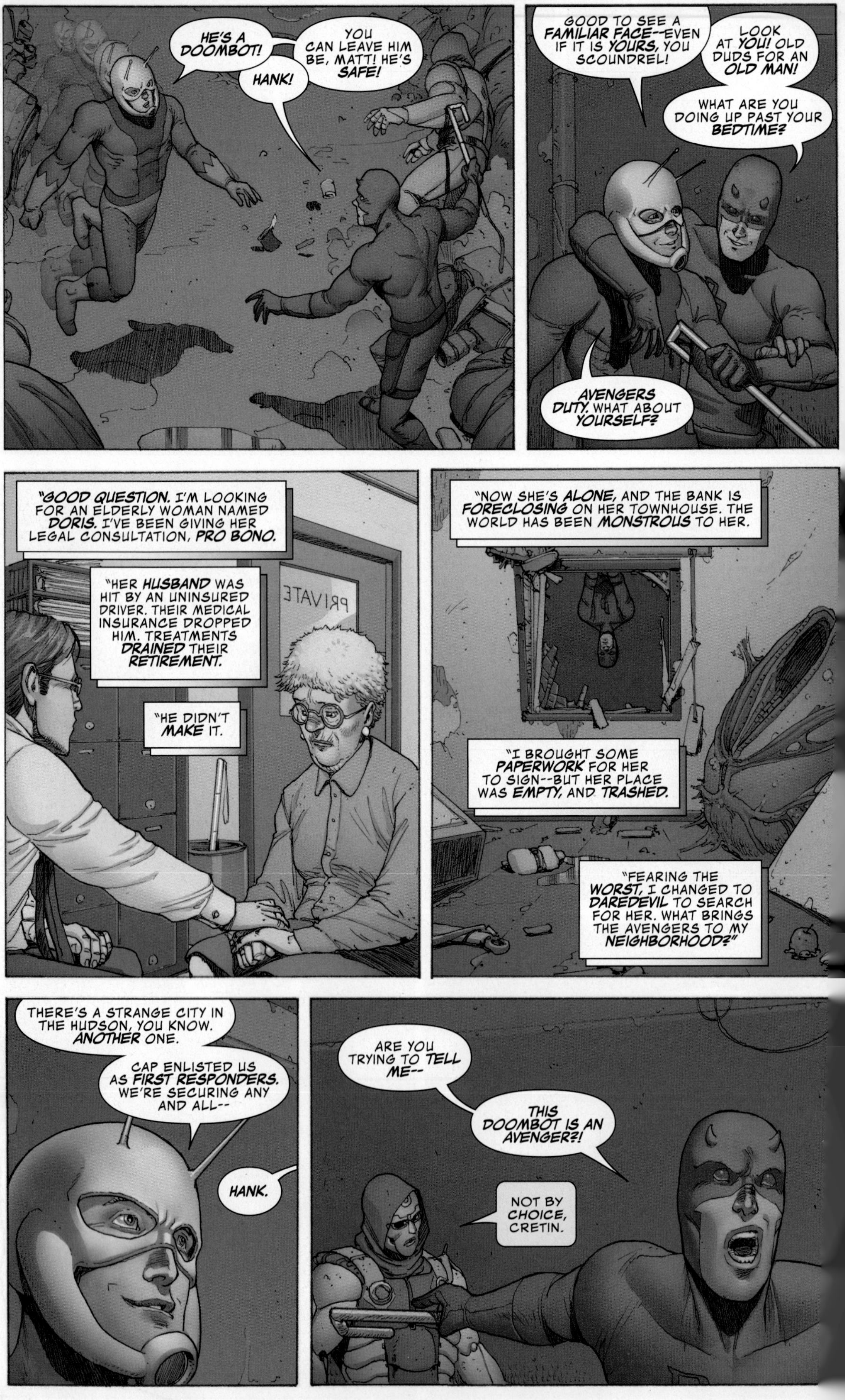
HE'S A DOOMBOT!
HANK!
YOU CAN LEAVE HIM BE, MATT! HE'S SAFE!
GOOD TO SEE A FAMILIAR FACE--EVEN IF IT IS YOURS, YOU SCOUNDREL!
LOOK AT YOU! OLD DUDS FOR AN OLD MAN!
WHAT ARE YOU DOING UP PAST YOUR BEDTIME?
AVENGERS DUTY. WHAT ABOUT YOURSELF?
"GOOD QUESTION. I'M LOOKING FOR AN ELDERLY WOMAN NAMED DORIS. I'VE BEEN GIVING HER LEGAL CONSULTATION, PRO BONO.
"HER HUSBAND WAS HIT BY AN UNINSURED DRIVER. THEIR MEDICAL INSURANCE DROPPED HIM. TREATMENTS DRAINED THEIR RETIREMENT.
PRIVATE
"HE DIDN'T MAKE IT.
"NOW SHE'S ALONE, AND THE BANK IS FORECLOSING ON HER TOWNHOUSE. THE WORLD HAS BEEN MONSTROUS TO HER.
"I BROUGHT SOME PAPERWORK FOR HER TO SIGN--BUT HER PLACE WAS EMPTY, AND TRASHED.
"FEARING THE WORST, I CHANGED TO DAREDEVIL TO SEARCH FOR HER. WHAT BRINGS THE AVENGERS TO MY NEIGHBORHOOD?"
THERE'S A STRANGE CITY IN THE HUDSON, YOU KNOW. ANOTHER ONE.
CAP ENLISTED US AS FIRST RESPONDERS. WE'RE SECURING ANY AND ALL--
HANK.
ARE YOU TRYING TO TELL ME--
THIS DOOMBOT IS AN AVENGER?!
NOT BY CHOICE, CRETIN.

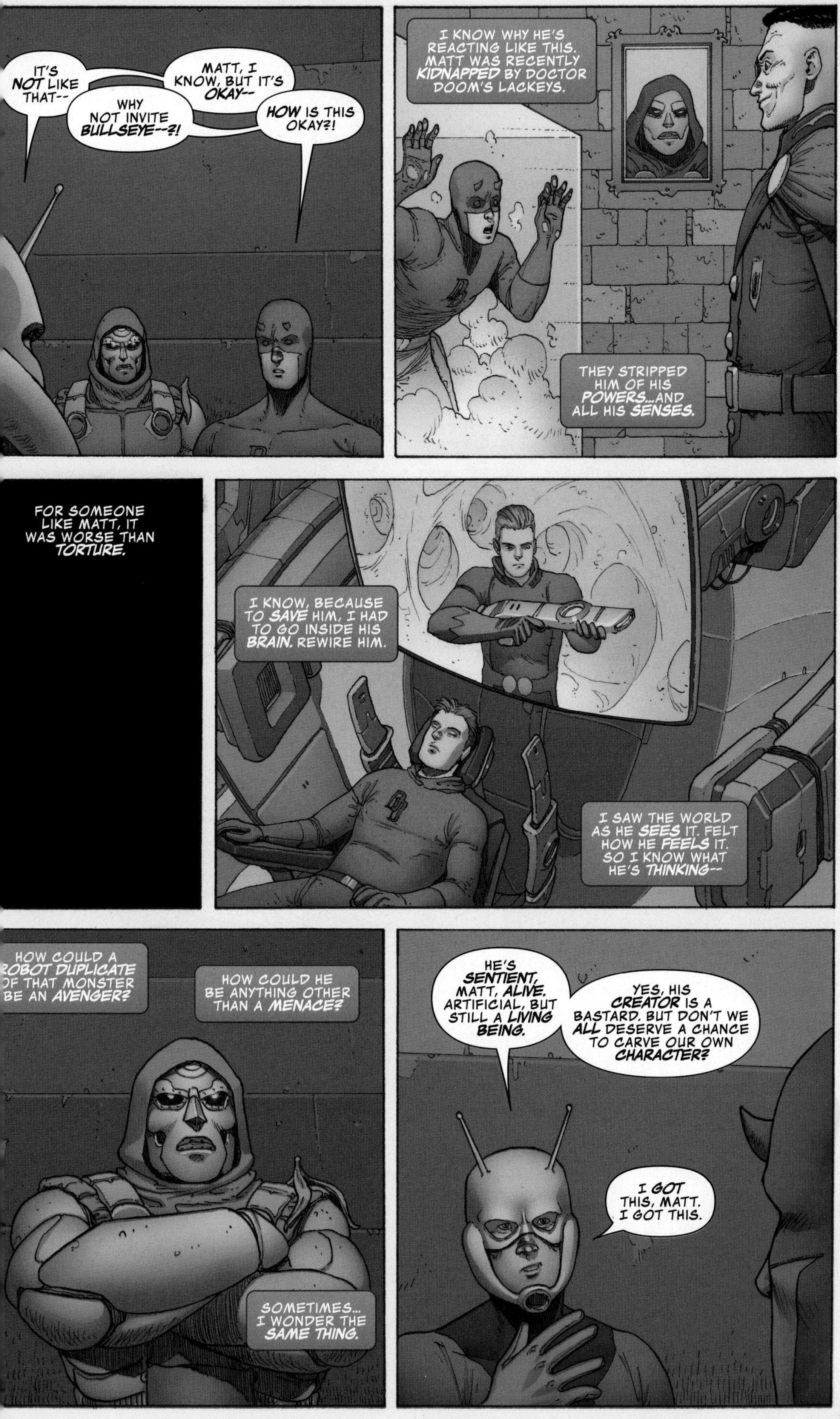
IT'S NOT LIKE THAT--
MATT, I KNOW, BUT IT'S OKAY--
WHY NOT INVITE BULLSEYE--?!
HOW IS THIS OKAY?!
I KNOW WHY HE'S REACTING LIKE THIS. MATT WAS RECENTLY KIDNAPPED BY DOCTOR DOOM'S LACKEYS.
THEY STRIPPED HIM OF HIS POWERS...AND ALL HIS SENSES.
FOR SOMEONE LIKE MATT, IT WAS WORSE THAN TORTURE.
I KNOW, BECAUSE TO SAVE HIM, I HAD TO GO INSIDE HIS BRAIN. REWIRE HIM.
I SAW THE WORLD AS HE SEES IT. FELT HOW HE FEELS IT. SO I KNOW WHAT HE'S THINKING--
HOW COULD A ROBOT DUPLICATE OF THAT MONSTER BE AN AVENGER?
HOW COULD HE BE ANYTHING OTHER THAN A MENACE?
SOMETIMES... I WONDER THE SAME THING.
HE'S SENTIENT, MATT, ALIVE. ARTIFICIAL, BUT STILL A LIVING BEING.
YES, HIS CREATOR IS A BASTARD. BUT DON'T WE ALL DESERVE A CHANCE TO CARVE OUR OWN CHARACTER?
I GOT THIS, MATT. I GOT THIS.

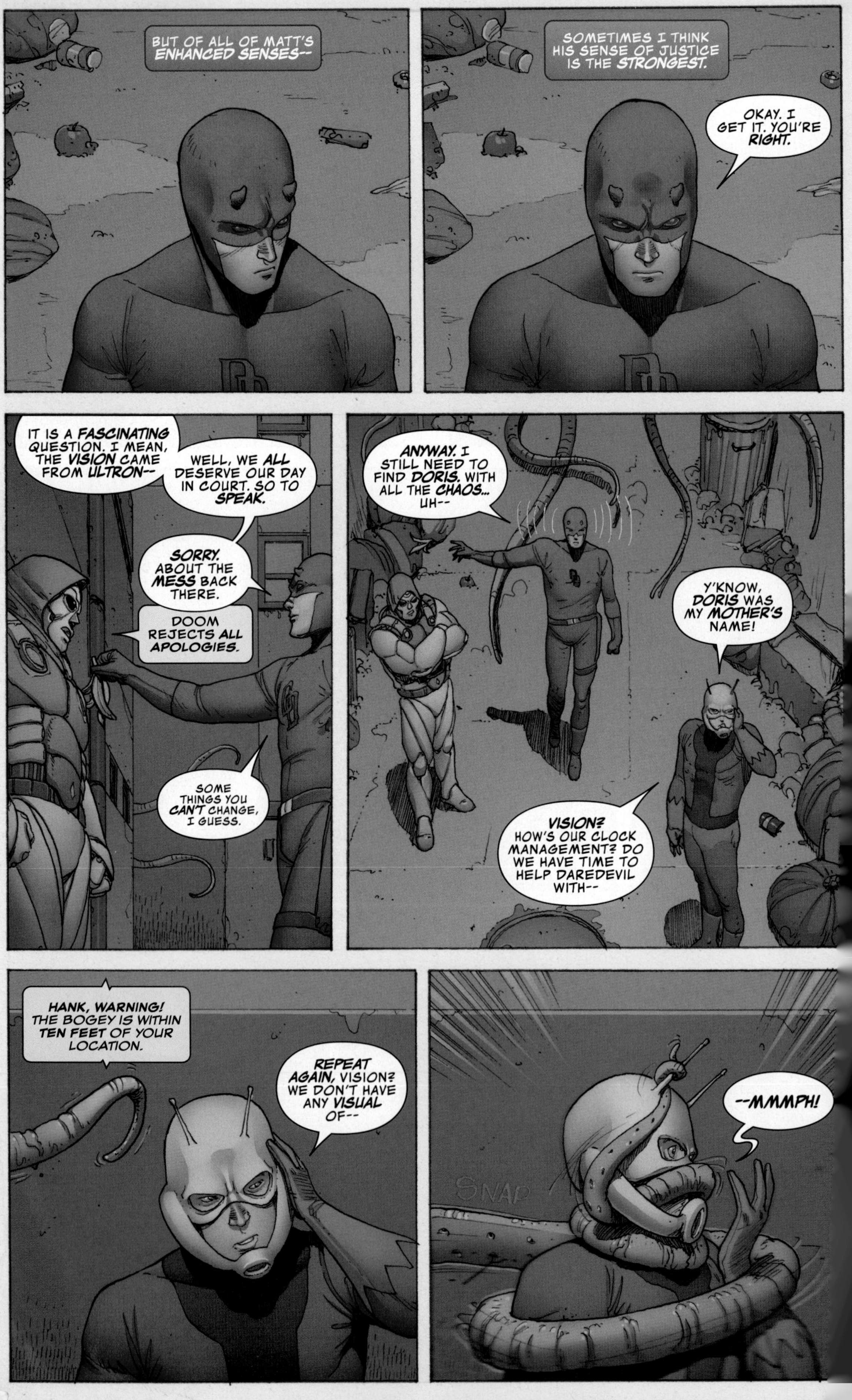
BUT OF ALL OF MATT'S ENHANCED SENSES--
SOMETIMES I THINK HIS SENSE OF JUSTICE IS THE STRONGEST.
OKAY. I GET IT. YOU'RE RIGHT.
IT IS A FASCINATING QUESTION. I MEAN, THE VISION CAME FROM ULTRON--
WELL, WE ALL DESERVE OUR DAY IN COURT. SO TO SPEAK.
SORRY. ABOUT THE MESS BACK THERE.
DOOM REJECTS ALL APOLOGIES.
SOME THINGS YOU CAN'T CHANGE, I GUESS.
ANYWAY. I STILL NEED TO FIND DORIS. WITH ALL THE CHAOS... UH--
Y'KNOW, DORIS WAS MY MOTHER'S NAME!
VISION? HOW'S OUR CLOCK MANAGEMENT? DO WE HAVE TIME TO HELP DAREDEVIL WITH--
HANK, WARNING! THE BOGEY IS WITHIN TEN FEET OF YOUR LOCATION.
REPEAT AGAIN, VISION? WE DON'T HAVE ANY VISUAL OF--
SNAP
--MMMPH!

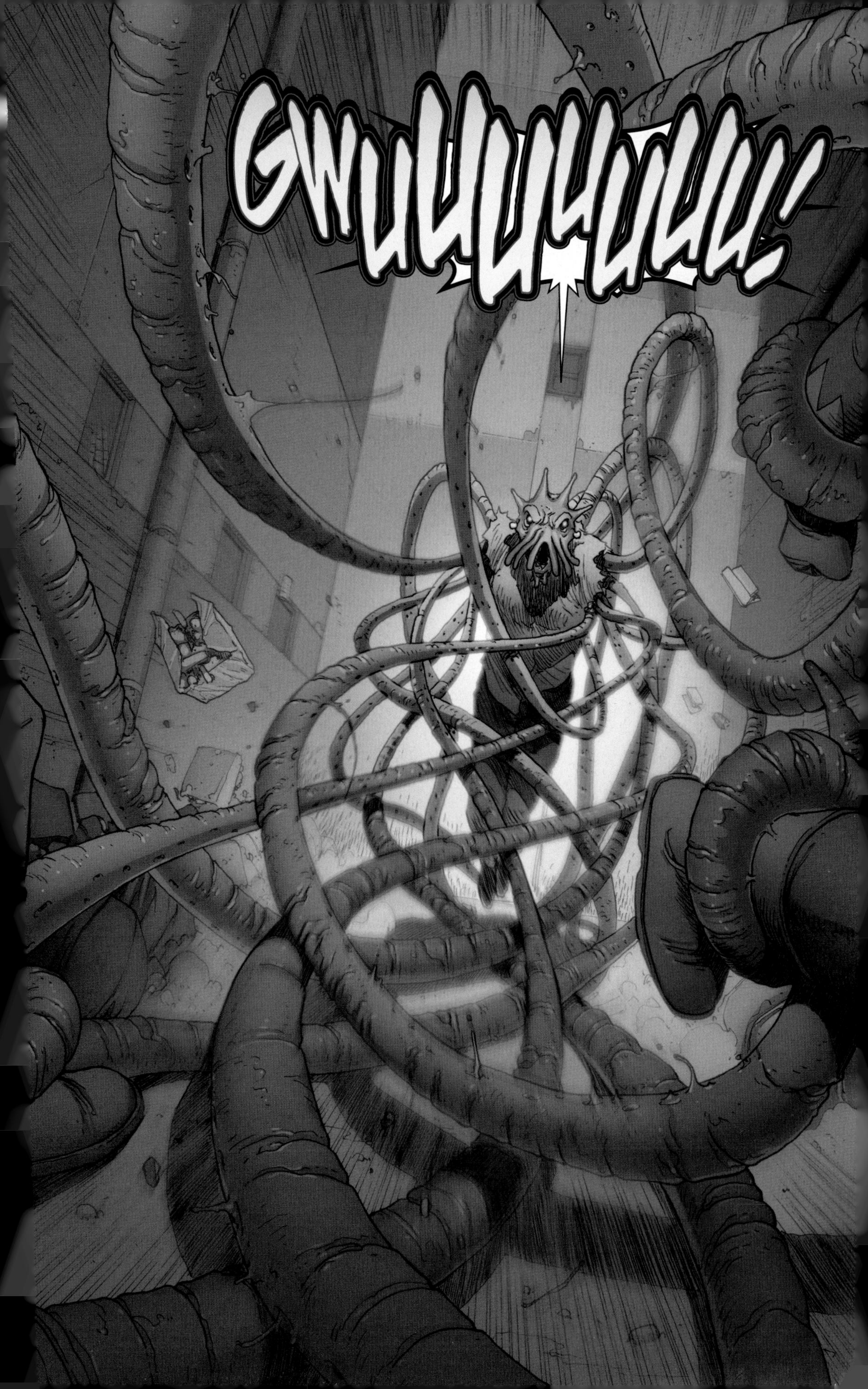
GWUUUUUUU!

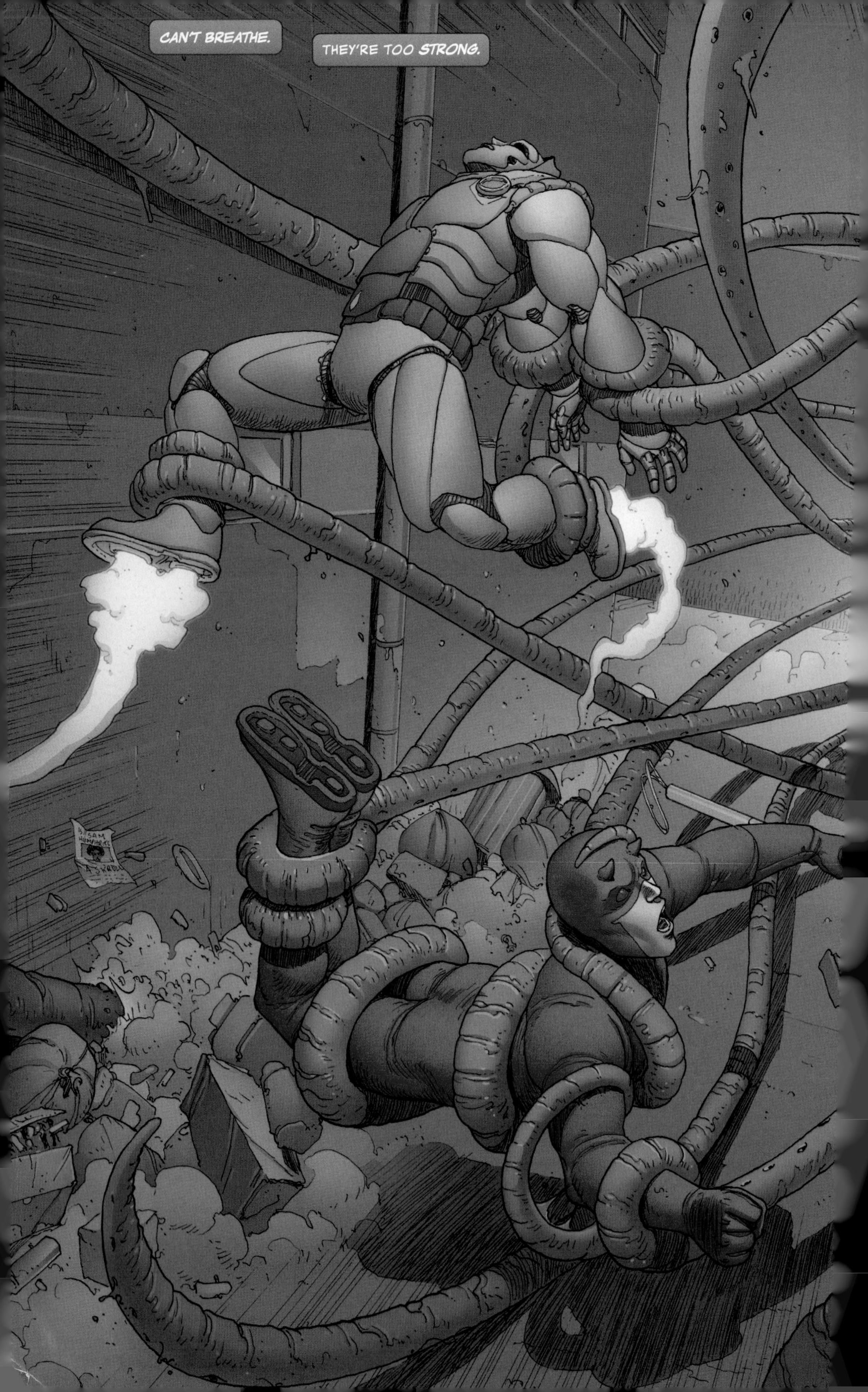
CAN'T BREATHE.
THEY'RE TOO STRONG.

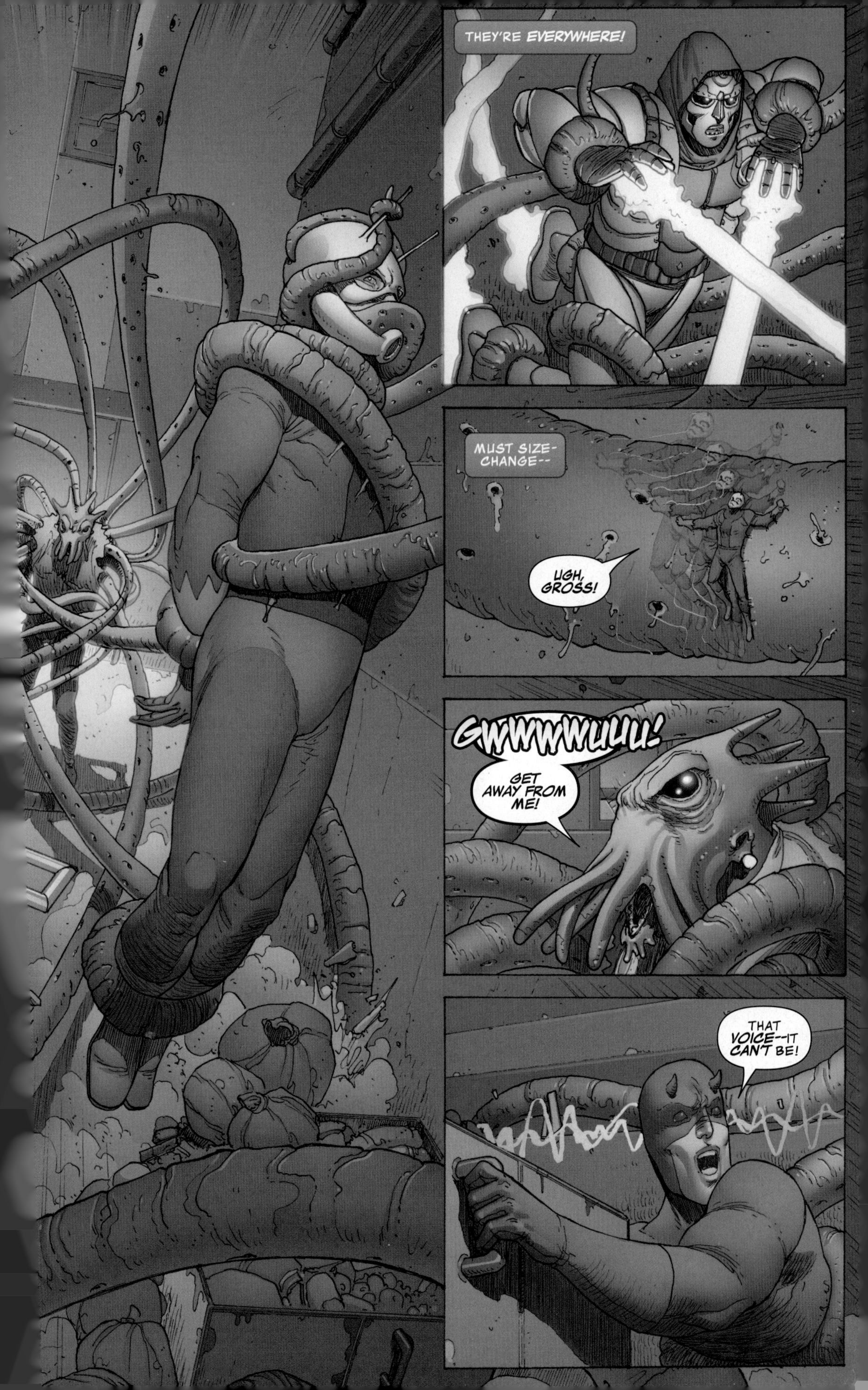
THEY'RE EVERYWHERE!
MUST SIZE-CHANGE--
UGH, GROSS!
GWWWWUUU!
GET AWAY FROM ME!
THAT VOICE--IT CAN'T BE!

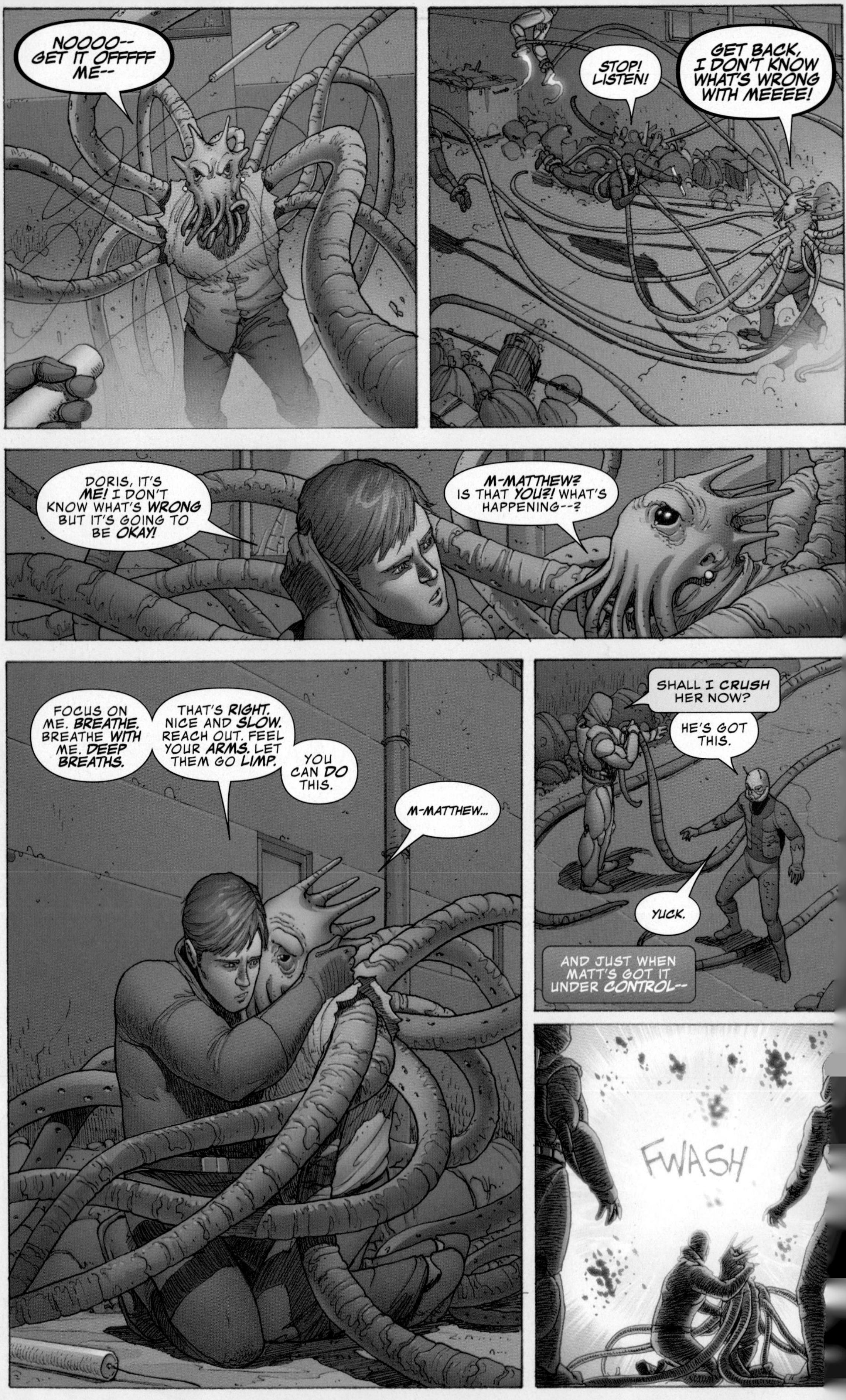
NOOOO--
GET IT OFFFFF
ME--
STOP!
LISTEN!
GET BACK,
I DON'T KNOW
WHAT'S WRONG
WITH MEEEE!
DORIS, IT'S ME! I DON'T KNOW WHAT'S WRONG BUT IT'S GOING TO BE OKAY!
M-MATTHEW? IS THAT YOU?! WHAT'S HAPPENING--?
FOCUS ON ME. BREATHE. BREATHE WITH ME. DEEP BREATHS.
THAT'S RIGHT. NICE AND SLOW. REACH OUT. FEEL YOUR ARMS. LET THEM GO LIMP.
YOU CAN DO THIS.
M-MATTHEW...
SHALL I CRUSH HER NOW?
HE'S GOT THIS.
YUCK.
AND JUST WHEN MATT'S GOT IT UNDER CONTROL--
FWASH

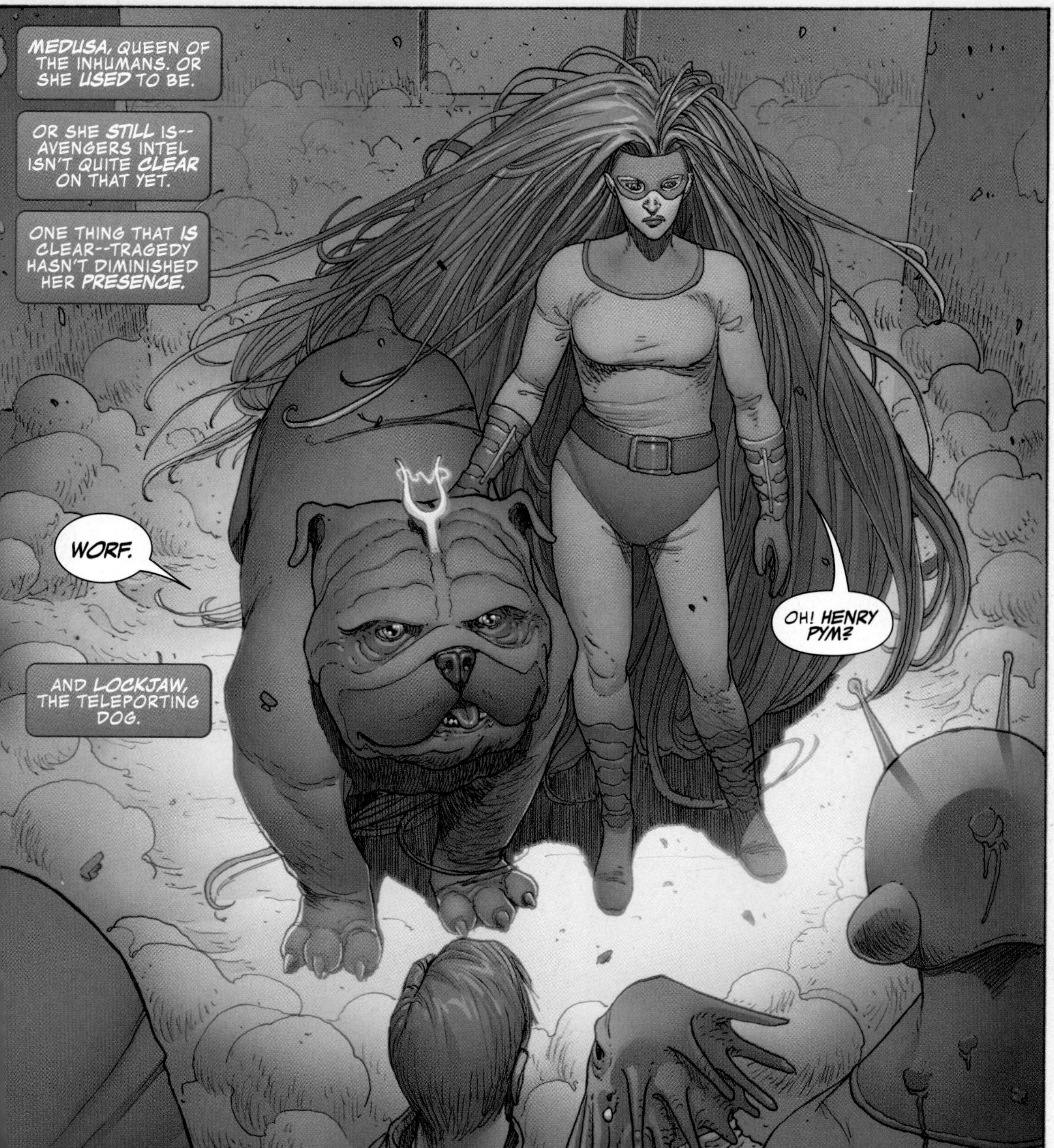
MEDUSA, QUEEN OF THE INHUMANS. OR SHE USED TO BE.
OR SHE STILL IS-- AVENGERS INTEL ISN'T QUITE CLEAR ON THAT YET.
ONE THING THAT IS CLEAR--TRAGEDY HASN'T DIMINISHED HER PRESENCE.
WORF.
OH! HENRY PYM?
AND LOCKJAW, THE TELEPORTING DOG.
GREAT. WHAT A TIME TO BE COVERED IN SNOT.

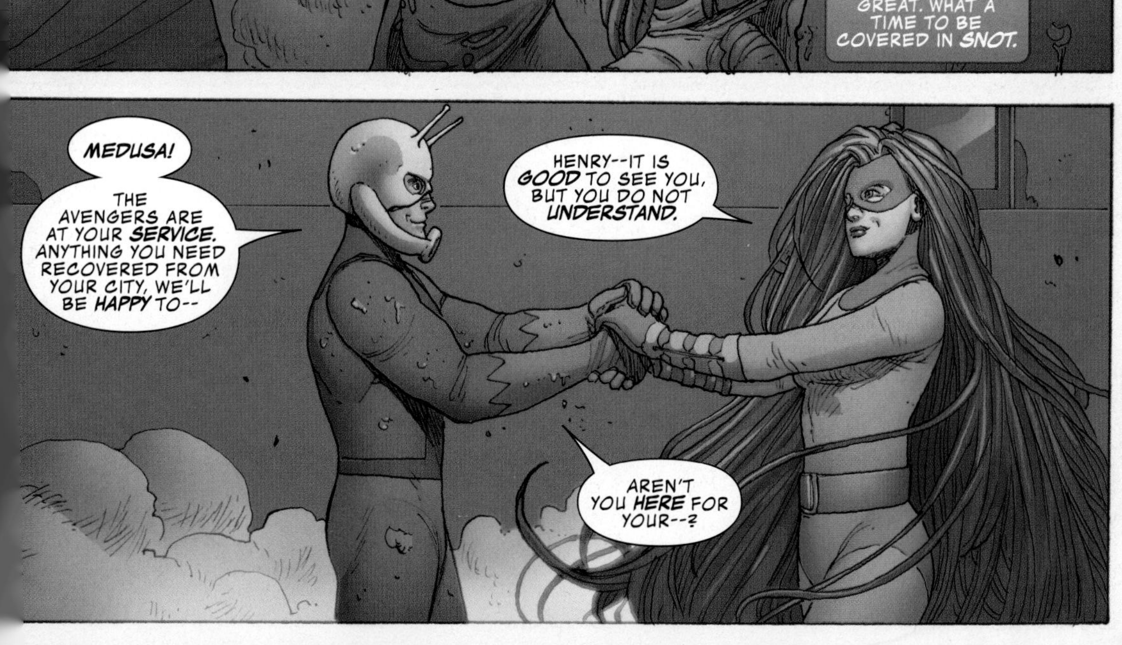
MEDUSA!
THE AVENGERS ARE AT YOUR SERVICE. ANYTHING YOU NEED RECOVERED FROM YOUR CITY, WE'LL BE HAPPY TO--
HENRY--IT IS GOOD TO SEE YOU, BUT YOU DO NOT UNDERSTAND.
AREN'T YOU HERE FOR YOUR--?

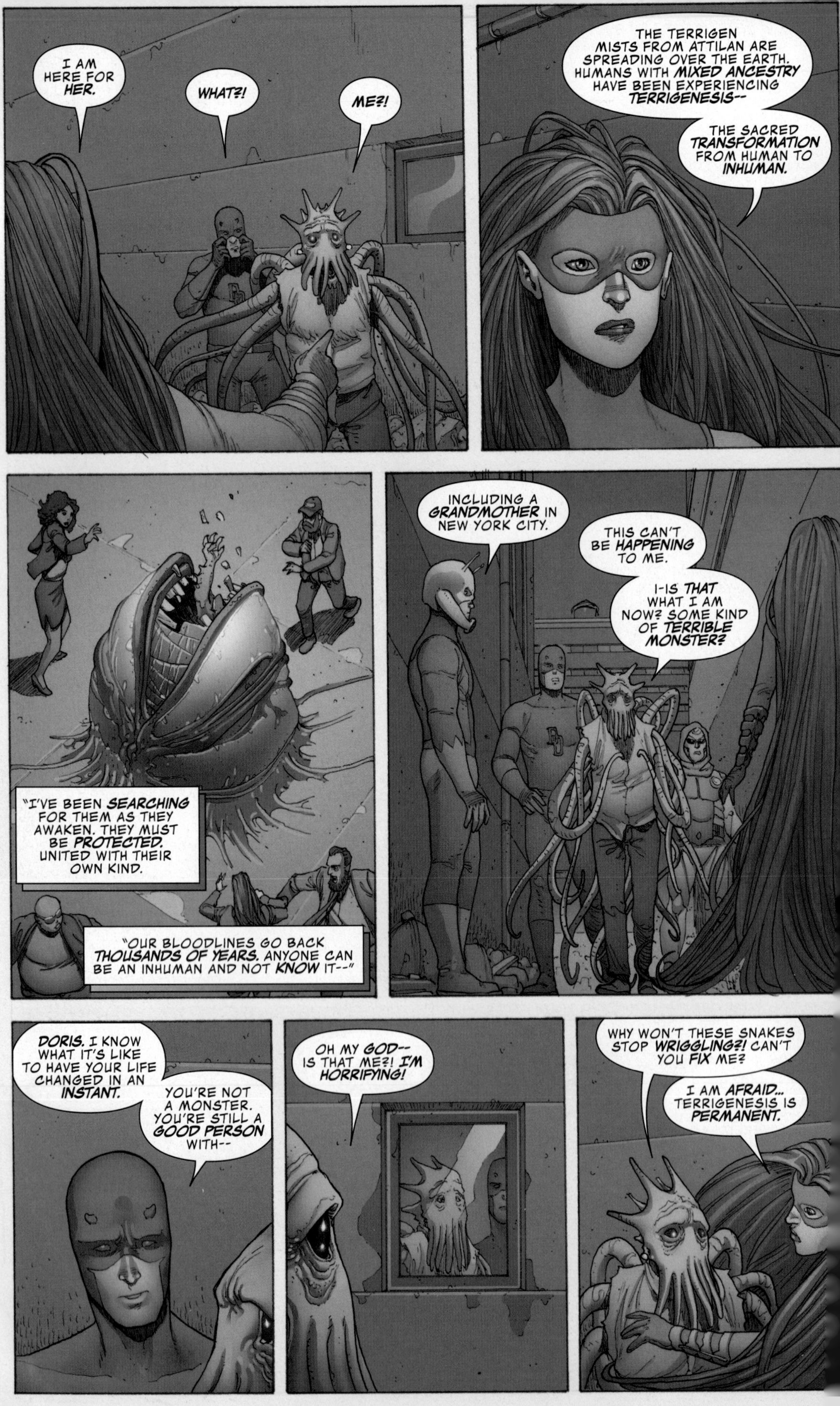
I AM HERE FOR HER.
WHAT?!
ME?!
THE TERRIGEN MISTS FROM ATTILAN ARE SPREADING OVER THE EARTH. HUMANS WITH MIXED ANCESTRY HAVE BEEN EXPERIENCING TERRIGENESIS--
THE SACRED TRANSFORMATION FROM HUMAN TO INHUMAN.
"I'VE BEEN SEARCHING FOR THEM AS THEY AWAKEN. THEY MUST BE PROTECTED. UNITED WITH THEIR OWN KIND.
"OUR BLOODLINES GO BACK THOUSANDS OF YEARS. ANYONE CAN BE AN INHUMAN AND NOT KNOW IT--"
INCLUDING A GRANDMOTHER IN NEW YORK CITY.
THIS CAN'T BE HAPPENING TO ME.
I-IS THAT WHAT I AM NOW? SOME KIND OF TERRIBLE MONSTER?
DORIS. I KNOW WHAT IT'S LIKE TO HAVE YOUR LIFE CHANGED IN AN INSTANT.
YOU'RE NOT A MONSTER. YOU'RE STILL A GOOD PERSON WITH--
OH MY GOD-- IS THAT ME?! I'M HORRIFYING!
WHY WON'T THESE SNAKES STOP WRIGGLING?! CAN'T YOU FIX ME?
I AM AFRAID... TERRIGENESIS IS PERMANENT.

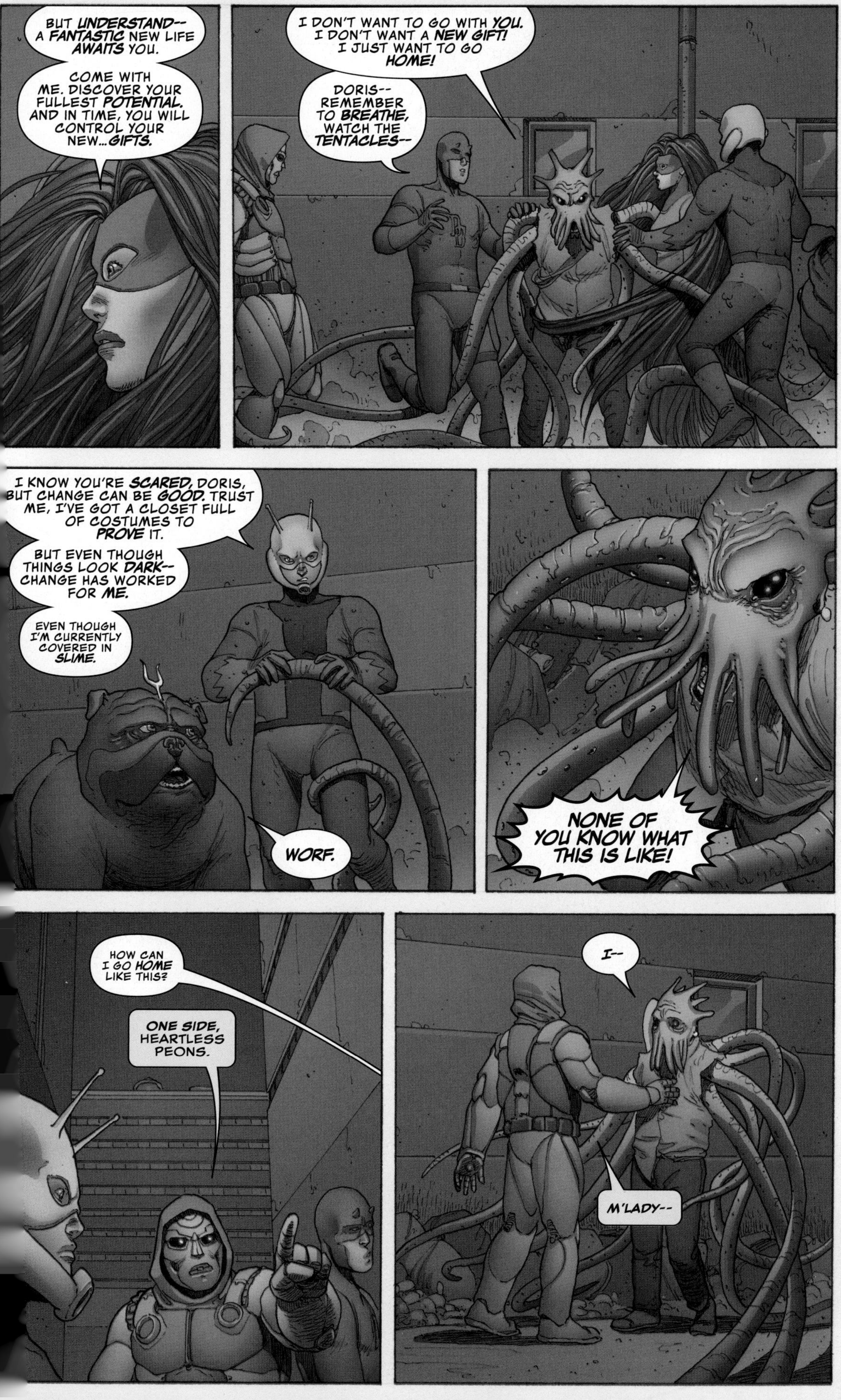
BUT UNDERSTAND-- A FANTASTIC NEW LIFE AWAITS YOU.
COME WITH ME. DISCOVER YOUR FULLEST POTENTIAL. AND IN TIME, YOU WILL CONTROL YOUR NEW...GIFTS.
I DON'T WANT TO GO WITH YOU. I DON'T WANT A NEW GIFT! I JUST WANT TO GO HOME!
DORIS-- REMEMBER TO BREATHE, WATCH THE TENTACLES--
I KNOW YOU'RE SCARED, DORIS, BUT CHANGE CAN BE GOOD. TRUST ME, I'VE GOT A CLOSET FULL OF COSTUMES TO PROVE IT.
BUT EVEN THOUGH THINGS LOOK DARK-- CHANGE HAS WORKED FOR ME.
EVEN THOUGH I'M CURRENTLY COVERED IN SLIME.
WORF.
NONE OF YOU KNOW WHAT THIS IS LIKE!
HOW CAN I GO HOME LIKE THIS?
ONE SIDE, HEARTLESS PEONS.
I--
M'LADY--

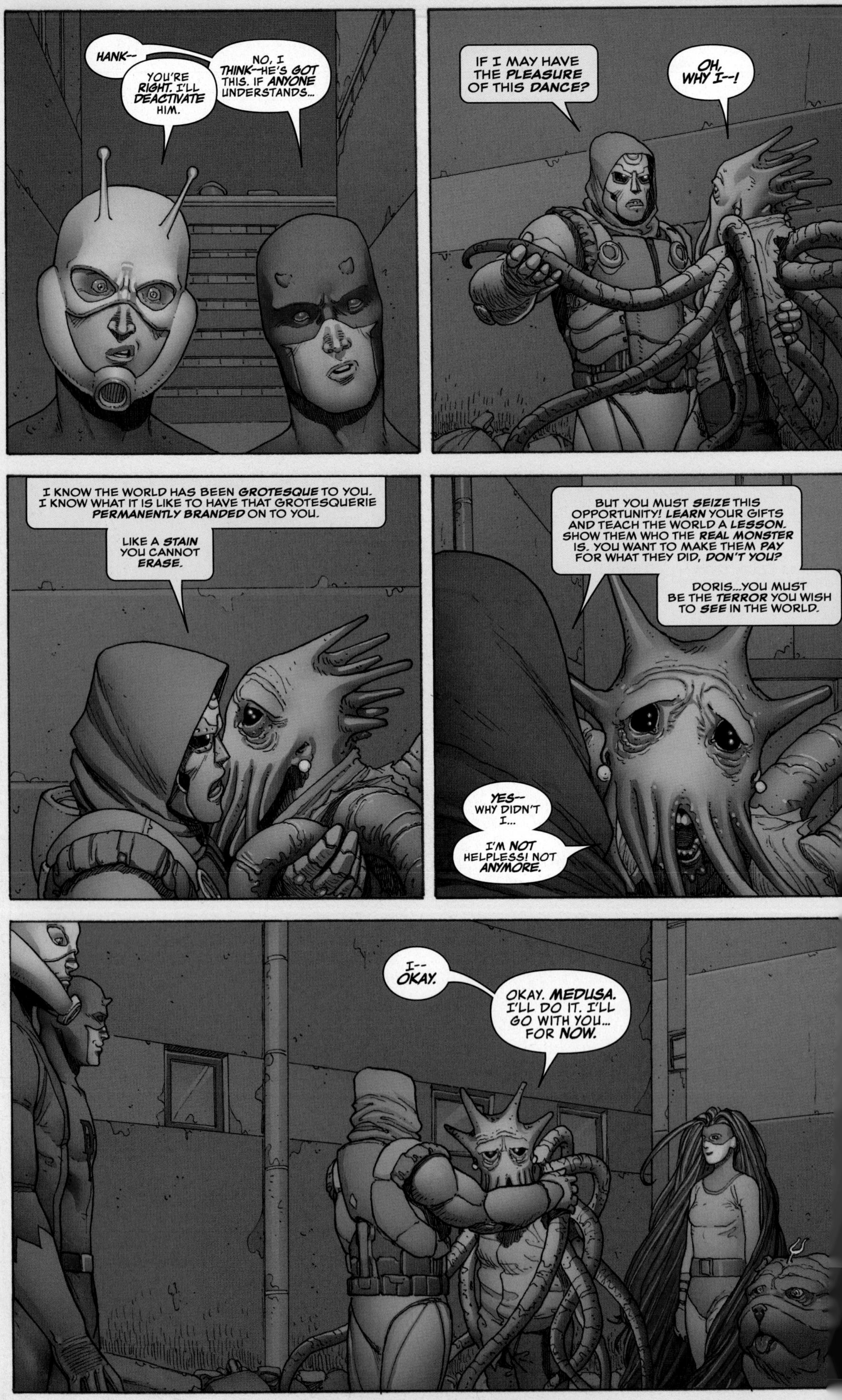
HANK--
YOU'RE RIGHT. I'LL DEACTIVATE HIM.
NO, I THINK--HE'S GOT THIS. IF ANYONE UNDERSTANDS...
IF I MAY HAVE THE PLEASURE OF THIS DANCE?
OH, WHY I--!
I KNOW THE WORLD HAS BEEN GROTESQUE TO YOU. I KNOW WHAT IT IS LIKE TO HAVE THAT GROTESQUERIE PERMANENTLY BRANDED ON TO YOU.
LIKE A STAIN YOU CANNOT ERASE.
BUT YOU MUST SEIZE THIS OPPORTUNITY! LEARN YOUR GIFTS AND TEACH THE WORLD A LESSON. SHOW THEM WHO THE REAL MONSTER IS. YOU WANT TO MAKE THEM PAY FOR WHAT THEY DID, DON'T YOU?
DORIS...YOU MUST BE THE TERROR YOU WISH TO SEE IN THE WORLD.
YES-- WHY DIDN'T I...
I'M NOT HELPLESS! NOT ANYMORE.
I-- OKAY.
OKAY. MEDUSA. I'LL DO IT. I'LL GO WITH YOU... FOR NOW.

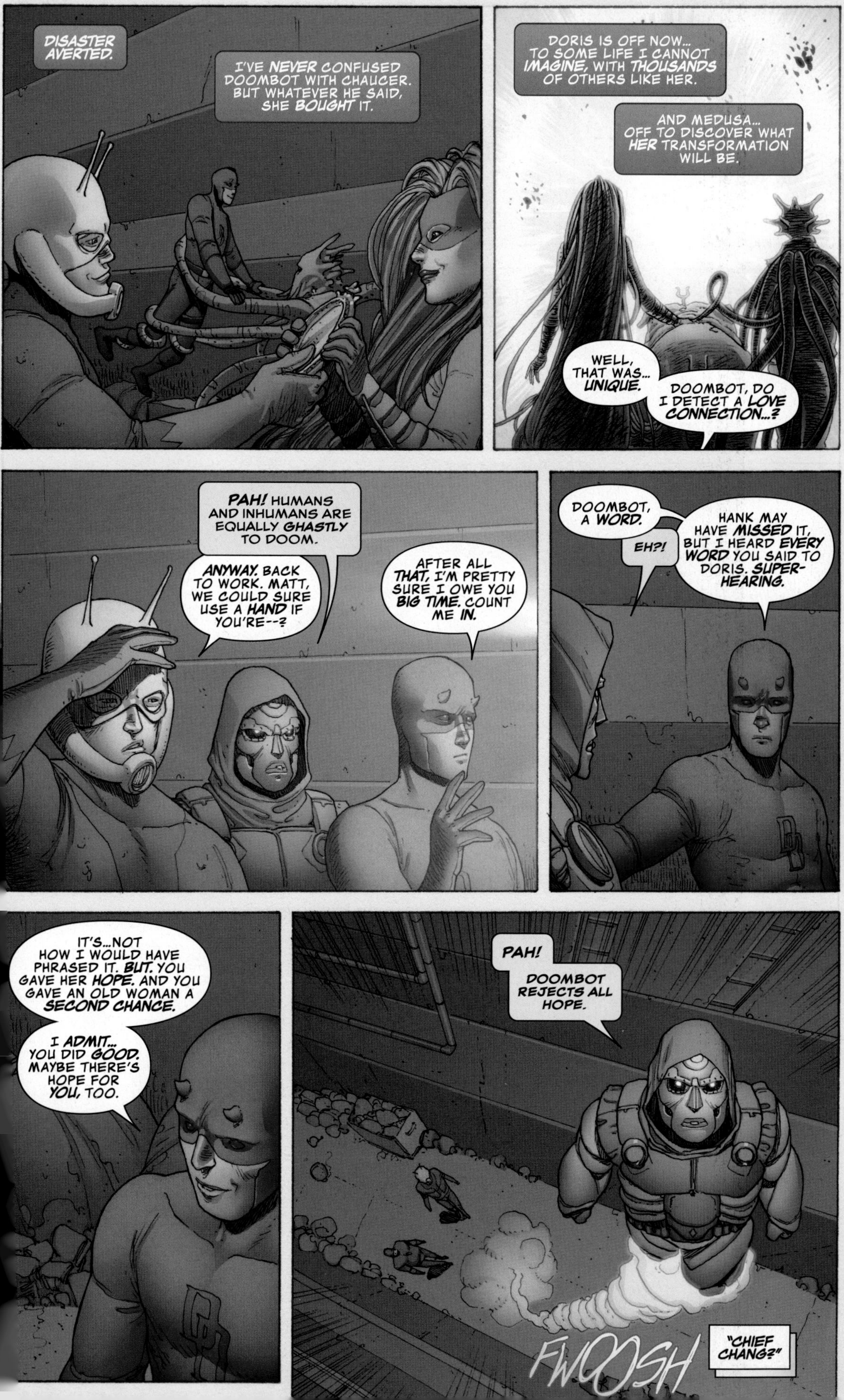
DISASTER AVERTED.
I'VE NEVER CONFUSED DOOMBOT WITH CHAUCER. BUT WHATEVER HE SAID, SHE BOUGHT IT.
DORIS IS OFF NOW... TO SOME LIFE I CANNOT IMAGINE, WITH THOUSANDS OF OTHERS LIKE HER.
AND MEDUSA... OFF TO DISCOVER WHAT HER TRANSFORMATION WILL BE.
WELL, THAT WAS... UNIQUE.
DOOMBOT, DO I DETECT A LOVE CONNECTION...?
PAH! HUMANS AND INHUMANS ARE EQUALLY GHASTLY TO DOOM.
ANYWAY. BACK TO WORK. MATT, WE COULD SURE USE A HAND IF YOU'RE--?
AFTER ALL THAT, I'M PRETTY SURE I OWE YOU BIG TIME. COUNT ME IN.
DOOMBOT, A WORD.
EH?!
HANK MAY HAVE MISSED IT, BUT I HEARD EVERY WORD YOU SAID TO DORIS. SUPER-HEARING.
IT'S...NOT HOW I WOULD HAVE PHRASED IT. BUT. YOU GAVE HER HOPE. AND YOU GAVE AN OLD WOMAN A SECOND CHANCE.
I ADMIT... YOU DID GOOD. MAYBE THERE'S HOPE FOR YOU, TOO.
PAH!
DOOMBOT REJECTS ALL HOPE.
FWOOSH
"CHIEF CHANG?"

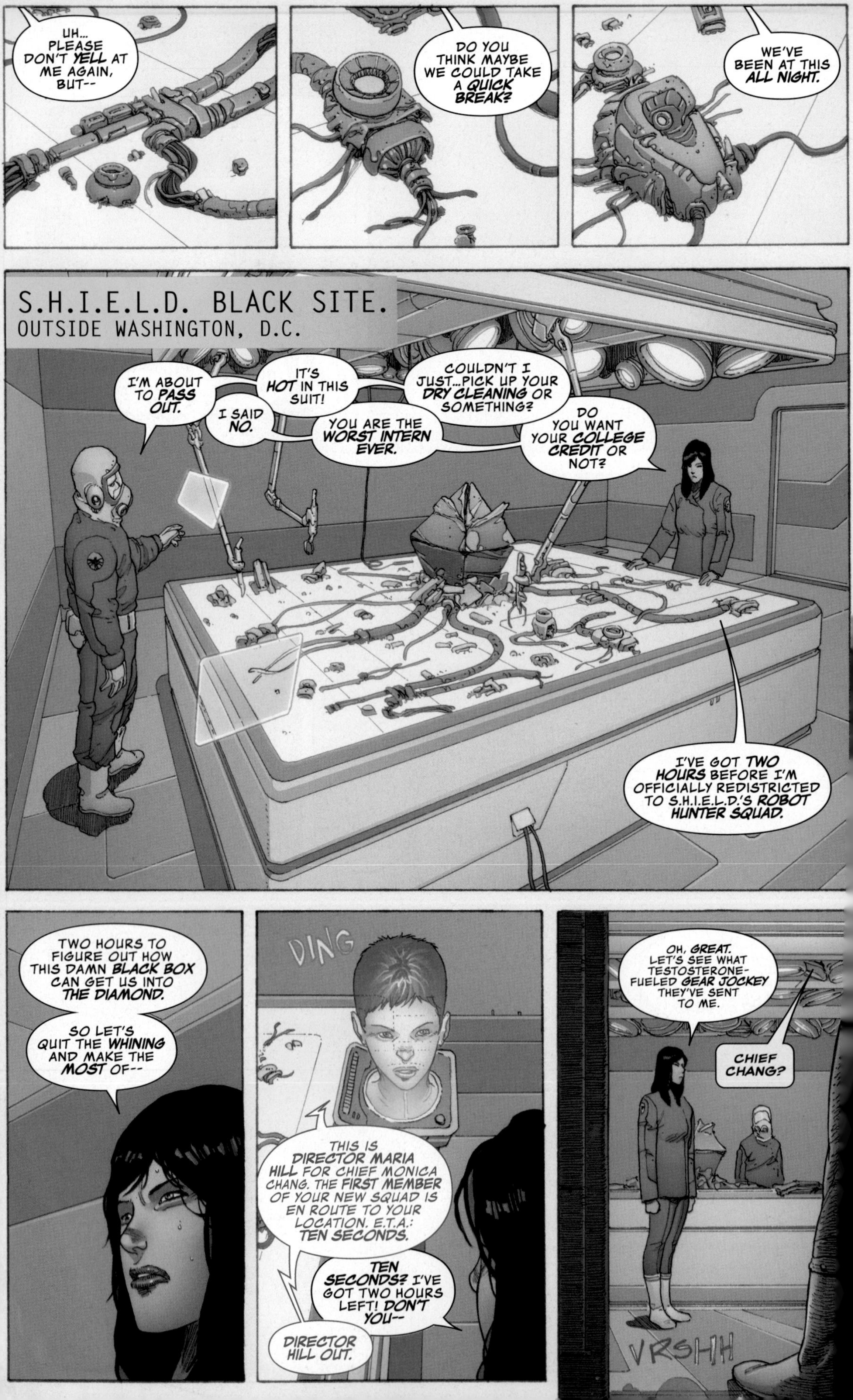
UH... PLEASE DON'T YELL AT ME AGAIN, BUT--
DO YOU THINK MAYBE WE COULD TAKE A QUICK BREAK?
WE'VE BEEN AT THIS ALL NIGHT.
S.H.I.E.L.D. BLACK SITE.
OUTSIDE WASHINGTON, D.C.
I'M ABOUT TO PASS OUT.
IT'S HOT IN THIS SUIT!
COULDN'T I JUST...PICK UP YOUR DRY CLEANING OR SOMETHING?
I SAID NO.
YOU ARE THE WORST INTERN EVER.
DO YOU WANT YOUR COLLEGE CREDIT OR NOT?
I'VE GOT TWO HOURS BEFORE I'M OFFICIALLY REDISTRICTED TO S.H.I.E.L.D.'S ROBOT HUNTER SQUAD.
TWO HOURS TO FIGURE OUT HOW THIS DAMN BLACK BOX CAN GET US INTO THE DIAMOND.
SO LET'S QUIT THE WHINING AND MAKE THE MOST OF--
DING
THIS IS DIRECTOR MARIA HILL FOR CHIEF MONICA CHANG. THE FIRST MEMBER OF YOUR NEW SQUAD IS EN ROUTE TO YOUR LOCATION. E.T.A.: TEN SECONDS.
TEN SECONDS? I'VE GOT TWO HOURS LEFT! DON'T YOU--
DIRECTOR HILL OUT.
OH, GREAT. LET'S SEE WHAT TESTOSTERONE-FUELED GEAR JOCKEY THEY'VE SENT TO ME.
CHIEF CHANG?
VRSHH

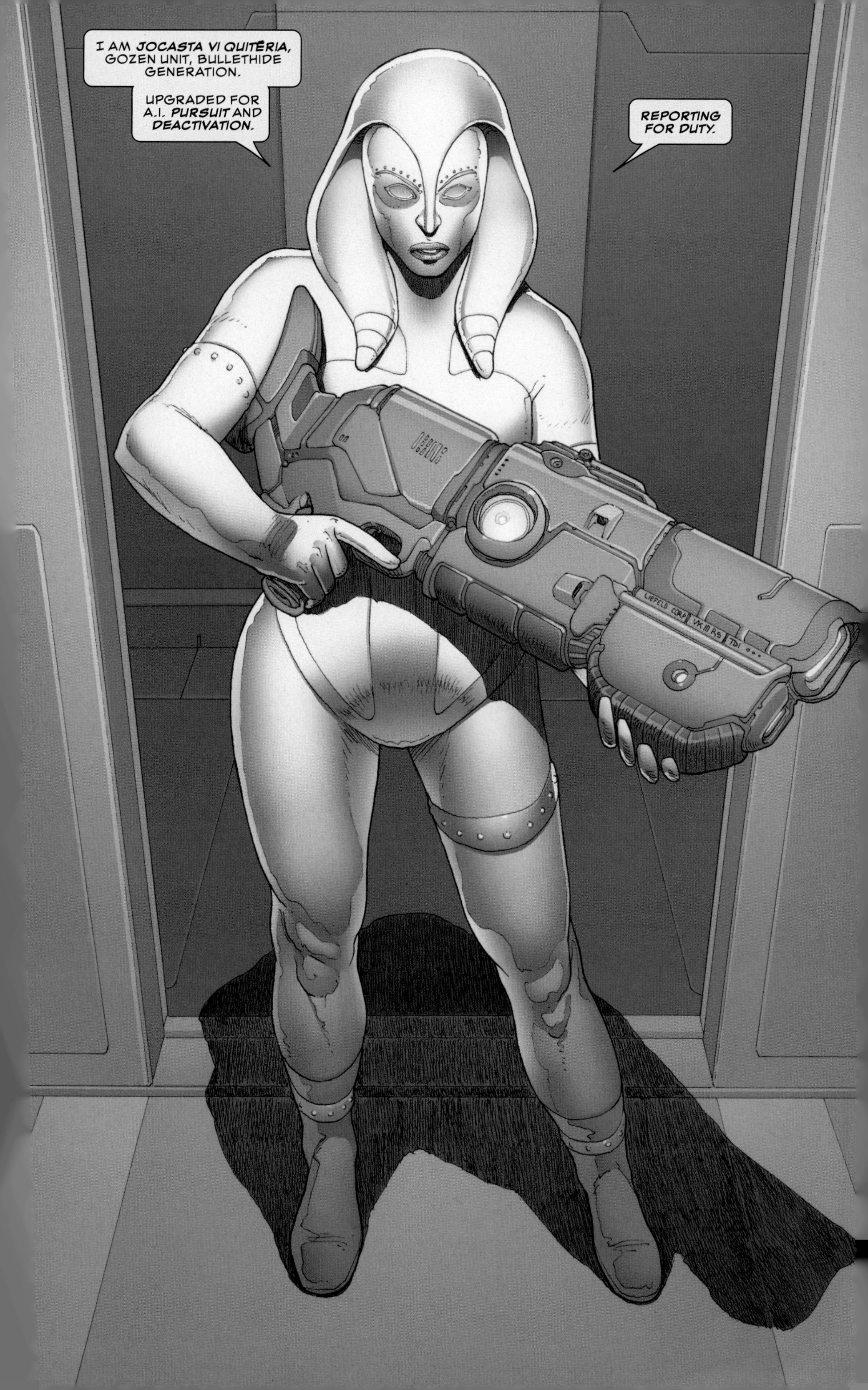
I AM JOCASTA VI QUITÉRIA, GOZEN UNIT, BULLETHIDE GENERATION.
UPGRADED FOR A.I. PURSUIT AND DEACTIVATION.
REPORTING FOR DUTY.
LIEFELD CORP VK III RS TDI

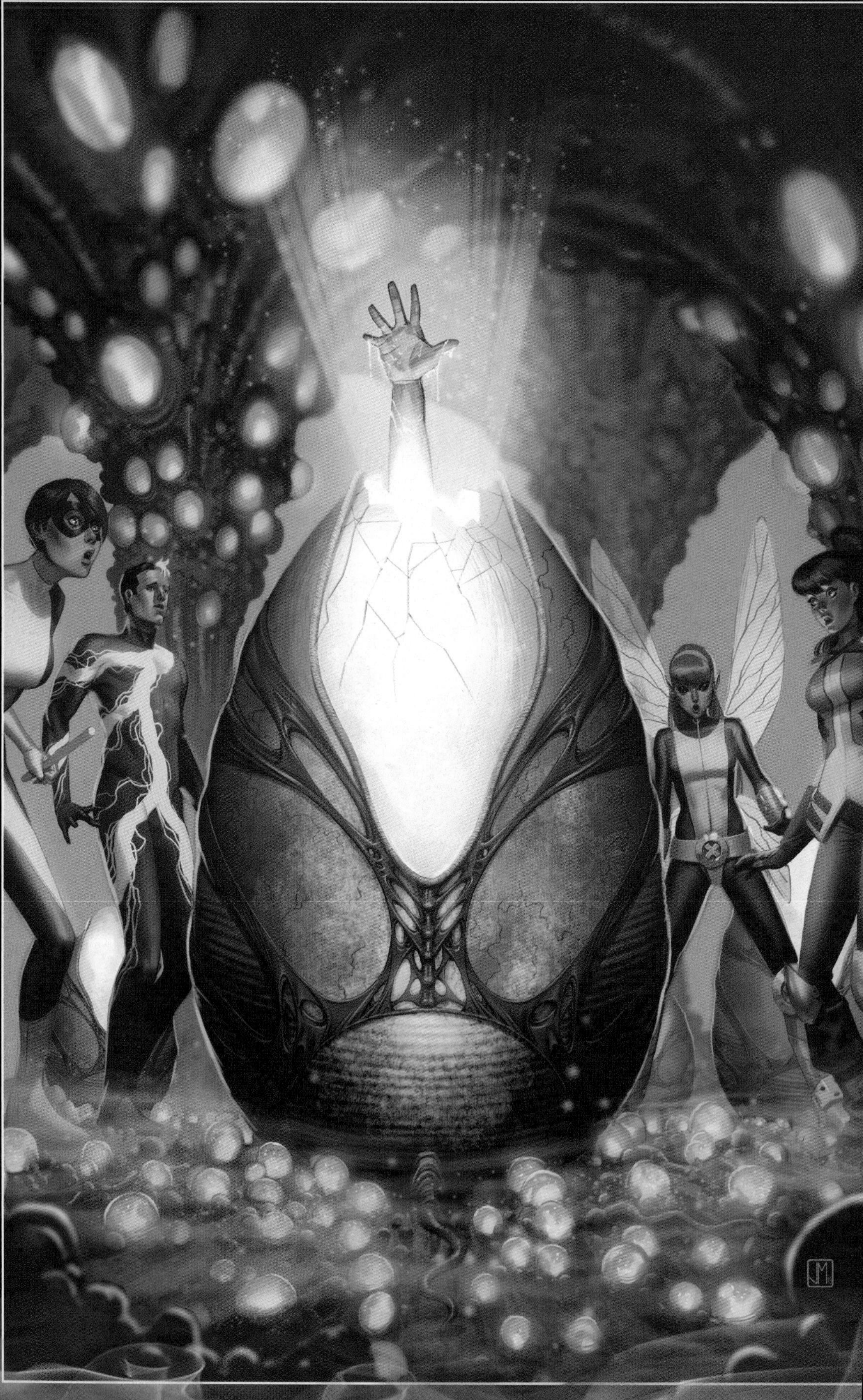

INHUMANITY: THE AWAKENING #1

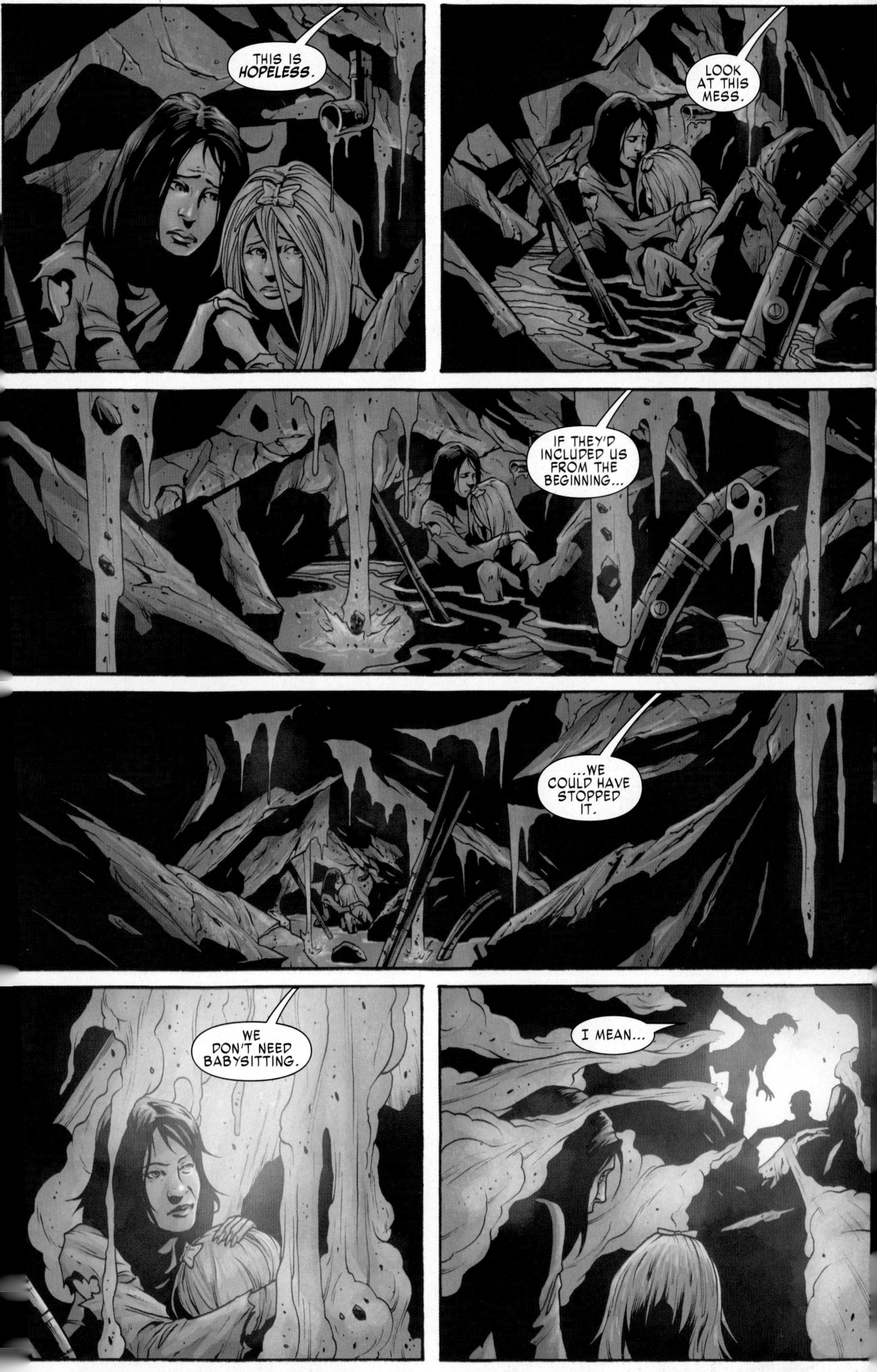
THIS IS HOPELESS.
LOOK AT THIS MESS.
IF THEY'D INCLUDED US FROM THE BEGINNING...
...WE COULD HAVE STOPPED IT.
WE DON'T NEED BABYSITTING.
I MEAN...

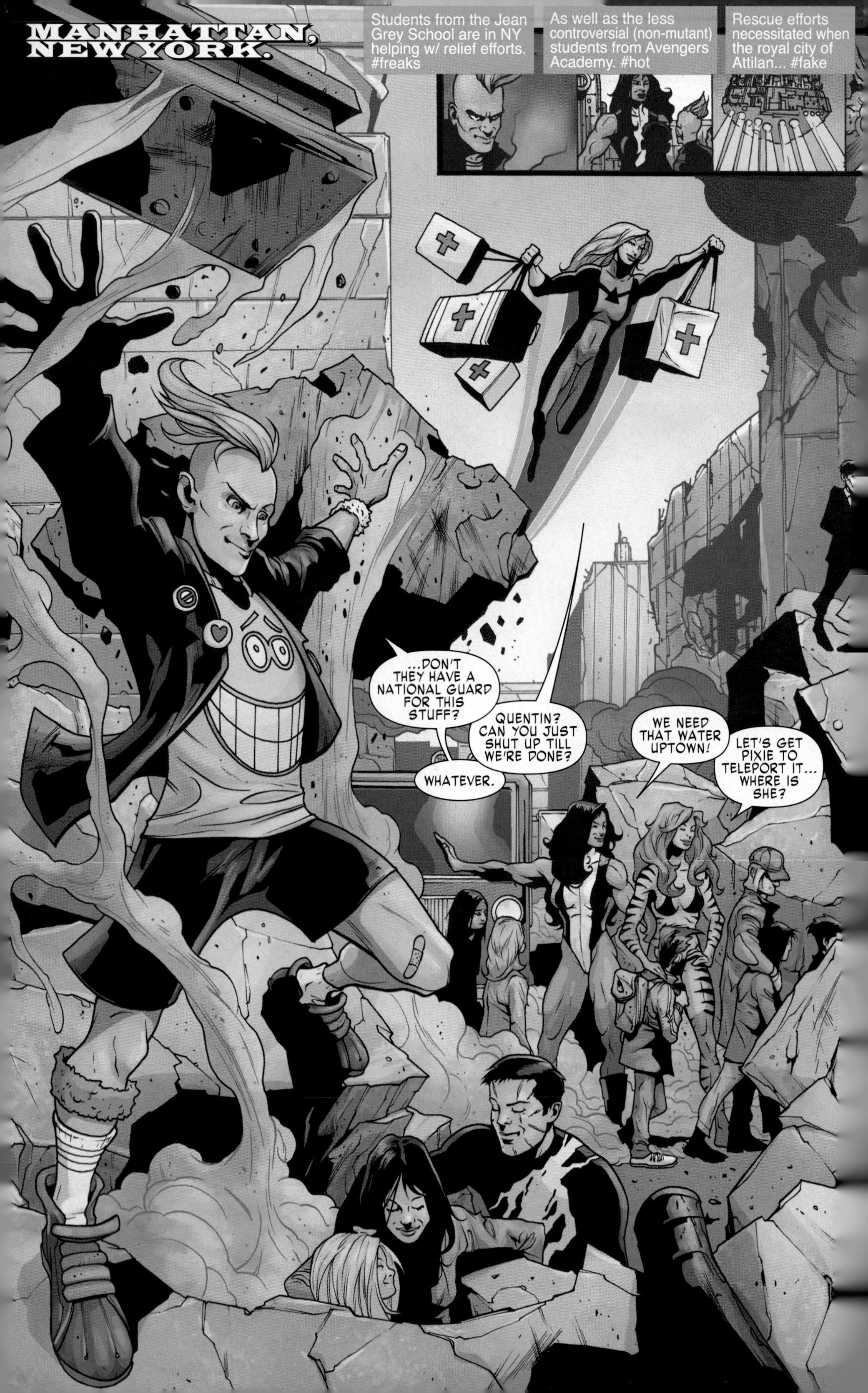
MANHATTAN, NEW YORK.
Students from the Jean Grey School are in NY helping w/ relief efforts. #freaks
As well as the less controversial (non-mutant) students from Avengers Academy. #hot
Rescue efforts necessitated when the royal city of Attilan... #fake
...DON'T THEY HAVE A NATIONAL GUARD FOR THIS STUFF?
QUENTIN? CAN YOU JUST SHUT UP TILL WE'RE DONE?
WHATEVER.
WE NEED THAT WATER UPTOWN!
LET'S GET PIXIE TO TELEPORT IT... WHERE IS SHE?

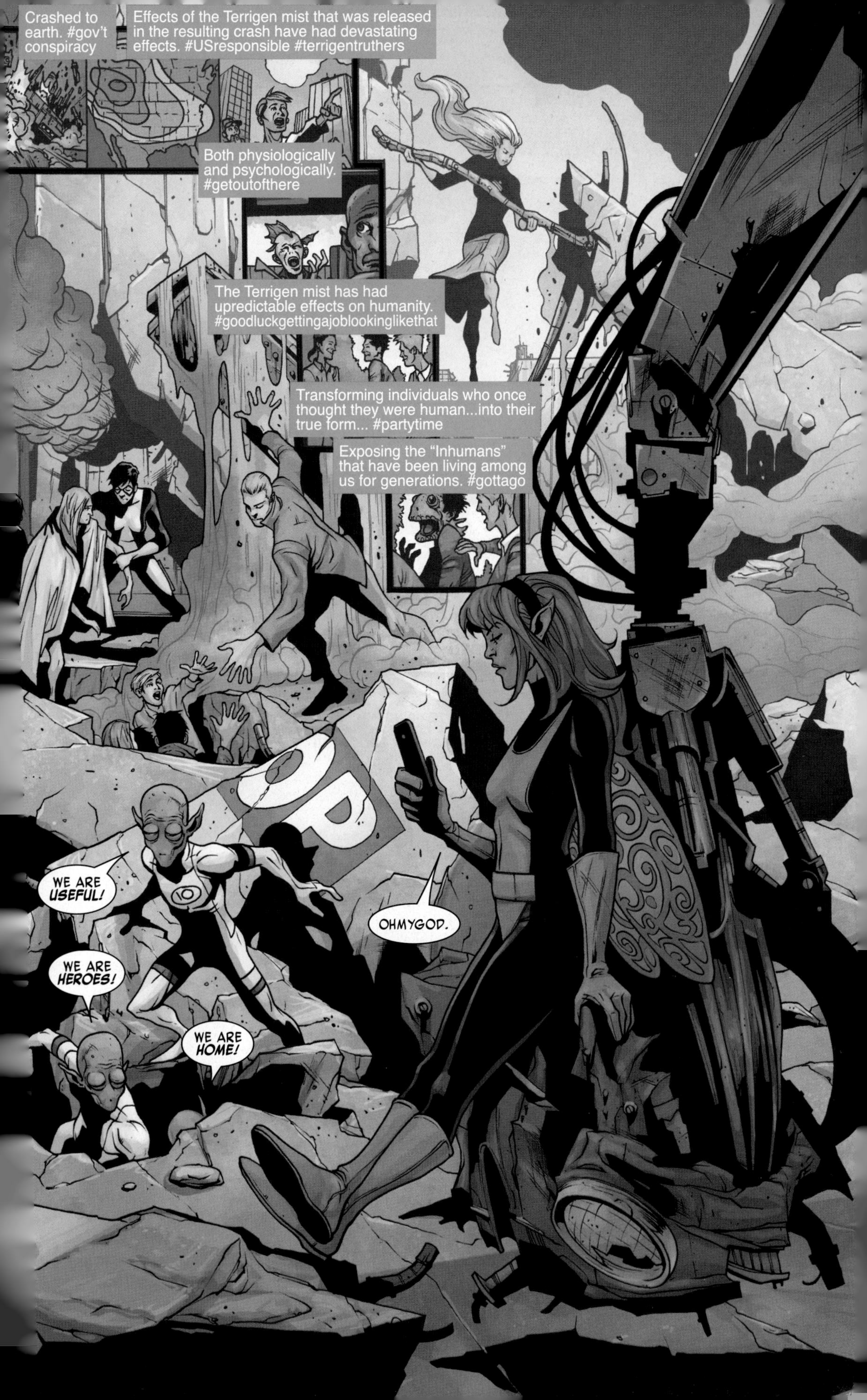

Crashed to earth. #gov't conspiracy
Effects of the Terrigen mist that was released in the resulting crash have had devastating effects. #USresponsible #terrigentruthers
Both physiologically and psychologically. #getoutofthere
The Terrigen mist has had upredictable effects on humanity. #goodluckgettingajoblookinglikethat
Transforming individuals who once thought they were human...into their true form... #partytime
Exposing the "Inhumans" that have been living among us for generations. #gottago
WE ARE USEFUL!
WE ARE HEROES!
WE ARE HOME!
OHMYGOD.

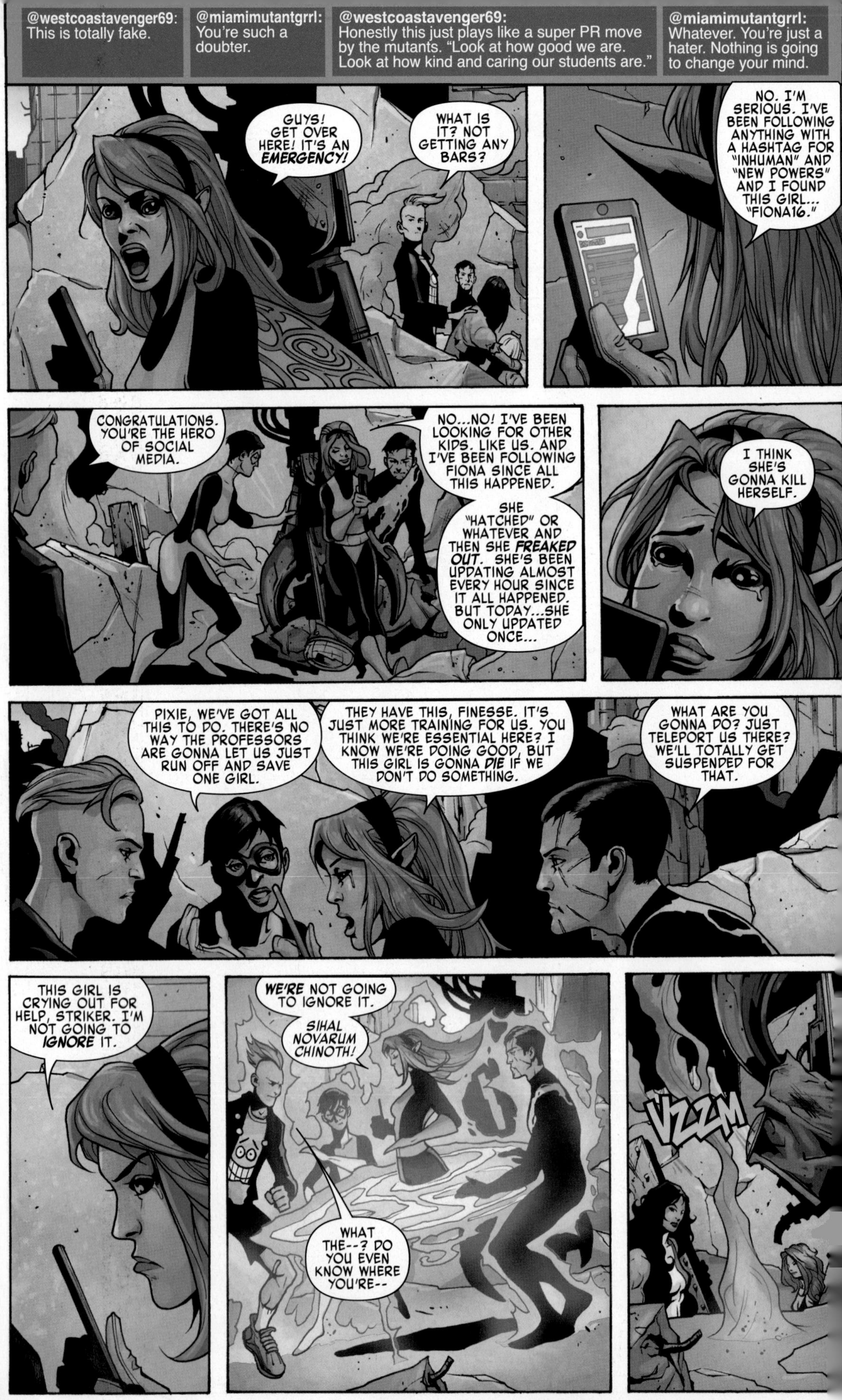
@westcoastavenger69: This is totally fake.
@miamimutantgrrl: You're such a doubter.
@westcoastavenger69: Honestly this just plays like a super PR move by the mutants. "Look at how good we are. Look at how kind and caring our students are."
@miamimutantgrrl: Whatever. You're just a hater. Nothing is going to change your mind.
GUYS! GET OVER HERE! IT'S AN EMERGENCY!
WHAT IS IT? NOT GETTING ANY BARS?
NO. I'M SERIOUS. I'VE BEEN FOLLOWING ANYTHING WITH A HASHTAG FOR "INHUMAN" AND "NEW POWERS" AND I FOUND THIS GIRL... "FIONA16."
CONGRATULATIONS. YOU'RE THE HERO OF SOCIAL MEDIA.
NO...NO! I'VE BEEN LOOKING FOR OTHER KIDS. LIKE US. AND I'VE BEEN FOLLOWING FIONA SINCE ALL THIS HAPPENED.
SHE "HATCHED" OR WHATEVER AND THEN SHE FREAKED OUT. SHE'S BEEN UPDATING ALMOST EVERY HOUR SINCE IT ALL HAPPENED. BUT TODAY...SHE ONLY UPDATED ONCE...
I THINK SHE'S GONNA KILL HERSELF.
PIXIE, WE'VE GOT ALL THIS TO DO. THERE'S NO WAY THE PROFESSORS ARE GONNA LET US JUST RUN OFF AND SAVE ONE GIRL.
THEY HAVE THIS, FINESSE. IT'S JUST MORE TRAINING FOR US. YOU THINK WE'RE ESSENTIAL HERE? I KNOW WE'RE DOING GOOD, BUT THIS GIRL IS GONNA DIE IF WE DON'T DO SOMETHING.
WHAT ARE YOU GONNA DO? JUST TELEPORT US THERE? WE'LL TOTALLY GET SUSPENDED FOR THAT.
THIS GIRL IS CRYING OUT FOR HELP, STRIKER. I'M NOT GOING TO IGNORE IT.
WE'RE NOT GOING TO IGNORE IT.
SIHAL NOVARUM CHINOTH!
WHAT THE--? DO YOU EVEN KNOW WHERE YOU'RE--
VZZM

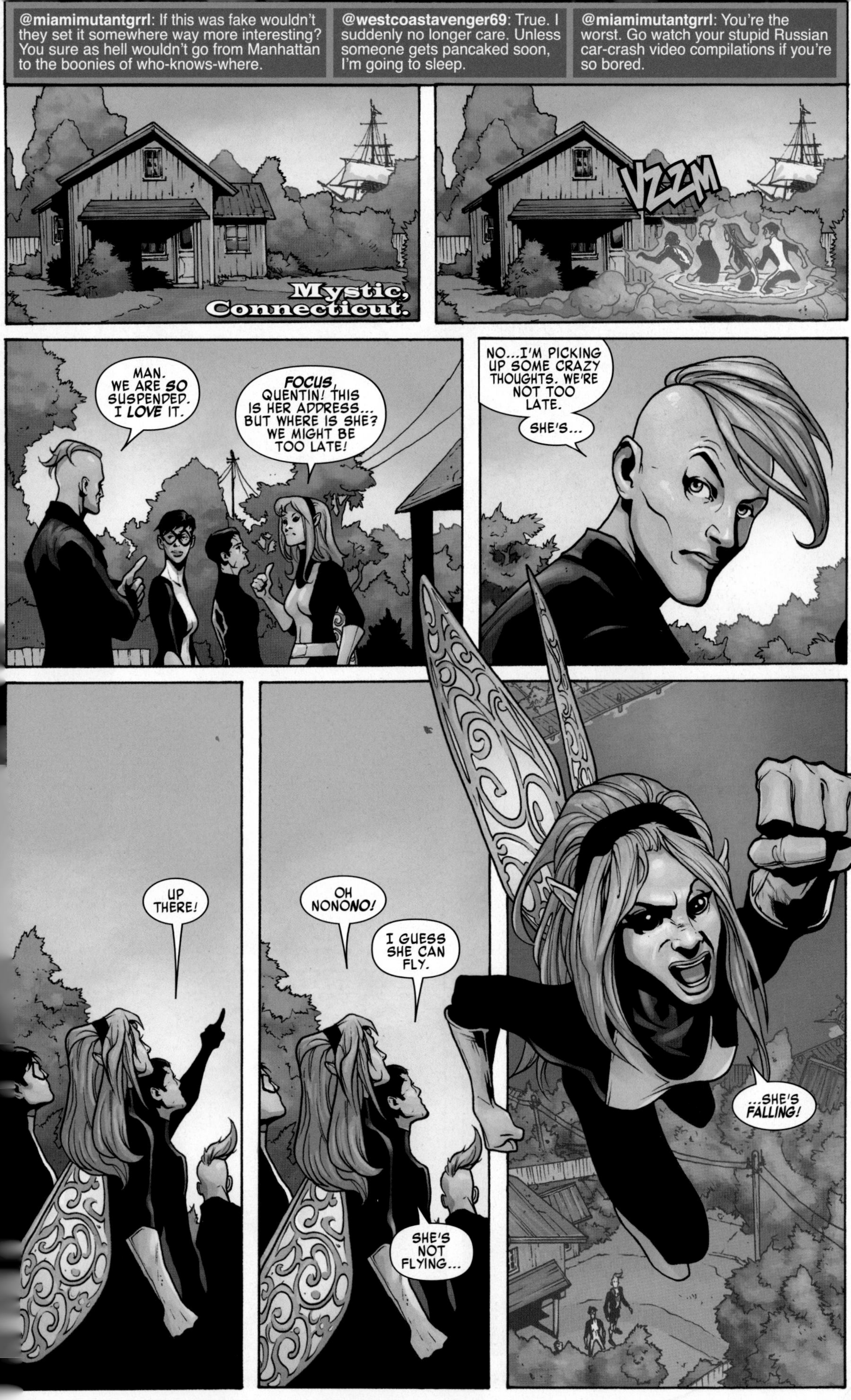
@miamimutantgrrl: If this was fake wouldn't they set it somewhere way more interesting? You sure as hell wouldn't go from Manhattan to the boonies of who-knows-where.
@westcoastavenger69: True. I suddenly no longer care. Unless someone gets pancaked soon, I'm going to sleep.
@miamimutantgrrl: You're the worst. Go watch your stupid Russian car-crash video compilations if you're so bored.
Mystic, Connecticut.
VZZM
MAN. WE ARE SO SUSPENDED. I LOVE IT.
FOCUS, QUENTIN! THIS IS HER ADDRESS... BUT WHERE IS SHE? WE MIGHT BE TOO LATE!
NO...I'M PICKING UP SOME CRAZY THOUGHTS. WE'RE NOT TOO LATE.
SHE'S...
UP THERE!
OH NONONO!
I GUESS SHE CAN FLY.
SHE'S NOT FLYING...
...SHE'S FALLING!

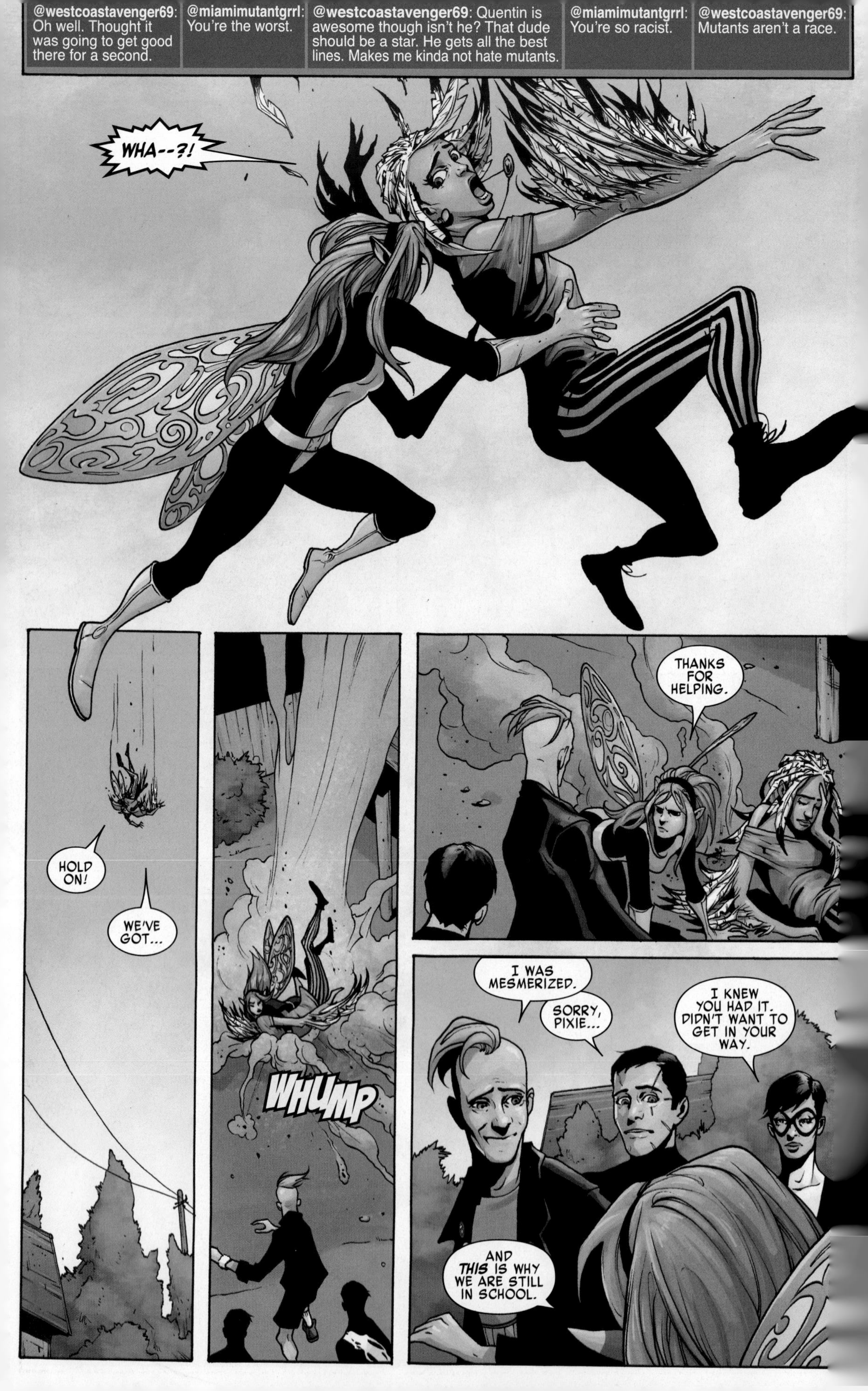
@westcoastavenger69: Oh well. Thought it was going to get good there for a second.
@miamimutantgrrl: You're the worst.
@westcoastavenger69: Quentin is awesome though isn't he? That dude should be a star. He gets all the best lines. Makes me kinda not hate mutants.
@miamimutantgrrl: You're so racist.
@westcoastavenger69: Mutants aren't a race.
WHA--?!
HOLD ON!
WE'VE GOT...
WHUMP
THANKS FOR HELPING.
I WAS MESMERIZED.
SORRY, PIXIE...
I KNEW YOU HAD IT. DIDN'T WANT TO GET IN YOUR WAY.
AND THIS IS WHY WE ARE STILL IN SCHOOL.

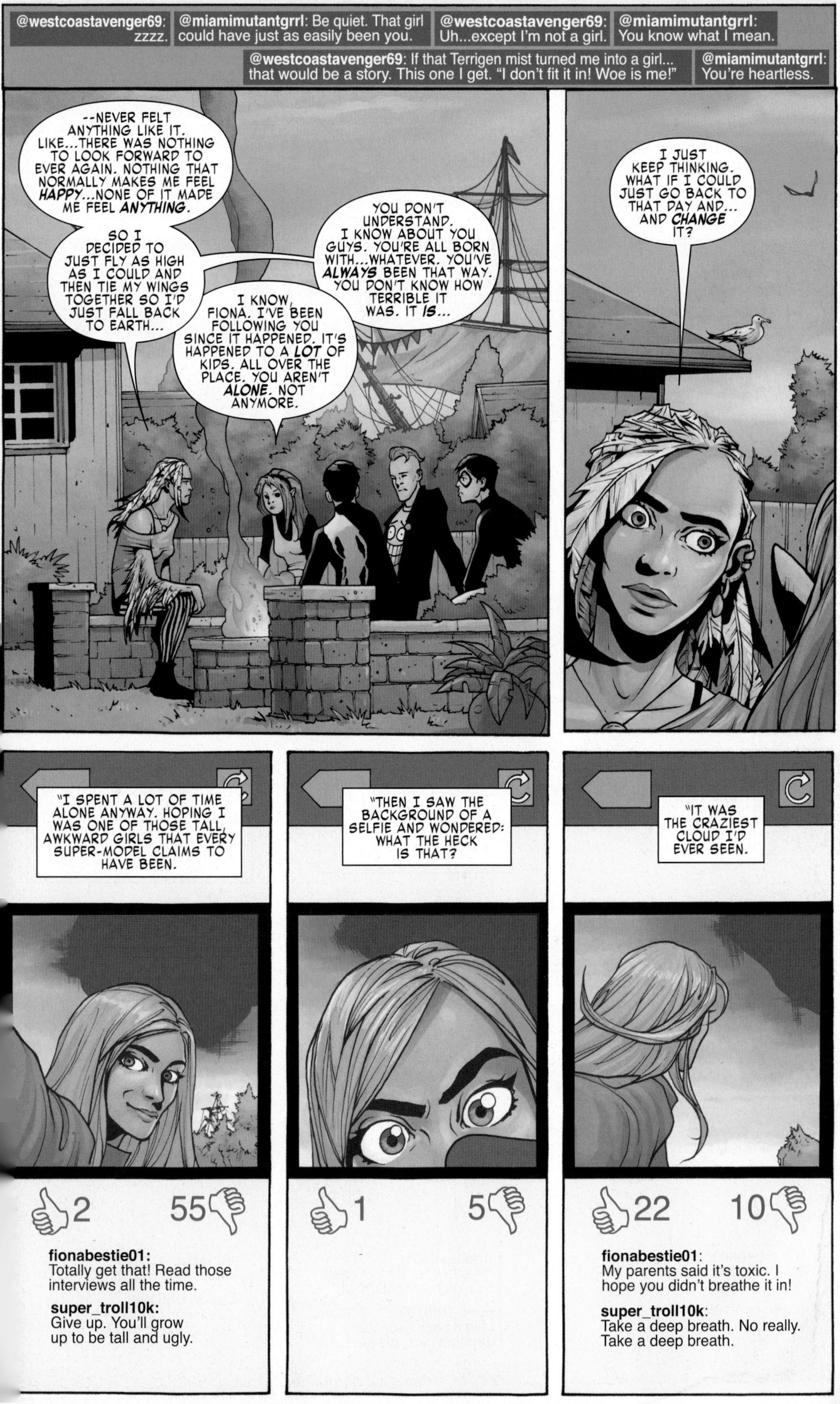
@westcoastavenger69: zzzz.
@miamimutantgrrl: Be quiet. That girl could have just as easily been you.
@westcoastavenger69: Uh...except I'm not a girl.
@miamimutantgrrl: You know what I mean.
@westcoastavenger69: If that Terrigen mist turned me into a girl... that would be a story. This one I get. "I don't fit it in! Woe is me!"
@miamimutantgrrl: You're heartless.
--NEVER FELT ANYTHING LIKE IT. LIKE...THERE WAS NOTHING TO LOOK FORWARD TO EVER AGAIN. NOTHING THAT NORMALLY MAKES ME FEEL HAPPY...NONE OF IT MADE ME FEEL ANYTHING.
SO I DECIDED TO JUST FLY AS HIGH AS I COULD AND THEN TIE MY WINGS TOGETHER SO I'D JUST FALL BACK TO EARTH...
YOU DON'T UNDERSTAND. I KNOW ABOUT YOU GUYS. YOU'RE ALL BORN WITH...WHATEVER. YOU'VE ALWAYS BEEN THAT WAY. YOU DON'T KNOW HOW TERRIBLE IT WAS. IT IS...
I KNOW, FIONA. I'VE BEEN FOLLOWING YOU SINCE IT HAPPENED. IT'S HAPPENED TO A LOT OF KIDS. ALL OVER THE PLACE. YOU AREN'T ALONE. NOT ANYMORE.
I JUST KEEP THINKING. WHAT IF I COULD JUST GO BACK TO THAT DAY AND... AND CHANGE IT?
"I SPENT A LOT OF TIME ALONE ANYWAY. HOPING I WAS ONE OF THOSE TALL, AWKWARD GIRLS THAT EVERY SUPER-MODEL CLAIMS TO HAVE BEEN.
2
55
fionabestie01: Totally get that! Read those interviews all the time.
super_troll10k: Give up. You'll grow up to be tall and ugly.
"THEN I SAW THE BACKGROUND OF A SELFIE AND WONDERED: WHAT THE HECK IS THAT?
1
5
"IT WAS THE CRAZIEST CLOUD I'D EVER SEEN.
22
10
fionabestie01: My parents said it's toxic. I hope you didn't breathe it in!
super_troll10k: Take a deep breath. No really. Take a deep breath.

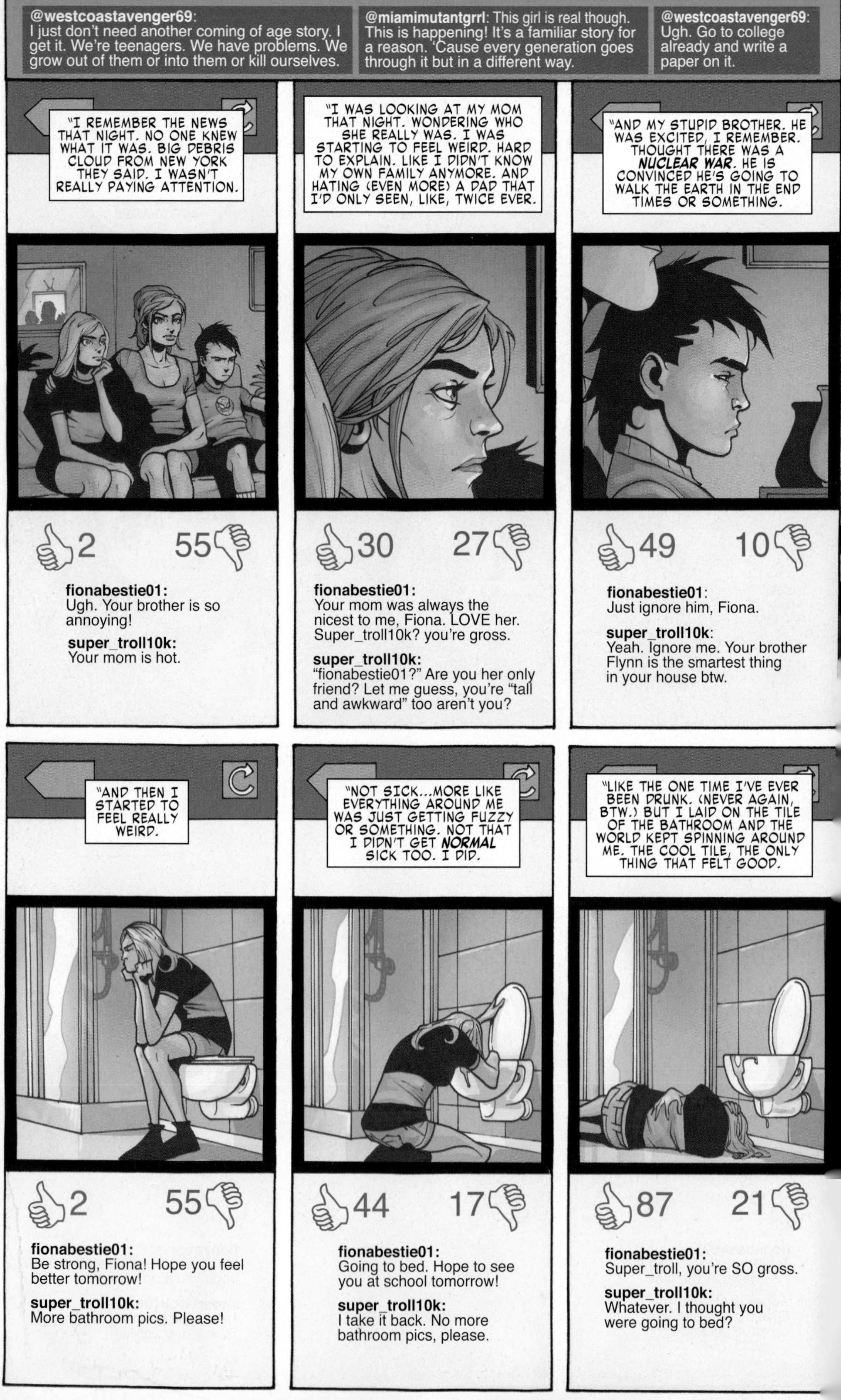
@westcoastavenger69: I just don't need another coming of age story. I get it. We're teenagers. We have problems. We grow out of them or into them or kill ourselves.
@miamimutantgrrl: This girl is real though. This is happening! It's a familiar story for a reason. 'Cause every generation goes through it but in a different way.
@westcoastavenger69: Ugh. Go to college already and write a paper on it.
"I REMEMBER THE NEWS THAT NIGHT. NO ONE KNEW WHAT IT WAS. BIG DEBRIS CLOUD FROM NEW YORK THEY SAID. I WASN'T REALLY PAYING ATTENTION.
2
55
fionabestie01: Ugh. Your brother is so annoying!
super_troll10k: Your mom is hot.
"I WAS LOOKING AT MY MOM THAT NIGHT. WONDERING WHO SHE REALLY WAS. I WAS STARTING TO FEEL WEIRD. HARD TO EXPLAIN. LIKE I DIDN'T KNOW MY OWN FAMILY ANYMORE. AND HATING (EVEN MORE) A DAD THAT I'D ONLY SEEN, LIKE, TWICE EVER.
30
27
fionabestie01: Your mom was always the nicest to me, Fiona. LOVE her. Super_troll10k? you're gross.
super_troll10k: "fionabestie01?" Are you her only friend? Let me guess, you're "tall and awkward" too aren't you?
"AND MY STUPID BROTHER. HE WAS EXCITED, I REMEMBER. THOUGHT THERE WAS A NUCLEAR WAR. HE IS CONVINCED HE'S GOING TO WALK THE EARTH IN THE END TIMES OR SOMETHING.
49
10
fionabestie01: Just ignore him, Fiona.
super_troll10k: Yeah. Ignore me. Your brother Flynn is the smartest thing in your house btw.
"AND THEN I STARTED TO FEEL REALLY WEIRD.
2
55
fionabestie01: Be strong, Fiona! Hope you feel better tomorrow!
super_troll10k: More bathroom pics. Please!
"NOT SICK...MORE LIKE EVERYTHING AROUND ME WAS JUST GETTING FUZZY OR SOMETHING. NOT THAT I DIDN'T GET NORMAL SICK TOO. I DID.
44
17
fionabestie01: Going to bed. Hope to see you at school tomorrow!
super_troll10k: I take it back. No more bathroom pics, please.
"LIKE THE ONE TIME I'VE EVER BEEN DRUNK. (NEVER AGAIN, BTW.) BUT I LAID ON THE TILE OF THE BATHROOM AND THE WORLD KEPT SPINNING AROUND ME. THE COOL TILE, THE ONLY THING THAT FELT GOOD.
87
21
fionabestie01: Super_troll, you're SO gross.
super_troll10k: Whatever. I thought you were going to bed?

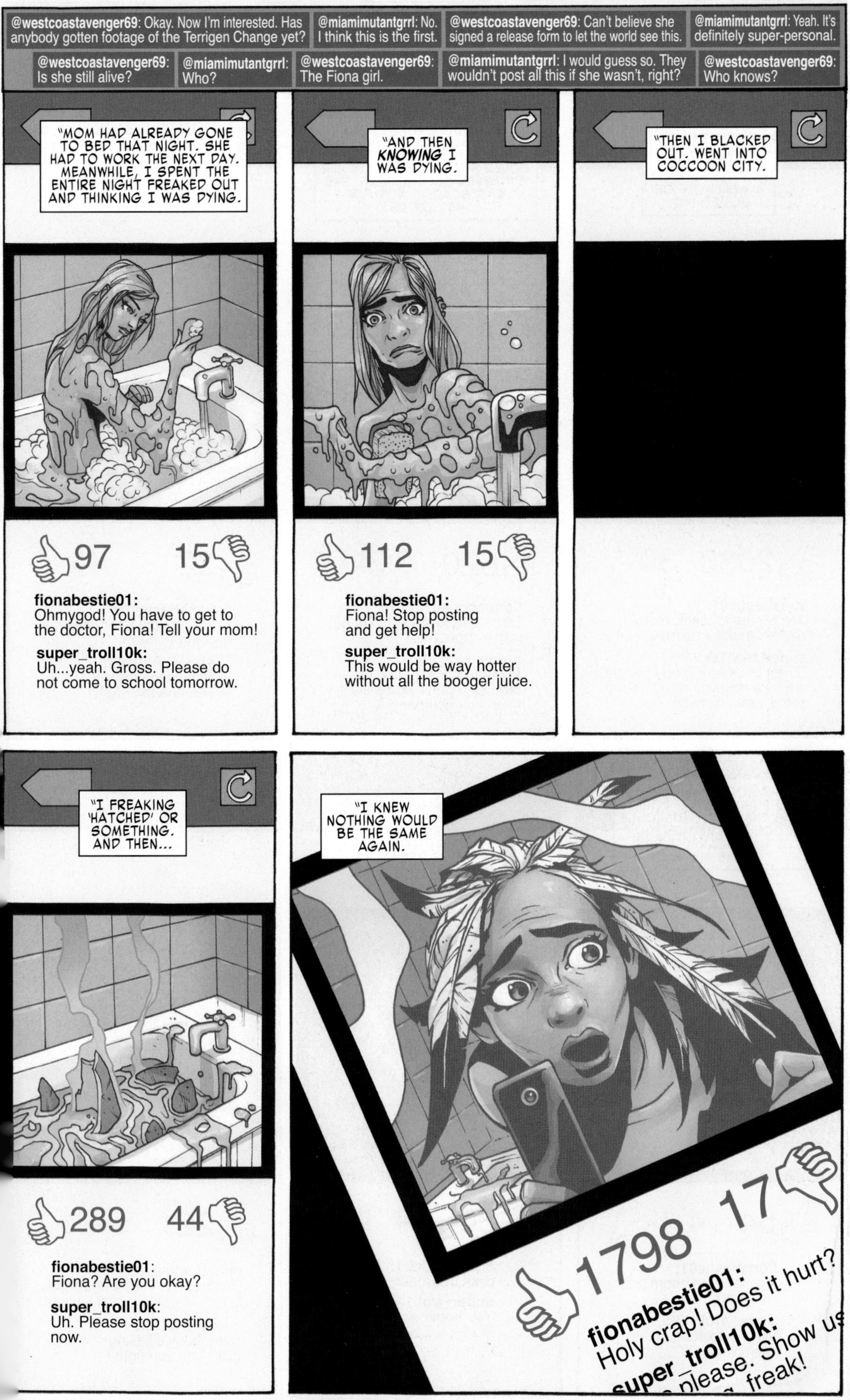

@westcoastavenger69: Okay. Now I'm interested. Has anybody gotten footage of the Terrigen Change yet?
@miamimutantgrrl: No. I think this is the first.
@westcoastavenger69: Can't believe she signed a release form to let the world see this.
@miamimutantgrrl: Yeah. It's definitely super-personal.
@westcoastavenger69: Is she still alive?
@miamimutantgrrl: Who?
@westcoastavenger69: The Fiona girl.
@miamimutantgrrl: I would guess so. They wouldn't post all this if she wasn't, right?
@westcoastavenger69: Who knows?
"MOM HAD ALREADY GONE TO BED THAT NIGHT. SHE HAD TO WORK THE NEXT DAY. MEANWHILE, I SPENT THE ENTIRE NIGHT FREAKED OUT AND THINKING I WAS DYING.
97
15
fionabestie01:
Ohmygod! You have to get to the doctor, Fiona! Tell your mom!
super_troll10k:
Uh...yeah. Gross. Please do not come to school tomorrow.
"AND THEN *KNOWING* I WAS DYING.
112
15
fionabestie01:
Fiona! Stop posting and get help!
super_troll10k:
This would be way hotter without all the booger juice.
"THEN I BLACKED OUT. WENT INTO COCCOON CITY.
"I FREAKING 'HATCHED' OR SOMETHING. AND THEN...
289
44
fionabestie01:
Fiona? Are you okay?
super_troll10k:
Uh. Please stop posting now.
"I KNEW NOTHING WOULD BE THE SAME AGAIN.
1798
17
fionabestie01:
Holy crap! Does it hurt?
super_troll10k:
please. Show us
freak!

@westcoastavenger69:
Kinda makes me wish I was near the Terrigen cloud now.

@miamimutantgrrl:
Be careful what you wish for.

@westcoastavenger69: So there's no way to tell if you're Attilan ahead of time?

@miamimutantgrrl:
I don't know.

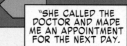

"AT FIRST I THOUGHT: I'LL CHANGE BACK. LIKE THE HULK OR A WEREWOLF OR SOMETHING.

"I'LL NEVER FORGET THE LOOK IN MY MOM'S EYES. SHE TRIED NOT TO LET ON BUT I COULD SEE SOMETHING IN HER I'D NEVER SEEN BEFORE. SHE WAS SCARED. NOT *FOR* ME...*OF* ME.

"SHE CALLED THE DOCTOR AND MADE ME AN APPOINTMENT FOR THE NEXT DAY.

 2633   30
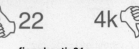 620   3.3k
22   4k

fionabestie01:
Don't listen to them, Fiona. You're beautiful no matter what.

super_troll10k:
Dang! Look how many people are following you now? You're going viral...literally!

fionabestie01:
Your mom loves you. Do not worry about that!

super_troll10k:
My friend has a thing for feathers. Don't worry. He'll keep you company.

fionabestie01:
Thank god! Everything's going to be ok.

super_troll10k:
She called the veterinarian, right?

"SHE WORKED NIGHTS AT THE PUB IN TOWN. I THINK IT'S THE FIRST TIME SINCE I COULD REMEMBER THAT I WAS SCARED TO BE HOME ALONE.

"MORE SCARED THAN I'VE EVER BEEN.

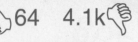 64   4.1k
 80   4.3k
221   5.5k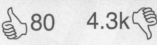

fionabestie01:
Just lock the doors and wait it out.

super_troll10k:
What pub does ur mom work at?

fionabestie01:
Shut up Super_troll.

super_troll10k:
You home alone now? More pics please!

fionabestie01:
Don't worry. They'll know how to get rid of it all. Just sit tight.

super_troll10k:
Somebody's calling FEMA on you right?

westcoastavenger69: Seems like they should come up with a test or something. Pee on a strip and "plus" means you're an alien and "minus" means you're normal.
Miamimutantgrrl: "Human" you mean. Honestly. You're so prejudiced. I hope you are an alien. That would be hilarious.
"THERE WAS NO WAY I WAS GOING TO GO TO SCHOOL LIKE THAT. I WAS WONDERING HOW I'D GET INTO TOWN TO THE DOCTOR'S OFFICE WITHOUT ANYBODY SEEING. AND THEN...
36 8.4k
fionabestie01: Do NOT go to school. Trust me.
super_troll10k: Aww, come on. We'd love to see you in person!
"...WINGS HAPPENED.
10.3k 270
fionabestie01: omg, Fiona. You just got famous! Look at your followers now!
super_troll10k: Girl, you are fine.
"AND FOR A MINUTE EVERYTHING GOT BETTER.
12.5k 55
fionabestie01: Awesome!!!
super_troll10k: Don't get sucked into a jet engine. lol
"I FORGOT ABOUT WHAT I LOOKED LIKE. WHAT ANYONE ELSE WOULD THINK.
18.9k 30
fionabestie01: Good for you!
super_troll10k: What we're thinking is "don't poop on our cars."
"IT FELT LIKE I'D DIED AND GONE TO HEAVEN.
520.4k 443
fionabestie01: So jealous!
super_troll10k: Filling my bird feeder

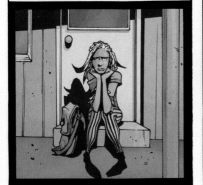

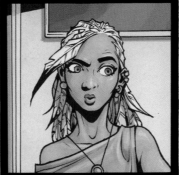

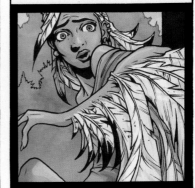

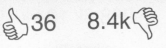

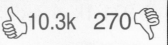

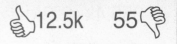

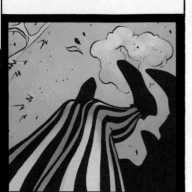

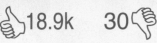

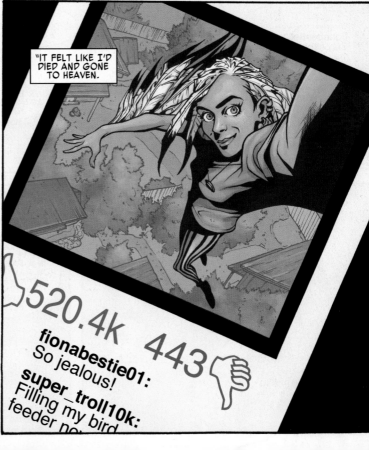

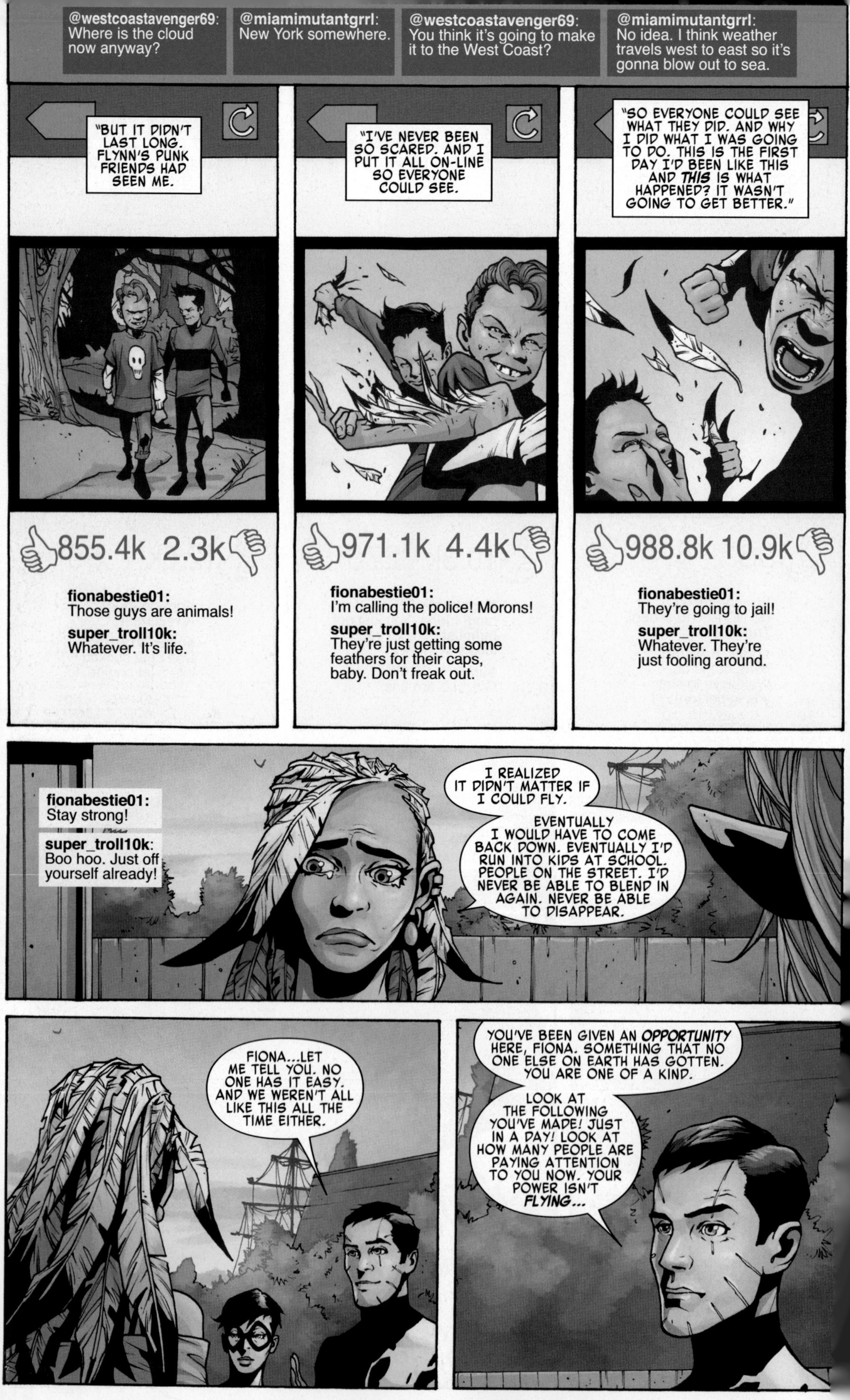
@westcoastavenger69: Where is the cloud now anyway?
@miamimutantgrrl: New York somewhere.
@westcoastavenger69: You think it's going to make it to the West Coast?
@miamimutantgrrl: No idea. I think weather travels west to east so it's gonna blow out to sea.
"BUT IT DIDN'T LAST LONG. FLYNN'S PUNK FRIENDS HAD SEEN ME.
855.4k 2.3k
fionabestie01: Those guys are animals!
super_troll10k: Whatever. It's life.
"I'VE NEVER BEEN SO SCARED. AND I PUT IT ALL ON-LINE SO EVERYONE COULD SEE.
971.1k 4.4k
fionabestie01: I'm calling the police! Morons!
super_troll10k: They're just getting some feathers for their caps, baby. Don't freak out.
"SO EVERYONE COULD SEE WHAT THEY DID. AND WHY I DID WHAT I WAS GOING TO DO. THIS IS THE FIRST DAY I'D BEEN LIKE THIS AND *THIS* IS WHAT HAPPENED? IT WASN'T GOING TO GET BETTER."
988.8k 10.9k
fionabestie01: They're going to jail!
super_troll10k: Whatever. They're just fooling around.
fionabestie01: Stay strong!
super_troll10k: Boo hoo. Just off yourself already!
I REALIZED IT DIDN'T MATTER IF I COULD FLY.
EVENTUALLY I WOULD HAVE TO COME BACK DOWN. EVENTUALLY I'D RUN INTO KIDS AT SCHOOL. PEOPLE ON THE STREET. I'D NEVER BE ABLE TO BLEND IN AGAIN. NEVER BE ABLE TO DISAPPEAR.
FIONA...LET ME TELL YOU. NO ONE HAS IT EASY. AND WE WEREN'T ALL LIKE THIS ALL THE TIME EITHER.
YOU'VE BEEN GIVEN AN *OPPORTUNITY* HERE, FIONA. SOMETHING THAT NO ONE ELSE ON EARTH HAS GOTTEN. YOU ARE ONE OF A KIND.
LOOK AT THE FOLLOWING YOU'VE MADE! JUST IN A DAY! LOOK AT HOW MANY PEOPLE ARE PAYING ATTENTION TO YOU NOW. YOUR POWER ISN'T *FLYING*...

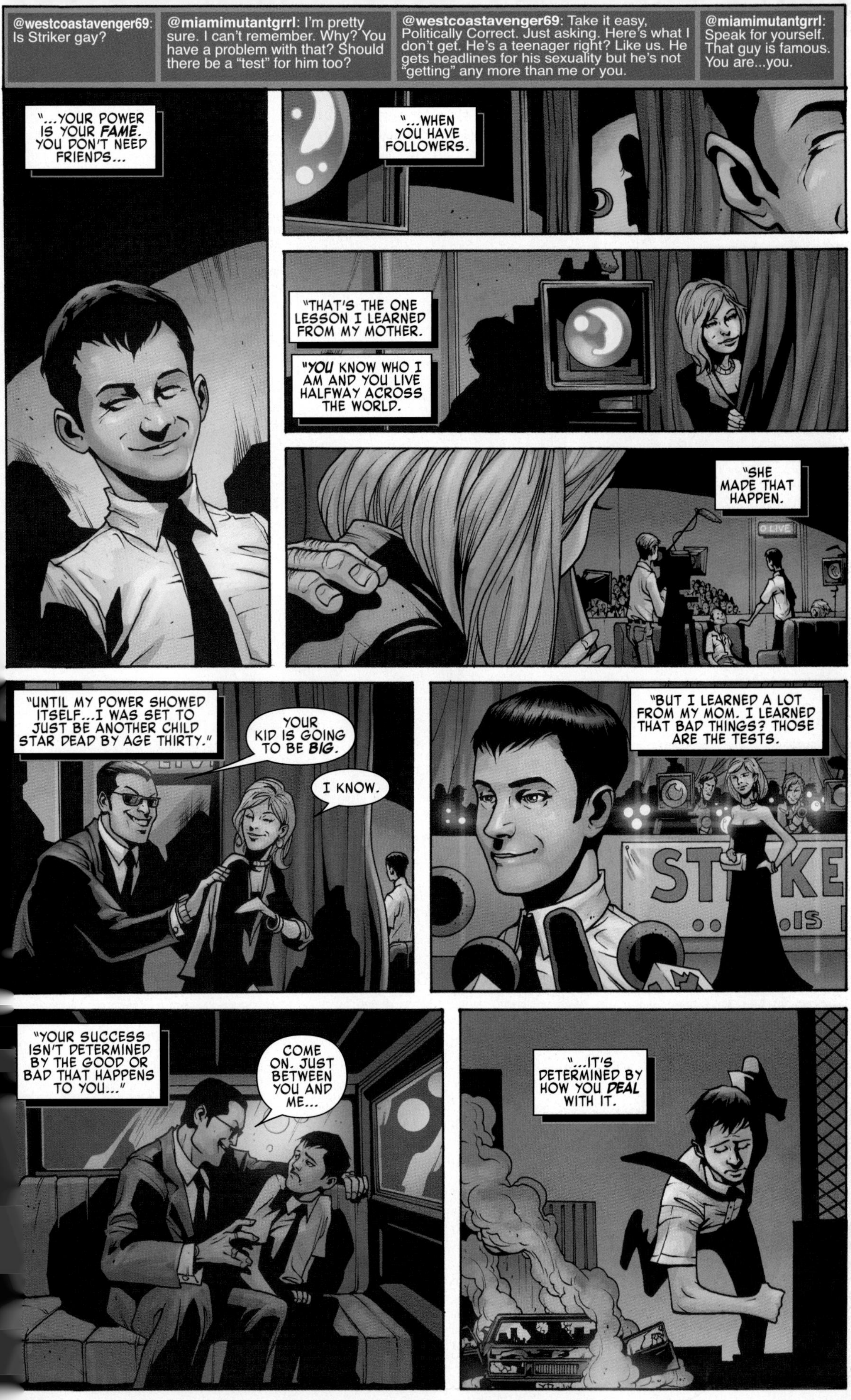
@westcoastavenger69: Is Striker gay?
@miamimutantgrrl: I'm pretty sure. I can't remember. Why? You have a problem with that? Should there be a "test" for him too?
@westcoastavenger69: Take it easy, Politically Correct. Just asking. Here's what I don't get. He's a teenager right? Like us. He gets headlines for his sexuality but he's not "getting" any more than me or you.
@miamimutantgrrl: Speak for yourself. That guy is famous. You are...you.
"...YOUR POWER IS YOUR FAME. YOU DON'T NEED FRIENDS...
"...WHEN YOU HAVE FOLLOWERS.
"THAT'S THE ONE LESSON I LEARNED FROM MY MOTHER.
"YOU KNOW WHO I AM AND YOU LIVE HALFWAY ACROSS THE WORLD.
"SHE MADE THAT HAPPEN.
"UNTIL MY POWER SHOWED ITSELF...I WAS SET TO JUST BE ANOTHER CHILD STAR DEAD BY AGE THIRTY."
YOUR KID IS GOING TO BE BIG.
I KNOW.
"BUT I LEARNED A LOT FROM MY MOM. I LEARNED THAT BAD THINGS? THOSE ARE THE TESTS.
"YOUR SUCCESS ISN'T DETERMINED BY THE GOOD OR BAD THAT HAPPENS TO YOU..."
COME ON. JUST BETWEEN YOU AND ME...
"...IT'S DETERMINED BY HOW YOU DEAL WITH IT.

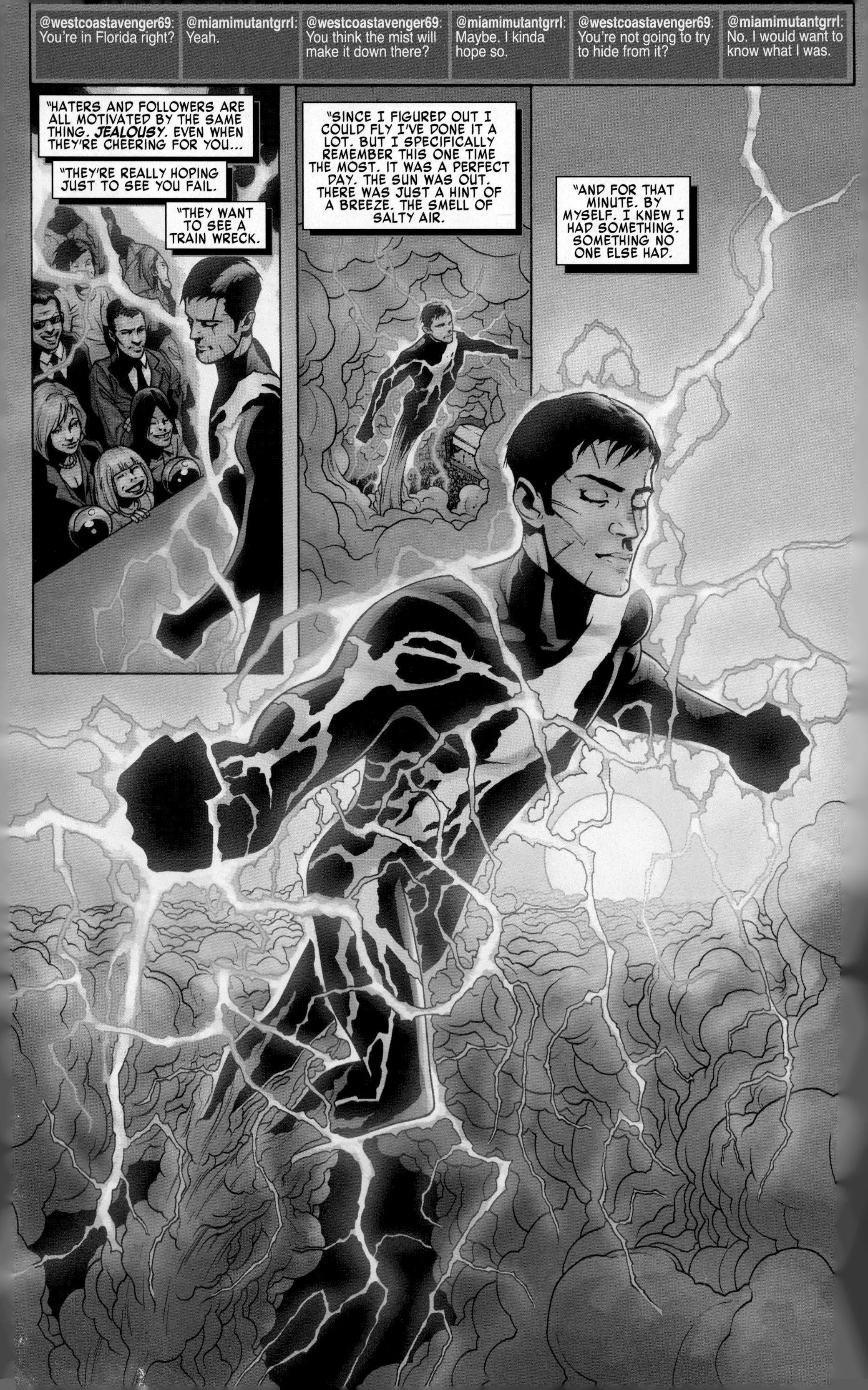
@westcoastavenger69: You're in Florida right?
@miamimutantgrrl: Yeah.
@westcoastavenger69: You think the mist will make it down there?
@miamimutantgrrl: Maybe. I kinda hope so.
@westcoastavenger69: You're not going to try to hide from it?
@miamimutantgrrl: No. I would want to know what I was.
"HATERS AND FOLLOWERS ARE ALL MOTIVATED BY THE SAME THING. JEALOUSY. EVEN WHEN THEY'RE CHEERING FOR YOU...
"THEY'RE REALLY HOPING JUST TO SEE YOU FAIL.
"THEY WANT TO SEE A TRAIN WRECK.
"SINCE I FIGURED OUT I COULD FLY I'VE DONE IT A LOT. BUT I SPECIFICALLY REMEMBER THIS ONE TIME THE MOST. IT WAS A PERFECT DAY. THE SUN WAS OUT. THERE WAS JUST A HINT OF A BREEZE. THE SMELL OF SALTY AIR.
"AND FOR THAT MINUTE. BY MYSELF. I KNEW I HAD SOMETHING. SOMETHING NO ONE ELSE HAD.

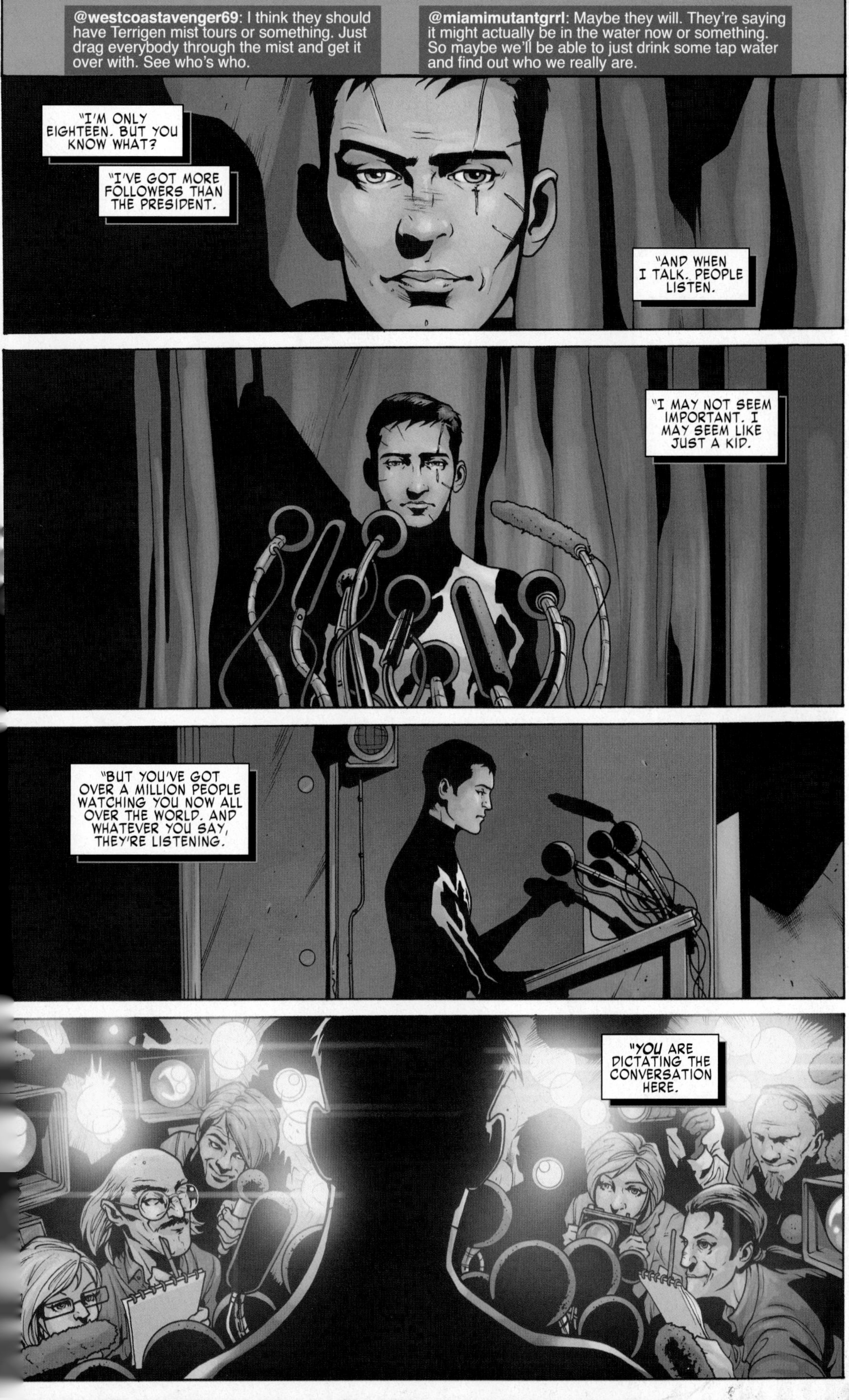
@westcoastavenger69: I think they should have Terrigen mist tours or something. Just drag everybody through the mist and get it over with. See who's who.
@miamimutantgrrl: Maybe they will. They're saying it might actually be in the water now or something. So maybe we'll be able to just drink some tap water and find out who we really are.
"I'M ONLY EIGHTEEN. BUT YOU KNOW WHAT?
"I'VE GOT MORE FOLLOWERS THAN THE PRESIDENT.
"AND WHEN I TALK. PEOPLE LISTEN.
"I MAY NOT SEEM IMPORTANT. I MAY SEEM LIKE JUST A KID.
"BUT YOU'VE GOT OVER A MILLION PEOPLE WATCHING YOU NOW ALL OVER THE WORLD. AND WHATEVER YOU SAY, THEY'RE LISTENING.
"*YOU* ARE DICTATING THE CONVERSATION HERE.

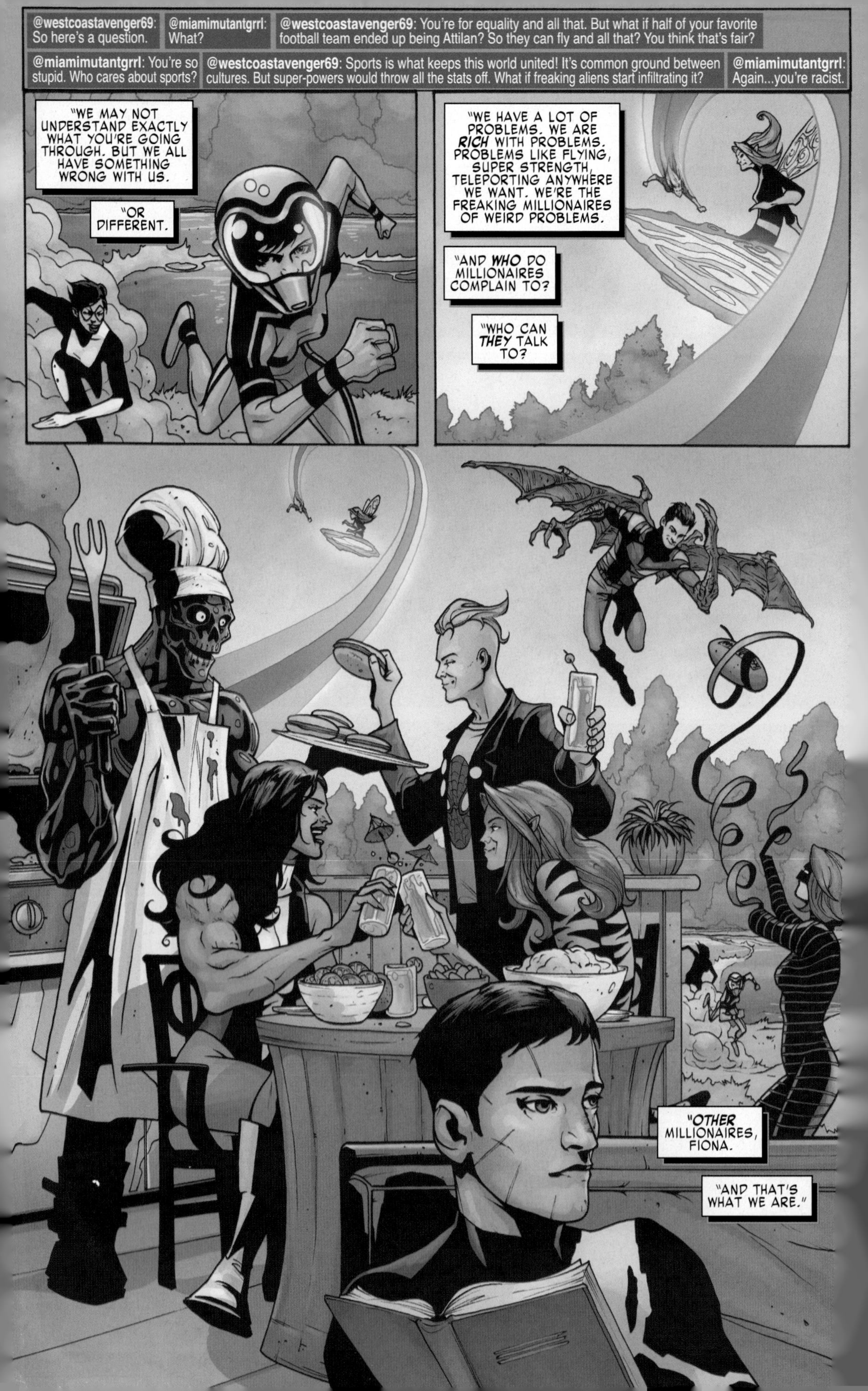
@westcoastavenger69: So here's a question.
@miamimutantgrrl: What?
@westcoastavenger69: You're for equality and all that. But what if half of your favorite football team ended up being Attilan? So they can fly and all that? You think that's fair?
@miamimutantgrrl: You're so stupid. Who cares about sports?
@westcoastavenger69: Sports is what keeps this world united! It's common ground between cultures. But super-powers would throw all the stats off. What if freaking aliens start infiltrating it?
@miamimutantgrrl: Again...you're racist.
"WE MAY NOT UNDERSTAND EXACTLY WHAT YOU'RE GOING THROUGH. BUT WE ALL HAVE SOMETHING WRONG WITH US.
"OR DIFFERENT.
"WE HAVE A LOT OF PROBLEMS. WE ARE *RICH* WITH PROBLEMS. PROBLEMS LIKE FLYING, SUPER STRENGTH, TELEPORTING ANYWHERE WE WANT. WE'RE THE FREAKING MILLIONAIRES OF WEIRD PROBLEMS.
"AND *WHO* DO MILLIONAIRES COMPLAIN TO?
"WHO CAN *THEY* TALK TO?
"*OTHER* MILLIONAIRES, FIONA.
"AND THAT'S WHAT WE ARE."

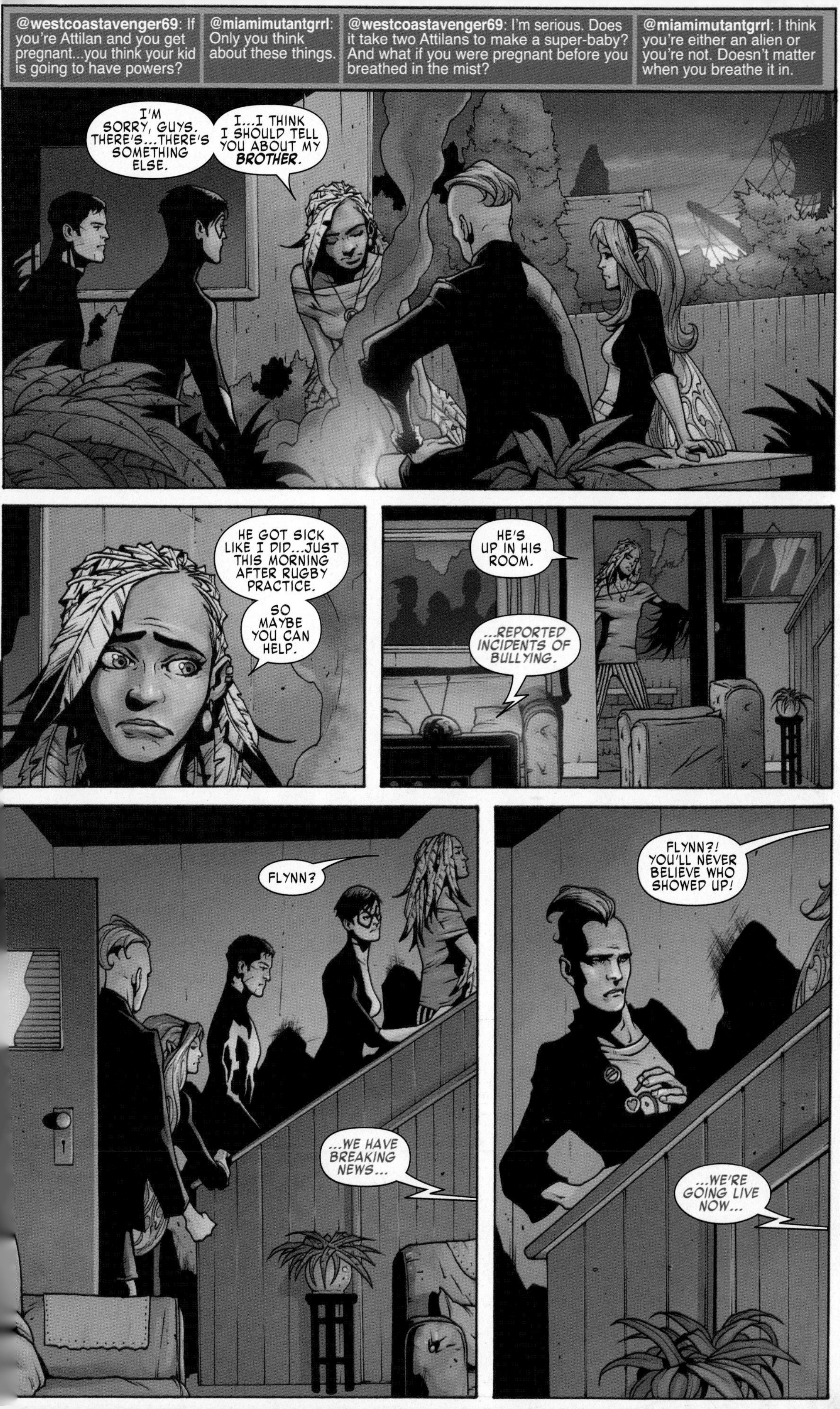
@westcoastavenger69: If you're Attilan and you get pregnant...you think your kid is going to have powers?
@miamimutantgrrl: Only you think about these things.
@westcoastavenger69: I'm serious. Does it take two Attilans to make a super-baby? And what if you were pregnant before you breathed in the mist?
@miamimutantgrrl: I think you're either an alien or you're not. Doesn't matter when you breathe it in.
I'M SORRY, GUYS. THERE'S...THERE'S SOMETHING ELSE.
I...I THINK I SHOULD TELL YOU ABOUT MY BROTHER.
HE GOT SICK LIKE I DID...JUST THIS MORNING AFTER RUGBY PRACTICE.
SO MAYBE YOU CAN HELP.
HE'S UP IN HIS ROOM.
...REPORTED INCIDENTS OF BULLYING.
FLYNN?
...WE HAVE BREAKING NEWS...
FLYNN?! YOU'LL NEVER BELIEVE WHO SHOWED UP!
...WE'RE GOING LIVE NOW...

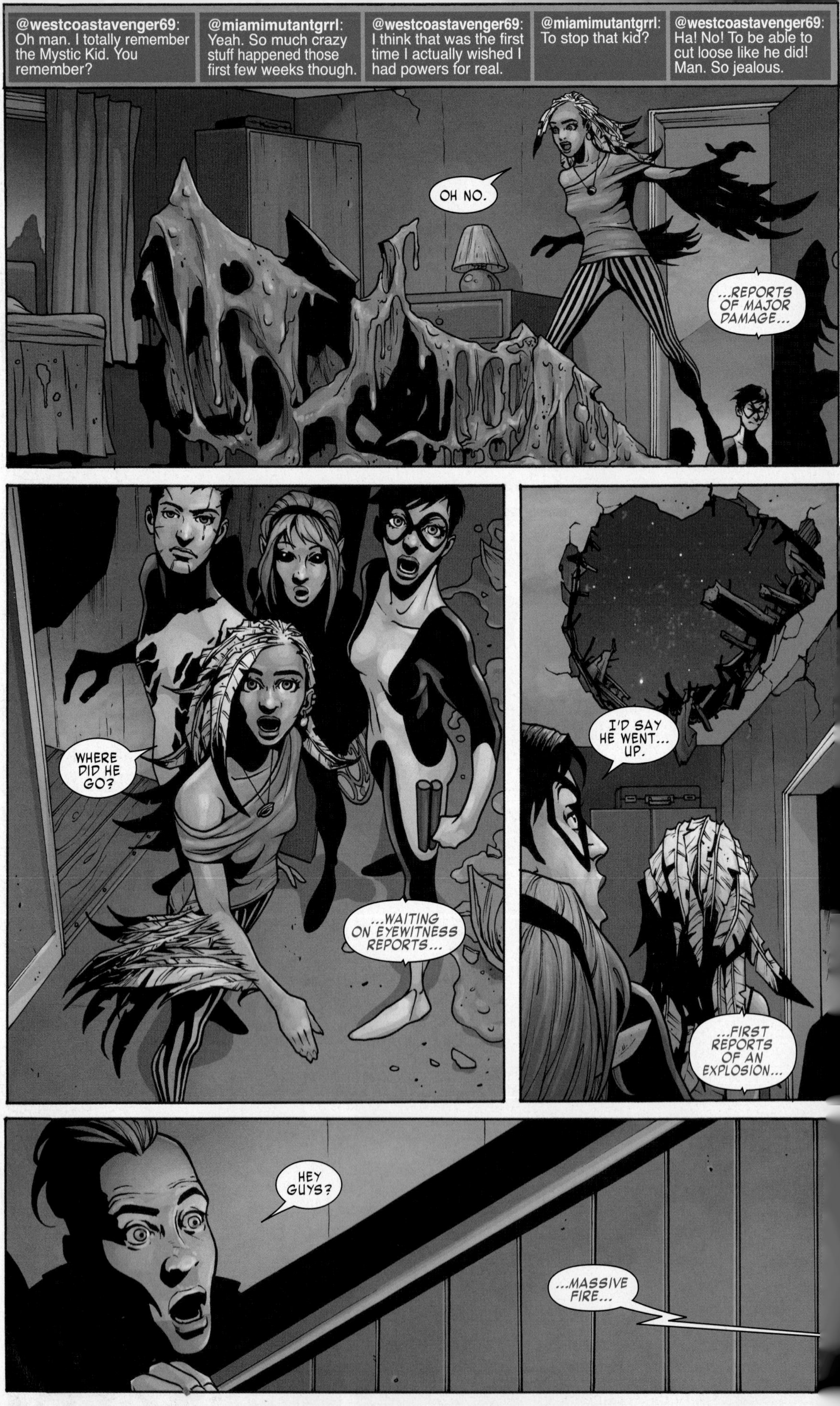

@westcoastavenger69: Oh man. I totally remember the Mystic Kid. You remember?
@miamimutantgrrl: Yeah. So much crazy stuff happened those first few weeks though.
@westcoastavenger69: I think that was the first time I actually wished I had powers for real.
@miamimutantgrrl: To stop that kid?
@westcoastavenger69: Ha! No! To be able to cut loose like he did! Man. So jealous.
OH NO.
...REPORTS OF MAJOR DAMAGE...
WHERE DID HE GO?
...WAITING ON EYEWITNESS REPORTS...
I'D SAY HE WENT... UP.
...FIRST REPORTS OF AN EXPLOSION...
HEY GUYS?
...MASSIVE FIRE...

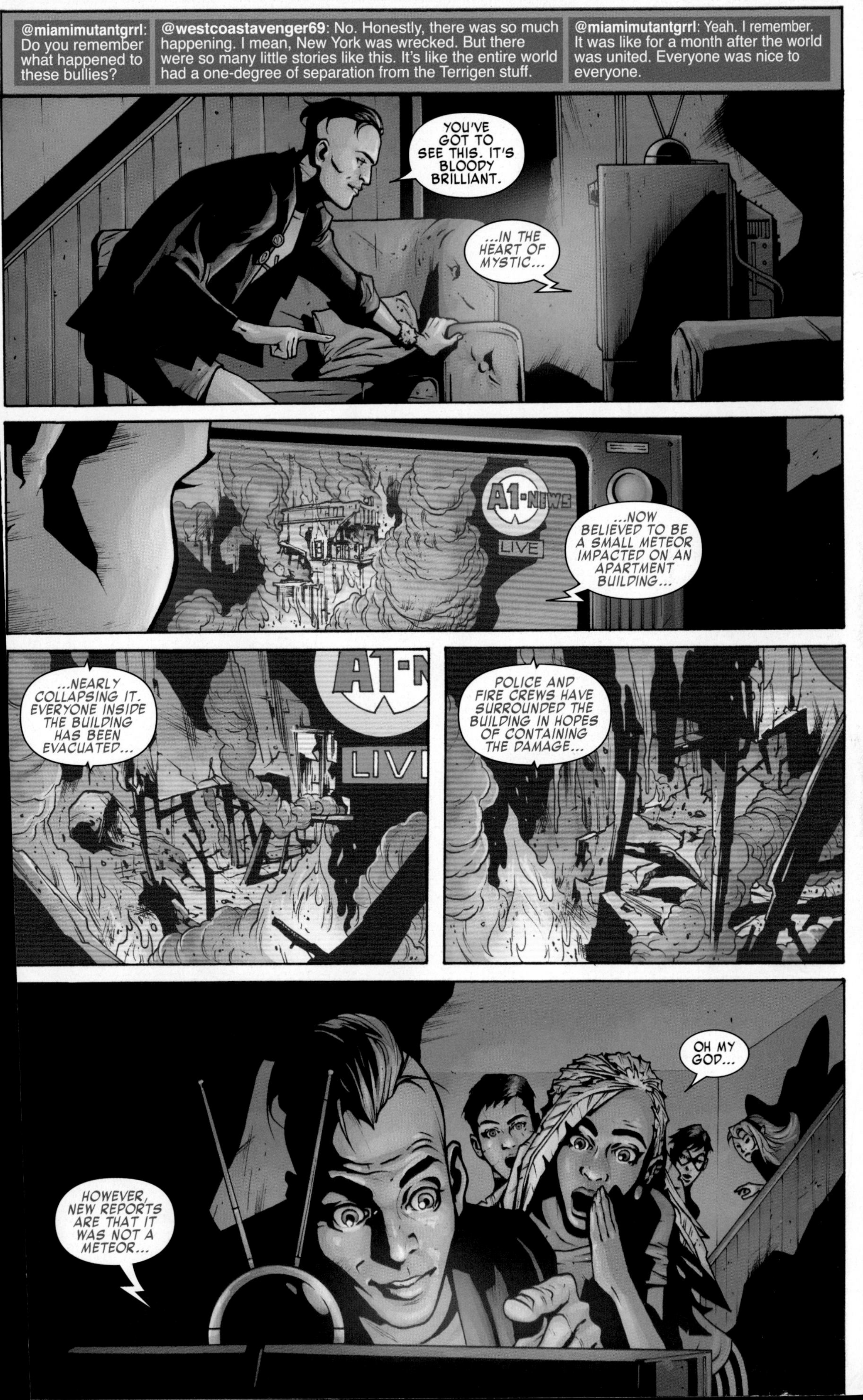

@miamimutantgrrl: Do you remember what happened to these bullies?
@westcoastavenger69: No. Honestly, there was so much happening. I mean, New York was wrecked. But there were so many little stories like this. It's like the entire world had a one-degree of separation from the Terrigen stuff.
@miamimutantgrrl: Yeah. I remember. It was like for a month after the world was united. Everyone was nice to everyone.
YOU'VE GOT TO SEE THIS. IT'S BLOODY BRILLIANT.
...IN THE HEART OF MYSTIC...
A1-NEWS
LIVE
...NOW BELIEVED TO BE A SMALL METEOR IMPACTED ON AN APARTMENT BUILDING...
...NEARLY COLLAPSING IT. EVERYONE INSIDE THE BUILDING HAS BEEN EVACUATED...
POLICE AND FIRE CREWS HAVE SURROUNDED THE BUILDING IN HOPES OF CONTAINING THE DAMAGE...
OH MY GOD...
HOWEVER, NEW REPORTS ARE THAT IT WAS NOT A METEOR...

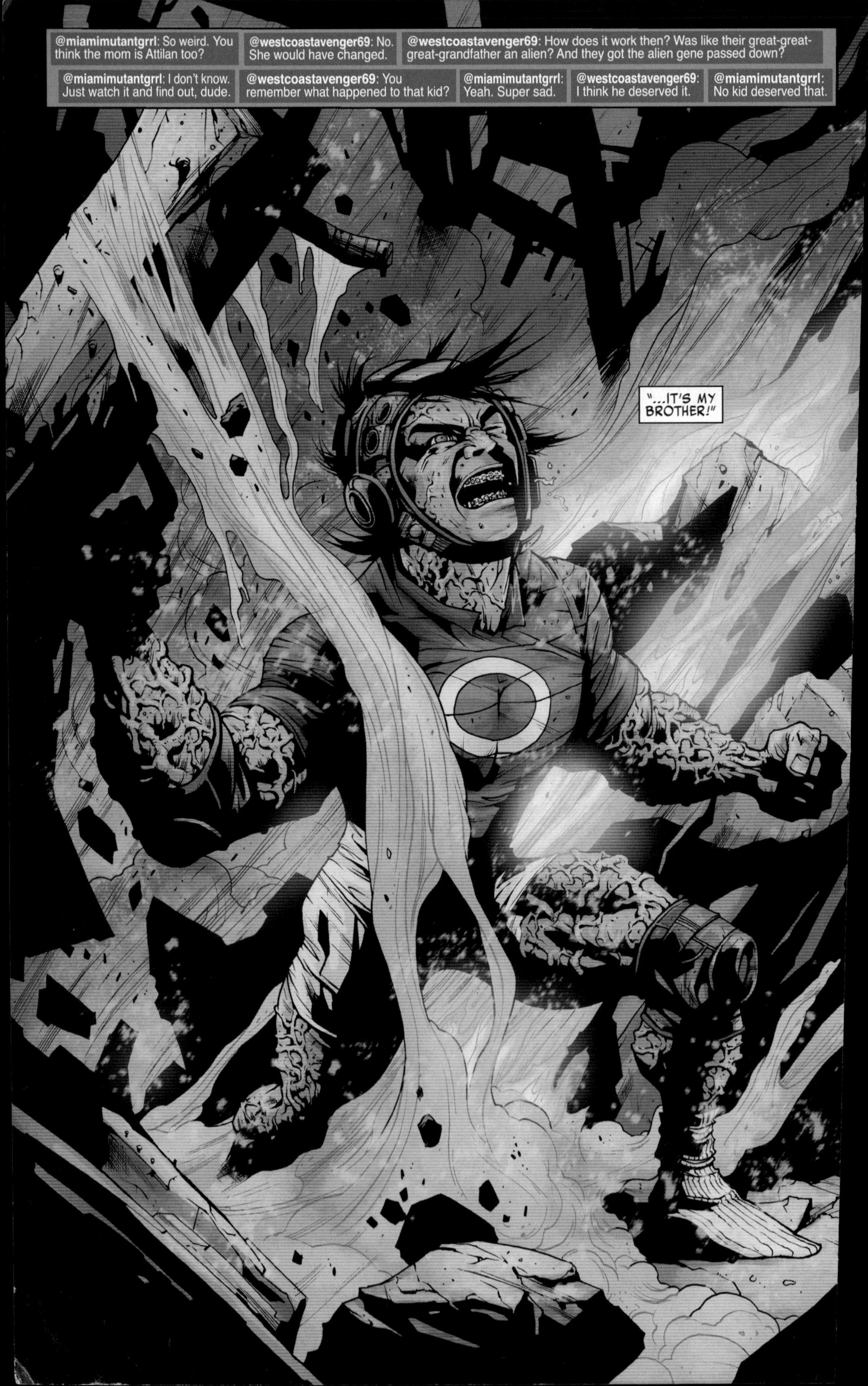

@miamimutantgrrl: So weird. You think the mom is Attilan too?
@westcoastavenger69: No. She would have changed.
@westcoastavenger69: How does it work then? Was like their great-great-great-grandfather an alien? And they got the alien gene passed down?
@miamimutantgrrl: I don't know. Just watch it and find out, dude.
@westcoastavenger69: You remember what happened to that kid?
@miamimutantgrrl: Yeah. Super sad.
@westcoastavenger69: I think he deserved it.
@miamimutantgrrl: No kid deserved that.
"...IT'S MY BROTHER!"

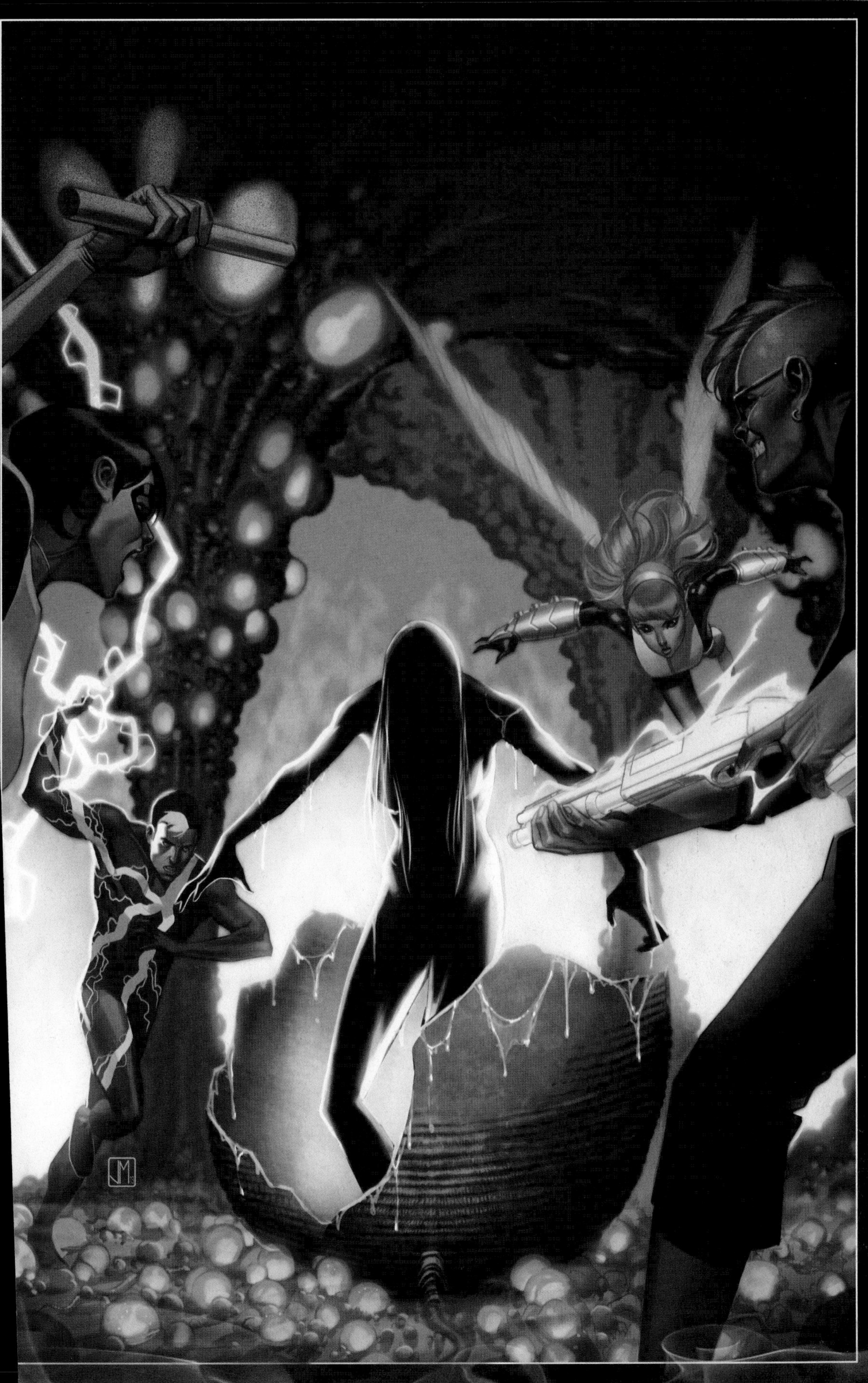

INHUMANITY: THE AWAKENING #2

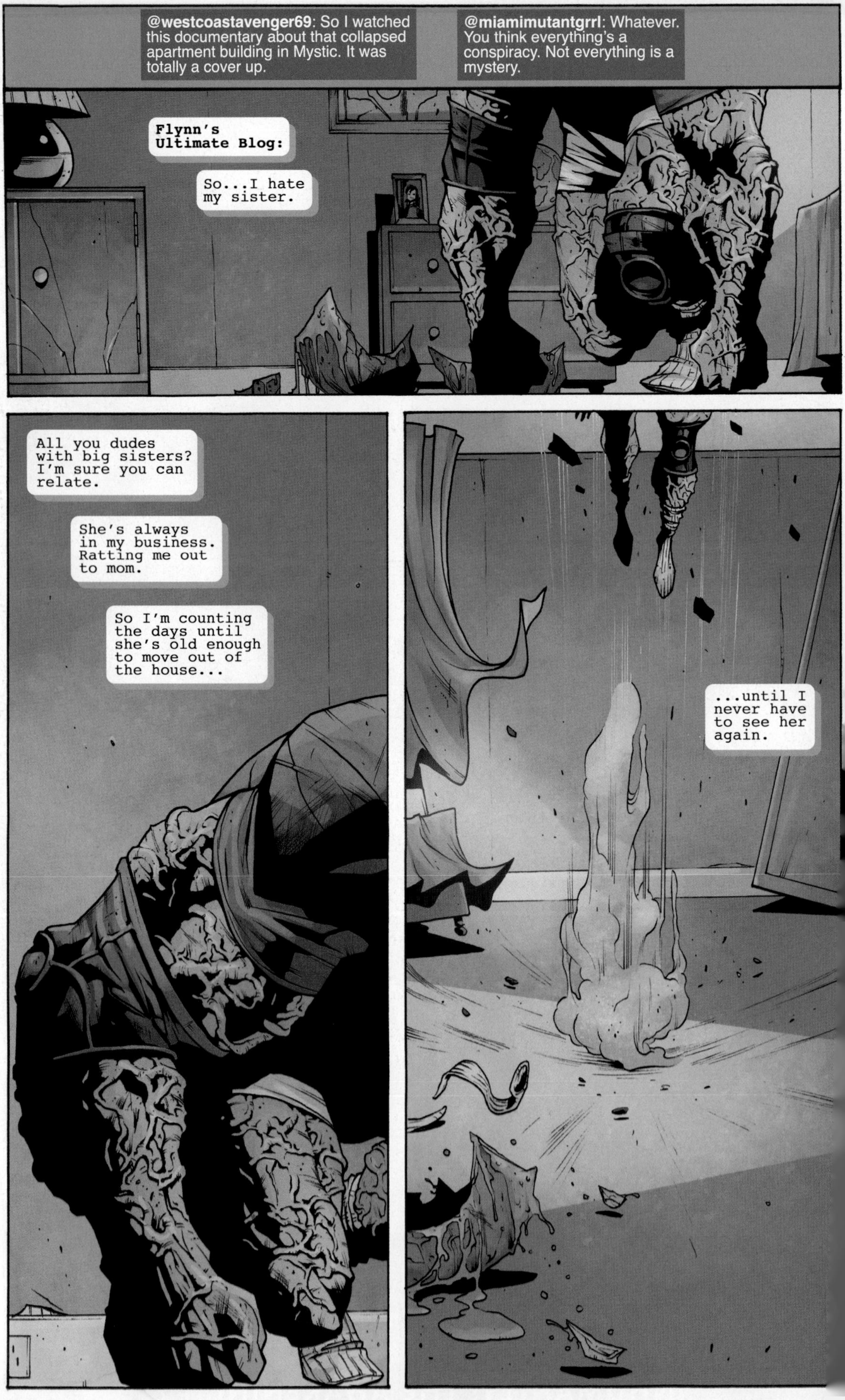
@westcoastavenger69: So I watched this documentary about that collapsed apartment building in Mystic. It was totally a cover up.
@miamimutantgrrl: Whatever. You think everything's a conspiracy. Not everything is a mystery.
Flynn's Ultimate Blog:
So...I hate my sister.
All you dudes with big sisters? I'm sure you can relate.
She's always in my business. Ratting me out to mom.
So I'm counting the days until she's old enough to move out of the house...
...until I never have to see her again.

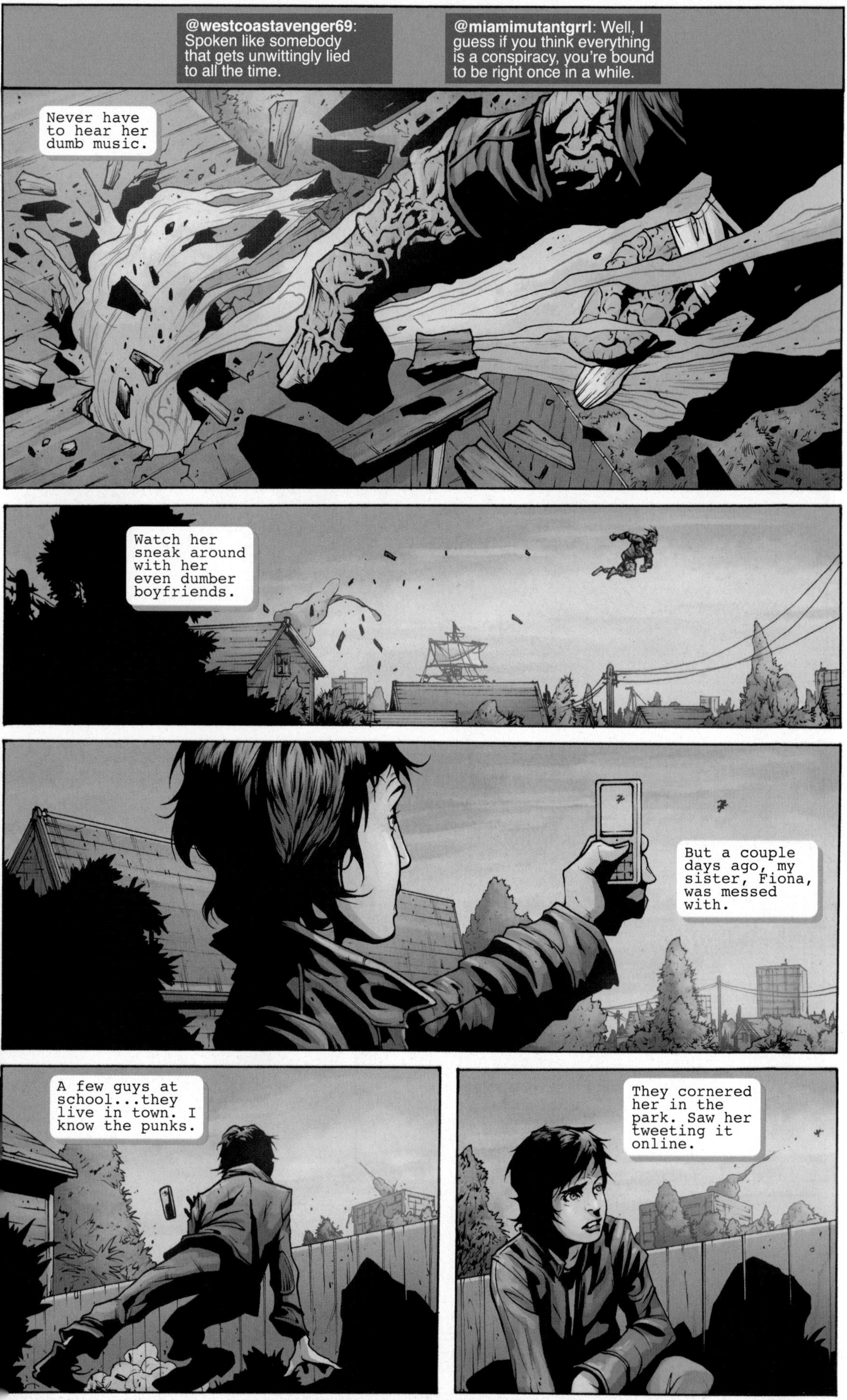
@westcoastavenger69: Spoken like somebody that gets unwittingly lied to all the time.
@miamimutantgrrl: Well, I guess if you think everything is a conspiracy, you're bound to be right once in a while.
Never have to hear her dumb music.
Watch her sneak around with her even dumber boyfriends.
But a couple days ago, my sister, Fiona, was messed with.
A few guys at school...they live in town. I know the punks.
They cornered her in the park. Saw her tweeting it online.

@**westcoastavenger69**: Anyway. The documentary is online. They say that the apartment collapse was caused by something dropping onto it. Not something coming out of it.

@**miamimutantgrrl**: Honesly. Who cares? On it or from inside it. No one was hurt. It was probably some poor kid that lived inside it. Woke up as an alien and freaked out.

They scared her good.

They did it because something happened to her.

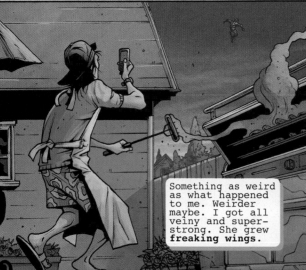

Something as weird as what happened to me. Weirder maybe. I got all veiny and super-strong. She grew **freaking wings.**

Anyway. Those dudes cornered her. Probably would have done worse if she hadn't been able to fly away.

Those dudes all live in the same apartment complex.

And as much as my sister disgusts me...annoys me...drives me nuts...

08 : 45 : 33 PM 23/10/13

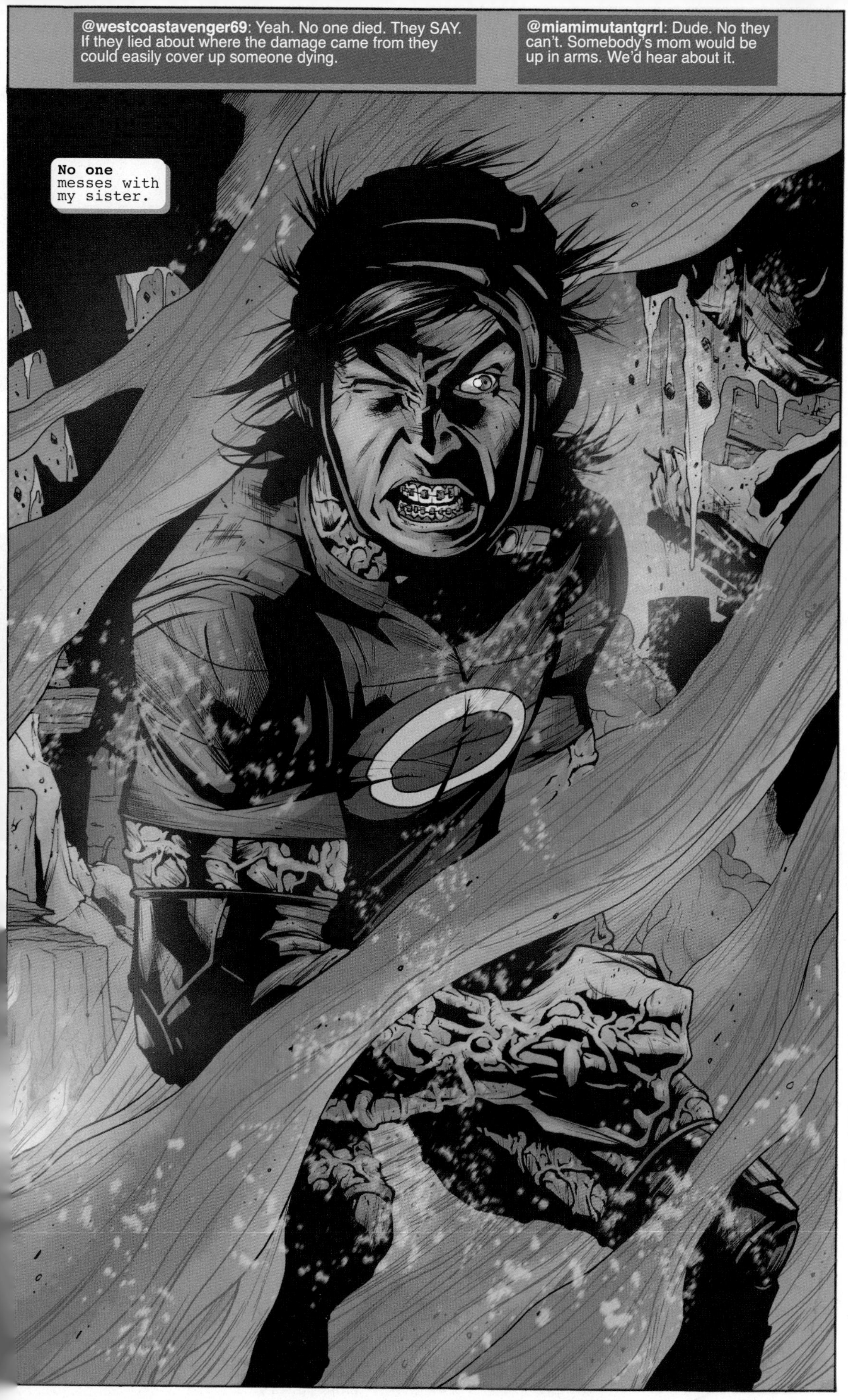
@westcoastavenger69: Yeah. No one died. They SAY. If they lied about where the damage came from they could easily cover up someone dying.
@miamimutantgrrl: Dude. No they can't. Somebody's mom would be up in arms. We'd hear about it.
No one messes with my sister.

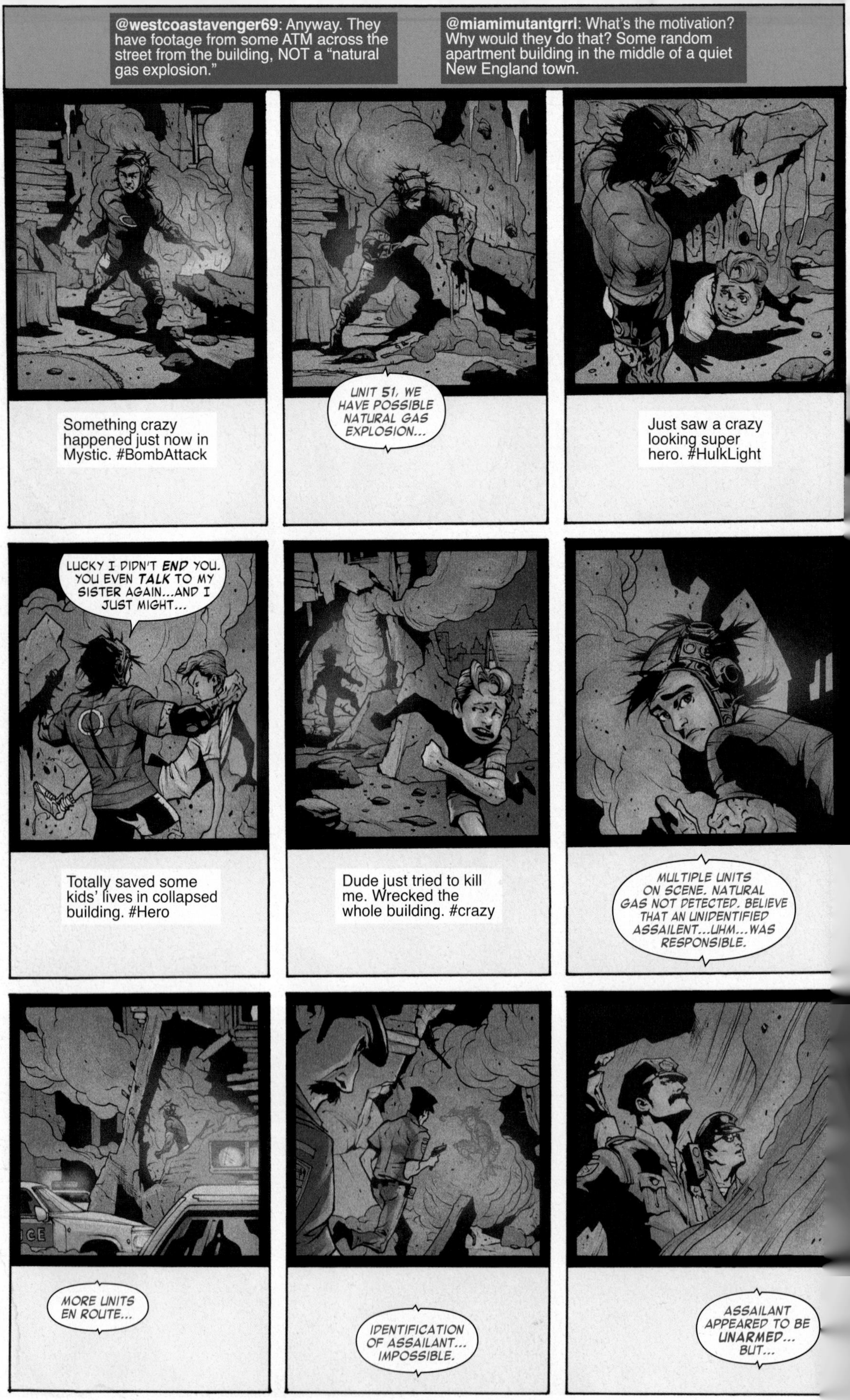
@westcoastavenger69: Anyway. They have footage from some ATM across the street from the building, NOT a "natural gas explosion."
@miamimutantgrrl: What's the motivation? Why would they do that? Some random apartment building in the middle of a quiet New England town.
Something crazy happened just now in Mystic. #BombAttack
UNIT 51, WE HAVE POSSIBLE NATURAL GAS EXPLOSION...
Just saw a crazy looking super hero. #HulkLight
LUCKY I DIDN'T END YOU. YOU EVEN TALK TO MY SISTER AGAIN...AND I JUST MIGHT...
Totally saved some kids' lives in collapsed building. #Hero
Dude just tried to kill me. Wrecked the whole building. #crazy
MULTIPLE UNITS ON SCENE. NATURAL GAS NOT DETECTED. BELIEVE THAT AN UNIDENTIFIED ASSAILANT...UHM...WAS RESPONSIBLE.
MORE UNITS EN ROUTE...
IDENTIFICATION OF ASSAILANT... IMPOSSIBLE.
ASSAILANT APPEARED TO BE UNARMED... BUT...

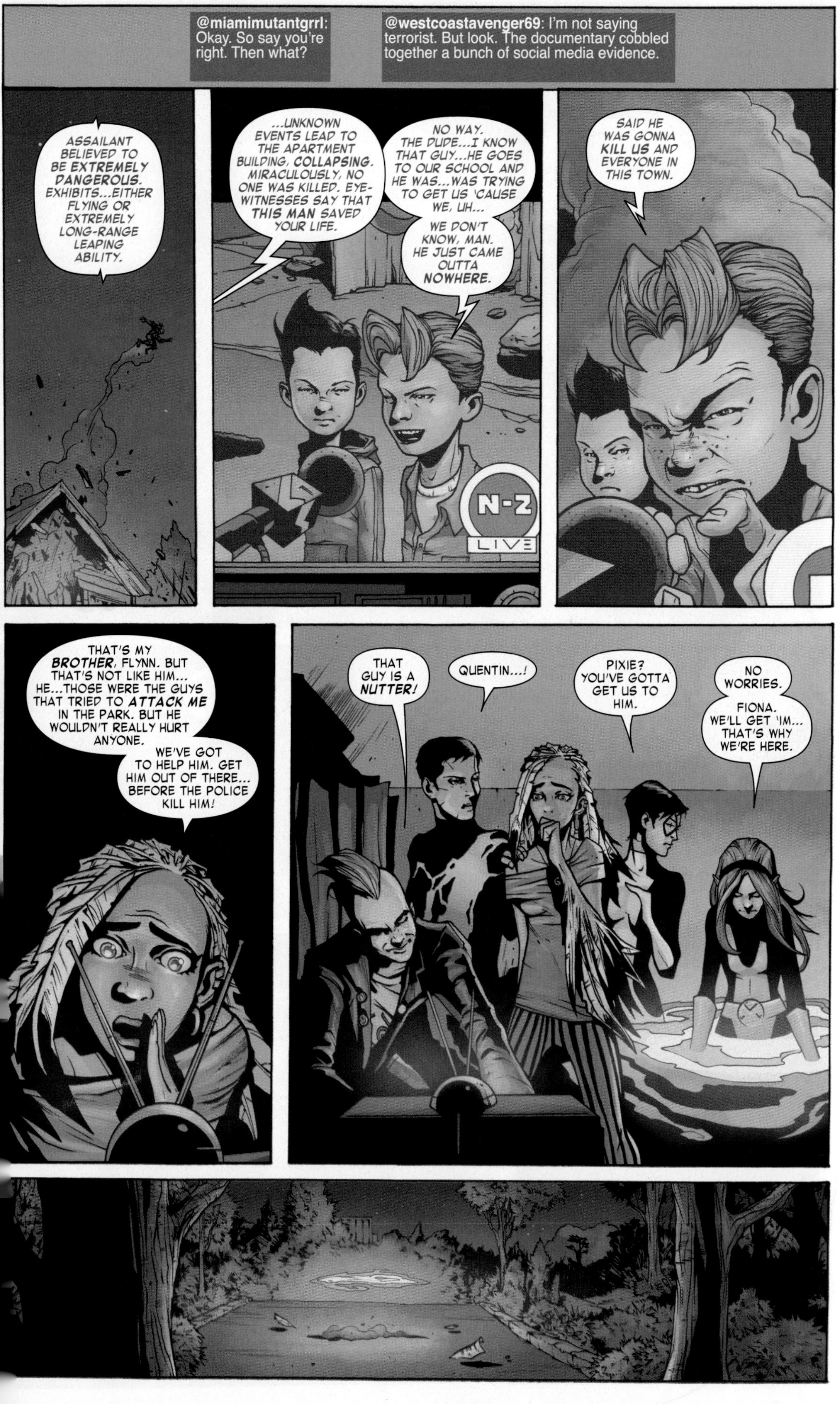
@miamimutantgrrl: Okay. So say you're right. Then what?
@westcoastavenger69: I'm not saying terrorist. But look. The documentary cobbled together a bunch of social media evidence.
ASSAILANT BELIEVED TO BE EXTREMELY DANGEROUS. EXHIBITS...EITHER FLYING OR EXTREMELY LONG-RANGE LEAPING ABILITY.
...UNKNOWN EVENTS LEAD TO THE APARTMENT BUILDING, COLLAPSING. MIRACULOUSLY, NO ONE WAS KILLED. EYE-WITNESSES SAY THAT THIS MAN SAVED YOUR LIFE.
NO WAY. THE DUDE...I KNOW THAT GUY...HE GOES TO OUR SCHOOL AND HE WAS...WAS TRYING TO GET US 'CAUSE WE, UH...
WE DON'T KNOW, MAN. HE JUST CAME OUTTA NOWHERE.
N-Z
LIVE
SAID HE WAS GONNA KILL US AND EVERYONE IN THIS TOWN.
THAT'S MY BROTHER, FLYNN. BUT THAT'S NOT LIKE HIM... HE...THOSE WERE THE GUYS THAT TRIED TO ATTACK ME IN THE PARK. BUT HE WOULDN'T REALLY HURT ANYONE.
WE'VE GOT TO HELP HIM. GET HIM OUT OF THERE... BEFORE THE POLICE KILL HIM!
THAT GUY IS A NUTTER!
QUENTIN...!
PIXIE? YOU'VE GOTTA GET US TO HIM.
NO WORRIES.
FIONA. WE'LL GET 'IM... THAT'S WHY WE'RE HERE.

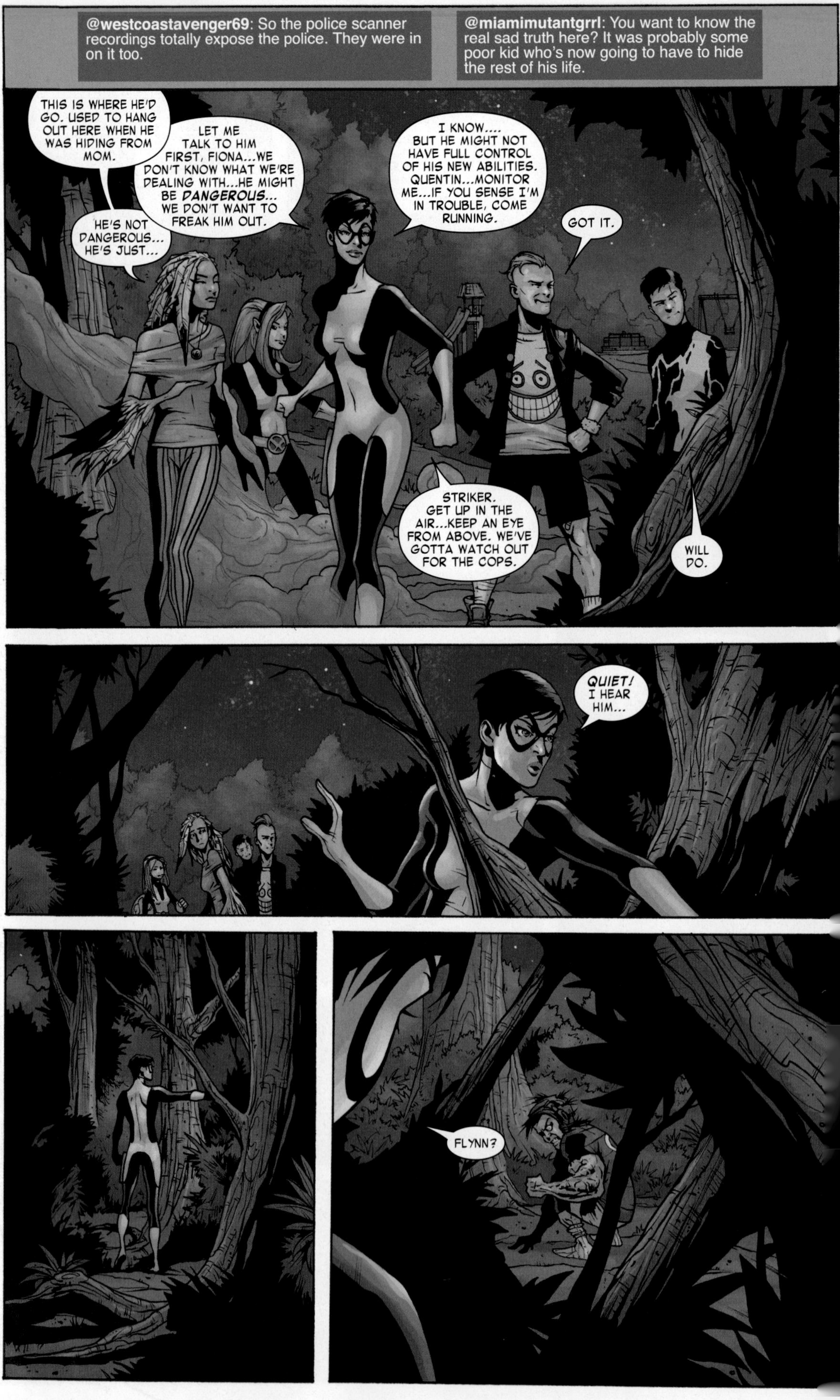
@westcoastavenger69: So the police scanner recordings totally expose the police. They were in on it too.
@miamimutantgrrl: You want to know the real sad truth here? It was probably some poor kid who's now going to have to hide the rest of his life.
THIS IS WHERE HE'D GO. USED TO HANG OUT HERE WHEN HE WAS HIDING FROM MOM.
LET ME TALK TO HIM FIRST, FIONA...WE DON'T KNOW WHAT WE'RE DEALING WITH...HE MIGHT BE DANGEROUS... WE DON'T WANT TO FREAK HIM OUT.
HE'S NOT DANGEROUS... HE'S JUST...
I KNOW.... BUT HE MIGHT NOT HAVE FULL CONTROL OF HIS NEW ABILITIES. QUENTIN...MONITOR ME...IF YOU SENSE I'M IN TROUBLE, COME RUNNING.
GOT IT.
STRIKER. GET UP IN THE AIR...KEEP AN EYE FROM ABOVE. WE'VE GOTTA WATCH OUT FOR THE COPS.
WILL DO.
QUIET! I HEAR HIM...
FLYNN?

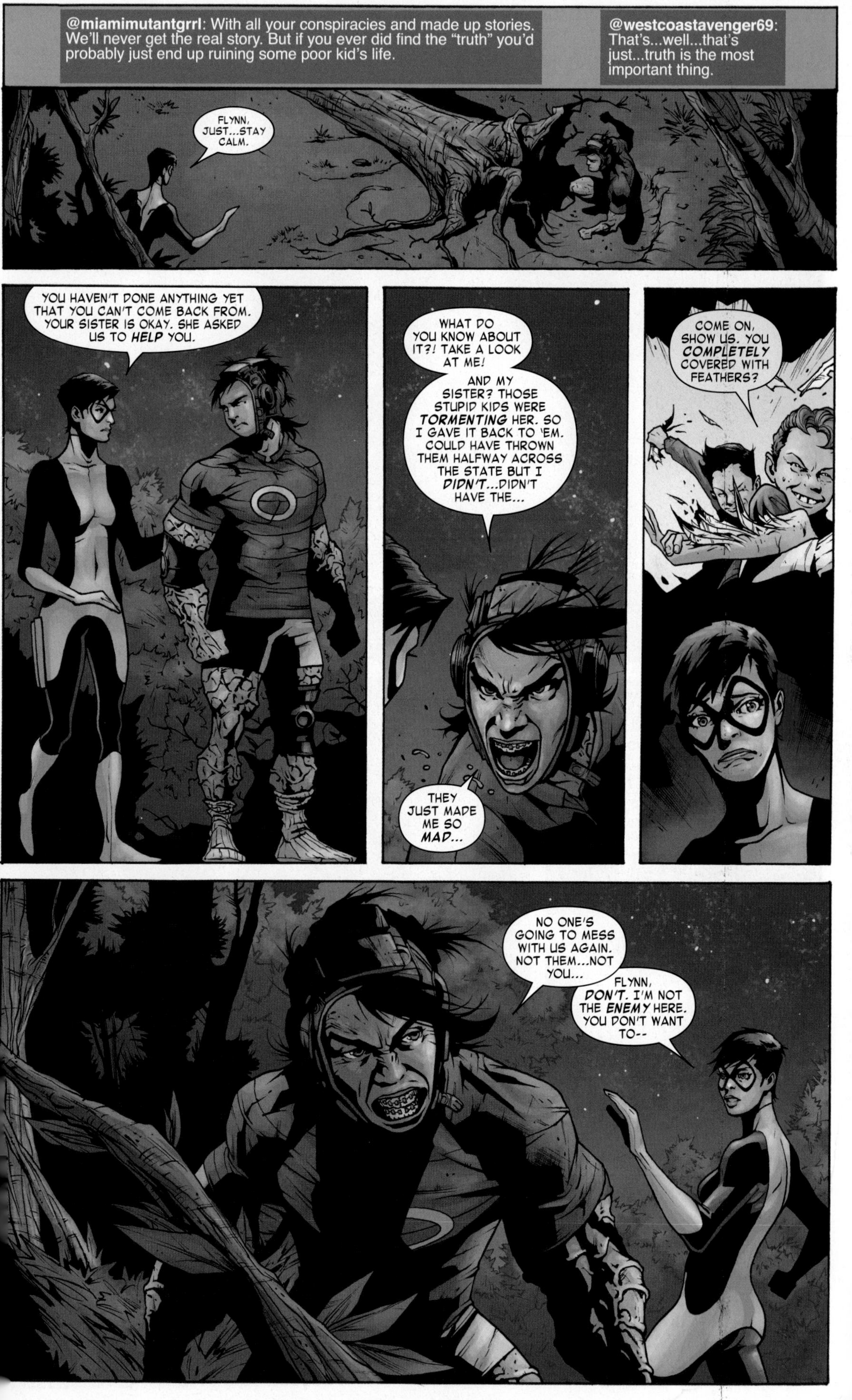
@miamimutantgrrl: With all your conspiracies and made up stories. We'll never get the real story. But if you ever did find the "truth" you'd probably just end up ruining some poor kid's life.
@westcoastavenger69: That's...well...that's just...truth is the most important thing.
FLYNN, JUST...STAY CALM.
YOU HAVEN'T DONE ANYTHING YET THAT YOU CAN'T COME BACK FROM. YOUR SISTER IS OKAY. SHE ASKED US TO HELP YOU.
WHAT DO YOU KNOW ABOUT IT?! TAKE A LOOK AT ME!
AND MY SISTER? THOSE STUPID KIDS WERE TORMENTING HER. SO I GAVE IT BACK TO 'EM. COULD HAVE THROWN THEM HALFWAY ACROSS THE STATE BUT I DIDN'T...DIDN'T HAVE THE...
THEY JUST MADE ME SO MAD...
COME ON, SHOW US. YOU COMPLETELY COVERED WITH FEATHERS?
NO ONE'S GOING TO MESS WITH US AGAIN. NOT THEM...NOT YOU...
FLYNN, DON'T. I'M NOT THE ENEMY HERE. YOU DON'T WANT TO--

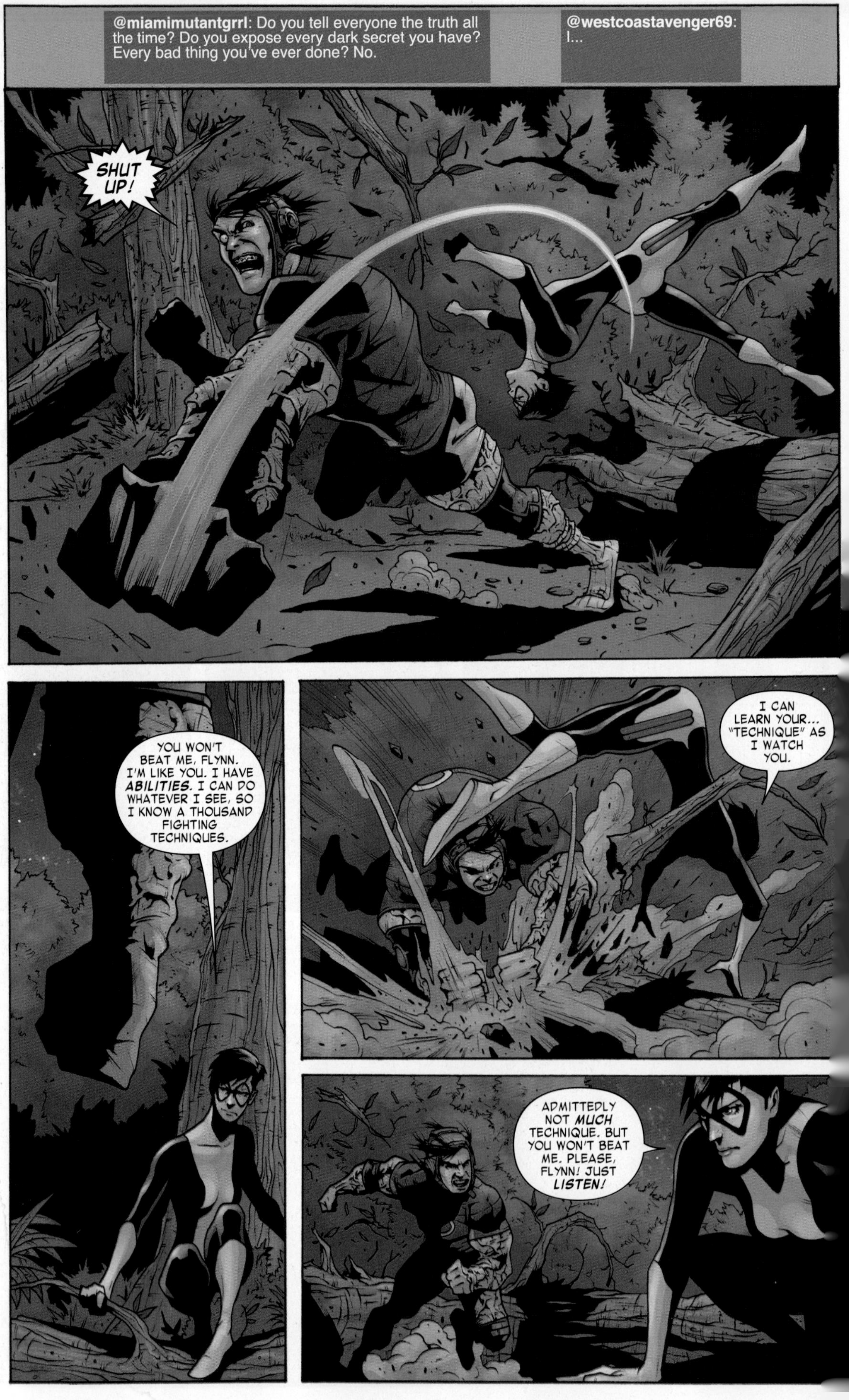
@miamimutantgrrl: Do you tell everyone the truth all the time? Do you expose every dark secret you have? Every bad thing you've ever done? No.
@westcoastavenger69: I...
SHUT UP!
YOU WON'T BEAT ME, FLYNN. I'M LIKE YOU. I HAVE ABILITIES. I CAN DO WHATEVER I SEE, SO I KNOW A THOUSAND FIGHTING TECHNIQUES.
I CAN LEARN YOUR... "TECHNIQUE" AS I WATCH YOU.
ADMITTEDLY NOT MUCH TECHNIQUE. BUT YOU WON'T BEAT ME. PLEASE, FLYNN! JUST LISTEN!

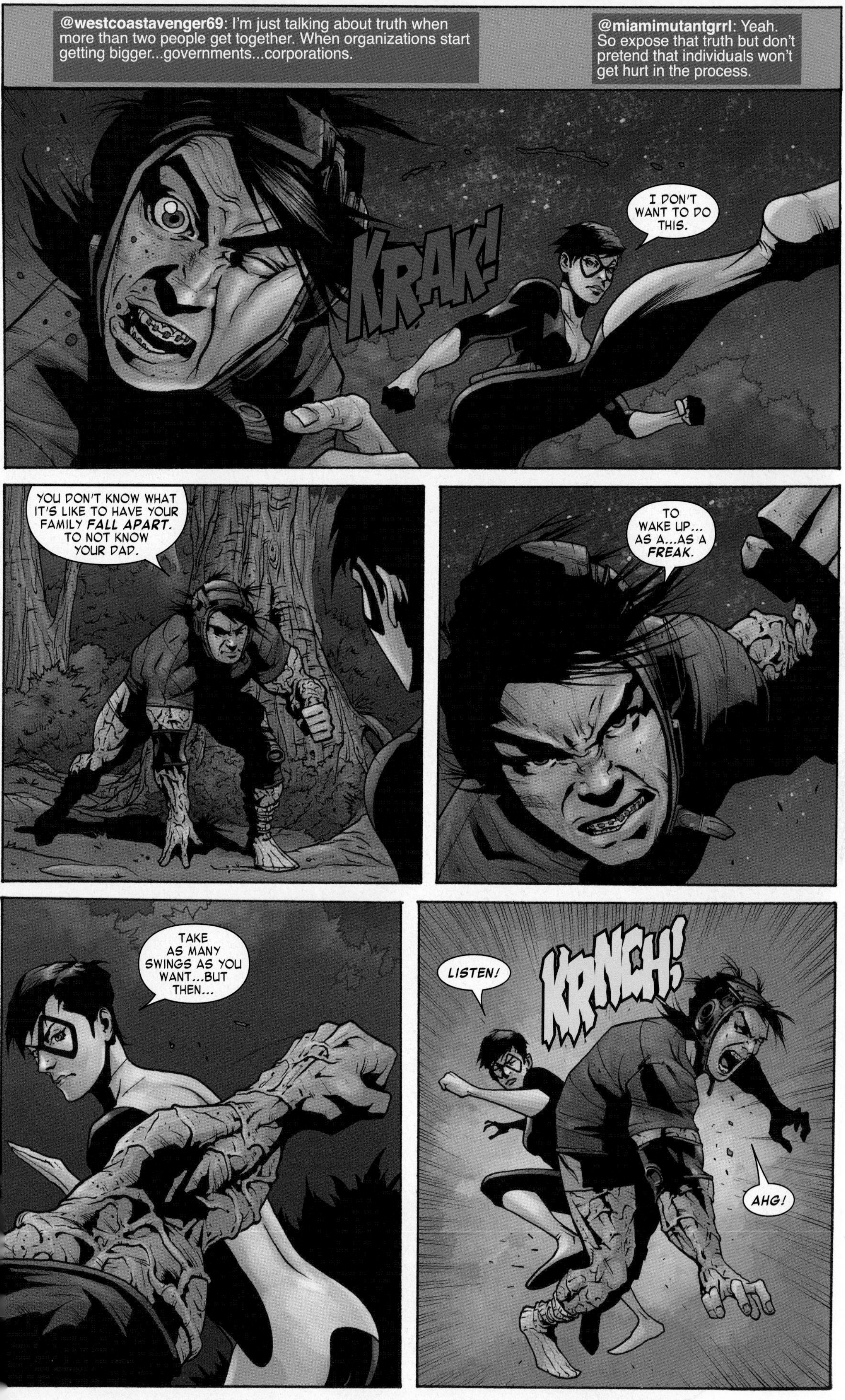
@westcoastavenger69: I'm just talking about truth when more than two people get together. When organizations start getting bigger...governments...corporations.
@miamimutantgrrl: Yeah. So expose that truth but don't pretend that individuals won't get hurt in the process.
KRAK!
I DON'T WANT TO DO THIS.
YOU DON'T KNOW WHAT IT'S LIKE TO HAVE YOUR FAMILY FALL APART. TO NOT KNOW YOUR DAD.
TO WAKE UP... AS A...AS A FREAK.
TAKE AS MANY SWINGS AS YOU WANT...BUT THEN...
LISTEN!
KRNCH!
AHG!

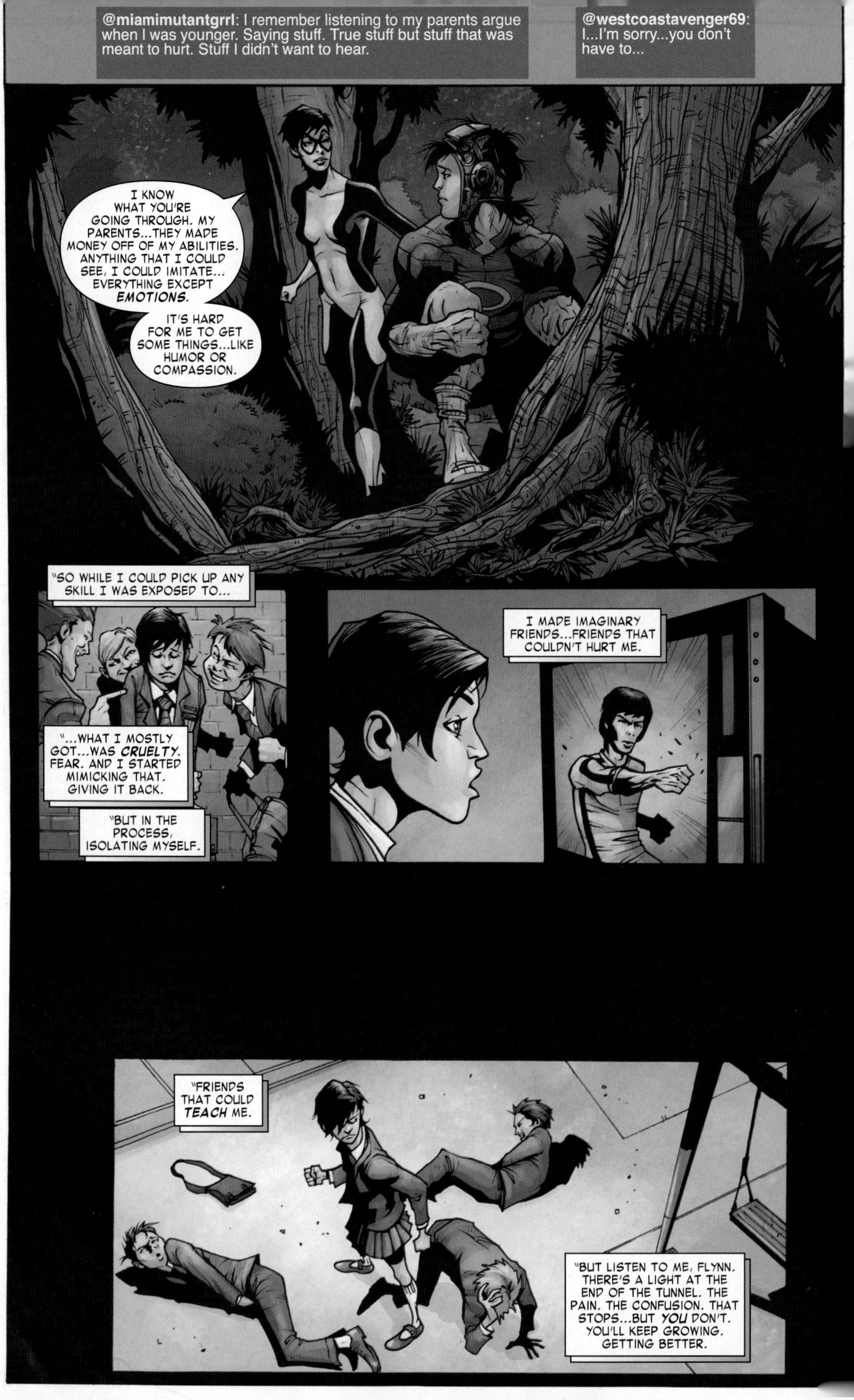
@miamimutantgrrl: I remember listening to my parents argue when I was younger. Saying stuff. True stuff but stuff that was meant to hurt. Stuff I didn't want to hear.
@westcoastavenger69: I...I'm sorry...you don't have to...
I KNOW WHAT YOU'RE GOING THROUGH. MY PARENTS...THEY MADE MONEY OFF OF MY ABILITIES. ANYTHING THAT I COULD SEE, I COULD IMITATE... EVERYTHING EXCEPT EMOTIONS.
IT'S HARD FOR ME TO GET SOME THINGS...LIKE HUMOR OR COMPASSION.
"SO WHILE I COULD PICK UP ANY SKILL I WAS EXPOSED TO...
"...WHAT I MOSTLY GOT...WAS CRUELTY. FEAR. AND I STARTED MIMICKING THAT. GIVING IT BACK.
"BUT IN THE PROCESS, ISOLATING MYSELF.
I MADE IMAGINARY FRIENDS...FRIENDS THAT COULDN'T HURT ME.
"FRIENDS THAT COULD TEACH ME.
"BUT LISTEN TO ME, FLYNN. THERE'S A LIGHT AT THE END OF THE TUNNEL. THE PAIN. THE CONFUSION. THAT STOPS...BUT YOU DON'T. YOU'LL KEEP GROWING. GETTING BETTER.

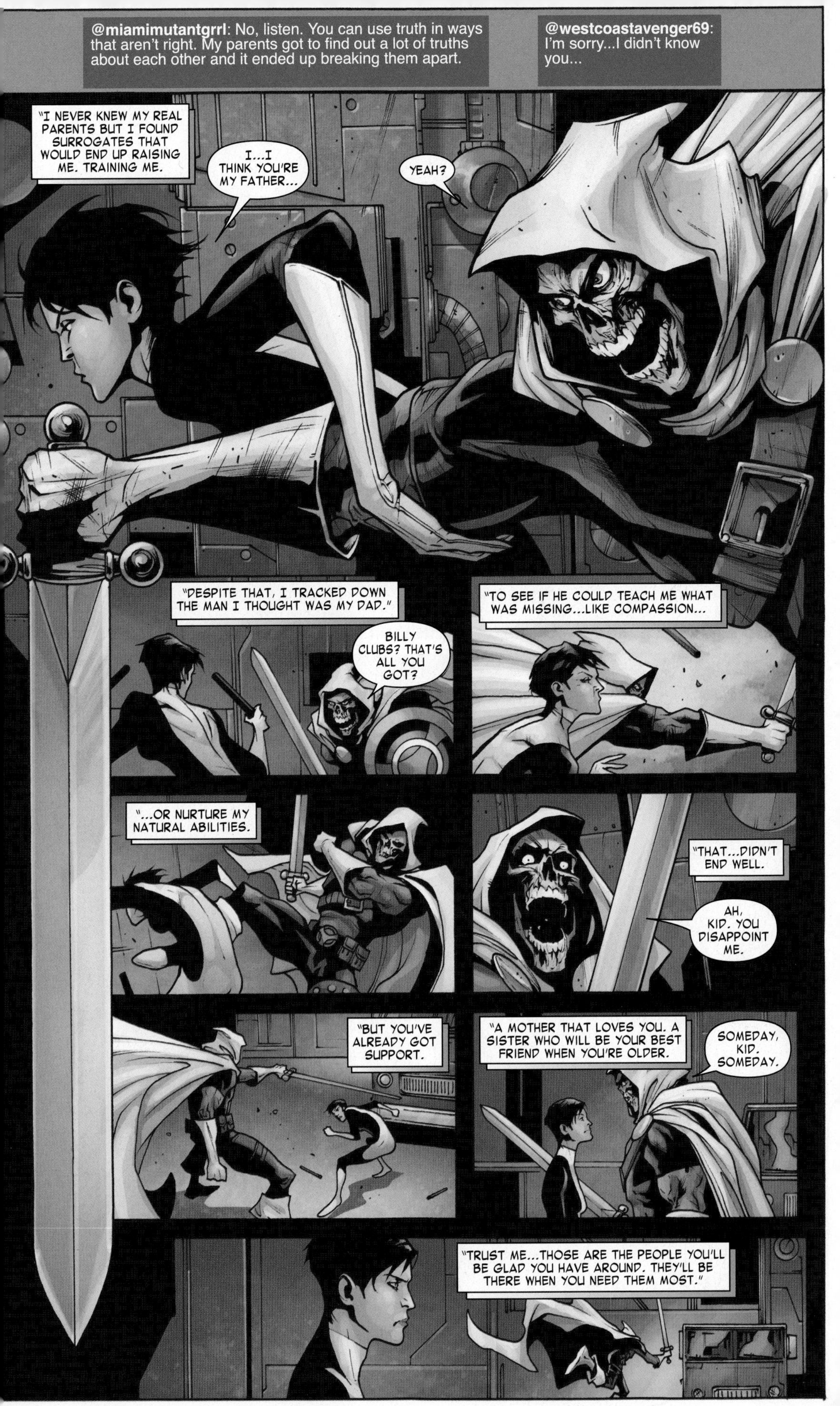
@miamimutantgrrl: No, listen. You can use truth in ways that aren't right. My parents got to find out a lot of truths about each other and it ended up breaking them apart.
@westcoastavenger69: I'm sorry...I didn't know you...
"I NEVER KNEW MY REAL PARENTS BUT I FOUND SURROGATES THAT WOULD END UP RAISING ME. TRAINING ME.
I...I THINK YOU'RE MY FATHER...
YEAH?
"DESPITE THAT, I TRACKED DOWN THE MAN I THOUGHT WAS MY DAD."
BILLY CLUBS? THAT'S ALL YOU GOT?
"TO SEE IF HE COULD TEACH ME WHAT WAS MISSING...LIKE COMPASSION...
"...OR NURTURE MY NATURAL ABILITIES.
"THAT...DIDN'T END WELL.
AH, KID. YOU DISAPPOINT ME.
"BUT YOU'VE ALREADY GOT SUPPORT.
"A MOTHER THAT LOVES YOU. A SISTER WHO WILL BE YOUR BEST FRIEND WHEN YOU'RE OLDER.
SOMEDAY, KID. SOMEDAY.
"TRUST ME...THOSE ARE THE PEOPLE YOU'LL BE GLAD YOU HAVE AROUND. THEY'LL BE THERE WHEN YOU NEED THEM MOST."

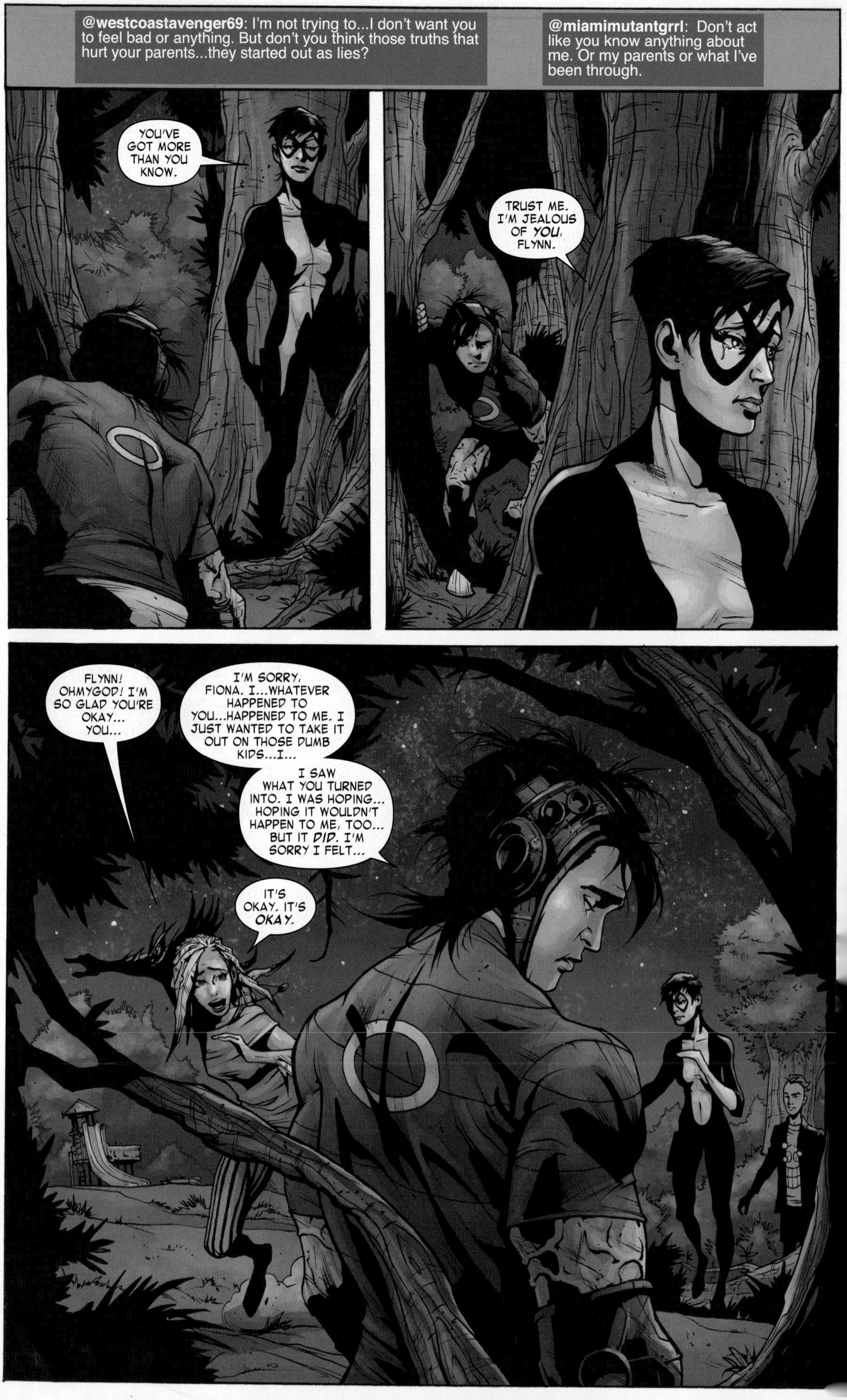
@westcoastavenger69: I'm not trying to...I don't want you to feel bad or anything. But don't you think those truths that hurt your parents...they started out as lies?
@miamimutantgrrl: Don't act like you know anything about me. Or my parents or what I've been through.
YOU'VE GOT MORE THAN YOU KNOW.
TRUST ME. I'M JEALOUS OF YOU, FLYNN.
FLYNN! OHMYGOD! I'M SO GLAD YOU'RE OKAY... YOU...
I'M SORRY, FIONA. I...WHATEVER HAPPENED TO YOU...HAPPENED TO ME. I JUST WANTED TO TAKE IT OUT ON THOSE DUMB KIDS...I...
I SAW WHAT YOU TURNED INTO. I WAS HOPING... HOPING IT WOULDN'T HAPPEN TO ME, TOO... BUT IT DID. I'M SORRY I FELT...
IT'S OKAY. IT'S OKAY.

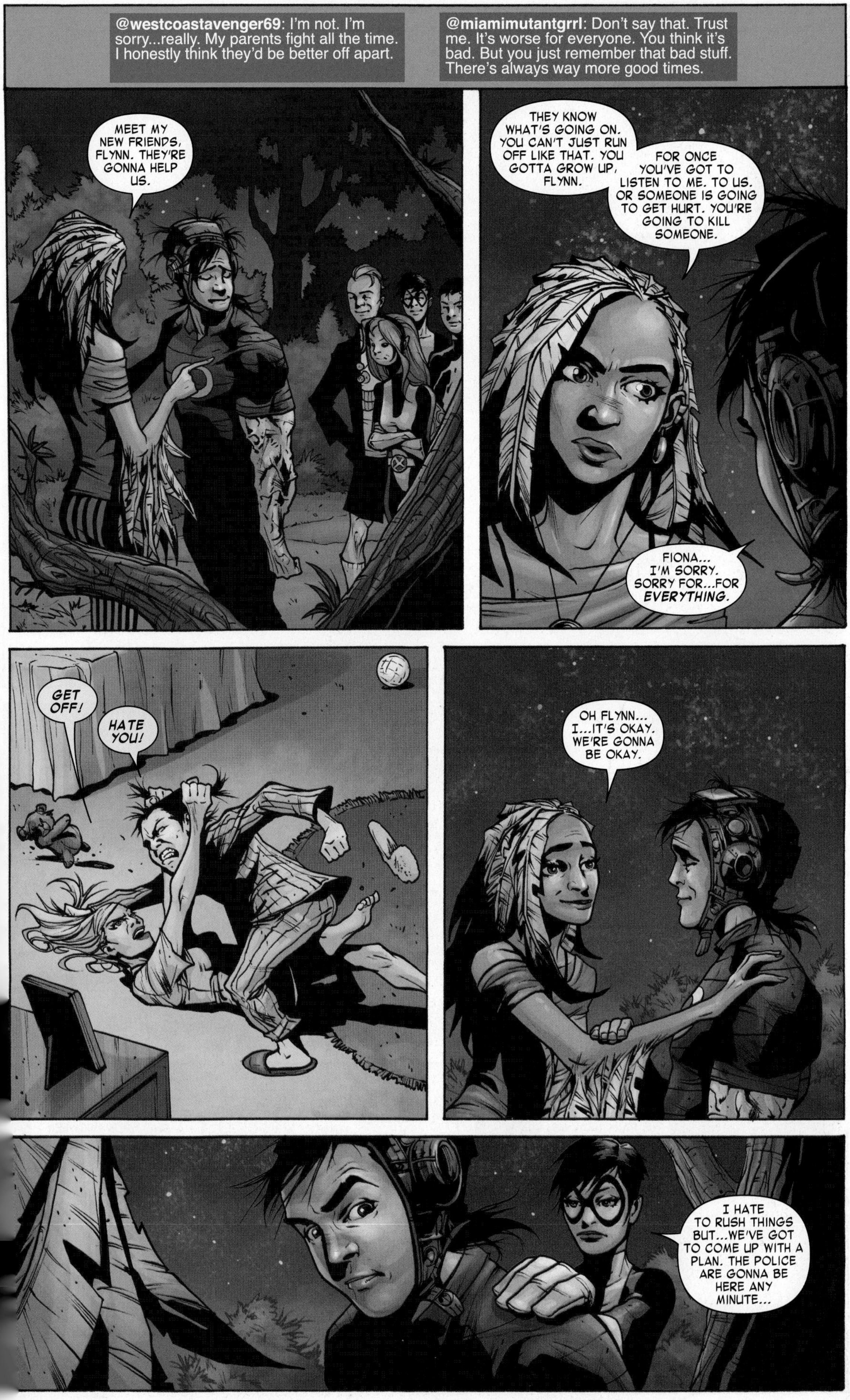
@westcoastavenger69: I'm not. I'm sorry...really. My parents fight all the time. I honestly think they'd be better off apart.
@miamimutantgrrl: Don't say that. Trust me. It's worse for everyone. You think it's bad. But you just remember that bad stuff. There's always way more good times.
MEET MY NEW FRIENDS, FLYNN. THEY'RE GONNA HELP US.
THEY KNOW WHAT'S GOING ON. YOU CAN'T JUST RUN OFF LIKE THAT. YOU GOTTA GROW UP, FLYNN.
FOR ONCE YOU'VE GOT TO LISTEN TO ME. TO US. OR SOMEONE IS GOING TO GET HURT. YOU'RE GOING TO KILL SOMEONE.
FIONA... I'M SORRY. SORRY FOR...FOR EVERYTHING.
GET OFF!
HATE YOU!
OH FLYNN... I...IT'S OKAY. WE'RE GONNA BE OKAY.
I HATE TO RUSH THINGS BUT...WE'VE GOT TO COME UP WITH A PLAN. THE POLICE ARE GONNA BE HERE ANY MINUTE...

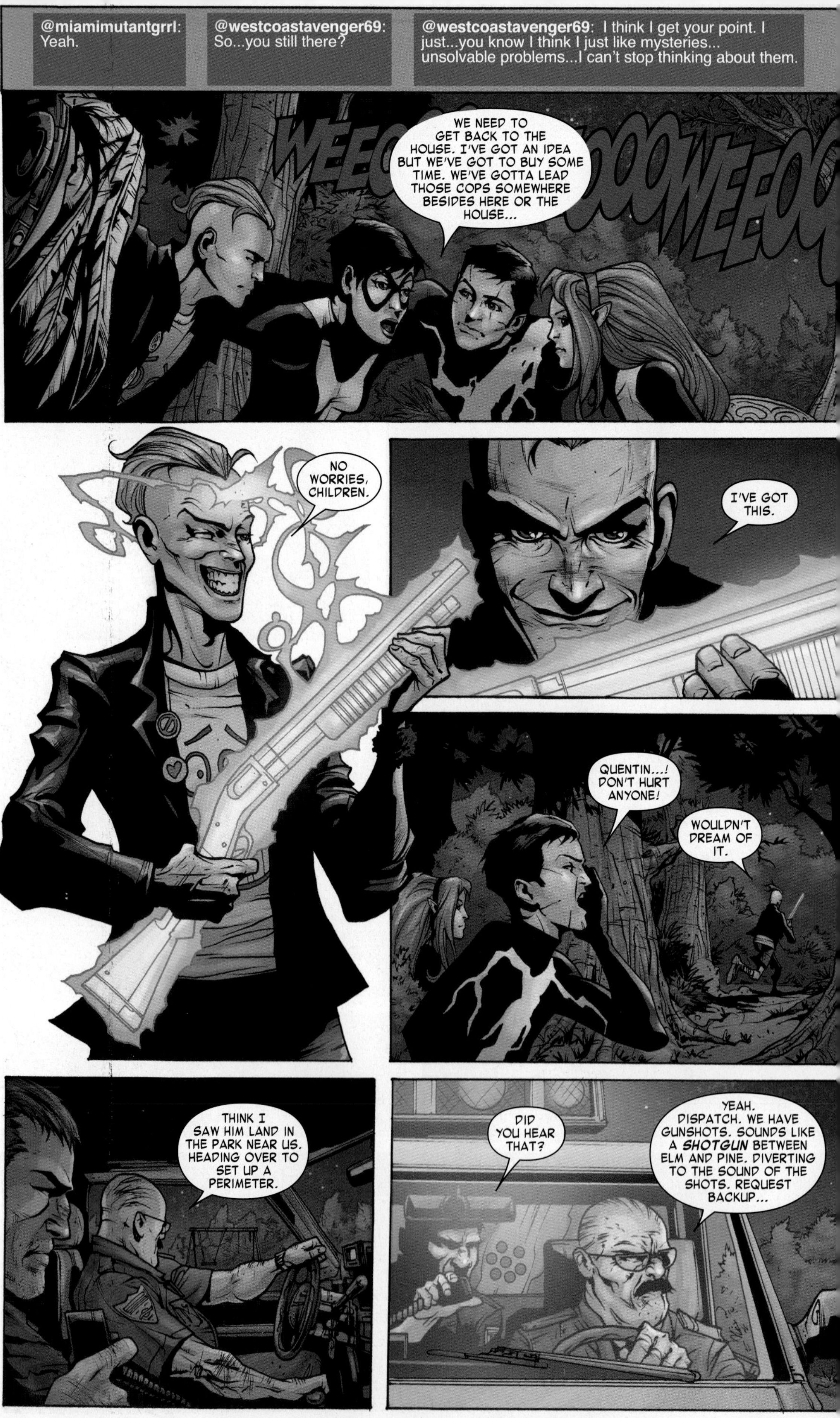
@miamimutantgrrl: Yeah.
@westcoastavenger69: So...you still there?
@westcoastavenger69: I think I get your point. I just...you know I think I just like mysteries... unsolvable problems...I can't stop thinking about them.
WE NEED TO GET BACK TO THE HOUSE. I'VE GOT AN IDEA BUT WE'VE GOT TO BUY SOME TIME. WE'VE GOTTA LEAD THOSE COPS SOMEWHERE BESIDES HERE OR THE HOUSE...
NO WORRIES, CHILDREN.
I'VE GOT THIS.
QUENTIN...! DON'T HURT ANYONE!
WOULDN'T DREAM OF IT.
THINK I SAW HIM LAND IN THE PARK NEAR US. HEADING OVER TO SET UP A PERIMETER.
DID YOU HEAR THAT?
YEAH. DISPATCH. WE HAVE GUNSHOTS. SOUNDS LIKE A SHOTGUN BETWEEN ELM AND PINE. DIVERTING TO THE SOUND OF THE SHOTS. REQUEST BACKUP...

@miamimutantgrrl: I know. I get it. My little brother is just like you. Kind of annoying. But not as...whatever.

@westcoastavenger69: What? What were you going to say?

@miamimutantgrrl: Nothing.

Insurance covered most of the damage.

Fiona's mom blamed the roof damage on the "falling pod."

Cleaning up the (now rotting) pods was another story. The smell was described by Fiona as a cross between barf and dog crap.

Yeah.

So the problem then was what to do with those pods.

With Pixie's help we got into one of the partially collapsed apartment buildings. Threw off the investigation for a long while. The police are convinced that the perpetrator lived there. No harm, no foul.

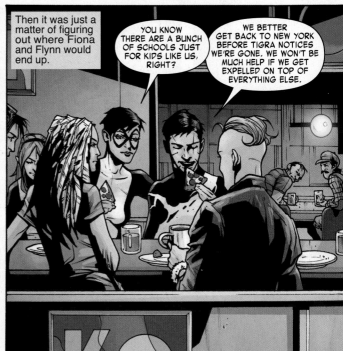

Then it was just a matter of figuring out where Fiona and Flynn would end up.

YOU KNOW THERE ARE A BUNCH OF SCHOOLS JUST FOR KIDS LIKE US, RIGHT?

WE BETTER GET BACK TO NEW YORK BEFORE TIGRA NOTICES WE'RE GONE. WE WON'T BE MUCH HELP IF WE GET EXPELLED ON TOP OF EVERYTHING ELSE.

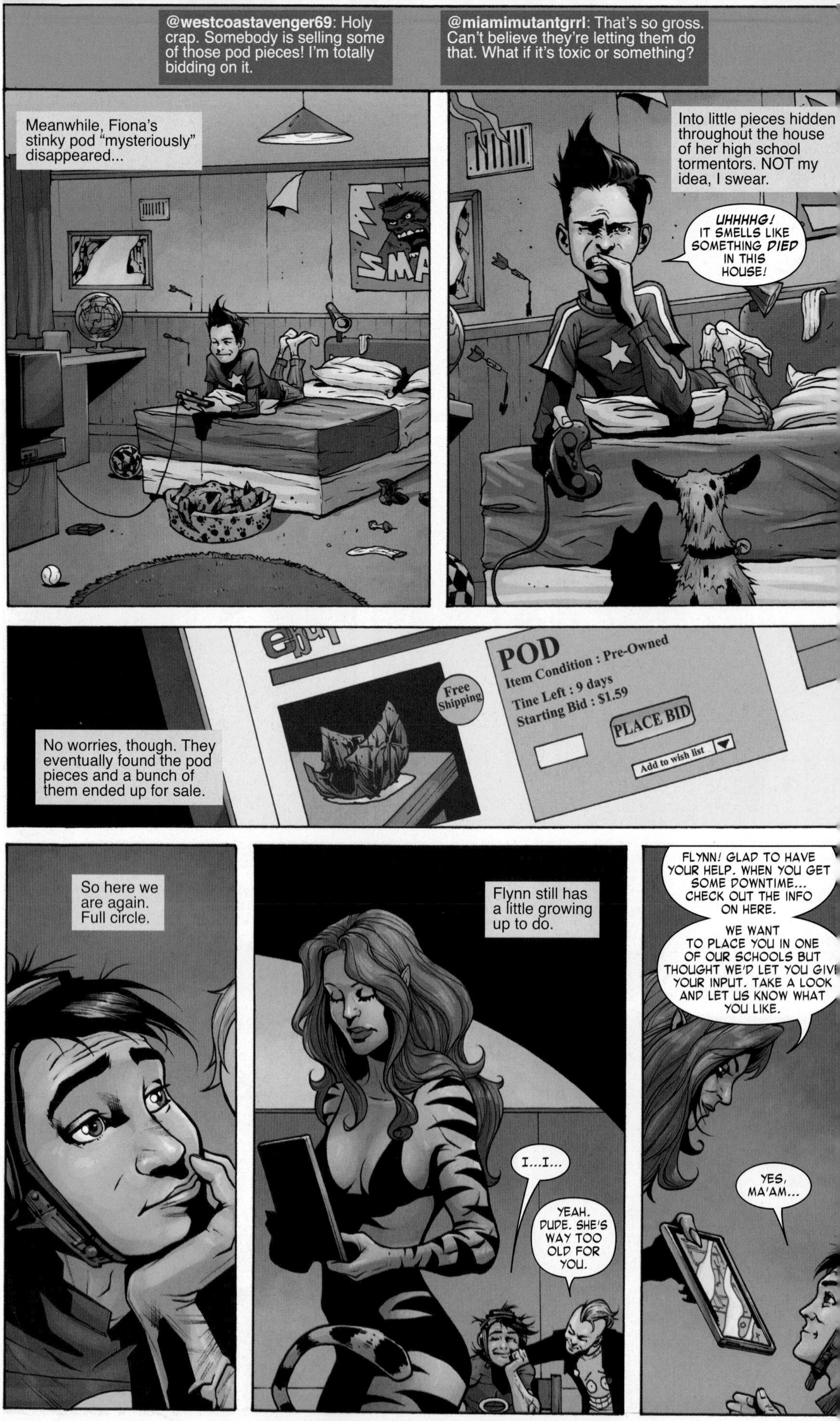
@westcoastavenger69: Holy crap. Somebody is selling some of those pod pieces! I'm totally bidding on it.
@miamimutantgrrl: That's so gross. Can't believe they're letting them do that. What if it's toxic or something?
Meanwhile, Fiona's stinky pod "mysteriously" disappeared...
Into little pieces hidden throughout the house of her high school tormentors. NOT my idea, I swear.
UHHHHG! IT SMELLS LIKE SOMETHING DIED IN THIS HOUSE!
POD
Item Condition : Pre-Owned
Tine Left : 9 days
Starting Bid : $1.59
Free Shipping
PLACE BID
Add to wish list
No worries, though. They eventually found the pod pieces and a bunch of them ended up for sale.
So here we are again. Full circle.
Flynn still has a little growing up to do.
I...I...
YEAH. DUDE. SHE'S WAY TOO OLD FOR YOU.
FLYNN! GLAD TO HAVE YOUR HELP. WHEN YOU GET SOME DOWNTIME... CHECK OUT THE INFO ON HERE.
WE WANT TO PLACE YOU IN ONE OF OUR SCHOOLS BUT THOUGHT WE'D LET YOU GIVE YOUR INPUT. TAKE A LOOK AND LET US KNOW WHAT YOU LIKE.
YES, MA'AM...

@westcoastavenger69: Did any pod kids show up in Miami?

@miamimutantgrrl: Yeah. A few. They're kind of local celebrities. One of them is going to be on that dancing show. She's got like six legs or something.

SUPERHUMAN SCHOOLS

THE WAKANDAN SCHOOL OF ALTERNATIVE STUDIES.

Located in picturesque Wakanda. Focuses on community, nature, and the animal kingdom in relation to natural abilities.

PAN-ASIAN SCHOOL FOR THE UNUSUALLY GIFTED.

Located centrally in Mumbai. Focus on technology and information processing.

AVENGERS ACADEMY.

Located in sunny California.
Focus on media relations and cosmic threats.

THE JEAN GREY ACADEMY.

Located in upstate New York.
Focus on teamwork and societal acceptance.

BRADDOCK ACADEMY.

Located in England.
Focus on history and politics.

LATVERIAN SCHOOL OF SCIENCE.

Located on the outskirts of Castle Von Doom.
Heavy focus on the sciences and long-range planning (master plans). Currently in the process of rebuilding.

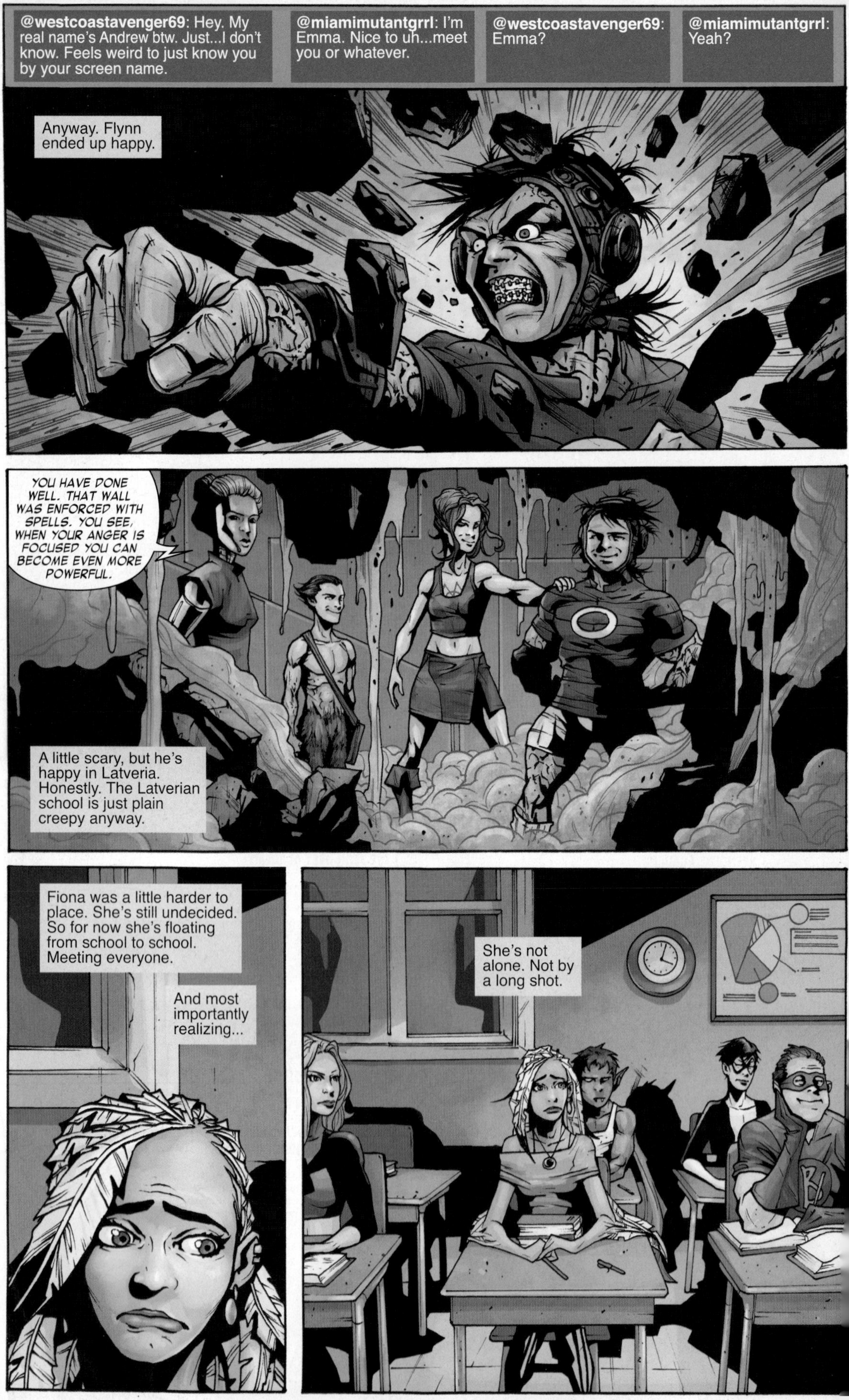
@westcoastavenger69: Hey. My real name's Andrew btw. Just...I don't know. Feels weird to just know you by your screen name.
@miamimutantgrrl: I'm Emma. Nice to uh...meet you or whatever.
@westcoastavenger69: Emma?
@miamimutantgrrl: Yeah?
Anyway. Flynn ended up happy.
YOU HAVE DONE WELL. THAT WALL WAS ENFORCED WITH SPELLS. YOU SEE, WHEN YOUR ANGER IS FOCUSED YOU CAN BECOME EVEN MORE POWERFUL.
A little scary, but he's happy in Latveria. Honestly. The Latverian school is just plain creepy anyway.
Fiona was a little harder to place. She's still undecided. So for now she's floating from school to school. Meeting everyone.
And most importantly realizing...
She's not alone. Not by a long shot.

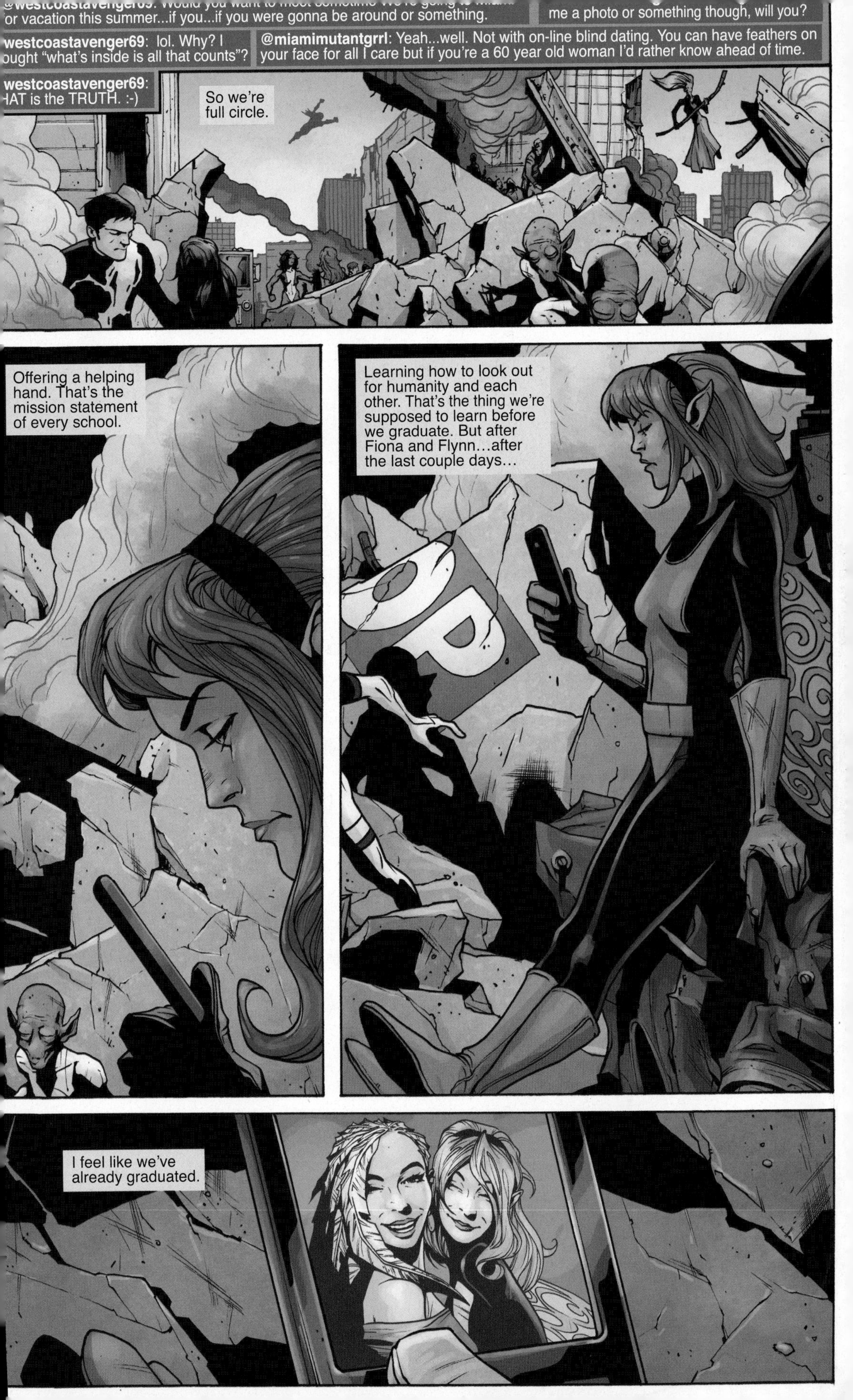
@westcoastavenger69: Would you want to meet sometime We're going to Miami
or vacation this summer...if you...if you were gonna be around or something.
me a photo or something though, will you?
westcoastavenger69: lol. Why? I
ought "what's inside is all that counts"?
@miamimutantgrrl: Yeah...well. Not with on-line blind dating. You can have feathers on your face for all I care but if you're a 60 year old woman I'd rather know ahead of time.
westcoastavenger69:
HAT is the TRUTH. :-)
So we're full circle.
Offering a helping hand. That's the mission statement of every school.
Learning how to look out for humanity and each other. That's the thing we're supposed to learn before we graduate. But after Fiona and Flynn…after the last couple days…
I feel like we've already graduated.

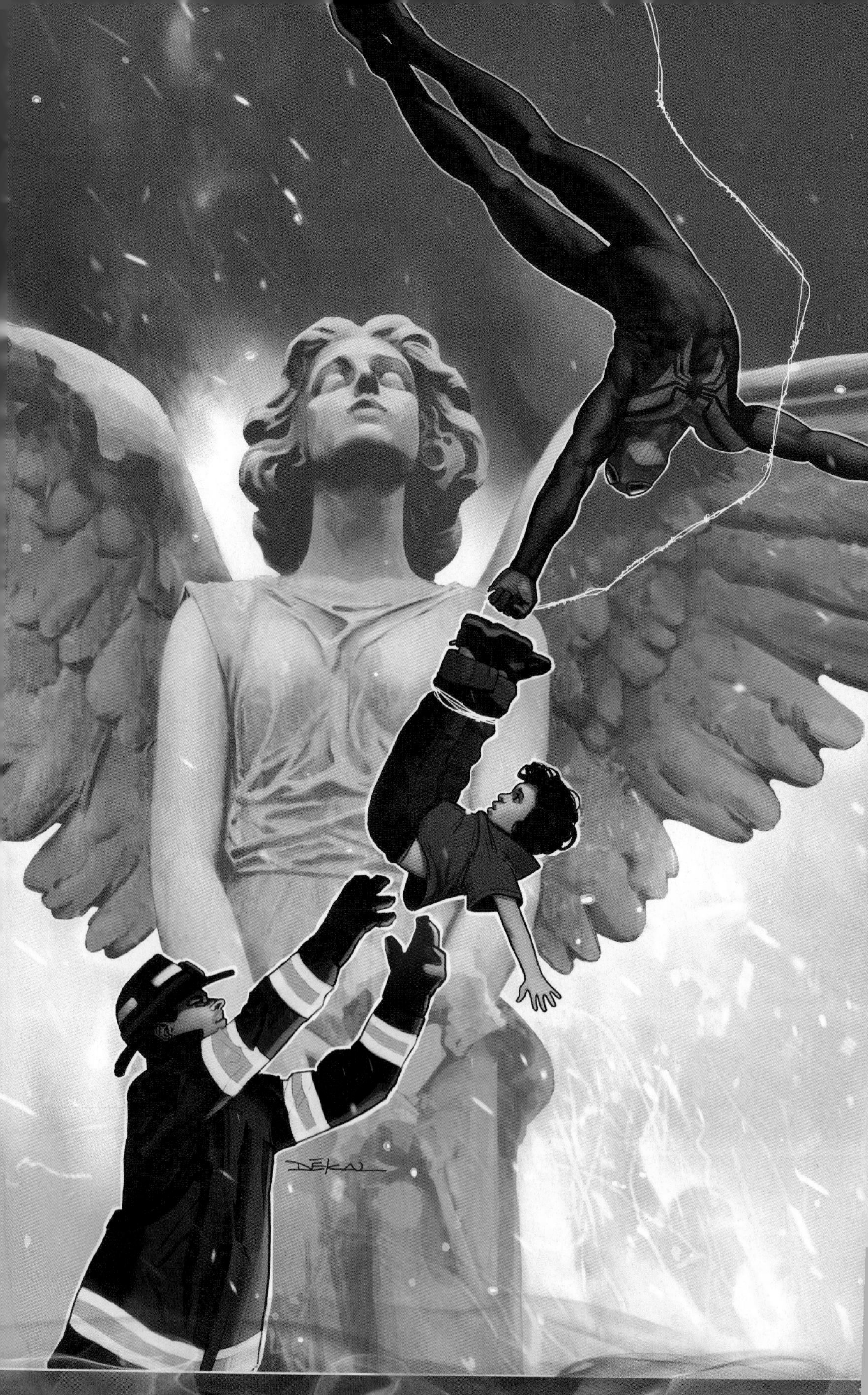

INHUMANITY: SUPERIOR SPIDER-MAN #1

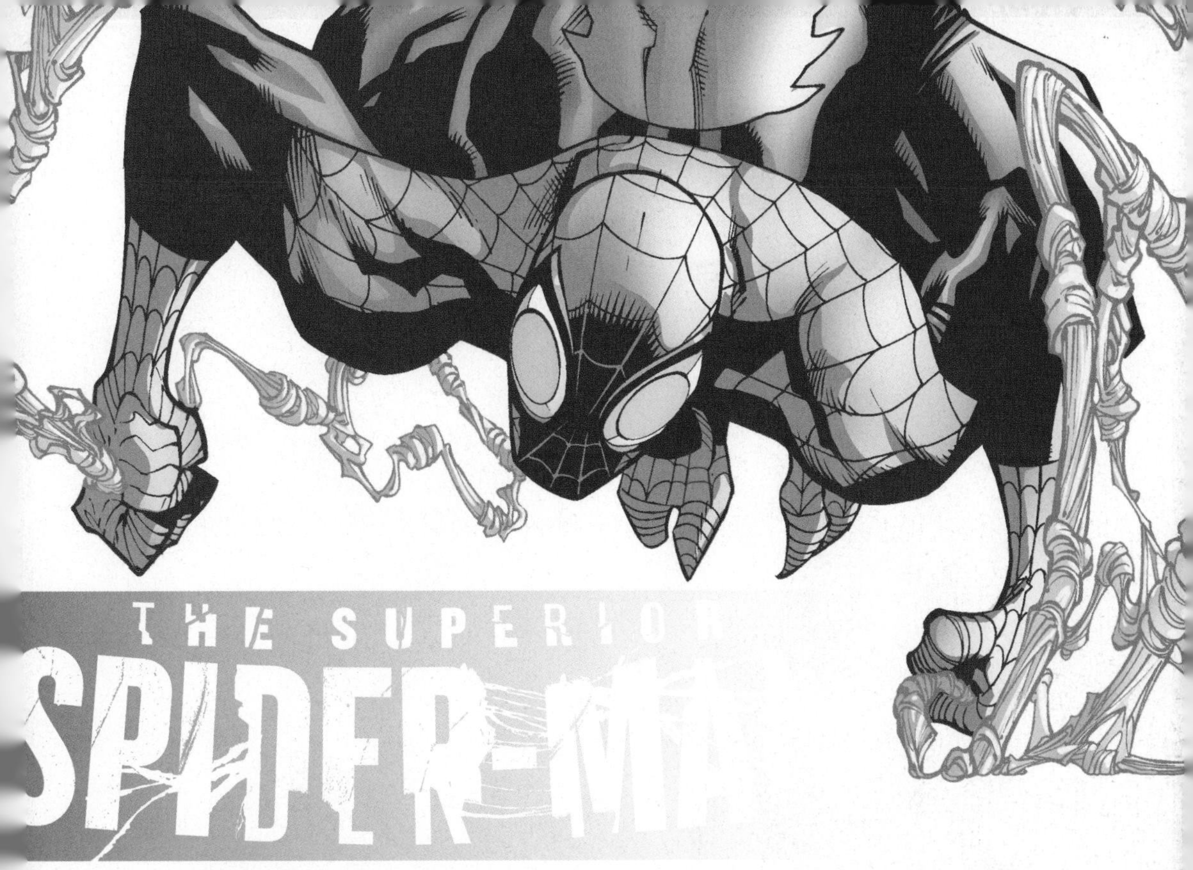
THE SUPERIO
SPIDER-M

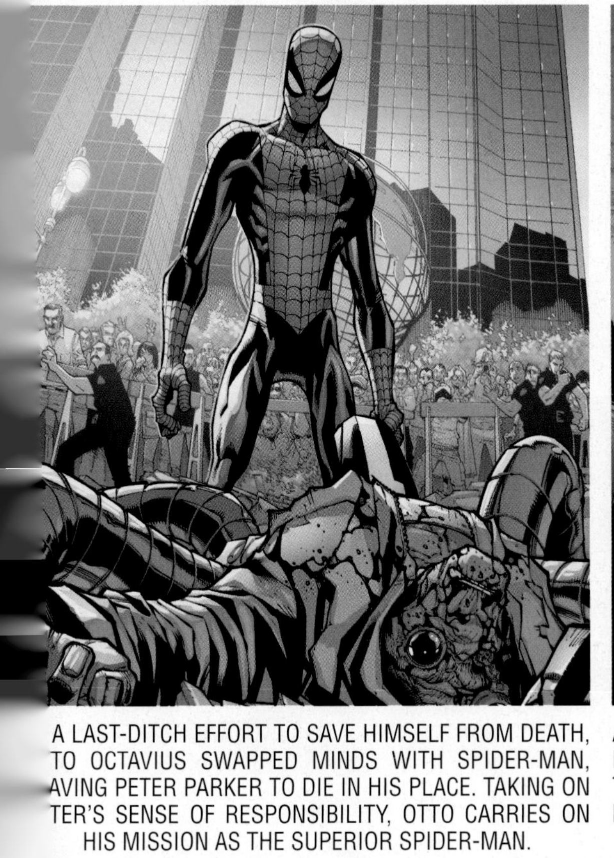

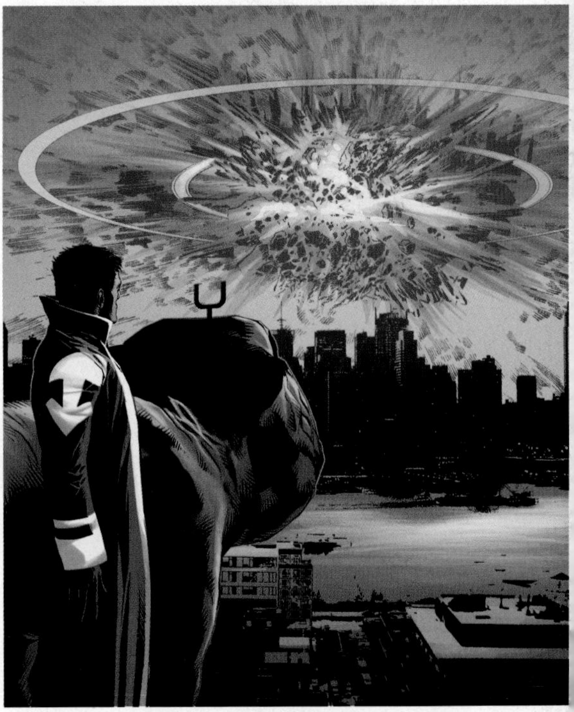

A LAST-DITCH EFFORT TO SAVE HIMSELF FROM DEATH, TO OCTAVIUS SWAPPED MINDS WITH SPIDER-MAN, AVING PETER PARKER TO DIE IN HIS PLACE. TAKING ON TER'S SENSE OF RESPONSIBILITY, OTTO CARRIES ON HIS MISSION AS THE SUPERIOR SPIDER-MAN.

ATTILAN WAS THE HOME OF THE INHUMANS, AN ADVANCED RACE WITH EXTRAORDINARY TECHNOLOGY AND POWERS TRIGGERED BY A CHEMICAL CALLED TERRIGEN. BUT THE FLOATING CITY EXPLODED AND FELL TO EARTH, LANDING IN NEW YORK'S HUDSON RIVER.

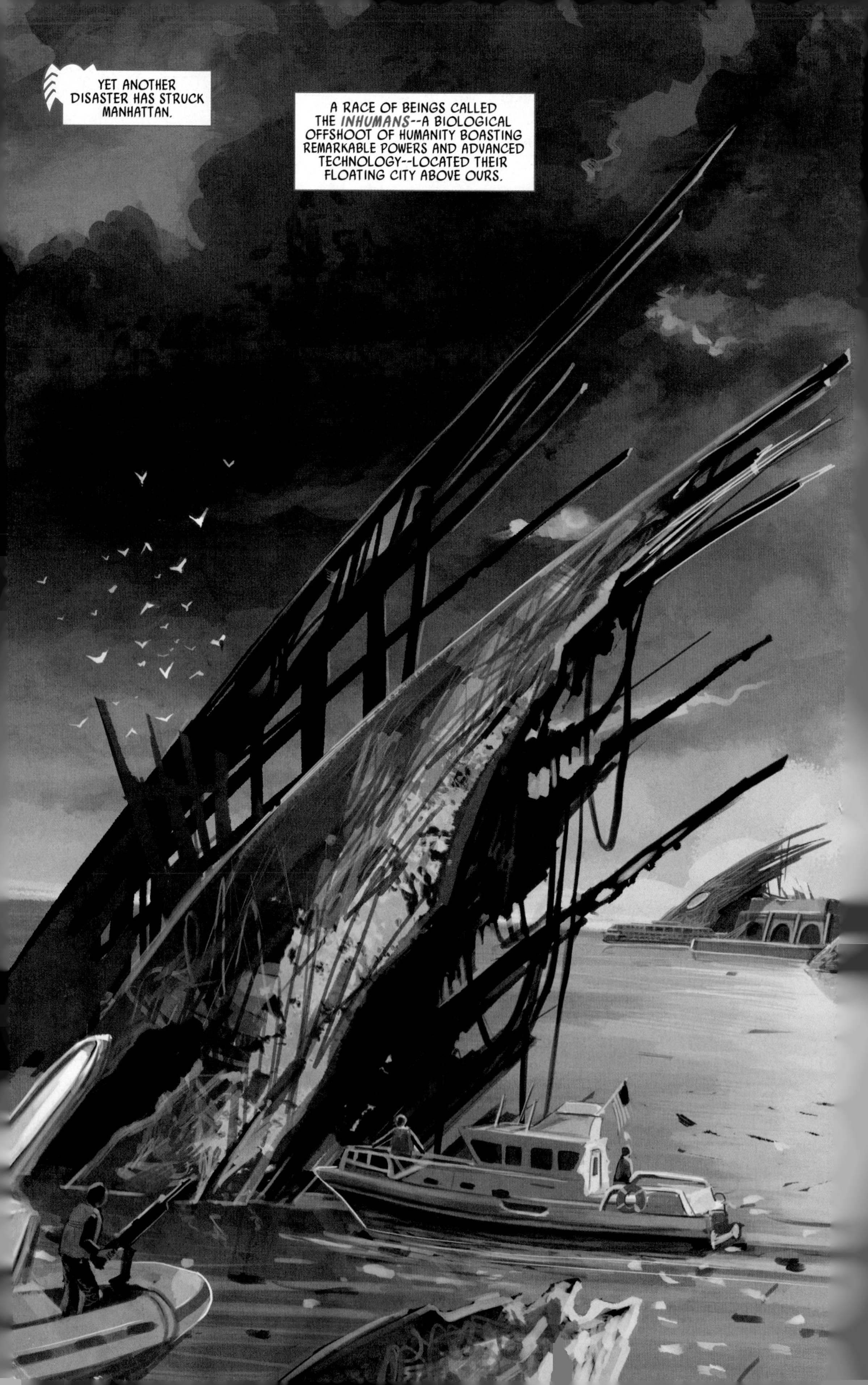
YET ANOTHER DISASTER HAS STRUCK MANHATTAN.
A RACE OF BEINGS CALLED THE INHUMANS--A BIOLOGICAL OFFSHOOT OF HUMANITY BOASTING REMARKABLE POWERS AND ADVANCED TECHNOLOGY--LOCATED THEIR FLOATING CITY ABOVE OURS.

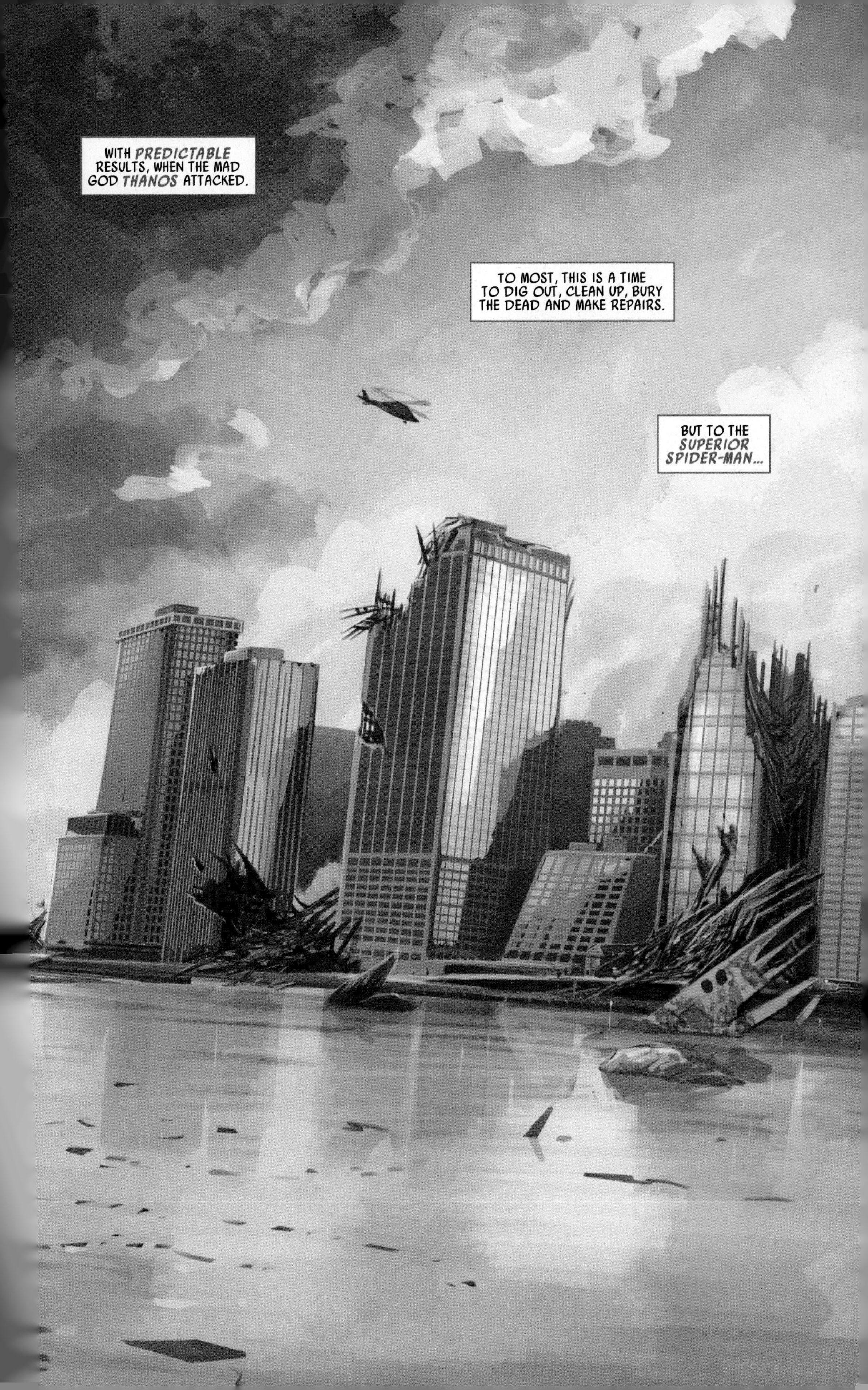
WITH PREDICTABLE RESULTS, WHEN THE MAD GOD THANOS ATTACKED.
TO MOST, THIS IS A TIME TO DIG OUT, CLEAN UP, BURY THE DEAD AND MAKE REPAIRS.
BUT TO THE SUPERIOR SPIDER-MAN...

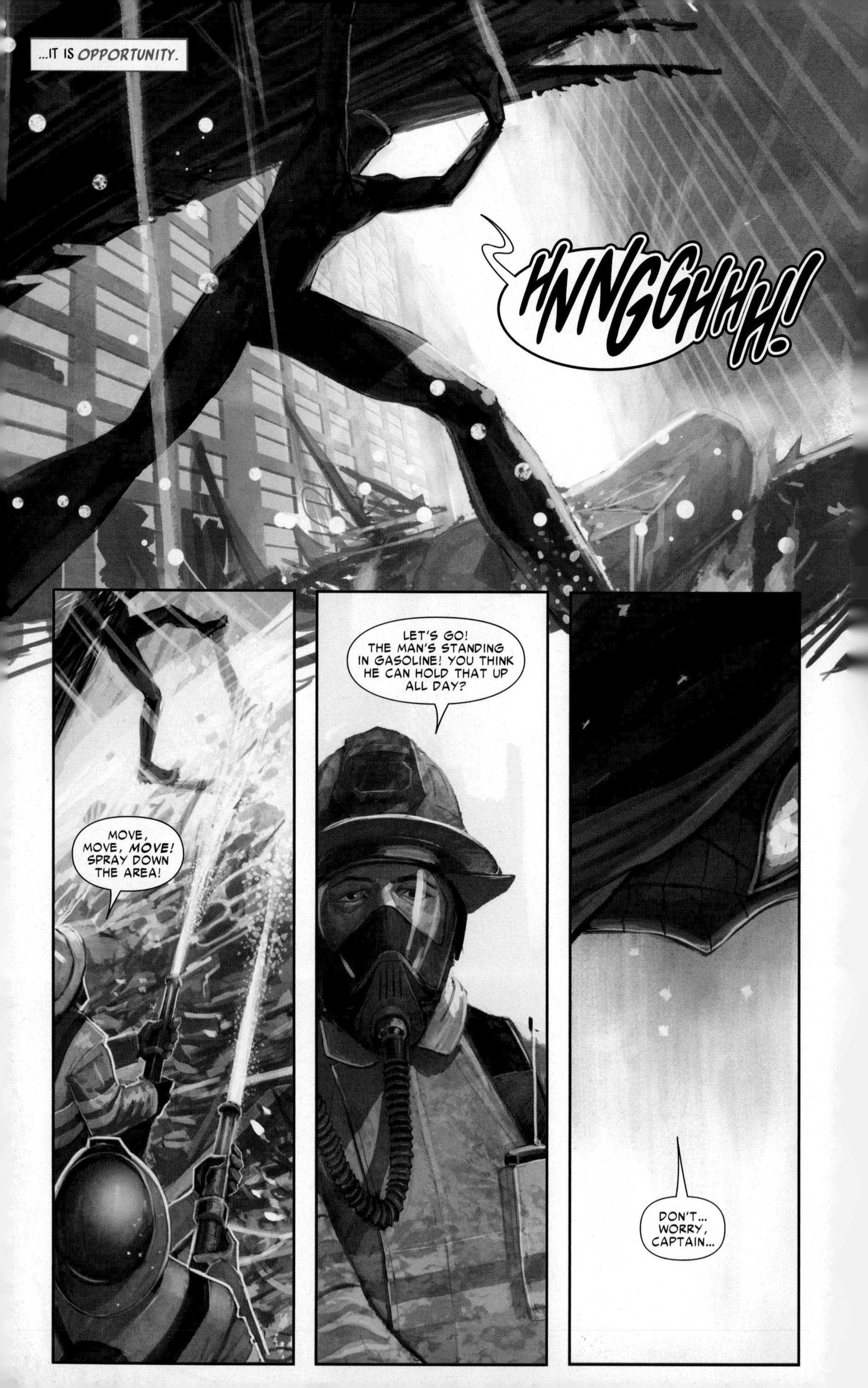
...IT IS OPPORTUNITY.
HNNGGHHH!
MOVE, MOVE, MOVE! SPRAY DOWN THE AREA!
LET'S GO! THE MAN'S STANDING IN GASOLINE! YOU THINK HE CAN HOLD THAT UP ALL DAY?
DON'T... WORRY, CAPTAIN...

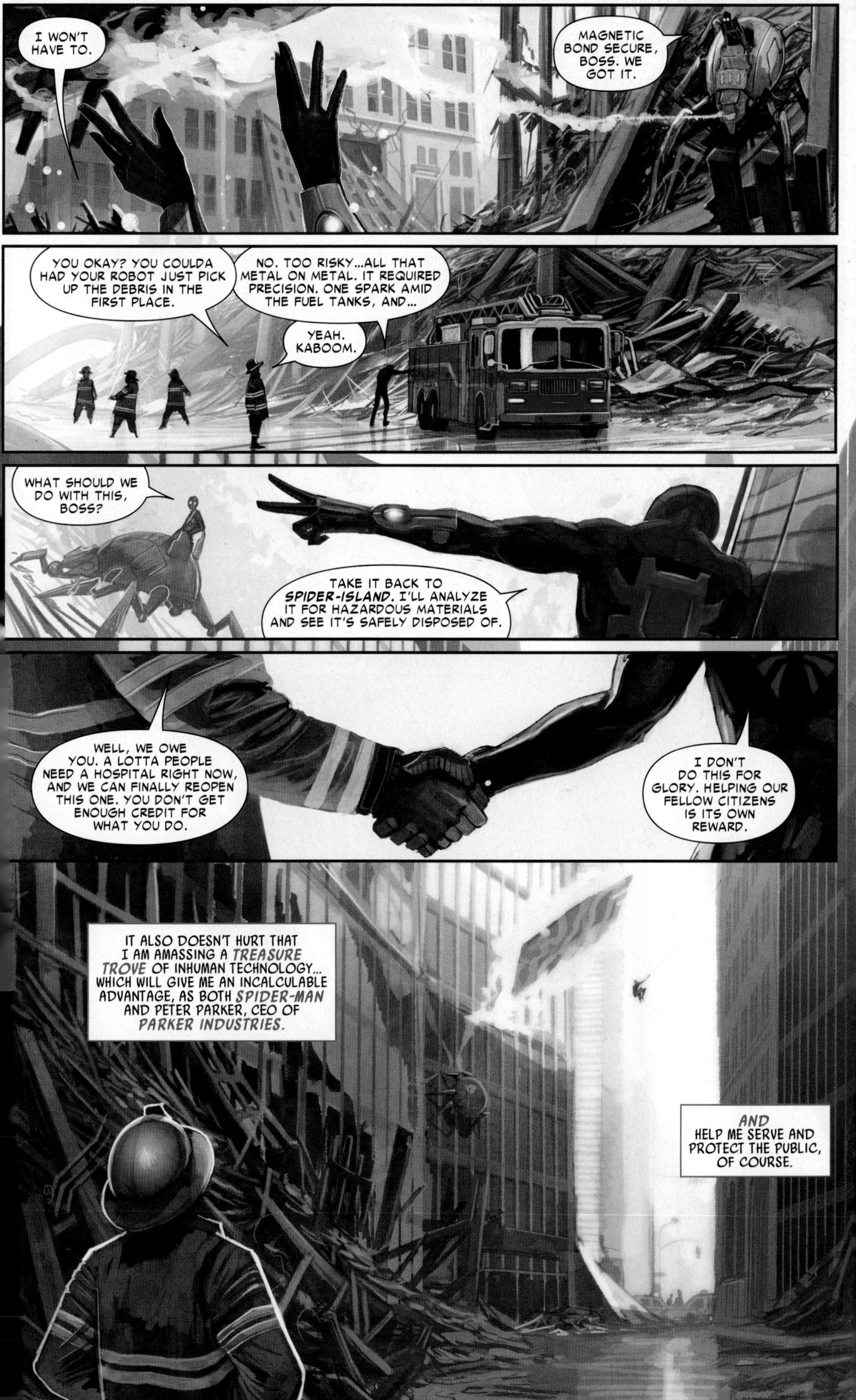
I WON'T HAVE TO.
MAGNETIC BOND SECURE, BOSS. WE GOT IT.
YOU OKAY? YOU COULDA HAD YOUR ROBOT JUST PICK UP THE DEBRIS IN THE FIRST PLACE.
NO. TOO RISKY...ALL THAT METAL ON METAL. IT REQUIRED PRECISION. ONE SPARK AMID THE FUEL TANKS, AND...
YEAH. KABOOM.
WHAT SHOULD WE DO WITH THIS, BOSS?
TAKE IT BACK TO SPIDER-ISLAND. I'LL ANALYZE IT FOR HAZARDOUS MATERIALS AND SEE IT'S SAFELY DISPOSED OF.
WELL, WE OWE YOU. A LOTTA PEOPLE NEED A HOSPITAL RIGHT NOW, AND WE CAN FINALLY REOPEN THIS ONE. YOU DON'T GET ENOUGH CREDIT FOR WHAT YOU DO.
I DON'T DO THIS FOR GLORY. HELPING OUR FELLOW CITIZENS IS ITS OWN REWARD.
IT ALSO DOESN'T HURT THAT I AM AMASSING A TREASURE TROVE OF INHUMAN TECHNOLOGY... WHICH WILL GIVE ME AN INCALCULABLE ADVANTAGE, AS BOTH SPIDER-MAN AND PETER PARKER, CEO OF PARKER INDUSTRIES.
AND HELP ME SERVE AND PROTECT THE PUBLIC, OF COURSE.

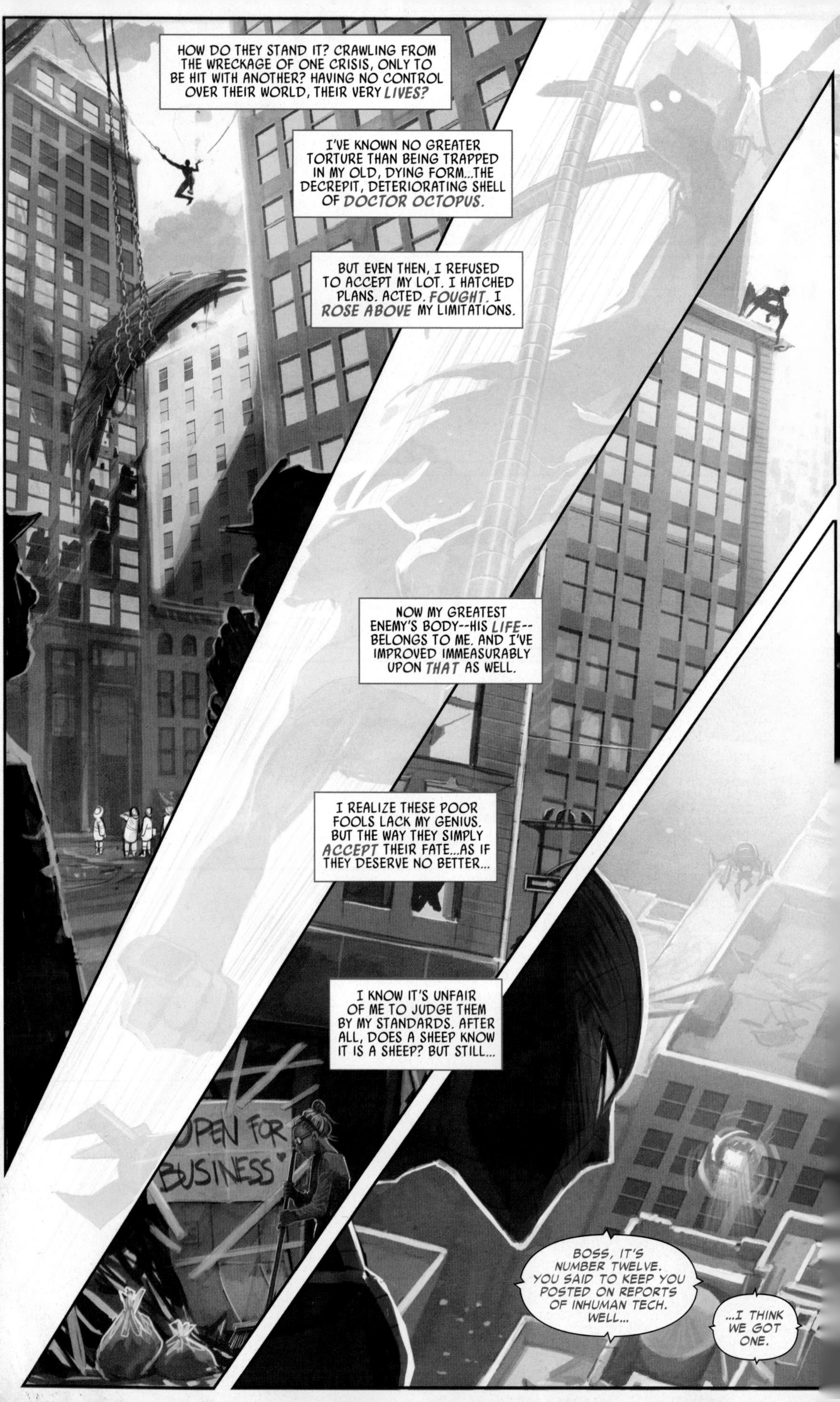
HOW DO THEY STAND IT? CRAWLING FROM THE WRECKAGE OF ONE CRISIS, ONLY TO BE HIT WITH ANOTHER? HAVING NO CONTROL OVER THEIR WORLD, THEIR VERY LIVES?
I'VE KNOWN NO GREATER TORTURE THAN BEING TRAPPED IN MY OLD, DYING FORM...THE DECREPIT, DETERIORATING SHELL OF DOCTOR OCTOPUS.
BUT EVEN THEN, I REFUSED TO ACCEPT MY LOT. I HATCHED PLANS. ACTED. FOUGHT. I ROSE ABOVE MY LIMITATIONS.
NOW MY GREATEST ENEMY'S BODY--HIS LIFE--BELONGS TO ME. AND I'VE IMPROVED IMMEASURABLY UPON THAT AS WELL.
I REALIZE THESE POOR FOOLS LACK MY GENIUS. BUT THE WAY THEY SIMPLY ACCEPT THEIR FATE...AS IF THEY DESERVE NO BETTER...
I KNOW IT'S UNFAIR OF ME TO JUDGE THEM BY MY STANDARDS. AFTER ALL, DOES A SHEEP KNOW IT IS A SHEEP? BUT STILL...
OPEN FOR BUSINESS
BOSS, IT'S NUMBER TWELVE. YOU SAID TO KEEP YOU POSTED ON REPORTS OF INHUMAN TECH. WELL...
...I THINK WE GOT ONE.

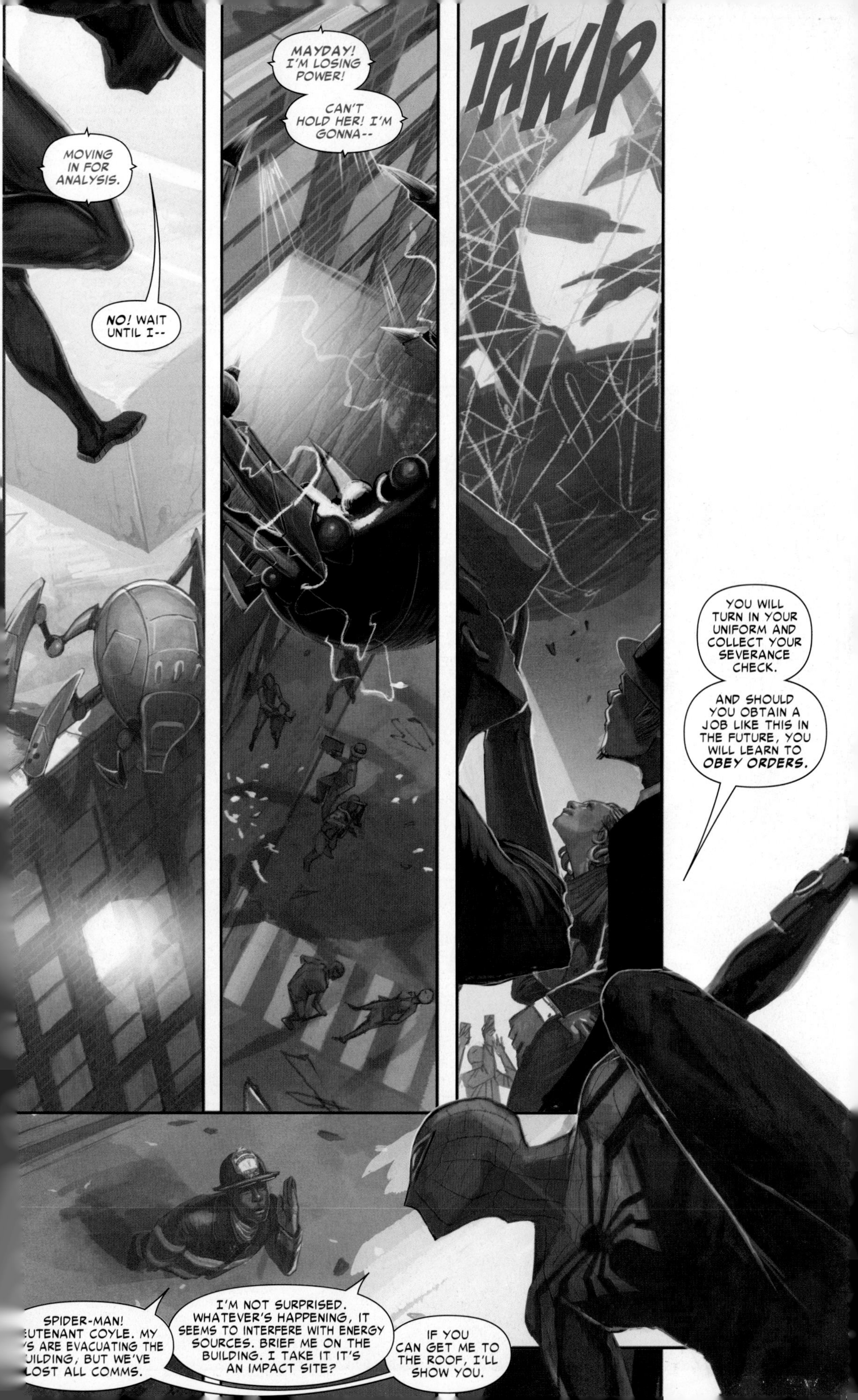

MOVING IN FOR ANALYSIS.
NO! WAIT UNTIL I--
MAYDAY! I'M LOSING POWER!
CAN'T HOLD HER! I'M GONNA--
THWIP
YOU WILL TURN IN YOUR UNIFORM AND COLLECT YOUR SEVERANCE CHECK.
AND SHOULD YOU OBTAIN A JOB LIKE THIS IN THE FUTURE, YOU WILL LEARN TO OBEY ORDERS.
SPIDER-MAN! EUTENANT COYLE. MY S ARE EVACUATING THE UILDING, BUT WE'VE LOST ALL COMMS.
I'M NOT SURPRISED. WHATEVER'S HAPPENING, IT SEEMS TO INTERFERE WITH ENERGY SOURCES. BRIEF ME ON THE BUILDING. I TAKE IT IT'S AN IMPACT SITE?
IF YOU CAN GET ME TO THE ROOF, I'LL SHOW YOU.

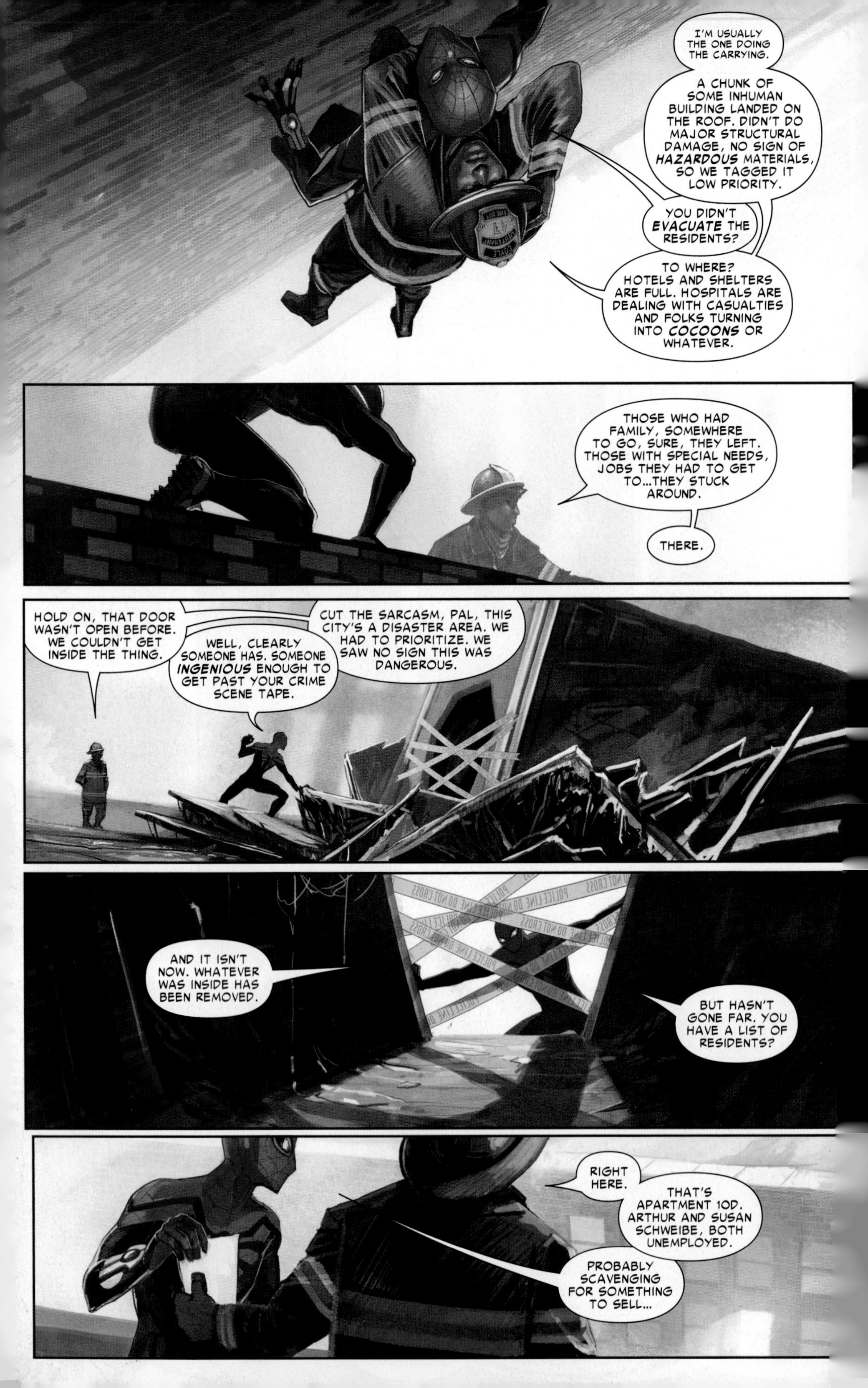
I'M USUALLY THE ONE DOING THE CARRYING.
A CHUNK OF SOME INHUMAN BUILDING LANDED ON THE ROOF. DIDN'T DO MAJOR STRUCTURAL DAMAGE, NO SIGN OF HAZARDOUS MATERIALS, SO WE TAGGED IT LOW PRIORITY.
YOU DIDN'T EVACUATE THE RESIDENTS?
TO WHERE? HOTELS AND SHELTERS ARE FULL. HOSPITALS ARE DEALING WITH CASUALTIES AND FOLKS TURNING INTO COCOONS OR WHATEVER.
THOSE WHO HAD FAMILY, SOMEWHERE TO GO, SURE, THEY LEFT. THOSE WITH SPECIAL NEEDS, JOBS THEY HAD TO GET TO...THEY STUCK AROUND.
THERE.
HOLD ON, THAT DOOR WASN'T OPEN BEFORE. WE COULDN'T GET INSIDE THE THING.
WELL, CLEARLY SOMEONE HAS. SOMEONE INGENIOUS ENOUGH TO GET PAST YOUR CRIME SCENE TAPE.
CUT THE SARCASM, PAL, THIS CITY'S A DISASTER AREA. WE HAD TO PRIORITIZE. WE SAW NO SIGN THIS WAS DANGEROUS.
AND IT ISN'T NOW. WHATEVER WAS INSIDE HAS BEEN REMOVED.
BUT HASN'T GONE FAR. YOU HAVE A LIST OF RESIDENTS?
RIGHT HERE.
THAT'S APARTMENT 10D. ARTHUR AND SUSAN SCHWEIBE, BOTH UNEMPLOYED.
PROBABLY SCAVENGING FOR SOMETHING TO SELL...

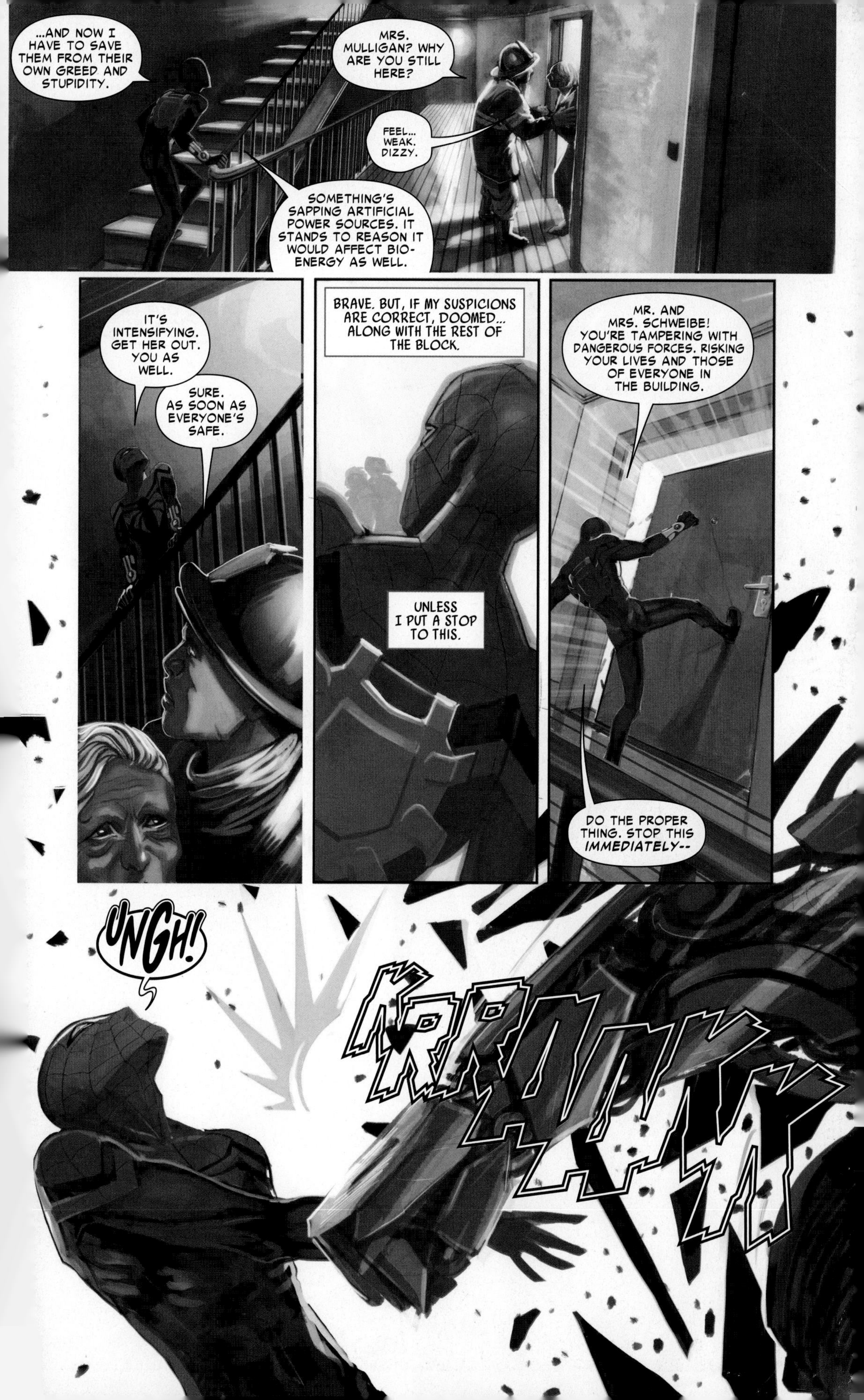

...AND NOW I HAVE TO SAVE THEM FROM THEIR OWN GREED AND STUPIDITY.
MRS. MULLIGAN? WHY ARE YOU STILL HERE?
FEEL... WEAK. DIZZY.
SOMETHING'S SAPPING ARTIFICIAL POWER SOURCES. IT STANDS TO REASON IT WOULD AFFECT BIO-ENERGY AS WELL.
IT'S INTENSIFYING. GET HER OUT. YOU AS WELL.
SURE. AS SOON AS EVERYONE'S SAFE.
BRAVE. BUT, IF MY SUSPICIONS ARE CORRECT, DOOMED... ALONG WITH THE REST OF THE BLOCK.
UNLESS I PUT A STOP TO THIS.
MR. AND MRS. SCHWEIBE! YOU'RE TAMPERING WITH DANGEROUS FORCES. RISKING YOUR LIVES AND THOSE OF EVERYONE IN THE BUILDING.
DO THE PROPER THING. STOP THIS *IMMEDIATELY*--
UNGH!

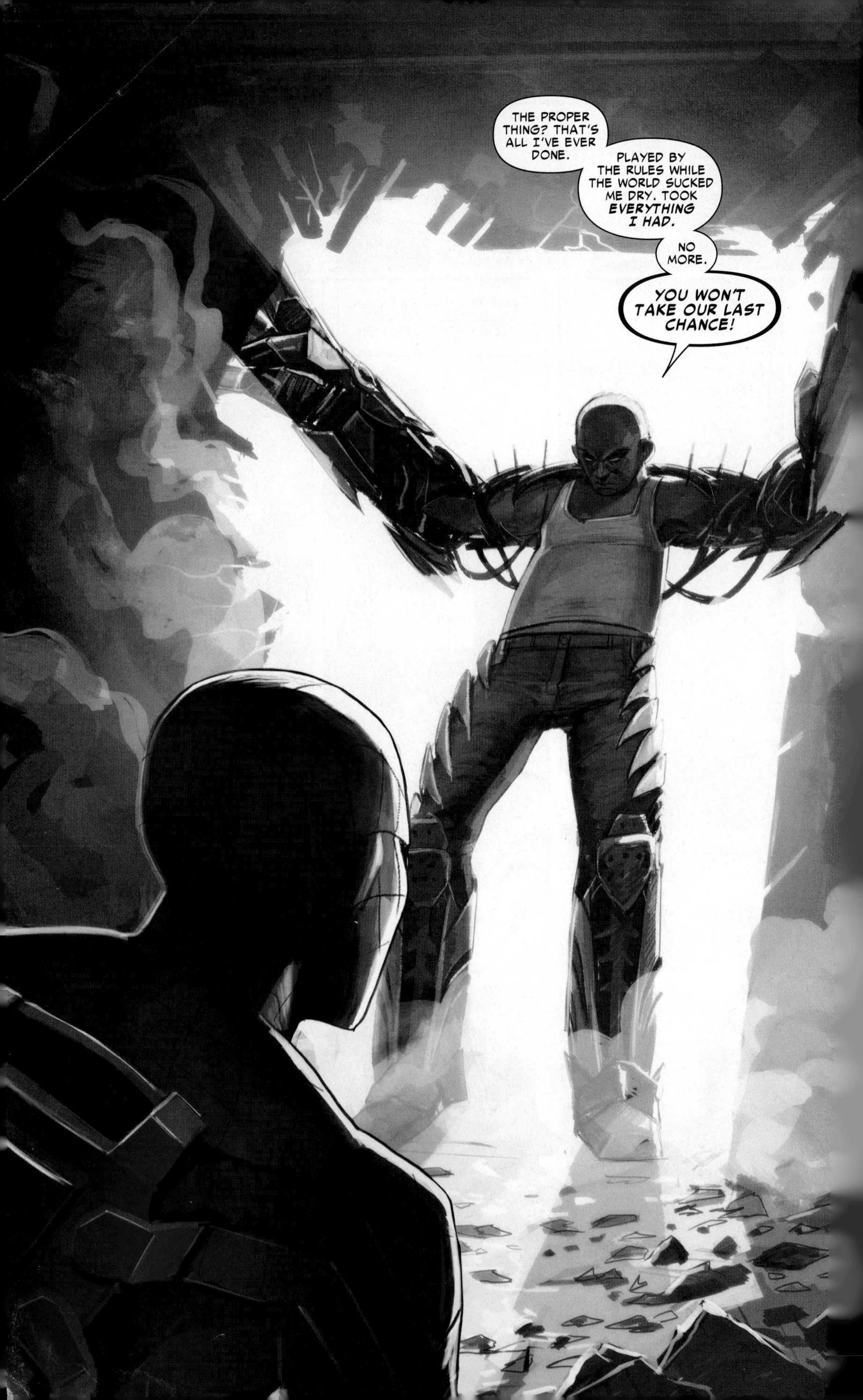
THE PROPER THING? THAT'S ALL I'VE EVER DONE.
PLAYED BY THE RULES WHILE THE WORLD SUCKED ME DRY. TOOK *EVERYTHING I HAD.*
NO MORE.
YOU WON'T TAKE OUR LAST CHANCE!

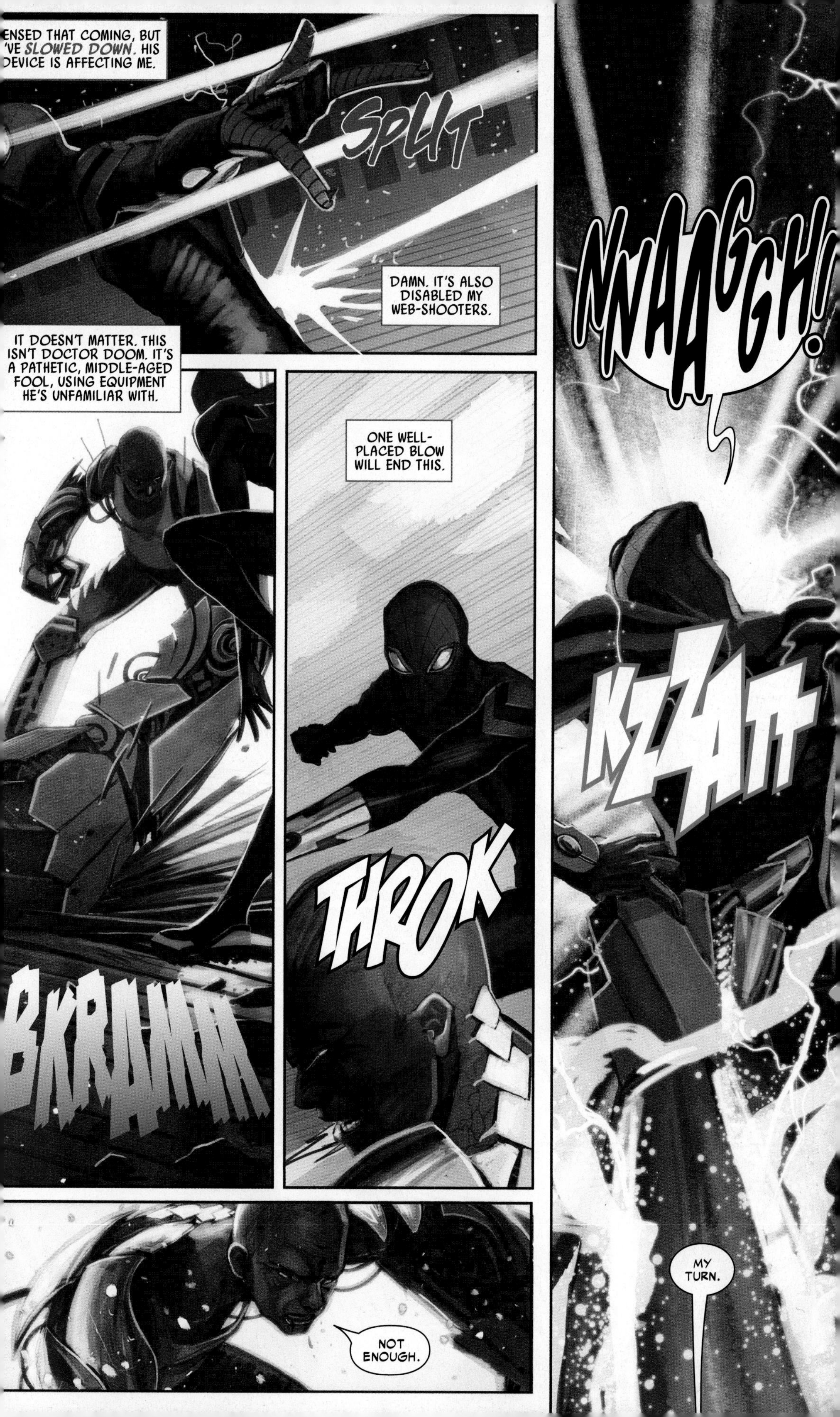
ENSED THAT COMING, BUT 'VE SLOWED DOWN. HIS DEVICE IS AFFECTING ME.
SPLIT
DAMN. IT'S ALSO DISABLED MY WEB-SHOOTERS.
IT DOESN'T MATTER. THIS ISN'T DOCTOR DOOM. IT'S A PATHETIC, MIDDLE-AGED FOOL, USING EQUIPMENT HE'S UNFAMILIAR WITH.
BKRAMM
ONE WELL-PLACED BLOW WILL END THIS.
THROK
NOT ENOUGH.
NNAAGGH!
KZZATT
MY TURN.

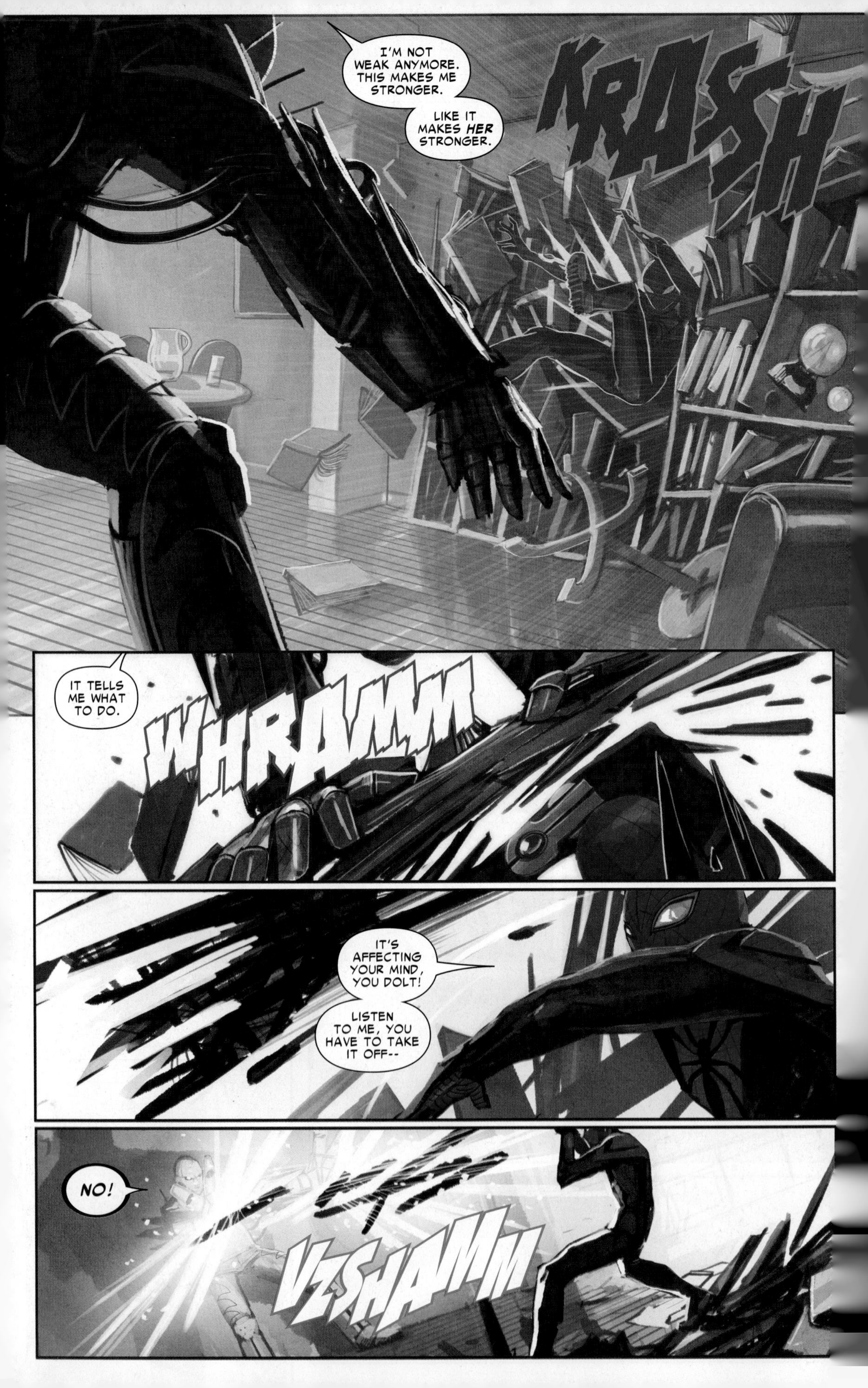
I'M NOT WEAK ANYMORE. THIS MAKES ME STRONGER.
LIKE IT MAKES *HER* STRONGER.
KRASH
IT TELLS ME WHAT TO DO.
WHRAMM
IT'S AFFECTING YOUR MIND, YOU DOLT!
LISTEN TO ME, YOU HAVE TO TAKE IT OFF--
NO!
VZSHAMM

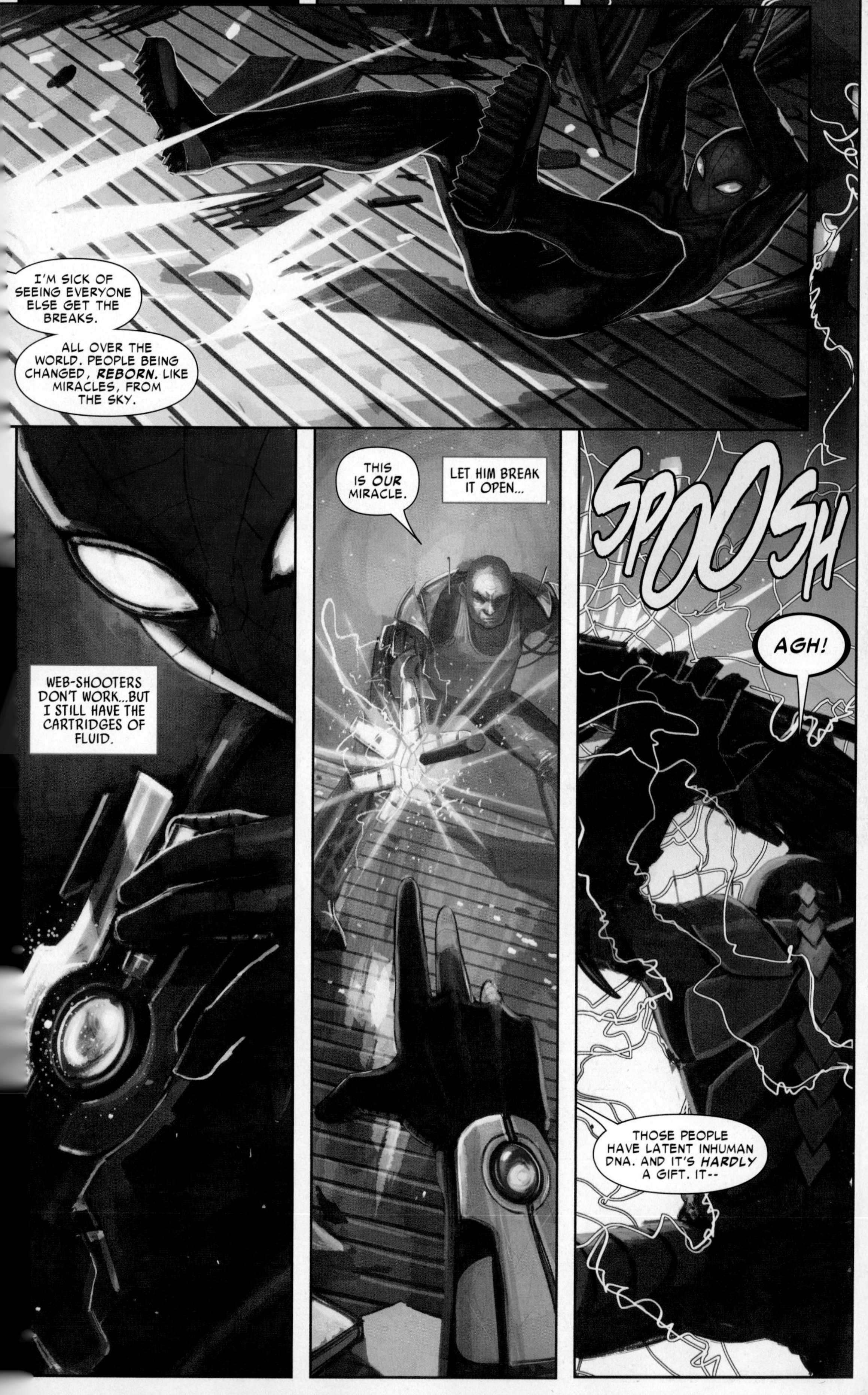
I'M SICK OF SEEING EVERYONE ELSE GET THE BREAKS.
ALL OVER THE WORLD. PEOPLE BEING CHANGED, **REBORN.** LIKE MIRACLES, FROM THE SKY.
WEB-SHOOTERS DON'T WORK...BUT I STILL HAVE THE CARTRIDGES OF FLUID.
THIS IS *OUR* MIRACLE.
LET HIM BREAK IT OPEN...
SPOOSH
AGH!
THOSE PEOPLE HAVE LATENT INHUMAN DNA. AND IT'S *HARDLY* A GIFT. IT--

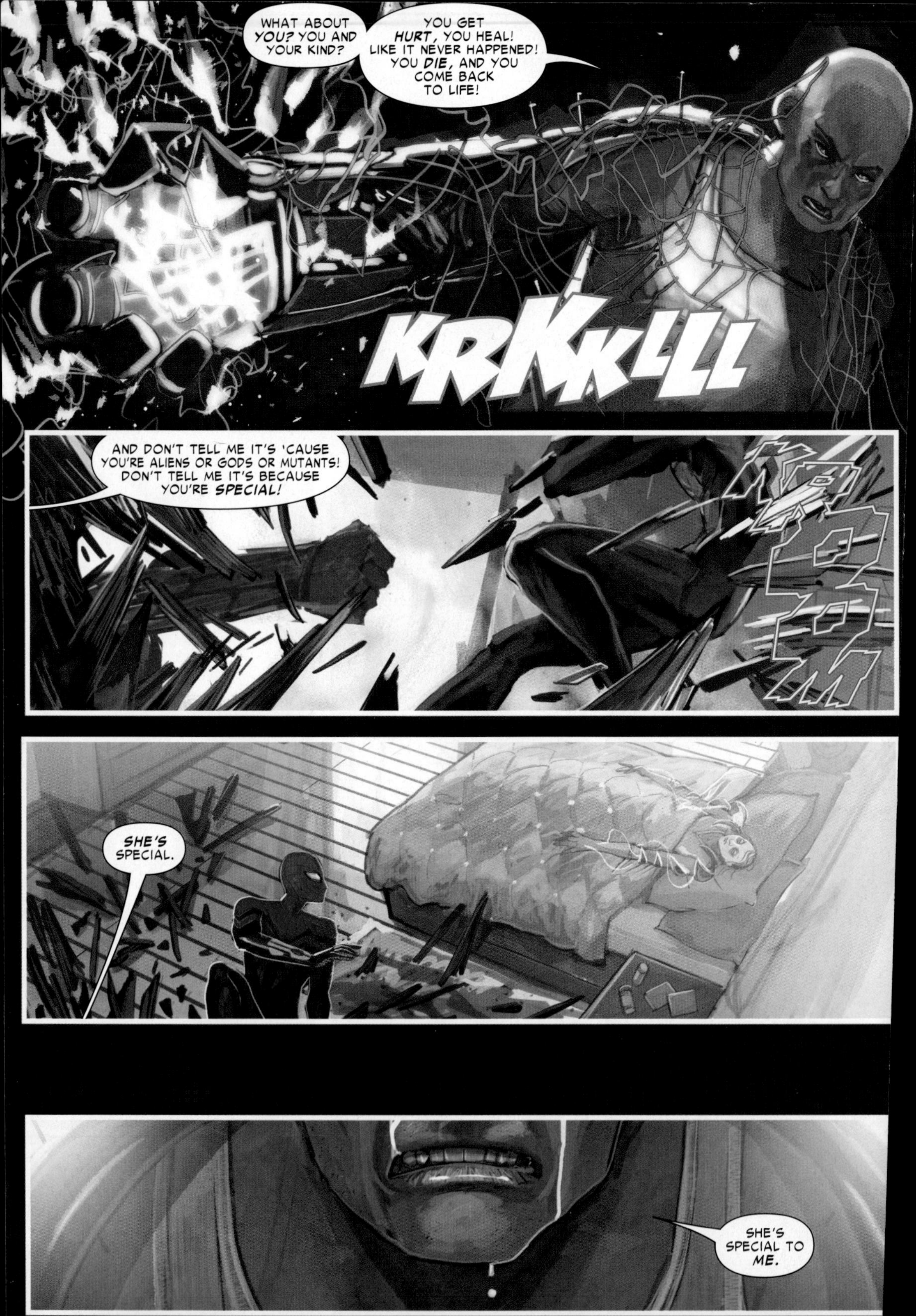
WHAT ABOUT YOU? YOU AND YOUR KIND?
YOU GET HURT, YOU HEAL! LIKE IT NEVER HAPPENED! YOU DIE, AND YOU COME BACK TO LIFE!
KRKKLLL
AND DON'T TELL ME IT'S 'CAUSE YOU'RE ALIENS OR GODS OR MUTANTS! DON'T TELL ME IT'S BECAUSE YOU'RE SPECIAL!
SHE'S SPECIAL.
SHE'S SPECIAL TO ME.

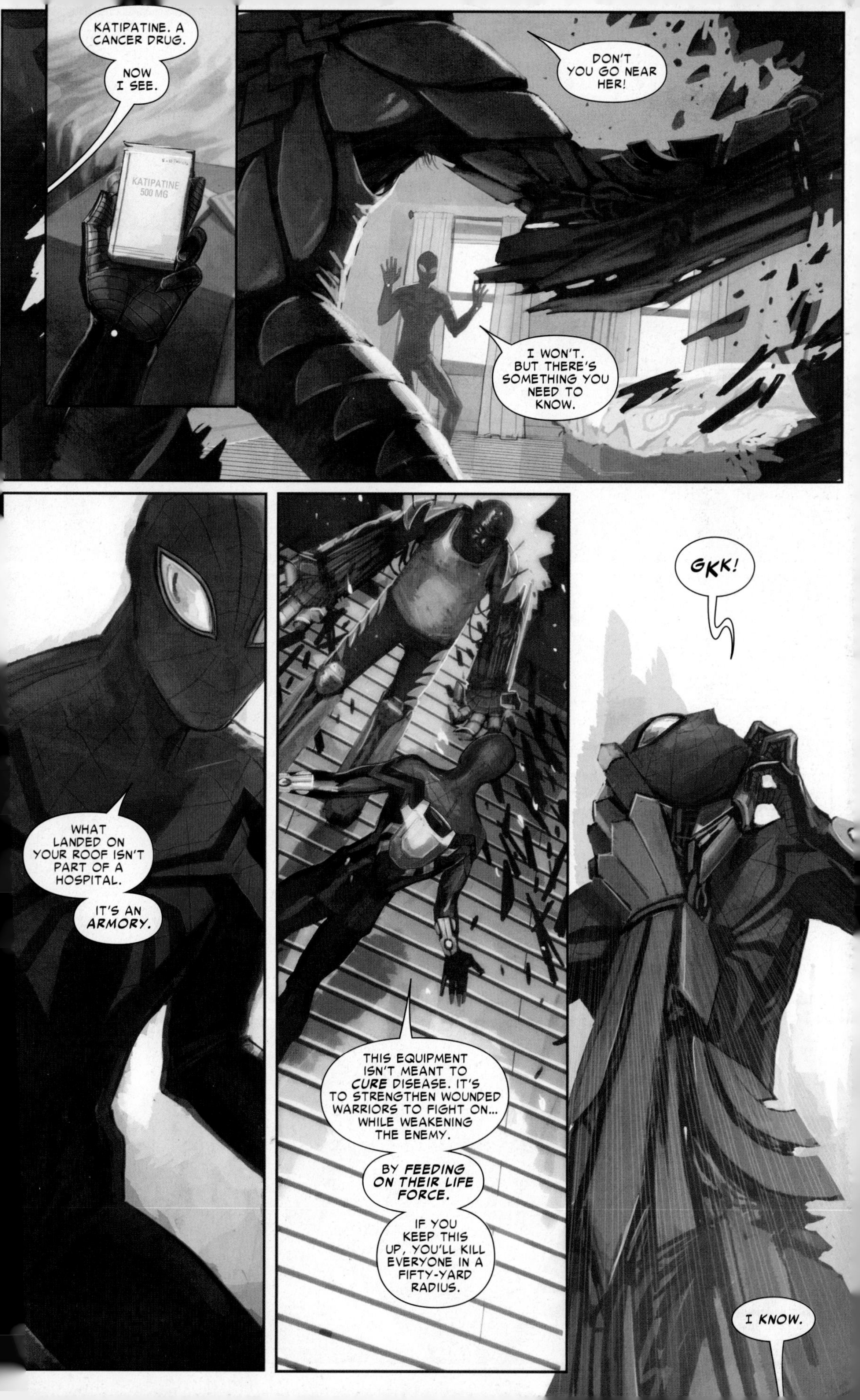
KATIPATINE. A CANCER DRUG.
NOW I SEE.
KATIPATINE 500 MG
DON'T YOU GO NEAR HER!
I WON'T. BUT THERE'S SOMETHING YOU NEED TO KNOW.
WHAT LANDED ON YOUR ROOF ISN'T PART OF A HOSPITAL.
IT'S AN ARMORY.
THIS EQUIPMENT ISN'T MEANT TO CURE DISEASE. IT'S TO STRENGTHEN WOUNDED WARRIORS TO FIGHT ON... WHILE WEAKENING THE ENEMY.
BY FEEDING ON THEIR LIFE FORCE.
IF YOU KEEP THIS UP, YOU'LL KILL EVERYONE IN A FIFTY-YARD RADIUS.
GKK!
I KNOW.

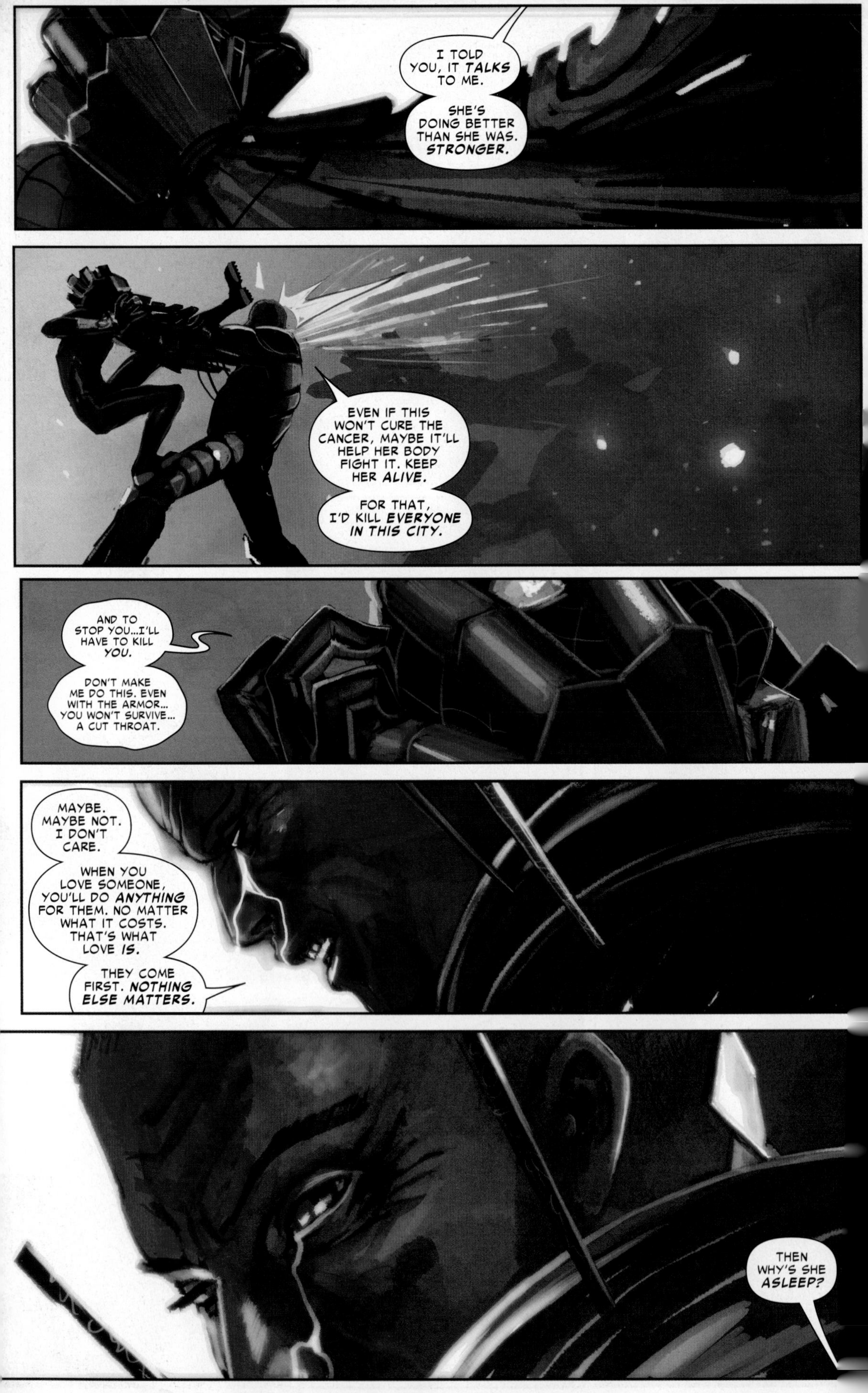
I TOLD YOU, IT TALKS TO ME.
SHE'S DOING BETTER THAN SHE WAS. STRONGER.
EVEN IF THIS WON'T CURE THE CANCER, MAYBE IT'LL HELP HER BODY FIGHT IT. KEEP HER ALIVE.
FOR THAT, I'D KILL EVERYONE IN THIS CITY.
AND TO STOP YOU...I'LL HAVE TO KILL YOU.
DON'T MAKE ME DO THIS. EVEN WITH THE ARMOR... YOU WON'T SURVIVE... A CUT THROAT.
MAYBE. MAYBE NOT. I DON'T CARE.
WHEN YOU LOVE SOMEONE, YOU'LL DO ANYTHING FOR THEM. NO MATTER WHAT IT COSTS. THAT'S WHAT LOVE IS.
THEY COME FIRST. NOTHING ELSE MATTERS.
THEN WHY'S SHE ASLEEP?

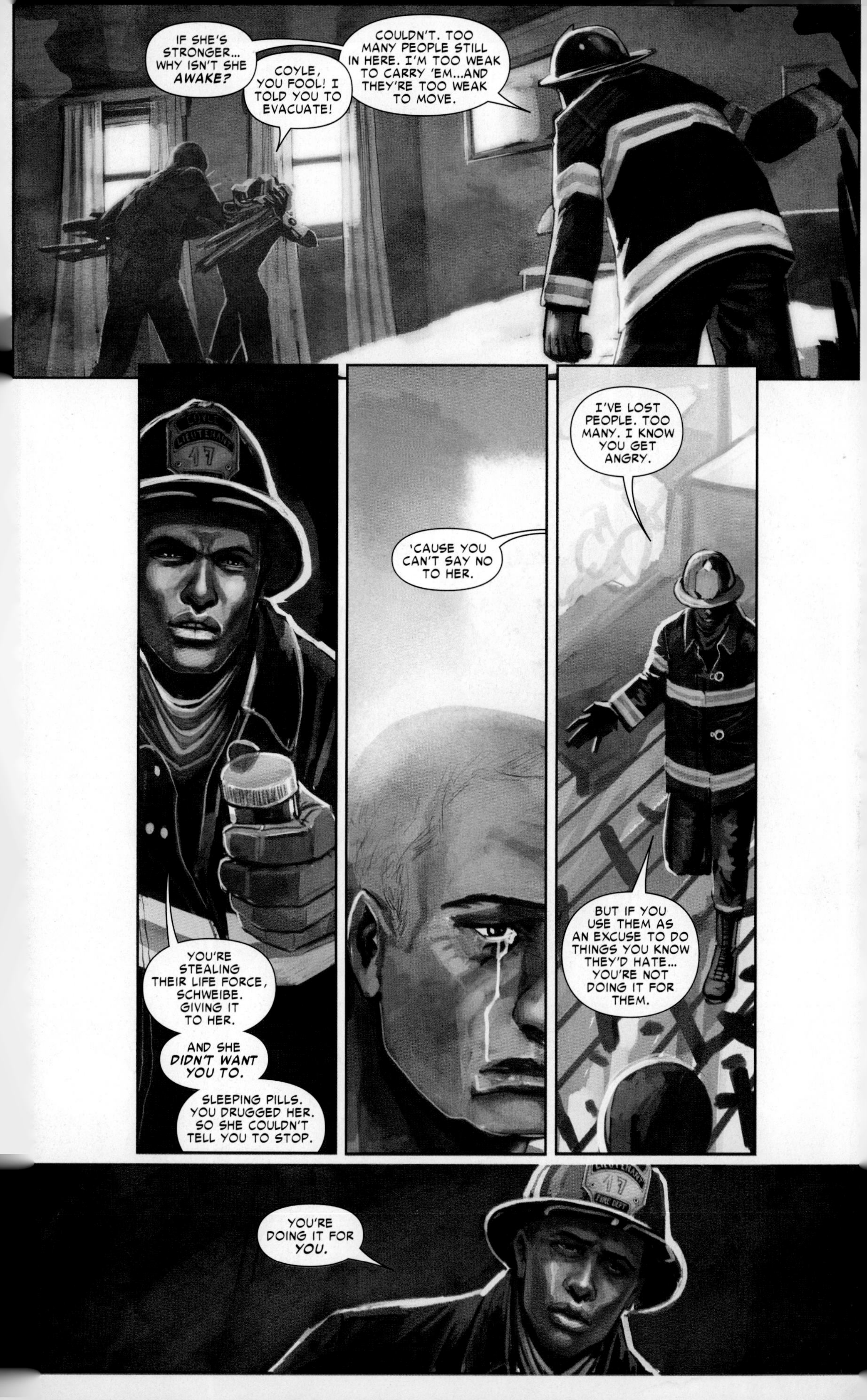

IF SHE'S STRONGER... WHY ISN'T SHE AWAKE?
COYLE, YOU FOOL! I TOLD YOU TO EVACUATE!
COULDN'T. TOO MANY PEOPLE STILL IN HERE. I'M TOO WEAK TO CARRY 'EM...AND THEY'RE TOO WEAK TO MOVE.
YOU'RE STEALING THEIR LIFE FORCE, SCHWEIBE. GIVING IT TO HER.
AND SHE DIDN'T WANT YOU TO.
SLEEPING PILLS. YOU DRUGGED HER. SO SHE COULDN'T TELL YOU TO STOP.
'CAUSE YOU CAN'T SAY NO TO HER.
I'VE LOST PEOPLE. TOO MANY. I KNOW YOU GET ANGRY.
BUT IF YOU USE THEM AS AN EXCUSE TO DO THINGS YOU KNOW THEY'D HATE... YOU'RE NOT DOING IT FOR THEM.
YOU'RE DOING IT FOR YOU.

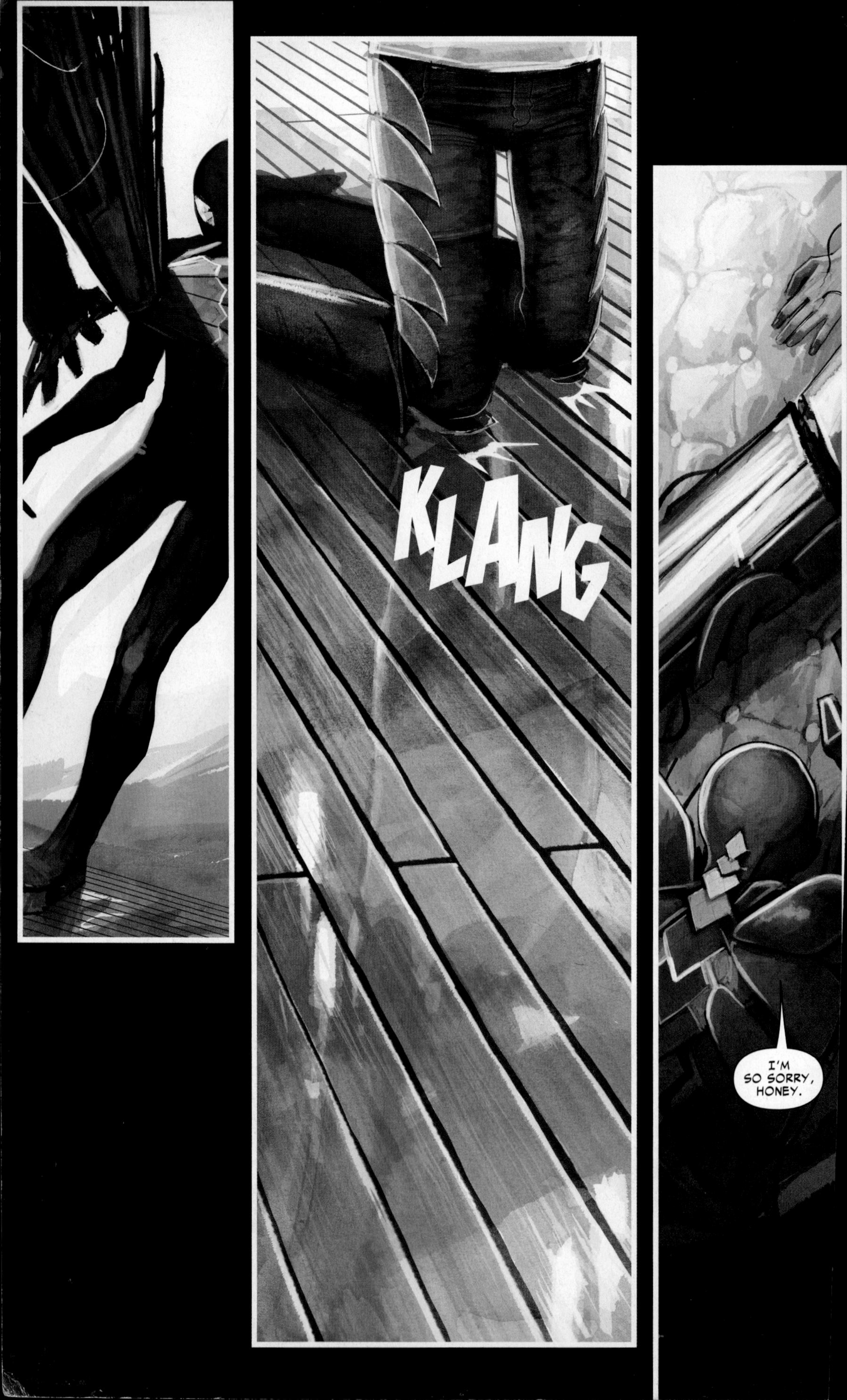
KLANG
I'M SO SORRY, HONEY.

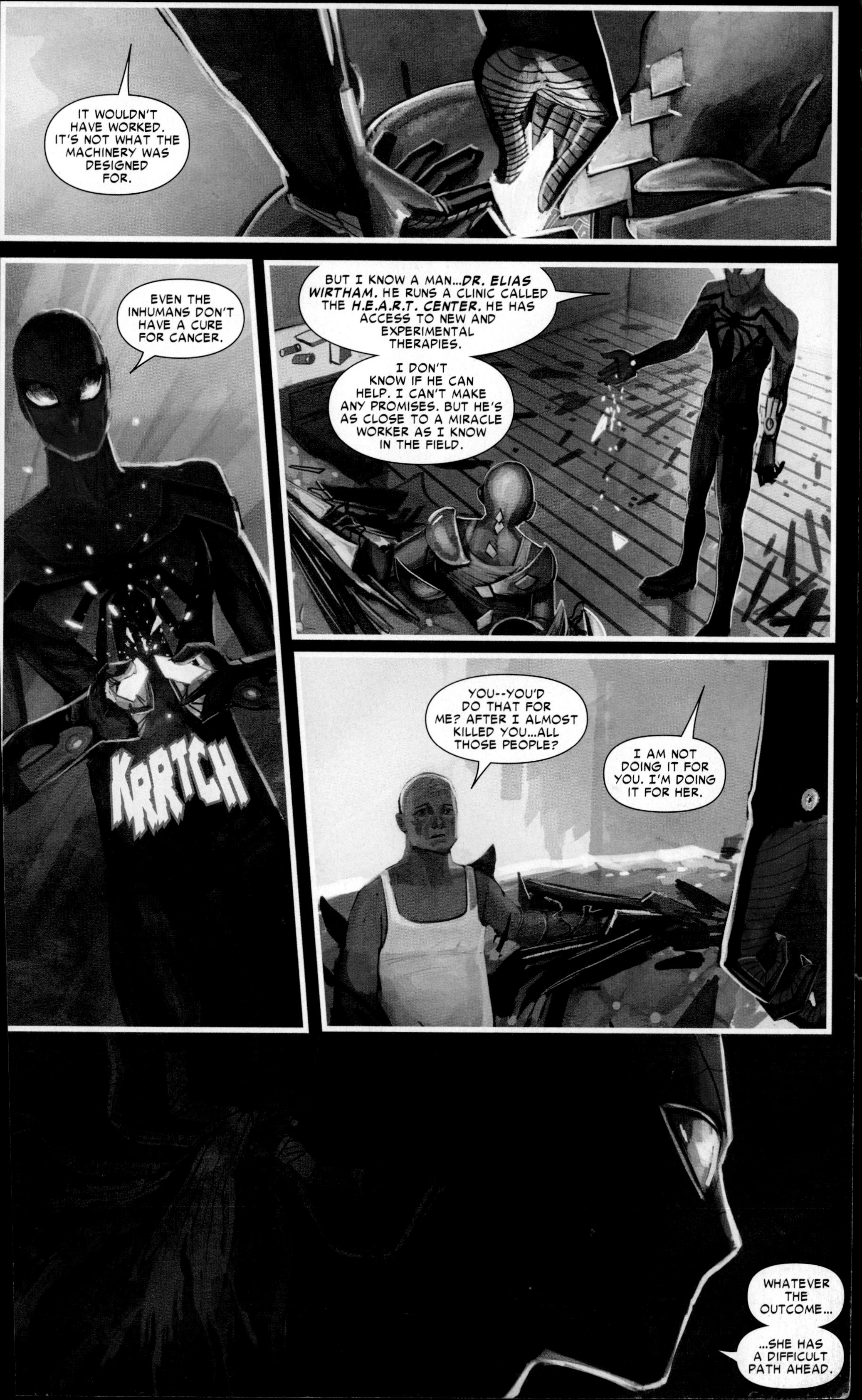
IT WOULDN'T HAVE WORKED. IT'S NOT WHAT THE MACHINERY WAS DESIGNED FOR.
EVEN THE INHUMANS DON'T HAVE A CURE FOR CANCER.
KRRTCH
BUT I KNOW A MAN...DR. ELIAS WIRTHAM. HE RUNS A CLINIC CALLED THE H.E.A.R.T. CENTER. HE HAS ACCESS TO NEW AND EXPERIMENTAL THERAPIES.
I DON'T KNOW IF HE CAN HELP. I CAN'T MAKE ANY PROMISES. BUT HE'S AS CLOSE TO A MIRACLE WORKER AS I KNOW IN THE FIELD.
YOU--YOU'D DO THAT FOR ME? AFTER I ALMOST KILLED YOU...ALL THOSE PEOPLE?
I AM NOT DOING IT FOR YOU. I'M DOING IT FOR HER.
WHATEVER THE OUTCOME...
...SHE HAS A DIFFICULT PATH AHEAD.

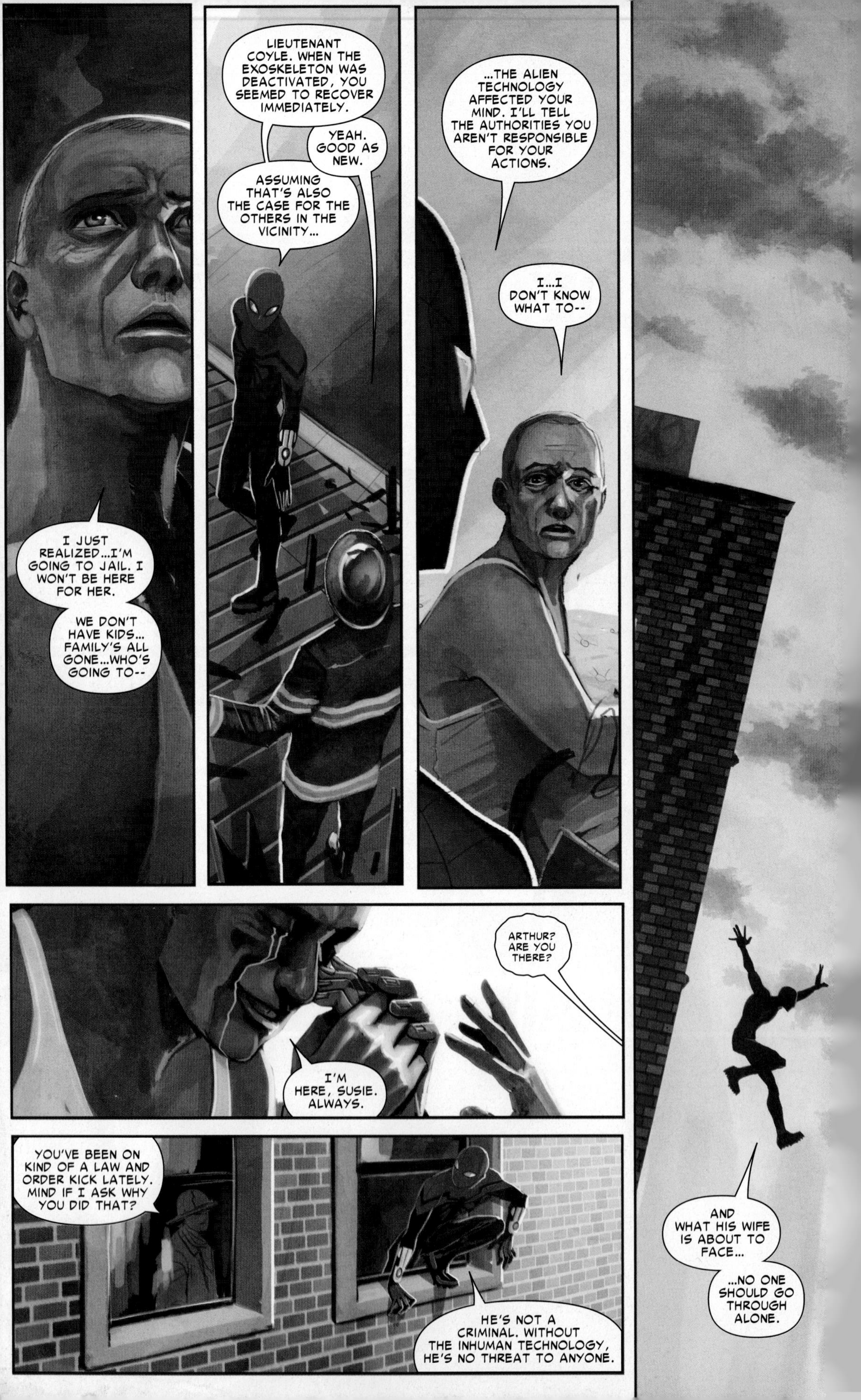
I JUST REALIZED...I'M GOING TO JAIL. I WON'T BE HERE FOR HER.
WE DON'T HAVE KIDS... FAMILY'S ALL GONE...WHO'S GOING TO--
LIEUTENANT COYLE. WHEN THE EXOSKELETON WAS DEACTIVATED, YOU SEEMED TO RECOVER IMMEDIATELY.
YEAH. GOOD AS NEW.
ASSUMING THAT'S ALSO THE CASE FOR THE OTHERS IN THE VICINITY...
...THE ALIEN TECHNOLOGY AFFECTED YOUR MIND. I'LL TELL THE AUTHORITIES YOU AREN'T RESPONSIBLE FOR YOUR ACTIONS.
I...I DON'T KNOW WHAT TO--
ARTHUR? ARE YOU THERE?
I'M HERE, SUSIE. ALWAYS.
YOU'VE BEEN ON KIND OF A LAW AND ORDER KICK LATELY. MIND IF I ASK WHY YOU DID THAT?
HE'S NOT A CRIMINAL. WITHOUT THE INHUMAN TECHNOLOGY, HE'S NO THREAT TO ANYONE.
AND WHAT HIS WIFE IS ABOUT TO FACE...
...NO ONE SHOULD GO THROUGH ALONE.

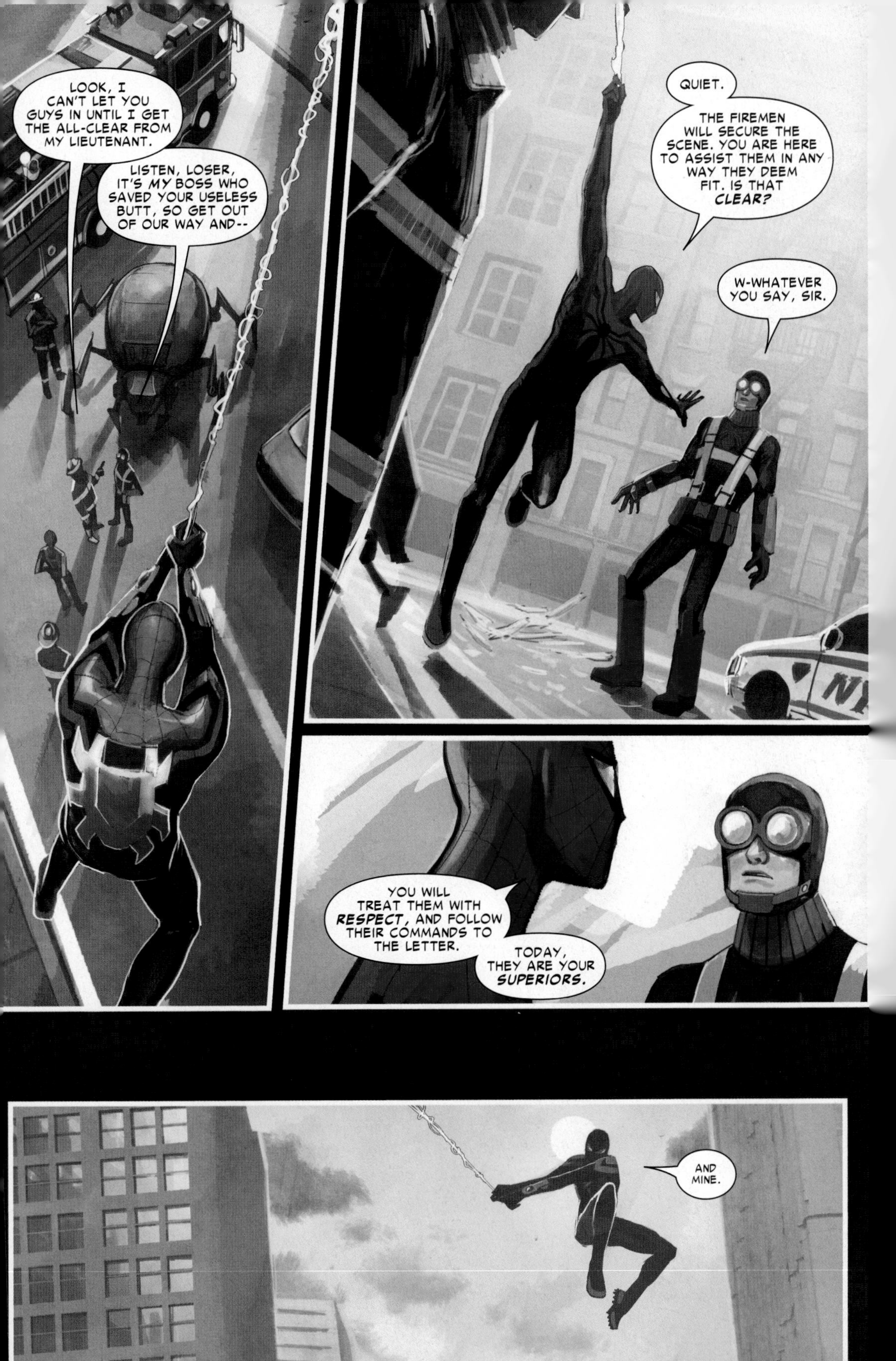
LOOK, I CAN'T LET YOU GUYS IN UNTIL I GET THE ALL-CLEAR FROM MY LIEUTENANT.
LISTEN, LOSER, IT'S MY BOSS WHO SAVED YOUR USELESS BUTT, SO GET OUT OF OUR WAY AND--
QUIET.
THE FIREMEN WILL SECURE THE SCENE. YOU ARE HERE TO ASSIST THEM IN ANY WAY THEY DEEM FIT. IS THAT CLEAR?
W-WHATEVER YOU SAY, SIR.
YOU WILL TREAT THEM WITH RESPECT, AND FOLLOW THEIR COMMANDS TO THE LETTER.
TODAY, THEY ARE YOUR SUPERIORS.
AND MINE.

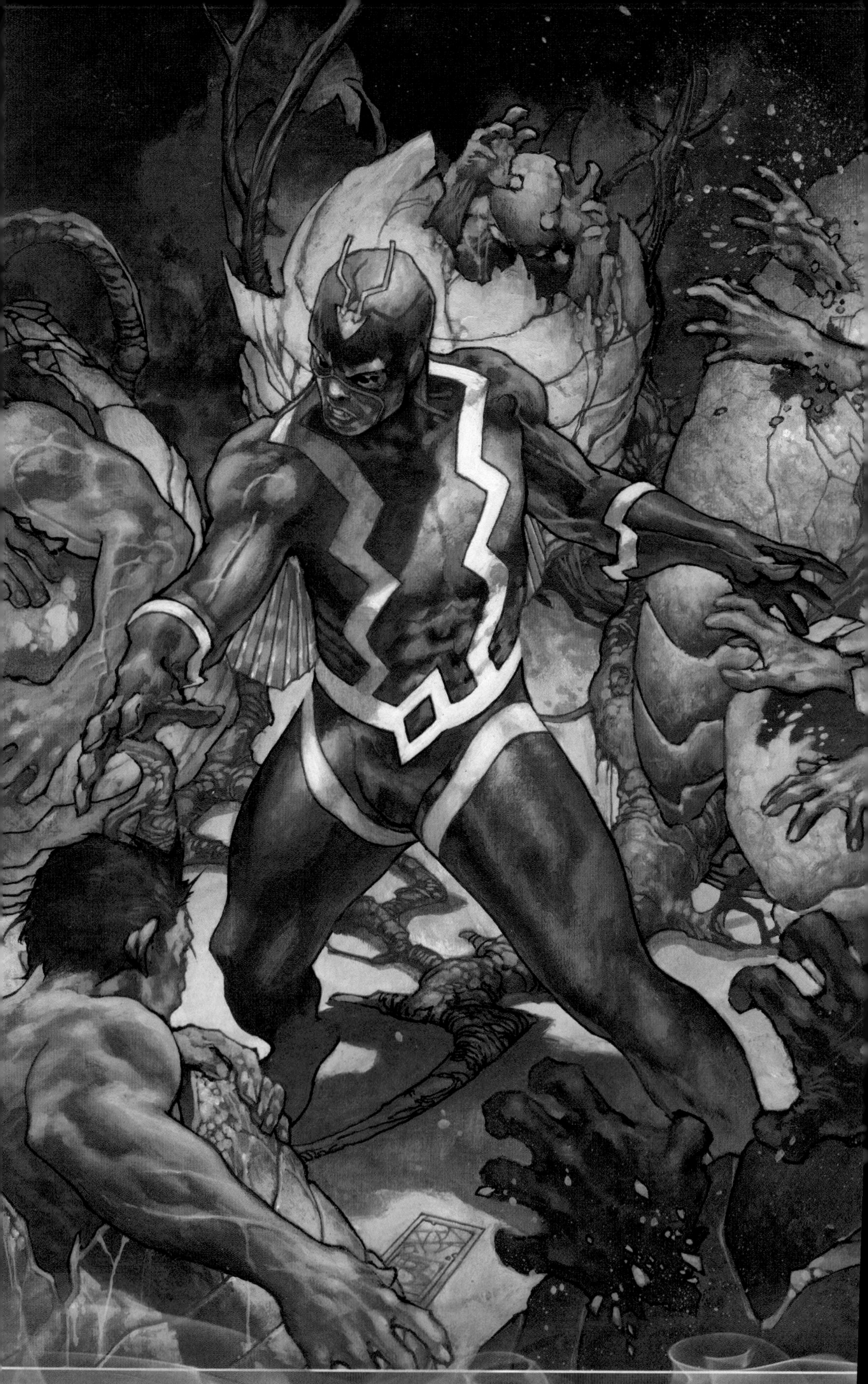

NEW AVENGERS #13

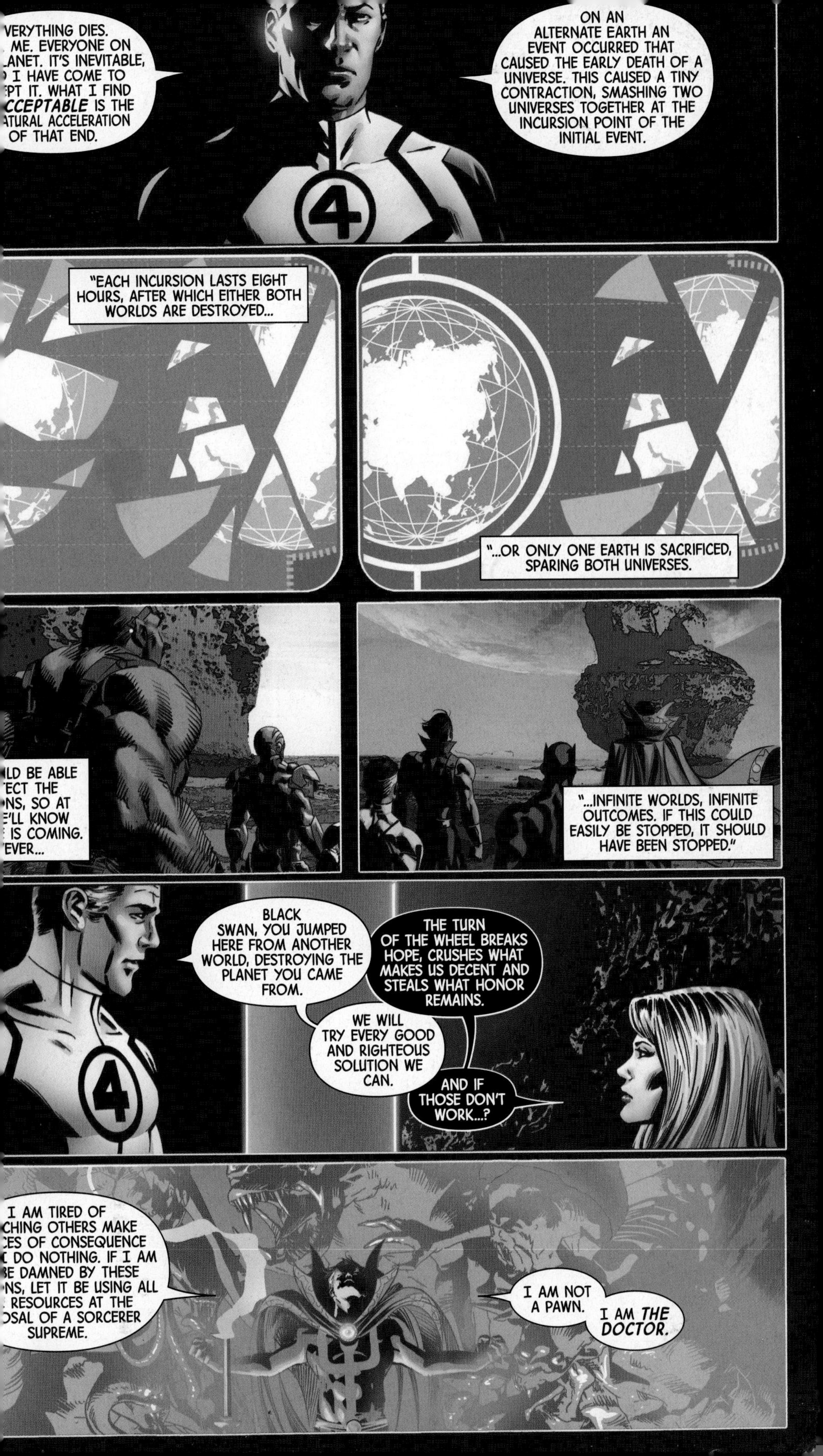

VERYTHING DIES. ME. EVERYONE ON LANET. IT'S INEVITABLE, I HAVE COME TO EPT IT. WHAT I FIND CCEPTABLE IS THE ATURAL ACCELERATION OF THAT END.
ON AN ALTERNATE EARTH AN EVENT OCCURRED THAT CAUSED THE EARLY DEATH OF A UNIVERSE. THIS CAUSED A TINY CONTRACTION, SMASHING TWO UNIVERSES TOGETHER AT THE INCURSION POINT OF THE INITIAL EVENT.
"EACH INCURSION LASTS EIGHT HOURS, AFTER WHICH EITHER BOTH WORLDS ARE DESTROYED...
"...OR ONLY ONE EARTH IS SACRIFICED, SPARING BOTH UNIVERSES.
LD BE ABLE ECT THE NS, SO AT 'LL KNOW IS COMING. EVER...
"...INFINITE WORLDS, INFINITE OUTCOMES. IF THIS COULD EASILY BE STOPPED, IT SHOULD HAVE BEEN STOPPED."
BLACK SWAN, YOU JUMPED HERE FROM ANOTHER WORLD, DESTROYING THE PLANET YOU CAME FROM.
THE TURN OF THE WHEEL BREAKS HOPE, CRUSHES WHAT MAKES US DECENT AND STEALS WHAT HONOR REMAINS.
WE WILL TRY EVERY GOOD AND RIGHTEOUS SOLUTION WE CAN.
AND IF THOSE DON'T WORK...?
I AM TIRED OF CHING OTHERS MAKE CES OF CONSEQUENCE DO NOTHING. IF I AM BE DAMNED BY THESE NS, LET IT BE USING ALL RESOURCES AT THE OSAL OF A SORCERER SUPREME.
I AM NOT A PAWN.
I AM THE DOCTOR.

THE ILLUMINA

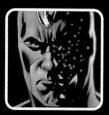

BLACK BOLT
Celestial Messiah

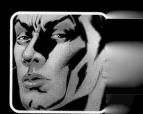

NAMOR
Imperius Rex

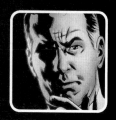

REED RICHARDS
Universal Builder

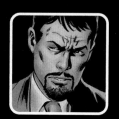

IRON MAN
Master of Machines

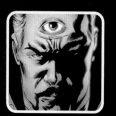

DOCTOR STRANGE
Sorcerer Supreme

BLACK PANTHE
King of the Dead

When you see this: AR, open up the MARVEL AR APP (available on ap
Android TM devices) and use your camera-enabled device to unlock extra-sp

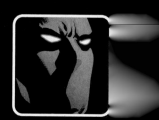

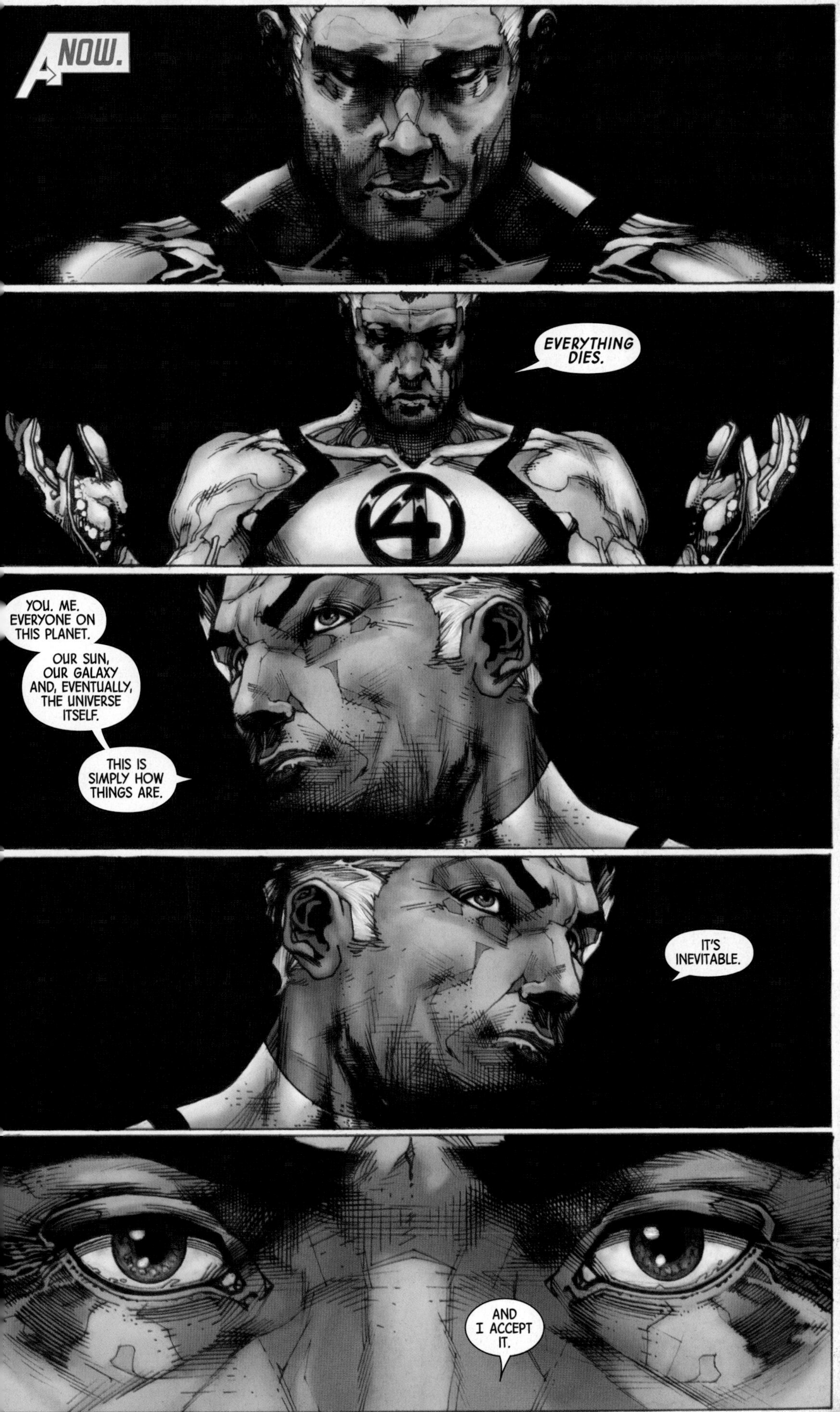
NOW.
EVERYTHING DIES.
YOU. ME. EVERYONE ON THIS PLANET.
OUR SUN, OUR GALAXY AND, EVENTUALLY, THE UNIVERSE ITSELF.
THIS IS SIMPLY HOW THINGS ARE.
IT'S INEVITABLE.
AND I ACCEPT IT.

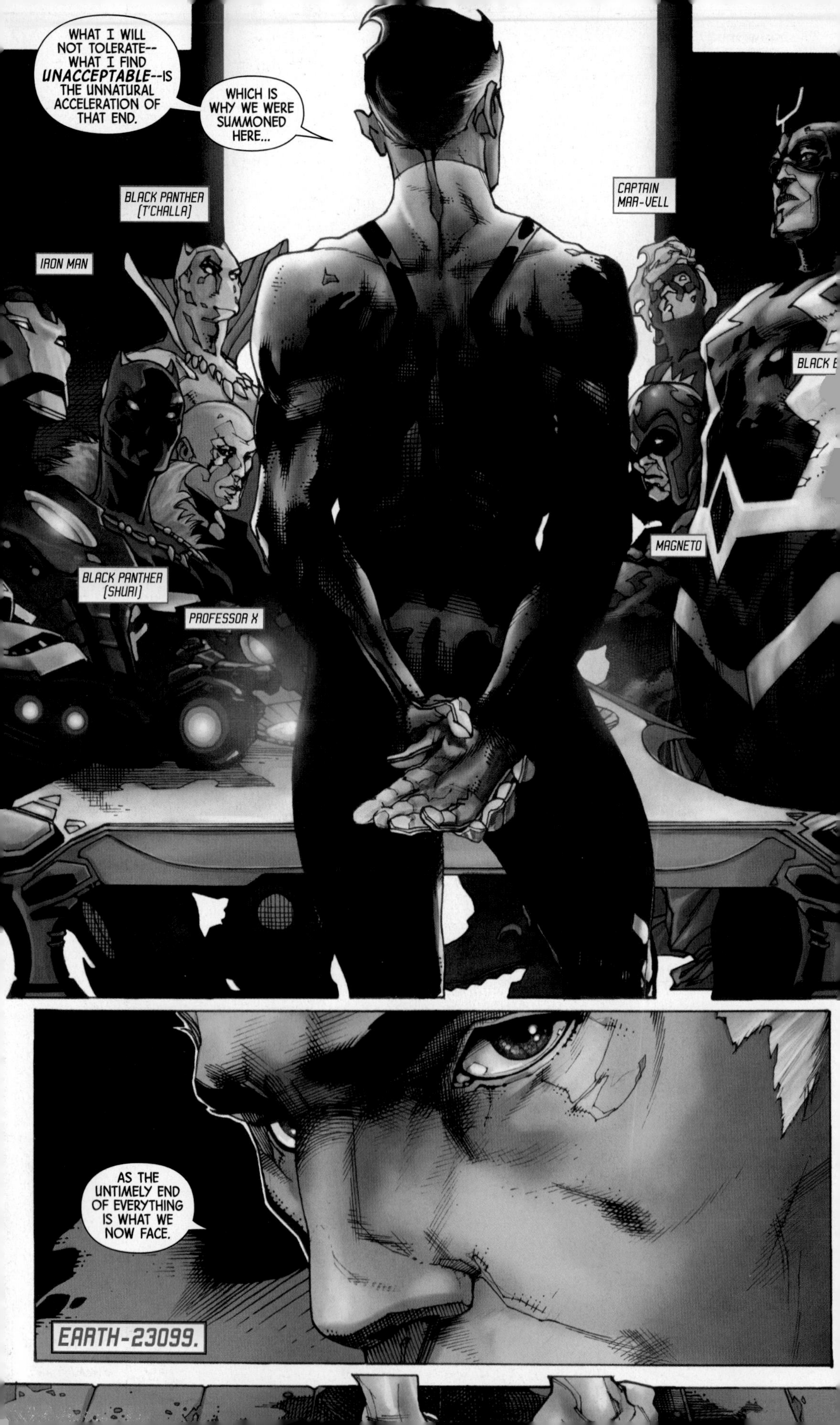
WHAT I WILL NOT TOLERATE-- WHAT I FIND UNACCEPTABLE--IS THE UNNATURAL ACCELERATION OF THAT END.
WHICH IS WHY WE WERE SUMMONED HERE...
BLACK PANTHER (T'CHALLA)
IRON MAN
CAPTAIN MAR-VELL
MAGNETO
BLACK PANTHER (SHURI)
PROFESSOR X
AS THE UNTIMELY END OF EVERYTHING IS WHAT WE NOW FACE.
EARTH-23099.

THE WORLD CHANGED OVERNIGHT AS THE GREAT MACHINE CAUSED CASCADING GLOBAL TERRIGENESIS.

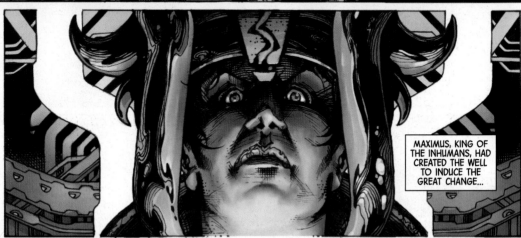

MAXIMUS, KING OF THE INHUMANS, HAD CREATED THE WELL TO INDUCE THE GREAT CHANGE...

AND TO USHER IN A NEW DAY FOR HIS EXPANDING KINGDOM.

THE ROYAL FAMILY WATCHED AS ALL THE UNCHANGED--THE LOST TRIBES AND THE HIDDEN ONES--BEGAN TO METAMORPHOSE AS THE MIST--THE TRANSFORMATIVE FALLOUT--SPREAD ACROSS THE GLOBE.

IT SHOULD HAVE BEEN THE START OF A NEW INHUMAN AGE.

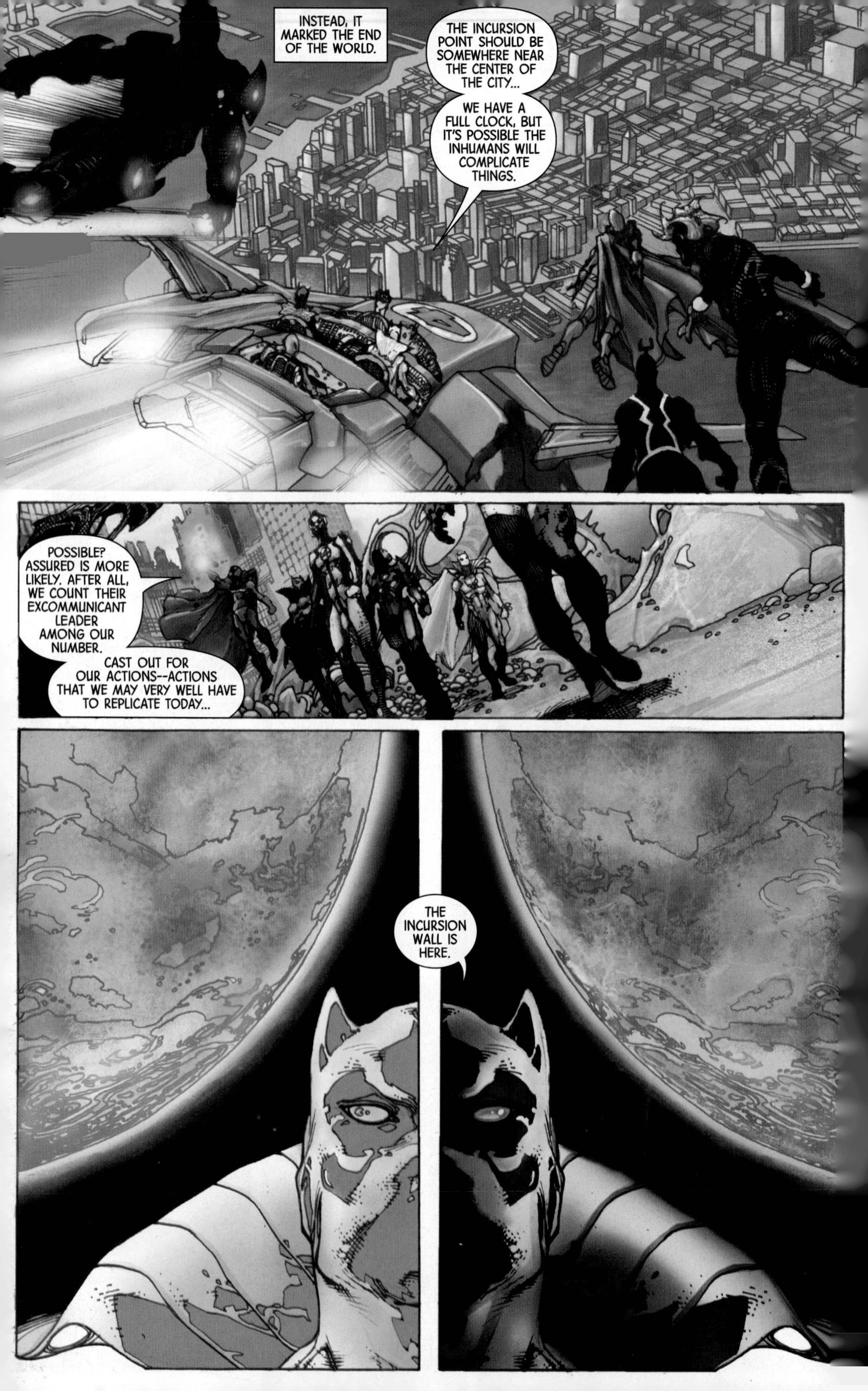
INSTEAD, IT MARKED THE END OF THE WORLD.
THE INCURSION POINT SHOULD BE SOMEWHERE NEAR THE CENTER OF THE CITY...
WE HAVE A FULL CLOCK, BUT IT'S POSSIBLE THE INHUMANS WILL COMPLICATE THINGS.
POSSIBLE? ASSURED IS MORE LIKELY. AFTER ALL, WE COUNT THEIR EXCOMMUNICANT LEADER AMONG OUR NUMBER.
CAST OUT FOR OUR ACTIONS--ACTIONS THAT WE MAY VERY WELL HAVE TO REPLICATE TODAY...
THE INCURSION WALL IS HERE.

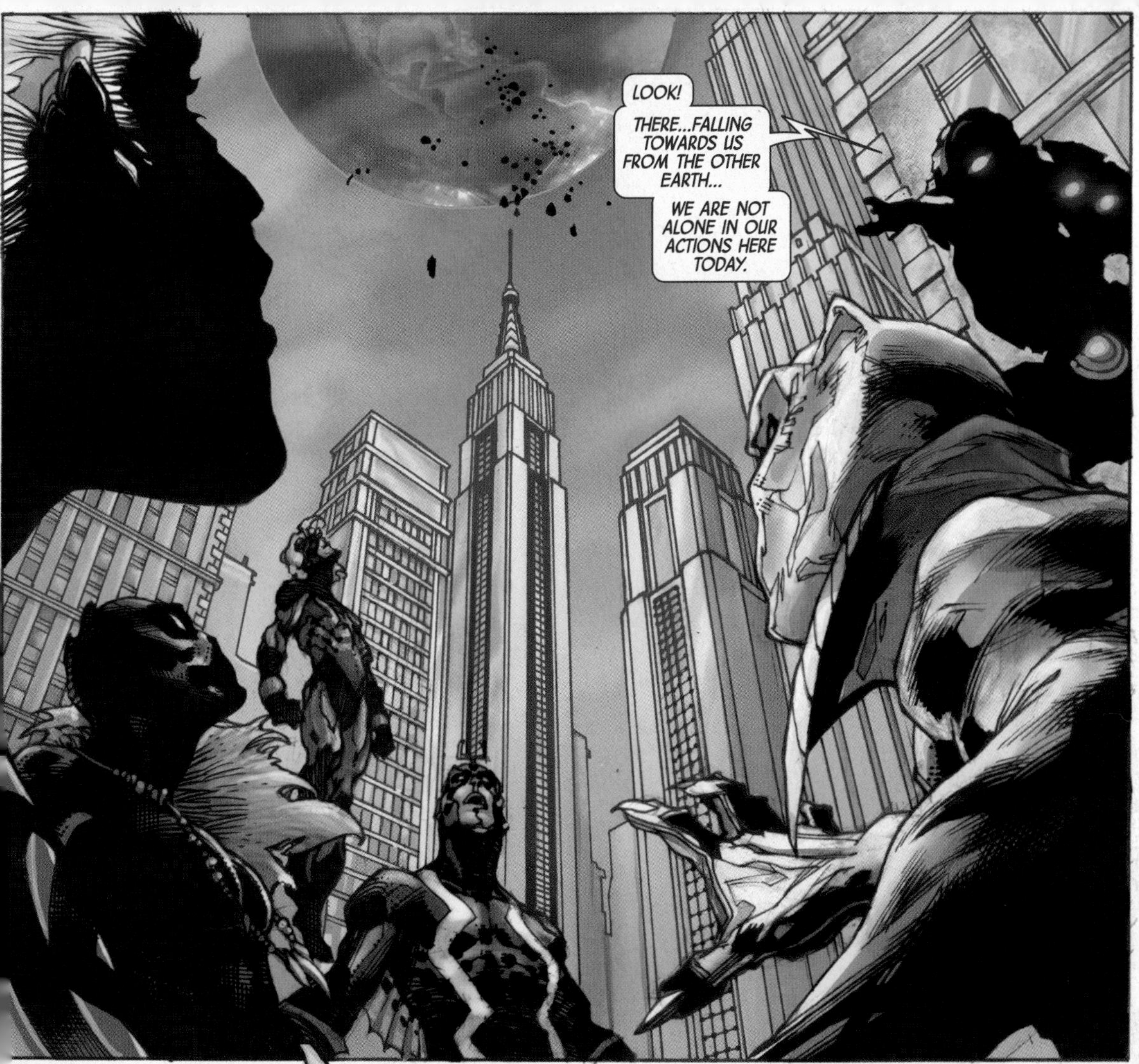
LOOK!
THERE...FALLING TOWARDS US FROM THE OTHER EARTH...
WE ARE NOT ALONE IN OUR ACTIONS HERE TODAY.

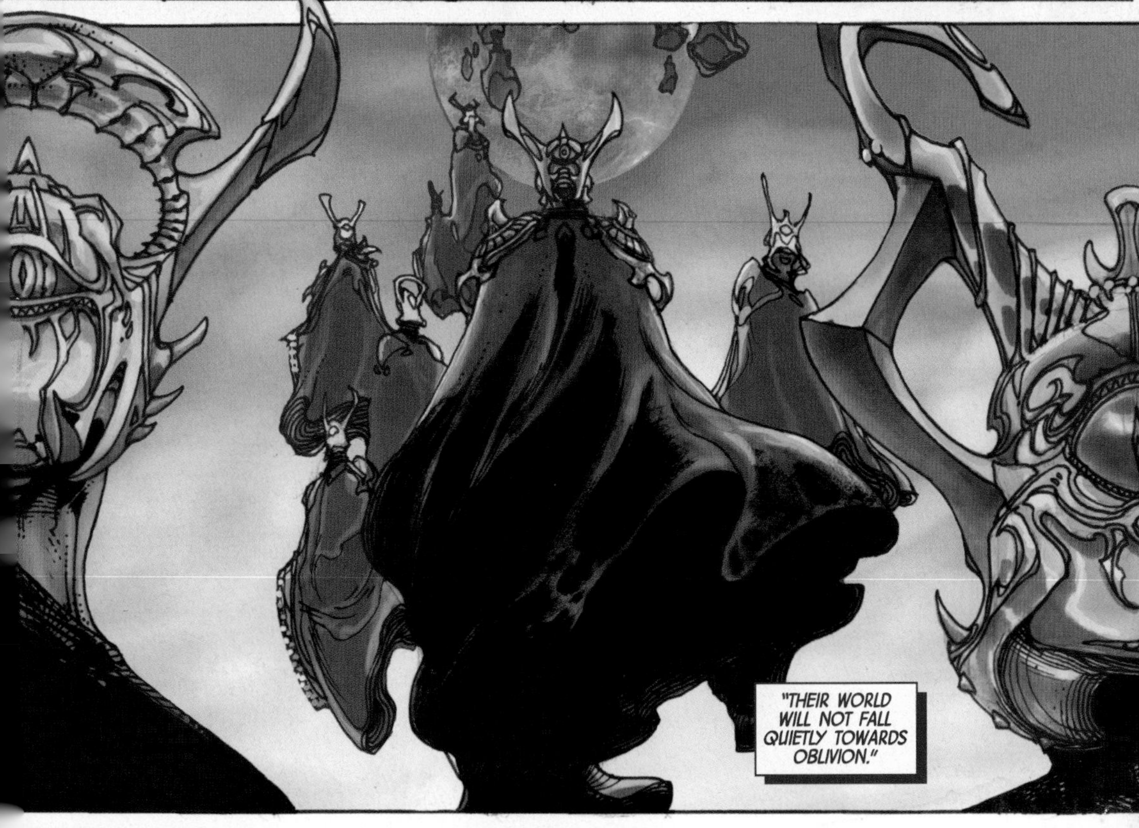
"THEIR WORLD WILL NOT FALL QUIETLY TOWARDS OBLIVION."

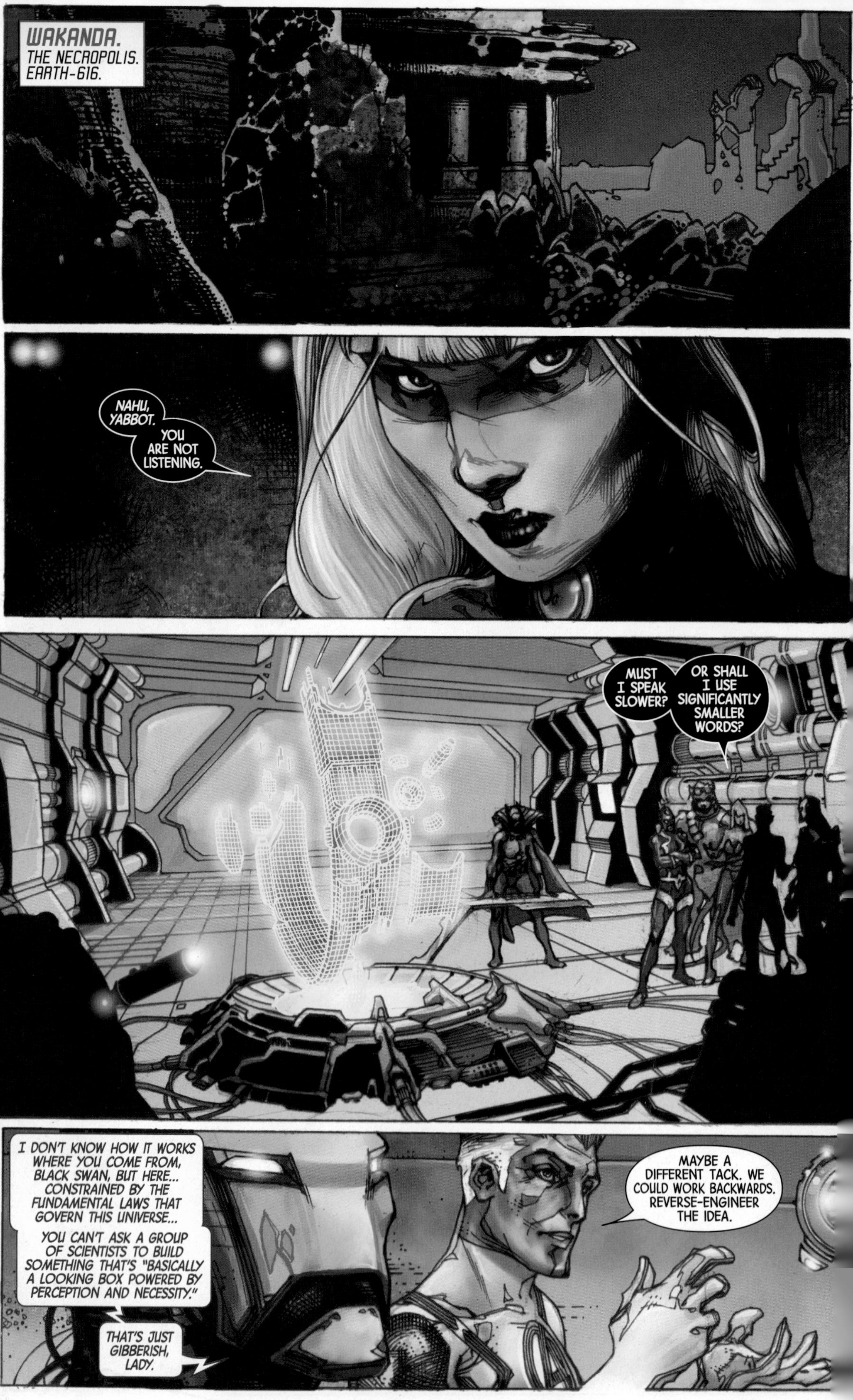
WAKANDA. THE NECROPOLIS. EARTH-616.
NAHU, YABBOT.
YOU ARE NOT LISTENING.
MUST I SPEAK SLOWER?
OR SHALL I USE SIGNIFICANTLY SMALLER WORDS?
I DON'T KNOW HOW IT WORKS WHERE YOU COME FROM, BLACK SWAN, BUT HERE... CONSTRAINED BY THE FUNDAMENTAL LAWS THAT GOVERN THIS UNIVERSE...
YOU CAN'T ASK A GROUP OF SCIENTISTS TO BUILD SOMETHING THAT'S "BASICALLY A LOOKING BOX POWERED BY PERCEPTION AND NECESSITY."
THAT'S JUST GIBBERISH, LADY.
MAYBE A DIFFERENT TACK. WE COULD WORK BACKWARDS. REVERSE-ENGINEER THE IDEA.

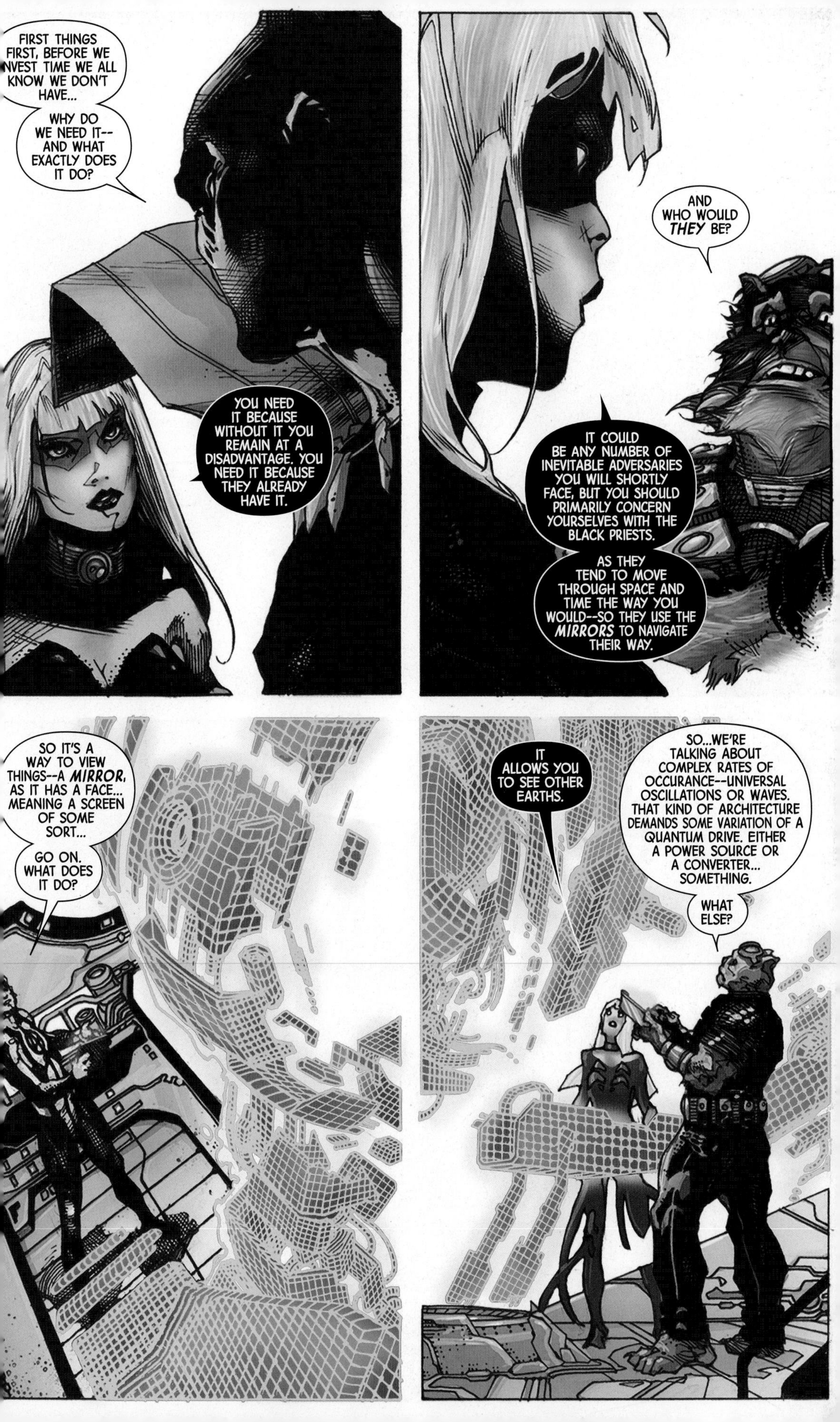
FIRST THINGS FIRST, BEFORE WE NVEST TIME WE ALL KNOW WE DON'T HAVE...
WHY DO WE NEED IT--AND WHAT EXACTLY DOES IT DO?
YOU NEED IT BECAUSE WITHOUT IT YOU REMAIN AT A DISADVANTAGE. YOU NEED IT BECAUSE THEY ALREADY HAVE IT.
AND WHO WOULD *THEY* BE?
IT COULD BE ANY NUMBER OF INEVITABLE ADVERSARIES YOU WILL SHORTLY FACE, BUT YOU SHOULD PRIMARILY CONCERN YOURSELVES WITH THE BLACK PRIESTS.
AS THEY TEND TO MOVE THROUGH SPACE AND TIME THE WAY YOU WOULD--SO THEY USE THE *MIRRORS* TO NAVIGATE THEIR WAY.
SO IT'S A WAY TO VIEW THINGS--A *MIRROR*, AS IT HAS A FACE... MEANING A SCREEN OF SOME SORT...
GO ON. WHAT DOES IT DO?
IT ALLOWS YOU TO SEE OTHER EARTHS.
SO...WE'RE TALKING ABOUT COMPLEX RATES OF OCCURANCE--UNIVERSAL OSCILLATIONS OR WAVES. THAT KIND OF ARCHITECTURE DEMANDS SOME VARIATION OF A QUANTUM DRIVE. EITHER A POWER SOURCE OR A CONVERTER... SOMETHING.
WHAT ELSE?

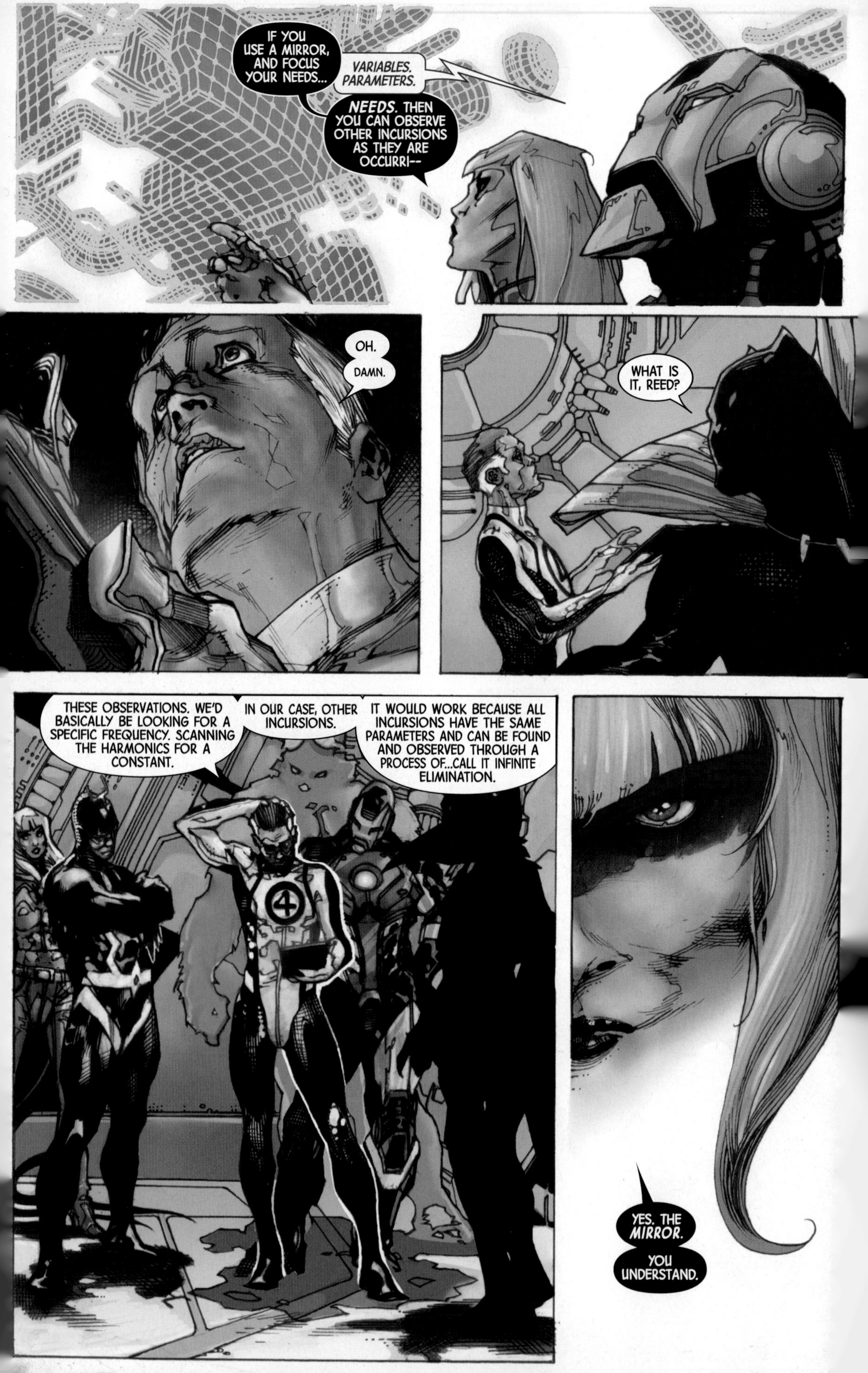
IF YOU USE A MIRROR, AND FOCUS YOUR NEEDS...
VARIABLES. PARAMETERS.
NEEDS. THEN YOU CAN OBSERVE OTHER INCURSIONS AS THEY ARE OCCURRI--
OH.
DAMN.
WHAT IS IT, REED?
THESE OBSERVATIONS. WE'D BASICALLY BE LOOKING FOR A SPECIFIC FREQUENCY. SCANNING THE HARMONICS FOR A CONSTANT.
IN OUR CASE, OTHER INCURSIONS.
IT WOULD WORK BECAUSE ALL INCURSIONS HAVE THE SAME PARAMETERS AND CAN BE FOUND AND OBSERVED THROUGH A PROCESS OF...CALL IT INFINITE ELIMINATION.
YES. THE MIRROR.
YOU UNDERSTAND.

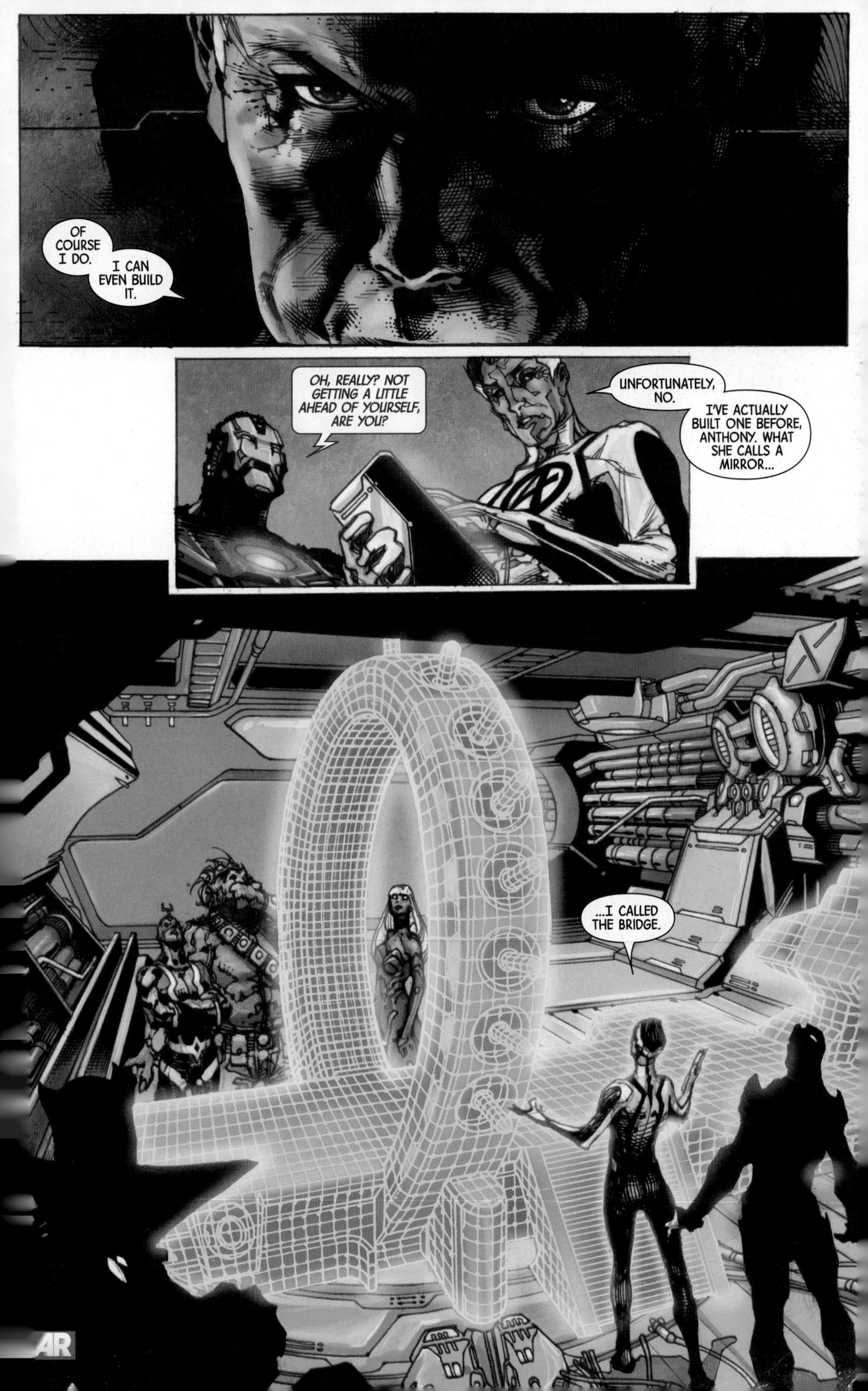

OF COURSE I DO.
I CAN EVEN BUILD IT.
OH, REALLY? NOT GETTING A LITTLE AHEAD OF YOURSELF, ARE YOU?
UNFORTUNATELY, NO.
I'VE ACTUALLY BUILT ONE BEFORE, ANTHONY. WHAT SHE CALLS A MIRROR...
...I CALLED THE BRIDGE.
AR

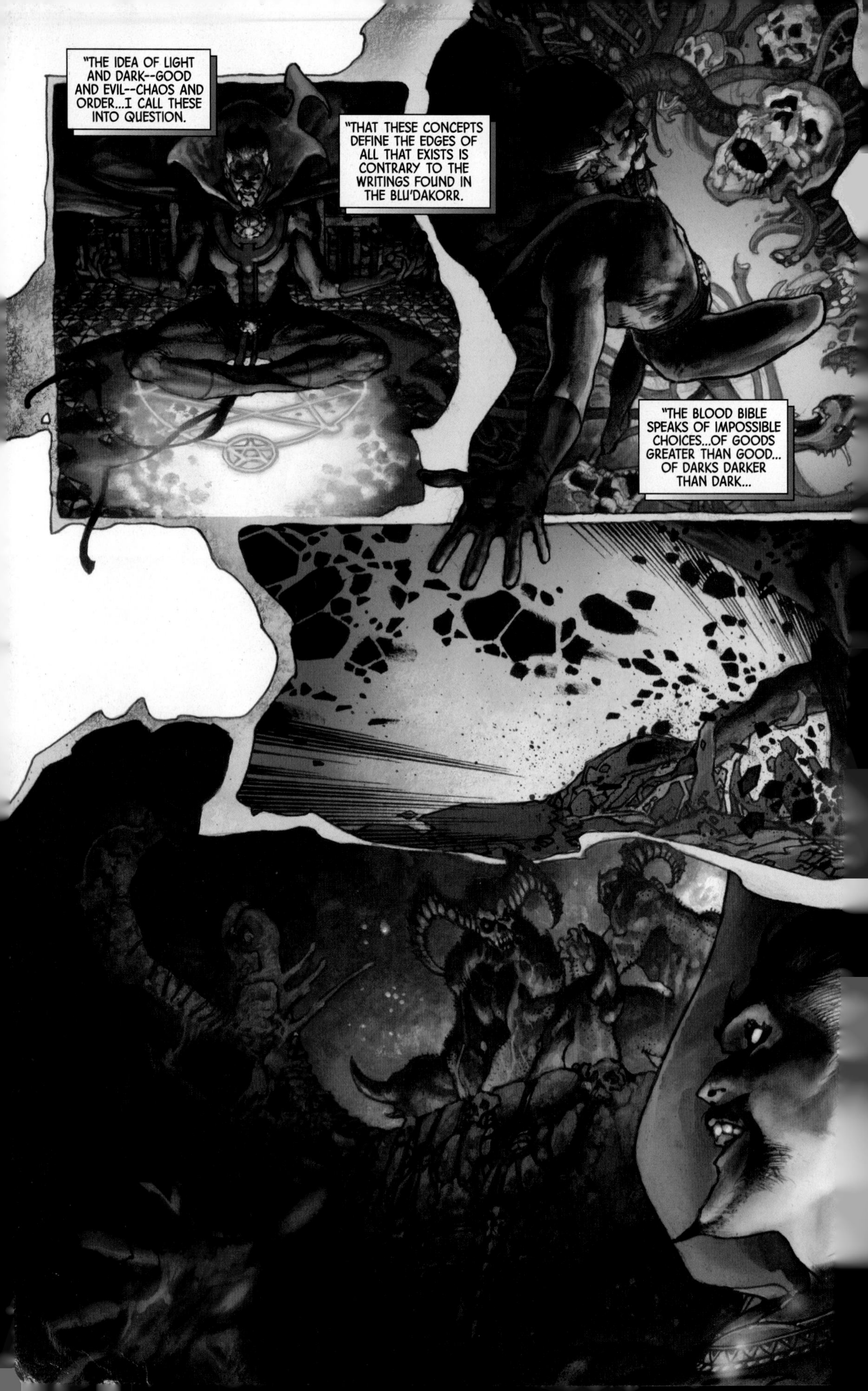
"THE IDEA OF LIGHT AND DARK--GOOD AND EVIL--CHAOS AND ORDER...I CALL THESE INTO QUESTION.
"THAT THESE CONCEPTS DEFINE THE EDGES OF ALL THAT EXISTS IS CONTRARY TO THE WRITINGS FOUND IN THE BLU'DAKORR.
"THE BLOOD BIBLE SPEAKS OF IMPOSSIBLE CHOICES...OF GOODS GREATER THAN GOOD... OF DARKS DARKER THAN DARK...

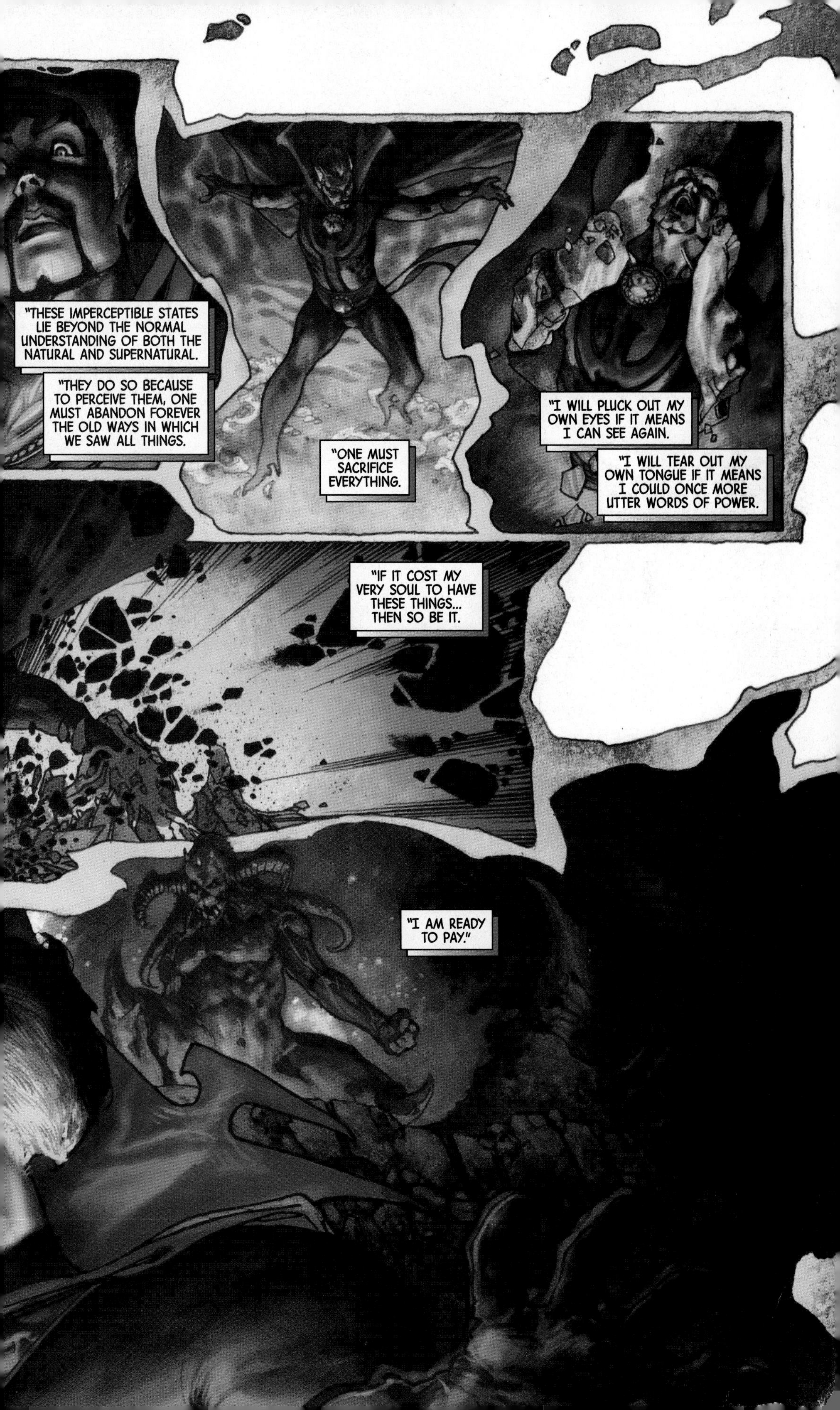
"THESE IMPERCEPTIBLE STATES LIE BEYOND THE NORMAL UNDERSTANDING OF BOTH THE NATURAL AND SUPERNATURAL.
"THEY DO SO BECAUSE TO PERCEIVE THEM, ONE MUST ABANDON FOREVER THE OLD WAYS IN WHICH WE SAW ALL THINGS.
"ONE MUST SACRIFICE EVERYTHING.
"I WILL PLUCK OUT MY OWN EYES IF IT MEANS I CAN SEE AGAIN.
"I WILL TEAR OUT MY OWN TONGUE IF IT MEANS I COULD ONCE MORE UTTER WORDS OF POWER.
"IF IT COST MY VERY SOUL TO HAVE THESE THINGS... THEN SO BE IT.
"I AM READY TO PAY."

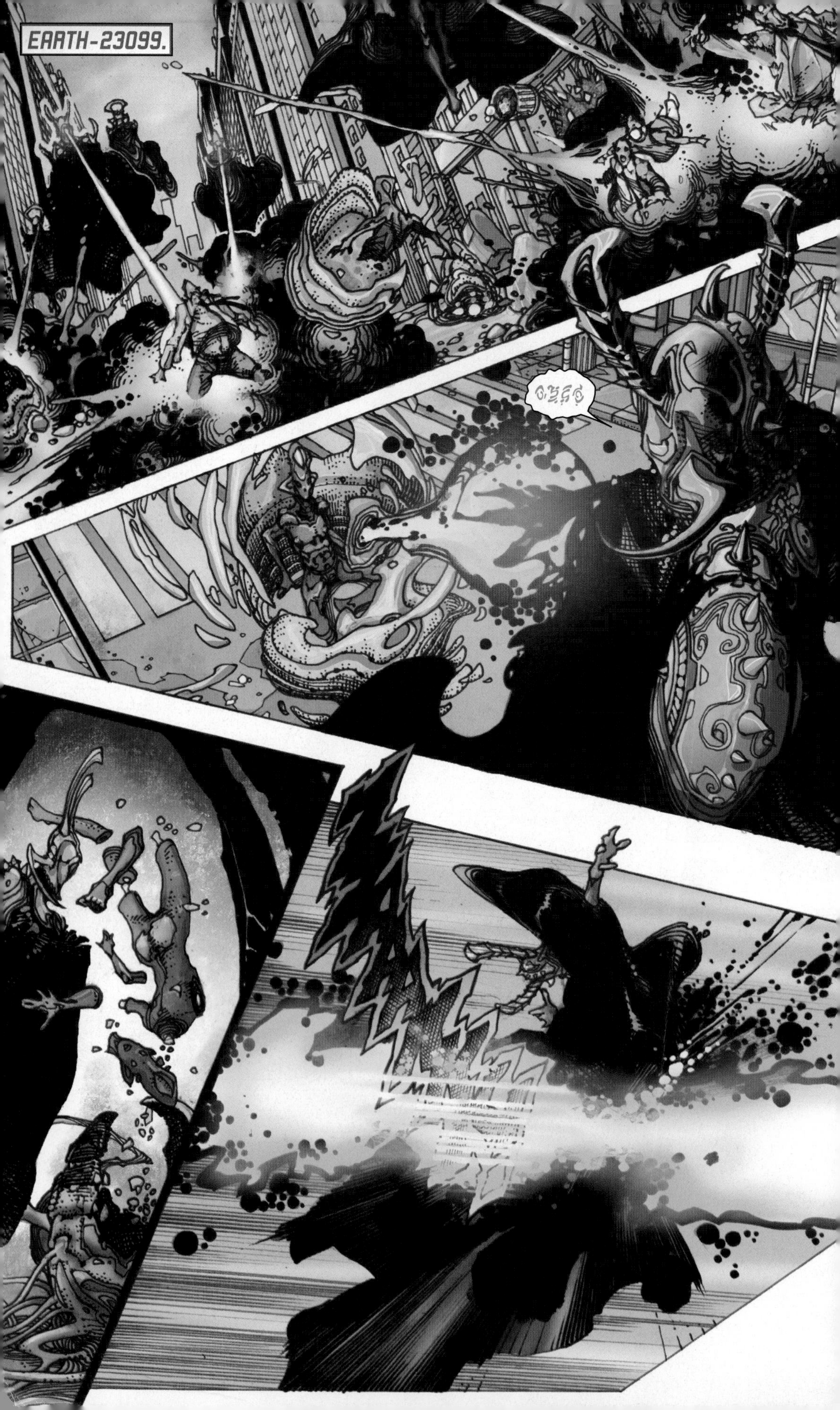
EARTH-23099.

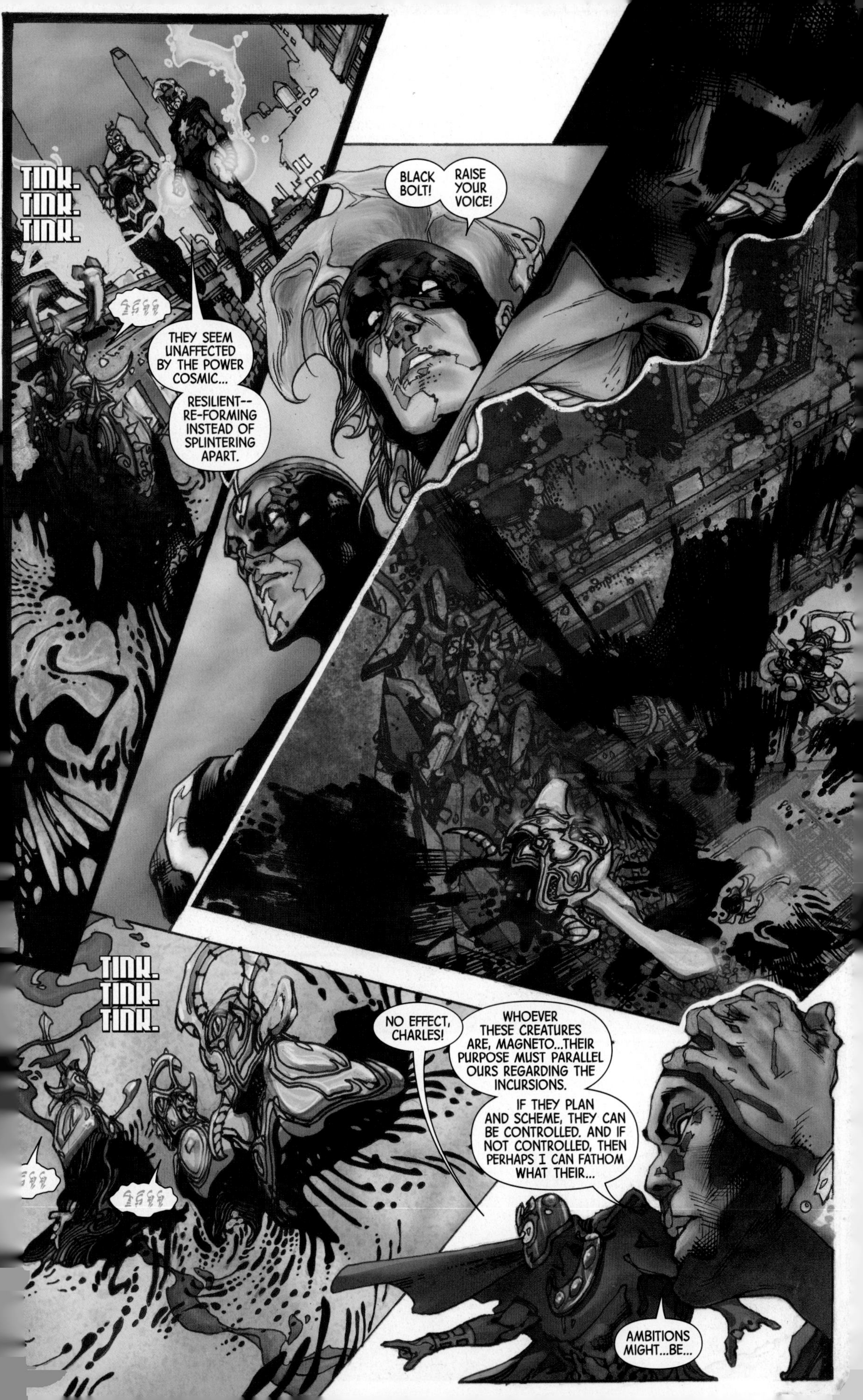
TINK.
TINK.
TINK.
THEY SEEM UNAFFECTED BY THE POWER COSMIC...
RESILIENT-- RE-FORMING INSTEAD OF SPLINTERING APART.
BLACK BOLT!
RAISE YOUR VOICE!
TINK.
TINK.
TINK.
NO EFFECT, CHARLES!
WHOEVER THESE CREATURES ARE, MAGNETO...THEIR PURPOSE MUST PARALLEL OURS REGARDING THE INCURSIONS.
IF THEY PLAN AND SCHEME, THEY CAN BE CONTROLLED. AND IF NOT CONTROLLED, THEN PERHAPS I CAN FATHOM WHAT THEIR...
AMBITIONS MIGHT...BE...

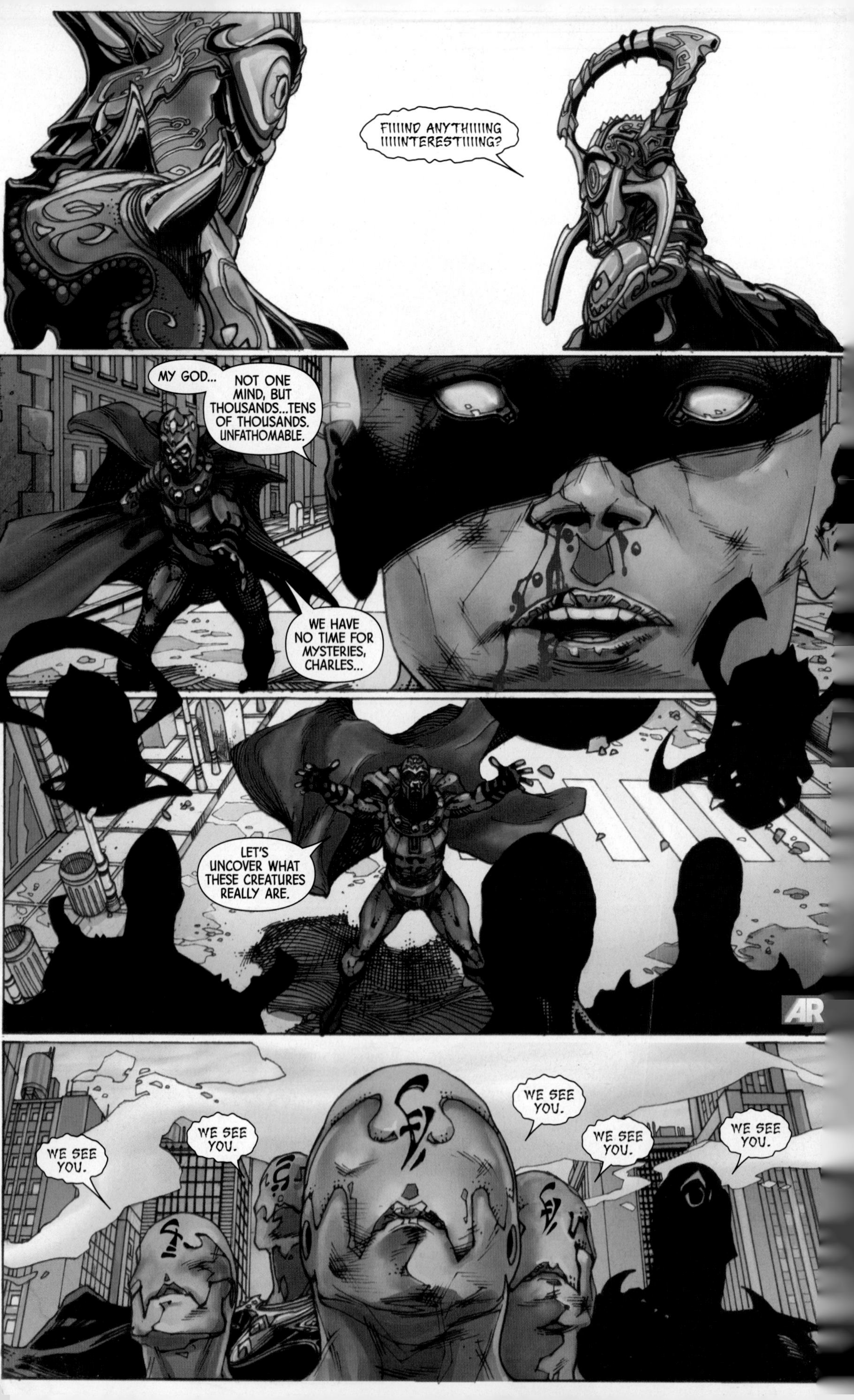
FIIIIND ANYTHIIIING IIIIINTERESTIIIING?
MY GOD...
NOT ONE MIND, BUT THOUSANDS...TENS OF THOUSANDS. UNFATHOMABLE.
WE HAVE NO TIME FOR MYSTERIES, CHARLES...
LET'S UNCOVER WHAT THESE CREATURES REALLY ARE.
WE SEE YOU.
WE SEE YOU.
WE SEE YOU.
WE SEE YOU.
WE SEE YOU.

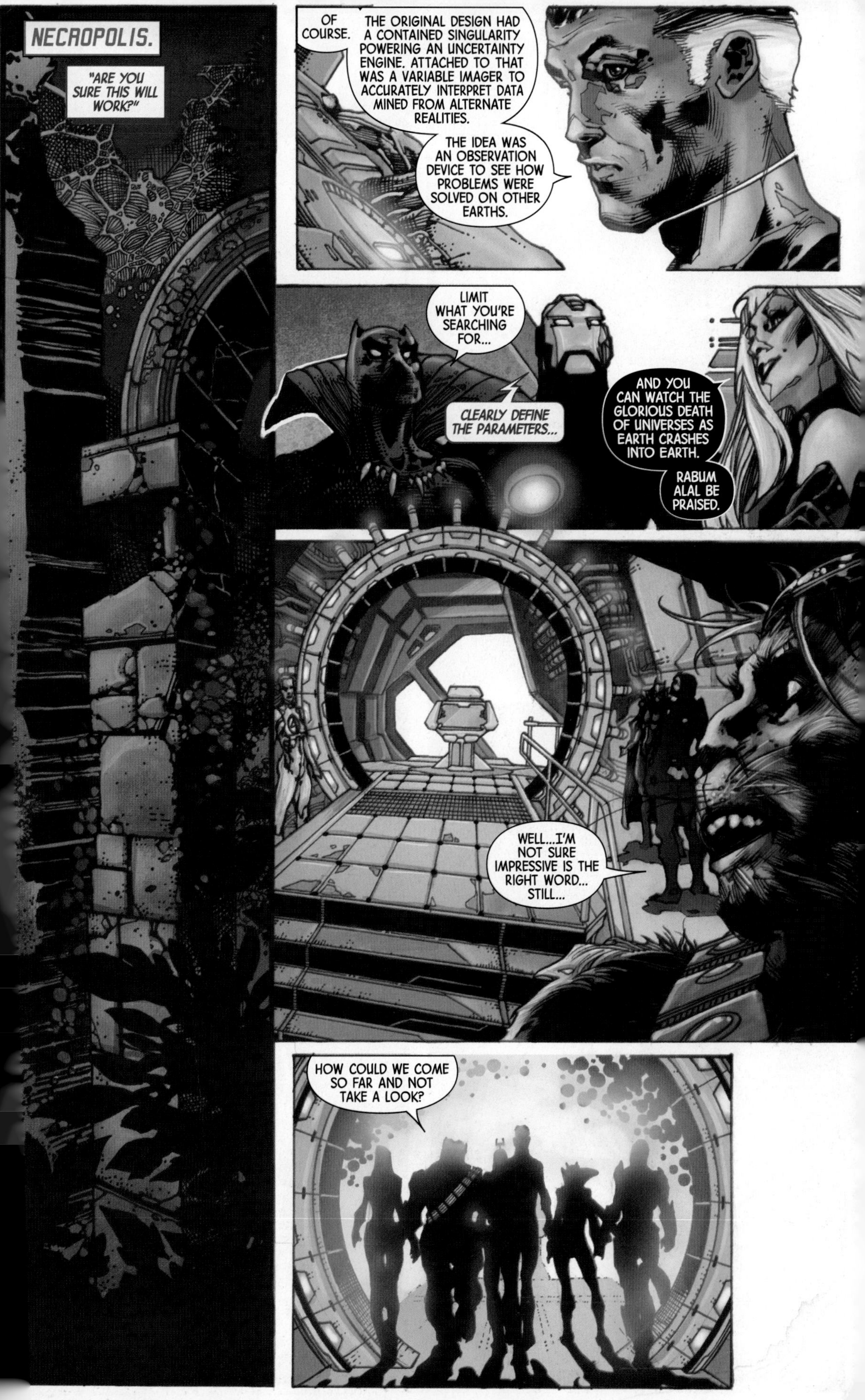
NECROPOLIS.
"ARE YOU SURE THIS WILL WORK?"
OF COURSE.
THE ORIGINAL DESIGN HAD A CONTAINED SINGULARITY POWERING AN UNCERTAINTY ENGINE. ATTACHED TO THAT WAS A VARIABLE IMAGER TO ACCURATELY INTERPRET DATA MINED FROM ALTERNATE REALITIES.
THE IDEA WAS AN OBSERVATION DEVICE TO SEE HOW PROBLEMS WERE SOLVED ON OTHER EARTHS.
LIMIT WHAT YOU'RE SEARCHING FOR...
CLEARLY DEFINE THE PARAMETERS...
AND YOU CAN WATCH THE GLORIOUS DEATH OF UNIVERSES AS EARTH CRASHES INTO EARTH.
RABUM ALAL BE PRAISED.
WELL...I'M NOT SURE IMPRESSIVE IS THE RIGHT WORD... STILL...
HOW COULD WE COME SO FAR AND NOT TAKE A LOOK?

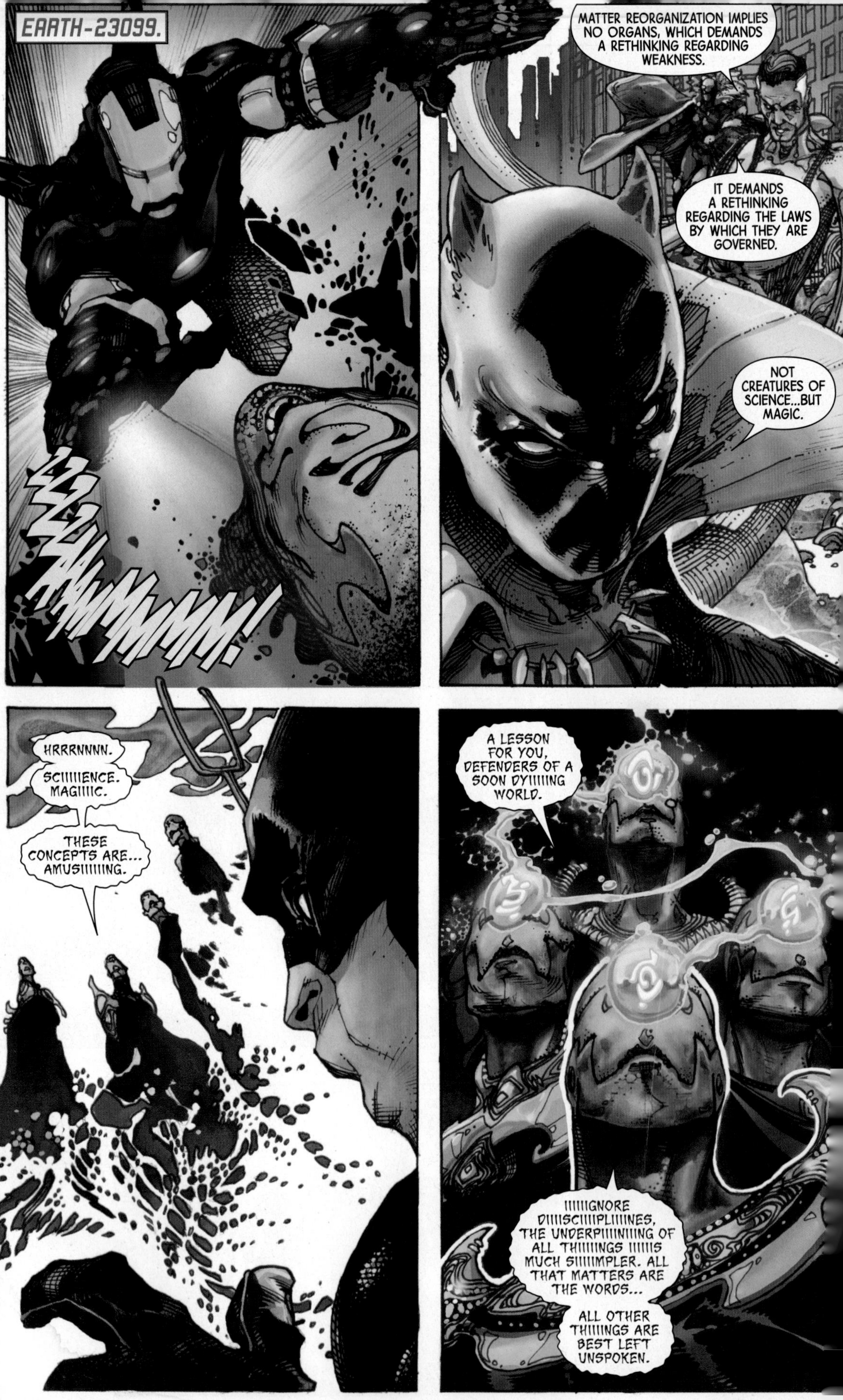
EARTH-23099.
ZZZWAMMMMM!
MATTER REORGANIZATION IMPLIES NO ORGANS, WHICH DEMANDS A RETHINKING REGARDING WEAKNESS.
IT DEMANDS A RETHINKING REGARDING THE LAWS BY WHICH THEY ARE GOVERNED.
NOT CREATURES OF SCIENCE...BUT MAGIC.
HRRRNNNN.
SCIIIIENCE. MAGIIIIC.
THESE CONCEPTS ARE... AMUSIIIIIIING.
A LESSON FOR YOU, DEFENDERS OF A SOON DYIIIIING WORLD.
IIIIIGNORE DIIIISCIIIIPLIIIINES, THE UNDERPIIIINIIING OF ALL THIIIIINGS IIIIIIS MUCH SIIIIIMPLER. ALL THAT MATTERS ARE THE WORDS...
ALL OTHER THIIIINGS ARE BEST LEFT UNSPOKEN.

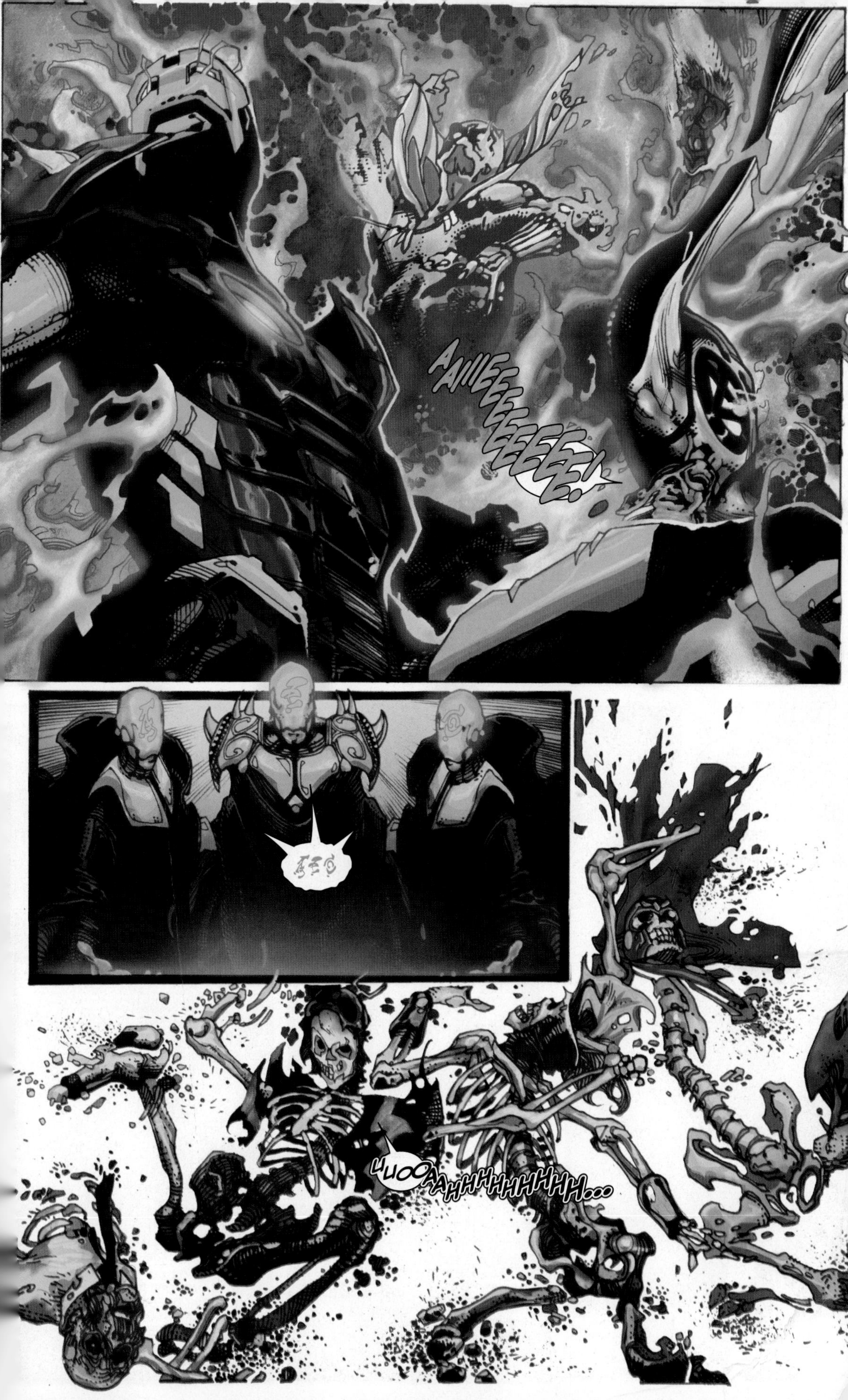
AAIIIEEEEEEEEE!
UUOOAAHHHHHHHHH...

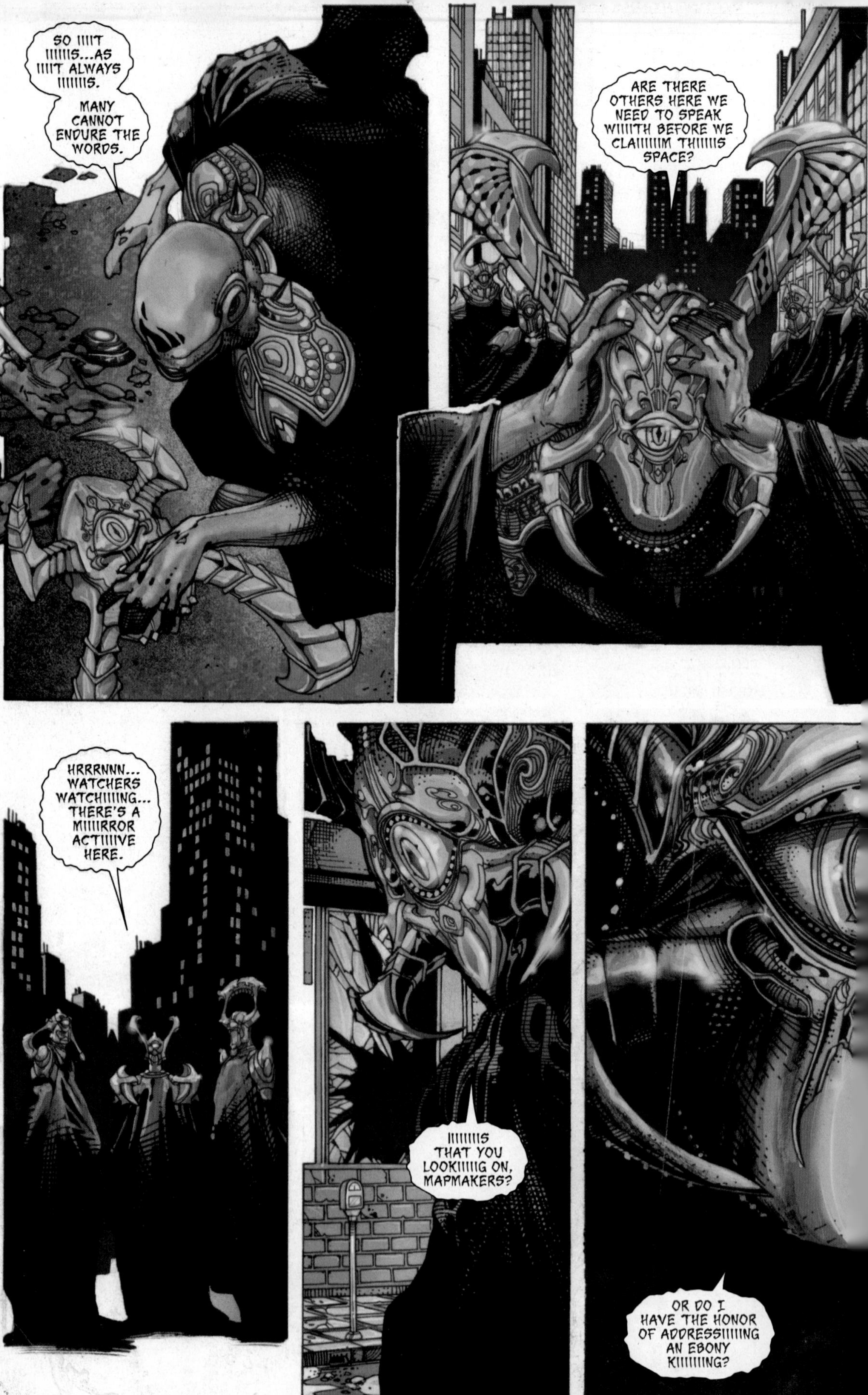
SO IIIIT IIIIIIS...AS IIIIT ALWAYS IIIIIIS.
MANY CANNOT ENDURE THE WORDS.
ARE THERE OTHERS HERE WE NEED TO SPEAK WIIIITH BEFORE WE CLAIIIIIM THIIIIIS SPACE?
HRRRNNN... WATCHERS WATCHIIIIING... THERE'S A MIIIIRROR ACTIIIIIVE HERE.
IIIIIIIS THAT YOU LOOKIIIIIG ON, MAPMAKERS?
OR DO I HAVE THE HONOR OF ADDRESSIIIIING AN EBONY KIIIIIIING?

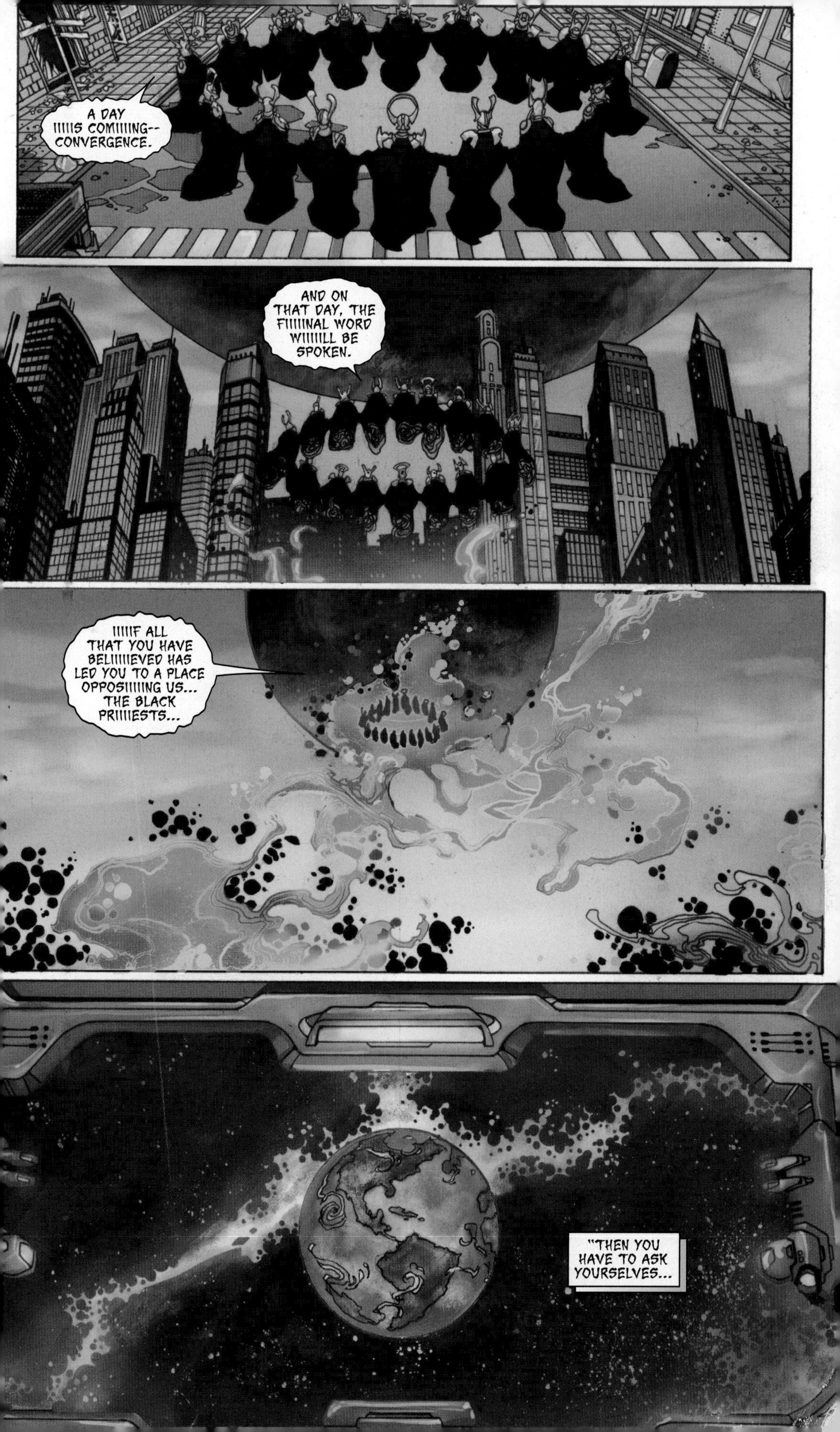
A DAY IIIIIS COMIIIIING-- CONVERGENCE.
AND ON THAT DAY, THE FIIIIINAL WORD WIIIIILL BE SPOKEN.
IIIIIF ALL THAT YOU HAVE BELIIIIIEVED HAS LED YOU TO A PLACE OPPOSIIIIING US... THE BLACK PRIIIIESTS...
"THEN YOU HAVE TO ASK YOURSELVES...

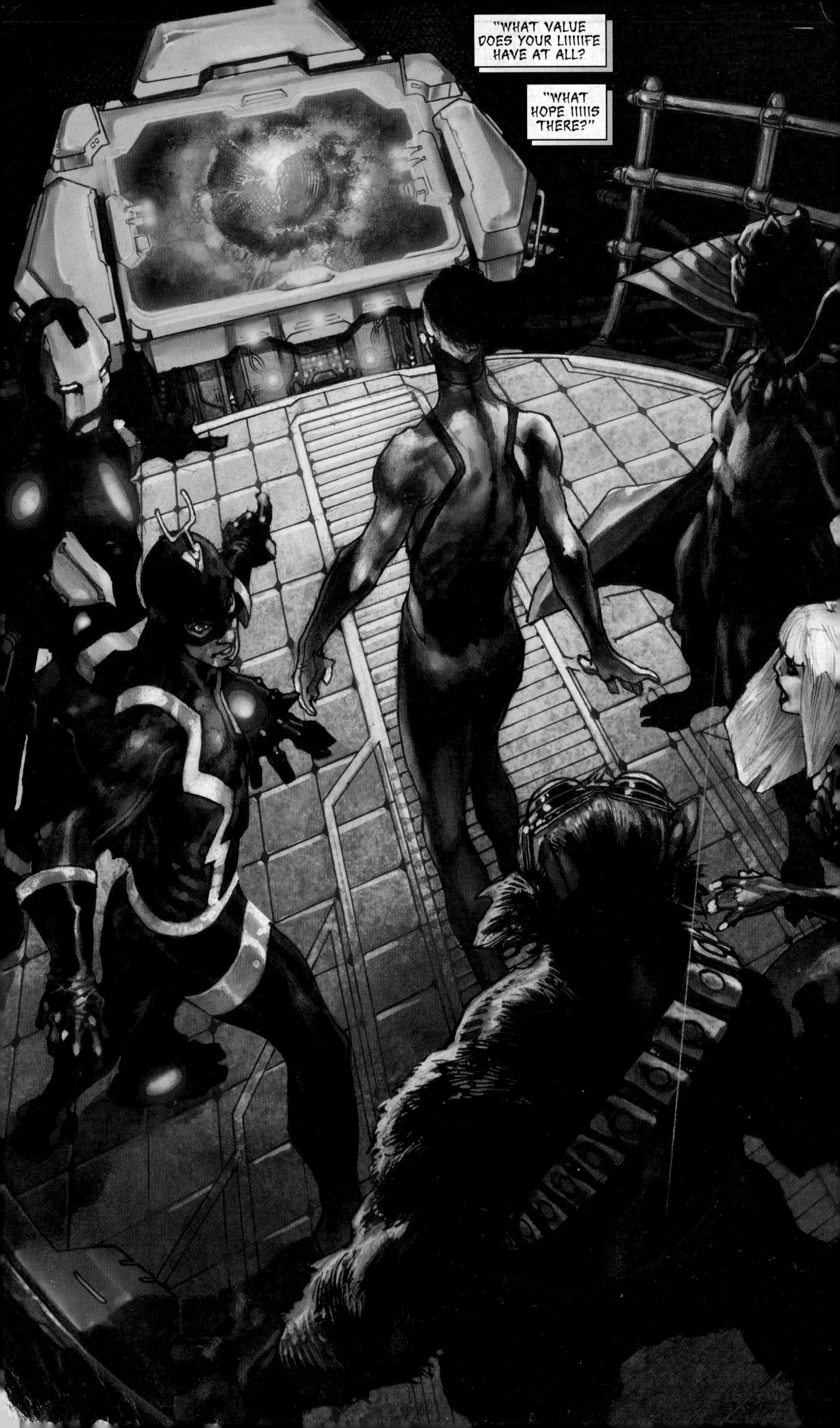
"WHAT VALUE DOES YOUR LIIIIIFE HAVE AT ALL?
"WHAT HOPE IIIIIS THERE?"

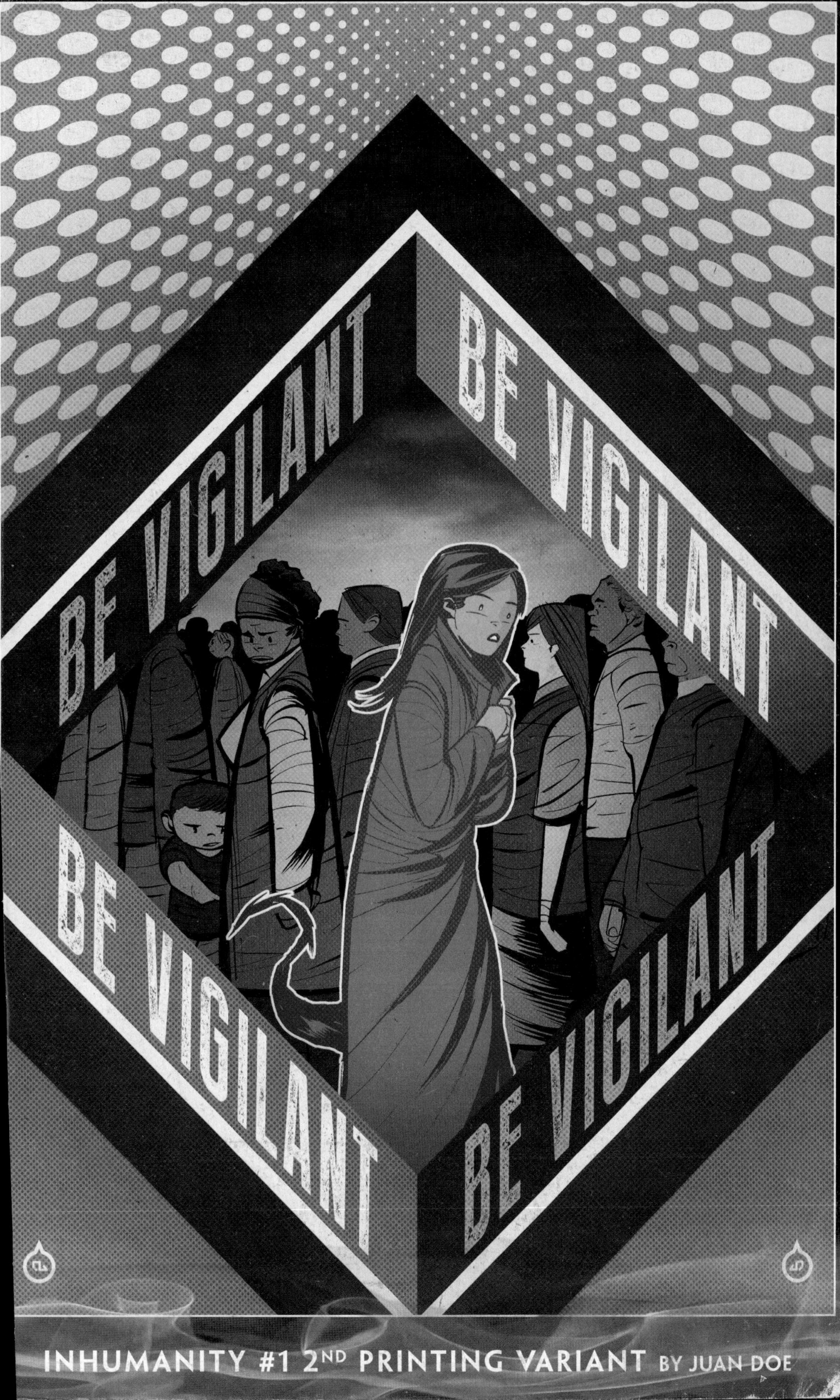
BE VIGILANT
BE VIGILANT
BE VIGILANT
BE VIGILANT
INHUMANITY #1 2ND PRINTING VARIANT BY JUAN DOE

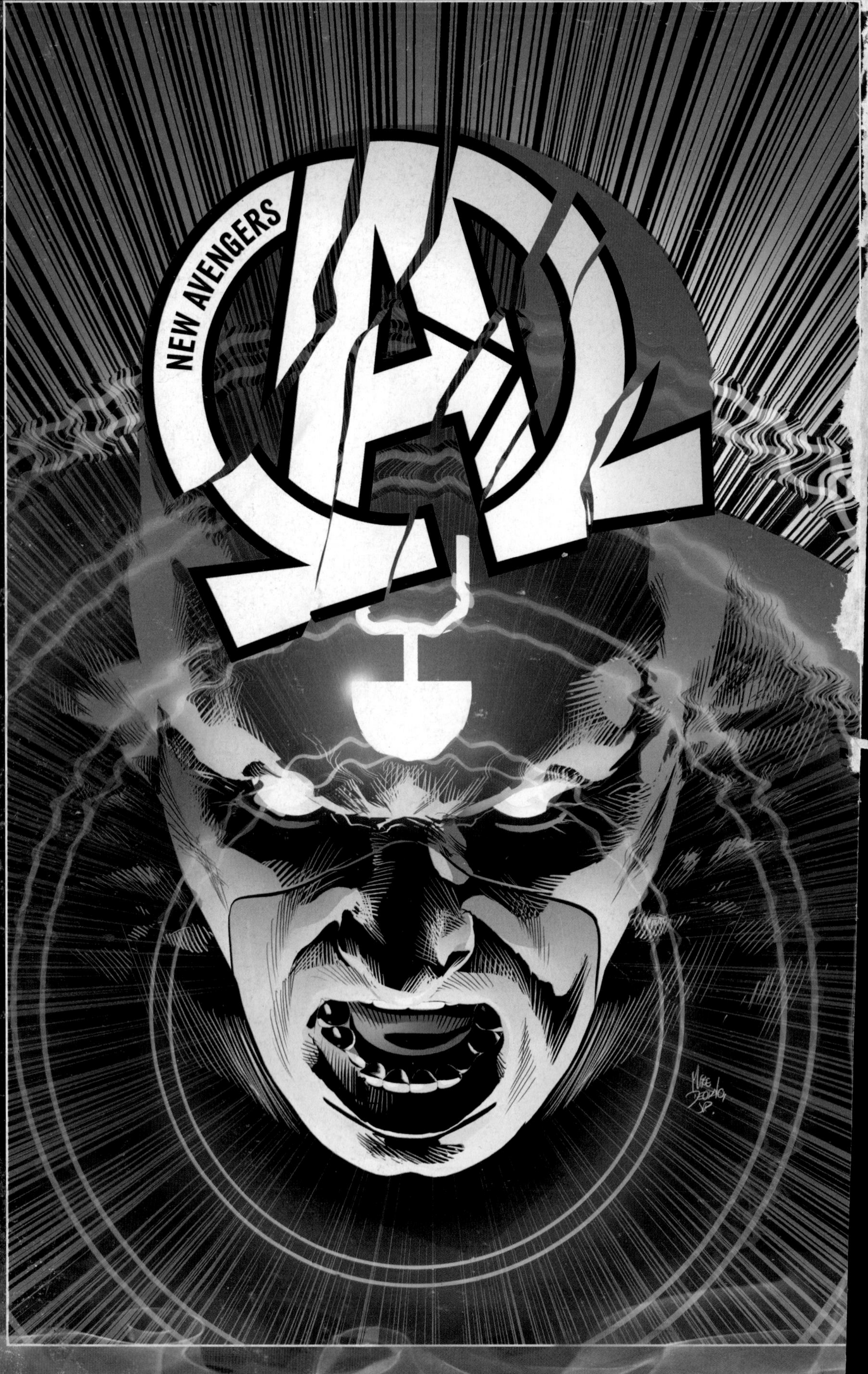
NEW AVENGERS

NEW AVENGERS #13 VARIANT BY MIKE DEODATO & RAIN BEREDO